ORPHEUS IN MANHATTAN

ORPHEUS IN MANHATTAN

William Schuman and the Shaping of America's Musical Life

Steve Swayne

UNIVERSITY PRESS

2011

OXFORD
UNIVERSITY PRESS

Oxford University Press, Inc., publishes works that further
Oxford University's objective of excellence
in research, scholarship, and education.

Oxford New York
Auckland Cape Town Dar es Salaam Hong Kong Karachi
Kuala Lumpur Madrid Melbourne Mexico City Nairobi
New Delhi Shanghai Taipei Toronto

With offices in
Argentina Austria Brazil Chile Czech Republic France Greece
Guatemala Hungary Italy Japan Poland Portugal Singapore
South Korea Switzerland Thailand Turkey Ukraine Vietnam

Published by Oxford University Press, Inc.
198 Madison Avenue, New York, New York 10016

www.oup.com

Publication of this book was supported in part by a grant
from the H. Earle Johnson Fund of the Society for American Music.

Library of Congress Cataloging-in-Publication Data
Swayne, Steve, 1957–
Orpheus in Manhattan : William Schuman and the shaping
of America's musical life / Steve Swayne.
p. cm.
Includes bibliographical references and index.
ISBN 978-0-19-538852-7
1. Schuman, William, 1910-1992.
2. Composers—United States—Biography. I. Title.
ML410.S386S93 2011
780.92—dc22
[B] 2010013551

1 3 5 7 9 8 6 4 2

Printed in the United States of America
on acid-free paper

Orpheus with his Lute made Trees,
And the Mountaine tops that freeze,
Bow themselues when he did sing.
To his Musicke, Plants and Flowers
Euer sprung; as Sunne and Showers,
There had made a lasting Spring.
Euery thing that heard him play,
Euen the Billowes of the Sea,
Hung their heads, & then lay by.
In sweet Musicke is such Art,
Killing care, & griefe of heart,
Fall asleepe, or hearing dye.

William Shakespeare, *Henry VIII*, act 3, scene 1

Who now is ready to begin that work for America, of
composing music fit for us—
songs, choruses, symphonies, operas, oratorios,
fully identified with the body and soul of the States?—
music complete in all its appointments,
but in some fresh, courageous, melodious, undeniable styles—
as all that is ever to permanently satisfy us must be.

The composers to make such music are to learn everything
that can possibly be learned in the schools
and traditions of their art, and then calmly dismiss all traditions
from them.

Walt Whitman, "Democratic Vistas"

to the Colvins,
Laura, Melissa, Richard, and Timothy,
who became my second family
and provided the material and emotional support
that made this book possible

CONTENTS

Acknowledgments *ix*

About the Companion Web Site *xvii*

Introduction: The Impact of a Single Symphony *3*

PART 1: THE EARLY YEARS

1. The Family Tree *9*
2. A Kid Grows in Queens and Manhattan *19*
3. Camp Cobbossee (and a Summer Abroad) *31*
4. A Flash in Tin Pan Alley *41*
5. Frankie *56*
6. An Unconventional Education *63*

PART 2: THE SARAH LAWRENCE YEARS

7. Sarah Lawrence and the Beginning of the Decade of War *79*
8. "The pupil is outdoing the master" *93*
9. Schuman, Copland, Koussevitzky, and Bernstein *108*
10. Populism, Progressivism, and Politics *123*
11. World War II and the Prize-Winning Composer *141*
12. The Modern Meteor I Sing *156*

PART 3: THE JUILLIARD YEARS

13. Wringing the Changes *179*
14. Dancing in the Dark *197*
15. Family Matters *216*
16. An Old Religion, Two Champions, and a New Symphony *225*

17. Delays and Diversions 241
18. Striking Out 255
19. The (Mostly) Off-Stage Ambassador 273
20. With an Eye on the Marketplace 290
21. International Man of Music 307

PART 4: THE LINCOLN CENTER YEARS

22. The Dream Defined 329
23. Something Old, Something New, Something Borrowed 345
24. One Nightmare after Another 358
25. The Potemkin Center 376
26. The Death of the Dreamers 391
27. The Death of the Dream 406

PART 5: THE YEARS OF COMPLETION

28. The Administrator Reinvents Himself 415
29. The Composer Reasserts Himself 430
30. Round and Round and Round He Goes 447
31. Bicentennial Fireworks 463
32. Reflections and Ruminations 478
33. Triplets 497
34. The Wind Was With Him 512
35. A Rare Vintage 530

Epilogue: William Schuman and the Shaping of America's Musical Life 551

Notes 557
Bibliography 653
Composition Index 663
Index 667

ACKNOWLEDGMENTS

The people who have helped me write this book are numerous. To thank as many as possible, I refrain here from relating most of their particular contributions. Both they and my readers should know that the greatest pleasure I derived from writing this book came from my interactions, in person and in writing, with these individuals.

Archivists and librarians with whom I spent countless hours. The staff at the New York Public Library for the Performing Arts takes pride of place: George Boziwick, Bob Kosovsky, Jonathan Hiam, Paul Friedman (Music Division); Charles Perrier, Patricia Rader, Philip Karg, and Susan Kraft (Dance Division); Sara Velez and Thomas C. Christie (Rodgers and Hammerstein Archives of Recorded Sound); and the many pages and security officers who welcomed, supported, and encouraged me. Next comes the staff at the Juilliard School: archivist Jeni Dahmus, head librarian Jane Gottlieb, Dan Yurkofsky, and Noah Opitz. Abby Lester and her colleagues, Sarah Pinard and Valerie Park, in the archives of Sarah Lawrence College have been peerless. The Library of Congress staff continually amazed me with their knowledge and helpfulness: Robin Rausch, Denise Gallo, Mark Eden Horowitz, Larry Appelbaum, James Wintle, George Kipper, Sam Perryman, Betty Auman, and Loras Schissel (Music Division); and Alice L. Birney (Manuscript Division). Judith Johnson, Jillian Matos, and their colleagues in the archives for the Lincoln Center for the Performing Arts opened up new vistas for me, as did Richard Wandel and Barbara Haws in the New York Philharmonic Archives. Jocelyn Wilk and Jane Gorjevsky, in different archives but both at Columbia University, have given help over the years, as did Bill Hooper at Time Inc. Robert Battaly and, especially, Erwin Levold (Rockefeller Archive Center) were patient and thorough and brilliant. Vivian Perlis and her staff at Oral History American Music (Yale University) cheered me on and helped me out. Jennifer Govan and John Carter (Teachers College, Columbia University) provided useful background information about Schuman's education. David Hunter (University of Texas at Austin) spurred my interest early on with rare recordings. Specials thanks also to: Suzanne Eggleston Lovejoy (Yale University); David Peter Coppen (Eastman School of Music); and David Sigler, Alice Kawakami, and Renee James (California State University at Los Angeles).

The librarians and staff members at Dartmouth College. No matter how often I called on these people, they came through. John Cocklin, Miles Yoshimura, Lucinda Hall (these three are saints), Laura Braunstein, Laura Graveline, Francis X. Oscadal, Amy Witzel, Bill Fontaine (Baker-Berry Reference); Pat Fisken, Pat Morris, and David Bowden (Paddock Music Library); Mark Mounts (Feldberg Business Library); Hazen Allen (another saint), Peter Collins, and Ray Marcotte (interlibrary loans); Catherine La Touche and Phyllis Nemhauser (Music Department); Jay Satterfield, Sarah Hartwell, Andrea Bartelstein, Peter Carini, Patricia Cope, and Eric Esau (Rauner Special Collections); and Robert Duff, Max Culpepper, and Matthew Marsit (Hopkins Center).

Archivists, librarians, and individuals who provided targeted information. In no particular order: Barbara Davis (New Rochelle Public Library); Maj. Sgt. Jane Cross (United States Marine Band Library); Nicole Williams (Englewood, New Jersey, Public Library); Jenny Romero and Warren M. Sherk (Margaret Herrick Library, Los Angeles); Gerhard Immler (Bavarian State Archives, Munich); Franziska-Maria Lettowsky (Salzburger Festspiele Archiv); Stuart Matlins (Woodstock, Vermont); Nancy Schneider and Trudy Wallace (Temple Shaaray Tefila); Diane Ota and Kimberly Reynolds (Boston Public Library); Jason Schultz (Richard Nixon Presidential Library at College Park); Jennifer Mandel (Ronald Reagan Library); Mary Hardy (Howe Library, Hanover, New Hampshire); Jens Boel, Sarah Thompson, and Alexandre Coutelle (UNESCO); Scott S. Taylor (Georgetown University); Dorothy Smith (Jacob Rader Marcus Center of the American Jewish Archives); Stephanie Bordy (Harry Ransom Center, University of Texas at Austin).

Elizabeth Jacques (bless you!), Alicia Estes, and Rachel Harrison (New York University); Cheryl Young, Michelle Aldredge, Baren Samspson, and Amy McLaughlin (MacDowell Colony); Laura Ries (Pueblo County, Colorado, Historical Society); Mark Hudson and James Duncan (Colorado State University at Pueblo); Susan J. Beattie and Kenn Thomas (University of Missouri at St. Louis); Kristen Castellana (University of Michigan); Chuck Barber (University of Georgia); D. J. Hoek and Greg MacAyeal (Northwestern University); Darwin F. Scott (Princeton University); Denise Monbarren (College of Wooster); Cheryl Gunselman and Patsy Tate (Washington State University); Christopher Harter (Tulane University); Liza Vick, Susan Halpert, Rachel Howarth, and Heather Cole (Harvard University); Carl Peterson and Helen Payne (Colgate University); Jeff Sauve (St. Olaf College); Judy Tsou and John Bolcer (bless you both! University of Washington); Monique Sugimoto, and Julie Graham (University of California at Los Angeles); Sara J. MacDonald (University of the Arts,

Philadelphia); Michele Mangione (ASAC Film Library, La Biennale); Nancy Shawcross and Marjorie Hassen (University of Pennsylvania); Mary Solt (Art Institute of Chicago); Millicent Callobre (Florida State Music Teachers' Association); Monica Syrette (University of Melbourne); Nanci Young (Smith College); Nicole A. Robinson (Muskingum College); Teresa Gray (Vanderbilt University); Vincent J. Novara (University of Maryland).

Bridget Carr (Boston Symphony Orchestra); Darrin Britting (Philadelphia Orchestra); Eric Schnobrick, Brittany Lesavoy, and Paul Kellogg (Glimmerglass Opera); Patricia O'Kelley, Louise Niepoetter, and David Bragunier (National Symphony Orchestra); Edward Yadzinski (Buffalo Philharmonic Orchestra); Susan Key (San Francisco Symphony); Klaus Lynbech (Danish National Symphony Orchestra); Steven Lacoste (Los Angeles Philharmonic Orchestra); David Winchell (Long Island Symphonic Choral Association and Orchestra); Jan Wilson (American Symphony Orchestra League); Michael Geller (American Composers Orchestra); Aurelie Desmarais (Houston Symphony Orchestra); David Eaton (NYC Symphony); Paul Lichau and Jane Church (Michigan School Band and Orchestra Association); Peter Nicholas Trump (Town Hall, New York City); Rob Hudson (Carnegie Hall); Gwyneth Michel (Moravian Music Foundation); LaRue Allen, Laura Raucher, Suzy Upton, and Bethany Roberge (Martha Graham Center of Contemporary Dance); Myra Armstrong (American Ballet Theatre); Molly McMullen (Kreeger Museum); Robert Tuggle and John Pennino (Metropolitan Opera); Barbara Petersen (BMI Classical); Laura Smith and Shelby Murphy (Aspen Music Festival and School); Mitch Berman (Wichita Symphony Orchestra); Trent Casey (Chamber Music Society of Lincoln Center); Victor Marshall (Dallas Symphony Orchestra); Reynold Levy, Cecelia Gilchreist, and Lesley Friedman Rosenthal (Lincoln Center for the Performing Arts); John Tafoya (St. Louis Symphony Orchestra).

Dartmouth College students, alumni, colleagues, and friends. My five Presidential Scholars: Patrick Handler, Ben Davis, Will DeKrey, J. Pendleton Vineyard IV, and Kelly Jackson; young alumni: Omar Pardesi, Brent Reidy, Bill Quirk, Andrew Haringer, Joshua Marcuse, Christian Wylonis; older alumni: David Schribman, Dan Zenkel, Nicholas Chamousis, Jeff Lazarus; staff, faculty, and friends of the College: Albert LaValley, Anthony Helm, Arthur Hanchett, Barry Scherr, Brian Miller, Bruce Duncan, Charles Dodge, Charles Hamm, Donald Marcuse, Evan Hirsch, Gerd Gemunden, Gregory Hayes, James Wright, Jane Carroll, Jason Nash, Jay Satterfield, Jeffrey James, Jere Daniell, Jill Savage, Lewis Glinert, Lynn Higgins, Margaret Funnell, Mark J. Williams, Mary Desjardins, Melinda O'Neal, Michael Casey, Michael Ermarth, Otmar Foelsche, Paul Christesen, Peter Saccio, Sally Pinkas, Scott Paulin, Spencer Topel, Susan Bibeau, Susan Blader, Susannah Heschel, Ted Levin, Thomas Garbelotti, Ulrike Rainer.

Other colleagues whose help and encouragement sustained me. Danielle Fosler-Lussier (The Ohio State University); Emily Abrams Ansari (University of

Western Ontario); David Schneider (Amherst College); Caldwell Titcomb and Daniel Stepner (Brandeis University); Peter Schmelz (Washington University in St. Louis); Edward M. Kliment (Columbia University); Annegret Fauser and Jeff Wright (University of North Carolina); John Graziano (Graduate Center, City University of New York); Rika Asai, Thomas J. Mathiesen, and Jonathan Plucker (Indiana University); Karla Prentice (American Society of Newspaper Editors); Beth Levy (University of California at Davis); Bob Golden and Evan Hause (Carlin America Inc.); Carol J. Oja and Anne Shreffler (Harvard University); Martin Brody (Wellesley College); Ralph Locke (Eastman School of Music); David Bonner (Austin, Texas); Wendy Miller and David Cook (Winthrop, Maine, Historical Society); David A. Dik (Metropolitan Opera Guild); David Schiff (Reed College); Melissa J. de Graaf (University of Miami); Joseph Kerman, Richard Taruskin, and Irina Paperno (University of California, Berkeley); Susan Feder, Peter Herb, Kate Hughes, Liz Keller-Tripp, Ed Matthew, and Christopher McGlumphy (G. Schirmer Inc.); Maria Iannacone, Debbi Oranzi, and Jacquelyn Nicklas (Theodore Presser Co.); Peggy Englebert (Arc of Camden County, New Jersey); George J. Ferencz (University of Wisconsin at Whitewater); Scott Sokol (Hebrew College); Geoffrey L. Shisler (London, England); Anthony Gilroy (Steinway and Sons); Gregory King (Baltimore); Gregory Nigosian (Chicago); Howard Pollack (University of Houston); Howard Stokar; Jack Gottlieb; Jacquelin Antonivich (Smith and Kraus Publishers); Janice Hale and Lauren Novak (Van Cliburn Foundation); Jennifer Freeman and Monique Parish (*Newsday*); Jennifer A. Geisheimer (Greater Cincinnati Foundation); Jennifer Rector Benjamin (University of Missouri at Kansas City); Jerome F. Weber; Jessica Rauch and Jim Kendrick (Aaron Copland Fund for Music Inc.); Joseph Horowitz; Thomas Cabaniss, Joseph W. Polisi, and Mary Belanger (Juilliard School); Judith Tick (Northeastern University); K. Gary Adams (Bridgewater College); Kathy Wilkowski; Kay Horton (Arizona State University); Kelly Buttermore and Sandra Bradley (American Council of Learned Societies); Karl Korte; Lawrence Doebler (Ithaca College); Neil Lerner (Davidson College); Leta Miller (University of California at Santa Cruz); Margarita Mazo (The Ohio State University); Levon Hakopian; Philip Barnes (St. Louis Chamber Chorus); Mark McMurray (St. Lawrence University); George Waterbury and Marty E. Miller; Mary Jane Dye (American String Teachers Association); Milan Vydareny (Chicago); Ron Schwizer (Pierre Monteux School); Paul Attinello (University of Newcastle upon Tyne); Paul Doherty; Paul Machlin (Colby College); Lee S. Shulman (Carnegie Foundation for the Advancement of Teaching, Stanford University); Steven P. Hill (University of Illinois); Paul Varnell (Chicago); Richard Crawford (University of Michigan); Robert S. Hines (University of Hawaii); Seow-Chin Ong (University of Louisville); Carl B. Schmidt (Towson State University); Scott Warfield (University of Central Florida); Eugene A. Swift (University of Essex);

Akihiro Taniguchi (Toyama, Japan); Denise Von Glahn and Charles Brewer (Florida State University); Thea Constantine (New York Public Library); Thomas Riis (University of Colorado); Barbara Heyman; Siamak Vahidi (University of Connecticut); William Rosar (University of California at San Diego); Gail Armondino (Stamford, Connecticut); Anne Mischakoff Heiles and Ruth Solie (Smith College); William Meredith (San Jose State University); Cathy Williams (New York Philharmonic); Jennifer DeLapp-Birkett (Silver Spring, Maryland); Margaret Mikulska (Princeton University); Craig B. Parker (Kansas State University); Tae Hong Park (Tulane University); Wayne S. Brown (National Endowment for the Arts); Maribeth Payne (W. W. Norton); Laura Matheson (Indiana University Press); Beverly Holmes (William Schuman Music Trust).

Grants and subventions. My research on the book was expedited first by the Dena Epstein Award for Archival and Library Research in American Music (Music Library Association) and then by a fellowship from the National Endowment for the Humanities. For the latter, special thanks go to Elizabeth Arndt and Jim Turner for their assistance. Publication of the book is unwritten in part by the H. Earle Johnson Bequest for Book Publication Subvention (Society for American Music).

Family and Friends, old and new, who helped out. David Barnathan; Rick and Susie Field; James Bonn; John and Lynn Wadhams; Kay and Dwight Camp; Josh Levinger and Laurie Levinger; Jon Sweeney; Milton V. Backman Jr.

Permissions. The quotations and photographs in the book appear with the kind permission of the following: David Beatty (Samuel Barber); Demetria Tobias (Merle Bateman); Kean McDonald (Robert Russell Bennett); Anne Rose Bergsma (William Bergsma); Marie Carter (the Leonard Bernstein Office Inc.); Robert Biddlecome; Robert Tuggle (Rudolf Bing and Eric T. Clarke); Richard Wandel (Floyd G. Blair, Carlos Moseley, Artur Rodzinski, and Albert K. Webster); Igor Blazhkov; Christopher and Stephen Davis (Marc Blitzstein); Harold Blumenfeld; Paul Lichau (Kenneth L. Bovee); Laura Kuhn, John Cage Trust; Kenneth A. Richieri, *New York Times* (Turner Catledge and Harold C. Schonberg); Elizabeth Todrank (Allan Knight Chalmers); Ward B. Chamberlin; Henry B. Chapin, Theodore S. Chapin, Samuel G. Chapin, and Miles W. Chapin (the sons of Schuyler G. Chapin); Alan Norton, St. Olaf's College (Albert Christ-Janer); Dianne K. Cahill (Howard L. Clark); Susan Cooper (David S. Cooper); the Aaron Copland Fund for Music Inc. (copyright owner of the letters of Aaron Copland to William Schuman); John Corigliano; Hiroko Sakurazawa and the David and Sylvia Teitelbaum Fund Inc. (Henry Cowell); Nicholas de Liagre (Alfred de Liagre); Erick Hawkins Dance Company (Lucia Dlugoszewski); Carnegie Corporation (Charles Dollard); Ilse Doráti (Antal Doráti); Sancho Soerio (Samuel Dushkin); Anna Crouse (John Erskine); Catherine Martensen (Frederick Fennell); the MacDowell Colony

(Louise Fillmore); Cornelia Foss (Lukas Foss); Richard Freed; Frank Gilroy; Stewart R. Manville (Percy Grainger); Ruth Sieber Johnson, Sigma Alpha Iota International Music Fraternity (Rose Marie Grentzer); Michael Gury (Jeremy Gury); Patricia Duffey Harris-Connelly (Roy Harris); Washington State University (Charles Haubiel); Houghton Library, Harvard University (Haubiel, Christopher LaFarge, Rosario Scalero); John Guertin of Theodore Presser Co. (Arthur Hauser and Isadore Freed); Raphael Hillyer; Anne Hobler; Ann G. Klein (Leta Hollingworth); Bill Hooper; Harold Ober Associates Inc. (Langston Hughes); Gerhard Immler; L. E. McCullers (Hunter Johnson); Marian Johns (Thor Johnson); Frances Kazan (Elia Kazan); the Rockefeller Archives Center (Howard Klein, John D. Rockefeller III, and Edgar B. Young); Wayne Koestenbaum; Robert A. Frank (André Kostelanetz); the Koussevitzky Music Foundation Inc. (copyright owner of the letters of Serge Koussevitzky); the Kreeger Museum (David Lloyd Kreeger); Gloria Hernandez, John Kaplan, and David Bearman (Paul Kwartin); Joseph Weiss/Frank Loesser Enterprises; Anne Lowendahl Jeliazkov and Fritzi Lareau (Walter Lowendahl); Catherine Luening (Otto Luening); Davis Dassori (Archibald MacLeish); Lora Martino (Donald Martino); J. D. McClatchy; Donald McInnes; Jens Boel (Max McCullough); Victor Parsonnet (Arthur Mendel); Bridget Carr, Boston Symphony Orchestra (Thomas Morris and Thomas Perry); Mark McMurray (Kenneth Munson); Shelley Mydans (Carl Mydans); Gail Kaufmann and Stephen Nauheim (Ferd Nauheim); Walter W. Naumburg Foundation Inc.; Middle States Association of Colleges and Schools (Ewald B. Nyquist); Bart Harrison (Eugene Ormandy); Juan Orrego-Salas; Bruce Paynter (John P. Paynter); Lauren Persichetti (Vincent Persichetti); W. Douglas Pritchard; James W. Pruett; Phillip Ramey; Vicky Bijur (Claire Reis); Robert A. Freedman Dramatic Agency (Elmer Rice); Gail Roberston and Joan Freeman Robertson (James Robertson); Gene Rochberg (George Rochberg); Alann Sampson of the Van Cliburn Foundation (Richard Rodzinski); Ned Rorem; Christopher Rouse; Robert Rudié and Kathryn Mishell; Lawrence D. Saidenberg (Daniel Saidenberg); Andrew Avery (Winthrop Sargeant); Svetlana Savenko; Elizabeth Gentry Sayad; Arthur Serating (Bob Serating); Elizabeth Pease (Roger Sessions); Linda Skelton (William Skelton); Nancy Smith Fichter (Lillian Eugenia Smith); Barbara Thanhauser and Ed Sonn (Howard Sonn); Rebecca Bilek-Chee, Ed Victor Ltd. (the Estate of Stephen Spender and Lady Natasha Spender); Joel Stegall; Mary Steinway (Frederick Steinway); Eileen K. Strang and Julien Musafia (Gerald Strang); Kelly Ryan, American Ballet Theatre (J. Alden Talbot); Craig Kridel, University of South Carolina (Harold Taylor); Isabel Brown (Antony Tudor); Michael Hurst, Film Society of Lincoln Center (Amos Vogel); Joan Warburg; Robert Ward; Helen DuBois (Edward Wardwell); Abby Lester, Sarah Lawrence College (Constance Warren); Michael Webster; Jonathan M. Weisgall (Hugo and Natalie Weisgall); Richard Wilbur; Harriet Koch (G. Wallace Woodworth);

Robert Birman, Louisville Orchestra (John Woolford); Herman Wouk; and Charles Wuorinen.

Oxford University Press. My editor, Norm Hirschy, ran this marathon with me and helped me to keep pace and stay sane. Thanks also to Katharine Boone, Madelyn Sutton, Christine Dahlin, Samara Stob, Brady McNamara, Woody Gilmartin, Michael O'Connor and the others in the New York office. My copyeditor, Norma McLemore, has been a wonderful guide and teacher.

Special thanks. To Karl Miller, for a window into a recording world I hardly knew existed; Walter Simmons, for making me hear and see music in new ways; Heidi Waleson, for your graciousness and generosity; and Wayne Shirley, for your excitement from Day One and your supererogation on my behalf.

Mike Backman. Everything I have done in the last twenty years draws upon your strength and steadfastness. Thank you for believing in me. Thank you for loving me.

Relatives and friends of Bill and Frankie Schuman. Inge Heckel, for that early interview about Frankie; Jean Carolene Marks, for your infectious enthusiasm; Gail Kaufmann, for giving me a child's perspective on the Schumans and their peers; Vera Marks Barad, for the treasure trove of materials you provided; Henry Heilbrunn, for your thorough work on your family history; John Israel, for your insights into your uncle.

Three final thanks. Judith Israel Gutmann (and her husband, Stephen): for your early confidence in me and your untiring assistance; Andrea Schuman: for sharing so much of your life with someone you have yet to meet; and Anthony Schuman: from our first exchange in August 2003 to today, you invited me on the journey of a lifetime, traveled with me at various points, and trusted me to make my own discoveries.

I cannot thank you enough.

ABOUT THE COMPANION WEB SITE

http://orpheus.dartmouth.edu/schuman/

The author has created a Web site to accompany *Orpheus in Manhattan*, and the reader is encouraged to take full advantage of it. Audio examples, real-time analyses, webcasts, and supplemental readings provide the reader additional opportunities within a dynamic environment to explore Schuman's life and music.

ORPHEUS IN MANHATTAN

INTRODUCTION

THE IMPACT OF A SINGLE SYMPHONY

Over the course of his lifetime, William Schuman received many letters from family members and old friends and fellow musicians and new acquaintances and perfect strangers. Some of these letters are forever lost. The letters he saved, and his answers to those letters, fill more than two hundred boxes that, stacked one on top of the other, would rise to the height of a four-story building. Of these letters, many of them speak to the impact Schuman's music had had upon the writers. Fellow composer Morton Gould parried and thrust with Schuman in witty repartee. Irate radio listeners expressed their indignation at the insult his music hurled at their ears and sensitive psyches. A teenage fan who one day would win the Pulitzer Prize in Music sent him annual birthday greetings and running commentary on the latest Schuman composition or recording or performance. Nephews and nieces and cousins and aunts and a doting sister and a supportive father and daughter and son all weighed in from time to time in epistolary fashion.

The Rev. Dr. Allan Knight Chalmers understood that his letter was but one of many that Schuman received on the occasion of the premiere of his Eighth Symphony in October of 1962. Chalmers may not have known of the letters that accused Schuman of institutional nepotism; the composer's symphony was being performed in a new concert hall that he indirectly administered. Those writers had no idea how long it takes a symphony to go from bud to full flower; they probably didn't care that Schuman received his commission for the symphony more than a year before he was approached to become the president of the Lincoln Center for the Performing Arts. Chalmers probably did not know of the numerous missives Schuman was fielding concerning the acoustical properties of the new Philharmonic Hall, as though he himself was fully to blame for its less-than-stellar sonic debut. If Chalmers had had previous contact with Schuman, the documentary evidence that remains does not demonstrate it. It appears he wrote only one letter to Schuman, and Schuman's response—and it is almost certain that there was a response, as Schuman answered nearly all of his mail—must have been a private one, as no carbon copy survives. But Chalmers's letter shows the impact one symphony can have on a perceptive listener, one who, at the time of the premiere of the Eighth Symphony, bore heavy burdens on his shoulders as he entered Philharmonic Hall.

> Dear Mr. Schuman:
>
> Let me add one more in the flood of thanks which must be coming to you after the world premiere of your Symphony No. 8 last night. It was a grand job.
>
> I used to tell my classes at Boston University, when I was teaching there, that a book is a confrontation of the writer and the reader, and if the reader bring nothing to the experience he may miss the value entirely. I know it is true that I brought something to your Symphony last night. We, here, have been sweating out a 17-month long job in helping James Meredith get his wanted rights in Mississippi, and the last two weeks have been pretty strenuous.
>
> It seemed to me that you were interpreting a truth in and to a generation pressured and determined.
>
> This may or may not have been what you meant, but anyway it was helpful last night to me. I was sorry for the old lady beside me, who was shocked and wouldn't clap. There are a lot of us, too, who want to say: thanks a lot.
>
> Sincerely,
> Dr. Allan Knight Chalmers
> Executive President
> NAACP Legal Defense and Educational Fund[1]

Chalmers's reference to "the old lady beside me" is beguiling, given that he was 65 years of age himself. And he had done much in his day. From 1930 to 1948, he was the minister of the Broadway Tabernacle Congregational Church, whose building on the corner of Fifty-sixth Street and Broadway in New York City was a stone's throw away from the site of the stables that Schuman's grandfather once ran on the corner of Fifty-seventh and Seventh Avenue, the place where Andrew Carnegie built a concert hall. Chalmers left midtown Manhattan to become professor of homiletics at Boston University's Divinity School. (One of his students there was Martin Luther King Jr.) Because of his fine work as chair of the Scottsboro Defense Committee, Chalmers was asked to serve as treasurer for the National Association for the Advancement of Colored People (NAACP), the venerable civil rights organization founded to seek justice for African Americans. In his capacity overseeing the NAACP Legal Defense and Educational Fund, it fell to him in New York City to help coordinate the effort to force the University of Mississippi to open its doors on October 1, 1962, to James Meredith, the first black student to enter Ole Miss. President John F. Kennedy sent federal troops and U.S. marshals to Oxford, Mississippi, to uphold Meredith's rights and to ensure the peace. Even so, two people were killed and dozens injured in the melee that enveloped Meredith's matriculation. These were the burdens that Chalmers brought with him to Philharmonic Hall on October 4. And Schuman's symphony helped him to lay them down.

In looking at the roster for the NAACP Legal Defense and Educational Fund's National Committee, one suspects that Chalmers may have written to Schuman in part because the conductor of the New York Philharmonic that evening, Leonard Bernstein, was on the committee. So was Leopold Mannes, president of the Mannes School of Music and Schuman's erstwhile colleague when Schuman headed the Juilliard School. The full-page ad in the *New York Times* that lists these men and chronicles the efforts of their organization features the words that Meredith spoke on October 2: "At this point it is more for America than for me."[2] More for a generation pressured and determined than for the old lady beside Chalmers.

Schuman himself was not a civil rights leader, though one of his first acts as president of the Juilliard School of Music was to establish race-blind admissions. He did not trumpet Jewish causes, though he himself was Jewish. He did not speak out for the handicapped, though his life was touched by disability. In general he eschewed lending his name to causes, whether or not he believed in them. But by virtue of his role as composer and educator and administrator and speaker and spokesman for organizations and institutions, he could not escape the swirl of events around him. And at times, his music and his words and his manner and his actions placed him, if not at the center of the world's events, in the flow of them: at times like King Cnut, unable to control the tide of history; at other times slipping into its stream; and at other times harnessing its power and redirecting its course. Chalmers was moved by the symphony. Perhaps he also intuited that the symphony's creator was, like him, a man who sought to change the world around him.

From the days in his youth when he organized neighborhood boys into athletic clubs to the day before he died when he composed letters to his protégés, William Schuman not only *sought* to change the world around him. He *did* change the world around him. New Yorkers especially enjoy the fruits of Schuman's many labors. He helped bring about the world-class reputation of the Juilliard School, with its famed String Quartet and Dance and Drama Divisions as well as its proximity to one of the world's great performing arts complexes; the programming at Lincoln Center, with its Mostly Mozart Festival, Film Society, and Chamber Music Society; and even the names of some of the city's spaces, such as Alice Tully Hall. Those outside of New York also experience his impact through his advocacy for quality musical education; his promotion of arts and artists; his lobbying of local, state, and federal governments on behalf of the arts; his efforts in the realms of recording and publication; his commissioning of music, plays, dance, and sculpture; and his many appearances in classrooms and lecture halls, on radio and television, in print and in person. He had his failings and failures, his blind spots and biases and weaknesses. He charmed many and injured a few. His self-assurance inspired those in his thrall and unsettled and puzzled and enraged and overwhelmed and amused those in its wake. By virtue of the positions he held—professor at Sarah Lawrence College for ten years, president of Juilliard for sixteen years, president of Lincoln Center for seven years, director of the Koussevitzky and Naumburg Foundations, chairman of the MacDowell Colony and of the BMI Awards to Student Composers—Schuman touched nearly every aspect of America's artistic life in ways that continue to reverberate through the ages. And not the United States alone. His travels on behalf of UNESCO and his work on behalf of the Department of State allowed him to disseminate his beliefs around the world. One can argue whether Schuman's cultural impact was great or small, lasting or fleeting. One cannot dispute that his impact was real.

My goal in this book is to gauge that impact at the time it was first felt. The echoes of the future may be heard in the soundings of the present, and the currents of legacy will occasionally eddy through these pages, but my principal concern drives me first to position Schuman in the times he acted. This requires an appreciation not only for Schuman's life and his music but also for the times in which he lived. My intention throughout is to remind the reader of those times by drawing upon their words and sounds and sights whenever possible. The evidence intermittently grows cold as it relates directly to Schuman, at which points I have to rely on his testimony and the testimony of others who were witnesses to the events or are keepers of the oral history. Elsewhere such recollections serve as a useful prism to examine the near and distant pasts with their coincidences and collisions and collusions. The larger aim remains to understand Schuman against the backdrop of the world in which he lived and moved and had his being and to appreciate the forces weighing upon him as he strove, by personal choice and by luck of the draw, to be a twentieth-century Orpheus, calming the furies of the world by dint of his many gifts—and primarily by dint of his music.

Thirty months before he heard Schuman's Eighth Symphony, Chalmers felt compelled to write to his former student King, who was quickly rising to prominence in the struggle for justice. "A man gets thin if he does not read, becomes inaccurate if he does not write, but most of all loses a profoundness if he does not think."[3] Chalmers's counsel is universal and applies to women and men in all walks of life. Schuman did not see Chalmers's letter to King, but from a young age he practiced its advice. He read widely. He wrote extensively. And he thought deeply. Here, then, is the story of a man who cultivated and spread profundity and precision and abundance, who helped to transform—for better and for worse—the ideas and institutions that support the musical fabric of the nation he loved so deeply, who sang a song that has shaped our lives, whether we know it or not.

PART I

THE EARLY YEARS

ONE

THE FAMILY TREE

Scherman. Schiemann. Schuhmann. Shuman. Schumann. The number of ways that others would spell the last name abound. An indexer who could not read the handwritten 1920 U.S. Census form offers the first. The second variant appeared in a 1956 newsletter of an organization for which Billy's childhood violin teacher served as treasurer. The third rarely appeared in Schuman's lifetime, but had his father not petitioned a court for a name change, this spelling would have been correct. Composer Walter Piston and conductor Artur Rodzinski began their correspondence with their colleague using the fourth misspelling—another writer would embellish it with a second terminal consonant—as if they knew the spelling was unusual but couldn't quite remember how it differed from the last variant. This final one, of course, was by far the most common gaffe, and understandably so, given that a homophonic musician born exactly a century before Billy spelled his name this way. But Schuman, who rarely addressed his correspondents' misspellings, did correct an interviewer on pronunciation. "I say Schuman [with a schwa for the second syllable]. When you said Schuman [with "ah" for the second syllable] I was so impressed, but it's really Schuman."[1] His preference bequeaths to us a pronunciation that distinguishes the twentieth-century American from the nineteenth-century German, a name that rhymes with "Truman," one of several U.S. presidents with whom the American composer, educator, and administrator had the opportunity to correspond during his professional career.

William Howard. According to Bill—and just about everyone who knew him called him Bill—the justification for a presidential name was an afterthought. His father, Samuel, had wanted to call his son Billy, in part because he wanted to distance his family from its German Jewish roots. Sam's parents, Moritz (Morris) Schuhmann and Rosa Kramer, came separately to America: Rosa from Olnhausen in the Heilbronn district of Baden-Württemburg; Moritz from the Bavarian capital, Munich. The how and why of their immigration remains unclear. The manifest for the *Teutonia* lists one 24-year-old Rosa

Kramer reaching New York City from Hamburg in June 1866; Rosa was born in 1840, and discrepancies of a year or two are not unknown in a ship manifest or a national census.[2] As for Moritz, Bill grew up hearing that Moritz's father, Abraham (Anton), served as a jeweler for the king of Bavaria. Gerhard Immler, director of the Privy Archives of the Bavarian State Archives in Munich, suggests that Abraham may have been "a [low-ranking] court servant responsible for keeping the crown jewels (official of the 'Schatzkammer' or 'Silberkammer') or a 'Hofjuwelier,' i.e., a self-employed jeweler, who, among other customers, received orders for new jewels or the repair of old ones from the crown," but confirmation of either of these possibilities may prove impossible, given than many of the pertinent records were destroyed in World War II.[3] Family lore also has Moritz landing in New Orleans at the time of the Civil War, being pressed into service on behalf of the Confederacy and, in some sort of accident, having his toes shot off. "Whether it was actually true or not we don't know," Bill Schuman once said in an interview, "But we do know he played the flute, and he earned his way by playing the flute at the Edison Flicks when they changed the reels," which could not have been earlier than 1894.[4] Before his forays in film music, Moritz briefly set up shop in Cincinnati as a haberdasher, a destination and trade very much in keeping with the history of Jewish immigrants in the 1860s.[5] As the tale of his induction into the Confederate Army suggests, he may have been a wild character. His younger brother, Wilhelm, followed in his father's footsteps and became a jeweler in Munich, but Moritz was intent on finding his own way, so much so that his mother, Fanny (née Franziska), wrote to his older married sister Peßla (Pauline): "We have the best letters from Moritz [from the States]. Perhaps dear God will delight us by making him come to his senses."[6] Whether his mother longed for him to be wed or devout is unclear, but not long after her prayer Moritz married Rosa and settled in New York City, where their eldest son, Samuel, was born in 1871 (siblings Sophie and Henry would arrive in 1873 and 1876, respectively) and where he established himself as a furrier beginning as early as 1872 and continuing until at least 1905.

Moritz and Rosa continued to speak German until their deaths (1913 and 1929, respectively). Bill fondly recalled Rosa quoting Goethe and Schiller to him *auf Deutsch*, even though he understood little of it. Sam, in contrast, sought to be identified as an American first and foremost. The obituary his son submitted to the papers in November 1950 lists two primary accomplishments of Sam's life, one of which was his status as a veteran of the Spanish-American War.[7] That military service defined Sam's understanding of himself. Like his father, Sam was a spirited fellow. He once was sent to New Orleans for three days on some assignment and, according to Bill, "got in with a lot of fast women and fast horses so he stayed for six months."[8] He was a lifelong gambler, and his 1892 enlistment into Company G, 22nd Regiment Infantry, New York State National Guard, was something of a crapshoot. His initial service was to last five

Moritz (Morris) Schuhmann, Schuman's paternal grandfather.

Rosa (Kramer) Schuhmann, Schuman's paternal grandmother.

years; he went in as a private and came out no higher than a corporal. But he later rejoined his company in May 1898, succumbing to the war fever that newsman William Randolph Hearst had inflicted upon the nation. Sam's papers reveal the modest extent of his service: he experienced no battles and received no wounds; his service was "honest and faithful," and his character was rated "excellent"; and as for "Distinguished Service," his papers blandly say, "None."[9] But the unexceptional nature of his service belies his devotion to country and the other men of his company. Bill would thank the men of the United Spanish War Veterans for their condolences when Sam died. "I need not tell you what an enthusiastic member my father was of the United States Spanish War Veterans and how much his comradeship with all of his old buddies meant to him."[10] Sam's service to his country at a time of war—and the importance of that service—reemerged when Bill attempted to offer his services to that same country at a time of war. The twentysomething Sam had found himself, courtesy of the armed services. When a similar situation arose almost a half-century later, it appears that his thirtysomething son felt the same might be true for him.[11]

Sam's other major accomplishment concerned his employment history. Unlike his younger brother, Henry, who earned M.D. and B.Phil. degrees from New York University in 1902 and 1903, Sam was no academic. Bill's first biographer suggested that Sam "had an almost abnormal interest in formal education probably because he never had any."[12] His discharge papers already indicate that he was a bookkeeper by profession, and shortly after he was mustered out of his regiment in November 1898 he found himself at Oberly & Newell, a lithography and printing firm that started out in 1878 and grew to such esteem that American Impressionist painter Childe Hassam would bring his work to them in 1917.[13] In later life, Bill would object to his family's being described as "prosperous." "My father was a salaried employee of a printing company, and

Samuel Schuman in his Spanish-American War uniform.

we lived modestly, but well."[14] Sam started at Oberly & Newell as bookkeeper and retired as vice president; his was the classic Republican success story in a day of progressive Republicans—Theodore Roosevelt and, initially, Taft—so Sam's decision to name his son after the then-current president was both a nod to his nation and to the policies its leaders pursued. Surely Sam could not have guessed that his William Howard would become a president himself, one who would stick to his convictions, even if they made him unpopular, and one who would be called upon to settle disputes at the highest levels of the music world, just as Taft would go on from his electoral loss in 1912 to be appointed by President Warren G. Harding to serve as chief justice of the U.S. Supreme Court.

Sam's pro-American bent exhibited itself in other ways. In 1909, three years after his marriage to Rachel Heilbrunn ("Ray") and two years after the birth of their first child, Audrey, Sam legally changed the spelling of their last name, well before many German Americans did so to disguise their heritage. He disassociated himself not only from the eastern European Jewish immigrants, whose interest in trade unions would run counter to the instincts of a self-made businessman,[15] but also from the German Jewish community in which he grew up. He attended temple only when Ray insisted, which was about once a year. He ate bacon and ham in restaurants, since he could not get it at home. And by word and example he brought up his children—to whom he gave names of indeterminate European ethnicity—to pledge allegiance to the United States of America.

In doing so, Sam was like many German Jewish men in the early 1900s. As one historian puts it, these men were "meliorists who expressed more fear at the prospect of socialism than horror at the excesses of capitalism."[16] Bill would similarly develop a healthy disdain for communism, even when his peers and mentors succumbed to its allures and tried to entice him to join them. As for religion, there could be three times as many women as men involved in the life of a Reform temple,[17] so men who weren't heavily active in leadership tended to stay away. This, too, would influence Bill, who suffered through Sabbath school and was never even a twice-a-year Jew. And the anti-Zionism that marked much of Reform Judaism in America found an echo in Bill's life, as he at times would turn away appeals to help Israel with explanations that bordered on casuistry.

Bill was his father's son, a man of unmistakably German-American Jewish stock, with the strengths and prejudices that came from that heritage. Those prejudices that could be rationally addressed and overcome, Bill overcame. Others, such as his personal opinions about organized religion, he would hold onto until the grave.

Manhattan. While it seems that nearly all East Coast composers of the twentieth century would spend part of their lives in Manhattan, few were actually born on the island. Dello Joio, Creston, and Reich join Schuman in this distinction; Gershwin, Copland, and Sessions came from the other side of the East River; and Rodgers came from still farther east. Bernstein, Harris, Piston, Porter, and Hanson were born in other states; Berlin, Herbert, Bloch, and others became naturalized Americans. But if New York is quintessentially American and Manhattan quintessentially New York, then Schuman, born on the island of Manhattan on August 4, 1910, is arguably one of America's most famous "American" composers. Furthermore, the nation (and Manhattan) feature prominently in the titles of his work—*American Festival Overture*; *George Washington Bridge*; *American Hymn*; *New England Triptych*; Symphony no. 10, "American Muse"; *On Freedom's Ground*—and he used distinctly American texts in his works, from the poetry of Walt Whitman and Archibald MacLeish to the 1897 Sears & Roebuck catalog and Ernest L. Thayer's poem "Casey at the Bat." Bill was unquestionably born and bred a Manhattanite.

But his quintessential Americanness was something of a fluke, considering the early peregrinations of the Schumans. In 1980 his older cousin Howard Sonn colorfully related the story of Bill's first abode:

> Seventy years ago I welcomed the advent of my only male cousin on the Heilbrunn side after all those females, Mildred, Hazel, Lucille, Audrey, Ruth & Evelyn.
>
> I understand that no one knew the place where the stork had dropped you. It was at 350 West 71st Street—the last building on the block with a marvelous view of the Hudson River and the N.Y. Central freight yards. The winter winds blew their icy breath in season and the hot winds in summer, all laced with the cinders from the trains that clanged back and forth day & night. Both the noise & the cinders penetrated the closed windows to Grandma's distraction. Grandma, Grandpa, Aunt Hattie and Henry moved from there to 112th Street about a year later & the Schumans to Morse Place where Grandpa had less opportunity to let you drink from his beer glass.[18]

His mother was the likely cause for some of the moves in Bill's first decade. Like Sam, Rachel Heilbrunn was a daughter of German immigrants. Her father, Louis (pronounced "LOO-ee," né Leopold), came from Liederbach bei Netra in the Eschwege region; his future wife, Julia Kahn, emigrated from Riedselz bei Weisenburg in the Alsace region. They arrived to America separately in the 1860s, married in New York in 1873, and had eight children over the course of fifteen years. Rachel was the fifth child and the third to survive into adulthood, and throughout her life she remained close to her family. Bill's dad would write to his son in 1942 about how his wife's sisters Lizzie and Hattie joined them on an outing at which they met Creston and heard works by Creston and Gustav Holst. (Dad also offered his opinion on what his son ought to do with his latest work, *Newsreel*: turn one of the movements into a patriotic march.)[19] Perhaps this familial closeness partially explains why, in the early 1910s, Ray—like all the Schumans, her name was truncated into a boy's moniker—took the family from Manhattan to live in Englewood, New Jersey. The Heilbrunns owned property there, and she and Sam could serve as overseers.

Julia (Kahn) and Leopold (Louis) Heilbrunn, Schuman's maternal grandparents.

Around 1900, Louis purchased a farm on Liberty Road in Englewood, and the Schuman clan was on that side of the Hudson shortly after Bill's birth. In 1913 Morris died in Jersey City and was interred in the Linden Hill Cemetery. Bill's younger brother, Robert, according to the 1915 New Jersey Census, was born in the Garden State that year. (His older sister, Audrey, was born in New York in 1907.) Bill fondly remembered riding with Louis from Morse Place in Englewood to New York in a horse and buggy; perhaps Louis was checking out his holdings in person. And though the family's stay in Englewood was relatively brief, Billy Schuman made a lasting impression on one neighbor, who took the time 45 years later to tell Bill how her eldest son, Bill's childhood playmate, "married the little girl who lived next door to us on Knickerbocker Road, and with whom he fought constantly when they were small."[20] The Liberty Road property apparently ended up in Ray's possession, as Schuman became the executor of the estate that held the mortgage after Ray's death in 1947.[21]

Like his son-in-law, Louis was a businessman, but unlike the bookkeeper Sam, Louis got his hands dirty.[22] Having arrived in New York as a teenage laborer, 20 years later he is listed in the *New York Times* as a cattle dealer working out of stables on the corner of Sixtieth Street and Eleventh Avenue, where he sold horses as well as cows. He supplied Sheffield Dairy with horses for its deliveries. And he prospered. He bought property (vacant lots in 1894 and 1906, and a four-story tenement building in 1896 that he sold four years later for a 33

Louis Heilbrunn and his grandson Billy.

percent profit) and businesses (he forced his brother Heneman to liquidate Heneman's share of a joint business in Louis' favor). One of Bill's earliest memories was hearing Sam and Louis talk about mortgages: "My father helped my grandfather take care of these books. My grandfather, somehow or other, got involved with Staten Island and went out there and lent money [to] people on Staten Island so he was very well liked."[23] He made his young grandson a partner in business, buying a cow for $60 and splitting 50–50 the $30 profit Louis made on the cow in just three days. No wonder that, since his dad was in the printing business, Bill had business cards made.[24]

Bill loved the countryside in New Jersey and would rediscover some of its verdant calm at summer camp in Maine. But the country boy soon became the city boy again, as the family moved back to the Upper West Side, where Bill attended P.S. 165, then out to Far Rockaway, Queens (1334 Beach Twelfth Street, where Sam, Ray and the three kids were for the 1920 U.S. Census and which Bill remembered fondly), and then back to Manhattan—first 532 West 111th Street, then 220 West 107th Street, then 605 West 112th Street, and finally the Hotel Franconia at 20 West Seventy-second Street. When confronted, at age 80, by the number of locales the family called home in his youth, the composer brushed it aside with the words from a Tin Pan Alley song. "There's a Rodgers & Hart song: 'In the month of May, it is moving day.' People would move on

May 1st or October 1st, and they did it frequently, because moving wasn't expensive in those days, and people rented apartments. . . . I don't know why. I don't know if all families moved as frequently as we did, but we moved a lot."[25] Bill slightly mangled Hart's lyrics: "On the first of May / it's a moving day." But that doesn't detract from the wonder that, in 1990 and at age 80, he could recall the *verse* to "Mountain Greenery," which appeared in 1926, right before he tried his hand at becoming a Tin Pan Alley composer and lyricist.

It would always be Manhattan—the great big city, that isle of joy—that would be a wondrous toy just made for Bill. Consider this typical Saturday for Bill, Audrey, and their cousin Lucille Sonn, who penned this recollection:

> Temple in the morning at Shaaray Tefila at 160 W 82nd St., followed by lunch. Then, trolley from 112th St. to 96th St. and Broadway to Riverside Theatre. The group would then walk up Broadway to 112th St. to Louis' apartment, where a meal was prepared by Hattie [Ray's sister]. They would gather around the piano played by Rachael [*sic* Bill's mom], Mildred [Lucille's sister] and Ruth Greenebaum [another cousin].[26]

Temple was a duty for Bill, but the theater, as he says in this excerpt from an interview conducted when he was in his late sixties, was a pleasure.

> [The Riverside Theater] was a vaudeville house, and every single Saturday my grandfather took me to the matinee, and to this day I remember all the acts. . . . It was my first real venture into the theater, and I just absolutely loved it. I still love vaudeville. I think it's a

Rachel (Heilbrunn) and Samuel Schuhmann, Schuman's parents, ca. 1906.

> great form. They had marvelous entertainers, and that's the first conscious recollection that I have of listening to people sing and perform and act. . . . The music was all the popular songs of the day, plus the so-called semi-classics . . . like "The End of a Perfect Day" of Cary Jacobs Bond [*sic*: Carrie Jacobs-Bond]. Victor Herbert would sort of be semi-classic. . . . Songs such as "Hanging Apples on the Lilac Tree" and similar gems were the semi-classics.
>
> So we used to sing, and I was considered a very good singer, and they always used to like me to sing a solo, which I'd do.[27]

And Bill would confirm Lucille's recollection independently in a letter to someone who assumed that Schuman was weaned on classical music and was thus unfamiliar with popular music. "The only music that I knew from my parents were songs from the Spanish-American War days that my father taught me, and from musical shows that we all sang on Sunday nights with my mother at the piano."[28]

Whether it was Saturday or Sunday or both, William Howard Schuman was enamored of the Big Apple and made its entertainments and enticements his own. No doubt he was inclined that way because of his father, the stolid manager who loved to gamble, and his father's father, a raconteur he met through the memories of his relatives. Bill's love for theater and music would mean that religion would take a back seat. His mother's father was far more devout than either Morris or Sam—at the time of his death in 1930, Louis was on the executive board of the Shaaray Tefila Sisterhood—Louis seems to have taught Bill more about business and the stage than about faith. Though by the 1930s, Bill's tastes would lean more toward Minsky's burlesque than vaudeville, the men in his life had unconsciously set Bill's course for him, one that would lead to the performing arts.

Even the littlest man, his younger brother, Robert, had a role to play.

TWO

A KID GROWS IN QUEENS AND MANHATTAN

Bill not only loved to sing in the parlor to his mother's accompaniment on the weekends. He also liked to sing during the week to his younger brother, Robert Monroe, who was born on May 3, 1915, just shy of five years after Bill.[1] (Bill didn't know where the middle name came from; could it have been Sam's continued fascination with presidential names?) There in Far Rockaway, Bill serenaded Robert with the hit songs of the day: "I Don't Want to Get Well (I'm in Love with a Beautiful Nurse)"; "Come On Papa"; "Keep Your Head Down, Fritzie Boy" (to the tune of "Pull Your Shades Down, Mary Ann"); "How 'Ya Gonna Keep 'Em Down on the Farm (After They Seen Paree)?"[2]; "Keep the Home Fires Burning"; "I Got the Guy Who Used to Be My Captain"; "Pack Up Your Troubles in Your Old Kit Bag"; "Give My Regards to Broadway."[3] From Bill's recollections, one senses that both boys sang and enjoyed the songs very much, a sentiment easily understood given the rapid, silly, and slightly risqué lyrics of several of these songs. But their friends weren't as amused. They noticed that Robert was not like them. They teased him. They were cruel to him. Why? Because Robert was retarded.

Was it Down syndrome? The result of encephalitis or meningitis? A mild form of cerebral palsy? If Bill ever knew, he never said, for in those days, it was "Don't ask, don't tell." No one in the family talked about it, so great was the stigma that surrounded families with developmentally disabled relatives. "My parents were advised that it would be better if he went away to school—to a school that took care of such children. . . . I used to cry myself to sleep every night, I remember, because my brother Robert wasn't around anymore."[4]

Robert was first institutionalized in a facility in the Pinelands of New Jersey—most likely the New Lisbon Developmental Center, which opened its doors in 1914—and then was relocated to facilities in New York State. He would live to be 42 years old and died on Ward's Island in the Manhattan State Hospital, the same hospital in which Scott Joplin had died 40 years earlier. Over the course of his life, his parents and sister would visit him. Even Frankie, Bill's

The three Schuman children: Robert, Audrey, and William, 1919.

wife, saw Robert. The nephew he never met, Bill's son, Tony, recalled that his mother "used to talk about how much he looked like my father, the more so since she brought him my father's old clothes."[5] But after their separation, Bill never saw Robert again. His parents and sister thought it would be too difficult emotionally for Bill to see his brother, and Bill never made any attempt to see Robert on his own.

But the older brother never completely forgot his younger brother. By the time the wider world had changed in its attitudes toward mental retardation, Robert was long gone, and Bill had little reason to comment publicly that he once had a brother. But he quietly paid homage to Robert twice near the end of his own life. He dedicated his fourth and last cantata, *On Freedom's Ground* (1985), to "my family: my wife, son, daughter, grandson, sister, and to the memory of my parents and brother"; a work celebrating the resplendent Lady on Liberty Island will forever resurrect a young man who lived and died on another island not far from the torch of freedom. And when, five years later, Bill was asked to dream up a list of songs he would like to hear as part of a cabaret-like fundraiser for the American Composers Orchestra, he gave Francis Thorne, the orchestra's cofounder, fellow composer, and cabaret pianist extraordinaire, six songs from the World War I era. Bill didn't tell Thorne the reason for the choice, but he did tell his son. "He remembered singing these songs to his brother during the period of the Great War," Tony said.[6]

So music played a significant role in Schuman's life well before he started lessons on the violin, the first of many instruments he would learn to play and the one he learned to play the best. Music lessons for both Bill and Audrey began in earnest after the family's return to Manhattan and, in keeping with the custom of the day, the daughter learned to play piano, and the son was given a violin. His first public performance as a soloist occurred on May 23, 1924, on a program featuring the students of his young teacher, Blanche Schwarz.[7] By the 1950s, she would become the president of the Violin/Viola/Violoncello Teachers Guild, based in New York City.[8] But in 1924, then in her early twenties, Schwarz was teaching young German-American Jewish boys how to play the violin. The finale of the 1924 studio recital featured Masters Schuman (age 13), Schuler, Jorgensborg, and Fischer performing a largo by Haendel (so spelled in the program and presumably the one from *Xerxes*). But Bill would remember the occasion neither for that piece or for the serenade by Pierne that the program says he was to play accompanied by Audrey. His debut piece, MacDowell's "To a Wild Rose," made the lasting impression when Audrey, seized with stage fright, failed to coax any sound whatsoever from the piano. Bill, undaunted, played the piece as a solo. Given that he, by his own admission, was "a marginal fiddle player, at best," one can surmise that this was not the finest performance ever of the drawing-room chestnut.[9] But in this seemingly insignificant moment in an otherwise forgettable violin recital, one catches an early glimpse of the man Schuman would become: prepared to go forward, alone if necessary, while others temporized at best or obstructed at worst. And the violin itself would play a pivotal role in Schuman's life as a composer, ranging in time from one of his earliest instrumental works to the Violin Concerto in the middle of his career to a commission for a solo violin piece that lay unmet at the composer's death. Both the instrument and the debut presage Schuman's career.

The manuscript of that early work, the *Three Songs Without Words for Violin and Piano*, bears no date, but the crude penmanship, the unfamiliarity with standard musical orthography (e.g., stems going in the wrong direction, use of sharps and flats in unorthodox ways), the unidiomatic writing for the piano (e.g., the right and left hands playing the same notes at the same time), and the simplistic melodic and harmonic language suggest a date earlier than Schuman's Tin Pan Alley songs of the late '20s and early '30s. The first, "Cradle Song," is a pale cousin of "To a Wild Rose," using the same metrical, melodic, and harmonic gestures found in the MacDowell piece. The first unmemorable 16 bars are heard twice, with the only changes the second time being the transposition of the violin up an octave and the piano occasionally breaking away from block chords to trace a contrapuntal line that awkwardly tries to hide the foursquare nature of the song's construction. Schuman followed these with a coda that sounds at first like yet another repeat but which compresses the 16 bars into 10. The most notable feature of the "Cradle Song" is its double tempo markings.

The English "Softly and Gently" echoes MacDowell's "With simple tenderness," but more interesting is the Italian marking largo, for the musical material is too static to be played this slowly; in his mature works, Schuman loved to use the particular term "largo."

The second song, "Melody," is marked Andantino and, in keeping with its earlier title, "Symphonic Song" (crossed out on the separate violin part) is more ambitious in every way. The violin part in particular engages in ornamental curlicues that resemble the embellishments of an Irish tenor on an old sentimental tune. The accompaniment is more active, though its hammering away at an inner voice when nothing else of interest is happening gives the impression that Schuman did not know how to keep the pulse moving. The harmonies are definitely more adventurous than those in the "Cradle Song," although they do not move much beyond the parlor music of the day. And the ending is abrupt; just as he had difficulty keeping the music moving, he had difficulty getting it to stop.

Though it has fewer measures than "Melody," the final "Serenade Appassionato" (marked moderato) is the most ambitious song of the set. Its more elaborate piano part begins to treat the accompaniment as an integral part of the work's conception, and its indications to repeat various two-and four-bar sections show a concern with the overall form of the piece. Schuman thought enough of this movement to expand and orchestrate it in 1932, at which time his penmanship and orthography were much improved. But like the other two songs, the melodies and harmonies are anodyne, and Schuman struggled to hold the piece together, interrupting its flow from time to time with static motion, ritardandos, and fermatas. However, the presence of the eight-page manuscript in ink, the separate three pages for the violin part, the orchestration of the last movement and a six-page pencil sketch collectively suggest that this early composition, slight though it is, held a special place in Schuman's imagination.

He would go on to explore instruments other than the violin before his music education training gave him familiarity on every orchestral and band instrument.[10] He bought a clarinet at a pawn shop and taught himself to play it; he signed up in high school to learn the double bass (it got him out of his Latin class) and found himself in demand as the sole bassist at a high school orchestra festival, playing the bass part in Weber's overture to *Oberon* more than a dozen times that day. He picked up some piano skills along the way, and he knew enough about the banjo to play it in public on rare occasions during his high school escapades organizing "Billy Schuman and His Alamo Society Orchestra." This last venture began when he was around 16 and continued into his college years. Thanks to his father, Schuman had business cards: WILLIAM HOWARD SCHUMAN/MUSIC FOR ANY OCCASION/Cathedral 3937.[11] As bandleader, he would secure the gigs (one and sometimes two per weekend; usually proms and dances at small colleges and other high schools, and occasionally the band played for a temple social gathering), contract the players (anywhere from 5 to 12 men, with the core ensemble of piano, trap set, two saxophones and, of course, the violinist-cum-vocalist), and obtain arrangements that publishers provided back in those days for free. He also tried his hand at arranging himself, with less than spectacular results, since at the time he did not fully understand the concept of transposing instruments.[12] At least one of his band members went on to bigger things: Burton Lane, composer of *Finian's Rainbow* and *On A Clear Day You Can See Forever*, was his pianist.[13] Schuman pithily summarized the band's efforts: "We made up in enthusiasm what we lacked in finesse."[14] But however skilled or unskilled he was as a violinist, he was good—or self-deluded—enough to entertain the possibility of dropping out of school to play violin and sing for a band that played regularly in a Chinese restaurant.

> I would have left college, but I probably would have been paid $10.00 a night to play the fiddle and sing, maybe $12.00 or $13.00, I don't know. My father said, "You know, I've always agreed with everything you've done, but I don't think you should do this because it interferes with your education. If you want to do it after you're 21 and have finished your formal education, it's okay with me, but I urge you not to do it. I urge you not to." So I didn't. And of course he was right.[15]

The idea of making his living as a professional vocalist wasn't the only career Schuman pondered back in those days. "As a boy I was an active school athlete in baseball and boxing and had at one time considered a career as a professional ball player. By the time I reached my early twenties, however, the importance of music in my life had manifested itself and other ambitions fell by the wayside."[16] His interest in baseball began to blossom shortly after the United States entered the Great War in 1917. There in Far Rockaway, Bill and the other boys organized the Crescent Athletic Club, named after the street in Inwood just north of Far Rockaway where some of the boys may have lived. Perhaps they also sought to emulate the Crescent Athletic Club in Bay Ridge, Brooklyn, which had been well known for its football, lacrosse, and, especially, hockey teams, and where baseball was regularly played on its grounds until the onset of the war.[17] According to Vincent Persichetti, Schuman's first biographer, at the Far Rockaway "branch,"

> the prime interest was baseball and Bill became alarmingly good at the game.... His sister Audrey loved looking out for her brother, three years her junior. At the end of each school year her notebooks were carefully handed over to him to facilitate his learning. It wasn't until Audrey discovered baseball pictures pasted all over her bequeathed books that she realized to what little use they had been put and how little effort Bill spent on his studies.[18]

Baseball crowded Bill's teenage life in Manhattan. He had formed the Milray Outing Club for Boys, so named because it combined the first name of his mother (Ray) with the first name of his codirector Herbert Blumberg's mother (Millie). The rationale behind the club on the directors' part was to find a way to earn some money. It also functioned so that its organizers could "have the exquisite pleasure of blackballing our enemies or putting them through a gruesome initiation ritual."[19] At the same time, though, it served a community need and scratched a personal itch. "It was an active baby sitters' league designed to care for children from the ages eight to twelve, daily between 3:30 and 5:30 and all day Saturday. The fee of $15 per season per kid included boxing lessons, wrestling, running, but mostly baseball."[20] The club ran for at least two seasons—a flyer for the second season remains among Schuman's papers—but playing baseball with kids sometimes half his age could not have brought Bill much satisfaction.

It was with friends like Frank Loesser, Ferdinand Nauheim, Eddie Marks Jr., and other boys his own age that he indulged his love of baseball and honed his skill. Grandfather Heilbrunn summed up Schuman's life in the 1920s. "I remember hearing him say to my father, with his German accent, . . . 'That boy is only interested in two things: the fiddle and baseball.' He was absolutely right."[21] And to Schuman, the two weren't at all equal: "Music was an enormously important part of my early youth and was second in importance only to baseball."[22]

Traces of baseball's importance would emerge from time to time in Schuman's life. He would forever defend the seemingly aristocratic tendencies of the performing arts by evoking the selective nature of a professional baseball team, where only the best get to perform at the highest levels, and even there catchers cannot replace pitchers on the field.[23] He felt that schools were failing students when it came to inculcating them with a love for the American way of life. "To interest boys and girls, Democracy has got to be made as exciting as a baseball game."[24] If Schuman was not so naïve as to believe that all boys and girls instinctively found baseball exciting, he did naively believe that one could learn to appreciate and understand baseball—or music. To an audience of music educators, he compared music with baseball to bring home this point.

> You need [training and discipline] to appreciate a baseball game. You miss the point if you watch a man bunt and be thrown out at first unless you know he's sacrificing himself to get a man on second. And each of the performing arts has its own myriad points—from the obvious to the subtle—each of which must be perceived to be enjoyed. It's not enough to watch and hear—the point is that you must see and listen.[25]

Baseball was even more important at times than the business seemingly at hand, as when a secretary interrupted a board meeting of the Film Society of Lincoln Center to hand Schuman a note: "Mets won 7–6."[26] And, of course, his 1953 opera *The Mighty Casey* celebrates the national pastime.

Baseball was also a critical component in the life of father and son. Bill sent Tony, who was away at camp, a newspaper clipping when their beloved

New York Giants announced that they would move to San Francisco. Bill added a short note. "When you read their history you will notice that from 1921 through 1924 they won the pennant. During those years I was eleven to fourteen respectively. Perhaps this can explain to you why I am such a Giant fan."[27] Together they would take in Game 3 of the 1967 World Series, flying out to St. Louis, praying for good weather, and watching as the Cardinals beat the Boston Red Sox, 5–2.[28] Independently, they would suffer leg injuries playing the game: Bill, a ruptured saphenous vein in a pickup game on Martha's Vineyard in June 1950; Tony, a compound fracture that was set temporarily with a baseball bat as a splint in a Riverdale/Polytechnic high school game in May 1961.[29] Tony neither inherited nor developed his father's ear and passion for music. But the source of Tony's baseball fever is obvious.

Grandpa Heilbrunn's assessment of Billy's obsessions, and Schuman's agreement with him, overlooks a component of Schuman's early life beyond the fiddle and baseball that made him the man he became: he was a reader. His 1916 certificate declaring him a member of the Order of Ropeco provides the earliest evidence of his literary proclivities. The monthly *Ropeco Magazine* was distributed free to boy customers of the clothiers Rogers, Peet & Co. ("Ropeco," pronounced "roh-PEE-koh," is an amalgam of the first two letters of the company's name.) A call for writers proclaimed: "Stories for our magazine should be from 3500 to 4000 words in length, and must be of a typical boyish type with a good moral trend."[30] Camping and sports stories were magazine staples, and boys sent away for the certificate of membership and the lapel button that signified that they, too, were proud Ropecs.[31] Copies of the magazine are hard to come by nowadays, and Bill saved none, but another recollection shows that stories like those in *Ropeco Magazine* appealed to him. When he was president of Juilliard, he wrote to conservationist and children's author Thornton Waldo Burgess.

> About 30 years ago I read four books of yours which made a lasting impression on me. Now my son is anxious to read these books for I have been telling him about them for some time. Unfortunately, however, they would appear to be out of print, judging from the report I get from my local bookseller. I cannot recall all four titles—one was "Boy Scouts on Lost River," and "Boy Scouts in a Trappers' Camp." Does my memory serve me well?[32]

The four titles were *The Boy Scouts in Woodcraft Camp* (1912), *The Boy Scouts on Swift River* (1913), *The Boy Scouts on Lost Trail* (1914), and *The Boy Scouts in a Trapper's Camp* (1915). "I loved those books. And so Tony tells me, I used to make up stories and I scared him to death about camping, which was never my intention."[33]

Schuman was a voracious reader. When he was laid up with hepatitis for the summer of 1954, he was unable to compose, but he saw a silver lining in his convalescence: for the first two months of his confinement, he read on average a book a day.[34] He received manuscripts to review for publication, prerelease copies to solicit a jacket blurb, complimentary books from grateful authors and editors. And he read them all. He wrote at least seven book reviews, two of which appeared in the *New York Times*, but he turned down a request to review a book by his good friend Jacques Barzun because he found the slim work "far beneath his abilities."[35] Though he preferred biographies and espionage thrillers—perhaps a later-life echo of the stories of derring-do he read as a child—he was as omnivorous as he was voracious. He thanked James Warburg for sending him a paper on the Marshall Plan, Glenn Seaborg for the Annual Report to Congress of the Atomic Energy Commission, and Herman Wouk for getting Schuman to reread *Aurora Dawn*. (The book, Wouk's first novel, was published in 1947; Schuman reread it by April of that year.)[36] He received both the *Herald-Tribune* and the *Times* and occasionally looked at the *World-Telegram* and the *Sun*. He kept abreast of what was going on in the music education journals as well as *Variety*. He tried to rescue *Modern Music* (1924–46) when it hit the shoals. He started and shepherded a journal—*The Juilliard Review* (1954–62)—to address an audience he felt the musicology journals missed. He praised the authors of, and referred others to, articles in the *Saturday Review*, the *New Republic*, *Commonwealth*, the *New Criterion*, and other journals and magazines. Colleagues, acquaintances, and strangers sent him libretti to set, poems to ponder, manuscripts to forward. And he read them all.

The depth and breadth of his literary exposure no doubt helped him develop into the orator whom everyone praised for his wit, wisdom, and winsomeness. Although he would have access to speechwriters during his Lincoln Center years, his preferred manner of addressing an audience would be to have people pose questions that Schuman insisted he not see in advance. Of course, he had stock answers and anecdotes to draw from, but his skillfulness in these settings came from more than his ease in front of crowds. He also had a well of reading from which he could draw, and his fertile and searching mind found sustenance in the books and articles and poems.

Given his strengths as a speaker, the comprehensiveness of his reading, and his own steady output of reviews and articles, it may come as a surprise that Schuman had great difficulty when it came to recording his memoirs. He tried to put virtual pen to paper by dictating his thoughts, only to find the process tedious. He tried to interest publishers in his life story, only to be turned away. He tried to work with other writers to help him shape his autobiography, only to be distracted by other projects that interested him more. And at the end of his life, time and energy were in too short supply to enable him to finish telling his story the way he wanted it told. But the hurdle was not simply the failure to secure a publisher or to see the earlier efforts to their conclusion. Schuman's literary standards stood as a challenge to his own literary efforts. He preferred being the protagonist in his own ongoing story to reflecting on that story. As keen as his mind was, he was first and foremost a man of action. He had no time for writing his story because he was living it.

The vivacity of his later years finds a parallel in the ebullience of his early educational experiences. He attended Speyer Experimental Junior High School, experimental in part because the idea that there should be a separate institution called "junior high" was a novelty in the early twentieth century. Thomas Briggs, a proponent of junior highs across America, was also a faculty member at Teachers College in New York City and a consultant to the Speyer School. In his study of 60 such schools, he waxed prophetic about the hidden potential resting in Speyer and its ilk.

> The physical redistribution of the grades seems assured; but if, having accomplished that, schoolmen rest content, they will have missed the one great educational opportunity of their generation for real educational reform. There is a demand for purposes so clear and so cogent that they will result in new curricula, new courses of study, new methods of teaching, and new social relationships—in short, in a new spirit which will make the intermediate years not only worth while in themselves, but also an intelligent inspiration for every child to continue as long as profitable the education for which he is by inheritance best fitted. In its essence the junior high school is a device of democracy whereby nurture may coöperate with nature to secure the best results possible for each individual adolescent as well as for society at large.[37]

Teachers College was so bullish on the innovations being advanced at Speyer that it published the school's curriculum in 1913, believing that other schools would benefit from this novel approach to elementary and secondary education.[38] (It is unlikely that Schuman knew about this publication, but the similarities between it and *The Juilliard Report on Teaching the Literature and Materials of Music* from 1953—another tract touting progressive education—draw themselves.) The administrators and teachers at Speyer were particularly high-minded.

Schuman met their high-mindedness with high-spiritedness. Though the curriculum at Speyer was designed to be completed in two years, Schuman claimed to take an additional six months, owing in part to the fact that he was suspended for disruptive behavior. "I saw in a movie where Charlie Chaplin went into some restaurant and poured some coffee into a sugar bowl or some such thing and made jelly, and I did it at Speyer, but I did it in the teachers' lunchroom." (A similar stunt appears in the movie *Sunnyside* [1919].) Schuman was also involved in other actions that needled the administration. For example, on Tuesdays the students were to go from class to class without saying a word. The administrators hoped that it would teach the students discipline. Bill responded with a discipline of his own: a highly choreographed handshake that eventually involved sixteen different movements. Students exchanged Schuman's Complicated Handshake in the hallways on their way to and from class, preserving the silence only by stifling their giggles at subverting the administration.

And, according to Schuman, these episodes were among the tamer ones. "I think a lot of them don't bear retelling."[39]

Schuman expressed his high spirits in other ways at Speyer. He played indoor baseball at the gym and was a member of the 90-lb. boxing team (he lost every single fight and stayed on the team only out of sheer bravado).[40] He was voted best orator in the school's yearbook, though he didn't remember speaking much "except to try to raise nickels and pennies to buy the makeup for the shows that I put on." One of those shows was his first original work, a three-scene play called *College Chums*. The extant copy looks too professional for a junior high school kid to have typed it, and one suspects that Bill's mother, Ray, listed as a "type-writer" in the 1900 U.S. Census, helped her son with the script. Schuman would later dismiss the play as treacle and its message of moderation as bunk. But in pitting two roommates of differing temperaments and skills against each other, the young playwright appears to be wrestling with two sides of his own nature.

> *Sam is sitting at desk reading a book. He puts the book on the desk and after several minutes of thought, starts to speak.*
>
> SAM: This sure is hard on a fellow, this darn old grind of getting a scholarship. All George does is to play baseball all day. I can't see a thing in it. (pauses) Well, I better start reading again, if I want to finish this book by tomorrow.
>
> *George suddenly bursts into the room, looking very hot and excited. He starts to speak as soon as he enters.*
>
> GEORGE: O'Boy! That was some game. Can you imagine the ninth inning, two out, bases full, and we needed four runs to win. I was at bat and hit a triple, then stole home, and we won. Yeh! Gee, I can't imagine anything more exciting than that.
>
> SAM: Maybe you think that's exciting, but I'm reading the History of Mankind, by Van Loon.[41]

Schuman's choice of Hendrik Willem van Loon's 479-page *The Story of Mankind*, first published in 1921, allowed him to be both funny and brutal in sketching Sam's intellectual prowess: van Loon's book was written for children.

The high-spirited athlete and class cutup would continue to get the skilled orator and so-so scholar in trouble. He was occasionally thrown out of his Sunday school classes at Shaaray Tefila for various sophomoric activities. Changes in Reform Sunday School came shortly after Schuman's stint as confirmand, and had he been exposed to that revised curriculum, spearheaded by Emanuel Gamoran, Schuman may have had different opinions about the place of organized religion in his own life. As it was, Reform education at Shaaray Tefila in the 1920s meant little to Bill, in part because of the distraction his antics introduced into the mix. One observer of the distinctions between the public school and temple school lamented the difference. "*There* attention and quiet, *here* indifference, often wild noise; *there* decent respectful behavior toward the teacher, *here* only the opposite." (Clearly, the observer hadn't seen Schuman at Speyer.) The temple school curriculum was often unchallenging and often reduced to rote recitation of a catechism in preparation for the confirmation ceremony.[42]

The fact that, at his confirmation, Schuman was asked to deliver words written for him by the Rev. Dr. Nathan Stern, the rabbi at Shaaray Tefila, is thus not as scandalous or hypocritical as it may have seemed to Schuman at the time. Certainly Schuman's skills as an orator at Speyer now worked in his favor as Stern chose him to address the congregation. And while Bill may not have been able to recall his oratorical exploits at Speyer, probably done mostly before and with his peers, the pleasure that his confirmation speech gave him, as he surveyed the congregation and delivered Stern's words, stayed with him for decades.[43] But save for his later appearances with the Alamo Society Orchestra and his sole and tragicomic experience of writing a service anthem less than a decade later, Schuman's affiliation with Temple Shaaray Tefila and Reform Judaism ended the day after he was confirmed. He had had no bar mitzvah; Reform Jews didn't have bar mitzvoth in those days. But he had become a man all the same, and to him the ways of the temple were part of the childish things he was destined to put behind him.

His junior high and high school chums would also help him become a man. In his innocence and excitement, Bill related to his father something his buddy Meyer Rosenthal had taught him: how to masturbate. (Rosenthal would become a famous actor who went by the stage name Anthony Ross.) Too embarrassed to speak to his son about this rite of passage, Sam promptly shipped his son off to Uncle Henry, M.D. "So I went out to Uncle Henry and I told Uncle Henry, and my Uncle Henry said, 'Whenever you have that feeling come on, you must take a cold shower.' So I went back and told the boys. If we had followed my uncle's directions, we all would have died of pneumonia!"[44]

Schuman did not relate as many colorful tales of his years at George Washington High School as he did of his days at Speyer, perhaps because GWHS wasn't billed at the time as an experimental school. Still, it is worth noting that Speyer and GWHS both were relatively new schools—GWHS was built in 1917—and, along with Sam Schuman's decision to send Robert to a modern facility in New Jersey, one senses that the family sought out the newest and the best. Bill and his wife, Frankie, would both be inducted in GWHS's Alumni Hall of Fame, although they did not know each other during their high school years.[45] And it's not hard to imagine why. Frankie was industrious and dedicated. Schuman was, at best, average. His matriculation into Speyer seemed unusual from the start.

> You were given an intelligence test, and you were rated A, B, C & D. I was rated C, the third lowest, and after two weeks I was demoted to D. This was especially interesting to me because I *knew*, even then, that this was crazy, because I couldn't spell, and I couldn't write legibly, and it had nothing to do with intelligence whatsoever.[46]

Schuman had made the honor roll at P.S. 165 four times between February and May 1922, so perhaps his continuation at Speyer rested in part on his performance in elementary school. The honor roll certificates he preserved indicate his rank in Ms. Susan Squier's 6-B² class: as high as fourth one month, as low as fifteenth in another. And the certificates themselves, with their rubber-stamp "signature" from the principal of the school, give the impression that they were designed more to enhance student self-esteem than to measure intellectual acuity: his ranking was in one sixth-grade class, and there is no indication whether there were other sixth-grade classes with similar certificates.[47]

Schuman made his way through school, neither at the top nor the bottom of his classes. At George Washington, he joined the school orchestra, first as a violinist and then as a double bassist. His limited instruction in music came from a forgettable course on theory, but a term paper on Tin Pan Alley ("a place of shocks, surprises and paradoxes") gives an early indication of where he would go after he graduated. He also sang, in high school, the standard high school fare of the day, which included Gilbert and Sullivan. His early biographer indicates that he was a fixture in the school chorus as well as the orchestra, stolidly holding his section together and having no difficulty memorizing his music. "To this day he can sing the bass parts of all his choral acquaintances in high school. . . . This is due to a specialized type of detailed memorization that keeps him from forgetting what people have said to him since he was three."[48] Here again is a window into the man Schuman would become. His pranksterism almost got him kicked out of school. His preternatural memory coupled with his tenacity and spirit of adventure—the other side of the pranksterism—got him through.

So did his gang of friends, with whom he bonded not only in Manhattan but also in Maine.

THREE

CAMP COBBOSSEE (AND A SUMMER ABROAD)

Meyer Rosenthal, 18 months older than Schuman, not only taught his younger playmate things that embarrassed Schuman's father. Meyer also told Billy about a summer camp in the wilds of Maine, this at a time when camps in the Adirondacks, Catskills, and Poconos were far more popular and well known.[1] The camp in Maine, founded in 1902, was still relatively new when Meyer and Billy went there in the early 1920s, but it was aggressive in establishing its place within the camping community. A 1917 ad in *Good Housekeeping*, one of many ads in the issue promoting camps from coast to coast, spells out this camp's distinctive features.

> Camp Cobbossee
>
> For Boys. 15th Season. On beautiful Cobbossee-Contee under fragrant Maine pines. Give your boy a chance to enjoy wholesome out-door sports under ideal conditions, where his natural manly instincts will develop into firm character under the supervision of leading college men as councilors. Unsurpassed by any camp in America for equipment, healthful environment and popularity; refined surroundings and influences. Write today for interesting booklet and full information.
>
> H. R. Mooney, Advisory Director.
>
> R. L Marsans, Director
>
> NEW YORK, Shandaken, Shandaken Institute.[2]

A contemporaneous account augments the advertisement by shedding some light on the Institute that fielded inquiries about Cobbossee, the two men behind the camp, and the community around the lake.

> Camp Cobbossee, Monmouth, on the shores of Lake Cobbosseecontee, Kennebec County, is a large, well equipped camp, maintained for fourteen seasons by Harry R. Mooney, who is in the insurance business in New York City. R. L. Marsans, the director, is principal of Shandaken Institute, Shandaken, N.Y. In connection with the camp is Cobbossee Colony of private bungalows and a farm. Boys from nine to twenty years of age are accepted, and a large proportion return from year to year. The boys, largely from New York, are encouraged to spend some time each day in study.[3]

In fact, Cobbossee had gained a following among boys from New Jersey (East Orange and Newark, specifically) as well as New York. And though the camp was not affiliated with any Jewish organizations, a good portion of its clientele came from the German-American Jewish middle class that Schuman and his family and friends belonged to. Marsans actively sought out this clientele by advertising not only in mainstream magazines but also in specialty magazines, one of which was the *Menorah Journal*.

There was no ad for Camp Cobbossee in the *Journal* of the spring of 1922, the time right before Schuman would become a camper, but Marsans did advertise in the April 1930 issue of the *Journal*, highlighting the "expert instruction in field and water sports, horses, wireless, tutoring" and the fact that the camp sought "boys of fine character." A historian of Jewish summer camps notes:

> There was no mention of kashruth or any other Jewish aspect, and this is significant. Early in the century established Jews here placed emphasis on "being Americans"; they wanted their sons and daughters to feel at ease in the community at large and become psychologically prepared for college years and then professional or business careers in a predominantly non-Jewish society. They were drawn to Maine and the Adirondacks for their children's summers—there the dust of the city and confines of the suburb could be shaken off and lungs filled with pure, sweet air of American mountains, lakes and forests.[4]

Camp Cobbossee was, in short, a place for Jews that was free of Judaism. It was also a place where German-American Jewish boys could go that kept them separate from their poorer eastern European co-religionists. Of course, it was a place for other boys as well, provided they were athletically oriented. Consider this eyewitness account from 1923 of two unnamed camps, one of which sounds as though it must be Cobbossee.

> We recall a very strenuous boys' camp on Lake Thompson [near Poland, Maine] which has athletic teams of prodigious success in matches with other camps; another on Lake Cobbossee Conte which wallops everything round about. They are among the most popular boys' camps in the region. One must admit that virility and courage are the stuff of which we make our heroes in the flesh. As raw meat with a bat in their fists we do not require them to be poetic or romantic. If they can swat a homer—that's "de stuff." And a boy mentally and bodily robust worships the physical hero in his presence—not always the finer hero limned on the pictured page of fiction.[5]

In truth, Camp Cobbossee allowed time for boys to worship heroism on the athletic field rather than exclusively on the pages of fiction. Sam Schuman could hardly find a better camp for his all-American boy.

Schuman's six summers at Cobbossee loom large in his own accounts of his adolescence. Stories about junior high are few; those about high school are even fewer. But camp was the place where Schuman's interests in baseball, reading, and music all came together. No wonder he put up such a protest in 1925 when his parents suggested that he not go to camp that summer. Cobbossee, in many ways, was where the boy found himself.

Schuman so enjoyed his first summer at the camp that he sought the following year to persuade other boys to join him. He had other motives for his proselytizing: he would get free access to a canoe if he brought four boys to camp. He brought a dozen.[6] And one of those 12 was Eddie Marks, who would also fall in love with Cobbossee. Schuman also pledged the D.V. fraternity at the camp, and he would never forget "the sadism of fraternity initiations at night on a lonely island in the middle of Lake Cobbossee."[7] By 1924, both Marks and Rosenthal were officers of the fraternity, and every year at camp the brothers had a banquet, complete with menus and a program. Fraternal activities were not limited to the summers; Schuman preserved an invitation to join his brothers for a 1924 meeting on Halloween at Marsans' home in Brooklyn, perhaps to play pranks on their beloved camp director.

The number of activities at camp seemed to go on forever. One contributor to the camp newsletter, the *Almanak*, joked about the nonstop pace.

> For the week before the first printing I was extremely busy. In the morning there was life-saving, canoe tests, swimming, office duty, morning activities, junior chorus rehearsal, life-boat duty, and nature. Then in the afternoon came baseball practice, tennis practice, swimming practice, life-boat duty, and senior chorus rehearsal. And after supper was more baseball practice, indoor league, council ring, amateur night, and senior, junior, and whole cast rehearsals. The only reason I'm free to write now is that I am O.D. and have nothing to do.[8]

Schuman wasn't nearly this busy, but he did concentrate his efforts in four principal areas: baseball, canoeing, music, and dramatics.

An undated article in the *Almanak* shows the extent of Schuman's athletic prowess at the time, as another contributor opined about Schuman's feats.

> One of the finest plays seen at camp in indoor baseball in many a day was the double play that ended the Senior game. The ball was hit to Schuman who threw it home to Jonas retiring the runner. Jonas on a quick relay managed to get his man at first completing a snappy double play. . . . Billy Schuman yesterday accomplished a fact [*sic*] that many major league pitvhers [*sic*] try but that very few succeed in doing. Namely pitching and winning a double header.[9]

It would also be at Cobbossee that Schuman discovered that he suffered from a form of muscular atrophy that would bring his dreams of becoming a baseball star to an end.[10] But his exploits as a baseball player at camp were celebrated far and wide.

His canoeing skills were, by definition, exhibited in a less public forum than his baseball skills, but in both sports he earned the right in 1926 and 1927 to wear a sweater emblazoned with the letter "C" as an honor for excellence in these two endeavors. His "free" canoe was named the Billy Schuman canoe, so many campers had he brought to Maine and so often was he on the water. The freedom the canoe provided also gave him the privacy to continue to indulge his love of reading. Rupert Brooke, the dashing young World War I poet who died a romantic (and noncombat) death, was among his favorites at the time. And if Marks is to be believed, Schuman's love of baseball poetry, including Thayer's *Casey at the Bat*, also began at Cobbossee, publicly at first but no doubt ruminated upon in those quiet moments on the lake alone.[11]

While athletics brought Billy much acclaim among his fellow campers, his musical accomplishments would be the more significant and long lasting in terms of the effects that camp had on him and others. Most of these musical and dramatic activities occurred during his second three-year stint at Cobbossee, and had he had his wishes, Schuman would have been at camp for seven straight summers in a row. But an opportunity arose in 1925 that his parents insisted he pursue.

In an attempt to curry favor with the American people, the Department of Education in Paris and the Committee Accueil des Étudiants extended an invitation to students from the New York schools to come to their city and

Billy Schuman, the rower.

country. The bureaucrats wanted the young Americans not only to see for themselves the toll that the fighting of WWI had taken upon the French countryside but also to better understand how resilient the French people were. Most of the American students were selected because they had studied French during their secondary education. And while most of the students came from Horace Mann and the Ethical Culture School, other students were also invited to travel. Schuman was among them.

But he didn't want to go. He had won the All-Around Camper's Cup the summer before, and he begged his parents not to send him away to France. But Sam and Ray felt that their son's horizons needed expanding beyond the reaches of the Maine woods. They would miss him, they assured him, since they came to visit him at Cobbossee. It would be hard to have him gone that long. (His parents saw the ship off from the deck of a ferry accompanying the ship out of harbor; Schuman recalled seeing his mother cry.)[12] But they stressed to their son that he would be grateful that they insisted that he travel abroad.

They also insisted that Billy visit Uncle Henry again, and the nephew received a pamphlet with a vivid red cover titled *The Boy's Venereal Peril*. It was unclear if Schuman would have enough free time in France to make the pamphlet worthy of his attention. (He did visit his great uncle Robert Schuhmann, who had migrated from Munich to Paris.)[13] But given that the ages of the boys ran from fourteen to twenty,[14] Billy was on the youngish side, and since Meyer had taught him certain things about sex, perhaps the adults were concerned that other older boys on the trip might similarly attempt to introduce Schuman to new pursuits. Billy was, after all, Sam's son, and like his father, the teenage Billy seemed to take his cues more from his peers than from his relatives. Indeed, later in life, in specific reference to the pamphlet with the bright red cover, Schuman coyly said: "I didn't say I had taken [Uncle Henry's] advice; this was the advice that was given."[15]

Since Schuman went to France against his own wishes, he must have been surprised by how much he enjoyed the trip, his first overseas. For starters, his mother composed "boat letters," enough to cover every day that her son was aboard the ship. "I was the envy of all because I had mail deliveries at sea."[16] Once they reached Europe, the boys saw the battlefields at Verdun; they heard from one of Marie Curie's assistants at the Radium Institute (later, Institut Curie) in Paris; they took tea in Strasbourg with Alsatian students extending their hands in friendship; and when they were ready to journey home, they were bid bon voyage by the mayor of Havre and the American consul for France. Their comings and goings were followed in the New York press; Schuman's scrapbook contains six clippings from the various newspapers. They were, for July and August 1925, American celebrities.

Schuman gathered his souvenirs, programs, diary, postcard pictures, and other items and placed them in box marked "France," which he stored on the top shelf of his closet.[17] To date, the box and its contents have not been located. But Schuman's memory of the trip was keen: "It was an extraordinary experience for someone from my narrow background suddenly to be in every major city of France and staying in the lycées and universities."[18] Perhaps it did open his eyes more to the larger world around him. But upon his return, he went back to baseball and music, at school and at camp.

The year 1927 would see Schuman's first big musical and dramatic success at Cobbossee, but even 1926 brought mention of his talents. The camp newsletters reveals that on two separate nights in late July, Schuman was in fine fettle as a musical showman.

> July 26: The Melody Boys, Herb Blumberg and Billy Schuman, entertained with a few selections on their banjos. . . . Herb and Billy reappeared as impersonators of two hobos. They sang several numbers in close harmony which were favorably received.
>
> . . . July 29 . . . Billy Schuman and Bert Levy played two beautiful selections, "Orientale" and "Ave Maria." [One presumes Schuman played the violin and not the banjo on this evening.]

But the next year brought Cobbossee something never seen before at camp.

> On August 7th, 1927, Billy Schuman and Eddie Marks, Cobbossee's famous authors and producers, came out with something new in the form of a monster minstrel show. This successful production met with a wonderful response. Everything in it measured up to the high standards set by the big shows of past years. . . .
>
> Much credit is due Mr. and Mrs. Marsans for their wholehearted co-operation, which they display so often; to Ross Whytock and Ted Adler for their invaluable aid in coaching the chorus, and also to the latter, Ted, for his assistance at the piano; but, above all, to Billy and Eddie, because it was their show, and their initiative which mean so much to the Winthrop Hospital Fund.[19]

Whatever comparison it had to "the big shows of past years," the Winthrop community treated the minstrel show as the first of its kind. Certainly it was Cobbossee's first "off-Broadway" show to transfer to Winthrop's Great White Way. A local paper ran a review: "A most successful minstrel show was presented at the Town hall [August 24, 1927] . . . Although the show was originally intended for camp production only, the first presentation at the camp for the aid of the hospital was so successful that it was decided to give a second performance at the Town hall."[20] Admission was 25¢ for the town hall performance, so the show did not prompt the hospital's coffers to overflow. But, as Schuman would later say, it gave him his first real taste of directing and producing.

The program for the first presentation of the *Monster Minstrel Show* places the action in part 1 at "Casa Cobbossee in August of 1943 (Daylight Savings)." Part 2 featured the Casa Cobbossee Cabaleros [*sic*], a six-piece orchestra with "Don Schuman" on the violin and Marks as the Casa Cobbossee radio announcer. Prior to part 2, there were 12 specialty numbers, and "the Minstrel will be interspersed with these acts." The program also lists a "Tango composed by William Schuman." Schuman would later say that the first piece he composed was a tango called *Fate*, written with words by Marks around the time he was sixteen.[21] But the only tango listed in the program, the eleventh of the 12 acts, is listed as "Pampa" and featured two of the campers, one in drag. "Freddie 'Lightfoot' Bashwitz . . . tangoed with 'Miss' Buddy Gans to music written by Billy Schuman."[22]

In his own recollections of the minstrel show, Schuman never fully divulged what his role was in the production, but both the camp newsletter and Marks's memoirs make clear that, with Marks, he was a writer, director, and producer. The two of them, along with Meyer Rosenthal/Anthony Ross and a fourth camper were also the end men. And as was the custom of the day, they appeared in blackface for the performance. "We thought nothing of blacking up and going through the end man routine."[23] And for his efforts on the show, Schuman made the camp honor roll that year, winning the cup in dramatics. (Marks won the cup for the *Almanak*.)

The following year would bring even a more auspicious success, the musical farce *It's Up to Pa*.

> The book, lyrics, and music were the work of Eddie Marks and Billy Schuman, the authors of last year's merrymaking Monster Maine Minstrel. It is significant that this is the first time the score of any Cobbossee show has been entirely original. Much credit is due Eddie and Billy for their adroitly written play and catchy musical numbers, upon which they spent considerable time and energy.[24]

The idea for the show came from their studies in French class, where they had read *Le voyage de Monsieur Perrichon*, "a delightful comedy . . . particularly suitable for use in the class room" written in 1860 by Eugene Labiche and Edouard Martin.[25] Marks and Schuman updated and transferred the action; in doing so, they not only made the French farce relevant to an American audience but also geared it explicitly for their fellow campers, particularly by including within the show a prize-winning song they had written together the summer before, "Red and White Aloft."[26] Marks wrote later in his memoirs:

> The campers were divided into two teams that competed on the athletic field, in the water, on the stage, and in a complicated all-day flag hunt (a kind of treasure hunt). When Bill and I were both on the Red team, we wrote, produced, and acted in a musical called *It's Up to Pa*. It had two performances for the benefit of the Winthrop Community Hospital, one held at Camp Cobbossee Lodge and the second in the Town Hall of Winthrop, Maine. The hit song of the show was *I Want to Be Near You*.[27]

Either Marks misremembered the color of their team or they were equal-opportunity dramatists, for less than three weeks later the Whites of Camp Cobbossee presented *Tell It to the Judge*, "A Mystery of a Mysterious Mystery (A Mystery Musical)." Marks and Schuman once again collaborated on book, lyrics, and music, and both boys had starring roles in this show.

But *Tell It to the Judge* seems either to have been an afterthought or a vehicle to present the songs the two writers had cut from the big show of the year. And the *Almanak* and the *Daily Kennebec Journal* both agreed: *It's Up to Pa* was a fine show. The latter noted that this was

> the second successive year Camp Cobbossee presented a successful musical show for the benefit of the Winthrop Community hospital. . . . This tuneful farce was written by the author of last year's successful minstrel show, Edward B. Marks, Jr., who was responsible for the clever lyrics while William H. Schuman supplied the catchy melodies and also directed the orchestra.[28]

The *Almanak* gives a fascinating peek into what took place in the hall as well as on stage. "An amusing printed article, relative to the plot, was handed to everyone in the audience at the end of the first act, and after the show, the sheet music for the two song hits of the show—'I Want to Be Near You' and 'I Can't Say Yes to You' were placed on sale."[29] Schuman was a published songwriter.

As it happened, Marks had the same kinds of connections when it came to music as Schuman had when it came to business cards. Both songs were published by Globe Music Co., a business that had the same address as Edward B. Marks Music Co., Eddie's father's business. The cover not only names Marks and Schuman but also gives credit to four other campers: Bernard H. Grad for the dances; M. C. Rosenthal (Meyer) for the staging; and Edwin L. K. Gilmore III and Herbert P. Blumberg (Schuman's Milray Outing Club partner) for the settings. A photo of three tents, presumably at Cobbossee, graces the cover, as does a list of the songs from the "tuneful summer farce" that weren't published. In short, the publications were vanity items made expressly for the campers, their parents, and anyone else who wanted to support both and remember the evening, and Schuman recalled that they paid for the publication.[30] (Marks the publisher used the back page of the folio to advertise many of his other, more lucrative wares.)

"We borrowed shamelessly from Gilbert and Sullivan and Rodgers and Hart," Marks would later say,[31] and the hit song of the evening certainly shows its indebtedness to the latter pair. Marks's lyrics throughout aim for, and occasionally overshoot, the witty repartee of Lorenz Hart ("I've a hankering to be anchoring/Close in your arms/Helter-skeltering to be sheltering/Far from alarms.") Schuman's music is much improved on the *Three Songs Without Words for Violin and Piano*. Here, the phrase lengths and harmonies are foursquare and assured, with little of the gangly unsteadiness of the violin pieces. The chorus, especially, is skillfully composed, with a two-bar motive generating all of the musical material for the remaining 30 bars, including the bridge, whose melody is an inversion of the motive. It is most definitely tuneful, and while not in the league of the melody for "My Heart Stood Still"—Rodgers and Hart's hit song from the year before—one can hear the echo of that song in this early effort by Schuman, who would later count Richard Rodgers as a dear friend.

Billy would return to Cobbossee as a full-fledged counselor at least once—in 1932, he wrote a story for the *Almanak*—and the following two summers would find him at other camps: Camp To-Ho-Ne in Great Barrington, Massachusetts, near the end of the summer of 1933; and Brant Lake Camp, just west of New York's Lake George in 1934.[32] But it was his days at Cobbossee as a camper and a junior counselor that stayed with him.

And not with him alone. Some of the old-timers pulled together a reunion in 1952 to celebrate the golden anniversary of the camp, with homemade movies made 25 years earlier just one of the highlights of the evening. And Schuman was crestfallen: the night of the reunion was also the day of his sixteenth wedding anniversary. He wrote to the reunion's organizers: "Although Cobbossee has meant a great deal in my past, Mrs. Schuman is very much my present and future, and it would be unthinkable for me to go carousing at the Cobbossee stag on that particular evening. Please, can't there be a 51st Anniversary celebration next year on an evening other than March 27?"[33] A second reunion would have to wait until the diamond anniversary year, when Edwin Gilmore was back in the United States. Gilmore had become a foreign correspondent for the Associated Press, and he won the Pulitzer Prize in 1947 for his reporting from Moscow. He had written a book, *Me and My Russian Wife*, and was coming to America for a lecture tour. And he wanted to pull together the old Cobbossee crowd, making a special request to invite Schuman and Marks. The invitation to Marks went astray, but Schuman was there along with 17 other men, one of whom had traveled from Alabama to New York City to be there for the evening. Schuman wrote out from memory the opening song from *It's Up to Pa* and distributed it that night for the men to sing. The experience was so moving that, in recalling it less than a decade later, Schuman would magnify the number of people there and forget about the golden anniversary reunion he had to miss.

> I don't know how many were reached, but I do know that some thirty or forty of us met together and some came from distant points. It was of course the kind of reunion that you can only have once, but it was a wonderful affair. We sang some of the old songs from our shows, and in turn each man got up and stated, usually with considerable wit, what he had been up to since camp days. Of course many of us had kept up our camp friendships throughout the years on a sporadic basis, but this was the first formal get-together, and really it was in tribute to the late R. L. Marsans . . . [who] instilled in each one of us his own sense of awe for the great outdoors and the spirit of working together, and everything emanating from him was one of good fellowship with emphasis on character and learning.
>
> . . . I can only say that, for me, the experience of camp was a principal enrichment of a lifetime.[34]

And beyond a lifetime. David Straus sent Bill's wife a letter of condolence upon hearing of his death in 1992. "Our friendship began in 1928 with Billy as my counsellor [*sic*] at Camp Cobbossee and when, in my scratchy boyhood soprano I sang the first song he and Eddie Marks composed. Thus began a cherished relationship which continued as we matured and the age separation narrowed." If Dave was mistaken about which was Eddie and Billy's first song, the story in the *Almanak* shows that he was not mistaken about the role he played. "The midget camp was represented in the show by Dave Straus and Billy Black. Their rendition of the opening song, 'We're Dressed Up for the Visitors,' was instrumental in making that number the smashing hit it was."[35] Not only did Schuman come away from Cobbossee having made memories of his own. He—and particularly his camp songs—gave many other boys memories they would cherish all their days.

FOUR

A FLASH IN TIN PAN ALLEY

On one of his Cobbossee scrapbook pages, Schuman typed out the briefest of biographies of his life at that time:

> WILLIAM SCHUMAN "Billy"
> New York City
> New York Univ. '31
> Camp '22–'24, '26–'28
> In charge of: Orchestra, Dramatics

Nothing in the scrapbook dates from any later than August 1928, so his self-identification as a member of the class of 1931 at NYU shows Schuman looking to the future from the vantage point of his summer triumph with *It's Up to Pa*. But some background information of what happened before that summer is necessary to understand what transpired after it.

Bill had gone uptown to George Washington High School in Washington Heights and graduated in January 1928. For his senior speech the month before, Schuman held forth on the popular song. "It is my contention that a song, in order to become a popular hit must possess one or more of four requisites; a pretty or attractive melody, an original universally appealing theme, a set of clever, well-constructed lyrics, and a 'Punch.'" His teacher was impressed enough to give him an "A" on both the speech and its accompanying paper.[1] Schuman, the impresario behind and the headlining singer for the Alamo Society Orchestra, knew the hits of the day, and his success at Cobbossee whetted his appetite for more success. There was one small problem: Schuman's inadequate knowledge of harmony meant that he didn't know how to undergird his attractive melodies, appealing themes, and clever lyrics.[2] Never mind the je ne sais quoi of "punch": Schuman couldn't "chord" his own songs or write a decent arrangement for his band. He was hampered musically, and he knew it. But before addressing this shortcoming, he would first take a serious detour after graduation. Besides, could he even make a living in the music business?

And was that a respectable career for him? He had grown up hearing his parents extol three vocations above all others: doctor, minister, and teacher. Unlike his Uncle Henry, Bill did not seem to have the scientific aptitude to become a doctor. However noble it was to be a minister—and Bill's parents used that word and not "rabbi"—Bill was disinclined from that direction. Perhaps teaching would be in the future, he must have thought, but not before he could take a stab at a career in business. After all, he came from a family of businessmen: his paternal grandfather, the haberdasher and furrier; his maternal grandfather, the cattle and horse dealer; his father, the bookkeeper who became a vice president and general manager of his firm. Bill had heard stories about the first and deeply admired the other two. A degree in business administration, then, could cover several bases: it could prepare him for a front-office job in the music industry should he wash out as a singer or composer. And he would be prepared for other, more lucrative jobs outside of the music industry. So within days of his graduation in late January, Schuman began classes in business administration at New York University's School of Commerce.

Bill's decision set him apart from two of his closest friends. Like Bill, Eddie Marks also graduated in January. (He went downtown to Dewitt Clinton High School, located in those days in Hell's Kitchen.) But Eddie and Ferd Nauheim, another member of the neighborhood gang who was also out of school by then, decided to spend their winter and spring working. So while Eddie and Ferd were making money and leaving the job behind them at the end of the day, Bill was enrolled in four intensive courses—Economic Principles and Problems, Industrial Organization and Management, Markets and Marketing Methods, and Foreign Trade Principles—as he attempted to cram one year of university work into one semester. Bill struggled at NYU that first semester; he earned no grade higher than a "B," and he would have to repeat the latter half of Economic Principles and Problems if he wanted credit for that part of the intensive course. No wonder that around this time he and his buddies started the United Musical Poker Players Association of America, gathering together every Sunday for penny-ante poker and singing while they played.[3] And no wonder that, in the summer of 1928, Bill was ready to go back to camp. Even if, as a counselor, he no longer had the opportunity to play baseball as fervently as he did as a camper, there would be other pleasures and pursuits at camp and its environs. Eddie Marks was also at Cobbossee that summer, working on the *Almanak*:

> Bill had a beat-up car, and would ferry me to Lewiston where we had the sheet printed on a small letterpress.... We would leave camp after breakfast on printing day, deliver the copy to the printer, and enjoy a lazy lunch and convivial afternoon before retrieving the copies and heading back to camp. We met a couple of summer students from Bates College who helped us pass the time agreeably. Mine had the euphonious name of Kay Way.[4]

Bill wanted anything that would distract him from the challenges and tedium of business school, which he knew awaited him after he decamped from Maine.

For decades, mystery has surrounded what exactly happened between Bill's return from Cobbossee at the end of August 1928 and his contrapuntal studies with Charles Haubiel beginning in November 1932. We know the date of the latter because of the voluminous notebooks Schuman kept of his exercises with Haubiel. But the years immediately before those lessons have eluded scholars for two reasons: a lack of documents from those years and the presence of a myth about those years.

When Schuman considered his autobiography in 1970, he crafted a table of contents that consisted of 13 chapters. He managed to draft the first five and nearly all of the last six chapters, but two central chapters—those on George Washington High School and Tin Pan Alley—either were never drafted or were lost or destroyed. What Schuman had to say about these years are contained in various interviews and oral histories, which brings us to the myth.

Like most myths, the myth of Schuman's Tin Pan Alley years is an amalgam of fact and fantasy. And the mythmaker was none other than Schuman himself. Here are his words from the first chapter of the 1970 autobiography. Note that the proposed title for the chapter—the very first chapter of the memoir—attempts to cement the myth in place.

> April 4, 1930
>
> Finally I was prevailed upon to attend a concert of symphonic music. My sister Audrey had an extra ticket and she and my mother persuaded me to go. It turned out to be quite a day.
>
> I was nineteen years old, and my background in music was limited to popular songs and occasional exposure to light classics. When I was a small boy, I can recall my father playing the William Tell Overture on the pianola; he played it each morning before he left for work. And we did have Sunday night sings around the piano. My mother played, and the songs were from current musical shows, so-called "semiclassics"; i.e., Hanging Apples on the Lilac Tree, Victor Herbert and, more often than not, the peroration. The peroration was our most high-flung selection; we all sang—mother, sister, brother, grandma, cousin—Welcome Sweet Springtime. These were words set to Rubinstein's Melody in F, which later, with my newly acquired musical erudicion [*sic*], I realized my mother had played in the key of C. . . .
>
> Before that fateful Sunday afternoon symphonic concert, I had already made beginning gestures as a composer. At Camp Cobbossee I began to write songs, and with my friend, Edward B. Marks Jr. as lyricist, we wrote two musical comedies for the camp. The music reflected the discernible influence of Gilbert and Sullivan and Rodgers and Hart, the darlings of the day. . . .
>
> The program of the New York Philharmonic on April 4, 1930 included the Funeral Music from Gotterdammerung [*sic*], a work of Kodály, Summer Evening, and

Robert Schumann's Symphony No. 3. It is difficult to describe to you the electric effect of that concert. I was as excited at what I saw as at what I heard. It was simply incredible to me to observe a sea of stringed instruments bowing together. The precision of the entries of the various instruments was breathtaking. I couldn't understand for a long while why the percussionists (never silent for a second in the popular music I knew so well) played so rarely. To say that it was an afternoon of high excitement and discovery is not to exaggerate but to understate.

I knew that I had to spend my life in music. That night was a sleepless one. With the resumption of the school week I immediately withdrew from N.Y.U. Being a practical lad, my head was not so much in the clouds that I didn't go to the registrar's office for a refund. Now what should I do? I started to walk uptown from Washington Square, thinking about the music I had written. A few of the songs composed for the camp shows had been publisher [*sic*] and I was discouraged because they didn't sound right. Someone else had put in the harmonies, the "chording," because I did not know enough to do this myself; I couldn't write the music down. It is true that I had studied a little music theory in high school, poorly taught, and could more or less write out the melody line, the "lead sheet." My piano playing ability was virtually nil. But as I continued my walk uptown I somehow knew that all that had gone before was merely a prelude and that that Philharmonic concert was for me the beginning. In my inner ear I carried the astonishing perfection of the remarkable world of sound into which I had been introduced at the concert.

As I walked on and on toward our apartment on West 112th Street, the conviction and resolve became clearer. I noticed out of the corner of my eye a sign on a building at the northwest corner of 70th Street and West End Avenue which proclaimed the Malkin Conservatory of Music. I walked in and the woman at the reception desk asked me what I wished. I told her I wanted to study to be a composer. She replied that I would have to take harmony lessons and that if I wanted to do so privately it would be $3 an hour. It was a matter of the greatest good fortune that the teacher assigned to me was the remarkable Max Persin, about whom more later.

And so it began in 1930. Five years later I was teaching composition and introductory courses in music and the other arts at Sarah Lawrence College and had completed my First Symphony.

The stories about Persin must have been reserved for the missing Tin Pan Alley chapter, for Schuman does not give the full measure of their lessons together in the other chapters of the autobiography. Though April 4, 1930, in fact fell on a Friday,[5] Schuman's recounting of "that fateful Sunday afternoon" displays his knack for storytelling, a skill both his father and father's father shared with him. And like their stories, the admixture of fantasy and fact makes the stories resonate. In Bill's case, the basic facts as told by him are all true. The concert did take place. The repertoire was exactly as Schuman remembered it. He did voluntarily withdraw from NYU. The Malkin Conservatory was located on the Upper West Side during these years. And Max Persin taught Schuman harmony. The fantasy derives from Schuman's decision to put the concert first in the chronology of these events. In fact, he had withdrawn from

NYU and begun his studies with Persin under the aegis of the Malkin Conservatory well before April 4, 1930. His NYU transcript and more than a dozen letters he wrote to Eddie Marks help to pinpoint his activities during these years, as do a handful of his published songs and arrangements. An article from 1944 further enlarges the ambit of the Tin Pan Alley years. And his first biographer, writing in 1948, both helped to create the myth of Schuman's epiphany and tried to present these years in all of their riotous complexity, only to be told that his account risked turning Schuman into "nothing more than a campus cut-up."[6] The fact is that the flash in Tin Pan Alley that Schuman claimed to have, a musical experience of the road-to-Damascus variety, was far more complicated than he allowed, and for good reason. The evidence strongly suggests that he *was* the equivalent of a campus cutup during these years, a flash in a different sense, a man, according to his good friend Ferd Nauheim, whose "most marked traits were his sense of humor, lack of inhibitions and dominant personality. A good looking boy, he never had any trouble getting dates whenever he wanted them."[7] Enough evidence exists, in other words, not only to set the myth aright but also to help us understand why and how the myth came into being in the first place.

Eddie Marks followed in his brother Herbert's footsteps and attended Dartmouth College, where the journalistic experience he received on the Cobbossee *Almanak* was put to use on the school newspaper. Bill returned to NYU, where he enrolled in six two-semester courses: Business Finance; News Writing (journalism); Elementary Composition (English); Reading, Conversation, and Communication (French); Medieval and Modern Europe (history); and a course titled "Contracts; Formation of Agencies and Employments." His poor showing the previous spring was exemplary compared with his work in the fall of 1928. He missed so many history classes that the instructor didn't even bother issuing a grade, indicating only that Schuman was absent. He earned "C's" in three classes; two more classes were added to the list of those he would have to repeat to graduate. The spring of 1929 saw the end of Schuman's academic career at NYU, when by March his academic performance sank so low that he was placed on probation. Rather than complete his courses that term, Schuman elected to withdraw from them, which he did on two separate days: March 25 and April 3, the latter date a fascinating pre-echo of the Carnegie Hall concert a year and a day into the future. (At the time, the Commerce School was in Washington Square, and the College of Arts and Science was part of the University Heights campus in the Bronx. Schuman was taking classes on both campuses, which might explain why his withdrawal took place on two separate days.)[8]

Schuman would not enroll again into a formal program until he matriculated at Teachers College, Columbia University, in the fall of 1933. But he was considering continuing his education elsewhere. Between May and July 1929, he had his NYU transcript sent to the Universities of Georgia, Michigan, Maryland, and Virginia, and although no evidence exists to show that he applied to these schools, their locations suggest that the problem with his university education wasn't New York University. It was New York City.

Bill was having a lot of fun in the Big Apple. Sure, he had to work. He wrote copy for the Paramount Advertising Company, "Creator of Advertising Ideas," and "during these years, which were roughly from my 16th through 21st, I also worked for a time as a salesman for a lithographer" (his father's firm, Oberly & Newell).[9] But he was a handsome young man coming of age at the end of the Roaring Twenties, hanging out with friends who liked to get drunk and hoped to get laid. Pursuing a career in Tin Pan Alley would not interfere with either of these enterprises. If anything, such a career might enhance them.

And so, in addition to his part-time job at Paramount Advertising, Schuman sought to further his reach into songwriting. He turned to his best friend and collaborator for more lyrics, and he turned to Eddie's father's firm for support. In late October 1928, on NYU stationery, Billy wrote to Eddie, telling him that Herbert was interested in "I Want To Be Near You" but was even more interested in something new from the songwriting duo. "How would you like to come home from college and find a Sch-Marks product flooding the market. Now lets see a good lyric." After boasting of the prowess of the NYU football team, which had gone 5–0 that season, Schuman signed off with this P.S.: "See you Thanksgiving. How are the women? Remember me to all the Jews."[10] By this time, Schuman was staying away from his former girlfriend

Bill Schuman, 1929.

Louise (immortalized in *It's Up to Pa*) and had embarked on a relationship with another girl, Désirée (or Dez, for short). Schuman invited Marks to join them on a trip to Washington, D.C., over the Christmas holidays. He also went to the NYU Library, but not to study. "Don't get excited, I only got a Philadelphia Phone book to find out Jeanne's address, I just wrote to her."[11] ("Darling" Jeanne was a mutual female friend who later may have been one of Marks's girlfriends.)[12]

The New Year back in New York City brought new opportunities for Marks and Schuman as songwriters. Schuman dropped Marks a line. "Listen babe—Do you object to St. Joseph's church of Brooklyn using 'Near You' in their annual charity show this year. All the other numbers are taken from current musicals." At NYU, Schuman had met Stanley Adams, the future lyricist for "What a Diff'rence a Day Makes" and future president of the American Society of Composers, Authors, and Publishers (ASCAP). Adams was writing the book for the St. Joseph show and looking for numbers to incorporate into it. Although Schuman personally disliked Adams—"a loud kike, uses don't incorrectly, talks a lot and I don't think you'll like him much more than I do"—he felt Adams could open doors for them. "I showed him all our stuff, he likes the tunes and thinks the lyrics are swell. All I can say at present is that its [*sic*] very possible that we'll get a break through him. . . . Please excuse many errors but I'm in a hell of a rush. The letters this boy gets from Dez Mmmmm."[13] Schuman sent Marks a second letter a few weeks later, stressing the urgency of matters. Herbert had floated the idea of doing an orchestration of "Near You," and Adams couldn't use the song unless it was orchestrated. Couldn't Eddie do something? "About three thousand will hear the number. Ed, you certainly ought be close enough to your brother to present these simple facts—there will be no dissapponitment [*sic*], or anything like that on my part—but you can never tell—"[14] Both Eddie and Herbert came through, and by mid-March Schuman had the orchestrations in hand. "The [show] is going to be given at the Waldorf-Astoria on the eve of April 2nd. 'Near You' is the second number of the show and it is reprised for the finale of the first act." That was the business news Billy had for Eddie. He also had some "Monkey Business (Wimmin)": "Oh, Désirée . . . To think that you have been in the city for the past 15 days and I have only had 17 dates makes me despair, I'll forget what you look like. Mmm you sweet thing."[15]

The St. Joseph's show coincided with Schuman's flagging interest in school, and by May 1929, all he could think about was breaking onto Broadway, either with a song or (preferably) with a show. Désirée had a cousin who had a libretto titled "Rain or Shine"; Schuman hoped he and Marks would have a chance to write the music for it, but Dez's cousin didn't have time to get the book in shape and was instead focusing on getting another book produced with the Gershwins. "I could hardly say that we could do a better job then [*sic*] Ira and George, even though you write a better lyric then the former."[16] Marks and

Schuman also wrote a standalone song that, according to Schuman, was generating some excitement.

> "This Business of Loving You" is being complimented on all sides. Some (including Meyer) say it is our best endeavor, but really boy I'm beginning to think its [*sic*] not bad. I think the verse is the nuts and the chorus gets 'em by the balls (the last three words not connected with the meaning of the title). In short the song has made a hit where ever played. I'm telling you this because it shows we can do some good stuff and if your enthusiasm is equal to mine there's no stopping us. I can't wait to start turning out a couple of good hits or a twenty or thirty we can do it boy! What say?[17]

After the summer of 1929, Marks and Schuman drifted apart as collaborators. But one of the important things that the Marks-Schuman correspondence from this time preserved is not just the saltiness of their missives. (Not as many Marks letters survive, but they, too, are very colorful, as is his memoir.) Schuman's choice of stationery helps to piece together what he was doing at various points of his life. His October 28, 1929, letter to Marks is less interesting for its content—more talk about football—and more interesting for its letterhead: the Malkin Conservatory.

Music historians tend to associate the Malkin Conservatory of Music with Boston, given that Arnold Schoenberg's first teaching post in America was at that institution. But almost two decades before the establishment of the Boston-based school by cellist Joseph Malkin, his pianist brother, Manfred, had opened a New York–based school. Founded in 1913, the Malkin School of Music (renamed Malkin Conservatory in 1924) was something of a gypsy. When Schuman walked home from NYU in the spring of 1929, the conservatory was at the corner of Seventy-eighth Street and West End Avenue; by the fall of that year, it had moved to Riverside Drive, the address on the masthead of Bill's letter to Eddie. The school consisted of a faculty more than a building, and one of the primary faculty members was the man who would become Schuman's first serious harmony teacher. The school catalog gives his credentials:

> Max Persin is a graduate of the Odessa Conservatory, where he studied theory and composition. He also studied composition under the Russian composer, Arensky. Mr. Persin has for many years been choir-master of one of the leading temples in New York, and has written some of the most beautiful services for choir and organ. He has been associated with the school since its inception, and has lent his fullest co-operation to the director in working out the latter's plan of musical education. Mr. Persin's courses are so arranged as to develop the pupil from within, and to lead him step-wise to the highest goal in musical education, namely, musical expression.[18]

According to Schuman, Persin would come to his home and begin each lesson by sitting down at the piano and improvising for an hour or longer. They would discuss the harmonization of Bach chorales or the latest piece by Ernest Bloch.

Persin, who approved of Schuman's efforts to write popular songs, would also ask to see his most recent tunes. He would arrive early and leave late, smoking his cigars the entire time and not accepting Schuman's offer of food.[19] As the Malkin catalog stated, Persin's role was to foster musical expression and "to develop the pupil from within," and one can trace the hand of Persin in Schuman's popular songs from late 1929 forward as the harmonies and structures get increasingly complex.

The pre-Persin song "I Want to Be Near You" (1928; lyrics by Marks, published by Globe Music) consists of a four-bar introduction, eight-bar verse, and a standard 32-bar chorus (here, AABA), and while the bridge section (B) employs a few accidentals, the harmonies never veer far from the song's home key of F major. In *Doing the Dishes* (ca. 1930; lyrics by Frank Loesser, unpublished), the structure of the introduction, verse, and chorus are identical to the earlier song, and the harmonies are hardly adventurous. Then, instead of a repeat of the verse, the song unexpectedly features a "song-within-a-song," a 25-bar break (AABA). Not only are the A phrases unusual with their truncated seven-bar length, but their harmonies slip and slide down the chromatic scale using the same progression that Jean-Philippe Rameau employed exactly 200 years earlier when he wanted to portray, in harmonic terms, sheer horror.[20] *Lovesick* (1930; lyrics by Marks, published by Marks Music), while adhering to a conventional structure, also uses more advanced harmonies throughout, showing Schuman's desire to portray in musical terms the malady the singer is suffering. And in *Waitin' for the Moon* (1932; lyrics by Schuman, published by Marks Music), both the words ("I'm feelin' blue and low") and the music draw heavily from jazz and the blues, with bent melodic notes, thick chocolaty chords, tangy harmonic progressions, and a surprise of a radiant major chord after the relentless minor mode. The song makes one imagine that Persin asked Schuman if he was listening and singing Gershwin as well as Rodgers, so strong are the similarities to "The Man I Love" (1927) and even to moments in the yet-to-be-heard *Porgy and Bess* (1935). Indeed, an in-house publication called the song "the latest example of that particular type of semi-negroid music at which American composers seem to be so talented."[21]

All of this illustrates Schuman's flourishing talents at the time and that Schuman did more than compose music to the lyrics of others. According to a notebook in which Schuman listed more than 110 songs he helped to create, no fewer than 12 have lyrics that he wrote. In addition, he also wrote lyrics for other songwriters' tunes. His listing indicates that he collaborated with at least ten different people, two of whom were female, and four of whom were his childhood friends: Marks, Rosenthal, Nauheim, and Loesser.

After both Schuman and Loesser began to achieve fame independently, their youthful collaboration rose in prominence, overshadowing nearly all of Schuman's other Tin Pan Alley efforts. The two boys met when the Schumans moved back to Manhattan from Far Rockaway, but after Bill enrolled at Speyer and became close friends with his Cobbossee companions, he and Loesser saw little of each other. Their mutual interest in songwriting brought them back together in the late 1920s, when they managed to publish one of their songs ("In Love with a Memory of You," Feist Music, 1931) and record two others, perhaps the sole artifact of Schuman's short-lived career as a singer.[22]

Loesser was indisputably Schuman's steadiest partner after Marks turned his attention to his studies, and Schuman's popular song notebook contains a list of 12 of their songs by title and implies, through the numbering of those songs, that their projected *Da Vinci Opera Comique* would also consist of 12 independent songs. But the later assertion that he and Loesser composed around 40 songs finds no support in the song notebook.[23] Loesser's recollection of their partnership is also silent on how many songs they wrote together, focusing instead on the futile industry Schuman displayed in his music making. Loesser commented on the pathetic quality of Schuman's playing on both the violin and the piano. But what stuck in Loesser's mind was Schuman's vibration of the piano key in emulation of what a skilled violinist is taught to do.

> I should have known then and during the year that followed that he'd never be happy as a Tin Pan Alley songwriter. I should have known that he would always have the little finger wiggling vainly on the keys in a desperate wish to hear music that couldn't possibly be produced through such a medium. . . . At the time Bill was not at all well educated musically, but he could already see his own path beyond such accomplishments as "In Love With the Memory of You," "Waitin' for the Moon," etc.[24]

Had Loesser forgotten that he didn't write the words for *Waitin' for the Moon*? Was he simply referring to one of the few Tin Pan Alley songs that Schuman got published? Or was he distancing himself from all of those unsuccessful efforts, not unlike Schuman's quip that Loesser's only real flop was their one published song?[25]

Though Loesser saw Schuman's path forward, Schuman himself was a bit slower to abandon Tin Pan Alley. Marks Music published at least two of his arrangements for flute and piano in 1931 (*Glow-Worm* and *Parade of the Wooden Soldiers*), *Waitin' for the Moon* the following year, and then the art song *God's World* in the year after that. His activities during these years are recounted in a 1944 feature in the magazine *Musical America* called "Meet the Composer."

> Schuman worked for popular music publishers writing songs, preparing night club and vaudeville material and even engaging in that bizarre nocturnal enterprise known as song-plugging in which he covered a nightly beat of clubs, hotels, dance halls and all other "spots" where popular music is performed, drumming business for new songs, his own and others. He lived and worked in this hectic atmosphere for several years. . . .

> When he reached his majority, Schuman began the study of counterpoint with Charles Haubiel and, at 23 entered Columbia University, where he subsequently received Bachelor's and Master's degrees in music.
>
> For a year and a half he experimented with a kind of dual life in which he tried to spend half the year in Tin Pan Alley and the other half closeted with his more serious musical projects. But the combination refused to jell. He found himself unconsciously writing down to the commercial standards in his popular compositions and he also found himself more and more at odds with the banalities of the Alley, which, despite its reputation for frenzy and unpredictability, is one of the most conservative, conventional and tradition-ridden communities in music.
>
> So Schuman, severed at last from the commerce of Broadway, went back to Columbia.[26]

Even with this report, the chronology of the Tin Pan Alley years is difficult to fix with certainty. Did he turn his back on the Alley in November 1932, when he began lessons with Haubiel, or in the fall of 1933, when he began his studies at Columbia? (The article author seems to infer that Schuman went back to Columbia on two separate occasions, which is inaccurate.)

Here again, the letters Schuman sent to Marks provide clues. In May 1931, after the publication of their *Lovesick*, and well after the life-altering concert of April 4, 1930, Schuman writes to Marks about their latest efforts.

> I thought the lyrics on the whole were good; not however consistantly [*sic*] so. Considering the time you did them and your mental attitude I think you did marvels but really you have done and will do much better. The only one that I didn't care for at all was "TELL ME WHERE I STAND." You asked me to express myself on the subject and I have been truthful. I've as much confidence as ever in your lyrical ability and look forward to the day when we'll share a mutual enthusiasm, which I am convinced can and must be present for SchuMarks to produce something really good.[27]

It is the last mention of collaboration that Schuman or Marks makes. A letter from Marks on a 1932 summer sojourn to Europe survives; addressed to "Naushu" (Nauheim and Schuman), there is no mention of songwriting whatever.[28] By then, all of Schuman's Tin Pan Alley songs and arrangements had been published; yet to come would be his last effort with Marks Music, *God's World*, a setting of a poem by Edna St. Vincent Millay. He would write some new songs and recycle one old one for a camp show when he was a counselor at Brant Lake in 1934. But by the summer of 1932, when he began his studies at the Juilliard School of Music's Summer Institute, Schuman's Tin Pan Alley days were receding in the distance.

One thing is clear, though, from this distance: with the list of their forty songs at the head of Schuman's song notebook, Marks was the lyricist Schuman had foremost in his mind as the Hart to his Rodgers, the Gilbert to his Sullivan. The stories of Loesser and Schuman working together on variety material in the offices of Feist Music Co. are compelling, and it is indisputable that the two worked on a musical of the life of Leonardo da Vinci that, given the numbering in Schuman's notebook, may have included as many as 14 songs. But that same notebook lists 20 songs from the "unproduced musical satire *With All Due Respect*," with lyrics by Marks, and among Marks's papers is a 90-page, two-act script for the show, with dialogue by F. A. (Ferd) Nauheim and David Geldman, lyrics by Marks, and music by Schuman. The script clearly indicates that this musical was based upon the second of the two Cobbossee shows from 1928, *Tell It to the Judge*, and the date on the title page—1931—shows that Marks and Schuman believed enough in that earlier sketch to elaborate on it three years later.[29] The Loesser collaboration makes for entertaining storytelling; the Marks collaboration was just as important, if not more so, to Schuman.

Equally entertaining and important is how the "creation myth" emerged, the tale of Schuman being dumbstruck at the sound of the New York Philharmonic and of his deciding then and there to become a serious composer. For starters, there was always a kernel of truth to it, as there is in every good story. And the closer in time one gets to the events recounted in the myth, the closer one gets to the truth. The 1944 profile on Schuman provides a thorough account of that seminal moment in Schuman's life.

> At the suggestion of his mother, Schuman decided to investigate the mysteries of symphonic music and, at the age of 19 he made the acquaintance of the New York Philharmonic-Symphony. The main impression he carried away from the first concert was wonderment at the ability of so many people to bow stringed instruments in unison. He virtually haunted Carnegie Hall thereafter for five or six years. He attended all the orchestral performances, including repetitions, and took to carrying scores with him. This could be a very expensive routine, but, according to Schuman, "there are ways for students to hear concerts in Carnegie Hall without parting with money." For example, it is possible to tarry over-long in the lounge after a matinee and emerge just in time for the evening performance.[30]

Schuman was not alone among his friends to appreciate the Philharmonic. Marks and Woodrow Sandler, another poker-playing buddy, had subscribed to the Philharmonic at some point during the Toscanini years (1928–36).[31] Schuman, however, was obsessed with both Carnegie Hall and the Philharmonic in those early years, for his early knowledge of the symphonic repertoire rested on his knowledge of Carnegie Hall's hideaways and his keen hunger for the sound of the orchestra. He recalled that period of his life for Isaac Stern, the man who almost singlehandedly kept Carnegie Hall from being bulldozed.

> Carnegie Hall became my second home. My education in music revolved around the offerings of the Hall where I spent four or five evenings per week, hearing the repeat performances of symphonic concerts and many other events as well. . . . The personal drama of going to the Hall first as a neophyte student and later as a composer completed the circle and has left me grateful beyond measure.[32]

There is no reason not to believe that Schuman haunted Carnegie Hall after his sister took him there on April 4, 1930, and that it was a seminal event in his life.

But the "creation myth" as Schuman spun it permits other stories to emerge unchallenged. One is the importance of his work with Loesser, playing up the amazing coincidence that these two geniuses would go unrecognized in their early years. In contrast, throughout his lifetime Loesser worked to puncture what he felt were Schuman's inflated views of the performing arts. His 1948 letter to Vincent Persichetti was the source of much of the "campus cutup" material that got Persichetti cashiered as Schuman's first biographer and led the management at G. Schirmer, the publisher of the biography, to commission Flora Rheta Schreiber to write the biographical portion of the book and leave the analytical portion to Persichetti. (At the time, Schuman was a publications advisor to Schirmer.) In that letter, Loesser skewered Schuman's uptown/downtown personae and how he adopted the former for the performing arts elite and the latter for his childhood buddies. And in a 1965 letter, Loesser again took a shot at Schuman and the artistic enterprises Schuman represented, making it clear that although he admired his friend's industry, he questioned the ideology behind the industry. (Loesser: "THE PERFORMING ARTS ARE NOT NECESSARILY THE NIFTY PERFORMING ARTS, or THE DIVINE PERFORMING ARTS or THE ACCREDITED PERFORMING ARTS.")[33]

Schuman would later attribute Loesser's veiled hostility to Schuman's forays into concert music as demonstrating tensions within Loesser's psyche.[34] But what makes Loesser's wrestling with his past germane to Schuman's "creation myth" is a small incident that happened shortly after Schuman saw Loesser's 1948 letter. Later that year, a journalist from the *Saturday Evening Post* wrote to Schuman. "I'm getting together some dope for a story on Frank Loesser and wonder if you remember a couple of anecdotes from the days when two brash but apparently talented youngsters named Schuman and Loesser tried to sell your first songs to vaudeville performers and so on?" Schuman wrote back a letter that is unbelievable, if one accepts the idea of Schuman's fantastic recall for conversations and events. "I can think of no anecdotes about Loesser and I am not sure in general what it is that you would like me to tell you about him. If you will call me some afternoon, I will do my best to answer your questions." The ensuing article contains but one paragraph that mentions Schuman (on the last page of the story) and no dope whatsoever from him. After Loesser's letter to Persichetti, perhaps Schuman recalled the adage, Once burned, twice shy.[35] Schuman, too, had issues.

By the time Schuman assumed the Juilliard presidency in 1945, he had begun to burnish his image. This required finding a way to fold his NYU experience into a larger narrative without revealing his abysmal performance there. Linking arms with Loesser and stressing the ground-shifting effect of the Philharmonic concert helped to clothe the Tin Pan Alley years in more virtuous vesture. Schuman also actively chose to make it difficult for scholars to examine his Tin Pan Alley efforts. In sending some of his materials to the Library of Congress, he wrote words that would mortify any student of history. "I am glad you liked my [published] popular song, but regret to tell you that I carry most of them in my head, since some years ago I took the precaution of destroying the manuscripts."[36] Still, some manuscripts may survive in private collections, such as the undated waltz song *Once More*, whose lyrics were sent to the Library of Congress and whose manuscript turned up in the papers of Eddie Marks.[37]

Between the destruction of the scores and the *mésalliance* of Loesser and the Philharmonic, Schuman's efforts to recast the Tin Pan Alley years also sought to bury his rowdy activities. Like Loesser, Ferd Nauheim gave Persichetti plenty of material to paint Schuman and himself as frat boys in search of a frat house.

> It was the Speakeasy era and we enjoyed the atmosphere, the feeling of lawlessness, the things that happened in speaks. Billy and I especially enjoyed going to one, particularly with a couple of girls, with the full knowledge that we had no money between us, just to see what would happen. Something usually did. . . .
>
> Looking back, it seems to me that most of the time we went places and did things sans females, at least that would be true in the early evening. . . .
>
> Bill and I rented a furnished apartment in the village. We lived at our respective homes but the apartment was a grand spot for parties and bull sessions. When we were thrown out of there because we had bleached the piano white with a spilled bottle of whiskey, we found a basement apartment on West Seventy-sixth Street near Riverside Drive. That was more convenient to our homes and we made more use of it. (Schuman volunteered that his parents didn't know about these bachelor apartments.)[38]

Schuman would often say that his parents avoided gossip of all kinds, and he once joked with Leonard Bernstein about the propriety his parents had taught him. Bernstein's letter had contained a profanity; Schuman responded: "Your marvelous letter . . . is being framed and will soon be placed in Macy's window. The reason: My mother told me never to write anything in a letter that couldn't be placed in Macy's window."[39] Some of the letters Schuman sent to Marks would have horrified his mother, and while his buddies continued well into their adulthood being fairly forthright about their escapades as young adults, Schuman was much more circumspect. The sheer number of his girlfriends would have probably caused some embarrassment and consternation among the administrators at Sarah Lawrence, an all-women's college that would be his employer a few years after his Tin Pan Alley days. His circumspection toward these years seems drawn from a combination of his upbringing, his professional engagements, and his rapid elevation into an elite society where certain fictions were expected and tolerated. By the end of his life, Schuman had so bathed the

Tin Pan Alley years in the light of the Philharmonic concert that he himself believed the fiction: "College—I quit after I heard the symphony." "I *know* it was the next day."[40] But the facts that do remain show Schuman at this time to resemble the characters and the stories Loesser would immortalize in *Guys and Dolls*. Schuman said in an interview when he was in his sixties:

> I drank too much at night, bum gin, and I wore a dirty hat, and I was an absolutely loathsome character. . . . If I give you the impression that I was wild, it's true, it's true. But I was not wild ever in the sense of breaking a law, nothing like that. . . . I was a perfectly normal young man growing up in that ambiance in New York, nothing more—but certainly nothing less.[41]

Unlike the ending of *Guys and Dolls*, the prospect of marriage was still somewhat in the distance. But not too far.

FIVE

FRANKIE

Frances Prince came by her nickname legitimately.[1] In letters to her parents while she was away at camp in the summer of 1927, all of which are signed "Frankie," the 14-year-old was direct and unsentimental as she wrote about relatives, counselors, acquaintances, fellow campers, and herself with little embellishment.

> Just got a letter from Harriet—she took four pages to tell me she had nothing to say and that she was on the toilet writing the letter. That's what you call news.
>
> In daddy's last letter he said that my questioning whether he had his vacation yet meant that I wanted you to come here. Well it didn't. I consider it a nuisance having parents come to see you, especially so late in the season.
>
> There's really nothing much to say but I feel like writing letters so I'm taking it out on you.
>
> In case you didn't notice on the post-card please send stockings for me to come home in. Do not delay.[2]

One can understand Bill's hesitation in writing to her shortly after he met her four years later.

> This is the third attempt I've made this eve at sending you these tickets. I thought I ought write one of those clever notes to properly impress you.
>
> Please take my word Frankie, this is a clever note; for the way I feel right now it is, in fact, brilliant; but as I hear you say "uh'huh" I seem to lose all confidence.[3]

These letters and her educational career together give the impression that Frankie was not easily impressed.

Born on June 12, 1913, Frankie had earned her bachelor's degree from Barnard College before turning 20. Her early IQ scores earned her a place in accelerated and experimental classes, and, in a strange twist of fate, Leta S. Hollingworth, the Columbia professor and child psychologist who worked with Frankie and other "fast learners" at P.S. 165, would later restructure the Speyer School that Bill attended. Given Schuman's tendency to embellish stories, it may be wise to discount his claim

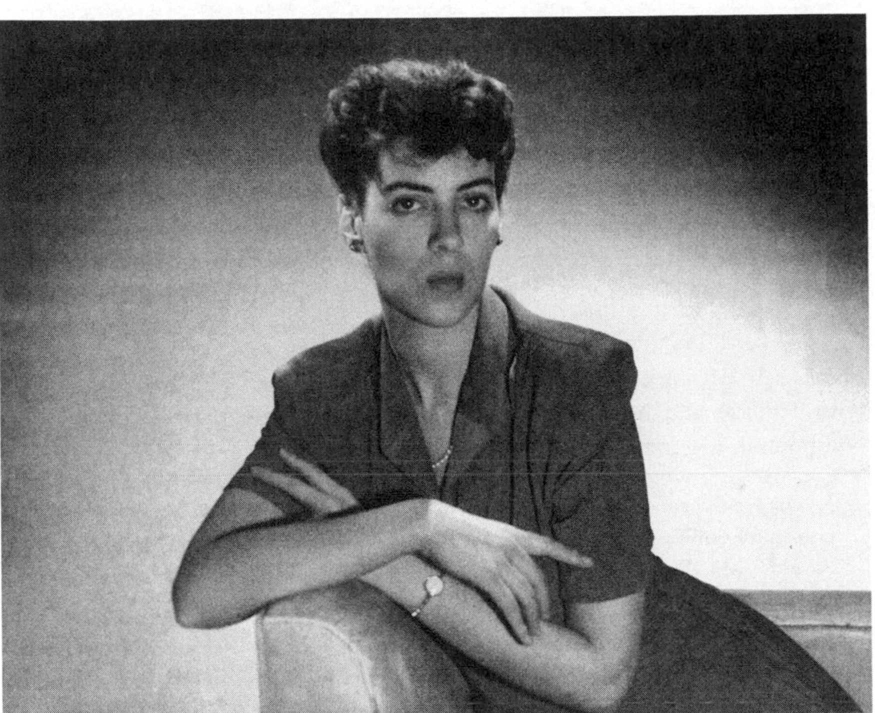

Frances Prince Schuman.

that Frankie's IQ was as high as that of Albert Einstein, but she probably did score above 150 and may even have been one of the three Jewish students whom Hollingworth identified as having IQ scores above 180.[4] Bill certainly had his own legitimate claims to being a bright student—and an occasionally indolent one as well—but Frankie eclipsed him academically in those early days. And although they once lived in the same apartment building, attended the same elementary and high schools, and had cousins who were close friends, the two of them didn't know each other prior to their college years. Besides, "he was three years older than I—and you know what that meant then" (presumably, that they ran in different social circles).[5]

Frankie wasn't the kind of girl Billy seemed to be interested in at the time. She graduated from George Washington High at the age of 16, with a New York State Regents' scholarship in hand that she sought to use at Cornell. Her parents, Leonard and Gertrude, were liberal, secular German American Jews and far more progressive than the Schumans were. Gertrude had graduated from Hunter College; Leonard had a law degree from NYU and was known as a scholar of Latin. But they objected to the idea of their only child attending a coed school, so Frankie went away to the North Carolina College for Women in Greensboro. After a year there, the culture clash was too much for her, so she transferred to Barnard and lived at home when she began her studies there in the fall of 1931.[6]

The Princes and the Loessers knew each other, and the sequence of events of when Billy met Frankie is forever lost in a fog of memories and their elaborations. Frank Loesser recalled the circumstances rather blandly and got the timing wrong. "[Bill and I] met again when we were about eighteen through a mutual friend named Frances Prince to whom, as you know, he is now married."[7] Schuman remembered Loesser playing a more theatrical role in bringing the two together. "[He] said to Frankie Prince that he was working with the young man that she was going to marry. And if he didn't, that he was going to marry her. And I met Frankie, not through [him] but through a friend."[8] That friend—Ferd Nauheim—remembered yet another aspect of how Bill met Frankie. At Barnard, Frankie would invite her classmate Bea Strasburger to visit with Frankie and her parents at the Princes' apartment. Bea married Ferd Nauheim in the summer of 1934. Ferd:

> I think I am accurate in recalling that Frankie and Bill met for the first time when I arranged a double date and the four of us went to a speakeasy called Ralph's at 124th St. and B'way. [Perhaps Nauheim meant either La Salle St. or 125th St., since 124th St. does not intersect Broadway. Assuming he had the general proximity correct, the speakeasy was in Harlem.] We ran up a bill of about $15 and Bill and I had $1.50 between us. The girls paid. After we took them to their homes we went to Tip Toe Inn and ran up another bill, then sat around till four in the morning before somebody we knew came in and bailed us out. That was the auspicious beginning of his romance with Frankie Prince.[9]

And after such an auspicious beginning, Frankie's "uh'huh"—the one Bill recounted in his letter to her—must have been withering.

In comparison to Schuman's upbringing, Frankie's had far more highbrow culture. She took piano lessons with a highly respected New York teacher. She and her parents attended orchestra concerts and piano recitals well before meeting Bill. At his camp, he was reading about Boy Scout adventures; at her camp, she was reading the latest offerings by Fannie Hurst and Heywood Broun, two popular writers of the day.[10] So in setting his sights on Frankie, Bill was aiming higher than he had aimed with Louise or Désirée or Evelyn, his other girlfriends of the time. Frankie was a catch, and he tried his best to catch her.

Take, for example, the end of his "clever note": "Je perds le paix sans trouver le bonheur." Schuman's attempt at elegance displays his somewhat limited grasp of French—"paix" is feminine—but also hints at some hidden message between him and Frankie. Had they encountered the Beethoven romance (WoO 128) that uses this anonymous text?

> Plaisir d'aimer, besoin d'une âme tendre
> Que vous avez de pouvoir sur mon coeur.
> De vous, hélas, en voulant me défendre
> Je perds la paix sans trouver le bonheur.

(The pleasure of loving, the need of a tender soul,
what power over my heart you have!
Wanting to protect myself from you, alas,
I lose my peace of mind without finding happiness.)

And the tickets he included may have been for Eugene O'Neill's new play that had opened a few weeks earlier at the Guild Theatre on West Fifty-second Street (now the August Wilson Theatre). By then, the Princes had moved out of the Hotel Franconia on West Seventy-second Street. Bill and Frankie saw the play, a six-hour trilogy that made for a psychologically intense experience so early in their relationship. In his review of the production, Brooks Atkinson remarked that "the curse that the fates have set against the New England house of Mannon is no trifling topic for a casual dramatic discussion, but a battering into the livid mysteries of life."[11] Decades later, Bill recalled that evening and its ramifications.

> We went and saw *Mourning Becomes Electra* and I walked her home, from the 40s [*sic*] to 96th Street, and we began to, as the phrase went in those days, "keep company." Obviously, our attraction was very strong, and both parents said, if we got married, we could come and live with them, but they both said this is not a good idea, but if we wanted to do it, it was our decision. . . . I wanted to wait until I had a job, Frankie also said I wanted to wait until she "made good."[12]

He pursued Frankie when they both spent summers on Martha's Vineyard, and back in New York he concocted a way to spend concentrated time with her by roping his old violin teacher Blanche Schwartz into the picture. Schuman reminded Schwartz about the setup: "I wanted to take violin lessons again, and we had a three-way barter. You taught me violin, I taught Frankie harmony and counterpoint (What a way to go after a girl!), and I believe Frankie taught you some Italian."[13]

As it happened, Frankie "made good" a lot sooner than Bill did. She held a series of odd jobs after graduation before she landed a position in 1935 as a counselor for the Vocational Advisory Service in New York City, a job she would hold for the next 14 years.[14] She worked primarily with handicapped individuals, though she also counseled youth. And she was restless, looking for some other work where her ideas might be better put to use. In early 1937, she sought out Hollingworth for some advice. Hollingworth had had to battle the strictures that male chauvinism imposed upon her in her own career, so she gave her young protégé—by then a year into her marriage—some counsel on being a working woman in urban America.

> Dear Frances:
>
> I was much interested to hear of your contact with the Girl Scouts. Of course nothing may come of such contact, but it is interesting, in any case, to elicit the attitudes of people toward one's ideas.

> The way upward, toward finally reaching what one wants in professional endeavor is often thro' manual work (at least so I found it, in my own youth); doing housework at home, and studying a few courses at a time. It is an absolute principle of mine that a woman should carry her own weight economically, in a marriage, either by doing the work of the home, or by earning a salary outside. Sometimes it's best to do the one; sometimes, the other. It all depends on individual circumstances, as to which is best.
>
> The job you already have seems quite good to me. There probably aren't many better jobs in that field for a person of your age. Couldn't you keep it, and "take" additional courses, evenings?
>
> . . . After May 10th, I should like to have you and Mr. Schuman take dinner with me, at the Faculty Club, and we can have a good visit afterwards. I will write to you about it.
>
> Sincerely yours,
>
> Leta S. Hollingworth[15]

Bill's career hadn't mushroomed yet, so Frankie's pursuit of her own career options both suited the practical purpose of bringing in income and provided Frankie a chance to explore her personal ambitions. And it was relatively easy, living on Riverside Drive and having no children, to be in the workforce alongside her husband.

Their visit to see Frank Loesser in 1940, then living in California, would change that. Loesser lived in a house, and Bill returned intent on living in a home of his own as well. At the time, Frankie put a good face on the decision to move to the suburbs. "We came back, found a house and were settled in it within two months. . . . We knew so many people and there was so much going on, we decided the distance would be a good barrier."[16] But later in their lives, Bill provided a different take on how Frankie felt about leaving Manhattan.

> Frankie can wax eloquent on the horrors of growing up in the suburbs. It all started when we visited Frank Loesser, and I said, "Frank has a house, why are we living in New York?" And Frankie claims that for twenty-one years she hated living in Westchester; I never knew that. Even today, I think, she would elect to stay in New York with children.[17]

Part of staying in New York with children would have probably meant staying employed and having her own career. But she accepted and adapted to the demands of suburbia, by scaling back her job and then giving it up entirely, by finding worthy causes to volunteer her time and talents to, and by supporting the aspirations of her husband, whose fame emerged not long after the move first to Larchmont and then to New Rochelle.[18]

"They had a joke that there were only two things that Bill was responsible for in terms of the household: filling the car with gas and keeping the bar stocked. Frankie ran everything else."[19] And she would not allow herself to get run over, either. "My first move after our marriage was being firm about a six-day, not a seven-day working week. [Bill] fought for a while, but when he discovered the delights of a day off—it's worked ever since."[20] Her choice of charitable outlets went beyond the white-glove, garden-club type that the wives of successful businessmen might be expected to join. Indeed, it's striking to read the extensive profile given her in a Westchester County newspaper in 1962 and find no mention of the organizations to which she gave her time. (The article does mention how Frankie, a third-generation New Yorker, "discovered in the suburbs the valid joys of gardening.") One may conclude that the readers might have found the organizations unconventional at best and subversive at worst. She was a founding member and officer of: the South Westchester Cerebral Palsy Association; the Volunteer Service Bureaus of the City of New Rochelle and Westchester County; and the Urban League of Westchester County, the local affiliate of "the nation's oldest and largest community-based movement dedicated to empowering African Americans to enter the economic and social mainstream."[21]

In her politics and her progressivism, she was generally ahead of Bill, who tended to be more conservative than his wife. Tony Schuman recalled the story that when the radio broadcast the news that Franklin Delano Roosevelt had died, his mother was so overcome with emotion that she dropped him, then 16 months old, from her lap. She later suggested to him that he base his senior high school speech on school segregation in New Rochelle, and it would be she who would assuage her husband's mind when Tony became more radical in outlook than either of his parents.[22] When they moved back to New York City in 1963, she immediately renewed her affiliation with her former employer, the Vocational Advisory Service. And after a brush with death—Frankie was treated for breast cancer in 1965—she became even more active as a volunteer in organizations that she helped found and that live on to the present day.

Frankie also became something of a musical confidante to her husband, as he shared his creative work with her and she unflinchingly gave her impressions.

> It never occurs to me not to play music for Frankie. She is the best critic that I've ever had, including Copland and Harris and everybody else because she loves me, and therefore she knows sort of instinctively and intuitively what it is I am up to and what I can do. She has always been able to express it, even to this day. I was playing her the introduction the other day of a new piece that I am fussing with—a new chamber music work [most likely *In Sweet Music* (1978)]—and she said: "I find it amorphous," and we had a long discussion about it, and I would try to explain to her why it wasn't amorphous. But I've been doing it with her for so many years . . . and being best friends for so many years and sharing everything, we naturally share that—and every kind of idea, whatever it is. As I say, we never stopped talking together, which is, I am sure, not unusual with happily married people, but this certainly extends to the area of ideas—every kind of idea. Lord, we never stop—she telling me about what she is doing, and my questioning it and this and that. That is the way it goes on.[23]

And as Bill's best friend, she was a confidante in other areas, telling him which girls in the Sarah Lawrence Chorus had crushes on him and kibitzing with him about which of their acquaintances might be gay.[24]

Mark Schubart—one such gay man, an early and devoted friend to both Bill and Frankie, and Bill's lieutenant in so many endeavors at Juilliard and Lincoln Center—reflected upon Frankie's life shortly after she died in 1994, two years after Bill:

> Yes, there was wifely devotion and wifely admiration. But there was also a strongly individual mind at work there, a whole person with other interests and other dimensions, and an exceptionally engaged way of sizing up the world. . . . [She was] a friendly but analytical counselor who always managed to combine tough, practical advice with great warmth and great understanding.[25]

Inge Heckel, Frankie's assistant in the 1960s at Channel 13, New York City's public television station, recalled the words of Sir Walter Scott when it came to Frankie: the will to do, the soul to dare. And in his decision to "keep company" with Frankie, to woo her, and to make her his companion for life, Schuman strove to make himself worthy of her. He had to elevate himself, curtail the Tin Pan Alley habits, and reinvent himself as a serious man with serious intentions. (Eugene O'Neill, after all, was a step up from Harry Lauder, the vaudevillian Bill adored in his childhood.) And while his courtship of Frankie cannot bear the full weight of Schuman's redirection and newfound industry, it is worth remembering that one of his last collaborative endeavors with Eddie Marks came around the same time that Ferd and Bill went out with Bea and Frankie. If there was an epiphany that radically changed Schuman's life, it wasn't the New York Philharmonic in the spring of 1930. It was Frankie in the fall of 1931.

SIX

AN UNCONVENTIONAL EDUCATION

March 4, 1933, was another red-letter day in Schuman's life. The year before had presented him with his first opportunity to vote in a presidential election. To celebrate the momentous change sweeping a downtrodden nation, he, Eddie Marks, and Ferd Nauheim attended the inauguration of Franklin Delano Roosevelt on that March day. "We stood a long way off, but we were there."[1]

The Schumans neither had great investments to lose during the Great Depression nor did they struggle during those years. The 1930 U.S. Census shows that, unlike most of their neighbors at 605 West 112th Street, they had a live-in servant. Ray's family had holdings in real estate, and Sam kept his job at Oberly & Newell throughout the Depression. The two of them had enough money to take Audrey and Bill and their niece Lucille Sonn in May 1931 to Europe first-class on the SS *Resolute*. Whether they had been saving for the trip or were taking advantage of a rate cut advertised a few months before they embarked, the fact that the five of them could travel at all in 1931, let alone in comfort, makes it plain that the Schumans did not want for much during the Depression.[2]

In 1932, when the average weekly wage fell to $17, Bill was pulling down nearly that in an allowance. "My father gave me $60 a month, and that doesn't sound like very much, but I lived at home and . . . $60 a month, if you didn't have any rent to pay, was enough to take care of your needs, and that was considered very liberal."[3] It was certainly enough to cover the bachelor pads that he and Ferd rented. And it was also enough to enable him to pay for private lessons in composition, first with Max Persin beginning in 1929, and then with Charles Trowbridge Haubiel from November 1932 to April 1934.

Schuman did not preserve his exercises with Persin, so it is difficult to know precisely when he ended his studies with him. But the song *God's World*, so

Ray, Audrey, Sam, and Bill Schuman in Bellagio, Italy, 1931.

different from the other Tin Pan Alley songs in sound and scope and text, sets the composition apart as a masterpiece in the original sense of the word, as though the journeyman composer offered this work as evidence that his apprenticeship is over. The earlier blues-inflected "Waitin' for the Moon," whose contract was signed on January 28, 1932, does little to prepare the listener for the daring of this song, finished before summer arrived that year.[4] In choosing words by poet Edna St. Vincent Millay, Schuman turned his back on the popular lyricists of the day. The melody is almost entirely through-composed, with few repetitions and myriad unexpected leaps and accidentals strewn across its 57 bars. Simple triads are few and far between, with Schuman preferring five- and six-note chords that defy traditional analysis on their own and in juxtaposition with their jangly neighbors. The music begins in one key (F major) for the first stanza, moves to a second, related key (B♭ major) for the second stanza, and ends with a harmony that refuses to privilege one key over the other. And the markings in the score—*con desiderio, libermente, con fervore, con brio, dolce e cantabile, morendo*—all signal an escape from the world of commercial publishing.

It is a wonder that Marks Music published the song at all. The bare-bones cover and the absence of any advertisements of the company's other wares suggests that this, like the songs from *It's Up to Pa*, was more of a vanity publication than one meant to make any money for the company. But for Schuman, it began a new approach to composing, as seen in two other works from 1932.

His *Adoration*, a setting of the *Aleinu* from the *Union Prayerbook for Jewish Worship*, borrows the same key scheme from *God's World*, and while the harmonies and melody are much tamer than the earlier song—Schuman suggested that *Adoration* was reminiscent of Saint-Saëns—one can easily understand how the cantor at Temple Shaaray Tefila had a difficult time bringing life to Schuman's setting. The entire experience further darkened Schuman's already negative views toward the synagogue. Two of the three versions of *Adoration* have the words from the Jewish service, but the third is stripped of the text and rearranged for string quintet, an early indication of Schuman's difficulties with organized religion generally and Reform Judaism in particular. He would be approached later in life to write something specifically for the Yom Kippur service, but he found no sympathy with the words in the *Prayerbook* and could not find a suitable substitute. His celebration of the divine was more earthbound, more pagan, more like that of Millay and like another poet to whom he would turn later in life, Walt Whitman.[5]

The other work from 1932, *Potpourri (Impressions of Bohemian Life)*, was an outgrowth of Schuman's first serious classroom study of music. After his Carnegie Hall baptism in 1930, he had regularly attended orchestral concerts with scores in hand. And he would listen to orchestral music with some of his buddies, including Frank Loesser. But although he was learning harmony with Persin, he remained untutored in other aspects of music. To rectify the situation, he enrolled in the Juilliard Summer School in 1932, taking two courses, each six weeks long, in orchestration and advanced theory. The latter was a stretch for him: he earned a grade of "C." But he excelled at orchestration and received an "A" for his work in that class. The teacher, Adolf Schmid, assigned piano pieces for the students to orchestrate, and Schuman did work up part of Chopin's Etude in E major, op. 10, no. 3, transposing it to F major. Schuman was somewhat self-conscious about his effort, though—perhaps Schmid hadn't assigned this particular piano piece or had spoken of its pianism being hard to transfer to an orchestral palette—so he attached a short note to the assignment. "I did not intend this Etude (scored for wood winds and strings) to be a practical orchestration. I did it only as a theoretic exercise and for the personal benefit derived." Note or not, Schmid liked Schuman's effort here. As for his other work in the course, Schuman apparently eschewed the assignments handed out by Schmid. Some years later, James Robertson, a former fellow student in Schmid's class who was by then musical director of the Wichita Symphony Orchestra, reminded Schuman of Schuman's unusual approach to assignments in the class. "I remember distinctly that on several occasions you brought in orchestrations of pieces you had written instead of doing the piano works that Schmidt had assigned."[6] And indeed, two other scores from that summer are the *Adoration*, sans vocalist and arranged for string orchestra, and the "Serenade Appassionato," the last of the three violin-piano Songs without Words, arranged for full orchestra. While Schmid's red pen is nowhere in evidence on the *Adoration* score, the serenade received the same notation as the Chopin etude: VG (very good).

So *Potpourri* is as much an essay in timbre as a composition in its own right. An oleo of various moods and gestures, it starts out with a rhythmic tattoo similar to the vaudeville song "Ta-ra-ra Boom-de-ay" and continues in a herky-jerky fashion through a parade of different episodes that are delineated by changes in tempo and a forest of fermatas. Someone (perhaps Schuman) identified ten sections using Roman numerals and a red pencil, and the overall form is that of a modified rondo, not unlike another bohemian musical impression, Gershwin's *An American in Paris* (1928). One of the work's notable features, given Schuman's later predilection for this sound, is an extended solo for bass clarinet in the second and sixth sections. Harmonically and melodically, it is less adventurous than *God's World* or *Adoration*, but, strikingly, like both of those works, it begins in the key of F major. And the occasional presence of parallel octaves in the more linear sections—a mortal sin to the pure contrapuntalist—demonstrate that although Schuman made great strides in harmony and orchestration in 1932, counterpoint still eluded him. *Cradle Song* for piano, dedicated to the firstborn of Hazel S. and Sidney M. Wittner and dated January 31, 1933, similarly shows a lack of contrapuntal engagement, featuring instead a rocking figure of undulating arpeggios in the left hand, sustained chords in the right hand, and occasional parallel motion in both hands over the course of its foursquare 32 bars.[7] (This song bears no relationship to the earlier "Cradle Song," the first of the Three Songs without Words for Violin and Piano.)

Studies with Haubiel would address Schuman's contrapuntal shortcomings. He remembered that it was Blanche Schwarz, his violin teacher, who recommended Haubiel to him, and though Haubiel taught at New York University, it is doubtful Schuman would have made any contact with him during Schuman's business school years. In the '20s, Haubiel (1892–1978) studied composition with Rosario Scalero (1870–1954), a brilliant contrapuntalist in his own right who would later go to the Curtis Institute, where he became Samuel Barber's principal composition teacher. Scalero's letters to Haubiel reveal the younger man to be a challenging and demanding student.

> . . . I am very glad in seeing your intense work, but, please, keep a rest before you begin again, because the work of next winter will be most important for you.
>
> Concerning all questions you speak from in your letter, I think they are too important for being treated in a letter, expecially [*sic*] I am very busy in these last day of my remaining in Europe. . . .

> We will speak exaustingly [*sic*] of all questions when I am in New York.
>
> In every case keep your mind quiet; everything will be all right, I am sure, because, after all, you are more advanced than you think.[8]

Schuman proved to be every bit as intense as Haubiel. Schuman remembered that Haubiel would say, "'Bring in eight or ten examples of this next week,' and I would bring in a hundred. I would stay at my desk all day, writing out strict counterpoint—whatever it was. (I hope this doesn't sound like I'm bragging; I'm not, I'm being descriptive.) When you've started later, you have to make up for lost time, and that propelled me to do this."[9] The five counterpoint notebooks Schuman numbered and dated back up his recollection nearly 60 years later. Lessons were often only days apart, and Schuman would manage to produce dozens of exercises between their sessions together. Throughout the notebooks, Haubiel passed his judgment on Schuman's work: "good"; "okay"; "bad"; "exposed points"; "reserve crossings for 4 parts"; "unprepared." And Schuman mastered the material at an astonishing clip. In little more than a month, Schuman advanced from writing first-species counterpoint to composing two free voices over a cantus firmus, and the last two notebooks contain the beginnings of double canons and double fugues. Schuman would later defend his approach to counterpoint as focused on the procedures and not on the forms, disputing the notion that terms such as *passacaglia* or *fugue* connoted certain conventions that dictate the architecture of a piece of music.[10] Whether his preference for procedure over form echoes Haubiel's words to him is impossible to know, but the 288 pages of exercises and compositions found in his notebooks give ample proof that Schuman left few things unexplored when it came to weaving together multiple lines of music.

Among the compositions from this period are *Cinq petits préludes a deux voix*, sketches for which appear early in the notebooks. Schuman extracted the preludes in April 1933, dedicating them to Jean Carolene Marks, Eddie Marks's niece, who was born the month before.[11] Schuman wasn't as close to her parents as he was to her uncle, but he was in business with her grandfather, Edward B. Marks Sr., publisher of most of Schuman's music up to this point. Clearly Schuman set his sights on bringing these pieces to a wider public as well. Raymond Burrows, a lecturer in music education at Teachers College, wrote a foreword to the preludes, and given his remarks about Schuman's compositions he must have written the foreword some years after the preludes were composed.

> As I have been impressed by some of the more radical works of this young American composer, I was naturally very much interested in examining these preludes which at a glance seemed to be more conservative numbers. The surprising fact is that they are not conservative at all. The harmonic progressions and the style of the cadences are quite unusual in a group of pieces which avoid obvious dissonance.

> While I think of these numbers chiefly as an interesting short group for concert purposes, they should prove valuable for piano teaching as well. My criticism of most so called "teaching interest" is that it cannot prove its musical as well as its educational value. These pieces are recommended because they have musical worth, because they employ the contrapuntal style, and because they show that music can be constructed along other lines than tonic and dominant harmonies. They should be presented after a student has gained considerable keyboard familiarity, as they have several little technical problems.[12]

The notebooks also contain the manuscripts for a number of other complete works, including the *Four Canonic Choruses* (originally called "Chorale-Canons"), the earliest appearing on July 11, 1933, and the last dated February 16, 1934. Shortly after he completed the first two choruses, Schuman matriculated at Teachers College of Columbia University, where he began studies toward a Bachelor of Science degree. The knowledge he had gained through harmony lessons with Persin, counterpoint lessons with Haubiel (which would continue until at least April 1934), and his haunting of Carnegie Hall enabled him to shave two years from the requirements for the degree. Still, during the summer before his formalized music studies began, Schuman was a restless young man. He had returned to the Juilliard Summer School to study conducting, to learn to play brass instruments, and to sing in the summer chorus. But he also schemed with Eddie Marks to get pretzels, smokes, and beer for some big blowout, and he shared some juicy stories with Woody Sandler, who was a counselor at Twin Lake Camp in Brandon, Vermont. Frankie was in the picture, but Bill hadn't settled in on her yet; her birthday letter to him that summer is signed "Your very good friend."[13] That year she had graduated from Barnard and was entering the workplace. Schuman was doing the opposite. He was putting advertising, printing, and Tin Pan Alley behind him. His dreams of being a composer had to be tempered by the reality that he needed to earn a living, which he determined he could do as a teacher, one of the three vocations (along with medicine and the ministry) he knew his parents revered.

Many of his student peers were several years younger than he, so it is no surprise that at times he chafed against his studies at Teachers College, finding many of the instructors inflexible in approach and ideology. But he also befriended other teachers and profited from the intellectual and philosophical engagement that the best of them had to offer. He particularly enjoyed his course on the aesthetics of music with Peter Dykema, one of the college's most prominent instructors in music. Dykema chose to base the entire course on the newly published *Art as Experience* of John Dewey, and at least one of Dewey's ideas—that "art can be understood only by studying the *interaction* between art object and the audience in experience"—would become a lifelong tenet in Schuman's own approach to music, evident in his insistence that an informed and attentive audience is a key ingredient to the promulgation of all music and particularly contemporary American music.[14]

Schuman was a well-respected student at Teachers College. One of his surviving term papers, "Shakespeare as Chronicler," shows him winning the admiration of his professor through his deft handling of Eliot, Hobbes, and Machiavelli in addition to Shakespeare. In the spring of 1936, in the middle of Schuman's studies of the Master of Arts degree, Dykema approached him to ask if he would be willing to teach a course on acoustics during the summer term. Schuman balked, citing his own limited exposure to the material, and Dykema responded by giving Schuman a course in orchestration and arranging instead.[15] But much of Schuman's éclat at Teachers College came from the steady stream of performances given to his music at the college and beyond.

The end of his first year at the college also marked the end of his studies with Haubiel, and two of the compositions he wrote under his supervision—the first pastorale and the Canon and Fugue for violin, cello, and piano—were performed in a recital of original compositions by Teachers College music education students in May 1934.[16] The first pastorale had a particularly interesting genesis. Having originally conceived the work in the key of B♭ minor for wordless contralto and B♭ clarinet, Schuman re-orchestrated it no fewer than three times: for oboe and clarinet; for violin and clarinet (in which version it was heard over the radio on December 27, 1942); and for two violas, the version first heard in 1934, which was transposed to the key of A♭ minor. Both works appear in the last of the five counterpoint notebooks, and their highly contrapuntal construction—the two-voice pastorale, the three-voice canon, and the five-voice fugue—serves as an artistic summa to Schuman's lessons with Haubiel. But when he was later asked to comment on those lessons, Haubiel had remarkably little to say.

> I am sorry not to have been able to help you with some interesting anecdotes about William Schumann [*sic*]. It happens our association of three years in the 30s when he studied counterpoint with me were exceptionally pleasant. He was one of the pupils for whom I had sincere liking. He was never argumentative, as some of my pupils have been, and in consequence there were no colorful duelling discussions between us. . . . I am really very happy to have had so important a part in the musical education of one of our really successful musical personages.[17]

Their relationship never gelled as either friends or colleagues. Just as Haubiel's intensity led his teacher Scalero to back away from him, so it appears that his most famous student similarly kept him at arm's length. Upon hearing that Schuman had been appointed president of Juilliard in 1945, Haubiel wrote Schuman to ask whether the school might have need of his services as a teacher of counterpoint. Schuman deflected the request by thanking Haubiel for his interest.[18] Several times Haubiel would ask Schuman whether he might persuade someone to publish or perform his music; as Schuman would write to others who had asked him to intercede on their behalf, he told Haubiel that he could not use his position in that way. And when Haubiel sought Schuman's permission to "mention, in my advertising in papers and magazines, the names of my most famous pupils," Schuman responded with "an absolutely frank reply" that under no circumstances would he allow his name to be used toward that end.[19] Further complicating their relationship was Haubiel's separation from NYU in 1947 because of accusations that he was anti-Semitic. Haubiel protested that he was being railroaded by his opponents, but his attitudes, as expressed in a 1946 letter to Marian MacDowell, do nothing to acquit him of the charges against him.

> They are now 100% of a certain persausion [*sic*] in the dept.—which suprised [*sic*] me very much when it was brought to my attention by one of my pupils whom they could not buy, when he gave me a photostatic copy of a page from the Jewish Year Book listing Philip James [then chair of the Music Department at NYU] as a prominent Jewish composer. Or course I can't see why Jews and Christians cant live amicably together, and they do so so frequently (we have a Jewish gentleman living with us in the apt. these past two years). So I'm constrained into supposing the opposition to me in the dept. is purely political (I'm on record as against Communism and the New Deal) or on professional grounds (I'm against all the atonal and politonal [*sic*] principles.[20]

Haubiel's conservatism in musical language and political beliefs, and his extremism in expressing his views, kept him from becoming more to Schuman than a prominent teacher. But Schuman was always gracious in thanking his former teacher not only for his instruction but also for the foundation he laid on which Schuman built nearly all of his subsequent music: "The contrapuntal work I did with you has, of course, remained a mainstay of my compositional technique."[21]

The *Canonic Choruses* completed under Haubiel's tutelage not only exhibited Schuman's mastery of counterpoint but also served as the first work to gain him national, even international, attention. Their premiere on May 8, 1935, took place in another concert featuring original compositions by Teachers College music education students. As with his violin debut with Blanche Schwarz, Schuman held the coveted position of being last on the program, with his "Chorale-Canons" being immediately preceded by two new art songs—*At Daybreak* (no date; text, Walter Conrad Arensberg) and *Sonnet* (April 1935; text, Millay)—and both of his pastorales, played by a trio of violin, clarinet, and flute. (The original instrumentation for the second pastorale in A minor was flute, oboe, and clarinet; the score indicates Schuman substituted the violin for the oboe.) But the choral pieces were the climax for the evening, and Schuman already had a sense of their importance. He had earlier submitted them for the

Joseph H. Bearns Prize in Music, administered by the Music Department of Columbia University and established to encourage American composers under the age of 25. He failed to win the award that year; in fact, the judges decided that none of the entries was distinguished enough to merit the prize. But Schuman received an unsolicited letter from one of the judges, the highly esteemed (if also very conservative) composer Daniel Gregory Mason. While Mason felt that the works were "rather slight and hardly justify the award of a prize," he also found them "poetic" and said that they "showed unusual musical feeling." He wanted Schuman to know "of the pleasure that your Canons have given me personally." Mason also encouraged Schuman to enter another year with "something more extended by you." Schuman would oblige Mason, but Mason would hardly be pleased the second time around.[22]

His successes as an undergraduate at Teachers College led the administration to grant him a scholarship that enabled him to study conducting at the Mozarteum in Salzburg, Austria, in the summer of 1935. In the 1930s, an informal relationship existed between the two institutions, as faculty from one would travel and visit the other. An American Study Group of Teachers of Music, complete with a student choir, traveled to Salzburg that very summer and was written up in an English-speaking paper. "The music group of Professor Peter Dykemas [*sic*], of Teachers' College, Columbia University, gave a successful concert of American compositions in the Mozarteum. Choral canons by William Schuman, who attends the Mozarteum Music Academy, and 'Indian Serenata' by H. A. Murphy were especially well received."[23] So Schuman's presence in Salzburg was both propitious and slightly propagandistic, though he delighted in the first performance of his music abroad.

Schuman had done passably well in his conducting courses at Juilliard and Teachers College, and he devoted his energies that Austrian summer to improving his own skills, though he also enjoyed imitating the mannerisms of the people he encountered, including his principal conducting teacher, Bernhard Paumgartner, the director of the Mozarteum. He found the principal value of his Salzburg experience in three areas. First, the wide exposure to music gave him a chance to hone his opinions on what good music was. For example, on his way to Salzburg, he took in a concert at Paris's Salle Gaveau and wrote down his impressions of each piece on his program (e.g., Chabrier's *Suite pastorale* was "cleaning music"; the first movement of Weill's First Symphony was "good, especially [the] Sostenuto [section]," but the second movement was "endless, confused in style but always coherent").[24] Once he reached Salzburg, he had the opportunity to hear world-class conductors in rehearsals and performances. Though the festival would harden his attitude against opera in general—the operas that summer were *Fidelio*, *Falstaff*, *Die Entführung aus dem Serail*, *Così fan tutte*, *Le nozze di Figaro* (sung in German), *Don Giovanni*, *Tristan und Isolde*, and *Der Rosenkavalier*—the opportunity to watch Arturo Toscanini,

Bill at Brant Lake Camp, July 18, 1934.

Felix Weingartner, Bruno Walter, Erich Kleiber, and Adrian Boult conduct orchestral concerts provided an experience he raved about for years. Second, it gave him his first exposure to a summer festival, one devoted primarily but not exclusively to music. Salzburg later became a model for a similar festival at Lincoln Center, and even before he became president of the center, he had laid out for himself the scale of his vision. "The Festival . . . will be an annual presentation of the Center. It should take its place and hopefully in time exceed the reputations of such long established summer festivals as Salzburg, Bayreuth and Edinburgh."[25] Third, and most important to him, he carved out time in his schedule to compose his most extended work to date: his First Symphony.

He wrote to Eddie Marks from his flat on Auerspergstraße, complaining that Eddie was a "bastard for coming through with such a long letter," regaling him with stories and jokes, marveling at the local *Hefeweizen*, and giving him a detailed account of his industry that summer.

> I love every minute here and I wish I could stay a year. . . . My working day is from eight (breakfast and a walk comes before that time) to my dinner hour at eight in the evening. In addition to my classes at the Mozarteum, attending rehearsals, studying a bit of German, occaisional [*sic*] swims and <u>regular</u> tennis games, I am working on my symphony. The symphony is giving me a great deal of pleasure (as I hope it will others) and somehow I've sneaked in enough time to be half way through the first movement at this point. The rest of the first part is clearly in mind and if I can get the requisite minutes for the physical work of writing I feel sure that I'll come home with

> one completed movement. I'm scoring the composition for a small orchestra of eighteen instruments (no piano) and the problems of orchestration involved completely facinate [*sic*] me.[26]

In a letter to Frankie a few weeks later, he revealed more about the symphony then in progress.

> The first movement of the symphony is finished and needs a bit of revision and editing, the second movement must wait although the main ideas are beginning to form, the third section, as you know, will be a revised version of the Choreographic Poem. When this project is over I must start my string quartet—when I don't know but it shall be. I can't explain how I feel about all this but I do have a vision and I like its looks.[27]

At its first—and apparently only—performance the following year, the program gave this further explanation of the intersections of dance and symphony.

> On the title page of the score for this symphony there is a note which reads: "The appellation 'Choreographic' was not included in the title because it was felt that to some it might suggest a program. There is no literary basis; it is intended as a concert piece but it is hoped that the music may also serve as a setting for a choreographic composition—in fact, the last movement is a revised version of the composer's 'Choreographic Poem' which was designed for a definite dance pattern." The note concludes with some remarks of interest only for the prospective choreographer.[28]

Schuman had frequented performances of modern dance during the early 1930s, and while the music that Billy Schuman and his Alamo Society Orchestra provided for dancing in the late 1920s was a distant cousin to the kind of music he would later write, rhythm and movement of the body were a constant in Schuman's life. The manuscript for the earlier *Choreographic Poem for Seven Instruments* (dated March 1935) has a later annotation in Schuman's hand. "Student work/First dance composition/Not to be played!"

There were those who told Schuman that those last four words should apply to the symphony he crafted in part from the *Choreographic Poem*. First came the verdict of Daniel Gregory Mason in March 1936, who wrote Schuman a personal note in response to Schuman's submission of the symphony for the same competition for which he had entered the *Canonic Choruses* the year before.

> We had our meeting of the Bearns Jury yesterday, and I found that without a word from me the other judges felt as I did about your composition. It seems so fragmentary, and so acrid and bitter. The only way I explain it is that you must have "gone modern"—and you seemed too sincere for that. I am puzzled and unhappy about it. I cannot help hoping that you will still be disposed to give up the effort to register with the modernists, and go back to writing melodic music for your own satisfaction. Your canons certainly show a true talent.[29]

Schuman recalled that Frank Loesser's brother, Arthur, a concert pianist and critic of note, was "cruelly imperious" when Schuman asked for Arthur's informed opinion of the work. And even Roy Harris, his future teacher and mentor, "proceeded to criticize the symphony severely and in detail" when Schuman brought it to him for advice, according to the writer of a 1945 article on Schuman's music.[30] But despite the discouragement he received from others, Schuman pressed on for the symphony's first performance as part of a Composers' Forum-Laboratory concert.

The Federal Music Project of the Works Progress Administration had begun the Forum-Laboratory as a way to let composers try out their new works on a generally sympathetic audience that was invited, after the performances, to enter into a conversation with the composer. Harris inaugurated the series in the fall of 1935; Schuman's turn, after a postponement from June 1936, would come the following fall in a program that featured the *Canonic Choruses*, the First String Quartet, and the First Symphony. The transcript of the event—a stenographic wonder mandated for the Federal Music Project—provides an eyewitness account of the evening.

> On October 21st, 1936, at 8:25 P.M., the Auditorium of the W.P.A. Federal Music Project Headquarters was filled to capacity and people had to be turned away despite the fact that the evening was scheduled to begin at 8:30. . . .
>
> The Symphony #1 was met with a great deal of enthusiasm. The composer comes upon the stage to thank Mr. Jules Werner, the conductor, and Mr. Kass, the concert master. . . .
>
> Q13: Are you consciously or unconsciously influenced by Stravinsky in the Symphony?
>
> A: I am not influenced any more by Stravinsky than Roy Harris. I studied all composers, past and present, with Mr. Charles Haubiel. I think it is absurd for anyone writing and not getting anything from the best and if the expression is eventually to become an individual one, the fact that it is [not?] based on any one person is an advantage more than anything else.[31]

The conductor would write to Schuman days after the premiere, apologizing for the poor performance and promising that "my conception of your first symphony will surely be given its most genuine re-creation when I am in the position to minister to a first rate group that I aspire to."[32] Far more revealing is the opinion of Howard Murphy, a professor at Teachers College who had had Schuman in no fewer than seven courses.

> My dear Bill:
>
> . . . I know that you would want me to give my candid opinion of the work aside from performance. As you know, I like the canons although I think some are better than others. As regards the quartette and the symphony, I felt that they both are transitional and experimental works containing many beautiful and effective passages, interspersed from material which was not so satisfactory. Specifically, I liked the

opening of the quartette to the second theme, the middle of the slow movement and some portions of the finale but I was sometimes unable to feel the underlying unity, especially at a first performance and I also thought the use of the high register of the quartette somewhat monotonous, especially in the scherzo. In the symphony, I felt that the finale did not belong with the first two movements as a difference in style and the slow tempo did not make it particularly effective as a final movement. You know, of course, that all these criticisms are very tentative and might be changed completely by a second and more adequate performance. I believe in you and your work and am sure that you will write many more works which will express your individuality more completely. I also had a feeling that if you had put these works away for a year before having them performed you would have changed some parts of them, but I know that you prefer in general to write new works rather than to revise old ones and that is entirely a matter of temperament.[33]

Murphy's comment on Schuman's temperament and the incorporation—and apparent disjuncture—of the earlier *Choreographic Poem* into the symphony's finale serve as an early indication of Schuman's compositional methods. Schuman rarely engaged in revising his existing compositions; the Violin Concerto (1947–59) is the notable exception that proves the rule. More commonly, Schuman would do one of two things: shelve one piece only to rework it into an entirely new piece later on (as he would do with the *William Billings Overture* of 1944, which became the *New England Triptych* of 1956), or recast a portion of one piece—and occasionally an entire piece—in a new medium for another composition: the second of the *Three-Score Set* of 1943 and the second movement of the Symphony for Strings of the same year; the last movement of the String Quartet no. 4 of 1950 and the last movement of the Eighth Symphony of 1962; the three Orpheus pieces (*Orpheus with His Lute* from 1944, *A Song of Orpheus* from 1961, and *In Sweet Music* from 1978); and the multiple versions of *American Hymn*, *Amaryllis*, *The Lord Has a Child*, and *Voyage*. Murphy's remark also carries a criticism that could be extended to Schuman's oeuvre: that good works, like good plays, are not written but rewritten, and that some of Schuman's mature works would have benefited from more scrutiny on the part of the composer.

But the experience of hearing his music, however inadequately performed, however unfavorably received, steeled Schuman in his quest to compose. He wrote to thank Ashley Pettis, the director of the New York Composers' Forum-Laboratory, for the spotlight on his music, which Schuman later called "too much—much too much."

Through the Composers' Forum-Laboratory I have gained the knowledge of my writing that actual performance alone can give. I feel that my next works will be rid of all the crudities I felt in my work when it was performed. These things were, to be sure, to be observed in the score but it was actually hearing my mistakes that has given me an added feeling of confidence concerning the next compositions. I now consider

> my first symphony fragmentary and with material that does not please me. The quartet of course was very, very badly [played] but you have already termed this an "unavoidable shortcoming."[34]

The Forum-Laboratory concert led him to shelve the quartet and the symphony, although Harris may have tried to secure a second performance of the latter work a few years later in Pueblo, Colorado.[35] The discussion after the concert built on the positive experience he had known at his confirmation, as he discovered he knew how to command an audience and showed promise as an extempore speaker. But the overall lesson for Schuman was that he had to be a composer. As he had written to his future wife from Salzburg the year before:

> Frankie, if I ever had any doubts that I was a composer they are shattered once and for all—I'm not referring to the quality of my work (that is unimportant since the good will always live and the other die) but to my desire to create music and the abundance of ideas that are always in my head.[36]

His life as a college professor would begin in 1935, and his final courses toward his graduate degree would be completed by 1937, but his future career was adumbrated in the amateur and subpar performances his compositions received in Milbank Chapel, at the Mozarteum, and in the auditorium of the New York City Works Progress Administration Federal Music Project Headquarters. His unconventional education was drawing to a close. And just as his progress as a composer in the early 1930s was steady and swift, so his climb to the top of the field of American composers would be sudden and convincing. Even Mason would come around eventually. Schuman was on his way.

PART 2

THE SARAH LAWRENCE YEARS

SEVEN

SARAH LAWRENCE AND THE BEGINNING OF THE DECADE OF WAR

Comrades, the battle is bloody and the war is long:
Still let us climb the grey hills and charge the guns,
Pressing with lean bayonets toward the slopes beyond.
Soon those who are still living will see green grass.
A free bright country shining with a star;
And those who charged the guns will be remembered;
And from red blood white pinnacles shall tower.

Samuel Harold Levinger (1917–1937)

A student newspaper can tell you a lot about the mores of a student body. Look at the issues of the *Campus*, Sarah Lawrence College's newspaper, from 1935 to 1945. They teem with fascinating insights into the lives of the well-to-do young women attending this elite school. The advertisements for Chesterfield cigarettes alone hark back to a time and place long forgotten, even if some 70 years later the campus still holds the somewhat dubious distinction of being a smoker's paradise. (In 2008, 64.1 percent of the students smoked, compared to 50.4 percent nationwide.)[1] From the mid-'30s to the mid-'40s, the burning concerns that the writers for the *Campus* brought to light tended to be rather mundane: who married whom, who was vacationing where, and who favored whom as a presidential candidate (Alf Landon was the favorite among students, but the faculty and staff overwhelmingly supported FDR).

It was a venue that didn't arouse readers' expectations of finding story after story about a young man from Columbus, Ohio, who died on September 8, 1937, at the Battle of Belchite on the Aragon Front in the Spanish Civil War.[2] The women of Sarah Lawrence were, generally speaking, socially aware but politically naïve. In one of Schuman's classes, a discussion on Sinclair Lewis's *It Can't Happen Here* led one student to assert that it had already happened here because FDR's administration was a fascist dictatorship—or maybe a communist one, she wasn't quite sure which.[3] Another woman at a school party came to Schuman and his wife and asked them to escort her outside for a breath of air after she had "just danced with a Negro boy."[4] And yet the school newspaper covered the death and memorialization of a 20-year-old male Jewish Socialist that most of the female students at Sarah Lawrence had never met.

The simplest and most obvious reason for the coverage on Samuel Levinger was that his sister Leah was a student at Sarah Lawrence and worked on the newspaper. Behind this grieving student stood her grieving advisor (or "don," as they were called). In recalling the role that the advisor, Genevieve Taggard, played in her life, Leah Levinger spoke fondly of her as "a good friend who helped me when my brother died." Taggard (1894–1948), better known as Jed, had met Sam and had a rapport with him, according to Leah:

> The year before he went to Spain my brother Sam was in the seamen's union; he came to see Jed with me in her home once or twice and they liked each other immensely. Then, when he went to Spain, she was one of the first people I told, and showed her some of his letters. . . . Then when he died she and another friend of mine brought me the news, and it wasn't a time where political perspective could matter at all. She cried for him. . . . What Jed helped teach me about suffering is all of a piece with what she helped me learn about poetry; neither grief nor art are to be taken in one's stride, labeled, understood, put in the appropriate mental compartment; they are real and must be experienced uncritically and wholeheartedly if one is to grow as a human being.[5]

Leah and Jed would smoke their cigarettes together and talk about progressive politics, proletarian literature, and literature as a social weapon. "Jed was the person who could listen, since she had been working so long on the relationship between 'pure' and 'socially useful' literature."[6]

At this distance it is impossible to know whether Schuman had met Sam or how well he knew Leah. He was keenly aware of what it meant to be a liberal Jew in the conservative Gentile environment of Sarah Lawrence, where he began teaching in 1935. A few years into his time there, the president of the college, Constance Warren, asked for his opinion on whether she should lift the unofficial quota on Jewish students, since Schuman, as one of a handful of Jewish faculty, might have better counsel than others. (Schuman recommended that the quota be kept in place for the time being.)[7] He also unquestionably knew Taggard, his colleague at the college, for she provided texts for Schuman to set, two of which openly express progressive and even socialist sentiments. And he was sympathetic to the cause of the democratically elected government of Spain, as were many of his faculty colleagues. Leah's articles about her brother may have comforted some and upset others when it came to the issue of the unofficial quota. They certainly put Jews front and center: Sam and Leah's father was a rabbi, after all. The *Campus* provides this and more information about the Taggard-Schuman collaborations and the various faculty and student efforts to give time and money to the Republican cause in Spain. The *Campus*, in other words, serves as a real-time account of Schuman's life and the lives of many of the professionals and students who populated his circle for the better part of a decade.

Much of Schuman's early career is inexorably tied to the Allies' fortunes in World War II, given his devotion to the democratic cause in America and his compositions that he himself called propagandistic and that he wrote with the intent of helping out in the war effort.[8] But the importance of war to Schuman's career began shortly after Francisco Franco staged his coup in the summer of 1936. In fact, Schuman's response to the Spanish Civil War and its repercussions in the United States is as much a part of his history as are his ties to WWII. The era finds Schuman at his most progressive. If the significance of the earlier conflict is somewhat obscured as a part of Schuman's own history, it is because, in part, that Schuman, in hindsight, wanted it that way.

This was an era when many composers were flexing their bona fides when it came to joining the masses. Aaron Copland's speech to "farmers who were Reds" in Bemidji, Minnesota, and Marc Blitzstein's articles for *New Masses* and *Daily Worker* are but two examples of the many composers who found comradeship with the proletariat, often those expressly with communist identifiers.[9] Schuman's intersections with the political Left provide a different understanding of how composers of this decade married ideology and aesthetics.

The extant letters to and from Schuman prior to his teaching at Sarah Lawrence are short on political rhetoric and philosophizing; they are mostly about music, women, jokes, and booze. But occasionally someone lets down his guard, as Woody Sandler did in a 1935 letter sent from Brant Lake Camp, the same camp at which Schuman was a counselor the year before. He gave Schuman his rundown on his fellow campers and regaled him with an account of the phenomenal spread that was laid out for the Brant Lake staff, which included "pickles, tongue, rye bread, beer, soft drinks, etc." He and a friend started drinking there and then "proceeded to the Carnegie Tavern where we further proceeded to load up on beers. After six apiece, we staggered out and headed unsteadily towards Columbus Circle . . . [where] we joined a group of communists and made some fast friends by delivering violent tirades against capitalism." Schuman must have known that Woody wasn't entirely kidding about the communists, and Woody later in the letter underscored that it wasn't all in jest.

> I had the very great pleasure of seeing two of Clifford Odet's [*sic*] plays ("Waiting for Lefty" and "Till the Day I Die") which had a tremendous effect on me. They are certainly marvelous propaganda. I walked out of that theatre swearing that the only thing that prevented me from considering myself an out-and-out communist was the fact that I still lacked too much knowledge of precisely what it implies to be such. My next step is going to be to read the Manifesto, which Lader [one of their female friends] is lending me, and if that suffices I will take my stand at that time.[10]

Sandler would later be named as one of 16 attorneys who were part of an alleged Communist Party cell within the National Labor Relations Board, so his earlier flirtation with communism may have been more than a passing fad.[11]

Whatever Schuman's exposure to or predilection toward communism, his attitude toward isms of all kinds was likely summed up in a clipping in one of his scrapbooks. Though the article by Herbert Little has no date, it must have been published around 1938, given its references to the Spanish Civil War. The wire services article, titled "Communism, Fascism, Nazism," argues that

> basically Fascism, Nazism and Communism as practiced are alike. "The state is all"—this is the theory of the corporate or totalitarian state setup, like a big corporation in this country. The methods of the three countries are similar—suppression and censorship of press, radio, cables, mails; use of force and violence to suppress protesting minorities.
>
> There are major differences, however, which go far to indicate that the struggle between the Communist and Nazi-Fascist philosophies will be unceasing.
>
> Chief of these is the fact that the Communists bend every effort to abolish private property and profit.
>
> Fascists and Nazis seek to preserve the profit system, although subjecting it to government control.
>
> The Communists despise religion and superstition and work hard through education to eradicate it. In Italy and Germany the governments use religion to intensify patriotic fervor for the state's aim and efforts.[12]

Perhaps Schuman kept the short article as a primer on these three ideologies that competed with democracy. But much of the terse article summarizes Schuman's own political philosophy. He was at best cool to religion, so its use by the Fascists and Nazis appalled him, as did their quests for purity at all costs. But his German Jewish heritage and his small-businessmen-made-good upbringing inclined him to be suspicious of communism, setting him apart from his composer colleagues who came from eastern European Jewish backgrounds—both rich ones (Blitzstein) and ones less well-off (Copland)—and who tended toward more radical leftist politics than did many American Jews of German extraction.[13] Schuman once chose not to join a panel of artists that included Communists and Communist sympathizers, perhaps less out of political conviction than out of propriety. At the time, he was president of Juilliard, and just months earlier he had lent his name as sponsor to an event in support of black artists that had been construed as organized by Communists. (Paul Robeson was also a sponsor.)[14] In his general refusal to affiliate with groups and individuals with political agendas on the Left and the Right, Schuman managed to keep himself above the fray, as his nearly blemish-free FBI file shows. But his views—and just as important, the views of the people with whom he associated—were progressive and ameliorative, and while Schuman himself may not have subscribed to the tenets of socialism or communism, his compositions during the first half of his Sarah Lawrence decade would give his colleagues on the Left encouragement and succor.

Indeed, notwithstanding the conservatism of the student body, Sarah Lawrence was dedicated to progressive ends from the beginning. Although "a central goal at the founding was to educate young ladies of good families to take their proper place in polite society," the early administrators of the college looked to the same educator and philosopher that Schuman had found so stimulating at Teachers College. They "were influenced by John Dewey and the progressive education movement. . . . For Dewey, the act of making knowledge one's own was the central goal of education, the creative act he saw as crucial."[15] The particular emphasis on the individual, that there was no one single path to becoming educated, struck a powerful chord in Schuman, who had cobbled together an unorthodox path to his own baccalaureate degree and who responded powerfully to Dewey's ideas. And so he, emboldened by what he had read in the school's catalog and convinced that his educational philosophy and experience would find a match with that of the college, called upon President Warren on April 1, 1935.

Warren's comments on that visit for the most part are unremarkable, but some of what she noted beggars belief. Either she misheard Schuman, or she misremembered the conversation, or Schuman misrepresented himself—or some combination of all these.

> Mr. Schuman called on me this morning. He has been taking his Ph.D. at Teachers College [he was just finishing his B.S. degree; the sentence was later circled and marked "incorrect"]. Is a graduate of Columbia [he hadn't graduated yet], and studied at the Juilliard School. He is a perfectly delightful young man to talk with. Has had a little teaching experience, but not much [perhaps a reference to Cobbossee; his teaching experience at Columbia would occur in 1936]. Has a fellowship from Columbia at Salzburg this summer to study conducting. He has done a good deal of composing. Is learning to play every instrument himself, but is not a professional in any instrument. His interest lies largely in teaching history and theory of music and composition, and he has many ideas as to how he wants to teach those. He has had considerable connection with work in the dance and with the theatre [Billy Schuman and His Alamo Society Orchestra? *It's Up to Pa*?]. Did a little work several years ago with the Theatre Guild. I think it is worthwhile for Mr. Swinford, at least, to see him. I am sending to Teachers College for his references.[16]

Jerome Swinford was the head of the small music department. He was a vocalist by training and probably had nothing like Schuman's vision for education. Swinford informed Warren of his meeting with Schuman. "Cannot see any opening for him here but is suggesting him for some other work. Thinks he would be wonderfully trained to teach instruments and had fine ideas about teaching music appreciation, but would be competent to teach only first year piano."[17] Schuman's training had prepared him to be a teacher at a junior high or high school, not a professor at a college, and Schuman recalled his experience of auditioning for a position at the Brooklyn Ethical Culture Schools at Swinford's behest. The results were dreadful all around.

But Swinford and others at Sarah Lawrence were working to secure a grant from the Rockefeller Foundation to give them some cushion to pursue their progressive educational philosophy. Miraculously for Schuman, the grant came through before he had to leave for Salzburg, and just two months after his visit with Warren, he was offered a job at Sarah Lawrence "to be in charge of exploratory work in the arts with freshmen, to assist in music in the general dramatics work and in the music department, and to act as don, or adviser, to a few students, at a salary of $2,400."[18] His entering freshman class of faculty included Taggard; dancer and choreographer Martha Graham, with whom he would create four works; and Jacques Barzun, historian and philosopher, who would remain a lifelong confidante. Rene d'Harnoncourt, the future director of the Museum of Modern Art, had joined the faculty the year before.

One can easily imagine, in those politically incorrect days, that Warren and Schuman talked about women as well as education. By 1935, Frankie was very much a part of Schuman's life. The year before, she came up to visit him at Brant Lake Park, and during his summer in Salzburg they exchanged letters filled with the endearments and teasings that lovers of all ages employ. Years later, Schuman said that he wished he had married Frankie before the Salzburg summer, but neither one of them knew how stable Schuman's job was, dependent as it was on foundation money. When, however, Warren offered Schuman a contract for the 1936–37 year, Bill and Frankie sprang into action and tied the knot on March 27, 1936, during the college's spring vacation. They moved to an apartment on Riverside Drive, and Frankie commuted downtown to her job while Schuman drove north to Bronxville for his.

In his first four years at Sarah Lawrence, Schuman helped to revolutionize the college's music offerings, especially in extracurricular areas. With his colleagues he started a Music Forum at which faculty and students discussed various aspects of music making, and it was at a series of these forums that Schuman demonstrated his ability to play every instrument in the orchestra.[19] Schuman worked with his colleague Horace Grenell to codify that ability in a draft proposal for a music appreciation handbook. Their joint effort—*Sounds: A Study of Orchestral Color*—was designed in partnership with Musicraft Records, which initially agreed to develop recordings to help demystify the modern symphony orchestra for the listener who "is easily troubled by the profusion of its resources. . . . In producing this volume the authors are aware of the impossibility of a complete survey. They have striven to assist the reader by illustrating the main body of orchestral sounds and the manner in which these sounds are organized."[20] Schuman also helped to persuade the administration to bring Ashley Pettis, pianist and director of the New York Composers' Forum-Laboratory, to teach there beginning in 1937. He and

Pettis worked to include student compositions in the Forum-Laboratory, thus providing a platform for the classroom work Schuman was doing with his "girls" (as he called them and as they liked to be called). All of them together started the Intercollegiate Music Forum, whose member schools were Sarah Lawrence, Vassar, Bard, Bennington, Columbia, and the Westminster Choir College, and whose first gathering, in March 1939, was on the Sarah Lawrence campus. Schuman also invited composers to talk to the students; among these composers were Aaron Copland and Roy Harris, the latter of whom wrote a piece expressly for the school chorus, which Schuman began conducting in 1938.

The leadership of the chorus fell into Schuman's lap unexpectedly. Prior to 1937, Grenell and Paul Velucci had led the chorus with less than spectacular results. The 1937–38 year looked to be a breakthrough one, as Lehman Engel, founder and conductor of the Madrigal Singers, was signed to lead the chorus. Schuman invited Engel to bring the Madrigal Singers to campus. The concert on March 2, 1937, complemented the course "History through the Ages," with choral music from the sixteenth century to the present day (appropriately for Sarah Lawrence, Schuman's *Canonic Choruses*).[21] The enthusiastic response came not only from the student body but from the administration as well, though Engel's services for 1937–38 weren't secured until late September.[22]

Schuman initially saw Engel as a composer colleague, praising the latter's Sonata for Piano for its vibrancy and clarity and inviting Engel over to Riverside Drive to critique Schuman's yet-unperformed First Symphony.[23] Engel's real skill, though, was in working with performers, first by founding the Madrigal Singers and then, not far into the future, working on Broadway. Schuman came to depend on him during the first half of his Sarah Lawrence years, offering Engel the first performances of the *Prelude for Voices* (completed in 1936 but not premiered until 1939) and the *Choral Etude* (also 1937, premiered in 1938) as well as repeat performances of the *Canonic Choruses*. From 1936 to 1939, Schuman wrote at least 20 letters to Engel, in which he extolled the Madrigal Singers' all-American program as "the most enjoyable evening we've [Frankie and I] spent the entire year," invited him to join them in Paris during the summer of 1937, and browbeat him for failing to bring the *Choral Etude* up to performance level ("I hope never to allow a piece I have composed in all sincerity to be presented in a perfunctory manner unworthy of noble traditions"). Engel's side of the correspondence—occasionally referenced in Schuman's letters—is missing, but one senses a deep camaraderie between the two young men (Schuman was one month older than Engel) with little competition between the two, especially when it came to conducting a chorus. To the contrary, they collaborated on a recording.

> In talking with Mr. Wise at Columbia Records about your recording the Choral Etude, he suggested that I write something for the other side for you to perform. I am writing Four One Minute Songs. These I would like to publish with Arrow Press issues. The four songs are very easy and will be ready very shortly.[24]

A later letter partially explains why these four songs never were completed: Wise had forgotten that he had spoken to Schuman about writing them and had approached Engel to fill out the recording with works of his own. Schuman was philosophical about the oversight: "We may as well have two American composers on records to help swell the pitifully small representation."[25] And another American composition did fill out the disc: Charles Ives's *Psalm 67*.[26]

Engel advanced Schuman's career not only by giving the choral works wider exposure: his failure to get the Sarah Lawrence College Chorus to thrive gave Schuman an opening. Ostensibly the rationale to let Engel go after only one year of conducting the chorus was to consolidate the college's performing outlets under the academic departments and not to continue them as independent extracurricular organizations. But Schuman, who had studied orchestral conducting and not choral conducting, was uncertain that the arrangement going forward would be to his liking.

> Since we all seem to feel it would be to our advantage to have the chorus directly a part of the music department, I am ready to accept the job. I do so with the reservations we mentioned on the phone yesterday—that this work be entirely aside from my other teaching at the college and that this be a trial year. We must see if I am able to do this job in a satisfactory manner on the one hand, and on the other whether this work proves to be an activity suited to me. . . . I am greatly appreciative of the confidence you have shown in me by offering me the additional work of the chorus. I shall try my best not to disappoint you.[27]

Schuman would end up frustrating Warren, but did so by his incredible success rather than any failure.[28] He turned the day-to-day leadership of the chorus over to the students. They were responsible for keeping attendance and enforcing discipline during their twice-weekly two-hour rehearsals. The chorus was open to any student who could carry a tune; the majority of the choristers could not read music. And Schuman decided that, if he was going to lead the group, he was going to give it his all. And the girls responded. Approximately 44 students participated in the chorus under Engel; Schuman added 14 more in his first year, a 32 percent increase that was remarkable in its own right. But the years 1939 through 1945 were far more impressive. In the spring of 1939, when he received word that his application for a Guggenheim Fellowship was successful, Schuman petitioned the foundation for permission to continue to conduct the chorus.[29] He didn't want to let his girls down: he had already told them that he hoped for 100 members the following October. Nor did they let him down: there were 98 girls in 1939–40; 113 in 1940–41; 109 in 1941–42; 94 in 1942–43; 89 in 1943–44;

and 85 in 1944–45. (Competing volunteer activities during WWII may account for some of the attrition in later years.)[30] Given that the student body broke 300 in only one of the years Schuman conducted the chorus, he had one-third of the student body in his ensemble. In addition, Schuman helped to organize the chorus's first extended tour, one that resulted, after expenses were paid, in a $1,200 profit that was turned over to the college's Scholarship Fund. Under Schuman, the chorus made its Town Hall and Carnegie Hall premieres, performed regularly on national broadcasts, and sang with the Boston Symphony under the baton of Serge Koussevitzky. No wonder that when the *Campus*'s editorial board summarized Schuman's role at Sarah Lawrence, they not only compared him to a legend at an all-male school but also positioned music as the equivalent of sports: "They Had Knute, But We Have Bill."[31] (Knute Rockne coached the Notre Dame football team from 1918 to 1930, leading the men to 105 victories, 12 losses, five ties, and six national championships. George "The Gipper" Gipp was one of his players.)

If Engel's misstep at Sarah Lawrence turned Schuman into a campus hero, it was Engel's connections away from Bronxville that helped to extend Schuman's fame. In addition to his work on Schuman's behalf with the Madrigal Singers, Engel was the president of Arrow Press and one of its four founders (Aaron Copland, Virgil Thomson, and Marc Blitzstein were the others).[32] Schuman hoped to place at least four works with Arrow. One, the *Four One-Minute Songs*, was never written. Another, a Concerto for Piano and Orchestra (1938), was actually published but was later withdrawn and rewritten. A third, the String Quartet no. 2, was begun when Bill and Frankie were enjoying a belated honeymoon in England and France during the summer of 1937. In a letter to Bill's parents, both Bill and Frankie wrote about how, despite their being ensconced along the shore of Lake Annecy and taking swimming expeditions daily, Bill managed to carve out five hours a day on composition, which resulted in the completion of a Prelude and Fugue for Orchestra and the start of the quartet.[33] The latter work was completed stateside that fall, and, in addition to its premiere the following spring at a Composers' Forum-Laboratory concert, it was featured at the Yaddo Festival at Saratoga Springs in the summer of 1938. (Composer Quincy Porter worked with an eager Schuman to bring the work to Yaddo.)[34] Although the work was published by Arrow Press and later reissued by Boosey & Hawkes, Schuman would later regret having let this composition see the light of day. When he received word that it would be performed in 1956 at two Southern California university campuses (UCLA and USC) on a program devoted to his works, he dispatched a telegraph to the organizers. "Please, please do not perform my String Quartet No. II. Early work; not representative." His request to schedule the Fourth Quartet instead of the Second went unheeded.[35] And near the end of his life, he repeated that "I wished I'd never published" the Second Quartet.[36] (The Prelude and Fugue, in contrast, was

Frankie and Bill on the boat for their European honeymoon, 1937.

withdrawn, even though orchestral parts were extracted from the score in anticipation of a public performance. Its material comes from the second and fourth movements of the First Quartet, which helps to explain why the orchestral reworking met the same fate as its chamber music source.)[37]

The fourth work that Schuman hoped would be published by Arrow Press was the Second Symphony. Arrow, however, was his second choice for a publisher, as letters to and from Schuman show. Possible publication, public performance, critical reception, personal whim, and local and world politics all inform the symphony's complex creation and legacy. Schuman's motivation for composing the work, his unsuccessful attempts at publishing the work, and the politics that surrounded the work then and now make for a fascinating study.

Schuman wrote to the offices of the Composers' Forum-Laboratory in the early fall of 1937, requesting another evening of his music. In response, he was told that, "according to the wishes expressed in your letter of October 2nd, we are scheduling you for Wednesday, May 21st, for an orchestra program not to exceed thirty minutes." (May 21 was a Saturday; the concert did occur on Wednesday, May 25.)[38] The Prelude and Fugue did not last a half-hour, and his only other extended orchestral work—the First Symphony—had been performed the previous October. So Schuman set to work on his new symphony. The manuscript's title page not only gives the dates of composition (November 1—December 23, 1937) and the place (New York City) but also identifies the work as "in one movement of 18 minutes," suggesting that Schuman tailored his symphony to fit the dimensions of the upcoming concert. The symphony opened the second half of the concert; the first half consisted of an arrangement of a Bach chorale, a Bach suite, and the Grieg piano concerto, and the concert concluded with Dvořák *Carnival* Overture. For unknown reasons, the Prelude and Fugue were not played that evening, but it is known that Schuman's reliance upon the resources of the Forum-Laboratory to copy that work left him unable to turn to them to do the same for the symphony. The copyists at the Edwin A. Fleisher Collection of the Free Library of Philadelphia had to rush to get the parts ready in time for the May performance.[39]

Three events prior to the May 1938 concert—one cumulative, the others singular—bring the premiere of the symphony into greater relief. During the 1937–38 school year, Roy Harris and Ashley Pettis tried to leverage the New York Composers' Forum-Laboratory into something national. With Schuman serving as secretary, they approached Copland, Howard Hanson, Douglas Moore, Quincy Porter, and Bernard Wagenaar to see if they would be interested in a loose confederation that they eventually called the American Composers Committee (ACC).

> There is need now for activity outside the federal project which will bring contemporary music to the people through schools, colleges, broadcasts, recordings, concert halls, and publications. Composers' Forum-Laboratory exists in other cities besides New York, and the time was never more propitious than now for a national organization of composers which, unlike special interest groups, would function with regard to a composer's competency and seriousness of purpose—not school of thought.
>
> Whatever ideas the writer has will perhaps merely serve as a basis for discussion when the Committee holds its first meeting. Roy Harris and Ashley Pettis have definitely assured me of their desire to cooperate in this venture. I hope you will join with us in working out these important problems.[40]

Their efforts would come to naught and would be undercut by the establishment in early 1938 of the American Composers Alliance, but for six months, Schuman, the young and somewhat unknown composer-professor at Sarah Lawrence, became a conduit for more famous composers to explore their collective options.[41] During this time, Schuman not only corresponded with the composers mentioned above but also with Nicolai Berezowsky, John Alden Carpenter, Louis Gruenberg, Frederick Jacobi, Werner Josten, Otto Luening, Harl McDonald, Walter Piston, Roger Sessions, Arthur Shepherd, and Randall Thompson, working to secure recordings and broadcasts of their music. The project may have come up short—the decision of the Columbia Broadcasting System not to allocate any money for Forum-Laboratory transmissions seems to have been the ACC's death knell[42]—but because of his industriousness, Schuman was becoming better known in the composer community.

The two singular events were announcements that Schuman's works had won prizes. First came word in January 1938 that his *Choral Etude* was chosen as one of the winners of the Federal Music Project's Choral Contest that year. The judges included Engel, Hanson, and Harris, and in listing the works in order of importance, the judges placed Schuman's work first. (The other winners, in the order given by the judges, were Armin Loos, David Diamond, John Vincent, and Elliott Carter.)[43] Then, three months later Schuman's new symphony received a similar accolade.

> The first prize in the composers' competition conducted by the Musicians' Committee to Aid Spanish Democracy has been won by William Schuman with his second symphony. David Diamond received honorable mention for an overture for full orchestra. . . . Roy Harris, Aaron Copland, Roger Sessions and Bernard Wagenaar were the judges. Over twenty composers submitted scores. The performance of the winning work was originally scheduled for this spring, but, owing to the present critical situation in Spain, this has been postponed until next fall.[44]

Schuman was now a two-time winner, and these awards stand at the vanguard of the many honors he would receive during the Sarah Lawrence years.

The writers for the *Campus* echoed and amplified what the Boston and New York papers were saying about Schuman and his music. In an issue whose front page, above-the-fold stories touched on the orphans of Spanish Loyalists; on the Westchester Security League "which wants to stamp out Communism, which wants to 'keep America American,' and which regards Hoover as the modern messiah"; and on the Socialist Party, "the one legal radical party in New York State," a below-the-fold story told students that "the first public performance of Schuman's Symphony No. 2 (yes, William Schuman of the Music Department)" was to take place in a few days. "This is the Symphony which was awarded a prize recently by the Musicians' Committee to Aid Spanish Democracy."[45] Two weeks later, the signed review of the symphony's premiere praised the work, pointed to the shortcomings of the performance, and once more stressed the work's connection to the Spanish Republican cause.[46] And an astute reader of both of those stories would have remembered that, a few months before, the *Campus* reported that Martha Graham had similarly brought leftish politics to the fore when she took part in a recital sponsored by the Dance Committee to Aid Spanish Democracy.[47] The honor the symphony garnered put Schuman in the thick of progressive politics at Sarah Lawrence.

The prize was to include both a fall performance and publication of the winning work. Both fell through. But Schuman pursued both on his own. He managed to secure a second performance with Howard Barlow and the CBS Symphony Orchestra. Despite the many negative letters that the network received as a result of the broadcast and that it forwarded to Schuman, he was undeterred in his belief in the work. He obtained a recording of the broadcast and used it to stimulate a discussion with a group of New York music teachers about the work specifically and contemporary American music more broadly.

He "wrote his symphony's principal motive on the blackboard and had the audience sing it."[48] He also sent the work to Gerald Strang, managing director of New Music, the West Coast publishing venture founded by the ultramodernist composer Henry Cowell. Strang was enthusiastic about the prospect of including the work in New Music's Orchestra Series and even prepared a letter of intent for Schuman to sign. Financial hardship on the part of New Music, however, necessitated a change in plans, and Strang, "with the deepest regrets," wrote to Schuman to tell him that New Music would be unable to publish his symphony. "I shall, therefore, return the score you submitted with the hope, however, that we shall be able to raise the money later to go ahead with its publication. If you have a chance to make other arrangements, you are, of course, released from any obligations to us."[49] Perhaps as a consolation, the recording arm of New Music offered Schuman an opportunity to compose a work for them. No documentation has emerged surrounding the reasons why Schuman wrote the Quartettino for Four Bassoons in 1939, but he dashed it off in two days the week after he received Strang's letter. Similarly, a recording of the work, which fits neatly on one side of a 78-rpm disc, was released under the auspices of New Music Quarterly Recordings that same year.[50]

The symphony, meanwhile, would receive two more performances: one in February 1939 with Serge Koussevitzky and the Boston Symphony, where the work received blistering reviews; and one 13 months later with Barlow and the Baltimore Symphony, where the work received an even mix of positive and negative reviews. In between those two performances, Schuman wrote to Engel to negotiate the terms of publication for his Concerto for Piano and Orchestra, who supplies scores and parts, what percentage of performance fee goes to whom, who holds the copyright, and the like. And then, rather nonchalantly, Schuman added: "I would like to give you my 2nd Symphony et al. on this basis."[51] In other words, the reception of the work in Boston did not deter Schuman from entertaining the possibility of releasing the work. But after Barlow's Baltimore performances, the not-yet-published work was shelved and never again performed. Fortunately, the Barlow CBS Symphony Orchestra broadcast has been preserved and provides an aural record of the work's early history.

The musical elements and the critical response the Second Symphony generated will be explored in another chapter, as will the Schuman-Taggard collaborations. Here, let it be noted that, as 1939 dawned, Schuman held high hopes for his Second Symphony. He most certainly put constraints upon himself in terms of the length of the symphony as well as on its overall tempo; he later said that he gave the symphony its larghissimo pace because copying costs are less for slow music than they are for fast music.[52] And it is possible that, as with the Second String Quartet, Schuman would have later regretted his decision to disseminate the work had he persisted in sending it out into the world. But the record shows he actively sought out performances and publication of the work and talked about it with knowledgeable colleagues. The work, moreover, had won a contest adjudicated by men whose opinions on musical matters were considered impeccable. Schuman was also obdurate with these men, seeking out Sessions, who initially was less favorably disposed to the symphony than were his fellow judges, and imploring Copland, who apparently had doubts about the single-movement conception: "Please change your mind and feel it with me—complete in one mv.—also feel it a symphony."[53] Throughout 1938, Schuman fervently believed in this work.

The symphony's association with the Spanish Civil War, then, becomes more than a matter of fact. Like the fate of the democratically elected Spanish Republicans, the fate of the symphony was determined in early 1939; no subsequent pushback could restore its fortunes. Their opponents wanted to turn the clock away from reform and away from the new; their supporters rallied too late and too weakly. Add to this the fact that Schuman no doubt knew that many American supporters of the Spanish loyalists weren't merely anti-Fascist but were also actively pro-communist; later, the North American Committee to Aid Spanish Democracy would be labeled as a front organization for the American Communist Party, in part because the Soviet Union, alone among industrialized nations, supported the Republicans against Franco.[54] Schuman knew there was a difference between fascism and communism, but he also seemed to sense, well in advance of many of his colleagues, what the ramifications might be if he were associated with true political radicalism, legal or not, popular or not. And so it is difficult to know whether we should believe Schuman's word that the decision to withdraw the work was based solely on the work's musical shortcomings. A progressive work, so marked internally by its modernist music and so identified externally by a prize, became a casualty in a larger battle. In light of Schuman's latter-day wishes, his Symphony no. 2 may never be heard again in concert. But in light of the idealism of the young Schuman, who took pride in a work that indirectly reminded men and women in his day of the fragility of democracy, perhaps it is time to rediscover the work—and others like it—to remind us of those earlier, tumultuous days and to keep alive the memory of men like Samuel Levinger, whose commitment to aid Spanish democracy was total.

EIGHT

"THE PUPIL IS OUTDOING THE MASTER"

In the summer of 1939, the influential critic Paul Rosenfeld surveyed the music scene. He linked three composers who, up until that time, had not been drawn together, in part because one so dominated the musical life of America that he seemed to have few peers, and another because he was a relative newcomer. Titled "Copland–Harris–Schuman," Rosenfeld's article is both humorous and disorienting in hindsight. He began by conceding that, "Copland probably is the most generously gifted composer among living Americans."[1] But upon examining the music for the film *The City*, the orchestral work *An Outdoor Overture*, and the ballet *Billy the Kid*, Rosenfeld found each score deserving of withering criticism. He voiced concern that the newly "popular" vein Copland was mining would overshadow the "artistic" works, from the Organ Symphony to the Short Symphony. For Rosenfeld, Copland "seems still to be standing at the fork in the highroad," and it is clear which branch Rosenfeld expected Copland to take. At this juncture, Copland was a disappointment to Rosenfeld; the Brooklyn Stravinsky was failing to make good on his vast potential.

Not so Harris. Save for its "slightly anticlimactic" short finale (which Harris would later lengthen), the Third Symphony elicited nothing but praise from Rosenfeld. His encomia only increased for the Soliloquy and Dance for viola and piano: a piece "wholly beautiful, allowing the listener the opportunity for complete absorption. . . . The sustained Soliloquy is full of passion and poetry. . . . The Dance is a wonder . . . the vitality and variety seem well-nigh inexhaustible." He ended this section thus: "If Harris can maintain himself on the level he has attained in it and continue giving us music of a quality as high, he may well awake some fine morning to find himself in the great company of the masters."[2]

As for the third man, Rosenfeld began: "Two other exceptional new American compositions presented during the season have doubled our impression of the talents of a young composer recently the recipient of a Guggenheim scholarship.

This is William Schuman, a New Yorker born in 1910."[3] The two pieces in question are the Second Symphony and the Prologue for chorus and orchestra, though Rosenfeld also used the column to praise the Second String Quartet that had debuted in the previous season.

> The raucous and sensuous sound [of the symphony] reflects the world of mechanism and industrial techniques; its closer parallels are in Varèse and Chávez; but it is clear and firm in its own way. One hears it in the lowing, groaning ox-horn like onset of the piece and the jagged principal subject. The Symphony testifies to the presence of something primitive in the composer's feeling, a fierceness and an earthiness. Indeed, a fixed and almost murderous vehemence seems to express itself in the *ostinato* of the initial movement.[4]

Rosenfeld's handicapping of the composer horse race at the end of the 1930s has Harris in the lead, Copland fading, and Schuman gaining on the inside. Such a ranking may seem improbable from the perspective of the early twenty-first century, so it is good to recall a nationwide poll conducted by the Columbia Broadcasting System a year after Rosenfeld's article, which put Harris in first place among American composers of the day.[5] Rosenfeld had a lot riding on Harris. Three times in 1934 he implicitly concurred with John Tasker Howard that Harris was the "white hope of American music," and Harris generally did not disappoint in the 1930s.[6] Yet his star would soon dim, and it wouldn't be Copland and his now well-known Americana works that would outshine him in the short run. In the long run, of course, Rosenfeld's musical trackside calls in his chronicle would come a cropper; the composer he filleted went on to become the dean of American composers, the man who comes after Ives and before John Adams as one of the best America has produced. In the 1930s and early '40s, though, Copland's primacy was not as assured as it is today. In many critical corners of yesteryear, it was Harris who ruled the '30s and Schuman the '40s.

Harris's own history resembled the cowboy myth in so many ways that it was almost predetermined that he would emerge as the premier American composer in the 1930s.[7] He was born in a log cabin in Lincoln County, Oklahoma, on February 12—Abraham Lincoln's birthday. His family would migrate west to the more fertile farmlands of rural Covina, California. While he would travel to Paris to study with Nadia Boulanger, Copland's teacher, Harris resisted Boulanger's method so strenuously that she would refer to him as her autodidact. Like Little Johnny Jones (and his creator, George M. Cohan), Harris crossed the Atlantic and never wavered in being "Yankee Doodle do or die." Thus he could return to America in 1929 claiming to be relatively untouched and untainted by European musical mores. Upon his reintroduction to American society, he soon became the subject of commentary that posited that his music was western to its core. Seeing the potential for such a niche in the critical and popular imaginations, Harris encouraged and fueled the western trope relative to his music and life, even in works that ostensibly have no claim on the American West, such as the Third Symphony (1939).

There is no question that Harris studied music assiduously, especially Bach and older masters.[8] He was especially fond of counterpoint. In his chronicle, Rosenfeld noted that "the fugue [of the symphony]—fugues are almost the hallmark of Harris's compositions—has immense vigor," and he lauded the "joyous double fugue" in the piano-viola Dance that was built "on *gigue*-like subjects" and underwent all kinds of contrapuntal elaborations.[9] Harris's emphasis on fugue and counterpoint resonated in Haubiel's zealous pupil.

Not only was Harris a master of counterpoint: he was also a master of self-delusion, with an overinflated opinion of his skills and talents that he never overcame. As early as 1933, a future biographer would despair of Harris's egotism. "Poor Roy Harris with his ideas of a growing demand for his music!! On what planet does he live?"[10] In the 1930s, many of his technical shortcomings were glossed over; he had come to composition relatively late in life (that is, his late twenties), and the sheer force of his originality could not be denied. By the 1940s, however, when musical technique became analogous to wartime industry, and efficiency and reliability mattered, Harris's deficiencies could no longer be ignored as easily. Coupled with his unapologetic American nationalism that was saturated, somewhat against his will, with concepts of racial supremacy, Harris's star steadily sank during and after World War II.[11]

The 1930s, though, was Harris's decade, in part because of his first symphony, *Symphony 1933*, which Serge Koussevitzky and the Boston Symphony Orchestra premiered in January 1934. Even before its premiere, excitement grew around this work. Koussevitzky himself wrote to John Erskine, president of the Juilliard School of Music, to express his wonder.

> I have just examined the score of a new symphony by Roy Harris. I can hardly find words to say how deeply impressed I am by his work. Indeed, this Symphony will enrich American musical literature of our day. And needless to say, I shall perform it both in Boston and in New York as soon as the orchestral material is completed.
>
> May I add that by supporting Mr. Harris at this time would mean more that [*sic*] merely help him personally: it would contribute to the promotion of American music, at large.
>
> Believe me.[12]

The symphony was a thunderbolt for many young musical mavericks, Schuman among them. In the mid-1930s, Harris taught summer classes at the Juilliard School of Music, and Schuman went there to study with him in the summer of 1936. (He earned three A-pluses for his work.) As for the *Symphony 1933*, Schuman either knew the recording that the Columbia Phonograph Co. made from the February 1934 Carnegie Hall performance—it would not be heard live again in New York until the Composers' Forum-Laboratory concerts in the fall of 1937—or encountered the work live at that Carnegie Hall performance, for in early 1937, a few months after his summer studies at Juilliard, he asked Harris for a score of the work so that he could inspect it more closely. Harris responded:

> My dear Schuman:
>
> Schirmer has a Symphony 1933. Take this letter with you and they will give it to you or at least let you look at it. I have only one copy. It is not published yet.
>
> I might tell you that the first theme is made of rhythmic device of three plus two, which you hear at the very opening. All material generates out of this device in one way or another. The second movement is a rondo or rather I should say a free adaptation of the rondo principle. The last movement is a study in variations of the principal theme which is announced in the beginning.[13]

In this, the earliest extant letter in the Schuman-Harris correspondence, one hears Harris not only instructing Schuman in the particulars of the piece but, more important, indoctrinating Schuman into Harris's notion of musical organicism, famously summed up in the word associated with Harris: autogenesis. Dan Stehman best defined this almost undefinable term.

> The fundamental formal principle in Harris's music is autogenesis, by which a melody is generated by a seed motif out of which the first phrase grows, each succeeding phrase either germinating in like fashion or launching itself from a figure in the last bars of the preceding phrase. His aim was to produce an effect of gradual organic growth, and thus the music often unfolds additively in blocks of gradually differing textures.[14]

At its core, autogenesis represents an anti-European mode of musical discourse; autogenetic musical material doesn't so much develop as it unfolds or blossoms. It also is less subject to criticism: the music is doing only what the materials seem to demand. It is a marvelous tautological situation where the composer can be both naïf and savant at the same time.

Both aspects of Harris's persona—naïve freshness and bold conception—abound in his *Symphony 1933*.[15] Like Schuman, the Boston critics loved the work. It had "rugged, driving sincerity"; it exhibited "breadth and vigor" and an "important and forceful expression." Moses Smith, the most perspicacious of the Boston critics, said, "The symphony speaks the American language. This music is virile. It has a destination."[16] Henry Taylor Parker of the *Boston Evening Transcript* went out of his way to position the symphony as the clarion to a new American music.

> Mr. Harris's symphony is unmistakably American—American of the Far West that nourishes itself rather than of the East that naturally and inevitably draws from Europe a part of its esthetic sustenance. . . . The new symphony is American, first, in a pervading directness, in a recurring and unaffected roughness of speech—an outspoken symphony. . . . In the second place, Mr. Harris's symphony is American in the nature of its rhythms, the scope of its melody . . . They seem to derive, besides, from the West

> that bred Mr. Harris and in which he works most eagerly—from its air, its life, its impulses, even its gaits.[17]

The New York critics, in contrast, were not so kind. Olin Downes, music critic for the *New York Times*, was particularly harsh, hitting Harris hardest where Harris was most vulnerable: right in the autogenesis. "There is little genuine organic development in this symphony. It sometimes repeats, but seldom progresses." He ended his review by saying that "the performance of Brahms [Fourth] symphony brought substantial relief from a program which had begun with a European futility [Stravinsky's *Apollon musagète*] and ended with an American ineptitude."[18] Downes's comments were fighting words for the newly anointed Western musical cowboy, and Harris and his claque took aim at Downes. Harris's supporters "reprinted the Downes and Parker reviews side by side and distributed them to libraries, journalists, and other musicians 'so the people could decide.'"[19] In addition, Arthur Mendel, an early supporter of Harris's, wrote a rebuttal that answered Downes's review point by point.[20]

What makes this particular skirmish fascinating is how a later Harris work would draw Schuman into the fray. On February 14, 1937, New York heard the premiere of what, in retrospect, is considered one of Harris's finest works, the Quintet for Piano and Strings. The reviewer in the *New York Times* wasn't Downes—N.S. (presumably Noel Straus) wrote the piece—but it echoed Downes's review of the *Symphony 1933* three years earlier. By this time, Schuman was studying privately with Harris. Whether or not Schuman had read the Quintet review on his own, Harris made sure that Schuman saw it.

> My dear Schuman:
>
> If after reading the enclosed [review] you find it befuddled and intellectually dishonest and misleading—I would appreciate you answering it by sending a critique of the criticism to Olin Downes who I believe welcomes comments which he can publish in Sunday papers—
>
> Cordially,
> Roy Harris[21]

Clearly Harris is referring to the rebuttal that Mendel penned, and Schuman must have been familiar with it, for Schuman drafted a lengthy, Mendellian response.[22] Harris would often manipulate those around him in what things they were to write about him, and Schuman was an early pawn in Harris's chess game of prestige and honor.[23] In the present case, the more men Harris could advance against the critics of the *New York Times*, the greater his chances of carrying the day for American music as he understood it. And while N.S. gave him reason to attack, it was Downes who was most in Harris's sights.

The tension between Downes and Harris came to a head in a radio debate that was broadcast on May 19, 1937, on WQXR's "Exploring the Seven Arts" program. Harris was invited by Ashley Pettis to appear with Downes in a free-for-all on contemporary music. Pettis, the organizer of the Composers' Forum-Laboratory concerts, immediately thought of Harris when the program was suggested; he told Harris he envisioned him "with feathers in your head and a tomahawk in your hand. . . . Perhaps the 'jawbone of an ass' might be a better weapon–that is more suited to the occasion."[24] Responses to the station suggest that the debate was a draw. One man wrote into WQXR to say that "Mr. Harris was too personal and at times overbearing and hinging on discourteousness." But another—Schuman—wrote in to "register my vote and the votes of three others who listened in with me as emphatically in favor of Roy Harris, and to express the hope that this debate be given as much publicity as possible."[25]

Despite Schuman's later reservations about Harris as a composer, he remained devoted to his teacher throughout the 1930s. The titles of the three movements of Schuman's Second String Quartet, written in the summer of 1937—Sinfonia, Passacaglia, and Fugue—recall those of Harris's Piano Quintet of early 1937—Passacaglia, Cadenza, and Fugue. A still earlier Harris work, the 1935 Symphony for Voices, made a particularly powerful impression on Schuman. He wrote to Harris:

> We [i.e., the library at Sarah Lawrence College] have the recordings of the SYMPHONY FOR VOICES. In the last two days I have listened to it eleven times and with each new hearing become more and more thrilled. Believe me when I say I have never heard choral music more magnificently wrought and more brilliantly conceived. The figures in the first movement are amazing—an ostinato idea which with each statement seems to take on added significance. The second movement of course is the most perfect single choral movement in the literature. What an idea for the word Tears. And then that fugue—YOU MUST GET THE CHORAL SYMPHONY PERFORMED.
>
> I wanted you to know what a great experience I've had from this music but I can't possibly say this in a letter. With each work I'm more firmly under your banner. . . .
>
> The modern man you sing.[26]
>
> schuman
>
> I could do a better teaching job on the Symphony for Voices if you'd get me a copy of the score. Would you try to do this.[27]

Schuman's love affair with Whitman can also be traced to Harris. "Although my *Prelude for Voices* was accepted by the Westminster choir for the festival this Spring [of 1937], I am taking a cue from Roy Harris and doing a longer work for them for next year and as a consequence I perhaps will withdraw the Prelude if I get another first rate group to give the first performance."[28] The Prelude, set to the words of Thomas Wolfe, was shelved until 1939, and Schuman composed *Pioneers!* (his first Whitman setting) for the 1938 Festival. For a time, Harris's word became Schuman's duty. Harris, in turn, ingratiated himself to the Sarah Lawrence campus. He came and spoke to the students in the spring of

The participants in the 1938 Westminster Choir Festival. Standing, left to right: Harold Frantz; Harry Becker; Wray Lundquist; David Felt; Elvin Etner; Mary Louise Wright; Schuman; Hubert Taylor; Robert Rudolph; Reuel Lahmer; and George Lynn. Seated, left to right: Harrington Shorthall; Harl McDonald; John Finley Williamson, director of the festival; Arthur Farwell; Aaron Copland; and Roy Harris. A portrait of Mrs. H. A. Talbot appears at the upper right.

1937, and eighteen months later came the announcement that he would write a piece for the chorus. In the wake of that news, a reporter paraphrased Schuman's attitude toward his mentor: "No music is being written abroad that in any way compares to the American School which Harris, in [Schuman's] opinion, heads."[29]

The critical success that greeted Harris's Third Symphony would mark the last time that Harris stood atop American music as its unrivaled leader. Harris had written a violin concerto for Jascha Heifetz, who liked Harris's melodies but didn't care for his harmonies. Rather than rework the concerto to Heifetz's specifications, Harris recast the material into a one-movement symphony. Its premiere was delayed because Harris could not interest any orchestra in performing the work—his Second Symphony had been poorly received—which led Harris to publish an article in the *New York Times* on New Year's Day 1939, that, according to Nicolas Slonimsky, a Harris biographer, "was sure to antagonize the greatest number of managers and conductors, music critics and symphony patrons." Koussevitzky read Harris's article and swore never to do another Harris work. But when he saw the composer with a large package under his arm—the Third Symphony—Koussevitzky asked to hear it. Harris played it for him, and Koussevitzky scheduled it for a concert the following month.[30]

The young Harvard student Leonard Bernstein, who reviewed concerts of the Boston Symphony Orchestra that winter, praised Koussevitzky for presenting three American works in close succession: Carpenter's new one-movement Violin Concerto (March 3–4), which, to Bernstein, "got steadily drearier, cloudier, more involved, and fancier . . . until the pianissimo ending found several good friends of modern music asleep in their stalls";[31] the one-movement Harris Third (February 24–25); and yet another one-movement work that was performed before either the Carpenter or the Harris, Schuman's Second Symphony (February 17–18).[32] Although Harris was one of Koussevitzky's favored composers, it was Copland who encouraged Schuman to send his symphony to the conductor.[33] Koussevitzky promised to perform the work, feeling that the young composer needed to hear how a first-rate orchestra made his music sound. In a Valentine's Day letter to his young wife, who had remained behind in New York until the actual performances, Schuman was equal parts awed and dismayed with Koussevitzky's interpretation of the symphony.

> It is an unbelievably exciting experience to have your music performed by a great orchestra. The Boston Symphony leaves nothing to be desired. Koussevitzky is wonderful to me & very considerate. He asks me my opinion on every detail then does it his own way. He believes so thoroughly in his own convictions that he is incapable of changing his idea of interpretation. This works both ways. The first portion of the work is done just as I should wish. The middle section is fast—faster than Schenkman. He insists on this! I've asked him several times to keep the same tempo—but no use. The rest of the work is also too fast. The results are very exciting but produce an effect different from what I should really have wished. The marvelous part is that he plays the work with real fire & conviction & wonderful regard for dynamic markings. My first experience at being "interpreted"—thank God by a great orchestra & an inspired leader. Of course, there are two more rehearsals & I'm in hopes that certain things will clear up. As a whole I'm thrilled & my admiration for K. is increased no end by his zeal & great ability.[34]

The Boston audience, however, loathed the work.

> Krenek's Second Piano Concerto . . . with the composer as soloist, and William Schuman's Second Symphony ran a close race for the questionable honor of being the most unpopular new music in the recent history of the symphony concerts. . . . When the [Schuman] went into rehearsal Koussevitzky introduced the composer proudly to the orchestra. Koussevitzky kept asking the young composer during the rehearsal whether everything was all right, in accordance with his wishes. As to the effect on the audience, Koussevitzky told Schuman, "The performance will not be a *succès*, but with me it will be a *succès*."[35]

Warren Storey Smith of the *Boston Post* can stand in for the other critics. Nearly all took note of the long-held C by the trumpets; indeed, Schuman's program notes for the Boston Symphony made note of this feature. How did this critic react? "When in the course of the single movement this pedal tone . . . is dropped, the listener experiences a blessed sense of relief, as when a dentist removes his drill."[36]

Only Moses Smith of the *Boston Evening Transcript* came to the work's defense (and Koussevitzky's as well), not once but twice. In his first review of the concert (which also included Sibelius's Third Symphony), Smith told his readers:

> I found the [Schuman] healthy and stimulating. In one long movement, which could discernibly be broken up into three sections, the symphony had muscular drive as well as intellectual conviction. Perhaps the language it employs and the form in which it is cast take it inevitably out of the category of music for large numbers of listeners. But I am not ready to concede even so much. It seems to me rather that Dr. Koussevitzky, far from having made a mistake in placing it on one of his programs, is actually disclosing to Boston audiences a genuine American talent.[37]

Not to be cowed by the audience or his fellow critics, Smith restated his opinion two days later in even stronger terms. "A second hearing of the Symphony by William Schumann [*sic*] . . . left this attestant with a feeling of renewed pleasure. The young composer clearly knew what he wanted to say and how to say it. Furthermore—and this is more obviously a matter of opinion—what he had to say was worth saying." The fact that Smith used almost one-fourth of his review of another unrelated concert to voice his "Second Thoughts" (so subtitled in the review) makes his opinion even more remarkable. Schuman clearly appreciated Smith's verdict; in his scrapbook of clippings, he underlined Smith's second thoughts and later wrote to Smith's daughter to tell her that "it was only your father who brought the note of encouragement and confidence."[38] And Smith's "second thoughts" weren't his last. In his review of the Harris Third a week later, Smith brought up Schuman's name repeatedly, beginning in the second sentence of a review ostensibly of the new Harris work.

> Last Friday and Saturday [Koussevitzky] presented the Second Symphony of William Schuman, one of the younger and more talented American composers. At yesterday's matinee concert . . . he directed the first performance of the Third Symphony of Roy Harris. . . . At the concerts of next week Dr. Koussevitzky will provide Bostonians an opportunity to make first acquaintance with the Violin Concerto of John Alden Carpenter, who will achieve the age of 63 next Tuesday and who was a modern composer before Schuman was born. . . . What the grumblers sometimes fail to consider is that the conductor is too conscientious and too honest to palm off the latest mellifluous product of an American pen, saying absolutely nothing, as a worthy expression of native talent. Instead he has sought out fresh eager voices, like those of Walter Piston and Roger Sessions and Aaron Copland; like that of Roy Harris in the two previous Symphonies by which his rugged imagination was made known here; and like that of the gifted Schuman last week.[39]

So although Bernstein had declared that "the most important music heard [that February in Boston] was the Harris *Symphony*," Smith was already reaching an opinion like the one Rosenfeld would reach a few months later: Schuman was the man to watch.

Given the paucity of correspondence between Schuman and Harris from 1937 to 1938, it is unclear when Schuman showed Harris his one-movement Second Symphony. He had taken the First Symphony to Harris shortly after he began studying with him. "He pointed out all the things he didn't think would work," Schuman said, "and then, when I eventually heard the thing, he was absolutely right."[40] Harris came to hear the May 1938 performance of the Second Symphony, which leads to the question: Whose idea it was to write a one-movement symphony first? Both Harris and Schuman endured comparisons of their music to that of Sibelius, likely abetted by the structure of Sibelius's Seventh Symphony and its surface similarity to their one-movement symphonies. But did Harris and Schuman decide independently of each other to write a one-movement symphony? Was the pupil emulating the master? Or did Harris, in recasting his concerto and completing the symphony in January 1939, steal a page from Schuman the way that Schuman stole a page from Harris's Quintet for his Quartet?[41] This much is clear: the hostile reception Schuman's Second Symphony received, coupled with Koussevitzky's and Smith's resolute belief in him, suddenly set him apart from his elders.

This support didn't keep Schuman from seeking Harris's approval or Harris from trying to steer Schuman. Koussevitzky had announced a festival of American music for the fall of 1939, and Schuman was determined to be a part of that festival, notwithstanding the negative reception his music had received earlier that year and (according to Schuman's recollection) Harris's slightly unsupportive stance. Recall that it wasn't Harris's idea that Schuman show the Second Symphony to Koussevitzky; Copland was the one to build that bridge. Now, with an American festival on the horizon, Harris seemed much more wary about his protégé.

> Roy was arranging the program, and I said: "Roy, I've got to write an overture." And he said: "They'll never accept it after the Second Symphony." And I said: "I have to do it, and it's going to be called American Festival Overture because that's what this is all about." So I got the idea and I remember taking it out to him—I remember this so vividly—out to Montclair, and I sang it to him while he was shaving, and he said: "Great." I sang him the fugue theme of the opening, and he liked that.[42]

According to Flora Rheta Schreiber, Schuman's second biographer, "this was the first time Harris had unreservedly approved a Schuman musical concept at first hearing."[43] The *American Festival Overture* is the stuff of the next chapter, but its success opened a fissure between Schuman and Harris, as the latter was proving to be professionally difficult and musically uneven.

Professional challenges would emerge as Schuman worked with Harris and Pettis on a grant proposal for the Rockefeller Foundation.[44] Submitted on May 1, 1940, and representative of 125 surveys that the authors received (out of 600 solicited), the proposal sets forth a rationale for a Composers' Institute "of men who represent a sectional cross-cut of America as well as the prevailing tendencies in American composition," to be established in Washington, D.C. At a cost of $150,000 per annum "for a period of two years, with necessary additional funds to continue three more years," the proposed institute was a pipe dream for the proposal's authors. Pettis saw that funding for the Composers' Forum-Laboratory was running out; this was his attempt to continue his brainchild in the nation's capital. (He would later try to establish it in San Francisco, again asking the Rockefeller Foundation for financial assistance, which it would deny.) Harris, for his part, wanted something more stable than the occasional festivals he organized. Two years earlier, he had resigned his position at Westminster Choir College because of the "undesirable conditions" (his words) he found at the school and the school's unwillingness to address the list of remedies he issued to its administrators.[45] While the proposal doesn't state this, it is likely that Harris—whose only job is listed in the survey as "Professor of Composition, Juilliard Summer School"—hoped that the $6,000-a-year post as director of the Institute would fall to him. (When the Rockefeller Foundation elected not to approve the institute, Harris would try again for funding, this time to help develop the music department at Cornell, where he was appointed composer-in-residence in 1941.) Schuman clearly was the odd man out in this triumvirate of authors. Given his bachelor's and master's degrees in music education from Teachers College at Columbia University, he was indisputably the expert on what institutions of higher learning were doing toward meeting the needs of American composers. But he was treated as a junior partner in drafting the proposal. Like Pettis and Harris, he, too, would write to the foundation for a second hearing.[46] And like Pettis's and Harris's requests, his went nowhere, mostly because his correspondent was out of the country until May, and by then Schuman was busy with other interests.

As was the peripatetic Harris. By 1941, he had published *Singing through the Ages*, an anthology of choral music.[47] Apparently he made some backroom deals with some of his contributors and failed to make good on his promises. Copland wrote three times to acquire his complimentary set of the anthology, and Virgil Thomson also repeatedly contacted the American Book Company for his set, but Harris had made no arrangements for free copies. In exasperation, the publisher wrote: "What are you trying to do—pass the buck? I do not understand for the life of me how you can blandly ignore these men. . . . It is very annoying to have these dunning letters keep coming to us when we had no arrangements whatsoever with these men."[48] Perhaps Harris wasn't yet someone to hate, but with the collapse of funding for his enterprises and the strained relationships he created with his colleagues through his absentminded business dealings and his high-handed polemics,[49] Harris was slowly turning himself into someone to contain if not shun outright.

His next major work—the *Folksong* Symphony for amateur chorus and orchestra (1940)—didn't help his fortunes among his peers.[50] At the time, though, Harris viewed his future very differently. Audiences applauded his new symphony—his fourth in Harris's enumeration—in part because of its immediate accessibility, and Harris believed that his star was continuing to rise.

In late October 1942, Harris wrote ecstatically to Schuman about the symphony that was then on his composing desk. "The fifth Symphony is turning out beyond my wildest hopes. I suppose that it will be my Opus Magnus [*sic*]. I'm not going to show it to anybody until after it has been performed."[51] Downes was at the premiere in March 1943, and he panned the work.

> Mr. Harris says that he has hoped to express in this symphony "qualities of our people which our dance music, because of its very nature, cannot reveal—heroic strength, determination, the will to struggle and faith in our destiny. . . ." We do not question his sincerity and loftiness of purpose in the work heard last night. . . . [But] we find it a weak symphony, weak in invention, weak in statement, undistinguished by original ideas. . . . The symphony, for this writer, is a labored piece of work and empty of important musical inspiration.[52]

By this time, Schuman had received two Guggenheim awards and the first-ever New York Music Critics Circle Award for his own Third Symphony (1941). The following month, he was notified by the American Academy and the National Institute of Arts and Letters that he would receive one of the ten $1,000 grants for outstanding American artists. Days later, he found out that he, not Harris, had been awarded the first-ever Pulitzer Prize in music. (The Pulitzer music jury had explicitly asked Harris to submit his new symphony.)[53] Why is Downes's review of the Fifth Symphony important? While Schuman's scrapbooks almost exclusively contain clippings of his own successes and failures, there are at least three Harris clippings in the scrapbooks: the one of "N.S." panning the Piano Quintet, which Schuman defended; one praising the Third Symphony, in which Moses Smith had mentioned Schuman; and Downes's pan of the Harris Fifth.

Harris, of course, would have a self-serving explanation as to why the Fifth failed to receive a sympathetic hearing.

> Koussevitzky, who knows my output well, my own wife Johana, a most astute musician, many of my musical friends, and all of my most gifted pupils are agreed that my <u>Fifth Symphony</u> is more important in scope, materials and realization than my <u>Third</u>. But the <u>Fifth</u> is ten minutes longer, requires more rehearsing, and in consequence has not been published or recorded. So it remains unknown—is practically non-existent

> to Americans. Such circumstances attend the slow death of much of America's best music.[54]

Schuman, however, was not one of those "most gifted pupils" who liked the Fifth more than the Third. In a lengthy letter to Copland, in which he spoke of lots of music, including his own *A Free Song* (which had not yet won the Pulitzer), Schuman spent an entire paragraph on Harris and the Fifth:

> Roy's work sounded much better in [Carnegie Hall] than you could have guessed from the radio. That is[,] the difference in sonority was greater than it usually is. The piece is a great disappointment to me as I think it is to most of R.H.'s admirers. Mills, for instance, was quite bitter about it, Rosenfeld (who is less reliable and as far as I can see likes only esoteric items—as soon as they become understandable to the crowd his interest wanes—is this fair?) also did not believe the symphony. Like all Roy's music it has wonderful things but the defects are much worse than some earlier compositions. The most perfect large work I believe is the Piano Quintet. But no composer writes at his best all the time. I think this work is a failure but I still believe in the value of R.H. To me the '33 symphony (with all its defects) has things that were not in music that way before. I felt able to take flight from these things and shall remain always grateful for this music. But I am so very disappointed with this work that I can scarcely begin to say all I have on my mind. One thing seems clear—there must be a real personal adjustment or the adjustment must come from the composing for healthy music to be produced. The personal problems of our friend must be very deep. I wish he could be helped. I'm not sure the real and full promise of his genius will come to light ever if the way is not made less confused.[55]

According to Harris, Schuman gave a lecture in 1942 about Harris's music, for which Harris thanked his former pupil.[56] Less than a year later, Schuman sharpened his opinion of his teacher, choosing works from 1937 and earlier as Harris's best. And when, in 1957, Schuman was asked to draw up a list of recommended works for a World Music Bank, the only work from these early years that merited Schuman's vote was Harris's Third Symphony from 1939.[57]

After Schuman's sweep of prizes and honors between 1941 and 1943, the gulf between him and Harris widened. Alfred Frankenstein would write in 1944 for the readers of *Modern Music*: "The evidence is accumulating on all sides and the conclusion is inevitable: William Schuman has caught the boat."[58] By this time, comparisons between Schuman and Harris were drawn that inevitably found the latter wanting. Frankenstein remarked:

> "Enthusiasm" is the word for Schuman, and his faults are the faults of enthusiasm. Some of his virtues stem from the same quality. . . . Schuman's big instrumental pieces employ a far freer, subtler, more intricate and kaleidoscopically shifting tonal plan that his choral works. Here he is closer to Roy Harris, with whom he once studied, than to anyone else, although he has much more rhythmic fire, variety and vivacity than

> Harris. . . . Harris writes a quintet in the form of passacaglia and fugue, chorale and toccata, Schuman a symphony in the form of passacaglia and fugue, chorale and toccata. But the lithe and aerated draughtsmanship of Schuman's polyphony and the luminous quality of his orchestra, which always glows and never glitters—these things, plus the rhythmic variety, give his music its own strong profile.[59]

One reason why Schuman seems to have caught the boat is because he, more than Harris and even Copland, understood the musical Zeitgeist. His music was generally more frenetic, more boisterous, more like the sleek and noisy assembly line than was that of his peers. Even the "quiet and expressive" aspects of his music were singled out for their workmanship and effectiveness. At a time when the nation was at war, precision and passion were among the watchwords for the nation, and Schuman's music delivered those in spades. While some of the works best known from that era—*Rodeo*, *Oklahoma!* and *Appalachian Spring*—draw from a river of sentimentality that runs throughout American history, the 1940s was also a time for newer, more modern and urban sounds, such as those found in Bernstein's *Fancy Free* and *The Age of Anxiety*. Schuman fit this more modern niche brilliantly, making him a force to be reckoned with.

By 1945, Schuman was considered by many to be the most powerful man in musical America. That summer he left his teaching position at Sarah Lawrence to become the full-time director of publications at G. Schirmer. (He had taken on some of the responsibilities part-time after Carl Engel's death in May 1944.) With full knowledge of Schuman's access to the movers and shakers in New York, Harris contacted his former pupil. Schuman recounted that phone call.

> And I remember that summer that Roy Harris called me, and he said: "You know the Steinway family well." I said: "I don't know them at all." He said: "That's too bad." I said: "Why?" He said: "I understand they are going to name the next president of Juilliard, and I want you to put my name in." I said: "I don't know that the Steinway family have anything to do with it." I already knew I was going to go, and I couldn't say anything. I don't know whether he would ever believe me or not. It was really very strange.[60]

No corroboration of this anecdote exists outside of Schuman's comment, and, as has been established, Schuman embellished his yarns. Assuming this yarn's veracity, here was Schuman, aware of the impending announcement that he would assume the presidency of Juilliard beginning in the fall of 1945, fielding a call from his former teacher to put in a good word for him for a position that would have suited Harris poorly.

Noted Harris scholar Beth Levy succinctly summed up the remainder of Harris's career. "For the forty years that stretched from the symphonic triumphs of 1939–40 to his death, Harris wandered in an American desert of his own creation, driven by a legend he had helped to create, but encumbered by its questionable assumptions and attendant stereotypes."[61] His most gifted pupil would devote much of the rest of his life to improving music education in America, working with the federal government to take American music beyond the 50 states, and nurturing structures and societies that would serve creative artists worldwide. They stayed friends, but professionally they traveled different paths.

In 1939, Rosenfeld was fighting an uphill battle when it came to recognizing Schuman as coeval to Harris and Copland. He used the Second Symphony as proof of Schuman's rising arc. Another commentator took issue with the same work, linking both Harris and Schuman to a third American iconoclast.

> Much has been written of Ives as an authentically American composer; and as much, I fear, is going to be written of Schuman. But I doubt that Americans will recognize themselves in the piercing dissonances which Ives goes in for; and Schuman seems to have adopted the method of Roy Harris in which one postulates a rawboned America and expresses it with rawboned music. With this method even a man apparently without a spark of inner musical impulse and with no more than a spark of musical ability can set an orchestra to blaring out one gigantically distended figure for twenty minutes and convince himself and one or two other persons that he is expressing America, as Schuman did in the symphony which C.B.S. broadcast last September. The method is Roy Harris's, but the pupil is outdoing the master.[62]

By the 1940s, the pupil was outdoing the master in nearly every measurable capacity, be it prize money or press coverage or the prestige of position. Schuman had not merely gained ground on Harris—and Copland, too—but was taking the lead.

NINE

SCHUMAN, COPLAND, KOUSSEVITZKY, AND BERNSTEIN

Aaron Copland was not only generously gifted, as Paul Rosenfeld volunteered in his overview of Copland, Harris, and Schuman. Copland was also generously inclined when it came to his fellow composers. Like Harris, Copland worked to secure a place for contemporary American music within America's musical life. One major distinction between the two men: Copland invested far less ego into his place within that life than Harris did in his own.[1]

That generosity of spirit enabled Copland to laud Schuman publicly in a 1938 review that echoes Robert Schumann's famous review of Frédéric Chopin's op. 2 that appeared more than a century earlier.[2] Copland had before him the music of his younger contemporary, and even though Copland's words are less immortal than Schumann's (and also more critical of the composition in question), they were no less effusive.

> Schuman is, so far as I am concerned, the musical find of the year. There is nothing puny or miniature about this young man's talent. If he fails he will fail on a grand scale. His eight part chorus *Pioneers* . . . tries characteristically for big things. It is carefully planned music—music of design rather than melodic inspiration. When the planning is too evident, as it sometimes is, the effect is unspontaneous. But for the most part, this is music of tension and power—a worthy match for Walt Whitman's stirring text. From the testimony of this piece alone, it seems to me that Schuman is a composer who is going places.[3]

Like so many other of his early works, *Pioneers!* had pleased Schuman initially. On the strength of its anticipated premiere at the 1938 Westminster Choir College spring festival, the esteemed British firm J. & W. Chester agreed in the fall of 1937 to publish the work and make it available on both sides of the Atlantic. (Marks Music, Schuman's principal Tin Pan Alley song publisher, distributed the work in the United States.) The work received a positive review in a London-based trade magazine: "[Schuman] has captured something of the rugged strength of the American author's words, and incidentally given his choir something to 'get their teeth into.'" Schuman asked Claire Reis to include information of its publication in her upcoming volume on American composers, and he proudly sent Lehman Engel a copy of the published score.[4] But neither the composer nor the publisher fully contemplated how the failure to provide a piano reduction for rehearsal purposes would depress sales. After more than ten years in circulation, *Pioneers!* realized for Schuman a net profit of just over £2.[5]

Copland's public acclamation, though, was worth far more than any royalty, and his praise enveloped more than just *Pioneers*! The industriousness that Schuman had shown with organizing the Composers' Forum-Laboratory concerts and the American Composers Committee had brought Schuman more closely into Copland's orbit. And Copland and Schuman became friends. Whereas Schuman preserved a formal style of address with Harris during the years of their lessons together (1936–38), he and Copland quickly moved to a first-name basis. Copland did not try to usurp Harris's role in Schuman's life, but he did offer ideas on what the up-and-coming composer ought to write next. And Schuman listened.

> I want to tell you how seriously I have taken your advice of last winter. You suggested I write some pieces for Piano and not restrict myself as to form. I report now the completion of two movements of my Concerto for Piano and Orchestra. The final mv. now under way but will be delayed with college coming up. I'm very anxious to have you hear it as soon as possible on two pianos. I've enjoyed writing for the Piano although it makes me furious that I can't play any of it myself.[6]

Schuman's love-hate relationship with the piano ran through his entire career. He gave the purest expression of his challenges with the piano when he wrote to Isadore Freed, editor of Theodore Presser's series, Contemporary Piano Music from Distinguished Composers. Freed had asked Schuman in the spring of 1955 to contribute to the series; it took Schuman more than three years to write something. "Frankly, piano writing is not my specialty—I find the instrument exceedingly difficult to write for, perhaps because I myself am not a pianist."[7] These pieces—the *Three Moods for Piano* (1958)—are but one of four works that Schuman published for the piano, far fewer than Harris or Copland.

Another measure of the struggle Schuman had when it came to writing for the piano is that he completed at least four other works for piano solo but chose not to polish or publish them. The *Five Little Preludes* from April 1933 were followed by a canon (with introduction and coda) from June of that year. The 1938 Piano Concerto was preceded by *Three Pieces for Piano*, which were performed at the same June 15, 1938, Composers' Forum-Laboratory concert that featured the *Choral Etude* and the Second String Quartet. Schuman's Sarah Lawrence colleague Judith Sidorsky premiered the three pieces (Fugal Prelude, March, and Ostinato Variations), which Schuman later called *Three Studies for a Piano Concerto* when he offered them to Quincy Porter for the 1938 Yaddo Festival.[8] Most tantalizing among the unpublished piano scores is a 1959 set of variations on a 12-tone theme. As with the *Three Pieces for Piano*, Copland appears to have been the proximate stimulus for the 12-tone variations, as Schuman pored over Copland's *Piano Fantasy* during the summer of 1957 and was fascinated that 12-tone means could be put to such individual ends (Schuman wrote to Copland, "If you are nodding in the direction of the serial technique I'd say that the result is nevertheless pure Copland.")[9] And like the 1938 pieces, the 1959 work served as a study for another larger work, in this case the first movement of the Seventh Symphony (1960).

In the case of the Concerto for Piano and Orchestra, Schuman devoted the latter half of 1938 to its completion. By this time, Schuman had adopted the habit of putting dates and places of composition on the last pages of each movement, and in the case of the concerto, all three movements were composed in New York. (Often, Schuman would mark only the end date of a work and not its start date. He explained to his publisher, "The dates of completion of compositions should always be on my works since I use these in lieu of opus numbers.")[10] The length of the movements, particularly the first one, makes clear the extent to which this work was quite different from the Piano Concerto he would compose four years later, whose three movements take approximately eight minutes each to perform.

I—Sinfonia (June 15–July 12, 1938; approx. 15–16 min.)
II—Fantasia (July 13–20, 1938; approx. 6 min.)
III—Ostinato Variations (December 22, 1938; 8 min.)

With its extensive unaccompanied solos throughout the concerto, Schuman exerted himself mightily in bending his talents in Copland's direction. He believed enough in the concerto that he allowed it to be published by Arrow Press, and given that Copland was one of the founders, Copland would have likely known that the work would bear Arrow's imprint. It is less clear who paid for the "fifty scores all bound and published looking" that Schuman offered to Arrow prior to Engel agreeing to publish the work.[11] However Schuman and the press came to pay for the copies, they clearly were made available for purchase, as several libraries own the publication. Just as clearly, Schuman became dissatisfied with the work and told Copland how the 1942 version differed from the 1938 one: "I have completely new first and second movements with the third movement alone using material from the discarded concerto of '38."[12] And in describing the new work, Schuman exposed both his approach to his newly composed work and Copland's attitude toward Schuman's compositions.

As usual I am excited about the work, especially the slow movement and I'll bring it to you for one of the rememberable sessions of hearing how Copland thinks my music is noble if-/ uneven-full of holes and lacking in objectivity. But you'll see Aaron-you'll love the 2nd mv. The first is straight forward and the last for [Rosalyn] Tureck [soloist for the work's premiere].[13]

If 1938 was a year of work aborted, it was also a year of work rewarded. The WPA prize for the *Choral Etude* and the first-prize designation for the Second Symphony from the Musicians' Committee to Aid Spanish Democracy come from the first half of the year. Copland was one of the judges of the latter contest, and in typical Copland fashion, he praised the piece while harboring misgivings about it. But Schuman's request that he accept the work as a full-fledged symphony (if only one movement in length) and Howard Barlow's performance of the Symphony that September with the CBS Symphony Orchestra affected Copland. He wrote to Victor Kraft after the broadcast: "What I like about it is that it seems to be music that comes from a real urge, which gives it an immediacy of feeling that gets everyone who hears it. If he can build on that, we've got something there."[14]

The broadcast did give many of the listeners an immediate feeling, and they wrote the network to unburden themselves. Schuman remembered the letters CBS received as uniformly devastating.

There was some farmer in Iowa who said: "For two days I've had a headache and aspirin wouldn't take it away. That awful music!" And one letter was worse than the next, so I called Barlow, and I said: "I am terribly sorry I got you into all that trouble." He said: "Trouble? What we want is audience reaction. I am going to program it again."[15]

Barlow would program it two years later with the Baltimore Symphony, but none of the eleven letters from 1938 mentions a two-day headache. One does mention aspirin, though, and eight of them have no kind words for the prize-winning symphony.

I have never felt such physical pain in my ears. All I have for careful listening is a headache due to the impact of excruciating tones & combinations of tones on the tympani of my ears.

Not knowing one note from another perhaps I am not in a position to voice any opinion, but I do wish to say that I thought the second symphony of Mr. Schuman atrocious, meaningless, noisy, tuneless and terrible. . . . I hope you will forgive me for being so crude about it, but truthfully I felt mad enough to "cuss."

If you ask us—we think that kind of a composition kills music rather than encourages.

I rise to remark that the "Second Symphony" of William Schumann . . . seemed to me unspeakably awful. Its meaningless jumble of discordant noises was bad enough in itself—but it was the persistent measured thud in the bass that pounded my nerves to the quick and made me want to howl. I tried to be a sport and stayed with the thing to the bitter end, hoping that somehow, somewhere, there might be a fleeting moment

> of harmony—or that in the end, the journey through purgatory might be justified by a glimpse of a "lost chord" that would seem like Paradise, by comparison. But there was no such happy interval and the instrumental contortions came to no end. They just suddenly stopped. "For this relief, much thanks," I said, and after taking an aspirin tablet, was able to enjoy the second second symphony—by Beethoven. What a nerve to present both on the same program!

Copland and Barlow, however, weren't the only ones who were favorably impressed by the symphony. Listeners from more ordinary walks of life, too, praised the work:

> It was with great pleasure that I listened to the symphony played on Sunday composed by a young American named Wm Schuman. . . . It was refreshing to hear such a fine composition by one in our own midst. Hope we may be privileged to hear more from this same source.
>
> I heard your "Second Symphony" yesterday and enjoyed it very much, as did several of my friends who listened in. We thought the long organ-point near the beginning quite thrilling, and admired the stark, austere quality of the work and the sustained melodic lines. Of course it was impossible to grasp it completely in one hearing, and I hope we get to hear it again, as well as some of your other works.
>
> On Sunday last I heard the performance of Wm. Schumann's Second Symphony. I would like to convey accurately the impression it made upon me, but words are little enough tools, after all. I believe that here is a true enduring modern work, elemental and direct, if brutal, in its approach; and the orchestration is superb. I would like at some future date that you repeat this work if enough listeners feel as I do about it. Mr. Schumann appears to be a composer of worth.[16]

Just over a month later, steeled by the affirming comments of these listeners and prodded by a postcard from Copland, Schuman sent his symphony to Serge Koussevitzky, conductor of the Boston Symphony Orchestra.

The road to Boston for Koussevitzky (1874–1951) was surprisingly direct.[17] He studied the double bass in Moscow, joined the Bol'shoy Theater Orchestra in 1894, and became its principal double bass player in 1901. In 1905, he married into money, which allowed him the opportunity to study conducting with a student orchestra at his home. His debut in 1908 featured Rachmaninoff at the piano and the Berlin Philharmonic under his baton. His career then alternated between his appearances as a double bass virtuoso and a conductor until in 1920 he and his wife left the Soviet Union, taking much of their fortunes with them and founding the Concerts Koussevitzky in Paris (1921–29).

On the other side of the Atlantic, the Boston Symphony Orchestra, founded in 1881, had favored German conductors for its first 37 years, but the anti-German backlash precipitated by World War I resulted in a turn to French conductors and an increase in French-trained musicians among the players. Koussevitzky's immediate predecessor, Pierre Monteux (1875–1964; conductor, 1919–24), introduced contemporary Russian and French music to Boston audiences; he had, after all, conducted the premieres of Stravinsky's *Petrushka* and *The Rite of Spring*, Debussy's *Jeux* and Ravel's *Daphnis et Chloe* (between 1911 and 1913). Koussevitzky also promoted contemporary music, and in his 25 years at the helm of the Boston Symphony Orchestra (1924–49), he would do for American music what Monteux had done for the Europeans. Koussevitzky premiered 99 works with the symphony, and the American composers he honored included Barber, Copland, Diamond, Gershwin, Hanson, Harris, Piston, and, on three occasions, Schuman.

If Koussevitzky had a musical Achilles heel, it was that he could not learn a new score simply through studying it on his own. Instead, he used his wealth to hire pianists to play the scores for him as he conducted the "orchestra." He was therefore reliant on the skills and (to some degree) opinions of other musicians to determine whether a new work was worthy of his ministrations. Even so, he was confident enough in his own judgment that he could and would turn down the recommendations of others, including Copland's.[18] So though Copland opened the door for Schuman, he and the music would have to walk through it.

Schuman's first letter is pure deference, saying nothing about the possibility of a performance. "I sincerely trust that you will find the time to look at this score." When Koussevitzky's secretary wrote back two weeks later to ask for the parts, Schuman dispatched them the next day, with the breathless admission that "any news of the piece, as regards possible performance by Dr. Koussevitsky [*sic*], cannot possibly reach here quickly enough." (Schuman wouldn't master the spelling of Koussevitzky's name until early 1941.) The news reached Schuman obliquely, as John Burk, program annotator for the Boston Symphony Orchestra, wrote to Schuman in late January 1939 to request information about the symphony, then scheduled to be performed in mid-February. Schuman remained breathless.

> Dear Dr. Koussevitsky:
>
> . . . I wish there were some adequate way in which I could express my feelings to you.
>
> In your long and distinguished career as champion of new music you have surely encountered every kind of composer. Yet I feel that no one before could ever have experienced more inner glow and excitement than I now feel at the prospect of your performance. The mere thought of the experience is so great that I must keep assuring myself that it is real.
>
> The only way I can really thank you, I know, is that my music prove worthy of the great honor you have chosen to give it.[19]

According to Schuman, Koussevitzky delivered a prophecy about the symphony. "During the period of rehearsal and before the performance, he said that the music with him was a *succès* and that of course I must hear a great orchestra perform it but that he didn't think it would be a *succès* with the public."[20] And, as has already been chronicled, the Boston critics, with the exception of Moses Smith, savaged the work. But in the afterglow of the experience, Schuman seemed to take the criticisms in stride. Schuman wrote to Koussevitzky on the Monday after the performance:

> The experience of your performances of my work has enriched my entire conception of composition. There is no adequate way in which I could tell you my present state of elation. I only know that during one short week I somehow managed to grow many years wiser. Now I am going to work to the end of bringing you a worthy piece next Fall. I trust that this composition will not cause you to regret the great encouragement you have so generously given to me.[21]

This letter complicates Schuman's recollection that Harris was cool to Schuman's idea to write a piece for the American music festival that Koussevitzky and Harris were organizing for the fall of 1939. Harris may have been reluctant after what he perceived as the towering failure of Schuman's Second Symphony. But if this letter is to be believed, the Boston performance of Schuman's Second Symphony provide the impetus for Koussevitzky to extend an invitation to Schuman to compose a new piece for the symphony to be premiered that fall.

And again, it is important to recall that not everyone was hostile to the Boston performance. The write-up in the Sarah Lawrence College newspaper was especially effusive in praising the school's local hero and noting that roughly 7 percent of the student body traveled to Boston to hear the symphony.[22] And on the same day the story in the *Campus* appeared, president Constance Warren wrote Schuman an effusive note to invite him to conduct the chorus the following year. "I cannot begin to tell you how exciting the development of the Chorus has seemed to us all. I wouldn't have dreamed that girls of that age could perform as they have."[23] Schuman remained loved and respected in Bronxville.

He also gained some new fans in Cambridge, most notably a junior from Harvard who was dispatched to meet Schuman at the train station. The accounts of the exchange between the 28-year-old composer and the 20-year-old student relate the encounter thus: Leonard Bernstein escorted Schuman back to the Eliot House and had a few beers with him before persuading Schuman to let Bernstein look over the score of the Second Symphony prior to the Boston rehearsal the next morning. Bernstein's one-word verdict of the work, uttered with the sleep-induced stupor every collegian exhibits at seven in the morning: "Seeeebeeeelius!" And then he more than likely went back to sleep. Schuman also remembered that Bernstein and his friends attended the concert and shouted "Bravo!" from their seats in the balcony. "The Schuman symphony," Bernstein wrote in his review, "was for the most part a joy to hear."[24] So in the space of 15 months—from December 1937 to February 1939—Schuman met three men whose influence would far exceed that of Persin or Haubiel or even Harris: Copland, one of his closest composer colleagues; Koussevitzky, his earliest and staunchest champion; and Bernstein, the supernova who would brighten all of American music—and cheer both Bill and Frankie—in countless ways. Years later, Schuman would recount in his autobiography how the Boston performance of the Second Symphony shaped his life. The distance from the event inevitably clouded some of his memories, but the combination of Copland's introduction, Koussevitzky's enthusiasm, and Bernstein's support never left him.

> Most important, I felt that for the rest of my life, no matter what else I did, I would have to express myself through music. Of course I was deeply hurt by the hostile reactions of public and press, but the encouragement of Lenny, of Koussevitzky, and of a few others more than made up for it.[25]

Another person who lived in New York City also was moved by the symphony. Margaret Naumburg (1890–1983) was, like Schuman, an educator who had serious qualms about the educational establishment. Her own experience was so unsatisfactory that she did not initially pursue education as a career.

> Only when a fundamental change in our present system became a practical possibility to me did I find myself committed to education. From the very beginning, I saw that there might be ways of modifying orthodox education, either to enter the system and work from within, or to make a fresh start, outside of all accepted institutions, and construct a plan with new foundations.[26]

She chose the latter course, starting a modified Montessori class in New York City with Claire Raphael in the fall of 1914. Naumburg developed the curriculum and was the principal teacher; Raphael was the assistant teacher who focused on music. The class grew both in size and scope and within a decade was renamed the Walden School.[27] In many ways, the Walden School, with its emphasis on progressive education, was the mirror and model, at its own educational level, for Sarah Lawrence College. The description of the former institution at the time of its closing in the late 1980s (given below) sounds much like a description of the latter.

> The school stressed allowing students to develop their identities, in large measure through the visual and performing arts. Individual contact with teachers is emphasized, and competition minimized. . . . Teachers are called by their first names. There are no grades and no formal preparation for college-entrance examinations.[28]

Naumburg left the school in the mid-1920s, and by the mid-'30s her focus had shifted to the role of art in the therapeutic treatment of children.[29] Raphael had since married Arthur Reis and, using her musical connections, founded the League of Composers in 1923. Schuman had begun to write for *Modern Music*, the league's journal, in early 1938, and at Reis's invitation had shared with her his vision on the future of the league in a detailed letter in May of that year.[30] Whether Reis brought Schuman to Naumburg's attention is speculation at this point, but in the month after Barlow's broadcast of Schuman's Second Symphony, Naumburg worked out with Schuman the details of what was his first serious commission: a musical score to accompany Naumburg's dance drama/ballet "Playground."

John Burk's program notes for the February 1939 Boston Symphony Orchestra performance of the Second Symphony state that "a ballet, 'Playground,' is now in process of composition," and it was likely this work that Schuman had in mind when he spoke of his early encounters with Copland. "Once when I was very much the neophyte, I showed him fifteen or twenty measures of music for a ballet (later abandoned), and he said: 'Well, when you have some music, I really want to see it. It looks like a good beginning.' Aaron was always tactful."[31] Naumburg spelled out the nature of their collaboration in her commissioning letter. "We decided to work jointly in whatever way seemed advisable in order to create together out of my word material and your musical material, a unified work of art, for a choreographic dance drama with orchestral accompaniment." Although Naumburg reached out to Schuman, he had confirmed his interest as early as the spring of 1938 and reaffirmed it that September. "You must know that your playground idea for ballet gets better with time to think about it. I wasn't properly enthusiastic last Spring because I was so tired out. I've come to believe very much in its possibilities."[32] Naumburg later explained to Schuman how she came to select him. "When I asked you to read and consider working on the music of 'Playground' it was . . . because I had heard some of your music and did believe that you had an essential purity of feeling and a scope to your orchestral understanding that was unique." But Schuman was busy with other projects, and the nature of the project "no longer sustains in me the creative impetus it impelled." Even though Naumburg, in an act of faith, gave Schuman the entire amount of the agreed-upon commission (a rather meager $200), Schuman felt compelled to return the money and to free himself from his obligation, promising to find another composer for Naumburg, should she wish his help, and to continue to contemplate the possibility of writing the score again, should his spirits quicken toward the ballet.[33]

Clearly they did not. What is less clear, given that no manuscript survives of "Playground," is whether some or all of its musical ideas made it into Schuman's breakthrough composition, the one he promised Koussevitzky for the fall of 1939.

> The composer writes as follows about his [American Festival] Overture: "The first three notes of this piece will be recognized by some listeners as the 'call to play' of boyhood days. In New York City it is yelled on the syllables, 'Wee-Awk-Eee' to get the gang together for a game or a festive occasion of some sort. This call very naturally

> suggested itself for a piece of music being composed for a very festive occasion. From this it should not be inferred that the Overture is program music. In fact, the idea for the music came to mind before the origin of the theme was recalled. The development of this bit of 'folk material,' then, is along purely musical lines.[34]

Three years after the premiere of the overture, Schuman said that the work's boisterousness came from the excitement he felt at the prospect of Koussevitzky devoting "two entire programs to the works of our own boys. This though was very much in mind when I started working on the piece. I kept thinking of it in terms of a kind of pep talk. 'Here it is at last—come and get it—'"[35] But by this time Schuman had begun to exhibit his recycler tendencies, turning the *Choreographic Poem*, for example, into the last movement of the First Symphony and the *Three Pieces for Piano* from 1938 into the first version of his Piano Concerto. To go from a ballet about a playground to the incorporation of a playground cry into an overture is not a far distance, although without any evidence the connection must remain speculative. As it happens, Schuman's final letters to Naumburg were sent just as the semester was ending at Sarah Lawrence and his time for composing, abetted and increased by his receipt of a Guggenheim Fellowship for 1939–40, was about to begin. "Playground" was far less important to Schuman and his career than delivering to Koussevitzky the promised piece, one that would be a *succès* to conductor and audience alike.

But first attention had to be paid to Harris. According to the manuscript, Schuman completed the overture on July 28, 1939, but there were changes ahead. That September, Schuman met with Harris to go over the score. Schuman's letter to Koussevitzky provides some insight into what the two composers discussed. "Roy Harris told me some of your observations on 'American Festival Overture.' These comments were very helpful to me. As a result I have reconsidered and changed the harmony in several places, particularly the brass sections. I feel confident you will find these changes to your liking."[36] Whether Harris was relating Koussevitzky's concern or conveying his own cannot be known, but Koussevitzky would later have some choice words about Harris for Schuman.

Next came the shattering development that the world premiere would not take place in Carnegie Hall, as everyone had assumed. The concerts that Harris and Koussevitzky had scheduled for Boston as a salute to the American composer dovetailed neatly with plans the American Society of Composers, Artists, and Publishers (ASCAP) concocted for New York. In conjunction with the Mayor La Guardia's office and the organizers of the 1939 World's Fair in Flushing Meadow, ASCAP announced a music festival to celebrate its silver anniversary and in response to Germany's aggression in Europe. The Boston Symphony Orchestra was to be part of the New York City festival, but the presence of nonunion players in the orchestra drew the wrath of the local Musicians' Union, and it was uninvited. The New York Philharmonic stepped in to take the place of the Boston Symphony Orchestra, and Schuman, had he pressed his luck, might have been able to hear his newest composition with that orchestra and one of its guest conductors. But he stood by Koussevitzky. "I have no desire or intention of hearing it in this Festival save by your organization. . . . It was composed with your knowledge and with the thought always in mind that if it turned out well[,] you and the Boston Symphony would perform it. This is what I still want more than anything else for the Overture."[37] And so it was that, on the afternoon of Friday, October 6, 1939, Koussevitzky and his orchestra premiered Schuman's *American Festival Overture* at Symphony Hall in Boston.

But still more changes were ahead. In his unfinished autobiography, Schuman recalled what happened after the performance:

> When the work was finally played in Boston I was very unhappy with the ending and afterwards I asked to see Koussevitzky alone. He said to me, "Now what do you think of your work?"
>
> After praising his wonderful performance, I said, "The ending is not right and I'm so unhappy to have it played in New York before I can change it, for I realize that there will be no opportunity to rehearse it.
>
> He then said: "You and I are the only ones who know that the ending isn't right. Compose the new ending you wish and I will find the time to rehearse it before the New York performance."
>
> This is exactly what took place.[38]

At its premiere, the *American Festival Overture* shared the program with George Gershwin's Concerto in F, Randall Thompson's Symphony no. 2 in E minor, and, most tellingly, Roy Harris's Third Symphony. And Schuman's original ending for the overture, with its block chords and insistent timpani, must have seemed not only a letdown but also an echo of the ending of the Harris work (which was, as it happened, a rewrite of the symphony's original ending and which, in its rewritten version, sounds suspiciously like the ending of Schuman's Second Symphony). The ending wasn't right for the piece or for Schuman's need to emerge from Harris's shadow. The new ending, comprising the last minute of the performed overture (mm. 326 on in the score), keeps the energy surging ahead, with its scurrying strings and soaring winds, and ends a work that had ostensibly seemed to be in B♭ major with a brass-heavy blaze of bitonality with major triads build on E♭ and C. It was a trial run for the end of the Third Symphony. It was audacious and brash. And it was nothing like Harris.

Schreiber asserted that "at the Boston première (Oct. 6, 1939) the overture was a success with conductor and audience alike. 'Fine!' said Koussevitzky. 'Now you must begin to hate Roy Harris.' Schuman knew that this was Koussevitzky's way of saying that he had come of age musically."[39] But Koussevitzky's comments about the original ending give the lie to part of Schreiber's assertion.

So do Schuman's words in a telegram to friends after the performance the next month, with the new ending in place. "Concert over. Exciting performance but cold reception. Am completely depressed by stupidity and intolerance of our blue bloods. Stravinsky came especially to hear the piece and was late and as a final insult an objectionable young lady asked me how I liked teaching at Bennington."[40] As for hating Harris, Schuman was never one vehemently to hate anyone. But after Harris's interventions allegedly on Koussevitzky's behalf and the mutual agreement between conductor and composer to make the ending of the overture less Harris-like, Koussevitzky's remark sounds in equal parts a validation of Schuman's compositional voice and a warning that Schuman's dependence upon Harris was no longer serving Schuman's best interests.

So even though the Harrises were in New York City from 1938 until they moved to Ithaca, N.Y., for Roy to take a post at Cornell University in 1941, Schuman began to gravitate more and more to Copland, Koussevitzky, and Bernstein for camaraderie and counsel. Schuman paid special deference to Koussevitzky, who had by this time asked Schuman to compose a major work for the Boston Symphony Orchestra. Other works required his more immediate attention—the Third String Quartet and what he called his Secular Cantata no. 1—but Schuman sketched out for Henry Allen Moe, the administrator for the Guggenheim Fellowship, what works he anticipated composing from April 1940 forward. One was "a piano work which has been ordered by a publisher"; which publisher and which piano piece, Schuman did not say, and it would appear that this piece was never completed. Neither was the second anticipated piece: "a Concertino for Bass Clarinet and Chamber Orchestra. This latter work will be written for Mr. Mazzeo of the Boston Symphony Orchestra." But the vestige of that work can be found in the Toccata movement of the Third Symphony, in what Schuman called "*the* passage," which Rosario Mazzeo played flawlessly at the first rehearsal of the Third Symphony, eliciting bravos from his fellow players and confounding Koussevitzky, who didn't understand what the huzzahs were about.[41]

Schuman had written two symphonies, one overture, one concerto, and several smaller pieces for orchestra when he turned to the Third Symphony. Notwithstanding these previous essays, Schuman felt that, with the Third, he was starting anew. He wrote to Koussevitzky:

> It is difficult to tell you what excitement and joy I feel in this new work. I know that in a sense it is my first orchestral composition. For the symphony you performed was, as you said at the time, experimental. The Overture, while an advance over the symphony, had the necessary limitations in emotional gamut of a short and special piece. In this new work I feel that the melodic writing is sustained. It is my fervent hope, and I must confess my belief, that this work will justify your faith in my progress. For these reasons I am taking the liberty of dedicating my first composition to you and your orchestra.[42]

It took him the better part of 1940 to compose the symphony, in part because he had also returned to teaching composition and advising students at Sarah Lawrence. He received a second Guggenheim Fellowship for 1940–41, but the prospect of having his days free to do nothing but compose positively terrified him, so he proposed extending the funding for the Guggenheim over two years while he taught half time. The Guggenheim offices more than met him halfway: they fully funded him for that year and gave him a special dispensation allowing him back into the classroom for two days a week instead of the one day he enjoyed the year before when his only college responsibility was the leadership of the chorus.[43]

The Third was completed in early January 1941, and Schuman turned immediately to his Fourth Symphony, which was completed by August of the year. Artur Rodzinski and the Cleveland Orchestra elected to premiere that work based on an audition he had organized for a committee selected to screen new American works. The Schuman symphony won out over works by Diamond, Van Vactor, Sowerby, and Harris.[44] But prior to the work's completion and its successful audition—indeed, prior to the successful premiere under Koussevitzky of the Third Symphony—Schuman showed the Fourth to Copland at the Berkshire Music Center, the educational arm of the Tanglewood summer music festivals at which Copland soon became a fixture.[45] Bernstein was also at the center that summer, and Schuman, in his nearly indecipherable scrawl, jotted down his impressions of the day on a mimeographed program. Like Koussevitzky's prophetic remarks about the Second Symphony, Schuman could also see into the future.

> The orchestra played like no professional group ever would. They gave all. Wonderful spirit of Berkshires among the kids.
>
> A most remarkable performance—Bernstein should develop into the first sensational American conductor. He has everything. [Bernstein conducted the *American Festival Overture*.]
>
> Koussevitzky so excited by Bernstein performance—he walked up to the stage & kissed us both in public!
>
> Weekend spent with Copland—a slap on the back for Sym. No IV (mv. 1 & 2)—[46]

Copland had never fully critiqued one of Schuman's scores before, and the physicality of his approval caught Schuman by surprise. He wrote to Copland shortly after returning home to repeat his prophecy for Bernstein and his wonder about his time with Copland.

> We know we've never spent a more enjoyable 24 hours. And exciting too. Friday night and wonderful Lenny. It's too much to ask us to wait until he gets more experience and an orchestra. Can't some rich patron but [*sic*] him 100 musicians.
>
> Your questioning the ending of the second mv. has resulted in a better finish-a few bars added and better rounded off I think. That slap on the back-was it supposed to make me feel as good as it did Aaron? I'm feeling pretty high and talking myself into a terrific last mv.[47]

The great triumph of the Third and the lesser success of the Fourth were still to come. But Copland, along with Koussevitzky and Bernstein, were already showing themselves to be far more supportive and indispensable to Schuman than anyone else in his musical life had ever been. It would be the young Bernstein who would recommend to Koussevitzky some cuts in the Third to discuss with Schuman, only to discover that Schuman also had cuts in mind, some of the very ones that Bernstein had suggested. It would be the seasoned Koussevitzky who would recommend Schuman for the job as director of publications at G. Schirmer, and Schuman would not agree to the position at Juilliard until he received Koussevitzky's advice.

Schuman returned Copland's generosity in spades. Schuman would be the preferred host and emcee for nearly every major Copland celebration that took place in and around New York City. He gave Copland, the composer of *Lincoln Portrait*, the first opportunity to serve as narrator of his own work. He announced a $250,000 gift to the MacDowell Colony in honor of Copland's seventy-fifth birthday. He provided a new introduction to Copland's *What to Listen for in Music*; in fact, Schuman was Copland's first choice to bring out a revision of the best-selling book.[48] And the two men lovingly complimented each other on their music. At times, as in the works from the late '50s and early '60s—Schuman's Seventh and Eighth Symphonies (1960 and 1962), Copland's *Piano Fantasy* (1957), *Connotations* (1962), and *Music for a Great City* (1964)—their compositions seemed to be engaged in conversations with each other. Certainly the history of music is filled with composers who were friends, but that history is not rich with examples of the kind of friendship that Copland and Schuman had.

Either would have become famous without the other, and Copland would have emerged as the more famous regardless of their friendship. But Copland's standing owes much to Schuman. On the occasion of Copland's eightieth birthday celebration with the National Symphony Orchestra at the Kennedy Center, Schuman offered these remarks: "Contrary to the ancient wisdom that holds 'two vinegar salesmen can't be friends,' composers of serious art music do have a spirit of camaraderie and nowhere is the letter and spirit of this communal concern so apparent as in the person of our *dean*."[49] Perhaps alone among Copland's colleagues, Schuman had the stature to make good on the words he spoke. The spirit of camaraderie owes much to both men, and maybe more to Schuman, who throughout much of his life ended up playing second fiddle to Copland—and doing so with great joy and affection and support.

Schuman joked how Copland found Schuman's music "noble if-/ uneven-full of holes and lacking in objectivity." Publicly, Copland was far more generous. "Schuman's work reflects his personality—full of drive and conviction, not lacking in emotional content, with a love of the grandiose and a wonderful eloquence."[50] Privately, he both slapped Schuman's back and prodded him to be more critical of his own work. Witness what occurred a few months after the premiere of the Fourth Symphony. Schuman returned to Copland to talk things over.

> I felt very fine indeed after the session with the 4th Symphony yesterday. I really get what you're driving at about my music—I think for the first time with any great clarity. The effect of your comments will show in a greater awareness of the problems. And some day I'll write a work that'll make you spin—no corn—and all very elevated like you said my best music was, so there.
>
> I am very much in your debt.[51]

Schuman was in Copland's debt. And Bernstein's and Koussevitzky's, too, as the years ahead would show. His fortunes would be tied to these three men in ways he could hardly foresee. He had begun to forget Harris.

TEN

POPULISM, PROGRESSIVISM, AND POLITICS

(*Knocking*)
On this rock, change
From this insolence, rage.
In this chaos, plan.
Here, here, here.
Open tomorrow's door.
(*Knocking*)

Genevieve Taggard—poet, Schuman's faculty colleague at Sarah Lawrence, onetime Socialist, and lifetime protester against social injustice—spoke at an assembly at New York City High School of Music and Art in the early spring of 1942. She began: "I am here to talk to you on a very solemn subject—The Arts and War." America's entry into the theater of battle had begun a few months earlier that school year. The peacetime conscription that had begun slowly in 1940 accelerated after the bombing at Pearl Harbor on December 7, 1941, and the minimum age for draftees had been lowered from 21 to 18. Many of the young men in her audience would be called to serve in the Armed Forces; other men and women would soon volunteer to do so. Taggard chose to address the seeming incongruity of artists engaging in combat.

> We all know that there must be a great deal more war than arts in the time just ahead. We love the arts. We hate war. We know that arts are the arts of life. And that war is the art of death. . . .
>
> How can I make sense of such complexities—for myself or for you? And in a few minutes when it takes years & years?
>
> . . . We who study the art of giving people pleasure, happiness, new energy, a sense of form—whatever it is we do—composing music, playing the flute, drawing and painting pictures, writing poems . . . we come to see that the artist is a social person. . . . This person fights for human life all the time. Even during peacetime. He makes life alive. Now this socialized person must at times throw hand grenades and fly bombers.

> He won't do it with all his heart until he knows that the person he must kill is really the enemy.
>
> We have known for a long time that the fascists are the enemy. . . .
>
> My slogan is Defeat Fascism in 1942. Rebuild the world on a just basis. We must be a part of a social unity that will do two things—wage war and keep art and life and light alive. . . .
>
> The words I wrote in 1934—after our depression, and after the riots in France, when fascism first began to penetrate there—those words are still full of meaning. . . . You will sing those words on May 7th at Carnegie Hall. Sing them hard, for the sake of our country. For the sake of each other.[1]

In fact, this was not the first time a chorus from the New York City High School of Music and Art had sung—in Carnegie Hall, no less—Taggard's words to music of William Schuman. But the months before the early spring of 1942 made it clear to all who were taking note of world events—and many of the faculty at Sarah Lawrence most certainly were—that insolence and chaos reigned, as evidenced by the *Anschluss*, the Munich Agreement, *Kristalnacht*, the final victory over Republican Spain by Franco's legions, the occupation of Bohemia and Moravia by Nazi Germany, and the invasion of Albania by Fascist Italy. In singing Taggard's words in both 1939 and 1942, Taggard and her collaborator wanted these youths from this American high school to understand that they represented the youth of a free and democratic nation with their defiant proclamation: "Tomorrow belongs to me."

Schuman certainly understood this, for whereas his previous choral works had been written with skilled singers in mind—the contrapuntal *Canonic Choruses* of 1933; and the textless *Choral Etude* and the impractical *Pioneers!*, both from 1937—he now deliberately and unapologetically wrote for young singers, as he had in the case of the *Prologue*. His intent to write for relatively untrained voices lead him to rethink some of his earlier efforts. For example, the *Prelude for Voices*, with a text by Thomas Wolfe (from his 1929 novel, *Look Homeward, Angel*), underwent drastic simplification. Schuman had completed the original eight-part version in December 1936 and was eager to show it to Lehman Engel. "Unlike the canons it is in the idiom I am thinking in now as distinguished from the textures of five (or even three) years ago. I will be most anxious to show you this work directly I get it from my copyist."[2] When no performance of the work materialized for the spring, Schuman withdrew the work, revised it extensively for the Sarah Lawrence College Chorus in 1939, and didn't issue another mixed chorus version until 1942. Even this work was far more complex than the other nonsymphonic music Schuman would write between 1939 and 1942. Compared to his peers, Schuman came belatedly to music for the masses. But he more than made up for his tardiness, not only with music that spoke to critics, audiences, and performers alike, but also with efforts to ensure that high-quality music for amateur forces became a priority for all those involved in the arts.

One of the first works that showed Schuman's turn to the accessible was *The Orchestra Song* of 1939. According to the promotion put out by G. Schirmer, its publisher, it is a "Traditional Austrian Song arranged for any combination of changed or unchanged voices." The text was a translation rendered by Marion Farquhar, a longtime friend of Sarah Lawrence College who became widely known for her "skill, ingenuity, knowledge of English diction and . . . poetic imagination" in translating song texts and opera libretti.[3]

> She sang it to me over the telephone. Well, she sang it to me at a party and I loved it so much that I called her and she sang it to me again over the telephone, and I put it down, and then I asked her whether she would write English words for it, and she did. I made a little arrangement, and I taught it to my chorus by rote. Every place we would play it, people absolutely loved this piece.[4]

Schuman's skills as an arranger, going back to his Tin Pan Alley years, resulted in a publication that Schuman dismissed as a trifle but that sold thousands upon thousands of copies. It is doubtful that the wartime straits of Austria contributed to its success. What is less clear is the degree to which the emergence of the Trapp Family Singers, whose New York City debut took place on December 10, 1938, as part of their first American tour, may have whetted the appetite of choruses across the nation for Austrian folk material.[5]

The major choral piece from 1939, *Prologue*, was in conception and execution a towering achievement for the young composer. According to a story in a newsletter from the High School of Music and Art, the work began with a poem that Taggard had written and had set aside as a "useful failure." She showed it to Schuman, who saw in it the potential for a work "suitable for an audience of young artists and musicians about to face the responsibilities, the pleasures, and possibly the disappointments of life."[6] The first four lines of the poem are set against a militaristic and insistent march, ending with the chorus emphatically shouting "Here!" followed by a lumbering passacaglia whose materials are extracted from ideas that appeared in the first section. Over the passacaglia, the chorus sings the last three words of the poem, with the lugubrious tempo providing a sense both of the effort and the seriousness involved in opening tomorrow's door. The work ends with a brief coda that integrates the march with the final three words, ending with a major triad that signals affirmation and hope.[7] The materials of *Prologue*—its jerky march rhythms, quartal harmonies, contrapuntal devices, and feints toward bitonality—will all reappear in the *American Festival Overture* and the Third Symphony with seemingly nonprogrammatic overtones. But the locus of these devices in this work at the very least suggest that these later works also share in Schuman's project to appeal to a wider audience.

The commissioning of *Prologue* places this wider audience front and center. Along with Copland and Harris, Schuman was invited to compose a work expressly for the students of New York City's High School of Music and Art.

The principal, Benjamin Steigman, took such pleasure in the commissions that he wrote to Winthrop Parkhurst, music editor for *Newsweek*, inviting him to the school for a program.

> I believe you will be interested in our forthcoming spring concert on Saturday, May 13 (to be repeated on Saturday, May 20), for no less than three American premieres will be given:
>
> PRELUDE AND FUGUE, for Strings and 4 Trumpets.................Roy Harris
> AN OUTDOOR OVERTURE..Aaron Copland
> PROLOGUE..William Schuman
>
> These works have been written especially for the High School of Music and Art. The scores of thousands of high school orchestras in our country may prove to be an important outlet for American composers.[8]

Steigman was mistaken about the Copland; the high school orchestra had already premiered the work the previous December.[9] And Parkhurst came, but not to the high school. The Composers' Forum-Laboratory had made arrangements for "An All-American Concert" of orchestral works by recipients of the Guggenheim Fellowship. That program consisted of the Copland; Harris's ill-starred Second Symphony; a Concertino for Piano and Chamber Orchestra by Walter Piston; a Concerto for Two Pianos and Orchestra by Paul Nordoff; and Schuman's first composition for chorus and orchestra. Instead of the high school's orchestra, the Federal Symphony Orchestra of New York City would perform. Conductor Alexander Smallens, who premiered Thomson's *Four Saints in Three Acts* (1934) and Gershwin's *Porgy and Bess* (1935), had the lion's share of the duties that evening. Alexander Richter, head of the high school's music department, led the orchestra and his chorus of 200 singers in the Schuman. Parkhurst's focus on *Prologue* is thus understandable, but even so his words are more than gracious.

> The work of your school chorus last night, it seemed to me, laid fresh emphasis on the significance of such an institution, not only for the city but for the nation. In the rendering of William Schuman's "Prologue for Chorus and Orchestra" your students brought the concert to a vivid and memorable climax. Under the vital direction of Mr. Alexander Richter, the disarmingly young singers compassed with superb ease a work that bristled with problems of intonation. The clarity of diction was as notable as the incisiveness of attack: the entire work was, in fact, projected in inspiriting fashion that could make many a mature chorus look to its laurels, in point of sheer musical craft as well as of heart-warming enthusiasm.
>
> Although I added to the cheers and applause last night, I was so stirred that I now send you this echo.[10]

Richter similarly felt that his forces had acquitted themselves well, but he gave most of the credit to *Prologue*. In his letter to Schuman, Richter obliquely recalled the state of the world in May 1939, with its myriad conflicts and the need to act, to "open tomorrow's door."

> By now I have been so swamped with telephones, telegrams, letters, and other personal good wishes that I cannot but tell you again how much I appreciate the efficiency of your composition, its musicianship and sincerity. I guess the critics quite agree with what I whispered into your ear last Saturday concerning <u>your</u> work. I say again that a composer who can come down from the clouds and write a piece of music for us lowly mortals is entitled to continue his craft, and that is why your music will be worth something. You can send a people to war with a brass band and you can support and give stimulus to almost anything with the right kind of tune. You certainly have done it for the youth of this country in your "Prologue". (Genevieve Taggard should certainly have been with us on the platform.) Musicians are no good without music and composers can't do without musicians, and believe me it was only the quality of your work that touched us off into being "a new and fresh voice". I feel greatly honored to have been of assistance to you.
>
> One critic, Richard Moses, now manager of The New Friends of Music, called me on the 'phone and began gushing, saying that it was nothing short of "fantastic". . . .
>
> I will want to see you about several things. In the meantime you must know that I now feel about your music as I did before the savants decided that it was good.[11]

The savants had decided that *Prologue* was very good. Irving Kolodin, years before he would rise to fame as music critic for the *Saturday Review* and program annotator for the New York Philharmonic, wrote in the *New York Sun*:

> For nearly two hours last night the orchestral program of American works sponsored by the Federal Music Project in Carnegie Hall followed a predictable course with music by Aaron Copland, Walter Piston, Roy Harris and Paul Nordoff. But with the opening measure of William Schuman's "Prologue" for chorus and orchestra, one became aware of a new and challenging voice, a fresh and venturesome spirit.

Kolodin praised Schuman's "forceful rhythms, his bold harmonic writing, his basic earnestness and musicality." And he was not alone. The critic for *Musical America* weighed *Prologue* against the other works on the program. "Mr. Schuman's opus . . . had a clarity of structure and intent that was not discoverable to any marked degree in any other music played, with possibly, the exception of Copland's Overture." The critic for the *New York Times* also drew comparisons, proclaiming that *Prologue* "possessed the most positive and straightforward ideas of any of the composers represented. There was a clarity of line, a transparency in every phrase of this richly promising piece of writing that showed how rapidly Mr. Schuman is forging to the front among native composers of the day."[12] Douglas Moore, a Guggenheim winner himself and professor of music at Columbia University, put pen to paper as soon as he got home. Although the Music Education Department at Teachers College and the Music Department at Columbia went their own ways, Moore knew of Schuman and his accomplishments, perhaps through serving on the juries that had evaluated Schuman's earlier scores for the Bearns Prize. "Congratulations on your Prologue which I heard this evening. It was the first music I have heard of yours and I liked it a lot. It was the same energy and forthright quality which I have admired in you and I am delighted to find it so."[13] And in what was the highest compliment of all, Smallens told Schuman that he wanted to perform *Prologue* that summer—on Independence Day, no less—as part of the Stadium Concerts. "I told the children before the concert that you had mentioned this idea. They broke out in cheering and one boy yelled, 'ya mean the Yankee stadium', to which 199 others shouted, 'naw, the Lewisohn ya dope.'"[14]

The kids were no dopes when it came to understanding the meaning of Taggard's poem. "Up to the words, 'Here, here,' the composition depicts the conditions of the world today and what is to be done to remedy them."[15] And the adults understood, too. Richter made a statement to the audience when the music was performed at the high school the following week. He told them that he had approached Copland, Harris, and Schuman about writing for the kids, and they not only came through with performable scores but also lent their hand in helping to prepare the works for performance. But Richter's larger message was one of solidarity and camaraderie in a cause that went beyond music.

> In asking American composers to write for amateur groups, I believe we can do a great service to music in this country. . . . Music must be brought closer to the people, for the people are now demanding it—and I am gratified more than I can tell you, that we have young-minded and able composers who are willing and ready to take up the challenge. . . . For such music as they have written and such personal help as they have given, let me thank them in the name of American Music and American youth.[16]

Not merely music for American youth. *The people* are now demanding modern music. Composers had to answer *to the people*. And Richter, Copland, Harris, and especially Schuman had made good on their demand.

The proletarian nature of *Prologue* must have been a source of amusement between Schuman and Lehman Engel, for shortly after its Carnegie Hall premiere, Schuman thanked Engel for the latter's invitation to write something for the Soviet Pavilion at the 1939 World's Fair, which had opened just weeks before across the East River in Queens.[17] Neither man had any known connections with the Soviet Pavilion, nor did the Soviets feature any American music in their display for the 1939 World's Fair.[18] But as it happened, Schuman did write something for the fair: an unpublished four-voice anthem, in his simplified proletarian style, to the first stanza of *At the Crossroads*, an appropriate sentiment for the gathering of the world's peoples in New York. (The poem, by

Richard Hovey [1864–1900], first appeared in 1900.) And this fellowship-of-all impulse, writ small in *At the Crossroads*, is writ large as Schuman, in the *Prologue* and the other two major choral works from this period, laid claim to a form of "cultural communism" that was the coin of the realm in artistic circles in the late 1930s.

There is no evidence that Schuman himself ever joined the American Communist Party or actively supported its aims as a fellow traveler. The mercantile aspects of his upbringing may have made him sympathetic to some of the claims of the underclass during the Great Depression, but his relative insulation from the ravages of the economic downturn coupled with his father's ascension into the professional class seem to place him apart from those who adopted redistributionist language in the financial realm. But he certainly spoke in these terms in the artistic realm, as evidenced in the events and writings surrounding his Secular Cantata No. 1, *This Is Our Time* (1940).

The impetus for the cantata is somewhat unclear. Smallens's performance of *Prologue* at Lewisohn Stadium on July 4, 1939, whetted Schuman's desire to have another work performed under Smallens's direction, and in a letter of November from that year, Schuman offered Smallens "the next piece on my composition list . . . if you so choose. I have several things in mind that I should like to discuss with you soon." In a letter two months later, Schuman outlined for the Guggenheim administrators his progress thus far. His work included the following: "Mr. Alexander Smallens has invited me to compose a work for the Philharmonic Symphony Society's Stadium Concerts next summer."[19] However Schuman inveigled Smallens's assent, by the end of 1939 he and Taggard were hard at work crafting the words for the cantata. Though the final version would consist of five movements, originally they considered a sixth, as Schuman indicated in a postcard from late December.

> Your words are beautiful and strong. I keep reading them over and over. I like the No. 1 in this morning's mail. This makes 1,4,5 and 6 OK. I'm not sure of all of 2 and 3. Don't change them—I need much time to read them and consider—they too may stand unchanged after they permeate this dull brain of mine. Titles x 4 and 6 seem right—maybe the others too—no hurry with them we should talk about titles for separate choral works.
>
> Thanks for a very pleasant visit and most of all for your wonderful words.[20]

The drafts of the text indicate that the two sharpened each other's work. Notations in Schuman's hand indicate a preference for certain words; notations is Taggard's hand show her awareness of Schuman's intentions when it came to orchestration.[21] But what the drafts cannot fully reveal is the degree to which Schuman understood that his collaborator was very politically engaged, so much so that there is reason to wonder whether she would have been subject to questioning by the House Un-American Activities Committee or the Senate

Permanent Subcommittee on Investigations had she not died in November 1948. Her second husband, Kenneth Durant, had served as the American director of the Soviet news agency TASS and was named in hearings of the Senate subcommittee as being a member of the Communist Party. Taggard herself had served on the editorial board of Young People's Records—as had Schuman for a few months—which was later implicated as being a Communist-front organization.[22] As with Schuman, there is no evidence that Taggard herself was a member of the Communist Party, but her sentiments and affiliations were much further to the left than Schuman allowed himself in public.

But what Schuman did allow in public was a full-throated defense not only of the sentiments of his first cantata but also for the makeup of the people performing it and the person who composed it. In a preview article in the *New York Times* on the Sunday before the cantata's premiere—again, Smallens would favor Schuman with a Fourth of July performance—Schuman himself laid out his views for all to read and parse.

> Although the performance of Thursday night of "This Is Our Time" is a world première, it is also a "first time" in another respect. For the first time in its long history the Philharmonic-Symphony Society will perform with a chorus of amateurs whose entire personnel is made up of workers. The members of the People's Philharmonic Choral Society are iron workers, painters, carpenters, workers in shoe factories, laundrymen, furriers and workers in the needle trades. They include, too, a few white collar and intellectual workers as well as a group of housewives.

Schuman assured his readers that "the People's Philharmonic Choral Society is non-political and functions purely for musical and social reasons" even as he singled out the society's conductor, Max Helfman, as "an exceptionally sensitive musician with a genius for making people sing."[23] It wouldn't be until 1948 that the society officially changed its name to the Jewish People's Philharmonic Chorus, but Schuman spent quite a bit of time with the chorus and Helfman prior to the work's premiere, according to a feature story in the *Sunday Worker* that appeared on the same day as the story in the *Times*. Surely Schuman knew of the organization's roots in the Freiheit Gezang Farein of 1923, a confederation of choruses whose concerts routinely included "The Internationale." In a biographical essay on Helfman, Neil Levin provides additional information about the political caste of the chorus:

> The Jewish People's Philharmonic Chorus [JPCC] was loosely federated under the national umbrella of the Jewish Workers Musical Alliance. . . .
>
> By the end of the 20th century, many of the aging alumni of Freiheits choruses from that era (at least through the 1950s) often preferred to remember them as "humanistically" oriented groups of "the folk." But in fact they were commonly, if informally, known all during that period as the "communist Yiddish choruses," or at least communist-leaning—labels they made no particular effort to reject or protest.[24]

Another scholar states that, "when it was most vital, in the 1930s and 1940s, the JPPC . . . appeared throughout the year at rallies, marches, and events associated with particular political causes."[25] So Schuman's claim that the society was apolitical was at best wishful thinking and at worst a prevarication.

As for his own allegiances, and notwithstanding his collaboration with Taggard, Schuman may have seen himself at the time as apolitical. He nevertheless eagerly and emphatically donned the mantle of the progressive.

> The opportunity of composing a score serviceable for an amateur group naturally appealed to me as one of the growing group of American composers who are conscious of their privileges and duties as composers in this democracy. While, for the complete practice of our art, we must continue to write string quartets and symphonies, admittedly requiring performers of the highest skill, we recognize, too, that music which the layman can perform is essential if we hope to reach a wide audience. Only in this manner can we communicate to our countrymen in intimate fashion the unique feelings of the contemporary composer. For regardless of one's opinion concerning the merits of modern American works, the fact remains that only these compositions and these alone are the result of direct contact with the present American scene.[26]

With such sentiments it may seem uncharitable to discuss whether *This Is Our Time* succeeded as a piece of music, given how Schuman himself situated it in a particular time and place. Audiences by and large from that time and place responded to the work with great enthusiasm, no doubt in part because they were family and friends of the choristers. Henry W. Simon, hearing the same chorus later in 1940 in a concert that featured both the cantata and the *Prologue*, enthused that "*This Is Our Time* says just what the title means. It is the American people's time to work, build foundations, laugh and dance. The music . . . says exactly that as well as the words, and the workers' chorus sang it just as hard as it could. The thunderous applause showed that the idea got across, no mistake." Still another opined that Schuman "has written one of the most forceful choral works since Kodaly's 'Psalmus Hungaricus.'"[27] But another of the cantata's earliest critics, Schuman's fellow composer Colin McPhee, astutely measured the work and found it wanting.

> In spite of the admirable vocal writing in *This is Our Time* of William Schuman, I don't feel convinced about the work. It seems to me somewhat too earnest, rather sombre, and definitely grandiose. . . . The musical approach is sincere enough, the writing direct and logical, but somehow it seems more like propaganda than a moving piece of music.[28]

This Is Our Time would go on to have other performances, but in later years Schuman would tell others frankly: "I do not regard it as one of my most successful compositions."[29]

What remains, though, is Schuman's focus at the time on writing music for the masses and his rallying of forces toward bringing contemporary American composers and the people together. Schuman spoke to a West Coast reporter in the middle of a fact-finding tour he was conducting in early 1940 for the Rockefeller Foundation. His words are again populist and progressive.

> American composers have finally come down from their "ivy towers" and are really producing living music for living people. . . . They have learned they can achieve more success for themselves and for the common good of American music by pulling together than by boosting their own works. . . . With over 30,000 high schools maintaining symphony orchestras averaging fifty musicians each, our immediate task is to urge American composers to write music for American youths, in an idiom they can feel and play emotionally and successfully.[30]

For composers to have the freedom to write for America's youth, however, there had to be financial incentives in place. The "Musical Survey" that Schuman, along with Ashley Pettis and Roy Harris, submitted later that spring to the foundation laid out a strategy for the American composer. After asserting that at least 60 percent of the 125-plus composers they had surveyed realized an average of only 5 percent of their annual income through composing, the three men enjoined the foundation to establish a Composers' Institute in Washington, D.C.

The objectives of the Composers' Institute would be:

1. To develop a representative musical literature of high standing serviceable to concerts, broadcasting, recording, and schools.
2. To promote an understanding and use of American music.
3. To create a much-needed social attitude that the composer is also a workman worthy of his hire and entitled to economic citizenship, preferably provided for in the budget of established institutions.[31]

Neither Harris nor Pettis at this time had steady employment. The WPA and its offshoots were shutting down by 1940, so Pettis was looking for work. Harris was also between jobs, and the report as written suggests that Harris envisioned himself as the future director of the Composers' Institute and Pettis as his executive secretary. Yet despite the transparent solipsism of the report—and the subsequent discovery that portions on music education that Schuman wished to include were omitted[32]—the officers of the Rockefeller Foundation were favorably impressed with the idea, choosing not to fund it because of its scope and precedent-setting potential while at the same time recognizing that "perhaps outright subsidizing American composition is the way of giving music in this country a lift . . . when and if present pressures ever let up."[33]

Having received a negative answer from the Rockefeller Foundation, Schuman on his own approached a source with even deeper pockets: the federal government.[34] On the same day that saw the premiere of *This Is Our Time* in New York City, U.S. Secretary of the Interior Harold Ickes delivered what the *New York Times* called a "striking Independence Day address," in which Ickes "called upon the American people 'to yell down the west wind' their 'great, hard, angry, shouting, razzberry laugh' at the 'superior people' across the Atlantic who call the United States a 'decadent, worn-out nation.'"[35] If Schuman saw the *Times* article about the speech, he did not comment publicly on it. When, however, *Life* magazine later ran excerpts of the speech—saying that it "easily topp[ed] all other 1940 Fourth of July rhetoric and match[ed] the eloquence of Britain's Churchill"[36]—Schuman took notice, so much so that he was compelled to write Ickes personally.

Schuman told Ickes how he had been so moved by the speech (as reported in *Life*) that he wanted permission to set portions of the speech to music. Figuring that Ickes was unfamiliar with him and his work, Schuman offered Ickes references that could vouch for his caliber as a composer. But the request for permission served as a pretext for a different agenda.

> What I have in mind has to do with schools, colleges and community groups in connection with instilling in them the democratic ideal. Many schools have been holding "Assemblies for Democracy". It is my understanding that for the most part these assemblies prove very little and often degenerate into mere flag waving instead of truly vital and dramatic presentations of the things Americans should fight for. To interest boys and girls, Democracy has got to be made as exciting as a baseball game.

The Rockefeller survey had fired Schuman's imagination, and Ickes's speech further fueled it. He related to Ickes his travels and his assessment of what he saw and heard.

> I had the opportunity of traveling over the country and hearing various high school dramatic and musical organizations. The quality of the performing abilities of our boys and girls is simply phenomenal, but the material they use is often of the most trite and banal description.

Schuman was far blunter in his *New York Times* piece a few weeks earlier. "Unfortunately the original music used by the large majority of our amateur groups (including, alas, the schools) has been written by hacks or by casual composers with questionable, if any, artistic convictions."[37] Schuman was trying to raise the quality of composition for these forces in his choral works. But now he hoped to enlist the powers of the Department of the Interior in a greater cause. Something far more important than the quality of music hung in the balance.

> Briefly, would something like this be feasible: could we get together a group of our best composers and writers who would agree to turn out material which would deal with the vital issues in the life of people living in a democracy and include as well a real educative message as to the genuine threats to the democratic way. I mean the

> composers whose works are played by the great symphony orchestras of the country, the best men we have; I mean too our best authors. This is vitally important so that the quality of the material turned out will be acceptable to the school administrators. The cooperation of educators would be sought in endorsing the material and indicating its suitable place in the curriculum.
>
> This material could be issued through normal commercial publishing channels. The group of men and women who are writing it might come together simply through their desire to help in this very real aspect of national defense. Wouldn't it then be possible for the branch of your department which has to do with education to endorse these specially created works and publicize the fact of their existence to the parties most concerned?[38]

The governmental role Schuman envisioned went well beyond the arrangement of the Composers' Forum-Laboratory, in which a composer received a subsidized performance in exchange for stimulating conversation. By August 1940, much of France had fallen to the Nazi army, and Mussolini had allied his nation with Hitler's. Schuman wanted to rouse his fellow citizens from the torpor that had overcome them in the wake of Germany's triumphs, and after his positive experiences with the Forum-Laboratory, it was natural for Schuman to turn to the government and ask it to deliver the wake-up call. Who better than American composers, underwritten by the federal coffers, to deliver "a real educative message as to the genuine threats to the democratic way" and "to help in this very real aspect of national defense"?

Implied in Schuman's suggestion is the idea that many of these propaganda pieces would require texts. How else to inculcate into these young women and men the virtue of democracy and the vileness of fascism? And Schuman tried to write explicitly propagandistic music with texts.

It is important to remember that during the 1940s the word "propaganda" did not have the exclusively negative connotations it currently has. Enemy propaganda was dismissed, but propaganda for our side—encouraging ("Rosie the Riveter") or minatory ("Loose lips sink ships")—was considered an important part of the war effort. These shifting meanings of "propaganda" may be seen in Schuman's use of the word. Before the 1950s, Schuman used the word positively to describe the political intent animating his own music. But by the mid-1950s, he used the word mostly in a pejorative fashion, referring to the negative things others were doing, both overseas (such as the need to "counteract Soviet propaganda belittling American cultural achievements") and in the United States (such as in his opposition to the "propagandists of the experimental left [or right, depending on your point of view"]) who promoted certain rigid musical aesthetics.[39]

In July 1943, Schuman wrote to poet Archibald MacLeish, who had spoken the month before at Sarah Lawrence's commencement ceremonies. Schuman hoped to enlist MacLeish into participating in

> a theatrical production for Radio City to be know [*sic*] as, "This Is the Civilian." . . . I have agreed to write an American Anthem. It is the hope that this piece will become a standard of its kind. The original thought was to set words of Whitman. The situation has changed because I have written a melody which I believe is right, to no words. And this is where I hope you come in. . . . Would you be interested in attempting words for this anthem.[40]

MacLeish declined Schuman's invitation, but the anthem idea stuck with Schuman. An unpublished and undated song for voice and piano, *Fair Land of Hope*, has written on the title page, in Schuman's hand, "war propaganda piece." The unrelenting tonal caste and Edwardian stride of the music make it Schuman's art-song answer to Irving Berlin's "God Bless America."[41] Beyond these attempts to compose an infectious song for the war effort, Schuman explicitly identified three other compositions as propaganda pieces—the second Secular Cantata, *A Free Song*; *Prayer in Time of War*; and music for the Office of War Information film *Steel Town*—none of which had been written at the time he corresponded with Ickes.[42]

Yet only two of these compositions that Schuman identified as propaganda—*Fair Land of Hope* and *A Free Song*—feature a text set by the composer. Vocal music has an inherent ability to convey a message through its texts, so it is remarkable, given the time and effort he had spent in 1939 and 1940 on choral music, that Schuman's interests after the summer of 1940 began to shift toward instrumental music. The unpublished and triadic *Choral Fanfare for Women's Voices* neatly illustrates this choral-to-instrumental shift. According to the copyist's score, the 14-measure piece was completed on January 17, 1941, less than a week after the completion of the Third Symphony, and both its heraldic function and its use of the syllables "la" and "lo" mark the short work as more instrumental than choral in sound and function. By the time he wrote the Choral Fanfare, Schuman was more engaged in writing for instruments, and his letter to Ickes hints at this more symphonic future, given that the composers he had in mind—"the best men we have"—were writing for the "great symphony orchestras of the country." (No doubt Copland and Harris were foremost in his mind.) His remarks about "over 30,000 high schools maintaining symphony orchestras averaging fifty musicians each" also suggest that choral music did not hold a monopoly on the imaginations on the young people he hoped to reach with his democratic message of top-drawer music composed by the finest composers for amateur performers.

With this in mind, one of the instrumental works Schuman completed after his letter to Ickes provides a fascinating chronicle of his own attempts to answer the message he asked Ickes to disseminate. *Newsreel in Five Shots* (1941) seems on its surface to offer little in support of democracy or in opposition to fascism. The first four movements in particular—"Horse Race," "Fashion Show," "Tribal Dance" and "Monkeys at the Zoo"—have neither clear titular nor musical references to the events of the day, and the fifth, "Parade," uses few of the signifiers (high flutes and piccolos, extensive percussion battery) that are usually associated with a military marching band.[43] But the circumstances surrounding *Newsreel's* composition give evidence of its place in fulfilling Schuman's democratic ideals.

> One of the things I wanted to do was to write music that could be performed by kids, because I love kids. I always have. . . . I knew that I could do it with chorus, and I thought the band was another way that I could do it. I wanted to have some outlet for another side of my desire to write music, which was to write for large numbers of performers who weren't necessarily of professional caliber. . . . [Newsreel] was my first experience. I got better at it after that because the Newsreel is too difficult to play in terms of its musical content, I would say . . . the materials [are] much more difficult than the subject matter would indicate. . . . I haven't written simple band pieces, but some of them in later years have been very, very popular and have been played all over the place, and that still goes on. Newsreel, I guess, was the first one I did.[44]

If, by his own account, Schuman failed to provide a work that could be navigated by the high school musicians he had visited the year before, it was not because he did not try to do so. *Newsreel* provides a template for the type of work that Schuman wanted his colleagues to produce and the government to distribute: musically substantive, comprised of short and variegated movements, illustrative without being either parodistic or jingoistic, participatory in American democracy by inviting youth to join more seasoned adults in the serious enterprise of making music.

Ickes, though, would not be drawn into helping Schuman reach his fellow citizens through music. Walter Onslow, supervisor of press service for the Division of Information within the Department of the Interior, answered Schuman on Ickes's behalf. He enclosed the Independence Day speech, informing Schuman that, "provided it is for a noncommercial purpose," he could use Ickes's speech, but "if any composition embracing portions of his text is to be published and placed on sale other arrangements will have to be made." As for the larger purpose that animated Schuman's letter—enlisting composers under the Department's sponsorship—Onslow redirected Schuman.

> The Office of Education no longer is a part of the Interior Department. . . . The Secretary, therefore, no longer has connection with educational activities. It would not be possible, therefore, for him to follow up your suggestion as you have outlined it. Perhaps you would want to take up this matter directly with Dr. Studebaker, the Commissioner of Education.[45]

If Schuman wrote to Studebaker, no letter has yet come to light. For the moment, then, Schuman's grand idea was shelved, and his own commitment to use music to promulgate democratic ideals muted as he continued to write compositions without texts and (mostly) without programs and to call on musical language that carries a range of significations, at times clear, at times open to multiple interpretations.

Before his days as a self-styled occasional progressive were through, though, Schuman composed one more major choral work. The history of *A Free Song* (1942)—its genesis part of an intricate web of patriotic and personal motivations, its singular distinction of winning the first-ever Pulitzer Prize in Music—has been treated in depth elsewhere.[46] In the context of *Prologue* and *This Is Our Time*, Schuman's choice of text deserves greater scrutiny. Rather than turn to Taggard again, Schuman now drew from Walt Whitman, a poet he had set only once before (*Pioneers!* of 1937) but who was a favorite of American composers immediately before and during World War II. Roy Harris was particularly fond of Whitman, so it is surprising that it was Koussevitzky who suggested to Schuman that he look at Whitman for inspiration, given Koussevitzky's conviction that Schuman needed to move beyond Harris. But in directing Schuman to Whitman, Koussevitzky was tacitly saying that, to find words that might be both timely and timeless, Schuman needed to move beyond Taggard as well.

Schuman believed that he had accomplished that task in the poems he chose from the "Drum Taps" section of *Leaves of Grass*.

> As you see by the text selected, which I enclose, the two movement cantata has an immediate meaning for us now, as well as an enduring message. This seems to me an essential element for a choral work composed at this time. The first movement is a kind of requiem but more than just a prayer for the dead—it points a lesson. The 2nd movement is in complete contrast and is in the nature of a very militant "pep talk."[47]

In his study on musical settings of Whitman, John Samuel Wannamaker suggested that Schuman had skillfully avoided turning his text into jingoistic parody.

> Whitman's participation in expansionist and isolationist sentiments of his time is but sparsely represented in the musical settings, indicating a general lack of interest in that aspect of his thought. All examples in the collection [of works set to Whitman] were written in times of war and thus tend to reflect a heightened sense of patriotism. As an example, the finale of Ernest Bryson's *Drum Taps* (1918) makes a particularly aggressive exhibition of saber rattling by combining two poems, "Race of Veterans," and "World Take Good Notice." As an example of complete contrast, William Schuman's *A Free Song*, for which he was awarded the Pulitzer Prize in 1943, combines lines from "Long, Too Long, America" and "Song of the Banner at Daybreak," poems which have elements of the same patriotic fervor. By careful editing of phrases and lines, Schuman achieves a text that expresses only a desire for freedom for all mankind.[48]

But not everyone agreed that Schuman's choice and editing had felicitous results. Fellow composer Arthur Berger, writing privately to Copland, took Schuman to task over the work. "Schuman has achieved a real low in his Free

Song. An indication of his musical taste is his choice of words. I don't think Whitman ever wrote anything worse than the words Schuman singled out from all the good stuff to choose from. . . . Schuman duplicates the feeling of the words he picks, instead of attempting to improve upon them."[49] And Copland, shortly after hearing a broadcast of the work, had voiced his own reservations toward the cantata even before he received Berger's letter. "Typical Schuman in conception and orchestration; full of imagination on the instrumental side (I loved those clarinets);–but the choral writing not my dish, giving the whole a somewhat forced impressiveness." Schuman responded a few days later.

> I don't agree that you would have had the same opinion of the Cantata had you heard it in the flesh. Piston thinks it my best composition and told me so and then wrote a letter to tell me again. It can't possibly sound forced because it isn't. Take it from me Aaron it's a swell piece and it would have swept you right along. When you do hear it all this will happen to you and if it doesn't you can't blame me for trying.[50]

Schuman seemed to miss the irony of his words here, as Copland spoke about a certain forced quality to *A Free Song* and Schuman responded that he was faultless even as he exerted real effort on the work, but the exchange provides a useful example of Schuman's earnestness and seriousness that created its own set of challenges. Henry Allen Moe, the administrator of the Guggenheim awards when Schuman was a fellow, was once asked for his assessment of Schuman. "Moe thought that . . . if [Schuman] had any weakness, it was a certain humorless intensity and an almost too serious approach to his work."[51] The intensity and seriousness, the defensiveness and assertiveness would become more and more evident as Schuman became more and more successful. He genuinely sought the counsel of others and often took criticism to heart. But he could bristle when he felt misunderstood or wrongly represented. Not even Copland, the man whose musical counsel he appreciated above all others, was spared, as both would discover a few years later when the stakes were higher.

Schuman, however, did not lord his accomplishments over his peers (at least not in writing). He could have tried to shame or punish those who disagreed with his opinions or disliked his work. His intensity and seriousness generally left him no time to gloat.

The three choral *pièces d'occasion* could have served as a platform for Schuman's self-aggrandizement. Their immediate public and critical acceptance helped to catapult Schuman to the forefront of American composers. And the politics they represented were equally *au courant*. But for all of Schuman's demonstrable pride in them, he seemed also to take pleasure in his more modest accomplishments. His other two choral works from 1942 neatly parallel the journey from lament to celebration that *A Free Song* traces. The wordless *Requiescat*, written mostly in two voices and composed in memory of his Sarah

Lawrence colleague Henry Ladd (1895–1941), was completed on February 4, 1942; his *Holiday Song*, a setting of words by Taggard extolling the joys of time spent in the countryside, was completed on May 26, 1942. While Schuman had little to say about the former piece, he did give some perspective on the latter some years later to San Francisco-based critic Alfred Frankenstein.

> "Holiday Song" was the result of a request that I received from a group of New York City schools to write a work for their annual field day. I presented the problem to . . . Genevieve Taggard . . . and she turned up the words to order. I might add that it is by far the most popular piece I have ever written. Printed copies are now into the second hundred thousand and the work is performed hundreds of times each year. All this does not make it good—it makes me awfully happy.[52]

Requiescat, *Holiday Song*, and *A Free Song* mark the end of Schuman's extended foray in composing works for amateur choruses. (The Sarah Lawrence Chorus premiered the shorter pieces; the Harvard-Radcliff Chorus performed the cantata with the Boston Symphony Orchestra.) He would write many other choral works, but never again would he write so many in a single stretch. And while he would encourage performances of *A Free Song* and even invite performers to consider making a commercial recording of the cantata, he also recognized that, as Frankenstein said about this and his other early choral works, "in some cases he cannot be absolved from the charge of plunging over the boundary line between the hortatory and the bombastic."[53] The same assessment could obtain for the instrumental works as well. But with them, their textlessness partially obscures the bombast.

As for Schuman the progressive, politics began to hem him in. Whether consciously or not, he began to distance himself from those whose political ties might come back to haunt him. *Holiday Song* was his last Taggard setting; Whitman, Chaucer, Latin mottos, American aphorisms, and commercial advertisements would be his textual fare until the last years of his life. At this point, near the beginning of his career, the burgeoning success of his less overtly political works—the *American Festival Overture* and the Third Symphony being at the head of this line—allowed him quietly to entomb those that were more overtly political. The *Prologue* and *This Is Our Time* were both published, so he could not defenestrate them. But the Second Symphony, and the politically motivated award it received, began to appear less and less in his biographical materials. Schuman was a political man, and he played his politics during these war years impeccably well. He thrived.

Taggard, in contrast, ebbed away. She left Sarah Lawrence in 1946, in the hope of devoting more time to her own pursuits and avoiding some unpleasant interactions with some of her colleagues. But her hypertension eroded her health, and she died in late 1948. One of her students remembered her as a profoundly sad person, who

> carried the troubles of the world on her shoulders. . . . The fighting in Spain, the late-thirties' rumblings of fascism in Europe and Asia, left their imprint in her sorrowing and in her philosophy. She would not wall herself off, so she espoused all their causes—the hollow-eyed, starving Chinese peasant, the persecuted Jew, the struggling worker.[54]

She sought to make the world's troubles her troubles. She sought to enlist Schuman in that struggle. She succeeded in doing so for a season or two. But where Taggart, who grew up as one of the rural poor, saw systemic social injustice and sought to correct it, Schuman, who grew up as one of the urban well-off, saw individual and collective opportunity and wanted to seize it. Her approach was more confrontational; his was more optimistic and positive. And in the first half of the 1940s, at Sarah Lawrence, in the concert halls, in the halls where prizes were awarded, and in the offices where positions were filled, optimism was what people preferred. Schuman was a natural fit.

ELEVEN

WORLD WAR II AND THE PRIZE-WINNING COMPOSER

It remains unclear whether Claire Reis played a part in introducing Schuman to Margaret Naumburg, thus helping him in 1938 procure his first commission. But by her own account, Reis played a prominent role in securing for Schuman one of his first major prizes. The honors he had received for the *Choral Etude* and the Second Symphony brought Schuman favorable press among those musicians and artists and audience members attuned to the Federal Music Project or the fight for Spanish democracy. His views were also known among the readers of *Modern Music*, the house journal for the League of Composers. But for many in the wider world of New York concertgoers, Schuman still was relatively unknown. Reis's proposal in the spring of 1939 began to change all that.

> As I sat one day with the Music Committee of Town Hall and listened to the account of the Artists' Awards that had been given, I realized that here was another opportunity to crusade further for composers' commissions. So I raised the question, "Why should Town Hall give awards for interpretive artists only, and not for composers?" . . .
>
> Walter W. Naumburg, chairman of the committee, and president also of the Walter W. Naumburg Music Foundation, then asked to whom a commission should be given. Because a main purpose in establishing Artists' Awards had been to encourage young artists, I suggested William Schuman, a young composer of twenty-eight who was at the time teaching composition at Sarah Lawrence College.
>
> No one on the committee seemed to know his work . . . I described Schuman's ability at length, and a few of the performances of his work that had been given, including a symphonic work conducted by Koussevitzky. . . .
>
> As the meeting broke up Walter took me aside and said, "Well, Claire, now the responsibility is on your shoulders. It is due to your confidence in this young Schuman that we have been won over."

Reis continued the account of her accomplishment with a look to what happened next.

> The next season William Schuman's Third Quartet was played in Town Hall by the Coolidge Quartet. The Town Hall committee, as well as the general group of critics, seemed very pleased that this young man had been selected for the award.
>
> A few years later Schuman was in the forefront of musical activities, not only as a composer whose works were being widely played but also because of the fact that he was Director of Publications of G. Schirmer and President of the Juilliard School of Music. I have never needed to explain since, who William Schuman is![1]

Schuman would never dismiss completely the awards he received before 1939. But the avalanche of honors bestowed upon him between 1939 and 1943—two Guggenheim Fellowships, the first-ever Town Hall/League of Composers Award, the first-ever New York Music Critics Circle Award (for the Third Symphony), the first-ever Pulitzer Prize in Music (for *A Free Song*), a grant from the National Institute of Arts and Letters (his induction would come in 1946), one of the first American composers to receive a commission from the Koussevitzky Music Foundation established to honor the memory of Koussevitzky's wife, Natalie (which resulted in the *Symphony for Strings*)—may be unprecedented in the history of music in the number and prestige of major awards in so short a time. Copland, who was no fan of *A Free Song*, understood the significance of Schuman's triumphs. "In the old days," he wrote to Schuman, "all the awards used to go to the dull little boys. Either you're a sheep in wolf's clothing, or new times bring new customs. In any case the Pulitzer people made a right smart start for themselves, and we're all proud of you."[2] The words in public journals and the newspapers and the private letters don't all corroborate Copland's words—not everyone was pleased or proud—but Alfred Frankenstein was more right than not. Schuman had caught the boat.[3]

The invitation from the League of Composers provided the parameters of the work Schuman could compose: "either for solo instrument, or a small group, or a choral work."[4] Schuman may have felt that a work for the League of Composers may have required more technical polish on the part of the performers than his choral works for amateurs. Perhaps the fact that he wrote this work after having completed his revision of his *Prelude for Voices* and before he had started in earnest on *This Is Our Time* made him choose a medium other than the chorus. Whatever the motivation, in late fall of 1939 Schuman wrote to Bernstein, "Jesus I'm writing a lovely 4tet. No. III," and gave the designations for the three movements—I Introduction & Fugue; II Intermezzo; III Rondo Variations—as though they themselves were proof of the quartet's loveliness.[5]

Though the manuscript for the last movement indicates that the entire work was completed in December 1939, Schuman was not pleased with what he heard after the first rehearsal. The ending of the first movement wasn't to his liking, and he told William "Fritz" Kroll, first violinist of the Coolidge Quartet, of his displeasure. Kroll invited Schuman to rewrite the ending, and even if the quartet had to rehearse the new part on the day of the premiere, it would do so.[6] The manuscript for the new ending (beginning at m. 179) is undated, so it is unknown how close Schuman came to the Town Hall premiere on Tuesday, February 27, 1940, before completing the revised ending. Some version of the work was performed that evening, the first piece on the second half of a program that included quartets by Mozart, Schubert, and Brahms. In his review for the *New York Times*, Olin Downes elected not to pass judgment, stating rather blandly that "the composition heard last night would be better discussed after further hearings."[7] But the quartet's overall "broadness of line, rhythmic diversity, and emotional intensity," to quote Vivian Perlis, pointed forward to the other instrumental works that Schuman would produce over the next few years.[8] And Schuman was sufficiently proud of the Third Quartet that, years after its premiere, he did not blanch at the prospect of the work's performance the way he did with the Second Quartet.

Composing, of course, wasn't the only thing Schuman did. From 1938 on, he directed the Sarah Lawrence College Chorus. On the chorus's April 1940 tour, it performed in Boston, Greenwich, Haverford (near Philadelphia), and at the Heckscher Theatre in New York. Part of the novelty of the tour for the girls was that it represented the first time that they contracted buses for their travels. For Schuman, part of the reward came from the first performances of his *Prelude for Voices* and *The Orchestra Song*. The chorus also sang three Old English rounds, at least one of which would be incorporated into a Schuman composition four decades later.[9]

The success of the chorus with the students, the Sarah Lawrence alumnae, and the larger concertgoing audience prompted Schuman to renegotiate the terms of his contract almost every year with the college administration. Some years he would ask for more time free and forgo a salary increase; other years he would argue that his contribution to the college merited monetary reward; and still other years he would angle for both. While his lengthy letters to Constance Warren were always deferential, Schuman recognized how important the chorus was to the life and reputation of the college, and he was more than willing to use the chorus as a bargaining chip. Schuman also recognized that he was not indispensable. He notified Warren in the fall of 1944 that it would be his last year at the college. Warren tried to secure Schuman's services to direct the chorus beyond the 1944–45 academic year, but Schuman declined: "There is no way in which I can now gauge the demands of the new position to the extent of knowing whether it would be possible for me to do both jobs and still have the freedom I need for my own work."[10]

Both the success of the chorus and Schuman's friendship with Serge Koussevitzky led the conductor to engage the chorus to sing with the Boston Symphony Orchestra in a performance of Debussy's *La damoiselle élue*. Schuman loved to tell the story of how Koussevitzky asked whether his chorus of virgins might be available for the engagement. Schuman responded that he could not vouch for their virginity but that the women did sing like angels. And Olin Downes's positive reviews of their February 1943 performance proved Schuman to be right.[11]

Schuman's own music, both old and new, continued to excite and provoke. More and more orchestras performed his *American Festival Overture*, to the consternation of some ordinary listeners, including the one who wrote the following note:

> Just how an awkward, discordant piece of surrealistic trash such as this could be considered an important piece of American contemporary music, is one of those things that strikes us as thoroughly incomprehensible. This Schumann [*sic*] should have submitted his score to a psychiatrist before making it public, thus we would have been spared this and other cacophonious [*sic*] bleatings.[12]

A reviewer for the *New York Post* attended a performance of the overture that was greeted with "a faint but unmistakable hiss. . . . I do not by any means endorse the hisser's opinion of the Overture, but I would defend his right to hiss. . . . We shall not be a truly musical nation until our listeners have violent, passionate convictions about this and every work on the program."[13] Schuman's next big orchestral score would see its share of violent and passionate convictions, with amateurs and cognoscenti lining up on both sides to cheer and dismiss the work.

Schuman had completed his Third Symphony by January 1941 but had to wait until the following fall for Koussevitzky to premiere it. Part of its fame stems from the companion third symphonies of Harris and Copland, which most scholars and critics believe are among the finest symphonic utterances from these two composers. Antal Doráti, conductor of the National Symphony Orchestra from 1970 to 1977, opened his 1974–75 season not only with the "three Thirds" but also with the composers in attendance. Bernstein repeated the same program with the New York Philharmonic in 1988, by which time Harris had died and Copland was suffering from dementia. All three works begin quietly, with a single melodic idea; all three end with full orchestra. But whereas the Harris (1939) ends slowly with a dark and insistent G-minor triad, and the Copland (1944–46) ends in a blazing, affirmative D-major crescendo, Schuman's Third concludes with the superimposition of a C-major triad over an E♭ major one, with the E♭/E♮ dissonance giving the ending less a sense of affirmation than of defiance.

The work, from start to finish, defies convention. Cast in two large parts, each subdivided into two distinct sections, the symphony evinces Harris's influence not only in the harmonies and melodies Schuman created but also in the forms (or lack thereof) that he employed. The first part, a passacaglia followed by a fugue, conjures up images of Bach and Brahms. But Schuman's take on these old forms is flexible and (to use Harris's favored term) autogenetic. The passacaglia theme is stated and then repeated six times, with each iteration entering a half step higher than the previous one (from E to B♭). It is then followed by four free elaborations on the passacaglia theme and then leads seamlessly into the fugue. And all of this is far harder to trace on first and even subsequent hearings than are the passacaglias of Bach and Brahms (or even Copland).

The fugue similarly has seven half-step entrances, from B♭ to E, followed by its own set of free variations. In both sections, an aspect of Schuman's writing that will mark nearly all of his orchestral music comes into sharp relief: the separation, rather than the blending, of the choirs of the orchestra (e.g., horns against strings at the opening of the fugue), here abetted by his use of four each of horns, trumpets, and trombones, which allowed Schuman to create separate choirs within the brass family (e.g., trombones in the fourth variation of the passacaglia, trumpets in the first free variation of the fugue). The inventive use of percussion also is a signal feature of Schuman's music, here exemplified by an extended timpani solo in the fugue section and, later, the introduction of syncopated rim shots on the snare drum near the end of the symphony. (So novel was this effect in orchestral music that the publisher felt obliged to describe in the score how the sound is produced.)

Just as the passacaglia and fugue depart from conventional understandings of the forms, so do the two sections of the second part, marked chorale and toccata, fail to follow historical norms. Expectations of four-part, hymnlike writing are dashed at the outset with Schuman's two-part counterpoint that leads to a solo trumpet melody intoned over block chords. It is the solemn spirit rather than the standard operation of the chorale that obtains here. When the chorale does behave in a more Bachian way—at mm. 91 on, where the voices move homophonically—the melodiousness of the trumpet solo is lost. The moment points to another paradoxical feature of Schuman's music: a linearity that unfolds as both melody and counterpoint, coupled with a waywardness that often makes the content and contour of Schuman's lines difficult to remember. Schuman insisted that he wrote his music by singing it rather than playing it at the piano, and nearly all of his non-accompaniment figures are reproducible by the human voice. The challenge, however, is that many of these "melodies" are not easily reproducible, either because of their intervallic content or their range or their length or some combination of these three. And as they are not easily reproducible, they are not easily retained in the memory. This does not negate the impact of these musical statements, which can only be described as melodic, and the themes in the passacaglia, fugue, and chorale all give ample evidence of Schuman's style of melodic writing.

The toccata, like the previous three parts, resists easy alignment with its similarly named forebears. It lacks the perpetual motion aspects of toccatas by Bach, Widor, or Ravel. Here, the emphasis is more on the tactile nature of the materials as they are played. One senses the feats of legerdemain being executed by the bass clarinet with its virtuosic opening and by the skittering winds throughout the section. The toccata accentuates a feature of the entire symphony that has made the work both popular and historically significant. Though there are times in the symphony where the complexity of the various contrapuntal lines results in a rather muddy sound, Schuman's prowess as an orchestrator is on full display in this work and stamp him as America's first great orchestral composer in terms of the sheer sonic possibilities of the orchestra. Neither Harris nor Copland nor any other American composer preceding Schuman—including Ives—had deployed an orchestra with as much variety and skill as Schuman did in the Third. Add to the sonic inventiveness its contrarian formal structure that both acknowledges the Old World and breaks free from it, all of which anticipates other orchestral works that would come a few years later, such as Bartók's Concerto for Orchestra, which Koussevitzky premiered in 1944, and Stravinsky's Symphony in Three Movements, also from 1944. On the eve of America's entry into World War II, Schuman's symphony was both precocious and audacious. And the audiences and critics at the time seemed to grasp the singularity of Schuman's opus.

What those first audiences and every subsequent audience heard until 2005 was a truncated version of Schuman's original score. He sent the manuscript of the Third to the Library of Congress with an explanatory letter that, lacking his usual secretarial assistance, he himself typed.

> Before the symphony was performed I made a number of cuts, most of these are in the manuscript but perhaps not all. After the work was completed I had it copied in ink and made corrections in that copy and for the first edition of the score. . . . There were no changes made in the symphony after performance—only before. I have left all the cut music (indicated as such) in the mms. I have no objection to showing what I deleted after a few months of perusal and before the first performance.[14]

In an article in *Modern Music* that appeared shortly after the premiere, Bernstein spoke of Schuman's tendency toward "'Plauderei,' a rather ignoble word to bestow on music so sincerely written. Yet a few examples of what was cut from the *Third Symphony* before performance would almost justify that word; and the fact that such material was cut indicates the decline of this unfortunate tendency."[15] Schuman's rationale for having cuts in mind was simple: "I always overwrote because it's very easy to make a cut. I would always have a cut in mind if I was unsure of a certain section."[16]

In 2005, the National Symphony Orchestra under Leonard Slatkin performed the uncut Third Symphony as it appears in Schuman's manuscript at the Library of Congress. Unaware of the history of the symphony, the program annotator erroneously asserted that the audience for the Washington performances were hearing the symphony "in the form in which Koussevitzky introduced it in

1941, before the score was published with the cuts Schuman made following the premiere. . . . [The cuts are] the kind of polishing that is frequently done once a composer hears his new work actually performed."[17] If Schuman is to be believed, he himself never heard the version of the Third that the audiences at the Kennedy Center heard the first week of February 2005. Those performances, however, make a compelling case for the original version of the symphony. Schuman remembered making a big cut in the first part, but the largest cuts by far occur in the toccata.[18] He excised a brooding recollection of the opening passacaglia theme (at m. 253), a lumbering double bass cadenza (at m. 286), and numerous shorter passages that extend the brilliance and virtuosity of the toccata. The published version is unquestionably Schuman's final thought on the symphony. His earlier thoughts before that first performance are not all "Plauderei" and, in the case of the return of the passacaglia theme, offer a better understanding of the Third's overall architecture and pace as well as of Schuman's youthful, "unpolished" urge to construct such an unusual work.

New York Times critic Olin Downes, who had been noncommittal with the Third String Quartet, was far less reticent about the Third Symphony: "For this chronicler, [the symphony] takes the position of the best work by an American of the rising generation that he has heard." Schuman was so enraptured by Downes's verdict that he wrote to the critic that very day and suggested that the two meet. "Personally I'm sick to death of the divisions in our music: critic-performer-composer-all going their independent ways with hardly a thought to the truly complementary possibilities of their activities. I'm sure I will gain a great deal through a frank exchange of ideas with you and I'm even bold enough to hope that the profit will be mutual." Downes answered with still more praise for the new work. "I am frank to say that it is the first symphonic work by what I will call the post-John-Alden[-Carpenter] generation I have heard which impressed me as the product of a composer who could really deal with a big form and who was already handling that with an audacity and originality of detail which contained enormous promise." Downes was so overcrowded with work, however, and Schuman never made available to Downes the score to study the work at greater length, so their meeting of minds would have to wait.[19]

Other critics did not share Downes's opinion, either in part or in whole. Robert Lawrence, apparently unaware of Schuman's educational history, wrote that the symphony is "a gallery of counterpoint exercises on a gigantic scale. . . . [It] points to a fundamental weakness in our modern conservatory methods—the fostering of virtuosity without an accompanying demand that the musician look well within himself."[20] The anonymous critic for the *New York Sun* also found fault with the work. "Rather than acquainting us with some new facet of human experience, Mr. Schuman communicates, and defiantly, that he has nothing to communicate, that the aura of his times is bleak, that they are truly out of joint. . . . To this taste it was as respectable a work as it was a repelling one."[21] The composer Lou Harrison drily remarked: "I do not respond to this kind of music. It seems to me formless and stuffy. . . . There is also a perfectly good name for a composition involving a passcaglia [*sic*], chorale, fugue and toccata. It is a suite, not a symphony."[22] Henry Simon, a critic and future editor who became Schuman's friend in later life, split the difference between Downes and the naysayers.

> Is it great music? I don't know. You can't tell about those things, especially not after a single hearing. I didn't, for example, take much to the themes: they are angular, full of uncomfortable intervals, and hard to whistle or remember. I like music that sings more. But maybe we'll catch up with Mr. Schuman's idea of a tune and learn to whistle it; or maybe his next symphony will respect our limitations. I do know, though, that I heard very good American music on Saturday afternoon and that I'd like to hear more of the same.[23]

When the New York critics came together six months later to decide which new work deserved their new Critics Circle award, "the first ballot was only 3 votes short of being unanimous. Aaron Copland's *Statements* received 2 votes and Henry Cowell's *Tales of Our Countryside* 1."[24] The critics had caught up to Schuman's Third.

The Fourth, in contrast, received a more muted welcome. It was the first piece of Schuman's music that Virgil Thomson heard, and his review of the New York performance shows his keen ear and intellect in identifying in one hearing the strengths and weaknesses of the work.

> I found it vague and more than a little diffuse. Its musical thought flows without hindrance, but it assumes its precise form with great difficulty. It takes the author quite a time in each movement to get around to saying what he has to say. Until that time comes, he writes pleasant little exercises in free counterpoint that go along nicely but that lack definition. The proof that the young man is a real talent, for all his turgidity and his demagogic predilections, is that at some point before the end of each movement he does get down to business and writes a brief passage or two that can be remembered.[25]

The Cleveland critics were similarly mixed in their opinions. Arthur Loesser—Frank's brother, who had imperiously dismissed Schuman's First Symphony—wrote, "Certain obvious features convinced me most readily, for instance the impressive 'ostinato' at the beginning and the brilliant tonal pyramid at the end. However, the entire work arouses admiration, give a feeling of strength, and inspires a desire for rehearing." But Herbert Elwell was less convinced, dismissing the Fourth as though it were slightly diseased. "It seemed to me to suffer from a sort of contrapuntal eczema common to much modern music."[26]

One review of the Fourth particularly rankled Schuman. A young man named Donald Fuller gave an overview of New York concert life in the spring of 1942, and he had the temerity to open with this sentence: "The premiere of William Schuman's *Fourth Symphony* by the Philadelphia orchestra revealed what appears to be a peculiar need in this composer for the strict forms whose use in the *Third Symphony* I deplored."[27] Schuman unleashed a fusillade against the hapless young man, correcting him as to which orchestra gave the premiere and badgering him about the precise meaning of "strict forms." In many ways, Schuman's disagreement about premieres and form constituted the kinder portion of his letter.

> This is not a note to you as a critic, for as a young composer I can't honestly think of you in such completely hopeless terms, but it looks very much as though you are willing, inspite [*sic*] of the fact that you should know better, to play their superficial game. . . . This note is meant in a friendly way, because I think of you as a sincere young person in music. It's very disappointing to me to see you writing trash. . . . What you will prove as a composer I do not know, but I do know that your start as a critic is not very promising. Please try to be a bit more humble in your evaluation of major works which you hear for the first time.

Fuller remarkably stood his ground. "I frankly don't get too clear an idea of what you're chastising me for, except that I haven't been completely enthusiastic about your work." So Schuman chastised him a second time, again in a take-no-prisoners style. Fuller waited more than four months before he would venture a response. "Please don't believe, as you wrote, that your music doesn't reach me, for it does. In fact it's just because it does that certain external attributes might cause me to criticize—with any real interest."[28] It is impossible to know how frequently and how vehemently Schuman engaged in arguments about music in general and his music in particular. But other evidence from this period, such as two letters to his Sarah Lawrence colleague Judith Sidorsky in which he apologized for losing his temper, suggest that Schuman could be not only passionate but also volatile. In reference to the argument he had with Sidorsky's husband, Horace Grenell, Schuman volunteered, "It seems that we feel we should agree to disagree (wherein necessary) with less enthusiasm."[29] Schuman displayed a great deal of enthusiasm with Fuller, and he would lock horns with others later in life.

Fuller's review of the Fourth Symphony was sketchy and allusive. Robert Sabin's review provides both a useful description and a fair assessment of the symphony.

> The opening movement begins, characteristically, with an ostinato, stated first in the double basses, with the English horn announcing a long-breathed theme against it. This persistent figure plays a dominant role in the entire symphony. The work is essentially contrapuntal throughout, which enables Mr. Schuman to hammer this ground bass into a dozen different shapes and to weave it into a great variety of textures. . . . Here, as in the *Third Symphony*, he builds up a series of closely related

episodes with cumulative power. . . . The second movement brings a sustained mood. Muted strings and brass are skillfully used to create atmosphere. . . . In the final movement Mr. Schuman turns again to hammering logic. We are out in the jazzy, brazen, chaos of the modern world. . . . The *Fourth Symphony* is not as entertaining, as spontaneous, as the memorable *Third* (which represents a high-watermark in American music), but it is an impressive work eminently deserving attention.[30]

Sabin wasn't the only person to hear flecks of jazz in the last movement. In his study on jazz in concert music in the mid-twentieth century, David Ross Baskerville pointed to this same movement, feeling that it "demonstrates how thoroughly assimilated the jazz impulse is in Schuman's own rhythmic style."[31] The movement also demonstrates how flexibly Schuman could treat his musical materials, for the main idea for the last movement comes from the last movement of the Third String Quartet, where the music heads in a markedly different direction. The Third Quartet has established itself as Schuman's most recorded chamber work; the Fourth Symphony, in contrast, has languished in the shadow of its symphonic neighbors. It is accomplished, but it is not as distinctive as some of Schuman's other works. It is as though Schuman felt the press of needing to complete yet another major work before his Guggenheim Fellowship ended. The last page of the Fourth bears the date of August 17, 1941; the premiere of the Third took place exactly two months later. Schuman later voiced his opinion of both works. "When I heard the recording recently, [the Fourth] seems much more a young piece than does the Symphony No. 3."[32] Had he waited to hear the Third first, the Fourth might have sounded very different than it does today.

By the time the Fourth Symphony was premiered, the nation was at war. Shortly after the bombing of Pearl Harbor, Schuman was in Pittsburgh to give a lecture on modern music. (The publisher Boosey & Hawkes had circulated a flyer advertising Schuman as a lecturer, and a number of institutions had hired him to speak during this period.) The writer for the *Pittsburgh Press* posed a question that Schuman himself must have contemplated over the years.

When war comes, does music go out the window?

"No," says William Howard Schuman, one of America's foremost composers who is spending today in Pittsburgh. "England has shown us that music and the theater are very important to morale."

War, of course, may bring a re-direction of music, he says, with the emphasis on morale.[33]

The war would redirect Schuman temporarily, as he sought to find a way to serve in the armed forces. Letters from Copland and Bernstein show those two men in near-mortal fear of the prospect of being called up: the former confided to Schuman that, as late as September 1942, he had not registered as required by law; the latter, after being declared ineligible for service because of his asthma, breathed a two-page sigh of relief to Schuman.[34] In contrast, his buddy Ferd Nauheim enlisted in the Army, went overseas, fought in the Battle of the Bulge, and distilled some of his experiences in a novel, *Behold the Upright.*[35] Schuman also felt compelled to serve in some capacity, and he saw the Army Specialist Corps as a way that his musical skills could be put to good use. The corps, however, was oversubscribed and eventually terminated, so Schuman's chances of obtaining an officer's commission were slim from the outset. What brought his chances for a commission down to zero was his history of progressive muscular atrophy, a condition he discovered in his late teens, thus dashing his dreams of a professional baseball career and later making it difficult for him to find life insurance. He would have to serve the nation some other way.[36]

Though he could not go to war, his music did. Schuman had written *Newsreel* at the request of educational administrators in Pennsylvania, and, soon after its publication, the suite of five pieces was required material for all class "A" bands in the state.[37] He had also arranged the work for orchestra and dedicated it to Alexander Smallens, the conductor who had introduced *This Is Our Time* in 1940.[38] But *Newsreel* also became a staple of Army, Navy, and Marine Corps bands. Yeoman Third Class Lehman Engel directed a Navy band in Chicago and programmed *Newsreel* within months of its appearance. "The fellows liked it & I do also," Engel wrote to Schuman. "It was easy to do & very effective. I must say I was frightened because I am not allowed much freedom that way but so far I haven't received sailing orders."[39] Other military men wrote to Schuman to tell him that the men of the United States Military Academy Band and the U.S. Marine Corps Band were also performing the work.[40] Yet it retained its appeal to educational institutions. In a touching letter to a nun at the Ursuline School of Music in Windsor, Ontario, Schuman laid out not only his vision for *Newsreel* but also his broader vision of music education.

> It was my hope to write a piece which would not be "writing down," but which would, at the same time, be suitable to the intellectual, emotional and technical plane of young performers. The principal thing in performing the music is to worry less about the notes than that the piece be performed with great élan. This is a dangerous statement for a composer to make and I would not have it misinterpreted as a disinterest on my part in the accuracy of musical performance. I merely mean that the accuracy of musical performance includes as a primary objective the achievement of the spirit of the composition. If technical accuracy precludes the achievement of this goal, all is lost.[41]

Newsreel was not conceived with the war in mind, unlike three other pieces from the early 1940s. But before Schuman turned his full attention to writing what he unabashedly called "war propaganda," he decided to rework his 1938 Piano Concerto. His reasons for doing so remain shrouded in mystery. Later in life he would refer to it as "a juvenile piece," even though the revision came well after his success with the Third Symphony.[42] The extant correspondence from the first half of 1942 contains almost no mention of the concerto. The months were filled with other pursuits: Schuman's endeavors to join the armed forces; an ill-fated attempt at composing an opera with librettist Christopher LaFarge that nevertheless netted Schuman $2,500; and a humorous back-and-forth with Hollywood producer Carl Winston about the possibility of writing a commercial film score for a Russian-themed movie, given how (to Winston's ears) the Third Symphony sounded Russian.[43] In late January, Schuman told Bernstein in the last of three postscripts to a long letter, "I'm writing a brand new Piano Concerto," and the next mention of the work is when Schuman spoke with Copland about the nature of the newness (the first two movements) and some aspects about the writing. At some point, Schuman must have spoken to Rosalyn Tureck about the work, as she received an early glimpse of the concerto.

> Tureck seemed genuinely enthusiastic. Thought the Piano writing was unconventional. It is not, of course, unconventional for us here now modern boys. Truth is I don't think I know enough about the instrument to write a really conventional piano part unless I cultivated the arpeggio system. Is there any P.C. that doesn't have at least one arpeggio. It seems to me that this new piece of mine hasn't a one which should certainly help it from becoming popular.[44]

Conductor Daniel Saidenberg wrote to the organizer of the concert at which the piece would premiere asking him to "tell Schuman if you see him that I'm crazy about the Concerto."[45] But Schuman accurately predicted the limited appeal of the concerto. Part of its challenge, strangely enough, is its requirement for reduced forces. Schuman chose to call it "Concerto for Piano and Small Orchestra," but "small" in this case meant single winds, no bassoon, two each of horns and trumpets, one trombone, and no percussion, all of which was considerably smaller than the orchestras Schuman's symphonies demanded. The smallness cuts both ways. Schuman would complain about some performances where the strings were also reduced, and he would later recommend a minimum number of strings and suggest larger numbers "at the discretion of the conductor" for larger halls.[46]

The concerto's Town Hall premiere on January 13, 1943, was part of a mostly Schuman evening, resembling the Composers' Forum-Laboratory concerts in their inclusion of an audience feedback session after the concert had ended. Virgil Thomson hosted the postconcert discussion, and Schuman quipped that it was nice to have his music appear alongside that of Johann Sebastian Bach and wished that Bach had shown up for the Q & A. (Tureck played a Bach concerto to open the concert.) Thomson also goaded the audience.

> Mr. Thomson's remark about Mr. Schuman's "choral writing being largely of an instrumental kind" brought several dissenting replies. One man said Mr. Schuman "does such fine choral work he should write an American Boris Godounoff."

> The composer himself said he was amused to hear his choral style called instrumental. "Fritz Reiner just saw a new piece of mine," he said, "and his remark was that I was trying to apply a choral technic to the orchestra." [Reiner premiered *Prayer in Time of War* the following month.][47]

Schuman's fellow composers once again had less charitable things to say about the new concerto. Paul Bowles asked "what emotional relation there was between the finished product and the original impulse that had made Mr. Schuman write it. It was cerebral music unfairly pushed into the uniform of direct, emotionally conceived music."[48] And Arthur Berger had little positive to say about the work, which explains in part his criticism three months later that *A Free Song* marked "a real low" for Schuman.[49]

The big news of the evening, however, wasn't the new Schuman concerto, nor was it Tureck's brilliant playing of it and the Bach, nor was it a revisiting of some of Schuman's choral music. The event of the evening, all the critics proclaimed, was the performance of the newly formed Collegiate Chorale under the direction of Robert Shaw. Schuman himself seemed to recognize in advance that Shaw's group would prove to be the star attraction of the evening, as he wrote enthusiastically about the chorale for the readers of the *New York Times*. Schuman had heard about the group in the summer of 1942 and had recommended it to Koussevitzky for the New York performance of *A Free Song* should "the management [find] the expense of bringing down a group from Boston too much . . . [the Collegiate Chorale] is one of the best groups of its kind I've ever heard. It is made up of young men and women of all kinds, a truly democratic concept."[50] Shaw had worked with the popular choral conductor Fred Waring, whose Fred Waring Singers were well known through their nationwide broadcasts of lighter fare. (In fact, in his teens Schuman had collected Waring's autograph.)[51] Shaw had something else in mind for the Collegiate Chorale, including developing a performance roster that was diverse racially, ethnically, and religiously. Shaw outlined the rationale and aims of the chorale in a four-page letter to Schuman, from which Schuman derived his article.

> We're as mongrel a make-up as can be assembled in the world's great cosmopolis. I should like to develop an instrument, available to all serious American composers (serious does not mean esoteric; maybe sincere is the best word) which should be technically equal to their most stringent demands and sympathetic without reservation to their mood and intent.
>
> If American composers could feel that there is a great American chorus as anxious to perform great American music as the composers are to write it. . . . then that ought to be worthwhile.[52]

The Town Hall audience was incredulous that Shaw, steeped in the commercial world of the Fred Waring Singers, could achieve such remarkable ends with the chorale. Although Shaw was beginning to outgrow the Waring approach, he was not inclined at the time to dismiss it out of hand.

> Mr. Shaw, whose first-rate chorus was generally regarded as the night's real news, was asked how he could reconcile working for Fred Waring's outfit and leading "serious music."
>
> "I think Mr. Waring tries to say in the music of entertainment what we are trying to say here in serious music," he said, getting the night's biggest ovation. "Fred tries to make sense and tries to make it simple and honest."[53]

Waring would later become a shibboleth for Schuman in his attempts at G. Schirmer to redefine the nature of choral music in the nation's schools and colleges.[54] But Shaw shared with Schuman the intersections between highbrow and middlebrow, and Schuman saw in his younger protégé the makings of a great conductor. Schuman introduced Shaw to George Szell, at the time a refugee conductor living in New York City, and Koussevitzky; he later brought Shaw to Juilliard, insisting that choral music needed as serious an approach to performance and composition as did instrumental music. And Shaw's career with the Collegiate Chorale, his eponymous chorale, and the Atlanta Symphony Orchestra comprise one of the great success stories of American music in the latter half of the twentieth century. Schuman helped launch Shaw's career, one of the many ways he indirectly shaped music in America.

Yet another significant thing occurred at Town Hall when Schuman's concerto premiered. While the more progressive composers disdained the work, a more conservative one found much to praise in the work. Douglas Moore, who had earlier written to Schuman after hearing the *Prologue*, wrote to him again after the Town Hall performance. He, too, found much to admire in the Collegiate Chorale, but his words about the concerto contained auguries of their own.

> The performances were all excellent and I was delighted by the breadth and technical brilliance of your choral work. I especially liked the last Requiescat. The concerto at a single hearing is a dashing and effective piece. I look forward to further acquaintance with it and I am sure I shall have many opportunities in the future.[55]

As chairman of the Music Department at Columbia, Moore ensured that he would reacquaint himself and acquaint others with the concerto. And less than two weeks later, Frank Fackenthal, Columbia's provost and administrative liaison for the Pulitzer Prizes, wrote to Schuman and invited him to submit the concerto for consideration.[56] The events of the next three months would upstage the concerto entirely, but Schuman had much to celebrate in the winter of 1943. Town Hall had been completely sold out for the January concert. The Office of War Information had requested 60 records to be distributed throughout the world "for propaganda purposes."[57] A good number of his musical colleagues had commented favorably on his revised concerto. He was speaking throughout the nation on behalf of modern music. The Pulitzer Prize committee had sent him a personalized letter. And after years of trying, Frankie was about to conceive a child. All in all, it was a propitious winter, one that would unfold into a radiant springtime of music and acclaim.

TWELVE

THE MODERN METEOR I SING

Copland invited Bill and Frankie to come once again to Tanglewood during the summer of 1942. The summer before, they heard Bernstein conduct the *American Festival Overture* there, and Bill got the slap on the back from Copland for the Fourth Symphony. In 1942, the United States was at war, and rationing meant that there was no gasoline to take the Schumans' Pontiac to northwestern Massachusetts and back. But they were grateful that summer for the invitation, knowing how busy Copland must have been.

> Don't bother writing if you're too rushed but it is always a great pleasure to hear from you. What about Lennie? Is Kousse really sold on that Russian's 7th [Shostakovich's Leningrad Symphony]? Will you tell him (Kousse) that I've started on his orch.-choral work for next year and happy to report that I'm following his idea and using "that great American poet—Vittmann". We both miss seeing you and visiting the Center this summer but it looks like that's the way it's gotta be.[1]

Frankie and Bill loved Copland. They had given him the keys to their house for all of March 1941, during which time Copland worked on his book, *Our New Music*. It was near the end of Schuman's second year as a Guggenheim Fellow, and he and Frankie decided to spend some of that time staying in New York City at the Fifth Avenue Hotel on the corner of Fifth and Ninth Streets. The arrangement delighted Copland. "On the verge of leaving," he said, "[I] thought I should tell you what a <u>wonderful</u> 5 1/2 weeks it's been in the house and how very grateful I am to you for turning it over to me. I've seldom spent a more concentrated and productive time."[2] Schuman's communication with Bernstein was also warm and affectionate, but it waxed passionate, in keeping with Bernstein's ever-changing temperament. His correspondence with Copland tended to be terse and yet revealing of both men's thoughts and desires. How much each man shared with the other of their private lives cannot be ascertained from the letters. But Copland knew more about Schuman's music and moods than probably anyone save his wife.

Aaron Copland and Schuman (at podium) at the Lotos Club, November 1, 1978.

During the spring of 1943, Schuman was unusually garrulous. Copland was in Hollywood, working on the score for *The North Star.* He wrote to Schuman after having heard the radio transmission of *A Free Song.* Along with his mixed review of the cantata (see chap. 10), he invited Schuman to fill him in on the news from the East Coast.

> What we need is a nice long evening with Frankie so's I can get all the dirt about everything—the ACA [American Composers Alliance], the League [of Composers], the concert of Feb 17, etc. But I'll settle for your impressions of the Lincoln piece. How does it seem in concert hall? Or were you too excited—as per usual—with your own piece to have any idea? Oh yes, and what did everyone think of Roy's Fifth—including you?
>
> I know you must be sumpin' awful busy—but try to write.[3]

Schuman did more than try. He answered Copland with a three-page, single-spaced, comprehensive overview of the world of music as seen through his eyes.

> Let's see—the agenda must include—Copland's Lincoln piece, Copland's Town Hall evening, Copland's (and Schuman's) friend Bernstein, Copland's admirer from Brazil—Guarnieri, Copland's baby the ACA, Copland's opinions (and

> Schuman's) of Schumans [*sic*] music. (You know—let's talk about you—how do you enjoy my last concert), Copland's question on Schuman's opinion of Harris's Fifth, Copland's influence with the Koussevitzky Foundation resulting in the awarding of a commission for next year of a Schuman work which of course is brand new news to Copland and finally, any other little items of new business that are raised from the floor.

Schuman dug in and dished out. He praised and pulled his punches over *Lincoln Portrait*. He bemoaned the fact that the Town Hall concert on February 17 was not as scintillating as it should have been, all because Copland couldn't be there. He detailed all the goings-on with Lenny and Kousse. He ran Paul Bowles's opera, *The Wind Remains*, into the ground: "It was this little trashy super duper arty pussy footing and chasing which made me all the sorrier because it wasn't strong enough to hiss." (Perhaps Bowles's negative review two months earlier of Schuman's Town Hall evening colored Schuman's views of the opera, although Schuman would have no doubt disagreed vehemently.) He warned Copland of some of the hazards ahead for the ACA. He concluded, with some sadness, that Harris' Fifth was a seriously flawed work. And only in the last paragraph of "the longest letter I've ever written" did Schuman "come to my favorite subject—the music of W.S.," defending *A Free Song*, singing the virtues of *Prayer in Time of War* (then still called *Prayer—1943*), and admitting that "there is something wrong with the Piano Concerto and I'm thinking about [it]. . . . It was wonderful to hear from you. Please write again. Frankie sends her love."[4]

Five weeks elapsed before Copland answered. "That was a wow of a letter you sent me some weeks ago. Just the kind I need to make this Hollywood jaunt seem less like an enforced exile." And a lot had taken place in Schuman's life in those five weeks, the most stunning of which was the selection of *A Free Song* for the first-ever Pulitzer Prize in Music. Though Schuman would acknowledge at the time of the news how pleased he was by the award, April 1943 was one of Schuman's cruelest months. The premiere of *A Free Song* had gone well in Boston, with the reviewer from the *Christian Science Monitor* writing two sentences that so encouraged Schuman that he underlined them in red.

> Mr. Schuman's cantata was "adapted" from poems of Walt Whitman. . . . The score made a very favorable first impression. The composer seems to have caught the spirit of Whitman's poems, whose appositeness to today's situation he has discerned and contrived musically to express. [The next sentences are set off by red felt-tipped pen:] The themes are pregnant and the texture is rich. Its contrapuntal firmness seems to body forth the thought and character of the poet.[5]

But his dream of employing the Collegiate Chorale for the New York performance fell victim to the success of the Harvard and Radcliffe singers to secure funding to travel to New York.[6] As much as Schuman respected the skills of G. Wallace Woodworth, the conductor of the Harvard Glee Club, as well as the skills of the collegians who performed in Symphony Hall, Schuman had wanted this showcase for Shaw and his multiethnic, interfaith, and fully adult chorus. Add to his disappointment the dismay that orchestra and chorus would perform in Carnegie Hall without the benefit of a rehearsal together. Whether Schuman expected the worst, he felt he had received the worst by the time the concert had ended. Schuman poured out his despair to Copland.

> I write to you in the blackest of black moods—the performance of the Cantata was very, very poor. But so poor that the audience got little idea of the work. Naturally it was the chorus that caused this and I know that Kousse was displeased. I can't imagine what happened but the kids just didn't sing. It was awful. It made no friends and that was too bad. In Boston even Friday afternoon loved it. I am down at the moment with full hopes for an early recovery. After the concert I had a tooth pulled and it turned out to be the most pleasant experience of the day.[7]

Schuman also felt a cold wind blowing from his publisher Carl Engel, who attended the Carnegie Hall performance. Schuman attributed it to the chorus's ineptitude, but Engel paid the cantata his highest compliment: he wanted to hear it a second time. His chief performance-related displeasure came from a premature entrance from a string player, but he also had a criticism of the work. To Engel, Schuman "had apparently broken the continuity of the work by a learned but not immediately convincing instrumental interlude. This may be no more than a snap judgment. On rehearing the piece I may easily revise my opinion. At any rate forgive my frankness."[8] Engel's opinion was echoed by Olin Downes, who called the interlude one of Schuman's "sandier stretches" where "the use of the fugue formula does not recompense for the absence of a commanding utterance."[9] Virgil Thomson faulted both the chorus and the piece, with "the chorus's effective enunciation of the text being zero in row U. The music's intrinsic interest seemed also to this listener to add up to a not high figure."[10]

And by early May, *A Free Song* had won the Pulitzer Prize.

Such was the success of the first of Schuman's three war propaganda pieces (not counting the unpublished song, *Fair Land of Hope*).[11] The second one, *Prayer in Time of War*, carved a different path. Begun shortly after the completion of *A Free Song*, Schuman had originally referred to the work as "Prayer for Freedom."[12] In all likelihood, this was the name Schuman appended on the header of the title page of the vellum score. At some point after the work was completed by early January 1943, the original title was excised and, in the space beneath the resulting hole in the vellum, Schuman wrote "Prayer—1943." Schuman must have also related the original title to Fritz Reiner, the conductor of the Pittsburgh Symphony for whom Schuman was writing the piece, given that Reiner, tongue in cheek, referred to the work as "my 'Prayer for Schuman.'" Schuman must have also conveyed to Reiner his disappointment at having failed the physical and thus being sidelined from active service in the military.

Reiner took the privations and demands of war with a lighter touch than did Schuman. "I am sure that General Eisenhower will get along well enough without you in Africa, so don't worry about it. We shall be in Westport for a week from December 21st and I hope that you will find time and Gasoline to visit us with the finished 'Prayer.'"[13]

With its slow-fast-slow archlike form, the parallelism of its first and final sonorities, its plainchant-like melodic efflorescence, and its progression from anguish through hope to quiet resolve, *Prayer in Time of War* is one of Schuman's more conventional pieces and, as a result, one of his more accessible works. Schuman insisted that the work was not in any way programmatic. At the same time, he resisted any and all attempts after World War II to drop the work's reference to war. (While Schirmer did not publish the score until 1950, the title *Prayer in Time of War* was used as early as August 1945.[14]) He also volunteered later that "if the fast-moving and vigorous middle section of the work seems unprayerlike, I consider exhortation in time of peril not far removed from prayer of a quieter sort."[15]

For the most part, performers, audiences, and critics readily took to the work. Its premiere in Pittsburgh had a visual element that likely contributed to the positive reception the work received. "The composer was twice called to the stage to acknowledge the ovation. . . . Preceding the performance Mrs. John P. Hoelzel, dressed in Red Cross field uniform, made a stirring plea for contributions of blood and funds for an organization that is doing noble service for the men and women in our armed services."[16] Leopold Stokowski, conductor of the NBC Symphony Orchestra, wrote to Schuman to thank him for composing the work. "I was deeply impressed by several things in your PRAYER—its purely musical qualities, its mastery of orchestration, its clarity, its deep expression. Thank you for such a wonderful experience."[17] And fellow composer Hunter Johnson exclaimed: "At last our American music has reached the point where manner and craftsmanship no longer outweigh substance and intensity of feeling." But again, not everyone found the *Prayer* to his or her liking. Composer Irving Fine found the same weakness—a tendency toward sectionalism—that Bowles had attributed to the Piano Concerto. But Fine's appeared to be a minority voice, with Johnson's final verdict an apt summation of the place of the *Prayer in Time of War* within the larger American canon. "We need more music of this 'inner' variety. The 'outer' variety is being amply taken care of. So more power to you!"[18]

The third of the three propaganda pieces came by virtue of Schuman's attempt to land a film job. How and when Schuman met Willard Van Dyke (1906–86) is unclear. With Edward Weston, Ansel Adams, and Imogen Cunningham, Van Dyke founded the f.64 group in 1932 in San Francisco, "devoted to making so-called 'straight' photographs of great clarity and sharpness—the opposite of hazy 'pictorial' photographs meant to approximate the effect of paintings." He worked as a photographer for the WPA's Art Project in the late 1930s and then shifted to making documentaries. He also relied on Hollywood to provide the scripts as he worked in New York even though he later said that the Hollywood writers "would write from their heads instead of *working with the realities of a location.* And we were never able to get a single script from them that was useful."[19] One film his unit, Documentary Film Productions, released was *Design for Education*, later known simply as *Sarah Lawrence*; Schuman was involved in that project.[20] Given the composers involved on some of the films, both with and without Van Dyke—Thomson (*The River*, 1938), Copland (*The City*, 1939), and Moore (*Power and the Land*, 1940)—Schuman would have also been aware of local opportunities for film composers of his professional stature. At first, these films were geared toward a domestic audience, but in the early 1940s Van Dyke joined the Office of War Information to make explicit propaganda films. Even with the earlier films, Van Dyke saw his artistic stance as that of a proselytizer. "We were aware that we were consciously being propagandists. The audience knew they were being told something and could reject or accept it."[21]

In his book that chronicles the genesis and development of the Office of War Information, Charles Alexander Holmes Thomson discussed the rationale behind the propaganda films. "Documentaries exploited favorable notions about America already existing abroad, corrected undesired ideas about America, and tried to establish new and desirable ideas and attitudes." He went on to examine the titles and content of production from July 1943 to July 1944. Amid movies such as *Swedes in America*, *Cowboy*, and *Autobiography of a Jeep*, Thomson gave all of four words to describe the documentary on which Schuman collaborated with Van Dyke—"'Steel Town' emphasized American industrial might"—making this one of the briefest accounts of the 29 films Thomson mentioned. In his book, he also explained a broader purpose. "Throughout these major topics with their propaganda themes were woven other propagandistically important themes, such as the demonstration of racial solidarity in the war effort, or solidarity of many important social groups in various activities relating to the war or to the postwar world."[22]

Steel Town—both the manuscript and the copyist's score use two words for the title—certainly engaged in these additional propagandistic messages. In a filmography for Van Dyke, the film is described simply as depicting "how American steelworkers live and work."[23] But the film had much more to say to perceptive viewers.

> The film shows a unified America where native-born and immigrant laborers work side by side in perfect harmony. Frank, the protagonist, is an immigrant man from the "Middle East," who came to the U.S. forty-five years before and who has been working in a steel factory in Youngstown, Ohio. Teamwork among men of different ages and backgrounds rules the factory. The perfect teamwork of steel workers does not stop in the factory. They have organized a town orchestra, since "steel men got a habit of doing things together." In private, Frank is raising a warm, Christian family

> "up on the hill." Frank's colleague, Fred, represents the union in the labor management committee, where the managers and workers cooperatively discuss "how to make more steel." *Steel Town* portrays a classless America, where everybody is assimilated into the mainstream.[24]

Steel Town was shown in Japan after the war, a fact that makes Schuman's 1975 comment all the more delicious. "I always remember [the film] because the first line was—it was a propaganda film of course—'More steel is made in Youngstown, Ohio than in the entire Japanese empire.' That was in 1944. Now, of course, Japan, if not the leader, is certainly number two in making steel."[25] Philip Dunne, chief of production for the overseas branch of the Office of War Information's Motion Picture Bureau, summed up both the impetus of these films—what he called the "factual film"—and their shelf life.

> The factual film is a legitimate descendant of the newsreel, often with a strong strain of the old-fashioned travelogue in its ancestry. . . . But the factual film is not the realm of the true documentarian, although many individuals with documentary experience have contributed to its development. . . . It is extremely doubtful if the form [these men] created—the emotional propaganda film—will survive in theatrical feature length the times which gave it birth. But there is no question that it has played an important and significant role in the winning of the war.[26]

Dunne's analysis may explain in part why Van Dyke, in discussing his own documentary efforts, rarely mentioned *Steel Town*. In one interview, he volunteered that the film "was done because of my experience with industrial processes." But for Van Dyke, "the goal of the documentary film is to change. To change an attitude, a concept, a misconception, even to change a whole condition that is hurting or hampering the development of man."[27] *Steel Town* fit these lofty criteria poorly, even as it did engage in the propaganda war.

Schuman's choice of paper also provides a window into the importance of *Steel Town*. With the revision of the Concerto for Piano and Orchestra in 1942, Schuman had begun to write his finished scores on vellum instead of manuscript paper. Only works done in some haste were committed to manuscript paper, and *Steel Town* was one such work. Schuman used shorthand to repeat whole sections from the earlier part of the score (identified as Reel 1) in the latter half (Reel 2), leaving it to the copyist to write out the music. There are few erasures and little evidence that he labored over the score, which he completed by April 1944.

What little Schuman said about the score later in life would usually include the fact that he turned some of the furnace music from the film score and "fixed it up" to use for the rape scene in the ballet he would write the following year, *Undertow*.[28] Schuman's fixation on this detail may be an inside joke between him and Copland, given that Schuman teased Copland about the music for the minister in *Appalachian Spring*. "The fact that Aaron Copland had previously told me that it was originally conceived for children at play added to my fun."[29]

As for Van Dyke, he and Schuman would rub shoulders in another life, as Van Dyke served as the director for the department of film at the Museum of Modern Art in New York, beginning in 1965, at the time Schuman served as president of Lincoln Center. Their initial interaction was filled with sparks and friction, as the two institutions jockeyed over which one of them deserved primacy in New York's burgeoning film scene in the 1960s.[30]

Vivian Perlis later explored with Schuman the nature of his patriotism. In the shadow of Watergate and Vietnam, Schuman volunteered that

> I am not a chauvinist or a flag-waving patriot, but I feel deeply patriotic not only because I was brought up that way but because I happen to think that way. One of the reasons I think that way is that I believe it's absolutely false to claim that there is any inconsistency between being an internationalist, which I am, and being someone who has a special appreciation for the local scene.

By then, Schuman's interaction with his twentysomething son had changed him. Schuman described Tony in the mid-'70s as being "as far left as you can be and still live within the law, which he does."[31] Throughout the decade of war (1936–45), Schuman eschewed the Far Left even as he knew and even socialized with some of them, just as he disdained the Far Right, even as some of his pieces brought them comfort. And at a time when many of his colleagues were expressing their love for country by donning a faux musical populism, borrowing the tropes of the agrarian heartland, and writing scores for rivers and plows that broke the plains, Schuman, the pragmatic East Coast urban-suburban man, celebrated playgrounds instead of prairies and factories over farms. When his would-be collaborator described Schuman as a "'cement-sidewalk' American," Christopher LaFarge may have meant the designation in a dismissive way.[32] Schuman loved his country, the grit as well as the dirt, and his patriotic and propagandistic works, which stretch all the way to his final years, express that love. The anthemic song, the prize-winning cantata, the somber tone poem, and the extroverted film score all are "patriotic music written in the midst of a national and world crisis . . . 'music [that] was meant to console and uplift, to encourage and exhort.'" They were also written to persuade and convince and convert, activities that music is ill equipped to do. It is difficult to judge such music by the same standards as music composed in relatively peaceful periods.[33] How did Schuman wish these propagandistic works to go forth into the world? The answer lies partially in his treatment of them after the war was over. The song was never published. *A Free Song* was effectively rewritten 40 years later in *On Freedom's Ground*. The tone poem that was initially identified with a specific year received a new name that made it more generic. And the film score was both shelved and cannibalized. Inasmuch as possible, they joined the other, less ideologically driven works that Schuman continued to write during the war years.

The symphony that Schuman wrote in 1943 is one of the more successful of the dogma-free works from this time period, and even its chosen name steers clear of easy ideological identification. He almost never referred to it by its number and never gave a clear reason why this was the case, although the success of Beethoven's Fifth and the failure of Harris's Fifth may have given Schuman pause in numbering his own Fifth. He and Koussevitzky had talked about an idea Schuman had for a work for strings alone, something that would pose an interesting challenge to a composer who had commanded a Mahlerian orchestra in his Third two years earlier. Before Koussevitzky could offer a commission, though, Artur Rodzinski, the incoming music director of the New York Philharmonic, had written to Schuman to ask whether he and the orchestra could have the premiere of "your new symphony No. 5, which you haven't started to compose yet, but which you might do wonderfully and give it to the Philharmonic and myself for next season. How about it?" Schuman rather blandly deflected Rodzinski, saying that as of April 23, 1943, "I have not started to write Symphony No. 5 yet." Perhaps Rodzinski's interest quickened Koussevitzky's determination, for less than three weeks later, the formal letter of commission from the Koussevitzky Music Foundation came. By this time, Schuman could afford to get into bidding wars with orchestras, and the fact that Koussevitzky was willing to offer him $1,000 for a work that Rodzinski wanted for free made the choice relatively simple. Schuman nevertheless did offer Rodzinski another work. "I may be doing an overture which could be ready for the spring of next year. I would be delighted to have you give the world première of this work with the Philharmonic should it materialize." The overture would materialize, and it would be the last work for orchestra that Schuman would write without the motivation of a commission.[34]

But the *Symphony for Strings*—rarely ever referred to as the "Symphony no. 5"—came first and progressed rapidly. Schuman told Koussevitzky that he had settled on "the work for string orchestra we discussed" on May 28; the first movement (according to the vellum original) was completed on June 28 and the second on July 11. Concurrent with the symphony, he contributed a set of three pieces to the *Festschrift* in honor of Carl Engel's sixtieth birthday. For the piano work, Schuman wittily made each piece 20 measures long, thus reflecting Engel's three-score years. The individual movements of the *Three-Score Set* were apparently composed out of order, with the last of the three completed on June 6 but the entire work completed on the same day as the last movement of the *Symphony for Strings*, July 31. (The first two of the piano pieces are not individually dated.)

The symphony and the piano pieces present something of a chicken-and-egg puzzle when it comes to their middle movements, as they share similar material. Is the piano piece a condensation of the symphony's slow movement (mm. 1–18 of the piano piece = mm. 1–4 and 78–91 of the orchestral work)? Or is the latter an expansion and elaboration of the former? Neither the manuscripts nor the pertinent correspondence provide a definite answer, although the piano piece was composed onto manuscript paper, suggesting that it was composed quickly. The last two bars of the second movement for the piano piece are crossed out and another two bars are added. Though the notes beneath the rejected ending are very difficult to read, their spacing suggests that the original ending for the second of the *Three-Score Set* more closely resembled the F♯ major ending of the slow movement from the symphony (mm. 94–5), hinting at the possibility that the piano work came after the symphony and was later emended to make it more distinct from that movement.

As for the outer movements of both works, there is little evidence that they are related beyond the features of Schuman's voice that they share: melodic materials built up of large intervals, tendency to avoid triadic harmonies until the final bars, tensile rhythms in the faster movements. The first of the piano pieces is an extended exploration of quartal harmony, the second of bitonality, and the third of rhythmic two-part counterpoint. They each also follow conventional structural designs, with the first two using ternary form and the third consisting of two statements of the same material framed by an antiphon that is slightly extended at its return. The brevity and formal coherence exhibited in the *Three-Score Set* make the work useful for analysis; the moderate difficulty makes it readily accessible to many pianists, although, as with the Piano Concerto, the writing for the piano is not always completely idiomatic.

Given that Schuman's principal instrument was the violin, it is unsurprising that the writing for the *Symphony for Strings* is as idiomatic as it is successful. What is surprising is how few string techniques Schuman used in the work beyond the standard *arco* (bowed) and *pizzicato* (plucked). There are no indications to play closer to the fingerboard (*sul tasto*) or near the bridge (*sul ponticello*), both of which change the sound of the instrument. Extended bowing techniques, such as *spiccato* and *col legno*, are completely absent. Other than the use of mutes in the slow movement, the string writing is remarkably conventional. Schuman achieved variety mostly through dividing the strings into as many as nine separate parts but also, as in the end of the first movement, having instruments play in unison (here, low violins reinforced by high contrabasses). It is as if, after the extensive choices he made in the Third Symphony, Schuman deliberately constrained himself here to focus on other aspects of the music.

The symphony's formal construction further suggests that Schuman was more interested in structural rather than sonic possibilities. As in the *Prayer in Time of War* completed earlier in 1943, the three movements of the *Symphony for Strings* follow standard patterns: a first movement in a loosely constructed sonata form; a second movement in ternary form; and a third movement a modified rondo form. In his willingness to subscribe to these conventions, even if not rigidly, Schuman was showing his independence from his former teacher Harris and his notions of autogenesis. The instrumentation may also be a bit unusual when compared to a symphony from the eighteenth or nineteenth centuries. But the architecture of its three movements would have been quite familiar to Haydn, Mozart, Beethoven, Brahms, and other Old World masters. Schuman, in short, wrote a classical fifth symphony.

Critics hailed the new work. Rudolph Elie Jr., writing for the *Boston Herald*, heard the work as the validation of all the awards Schuman had won in the previous months and years.

> It is evident that William Schuman is well on his way to becoming the foremost American-born composer of the day. In point of fact, after hearing the first performance of his Symphony for Strings played by the always astonishing string band of the Boston Symphony Orchestra, I can say that Mr. Schuman already is the foremost American-born composer of the day—and entertain no expectation of being called out for a dawn appointment at 12 paces.[35]

Moses Smith, the only Boston critic who admired Schuman's Second Symphony at its New England airing in 1939, reached out beyond the Boston public to offer his verdict of the work in the pages of *Modern Music.*

> Schuman's *Symphony*, a shorter, three-movement affair, seemed to me not only the clearest, best integrated and in many respects strongest of his larger works; it is, in addition, easily one of the best symphonies by any American to date. The writing for strings, while not particularly brilliant or original, is competent and varied. The moment the music gets started it is clear that the composer is busy saying things. The concentration of utterance, however, is not jerky. For despite what seemed momentary floundering in the slow movement the *Symphony* struck me as one of the most unified major orchestral works by a contemporary American. In this regard, it resembles the mature work of Walter Piston.[36]

Koussevitzky elected to play it twice in 1943, first at its mid-November premiere, and then again to celebrate a milestone in the Schuman household. Schuman had written to Copland in late September about the new piece and the family news. "As for the music itself I can only say it's a step forward. Around Xmas Frankie plans to produce a little thing of some sort—a little Aaron or Lenny or maybe even a little Frankie." Schuman asked Koussevitzky to schedule the premiere to accommodate Frankie's pregnancy, and Koussevitzky obliged. Then prior to the New Year, at which time the Boston Symphony Orchestra would take the *Symphony for Strings* on tour with them, Koussevitzky sent Schuman a telegram.

> DELIGHTED HAVE MADE A RIGHT GUESS AM PLAYING YOUR STRING SYMPHONY TONIGHT AND TOMORROW IN HONOR OF YOUR FIRST BORN BOY WARMEST REGARDS TO MRS SCHUMAN AND YOU
> SERGE KOUSSEVITZKY[37]

Anthony William Schuman, their only boy, was born on December 22, 1943.

Schuman so believed in the *Symphony for Strings* that he allowed it to be published before its premiere, a brash display of confidence after the middling response to the Fourth Symphony.[38] But his confidence was well placed, and the praise from his colleagues continued to flow in decades after the work's premiere. In 1947, Chilean composer Juan Orrego-Salas complimented "that perfect balance between skill and a human sense in the use of technical elements in music." In 1955, dancer and choreographer José Limón premiered his *Symphony for Strings* to Schuman's music. In 1975, Vladimir Ussachevsky sent the score to Schuman along with a letter, written on stationery from the Electronic Music Center of Columbia and Princeton Universities, asking Schuman to inscribe the score for him. "The other day I took out your score . . . to refresh my memory on some strong and intriguing things in it which impressed me years ago. It occurred to me suddenly that your score was the first score of American music I ever purchased." And in 1985, Schuman's protégé and young champion Ned Rorem complained to Schuman in a postcard about a concert he recently attended. "Your beautiful Symphony for Strings, being now a classic, was a bit elbowed out by DD's [David Diamond's] new opus. Please know that if it weren't for your piece, my new String Symphony would be quite different. Can I play it for you when I get back in early Dec.? Happy Thanksgiving to you & to Frankie." Oddly enough, the missives from Orrego-Salas, Ussachevsky, and Rorem were all written in the month of November, the same month the *Symphony for Strings* was premiered.[39] Decades later, the work, written after the news about the Pulitzer Prize and with the awareness of Frankie's pregnancy, continues to radiate an afterglow of optimism and hope.

Soon after his completion of the symphony and the piano pieces, Schuman turned his attention to the overture he had offered Rodzinski and the New York Philharmonic. Rodzinski made clear his preference for a larger work from Schuman if possible and also jested that, since the overture would be ready for presentation in the spring of 1944, it should be called the Spring Overture. Schuman replied in a similar lighthearted vein.

> Thanks for your letter, the congratulations on the Pulitzer prize and the suggestion that we call the overture the Spring Overture. I accept the first two gladly, but I feel that my namesake said the last word on the subject of spring even if my composition would not be in B flat. [Robert Schumann's Symphony no. 1 in B♭ major, op. 38, is known as the *Spring* Symphony.] I know that you want a larger work, and I can only say that there won't be time to prepare one for next season. It may be that the overture will turn into something else, but I doubt that it will be a really large work.[40]

The *William Billings Overture* that Schuman offered Rodzinski would indeed turn into something else, but that was more than a decade into the future. Billings's life and music becomes something of a thread in Schuman's own life and music. During his studies at Teachers College, he wrote a paper on the arts and music of the 13 colonies in the eighteenth century. While only a few pages survive of the paper, it may be no accident that the surviving pages discuss Billings. Schuman devoted the better part of one paragraph to outline the significance of one of Billings's hymn tunes.

> William Billings' song "Chester" has been called the "Over There" of the revolution. Although "Yankee Doodle" was used the most as a marching song, "Chester" was certainly sung by the Continental troops.[41] The melody was originally written by Billings as a hymn tune, but in his second book, The Singing Master's Assistant, "Chester" was published as a war song. It certainly is anything but a good piece of music, even of popular music. The melody is drab and banal and the accenting of the words is often ill chosen, (i.e., using the word "and" on the first beat of the fifth bar. It is also curious that in the last beat of the next to the last bar, there is no leading note. There seems to be no reason for this and the omission does not help the song much.)[42]

His harsh assessment of "Chester" as a young and brash student is greatly at odds with the notes he provided in 1944 for his *William Billings Overture*. "To an increasing number of musicians and laymen alike, Billings has become more than a mere reference listing in a history book. And for some of us who perform his music he remains, for all his shortcomings, a composer of great strength, with a deep religiosity and rugged individuality."[43] The change in attitude is probably attributable to Schuman's changed relationship to Billings. At Teachers College, he studied the music. At Sarah Lawrence, he performed it.

Before he taught the chorus some of Billings's music, Schuman had encountered it in at least two other places. On the same March 1938 evening that Lehman Engel and his Madrigal Singers premiered Schuman's *Choral Etude*, they also sang the music of other American composers. The first work on their program was "Chester." And a few weeks before that, Schuman had been arranging programs for radio broadcast. One of the proposed works was Otto Luening's *Prelude on a Hymn Tune by William Billings*, with the hymn tune in question being "Hymn to Music." Schuman would introduce Billings to the chorus some years later. In a joint concert with the Yale Glee Club on December 5, 1942, the combined choirs sang three "fuguing tunes" by Billings: "Creation," "When Jesus Wept," and "Be Glad Then America."[44] (None of these technically are fuguing tunes.) When the two groups came back together a year later, they omitted "Creation" but sang the other two Billings tunes. So Schuman's choice of two of the three tunes he incorporated for his overture would have resonated deeply among the students at both Yale and Sarah Lawrence.

The decision to include "Chester" thus may be read as yet another way to use music toward propagandistic ends. Choosing Billings for his work at a time when Harris chose folksong and Copland cowboy tunes and Shaker hymns unquestionably locates Schuman within that stream of American composers who were searching for an indigenous musical world. Choosing "Chester" further marks the *William Billings Overture* as a work associated with the prosecution of war. Schuman was quite explicit about this in his notes for the first performance. After stating that the tune, composed in 1770, began as a church hymn but was quickly adopted by the Continental Army, he quoted two quatrains associated with the tune, both bellicose, one explicitly militaristic.

Let tyrants shake their iron roads,
And slavery clank her galling chains.
We fear them not, we trust in God.
New England's God forever reigns.

The foe comes on with haughty stride,
Our troops advance with martial noise;
Their vet'rans flee before our youth,
And gen'rals yield to beardless boys.[45]

Harris had long before adapted another tune associated with war in his "American overture," *When Johnny Comes Marching Home* of 1934. Schuman's response to "Chester" in the '30s focused on the music, which he found wanting. In his notes to the Philharmonic audience in 1944, he spent more words telling about the history of "Chester" and providing its text than he did in describing his manipulation of Billings's music. Billings and "Chester" spoke to him during World War II in ways they did not speak to him before.

The overture didn't speak convincingly to Downes, who complained of the segmented nature of the work, its highly calculated contrapuntal effects, and its failure to "establish the sensation of cellular growth and organic development."[46] The work was performed sporadically over the next 12 years, but it never fully caught on. The executives at G. Schirmer had decided to rent the work and not make it available for purchase, which along with their decision not to publish a study score further depressed performances and interest in the overture. Thor Johnson conducted the overture in 1955 as part of a concert to welcome back to New York the delegates and staff of the United Nations. Johnson wrote to Schuman and encouraged him to see to it that Schirmer made the work more easily available. Schuman had already been in negotiations with his publisher about the work, and, dissatisfied with the outcome, he reluctantly declared his independence from Schirmer and joined the roster of composers that Arthur Hauser was amassing for Theodore Presser Co. in Bryn Mawr, Pennsylvania. Since the overture was never published, Schuman chose officially to withdraw the work, recast it, and give it as one of his first new works to his new publisher.[47] Schuman's embrace of "Chester" literally changed his life.

Two other commissions that Schuman received in 1944 were of a more popular nature. In 1942, Eugene Goossens, conductor of the Cincinnati Symphony Orchestra, wrote to Schuman and a number of other composers requesting fanfares that would be played at the beginning of each Cincinnati Symphony concert. On the bottom of Goossens's letter, Schuman wrote: "Will try but doubt that there will be time now."[48] One of the fanfares Goossens received was Copland's *Fanfare for the Common Man*, so, emboldened by the success of that project, Goossens wrote again to a number of composers, this time inviting them to write a variation on a theme that he himself had composed. This time, Schuman readily agreed, and Goossens thanked him for his "promptitude."[49] The composers whose efforts were stitched together were (in order of musical appearance): Paul Creston, Aaron Copland, Deems Taylor, Howard Hanson, Schuman, Walter Piston, Roy Harris, Anis Fuleihan, Bernard Rogers, and Ernest Bloch, with Goossens's theme heading the parade and a finale, also composed by Goossens, bringing the work to a rousing finish. In his review of the work, Robert Tangeman noted that

> a surprising degree of continuity and unity has been maintained, despite the individual personalities clearly evident in most of the variations. Similar in character were the allegro movements by Copland and Piston, both of them polyphonic and strongly rhythmic. Schuman wrote an effective four-part canonic piece for strings, the most quiet and expressive section of the work. Harris came dangerously close to overworking an ostinato figure derived from the opening notes of the theme. Rogers caught the fancy of the audience with the esoteric Oriental coloring of his *Variation alla Cinese*.[50]

The other, more substantial, work was an overture for the second half of Billy Rose's revue *The Seven Lively Arts*. According to Schuman, Rose needed music

NBC Symphony Hour, December 16, 1943. From left: Leopold Stokowski, Deems Taylor, Paul Creston, Aaron Copland, and Schuman. Photofest.

for a poem he had found in *The Nation* and wanted to use in the show. He asked Robert Shaw, who was directing the choral music for him, to recommend a composer, and Shaw gave Rose Schuman's name. Schuman wasn't interested in the poem, but Rose made him a different offer: to write an orchestral work that would be performed as part of the arts extravaganza *and* to provide the incidental music for a play he was producing on the life of King Henry VIII. Schuman wrote the orchestral work, which he titled *Side Show*, during the first half of the summer of 1944. Schuman wrote to Copland some months later about the work and its prospects.

> The Billy Rose piece was finished last July. It is an 8 (approx.) minute affair which I have called SIDE SHOW for orchestra. I give you fair warning that you will like it very much—just as my large choral pieces are, you tell me, "not your dish" so is this piece up your alley, and I mean right up. It opens will [*sic*] a great grandiose musical announcement which says—Ladies and Gentlemen—there follows fast music from there on in which is a work out for a symphony orch. like a jam session. Only everything is, I trust, highly organized. For me the piece (with its soupy waltz and snare drum rolls—and oriental sounding dance) is very funny and highly satirical. But F. Reiner, who plays the first symphonic performance this year, finds it fresh but not funny or satirical. I told him I probably had an over developed sense of humor to which he replied that it was probably under developed. But B. Rose loves it and will open his second act of Seven Lively Arts revue with it. It remains a question of audience reaction of course. If people talk during it (his great fear as showman) out it comes. I also started music for the Margaret Webster–Billy Rose production of Henry VIII and got half through when the play was put off for a time because of actor trouble. It may go on later this year.[51]

Side Show—later renamed *Circus Overture*—was put into the show during its out-of-town tryouts where it stayed for a handful of performances. Rose needed to trim the length of the show, and Schuman's overture was probably five minutes too long. As for the incidental music for *The Famous History of the Life of King Henry VIII*, a working script dated July 27, 1944, lists approximately 30 music cues. Based on the limited annotation in Schuman's copy of the script, the discussions about where there would be music and how much music there would be were spare. The production came to naught, though, as Laird Cregar, the actor who was slated to play King Henry, died on December 9, 1944. Schuman did manage to complete two short works that were to be used in the play: a Te Deum that would have been sung during the coronation scene; and a song to a text of Shakespeare, *Orpheus with His Lute*, which Schuman would revisit twice more as the basis for *A Song of Orpheus* (1961) and *In Sweet Music* (1978).[52] His time with Rose gave Schuman a host of stories. He talked about the meeting at which, with conductor Maurice Abravanel at the piano, Schuman sang *Orpheus with His Lute* for Rose and Mary Martin; the manner in which Rose reneged on the money he had promised for the incidental music; and

Schuman's small part in Rose's negotiations with Igor Stravinsky on how to make the latter's *Scènes de ballet* a "great success," namely, should Stravinsky agree, Schuman—and not Robert Russell Bennett—would reorchestrate a portion of the ballet.[53] But the concert premiere and broadcast of *Side Show* gave Schuman greater satisfaction than anything connected with Rose. Reiner chose not to send Schuman clippings from the Cleveland critics, electing instead to summarize their comments.

> One admitted that although it was a bombastic piece it proved you to be an "adroit weaver of orchestral colors"—another conceded that while it "might have some merit it was hidden in the loud orchestration" etc. etc. I didn't think you were particularly interested and therefore didn't order a set to be sent you. I am sure that you heard the audience's very definite approval over the air.[54]

One more work that was begun in 1944—Schuman's first extended dance work and only ballet—will be discussed in a subsequent chapter. But the big news of the year had nothing to do with prizes won or works composed. On September 22, Schuman entered into an agreement with Gustave Schirmer, president of the publishing firm, to become the director of publications, a position that prosaically demanded "the giving of counsel and advice to our Publication Department" but that carried enormous power far beyond counsel and advice. Carl Engel, who had been president of G. Schirmer from 1929 on, died suddenly in May 1944. He had hired Gustave Reese in 1940 to become the director of publications, but after Engel's death Schirmer wanted a change. He approached Koussevitzky to ask for advice, and in parallel to Robert Shaw's proposal to Billy Rose, Koussevitzky recommended Schuman for the job. Once again, a letter from Schuman to Copland contains many of the details and Schuman's attitude about his new career.

> Our great friend Serge Koussevitzky was largely instrumental in my being offered this post. Let me hasten to add that aside from the opportunity of doing a progressive job with the largest publisher it will also give me the kind of flexible schedule I have never enjoyed in teaching. Mr. Schirmer does not think the work should take me more than a few afternoons each week once it gets under way. That remains to be seen. At any rate I will keep my mornings always free for writing. Are you surprised—not nearly the way I was. It just never entered my head. Letters have been coming in from all over the country from composers. The first paragraph is one of congratulations, the second calling attention to their works and the third asking about my job at SLC. That is the general form.[55]

Schuman hoped to use his position at G. Schirmer to shake up the status quo. Though the position wouldn't begin full time until his duties at Sarah Lawrence ended in May 1945, Schuman began to assemble a panel of advisors who were active in education who could help him counter what he saw on his nationwide tour for the Rockefeller Foundation in 1940 and which he bemoaned in his letter to Harold Ickes that summer: a wealth of student performers who had a dearth of good music. Schuman met with G. Wallace Woodworth, conductor of the Harvard Glee Club, to discuss the creation of the Harvard-Radcliffe Choral Series at Schirmer. Schuman told Woodworth that he intended "to throw all his influence at G. Schirmer's in the interest of publication of good music realizing at the same time the commercial necessity of publishing along side the good music inferior material."[56] Good music, he assured Woodworth, lay more in the Harvard-Radcliffe series than in Fred Waring's more popular arrangements, a belief that could have worked against Robert Shaw, since Shaw came from the Waring organization. But during his tenure at G. Schirmer, Schuman shrewdly launched not only the Harvard-Radcliffe Choral Series but also the Robert Shaw Choral Series, finding good music from both Woodworth and Shaw.

Shaking up the status quo would also mean doing something about how people wrote about music. In addition to publishing music, at the time G. Schirmer published the journal *Musical Quarterly*. Founded in 1915, the journal was the flagship publication in the United States for serious writing about music, far surpassing the trade press in the depth and breadth of its coverage. Schuman admired *Musical Quarterly*'s reach, but he found the prose stodgy. More egregious to Schuman was the journal's noncoverage of the contemporary American music scene. As director of publications, he could not only have a say in what kind of music was being published but he could also have a say in what people said about the music.[57]

He also would have a say in whose music got published. The congratulatory letters made that clear. Samuel Barber, already a Schirmer composer, had no need to curry favor with Schuman, but in his letter of best wishes he expressed his views of what Schuman's appointment would mean. "Certainly there is a great deal to be done there, and you who are younger and not *lebensmüde* [world-weary] as Carl was, should be able to put it over. Such an appointment can be of greatest importance to American music."[58] Schuman took great pride in the fact that Roger Sessions's Second Symphony was published on his watch at G. Schirmer, and he saw his work with a publisher as an extension of his college career: his position gave him "the opportunity of teaching by publishing composers who hadn't been published."[59] Both David Diamond and Lukas Foss became Schirmer composers during Schuman's tenure. Schuman joked that Foss was all of 15 years of age when he came to see Schuman at Schirmer's with a sheaf of piano music tucked under his arm; in fact, Foss was in his early twenties, by which time he had composed a piano concerto as well as a number of piano works.[60] Diamond's encounter with Schuman was, if anything, more dramatic than Foss's, and both composers relived the moment if only to make amends. Diamond recalled that Schuman rejected all of his music. Schuman corrected his colleague.

> Your memory on the Schirmer luncheon is faulty. I invited you to tell you that I wanted Schirmer to publish your music and suggested that we begin with some short songs or choral pieces. Your screaming, "Fuck you", was to register your objection to our not beginning immediately with big works. But all of this is so unimportant now.[61]

Schirmer could not live on contemporary music alone, of course, and Schuman was philosophical about the business aspects of publishing when he was dictating his memoirs.

> At Schirmer's, it was obviously my task to see that the selections I made would not soon put the firm out of business. As I examined the huge catalogue of the house, it was clear to [me] that its famous library of "musical classics"—the composers of the past—was its principal mainstay. It was also clear that of the contemporary works published each year, 99 per cent were chosen solely with dollar signs in view.

He took it as his mandate to eliminate the "bad to mediocre works (the so-called semi-classics)" from the house's holdings and to focus on the old masters and modern composers. Even though Gustave Schirmer personally did not care for most twentieth-century music, "he understood that contemporary composers had to be tolerated if Schirmer was to continue to be, as he described it, 'the Tiffany of music publishers.'"[62]

Schuman also had sound financial reasons for joining this gilt-edged firm. The starting salary at Schirmer was more than double what he was making at Sarah Lawrence, and it came with greater certainty for increased compensation

Schuman during his Sarah Lawrence years.

than academia held. He had become a father in late 1943, and he and Frankie wanted a second child. He had been unable to purchase life insurance because of his muscular atrophy, so he needed to arrange his investments in such a way as to guarantee that his wife and children would be provided for in the eventuality of his death. It was a smart move on many fronts.

It didn't take long, however, for Schuman to conclude that he had made a mistake. When Koussevitzky had approached him to see if he might be interested in the presidency of the firm, Schuman demurred. "I said: 'But I am not a businessman.' And he said [imitating accent]: 'Villiammm, through de night you have become aaa businessman.'"[63] Schuman settled for a lesser position, but it still felt like the wrong position. With a wife and son, however, he could hardly afford not to continue. He was 34 years old, and he felt trapped.[64]

However momentous Schuman's impact on the world of music was before the summer of 1945, however significant he imagined it might be at G. Schirmer, that impact was about to increase exponentially. What happened next led Harvard's "Woody" Woodworth to exclaim: "You are the modern meteor,—no question!"[65] Meteors, though, often come one after the other and appear reliably, as in the Orionid meteor shower. Schuman was a modern comet, a singular body that doesn't come across the horizon every year. Wondrously enough, Halley's Comet—the sire of the Orionids—appeared in 1910, the year of Schuman's birth, and the famous comet, like Schuman, to this day continues to draw a host of meteoroids, some minuscule, some magnificent, in its orbit. The musical comet was about to come fully into view.

PART 3

THE JUILLIARD YEARS

THIRTEEN

WRINGING THE CHANGES

Some of Schuman's stories are simply too entertaining not to repeat in full, using his own words. His tendency to embellish and elide the facts is on display in this revealing tale, which gives us Schuman's perspective on an event as seminal as that of the Carnegie Hall concert in April 1930.

> The New School—I think it was called the New School for Social Research—on 12th Street, wanted to raise some money, so they were having a dinner in which modern music was being discussed. Either Aaron Copland or Erich Leinsdorf—one or the other—was the master of ceremonies. I don't remember which one. I don't even recall who all the other participants were except that Erskine [John Erskine, president of Juilliard] was one, and I was one, and we agreed to give our services in the cause of raising money for the school, thinking that this dinner on the subject of modern music would be intriguing for the public. And it was. They had a big crowd there.
>
> I was called on first, and I didn't know I was going to be called on. So I said: "Mr. Chairman, I am not prepared with any opening remarks and I will give up my time as long as you promise me the first question from the floor" or something else that was mildly amusing. And I sat down.
>
> Erskine got up, and in his usual marvelously witty way said: "Modern music has two problems. The first is it's not heard. The second is it's heard." Isn't that marvelous? And then he went on to say that modern music had no melody, all the cliché arguments. So suddenly I found myself on my feet, and I said: "Mr. Chairman, I want my ten minutes back because somebody has to answer John Erskine."
>
> I had never met John Erskine before, and I said: "John Erskine wrote books that I wasn't permitted to read when I was an adolescent by my parents, which I promptly devoured, and he is a man of great learning, and I can't do him battle in any field except music, which is the field of my professional equipment and obviously not of his." The reason I remember this so well is that others have told the story many times, and so have I.
>
> Then I said: "As to the question of modern music not being melodic,"—and I gave a definition of what melody is—"if the audience will forgive me, I'd like to sing a little

> modern music. I'll start with Mathis der Maler of Hindemith," which wasn't very old at that time, and I sang some of that. We had a great time. Everything was fine.[1]
>
> At the end of the evening I remember Aaron said to Frankie: "You simply have got to tell Bill he can't do this kind of thing in public because he antagonizes people." Erskine came over to me and he said: "Now, I want you to know, Schuman, that I wasn't always an old fuddy-duddy, and I loved the way you came at me tonight. Will you have lunch?" So he invited me to have lunch at the Century [Club].[2]

So began Schuman's ascendancy to the presidency of the Juilliard School of Music.

Erskine did not repeat this particular story in his memoir. He had served as Juilliard's president from 1926 to 1937, having left his position as a professor of literature at Columbia University to lead the school. In his memoir, *My Life in Music*, he volunteered that "before we chose Mr. Schuman as our new president, the School Board considered a number of other candidates, or perhaps we should say, other possibilities." One was the conductor Bruno Walter, who was approaching 70 years of age. Erskine invited Walter and some board members over to his home for conversation. "At the end of the evening my colleagues on the Board when away convinced that they had met a great man—but convinced also that his heart was in Old Europe, and he was not for our School." Erskine made his preference and rationale clear.

> I happen to know more about [Schuman's] work than most of the other members of the Board, some of whom felt at first that we were taking a risk to put the School in his charge. All that they knew about him was that his previous teaching had been done in a small school, he composed in the modern manner, and he was extremely youthful. I held out for Schuman on the ground that youth more than anything else was what the School needed.[3]

James Warburg, one of the directors on the Juilliard Board, had far less to say about Juilliard in his reminiscences than did Erskine. Scion of the German-Jewish banker Paul Warburg, he served in the FDR administration as a financial advisor. As his more than two dozen books attest, he was more interested in domestic and foreign affairs than in the intrigues of the Juilliard position. His youngest daughter, Kay, attended Sarah Lawrence from 1941 to 1945 and sang in the chorus all four years, so Warburg knew of Schuman's work and was impressed. Schuman and Warburg would become close friends: Schuman's country home was built on property that was once a portion of Warburg's Greenwich estate, and Warburg and his third wife, Joan, would continue to follow the New York music scene more out of loyalty to Schuman than because of personal interest. In his memoir, Warburg's sole mention of Juilliard in this period focused upon his decision to resign from the various directorships that he held with the exception of the Polaroid Corporation and the Juilliard School of Music.[4]

Both men wanted Schuman to throw his hat into the ring for the presidency of the Juilliard School of Music. After Erskine stepped down as president in

1937, Ernest Hutcheson, a composer, pianist, and educator who was born in Australia and who had served as the school's dean for more than a decade, stepped in. Erskine was 46 when he assumed the presidency, 57 when he bowed out, and 65 when he sparred with Schuman. Hutcheson was retiring at age 74, Warburg was a relatively young 48, and Schuman, at the time of the interviews, was a few months shy of his thirty-fifth birthday. Copland, in his remarks to Frankie, showed concern that Schuman wasn't paying proper homage to his musical elders. Some of those elders wanted Schuman to know that they were looking for something radically different.

Not all of them, though. Hutcheson offered a less supportive perspective. In a journal that consists of letters that he composed to his deceased wife, he noted that, by June 5, 1945, Schuman had assented to allow his name to go forward. Along with him, the board hoped to interview: violinist Albert Spalding (b. 1888), whose autobiography *Rise to Follow* had appeared in 1943; pianist Edwin Hughes (b. 1884), who had taught at the Institute of Musical Art; and pianist and conductor Reginald Stewart (b. 1900), who was the director of the Peabody Conservatory in Baltimore. Spalding declared himself unavailable, but the others "are thinking it over and I think they will let their names be presented." For some reason, Hutcheson's favored candidate for president never came for an interview: Paul Hindemith.[5]

Schuman, according to his own testimony, reluctantly agreed to meet with members of the Juilliard board and initially insisted that he not be considered a candidate for the position. He could see no possible marriage between Juilliard's hidebound, rote education and the progressive, student-oriented approach that he enjoyed at Sarah Lawrence. He had set out his approach to education in the opening paragraph of one of his earliest published essays.

> There are many reasons why the present public is without aggressive and intelligent interest in the music it so apathetically absorbs. One of these, perhaps outstanding, is an obvious deficiency in the quality of its education. Increasingly clear is our need to understand the points at which this education fails. But it is even more important that we examine carefully and with open mind any fresh approach in music education for the new generation. So long as the public lacks curiosity about what is untried, the contemporary composer of vision will be ignored, and so long as that public is educated through a system which imposes rigid formulae of esthetic norms unrelated in any vital way to the experience of the individuals that make up its collective entity, the growth of a healthy curiosity will be thwarted.[6]

His disdain for conventional education was palpable, and though he may not have had Juilliard in mind as he wrote these words in 1938, the Juilliard of his imagination in 1945 certainly made a convenient foil for all that was wrong with the teaching of music.

Schuman's own unconventional and individualistic education convinced him that learning came in doing and not hearing, that the best instructors were those who were active in the nuts and bolts of their discipline and not theorists of it, and that dead wood should be gathered and dispatched. He was uninterested in the position, so he pulled no punches in his critique. However ill fitting the Schirmer job was, the Juilliard job would be even more ludicrous. And so Schuman gave the elderly board members the same treatment he gave Erskine, telling them everything that was wrong with their attitudes about contemporary composition, about education, about music, about their school.

Hutcheson vividly recalled what Schuman said and how he said it.

> Schuman talked very openly and aggressively; in fact he laid great stress on aggression as the main point of his policy if made president. He seemed to disapprove of what the Juilliard had done so far, and said it had never taken a leading position in the country as it should have done. He repeated a good deal of the well-worn criticism and was ready to quote the Juilliard will with the interpretation that "American music" meant "the American composer". He thinks the orchestra should record little known works and contemporary American composers. He thought we had quite a wrong set of composition teachers; nor does he like the "virtuoso" teaching of other branches. He wouldn't be at all interested to become president of the Juilliard as it now is, but thinks that it could become worth while under "aggressive" direction. He seemed to refer rather vaguely to a group ("a little group of earnest thinkers"?) to which he belonged and which he considered rather final in its opinions. He didn't really know much about what the Juilliard has been doing. But he didn't ask a single question—he just told us.[7]

Despite Schuman's apparent lack of curiosity and his attacks on the school on whose board Hutcheson and the other men served, the trustees voted to offer him the presidency.

Before the die was cast, Schuman turned to his champion and mentor Koussevitzky. Kousse, after all, had recommended Schuman for the Schirmer post, and Schuman did not wish to alienate him by making a rash decision. At the same time, Schuman felt that he should take the position, and while his request for Koussevitzky's counsel was more than a pro forma gesture, it is clear that, by mid-June, Schuman had made up his mind.

> As you can realize, it has not been an easy problem for me to decide. After weeks of thought, I have arrived at the point where I feel that the Juilliard School is a challenge and opportunity to put my philosophy and ideals into practice. It seems to offer genuine scope to deal with many of the specific problems which you and I have long discussed.

Koussevitzky called the next day—it is worth noting that Schuman's letter was written and dispatched on a Sunday—and offered his encouragement and blessing. Schuman responded:

> Your enthusiastic support and real understanding of my problems and objectives are things which I value most highly. As you know, much prayerful thought went into my

> decision. It constitutes a very important and rather final step in my career. Your endorsement of it helped confirm my conviction about it.[8]

It is difficult to know at this distance what Schuman meant by a "rather final step," but in light of his father's long tenure with Oberly & Newell and his grandfathers' similar experiences with their careers, Schuman may have seen the Juilliard presidency as the highest and last pinnacle that a man of his education and accomplishments could reach. The prospect for longevity in the post, given the ages of Erskine and Hutcheson when they stepped down, was great, and around the corner, Schuman had another example in the retirement that year of Nicholas Murray Butler, the 83-year-old president of Columbia University who had served in that capacity for 43 years.

Butler was far more tested when he assumed the Columbia presidency than Schuman was as he contemplated heading what was already considered the leading conservatory of music in the United States. His inexperience in administration was a concern for some. But he pondered how to move forward and how fast to move. "I think of the first year at the School as a time for study, exploration and minor adjustments and innovations. No major changes can be contemplated until the materials at hand can be weighed and evaluated and until the staff has some grasp of my thinking." In fact, Schuman moved much faster than this, and a January 16, 1946, press release from the school, titled "Plans for an Extensive Reorganization of the Juilliard School of Music," outlined some of Schuman's far-reaching goals:

- the consolidation of the Juilliard Graduate School and the Institute of Musical Art "into a single unit to be known as the Juilliard School of Music";
- orchestral and choral concerts that will be for the community as well as for the students, taking place in public concert halls and over the radio;
- commissioned works written to complement the teaching of music and opera: "Through these commissions, composers will be able to develop a repertoire of contemporary music meeting the technical skills of students at various levels of proficiency";
- the release of recordings of the commissioned works to the general public. "Other contemporary music, and less familiar works of the past, will also be recorded";
- the creation of a Placement Bureau "to serve the students and alumni, and to provide means of evaluating current standards of employment";
- a shift in scholarship allocation whereby "the actual amount of financial assistance will now be determined only by the economic status of the prospective student."

The release summarized the rationale for these changes in language that sounds strikingly similar to Schuman's views of education that he aired in 1938: "The broad objective of this program is to achieve the highest goals of individualized instruction and, at the same time, to maintain the Juilliard School as a progressive force in music."[9]

The consolidation of the two separate educational entities was one of the most contentious changes Schuman sought to implement. The graduate school was highly selective and heavily subsidized; the institute took all comers and generated lots of income. The faculty and students of the former looked down upon those in the latter. But Schuman's feeling was that the Juilliard name covered them both, and to ensure the quality of all the students and faculty, the two entities needed to be made one. The ringing of the changes brought the wringing of many hands. "I remember when someone called me and said: 'The faculty is up in arms,' and I said: 'Let me know when the first one submits his resignation.'"[10]

John Perry, one of the eldest members of the board and the former lawyer of Augustus Juilliard, asked Warburg to deliver the following message to Schuman on the eve of the announcement that he had been appointed as president of the school. "[Our decision is] either the greatest thing that has ever happened to the Juilliard School or the most colossal error of [the board members'] collective lives."[11] Depending on who traces Schuman's time at Juilliard, the decision was neither great nor a disaster, or it was both, or it was one or the other. Andrea Olmstead, in *Juilliard: A History*, described Schuman's early months in terms that resemble the Night of the Long Knives, and throughout her text she painted Schuman in mostly unflattering ways. Joseph Polisi, whom Frankie described as a man "in whom my husband had great faith and whom he considered his musical son," did not shy away from discussing the controversies of the Schuman years but generally gave Schuman high marks for his leadership of the school.[12] Both Olmstead and Polisi have ties to Juilliard: Olmstead as a former music history faculty member during Peter Mennin's administration; and Polisi as Mennin's successor in the corner office. Both have their reasons for accentuating the side of Schuman they find most compelling during this period—and doing so in such comprehensive fashion—that it is challenging for writers to achieve a sense of balance.

An exchange of letters between Erskine and Schuman sheds some light on how a former administrator viewed the activities of the new man and how the new man operated. At issue was the position of Carl Friedberg, the principal teacher on the piano faculty. Friedberg, a student of Clara Schumann who had played for Brahms, began teaching at the Institute of Musical Art in 1923. By the time Schuman was named president of Juilliard, Friedberg was 72 years old, more than twice Schuman's age. Schuman intended to ask Friedberg to retire at the conclusion of the 1945–46 academic year. To Erskine, Schuman's decision smacked of ageism and overweening ambition and showed little deference to a man of Friedberg's stature. Erskine not only upbraided Schuman for what he perceived was haste "in your feverish decisions," but he also warned Schuman that he was showing symptoms of an "over-taxed nervous system," evidence of which was his inability to sleep "without the aid of drugs."

> For your own sake, Bill, as well as for the School, remember that Carl Friedberg is a teacher with a name through the western world, and that you are still a young musical educator with your name to make. Don't be impatient. We old fellows shall be gone soon enough.[13]

Schuman would have none of it. He cited the action of the board two months earlier, at which time Schuman brought up his intention not to reengage Friedberg and three other faculty members. "You were present at that meeting and raised no objection." (The agenda for the meeting indicates that Friedberg was one of five faculty members who were slated for retirement.)[14] He informed Erskine that he had read the Friedberg letter to one trustee prior to the recent meeting, "and at the Board meeting, before you came, definitely showed it to one and possibly two other members." (Read: Had you arrived earlier, you would have seen the letter as well.) These other men found the letter to be excellent,

> but after reading your criticism of it I am ready to agree that it leaves room for improvement. But please do not think that the reason for this is any over-taxed state of my nervous system. Whatever its shortcomings, I assure you the letter was not written in haste.

The most telling part of Schuman's letter showed that a gulf had emerged between the old guard and the young bucks. As would be evident later, age was no predictor of which camp a person might occupy. Friedberg's contract was not renewed, but Rosina Lhevinne, a member of the piano faculty who was 65 when Schuman arrived, stayed on the faculty until her death at age 96. Schuman perceived that the old guard sought out Erskine to help them bank Schuman's fire. Schuman, in turn, made it clear to Erskine that Erskine wasn't hearing everything there was to hear.

> Since you are kind enough to be concerned about the tension and worry of the job here I know you will be happy to hear me say that in my opinion the most difficult period has passed. Naturally enough the people who would come to you are not necessarily those who are overjoyed at the turn of events. For this reason I am afraid you have been given a warped picture of the actual state of affairs. As things stand now, I feel that the students and the faculty are, in overwhelming majority, strongly behind our announced plans. Until your letter came I thought that the major crisis had passed and that from now on we could proceed in more normal fashion. If this letter does not satisfy the issues you raise we must certainly pursue the matter further and if necessary review all these things with the Board.[15]

This last sentence mediates between the positions that Olmstead and Polisi and others advance. Juilliard's Board of Trustees was ultimately responsible for the actions of the president, who served at their discretion. At any time and for any reason, they could ask for Schuman's resignation. They could also upend the president's agenda or hand him his remit, at which point the president would have to choose between obeisance and rebellion. For most of his administration of the school, the trustees helped Schuman execute his vision. (Even Erskine later helped Schuman draft a sensitive letter.) Those trustees gave Schuman more than 16 years at the helm of Juilliard, at that time the longest term any president had served the school. And at the time of his resignation, several trustees expressed regrets that he was leaving. However one views Schuman's leadership of the school, that leadership was enabled by his boards, whose courage and fecklessness and shilly-shallying and brilliance must be noted along with that of Schuman.

This is not to say that Schuman always kept his trustees apprised at the time he was hatching plans. Soon after his presidency was announced in August 1945, he contacted Fritz Reiner to see if he might interest the famous conductor to lead the Juilliard Orchestra and teach courses on conducting. While their scheme never materialized, Reiner did express interest in the position and wrote in explicit detail what he would hope to do at Juilliard.[16] When Reiner turned him down, Schuman turned to Thor Johnson, a young conductor who, like Schuman, had spent a summer in Salzburg. Though Johnson stayed only nine months (1946–47), he was unstinting in his praise for Schuman. "There is no doubt in my mind that this past year under your aegis has been the most important thus far for me and I fully realize my indebtedness to you for making it possible."[17] The next academic year, Edgar Schenkman led the orchestra. He had previously conducted the premiere of Schuman's Second Symphony in 1938 and recorded the *Symphony for Strings* in 1946, so Schenkman was no stranger to Schuman. His year with the Juilliard Orchestra, however, ended unhappily. Schuman had persuaded both Schenkman and Koussevitzky to allow the latter to lead the ensemble in a Carnegie Hall appearance in May 1948. The rehearsals and concert earned Schuman one of the few letters of criticism he received from Koussevitzky.

> I must tell you that the standard of your Student Orchestra is not up to the mark. My impressions of the rehearsals was one of profound disappointment and astonishment, for I had to teach the students some elementary principles, for which not only their teachers are to blame, but also the Director, who is responsible for the engagement of the teachers and for establishing the reputation and basic standard of the School.
>
> . . . As I once told you,—only if you have great teachers will you have great pupils. Mediocre teachers are deadly to a School.[18]

Schenkman resigned; whether he jumped or was pushed is unclear.[19] Guest conductors led the orchestra the following year (1948–49). In the course of the year, Schuman saw Jean Morel, whom he promptly invited to organize a French festival at the school. Morel remained on the Juilliard roster until 1971; his pupils included James Levine, Dennis Russell Davies, Jorge Mester, Leonard Slatkin, and James Conlon.

The loss of Schenkman and the choice of Morel points to one of Schuman's great strengths: his ability to surround himself with effective, driven, and loyal deputies to join him in the enterprises he envisioned. The January 1946 press release announced a number of new hires for the subsequent academic year. Norman Lloyd, Schuman's colleague at Sarah Lawrence, would "supervise general student activities and be responsible for the integration of the students' individual program of study." Lloyd would go on to become dean of the Oberlin College Conservatory, and from there he joined the Rockefeller Foundation as director of arts programming.[20] Also announced in the press release was Mark Schubart, who would oversee public relations. Schubart, a music editor for the *New York Times*, had met Schuman through their work on bringing Max Rudolf's book, *The Grammar of Conducting*, to print. Like Morel, Lloyd and Schubart stayed at Juilliard for Schuman's entire tenure. Schubart, who followed Schuman to Lincoln Center, reflected years later on his relationship with Schuman at Juilliard. "I always saw myself as trying to help Bill implement his really innovative ideas about the school. But my mission was, in a way, to preserve the great performing tradition and not to let that get swept aside. In other words, to preserve the old along with the new."[21]

Schuman's interests at Juilliard did lie more with the new than the old. He initiated music festivals sometimes focused on composers (Hindemith, Bloch, Copland), sometimes focused on geography (Great Britain, France, the United States), but always featuring new music. In commissioning new works, his administration was declaring that the repertoire for Juilliard students was far from closed. And while he did not exercise veto power over the choices of the various ensemble leaders, through his tenure he ensured that they regularly programmed contemporary music in general and American contemporary music specifically. At various

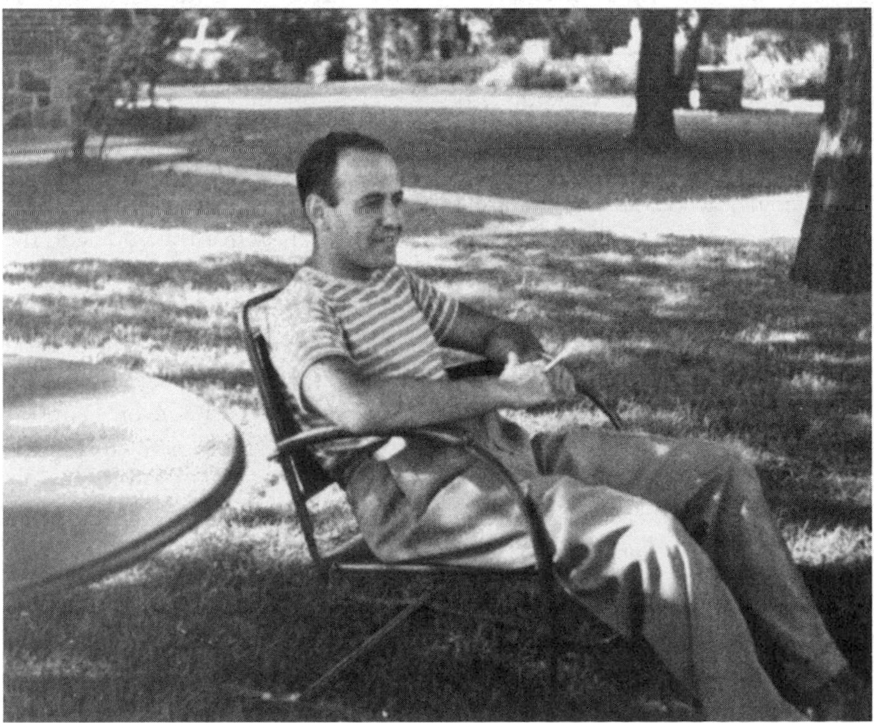

Mark Schubart.

times throughout his administrative career, some uninformed critics would accuse Schuman of using his post to encourage performances of his own music. A memo to Frederik Prausnitz, at the time an assistant dean, provides an example of Schuman's approach to the problem of being a famous composer and the head of an institution at which his works might be showcased.

> Since we have so few opportunities of presenting American composers on our orchestral programs (really only five a season) it seems to me that we should not have two works of the same composer unless there is some special over-riding reason such as the one-man Copland evening. Next year there are two works of William Schuman listed. May I request that one of them be deleted.[22]

While the Juilliard Orchestra remained one of Schuman's principal concerns over the years he was at the helm of the school, he was also keenly involved with two other major student performing ensembles. His prior experience with Robert Shaw and choral music motivated Schuman to carve out a place for both at the school. Though choral conducting instruction had been a part of Juilliard since 1905, it was in the 1946–47 academic year, concurrent with Shaw's employment, that the school officially offered a choral conducting major.[23] Schuman also focused on the Juilliard Opera Theater, the name given to the opera department shortly after his arrival. Schenkman was originally hired in 1945 to serve as musical director for opera, but his departure in 1948 led Schuman to turn the Opera Theater solely over to Frederic Cohen, who directed it until the early 1960s.[24] Schuman generally refrained from dictating to his various conductors and directors the repertoire they might perform, but he did let Shaw know of his soft spot for the Berlioz Requiem, a piece that apparently was never performed at Juilliard during Schuman's tenure.[25]

Without question, the Juilliard String Quartet best represents Schuman's industry and imagination in the realm of ensembles. "When I knew that I was going to the school that summer," Schuman later recalled, "I carried a little black notebook around in which I put down things, and the first thing was 'Fix theory,' and the second thing was 'A resident string quartet.'" (Earlier, Schuman said that "the very first item I had in my memo book when I started at Juilliard was about a resident quartet.")[26] Robert Mann, a young violinist recently released from the Army, was unaware of Schuman's idea, but he longed to found a quartet, this at a time when few professional string quartets were active in the United States and when the most famous of those—the Budapest Quartet—was staffed by eastern Europeans. Schenkman, who knew of both men's ambitions, arranged for them to meet. Schuman knew what he wanted:

> We needed a quartet that would play the standard repertoire with the sense of the excitement and discovery of a new work . . . and would play the new works with a sense of reverence usually reserved for the classics. It should embrace the entire repertoire of music, and I would try to find a leader in whom I had great confidence, someone I could back to the hilt.[27]

Those words—"that it was important to play old music as if it had been just written and new music as if it had been around for a long time"—originated with Mann; Schuman loved the idea.[28] And he gave Mann his confidence, generally excusing the youthful exuberance of the members of the quartet while drawing the line on their clothing and grooming, a recurring bugaboo in Schuman's dealings with his subordinates.[29]

Others have chronicled the founding and the history of the Juilliard String Quartet and the impact it has had on musical life in the United States.[30] Nearly all the stories tell of how Mann came to Schuman with two other members of the putative quartet and how they poached Raphael Hillyer from Koussevitzky and the Boston Symphony Orchestra when Eugene Lehner, a former violist for the Kolisch Quartet who also played in the orchestra, turned them down. Schuman volunteered that "they [presumably Mann, Arthur Winograd, and Robert Koff] heard many, many people play" before deciding on Hillyer. One of those persons was Louise Rood, and her story deserves a bit more play in understanding Schuman's mind-set at Juilliard.

How and why Rood came in contact with Schuman may never be fully discovered, but clearly she either knew of, or found out about, Schuman's notion of a resident quartet. Schuman and Rood seemed to hit it off—she, too, taught at a progressive women's college, Smith—but she was not going to be asked to join the quartet. Why? Ostensibly because she was too old.

> Let me tell you how much I enjoyed our talk of a few weeks ago and how much I regret that, despite my hopes of inviting you to Juilliard, nothing can materialize for next year. You will recall that the basis of your coming was to be membership in the string quartet which we hope to found. While the young men in question are not anti-feminists and would welcome a gifted woman performer, they feel that there should not be too much of an age differential within the group. I must say that in thinking the matter through I rather agree that as players in their early twenties it would be impractical in terms of the future to have any member more than ten years older. This may not be valid reasoning, but in any case it is a point.[31]

Given the later composition of the Juilliard String Quartet, when Mann was often the senior member of the quartet by a generation or more, the excuse of ageism is unfortunate if plausible, given the youth and brashness of Mann, Winograd, and Koff in 1946.

The claim of not being "anti-feminist" is more troubling, though, given Schuman's tenure at Juilliard. While it appears that he did not actively discriminate against women, neither did he actively work to secure them prominent roles in his administration or on the wider faculty. His vision of American composers, for example, seemed to accept as a given that those composers were male. Consider his response to Julia Smith, who had complained at the complete lack of representation of female composers in the announcement of Juilliard's American music festival of 1955–56.

> Please understand that in awarding the commissions for our Festival it was our thought be be [*sic*] as inclusive as possible of all the principal current trends in American musical composition. We made, however, no pretense at comprehensiveness for this would be quite impossible with the sizeable number of composers of merit now writing in this country. I do wish you to know that I realize full well that many gifted composers including some famous ones have not been included in our commissions simply because one Festival could not absorb so many works. Let me assure you that we have prejudice [*sic*! **no** prejudice!] whatsoever against women composers and the fact that none were commissioned should not mislead you.[32]

The carbon copy is uncorrected, so one hopes that Schuman or his (female) secretary caught the second error prior to sending Smith the letter.

Schuman generally felt no need to single persons out because of their race or gender or sexual orientation. Later in life, he protested against such ghettoization. "What bothers me [is] when they compare somebody like Joan Tower and Ellen Zwilich because they're both women—It's just ridiculous."[33] At the same time, he was subject to the prejudices of his time and place. The same man who brought color-blind admissions to Juilliard was the same man who, several years before, confided to Bernstein that Juilliard graduate and African-American conductor Dean Dixon "is a nice chap and I'm glad to see a colored man have a chance. I don't know his work but after all he is no 'Missionary' (remember?)" (The same letter finds Schuman referring to Dmitri Mitropoulos as "the Greek.")[34] He deplored discrimination while, at times, unconsciously expressing his own biases, one of which was against "missionaries" advancing their grievances. There is no evidence that Rood aired any disagreement to Schuman. But she was all of 35 years old. Lehner, who took on the role of coach to the Juilliard String Quartet, was 40. Schuman's attitude toward women and their role in the professions seems to enter into this exchange. By the early 1950s the Dance Division had more than its share of talented and powerful women, and Schuman freed them to do remarkable things (see chap. 14). By then Frankie had adjusted to the life of a full-time suburban, stay-at-home wife and mother, having been asked by her husband to quit her job. So Rood's age probably did have something to do with her not being offered the violist slot for the Juilliard String Quartet. So, too, did the age in which she sought the position.

If the Juilliard String Quartet broke no new ground when it came to the gender and race of its members, it certainly reshaped the landscape of chamber music in the United States. Schuman said that "when I do permit myself the luxury of reminiscing—which I rarely do because it's not my nature—I think of the Juilliard with the greatest, greatest satisfaction."[35] And had he made no other substantive change at Juilliard in his tenure there, the founding of the Juilliard String Quartet would earn Schuman a place in music history.

"Fixing theory" was also noted in Schuman's little black book, and he set to fix this with a vengeance. He and Norman Lloyd retreated to Atlantic City in the fall of 1946, where they spent four 12-hour days laying the groundwork for the changes Schuman wanted. Vincent Persichetti, not yet a member of the Juilliard faculty, came north from Philadelphia that fall to consult with Schuman and Lloyd. And in December, Schuman presented his proposed curriculum on the literature and materials of music to the board of directors for their approval.

Eighteen months later, Schuman spelled out the curriculum changes in the pages of the *Musical Quarterly*. To Schuman,

> conventional theory education shows a consistent lack of concern with the entire work of art, and it is largely because of this that it has failed to develop intelligent listening. . . . In order to give musicians the best equipment to meet the demands of this expansion, we must produce more performers who have a composer's knowledge of music. . . . If what we are doing seems too "progressive" to some educators, I think the reason is not so much that it is daring but that education in the theory of music has for a long time been in need of thorough rejuvenation.[36]

Schuman was always generous in sharing the spotlight with his colleagues, taking care to name them in the article and the subsequent book—*The Juilliard Report on Teaching the Literature and Materials of Music* (W.W. Norton, 1953)—that laid out the philosophy of the new theory curriculum. His aim in doing so was to show that this was not one man's idea imposed upon a recalcitrant institution but that it came organically through the amassing of a talented and caring faculty who believed in a holistic approach to music and distrusted teaching music theory in an atomized, rote, mechanical fashion. The approach also allowed for great variety among teachers who would respond to the wide range of interests among students. "This lack of uniformity has caused some confusion in minds accustomed to the usual rigidity of courses in music theory, and students who have been trained through such courses expect and even demand the authority of a 'system' that supplies undisputable answers." The confused minds, in this case, belonged not to students alone; teachers in other institutions longed for a syllabus that Schuman and his colleagues must have developed for this revolutionary program, only to be told that no such syllabus existed or could exist.[37]

What was beyond confusion, as he made plain in his introduction to the 1953 book, is that Schuman wanted to replicate at Juilliard what he had experienced at Sarah Lawrence. In addition, the very title of the theory program he created—The Literature and Materials of Music, which quickly became abbreviated to "L&M"—was a repudiation of his education at Teachers College, where concepts were presented unattached to the real-life situations to which they supposedly applied. Inasmuch as it was possible within the structures and strictures of an academic institution, Schuman sought to re-create the best parts of his own educational experience: the individualism of his lessons with Persin, Haubiel, and Harris; the focus on examining compositions to unravel the compositional problems that Schuman had faced; the open-ended nature of his

Sarah Lawrence classes coupled with the regular one-on-one meetings with his donnees there; the embrace of rigor and the rejection of rigidity. L&M was designed for the young William Schuman and those students who resembled him.

Because of its amorphous nature, it would be almost impossible to judge definitely whether L&M was mostly successful or not. Without question, Schuman succeeded in altering the conversation about music education through the introduction of L&M at Juilliard. Schuman's reform addressed an imbalance he saw in music education in his day. Schuman's office sent out complimentary copies to no fewer than 50 schools and countless other individuals involved in the music world.[38] Through that dissemination, the teaching of people trained in the L&M system, and the speeches that the publication of Schuman's article and book afforded him, the gospel of L&M spread far and wide.[39] At this writing, Juilliard continues to offer courses under the rubric "LMM," although their disposition looks more like the type of theory curriculum against which Schuman inveighed ("Counterpoint and Harmony," "Form and Analysis," etc.). With a focus on composing and compositions, though, the original curriculum continues to echo today at Juilliard and in other schools across the nation and the world. L&M was meant to be a shot heard round the world. And Schuman did everything in his power to make sure that it was.

The fact that the 1948 article appeared in the *Musical Quarterly* points to another realm in which Schuman was changing the status quo. Though he relinquished his position as director of publications at G. Schirmer upon his appointment to the Juilliard presidency, he did continue to work for Schirmer as a special consultant in the Publications Department. His responsibilities included oversight of Schirmer's house journal, the *Musical Quarterly*, and in his capacity as consultant, Schuman hired Columbia musicology professor Paul Henry Lang to serve as its editor. Schuman and Lang were witnesses to a cataclysm in high-end music journalism and scholarship. The League of Composers' journal, *Modern Music*, went dark in 1946, and although Schuman tried to get Gustave Schirmer to take over that journal, complications prevented a successful merger. Two years later, the American Musicological Society produced the first issue of its journal, and Lang, as a member and officer of the society, was party to that development. The shifts in publication led Schuman to enjoin Lang to orient the *Musical Quarterly* to cover contemporary music events, resulting in the creation of the feature "Current Chronicle"—an idea Schuman imported from the defunct *Modern Music*[40]—and the publication of articles such as Schuman's on the Juilliard curriculum. Schuman also wanted to change the tone of the quarterly. While he was willing to keep the "high level of scholarship" that had marked the journal for years, Schuman demanded that "the base of the magazine be broadened; that the style of writing be somewhat less deadly and that the subject matter not eschew important issues of our times in music, however controversial these may be."[41] His role as special consultant was terminated before he could complete his makeover, but he tried again, this time at his own institution. The *Juilliard Review* began publication in the fall of 1954. It was a journal devoted, according to Richard Franko Goldman's inaugural editorial, "to a serious view of music in our day, as we find it, and in terms of the idea that music is a high art, neither trade, nor entertainment nor commodity."[42]

Changing the complexion of a journal proved harder for Schuman than changing the curriculum of a conservatory, and neither the *Musical Quarterly* nor the *Juilliard Review* measured up to what he had envisioned. The *Review* in particular struggled to find the right tone. It never found a loyal audience. And it folded in 1962, the year after Schuman left Juilliard. He had particularly harsh words when reminiscing over the *Review*.

> I always thought that was sort of a flop. It seemed to me to be a rather lugubrious magazine and excessively INTELLECTUAL in capital letters. . . . It was a magazine that couldn't be understood by the Juilliard faculty, which could be as much a comment about the faculty as about the magazine, but it really didn't carry out my hope for it, so I was always rather disappointed in it.[43]

Far more successful was yet another change that Schuman instigated at that time. In March 1946, Walter W. Naumburg—banker, amateur cellist, and benefactor to young musical artists—invited Schuman to have lunch with him. It was Naumburg, according to Claire Reis, who in 1939 asked whether it was wise to commission a work from the relatively unknown composer.[44] Now Naumburg invited the young Juilliard president to join the board of the Walter W. Naumburg Music Foundation. Naumburg was 78 years old at the time, and he saw in Schuman a possible guardian of his legacy. Naumburg, looking to the future, saw the need to bring some younger men onto the foundation's board. Between the end of 1950 and the end of 1953, five members of the nine-member board would die, including Naumburg's wife, Ernest Hutcheson, and Daniel Gregory Mason, the Columbia composer who had praised Schuman's *Canonic Choruses* and recoiled at the First Symphony. Naumburg wanted Schuman on the board, and he also asked if he knew anyone (young, of course) for another place on the board. Schuman recommended two people to Naumburg: Quincy Porter (born 1897), a composer who was heading to Yale that year; and Schubart, Schuman's deputy at Juilliard. Hutcheson suggested Copland (born 1900), and Naumburg acted on Hutcheson's suggestion. At the fall 1946 meeting, Schuman and Copland represented the new guard for the foundation.[45] Naumburg would later reflect upon the impact of inviting them onto the board. "The Foundation has undoubtedly done good work since its inception," he said in a letter to Schuman, "but it was because we felt that it should advance into new fields of endeavor, that we were so anxious to obtain your membership on the Board, as well as Mr. Copland's."[46]

Schuman and Copland began to explore those new fields at their very first meeting. The foundation had made it possible for young artists to have a Town Hall debut recital that would be reviewed by the local press. Schuman wanted to make sure that the artists demonstrated "knowledge of the general literature of music, past and present." Copland was more specific: all artists should include a contemporary American work on their recital programs. His motion was passed unanimously. Then Schuman suggested the creation of an award for composers in addition to those already offered to singers and instrumentalists. Naumburg appointed Schuman chair of a subcommittee to explore the possibility; Schuman's fellow committee members were Copland and Mason.[47] It would take Schuman more than a year to craft a proposal to the board, his delay attributable to a rash of changes at Juilliard, Mason's illness, and Copland's travels, but in April 1948 he presented his idea to Naumburg: the creation of the Naumburg American Composers' Recording Prize, with $500 allocated to a panel of judges who would select "a major work by an American Composer deemed most worthy of recording" and an additional $2,000 allocated to defray the costs of recording.[48] After unsatisfactory discussions with the executives at RCA Victor, Schuman turned to Columbia Record Co., whose people drew up a contract for Schuman to take back to Naumburg for his lawyer to review. Before a single recording had been issued, Mason offered Schuman his verdict on the award: "It is good that we can now go ahead with your interesting innovation, the best step that has yet been taken in the recording of American music."[49] Between 1949 and 1983, the music of 36 composers was recorded, and some of these recordings remain the only commercially released recordings of the pieces selected by the judges.[50] Schuman himself was a beneficiary of the award when the judges recommended that his Third Symphony be recorded. In typical fashion, Schuman wished to indemnify himself against all accusations, real or imagined, that Naumburg, the foundation board, or the judges were playing favorites by selecting his work.[51] Later, Schuman tried to talk Naumburg out of his idea of an all-Schuman album consisting of the Third and Sixth Symphonies.

> Inasmuch as the market for contemporary symphonies is limited, are we not therefore limiting it all the more in consideration of the fact that most of the buyers will undoubtedly be people who are sufficiently interested in my music to have already purchased the Third and would hesitate at being obliged to buy the additional copy of the Third in order to have the Sixth. Naturally, you know best and I will accept you verdict. incidentally, do you have anything planned for the other side of Piston's Symphony [the Fourth]? I greatly admire the work and Piston and feel that my own work would be in cosy surroundings.[52]

Taken together, the impetus to distribute the wealth of recording opportunities to as many composers as possible; to position contemporary music more centrally in the lives of the men and women who wrote and read about music;

to acknowledge the team effort behind L&M; to launch a chamber ensemble whose accomplishments, in many ways, would outstrip his own; to ensure that the major performing groups at Juilliard would feature American music; and to surround himself with younger deputies and older counselors who could help him realize all of these ideas: together these all point to a man who delegated, rather than aggregated, power. He had moments, such as his decision in the late 1950s to cancel the school's membership in the National Association of Schools of Music, when the power available to him got the better of him. But the tally of accomplishments from 1945 to 1950 alone and their reverberations for decades mark Schuman as something more than a very talented and accomplished composer.

He knew this as well as anyone.

> I spent *months* studying pension plans. Now, if you mentioned this to one of my friends in music, they wouldn't know what you were talking about. I find it just as intriguing as fugue writing, you know.... I had to equip myself with enough knowledge for my board. I went to large universities and large banks and others to find out what they have used, where and why, and it was extremely interesting.[53]

One sees in this interest in the nuts and bolts of business both Schuman's upbringing and, ironically, the business school education at New York University that he would now start to mythologize as insignificant and misdirected. But his acumen in business, his ability to isolate a problem and ferret out its solution, and his knack for juggling many issues at once and focusing, laserlike, on the issue before him at any given time made him into the highly successful individual, administrator, and educator that he became. His success as a composer also draws from this well, though his facility, both innate and learned, occasionally shows through his music when it turns facile (a complaint which was the nub of Engel's and Berger's comments about *A Free Song* and which will recur over and over again for many of his other works). Self-criticism was not a posture Schuman adopted. He didn't have time for reflection, so busy was he creating universes ex nihilo.

For the most part, his colleagues applauded his fecundity, methods, and manner. His string of successes led G. Schirmer not only to initiate a book on his career and one on Barber's (he and Barber, Schuman would say, were the firm's "white-haired boys," i.e., favored sons) but to squelch the first draft of his biography and abandon the author, Vincent Persichetti, in favor of someone who would be more deferential to Schuman the man and the myth.[54] At their worst, the man and the myth were nauseating. Schuman would say that the board vote for his coming was unanimous. Hutcheson remembered it differently.

> They proceeded to agree on William Schuman for President, and John [Erskine] and [John] Perry are to present his name to the Foundation, whose consent of course is necessary. I made objections, but of course to no effect at all. John and Warburg had

> absolutely made up their mind; in this matter they are in complete agreement, and the others just tag along—Perry and Benkard, I think with some secret misgivings, McCollester feeling (very justly!) that the possibilities had not been exhausted, and Edward Johnson just going with the majority. In the end I refrained from voting.... Things are certainly going Jimmy Warburg's way. As for John, I can't understand him at all. In all this business he has shown a terrible *Leichtsinnigkeit* [foolishness]. His reasons for backing Schumann [*sic*] and his airy dismissal of other suggestions are, it seems to me, positively flimsy.[55]

Schuman's early years at Juilliard were especially rocky. His occasional fits of anger were common enough that one journalist at the time called him "the aesthete with a social temper that now seems to be receding."[56] The stresses of Juilliard reversed the flow, as people there recalled that he would fly into a rage when anything displeased him. Hutcheson noted a faculty meeting in the fall of 1948 at which, in his opinion, Schuman's "position as president is at stake, and he is now sincerely anxious to cooperate with the faculty. We would all like to help him, and would much rather see him make good than contemplate the risks of a new president."[57] Hutcheson never fully warmed to Schuman, and those who confided in Hutcheson tended to reinforce his negative opinions.

At his best, though, Schuman was extraordinary. Four years after the decision to bring Schuman to Juilliard, Erskine reflected on the decision, no doubt with an eye to the Hutchesonians who would read his memoir.

> If we had no other reason for thinking highly of our young President, we should honor him in the very height of his inexperience for guiding the School safely through the difficult years immediately after the last war, when our halls were crowded with G.I.'s, when many of the faculty were temporarily scattered, and when the temper of the world was hardly favorable to the contemplation and study of an art. We have come through safely, and if in many respects we have now to begin again I am glad the School is so young and that it wears so few scars of time as it starts on its second chapter.[58]

The changes Schuman brought to the Juilliard School were not all successful, and even the successful ones were not always received well initially. Those that succeeded were significant. But he rung—and wrung—the changes at the School. Robert Mann sized up Schuman's tenure thus: "William Schuman, you might say, is the man who shaped the vision that became the Juilliard of today."[59]

And just as the school was starting on its second chapter, so Schuman also was entering a new chapter in his life as a composer.

FOURTEEN

DANCING IN THE DARK

Schuman kept up a lively correspondence with Walter Piston (1894–1976), who taught at Harvard for 34 years. Their first exchange occurred before Schuman had completed his bachelor's degree and reads as though Schuman was hoping to glean some information for a class assignment about Piston's use of "modal effects" in his music. Piston writes, "The subject is a big one and you might be interested to know that John Vincent, from Nashville, Tenn., is now working at Harvard toward a Ph.D. on aspects of the ecclesiastical modes as used by modern composers. He is developing a very interesting theory."[1] Schuman would similarly strike up a correspondence with Vincent (whose theory would be published in 1951 under the title *The Diatonic Modes in Modern Music*), and it was especially active during Schuman's Lincoln Center years, as Vincent (1902–77) tried several times to lure Schuman to join the faculty at UCLA and waxed ecstatic about the glories of fishing for albacore. Piston's correspondence with Schuman was sometimes even more workaday than the Vincent-Schuman exchanges, as he and Schuman discussed commissions that Schuman had swung Piston's way: one for the Sarah Lawrence College Chorus that ended in futility, another for the American Festival at Juilliard that resulted in Piston's Fifth Symphony. But just as often, the composers wrote in glowing admiration for each other's work, with Piston praising *A Free Song* and the Sixth Symphony ("I told Ormandy that nothing could please me more than to be paired [on a recording] with your no. 6, as he said he planned"), and Schuman requesting the score of the Fourth Symphony to read and, after having read it, to recommend the work to Jean Morel and the Juilliard Orchestra.[2] It was on Schuman's watch as chairman of the board of the MacDowell Colony, a retreat in New Hampshire for serious artists, that Piston received the colony's Edward MacDowell Medal in 1974. Theirs was a warm and collegial relationship.

Piston's handwritten letter of October 29, 1946, provides a brief example of their camaraderie, and although there is no extant response, one can imagine that Schuman either sent a private letter in response or thanked Piston in person for his kind remarks. "I listened to the broadcast of 'Undertow' and thought it strong, original, and expressive. Glad you are not being overpowered by administrative duties." Piston must have been unaware that *Undertow* had been written before Schuman had begun in earnest at either G. Schirmer or Juilliard, for the press of duties would stanch the flow of compositions from Schuman's pen. Still, it is remarkable that three of the major works Schuman composed between 1944 and 1949 were for dancers and that two of these were on topics as dark as Erebus.

Schuman, of course, was familiar with aspects of the dance world. His youthful band gave him practical experience with the social dance scene, and during his teens and early twenties he had seen such modern dance progenitors as Ruth St. Denis, the duo of Harald Kreutzberg and Yvonne Georgi, Doris Humphrey, and Martha Graham.[3] His 1935 *Choreographic Poem for Seven Instruments* was one of several works that Schuman had written for the dance in his earliest years. "I had created scores for minor dancers around town. Just young dancers, I don't even remember their names, who'd ask me to do things. It was a wonderful experience for me. They were all juvenile pieces that I've since withdrawn."[4] He discovered ballet later and was "shocked" by what he called "the dissonance of the curve, compared to the consonance of the angle," so accustomed had he become to the fluidity of modern dance.[5] It was that unfamiliarity with ballet, according to Schuman, that landed him his first commission for a dance work: a ballet by the great British choreographer Antony Tudor.

> I got a telegram from Tudor . . . asking if I would meet with him. He studies music through recordings. I guess I didn't have many recordings, but he went to hear a lot and he knew whatever there was, and he asked me whether it was true that I had rarely or never been to the ballet. I said: "Not very much. I was brought up more in modern dance." And he wanted me to do a ballet. . . . He described a lot about the ballet, and it intrigued me very much.[6]

Two years before he approached Schuman, Tudor had one of his most successful premieres with *Pillar of Fire*, performed by the American Ballet Theatre, his newfound home during the war years. His lover and principal male dancer, Hugh Laing, had initially tried to discourage Tudor from using the music that he eventually chose for that ballet. "He played the music for me in London and I told him he was a damn fool to try and use it," Laing said later.[7] Laing ultimately relented. One of Tudor's biographers writes:

> Long before [Tudor] started rehearsing or even selecting his cast he and Hugh would invite any of the likely prospects to their large room on Fifty-eighth Street and play the recording of [Arnold Schoenberg's] *Verklärte Nacht*. It was compelling music, music of overripe passions, splintering conflict and extraordinary tenderness. By the time he began putting the ballet together it had become familiar to all.[8]

One critic wrote of *Pillar of Fire*, which received 30 curtain calls at its premiere in April 1942, "Here is no glib talent but something very like a new force in the evolution of dance."[9] In many ways, the rapid ascendancy of Tudor in dance circles parallels Schuman's career in music, which may explain in part Tudor's decision to be the first to engage Schuman to compose a score for the ballet. Tudor's choice of early Schoenberg, as well as pieces by Prokofiev, Constant Lambert, Ravel, Holst, Bloch, Weill, and Delius, also shows a decidedly conservative streak when it came to twentieth-century music. (When Tudor used Copland's *Music for the Theatre* for the 1941 *Time Table*, one dance critic noted, "it is not altogether his kind of music.")[10] Tudor discovered much of the music he chose to set through the phonograph. Much of that music, understandably, was not overtly avant-garde, which would further explain Tudor's interest in Schuman. But nothing in Schuman's published catalog up to Tudor's solicitation gives any overt indication of the kinds of sexual tension that would mark his dances from the 1940s. First with Tudor, and then with Martha Graham, Schuman began to enter a Freudian universe.

Schuman understood the psychosexual complexities of his submersion into the dance world. At times, he joked about it.

> JOHN GRUEN (interviewer): How did you find—plumb your mind some more about working with Tudor . . . Anything that might in some way deepen our knowledge of this man as an artist and even as a person . . . Did you have personal contact with him in some way?
> SCHUMAN: When you say "personal contact with Tudor," that could be misunderstood.
> GRUEN: No, you know what I mean.
> SCHUMAN: I've had a very cordial relationship.[11]

Any desire to attribute homosexual panic to Schuman's remarks is quickly undercut by the long list of his gay collaborators, colleagues, and protégés. His decision to found the Dance Division at Juilliard may have concerned some who feared an increase of the number of gay male students at Juilliard; Schuman's invitation to Tudor to become one of the division's founding teachers would not have allayed that fear. Schuman did not seem to care. His views about homosexuality are mostly confined to interviews but occasionally peek out from his letters, such as when he asked Barber to "give my greetings to Gian Carlo, and I hope that we all may soon meet," using language that mirrors similar wishes to his heterosexual correspondents and that he would continue to use to the end of his life in writing to Ned Rorem and John Corigliano.[12] Schuman was comfortable with the exploration and expression of nontraditional forms of sexuality, perhaps more so than were others in his orbit. Schuman recalled Tudor's explanation for *Undertow* was "that it stemmed from an idea of [John] Van Druten . . . about a homosexual murderer and his redemption."[13] Others, including Tudor's biographer, see the end of the ballet as enshrining gay ostracism and self-loathing, much of which stemmed from Tudor's own view of himself:

> [In *Undertow*, Tudor] took himself as well as Hugh to account, demons and all . . . a ballet that seemed like a case study of all that he knew and came to believe.
>
> By those terms, it depicted homosexuality, at least its superficial genesis, as the consequence of child molestation—a sordid encounter between an old man and a boy. It traced the life from a painful childbirth, to a rejecting mother, to distrust of all people, to a climactic love/murder redolent with pathological eroticism. Included in this panoramic tableau were the rough street characters who compelled and disgusted Tudor as a boy; a female Elmer Gantry with a mania for seducing her congregants; a nymphomaniac who incites gang rape. Nothing quite like this had ever taken place on a ballet stage before.[14]

Artistic concerns, the exposure that would come from aligning himself with Tudor's rising stardom, and financial considerations no doubt contributed to Schuman's decision to write the score. But whatever view of the subject matter one takes, it remains compelling that Schuman, married with a newborn son at home and a job at a highly regarded school for young women, would agree to collaborate on this ballet choreographed by a gay Englishman and featuring that man's lover as the central transgressive character. Schuman's inclinations toward patriotism and propaganda did not preclude his embrace of the shadow side of human life.

The contract for *Undertow* stipulated that Schuman would "compose and orchestrate the music for a ballet (not yet titled) by Antony Tudor, to run from 15 to 35 minutes, working in collaboration with Mr. Tudor . . . [and] to make complete and final delivery [of the piano score] by January 1, 1945."[15] The "Choreographic Episodes for Orchestra" that Schuman extracted from the ballet score lasts between 25 and 30 minutes, a fact that surprised Schuman, since he recalled that "the entire ballet ran about 42 and it seemed to me that I cut out something like half."[16] *Undertow* was Schuman's longest and most involved score to date, and its emergence has been wonderfully preserved in long letters that Tudor sent to Schuman as they shaped the work together. Tudor also included diagrams of how he envisioned the music, and while some of Tudor's descriptions are elliptical, it is an overstatement to say that Schuman knew nothing of the story Tudor was attempting to tell in his ballet.[17] In addition to his prose attempts, Tudor telephoned Schuman, but he longed for time in person to explain his vision for the ballet, time that was difficult to come by given that the Ballet Theatre was on tour. Schuman had been sending Tudor music as it was composed, and Tudor complained that the music was overly sectional and wasn't developing in a wavelike fashion. Schuman wrote back in protest. "Your letter has been quite a shock to me. In fact my only comfort is that you felt free to write frankly. To begin with I think that your fears will vanish when you see the score as a whole. Often what appears arbitrary or sectional viewed in the light of a movement or portion of a work takes on entirely different meanings in proportion to the whole."[18] Tudor himself later said that he was "shocked" by Schuman's music, "because it was quite different from what I had expected. Still, everything functioned. The music obeyed the atmospheric demands" that Tudor requested from Schuman.[19] Tudor's proclivity to create based on recordings, coupled with the recent success of his use of Schoenberg's highly sectional *Verklärte Nacht*—in which the sections are brilliantly elided—seemed to make Tudor nervous as he received Schuman's score literally in sections.

Undertow was the only score Tudor ever commissioned, and the Tudor-Schuman letters provide a window into how stressful the creative process was for both men. The last of Tudor's letters to Schuman prior to the premiere of *Undertow* shows the disjunctures that characterized the approaches each took to the work. Tudor chided Schuman for (in Tudor's mind) abandoning the original idea that "the work should be approached not as stage music, but as though you were writing a symphony." Yet at the same time, Tudor instructed Schuman to write in rather nonsymphonic ways.

> Now that you are well away onto the last movement of the ballet, I am bringing you some of the worries that I have been saving up. Just in case of any possible divergence in our points of view regarding the last scene of the ballet, I will recapitulate our decisions as I remember them. It was to last about six or seven minutes, and we invented for ourselves its subtitle "essay in fear". It was to open with a crash of chords to synchronise with the lighting up of the space; then it was to progress through all the terrors of a hunted and haunted individual; quiet moments when he hears the beating of his own heart, spasms when he feels he is about to be caught, the fearsome times when he knows himself a total outcast, leprous and dirty; and so on. Near the end of the movement something akin to the opening movement of the ballet was to creep in while the main subject matter is still in process of development; and then right at the end it was to dissolve into our space feeling again. I have one additional thought on this. I would like to end the whole ballet with a strong and unmistakeable [*sic*] AMEN; or a series of them spreading out into eternity.[20]

If Schuman managed to appease Tudor in this final tableau, it would be because Schuman had followed Tudor's directives prior to the receipt of this February 21, 1945, letter, for the orchestral score—on manuscript paper—bears the completion date of February 22, 1945.

Yet another example of the two creators working at cross-purposes comes from the names that Tudor gave the characters. Critic John Martin was confused.

> Mr. Tudor has never been so difficult, indeed, and it will take half a dozen visits and the closest concentration to be sure exactly what he is driving at. . . . Except for the central figure of the Transgressor . . . all the characters bear names out of Greek (and in one or two instances, Roman) religious lore. They assume the functions of symbols, having to do with various aspects of sex, in the mind of the Transgressor where apparently the entire action takes place.[21]

Tudor would later say that this was an evasion on his part: "the classical prototypes rather than calling spades spades—whores whores—nymphomaniacs nymphomaniacs—dirty little bastards etc., etc."[22] But at the time, Schuman was less confused than indignant, writing to the conductor Alexander Smallens, who attended the ballet two days after its premiere: "I am in full agreement with you about the names Tudor gave his characters, but please believe that this was a complete surprise to me since he got the idea and inserted them into the program less than twenty-four hours before we opened."[23] (The names include Volupia, Polyhymnia, Ate, and Medusa.) Schuman would also later claim that he was unaware that the opening sequence would portray the birth of the Transgressor. (In one of his letters to Schuman, Tudor described the opening scene as requiring "a feeling that is spatial, and almost cerebral, but holding in it all the unsatisfied romantic desires, that start off our tale of destruction," but he did not mention anything approximating childbirth.)[24] Most of the early critics were confounded by Tudor's conception, especially its graphic depiction of the Transgressor committing murder as part of the sex act. A snuff ballet with homosexual overtones was certainly novel in 1945. Both audience and critics were bewildered.[25]

As for the music, all Martin would say was that it "is full and dramatic and requires considerably more listening to than a first performance allows." The reviewer of the Los Angeles premiere of the concert suite had no such reservations.

> It was pictorial, written for decadent ballet which did not emerge from its natural locale, the sophisticated New York night life where it was born. The young people in the large audience were prepared to applaud anything by this young American and they gave it an ovation. . . . The orchestra makes ugly sounds, there is little rhythmic variety, the long, low notes of the first episodes are as haunting as a foghorn and about as interesting. This is water-front music with occasional bright glimpses of Salvation Nell singing a humble song, hymnlike and accompanied by the big bass drum. It is supposed to evolve around a murder, psychological and premeditated. The listeners needed music therapy at its conclusion.[26]

The reviewer accurately reported the audience's response on the night of the premiere. Virginia Wallenstein, wife of the conductor of the Los Angeles Philharmonic, wrote to Schuman a week after the performances. "'Undertow' had a fine success out here—shrieks and yells Thursday night, gentle, ladylike applause Friday, and warm approbation in Beverly Hills."[27]

The following year, Artur Rodzinski opened the New York Philharmonic season with *Undertow*. Virgil Thomson, up to then a reluctant supporter of Schuman's music, overflowed with praise for the orchestral version and for the Tudor ballet, which he obliquely mentioned in his review in the *New York Herald Tribune*. Perhaps Thomson, another prominent gay artist on the New York scene, sought not only to congratulate Schuman for his music but also to thank him for his courage.

> The concert suite derived from Schuman's ballet, "Undertow," is no less powerful a musical work than its theater version. In either form it is the most expressive piece I know by this composer. His overtures and symphonies have always seemed to me talented but tame, striking for their facility but conformist in substance. This work is more straightforward, more acute. It has, in fact, an atmosphere. It is intense, psychologically upsetting, full of pain; and its violence is convincing. The beginning and the finale are static, and that is no doubt the fault of a libretto that is rather meaningless at the two ends. But the middle parts, which represents [*sic*] all the horrid things that can happen in a big city to a lonely and rather horrid young man, a future sex-murderer, are deeply absorbing. It is music of powerful and specific expressivity. What it means and what it sounds like are original, unique, not easily forgotten. Psycho-sexual disturbances have not previously been depicted in music in just this way.[28]

The story of *Undertow* is rife with explosiveness, and the music responds in kind throughout. At the same time, the music is equally notable for its soaring violin lines, so one understands why Schuman felt compelled to ask impresario Sol Hurok to augment the orchestra's string section for the performances and why, after Hurok refused to do so, Schuman engaged extra players from the NBC Orchestra and paid them out of his own pocket to bolster the sound.[29] Structurally, *Undertow* is composed of several nested arches of musical material, with the prologue and epilogue expositions of similar musical material, with the regular development and recapitulation of the "Salvation Army" material (whose original appearance Schuman recommended be played on a cornet "as I think the humor and over-all effect would be immeasurably enhanced")[30] and with regular reappearances of the music that accompanies the various violent episodes in the work (the opening birth, the gang rape, the murder). In comparison to *Verklärte Nacht*, *Undertow* shows its seams much more clearly; Tudor deserves credit for spotting the episodic nature of Schuman's score even before Schuman himself did. And in fact, cyclical and developmental procedures exemplify the music Schuman wrote after *Undertow*, most clearly in the Sixth Symphony of 1948 but also in nearly all of his subsequent larger works for orchestra. The reliance on old forms, be they passacaglia and fugue or sonata and rondo, was broken in *Undertow*. The long-breathed violin lines, present in the earlier works, also reached new heights here, and Schuman would develop this feature even more in the Violin Concerto he began writing in 1946. The new wine of *Undertow* required and received new wineskins. Not only Thomson sensed this, but so did another critic who was much closer to Schuman: his wife, Frankie. "For me *Undertow* is a seminal work, and I hear some of it in almost everything Bill wrote after that."[31] Of the many unjustly neglected works of this composer, *Undertow* may well stand as the score most in need of rediscovery.

From his début outing with a rising star in the ballet world, Schuman turned to an established figure in modern dance for his next terpsichorean effort. Or, rather, she turned to him.

> I can tell you when I first met [Martha Graham] personally, because it's something I will never forget. She was brought back to meet me after a performance of one of my symphonies with the Boston Symphony Orchestra under Koussevitzky: And Katharine Cornell brought her to me. Katharine Cornell came up to me and introduced herself. She didn't have to; I recognized her immediately, of course, and said, that Martha Graham wanted to meet with me. And Martha looked into my eyes, and if you've ever been looked by Martha's eyes, you are forever changed. They're like no other eyes in the world. [Laughter] They change you. She said, "Mr. Schuman, your music moves me." I wanted to scream, "Ma," and run. [Laughter] And I knew that whatever that woman ever asked me to do, I would do. I just knew. And I said that it was a great honor to meet her, and of course, it would be my privilege to compose for her.

Schuman continued the story by saying, "She asked me where I would be for the next month and I told her I would be at Martha's Vineyard, and I jotted down my address on a piece of paper, and she sent me a letter, which I'm sure I have, a long letter saying that she had two ideas for a work."[32] Graham's letter is dated August 12, 1946, which suggests that Schuman may have conflated his meeting of Graham with another occasion at which Koussevitzky performed one of his works, since he conducted no Schuman works of any kind in either Boston or New York between December 1944 (*Prayer in Time of War*) and October 1947 (Symphony no. 3). (He did conduct the *American Festival Overture* at Tanglewood on August 10, 1946, two days before Graham's letter, but it is doubtful Graham and Cornell attended this concert, as the letter begins with the words: "At long last this is ready to send.") Schuman also forgot that Harold Spivacke had been in touch with him prior to Graham's letter; Spivacke was head of the Music Division at the Library of Congress and overseer of the Elizabeth Sprague Coolidge Foundation. "I am writing you about the commission to write dance music for Martha Graham which we discussed by telephone last month. Did you have an opportunity to discuss this with her? At any rate I am naturally eager to know your decision and will be very grateful if you will write me at your earliest convenience."[33]

Schuman was correct, though, in remembering that Graham sent him two ideas: one for the Scottish ballad *Tam Lin*, which Graham had worked out in a 16-page script for which she envisioned the folk singer Susan Reed; and a three-page treatment simply called "Untitled: Jocasta's Dance." Graham's letter also suggests that she and Schuman discussed some practical ideas about the work, specifically about the orchestral forces that would be involved. "You spoke of an oboe and cello carrying the main line as I remember and of using the other instruments as under and around these two. I think that might well suit either of these ideas." Graham also gave voice to words that corroborate the intensity of their initial meeting, if not its timing. "I hope with all my heart that you can write something as I have wanted to work with you for such a long time. I shall await your reply with anxiety."[34] Schuman did reply with alacrity, and although his letter is lost, Graham's relief upon receiving his missive is palpable.

> I have been in the jitters until your letter came because I was afraid you would not like either of the ideas. I am glad you did choose the Jocasta's dance. I had started to work on the Tam Lin so that it was much more detailed and I finished it sooner. But the one I would like best to dance is the Jocasta. I think because I can hear your power and rich dark tragic sense musically. Of course it is all in my imagination. But I think I can feel on my skin what you will write.[35]

Graham also repeated the fact that the Library of Congress was commissioning the work, which, given the spaces in which the dance would be performed, required orchestration for a small ensemble. By late October, Graham had fleshed out her sketch on Jocasta and had sent it sans title to Schuman.

The dance tells the story of Jocasta at the moment she realizes that the prophecy has come true that her son would murder his father and marry his mother. In her scenario, Graham located the action of the dance within Jocasta's heart "when, behind the door of her room, she faces her death." The dance recalls Jocasta's seduction by her son Oedipus and the blind seer Tiresias's revelation of the crime the couple has committed. As with many Graham dances of the era, there is also a chorus of women who augment and complement the story, which ends with Oedipus tearing out his own eyes and Jocasta taking her own life.[36] Graham couldn't decide on a title; she suggested several to Schuman in the letter that accompanied the scenario, none of which was the title she decided upon at the end.[37] In an echo of *Appalachian Spring*, which Copland called "Ballet for Martha" and let her name be the title, so the vellum title page identifies this dance as "Work for Martha Graham," with the copyist's version bearing the title *Night Journey*.

The paucity of letters between Graham and Schuman about the dance is remarkable, and it suggests that the two conferred in person and over the telephone as the work developed. By the middle of January, Schuman apologized for his slow pace of composing, ascribable in no small part to the turmoil at Juilliard. "The outline you gave me, I find most sympathetic and what music I have already composed will, I am confident, please you. If you wish, toward the middle of February it will be possible to deliver eight or ten minutes of the score. The introduction and first chorus dance are already complete and the first solo is in process."[38] The entire ballet lasts approximately 25 minutes and premiered in early May, so Schuman had much work to do in the winter and spring of 1947. (There is no completion date on the vellum; the copyist's score has the indication "April 1947" at its end, and the Schirmer biography lists April 9, 1947, as the date of completion.[39] A set of undated sheaths titled "The Death of Jocasta" may be the pages Schuman sent to Graham, as they contain the opening of the dance.)

Challenges greeted the premiere, which took place in Cambridge as the final event of a three-day symposium on music criticism at Harvard University. One of these challenges was that the conductor and his musicians were at odds, Schuman would say later.

> I remember the first performance because they were players from the Boston Symphony. Louis Horst . . . was the conductor. And he was an old vaudevillian, and he treated those Boston Symphony men as though they were in the vaudeville pit; number one. And number two, as though they should have been able to sight-read the score. So, he was furious that they weren't right there. . . . And so there were great troubles between Horst and the musicians. But I happened to know them all because they were in the Boston Symphony, so they weren't going to let me down.[40]

The dancers were also showing signs of stress; the dancer Helen McGehee recalled one vivid example of the strain Graham and the others were feeling. "I remember when we got to Boston and it came to the final orchestra rehearsal of *Night Journey*—we had miserable room to get dressed in—there on the floor were a million of little pieces of a metronome. Martha had thrown it at Helen Lanfer, the pianist."[41] According to John Martin of the *New York Times*, what he saw at Harvard was "not one of Miss Graham's more inspired works." When the dance came to New York the following season, Martin had nothing to say about the music but noted that the choreography "has been greatly altered . . . and just as greatly strengthened. Last night's audience, indeed, greeted it with cheers and very genuine enthusiasm. This report, then, must be considered in a measure a minority opinion."[42]

The majority opinion seems to be that *Night Journey* is one of Graham's most successful dances, abetted by the 1961 film of the work that Robert Sabin called "superb" and Clive Barnes identified as "among the two or three successful dance films ever made."[43] Much of the praise has understandably fallen to Graham's dancing and choreography and Isamu Noguchi's design, but the music also received its share of acclaim from the start. Martin praised the score in its Boston performance, even if it seemed that he did not care for it. "Mr. Schuman's music is dark and portentous. As in his only previous score for the dance [*Undertow*], he relies for his dramatic effect largely upon persistence and iteration, which direct their attack upon the nerves. It is a substantial score, however, and a completely appropriate one." Two Boston critics had differing views, with the writer for the *Boston Sunday Globe* writing that "Mr. Schuman's music . . . speaks out with great power and deserves to be heard by itself" and the writer for the *Harvard Crimson* stating that "in the impression of a first hearing the use of the musical ideas is stronger than the ideas themselves." (Many years later, John Rockwell would concur with the anonymous Harvard reviewer, arguing that *Night Journey* "works better, given its gestural explicitness, for the stage than it does in the abstract.")[44]

Though it is a smaller score than *Undertow*, both in its original orchestration of 15 instruments and its overall length, *Night Journey* ventures further afield tonally and motivically than does the Tudor ballet.[45] Graham's lack of specificity allowed Schuman to write the kind of score that Tudor seemed to request, one where sections blur into each other and are not clearly demarcated in the music. The tempi are for the most part on the slow side, which explains the use of some form of the word "portent" by several of the critics. (According to Schuman's Schirmer biographer, he heeded his three-year-old son's advice that he needed to make the music scarier.)[46] This sense of foreboding is augmented by Schuman's decision never to use a simple triad anywhere in this work. Whereas *Undertow* employed triads in the Salvation Army sequence and at the very end with a luminous D♭ major chord accompanying the Transgressor as he walks offstage, in *Night Journey* Schuman makes no use of unadorned major or minor triads, instead stringing dissonant garlands of melody over the few minor triads that emerge in the more ponderous sections and undercutting the one major triad in the piece—also D♭—by superimposing upon it its E♭ neighbor. Here, Schuman often allows his linear writing to resolve into complex chords that have no clear harmonic function (e.g., at m. 30, G♭-E♭-A♭-D-F-C-E-B♭). The slow two-part counterpoint near the opening of the piece, with a slowly descending bass line over which an expanding intervallic wind melody eventually collapses back upon itself, returns at various moments either as a direct quotation or in shards subject to melodic and harmonic development. Ostinati in faster passages alternate with jagged wind ejaculations that refract their own upward-reaching melodic idea. The frenetic passages, few in number, do little to dispel the overall caste of gloom that shrouds the entire work. Though the title was Graham's, *Night Journey* aptly embodies the bleak darkness that runs through Schuman's first collaboration with Graham.

In a lengthy letter to Fanny Brandeis, program annotator for the Louisville Orchestra, Schuman described the genesis of his next work for Graham as well as his compositional intentions for the score, which remained unnamed at the time.

> About three years ago I had the privilege of collaborating with Miss Graham on the work known as "Night Journey" which was commissioned by the Elizabeth Sprague Coolidge Foundation in the Library of Congress, and was first performed on May 3, 1947 at the Harvard Symposium on Music Criticism. Working with Martha Graham was for me a most rewarding artistic venture and is directly responsible for the current collaboration. When I received a telephone call last spring from Miss

> Graham informing me that the Louisville Orchestra would commission a composer of her choice for her engagement, I had no intention of adding to my already heavy commitments. However, as the telephone conversation progressed and as the better part of an hour was consumed, my resistance grew weaker and suddenly I found myself discussing the possible form the work could take.
>
> Actually, my reason for wanting to do the work was not only the welcome opportunity of writing another piece for Miss Graham, but also the opportunity of employing the full resources of the modern symphony orchestra for a choreographic composition. Economic necessity customarily obliges the composer to limit the medium of his score to small ensembles, often totally inadequate for the tonal demands of the subject the dance has chosen and the acoustical requirements of the average auditorium.
>
> In the present work it was my hope to write a composition which would afford a satisfying musical experience by itself but which, at the same time, would be suitable for integration with the dance.[47]

By this time in his life, the demands at Juilliard required so much of his time that Schuman looked forward to uninterrupted summers during which he could fulfill the commissions he chose to accept. One such commission came to him officially in early May 1949 from Harold Spivacke, once again representing the Coolidge Foundation, this time requesting a 25-minute string quartet to be performed at a festival to be held in October 1950. Such a commission would unlikely have been formally offered without prior discussion as to the possibility of its acceptance, a fact that makes Schuman's three-week delay in responding to Spivacke unusual. What appears to have happened is that between the verbal agreement for the quartet and Schuman's formal agreement to the Coolidge commission, Graham called him about the opportunity the Louisville Orchestra was handing her. "The more I think about your idea," Schuman wrote to Graham in late May, "the more excited I become and I am going to move heaven and earth to clear the time. You have presented a really fresh idea and the possibility of a new medium which I am sure that other orchestras will want to emulate if I can do my part as well as you will do yours."[48]

In her dissertation on the commissioning project undertaken by the Louisville Orchestra, Jeanne Belfy devoted more than one-sixth of her text to the importance of this "new medium," the music Schuman wrote for it, and the effect the collaboration had on the Louisville Orchestra.[49] In February 1948, Charles R. P. Farnsley, previously the president of the Louisville Philharmonic Society, resigned that position to become the new mayor of the city upon the death of the previous officeholder. Farnsley had an idea that he believed would "make the Orchestra financially sound, artistically superior, and historically significant": the commissioning of new works to be performed on each of the six regular subscription concerts. After a shaky start for the 1948–49 season, Farnsley's idea "was continued a second year although, as the novelty wore off, it became evident that the commissioned music was not saving the orchestra from financial troubles," Belfy writes.[50] As Belfy has persuasively shown, the decision to invite Graham to create a dance concerto for the Louisville Orchestra did not save the ensemble from bankruptcy. What it did do, however, was to generate, for the first time, intense national interest in the commissioning project, as out-of-town critics descended upon Louisville for the work's premiere in January 1950. Interest was further whetted when Schuman helped the orchestra obtain a recording contract to document the commission, making it one of the first regional orchestras to be represented by a national recording company and opening up a discussion on the importance of regional orchestras. That same year, Graham and Schuman helped the orchestra secure a New York debut at Carnegie Hall in December, which included a reprise of Graham's dance concerto, her first appearance after injuring her knee on the company's spring European tour. The success of the Carnegie Hall concert led to another Louisville commission for a second solo dance from Graham, resulting in Norman Dello Joio's *The Triumph of Saint Joan* (1951). Two years later, the orchestra submitted a grant proposal to the Rockefeller Foundation "to commission 46 musical compositions a year . . . [and] to make records of such works available for purchase by interested schools, institutions, and individuals." The foundation funded the proposal, and it resulted in dozens of recordings of new music.[51]

Many of these events would have occurred had Schuman not been involved with Graham in creating what became *Judith: Choreographic Poem for Orchestra*. At a minimum, Schuman's association with these events shows how fortune smiled on him as he entered his fortieth year. But given the ways Schuman had already pressed to bring contemporary music to American audiences through commissions at Juilliard and the Naumburg recording prize, it seems more likely that Schuman is as much a catalyst of these events as a witness to them.

Consider a letter Schuman received a month after the premiere of *Judith* from John Woolford, manager of the Louisville Orchestra, as evidence to this likelihood. Woolford minced no words in his opening sentence: "There has been considerable agitation from our Directors, subscribers, etc. to try to get Columbia or Victor to record JUDITH." He went on to say that the conductor, Robert Whitney, feels that the orchestra is finally ready to take this momentous step, in large part because of "your enthusiasm for the performance . . . [and] what you said about the rather singular nature of the Louisville Orchestra's performance." Woolford, though, will not approach any of these recording companies unless Schuman gives him the green light. The letter ends: "Your countless friends down here are still singing your praises on several scores. The Bourbon and bray-nch water are waiting on you, so come back as fast as you can."[52] Upon receipt of the letter, Schuman called on David Hall of Mercury Records to gauge the soundness of Woolford's proposal. Hall proposed to Schuman that Mercury record the orchestra performing both *Judith* and

Undertow, news that Schuman eagerly related to Woolford, adding in a follow-up letter, "I would like very much to help the Louisville Orchestra launch a career in recording." Schuman proposed to Woolford and Whitney the idea that he, the composer, conduct the earlier work, thinking that this act would add to the cachet of the project. When the Louisville sessions failed to produce a satisfactory recording of *Judith*, Schuman elected to forfeit the fee he had earned as conductor and donate it to a fund to underwrite a recording session in New York. And in anticipation of the orchestra's New York appearance, Schuman wrote a story that ran in the *New York Times* praising the orchestra's policy of commissioning new works and making a direct plea for New Yorkers to contribute to the Louisville Fund so that the commissions and recordings could continue.[53] Graham was the spark, but Schuman kept fanning the flame.

As for the work itself, *Judith* was created with less of a story in mind than either *Undertow* or *Night Journey*. Like Tudor, Graham envisioned a symphonic composition to which she would set her solo. But she was unclear as to the content of that solo. "This has gone through a series of lives, this piece. It started as the Gospel of Eve but has grown beyond that into something else." Whatever else it had grown into, more important to Graham were the conversations she and Schuman had about the shape of the overall choreographic poem (to use Schuman's term).

> As I remember it you spoke as follows. . . .
>
> Broad introduction into a slow beautiful movement building to a dramatic climax. Repeating the opening motif and developing into an allegro, then into a scherzo. Returning to the opening (Andantino) ending affirmatively. I may have mistaken what you said but as I remember it was something like this. I had thought of the opening . . . the summons . . . as you related it . . . with the petition as the slow movement . . . the other dances as fitting into the allegro, that is the dance of gladness, with the temptation as something like the scherzo. The ending sweeping into the dance of sorrow and the final affirmation. [All ellipses are in the original letter.][54]

The four-part division that commentators have heard in the score was present from the beginning and has nothing to do with the drama of Judith beheading Holofernes on behalf of the Jewish people.[55] Schuman even checked with Graham about the nature of the divisions. "Am I correct in assuming that you do not wish a work in four or five separate dances, but a continuous symphonic development which would nevertheless allow for these separate sections?"[56] The resulting score, better understood as a five-part symphonic poem of slow-fast-slow-fast-slow, was finished in little more than two months; whether Graham had decided on the Judith story during this time remains unknown, although in a later letter she averred that "I gave William Schuman the idea for Judith—a script. I also gave him the Apocryphal quotations."[57] When exactly Graham determined to link her dance to the biblical story of Judith is unknown, but from the start she made known to Schuman the joy he gave her in consenting to collaborate again. "I think it is wonderful of you to do it. I was afraid to call you because I hated to have to face the fact that you might well say no. I had heard your music with it and I think the wonder of dancing to a bank of such music will be a great experience."[58]

The music of *Judith* returns to a more tonal universe than the one *Night Journey* had traversed. Chains of triads embellished by melodies that trade in pitches other than those in the accompanying triads open the work and reappear from time to time. Certainly the most significant triadic moment comes at the very end with the work's triumphal C-major close, reminiscent of the final moments of the Fourth Symphony (1941) and the Symphony for Strings (1943) but missing from the other large works between 1943 and 1949 (including the first version of the Violin Concerto). Indeed, Schuman's predilection for ending his works in a blaze of major-triad glory becomes more pronounced after *Judith*, and rare will be the extended composition after 1949 that does not undergo this cadential absolution for its highly chromatic sins. Also present in *Judith* is the organization of musical material by choirs, a feature heard in the Third Symphony, but here with less even distribution among the choirs and more reliance upon the string family. The timpani solo in the opening section also marks the music as from Schuman's pen, as do the skittish winds in the faster sections.

The success of *Judith* was tremendous, as were its hurdles. The very concept of a dance concerto was novel, and the decision to have Graham dance downstage with the Louisville Orchestra upstage behind a scrim meant that the solo would not engage the whole of the space a dancer might ordinarily encompass. Graham had already determined that she would not dance the entire time the music was sounding, so literally and figuratively she shared the stage with Schuman. Robert Sabin, writing for *Musical America*, produced the most in-depth analysis of the Louisville choreography as well as the music. His comments and comparisons astutely position *Judith* within the oeuvres of both Graham and Schuman.

> The dance of *Judith* is one of Miss Graham's greatest solos, one to rank with *Dithyrambic*, *Lamentation*, *Frontier*, and *Deep Song*. It lasts for twenty-five minutes and is as intense and cumulative in its effect as *Herodiade*, or the snake dance in *Cave of the Heart*. Yet neither the choreography nor the music is strident or melodramatic. Miss Graham and Mr. Schuman developed an understanding of each other's styles and personalities in working on *Night Journey*, a fact that reveals itself in the subtler integration of dance and music in *Judith*. The music is not as frenzied as that of *Night Journey*, but it is perhaps even more potent dramatically. It is music in blacks and greys, music of understatement and tremendous restrained power. Even in the section depicting Judith's dance of temptation, Mr. Schuman has scorned the obvious (as Miss Graham has) and delved into reaches of sensuality and sexual impulse barely hinted at

> in Strauss' Dance of Salome and other similar bits of stock theatre. This is no vulgar carnival-dance, in pseudo-oriental style, but a profound psychological study. . . .
>
> The choreography has elements of the percussive violence so prominent in *Night Journey*, but it is basically more lyric, with long phrases that are reflected in the score. Miss Graham uses the floor space with the utmost economy, so that one is never conscious of any limitations. *Judith* is probably the most taxing solo dance ever conceived, and her performance of it is an experience never to be forgotten.[59]

A year later, Sabin reviewed the New York premiere of *Judith*. "[Graham] has changed the choreography considerably in detail, but the general plan and the spiritual significance of the work are unaltered. She has made the opening episode less vehement and virtuosic in tone, and she has revised the ending to produce a quieter more heroic triumph than the frenzied finale of the original performance." On that night of New York premieres, with works by Thomson, Martinů, and Diamond, Sabin unequivocally called the Schuman "the best score of the evening."[60]

Judith triumphed throughout the world. At its Los Angeles premiere in February 1952, conductor Alfred Wallenstein had to take six bows to acknowledge the enthusiasm from the audience. Robert Russell Bennett wrote to tell Schuman he found it "about the finest of all modern ballets." Lucia Dlugoszewski, a dance composer championed by the New York School, voiced an opinion that was likely at odds with those of Cage, Feldman, and their cohorts. "I have always wanted to tell you how superb I thought your score for Martha Graham's Judith was. I feel no one in contemporary music has been so successful in expressing passion, drama and power as you did in that work. Only a Wozzeck is anything like it in power."[61] Graham herself continued to move audiences with her performance of the work. Agnes de Mille recalled one particular occasion. "Martha took *Judith* to Berlin in September 1957 and danced it at the opening ceremony of the Congress Hall. The critical reaction was tremendous. I personally saw Mary Wigman weeping, with her star dancer, Dore Hoyer, half fainting against her and close to collapsing from the emotional onslaught of what they had witnessed."[62] Anna Sokolow created her own choreography to the music, and with Pauline Koner dancing the role, *Judith* thrilled an audience of 3,000 delegates to an international conference sponsored by the Union of American Hebrew Congregations.[63] But by 1980, Graham had reconceived the dance altogether, choreographing it for two principals and the company. She also jettisoned Schuman's score, replacing it with a mélange of Varèse's *Integrales*, *Ofrrandes*, and *Octandre*.[64] A few years later, a new recording of *Judith* appeared, and Schuman sent it to Graham in hopes that it would rekindle her memory of the solo. "For me (and not because I was the composer) Judith was one of your greatest creations. Would it be possible for you to recreate it? . . . Next year is my 75th birthday, and this would be the greatest present you could possibly give, not just to me, but to the intervening generations who have never seen Judith in its original form." Graham, however, was unable to oblige Schuman, but she did offer him two memories she had of that time.

> One was the night before its premiere in Louisville. I was frightened and sleepless and I induced the guards in the building where we rehearsed, much against their will, to lock me and Helen Lanfer, my accompanist, in for the night so that in between waking and sleeping I could portray this woman Judith in a vivid way. My second lovely memory is of a performance in Berlin, my first since refusing an invitation to appear at the Berlin Olympics in 1936. I returned and performed 'Judith'. It was a rewarding, yet terrifying, experience and I owe it to you and the glory of your music.
>
> . . . Please forgive me that I cannot accede [to] your request. If I could, I would.[65]

Yet another memory Graham could have shared with Schuman was the fact that, after the 1950 Carnegie Hall appearance, she contacted Schuman to see if he would compose another solo work for her and the Louisville Orchestra. Schuman declined, and Graham wrote to tell him not only that she fully understood but that she appreciated his role in helping her achieve an artistic triumph at a time when her marriage to fellow dancer Erick Hawkins had come to an abrupt and deflating end and her future was far from certain.

> It has been a wonderful experience to work with you. Your strange white dedication and your intuitive utterance which you give to the urgencies of life and the beauty of that utterance all make it a rare privilege. This whole time struck across my life at a time which turned a personal terror into an exaltation. It could never have done that if the music and understanding behind its creative inception had been less great.[66]

Graham and Schuman would collaborate on two other occasions, neither one as successful as their first two efforts. A few months after his decision not to write another work for Louisville, Louisville basked in the glory he had enabled them to experience. *Undertow* and *Judith* were now available to the public, and not through the old technology of 78-rpm discs, but on a 10-inch long-playing album:

> This is the first record made by the Louisville Orchestra. It does itself proud. More than that, it gives its supporters—both moral and financial—reason for genuine satisfaction and the people of Louisville as a whole cause for pride. If there are any doubters, I can only suggest they listen to his record. It ought to convert them.[67]

Schuman had little time to celebrate with his friends in Louisville, for at Juilliard he was hatching his latest idea: a Dance Department. He had advanced the idea of "a School of Theatre and Dance as part of Juilliard" during his first year as president.[68] His work with Tudor and Graham, though, seemed to crystallize his vision and steel his intentions. He asked Mark Schubart, by then dean of Juilliard, for his thoughts about such a move. Schubart offered up a slew of objections. Schuman was undaunted.

> I think your reservations are well taken and I can even add some more myself. However, there will always be reservations concerning the addition of a Dance Department and I am well aware in trying to establish one that we are letting ourselves in for a lot of headaches. Nevertheless, there is one reason why as musicians we should strive to have a Dance Department. Dance uses music in a more fundamental manner than any other art outside of music itself. I need not tell you that the musical standards of most dancers are practically nonexistent and cannot be dignified by evaluation. If we are able to turn out a generation of dancers with first-rate technical training in the dance and professional musical insights, we will have contributed in an important manner both to music and the dance. Furthermore, since we are not a school of the dance, we can, if we are sufficiently skillful, avoid setting up a department of dance devoted to one style, be it Graham, Tudor, Balanchine, Limon, or what you will. We can actually give instruction with ample consideration of all significant contributions to the dance and therefore avoid getting bogged down in a motionless passion of cultism.[69]

By the following fall, the Dance Division had opened with a faculty that included Tudor, Graham, de Mille, Helen Lanfer, Louis Horst, Doris Humphrey, José Limón, and Jerome Robbins. Schuman had had contact, either through his own dance works or from his interest in the dance scene, with almost all of these people. (He and de Mille even joked about the fact that, based on her recommendation, he didn't see *Oklahoma!* when it was in rehearsals in Boston; by the time the Dance Division was founded, he had still not seen the show.)[70] Martha Hill, his choice for director of the Dance Division, was chairman of the Dance Department of Bennington College; the Sarah Lawrence Chorus often traveled with the school's Dance Ensemble, and the intercollegiate activities Schuman inaugurated at Sarah Lawrence brought him in contact with Bennington and Hill's Bennington Dance Festival. Once again, Schuman showed his knack in picking people: Hill served as director of Juilliard's Dance Division for more than three decades. Those years were not without turmoil, and the Dance Division was nearly terminated in the move to Lincoln Center. But the concept of a dance component at a conservatory of music was Schuman's, and he brought it to pass.

The world of dance, then, owes Schuman a debt of gratitude, and not only for his collaborations with Tudor and Graham. Pearl Lang, who danced in the chorus for *Night Journey*'s premiere, offered a pithy summary of Graham's range: "One certainly couldn't get a better repertoire than with Martha Graham—beheading, jealousy, murder, incest, lust."[71] Add prostitution and homosexuality, and Lang's words define Schuman's first three dance scores. By themselves, *Undertow*, *Night Journey*, and *Judith* would be impressive contributions to the world of music and dance. Their offspring—the Juilliard Dance Division, the Louisville Orchestra recording project—have had an effect far greater than the scores. Schuman the composer sought out occasions for these scores to be heard again. Schuman the creator took quiet pride in all of his children, musical and otherwise, often bringing them into being with a flurry of activity and then letting them find their own way into the world. Anyone who has ever listened to a recording by the Louisville Orchestra or seen a dance performance by a graduate of the Juilliard School has been touched by Schuman's reach. They—we—are all Schuman's artistic heirs.

FIFTEEN

FAMILY MATTERS

Bill wanted his own heir. It was during his 1935 summer in Salzburg that he wrote to his buddy Eddie Marks to see if Eddie had laid eyes on Billy's newest kin. "Have you seen my nephew yet? I can't wait to see the little one. I've been crazy about so many other people's kids in my day that I fear if I ever have some of my own the novelty will already be worn off." In a handwritten comment on the typewritten letter, Schuman added: "(I just heard that you paid [my sister] Audrey a visit.)"[1] From whom he had heard this, he doesn't say, although Frankie was writing him regularly that summer and may have conveyed the news about Eddie's visit to see Bill's sister and her newborn son, John. Audrey gave birth to Judy three years later. And throughout his life, Schuman stayed close to his sister, her two children, and their children.

As for his own offspring, the first one would come more than seven years after Bill and Frankie were married. In describing their first apartment, Schuman painted a somewhat idyllic existence.

> When we first got married, we found an apartment at 260 Riverside Drive on the northeast corner of 98th Street, and I remember it because we paid $55 or $65 for a beautiful bedroom overlooking Riverside Drive, a kitchen and dinette combination, a lovely living room and plenty of closet space. We had part-time help for $12 a week, our mothers thought we were paying too much, a part-time person to do the shopping and the cooking and the laundry. I was earning $2,400 a year at Sarah Lawrence and Frankie was earning $1,600–$1,800 working as a professional at the New York State Employment Bureau. So, for under $4,000 or so, we could live beautifully.[2]

Hired help was a part of the household from the beginning and was a reflection of Schuman's upbringing—his family always had domestic help—and the economies of yesteryear that made it possible for middle-class families to have servants.

The move to Westchester County in 1940 would seem to presage the intent to start a family, but it wasn't until the fall of 1943 that Frankie's pregnancy became a topic of conversation with Schuman's correspondents. He wrote to Copland out in Hollywood about the new symphonic opus—the *Symphony for Strings*—and Frankie's "Xmas-opus-to-be." Copland responded wittily, "It was hard to tell whether you were more pleased with the String Symphony or the Xmas-opus-to-be. Personally I was thrilled at the prospect of examining the latter. How nice to think that it doesn't have to be submitted to the critics for a long time to come!"[3] Three days before Christmas, the Schumans had a child at last.

Schuman needn't have worried about the novelty wearing off. Correspondence between his closest friends—Leonard Bernstein, Frank Loesser, and others—inevitably included greetings to and from Tony, the latter expressed by Tony's father. (His full name, Anthony, didn't gain traction in a household run by a couple who called themselves Bill and Frankie.) Bill often sang songs to Tony from the *Fireside Book of Folk Songs* before bedtime, and at other times they listened to recordings of Josef Marais, the South African folk singer who composed "Zulu Warrior." (Marais was under the impression that Schuman was thinking about writing a work based on his tunes, which, if true, may have been a bonbon intended for younger kids.)[4] Loesser songs also entered into the repertoire, so much so that Bill would joke with Frank that "'Baby It's Cold Outside' is now such a popular piece in our household that Tony thinks I wrote it."[5] Tony himself was developing an astute ear for timbre and rhythm, calling down from upstairs as his father was listening to a recording of *Circus Overture* and wondering where the bassoons were or being drawn to the study at the sound of the typewriter and adding his own glyphs when his dad stopped to ponder the next sentence.[6] Bill doted on his son.

While Tony grew stronger, Schuman's parents grew weaker. In later years, Schuman reflected on his mother, about whom he said very little in his correspondence while she was alive.

> My mother was a woman of astonishingly strong character who, beginning at about the time I was 9 years old through to her death when I was 37, gallantly suffered a series of difficult and devastating illnesses. She was a purist and since, aside from the experiences of any housewife, she was insulated from many of the practical problems of the world, my sister and I were able to gain by the splendid example she set for us of strength of character. She had a delightful light side on those infrequent occasions when she was "*ausgelassen*."
>
> Mother was a perfectionist, which found its outlet in compulsive housekeeping. If this was excessive and somewhat burdensome to live with in one respect, it certainly had its rich rewards when it came to the table. She was an excellent cook. While in retrospect one recognizes that her repertory was somewhat limited and in no sense in the tradition of the Cordon Bleu, she did, as the saying went in those days, set "an excellent table," and the memories of the marvelous meals that we had during our home life remain, and even to this day can start the juices flowing.[7]

The onset of Ray's illnesses coincides with the mental retardation diagnosis of her youngest child, Robert, and the decision to send him away, suggesting that her initial illness was psychosomatic in origin. But prior to that final illness, she was especially convivial. Schuman recalled the first decade in his parents' house. "So we used to sing, and I was considered a very good singer, and they always used to like me to sing a solo, which I'd do. It was just the family, but very pleasant evenings, and on such evenings my mother would be, in the German phrase, *ausgelassen*, sort of out of herself and very cheerful."[8] Singing to Tony thus echoed the singing in Bill's own childhood.

Near the end of his own life, as he endured his own physical suffering, Schuman drew particular lessons from the example of his mother. "I was very close to my mother, but my mother never called me darling or dear the way other mothers did. I always felt that. . . I came to appreciate my mother much later on in life than I did earlier. . . . She was a very heroic person and took her ill health in a wonderful way, and I got to understand her."[9] She was "quite lame" by her mid-sixties, and Bill and Audrey moved Sam and Ray from Chatham in upstate New York down to Rye in Westchester County so that they could better take care of them. Ray died at the age of 67 on September 3, 1947, the very day the move to Rye occurred, which led Schuman to bring his father to live temporarily at home with him, Frankie, and Tony in New Rochelle.[10]

His father was ill at this time, too, but he carried himself with greater equanimity than had Ray, one reason among many that led Schuman to feel more at ease with his father than with his mother.

> My father was a very optimistic man and had an excellent, wonderful disposition. I don't know what my mother's disposition could have been or would have been because she was very sick and she was a very heroic person. She was sick for many, many years. So she had, I would say, a more varying disposition, with ups and downs, and my father was much steadier.[11]

In fact, Sam was doing rather well for someone in his mid-seventies. He had had cataract surgery, which gave him greater acuity when it came to the racing forms. With Ray gone, he indulged himself in that pastime, which had gotten him into trouble on his honeymoon when his boss had to wire him money to cover his losses at the track.

The beginning of the end for Sam started with a successful day with the horses.

> He was leaving the Hotel Franconia, where he had a single room after my mother's death, and he wanted me to lend him money out of my savings to gamble with. I said, "I can't do that Dad. I'll do anything in the world for you, but I can't do that and you know I'm right." He said, "I know you're right." But he started to gamble whatever money he did have, and the day he was leaving the hotel this car hit him and knocked him down, I was in a board meeting. I was called out of the meeting and they told me

> he was at Roosevelt Hospital. So I went back into the board meeting and I said, "Gentlemen, I have to leave, my father was in an accident, I'll call you when I can," and I left. I went to the hospital, he could barely speak, "I had a good day at the races. Reach into my right pocket and take that cash away before somebody gets it."[12]

The day was October 11, 1949. Sam did not leave the Roosevelt Hospital until late March, over five months later, when he was transferred again to the Schuman house. By mid-June, Bill was cheered by his father's "miraculous if incomplete recovery."[13] By early fall, Sam was back at Roosevelt, this time diagnosed with cancer. He made Bill promise to send tickets to his attending physicians for the December 29 New York premiere of *Judith*. Sam didn't live to see the performance, but his son made good on the promise.[14] One of those physicians wrote to Schuman after Sam's death on November 29. "Your father took great pride in all your accomplishments and I know how much comfort he derived from your devotion to him. You have the satisfaction of knowing that your father's last days were made as pleasant as possible through your efforts."[15] Another physician provided a more colorful picture of Sam's last days. "I liked his fighting spirit and his refusal to let long and hopeless illness defeat his smile, his old & risqué jokes and his will to be a charming devil of an old man."[16] Perhaps it was this fighting spirit, this devil-may-care attitude, that allowed Bill to continue working without missing a beat. The day after Sam's death, Bill wired the people in Louisville to tell them of his intention to waive his fees to smooth the way for the anticipated New York recording session for the Louisville Orchestra. The chief work that the orchestra was to rerecord: *Judith*.[17]

Sam's accident as a pedestrian overlapped with another accident of sorts. In writing to Bernstein about his father's plight, Schuman went on with more from the home front. "To offset this news of gloom, you will be interested to know that last week Frankie and I adopted a four and a half months old daughter. Also, we think our dog is going to have puppies. There is nothing like living in capital letters!"[18] More than five years had passed since Tony joined the family, and Bill and Frankie concluded that they could no longer wait to have another child of their own. By the time they adopted Andrea, they were 39 and 35. Andrea spoke of the reasons behind the adoption: "My mother was an only child and did not want that experience for Tony. . . . They were relatively old parents for their time, and as it was the only way to assure 'one of each' (a boy and a girl), adoption seemed the answer."[19] But the adoption wasn't without its difficulties. One of the adoption agencies they turned to had stopped accepting new applications.[20] And after the initial placement, there were still hurdles to overcome. In early summer of 1951, Schuman plaintively said that "adoptions . . . involve court proceedings and we are still not in the clear."[21] But just as they had doted on Tony, they doted on Andy (the propensity for nicknames continued). Schuman wrote in a letter to a friend, "I can say, without fear of immodesty, that never was there a more beautiful child, since she is adopted."[22]

In terms of affection, Bill and Frankie strove never to privilege one child over the other.

> The thing that it taught us (we suspected this), but when you have an adopted child, especially when you get one in infancy . . . there is no difference between an adopted child and a natural child. It's hard to imagine that, vicariously, perhaps, but there isn't. The child becomes a member of the family. We adore her, and Tony feels the same way. Any thought to the contrary never came up. None. None.[23]

In a letter to her parents—with its typical abundance of dashes—Frankie confirmed that they treated their two children more or less equally.

> Yesterday was Andy's birthday and a real production. Started here at 7 o'clock a.m. with presents etc. and then lollypops to take to school for all the children. I went over to watch that and it was something to behold—she passed the candy very seriously and intent mostly on not spilling them—and her face when the class sang happy birthday was just one of those things—then home for lunch and the butcher had sent her a pint of ice-cream—when she telephoned to thank him he sang happy birthday to her—and then the party here—we collected ten kids by the time the ice cream and cake period came—and she had ordered a cake just like "the one you made for Grandma"—she got a terrific haul of presents but she has kept track of them all and knows what she got—we had some happy birthday napkins left over and to-day she said "how is it my birthday again?" anyway she had a wonderful time and is delighted not to be 2 years old any more. Tony is fine and didn't mind the birthday too much—after all he had the party too and some presents. I bought him a book on how to play chess and we're really down to business.[24]

In the 1950s, Bill and Frankie got down to the business of raising Tony and Andy. In the fall of 1950, Schuman sought to move the family back to New York City and actively looked for both an eight-room apartment for the family and a school for Tony, who would be entering the third grade in the fall of 1951. The difficulty of finding affordable housing and an appropriate school and the deterioration in Sam's health led Bill to give up this quest and to remain in New Rochelle.[25]

As Tony grew older, his father attempted to transfuse his passion for other aspects of life into his son. Summer camp was one, and Tony made the trek northward to Winthrop, Maine, for a half-dozen summers. Just as Cobbossee had worked its magic on the father, it did the same for the son. Tony recalled that

> I loved everything about it—the sports, the lake, Color War [Red Team vs. the White Team], theater. I was less enthusiastic about camping, but did love the canoe trips.
>
> We didn't do original productions at camp, having no Schuman and Marks to write them, but had fun nonetheless. As a great bonus, the American Savoyards, at the time the premier Gilbert and Sullivan troupe in the U.S., summered in nearby Monmouth, Maine, so I saw the complete repertoire. I relished the G&S trips with enormous enthusiasm.[26]

Trains were another place where father and son bonded. "I have vivid memories of a two-day trip to Tucson in 1959 (I was in 9th grade and reading *Ivanhoe*) when dad and I got off the train at every major city (St. Louis, etc.) and some small towns (Tucumcari, NM) to plant our feet and say we had been there and to buy a pennant to mark the occasion. I still have the pennants. It was a fabulous trip (*Ivanhoe* aside)."[27]

But it was baseball that truly glued the two together. Tony was away at Cobbossee in the summer of 1957 when his dad sent him the clipping containing the news that their beloved New York Giants were moving to San Francisco.[28] Three summers later, another letter from Dad to the Cobbossee camper came on the eve of father, mother, and sister heading off to Europe. In it, Schuman crowed about Tony's report card, which, he said, demonstrated "your usual excellent work."

> The only other news that you and I would have to discuss at great length if we were together is the expansion of the National Leagues into 10 teams each and the dissolution of the Continental League. I hope this move meets with your approval. . . . It looks as though we'll be getting a National League team here before too long.
>
> Once again, much love to you from your Mother, Sister and Dad.
>
> Love,[29]

Tony's career in baseball effectively ended in the middle of a 1961 game. In a description that would make his father proud, Tony recalled the day.

> I broke my leg covering second base on a steal attempt by a Poly Prep runner at a game in Van Cortlandt Park at the end of the regular season. I had had a good year, batting over .300. I had singled and scored and we were leading Poly in that last game. The break was bad—both bones clear through, but not compound (i.e., didn't penetrate the skin). I was splinted with a fungo bat and carried on a folded lawn chair to the school station wagon which took me to the New Rochelle hospital. The recuperation was very long—3 months in a cast to my hip, another month with a cast to my knee (they didn't put in metal plates and screws in those days). I got out of the cast just days before heading off to my first year at Wesleyan, on crutches with a limp.[30]

The entire family witnessed the accident.[31] The next day, Schuman wrote to thank the coach of the Polytechnic Preparatory Country Day School in Brooklyn for his ministrations and closed his letter with a nod to their shared love of the game. "Our family doctor said that you did a fine job with your improvised splint and, certainly, with our son's passion for the game, a baseball bat was wholly appropriate."[32]

Andrea's pursuits were less athletic but no less involved. She and her friend Misty Mydans created the *Three Star News*, an occasional neighborhood newsletter that initially cost 2¢ but quickly doubled in price. With Suzy Schuman (the family dog) as mascot, Misty and Andy wrote about the comings and goings of neighbors, of the fire at the Howard Johnson, and of other very local news. The *Three Star News* also gives a unique perspective on several of the Schuman family trips, including a Thanksgiving holiday trip to Atlantic City and a visit to Lake Como.[33]

Summer camp proved not to be as memorable an experience for Andrea as it was for her brother, mother, and father. One camp was highly regimented "as bells rang for activities that always seemed to call for clothing changes (as from horseback riding to swimming). And mustn't be late!" Another camp, reachable only by boat, proved much more amenable to Andrea's pace, especially with its focus on "sing[ing] in the little country chapels on Sundays—get in the boat, zoom along and sing some hymns. . . . It was great. But again, once was enough." Yet another camp that focused on horseback riding led to the ruination of Andrea's left knee. "End camp, enter summer school."[34]

Andrea provided the support for an embarrassing moment at Lincoln Center. One morning her father unwittingly donned her knee socks as he headed off to work. Frederick Steinway was present when calamity struck. "I was preparing to rush over a grounding strap and a spray can of anti-static!"[35] Schuman couldn't figure out why his pants were clinging to his legs and crawling up to his knees.

The stories of the Schuman family in the 1950s take on something of a Ward-and-June-Cleaver hue, but there were the unusual twists and turns behind the scenes. One was Bill's exercise regime in a strange lap pool he built in the basement of his home. Tony gives the details:

> The [New Rochelle] pool was built with a wooden frame enclosing the pool area, which was cinched in the middle to avoid a structural lally column, giving the pool the shape of a sigma. It was about 6' wide at both ends, 3' wide at the center, and about 30 feet long. No one used it much except dad, who swam laps pretty regularly. He used a giant tea heater (submersible electronic heating element) to heat the water. It was certainly an oddity rather than a luxury; this was no indoor patio!![36]

The quiet that needed to accompany the life of a composer also set the Schumans apart from their neighbors. Though his children attended classical concerts on occasion, neither Tony nor Andrea developed a deep appreciation for this music during their childhood years.

> Dad's composition time was sacrosanct, and mom was a gatekeeper, although we understood not to enter the study when he was composing. . . . As a typical adolescent more attuned to Buddy Holly (and later Dave Brubeck and Gerry Mulligan) than atonal symphonic music, my father's music was not easy for me. I took piano lessons for 6 years without ever really gaining an understanding of musical structure, so I was unable to make out the intricate contrapuntal or chromatic sequences my father was creating. I know he was disappointed that we (his children) did not express more interest in his music, but he did not go out of his way to press it upon us or to explain it. . . . My father and I really connected around popular music of his day, rather than mine. I still know all the lyrics to Rodgers and Hart and Gershwin.[37]

Andrea was slightly more attuned to her dad's music than was her brother, arranging to be with her dad on Thursdays when he drove out to the country in order to hear Robert Lawrence's opera broadcasts on the radio.[38]

Like many suburban families, the Schumans had a congeries of animals in the house. Tony vividly and humorously recalled a number of them.

> As for the pets, there was a string of dogs, starting with Muffin, an Irish setter bought when I was very little so we would have a large gentle dog in the house and I wouldn't be afraid of dogs. This strategy worked well; she was a lovely dog, but she ran in front of a car and was killed. Beauty was a beagle, also a wonderful dog, who ran off to join a pack of wild dogs in Larchmont. There was Ricky (née "Ricardo") a standard size brown poodle who was also very sweet; and several terriers (Corky and Suky, if my memory is right). The terriers snapped at the mailman and were given away.
>
> In addition to the dogs, there was one cat, Nicky, a white kitten, who early in his brief tenure with us jumped up on dad's bald head from behind the rocking chair, and that was the end of Nicky. There was a bird or two and several batches of fish (guppies, tetras, etc.). But the important pets were the dogs—Suzy (a cocker spaniel) being the champ, but Ricky and Beauty were great pets as well.[39]

Suzy was Andrea's responsibility and lived until 1974, the year Andrea's son Josh was born.[40]

In general, family took priority over other pursuits for Schuman. He would miss a concert to celebrate a child's birthday, and he did not go to a Cobbossee reunion that conflicted with his wedding anniversary.[41] Family mattered a great deal to him, even when it came to the troubled and troubling history of his interactions with his younger brother, Robert. The kids were told about their uncle for the first time in

Schuman and Suzy, summer 1963. Photo by Tibor Hirsch.

the 1950s, possibly because, at that time, Audrey decided to transfer her brother to the Manhattan State Hospital on Ward's Island, which was closer to her home in Queens Village. One reason they hadn't known about Robert before was because evidence of his existence, such as photographs, had been knowingly suppressed and destroyed.[42] Robert died on August 31, 1957, at the age of 42. The Schumans were vacationing on Martha's Vineyard at the time; one imagines that Audrey, who handled Robert's cremation, phoned to give her brother the news, but there was no move to memorialize their brother. Perhaps Audrey did not call, for the very next day, Schuman wrote to Bernstein: "Excuse this fast note but the sun is out on this beautiful island and I can't afford to miss a minute of these last precious days."[43] Whatever occurred in the days after Robert's death, 20 years would pass before Bill unburdened himself about Robert: "If my parents were still alive, of course I wouldn't be saying this [about Robert being developmentally disabled]. . . . I never told anybody before."[44] The secrecy and suppression and silence were choices that the family made. In light of the effect Robert had on his mother's health, Bill's choices become more explicable even as they remain inscrutable.

As the Schumans were about to head into the 1960s, the paterfamilias wrote a prescient letter about the decade ahead to Paul Henry Lang, who had announced his daughter's impending marriage. "It is hard for me to believe that we are all at the point where our children are ready for the big plunge. As I look at my fifteen-year old son, I somehow feel that he will give us a little more time at home than our ten-year old daughter, who is really something."[45] Before the '60s were through, Andrea would be married. She was the more liberal one of the two children, although Tone—another nickname given to Anthony—would try his wings and his parents' patience before long. But throughout his life, and in the '50s in particular, Schuman took great consolation in his family and Frankie in particular. The opening line on a postcard he sent to Frankie while he was on his 1952 trip to Europe for UNESCO speaks volumes: "*Venice sans tu stinkera.*"[46] Later letters from Venice include remarks about Tony and Andrea as well: "I miss you and the kids like anything."[47] And a 1956 Christmas Day note to Frankie encapsulates the simplicity and the profundity of Schuman's understanding of family:

> Not much this year. These four little trifles are hardly worth remembering. Perhaps you might open the smallest box first, then the one in silver paper, then the smaller green & finally the larger green. As I say it doesn't much matter but at least we can try to build up some sense of excitement—can't we? It's so difficult, you know, to give to those who have everything one could imagine—charm, material wealth & spiritual blessings—not to mention adorable children & a truly remarkable husband who loves you.[48]

Trifles were forgettable. What mattered was the moment, which he longed to savor just like those last days on the Vineyard. And Bill, like his wife, had just about everything one could imagine. He had music. He had children. He had Frankie. Who could ask for anything more?

SIXTEEN

AN OLD RELIGION, TWO CHAMPIONS, AND A NEW SYMPHONY

January 12, 1949, was the last time Serge Koussevitzky conducted a Schuman composition with the Boston Symphony Orchestra. At the end of the 1948–49 season, he stepped down after 25 years on the orchestra's podium. His influence on America's musical life is enormous, with Tanglewood standing as his most enduring creation. But his championship of American music is also legendary. For his final season, Koussevitzky brought the Boston Symphony Orchestra to Carnegie Hall for a festival of two programs devoted to American composers. According to *New York Times* critic Olin Downes, "Dr. Koussevitzky planned these programs as demonstration of the advances made by American symphonic composers in the last ten years."[1]

Schuman had made considerable advances over the decade. Ten years prior to the Carnegie Hall concert, Koussevitzky provided Schuman with the first professional orchestra performance of his Second Symphony. From there, Koussevitzky's fondness for Schuman and his music resulted in four premieres—the *American Festival Overture* (late 1939) the Third Symphony (late 1941), *A Free Song* (early 1943) and the *Symphony for Strings* (late 1943)—and performances of *Prayer in Time of War* (late 1944). Schuman tried to interest Koussevitzky in the *Circus Overture*, but Koussevitzky chose not to program the piece; as for the Fourth Symphony and *Undertow*, there is no correspondence that indicates that the two men discussed whether the Boston Symphony Orchestra would play either work.[2] Schuman did offer Koussevitzky the first performance of the Violin Concerto, but by the time it was completed and the complications surrounding its commission were resolved (see chap. 17), Koussevitzky's successor, Charles Munch, would lead the premiere in early 1950. But Schuman owed Koussevitzky an enduring debt for the conductor's support. The League of Composers hosted a dinner for Koussevitzky to celebrate his tenure, and Schuman wrote for the book of memories presented to the conductor: "As one composer who is proud to have you as musical champion and warm personal friend, I know better with each passing year how rare are your qualities as artist and man."[3]

With the retirement of Koussevitzky, Schuman was losing a musical champion. Fritz Reiner in Pittsburgh and Artur Rodzinski in Cleveland and New York premiered some of his works—*Prayer in Time of War* and *Circus Overture* for the former, the Fourth Symphony and the *William Billings Overture* for the latter—but neither conductor seemed as willing to correct what Schuman called the "sad state of affairs when American works which are well received by press and public alike are left unplayed after the novelty of their first presentation."[4] Alfred Wallenstein and Pierre Monteux on the West Coast introduced their audiences to Schuman, but they were too far away. Nor had Schuman cultivated the close relationship with these conductors that he had developed with Koussevitzky. Of course, Koussevitzky's young disciple Leonard Bernstein was a dear friend who would prove to be an advocate for Schuman and his music, programming the Third Symphony with the New York City Symphony in 1946 and leading premieres of his own in the 1960s. But he had no world-class orchestra at his fingertips in 1949, and as Schuman looked forward to the 1950s, he looked for his next Koussevitzky. He would find that new champion in Eugene Ormandy, and the correspondence between them—more than 200 letters spanning 38 years—provides a window into nearly all aspects of the music business. The letters also indirectly reveal when Ormandy replaced Koussevitzky as Schuman's champion: only seven letters predate Koussevitzky's retirement.

In addition to being a time to find another conductor who would encourage Schuman and perform his music, the late 1940s also presented Schuman with a challenge that was, at turns, political, philosophical, and spiritual: How involved would he become in nurturing Israel? In the years immediately after World War II, numerous musicians lent their names and skills in support of the nascent nation; many of these musicians were Jewish by heritage, and some were also practicing Jews. Koussevitzky conducted the Israel Philharmonic Orchestra (originally named the Palestine Orchestra) on its American tour in early 1951. His willingness to assist in this way was likely encouraged by Bernstein, who conducted the Israel Philharmonic Orchestra in the late 1940s. Bernstein sent Schuman a handwritten letter in which he exclaimed the wonders of what he was seeing and hearing in the fall of 1948 and his role in the midst of it all.

> I've been trying desperately to find a moment to write you from this miracle-land, and I finally find myself doing it between eggs & coffee at 9:30 A.M. before a rehearsal. That's the way it goes here: 40 concerts in 60 days, and I'm rather skinny as a result. But what an experience! It is a great people, these, with a magnificent sense of future & will to peace (you should understand that deeply), with a marvelous army, grown-up overnight, calm and sure and quiet. The beauties & variety of the land are breathtaking, & the potentialities unlimited.

> Last week we toured Galilee, fresh from the fighting (48 hours after), and saw the miracles personally. I've visited the Jerusalem fronts (and been decorated by the Area Commander! I'm as proud as a Silver-Star-owner.) Next week I'm going down to the Negev, Beersheba, Negbah, etc. to play for the soldiers. [Approximately 5,000 soldiers heard the concert on the Beer Sheba dunes on November 20, 1948.] One needs an endless supply of energy to do all this—with the extras, special concerts, Pension Fund, rehearsals, etc.—but somehow one finds the necessary strength in Israel.[5]

Less than a year later, Bernstein wrote to Schuman on behalf of the American Fund for Israel Institutions, asking if Schuman would consent to serve on the Fund's Musical Advisory Committee, which Bernstein was asked to form. "Please let me know that you will join me in this invaluable work, for which only you and a very small group of others are eminently qualified. Needless to say, I recognize (as does the American Fund) the value of your time, and you may be sure we would call upon you only at most infrequent intervals." Schuman took more than a week to answer Bernstein "because I wanted to consider my answer very carefully."

> May I start by saying that I make it an unalterable practice not to lend my name to any committee of the kind you envision unless I have the free time to devote to its activities. At the moment, it would be foolhardy of me to take on any other commitment, despite the assurances of the infrequent intervals at which I would be asked to come to meetings.[6]

An overview of invitations Schuman received and accepted suggests that other factors were in play when he declined Bernstein's invitation. In 1946, Schuman agreed to join the Board of Directors for the American Youth Orchestra with the understanding that his duties would be light. In 1948, he accepted Otto Luening's invitation that he become a director of the American Music Center, with duties consisting of "1 annual meeting, perhaps one other one—your advice occasionally, by phone." That same year, he agreed to become a corporate member in the MacDowell Association; "actual responsibility only one meeting a year—elections held, reports made, and usually quite a successful party—also minimum dues of five dollars." In 1949, the year of Bernstein's invitation, Schuman served on "a survey committee for the evaluation of the work done or proposed at the Baltimore Institute of Musical Arts . . . an interracial school which has been established within the last few years and which now wishes permission to award a degree."[7] Schuman did say no to invitations that had a political caste to them. When up-and-coming musicologist Arthur Mendel wrote to Schuman in 1947 to ask him to serve with Mendel on a panel that might include communist sympathizers, Schuman wouldn't even give Mendel an answer other than to commend Mendel for his "impressive letter."[8] Another organization Schuman decided against sponsoring or joining was the Toronto Jewish Folk Choir on the occasion of its twenty-fifth anniversary. His response in this case sounds strikingly similar to the answer he gave to Bernstein.

> As President of a well-known School of music I have discovered that any use of my name in support of another musical organization implies the endorsement of the School. I therefore have to make it a practice not to lend my name in support of any organization unless I am an active participant of that organization. I feel confident that you will understand that this reason and this alone causes me to decline.[9]

Yet, in 1951, Schuman accepted membership on the American Advisory Planning Committee for the Esco Music Center at Ein Gev, Israel, and agreed to be a sponsor of Music for Israel.[10]

The complications that emerge in evaluating Schuman's relationship to Israel and Jewish life exist in part because of others' expectations that Schuman should involve himself, given his own heritage. In 1946, he was approached by a woman doing a study titled *The Contribution of Jewish Composers to the Music of the Modern World*. She asked Schuman to tell her about his Jewish upbringing. His statement to her summarizes his own understanding of his religious practice and beliefs.

> I am afraid that my religious education was not a very effective one and the less said about it the better. I cannot honestly say that religion played any significant part in my childhood beyond the fact that going to Sunday School was pleasant in a social sense, even though I was expelled on more than one occasion. Also, formal religion plays no part at all in my life today. Nevertheless, I consider myself a religious person in the sense of religion as an ethical and moral concept. However, in the development of this concept it would be unfair to cite formal religious training as having played any important role. In other words, I find no need for any institutionalized religion for myself, while recognizing its value for others.[11]

While Schuman did not go out of his way to ensure that people did not view him as a Jew, he did not completely identify as a Jew himself. Nor did others readily associate him with Jewish life. For example, in his study on American Jewish culture, Stephen J. Whitfield discussed Copland and Bernstein—two of Schuman's closest musical friends and both from eastern European Jewish stock—but makes no mention of the German American Jew Schuman and how Schuman's life and music contribute to our understanding of American music.[12]

At the same time, Schuman spoke out against anti-Semitism, though his words were often muted. When the Juilliard Orchestra went on tour to Europe in the summer of 1958, the U.S. State Department helped them secure concerts in various cities. One of these cities was Beirut, Lebanon, despite the fact that an Israeli student was a member of the orchestra. Schuman wrote an eloquent letter to Anis Fuleihan, the director of the Beirut Conservatory of Music and a personal friend, stating that, under the circumstances, the orchestra would not go to Lebanon. "Our School will continue to welcome students without regard to citizenship and always with the assurance that they will be fully integrated into the activities of the School without prejudice because of race, religion, color or national origin."[13] And in giving his Ninth Symphony a subtitle that referred to the March 1944 massacre at the Ardeatine caves in Rome, Schuman reminded his audience of the horrors of the Nazis, although only 75 of the 335 who were slaughtered in Rome were Jewish, and, even more to the point, Schuman had composed a portion of the symphony before he visited the caves for the first time in April 1967.[14] In both instances, Schuman's stance could be construed as speaking out against fascism as well as anti-Semitism. His daughter, Andrea, recalled that "our family actually had its own foreign policy when we were growing up—no one was permitted to buy anything made in Germany (I remember shopping with my mother—she would turn things upside down to see where they were made), and they would not set foot in Spain."[15] His initial reluctance in the late 1940s to lend his support to Israel may have been because he could not yet clearly see where its policies and politics would take the young country and certainly was influenced by his reflexive retreat from engaging in causes that might be remotely controversial.

Oddly, Schuman's most sustained argument against anti-Semitism comes years before many of the opportunities to speak out against anti-Semitism came his way. In 1934, he wrote an article for the *American Hebrew and Jewish Tribune*, giving as his rationale "the fact that the past year was the fiftieth anniversary of Wagner's death, [resulting in] new books and articles about him. . . . But one of his many essays about music seems to have escaped current comment." The essay Schuman examined was Wagner's noxious "Judaism in Music." And yet Schuman treated Wagner's vitriol with studied detachment, never disclosing whether he had any emotional or personal investment in Wagner's argument. Schuman naively called on various "witnesses"—Joseph Conrad, Julian Green, Ernest Newman—to refute Wagner's insistence that Jews cannot master a foreign tone, as though such "witnesses" could have swayed Wagner. He defended Mendelssohn from Wagner's attacks with a curious feint of his own. "If Mendelssohn was not the genius Beethoven was, why lay the cause to Judaism? Berlioz was, without reasonable doubt, a great musician; he too was certainly no Beethoven, yet one would hardly seek to lay this blame to his religious belief." Indeed, Schuman's identification of Mendelssohn's Judaism to religious belief is doubly wrong, given Mendelssohn's identification as a Lutheran, but it is instructive to see how narrowly Schuman construed Judaism at this time. As for Wagner, later in life Schuman would unapologetically exclaim that he generally loathed Wagner's music, but in 1934, he was far more charitable, as demonstrated in the pseudo-psychoanalytical final paragraph of his article.

> Richard Wagner is rightfully entitled to high esteem as a great composer. If we cannot find excuses for his prejudicial insanity, it might be reasoned that his great musical powers encroached on his other faculties and made them weaker. Hence such an unfounded treatise as his "Judaism in Music."[16]

(Would Schuman have considered the possibility that his great administrative powers encroached on his other faculties?) Fourteen years after this article, Schuman was forced by the people around him to address issues of Judaism and music in far more personal ways than he had done for the readers of the *American Hebrew and Jewish Tribune.*

It is extremely difficult to know to what degree Schuman wrestled with these issues in his music at this period of time. The ideas and scenarios of *Night Journey* and *Judith* originated with Martha Graham, so the bleakness of the one and the triumph of the Jewish people in the other are incidents of Schuman's decision to work with Graham and are not necessarily representative of his intentions. The Sixth Symphony of 1948, in contrast, does suggest that Schuman found it difficult to write light and celebratory music at this time. One commentator said of the symphony that it sounds as though it may be "a reflection on the horror of the war just passed."[17] The compositional and reception history of the symphony as well as its relation to other symphonies written in the 1940s bolster this commentator's reading of the work as a statement of life in what Bernstein, in the symphony he wrote a year after Schuman's Sixth, identified as an age of anxiety.

The work's premiere was also swathed in nervousness. The Dallas Symphony Orchestra commissioned Schuman to write a work for its 1948–49 season. It would be the third and last commission the Dallas orchestra would extend under the leadership of its conductor, Antal Doráti. Doráti came to Dallas at the invitation of John Rosenfield, music critic of the *Dallas Morning News*, who was trying to persuade a number of influential businessmen to revivify the then-moribund organization. As a condition of his coming, Doráti insisted not only that the regular concerts feature contemporary music—his inaugural concert included *Prayer in Time of War*—but also that the orchestra commission one composition a year. Doráti reflected on Schuman's offering.

> Schuman gave us his Sixth Symphony, a complex, fine piece, its rich texture laid out in and woven across one huge movement. It was experimental enough to tax our young orchestra to its limits, but with assiduous rehearsals we mastered it—as I like to recall—rather brilliantly.[18]

At the time of the premiere, Schuman obligingly agreed with Doráti's recollection. "I'm very happy with everything. . . . No composer could ask for a better premiere."[19] But the politesse voiced among the Dallas doyennes quickly fell away after Schuman left the Lone Star State. For starters, the performance there added eight minutes to the length of the symphony as Schuman had imagined it. Schuman would later cut five bars from the end of the symphony, but that cut cannot explain why the Dallas performance clocked in at well over a half hour.[20] The reason for the bloated performance was simple, as Schuman recalled two years after the premiere: "The players in the Orchestra were for the most part of considerably less than outstanding ability." Schuman did not doubt for a moment that the men worked assiduously, but their playing was far from brilliant. "They tried hard and Doráti was most cooperative, but somehow the work missed fire. . . . [The audience] found the Symphony utterly without appeal. In fact, some were so incensed over the work that they questioned whether they should even complete payment of the commission."[21] Rosenfield knew that this would be the case, and the first three paragraphs of his review recited the fulminations that composer Carl Maria von Weber had voiced in 1807 against Beethoven's Fourth Symphony (one of the works on the program in Dallas), thus showing that such misunderstandings peppered the history of music criticism.[22]

The befuddlement that greeted the Sixth Symphony in Dallas can also be traced to the other two works that Doráti introduced in earlier seasons. Those works were, according to Doráti, completely without controversy, and for good reason: Hindemith's Symphony Serena (1946), "a charming, intriguing game of sounds"; and Piston's Suite no. 2 (1948), "patterned on baroque forms, a well-conceived, craftsmanlike but unremarkable work."[23] Schuman's symphony is magnitudes more difficult for performers and audience alike than either the Hindemith or the Piston. Schuman himself seemed initially to understand that something lighter befitted the occasion, as his original conception of the Dallas work envisioned a suite of pieces—he referred to them as a divertimento—that, by late July 1948, he had abandoned and may have destroyed.[24] So both the audience and the composer—and perhaps the conductor—were anticipating something less weighty than the work Schuman unveiled.

Schuman's thoughts during 1948, though, were on weighty matters. Beyond the challenges that Juilliard faced, beyond the tensions that arose between him and his associates surrounding Israel, beyond the joy and sadness that he experienced within his immediate family, there was yet another encounter that seemed to affect Schuman in profound ways. During the 1947–48 school year, Sarah Lawrence had the privilege of having the English poet, novelist, and essayist Stephen Spender as a guest lecturer. Joining Spender in Bronxville was his wife, pianist Natasha Litvin. The Spenders and the Schumans became friends, and the letters from Spender to the Schumans suggest that the friendship was particularly warm. The two men talked about the possibility of setting some of Spender's poems to music. Spender even wrote out two of them by hand and signed them:

Stephen Spender for William Schuman
April 1948

Stephen confided that Bill and Frankie "have really made a great difference to our visit to America and we appreciate this particularly because we know how very busy you both are." Natasha gushed that "we both feel more at home & happy chez Schuman than anywhere else in America" and dreamt of the summer of 1949 with the two couples cavorting "chez Spender by the English see" [*sic*]. And after the Spenders had decamped from Bronxville, Stephen felt compelled to apologize to Frankie for not getting together before their departure. Once again, he reiterated his devotion to the Schumans.

> I can take the opportunity to tell you how tremendously grateful Natasha and I were to you and Bill. I realize how difficult it is to have any friendships when one is leading a busy life. Further reason we appreciated and understood the devotion, in addition to the warmth, which Bill and you showed to us. It meant a very great deal to us both and is among the things which have touched me most closely in America.[25]

There are no surviving letters from either Bill or Frankie to the Spenders, and the reunion on the English shore never took place. But given Spender's virulent antifascist writings and activities, his public affiliation with and public abandonment of the Communist Party, and his soon-to-be published essay in the anti-Communist collection *The God That Failed* (1949), Spender and Schuman likely talked about their shared ideological perspectives and predilections. The clampdown on writers and musicians under Andrey Zhdanov in the Soviet Union was also playing on the world's stage—the purge aimed at Shostakovich, Prokofiev, and others began in February 1948—and despite his mixed feelings toward Soviet music, Schuman would have found the forced adoption of an aesthetic style to be inimical to his understanding of the artistic impulse. In other words, Spender and Schuman came into each other's life at a time of great portent in the world of ideas and culture.

For Schuman, the fruit of this time of great artistic ferment was the Sixth Symphony. Having abandoned the divertimento idea midsummer, he somehow found time throughout the rest of the year to work on the symphony. His letters reveal little of the compositional process, but he did divulge his enthusiasm for the new work to his nephew John Fitch. "I am now composing Symphony No. 6 and, if you will forgive an understatement, let me assure you it is a knockout!"[26] He also informed Koussevitzky of his progress on the work. "In whatever spare time I have been able to manage from the School I have been hard at work on my Sixth Symphony which I anticipate completing by early January. I look forward to seeing you at your next New York concerts and hope that I may have the pleasure of a visit with you."[27] Whether he showed the work to

Koussevitzky that January is unknown, but Schuman did manage to complete the score on December 31, which prompted him to write on the final page of the manuscript: "Happy New Year!"

That such a bleak musical statement—Robert Sabin described the Sixth as "a requiem for the twentieth century"[28]—could receive such a fizzy send-off demonstrates the detachment that Schuman often brought to the compositional process: writing music was more an exercise of craft than a realization of an emotion or affect. When Karl Miller invited Schuman to reflect on the deeper meaning behind the work, Schuman demurred. "I remember asking him what he was thinking about when he wrote it," Miller said. "He was reluctant to reveal such thoughts and simply replied, 'The melody came to me and I was on my way.' I pressed the issue some, and the more we talked the more I sensed he preferred to let his music speak for itself."[29] In terms of its formal construction, Schuman said little about why he cast the piece as an extended one-movement work, though the Sixth appears to have four clearly delineated sections framed by a slow prelude and postlude—what Schuman referred to as "two great big anchors at the beginning and end"—that share musical material. Schuman did choose, though, to talk about the concept of the one-movement symphony, provocatively comparing the form to a play he and Frankie attended early in their courtship.

> The purpose of the one-movement thing is not only to say what you have to say in a single utterance, but it is also like an act of a play. It's like going to the theater and have [*sic*] a continuum for an hour and a half; or Eugene O'Neill's *Mourning Becomes Electra* where you go out for dinner and come back two hours later to finish the play. . . . I think the principal problems with a one-movement symphony are those of form and audience interest. I think the particular reason for doing it is that you have materials that you do not wish to be interrupted, your musical invention just goes on and you want to do a whole evening's play or a half-hour symphony without an intermission.[30]

Theorist Richard Pye has exhaustively examined the Sixth, which he considered "music representative of an American symphonic tradition largely uncharted in the analytical literature"; in doing so, he has opened a wide window by applying techniques on Schuman's musical language that are used to understand the music of the Second Viennese School.[31] His analyses highlight the importance of the major-minor sonority that opens and closes this work, which Peter Dickinson called "[Schuman's] own type of tonic."[32] Indeed, the triad inflected by a fourth note appears in various guises throughout Schuman's career (cf. the major-minor sonority at the opening of the Eighth Symphony, 1962; the minor triad with the added minor sixth at the end of *A Song of Orpheus*, 1961; the viola embroidery on the final A-minor chord in the *Concerto on Old English Rounds*, 1973). Here in this symphony, the "tonic" triad gives a sense of harmonic underpinning, but throughout the work Schuman deflects all sense of harmonic arrival. Melodic motives, rhythmic gestures, and timbral effects appear and return in altered form, recognizable and unfamiliar at the same time, with the variety splayed across its half-hour canvas with such skill that Miller concluded that, for him, it "remains a high point in [Schuman's] creative output, one of the most profound expressions in 20th Century orchestral literature. I know of no other work quite like it."[33]

A survey of other American symphonies composed in the 1940s confirms Miller's observation. One-movement symphonies are oddities, with only a handful of American composers engaging in the form (most notably Harris in his Third, which may have been inspired by Schuman's one-movement Second). Equally odd, especially after the successful prosecution of World War II, are symphonies that end not with a bang but a whimper, as does the Sixth. The high-octane conclusion of Blitzstein's *Airborne Symphony* or the stirring reinterpretation of the *Fanfare for the Common Man* in the finale of Copland's Third (both 1946) mark these works as paeans to America and its victory. Schuman's first postwar symphony, in contrast, ends in disquiet, and its musical materials, while quintessentially Schumanesque, are deployed in ways that set them apart from the brash works he composed earlier that seem to wear proudly their American provenance. Its "Mourning Becomes Electra" seriousness, its musical homecoming thwarted by figures hunted and haunted, set this symphony apart from most of the other symphonies of its day, with the possible exception of two other works that sketch a similar musicodramatic trajectory: Bernstein's Symphony no. 1 (1942), which recounts the woes of the prophet Jeremiah; and Hanson's Symphony no. 4 (1943), written in memory of the composer's father and subtitled "Requiem." (In 1944, Hanson's symphony won the second Pulitzer Prize in Music.) Both the Bernstein and the Hanson symphonies are multimovement works; both use descriptive titles for each movement (Prophecy, Profanation, and Lamentation; Kyrie, Requiescat, Dies irae, and Lux aeterna); both start and end quietly. Their programmatic caste colors Schuman's nonprogrammatic Sixth. Knowing those works, knowing what was going on in the larger world, and knowing what was going on in Schuman's own world, it is difficult not to hear the Sixth as a rumination on events public and private, regardless of Schuman's intentions and wishes. One may also join Schuman's colleague Vincent Persichetti in a less imaginative impression of the work. Prior to heading off to Dallas, Schuman invited Persichetti over to sample the new work. Persichetti wrote to thank Schuman for the soirée. "The Sixth Symphony evening was a wonderful one. Tastes of the music keep coming back. I don't think you realize how packed with music it is. The Sixth is a big one."[34]

The Sixth also became something of an Ormandy staple. Hans Heinsheimer, head of the symphonic and operatic divisions of G. Schirmer, sent the conductor the score of the symphony while Ormandy was in Europe during the summer of 1949. In his letter, Heinsheimer offered Ormandy the Philadelphia and New York premieres of the Sixth. Ormandy's blunt and forthright response serves as an example of the kind of interactions he would have with Schuman. Instead of the mutual deference Koussevitzky and Schuman showed each other, Ormandy would be direct and, at times, slightly cruel and occasionally misleading.

> The Schuman 6th Symphony looks very good to me. It has only one fault—it was commissioned by an orchestra which also commissioned a work by Hindemith which I intend to play this year. For this reason, I would prefer asking Mr. Schuman to give me a first performance on a new work, if he has one. Otherwise, I am afraid I would have to postpone the performance to the following season. Had I received your letter, which went astray, I would naturally have chosen Schuman's 6th Symphony.
>
> With best wishes, and hoping to hear from you about the premier [*sic*] of a new Schuman work.[35]

What Ormandy failed to state, and what would prove to be an almost insurmountable hurdle for the next ten years, was the fact that the Philadelphia Orchestra had no funds for commissioning new works and that none of its benefactors would come forward (as they had in Louisville) to underwrite a commissioning venture. Ormandy wanted a new work for free, believing that his reputation and that of the orchestra provided sufficient compensation to the composer. Schuman believed otherwise, and though he eagerly sought out Ormandy to play his works from this time forward, he hedged when it came to writing a new work for Ormandy, expressing his sincere wish that the Philadelphia Orchestra would indeed introduce one of his compositions while at the same time waiting for the allocation of funds that would make such an enterprise remunerative. Until that day arrived, both Schuman and Ormandy profited from their mutual admiration for each other's talents.

The Sixth Symphony acted as a lodestone for their correspondence for much of the early '50s. Having been assured premieres on the eastern seaboard—Ormandy indicated he would take the work to Baltimore and Washington, D.C., as well as Philadelphia and New York—Ormandy chuffed at the news that a Naumburg recording prize had been given to Schuman's Third Symphony. He accused Schuman of being unhelpful in the matter of recording and suggested that he direct the Naumburg jury to change its decision to allow "an authentic and fresh performance of your *latest* opus." Schuman had to remind Ormandy that the jury was independent and that in no way could he contravene its verdict, so Ormandy reluctantly agreed to perform and record the Third Symphony during the 1950–51 season and to release himself from the first performance of the Sixth should Schuman wish to have another orchestra present it in the East. Schuman bided his time; he wanted Ormandy.[36] Ormandy meanwhile persuaded Heinsheimer and Schuman to allow him to present the work in September 1951 with the Danish National Symphony Orchestra.

> The Orchestra was in near-revolution. But I finally calmed them down and then, with 5 intensive rehearsals, we gave the first European performance of your Sixth Symphony. . . . There were several mistakes (bars missing, etc.), but everything went well last night. The audience was more than cordial and even the Orchestra began to like it at the end.

Schuman wrote to thank Ormandy not only for the news but also for the recording of the Third, which had been released that summer. As to the Sixth, Schuman understood the feelings of the Danish musicians; after all, he had experienced some of those same feelings in Dallas. "Frankly, I know that the work presents formidable problems both in performance and listening, but I have every confidence that these same problems will not seem so formidable years hence. At any rate, I feel most fortunate in having your warm support as a colleague and a friend."[37]

To help him prepare for the Philadelphia performance of the Sixth, Ormandy sent Schuman a recording of the Copenhagen performance, explicitly stating that he was aware that it was not an ideal representation of his concept of the symphony. Schuman was nevertheless profoundly moved.

> Your understanding of my music and the miraculous results that you achieved with an orchestra not always able to come up to your standards of execution have my unqualified admiration. Quite honestly, since the death of Koussevitzky, I have felt rather lost on the conductorial front because there seemed to be no one with real conviction about my music demonstrated through consistent performance. I now feel that I have such a conductor in you, if you want to play the part.[38]

Ormandy never answered Schuman's invitation with words. But in addition to the Third Symphony, he went on to record the Sixth and Ninth Symphonies, *Credendum*, the *New England Triptych*, and the Variations on "America."

Ormandy's advocacy for Schuman's music did not always meet with the approval of his audience, as evidenced in one "fan letter" he shared with Schuman.

> I wish to register a protest against any more works of Mr. William Schuman if they sound anything like that Symphony No. 6 which you and the orchestra performed, albeit admirably, last night in Carnegie Hall. What a waste of a good orchestra, and what a long time to make people feel ugly! One half hour—and not a beautiful bit of music in the whole business.
>
> The first part was all out of tune, and sounded like prisoners enroute to the mines in Siberia. Then the barnyard got loose, with quacks and clucks, and after awhile the war in Korea got really under motion, crazy intervals—supposed to be hung together from the sides of a bridge.
>
> If that had been the last thing on the program, I should have left and been home earlier. We were glad we have not heard the first five of the symphonies, if they are in a similar vein.
>
> Poor Juilliard School![39]

Ormandy and Schuman had a good chuckle over this woman's missive. Schuman's response to another opinion about the Sixth merited a more heartfelt response. Roger Sessions had been sent a score of the symphony for examination at Schuman's behest, but Schuman, in the rush of business at Juilliard, had forgotten all about it. Sessions, who had been the lone dissenting voice for giving Schuman the prize for the Second Symphony, sought to atone in a six-page handwritten letter for what he now felt was an error on his part.

> I like the Symphony immensely, and shall grab most eagerly at any chance to hear it. . . . Your Symphony convinced me once more that you are one of the leading composers of your generation. . . . The symphony is music towards which I feel especially sympathetic and with which I find a readier contact than I have felt with some of your earlier music. Either you have grown tremendously, both in the power of your ideas and the mastery of your means; or else I have come closer to your music. In any case I am sure that your music is much more personal, and its impact is more forceful than it has been in other works I have known or heard. Your full power punches and the music speaks more directly.
>
> . . . The Symphony impresses me tremendously—I shall send it back to Schirmers tomorrow with real regret, and will miss having it.[40]

The sentiments of the Carnegie critic, however, were more widespread than those of Sessions, and the history of the Sixth in the 1950s makes it appear that the work was jinxed. The management of the Philadelphia Orchestra tried to interest the cities on its February 1952 tour in the Sixth; not one chose the symphony, so the management sent the rented parts back to G. Schirmer. Some years later, Bernstein would similarly drop the Sixth from his 1958 South American tour because the audiences weren't receptive, the orchestra couldn't keep the work in their bones with so much time intervening between performances, and the altitude of Quito and La Paz made playing it nearly impossible for the brass section.[41] The challenges in getting the work recorded also provide a case study of the intersection of arts and business, as complications arose because of Schuman's decision to leave ASCAP and join Broadcast Music Inc. (BMI), ASCAP's upstart rival in handling performing rights for musicians, Ormandy's policy not to repeat works in consecutive seasons, and Columbia Records' desire to save money. Out of desperation, Schuman was prepared to turn to the New York Philharmonic and Mitropoulos just to get the work on vinyl, but Ormandy and Columbia finally came through late in 1953, and the Philadelphia Orchestra recording of the Sixth stood for nearly a half-century as the only commercially available recording of what many consider to be Schuman's finest work.[42]

Schuman and Ormandy agreed among themselves that the Philadelphia Orchestra would have the opportunity to introduce Schuman's next orchestral score, which Schuman hoped to deliver in time for the 1953–54 season. "I have no idea when I will feel ready to tackle another symphony, but I do know that the answer to your request for the first crack at No. VII is a wholehearted, enthusiastic yes."[43] As it happened, Ormandy's only premiere of a Schuman work—the Ninth Symphony—took place in the 1968–69 season, though in a manner of speaking, Ormandy did have the first crack at the Seventh Symphony, which was premiered by the Boston Symphony Orchestra in the fall of 1960 under Charles Munch. It just wasn't called the Seventh Symphony when Ormandy saw it.

On New Year's Eve 1958, Ormandy wrote to Schuman to inform him that the Academy of Music—an administrative branch of the Philadelphia Orchestra—had set up a commissioning arm and that the very first commission was being offered to Schuman for a work "between 8 and 14 minutes in length and it should be an opener, a symphonic poem, or a closing number," to be performed at the Academy's anniversary gala on January 23, 1960. Ormandy, moreover, wanted Schuman to deliver the work by May.[44] Schuman, for his part, had a longstanding agreement with the Boston Symphony to provide a work for its 75th anniversary and was already late in fulfilling that commission, but he eagerly set it aside for the Philadelphia work, stipulating that he could not possibly complete it any sooner than early September. By April, word came back to Schuman that, given the rest of the gala program, he needed to plan on a shorter, rather than a longer, piece; since Schuman had not written a note by that time, he voiced no objection to the stricture.[45] He, however, seemed to forget that he agreed to this time limit, for in late June he wrote to George Rochberg, then director of publications at Theodore Presser Music Publishers, that the work was "in the neighborhood of ten or twelve minutes and I am not sure yet what the title will be. It is something like Fanfare, Aria and Dance. Perhaps the language mixture isn't very attractive and I will think of something better."[46] Mid-July found him sending two of the three movements to the copyist, thinking that he would not be sending "the last section to you until shortly after Labor Day, but maybe I am overly pessimistic."[47] He also wrote to Ormandy.

> The work is two-thirds complete and I feel impelled to send you a progress report. It will be called:
>
> CELEBRATION CONCERTANTE
> I VIGOROSO
> II CANTABILE-INTENSAMENTE
> III SCHERZANDO BRIOSO
>
> The work I hope will please you, but I certainly know that you will be happy to learn that I am sticking within the time requirements that you originally projected for me (eight to fourteen minutes). Number I is three minutes long; Number II is five minutes long. The third piece will also be five minutes as I now envision it—hence that entire work will play about thirteen minutes.[48]

Frankie insisted that they take three weeks' vacation, so he did not complete the final movement until late September. Then, because of complications with the copyist, the score for the *Celebration Concertante* did not reach Ormandy until early November. Considering that he had wanted it much earlier, Ormandy could not have been pleased with this delay, and upon receiving the score, he sounded the alarm.

> It is like all your works–uncompromising. Whether it is the kind of work our socialites will appreciate is another matter, and the answer to that question will be learned at the performance. I am sure they had something more festive and melodic in mind, but as long as your piece turned out to be so fine musically we will just simply have to take the chance that the audience, 50% of whom are not the real music lovers in Philadelphia, will like it.[49]

Ormandy later wrote that, should it go on the program, it would have to open the concert, whereas Schuman felt it should not kick off the festivities. Further complications between the Academy and Presser about the performance fee led the orchestra manager, with Ormandy's full knowledge, to threaten not to put the piece on the gala program. Schuman was livid, as was clear in a letter he wrote to his publisher: "I am now so disgusted . . . that I hope we get the piece back and that they do not perform it. The heart has gone out of me where their performance is concerned."[50] Ormandy granted Schuman his wish, but he also suggested that the Philadelphians perform it at a regular concert in the 1960–61 season. By the time Ormandy had made his proposal, Schuman had already made his own decision to recast the commission into something else, as he told Rochberg.

> I am hard at work on an opening movement which when added to the former CELEBRATION CONCERTANTE will become Symphony No. VII. . . . The movements will stand and all we will have to do is to change page numbers and title. It is my hope that the muse will work overtime and that the new movement I am composing will be completed before spring.[51]

A look at the vellum for the Seventh Symphony bears all this out: the second movement of the symphony is numbered "Page 1," even though the first movement is 26 pages long; the third and fourth movements continue the sequential numeration begun in the second movement; and the original date on the last page—September 13, 1959—is scratched out and in its stead Schuman wrote "Spring 1960."[52] The music itself also reveals its original performers and purpose. The orchestration for strings alone for the "Aria" movement takes advantage of the Philadelphia sound that Ormandy, a violinist himself, made famous. And the heraldic "Fanfare" (featuring the brass) and the sprightly "Dance" (with its emphasis on the woodwinds) emphasize the other choirs of the orchestra—the concertante element of the title—as well as the celebratory nature of the gala concert (see, e.g., the work's blazing E♭ major conclusion). Schuman changed nothing in the three movements of the *Celebration Concertante*; he simply made them serve as the final three movements of the four-movement Seventh Symphony. Schuman returned to the Academy of Music the $1,000 commission he had received, a fee more than one-third less than his typical commission for such a work; he was doing this as a favor to, and out of appreciation for, Ormandy and the orchestra. Nine years would pass before Ormandy would get a world premiere from Schuman. And Ormandy never performed the Seventh Symphony with the Philadelphia Orchestra. (Lorin Maazel led the work with the Philadelphians in the winter of 1968 as a guest conductor.)

Though their correspondence cooled somewhat in the immediate aftermath of the *Celebration Concertante*, Schuman and Ormandy soon returned to their letter-writing ways and continued to stay in touch over the next 20 years. Schuman enjoyed Ormandy's "warm support as a colleague and a friend" even when the warmth turned incendiary, as it would around the acoustic problems with Philharmonic Hall at Lincoln Center. And Ormandy persisted in wanting Schuman to send him new works for first performance without having to commission them.[53] Ormandy was never a friend of Schuman's the way that Copland and Bernstein and Morton Gould were friends. They were friends the way that Schuman and Koussevitzky were friends. And that seemed to suit them both just fine.

Whether the two men ever talked about their common Jewish heritage cannot be determined from the letters. Neither man seemed to traffic much in that heritage. Upon Ormandy's death in 1985, "at his wife's request he was buried in the Old Pine Street Churchyard, Pine and Fourth Street, in his beloved Philadelphia."[54] Schuman would do Ormandy one better by being cremated and not having any religious identification attached to his death. Religion and ethnicity were not their point of contact. Their common heritage was music, and despite their occasional clashes, the two men worked together to serve that heritage from the 1950s through the '70s, just as Schuman and Koussevitzky did in the '40s. Younger conductors, most notably Leonard Slatkin and Gerard Schwarz, would pick up where Ormandy left off, just as Ormandy picked up where Koussevitzky left off. But Schuman was blessed to have two staunch champions for the better part of his creative life, one who helped to establish Schuman as a composer of the first rank, and the other who helped to disseminate Schuman's music throughout the world.

SEVENTEEN

DELAYS AND DIVERSIONS

Those who worried about the work at Juilliard cutting into Schuman's time as a composer must have been heartened by the stream of major works that he produced in the first five years of his presidency there, including three dance scores, a symphony, and a concerto. The next five years, however, were not nearly as successful in terms of compositional output or esteem. And the entire decade, 1945–55, when considered as a whole, had more than its share of strikeouts and squeeze plays for Schuman. Near the end of these ten years, Schuman suffered one of his greatest setbacks. It didn't come in the concert hall, however. It came as a virus.

Just before he assumed the Juilliard presidency, Schuman exchanged a series of letters with officers of the Michigan School Band and Orchestra Association. Early in 1945, both Schuman and fellow composer Morton Gould gave presentations in Ann Arbor to the association's membership, and the educators were so thrilled by what Schuman and Gould had to say that 60 of them signed a pledge promising "to purchase at the time of publication one band arrangement each of an original composition to be written by Mr. Gould and you."[1] In March, Schuman set the terms for a work he hoped to deliver by November 15. "My present plan is to write a six-minute overture. Do you like this idea, or do you have any other suggestion that you would care to send on? I know now that I will not get to composing until after the premiere of my new ballet next month."[2] *Undertow* premiered on April 10, 1945, and shortly after that Schuman was plunged into negotiations between G. Schirmer and the Juilliard School of Music. When the association from Michigan inquired again in September about his progress on the band piece, Schuman fessed up.

> Perhaps you have heard that beginning next month I am assuming the presidency of the Juilliard School of Music. I need hardly tell you that the last three months have been a series of endless meetings and discussions. During this period of turmoil, I have tried very hard to compose a band piece and actually have made several starts, but

> nothing that I have hit upon so far represents my best effort. Inasmuch as I can't be satisfied with anything less, I must wait for a period of some leisure. I assure you that this is the next piece on my composing agenda, and that I will try my best to have it for you by the spring of the year.[3]

One of those false starts may be the *Fanfare, Song & Dance*, an undated 70-measure fragment for band, one of whose unusual features is a sustained B♭ in the brass that is held for 25 measures and carries the notation "Breathe at different places to sustain unbroken sound." Clearly the long-held trumpet C in the Second Symphony had not completely been expunged from Schuman's compositional palette. Equally clear is the realization that, at the outset, Schuman was preparing this work for publication, as the first page contains instructions to the engraver. (Though the titles are similar, this fragment was not recycled into the "Fanfare, Aria, and Dance" that became the *Celebration Concertante*.)

Whereas Gould managed to complete his Ballad for Band the following year, it would take Schuman five years before he would return to his band piece. It was not the next work on his agenda, and he acknowledged his oversight in a January 13, 1950, letter to Edwin Franko Goldman, founder of the Goldman Band and Schuman's traveling companion, along with Gould, to the Ann Arbor gathering in 1945.

> The piece for band, which I am now in the process of finishing, is being written for schools and is called "George Washington Bridge." I hope you will consider it a good work. I will send you a copy the moment it is available which should be by the first of June. The premiere, I rather suspect, will have to take place in Michigan, since this piece is the direct result of the idea discussed there some five years ago when you, Morton Gould and I appeared at their biannual discussion. Remember? The plan was for a number of schools to get together and ask a composer to write a piece for them. This work is my belated answer to that request.[4]

How and why Schuman named the work after the man-made Hudson River landmark is not revealed in any of the extant correspondence, but an undated document contains his early draft of the statement that would eventually appear in the published score.

> GEORGE WASHINGTON BRIDGE
> An Impression for Band
>
> There are few days in the year when I do not see George Washington Bridge. I pass it on my way to work as I drive along the Henry Hudson Parkway on the New York shore. I am no stranger to this bridge for I have known it since my student days when I watched the progress of its construction. Ever since, it has had for me a personality of its own, an almost human personality. And this personality is varied and various, assuming different moods depending on the time of day or night, the weather, the traffic and, of course, on my own mood as I pass by.

> I have waked [*sic*] across it late at night and at midday. I have seen it dimly through the gathering fog and vividly with sunshine upon it. I have travelled over it countless times and passed under it on boats. Coming to New York City by air sometimes I have been lucky enough to fly right over it. It is difficult to imagine a more gracious welcome or dramatic entry to the great Metropolis.[5]

Le Corbusier shared Schuman's affection, calling the George Washington Bridge "the most beautiful bridge in the world. . . . When your car moves up the ramp the two towers rise so high that it brings you happiness; their structure is so pure, so resolute, so regular that here, finally, steel architecture seems to laugh."[6]

On the occasion of the bridge's fiftieth anniversary, Schuman admitted that a sense of loss accompanied his affection for the bridge. "I lived in Englewood and walked across it just after it was opened to pedestrians. . . . I always loved it, though I also loved the ferry, so I had mixed feelings for a while."[7] But near the end of his life, Schuman reaffirmed his love for the bridge, for bridges in general, and for comely bridges in particular. He expressed a fondness for another bridge associated with Washington, oddly enough the Tacoma Narrows Bridge, which earned the sobriquet "Galloping Gertie" because of the wind-driven oscillations that led to its collapse four months after it was opened in 1940.

> I like bridges to begin with. In contradistinction to tunnels, which I hate. I feel claustrophobic in a tunnel, I don't like being in a tunnel. . . .
>
> I got into a conversation with a man who told me he built bridges. I said, "How exciting and how wonderful. I would certainly hate to be the man who built that bridge that just [collapsed]. . . . He said, "Well, you're looking at the builder." I thought that was a beautiful bridge. I think it was the same as the Whitestone bridge, which I also think is beautiful, and the Throg's Neck. I think those are beautiful bridges, and the Golden Gate is a beautiful bridge. I think there is something about a bridge that's just so exciting. It's so graceful, it's a living organism to me. I think about a bridge the way I think about a railroad. I love railroads. I think of bridges in that same genre.[8]

Frederick Fennell, the esteemed conductor and founder of the Eastman Wind Ensemble, wrote to Schuman upon the occasion of Fennell's performance of the work in the summer of 1952. The repertoire for wind ensemble was still relatively thin, and Fennell would have an outsized effect over the next decades in improving the number and quality of that repertoire. Even so, at this early date, he recognized the nature of Schuman's achievement: "This is without question one of the few good works for band."[9] A few months later, he reinforced his point. "This piece has become so much a part of my life that I cannot speak in a detached way about it. . . . We are endeavoring to establish a repertory that the Wind Ensemble will record for Mercury Records in the Eastman Series and I insist that the *Bridge* be on that first LP."[10] It was on Fennell's first-ever long-playing record, whose potential influence Fennell likened to that of the Gutenberg press. After such a presumptuous comparison, Fennell explained what he had in mind.

> I am reminded of an incident concerning a rather well-known man, who shall be anonymous, who declared upon the first reading of your piece that he did not understand it from the first chord. I believe that if there are those who will take the time to hear a good performance such as we put on records, that we can have some chance of adventuring in the schools beyond the safe confines of what is know into the adventurous areas of the unknown and unexperienced.[11]

Those first bitonal chords—B♭ major/C major followed by E♭ major/G major—and their transpositions and permutations appear throughout the work and yield to a radiant C-major triad at the work's conclusion. The combination of rather mild dissonance sounded by brass and winds and punctuated by percussion provides a sonic cognate for the graceful cable and steel and concrete of the bridge that was begun in 1927 and completed in 1931. As with other quasi-programmatic works by Schuman, there are no one-to-one correspondences, no equivalent to honking taxi horns or braying donkeys on the trail. *George Washington Bridge*, like the Ninth Symphony of 1968, is exactly as Schuman subtitled it: an impression, not a portrait. And as Fennell predicted, it is an impression that has been heard and played by thousands upon thousands of high school and university wind ensemble players, in no small part because of Fennell's championship of the piece.

A far more modest effort on Schuman's part was the anthem he wrote for men's voices at the behest of Marshall Bartholomew (1885–1978), the founding director of the Yale Glee Club. Schuman and Barty became acquainted during Schuman's tenure as conductor of the Sarah Lawrence Chorus. During the war years, the two ensembles sang together on at least three occasions, including a joint Town Hall appearance in December 1942. Barty had also served as an advisor to the War Department in both world wars; during the Second World War, he carried on a lively correspondence with Harold Spivacke, the same individual with whom Schuman corresponded as he sought to join the Armed Services. Barty and Spivacke considered, together, who was well suited to serve as an Army song leader. Barty had reservations about redeploying veterans from the first global conflict. "They are almost without exception in their late fifties and that is a pretty advanced age for the very strenuous life that a first-class Army song-leader should live. If I had charge of the personnel choice in this matter I should greatly favor men between 35 and 50 on account of their physical advantages."[12] Schuman was a few years shy of Barty's ideal song leader, and there is no documentation that the two men talked about the possibility of Schuman serving in this capacity or of Barty using his influence on Schuman's behalf. But around the time of the Town Hall concert, Barty floated an idea past Schuman. Schuman subsequently wrote to Barty, apparently failing to mention the idea, but Barty brought it up in his whimsical reply. "Thanks for your note of January 18th and you need not apologize for your typing. It is quite original and in the spirit of the time; has a touch of Dali and surrealism about it. . . . Don't forget that piece you were going to write for the Yale Glee Club."[13] It took Schuman three more years to fulfill Barty's request.

Truth Shall Deliver, written for a three-part a cappella men's chorus (tenor, baritone, and bass), is striking on a number of fronts. First is its text from Chaucer, which is subtitled "Ballade of Good Advice." In its remonstrance against vanity, envy, greed, and the like, it points forward to the texts Schuman would later set for the *Five Rounds on Famous Words* (1956, with the fifth completed in 1969). Second is the anthem's clear ternary structure with its reliance upon a refrain, both somewhat unusual for a Schuman choral work. Last is the middle section, in which the three voices move "with precision" (as indicated in the score) in an extended vocal etude of stacked parallel fifths (resulting in major ninths as the outer interval). While not as harmonically daring as *George Washington Bridge*—something that would be difficult to achieve with only three voices—the anthem avoids major triads until the final measures, where Schuman engages in a plagal cadence that, like its counterpart in church hymns, adds a harmonic "Amen" to the stern counsel offered by Chaucer's words.

Barty loved the anthem enough to perform it extensively during his last years with the Yale Glee Club. He took it on tour to Europe in 1949 and the Caribbean in 1951. The latter occasion—and his impending retirement in 1953—led Barty to praise Schuman for the work. "It is a good piece and has the double virtue of an unusually good text. I hope you will have the inspiration to do something else for us before I leave these diggings."[14] Barty would have to be satisfied with the one work, but he may not have known that Schuman also held the work in esteem, if in a slightly different way. At a concert at which the anthem was performed in 1965, Schuman asked the conductor if he would do a favor for him. Schuman related that favor to Frederick Hart, Marion Farquhar's friend and companion. "At the request of the composer, the performance of 'Truth Shall Deliver' is dedicated to the memory of Marion Jonas Farquhar, a distinguished translator who translated the Chaucer into modern English for the work we are about to perform, and who was a close friend of the composer." Schuman felt that, in making this request, "in a small way I have carried out Marion's wish."[15] The exact nature of that wish is a mystery.

Another mystery of sorts—and one of the more unusual near misses for Schuman—is embodied in the Fugue for Strings. He wrote it in a week's time, completing it immediately after he had finished *Truth Shall Deliver*. (The manuscript of the fugue is marked "New Rochelle, May 20–27, 1946"; in a letter to Barty, Schuman indicated that he completed the choral piece on May 20, 1946.)[16] He was pleased enough with this work to write to Claire Reis, who was updating her book *Composers in America* (the previous edition appeared in

1938). He asked her to include the Yale piece and the fugue as new compositions and even anticipated a recording of the latter.[17] Less than a month later, he had second thoughts. "Please delete the listing of 'Fugue for Strings' which I mentioned last time. After hearing the work in rehearsal I decided to withdraw it."[18] The manuscript contains numerous markings in red ink as well as corrections (and one insertion) taped along the edges of the score on smaller pieces of manuscript paper. Most of the corrections concern spelling and ease of reading; none of them is in Schuman's hand. While the harmonic vocabulary of the fugue is very much in keeping with his other works from the time, that similarity is forced upon the subject of the fugue, which is a 12-tone theme. The rest of the work shows no overt signs of serial manipulations, and it ends with A as the tonic pitch, much as it began. Perhaps this early experimentation with a 12-tone row was Schuman's attempt to prove to himself that he could compose a work using some of the latest techniques and still make it sound like his nonserial works. Whatever the reason, the fact that the subject is a 12-tone row is likely not happenstance, as Schuman's experiments with serialism continued into the next decade.

In addition to *Truth Shall Deliver* and the Fugue for Strings, a major work occupied his time, he told Reis. "At present I am composing a 'Concerto for Violin and Orchestra' which is now under way and should be completed by the Fall of the year and therefore safe, I think, to list."[19] Samuel Dushkin (1891–1976), the Polish-born American violinist for whom Stravinsky composed his Violin Concerto (1931) and *Duo concertant* (1932), invited Schuman to write a concerto. The fee—$3,500—was one of the largest commissions Schuman had received to date.[20] And Dushkin's credentials as an advocate for, and performer of, contemporary music augured well for the project. Schuman eagerly looked forward to the collaboration and sought to bring one more collaborator on board: Koussevitzky, to whom he offered the world premiere even before a note of his concerto had been written.[21]

Problems soon beset both the composition and the composer. Schuman had promised Dushkin a finished concerto by October 1946; in mid-May of 1946, he still hadn't written a note.

> This is not the literal truth since I am beginning to develop quite an appealing formal concept: an extended one-movement work in well defined sections of varying speeds and feelings which would emerge in the natural course of musical development. School is coming to a close and I plan to begin work in a few days, limiting my time in the city to just one day a week.[22]

This description of a single-movement work sounds more like the Sixth Symphony than the Violin Concerto, although the first movement of the concerto also fits Schuman's prose. Later, in the midst of his revisions of the work, violinist Isaac Stern suggested that Schuman jettison the second half entirely and give the world the 15-minute first movement as the complete concerto.[23] Schuman rejected the idea, but his revisions demonstrate that the first movement was clearest in his mind from the beginning. (Of the 64 manuscript pages Schuman used for the last of the three revisions, the first movement requires only eight.) At some time during the summer of 1946, Schuman determined that he would write a traditional three-movement concerto. By September, he confided to his Juilliard colleague Beveridge Webster that "I have been deep in the composition of my Violin Concerto, which is still lacking a final movement."[24] The school year would bring composition virtually to a halt, and the entire concerto wasn't completed until July 13, 1947.

Schuman's delay was abetted by his opinion of Dushkin's playing. "Dushkin invited me to come to Town Hall to hear him play. And I was shocked! It was such terrible violin playing—awful!"[25] Schuman's recollection is bolstered by the *New York Times* review of the March 12, 1946, Town Hall recital.

> In general, Mr. Dushkin's recital was disappointing. He is, of course, an experienced musician, and most of his playing is marked by straightforwardness and vigor. However, last night he seemed to have difficulty playing in tune, and the tone he drew from his violin was often scratchy, uneven and forced. Despite rewarding moments scattered throughout the program, the recital was below Mr. Dushkin's proven capabilities.[26]

Why, then, did Schuman write to Dushkin two months later about his intention to work on a concerto that he may have felt Dushkin could not navigate? And why, if not a note had been put to paper, did Schuman not write a work that accommodated whatever skills Dushkin still possessed? There is little documentation between the summers of 1946 and 1947 that touches on the concerto, making it impossible to determine Schuman's rationale in composing a work beyond Dushkin's ability.

Years later, Schuman would recall the evening of January 12, 1947, when he informed Dushkin that he would not allow the violinist to perform the concerto Schuman had written for him.

> I remember it so vividly because we were going to a concert given in Koussevitzky's honor at the Museum of Modern Art, and we both went there, and I said: "Let's go, because I have to talk to you. Why don't we have dinner tonight or something?"
>
> So we went to the bar at the Hotel Plaza on 59th Street, and he ordered a cognac. It was not in a snifter, but it was in a small stemmed glass. I said: "Listen, Sam, this is the most difficult moment of my life in personal relationships, and it will be for you, too, but I can't go on with the Violin Concerto. I know you were a great performer at one time, but no one is going to play it, and this is what I have to tell you."
>
> He got white, and he broke the glass in his fingers. He was so tense that he snapped the stem of the glass. He didn't cut himself. And it was *just terrible*.[27]

The terms of the commission stipulated that Dushkin held exclusive rights to the concerto for three years after its completion. Dushkin held onto those rights, perhaps in the hope that he could master the work's demands. He never did. Schuman said, "I went up and I heard him play it a few times, Dushkin, and he was a wonderful musician. He made some excellent suggestions."[28] But it was Stern who performed the work with the Boston Symphony and Charles Munch on February 10, 1950, some 30 months after Schuman had completed the work. (Dushkin apparently waived his exclusive rights a year prior to the premiere.)[29] Schuman had also hoped to honor him in the final publication with the following words: "This work was commissioned by my friend, Samuel Dushkin, and during the course of its composition I had the advantage of his deeply perceptive musical insight."[30] By the time the work was published in 1960, however, Schuman's words were truncated: "*This work was commissioned by* SAMUEL DUSHKIN."

According to the Boston and the New York critics (the Boston Symphony Orchestra brought the work to Carnegie Hall a month after the premiere), the audience responded coolly to the concerto. Cyrus Durgin of the *Boston Globe* volunteered that he had done some eavesdropping. "Lobby conversation about it at intermission yesterday was probably a good deal more severe than any criticism of it that appears in the morning papers. The plain truth is that apart from the slow movement, the idiom is crabbed and harshly dissonant, and the public just doesn't like dissonance." He continued:

> A more patient and reasoned estimate would take into account the singing slow movement, which in my ears is quite pleasant; the unusual formal structure of the first and third movements, which are subdivided into several sections; the individual and often times powerful scoring of the first movement, and the ingenuity of the long cadenza in that movement. . . .
>
> Yet as pure sound, some pages are ugly, and some freakish, while there are those of much beauty. I can't say I was enthralled by a first hearing, but I would like to hear the score again. . . . Let us hear it again, meanwhile categorizing the Concerto as strongly individual and somewhat baffling.[31]

Things were no different in New York. Audience diffidence led Ross Parmenter in the *New York Times* toward a psychological description of the work as "a study of the individual, as represented by the solo violin, to maintain his integrity and balance—his personal music, so to speak—in the face of a harsh and often overbearing surrounding milieu." Parmenter was on more solid ground as he posited why the music itself may have failed to impress the majority of those who attended the concert.

> One of the factors that may have troubled some listeners was that there were many passages when there seemed to be little relationship between the music the soloist was playing and what was going on in the orchestra behind him. But it seemed the very point of the concerto that there should be disparity between the opposed forces. . . . It was in the more lyrical second movement that the violin part and the accompaniment seemed most in sympathy.[32]

Both Durgin and Parmenter recognized that the original second movement behaves much like many slow movements in concerto, serving as a respite between the high drama of the first movement and the flights of fancy in the third. Schuman himself understood that this movement carried a special appeal. Violinist Rafael Druian wrote to Schuman to ask if he had anything that he might perform on his October 1, 1950, Town Hall recital. Schuman lamented that he didn't have anything at the moment. "If you wish, I will fix up the second movement of the Concerto which could make a very effective short solo piece. It would be listed under its title in the work—'Interlude.'"[33] (Druian instead played William Flanagan's *Chaconne* as the sole American work on the program.)

Schuman's focus, though, was on the last movement. Some of the changes he envisioned apparently came about because of Dushkin, who wrote to Schuman that he was "very glad you are making the changes in the last movement of your Concerto. You know how I have always felt about that and I am now eagerly looking forward to seeing what you have done."[34] Schuman later wrote to Stern to tell him "about my decision to rewrite the entire last movement of the Concerto and to do this at such a time as I really feel fresh toward the work."[35]

That time of freshness fortuitously preceded a summer of sickness. In February 1954, Schuman scheduled the revised Concerto for the Festival of American Music that would take place at Juilliard in 1956, and Stern agreed to appear gratis. Before the summer arrived, he revised much of the last movement. But by June 1954, Schuman was waylaid with hepatitis. The following month he wrote to his copyists, Betty Sawyer and Stanley Wolfe, about his health as well as his work on the Concerto.

> I am sorry to have conked out on you—sorrier still to have done likewise on myself for these precious weeks. I believe, however, that the Concerto for Violin and Orchestra will provide you both with plenty of work. It is also my hope that the muse will not forsake my bed and that I may be able to proceed with the new work that I had planned.
>
> In regard to the Concerto, the following needs to be done:
>
> 1. I am making some revisions in the first movement which will be complete in another few days. I will send a corrected printing of the first movement together with the original tissues. The tissues of the score should be corrected.
> 2. I will inform Schirmer's that either or both of you will be in to pick up the tissues of the parts. The first movement should be corrected and the additional instruments added.
>
> The Concerto was originally in three movements. Since my revision of the third movement, I am deleting the second movement in its entirety and the work will now consist of two movements. The tissues of the new second movement [my secretary] has. Please note that some of the old copied pages have been retained and need not be recopied. My manuscript, of course, needs copying in beautiful script. Parts should also be prepared (all on tissues) for this new movement.[36]

The muse may not have forsaken his bed that summer, but most of his other composition plans—the commission for the Boston Symphony, a work for André Kostelanetz—went out the window. The hepatitis sufficiently sapped his strength that he lost what amounted to a year's worth of composition time. He spent 12 weeks in bed reading a prodigious amount that included "the complete works of Willa Cather, with all those masculine females."[37] And he completed the first revision of the concerto.

The new second movement was now longer than the original first movement and principally exchanged the amount of rhapsodic forgetfulness that permeated the original last movement for more pyrotechnics. The loss of the lyrical six-minute Andantino of the original was somewhat attenuated by the new movement's introduction, but whereas the former is more of an island of repose that finally rested on F major, the introduction features dissonant brass and violin arabesques instead of the long-breathed skeins of melody found in the original second movement. It is also much truncated, lasting less than half as long as the original Andantino before it launches into the finale proper. This abbreviated moment of lyricism is one of the most obvious differences between all three versions. For the third version, which Schuman undertook in 1957–58, he expanded the introduction to the (new) second movement, adding a longer orchestral passage of snarling brass and insistent percussion that comes before the violin enters with a far more lyrical idea than is present in the second version. The complete abandonment of the Andantino, though, strikes me as a miscalculation, and all the more so given its initial favorable impression on the professional critics. (Schuman later incorporated much of the Andantino into the final movement of his *Three Colloquies for French Horn and Orchestra*.)

Another noticeable change from the first to the final version is the concerto's ending. Whereas the old third movement ended with one of Schuman's trademark polytonal blats (a D-major triad over a F bass with an added C in the horns), both the second and third versions end with a pulsating F-major triad. The former comes from the same bleak world as the contemporaneous Sixth Symphony and *Night Journey*; the latter shares the more optimistic conclusions of *Judith* and the works of the 1950s (*George Washington Bridge*, *The Mighty Casey*, *Credendum*, *New England Triptych*, and the *Celebration Concertante*/Seventh Symphony). There is nothing inherently better in one kind of ending versus another kind, but it is instructive that Schuman chose not to preserve the more harmonically challenging original ending when he reworked the movement's materials. (His statement that "some of the old copied pages have been retained and need not be recopied" is ample proof that the final movement recycles older ideas.) Whatever his reasons for these and the other changes, he wrote to Rafael Druian as the third version was still being copied: "I have revised the work for the third time and now feel it is right."[38] Polisi provides an extensive analysis of the final version of the concerto, concluding that "Schuman's extensive editing of the concerto's second movement [*sic*] gave the entire work a focus and passion that merits consideration of the Violin Concerto as one of his most successful and masterfully composed works."[39] Without question, the revisions make the concerto stand apart from nearly all of his other works and conjure up the comments uttered after the premiere of the First Symphony by his professor at Teachers College, who recognized that Schuman preferred to write new works rather than improve old ones.[40] Clearly, the Violin Concerto held a special place in Schuman's creative life, perhaps because the solo instrument was the one he himself played best. A half-century has passed since the final version was premiered. Given how different the first and final versions are, an enterprising impresario may want to place the original and final versions on the same program and let the audience and critics revisit the process that led Schuman to create this remarkable work of focus and passion.

Schuman had three world premieres in 1950: the long-awaited airing of the Violin Concerto; the long-delayed delivery of *George Washington Bridge*; and the almost-postponed presentation of the Fourth String Quartet. Of the three premiere dates, only the one for the quartet was fixed at the time Schuman was given the commission. In his role as overseer of the Elizabeth Sprague Coolidge Foundation in the Library of Congress, Harold Spivacke invited Schuman in May 1949 to write a quartet for a festival to be held nearly 18 months later. Even then, Schuman knew that, because of his many other commitments, he would not have anything ready for Spivacke until the end of the summer of 1950.[41] Schuman was factoring in the composition of *Judith* and *George Washington Bridge*. He did not anticipate the challenges that would arise because of his father. As the summer of 1950 began, he wrote to Spivacke, telling him of the ordeal with his father's accident and the joy with Andrea's arrival. He then talked business with the precision of a drill sergeant.

> To get to the Quartet, the situation is exactly this. The day after tomorrow, June 24, we leave for Martha's Vineyard. I will have six weeks of freedom in which to compose. I will then come to New York for several days and I will be back at Martha's Vineyard for another three weeks of uninterrupted time for composition. It is my hope that within these nine weeks I can produce the work, but one never knows these things for certain. It seems to me that from your point of view you must either withdraw the commission because I have not delivered the music on time, or see what I can do over the summer with an idea of delivering the music before the beginning of October. While I can give you my assurances in terms of the effort I will expend in attempting to produce this work, if you absolutely have to count on it for the Festival, you probably have no choice but to withdraw the commission at this time.[42]

At the time Schuman wrote Spivacke, not a note of the Fourth Quartet had made it to paper. Before Schuman's fortieth birthday on August 4, the entire work was completed.

Tony Schuman offered an extended vision of summers at Martha's Vineyard:

> My mother's aunt Amy (Prince) Charak and her husband Walter Charak, a Boston-area furniture manufacturer, had a wonderful house on North Road nearby. That house had a one-room out-building with cold water and toilet that my parents gradually expanded into a small house with three bedrooms, living room, and eat-in kitchen. The whole house couldn't have been more than 800 sq. ft. if that. But it gave us a base on the Vineyard. We were up there for a month or so each summer, with the Charaks renting the house out the rest of the time. We all have powerful memories of those years, filled with beach, chowder, beach plum jam, fishing from the Menemsha jetty using clams for bait, riding the Flying Horses Carousel in Oak Bluffs, and playing softball on Sunday mornings in Chilmark. It was a big day for me when I graduated from the kids' game to the grown-up game (by then Dad had retired from the game).[43]

His father's recollection of this particular summer is no different. In an uncharacteristically chatty letter to Hans Heinsheimer at G. Schirmer, he recounted the circumstances surrounding the composition of the quartet as well as the summer on the Vineyard.

> I write to you today with a considerable feeling of smugness because I have finished my Fourth String Quartet. I know that you are not interested in anything I write for string quartet since this cannot be acted or sung or presented with lights and handsomely gowned females. But I feel smug because it fulfills my assurance to you that I would be prepared to begin writing for the theatre at age forty. I was forty on August 4 and finished the Quartet on August 3. This photo-finish was in keeping with the composition which went with astonishing speed, so much so in fact that by the time I was composing the last movement I had practically no recollection of what I had written in the first movement and had actually to reread that music in order to compose a movement which would bring the work to what I hope is a logical close. Partly, the reason that I wrote so swiftly was my ardent desire to get on to other things and, partly, because I was in love with writing a string quartet and writing it in the manner in which a composer should be privileged to live more often. This is to say that Martha's Vineyard Island is a wonderland and our life there is nothing short of idyllic. Whether you believe it or not, the truth is that I was never at my desk in the morning later than 7:30 or at the most 8 and was very often there shortly after 6. What is more, I remained at it for five, six or seven hours each day and still managed to get three or four hours out in the brilliant sunshine of the afternoon. So, if the Quartet equals my generally ebullient state of being, it will be all that I could ever hope for.[44]

What makes Schuman's ebullience all the more remarkable is that, on Sunday, June 25, less than 48 hours into the family's stay on the Vineyard, Schuman ruptured his saphenous vein in the first softball game of the summer. "The doctor tells me that it will be a matter of three to six months before my leg is completely well again. I must rest the leg as much as possible and keep iced dressings on it. I can get around only with difficulty and have resigned myself to an even more restful summer than I had planned."[45] Hobbled in body but not in spirit, Schuman began the quartet the day after his injury, and "if it were not interpreted as a slight against the marvelous climate of that wonderland, I would say it was composed in white heat."[46]

Its premiere was similarly feverish. Schuman later apologized to Alexandre Moskowsky, first violinist of the Hungarian String Quartet, for his behavior and demeanor at the time of the premiere, confessing that, given the fact that his father was in the hospital, Schuman wasn't even certain he would be present for the premiere. But even though some of the critics thought that the performance was authoritative, Schuman and the performers felt differently.[47] The Hungarians had a little more than a month to learn the work, and Schuman did not have the opportunity to hear them beforehand. Moskowsky complained about one passage in the last movement that was "all but unplayable"; Schuman agreed, but there was no time to rewrite it before the October 28 premiere. The Juilliard String Quartet gave the work its New York premiere in a performance for the League of Composers two months later.[48] Schuman addressed both problems that he had faced in Washington. Writing to Spivacke, he said that the Juilliard performance was destined to be better than the Hungarian one because "I have had time to work with them and to make a number of important adjustments in tempo and dynamics, in addition to rewriting a dozen bars or so." Those dozen bars included the unplayable ones that Moskowsky identified.[49]

Copland, who heard both the Washington and New York performances, was bowled over by the work. "A composition like the Fourth String Quartet makes one understand why Schuman is generally ranked among the top men in American music. . . . This is music written with true urgency: compact in form, ingenious in its instrumental technique, quite experimental as to harmony." Copland went on to suggest that the quartet marked a turning point in Schuman's oeuvre. "I cannot remember another work of Schuman that strikes so somber a note." (One can wonder whether Copland knew *Night Journey* or the Sixth Symphony at this time.) Copland's review, which he chose to reprint a quarter-century later in *Copland on Music*, was an unqualified rave, praising Schuman for the complex harmonic fabric that "teeters on the edge of the atonal," his "masterful handling of instrumental color and rhythmic ingenuity" ("There is nothing quite like these rhythms in American music, or any other music for that matter"), the instrumental writing that is "idiomatic, and at the same time original," and what he called Schuman's "greatest advance . . . the composer's handling of the formal problem in this work."[50] This was Copland's second—and last—formal review of Schuman's music. The first, of *Pioneers!* (1937), helped to launch Schuman's career. This second one confirmed it.

The Fourth, though, has been slow to establish itself in the quartet repertoire. It is perhaps the most demanding of Schuman's five quartets, for performers and audience alike. The Juilliard String Quartet recorded the work in 1952; no commercial recording of the work has appeared since then. The Juilliard took the work on its European tour in 1955. Raphael Hillyer wrote to Schuman from Copenhagen: "It has been a particular pleasure to find a great deal of interest in American music in each country we have visited. The response to your 4th Quartet has been most enthusiastic and the newspaper response, as in Berlin, has been impressive."[51] Schuman clearly believed in the work and in the music he wrote, so much so that he cannibalized the last two movements for his Eighth Symphony. During much of the 1940s, Schuman wrote pieces and let them be. In the 1950s, he increasingly recast earlier compositions, thus returning to his practices of the mid-1930s. Indeed, with the Fourth Quartet at the vanguard, it is rare to find a large Schuman score after 1950 that does not serve either as musical host or parasite.

The next major work certainly fits this description, as it spawned a set of choruses shortly after its completion and was completely reworked into a cantata for the American bicentennial. Yet *The Mighty Casey*—which Schuman would refer to as "my baseball opera"—stands apart from nearly every major work of Schuman's maturity in one significant way: it was written without a commission. Schuman devoted three years to his first opera, a genre that both enthralled and appalled him for his entire life. The story of Schuman's operatic exploits—from the ancient Native Americans to the actor Glenn Ford—deserves its own chapter.

EIGHTEEN

STRIKING OUT

The number and variety of stories and ideas Schuman considered as possible operas astonish in their scope and seeming haphazardness.

- In 1942, Billy Schuman got together with his childhood friend Marty Goldsmith and kicked around some ideas about turning Homer's *Odyssey* into a libretto.[1] Goldsmith was another one of Schuman's chums who found success in the arts. A few years after his lunch meeting with Schuman, Goldsmith turned his 1939 novel into a screenplay for the classic film noir *Detour* (1945).
- In 1943, Schuman approached Countee Cullen about the possibility of writing a libretto.[2] Cullen, one of the poets Schuman set in his early *Canonic Choruses* and an early and towering figure in the Harlem Renaissance, taught French at Frederick Douglass Junior High in New York City; one of his pupils was James Baldwin. Their slim correspondence does not reveal the subject Schuman had in mind and why Schuman felt the two men could work together. Cullen died in 1946, so their unconsummated collaboration might have been an unfortunate one had their work begun.
- In 1944, Schuman wrote to white southern writer Lillian Eugenia Smith about the possibility of turning her novel, *Strange Fruit*, into an opera. The arranged lunch between Schuman and Smith had to be canceled because of Smith's pressing engagements. Still, Smith sent Schuman a letter detailing her feelings about the possibility.

  > I do want to meet you sometime, not because I am interested in making Strange Fruit into an opera–for frankly I am not–but because I am interested in your work as a composer. . . . As for Strange Fruit as an opera, I don't hear any singing in Strange Fruit. It is too stark, too bitter in its essence, too close to every white and colored person in America today for it to be sung about. And the characters are not types or symbols, but people where roots are embedded in their families, in their culture so deeply, and because so ramifying and complex it just isn't the kind of theme that people can burst into arias about. I do see it as a dance in highly abstract form.[3]

  Schuman was hard at work on *Undertow* at the time.

- In 1945, Schuman persuaded conductor Alexander Smallens to introduce Schuman to playwright Elmer Rice. Schuman, who by that time had won the Pulitzer Prize in Music, hoped to convince Rice that he was the right composer to turn Rice's Pulitzer Prize–winning play *Street Scene* into an opera. Rice demurred, telling Schuman that "I am not sure that it would be wise for me to allow *Street Scene* to be done as a musical play at this time." Rice's letter makes plain the fact that he and Schuman were discussing a work for a Broadway theater and not an opera house, which presented insuperable problems as far as Rice was concerned.

  > The production of a musical play on a commercial basis presents many practical problems that can be met only by people who have experience in this field. I do not have this experience, and I gathered from our conversation that you do not either. . . . I feel it would be essential to the success of the venture to set up a production under the auspices of someone who is thoroughly familiar with the production of musical plays.[4]

  Rice would get his wish when, two years later, *Street Scene* opened on Broadway with lyrics by Langston Hughes and music by Kurt Weill. (Perhaps there is some poetic justice in Weill besting Schuman here, since Billy Rose had originally wanted Weill to write the symphonic music for *The Seven Lively Arts*, but Schuman got the gig.)[5]
- In 1946, after having completed *Aurora Dawn*, author Herman Wouk wrote to Schuman to see if they might get together. "We both were intrigued by the notion of writing an opera, and would lunch together and kick ideas around. I was strong for a Biblical opera, 'I Am Joseph' (Genesis 45:3). Bill wasn't."[6] Wouk then suggested that Schuman see if John Steinbeck would consent to give Schuman the rights to turn *Of Mice and Men* into an opera: "stunning theatre, colorful setting, passionate events, the action limited to a few strongly marked characters—an opera libretto, in a word, much more nearly than even 'Street Scene.'"[7] Schuman responded, using one of his favorite slang expressions: "I think your idea of 'Of Mice and Men' is probably a brilliant thought but not my dish."[8] (It was Carlisle Floyd's, though; his opera based on the Steinbeck novella appeared in 1969.) Wouk and Schuman later discussed whether Franz Kafka's novel *The Trial* could effectively be turned into an opera. They both concurred it could not. "Its principal qualities are certainly literary ones. Despite this, you would be surprised how many people have suggested this work to me."[9] Wouk, a former U.S. Navy officer, also suggested to Schuman that the activity on the flight deck of an aircraft carrier might provide the foundation for a ballet. "It is already a ballet without music, a stirring and slightly macabre dance of men and mortally dangerous machines." Schuman was intrigued but did not carry the idea any further.[10]
- In 1948, Douglas Moore wrote to Schuman to see if he would accept a commission to write an opera. Schuman responded: "As you already know, I have been searching for an opera libretto for something like seven years and have been spectacularly unsuccessful. . . . The medium you have selected for my work involves extra-musical considerations which are to a great extent beyond my control and which oblige me, however reluctantly, to decide negatively."[11]

- Also in 1948, Schuman wrote to his soon-to-be biographer Flora Rheta Schreiber, convinced that she might be drawn to his latest fascination. "You might be interested to know there are only four other examples of composers treating the Oedipus subject listed in the best opera reference book, namely: Sacchini, 1789; Leoncovallo [*sic*], 1920; Stravinsky, 1927; Enesco, 1936; —Schreiber-Schuman, 1956."[12] (The fifth example in the list is Schuman's projected collaboration with Schreiber, one he felt they could bring to the stage by 1956.) It would appear that he envisioned using *Night Journey* as the foundation for a larger dramatic treatment, for three years later he and Schreiber continued to discuss "the Jocasta idea for soprano and orchestra."[13]
- In 1949, his colleague Marion Bauer wrote to him about a brilliant new production of Lorca's *Blood Wedding*. Schuman's libretto search was apparently so well known among his colleagues that Bauer joked, "You will think that I have appointed myself as a committee of one to find you an opera libretto." Schuman wrote back in thanks as well as disappointment, as he was unable to see the Lorca before the production closed.[14]
- In 1954, Lincoln Kirstein sent Schuman a scenario for *Mr. Wind and Madame Rain*. Like *Of Mice and Men*, it was not Schuman's dish, but he did wonder what Kirstein had in mind. "Do you think of it as a ballet, or as opera-ballet?"[15]
- Others would send ideas and librettos Schuman's way (including a suggestion in 1963 that Schuman should read *Death in Venice*; seven years later, Britten began work on his opera based on Thomas Mann's novella).[16] Schuman dutifully read the librettos, but none of them slaked his operatic thirst. In 1965, he wrote to Claire Reis about his never-ending search for the perfect scenario. "Thanks so much for the continuing thoughts of my doing an opera. It all seems pretty far away these days. The truth is, given the choice, I'd rather do a string quartet or a symphony. Isn't that terrible?"[17]

The catalog of ideas and possibilities also includes at least three operatic treatments that Schuman pursued with greater vigor than those above. The first came unbidden, and as with *Street Scene*, Schuman was initially passed over for someone else. Administrators at the Metropolitan Opera approached the Carnegie Corporation of New York in the summer of 1941 with an idea: Would the corporation be willing to provide grants-in-aid to a composer-librettist duo that would shadow the Met for six months? At the time the idea was born, the Met hadn't presented an American opera for six years.

> American opera, if it is to be a valuable addition to the literature, should be born in the Metropolitan Opera House as the outcome of a season spent by composer and librettist in daily contact with the conductors, stage directors, and others familiar with the problems and pitfalls. Roles grow well when conceived for specific performances. Librettist and composer should have the run of the place.[18]

Administrators at the Carnegie Corporation agreed and gave the Met administrators $5,000 to split evenly between the librettist and composer. The Met, now assured of financial support, approached author Christopher LaFarge (1897–1956), whose novel in verse *Each to Its Own* had appeared a few years earlier and favorably impressed the Met administrators. After provisionally obtaining LaFarge's agreement, they then sought out a composer. ("Composers," they had confidently written to Carnegie, "are not lacking.") Their initial search led them first to Samuel Barber and then to Schuman.

In his diaries, LaFarge chronicled the arc of the project, from his initial September 1941 meeting with and impression of Barber ("pretty conceited, but intelligent") and his own intense interest in the project ("Barber or no Barber") to the demise of his collaboration with Barber's replacement some eight months later ("Too bad, very depressed, also steam [has] gone out of me").[19] Barber bowed out less than a month after his introduction to LaFarge, who felt somewhat slighted by the younger composer ("[He] is afraid my work won't inspire him. Too bad.")[20] A month passed before Schuman came on the scene. LaFarge drew some memorable sketches of Schuman in those post–Pearl Harbor days.

> He struck me as energetic, intelligent and sociable—obviously he is although but 31. Been over the bumps enough to know what life is all about & has a good idea of what a collaboration implies. All his questions & statements were forthright & to the point: and we found ourselves in good agreement on almost every major principle involved.[21]
>
> Schuman interesting & fun at lunch. Afterwards he & I talked till 4:30, exploring the ground & arriving at a better knowledge of each other & our possibilities as collaborators. I find we continue to agree on our general principles & approach, which is most heartening. He has, I think, integrity, as well as some humour, and he is not afraid to tackle anything. We agreed at least on one theme solidly (others we left to jell later): that we'd tackle nothing till we found something we could both feel excited about. Both of us rather want to get going, as time may be short, with the war.[22]

For a while, Schuman did hang around the Met along with LaFarge and attended some of the productions there, including the debut of Sir Thomas Beecham in a double bill of *Phoebus and Pan* (J. S. Bach–Picander) and *Le coq d'or* (Rimsky-Korsakov). Schuman also received regular $500 monthly payments from the Carnegie Corporation. (His Sarah Lawrence salary for the 1941–42 school year worked out to $300 per month.)[23] In the middle of the six-month incubatory period, in the middle of the money, Schuman agreed on an idea that LaFarge presented to him: a dramatization of the imagined life of the thirteenth-century American Indian cliff dwellers of Mesa Verde (in modern-day Colorado), with a prologue and epilogue featuring the powerful deeds of the Brother Gods Nayénezgani and Tobadzischíni.[24]

Whatever persuaded Schuman to consent to the development of an idea that was foreign to just about everything he had ever done up to this point in his life, he quickly concluded that he had made a horrible mistake. LaFarge bore witness to Schuman's change of heart and mind.

> I read him part of the opera, which he followed in the typescript. He said then that he was afraid of it: didn't see <u>how</u> he could set it to music or perhaps it was the Indian

> theme that was so alien to him, perhaps, he said further, he just wasn't ready to write or the person to write, an opera. . . . We talked in a circle for a half hour & he left, with the script & said he'd study it & reflect & perhaps try a few bars—the Dam Prayer, for instance.

LaFarge concluded that Schuman at this point was "discouraged."[25] He was also implacable.

> I have reread the first pages you left with me and find that I am in no way moved to make music for this story. Let me again stress the fact that I consider my reactions as a limitation on my part and not on yours. The work is obviously one of high competence, and the language is very moving. The fact that it doesn't "reach me" can only be chalked up, as I say, to some lack in me. Nevertheless, I cannot write an opera with this book, and I know you will agree that it would be suicide to try to force the issue.
>
> I can't tell you how much I regret that our first try should turn out this way because I found working with you extremely stimulating and pleasant. Try not to think too ill of me for turning down this book, but the decision as it stands is dictated by what I am and not what I would wish to be.[26]

In a handwritten note to the Carnegie Corporation, Eric T. Clarke, administrative secretary of the Met and the driving force behind the grant-in-aid program, not only summed up Schuman's decision not to move forward on LaFarge's scenario but also pithily provided two images of Schuman, one of his indecision toward opera libretti in general, and the other of the nation Schuman celebrated at a time when *Rodeo* and *Oklahoma!* were normative: "He just couldn't see La F's book as his meat. (He'd agreed to it some months ago, but I guess composers are much like women and have always the right to change their minds. La F, who's keen on the West, says he fears Schuman is a 'cement-sidewalk' American. Maybe La F was too good a salesman.)"[27] LaFarge, however, laid the collapse of the collaboration squarely at Schuman's feet: Schuman, after all, had green-lighted the Native American story in the first place. LaFarge also deduced that Schuman was no longer interested in working with him on any project, which further depressed him.[28] The administrators of the Met sought to find another composer for LaFarge—Schuman recommended Anis Fuleihan—but nothing more came of *Mesa Verde*.[29]

Schuman was abashed, not the least because he had pocketed $2,500 without having produced a note of music. He wrote to Clarke to assess the situation. Clarke responded:

> What pleases me most about your letter is that you "owe us a work when the right book comes along." I should indeed be sorry had the passing of the season left you disinclined to work in the operatic medium. Actually, you do not "owe" us any opera but if I can be of any help in steering stories your way I want you to be sure to let me know. It will be grand if something operatic emerges from the time you've spent with us no matter how long a period passes before it is ready.[30]

Some months later, Clarke wrote a long letter to the Carnegie Corporation that attempted to justify an opera-birthing program that had failed to conceive an opera. In it, Schuman momentarily grabbed the spotlight in his own epilogue.

> On December 30th Schuman came in, repeated that he felt he owed us an opera, said he'd found a subject, and would now prepare his own libretto and set it to music. All this he thought would take him three years, and what worried him was the question, how to get freedom from his duties at Sarah Lawrence? I told him I knew of no organized philanthropy that made such long-term grants for composition but that there occasionally were rich singers and others who commissioned works, and if any such opening appeared I'd let him know. I have not seem [*sic*] him since and fear he is reaching for a subsidy before committing himself to produce.[31]

The timing of Schuman's visit and of his queries to other collaborators suggests that his idea was one he thought would interest Countee Cullen. So it was that, with his rejection of *Mesa Verde*, Schuman's search for the perfect libretto began.

The other two opera projects that Schuman earnestly pursued came in the midst of his work on what would become his first completed opera, whose genesis is somewhat shrouded in mystery. How did Schuman come to choose an advertising executive as a librettist? One of Schuman's last collaborators, J. D. McClatchy, provided a clue.

> I asked him about Jeremy Gury, the librettist for *The Mighty Casey*. Bill had been discussing with Al Capp an opera on Li'l Abner, and Gury's name was suggested to him. A literary advertising man, he'd done a libretto for Alex North. First, Gury talked Bill out of a cartoon-opera. Bill then mentioned that years before as a camp counselor, he helped put on plays every week for the kids, and dramatized songs. He remembered "Yankee Rose" in particular. He mentioned the idea of Casey, and Gury came up with the text.[32]

Aside from writing a libretto prior to meeting Schuman, Gury had coauthored the children's book *The 'Round and 'Round Horse* (1943). But it was his collaboration with Alex North that was likely the proximate cause for Schuman and Gury coming together. North, who became well known in Hollywood and beyond for his film scores (15 Oscar nominations, including for *A Streetcar Named Desire*, *Spartacus*, *Who's Afraid of Virginia Woolf*? and *Under the Volcano*) as well as for his evergreen "Unchained Melody," was held in high esteem by Schuman, who wrote North a fan letter after seeing *Prizzi's Honor* (1985).[33] In a tantalizing series of coincidences, Schuman served on the editorial board of Young People's Records in the late 1940s and was thus listed in an advertisement for a recording of Douglas Moore's *The Emperor's New Clothes*, a work that "will introduce your child to the delights of the opera, and thrill him with a story that has already enriched the lives of many generations of children."[34]

Around this same time, Schuman traveled from New Rochelle to Manhattan for a 12:30 P.M. Young People's Records board meeting one Saturday in February 1949; that same day, a 3 P.M. matinee of the North/Gury collaboration—*The Hither and Thither of Danny Dither* (touted as "the hit musical for children!!")—was playing uptown.[35] Schuman saw *Danny Dither*, a fact confirmed in an early report on *Casey* stated that "he knew and liked Jeremy Gury's libretto for Alex North's children's opera, 'The Hither and Thither of Johnny [*sic*] Dither,'" and in later life Schuman called the musical "quite attractive."[36] Less than two months after *Danny Dither* ended its brief Manhattan run, Schuman and Gury began to talk about their collaboration.

The letters from Gury to Schuman that survive—among the Schuman papers there are only five letters from Schuman to Gury—show that it took the two men some time before they settled on the story of the slugger from Mudville. Gury may have dissuaded Schuman about turning Li'l Abner into an opera, but Schuman initially seemed drawn to the idea of creating a children's opera of his own. The Aladdin story was considered—"a delightful story wonderfully full of sex symbolism of the most transparent nature; underground caves, secret passageways, huge potency reactions when the lamp is rubbed"—before it was abandoned.[37] Adult-sized stories also crossed their minds. Schuman suggested that Gury read Vardis Fisher's *Children of God*, an epic novel that traces three generations of nineteenth-century Latter-Day Saints from Palmyra, New York, through Salt Lake City to the Mexican border. Gury found it all a bit daunting: "awfully big idea as it is in the book and I'm hoping it will simmer down to a clear set of impressions. Hasn't simmered yet."[38] Even after they decided on Casey, the question arose whether there should be a companion piece to make for a double bill. One idea—variously called "Flight 821," "Westbound Flight," and "Flight 242"—seems to have sprung from an idea Schuman had given to LaFarge about a public-address system at an airport. While Gury sent Schuman a rough sketch for this subject, the idea was also discarded.[39]

Their collaboration wasn't always smooth. Gury once apologized for yelling at Schuman on the phone while at the same time indicating that Schuman's volume had matched his own.[40] Gury also told Schuman not to be afraid of writing something that might end up being as popular as a Sousa march, an indication that Gury may have felt the music was too serious to make for a successful Broadway show. And Broadway clearly was the destination Gury had in mind for *The Mighty Casey*, as he imagined the kinds of aural and visual reinforcement of the story that would have been out of place at the Met of the 1950s.[41]

Schuman similarly had Broadway on the brain. In mid-July 1952, when work on *The Mighty Casey* was fairly far along, he attended the premiere of *Wish You Were Here*, the Catskills-summer-camp-meets-Ziegfeld-Follies musical with a book by Arthur Kober and Joshua Logan and music and lyrics by Harold

Rome. After the performance, he wrote to Saul Schechtman, one of the back-office musicians who was involved with the show and managed to obtain the tickets for Schuman. "We enjoyed the show very much and are sorry that it seems to be unsuccessful. I am enclosing the reviews of the morning papers in the unlikely event that you have not already seen them." Schuman went on to talk about *The Mighty Casey* audition that had just occurred for Alfred de Liagre Jr. (c. 1904–1987) and Donald Oenslager (1902–1975), two legendary producers. According to Schuman, they were "anxious to put it on. They have certain reservations about the leading female role and we are in the process of evaluating this reservation. We are all agreed that it would be better to put the work on at some point distant from New York where we will have a chance to get a look at it and see what we have."[42] Hans Heinsheimer, who ran the Dramatic and Symphonic Repertory Department at G. Schirmer, pitched *The Mighty Casey* to de Liagre as a "musical."[43] This was a time in musical history when numerous works that could be construed as "American opera" were appearing in Broadway theaters: shows by Weill (*Street Scene*, 1947; *Love Life*, 1948, with Alan Jay Lerner; and *Lost in the Stars*, 1950, with Maxwell Anderson), Gian Carlo Menotti (the double bill of *The Telephone* and *The Medium*, 1947; *The Consul*, 1950), Heitor Villa-Lobos (*Magdalena*, 1948), and Benjamin Britten (*The Rape of Lucretia*, 1948). Even the Old Masters—Verdi (*My Darlin' Aida*, 1952), Bizet (*Carmen Jones*, 1953), and Borodin (*Kismet*, 1953)—got some action. The time seemed propitious for highbrow music to be commercially successful on Broadway, but in Schuman's remarks about the new musical, already one can sense his unfamiliarity with the ways of Broadway. The words from the critics were indeed poisonous, but Logan and Rome rewrote the material, Eddie Fisher recorded the title tune, and *Wish You Were Here* went on to run for more than 17 months and racked up 598 performances.[44] Notwithstanding his own love of theater, Schuman's commercial Broadway instincts were untested. *Casey* would also need rewriting, and his vacillation over the proper venue for the work—opera house versus for-profit theater—was also at play in the composition of the work. He said as much to Bernstein.

> I am trying to pour my love for baseball and all that it means into my chosen medium of expression—which is, in case you have forgotten, music. Whether I will succeed is a moot point. My problem seems to be to write a work which I am willing to sign and which is nevertheless sufficiently "available" in terms of musical materials to be understood by the general public. This makes it all strangely fascinating.[45]

Box office draw requires more than strange fascination, as Schuman would discover, but the initial focus on Broadway informs Schuman's decision not to seek a commission for the work at the outset.

The disparity between commercial and not-for-profit venues plagued Schuman and Gury from the start. Schuman wrote most of the opera/musical during the summer of 1951, much of it during his escape to Martha's Vineyard. Gury came to visit him there, and the two argued so vehemently about the dramatic form the various scenes should take that Gury likened their disagreement to a "blood bath." Somehow, they came to see eye to eye on solutions to the problems, and Gury was especially heartened by Schuman's attitude about the nature of the work.

> When you re-defined the problem driving away from the airport saying that the music for Casey must be the best within the framework of its own natural theatrical appeal it was as if a huge dark cloud had suddenly lifted. Therein, I thought, lies greatness—to take a simple, homely, common idea and endow it with a wealth of imaginativeness and originality is what makes good art. And it was then that I felt sure that my office boy friends and ball fans and millions of others would come away from "The Mighty Casey" having had a totally new and wonderful experience. At this point Casey gives promise of reaching out far beyond the chic Menotti audiences and re-creating opera as a mass medium.[46]

Two weeks later, with Schuman still working on the Vineyard and Gury back at his desk in New York, they conferred over the phone, and once again the conversation grew so heated that Gury confessed to being "exhausted from shouting into the phone; the cat is hiding in terror and Lou [Gury's wife] suggested that I was really quite irritating. I had a mental picture of the volume of both our voices being drained off on all those party lines with precious words becoming muted in so many strange ears."[47] But by the fall, the work was sufficiently completed that the men were ready to audition for backers.

Schuman had tried to circumvent the need to go that route. Even before he had made much headway on the score, Schuman sought to give the work's premiere to the Louisville Orchestra. Members and patrons of the orchestra were interested, since short operas were already a part of the orchestra's commissioning project. Discussions went back and forth in the spring of 1951 about when the premiere might take place and how much money it would require. Movers and shakers in Louisville society even contacted the president of the National League to see if Major League Baseball would help to underwrite the work.[48] By the summer of 1951, though, the home of the Louisville Slugger was being passed over as the site for *The Mighty Casey*'s first outing.

Next came Dallas. Doráti had left as conductor of the Dallas Symphony, but Walter Hendl had taken over, and he and Schuman had already considered performing one of his new ballet scores in Texas. Hendl, one of Schuman's former Sarah Lawrence colleagues, had "initiated discussions about a possible *Casey*. General feeling was that [the Texas] State Fair (the big barn) might take it during the Fair Exposition, attended by 2,000,000 people. Either that, which would be strictly professional, or else a semi-pro production with college facilities etc."[49] Hendl had decamped for Europe before Schuman could work out all the details, but he explained to Hendl how the timing of the Dallas performance was important. "My reason for wishing to discuss all this with you is, among other things, my desire to bring you together with the potential producers for New York. My thought is that if all goes well, we might be able to schedule the time for the New York run (hopefully) when you could be here to conduct."[50] Negotiations once again fell apart, and Schuman looked elsewhere.

Hendl's suggestion of "a semi-pro production with college facilities" now became more viable, and the University of Michigan became the object of the opera's affection. The decision makers in Ann Arbor, though, were not speedy in their deliberation, and four months after Michigan expressed interest in the opera, Heinsheimer decided to give the work to Moshe Paranov and the Hartt School of Music in Hartford, Connecticut. The Hartt forces premiered Schuman's baseball opera in early May 1953, almost three years after Schuman finally decided to work seriously on his first opera.[51]

Paranov, in order to fill out the evening, paired *The Mighty Casey* with Douglas Moore's one-act "folk opera," *The Devil and Daniel Webster* (1939), another hybrid work that straddles the line between musical and opera.[52] Moore, whose proposed commission to Schuman to write an opera had come five years earlier, was effusive in his praise of Schuman's work.

> I want to tell you while I am still on the crest how much I enjoyed Casey last evening.
>
> There has never been any doubt in my mind that you were destined to write for the theatre. Your musical personality so vivid and intense, your gift as a choral composer and remarkable individuality with the orchestra all point that way.
>
> In choosing Casey you have taken a subject that you are really hot about and that is what makes communicative opera. The result is a magical distillation of genuine feeling in an American pattern spiced and seasoned by your skill and instinct as a composer. I found it tremendously moving, full of love and tenderness, exhilarating and entertaining. Your feeling for American speech and American behavior is original and genuine.
>
> I love opera more than anything else and to discover a fine new one is an exciting experience.
>
> Warm congratulations to you and thanks,
> Sincerely,
> Douglas[53]

Schuman's response demonstrates his characteristic generosity to his colleagues as well as his undying belief in the need for such "made in the U.S.A." works.

> It was especially nice, I thought, that "Casey" could be teamed up with your "Devil." . . . Your work went exceedingly well last night and will undoubtedly have the same splendid effect tonight when I shall again be there. It is heartening that your work continues to be performed in the repertory and I fully believe that the long run it is scheduled to

> have this summer will do a great deal toward establishing the possibility of using serious American theatre works as standard repertory of opera groups.

Schuman went on to tell Moore how "'Casey' needs work on the first and last scenes and I am already teaming [*sic*] with ideas for this. . . . The experience of writing for the theatre has been a thrilling one and I can't wait to get started on another work, although this time it will be different subject matter."[54]

He had started planning on that other work before *Casey* hit the boards. In December 1951, after he had finished his first version of *Casey* but before he and Gury agreed to some revisions and additions, Schuman wrote to Sara White Dreiser, widow of Theodore Dreiser, about his latest operatic vision.

> Along with much of the civilized world, I have long been a great admirer of the writings of your late husband. It has been my thought for many years to base an opera on "An American Tragedy". Preparation of a libretto to meet the peculiar demands of opera-theatre will entail long study and careful preparation and the selection of a highly gifted writer. This work, together with the composition of a score of major proportions will occupy a minimum period of three to five years. It is my hope that I may have your permission to proceed with this project. I feel confident that when the time for publication and production arrives there will be no difficulty in making satisfactory arrangements.[55]

In his subsequent communication with Mrs. Dreiser's representatives, Schuman stated that "the opera I plan will be on a scale requiring the resources of an opera company such as the Metropolitan. Although I have no way of knowing whether the Metropolitan Opera Association itself will be receptive to the work when it is completed I feel under some obligation to show it to them first."[56] Ten years after he failed to deliver an opera to the Met, he still felt that he owed it one.

By April 1952, negotiations of the terms of Schuman's option on the Dreiser novel had been completed. With *Casey* more or less completed, Schuman's compositional mind turned to this new prospect. "I am beginning to think of the structure of the opera and hope to have enough of an outline ready by next summer to begin searching for a writer. This is no easy task since a highly specialized talent is required."[57] At various points in the project, Schuman contacted or tried to reach: Harold Brown, poet, playwright, and coauthor of the screenplay for *A Place in the Sun* (1951), which was based on the Dreiser novel; Norman Rosten, poet, playwright, screenwriter, and future librettist for Ezra Laderman's opera *Marilyn* (1993); Howard Sackler, who wrote *The Great White Hope* (both play and screenplay); and James Agee, the author of *Let Us Now Praise Famous Men* and *The Morning Watch*.[58] By 1954, Schuman lost interest, though it wasn't until 1965 that he formally relinquished his exclusive rights to produce an opera based on *An American Tragedy*.[59] (Tobias Picker's opera based on the Dreiser novel premiered at the Met on December 2, 2005.)

The proximate reason for Schuman's waning interest in the Dreiser was his waxing interest in another property. *The Last Notch*, a "suspense western" by Frank Gilroy, appeared on television on March 30, 1954, as an episode of the *United States Steel Hour.*[60] Apparently Schuman saw it, because by the end of August he had signed a contract to turn *The Last Notch* into an opera with Gilroy as librettist.[61] The contract did not preclude film rights for the play, so Gilroy turned the work into the screenplay for *The Fastest Gun Alive* (1956), starring Glenn Ford. Gilroy expressed an initial dislike for *The Mighty Casey* that mellowed over time.[62] He certainly esteemed Schuman enough to turn down another organization that sought to acquire the dramatic rights to *The Last Notch*. "I still hope," he wrote to Schuman, "that one day we will be able to get together on the opera. I have an intuition that that will happen. Not for awhile but sometime."[63] It never happened.

Television gave *Casey* its next big break. After the Hartford premiere and despite the deficiencies that Schuman saw in the score, de Liagre was still making plans to bring *Casey* to Broadway for the 1943–44 season.[64] Gury wrote to Schuman, asking him to pass along some brochures to "Delly" (de Liagre) that Gury thought might help the producer raise money.[65] But nothing on Broadway panned out. For some unknown reason, all parties chose to forgo a lucrative option to license the show to Frigidaire, the home appliance manufacturer then based in Dayton, Ohio. The Frigidaire production for the company's employees and Daytonians was projected to reach "a potential audience of at least 25,000."[66] Instead, the next major production of *Casey* would reach more people than the folks at Frigidaire—and perhaps more than de Liagre—could have ever imagined.

Representatives of Ford Motors' *Omnibus* television program came calling in June 1954 to express their keen interest in televising *Casey* the following year. As the date for the March 6, 1955, broadcast approached, Schuman wrote to friends and family, urging them to tune in. De Liagre and Oenslager were invited to watch, as was Richard Rodgers, with whom Schuman had developed a cordial friendship. (Schuman wrote to him, "I happen personally to think that it belongs in the professional theatre. Maybe I should stick to my symphonies.")[67] Rehearsals in the studios, though, caused Schuman great angst. Two weeks before the broadcast, he wrote to composer Louis Gesensway: "Even at this late day the cast has not been finally assembled and I am in something of a tizzy."[68] He apparently lost his cool with *Omnibus* creator Robert Saudek and producer Paul Feigay, sending them separate letters of apology the morning after the opera aired. He also told Saudek that the first wave of letters, telegrams, and phone calls he received had nothing but "praise for the manner in which the work was adapted for television and presented by 'Omnibus.'"[69]

Friends and family continued to toss Schuman bouquets, but the brickbats weren't far behind. De Liagre called the entire production "wholesale, premeditated murder" and pledged to serve as a "full time witness" should Schuman elect to sue *Omnibus*.[70] In his note to Paranov, Schuman pinpointed the difference between what happened in Hartford and what people saw on their televisions at home.

> Most of the people who saw your stage production (Douglas Moore and others) were disappointed in the TV performance. Considering the limitations of the medium, I am satisfied that "Omnibus" did well by the work—certainly, they wanted to. I, of course, could never be happy with the kind of rushed preparation that the TV world demands.[71]

Saudek answered Schuman's letter of apology by reminding him that "the values contained in a television production do not happen to include that kind of final polishing which comes of weeks of rehearsals and out-of-town tryouts."[72] Schuman seemed to object to what he considered the slapdash nature of the television performance, and in comparison to the careful preparation that marked Paranov's New Haven performances, he had good reason to object. But the medium was so different from the theater that many of Schuman's supporters had little to nothing to say about the flaws in execution on *Omnibus* and nothing but praise for Schuman's accomplishment.

Most of the professional critics were also affirmative in their opinions of the work and its presentation. But the positive reviews in the *New York Herald Tribune*, the *Baltimore Sun*, and other papers meant relatively little, as Harold Schonberg in the *New York Times* was unforgiving. "Mr. Schuman's music . . . is essentially unfitting to Thayer's immortal, resounding lines. It is essentially unvocal. . . . Schuman is a skilled and resourceful composer of proved intellectuality. He orchestrates like a master, too. But he decidedly does not have the light touch."[73] Schonberg's review of the premiere had been far less harsh but still managed to identify what remains *Casey*'s biggest challenge.

> Some of [the music] is lively, amusing, tongue-in-cheek. Casey strikes out to an accompaniment that carries suggestions of Prokofieff's "Scythian Suite," Beethoven's Ninth Symphony, Times Square on Saturday evening, and the Queen Mary coming into dock, all rolled into one. . . . About everything, indeed, is present but relaxed melody. Mr. Schuman, one feels, tries too hard. His dry, often jerky melodic line, with all of its major sevenths and ninths, his austere harmonies and his rhythmic intensity somehow do not fit this pleasant little fable. . . . What one looks for, and what is missing, is the folkish flavor and the genial musical outlook of a practiced hand at operetta.[74]

Between the dramatically static choruses—which are even more static on television—and the absence of long-limbed melody, *The Mighty Casey* is far from being a home run for adults. The gangly melodies, the odd word accents, and the goofy repetition of words (e.g., nine iterations of "surprise," followed by eleven of "we can't," eight of "we must," and four more of "we can't") may, however, cast a more mesmerizing spell on children, and the reasons Schuman chose Gury in the first place had to do with Gury's prior work with children. Expending this much effort, in terms of creating and performing the opera, makes it difficult to assess whether *Casey* could ever be done solely or even primarily for a kids' audience, and those correspondents who wrote to Schuman about their successful productions would almost always volunteer: the work is extremely difficult.[75] But kids would not be as bothered as Schonberg was about the stylistic mélange or the quirkiness of the melodies and rhythms—or over how hard the opera is on its performers relative to the work's rewards.

Fellow composer and Juilliard colleague William Bergsma was far kinder than Schonberg in his overall assessment of the work, but sentiments similar to those voiced by Schonberg are couched beneath Bergsma's positive remarks.

> The problem was (as you undoubtedly realized before you started writing) an enormously tricky one—the blending of Schuman and Broadway—and I feel you tossed off most of the solutions with exemplary brilliance. . . . Once you get a good intense Schuman-like plot straightened out, you're going to go to town with an opera, and don't let anybody stop you, not even W. S.[76]

For the time being, Schuman had forsworn opera.

He hadn't abandoned music for the stage, although the opportunity to write his next dance work came from left field. In November 1950, Schuman accepted a commission from Sigma Alpha Iota, the international music fraternity for women whose publication *Pan Pipes* carries several stories about Schuman's music. "The composition is to be a piano composition, a concert work of any length and difficulty. However, we do hope that it will be easy enough for most concert artists to perform. The premiere performance of the piano work will be one of the highlights of the golden anniversary convention of the Fraternity in 1953."[77] By the late fall of 1952, Schuman had composed the first of what would become five interlocking movements of the as-yet-unnamed piece. Martha Graham had paid Schuman a visit to tell him about her upcoming performances of *Judith* and to help him decide what the overall title for the new work should be. Unknown to Schuman, Graham "needed a new work for herself for her Broadway season, [but] she had no money, no time, and no script."[78] Though Schuman was still in the early stages of his commission for the women's fraternity, Graham seized the opportunity. She gave him "the eye treatment" and asked Schuman to orchestrate the new work so that she could use it in her spring 1953 season. All of this presented formidable challenges to Schuman, the greatest of which was convincing the officers at Sigma Alpha Iota that having the world premiere of their commissioned work somewhere other than their golden anniversary convention in the summer of 1953 was desirable. Graham told Schuman: "Bill, you know perfectly well you can do that if you want to."[79] Schuman donned his diplomat's hat and wrote to the fraternity's officers.

> Since the purpose of your interest in American music is to help bring it into being and to disseminate it, you naturally would wish a work that you commissioned to have the widest possible use. However, I do not wish to press this thinking upon you, or to take any action with which you are not in complete accord; therefore, let us agree to decide nothing finally at this particular point. Let me see how I progress with the work.[80]

Graham got her dance score and premiered it on May 17, 1953—less than two weeks after the *Casey* premiere—and Sigma Alpha Iota got its piano score and premiered it on August 18, 1953. As with the previous scores for Graham, this one did not have a name until Graham gave it one: *Theatre for a Voyage*.[81] (The score of the Graham version bears the title *Five Pieces*; the title "Theater for a Voyage" is penciled in. Schuman lost track of the orchestrated version, and there is the possibility that he may have turned some of this task over to composer Henry Brant, whom he had earlier employed as a copyist on *The Mighty Casey* and who was engaged to assist Schuman "with the copying of the score and parts for the untitled work you are composing for Martha Graham.)"[82]

Bertram Ross, one of her partners in what was simply referred to as *Voyage* at its premiere, remembered various aspects of the dance and the history surrounding it.

> *Voyage* (1953) was my favorite piece of Martha's. It was the first dance she choreographed after Erick [Hawkins] left. I was "The Beloved." Martha kept running away from me, her true love. At one point Martha was mysteriously part of my body. She was hooked onto me. Bob Cohan used Martha as an instrument, a lyre, to express himself. Stuart [Hodes] was shadowboxing in the dark. He was the opposing side. We wore evening clothes—the latest in fashion—made of silk, or polished cotton. I wore blue, Bob wore green, Stuart wore red, and Martha wore an off-the-shoulder evening dress. They were form-fitting, like for riding. You undressed as you moved. These evening clothes, the height of sophistication, were stripped off, and you came to the barbaric, down to the skin, with savage hieroglyphics on our bodies. With *Voyage*, Martha was working out the fact that her dance partner and husband, Erick, had left her. She was experimenting and made me move in a way I had never moved before. Martha said, "I want you to move in a way that has never been seen in performance." I was new, and she was fascinated with me. She felt I was the most "dramatic" of the men. She was always prodding me for movement sequences, and I know she liked having me around. I remember in *Voyage* Martha developed this seemingly unmotivated turn which was like an explosion.[83]

John Martin's review of the production sketched the same scenario provided by Ross and added that "'Voyage' . . . may be taken to mean symbolically, and to a certain degree literally, a kind of luxury cruise." He concluded: "It is a curious piece, full of bewilderments and rather startlingly obvious symbols—so obvious, indeed, that one is inclined at first to disregard them. It has, however, the characteristic Graham absorption and, amid the many familiar technical devices, some stunning invention."[84] Graham, however, was displeased with her effort, if Schuman's letter to her the morning after the premiere is an indicator of her feelings. "You were disturbed, I know, last night because 'Voyage' did not live up to your hopes for it. This is to say that my confidence in what you are doing with the work is unshaken and that I know you will find a way to solve its problems to your own satisfaction."[85] That confidence induced Schuman to send a letter to the Rockefeller Foundation, imploring it to extend "a sizable grant to enable the making of documentary sound films of representative Graham repertory. . . . Such an achievement on films would be of inestimable value for future generations."[86] The grant was not forthcoming, and several more years would pass before Graham would have the chance to commit *Appalachian Spring*, *Night Journey*, and other expressions of her art onto film. As for *Voyage*, Graham used Schuman's music once more in her spring 1955 season and then shelved the score.[87]

Meanwhile, the impact of Graham's early appropriation of Schuman's piano piece meant that he now needed to address whether the work sought to convey, in sonic terms, a luxury cruise. He asked the Sigma Alpha Iota officers to add two parenthetical sentences to the commission description that appeared in the convention program. "(Miss Martha Graham has given the title 'Voyage' to her dance composition using an orchestral arrangement of these pieces. The cycle was composed originally for piano without a programmatic or extra-musical plan.)"[88] But after the premiere—which was overshadowed by Schuman's electric keynote speech titled "The Fiddlecase and the Football"[89]—he was faced with a dilemma. He wrote to Lillian Steuber, the California-based pianist who debuted the work at the Chicago convention.

> It seemed to me that the acceptance of the work would have been helped by a separate title for each of the five pieces under the general title "Voyage." While ordinarily I do not use programmatic titles, those pieces are recognizably, I believe, of a dramatic nature and the use of the single title "Voyage" is perhaps too abstract. Let me say immediately, however, that I am at a loss as to what to call the pieces.[90]

Though "at a loss," Schuman suggested five possible titles, only two of which—"Anticipation" (#1) and "Decision" (#4)—made it into the published piece. He and Steuber went back and forth over possibilities. Steuber came up with "Caprice" for the second section; her ideas tended to be flowery, with references to Baudelaire and Robinson Jeffers. She also suggested that Schuman should add tempo markings and not just metronome markings, an idea Schuman readily adopted.[91] Though it is Schuman's largest and most challenging piano score, it has remained something of a rarity among concert pianists, receiving only two commercial recordings since its debut in 1953 (one in 1955, the other in 1987).[92]

Schuman, of course, could not know what the reception of *Voyage* would be. His concerns focused not on its future performance history but on its immediate publication. Despite his being cashiered in August 1951 as the director of publications for G. Schirmer, Schuman had good relations with the firm. Those relations began to be tested in late 1952 when Schuman chose to leave ASCAP and join BMI, perceiving that BMI was better suited to handle the performing rights of serious composers. The score for *Casey* was in preparation before Schuman made the switch; *Voyage* came afterward, and at the time, G. Schirmer wasn't legally set up to administer the rights of BMI composers. Schuman created a holding company—Howard Music (based on his middle name)—to serve as the publisher of record for *Voyage*, although Schirmer took care of the details of printing and distributing the work, which appeared by mid-1954. Everything came to a head, though, by late 1954, as Schuman realized the firm to which he had entrusted nearly all of his scores was turning on him. He poured out his frustrations in a four-page letter to Heinsheimer.

> You, better than anyone else, know that I was prepared to give up the BMI contract if it meant that I couldn't stay with G.S. Don't think that it wasn't painfully clear to me that Mr. S was willing (after telling me that he could continue to publish my music although I was with BMI and advising me to sign that contract) without a qualm, to have me leave the firm after so many years of happy (Engel's regime and my own) association and a sizeable [*sic*] catalog.

Schuman wanted to see his unpublished works—the Quartettino (both its original bassoon version and a version for clarinets), the *William Billings Overture*, *Circus Overture*, and the Violin Concerto—finally make it to print. Moreover, he felt that the firm wasn't doing enough to promote his music. "I have a realistic understanding of the commercial value of my music at the present time and I realize too that your admiration and estimate of its worth is strictly qualified. The fact remains, nevertheless, that I must know where I stand on this important aspect of publishing."[93] For more than a year, Schuman, Heinsheimer and others at the firm would discuss Schuman's relationship and value to G. Schirmer, sometimes in businesslike tones and at other times venomously. By the end of 1955, Schuman was ready to bolt. Gustave Schirmer gave him a push. "Although we will always have an interest in your works, we cannot be committed to publish everything."[94] Schuman had recently cost the firm a lot of money: the issuance of *Casey* required a sizable outlay, and the work seemed not to be catching fire. In addition, orchestras were running away from the Sixth Symphony, and Schuman's most popular works (the Third Symphony and the *Symphony for Strings*) were yesterday's news. But however understandable Schirmer's position, Schuman felt an almost palpable blow at being separated from the publication house that still kept Barber and Bernstein.

Hepatitis kept Schuman from composing during the summer of 1954. But the dry spell of new pieces between *Voyage* (completed April 19, 1953) and

Credendum (officially commissioned on July 13, 1955) had other sources. The torrent of works that poured out of Schuman's pen after 1955—and the popularity of two of them (*New England Triptych*, 1956; *Carols of Death*, 1958)—has an almost I'll-show-you quality about them. *Casey* and Schuman may have struck out, but Schuman was determined to prove that he was still in the game.

NINETEEN

THE (MOSTLY) OFF-STAGE AMBASSADOR

Schuman's decision to leave ASCAP for BMI complicated matters for him in terms of his publications and the performing rights of his compositions. The switch, though, had immediate benefits, not the least of which was Schuman's $7,000 per annum compensation, guaranteed for five years, that he received in his role as consultant to BMI.[1] Beyond the financial rewards was one that, ironically, was off-limits to him at Juilliard: exposure to the music of younger composers.

When Schuman arrived at Juilliard in October 1945, the composition faculty consisted of Vittorio Giannini (b. 1903), Frederick Jacobi (b. 1891) and Bernard Wagenaar (b. 1894); he quickly added William Bergsma (b. 1921), Peter Mennin (b. 1923), Vincent Persichetti (b. 1915), and Robert Ward (b. 1917) to the roster, showing a preference for contemporary composers over established ones. Schuman also invited the more seasoned Copland to join the faculty, and Copland gave Schuman the impression that he would accept. Copland got cold feet, though, leading Schuman to tell Copland that "the fact that you changed your mind about coming here as a regular teacher has been a great disappointment to me."[2] As for adding himself to the faculty roster, there was no structural impediment preventing Schuman from joining his colleagues and having his own composition students. For Schuman, however, there was a moral impediment. His impartiality in adjudicating one student against another or in advancing one faculty member over another could be called into question if he had had a studio of his own at the school. One result of his self-imposed constraints was that he initially had less contact with young composers than he did during his days at Sarah Lawrence.

That early contact included an encounter with a 16-year-old student at New York City's High School of Music and Art. The principal of the school brought Seymour Shifrin (1926–79) and his compositions to Schuman's attention. In a letter in support of Shifrin's application to join the faculty at Brandeis University, Schuman spelled out what happened next. "He became my student, and during the years in which he studied with me, I had ample occasion to observe that I would not be surprised to see him develop into a mature scholar and artist of extraordinary capability."[3] Shifrin also "vividly remember[ed] our meeting at the High School of Music and Art and the happy issuance of it. I count that meeting as one of the most fortunate and crucial moments for me."[4] Their artistic relationship was akin to that of a father and a son, even down to its occasional tensions: "Despite some brash moments in the past, I remain your erstwhile student (I'm afraid you're stuck with me) and devoted friend."[5] Shifrin, in fact, was the only long-term student Schuman ever took on, and they worked together prior to the latter's move to Juilliard. In later life, Schuman would take great delight in listening to the tapes and reading the scores sent to him by his younger colleagues. Christopher Rouse (b. 1949) would have a Shifrin-like role in Schuman's life in terms of closeness—the two began corresponding when "Chip" Rouse was 12—but there were no formal lessons between the two that rivaled those of Shifrin and Schuman. To avoid choosing favorites, Schuman chose instead not to take on any private students.

He did, however, choose to assume the role of presiding judge in the BMI Student Composer Awards, which were founded in 1951 and were first awarded the following year. This, undoubtedly, was part of the consultation Schuman extended to BMI, and their financial investment in younger compositions helped to persuade Schuman to leave ASCAP for BMI. Schuman defended BMI to a correspondent who was accusing BMI of participating in the payola scandals of the late 1950s, using the Student Composers Awards as proof that BMI was not solely the horrible rock-and-roll-abetting entity that the supporters of ASCAP were making it out to be.[6] "These awards are given annually and judged by a group of publishers, composers and educators. The awards constitute cash prizes to help young composers continue their education at institutions of their own choice. To date, over $30,000 has been granted by BMI for those awards which the organization hopes to continue indefinitely."[7] At the time of this writing, BMI not only continues to offer the award but has also added the William Schuman Prize, to be awarded "to the composer whose work is judged 'most outstanding' in the competition."[8] Nearly 300 young composers received a BMI Student Composer Award during Schuman's 30-year tenure as presiding judge. They include Donald Martino, Dominick Argento, William Bolcom, Teo Macero, John Harbison, George Crumb, Mario Davidovsky, Philip Glass, Charles Wuorinen, Stephen Albert, William Albright, Charles Dodge, Joseph Schwantner, Stephen Hartke, John Adams, Christopher Rouse, Eric Ewazen, Aaron Jay Kernis, Tobias Picker, Daniel Asia, Larry Polansky, Steven Mackey, and David Rakowski.[9] Schuman wrote a letter on the occasion of the thirtieth anniversary of the awards to be used to spread the word about the awards still further. Addressed to Edward Cramer, president of BMI, Schuman sang the praises of everyone involved.

> In bringing together year after year juries of America's most distinguished composers, conductors, educators, and publishers, talented youngsters have been identified and helped through your scholarship grants to continue their studies. Some of the young winners of the past are now celebrated composers themselves and have served as judges.
>
> In a word, sir, BMI is to be congratulated on its splendid program in adhering faithfully to its principles and in providing adequate funding for their implementation. In a world not known for its hospitality to aspiring young composers, your laudable efforts are all the more welcome.[10]

Illness kept Schuman from serving as presiding judge in 1983, so Ulysses Kay stepped in. Schuman somehow thought that Milton Babbitt had substituted for him, and the following year he recommended that Babbitt continue as presiding judge and that he be relieved of his responsibilities and given the honorific of emeritus.[11] He may not have had another composition student after Shifrin, but in his work with BMI in starting and sustaining the Student Composer Awards, Schuman had a greater effect on the lives of young American composers than he would have likely had from a studio in the Juilliard School.

It was typical of Schuman to maximize his influence whenever possible. He and his colleagues created the *Juilliard Report* because "the school has received a steadily increasing number of written inquiries requesting detailed information concerning the actual operation of the [Literature & Materials] curriculum."[12] Sending copies out free of charge to various music educators increased the report's importance by highlighting Juilliard's magnanimity and support of its sister institutions.

Schuman's skills on the rostrum were also put to good use. He was no shrinking violet when it came to appraising this side of his life: "My real success as a performer has come about as a public speaker. . . . It would be falsely modest of me not to say that publicly and privately I have been the recipient of nothing but the most glowing praises about my ability as a speaker."[13] Letters he received after his addresses to various organizations describe his words as brilliant, witty, incisive, and timely. Not only musicians offered these encomia: the managing editor of the *New York Times* wrote to thank Schuman for his "significant and provocative" 1961 speech to the American Society of Newspaper Editors—Harold Schonberg volunteered that his boss was "bubbling with enthusiasm over your talk"—and his 1968 speech to the Economic Club of New York City was viewed by nearly all who heard it as the better of the two speeches on that particular evening, the other one given by Ronald Reagan, then governor of California. (One correspondent exclaimed: "To hell with Reagan—Schuman for President!")[14] Many of these speeches were reprinted—sometimes in esoteric organizational publications but just as often in widely circulated journals and newspapers—thus further disseminating Schuman's beliefs and approaches to a national and international audience.[15]

Given the opportunity, however, Schuman eschewed the higher profile of speeches and publications, and focused his energies instead on inventing or overhauling institutions and programs. His role in these efforts often went unsung, which did not seem to trouble him. While he was generally not interested in the kingdom and the glory, he did thrive on the power that such endeavors demanded. And with a few notable exceptions, Schuman wielded that power wisely and knew when to back away.

Schuman did not always get his way, however. After Koussevitzky's death, the directors of the music foundation that he established searched for an effective way to honor the conductor. Schuman brought an idea to the board, which found lacking. Undeterred, Schuman wrote to Koussevitzky's widow, Olga, who oversaw the foundation, and repeated his idea.

> There is need in the world of music today for a publication devoted to high level evaluation of the forces—esthetic, philosophical, economic, and, if you will permit, spiritual—that pertain to creative music. I believe that the Foundation should give serious thought to founding such a publication as a living memorial to a great performer whose concern for the music of his time was, to the best of my knowledge, without parallel in the entire history of the art.[16]

Olga also rebuffed Schuman, at which point he turned to his colleagues at Juilliard to bring his idea to reality. The troubled history of the *Juilliard Review* has already been recounted (chapter 13).[17]

The Koussevitzky Music Foundation was (and remains) well known for its commissions, and Schuman's experience on both the receiving and the giving end of the Koussevitzky commissions propelled him to create his own legacy of commissioning works.[18] There was the commissioning project for pedagogical pieces that was inaugurated at the beginning of his tenure as president of Juilliard (see chap. 13), one that left a number of tantalizing compositional projects—a string quartet from Stravinsky, a woodwind quintet from Harris, pieces from Bernstein and Barber—unfulfilled.[19] Schuman saw the fiftieth anniversary of the school as yet another opportunity to invite composers to write new works, and the precedent of previous Juilliard festivals devoted to French music and British music gave Schuman the compelling rationale to limit commissions to American composers and to marry the golden anniversary of the school to an American festival. As he wrote to Piston, Schuman hoped to have "a bang-up festival of American music" that would include older works but that would be focused on the new pieces composed expressly for the anniversary.[20]

Among the composers who were commissioned were Piston, Bergsma, Mennin, Shifrin, Moore, Persichetti, Diamond, Babbitt, Barber, and Bernstein. The latter two eventually bowed out because of other demands on their time. Harris was also to contribute a work, but his demands that William Warfield perform in it and that Juilliard pay Warfield led to some pointed accusations from Harris and some equal frank rebuttals from Schuman.[21] Harris proposed an alternative work, "something I already have planned out and sketched. It is a Folk Song Fantasy for a Capella [*sic*] Chorus and Solo piano, in five sections—about 25 minutes in length," and he delivered it in time for the festival.[22] Despite the contortions Harris would routinely demand of his former pupil, he and Schuman remained on good (but not overly friendly) terms for their entire lives.

Copland was another composer with high marquee value who was asked to contribute a work. In offering the commission to Copland, Schuman expanded the normal commissioning letter to include more history about the purpose and scope of the festival.

> We are planning to hold a year-long festival in 1954–55 celebrating the 50th anniversary of the School. Our idea is to give the most comprehensive American music festival of which we are capable—including historic perspective on all the branches—piano music, orchestral music, chamber music, choral music, lyric stage, etc., etc.[23]

Copland's original idea—"the creation of a Cantata in recognition of the hundredth anniversary of Walt Whitman's *Leaves of Grass*, which will occur in 1955"—stayed with him into the summer of 1954, at which time he began to hedge his bets. "I should prefer to let you have the work for chorus and orchestra if it materializes, but that, if it doesn't, the major piano composition will be a certainty."[24] Even that work was late, moving Copland to "throw myself on your (I hope) tender mercies."[25] Although it was delivered a year after the festival, Schuman gave it its own special concert, at which pianist William Masselos played the work in the first half of the program and then repeated it after intermission.[26] Prior to the premiere, Schuman gave Copland his impressions of the *Piano Fantasy*.

> This summer I studied your work and am no end impressed. If you are nodding in the direction of the serial technique I'd say that the result is nevertheless pure Copland, resembling a different kind of cereal—Wheaties, the Breakfast of Champions. Seriously, the work is a major Copland which, in my book, is something to cheer about. I do confess that I found it an exceptionally difficult work to hear without actual performance and therefore I am not certain that I have fully grasped what the effect will be when I finally hear it, even though I am able clearly to discern the structural mastery and ingenuity of thematic manipulation. It is a great honor for us at Juilliard to present the world premiere of this important composition and we are all greatly in your debt.[27]

Copland's foray into serialism stimulated Schuman to continue his own experiments before the decade was out.

Schuman also sought to expand the notion of commissioning organizations beyond the Koussevitzky Music Foundation and beyond Juilliard. Early in his tenure as a director of the Metropolitan Opera Association, he began to explore the possibility of the Met directly commissioning works. While once again it appears that he was attempting to atone for his aborted project with Christopher LaFarge, his new ties with BMI and his previous experiences with the Koussevitzky Music Foundation now gave him a platform from which to launch his idea of creating new American works expressly for the Met. He wrote to the president of BMI.

> Should the present plan that I have proposed to the Metropolitan Opera Association be adopted, the commissioning monies involved would be as follows: A short work, $3,000 for the composer, plus $1,000 for the librettist; a full work, $5,000 for the composer plus $1,500 for the librettist. In other words, if you undertake two commissions, you would be committing yourself to an expenditure of $8,000 to $13,000. If the idea is acceptable to your Directors, I would report your offer to the Metropolitan subject to mutually agreeable procedures.[28]

And he drafted a letter on the commissioning program to the board of the Met.

> The Metropolitan Opera Association in collaboration with the Koussevitzky Music Foundation, Broadcast Music, Inc. (and any other collaborating agencies) commissions five or more new operas. Upon completion, each of these works is given to some other production unit for presentation with a contribution by the Metropolitan of $5,000 to help defray the production expenses in such instance. If any of the works prove in trial performance to be suitable for the Metropolitan stage, they would then be presented at the Metropolitan. The Metropolitan reserves the right, of course, to produce the work immediately at the Metropolitan. . . . The organizations that I approached were the Koussevitzky Music Foundation, Inc., Broadcast Music, Inc., and the Alice M. Ditson Fund of Columbia University. The Koussevitzky Music Foundation, Inc., and Broadcast Music, Inc., have each agreed, subject to the working out of mutually acceptable details, to underwrite respectively three and two commissions for a total of five. The Alice M. Ditson Fund, while appreciating the possibility that the Metropolitan would enter more vigorously the field of contemporary music, could not lend support at this time.[29]

Schuman apparently did not send this letter, and after further consultation with other members of the Met board, he concluded that the commissioning program as he envisioned it might be unfeasible. The Met's Executive Committee concurred, and the idea of the Met collaborating with other funding organizations to underwrite the creation of new American operas for the time being came to a halt.[30]

Yet a new American opera was premiered at the Met less than five years later. Barber began work on *Vanessa* during the summer of 1954, and while other opera houses were interested and willing to mount the work, the Metropolitan Opera announced in March 1957 that they would give the world premiere of this opera, the first premiere at the Met of an American opera in more than ten years. (A decade later, Schuman would ask for and receive a list of American operas premiered at the Met.)[31] The Met, of course, had been interested in

Barber early on—recall that Schuman replaced Barber as LaFarge's collaborator when Barber withdrew—and given that Barber wrote his opera without a commission, it is likely that Schuman's 1953 commissioning idea for the Met had no direct effect on its decision to mount *Vanessa*. Indirectly, however, Schuman's reminders to the Met of what he felt was its responsibility to encourage the writing and production of American opera favorably coincide with that decision. Schuman certainly thought so when he wrote to Barber well in advance of the public announcement.

> Attempts that I have made in the past to get the management interested in contemporary opera in general and contemporary American opera in particular met with absolutely no success. And the announcement of the production of your work came as a wonderful surprise for I had never heard it mentioned at the Opera House. I hope and expect that your opera will be successful with the public as, I know beforehand it is bound to be with the many admirers you have for the splendid works you have given us in the other forms.[32]

A similar story could be told of Schuman's attempts to get the management of the New York Philharmonic interested in contemporary American music. On April 1, 1955, he wrote a no-nonsense four-page letter to Floyd G. Blair, president of the Philharmonic-Symphony Society of New York. In it, Schuman sought "to discuss the problems of the Philharmonic in relation to the performance of contemporary American music in general, and, specifically, with reference to the performance of American music and the use of American soloists in the forthcoming European tour of the Orchestra." Schuman had taken up these problems with Dimitri Mitropoulos, the music director of the Philharmonic; he had shared them with the members of the Music Advisory Committee for the American National Theatre and Academy, a panel that assisted the U.S. State Department in selecting musicians for overseas travel that was underwritten by the federal government. Now he was laying out for Blair his views on the problem. Schuman advanced evidence from the four previous seasons of total works performed and how many were written by Americans. "Nothing that I can write here could possibly be as strong an indictment of the slighting of contemporary American music by the Philharmonic during recent seasons than the actual list which appears above."[33]

Blair's initial response of umbrage—Schuman's secretary had sent Blair not the original letter but one of the mimeographed copies that was meant for the nearly 20 other individuals with whom Schuman shared his *J'accuse*—was followed by coolness, hoping that acknowledgment of Schuman's letter and the enclosure of Olin Downes's column extolling the "eclectic programs" of the most recent season would appease Schuman.[34] Downes was not named by Schuman as one of the additional recipients of the Blair letter, but his column strongly suggests that someone leaked the letter to him.

> There have been renewed complaints that in the season past, insufficient attention was paid to American composers. It is to be said that today the American composer has more opportunities—speaking, let us say, in terms of the last thirty years—than he had ever dreamed of in the first quarter of this century. At that time there was certainly a stricter choice of American works selected by our orchestras for public performance, and nowhere near the readiness to perform score of experimental and often immature workmanship that there is today. So many are these opportunities that it is hard to believe that any really meritorious score by a native son or daughter would be rejected by musical organizations anxious to discover new music—or old music, for that matter—that would interest the concert-going public.[35]

Schuman was not appeased and continued to press his point. "In my view, the Philharmonic and other American orchestras have a special obligation to the American public in the presenting of music by Americans."[36] Schuman wasn't the only one to hurl accusations; behind his back, people at the Philharmonic suggested that his reason for bringing up this issue was nothing but self-promotion. In one interoffice memo, a staffer wrote, "Did you notice that no work of Schuman's has been performed in the 5 years he writes of?" Someone else answered: "Yes, thank God!"[37] The staff also felt that Schuman, contra Downes, wanted American works no matter their quality. The officers of the Philharmonic practically gloated to themselves when Schuman voluntarily agreed that "merit [is] the only criterion for the performance of music, be it old, new, American or Hindustani." "At least we now have him on record as agreeing that merit should be the only criterion for the selection and performance of music."[38] But in light of his other activities on behalf of American composers, the backroom backbiting seems misplaced, although Schuman would have likely benefited had the Philharmonic been more aggressive in promoting and performing American works.

The imbroglio fizzled out, but its reverberations may have been felt when, two years later, Leonard Bernstein was named to head the New York Philharmonic. Surely the directors of the New York Philharmonic were familiar with Bernstein's three seasons at the helm of the New York City Symphony (1945–48). Upon Bernstein's taking the podium of the Philharmonic, Schonberg recalled Bernstein's earlier engagement with the New York City Symphony. "Bernstein put some classics on his programs, but he concentrated on twentieth-century masterpieces. Audiences heard major works of Stravinsky, Hindemith, Bartók and Berg. Important American composers were represented; so were Milhaud, Shostakovich, Chavez and many others."[39] This is what Schuman had sought for the New York Philharmonic. Another press report recorded: "Mitropoulos said that his successor's appointment was a sign that America was now so grown up musically that it could offer such an important post to an American-born and American-trained musician."[40] In his letter to Blair, Schuman was saying the same thing about composers. As with the Met approaching

Barber, Schuman cannot be directly tied to Bernstein's selection. But his intervention, as unwelcome as it was in 1955, found vindication in 1958.

Three mergers that Schuman proposed also attest to his ambassadorial instincts. Shortly after he came to Juilliard, Schuman was inducted into the National Institute of Arts and Letters. He would later say that he proposed the idea of merging the institute with the smaller and more prestigious American Academy of Arts and Letters "shortly after I became a member of the Institute in 1946."[41] In fact, it wasn't until 1954 that he made the suggestion, enumerating his rationale in a letter to the institute's president, Marc Connelly.

> 1. Hardly anybody has ever heard of the National Institute of Arts and Letters. Ignorance of the existence of the Institute is understandable, I suppose, among the great unwashed, but is not encouraging when it exists in the highest circles of education, the arts and the professions.
> 2. The American Academy of Arts and Letters is no better known but the very existence of two organizations is confusing. Could not something be done about making one organization instead of two?[42]

His proposal was strongly opposed by writer, journalist, and commentator Walter Lippmann, who served with Schuman on the committee that was asked to consider the merger.[43] The proposal languished, but from time to time Schuman would advance the notion of bringing the two institutes together. In 1976, more than 20 years after his initial suggestion, his idea came to fruition.[44]

Another proposed merger took even longer to go from suggestion to reality. At an assembly on December 11, 1958—the birthday of Fiorello H. La Guardia (1882–1947), mayor of New York City from 1934 to 1945 and patron of the arts—Schuman advanced the possibility of bringing the High School of Music and Art and the High School of Performing Arts under one roof. The former, with its full academic curriculum augmented with special studies in the arts, was created by La Guardia in 1936; at the time of Schuman's suggestion, it had an enrollment of 2,000 students. The latter, with a curriculum designed to prepare students for the stage, was established in 1947, and with only 600 students enrolled, it was much smaller than the High School of Music and Art.[45] Schuman even suggested a location: adjacent to Lincoln Center, which was still in the planning stages at the time.[46] The students at Music and Art, then located where City College of New York is today, voiced their opinion of Schuman's idea: they booed. Schuman recalled that raspberry at the cornerstone-laying ceremony for the Fiorello H. La Guardia High School of Music and Art and Performing Arts, whose campus is adjacent to Lincoln Center and which received its first students in 1984, more than a quarter-century after Schuman's assembly speech.[47] The span of time between his idea and its fruition led others to misstate the role he played in this merger. "You are mistaken in referring to me 'as an initiator,'" he said. "To be candid I was not an initiator; I was the initiator, and I will not soon forget those difficult, bloody days."[48]

The third merger took less than five years to consummate, but the acrimony it generated at its start rankled Schuman far more than any high school catcall could. In the fall of 1950, Schuman was approached to see if he would undertake a delicate task: Would he be willing to chair a meeting bringing together two subcommittees, one from the International Society of Contemporary Music (ISCM, U.S. Section) and one from the League of Composers, for the express purpose of determining the feasibility of a merger? Though he had published articles in *Modern Music*, the League of Composers' house journal, Schuman had been critical of that organization and of the ISCM for basically the same reason: the tendency of each organization to normalize certain aesthetic predilections and to minimize wide representation. Schuman never shied away from giving his opinion on a piece of music, but he resisted trying to make his own predilections universal.[49] From where he sat, the same could not be said of the league or the society.

What was playing out in the United States was no different from what was playing out elsewhere with the ISCM.

> From its inception the ISCM was plagued by internal disputes concerning its purpose and operation. There was conflict between those countries that felt that it should promote avant-garde music (principally Germany before 1933 and Austria and Czechoslovakia before 1938) and those that considered any contemporary music to be worthy of the society's interest (principally France, Great Britain and the USA).[50]

The history of both organizations in the United States revolves around the ultramodernist composer Edgard Varèse (1883–1965), whose insistence on the new and the unheard cleft his International Composers' Guild in twain, with the disaffected members forming the League of Composers. The U.S. section of the ISCM more naturally fit composers of Varèse's temperament, and with the influx of European émigré composers in the 1930s and '40s, the U.S. section began to show a preference for avant-garde music over more mainstream expressions of contemporary music, a tendency that the founding American members had fought since the society's inception in the 1920s.[51] On paper, both the ISCM and the league were created to serve the modern composer, regardless of aesthetic predilection, and their continued separation led to a duplication of efforts. Schuman, who had never been closely affiliated with either organization, seemed to be the logical person to broker a marriage.

Unfortunately, Schuman was affiliated with an organization that some of the ISCM composers did not trust: the Juilliard School of Music. Although the school had hosted a major concert for the society, several of the ISCM representatives felt that the merger idea was concocted by the Juilliard faculty and administration and would lead to the dulling of the society's cutting edge. The

ISCM contingent unilaterally pulled out of the merger talks. As a result, both Frederick Prausnitz, outgoing president of the ISCM (U.S. section), and Frederic Cohen tendered their resignations as members of the ISCM board to Milton Babbitt, incoming president. Both Prausnitz and Cohen worked at Juilliard, and both accused their fellow ISCM members of petty divisiveness.[52] Schuman tried to stay above the fray, telling Babbitt that he would be willing to discuss what Schuman saw as the sticking point that prevented amalgamation.[53] But it was in a letter to Shifrin, an ISCM partisan, that Schuman gave vent to his thoughts and feelings.

> This issue has absolutely nothing to do with the merits of amalgamation, but does have everything to do with human conduct. I am not concerned here with the internal organizational problems of either organization, or the question of whether or not they should have joined forces, but referring only to two things, the first being the cavalier and rude manner in which the negotiations were interrupted by ISCM and the second, the poisonous and unwarranted personal attacks made at the ISCM meeting. These attacks were shocking enough and resembled the kind of irresponsible leveling of charges which all right thinking men abhor in public life, but to have you fall prey to such charges and form opinions about men you do not even know based on them is more than the traffic will bear.[54]

Shifrin backed down.

Schuman pressed ahead on another front. Less than two years later, Schuman sailed to Venice, Italy, as a U.S. delegate at the International Conference of Artists sponsored by the United Nations Educational, Scientific, and Cultural Organization (UNESCO). Though he was not required to submit a report of his activities, Schuman took it upon himself to send his impressions to Max McCullough, executive secretary of the United States National Commission for UNESCO. Schuman devoted nearly an entire page of his seven-page letter to the problem of the ISCM. The problem, as Schuman told McCullough, was that

> the International Music Council recognizes [ISCM] as the official spokesman for the composers of each country. I stated at the meeting quite frankly that in the United States this group in no sense represented the American composer but only a small clique. To my surprise and delight a number of other delegates shared this opinion. As a consequence I was able to propose, and have accepted, wording which insists upon a composers group being sufficiently representative of the composers in each country to deal with governments and national and international bodies. Furthermore, it was agreed at the Conference that should it not be possible to reorganize the various national chapters of the International Society of Contemporary Music as truly representative groups, that some other organization be formed to represent the member country in the International Music Council.[55]

Schuman slightly overstated the outcome of the discussion in Venice. The ensuing Resolution No. 7, "Relations with Governments," reads: "The Conference expresses the hope that a recognized association of composers will be constituted in every country, sufficiently representative to negotiate directly with governments, as well as national and international organisations."[56] Even so, it indirectly gave Schuman leverage to bring the U.S. section of the ISCM to heel. Several months later, he wrote to Babbitt to ask about some changes being proposed by the central ISCM administration. Schuman tipped his hand.

> The [ISCM] came in for some good, healthy criticism at the UNESCO conference I attended last September. The feeling was that either ISCM, in terms of its local chapters, should become truly representative of the composers in each country, or another organization should be formed that would fulfill this function. It would greatly assist me if I could know from you, as President, what view you take of these sentiments.[57]

Babbitt wrote back to tell Schuman that Elliott Carter was now president, so this matter was in Carter's hands. He also added that a shakeup was under way and intimated that a greater variety of music would be forthcoming.[58] That wider representation made it possible for the ISCM and the League of Composers to resume talks about merger. By the spring of 1954, the announcement was made that the merger would take place, and by December of that year, the League of Composers–International Society of Contemporary Music, United States Section, was born.[59]

In the same letter to McCullough in which he took the ISCM to task, Schuman also indicated that the Venice conference quickened his belief in "the absolute necessity of official recognition of the arts by the United States Government." No time should be lost, Schuman felt, "on this vitally important need for making known here, as well as abroad, the existence and achievements of American artists as living evidence that we are concerned with something more than materialism."[60] Schuman's subsequent work from 1954 to 1960 as an advisor to the U.S. State Department gave substance to these 1952 affirmations. Given that this governmental service was closely tied to the development of Lincoln Center, Juilliard's place in the center, and Schuman's selection as the third president of the center, a fuller discussion of this aspect of his cultural ambassadorship shall have to wait for now. His time in Venice and his interactions with McCullough would have a more immediate effect on Schuman as a composer.

Three years after Schuman's initial exposure to the work of UNESCO, he was asked to contribute to its program in a way no one had ever been asked before. He became the first composer commissioned by the U.S. National Commission for UNESCO to write a work on its behalf. Schuman was very particular about how others referred to the commission. It did not come directly through UNESCO. Rather,

> the work was commissioned through the U.S. Department of State for the U.S. National Commission for UNESCO. The first time, as I was informed, that a department of the U.S. government has ever commissioned a symphonic composition. This

> fact (if it is one) has frequently appeared in reviews and is used both for and against the piece and also the State Department but I should hasten to add that most of the critics have praised the idea of the commission and I'm in no position to know how they feel about the State Department.[61]

It most certainly was not "the first musical work ever commissioned by an agency of the United States Government." The Works Progress Administration and the Office of War Information both commissioned scores, and the Library of Congress oversaw the commissions that were handed out by the Coolidge Foundation.[62] But it was the first commission of its kind, strangely akin to those musical extravaganzas that companies like Frigidaire would put on for employees and their families. And the commissioning letter itself is filled with the zeal one often finds in a government bureaucrat who earnestly believes his division has the power to change the world. McCullough was, apparently, such a man.

> On behalf of the U. S. National Commission for UNESCO I should like to invite you to accept a commission to compose a work for orchestra, which might be played for the first time on the occasion of the Fifth National Conference to be convened by the National Commission in Cincinnati in November of this year. . . .
>
> The National Commission extends this invitation because it believes that the spirit underlying UNESCO's work must be conveyed not in words or in visual symbols alone, but also through music and other art forms. . . .
>
> The National Commission hopes that it may be possible to convey in music something of the hopes of the peoples of the world that attended the founding of the United Nations, of the disappointments that have accompanied its growth and of the still present yearning of peoples everywhere for the growth of that intellectual and moral solidarity that will draw them together as a family of man.[63]

McCullough's hopes had an aura of uncertainty around them because, as the project was under discussion prior to the delivery of his official commissioning letter, he attempted to make the music serve as a conveyance for words. He asked arts patron, writer, and social activist Dorothy Norman (1905–97) to provide a text for Schuman to set. The diversity of sources from which Norman compiled her text proved to be an insurmountable obstacle for Schuman in terms of shaping a sense of consistency for the work, so he informed both her and McCullough that her text—and, by inference, any text—could not serve as the backbone of the work he would compose.[64] An instrumental work it would be.

Schuman had two large commissions already sitting on his desk: a work for André Kostelanetz "in a light vein with a ready appeal for many people [that] should run about eight to ten minutes in length"; and a 20- to 30-minute work for the Boston Symphony Orchestra in celebration of its seventy-fifth anniversary.[65] Hepatitis kept him from working on the first, which in turn led him to negotiate a delay on the second. The offer to write a work for UNESCO pushed the other commissions to the side, and the summer of 1955 on Martha's

Vineyard was devoted to the Cincinnati work. Schuman gave a detailed account of the new composition and his working methods to Lucien Wulsin, chairman of the board of the Cincinnati Symphony Orchestra.

> The more I worked on this project the more I realized that a short overture would not fill the bill. Consequently, I am spending the entire summer (my wife will tell you mornings, afternoons, nights, Saturdays and Sundays included) producing a work which will be approximately sixteen to seventeen minutes in length. It is to be called
>
> CREDENDUM
> Declaration—Chorale—Finale
> For Orchestra
>
> The word Credendum is used in its meaning "an article of faith." If you see [conductor] Thor Johnson would you pass this news along to him? I cannot promise that the work will be easy to perform, but then he knows my music and will not expect it to be. Incidentally, I should like to find better words for Chorale and Finale and if you have any suggestions, I would greatly appreciate your forwarding them to me.[66]

He also asked McCullough if he might suggest alternative titles for the last two sections; McCullough, unapologetically admitting his ignorance of music, asked Schuman what was meant by the term "chorale." Wulsin had no recommendations, but Johnson chimed in. "Would you consider the movement listings as Declaration–Hymn–Confirmation or is this too theological?" "Hymn" would not do, Schuman told Johnson, and he ultimately kept his original subtitles.[67] He also took great pride in this work: "It has a big sort of hortatory first movement, and then it has the second movement, which is one of the best I've ever done. . . . I love that. That really works very well. And then the third movement is, you know, whatever it is, a scherzo-like thing."[68] Even after 20 years, only "Declaration" seemed to work for Schuman.

Strikingly, not one of his correspondents said anything about the title for the work itself, but in light of the sentiments McCullough expressed in the commissioning letter, *Credendum* conveyed in a word something of the aspirations McCullough sought in this work. How Schuman fell upon this particular Latin word is a matter of speculation. It is doubtful that he recalled the word from his own Latin studies, which gave him "what little I know of English grammar."[69] In later life, he would repeat what he told Wulsin, that the Latin was a cognate for "article of faith." That no major work prior to Schuman's bore the name *Credendum* suggests that he consulted with others before deciding on a Latin word that both clarifies and obscures at the same time.

The word also obliquely reflects another cultural phenomenon of the day: Edward R. Murrow's program, *This I Believe*. Murrow invited men and women from all walks of life to write an essay about their own personal philosophy, their individual credo. The authors of the essays read their own words for the radio broadcasts. Newspapers syndicated the edited written versions. A 1952 compilation of 100 of the essays made it to the *New York Times* best-seller list for at least 29 weeks, an understandable phenomenon given that "thousands of people, including hundreds of educators and no fewer than sixteen publishers, after hearing 'This I Believe' on the air or reading it in the newspapers, wrote in to urge its appearance between covers."[70] A second volume appeared in 1954, and while Schuman was not featured in either the radio program or the published essays, a number of his colleagues did participate in *This I Believe*: Sarah Lawrence presidents Constance Warren and Harold Taylor; conductors André Kostelanetz and Dmitri Mitropoulos; composers George Antheil, Leonard Bernstein, Henry Cowell, and Roy Harris; dancer Martha Graham; and foundation administrator Olga Koussevitzky. Not everyone found the program inspirational; at least one minister inveighed against the spiritual pabulum contained in many of the essays.[71] But it was financial straits, not religious opposition, that forced the program to go off the air in April 1955, just a few months before Schuman wrote to Wulsin and told him the name of his new work.[72] It was a time, in the middle of the Cold War, when people wanted to believe in something if not someone. As it happened, Schuman said, "Ed Murrow was after me to do a 'This I Believe' program. I got hung up on trying to say what I am about. What I am about is what I have done and what I do."[73] Instead of using words, Schuman placed his marker down in music. *Credendum*: this I believe.

As far as the work itself, everyone scrambled to get *Credendum* ready in time for its November 4 premiere. Having begun the work at home in New Rochelle on June 20, Schuman worked furiously at Menemsha and completed it on September 6, two days before he was to leave Martha's Vineyard. Henry Brant, who once again served as Schuman's copyist, had to travel to Rome to receive the Prix Italia. "Before leaving he delivered 61 pages of the score, which is just about half, and promised me the remainder by air mail from Italy by the 1st."[74] Brant was more or less true to his word, sending the remainder of the score in two batches on September 29 and October 3.[75] A copy of the score was made and sent to Johnson, while a copyist stateside extracted the parts, which arrived less than two weeks before the premiere. Despite Johnson's enthusiasm for the work—"It appears to be your finest work to date"—the demands of *Credendum*, the time left to solve its demands, and the possible fatigue of performers working on "a two-show-a-day basis" (an afternoon subscription concert followed by the UNESCO evening concert open to the public) resulted in an outcome similar to the one Schuman had experienced with the Dallas Symphony and the Sixth Symphony. The reviewer for *Musical America* found the chorale "worthy" but the outer movements "labored and ineffectively hinged," which may have been as much the fault of the performance as the piece. All Schuman could bring himself to do was to congratulate Johnson for his "excellent conducting." The rest was left unsaid.[76]

Part of the fault lay with Schuman. One listener who served on the International Music Council of UNESCO told Schuman that the last movement felt overextended to him. Schuman concurred. "Your comment on 'Credendum' pleases me very much for I too thought the end was over extended. Ormandy is doing the work this March with the Philadelphia Orchestra and I have shortened the last movement."[77] Shortly after the premiere, Schuman sent *Credendum* to Ormandy and sheepishly asked him to consider changing his programs so that Ormandy could give the New York premiere. Schuman also told Ormandy that the U.S. Information Service, the overseas arm of the U.S. Information Agency, "is prepared to purchase records to send abroad. In other words, they regard this as suitable propaganda material in the United States cultural offensive."[78] Ormandy was a tough customer. He wanted a guarantee that someone would underwrite the recording; after Schuman was turned down by UNESCO (no money) and the Rockefeller Foundation (no immediate interest), his new publisher, Theodore Presser, agreed to assume the costs of the recording. Then, after he had heard the work in rehearsal, Ormandy demanded changes in the score itself.

> There is much too much percussion almost from the very start. At times it is almost ear-splitting. This can be corrected during rehearsals, but where the work seems to "leave the listener" is in the development part of the finale movement and this is where I think you will want to think about cuts. I would also urge you to cut down the excessive percussion because even my eardrums almost cracked, and I am certainly used to a lot of percussion.[79]

Ormandy may not have read the comments from the UNESCO Music Council member, but he had reached the same conclusion about the finale. Schuman wrote to Ormandy to tell him that "I have been considering cuts in the last movement of the work and agree that some adjustment is needed. Before receiving your letter I studied this movement with precisely this in mind and hope to come up with a solution before long." Five days later, he wrote to Ormandy again. "I believe the changes I have made will prove to be a big improvement. The cuts all come in the last movement and reduce the playing time by about one minute and a half. Included in the cuts are a number of bars with much percussion. In addition I have cut percussion in a number of other places."[80]

After having agreed to substitute *Credendum* on his March programs, Ormandy threatened to remove the work "because of the demands made on our Association by your publisher."[81] Ormandy felt that the special nature of *Credendum* warranted a special dispensation in terms of performance fees. Schuman and Arthur Hauser, president of Theodore Presser, didn't see things the same way. (Two years later, Hauser wrote Schuman a three-page letter explaining Ormandy's latest demands; Schuman responded: "Let Ormandy take

Credendum off program if he won't pay fee."[82] Two years after that, he did remove the *Celebration Concertante*.) Ormandy relented, and *Credendum*'s New York premiere was well received by audience members and critics alike.

Henry Cowell reviewed the work in the *Musical Quarterly* following the New York concerts. Cowell found the size of the orchestra exceptional: "four to five of each of the winds instead of the customary three; plus six horns, two tubas, etc., a seating usually required only for certain early 20th-century massive tone-poems. There is more than the usual number of percussion instruments, including a piano, steel plate, hard mallets hitting chimes furiously, etc." Cowell went on to praise Schuman's deft handling of the orchestra and singled out as a major aspect of Schuman's musical style the lyricism evident in the chorale.

> The second aspect of Schuman's style consists of chattering repetitions of tones and chords, usually highly dissonant, rapid and syncopated. This sort of passage occurs as a second theme in the first movement, and recurs throughout the piece. It gives the impression of being a sort of liaison between early Varèse and early jazz, subjects well known by this composer. It splutters and stutters, but agreeably, and induces a sort of static excitement which is a great contrast to the long lyric lines of the other side of the Schuman style.

(One is reminded of Copland's remark five years earlier in the same journal about Schuman's rhythm: "There is nothing quite like these rhythms in American music, or any other music for that matter.")[83] Cowell's conclusion echoed that of Thor Johnson when the conductor first saw the score. "The total work is impressive, large-scaled, Schuman's *magnum opus*."[84]

The winds were shifting in American music, with the necessity of *magna opera* being questioned by those a generation younger than Schuman and Cowell who sought a form of expression different from midcentury tone poems that require six horns and quadruple winds. At the premiere the following year of another musical milestone, Copland's *Piano Fantasy*, the reviewer turned his eye to the audience, "one of the most knowledgeable that could be assembled in New York. At the end of each performance it hailed composer and performer. There were a couple of boos. Someone who checked their source said they came from avant-gardists who regard Mr. Copland as an old conservative. They couldn't be more wrong."[85] Schuman, like Copland, was on the cusp of being supplanted—or, worse, ignored—by those young composers he was seeking to encourage. *Credendum* and his compositions of the next six years serve as a fascinating prism to see how Schuman's ambassadorial interests are refracted into particular, and even peculiar, creative choices. As he reached out to a wider and wider audience, he also quietly began to study the tricks of the musical illuminati. He tried to obscure his own avant-garde adventures from this era. But even if his exertions came to light much later, their impact can be seen in the music he would compose in the 1960s.

TWENTY

WITH AN EYE ON THE MARKETPLACE

Once he decided, at the end of 1955, to leave Schirmer and join Theodore Presser, Schuman understood that he could no longer count on Heinsheimer and others at Schirmer to promote his works. *Voyage* suffered from being the last work that Schuman placed with Schirmer just as his affiliation with the company began to sour. *Credendum* fell between two stools, as Schuman initially asked Schirmer to handle the first few performances before he gave it to Presser to publish. The legend on the retail version of *Credendum*—"Study Score No. 1"—succinctly identified Schuman's challenge going forward. The composer of four published symphonies and numerous smaller works suddenly needed to start all over again, needed to create a new catalog of music for a new publisher.

Schuman said as much to Arthur Hauser, the president of Theodore Presser. "As I told you during my visit last month, I am trying during the first month of this summer [of 1956] to turn out some pieces which your sales department can actually sell and which will satisfy, as well, my desire to write for the schools."[1] From the start of his affiliation with Presser, Schuman was focused on a more popular market than he had mined with Schirmer, and choral music seemed a logical place to start, given his success in the field from his "Holiday Song" to the two secular cantatas.

The first works Schuman sent to Presser after *Credendum* were arrangements for mixed voices and for women's voices of a composition he had written in January 1956. The impetus for *The Lord Has a Child* actually came when Schuman was in the throes of composing *Credendum* the previous summer. He was approached by Albert Christ-Janer, who with Carleton Sprague Smith, chief of the New York Public Library's Music Division, was "editing an anthology of American hymns. . . . It will contain an important section of contemporary hymns, some of which are already in use and others which will be composed for this hymnbook. We should greatly appreciate receiving hymns from you, composed for this publication." The honorarium was small—$100 per hymn—but Schuman was interested, perhaps because he knew Smith well. At the time he did not notice a caveat in Christ-Janer's letter: "The final selection of the hymns in the contemporary section is to be made by a board of musicians and scholars in the music profession."[2] Schuman would later balk about how "it never occurred to me that this hymn would then be 'tried out' with a number of others and the 'winners' used," but in referring to the hymn as a "commission" rather than an invitation for a submission suggests that Schuman misunderstood the original intent of the editors.[3]

It would also seem that Schuman had the chorale from *Credendum* in mind as a possible hymn, this even before he received Thor Johnson's letter suggesting "Hymn" as a subtitle instead of "Chorale." "I will be happy to consider the composition of a hymn, but would like to know whether such a piece must have a text or whether the music in and of itself would be sufficient. Also, would you wish to consider an excerpt from an orchestral work containing a hymn."[4] The guidelines were vague on the matter, but inasmuch as the hymns were meant to be sung, the editors did prefer the music to be texts, and they had a separate call to writers to send material that they would distribute to possible composers. Schuman was sent two lyrics by Langston Hughes and was given the option of choosing either one or both to set.

By mid-October, he had decided on using "The Lord Has a Child."[5] He later wrote to Hughes directly to tell him of his choice. "I like the one entitled 'The Lord Has a Child' very much indeed and have already set this to music. The other, entitled 'The Wonder of His Presence,' I am not using, although this should not be taken as adverse criticism, merely that I did not find a way of setting it to music." Schuman went on to inform Hughes of his intention to make and publish choral settings of the hymn and "to inquire whether you would wish to write other lyrics suitable for choral setting. I have no specific subject matter in mind, only to say that these need not necessarily be texts suitable for sacred music. I should like, for example, to write a graduation song for high schools."[6] Hughes reminded him of the graduation song in *Street Scene*—"Wrapped in a Ribbon and Tied with a Bow"—and related to Schuman how much trouble that particular lyric gave him. To write another graduation song would set off an allergic reaction. "But almost any other subject, I'd be willing to try."[7] Schuman invited Hughes to send whatever unpublished lyrics and scripts he felt inclined to send. "For my part, I promise to read them promptly and to be in touch with you soon."[8] Hughes answered immediately and sent Schuman a sheaf of materials that included "Hand Loved Best of All," "Journey Into Space," "Train That Took Wings" and "Love from a Tall Building." Schuman found none of these to his liking, telling Hughes that "I do wish that you would let me see some shorter verses." On his copy of Schuman's letter, Hughes underlined the last two words, but apparently he sent no other materials to Schuman, as their correspondence ceased after Schuman returned the scripts.[9]

Schuman would revisit the music he wrote for the hymn on several occasions: as the middle movement for the (withdrawn) *Three Pieces for Five Brasses* (1980); for the three different versions of *American Hymn* (brass quintet, 1980; concert band, 1981; orchestra, also 1981); for his *Showcase: A Short Display for Orchestra* (1986); and for the final work he completed, for mixed chorus and brass quintet, and also named *The Lord Has a Child* (1990).

As for its original version, Charles William Hughes annotated each of the hymns for *American Hymns Old and New* and had this to say about *The Lord Has a Child.*

> This poem, imagining the singer as a child tenderly watched over by the Lord as Father, has been set as a unison song with piano or organ accompaniment by William Schuman. There is more than a touch of the popular song in Schuman's setting, which perhaps departs more widely from the conventions of hymn writing than any other in this section.[10]

When Schuman sent the choral versions to Presser, he gently teased George Rochberg, who was the music editor at the time, in a long parenthetical aside. "Incidentally you did not comment on this gem of a composition and I can quite imagine what a surprise—if not a shock—it was to you. But composers are people and therefore many sided, and this is one side of me you do not know about."[11] That side was much closer to *God's World* of 1933 than to the Cobbossee songs of 1928. The two-bar introduction indicates that the hymn is in G major, even though there is no key signature for the hymn, and the reason why there is no key signature soon becomes apparent. The 16-bar refrain goes as far afield as D♭ major, and the eight-bar verse begins in B♭ major, reaches D♭ minor by its sixth bar, and then deftly modulates back to G major. One reviewer remarked about the "unusual harmonic progressions" in the mixed chorus version, which differs from the unison version in the contrapuntal elaborations the music deploys as the piece progresses. The accompanist for the choral version is also kept much busier than her church counterpart, with one passage with eighth-note parallel fifths in the left hand and parallel sixths in the right hand sure to tax most high school pianists.

Schuman was surprised and disappointed that the arrangements of "The Lord Has a Child" did not sell well. "I have been disheartened by the lack of enthusiasm for the choral pieces—disheartened by this because my choral catalog at Schirmer's continues to be requested and because I believe the rounds and perhaps the hymn I have given you should be the beginning of a catalog in this field of comparable standing to my Schirmer catalog."[12] Other contemporary choral anthems provide as much substance with fewer difficulties for the performers than does "The Lord Has a Child." Schuman's exploration of modulatory possibilities in this work, however, explains in part why he turned to it again later in life.

Though he despaired of the situation with the *Rounds* in 1958, they became better known as time went on. It is hardly surprising, given his intensive work with Haubiel on counterpoint in the early 1930s, that

> I have had a fine time composing these rounds. You will notice that they are all written out as choral pieces and that they include in each instance an added ending. The melodies are not too difficult to learn and once they are learned, choruses should have no trouble in handling the contrapuntal complexities that result.

Schuman himself compiled the texts of aphorisms for the *Four Rounds on Famous Words* and envisioned writing another whole set "if this first set does well."[13] He pushed to have them published as a set, not as individual pieces, and he got his wish. What he also got was a reshuffling of the numbers. "I noticed that you changed the order of the Rounds. Did you do this just by chance or on the basis of conviction? On whatever basis you did it, I find that the order is superior to my original order and will make the group more effective because it will end quietly."[14] Schuman's order was Caution, Beauty, Health, Thrift. Presser listed them as Health, Thrift, Beauty, Caution. And he never got around to creating another set, although in October 1969 he dashed off a fifth round, writing it on a torn-off piece of manuscript paper with the notation: "Excuse haste. Ha!" He also suggested a new order for the (now) *Five Rounds on Famous Words*—Caution, Haste, Health, Beauty, Thrift—though performers arrange their order in ways that suit them.[15] In sending the manuscript of the fifth round to the Library of Congress, Schuman wrote: "These rounds have become popular with choruses around the country and my publisher is planning to issue them in a new edition in which they will all be combined. It was in response to his request that I wrote the additional round."[16] What motivated Presser to request a fifth round and not an entirely new set? Calvert Bean, director of publications at Presser, explained to Schuman, "As we checked the layout of this proposed new issue of the pieces, the idea of your adding a fifth Round of not more than 3 pages of engraved music seemed to be still better, from the standpoint of promoting this new format."[17] Schuman exchanged the fifth round with Ned Rorem, who had sent Schuman a copy of *Critical Affairs*. Schuman commented on the rationale for the new round: "For reasons of pagination for the collection—is this a new one?"[18]

Schuman didn't set the maxim "Necessity is the mother of invention" in his *Rounds*, but the saying applies to what is probably Schuman's most popular original work. In February 1954, conductor André Kostelanetz offered Schuman a $1,000 commission for a work that (1) would not take long to rehearse; (2) "should be in a light vein with a ready appeal for many people, and should run about eight to ten minutes in length"; (3) might be programmatic in nature, "with an American background"; and (4) could be completed by the fall at the latest. Schuman negotiated for a 50 percent increase in the commission and tried to secure a recording in the deal, something that Kostelanetz was powerless to promise.[19] Schuman started on the work almost immediately, but he was dissatisfied with his initial efforts. "I have discarded all my ideas for the piece and have begun again and so have, at the moment, nothing to report. I do want to see you, however, again before I begin work on the piece in July."[20] He did write Kostelanetz in July, but with news of his health leaving him bedridden for the rest of the summer and the unlikelihood of completing the composition in time for a November performance.[21] He also wrote to Copland to say how incapacitating the hepatitis was, given how he wrote music.

> The act of composing for me involves a lot of physical energy—I sing, move about, conduct, yell and in short make about as much noise as my finished orchestral products which in the opinion of some is considerable. Perhaps if I had a nocturne in mind or even the slow movement of a quartet I would be more successful, but, truth to tell, I had hope to compose a rousing overture (on order from André K) this summer.[22]

At the time, the overture was known as "Plymouth Rock."[23] But even with a slice of Americana carved out in Schuman's mind, his slow recovery and the paucity of musical ideas found him chagrined when, in the winter of 1955, Kostelanetz had paid him the rest of the commission even though Schuman had yet to produce a single note. "I wish I could report progress, for I have no work to think about at the moment except yours and have put off all other commitments. Yet the muse remains stupid, blind, dumb and, what is worse, deaf. Let us hope that with the spring of the year I can get off the ground."[24]

By the early summer, he had made some progress with the "intention to compose a work called 'Sleepy Hollow Legend,' the spirit of which will be indicated in a program note quoting passages from Washington Irving's famous story 'The Legend of Sleepy Hollow.'"[25] In a way, Schuman was fortunate that *Credendum* interrupted his *Sleepy Hollow Legend*, for Kostelanetz wrote back to say, No Hudson River piece, please. Ferde Grofé's *Hudson River Suite* was new and was being heavily promoted in the press and was about to be recorded. Schuman's work, Kostelanetz felt, was too similar to Grofé's by implication if not musically, so he asked Schuman to find another idea.[26] It took Schuman another four months to shake off the ghost of Ichabod Crane (so he told Kostelanetz).

> Now I have a wonderful idea which I hope will please you. Here's the story:
>
> Beginning some years ago as part of my professional activities I conducted choral groups and the music of America's first professional composer—William Billings—came to my attention. I have been a Billings' fan ever since, finding in his crude utterances sentiments of great vigor which find in me a responsive chord. Some years ago I wrote an overture based on certain themes of his called, not unnaturally, "William Billings Overture." The first performance of this work was given by the Philharmonic under Rodzinski and it has been performed by a number of organizations since that

> time, yet I have never published the work because I have never been satisfied with it. I have finally determined to withdraw this composition with a view some day of re-writing it. Now, however, I wish to do a wholly new Billings composition which while employing some of the music I had used in the overture will be entirely new in concept and not an overture at all. What I plan is as follows: Some general title such as "Spirit of '76"—Three Pieces for Orchestra after William Billings:
>
> 1. "Be Glad Then America"
> 2. "When Jesus Wept"
> 3. "Chester"
>
> The first piece (words for the three pieces on which the music is based should be printed in the program book) would be a vigorous allegro of approximately 2½ to 3 minutes; the second piece would be based on "When Jesus Wept"—which is one of the most beautiful melodies I know and is in the form of a round. It would be scored for solo oboe (possibly bassoon, also) and strings. I feel confident that this will make a beautiful adagio of 3½ to 4 minutes. The final movement "Chester" would be based on the song of that name which was the rallying song of the American Revolution. The movement would open with a subdued choral statement of "Chester" soon giving way to a spirited treatment and gradually building up to a climax in which the fast music would be pitted against the return of the hymn. This movement I should also judge would be approximately 3–4 minutes in length. I am very excited about the possibility of doing these three pieces for I believe that I can write the kind of work you commissioned without compromise and at the same time supplying a link of sentiment which will help you with the pop audience.[27]

Schuman wasn't telling Kostelanetz the whole truth. At the time, he was in negotiations with Hauser about leaving Schirmer, and one of his grudges against his publisher was that it had declined to publish the *William Billings Overture*. The piece was the first one he had placed on his "Schirmer-must-publish-these-works-or-I'm-out-of-here" list.[28] "I will be flexible and agree to publish in the first half of '56 if you feel there are too many Study Scores of mine to come out in one year. . . . I cannot agree however to have the work languish in the rental library."[29] The overture was also being performed into the fall of 1955. Thor Johnson expressly asked Schuman to have the overture published after his successful performance in 1954 with the Cincinnati Symphony and in anticipation of his September 1955 engagement with the Symphony of the Air at a reception for United Nations delegates and Secretariat members in New York City.[30] And Ormandy was planning on performing the overture during the 1955–56 season; *Credendum* took its place.[31]

But negotiations with Presser consumed much of Schuman's attention in December 1955, and one of the points he wanted to discuss with Hauser was "Williams [*sic*] Billings Overture—will explain new idea."[32] Hauser gave the go-ahead, and by March 1956, Schuman could report to Kostelanetz that "I am making very good progress on your three pieces. The second is finished, the first is lacking but a coda and the third is beginning to take shape in that area above my shoulders that I refer to euphemistically as my mind."[33] For a while Schuman did not know what he would call the piece, but eventually he settled on *New England Triptych: Three Pieces for Orchestra after William Billings*. By mid-summer, he sent the score to Kostelanetz (again Brant served as copyist), well in advance of the projected October premiere. Thor Johnson also inquired after the piece, having heard that Schuman was writing "new music on William Billings." Schuman corrected him. "You will note that I hve [*sic*] used some of the material from the Overture, but I think you will agree with me that the new work is vastly superior."[34]

TABLE A A comparison of two pieces based on the music of William Billings

William Billings Overture	*New England Triptych*
BE GLAD THEN AMERICA	
mm. 1–39	mm. 1–75
40–100 timpani solo, 75–107	***76–136*** *timpani solo rewritten; changes in dynamics and some added notes*
101–139	
	137–171
140–239	***172–271*** *rewriting of melody at* 186/*218 addition of vla/vc @* 214/*247 to* 236/*268*
	272–330
240–259 (slow transition to:)	
WHEN JESUS WEPT	
260–291	
	1–43
292–323	***44–75***
	76–111
324 (fermata)	
CHESTER	
325–429	***1–105*** *rewriting @* 411/*87*
430–456	
	106–176

On the title page of the manuscript for "Be Glad Then America," Schuman wrote the following: NOTE As in all others of my manuscripts—no changes and correction are entered. The copied score & first publication of the score receive the attention. The mss. is in consequence an uncorrected edition—not reflecting recent thoughts or errors discovered. W.S. October, '56

Bold numbers are used for passages that are nearly identical between the two works. Schuman did not take the opening 39 measures of the *Billings Overture* and chose instead to compose 75 measures of new material. At m. 76 of the *New England Triptych*, he transcribes m. 40 from the *Billings Overture*. Materials related to the *Billings Overture* are in roman type; materials related to the *Triptych* are in italics, e.g., 411/*87*.

Within months of its premiere, *New England Triptych* was being scheduled on major symphony orchestra programs for the 1956–57 season, nearly half of which had already passed before word of the composition spread. Hauser was ecstatic. "You certainly called the turn when you said that this work was going to be a very popular number on symphonic programs. I hope, in fact I am certain, that it will be a permanent number in the repertories of all important orchestras from here on in."[35] Two years later, in a promotional letter designed to go to conductors and orchestra managers throughout the world, Hauser laid on the praises of the work, quoting critics and ticking off a list of cities where it already had been performed, including Ankara and Bombay. "New England Triptych is indeed a rarity: a seriously written work, playable by professional as well as community and school orchestras, acclaimed here and abroad, established in three short years in the orchestral repertoire of the day, in short, a 'hit.'"[36]

What makes it so is that, with the exception of the delivery date, Schuman stayed faithful to Kostelanetz's original request. The work doesn't require a great deal of rehearsal time and yet it displays the orchestra—especially the woodwinds—brilliantly. It is in a lighter vein than Schuman's symphonies and ballets and takes occasional forays into polytonality without ever losing sight of a plain triad. While it is longer than the eight-to-ten-minute work that Kostelanetz requested—it often runs closer to 15 minutes—its three movements are relatively brief, and the decision not to retain the continuous fabric of the *William Billings Overture* counterintuitively makes the longer work easier to follow, given its two caesuras between movements. Indeed, its formal construction makes it more like a sinfonietta than an overture, thus giving it a highbrow sheen for a popular audience. And though Billings remains relatively unknown in the United States, he can be cast as a quintessentially American figure. Schuman wrote as much in his paper on Billings for Teachers College, in which he called Billings's melody for "Chester" "drab and banal." That drab and banal along with its rough-hewn companions helped to spread Schuman's name and his music far and wide.[37]

Even before the first performance of the *Triptych*, Schuman had determined to transcribe some of the work for band, thus fulfilling a promise he had made years earlier. In 1952, Charles Hammond wrote to Schuman to ask whether he would accept a modest commission from the organization he represented, the Alpha Chapter at the University of Louisville of Pi Kappa Omicron, a band fraternity that had national aspirations at the time. The fraternity had earlier commissioned Persichetti's *Psalm for Band*, and Persichetti returned to Juilliard with glowing reports of his experience in Louisville. Schuman accepted the commission provisionally. "The next piece for band that I write, I will write for your group, and as soon as it is possible for me to do so, I will get in touch with you." Four years later, he wrote to tell Hammond that he had completed the piece.[38]

Schuman wrote to Hauser first to tell him of his new work, *Chester: Overture for Band*, and of his conviction that it would be a commercial success. "Please be assured that I shall do my best not to make excessive demands in this piece. My last 'Class A' band composition called 'George Washington Bridge' has done extremely well and I am hopeful that 'Chester' will do even better."[39] The word Hauser received from his colleagues confirmed Schuman's opinion, even though there were some markets that it might not penetrate. The London-based Presser agent wrote back after examining the score.

> My opinion about this work is that it undoubtedly has commercial possibilities, and particularly outside Germany I think that it should obtain a good number of performances without any difficulty. I say outside Germany rather advisedly because there the attitude may be so advanced that Schuman may be looked upon as 'out of date'—but we will see.[40]

Schuman had cast his lot with the educational audience in the work, so he could not have been overly concerned that the "advanced" Germans would not give the work a fair hearing.

"On first hearing, it seemed the best of the works this enterprising group of young men has commissioned over the past few years," is how the local Louisville paper heralded the overture's premiere on January 10, 1957.[41] Behind the scenes, a comedy of errors played out for more than a year. Hammond stopped writing. The president of the fraternity confessed that it didn't have the $250 it had promised for the piece, which was already less than Schuman's costs in preparing the score. In June, he wrote to the band's conductor, the one adult who was acting responsibly. "Incredible as it seems, I have still not heard from the Fraternity. Nevertheless, on the theory of turning the other cheek, I am listing the composition as I agreed in its published form (on the score and all parts) as having been commissioned by the Fraternity." Immediately the fraternity sent Schuman $100 and promised to send the rest later. Schuman wrote to the conductor again in February, telling him that he intended to put the matter behind him. "I am not pressing them for payment for life is too short and I prefer to think of the next piece." Another check, this time for $50, arrived a few weeks later, with a promise that the fraternity would borrow the rest if necessary. The correspondence is silent on whether Pi Kappa Omicron ever paid the remaining $100. What it does include are suggestions to Schuman on how to make the work more suitable for high school bands. With the exception of the second tuba part, the band director felt that the work needed no adjustments.[42]

Percy Grainger was on hand when the overture received its New York premiere. Schuman had met the composer-pianist during the period when Haubiel was teaching Schuman counterpoint; Haubiel and Grainger were colleagues at New York University. Grainger said to Schuman, "My wife and I were entranced with the inspired vitality of your *Overture, Chester* last night at the Goldman Band. As always in your scoring, you achieve a flaming brilliance that is quite unique. It was a great treat."[43] At roughly twice the length of its companion movement in the *New England Triptych*, the band version differs mostly in how Schuman elaborated the musical material. The opening chorale presentation in G major, winds only, occurs in both versions, but whereas the orchestral version immediately launches into the Allegro vivo main section, the band version repeats the chorale, now in E♭ major, brass alone. The woodwind curlicues in the orchestra version are more difficult than those in the band version, with their length, range and technical requirements in the orchestra version dramatically pruned for the band version. The orchestra version is also very succinct, getting to its final E♭ cadence with few modulatory diversions. The band version, while maintaining the propulsion of the Allegro vivo, meanders through harmonic and motivic glens with little concern for overall formal balance, and after sending the music through a polytonal filter midway through the fast section, most of the remaining music favors D♭ as the tonic, a perfectly manageable key for a high school band peroration.[44]

Some years after having created both the *Triptych* and the overture, Schuman toyed with the idea of rewriting the latter for orchestra. Schuman didn't say whether he was imagining high school or professional orchestras for his arrangement of an arrangement, though he did envision the possibility that, in addition to being a standalone piece, "it could also be offered as an optional (longer) Third Movement to the NEW ENGLAND TRIPTYCH." The press of other demands (and, apparently, his publisher's coolness to the proposal) prevented him from making good on his idea.[45] But he would revisit "Chester" one more time before he was done with this particular Billings tune.

A year after the premiere of the overture, Schuman turned his attention to the second movement of the *Triptych*. On the manuscript, he indicated the relationship between the overture and this new band arrangement.

> *When Jesus Wept
> Prelude for Solo Cornet, Solo Baritone (Euphonium) and Band
> Based on the round of the American composer William Billings (1746–1800), the Prelude is intended to serve as an introductory work to the composer's Overture for Band Chester which is based on William Billings' Hymn and Marching Song of the American Revolution. When performed together there should be no more than a momentary pause between the Prelude and the Overture.
>
> *transcribed by the composer from his New England Triptych—Three Pieces for Orchestra after William Billings

"Be Glad Then America" would wait 20 years before it made its definitive appearance as a band arrangement.

Schuman hoped that there was other band music in him. He and Hauser spoke of a work whose tentative title was *Piping Tim: Fantasy for Band*. Like the overture, it was earmarked for high school bands and was going to be constructed out of old music, this time from the Irish folk tune "The Galway Piper." He was hoping to squeeze in the writing of *Piping Tim* between *A Song of Orpheus* (1961) and the Eighth Symphony (1962), but the latter consumed so much of his time that he felt he couldn't put it aside to write the light band piece he had in mind.[46]

Another request also made the *Piping Tim Fantasy* less appealing. William Revelli, director of the University of Michigan Bands, had just returned from a successful tour of Europe, the Soviet Union, and the Near East. He and his band were given the spot of honor at the upcoming annual meeting of the Music Educators National Conference. And Revelli gave Theodore Presser the honor of promising to perform a new work for the occasion that the publisher would provide. Revelli knew Schuman was a Presser composer, of course, and it was no secret that Revelli was hoping that Schuman would not only be honored but would also find the time to write for the University of Michigan Band.[47]

Schuman knew that "the little work that I was dreaming up would not fill the bill" for the conference. At first he couldn't see a way to write an entirely new band piece, no matter how auspicious the premiere might be. Besides, he felt that "there is no point in writing a band piece unless it can have wide use for my basic purpose is to make my music practical for the schools and that is the reason why I am interested in the medium of band."[48] Then he had a brainstorm, which he shared with Revelli.

> Last night, instead of sleeping like any sensible man should after a hard day's work, I started thinking about Bill Revelli and the band piece. I do not like to turn Bill down. He has done so much to make the band a true instrument for artistic expression that I feel personally grateful to him for this as well as his own encouragement to me to write for the medium. The idea that I proposed for the Chorale from CREDENDUM let us put aside for future time. How stupid of me not to have thought before that I could make a very effective band work based on the first of the three NEW ENGLAND TRIPTYCH pieces: to wit: "Be Glad Then America." As a matter of fact, although it will require considerable rewriting (as did "Chester") I anticipate that it will be as effective as "Chester."

A fundamental problem remained. While rewriting an old piece would require less time than writing a new one, there were not enough hours in the day for Schuman to revise "Be Glad Then America" alone. The solution?

> I will prepare instead of a full score, a reduction which I will send on to you in a copied professional version. This reduction will have full instructions for instrumentation. . . . Normally, the editor would make the reduction from my score. Now, in the interest of time, I am suggesting that he make the full score from the reduction which I will prepare.[49]

Schuman worked closely with Calvert Bean to assemble the score, and Schuman stated more than once his full faith in Bean's ability to realize his intentions.[50] But the result failed to please Revelli, who reluctantly informed Schuman that "Be Glad Then America" did not work as a band piece, at least not in the version Revelli received, and as a result he would not be premiering the work at the national conference after all. Though he was disappointed as well as mystified at what went wrong, Schuman understood Revelli and agreed with him. "Your decision to include only the two other works from the 'Triptych' is a wise one. It would be foolish indeed to put on the other piece if it is not right. You can well understand that since the other pieces I have written for band 'sound', there must be something going on here that I don't know about."[51]

Schuman attended the conference and praised Revelli for his performance of the Prelude and Overture. "I can't let the concert of Saturday night go by without telling you again how remarkable I think your band is. This was the first time I heard 'When Jesus Wept' and I must say that you made me like it. Your performance of 'Chester' is superb." He also asked Revelli to do him a favor: play through "Be Glad Then America" again and tape it for him, so that he could hear what was not working. "If I can salvage this score, I will certainly do so, and it goes without saying that you will have the first performance."[52] By the time the corrected band version appeared, Revelli had retired from Michigan. For his last official concert in Ann Arbor in January 1971, Revelli sought to commission Schuman to write a work for the occasion, and Schuman eagerly accepted the assignment. Financial constraints, however, made it impossible for Revelli and the University of Michigan to meet Schuman's suggested fee of $10,000. Revelli acknowledged that premiering a new Schuman work "would have been one of the high points of my musical career." Schuman was also living in anticipation of writing an extended band piece. "I have become so enamored with the thought of doing a work for your last concert that I feel let down and therefore fully understand how keenly disheartened you are." Other commissions awaited Schuman, and bands didn't pay as well as orchestras or opera houses paid. After he finally revisited and revised "Be Glad Then America" in 1975, this after receiving a lackluster transcription by an admiring band conductor, one more band work lay ahead in Schuman's future.[53] Like the transcriptions from *New England Triptych*, *American Hymn* (1981) was an arrangement of a 1950s work: "The Lord Has a Child," Schuman's contribution to *American Hymns Old and New*.

Between the Overture ("Chester," completed July 30, 1956) and the Prelude ("When Jesus Wept," completed February 27, 1958), Schuman engaged in one of the more interesting escapades of his compositional career. In the fall of 1956, Schuman received a $2,500 commission to write "the complete musical score for our motion picture photoplay entitled 'The Earth is Born' (hereinafter referred to as the 'Photoplay') the normal running time of which will be approximately 25 minutes"; "our" was Transfilm, Inc., a production company working in tandem with Time-Life Pictures.[54] How and why Schuman was chosen is not revealed in the correspondence, but Schuman made clear that he wanted to have the option of recycling some of the film score into other future works. He would do so, but not until he finished the score under tight time constraints, barely completing it before Frederick Prausnitz was supposed to record the music in mid-March 1957.[55] At the time he sent the score to the Library of Congress, Schuman noted the following about *The Earth Is Born*:

> Of particular note, perhaps, is the fact that two orchestras were used in the composition. In the final result the listener cannot tell when one orchestra is used as distinguished from another. The reason for arranging the score this way was budgetary. The device of using the smaller and larger orchestras makes possible a full symphonic ensemble for some sections.[56]

Schuman was told that the work would be played approximately 50 times at the 1958 World's Fair in Brussels and that it had been provisionally selected for film festivals in Venice and Edinburgh; it was played at the former but not at the latter.[57]

Bill Hooper, archivist at Time Inc. Archives, provided an engaging overview of the history of *The Earth Is Born*.

> Time Inc. commissioned *The Earth Is Born* in 1954. It was initially intended to be one of four short films, based on the Life series *The World We Live In*. According to an early letter of agreement between Time Inc. and Transfilm Incorporated, it was envisioned as a twelve-and-a-half minute film. At that time Transfilm was also authorized to "commence the preparation of three additional storyboards tentatively agreed to be on the subjects of '*Creation of Life*,' '*Evolution of Life*' and '*The Universe*.'" The four films were intended for theatrical distribution and later use in schools.
>
> Progress on *The Earth Is Born* went slowly. During the expensive production process, *Life*'s editorial department requested a number of changes, greatly upsetting the folks at Transfilm, helping to send the film considerably over budget. Due to the production problems, and the significantly higher than anticipated costs, it was decided to discontinue three of the pictures and to complete a somewhat lengthier (20 minute) version of *The Earth Is Born*. Work does not appear to have been completed on the film until the Summer of 1957.
>
> According to a memo in our files, dated July 24, 1958, when the film was first completed "it was agreed that prohibitive costs made theatrical distribution unlikely and that some other form of exploitation would have to be found to recover even part of our expenses."
>
> Time Inc. and Transfilm spent years squabbling over who was responsible for the cost overruns. Time Inc. contended that Transfilm did not get advance approval for many of the expenses that approximately doubled the cost of the film. In a letter to Life's General Manager, dated May 9, 1961, Transfilm argued that "after the first year of production, when it became evident that the re-creation of the Earth, even in

miniature, was going to be a mammoth undertaking and that it had evolved into an experimental endeavor, an entirely new concept developed. . . . We were both fully cognizant that it would require a lot more money to complete. How much? It was impossible for anyone to estimate. Only one thing was certain—we were both anxious to accomplish what we had set out to do and to do it without changing the production technique." Transfilm refused to turn over the negative for *The Earth Is Born*, prompting Time Inc. to threaten legal action in June of 1961. Legal settlements were finally reached in late 1963/early 1964.

Documentation is sketchy, but it appears that the film was aired on CBS in 1960. We have a letter, dated January 19, 1960, from Life's General Manager to a co-producer at CBS Television Network, stating how the credit should be worded: "THE FILM YOU ARE WATCHING—THE EARTH IS BORN, PRODUCED BY TRANSFILM—WAS COMMISSIONED BY LIFE MAGAZINE AND BASED ON ITS AWARD-WINNING SERIES AND BOOK, 'THE WORLD WE LIVE IN.'"

In a memo dated July 5, 1960, Life's General Manager describes the film to Life's Publisher as "one of our distinguished failures. . . . Mr. Luce, I am told though I can't confirm it, regarded it as one of the dullest pictures he had ever seen." [Henry Luce was the publisher and creator, with Briton Haddon, of *Time* Magazine; his other publishing ventures include *Fortune*, *Life*, and *Sports Illustrated*.] The General Manager felt that "a little of the creation of the world goes a long way and the pictures of molten lava and steaming water tend to be repetitious and the music score is pretty Wagnerian and heavy." (NOTE: This comment is the only reference in our files to William Schuman's score.)[58]

Schuman would recycle some of the music in the first movement of the Seventh Symphony, but for the most part he chose to shelve the film and the music he wrote for it, and other than what he saw with his Moviola at home, it is uncertain whether he ever got to screen the finished film as he may have done with *Steel Town*. (There is no conclusive evidence that Schuman took up an offer to arrange a private screening of the earlier documentary.)[59]

After *The Earth Is Born*, Schuman rested from his labors as a composer, since the labors surrounding Lincoln Center were beginning to consume much of his time. The Boston commission, which was already overdue, vexed Schuman as he tried to find an appropriate text for the work for chorus and orchestra he hoped to write. The Violin Concerto required its final nip and tuck, and it is the only major composition Schuman essayed until the *Celebration Concertante* of 1959. The summer of 1958 offered few opportunities to compose, given that Schuman was traveling overseas with the Juilliard Orchestra. But when he returned home, he immediately got back to work on two sets of pieces in close succession.

The first had its genesis in the spring of 1955, when Isadore Freed invited Schuman to contribute a piece for his piano series, "Contemporary Piano Music by Distinguished Composers." Schuman provisionally accepted the invitation with the understanding that he could not have a piece ready any sooner than that fall.[60] The *Credendum* commission made the deadline impossible; besides, "the completion of this work [i.e., *Credendum*] . . . has left me devoid of musical ideas, a state which some will tell you I am in always. But, of course, you and I know how wrong they are and one of these days I might be able to come through for you."[61] He tried in the spring of 1956, to no avail. He tried again that summer, again coming up short. "I find this assignment extremely difficult in comparison to writing a symphony." The summer of 1957 also proved to be fruitless. "I filled several pages, but, after struggling for a long time, felt that I had to destroy them."[62] Finally, in late August 1958, Schuman had a breakthrough, more out of embarrassment than inspiration.

> I felt badly these last several years in not being able to supply you with piano pieces for your series. You know, I think, that I have made a number of attempts to write something for the series but have had no luck. Frankly, piano writing is not my specialty—I find the instrument exceedingly difficult to write for, perhaps because I myself am not a pianist.
>
> When I arrived home from Europe about ten days ago I found the catalog announcing your new series and including my name as contributor. Such a vote of confidence sent me immediately to the workbench in an effort to make you and Theodore Presser Company honest men. The result will reach you shortly under separate cover. I can only hope that you will find them possible to include in the series and that you will bring to bear your editorial acumen in clarifying some of the notation problems which I am sure can be improved for piano.[63]

Freed immediately recommended that Schuman lengthen the second piece. Doing so was a struggle for him, but he was greatly pleased with the results and commented that he could scarcely remember the original version. He also asked Freed, in consultation with Freed's wife, to help him come up with titles for the pieces.[64] (This became a standard operating procedure for Schuman: he allowed Martha Graham to name his dance works, including *Voyage*; he asked Lillian Steuber to assist him in coming up for subtitles for the five sections in *Voyage*; and he asked numerous people associated with *Credendum* to help him improve the subtitles for that work.) In "a somewhat long and rambling letter," Freed congratulated Schuman on the new version of the second piece and sent along his editorial comments and questions. As for the titles: "My wife has made some suggestions for titles using the word 'mood' in connection with each piece—Gentle Mood, etc. If none of these are to your taste perhaps they can help you nevertheless."[65] The works became *Three Moods*, with the subtitles "Lyrical," "Pensive," and "Dynamic."[66]

The motivation for the second set of pieces dovetailed with Schuman's desire to enlarge his choral holdings with his new publisher. Kenneth Munson, chairman of the Music Department at St. Lawrence University in Canton, New York, offered Schuman a commission as part of the school's Festival of the Arts to be held in the early spring of 1959.

> We have in mind a composition about 5-8 minutes in length, preferably for a cappella chorus, and in difficulty roughly comparable to your Prelude and Prologue, both of which our group has performed well. One of our purposes is to add a work of high quality to the limited repertory of contemporary pieces which can be undertaken by the moderately-skilled performers who make up the bulk of participants in a liberal arts music program such as ours.[67]

The invitation arrived on the eve of Schuman's departure for Europe, so Schuman hedged his bets with Munson, asking him and his colleagues either to suggest possible texts or to ask another composer to fulfill the commission. As Schuman was their first choice, Munson sent Schuman four texts: Dylan Thomas's "And Death Shall Have No Dominion"; T. S. Eliot's "Macavity: The Mystery Cat"; Chorus X from "The Rock," also by Eliot; and an excerpt from Stephen Vincent Benet's posthumous verse epic *Western Star.*[68] None of them excited Schuman, but in a torrent of activity, he finished the three *Carols of Death* less than a month after Munson had sent him the texts he rejected. As he had done with *Pioneers!* and *A Free Song*, Schuman once again turned to *Leaves of Grass*.

> The words of "Carols of Death" haunted me for years, because I think they're absolutely beautiful, beautiful words, and I never could find the music that I felt was right to go with them. The "Carols," of course, is my own title—"Carols of Death"—and I liked the title. . . . I don't mean it in an ironical sense at all, but just, I think they are songs about death, and I am not and have never been morbid about death. I always think that death is one branch of life, just to make up a new thought no one's ever mentioned or said before. There's nothing very special about it. But I thought the Whitman texts were absolutely special. I think it comes from *When lilacs last in the dooryard bloom'd*; I have to look it up, where it comes from. [The phrase "carol of death" appears in this Whitman poem; the text of the third setting is also in this poem and bears the heading "Death Carol."] Then I got the idea of making it into three pieces. I began thinking about it. I rarely have done that with a piece of music, but over a period of years I kept thinking about it. . . . (I don't know how many years it was). Then, the idea that I got to make the carols was the fast music in the second piece. That's what took me so many years to think of what to do. Because I couldn't have three slow pieces, and the first one, played alone, I think is considered rather severe. The second one has, of course, the rhythmic interest of all the chorus rhythms, and then it has a long slow ending, and I'm very fond of it. Then, the last one, "To all, to each" . . . I think makes a perfect ending for it. And people that know and like my choral music, such as Bob Shaw and others, think this is the best, this is the best I've done. And I like that.[69]

With its unison opening that blossoms stepwise in both directions, "The Last Invocation" deploys the same technique that Schuman introduced in his *Prelude* 20 years earlier and also used in purely instrumental pieces (e.g., the slow movement of the *Symphony for Strings*). In this and the other two carols, pedal tones appear over which the harmonies shift, with pure triads only occasional visitors until the last carol. "The Unknown Region," the second of the *Carols*, exhibits the characteristic traits of rhythmic propulsion and the seemingly endless repetition of a few syllables that one finds elsewhere in Schuman (e.g., *The Mighty Casey*), with the four-part slow ending reflected in a similar gesture at the opening of the last carol, "To All, To Each" which is mostly in three parts, with the altos and tenors providing the pedal tone as the outer voices move in parallel tenths throughout much of this section.

Schuman recognized that the *Carols of Death* were among his more difficult choral compositions. He assured one choral director that "you will have no problem in preparing [*A Free Song*]. Surely it is much simpler than 'Carols of Death.'" And when he was preparing to deliver the keynote address at the 1977 American Choral Directors Association convention, he looked with favor upon the programs being presented. "I do note, with pleasure, that the three choruses performing on Thursday morning will each be performing music of mine and I leave it to you to see that these selections are varied. I would hope that the best of the choirs would perform Carols of Death and I leave it to your judgement and the others what other pieces will be performed by the other groups."[70] He treasured the 1965 recording of the *Carols* that the Gregg Smith Singers made, not only commending it to those who asked but also, in at least one instance, sending it to an orchestra conductor as a keepsake, since the conductor—Peter Kermani of the Albany Symphony Orchestra—was a first-year student at St. Lawrence when the *Carols* premiered.[71] They are unquestionably important works in Schuman's oeuvre, but they point backward as much as they "point the way toward Schuman's most recent style," as Christopher Rouse asserted in 1980.[72]

The *Carols of Death* serve as a fitting conclusion to Schuman's brief but intense populist phase, in which he deliberately composed music for its marketplace potential. His interest at this time in *The Last Notch* as a possible opera subject and the telecast of *The Mighty Casey* further demarcate this period of his life as one where he consciously sought to reach out to all and to each. In contrast, his next work retreated from the Everyman stance that he adopted with Presser. So radically did he break with the popular skein in this work that he left it not only unpublished but uncatalogued in his own papers. That work holds the seed to the "rhetorical" and dramatic works Schuman wrote in the next decade, to use Rouse's terms, and though Schuman scoffed at some of the new music around him, he took note when two of his esteemed colleagues took the plunge into serialism. Schuman swam after them.

TWENTY-ONE

INTERNATIONAL MAN OF MUSIC

Roy Harris roped Schuman into serving on what Harris called an "international jury," tasked with the responsibility of drawing up a list of "names of those Occidental composers whom you think should be represented on this International Festival [the Pittsburgh International Contemporary Music Festival, held in November 1952]."[1] After some more wheedling from Harris, Schuman came through. "The following list of composers does not pretend in any way to be a complete catalog of contemporary composers of proved merit. It is a suggestion of a group that is fairly representative, but not all inclusive. I will be delighted to have the committee enlarge, subtract, amend and correct."[2] Schuman's tabular list:

Barber	Debussy	Milhaud	Sessions
Bartok	Hanson	Nielsen	Shostakovich
Berg	Harris	Piston	Sibelius (Symphony No. IV)
Bloch	Hindemith	Prokofiev	Stravinsky
Britten	Honegger	Ravel	Vaughan Williams
Chavez	Janacek	Schönberg	Villa-Lobos
Copland	Malipiero	Schuman	

Seven of Schuman's 27 "fairly representative" composers were dead. One—Sibelius—was no longer composing, and Schuman limited Sibelius's output to one "contemporary" work that was composed in 1911. The junior member on the list was Britten, who was just three years younger than Schuman and Barber. No Messiaen or Boulez or Stockhausen. No Varèse or Webern. No Charles Ives, whose Second Piano Sonata ("Concord") was recorded in 1948 and received wide circulation. "I'm an admirer of Ives as a great original. But in my judgment Ives will never have a truly exalted place in the history of music because technically he was an amateur."[3] No Elliott Carter, who was blazing new trails with his Cello Sonata (1948) and the First String Quartet (1951): "With repeated hearings of [Carter's] Piano Concerto and the Concerto for Orchestra. . . . I feel empty, empty, empty, empty. I don't feel any soaring need for him to write music. I heard a soaring intellect, not a soaring what?—heart? Whatever you want to call it. It seems to me the highest kind of music that can be produced by intellectuality."[4] And no John Cage, whose Sonatas and Interludes for Prepared Piano (1946–48) had tongues wagging, whose *Music of Changes* and *Imaginary Landscape no. 4 for 12 Radios* (both 1951) had heads shaking, and whose *4'33"*—which debuted on August 29, 1952, "a landmark date in American music history, as important here as the premiere of *Le Sacre du Printemps* was for Europe in 1913"—had people walking out of the concert. Kyle Gann wrote that Cage "would subsequently become the most influential and controversial, well-loved and widely ridiculed composer of the second half of the twentieth century."[5]

Cage presented a particular challenge to Schuman in the 1950s, as Schuman found himself with more and more power to help shape the views of American music not only within the United States but abroad. For six years—from the fall of 1954 to the fall of 1960—Schuman served on the Music Advisory Panel of the International Exchange Program (later renamed the International Cultural Exchange Service). The American National Theatre and Academy (ANTA), established by Congress in 1935, was the umbrella organization chosen to advise the U.S. State Department in its International Exchange Program. The opening paragraph in the minutes of the Music Panel's first meeting expressed the high calling envisioned for this program and this panel.

> ANTA was selected by the State Department as its professional agent to assist in the encouragement of international tours by American performing artists of outstanding ability. ANTA in turn has called together a panel of the MUSIC experts to serve in an advisory capacity to guide, advise and help select the proper talent that will best represent American art. This is the best type of representation to acquaint other countries with American cultural achievement. Panels have been arranged for Drama, Music and Dance to help set up this program.[6]

(Members of the initial Music Panel were Olin Downes; Edwin Hughes of the National Music Council; Jay Harrison, *New York Herald Tribune* music editor; Paul Henry Lang, *New York Herald Tribune* music critic and musicologist at Columbia University; Schuman; Carleton Sprague Smith, chief of the Music Division of the New York Public Library; and Virgil Thomson. In addition, there were three staff members who attended most of the meetings: Rosamond Gilder, U.S. director, International Theatre Institute; Virginia Inness-Brown, vice chair, International Exchange Program; and Robert Schnitzer, general manager, International Exchange Program.) As the inaugural minutes make plain, the Music Panel was charged with sending representative American artists and representative American music overseas. The Music Panel would wrestle throughout its existence with what the word "representative" meant.[7]

Was Cage, for example, representative? In the years that Schuman served on the Music Panel, Cage submitted proposals at least twice to be sent overseas under the aegis of the State Department. The first came within months of the panel's inception, but prior to that, Cage had written directly to Schuman to offer his services and those of pianist David Tudor for a concert at Juilliard. "I am also available for lecturing; a subject that interests me and has been proposed by the Dartmouth College Lecture Committee is 'The Relation of Music for Magnetic Tape to that of the Twelve-Tone Row.'"[8] If Schuman answered Cage, the letter is missing from the papers Schuman gave to the New York Public Library, but given Cage's negative reception at Juilliard in 1952 for a lecture sponsored by the International Federation of Music Students, Schuman may have been loath to invite Cage to campus again.[9] It is also difficult to know for certain what Schuman thought of Cage prior to early 1955, although a 1949 letter from his former Sarah Lawrence colleague Horace Grenell, who found the music of Cage "so completely decadent and little more than a curio," gives some idea of what those who had Schuman's ear thought of the iconoclastic composer.[10] What is known is that, when given the opportunity on the Music Advisory Panel to vote to support Cage's enterprises, Schuman initially voted against him. In February 1955, Schuman was outvoted 3–1 on a proposal submitted by Cage and Tudor, "who were forming a group with the Merce Cunningham dancers to go to Japan, Indonesia, Italy and Egypt." Schuman's objections were that "they are too esoteric," "they are experimental, and not good for this Program," and that "John Cage is not universally acceptable even to intellectuals in this country." Five years later, though, Schuman would vote to send Cage and Cunningham to the tenth anniversary of the Berlin Festival. On both occasions, the Dance Panel voted to turn down the projects.[11]

Cage in many ways is emblematic of the convulsions coursing through American music in the 1950s and how they affected those established and conservative members of the musical establishment. At the very first panel meeting he was able to attend, Schuman agitated to ensure that orchestras not only engage "outstanding American artists" but that they also program American music.[12] Schuman's spat with the New York Philharmonic and its slighting of American works for its 1955 European tour grew out of this belief, and it elicited something of an I-told-you-so from him once reports on their American-music-free performances came back to him. "In fact, the extensive programming of Shostakovich, Prokofiev and Kabalevsky has had repercussions in our consulates and has got all the 'bright boys' in Europe saying that we are playing Russians because we have no composers of our own. Anyway, that's what I hear via the mail."[13] Later in his tenure on the panel, he would repeat his position.

"Mr. Schuman feels that a representative American artist must represent America's creative efforts."[14] The entire panel similarly went on record numerous times about how this policy was fundamental to its work.

> It is the sense of this Panel that every artist going abroad under the sponsorship of this Program should recognize his non-professional responsibilities as an Ambassador of the American people, and prepare himself well beforehand as to the culture and music of the country to which he is going, as well as the music of his country.[15]

The music of homegrown composers needed to be heard and played and understood and talked about, Schuman and his colleagues felt. Yet the panel rejected Gershwin's *An American in Paris* as a representative work, dismissing it as a "second-class piece."[16] Jazz, both the music and its practitioners, so flummoxed these Brahmin that they recognized their own lack of expertise and selected another expert to join the panel.[17] And at first, for Schuman, someone like Cage was "not good for this Program," suggesting more delicately what Grenell had said: that decadent music wasn't American music. Schuman may have missed the irony when earlier in the decade he argued that the U.S. section of the International Society of Contemporary Music ignored the full panoply of American compositional effort and then asserted, after the merger between the League of Composers and the ISCM was completed, that there were composers and music that nevertheless remained beyond the pale.

One cannot fully fault Schuman, however, for the 1950s in the United States, musically speaking, was a disorienting decade. It saw the rise of rhythm-and-blues and its spawning of rock-and-roll. Cage and the New York School cultivated musical indeterminacy, while Babbitt and others explored total serialism. By the end of the '50s, Max Mathews at Bell Labs was creating new programs in electronic music, and Vladimir Ussachevsky and Otto Luening were teaming up with Babbitt and Sessions to found the Columbia-Princeton Electronic Music Center. If there had ever been a grand narrative of American music, it was shattering into a million bits during the period that Schuman and his co-panelists were trying to convey to the world what American music looked and sounded like.

Adding to the complications presented by the explosion in musical expressions stateside were the expectations overseas of what American music ought to be. According to the minutes of a panel meeting, Schuman took great pride in the fact

> that he can say, when talking about the operation of this Program, that our Government has never challenged an artistic decision made by the Panels. On purely artistic terms we have had no interference. Mr. Schuman believes that this statement on artistic freedom should be added to any release made to the press.[18]

But in the field, there was "a general feeling among . . . officials that ANTA's panels in music, dance and theatre are thinking too much in terms of New York, or European cities" and that the needs in other parts of the world, particularly

Asia, were different from those imagined by Schuman and his colleagues.[19] Asia hadn't been much on Schuman's radar prior to his work on the Music Panel, but he quickly became more attuned to how the federal government might use music as a propaganda tool in the Eastern hemisphere. Consider this exchange recorded from one meeting:

> [Pianist] Joel Rosen made a four month tour of Asia and around the world. . . . There was an informal aspect to his concerts and he feels strongly that tours should be directed toward the universities since the future leaders of the countries will come from the college students of today. The whole cultural program is just a trickle in comparison with the Russians. Mr. Rosen stated, for example, that only four American pianists have been to Japan, but six Russian pianists have given 60 concerts there this season. . . . After hearing Mr. Rosen's talk, it seems to [Schuman] that there is a level of population that is most important to reach, and that is the Asian student population.[20]

It is almost difficult to recall a time when Asian students in both hemispheres were not involved in Western classical music. And Juilliard would be one of the institutions that would profit from this shift in focus among Asian students.

Schuman himself also nurtured and benefited from Juilliard's growing national and international profile in Asia and beyond. The dissemination of the *Juilliard Report on Teaching the Literature and Materials of Music* brought the curriculum into greater prominence, and the roster of teachers on its faculty was unparalleled in the United States. Its image was burnished further when the school was selected to be the principal educational institution for the novel project being discussed for Lincoln Square. In late 1954, a convergence of dreams and plans began to emerge. Both the Metropolitan Opera Association and the Philharmonic-Symphony Society were looking to build new homes for their performers, and the area slated for redevelopment between West Sixty-second and West Seventieth Streets in Manhattan held promise as a future site for their facilities. Two representatives from the Met, two from the Philharmonic, philanthropist John D. Rockefeller III and some other men of distinction, including Lincoln Kirstein of the New York City Ballet, came together in late 1955 to form the Exploratory Committee for a Musical Arts Center. By this time, the men had determined that institutions beyond the Met and the Philharmonic needed to be invited to join in the Lincoln Square project. Questions arose as to what type of educational offerings the project would encompass. Columbia was planning to build a new arts center, a decision that would have to be revisited had its administrators come to an agreement with the Exploratory Committee to make Columbia the education constituent in the project. But neither Columbia nor New York University focused enough on the training of performers to become professional artists; Juilliard was far and away superior to these institutions in that regard.[21] In February 1956, Schuman wrote to Copland to say that the idea of Juilliard joining the Lincoln Square project was, at best, "a far-fetched possibility"; a year later, Schuman explained, in a meeting of the Metropolitan Opera Association Board of Directors "how in its plans for moving into the Lincoln Center group the Juilliard School would narrow its operations to cover only the most highly gifted graduate students and would expand its present curriculum to cover drama and the dance."[22] Twelve years earlier, Schuman had shaken Juilliard to the core when he arrived and started making changes. The move to Lincoln Square would further change the institution.

So would the successes of its students, the most stunning of which was Van Cliburn's triumphant showing in the inaugural International Tchaikovsky Competition, held in Moscow in 1958. Cliburn and Daniel Pollack, both students from Rosina Lhevinne's Juilliard studio, were accompanied by Mark Schubart, the school's dean, who sent an article back to the *New York Times* about the entire experience. That the president of Juilliard would send his dean to Moscow in itself speaks of how important Schuman viewed this international exposure; Schubart's article in turn sounds as though it could have been written by Schuman.

> It is hard for Americans to understand that, despite the exigencies of international relations, the attitude of the Russian individual toward the American individual is warm and friendly. Music, of course, really is an international language and a happily neutral ground for fruitful interchange.
>
> . . . The Russians are obviously starved for intimate contact with the Western world, and in a curious way the great popularity in the United States of touring Russian artists might be said to indicate the same instinct in reverse.[23]

At his very first Music Panel meeting, Schuman voiced his opinion that the State Department's policy of not sending American performers behind the Iron Curtain was misguided. Rather, the minutes say, "Mr. Schuman would like to invite an exchange of performing artists and believes this is the greatest way to break the iron curtain."[24] Cliburn's success, to Schuman, not only put a crease in that curtain but also tore off the blinders that, he felt, too many Americans had when it came to American artists and composers. He congratulated Cliburn:

> All of us at the School felt pride in your achievement and in the knowledge that the astonishing world-wide attention given your performances in Moscow would not only accelerate your own acceptance as an artist but could have broader implications as well. . . . Surely as Americans it is rewarding to have a joyous event of international scope stem from an American artist. Perhaps the surprise expressed in some foreign quarters that Americans have achieved distinction in music will awaken those Americans who do not fully appreciate the remarkable qualities and importance of our performers and composers. Perhaps we needed to be reminded that our musicians can be accepted with the best anywhere, that music is a national asset and enhances American prestige.[25]

The chairman of the piano jury for the competition was Soviet pianist Emil Gilels, who took the unusual step of going backstage after Cliburn's performance of Rachmaninoff's Piano Concerto no. 3 to embrace the 23-year-old Texan.[26] If Gilels had not met Cliburn before, he certainly was familiar with

Juilliard, as he had visited the school twice in the fall of 1955 and had received a package from Schuman in appreciation for his honoring the school with his presence. Given Schuman's focus on the Music Panel, the contents of the package are completely predictable. "This package will consist of a number of scores and recordings of contemporary American music, together with some material on Juilliard School. We hope, through you, to make this gift to the Moscow Conservatory Library."[27] Also unsurprising was Schuman's response to Gilels's invitation to come to the Soviet Union to participate in a Congress of Composers that Gilels was planning.

> Should the Congress actually materialize and should I be invited to attend, I am not at all sure that I would wish to do so. Assuming that my busy schedule here at Juilliard could be arranged so that I could be free to go, I would still not wish to consider this assignment unless the Department of State urged it upon me as part of their program and therefore in the national interest.[28]

Schuman did not travel to the Soviet Union in the 1950s—Khrushchev's "Secret Speech" and the Hungarian invasion put a damper on Soviet-American interactions—but he did join the Juilliard Orchestra on its 1958 European tour. In an issue of the *Juilliard Review*, half of which covered the tour, Schuman wrote about the invitation the orchestra received "to participate in the International Festival of Youth Orchestras which was being planned for the 1958 Brussels Fair." Traveling all that distance to perform one concert would have been extremely cost-inefficient, so Schuman and the school's Board of Directors came up with a proposal.

> It was decided to bring the invitation to the attention of the Government through its International Cultural Exchange Service which is administered by the American National Theatre and Academy (ANTA), in the hope that ANTA's panel of experts would approve the selection of the Juilliard Orchestra for an extended tour in which Brussels would be included. We all were immensely pleased and proud that, in due course, the ANTA panel gave the Juilliard Orchestra its stamp of artistic approval and recommended that on its tour it represent the United States at the International Festival of Youth Orchestras.[29]

In his recounting of events, Schuman failed to mention that he was on the ANTA Panel, that other American orchestras had received invitations, and that the question of which student orchestra would represent the United States—the State Department was willing to underwrite only one orchestra—had been a highly contentious issue over several panel meetings. Howard Hanson had asked at one panel meeting for the Eastman Philharmonia to be considered and promised to submit a written request to the panel to that end; for some reason, he never followed through.[30] E. W. Doty, president of the National Association of Music Schools, wrote a private letter to Robert Schnitzer, general manager of ANTA, suggesting that the makeup of the Juilliard Orchestra invalidated its classification as a student orchestra, an assertion that Doty later admitted he based on hearsay.[31] Schuman was so incensed at this breach of professional decorum that he sought a formal apology from the national association, and when Doty's successor suggested instead that the entire case be referred to the association's Commission on Ethics, Schuman peremptorily withdrew Juilliard's membership. Schuman further tried to rain opprobrium down upon the national association by circulating a sizable dossier of the contretemps among other institutions and asking an intermediary organization, the Middle States Association of Colleges and Secondary Schools, to render a verdict against the national association. The chairman of that organization counseled Schuman to cease and desist, suggesting that "by pursuing matters further [Juilliard] would only serve to sully its own name."[32]

All of these political machinations show how powerful a man Schuman was—and how powerful he thought he was. In the case of the orchestra's tour, however, his actions should not overshadow the historic success the orchestra enjoyed in England, Belgium, Germany, Denmark, Austria, and Italy. The orchestra played at a level that astonished the Europeans, and the orchestra members, decked out in Vera Maxwell–designed and donated outfits for the women and formalwear for the men provided by Aleck Gingiss of After Six and paid for by a wealthy chemical industrialist, created a visually stunning tableau on the stage.[33] Howard Taubman, music critic for the *New York Times*, translated for his American readers a review the orchestra received in Konstanz, Germany (on the Swiss border). "Let us speak frankly: What German, what European Hochschule, could put together such a highly qualified orchestra? None." Critic after critic repeated the same refrain: the Juilliard Orchestra was on a par with many professional orchestras.[34] Schuman gave a similar report in his remarks to the ANTA Music Panel. The minutes of the meeting tell of the orchestra's musical triumph.

> Mr. Schuman was with the Orchestra during three major concerts, in London, Brussels and Rome. Not being immodest, if he had tried to write a precis of what would take place in terms of reception and prestige, he could not have imagined anything like what actually did occur. There were encores, acclaim, and wildly enthusiastic notices in the press. The Orchestra played impeccably; it was the best Orchestra they have ever had, mainly due to the two weeks rehearsal time before departure. They did six different programs in Brussels, where they were highly praised. An editorial stated that there was no school in all of Europe equal to this.[35]

As for repertoire, the orchestra played the music of four Americans: Barber, Copland, Piston, and, of course, Schuman, but he received only five performances (one for *New England Triptych*, four for the *Symphony for Strings*), making him the third-most frequently performed American composer on the orchestra's tour. (Piston and Barber each received seven performances; Copland received four.)[36]

Cliburn the soloist had come to the Old World and conquered; now the Juilliard School's ensemble demonstrated that he was not a fluke. To Schuman, both of these conquests were further tools to propagandize on behalf of the government. In fact, his role on the Juilliard tour was one of reconnaissance and not merely as a doting father figure. David S. Cooper, head of the Music Branch of the Information Center Service within the U.S. Information Agency (USIA; overseas known as the U.S. Information Service, or USIS), wrote to Schuman prior to the orchestra's departure for Europe.

> It would be very helpful if you would be willing to call at the USIS posts in the cities you visit in order to confer with our field officers on various aspects of the music programs they conduct. Some of the specific situations on which we would appreciate your reactions are the status of performances of American music in Europe, the adequacy of our efforts to support and stimulate them, and the problems of selecting and assisting American performing artists or groups who do not travel under the President's Program.[37]

Cooper and Schuman had begun corresponding shortly after the premiere of *Credendum*, whose recording was purchased and disseminated by Cooper's agency to the overseas posts.[38] But Cooper's new request came with a weightier proposal: that Schuman consider service to the USIA as an advisor on music. Schuman accepted Cooper's offer, and after a background check turned up nothing untoward in Schuman's past, he joined the USIA Advisory Committee in 1959 as its first musician.[39] The correspondence between Schuman and Cooper during this year is nearly conspiratorial in tone as they searched for ways to cut through governmental red tape to make greater room to use music as a cultural weapon. They carved out a Music Advisory Panel that met for the first time in 1960, with Schuman as chair, which resembled the ANTA Music Panel both in function and, to some degree, in personnel.[40] How much more Schuman would have done remains a matter of conjecture, for in the fall of 1960, he curtailed his involvement with both ANTA and the USIA. "It seems that I have been overworking and have reached a point of fatigue which has resulted in an unmistakable warning. My physician has laid down the law and I must follow his advice if I am not really to become ill. For the foreseeable future I must give up my many extra-Juilliard commitments."[41] The commitments he kept beyond the day-to-day operation of the school were the ongoing development of the Lincoln Square project and his composing.

Most of his works from the 1950s, as has already been shown, were aimed primarily toward achieving wide distribution. The band pieces (*George Washington Bridge* and *Chester*), the choral works (*The Lord Has a Child*, *Four Rounds*, *Carols of Death*), the major orchestral work premiered by the University of Miami Orchestra (*New England Triptych*), the opera produced by the Hartt School (*The Mighty Casey*), a score for a film designed for commercial distribution (*The Earth Is Born*), and the short piano pieces meant for novice players (*Three Moods*) all cultivate easy accessibility. The success of the *Triptych* in particular cannot be denied; it remains popular with performers and audiences alike. This was also a decade when the copyrights for his published Tin Pan Alley songs needed to be renewed, and Schuman was unabashed at trying to exploit the youth market with these seemingly antiquated works. He pushed one song particularly hard. "My feeling about 'Waitin' For The Moon' is my hunch that it can make a successful piece in rock and roll arrangement. It lends itself to this type [of] treatment. To issue it as is would prove nothing. It requires a fine arrangement. I wish I had the time (or maybe you'll say the talent)." He scribbled a $\frac{12}{8}$ rhythmic treatment that was something of a cross between *Heart and Soul* and *Unchained Melody*.[42] And to his publisher's bemused remarks that the president of Juilliard and the composer of serious music shouldn't try to compete with Elvis and his ilk, Schuman simply replied: "among my large catalog of work I have no stepchildren."[43]

But when compared to other music composed in this decade that was held in high esteem by other composers (e.g., Boulez, *Le marteau sans maître*, 1953–55; Stockhausen, *Gruppen*, 1955–57; Stravinsky, *Agon*, 1953–57), Schuman's children were not only out of step but were also falling behind. Some years later, he wrote disparagingly about the kind of music that was achieving success. "If you want more performances, you had better write for 16 carefully selected instruments, each played judiciously in different parts of an auditorium, and at least half of which are of the bell-like percussion variety. Also, be very careful to avoid any semblance of step-wise melodic invention, or discernible rhythmic cohesion."[44] If Schuman wasn't predisposed to write this kind of music himself, nevertheless his increased visibility as a spokesman for music in the 1950s made it all the more imperative that his own works be more *au courant*. Neoclassicism was dying off and Cageian indeterminacy was not Schuman's dish, to say the least. Total serialism would have been too great a leap for Schuman, but the examples of Stravinsky, Dallapiccola, Bernstein, Copland, and Rochberg provided a more congenial route: find a personal expression within the 12-tone system.

Rochberg was one of the first to widen Schuman's 12-tone horizons by sending Schuman his essay, *The Hexachord and Its Relation to the Twelve-Tone Row*, which was published in 1955. Schuman struggled to get through the analyses and tables, but he was impressed enough with the essay that Schuman suggested that Rochberg "write a general text on 20th century compositional techniques in which the 12 tone would be one important facet but which would include other important departures."[45] The two men spent an afternoon together in which Rochberg played his Sonata-Fantasia for solo piano for Schuman, who was more impressed with "the overriding and inescapable emotional urgency of the music and the unimpeachable artistic integrity which motivated its creation" than the music itself, given that his own impressions were "unavoidably—however unwillingly—colored by personal predilections."[46] But Schuman took an opportunity to leak news to Rochberg about his receipt of a Koussevitzky Foundation commission to express his thoughts on Rochberg and dodecaphony.

> Now that distance separates us I have the temerity to express the hope that you do not write your next piece in any "system." Please understand that I do not refer to the technical procedures of composition, or the selection of a particular esthetic—rather to the inadvisability of a man of your talents limiting himself by attempting always to fulfill predetermined procedures. Don't do it, George. You don't have to. Let your talents ride. Since you have chosen to write in a certain technique you will do so anyway and with a welcome abandon of emotional drive if you cease to hamper yourself with contrived (however brilliant) limitations.[47]

Rochberg was moved by Schuman's interest and concern, but he reassured him that 12-tone composition was more than a "system" for him.

> I am really trying to say that 12-tone as a way of thinking & feeling is right for me; I am well aware, however, that it need not be & very often is not "right" for someone else. . . . I feel certain that you must know how strongly I want to write a music which is emotionally free and full of life; your faith in my gifts is very heart-warming and there is much more in your letter for which though implied I am very grateful.[48]

Perhaps they agreed to disagree in 1957, but three years later, Schuman gave Rochberg kudos for the accomplishment—and the music—represented in the Second Symphony (1956), which was written in the "system" from which Schuman sought to liberate the liberated Rochberg (or so Rochberg thought and felt at the time).[49]

The exchange with Rochberg also came just months before Schuman studied Copland's *Piano Fantasy*; he recognized the serial techniques in it yet also heard in it "pure Copland."[50] Days after its premiere, Schuman wrote to Copland to acknowledge the thank-you note Copland sent to him for the showcase treatment that Fantasy received. He assured Copland that "it was your music which made everything else seem right. Please know that I spent hours yesterday studying the score while the sounds were still so fresh. This work is for keeps."[51] Now two composers that he admired—not to mention Stravinsky—had shown that adopting 12-tone methods did not efface the composer's own unique voice.

Bernstein's music also proved this axiom. "Quiet" (*Candide*, 1956) parodied the avant-garde music of the era, skewering both Cage and serialism, yet the song, "especially as Bernstein himself conducted it at the end of his life, also happens to contain some of the most eerily beautiful music in the score."[52] And the 12-tone row that comprises the fugue subject in the center of "Cool" (*West Side Story*, 1957) finds Bernstein mingling jazz and serialism with audacity. When Schuman heard and saw the shows is uncertain from the documents, but in the case of *West Side Story*, he congratulated Bernstein on the out-of-town reviews and announced that he hoped to be in the audience on opening night.[53]

The Italian dodecaphonist Luigi Dallapiccola also made a cameo appearance in Schuman's life at this time. He was teaching at Queens College during the 1956–57 academic year, and Juilliard had arranged to premiere his *Cinque Canti* on February 1, 1957. As the head of the school, Schuman had to attend such an auspicious event.[54] Howard Taubman described his impression of Dallapiccola's motivation in a way that sounds as though Rochberg was writing about his own compulsion. "[Dallapiccola] uses twelve-tone techniques out of inner necessity. He is one of the few practitioners of this compositional faith who has turned it into an original and deeply felt communication."[55] Schuman didn't state his impressions of the songs in any of the letters he saved, so whether he liked the *Cinque Canti* is a matter of speculation. He did, however, obliquely express his appreciation for Dallapiccola when he acknowledged to his publisher that the reason *Credendum* was to be performed in Italy in 1959 was that Dallapiccola had heard it in New York and recommended it to his colleagues.[56]

With these living composers showing Schuman that it was possible to use the 12-tone method and yet sound distinctly original, Schuman decided to spend part of the summer of 1959 with the music of a deceased composer he had not thought to include on his 1952 list to Roy Harris. He wrote to Leonard Feist, then president of Associated Music Publishers to ask for a favor. "I should like to buy a few of the works of Webern, which I understand you handle. After you give me my professional discount, a discount for being your friend, and a discount for wanting this music, how much will you owe me when you send me the music."[57] His use of the scores was explained in a letter in answer to one sent by Benjamin Grasso, vice president of the firm. "Thanks ever so much for answering my letter to Leonard. Despite my joking, I certainly had full intentions of purchasing the Works of Webern. However, now that you suggest sending them to me as a gift, I must confess that this is the best price that anyone has offered yet. Actually, Webern's output is very small and I was hoping to get his Collected Works to study this summer."[58] This request for the Webern came just a month after Schuman had shared with Milton Katims, conductor of the Seattle Symphony, his intention to work on three commissions that summer:

> One is for a short work for the Philadelphia Orchestra which I have not yet begun, but which is to be performed January 23, 1960—God and the muse willing. The second work is for the BSO [Boston Symphony Orchestra] which, although already begun, is being put aside in favor of the shorter work for Philadelphia. It is promised for 1960–1961. The third work is for Leonard Rose on a Ford Foundation commission which should be available early in 1962.[59]

The first work, of course, was the *Celebration Concertante*, which was completed by September and was pressed into service for the second work, the Seventh Symphony, which was completed in the spring of 1960. Between those two works lies another work: a pencil sketch for an extended work built on a 12-tone row.[60]

The 14-page sketch bears two dates. One, November 9, 1959, may be when Schuman began work on the sketch. Though the manuscript is filled with snippets of various possibilities for the musical material, Schuman numbered the measures he intended to use, even indicating in one place that measures on another page needed to be inserted at a particular point and providing a conclusive double bar at the end of the work's 88 measures. At the start of these enumerated measures appears another date: August 23, 1960. Conceived for the piano, at points the writing is slightly unidiomatic, not unlike Schuman's published piano works. It unfolds in a fashion similar to that of a Bach invention: after the main theme is stated as a solo voice, its answer enters fugue-like at the interval of a perfect fifth while the original voice provides a contrapuntal underpinning to the theme. Other entries come at the octave and the perfect fifth above the octave. One can see yet again the influence of Haubiel's counterpoint lessons as the work continues mostly in a linear fashion, though on occasion the music moves homophonically in four-voice chords. Throughout the manuscript, Schuman identifies which permutation of the row he is using in each voice at every turn (e.g., RI-C, I-E♭, etc.; for some reason, Schuman chose the retrograde of the original row as his theme). Those chords that Schuman deployed also follow the constraints of the rows Schuman selected at any given time. In addition to the piece and its adumbrations, an additional two pages contain all 48 permutations of Schuman's 12-tone row. And one of those permutations—P_5 (or O-F, as Schuman identified his rows by the starting pitch of their original version)—Schuman rhythmicized and installed as the opening theme in the first movement of the Seventh Symphony, the work that fulfilled Schuman's commission for a work to celebrate the Boston Symphony Orchestra's seventy-fifth anniversary.

The *Celebration Concertante* already exhibited evidence of Schuman's 12-tone studies: the three-note fanfare of the *Vigoroso* is presented in its inversion, retrograde, and retrograde inversion forms before the movement has run its course; the opening measures of the *Cantabile intensamente* are so saturated with chromaticism that, unlike in their source material—the second of the *Three Moods*—all 12 notes are traversed by the downbeat of the third bar; and, as Rouse has already noted, the finale features a 12-note chord, albeit one arrived at through what Rouse memorably called "triad piles."[61] But there is no mistaking the 12-tone construction of the first movement's principal theme. Schuman excerpted that melody as the basis for a set of variations his Juilliard colleagues would compose for a dance work choreographed by José Limón.[62] Upon receipt of the melody in the summer of 1960, William Bergsma felt compelled to make a tongue-in-cheek comment about it: "Your theme, although a shade diatonic for my taste, is a good and workable one. I spent a pleasant half-hour harmonizing it à la Schuman."[63] Schuman had finished his large-scale harmonization of the theme by early May. "Last week I finished my Seventh Symphony (incorporating the unlamented CELEBRATION CONCERTANTE) and I am now having the first movement copied. You should be receiving the work in early June."[64] In writing to Rochberg about the new movement, Schuman chose not to divulge anything about the nature of the musical material. "It is my belief and fond hope that this new 1st movement puts the 2nd movement (previously the opening one) in a wholly different light. You will observe that the new piece has a lot to say about what is going to follow."[65] What he had done was to lift whole-cloth a homophonic section from *The Earth Is Born* and superimpose upon it the 12-tone row he composed two years after the film score, the combination of the two elements comprising the opening gesture of the first movement. As for the incorporation of the fanfare motive in the first movement, it may appear as though these three notes are the work's motto, as Rouse heard it,[66] but in fact the *Largo assai* is a consummate act of subterfuge as Schuman retrofitted all this disparate material to compose a movement that unmistakably speaks his lyric and harmonic language but one that also subtly engages in serial organization, including hexachordal organization of pitch materials, for example, during the duet between the clarinets near the end of the movement. And even the choice of instruments there partially disguises the fact that most of the symphony was written with the Philadelphia Orchestra in mind—recall the all-strings third movement—by now placing the spotlight on Rosario Mazzeo, the Boston Symphony Orchestra's bass clarinetist who had made a splash in 1941 with his flawless solo in the toccata of the Third Symphony.[67]

Schuman chose not to speak out about his experiments in serialism in the Seventh Symphony, perhaps not wishing to draw undue attention to his efforts, perhaps hoping that someone else would notice. If it was the latter, he hoped in vain. Karl Kroeger, reviewing the score in 1963, was withering in his criticism.

> One cannot deny that the score has some moments of brilliance, and even inspiration. . . . However, so much of the material has been heard so many times before in so many other Schuman works that it is no longer either appealing or interesting. . . . Frankly, one wishes that a composer of Mr. Schuman's distinguished reputation would recognize the fact that it is not sufficient simply to rewrite, over and over, the same piece with minor variations. If one's music is to live it must be reborn with every work. As it is, the Symphony was old-hat before the ink dried on the page.[68]

With its chromatic intensification and its 12-tone techniques, the Seventh represents a major variation in his style of composition and a definite—even defiant—break with the populist pieces of his immediate past. The 12-tone sketch served as the springboard into this new dimension of sound organization. Together, they mark Schuman's attempt to reaffirm his position as one of the leaders in American composition. Whether anyone else saw it at the time, in these works he was demonstrating his facility in the language of the day while simultaneously retaining his unique sonic signature.

What is also noteworthy is that the decision to recast all these materials as the Seventh Symphony liberated Schuman to return to being a symphonist. His original idea for the Boston Symphony Orchestra commission was a choral work with orchestra, possibly his third secular cantata.[69] Had he composed such a work, one can imagine how it, too, would have fit into his more populist project of writing pieces that universities could perform. His inability to find a suitable text of Americana, however, led him to abandon the idea of a choral-orchestral work and "to proceed this summer [of 1957] with the composition of a straight orchestral work for the BSO."[70] But nothing materialized in that summer or the following one. In March 1959, after news reached the staff of the Boston Symphony Orchestra that Schuman had accepted a commission for a concerto for cellist Leonard Rose, they asked more aggressively for their work. Schuman reassured Thomas D. Perry Jr., manager of the orchestra, that he had everything under control.

> I want you to know that in accepting the commission from the Ford Foundation I made it clear that I could not begin the work until I had completed my commission from the Boston Symphony Orchestra. Actually, work has been in progress on your composition for some time. A shorter work for the Philadelphia Orchestra—started later—will be finished sooner (no accounting for the processes of composers). According to my present calculations, your work should be ready for the season of 1960–61. At least this is my fond hope and I trust that my rash prediction will not jinx the muse.[71]

Perry quipped, with a nod to Loesser's *Guys and Dolls*: "At the rate we are going we've got the oldest established permanent floating 75th anniversary celebration in musical history."[72] Schuman, as it turned out, was correct both in predicting the order in which the works would be completed and in knowing in which season the Boston commission would appear. What he didn't know was how his engagement with serialism would unlock his symphonic impulse.

The commission after the one for the Ford Foundation showed this to be true. In the first time in the history of the organization, the New York Philharmonic Orchestra issued commissions to Schuman, Copland, and other composers in anticipation of its move to Lincoln Center in the fall of 1961.[73] Schuman had long wanted to write a major work for his hometown orchestra.

> Such knowledge as I have of the orchestral repertory has come largely from the good fortune I have had as a native New Yorker of hearing the Philharmonic. Please know that the execution of this commission I regard as a privilege. I hope it turns out to be my best work. At the moment, the statement sounds rash indeed for I have not a thought in my head and will not be able to begin even thinking about it until this summer [1960].[74]

On June 20, 1960, he wrote in his datebook: "Started to think of Symphony. Goal 150 Hours by departure for Europe Aug. 3." That summer he totted up the hours. He wrote to his publisher: "The new work goes slowly and I will have one movement to show for the summer's labor. This means that next year will have to be a real rat-race in order to finish the work by June. In June I must begin the cello work for Rose."[75] On July 31, he had reached his goal of 150 hours; by September 27, he had logged 29 more.[76] He also met that day with Carlos Moseley, associate managing director of the Philharmonic. Moseley told him that the move to the new Philharmonic Hall would be delayed until the fall of 1962. On the cover page of the symphony's manuscript, Schuman tersely recounted the story of this work and the subsequent one:

begun Symphony No. VIII	June 23, '60–August 6, '60 Sept. 12 to 27, '60 July 17, '61–June 14, '62	total hours 645:30

interrupted to compose
A Song of Orpheus
Sept. 28, '60—July 4, '61
total hours 184

Schuman received the commission for what would become *A Song of Orpheus* in February 1959. W. McNeil Lowry, director of the Program in Humanities and the Arts for the Ford Foundation, wrote to Schuman to tell him that violinist Michael Rabin and cellist Leonard Rose had expressed a desire to have Schuman write a composition. When Schuman proposed "a Duo Concertante for Violin, Cello and Orchestra" [cf. the *Celebration Concertante* just months later], or possibly a Double Concerto for these two instruments and Orchestra," Lowry indicated that the foundation intended to commission solo concertos and that he would need to choose between the two interested musicians. Schuman wrote to Rabin to say that, though he admired Rabin's artistry, "I cannot at this time undertake the composition of another violin concerto." So Rose the cellist became the beneficiary of Schuman's earlier protracted labors on the Violin Concerto.[77]

Vincent Persichetti had suggested to Schuman that *Orpheus with His Lute*, a song that was part of the incidental music Schuman composed for Billy Rose's stillborn production of *Henry VIII*, might serve as the basis for a set of variations. In his notes for the premiere of *A Song of Orpheus*, Schuman conceded that "although the composition is not in the form of set variations, all the music grows out of the melodic line of the song which is stated at the very beginning of the composition."[78] (In the score, that melodic cello line has Shakespeare's text printed below it, suggesting that Schuman expected the soloist to know the words as well as the notes.) Schuman joked with Ormandy about the instrumentation. "You will scarcely be able to believe it, Gene, when I tell you that the work is scored for woodwinds, horns, harp and strings, in addition to the solo instrument—imagine a work from me with no brass, timpani or percussion! The entire work will be melodic."[79] In fact, the work contains Schuman's first published use of the harp, an instrument he had admired in Piston's Fifth Symphony and that he was also exploring in his Eighth Symphony.[80] With its slow-fast-slow arch form (reminiscent of *Prayer in Time of War*), unforced lyricism, and mild dissonances emerging from embellishments on the triad, *A Song of Orpheus* serves as a backward-looking interlude to the more tumultuous symphonies that tried mightily to be truly contemporary.

In some circles, though, the more contemporary Eighth Symphony was greeted with the same diffidence that the Seventh encountered. Richard Franko Goldman reviewed the Eighth, and although he was kinder than Kroeger was about the earlier symphony, the sentiment remained the same.

> Technically, the Eighth reveals little change from Schuman's other works of recent years. The basic harmonic trademark is still the major-minor triad in wide-open position; the melodies are still more notable as "tunes" than as themes or motifs; and the rhythmic bounce and restlessness, the energetic punctuation of brass and percussion are still stylistically characteristic. In the Eighth Symphony, one feels this latter element of the Schuman style to be more of an overlay than it has appeared to be previously.[81]

Yet the harmonies and melodies do show traces of Schuman's 12-tone escapades. The opening of the symphony does indeed begin with the trademark major-minor triad, but then Schuman added notes one by one to the texture, and when analyzed along with the ensuing horn line, the opening of the symphony suggests that he was thinking serially, since 11 of the 12 tones emerge before any of the earlier tones repeat. Even in the last movement, which is a reworking of material from the finale of the Fourth String Quartet of 1950, Schuman found a way to integrate 12-tone techniques into this older material, such as in the bassoon-bass clarinet duet over a pedal-point D (mm. 115–18), where the material incorporates all 12 tones in a nonrepeating fashion. Serialism became one of the tools in Schuman's compositional toolbox. But for Goldman and others, it was not sufficient. Goldman also reviewed Copland's *Connotations*, another one of the Philharmonic's commissions and Copland's first 12-tone piece for orchestra.

> It almost seems a pity that Copland feels impelled at this stage, for whatever reason, to try on a new method (for it would be incorrect to describe it as a new style) that gives the impression of being uncongenial, even though it may seem important. The method itself is no longer new enough to arouse interest for its own sake. The interest must be in what the composer has found to bring to it, and in this case it is rather difficult to be certain what that is.[82]

The opinions of the Goldmans of the world may have led Schuman to remain quiet about his own glancing adoption of a system he once dismissed as stultifying. But in a letter to Edward Downes, Schuman subtly revealed that more was going on in the Eighth Symphony than met the eye or ear. Downes invited Schuman to prepare his own program notes for the premiere.

> Frankly, over the years I have become increasingly resistant about issuing play-by-play accounts of my own music. Perhaps I'm making a minor protest against the elaborate essays which these days so often accompany the launching of new works. Complicated polemics for particular aesthetic creeds or compositional procedures may be of value to scholars, but they confuse laymen. Techniques, after all, are work methods, which, in the mature artist, cannot be isolated from his creative process. Preoccupation with descriptions of techniques bears a direct relationship to the rather absurd length we go to in placing composers in categories and often pre-judging their work accordingly as though musical vocabulary itself had something to do with excellence.
>
> This is not to say that it is not desirable to help an active listener hear more in his first exposure to a new work (passive listeners are not receptive to help, since their particular joy is sound-bathing). Certainly, a writer can supply helpful guideposts and I am all for it, provided he sticks to the music and avoids philosophical meandering. In time, the music will be judged by its inherent worth. Fortunately, no propaganda, however skillfully contrived, can, in the final analysis, substitute for genuine criteria any more than prose explanations can substitute for musical clarity.
>
> Having divested myself of these gratuitous comments, I had better stop before I write the kind of essay I am complaining about.[83]

Downes chose to print Schuman's non–program notes in the program book. And in retrospect, the Seventh and Eighth Symphonies can be heard as attempts on Schuman's part to be less conservative and more progressive. He and Copland both were struggling to stay current; the symphonies are partners in dialogue with Copland's *Connotations* and *Music for a Great City* (1963), works that take more risks than might be expected from their creators and receive more criticism than they might deserve simply because they are neither truly avant-garde nor truly recherché. (Barber suffered far less hostility at this time; his Piano Concerto, commissioned by G. Schirmer for the company's hundredth anniversary and earmarked for the Lincoln Center performances of the Boston Symphony Orchestra, won the Pulitzer Prize in 1963.)[84] Later in life, Schuman was philosophical about the mixed reviews his work had always received and the trade-offs he made to write music his way.

> I would like to be loved through my music, as anybody would be. But I recognized that this was not necessarily to be the case, and it would be much better to be despised and write what you want than to be loved and write what you didn't want. . . . I was asked that question just the other day [in February 1977] . . . "Why—when you write these difficult symphonies that hardly anybody ever plays, and you can write the *New England Triptych* or orchestrate Ives' *Variations on America*—why don't you write a holiday overture that would make you a lot of money and would be played a lot?"[85]

He made a fair amount of money on the commissions and wrote the kind of music he felt compelled to write—even music with 12-tone rows in them.

Just as composition for Schuman took new turns in the late 1950s, so did his work at Juilliard. The decision to join the other constituents at Lincoln Center brought a host of challenges to Schuman and his board. The Preparatory Division of the School would not travel with them to Lincoln Center; though it had close to 800 elementary and secondary students enrolled by late 1961, it would have to find another institutional home. The regular student body would also have to be cut back, as space would be at a premium in Lincoln Center.[86] A Drama Division would have to be created from scratch, and how it would relate to the repertory theater constituent envisioned for the center was unresolved. The issue of primacy in the area of dance at Lincoln Center led to questions about the place of the Dance Division within the relocated school.[87] The specter of lost revenue and new expenditures resulted in proposal after proposal of what to eliminate, what to keep, and who would pay. There were many who felt that Juilliard should simply stay at its Morningside Heights location and not join in the Lincoln Square venture; Juilliard's reputation in the nation and beyond was solid, and the sacrifices that moving would demand were steep. Schuman deftly led his Board through the thicket while at the same time he educated Rockefeller and his associates of the peculiar needs an institution like Juilliard required. He remained convinced that the move to Lincoln Center would redound to Juilliard's benefit in the long run, a view that, in the opinion of later observers, has been acknowledged to have been correct.[88] He summed up his life at the time in a letter to Harold Spivacke at the Library of Congress.

Schuman poolside. Photo by Phillip Ramey.

> What with my growing catalog of works, my BMI contract, and my contract with Theodore Presser and Company, I could actually support my family (more modestly, to be sure) as composer. I mention this because the Juilliard position is one that I keep out of devotion and deep interest and not because I have to have the job. This is something I would not have known even five years ago, but I do now. I love the School and the opportunity for the really creative work that it provides. Right now, of course, with the Lincoln Center, it is all a fabulous experience.[89]

That was the summer of 1960. In the middle of the following summer, he wrote to Mark Schubart who was in Europe to give him an update on his composing and the ongoing challenges. "I swim my 20 laps at noon, have a slight lunch, rest, write some more music and swim another 20 before I start those pre-dinner drinks. This morning I delivered the last of my cello piece—'A Song of Orpheus'—to the printer and now in a day or two I will begin another work—that is if Lincoln Center calms down."[90] As Schuman anticipated, Lincoln Center was not about to calm down. What he did not seem to anticipate, amid his forty laps and aperitifs, was just how tumultuous his fabulous experience with Lincoln Center was about to become.

PART 4

THE LINCOLN CENTER YEARS

TWENTY-TWO

THE DREAM DEFINED

The Metropolitan Opera and the New York Philharmonic weren't the only institutions that were seeking new homes in the mid-1950s. Fordham University, whose main campus was on Rose Hill in the Bronx, dreamed of a midtown campus but couldn't afford midtown prices. Fordham's president, Father Laurence J. McGinley, related this dream to Robert Moses, whom the *New York Times* described as a master builder "who played a larger role in shaping the physical environment of New York State than any other figure in the 20th century."[1] Moses held many titles during his career, including chairman of New York's Committee on Slum Clearance, in which capacity he had power and money to raze entire neighborhoods for the sake of urban renewal. "One of the principal objectives of urban renewal," according to a professional in the field, "is to attract more middle-class families back into the central city and slow down the exodus of middle-class families from the inlying areas," and the convergence of wishes presented by Fordham, the Met, and the Philharmonic gave Moses a chance to create the kind of cultural campus that would further his extravagant vision for New York City.[2] Robert A. Caro, Moses's Pulitzer Prize–winning biographer, may be excused for imagining that all the stars had aligned early on in the Lincoln Square project. He nevertheless captures the horrific grandeur of what the project meant to Moses and to the city.

> By 1957, [Moses's] plan for the Lincoln Center for the Performing Arts included not only a four-square bloc Fordham campus, a Philharmonic Hall and a new Metropolitan Opera House but a ballet center, a repertory theater, a high school of the performing arts, a library and museum of the performing arts, a new home for the famed Juilliard School of Music, and such related facilities as 4,400 units of housing, a public school and playground, an underground parking garage, a firehouse, a park with bandshell for outdoor concerts, a headquarters for the American Red Cross and the Fiorello H. La Guardia High School, "not to speak," as Moses put it, "of the neighboring offices of *The New York Times*." . . . Moses was not making even a pretense of creating new

> homes for the families displaced; to replace the 7,000 low-income apartments being destroyed, 4,400 new ones were being planned—4,000 of them luxury apartments.[3]

More than 5,000 families and several hundred small businesses were forced to relocate as a result of the development of Lincoln Square; some of those businesses did not survive.[4] Fordham was a convenient target for residents' ire. The university technically was part of the Lincoln Square redevelopment project, although McGinley would become far more involved with Lincoln Center after his retirement as Fordham president in 1963; in fact, he would become one of Schuman's staunchest allies when Schuman was nearly bereft of support.[5] Having a Jesuit university affiliated with the project, though, complicated matters, and a lawsuit was filed stipulating that the separation of church and state was being violated, since Fordham was obtaining prime real estate at below-market rates.[6] But while plaintiffs were willing to fight the Catholic Church, fewer seemed as willing to inveigh against high culture. The week that Philharmonic Hall opened, Schuman opined about the tension between the underclass and the upper crust.

> At a time when so much attention is being given to urban renewal, we should remind ourselves that the arts are not merely ornaments to the great communities of the world—New York, London, Paris, Rome, Vienna—but central to their appeal. Communities suffer far more than is generally realized from malnutrition of the spirit—neglect of the cultural diet. The physical slums of any community are all too apparent, and their evil is plain enough. But a community in which the spirit is not fed—where it does not often enough encounter the perfection of the arts—is just as certainly underprivileged.[7]

By bringing Lincoln Center to New York City, Moses and John D. Rockefeller III and the men of industry surrounding them were doing war against a form of evil that wasn't as plain as the slums but was, in Schuman's mind at least, just as invidious. No wonder, then, that Schuman, a man from middle-class businessman stock who climbed the ladder of success, emerged as not only one of the most effective spokesmen for the Lincoln Center for the Performing Arts but also the president of the organization.[8]

Had it not been for the disastrous Bay of Pigs invasion, however, Schuman might not have made it into the corner office. Rockefeller was chosen as the first president of Lincoln Center in June 1956, though, considering that he was relying on others to help set the agenda for the burgeoning Center, he assumed the position mostly because the bylaws required that someone hold that title.[9] While his own artistic ambitions were slight, Rockefeller's artistic philosophy was expansive, according to Edgar Young, one of his closest associates. "Rockefeller made no pretense of professional knowledge or expertise in any of the arts. He was not an opera buff, a symphony fan, or a balletomane. But he believed that opportunities to experience the arts should be available to everyone; he

Schuman during his Lincoln Center years. Photo by Carl Mydans.

recognized that the arts could play a significant role in the lives of large numbers of people."[10] His administrative skills were more than adequate for the beginning of the enterprise, but soon the need for a full-time executive at the helm of the center became apparent. As Young said,

> By September, 1960, the search had focused on General Maxwell D. Taylor, the retired U.S. Army Chief of Staff, who was then serving as chairman of the Mexican Light and Power Company. . . . Taylor's keen analytical mind, his firmness in executive decisions, his ability for clear verbal expression, his reputation for fairness and integrity were qualities needed for the executive leadership of Lincoln Center. . . . He was a well-known educator, having significantly broadened the educational approach at West Point during his period of command there. In management and public-administration circles, he was regarded as a careful innovator and a strong executive. General Taylor was ready to return to the United States. He wanted an opportunity for leadership in civilian life and accepted the offer to become president of Lincoln Center, effective January 1, 1961.[11]

In his biography of his father, John M. Taylor noted the seeming incongruity of General Taylor leading Lincoln Center. "He had never had more than casual contact with the performing arts, and his taste in music hardly went beyond early Beethoven. But Lincoln Center was not looking for an artistic director; it was Taylor's managerial expertise that was needed during the construction period."[12] In short, those charged with the presidential search chose a military version of Rockefeller.

Taylor's initial contract was for five years, but four months had not expired when Taylor was summoned to the nation's capital to chair the Cuba Study Group that was convened to investigate what went wrong with the Bay of Pigs invasion of April 1961. President John F. Kennedy himself called Rockefeller to ask that Taylor be granted a two- to three-month leave of absence to complete the investigation. Rockefeller complied, although Taylor felt that, for all intents and purposes, his presidency of Lincoln Center had come to an end. His rapport with Kennedy's brother Robert all but insured Taylor's continued involvement with the federal administration, and on July 1 he assumed duties as military representative of the president.[13]

Brief though it was, Taylor's stint as president of Lincoln Center—and more tellingly, his choice by the search committee—colors the choice of Schuman as his successor. Both Taylor and Schuman were meticulous men who were accustomed to marshaling forces and directing them toward an articulated goal. Schuman, however, could hardly be described as a "careful innovator." Innovator, yes, but the weeping and gnashing of teeth that his early Juilliard reforms elicited in some corners of the school showed a certain brashness in his manner of implementing change. Similarly, the policies he sought as an advisor to the federal government rankled some of the career diplomats in Washington. There was no question that Schuman, like Taylor, was highly regarded in his field. But at a time when the leadership of Lincoln Center was still focused primarily on the construction phase of its development—and must have imagined that it could afford to do so for the five years that Taylor was contracted to preside over the center—the selection of Schuman radically shifted the ground beneath the concept of the center. Taylor's priorities, according to Young, were what one would expect if one viewed Lincoln Center as a collection of buildings: "a firm construction schedule, completion of fiscal planning studies and solution of financial problems related to constituents, a carry-through on operational plans, especially as related to the World's Fair [of 1964–65]."[14] While Young would serve as Acting President after Taylor's departure and would stay on to shepherd the construction at Lincoln Center, Schuman's priorities for the center were worlds away from Taylor's.

This may explain in part why Schuman did not know that he was seriously being considered as a candidate for the presidency until mid-August.[15] It is striking, according to entries in Rockefeller's diaries, that "there was a consensus that greater emphasis should now be placed on the program function of the Center" less than a year after the consensus had been that Taylor was the ideal president. But by early August, the search for a new president focused on finding "an individual basically from the arts field but who has administrative ability and experience," and on August 15, "the Lincoln Center Executive Committee met . . . [and felt] that it would be sound for us to go ahead now with an individual who combined both the arts background and the management ability and that William Schuman was the man."[16] In a letter that he sent to his closest friends and colleagues on the eve of the announcement of his acceptance, Schuman underlined his vision for Lincoln Center, one that could not in any way have been written by Taylor.

> Lincoln Center can have an influence of the first magnitude if it fulfills the hopes of all those associated with it. It can lead to a vastly increased interest in and support for the performing arts. It deserves—and has already gone far toward achieving—widespread support from all segments of our society, among performing artists, patrons of the arts, city, state, and federal governments, and the American people generally. I believe that the Center can provide leadership in bringing large numbers of Americans to a new interest in music, drama, and the dance and in giving them new opportunities to enjoy an experience with these arts. I believe it can lead the way in the development of new 20th century solutions to the problems of supporting and encouraging the creators, performers, and institutions of the performing arts. I want to do everything I can to help achieve such objectives.[17]

Congratulations for his selection came from all quarters. An old friend reminded him of how far he had come. "I'm sure that 112th and 72nd Streets, P.S. 165 & Camp Cobbossee are all bursting with pride at the success of their alumnus."[18] Composer Marc Blitzstein trenchantly expressed what many in the creative community thought and felt. "You really *are* the ideal choice for the Lincoln Center—who goofed?"[19] Schuman's secretary suggested that Blitzstein get the standard form letter: "Thank you ever so much for your thoughtful letter. The wonderful expressions of support that I am receiving from friends and associates is [*sic*!] a source of encouragement for which I am deeply grateful." But Schuman wrote two short sentences in response to Blitzstein's missive. "I greatly appreciate your letter. The opera, I trust, is all finished and scored and that you have nothing to do but to relax and await a magnificent production."[20] Schuman's response illustrates the fact that he insisted that, in his new position, he be identified first as composer and second as the president of Lincoln Center; throughout his tenure as president he would remain focused on what he and his colleagues were adding to the American music repertory. (The opera to which Schuman referred, *Sacco and Vanzetti*, remained unfinished when Blitzstein was murdered in January 1964.)

Another insightful letter came from Harold Taylor, president of Sarah Lawrence from 1945 to 1959 and an educator and thinker far more progressive than Schuman could ever dare to be. Taylor congratulated Schuman on the appointment and wittily outlined the difference between Schuman and his predecessor at Lincoln Center.

> The military man with the family name who was in there before was fine for giving people the sense of security that it was a going thing & they could give money to it, but what it had to have, & what you can give in such abundance, is the flow of creative

> ideas, the conception of what the arts can do & how they should be done, and the impact of a man with your kind of personal & aesthetic integrity. . . . P.S. You never could keep a job, could you.[21]

Bill and Harold had started their school presidencies in the same year; Bill bested Harold's tenure by two years. Every indication was that Schuman's tenure at Lincoln Center should be long, that he would keep the job just as he kept the Juilliard job. That was the hope, at least.

Days after the announcement, Schuman sketched out for himself what he hoped to accomplish as president.[22] He saw, as did General Taylor before him, that construction and the World's Fair were important stages in the development of Lincoln Center. But the bulk of his six-page memo to himself focused on projects: "It is only through the presentation of specific projects that Lincoln Center can realize its potential," he wrote. His imagination led him to name 15 projects in all that became less and less detailed as he dictated his ideas. In light of his accomplishments at Lincoln Center, it is instructive to compare the vision with the reality.

1. Lincoln Center for the Performing Arts, Festival '66. Schuman pulled no punches in terms of the scope he imagined. "It should take its place and hopefully in time exceed the reputations of such long established summer festivals as Salzburg, Bayreuth and Edinburgh." Schuman had experienced the Salzburg Festival firsthand in 1935; for him to hope that the Lincoln Center Festival could one day outrank that summerlong festival shows how audacious his hope was. He may have also temporarily forgotten that Sir Rudolf Bing, the general manager of the Met, was also a cofounder of the Edinburgh Festival. Bing would later prove to be one of Schuman's greatest nemeses in the struggle to define Lincoln Center, but Schuman's dream accommodated the Met—or at least the Opera House. "The commissioning of new works which will be an integral part of the Festival will encompass all the media: opera, dance, orchestral music, chamber music, choral music, drama. It may well be that art film should also be included." Less than a year later came word that $100,000 had been allocated from the Lincoln Center Fund to commission new works for the festival.[23] Here, again, the gulf between what Taylor might have brought and what Schuman did bring is enormous and is further illumined by how reality took hold of Schuman's grand commissioning scheme. "Four new works were premiered during [the festival] at Philharmonic Hall—compositions by Ned Rorem, Ezra Laderman, Gunther Schuller and Easley Blackwood, two of these being works specially commissioned by the Lincoln Center Fund."[24] The bulk of the earmarked commissioning money went elsewhere between the time of Schuman's announcement and the time of the inaugural festival, which was pushed back to 1967 due to construction delays. (What would become known as the Mostly Mozart Festival began in the summer of 1966 to have something going on in Philharmonic Hall.)[25] During Schuman's tenure, Festival '68 was held (though on a smaller scale than he had envisioned), contracts had been issued for Festival '69, and Festival '70 was on the drawing

board. The latter two festivals were ultimately canceled. Taylor would likely not have conceived of such a festival; Schuman could not give birth to the festival he had imagined.

2. Lincoln Center Teachers' Institute. Schuman advanced this idea years before he became president of Lincoln Center, and he had already won the approval of both the Juilliard Board of Directors and the Lincoln Center Council, a body made up of representatives from the various institutions, or constituents, that constituted the center.

> Each summer, there would come to Lincoln Center some 400 or 500 teachers from all over the country, mainly from high schools, but sometimes from colleges, junior high schools, and even elementary schools. The purpose in bringing them to Lincoln Center (to state it in its negative form) was not to discuss pedagogy or to offer courses in methodology or in teaching techniques. The positive goal is to give these teachers an experience in depth with the finest artists that we have. . . . As a result of this project, it is envisioned that in the course of ten years upwards of 2,000 teachers will have been given the inspiration and the techniques to improve their work and through them indirectly thousands of other teachers, and most importantly, over a million students.

Schuman was waiting for the right time and the right forum to give substance to his dream of a Teachers' Institute. Hiring Mark Schubart as executive director of the Lincoln Center Fund seemed to guarantee that he at least had the right man to enliven his idea. Schubart would prove to be immensely skillful in bringing music to schoolchildren throughout the Greater New York City area, but the task of bringing teachers to Lincoln Center would have to wait until 1976, long after Schuman had stepped down as president.[26] As with the festival, the lack of money dashed his plans. Whereas the Lincoln Center Fund was originally designated as the chief funding source, at the time of the institute's beginnings more than half of the money came from endowments and trusts external to Lincoln Center, and the balance was raised through private appeals.[27]

3. Intercollegiate Festival of Performing Arts. While Schuman envisioned a festival that would encompass all of the performing arts, his example turned to a field he knew well—choral music—and in that more limited form, the First International University Choral Festival took place in the fall of 1965. G. Wallace Woodworth—the conductor of the Harvard Glee Club and the force behind the Harvard-Radcliffe Choral Series that Schuman launched while at G. Schirmer—was the festival's music director. A second festival that took place in March 1969 was planned while Schuman was in office. Robert Shaw, whom Schuman had helped to discover in 1942 and who oversaw the eponymous choral series at Schirmer that Schuman established against Woodworth's wishes, was the music director for this and for the third and final festival, held in 1972, which featured Schuman's *Declaration Chorale* (1971) as the *pièce d'occasion*.[28]

4. Lincoln Center Chamber Music Series. "There is no constituent at Lincoln Center in the field of chamber music. Chamber music at Lincoln Center therefore can either take the form of separate bookings for organizations that use the Center's halls, or it can take the lead in organizing a series of its own." Here is the nucleus for the Chamber Music Society of Lincoln Center, which was

officially constituted in 1969. In many ways, Schuman's vision here resembled the vision he had for Juilliard when he assumed leadership there. But the challenges of bringing the Chamber Music Society into being dwarfed those that Schuman experienced in the mid-1940s over the formation of the Juilliard String Quartet. (See chap. 26 for the development of the Chamber Music Society.)

5. "Music Break at the Center." "Studies should be undertaken to determine the feasibility of presenting music for the public during the noon hour each week-day or late afternoon, or both. Lincoln Center can create the 'music break.'" This idea remained on the drawing board.
6. A Foreign Festival at Lincoln Center: "During the spring season when the Metropolitan Opera is on tour, the Center should develop a Festival of foreign performing groups and groups from other parts of this country." From 1884 to 1986, the Met company would go to various cities during the spring to bring opera to the hinterlands, and during its absence various groups and performers would take the stage at the Lincoln Center. But as with the noontime concerts, the vision of a special festival in the Opera House during the Met tours never materialized.
7. "It is anticipated that Lincoln Center will have a resident ballet company. But . . . the Center might well wish to be in a position to make it possible to create during certain periods of the year opportunities for the so-called free dances of a Martha Graham or a Jose Limon, and to present other companies, such as that of Jerome Robbins which combines the techniques of ballet and modern dance in a peculiarly American manner." Schuman in fact explored the possibility of creating a Lincoln Center constituent that he tentatively named the American Dance Theater. This resident company would be trained to perform modern dance, just as the New York City Ballet was trained in classical dance. Agnes de Mille was Schuman's confidante as he tried to animate this vision in 1963, but the inadequacies of the lay leadership and the challenge of bringing together the likes of Graham, Limón, Sokolow, Ailey, Cunningham, and their peers doomed the enterprise.[29]

The other projects included: a Lincoln Center Chorus, which he tried to launch;[30] a Lincoln Center Children's Theater; a marionette theater "along the lines of the petit guignol in the Tuilleries" [*sic*];[31] educational television programs developed by the center; a community arts school housed in the projected Lincoln Square high school; an education program that the center would run for local schools (Schuman labeled this project "most important"); a program for presenting new artists and new works; and a forum for creators in the various performing arts ("composers, choreographers, etc.") to come together and share their ideas with each other. Education in particular received Schuman's attention. Working in tandem with the New York City Board of Education and similar boards in more distant communities, the Lincoln Center Student Program by the fall of 1963 had touched more than a quarter of a million young people with special performances of the New York Philharmonic in Carnegie Hall and truncated presentations of opera in school auditoriums, courtesy of the Metropolitan Opera Studio. A select handful of students were invited to performances at Juilliard, where they were taught about the pieces, met the performers, and sometimes heard from the composers whose works were on the program.[32]

Education was an early and unqualified success, but it, like all of Schuman's proposed projects, cost a lot of money. "The Center, in my view, must recognize that its fund-raising efforts cannot stop when the monies are in hand for the erection of the buildings." The projects would be underwritten through a combination of endowments, constituent contributions, private gifts, and government support. Though he never used the term in the memo, he was making Lincoln Center a constituent on a par with the other constituents. Later in his term, the resentment from the officially chartered constituents—the Met, the Philharmonic, Juilliard, the Repertory Theater, the Library and Museum, the New York City Opera, and the New York City Ballet—would reach a boiling point: "The constituents feel that [Lincoln Center] programs are too ambitious, too costly, compete with them, and especially for fund-raising dollars."[33] In the view of the staff of these other organizations, Lincoln Center had become the eighth constituent by means of stealth. But Schuman believed from the start that the entire concept of Lincoln Center enveloped not only "the autonomy of constituents, but the possibilities that exist for 'making the whole greater than the sum of its parts,'" a sentiment his memo indicates he intended to make plain at the reception that would be given to honor his first days in office.

Schuman's memo left two particular areas unexplored: film and musical theater. In the case of film, Schuman provisionally imagined that filmmakers could be commissioned for the Lincoln Center Festival, but he had not conceptualized a vehicle for film within the Lincoln Center rubric at the time he let his initial thoughts take flight. A letter from Elia Kazan began to change Schuman's thinking. Kazan was serving as a consultant to the architects for the center's repertory theater space and would go on to have a more central role in the life of the theater constituent. Those early meetings seemed to expose a void that Kazan hastened to point out to Schuman. "There is a function that Lincoln Centre can perform and even an obligation that it must meet. . . . I think we should try to work out some kind of program for Lincoln Centre that can make it *the* place where films are recognized on a level with the other major performing arts in this country."[34] Shortly after his arrival as president, Schuman pulled together a group of film experts to produce the first-ever New York Film Festival, which was held in September 1963. If anyone had doubts about the potential for such an offering, they were quickly dashed. Bosley Crowther, the *New York Times* film critic, surveyed the impact of the first festival. "The tremendous public response to this first exposition of motion pictures in Lincoln Center's 2,300-seat Philharmonic Hall was nothing short of a full-blown cultural phenomenon. . . . Very few people, not excepting the Lincoln Center management, dared expect that it would draw such a turnout—close to capacity for every one of the 21 shows."[35] The festivals were not without controversy among the Lincoln Center directors, according to Schuman.

> I remember when [Amos] Vogel [codirector of the Film Festivals from 1963 to 1968] put on a picture with lots and lots of nudity in it, which was quite shocking, that was one of the times that John D. Rockefeller came, and he came with his young daughter. He didn't say a word because he is very disciplined about interfering with professional matters. But Father McGinley was there, and the next morning we were having an executive committee meeting, and I had just finished giving a report on Great Performers at Philharmonic Hall, and McGinley said great men had to leave the theater, and I said: "Larry, wait till next year. Our new series is called 'Great Genitalia in Philharmonic Hall.'" And that broke up the meeting.[36]

Shortly after the conclusion of the equally successful second Film Festival, Schuman began to push for the creation of a Film Society of Lincoln Center, in part to capitalize on the momentum generated from the Film Festival but also to get the deficits of the festivals off of the Lincoln Center books (and the heat off of the directors).[37] Though it was not one of his original brainchildren, the Film Society of Lincoln Center is one of Schuman's creative offspring.

How and when Schuman introduced the notion of musical theater is unclear from the documents. As with film, it was not listed among the ideas he imagined prior to his presidency, so it is a dubious proposition for Young to suggest that "Schuman brought to Lincoln Center ideas for new constituents, particularly for chamber music, modern dance, and music theater."[38] Nor was it considered as a possible constituent when the original Statement for Constituents was adopted, suggesting that no one—including Schuman—had thought about musical theater in the early years of Lincoln Center.[39] By September 1962, however, Schuman did report to the center's Executive Committee that he was having "discussions with leading figures in the musical theater field with regard to the possible creation of a musical theater constituent at Lincoln Center."[40] The chief leading figure was Richard Rodgers, who agreed to head what was first called the New York Music Theater and then adopted the name the Music Theater of Lincoln Center.[41] While Schuman had great respect for Rodgers, the principal rationale for the Music Theater of Lincoln Center was to keep the New York State Theater from being dark as well as to run a profit (or at least to not run as great a deficit as that of some of the other constituents). Initial discussions sketched out a four-month season, from mid-January to mid-May, in which Rodgers would produce "a series of four revivals of light opera and/or musical comedy masterpieces for the State Theater during the period in question." Later, it was decided that summer would be better, two musicals would be more realistic, and that after they played at Lincoln Center the works would go on tour. Rodgers also made a concession. "He acquiesced to Mr. Schuman's insistence that one of the two revivals be of a work by Richard Rodgers—very possibly 'Carousel.'"[42] Schuman even dangled in front of Rodgers the possibility of commissioning a new work for the inaugural season, which he then imagined would coincide with Festival '66.[43] Instead, the inaugural season occurred in the summer of 1964, coinciding with the World's Fair; *The King and I* played that year, with *Carousel* appearing the following summer. By 1967, storm clouds appeared on the financial horizon. By 1974, the Music Theater of Lincoln Center ceased to be a constituent. Schuman never mentioned this constituent at all in his lengthy 1977 interview with Vivian Perlis, and in his 1991 interview with Heidi Waleson, his only substantial comment was, "We started the Lincoln Center Music Theater, with Dick Rodgers, and that couldn't work for financial reasons, for a long period of time."[44] Perhaps its failure led Schuman not to talk about it, but though he himself loved and attended musical theater—and even fleetingly conceived *The Mighty Casey* for Broadway—he did not have a history of promoting musical theater. The Music Theater of Lincoln Center was born with commerce in mind, and most of Schuman's best ideas ignored the bottom line.

Somewhat more curious is the place of jazz in Schuman's planning for Lincoln Center. He made no mention of it in his September 1961 memo, but in a January 1962 Lincoln Center press release, the proposed summer festivals, in addition to including newly commissioned pieces, "will also include works from the standard repertory, will encompass opera, drama, dance, operetta; orchestral, choral, and chamber music; vocal and instrumental recitals; motion pictures; folk music and creative jazz, as well as educational programs relating to the festival."[45] In the interval between these two documents, an advisory committee consisting of Russell Sanjek, Billy Taylor, and Gunther Schuller was formed. The original Lincoln Center concept had not included jazz, and some in the wider musical community objected to this omission. The committee, which was convened in late 1961 and disbanded in late 1964, reported that commercial excellence did not necessarily track with artistic excellence and that jazz at Lincoln Center needed to fall in the latter category. Schuman's stance, as implied in a letter he sent to a fellow music educator, appeared to be that the venues at Lincoln Center were inappropriate for most expressions of jazz.[46] Benny Goodman and Dizzy Gillespie both played in Philharmonic Hall in the early 1960s, but, for the most part, jazz was a dead letter at Lincoln Center for decades.[47]

Those who wished to gripe about the offerings and approaches of Lincoln Center had a fairly easy target at their disposal. Schuman's childhood friend Frank Loesser called and gave what was to Schuman a "cavalier dismissal of our enterprise." Loesser intensified the attack by rattling off a list (all in capital letters) of the performing arts that Lincoln Center overlooked.

> Professional wrestling, bull fighting, auto races, burlesque, comedy, radio & TV announcing, news & weather reporting, political debate, religious oratory, figure

Schuman (right) and Richard Rodgers, October 22, 1962. Photo by Bob Serating.

> skating, strip tease, diving, auctioneering, stilt walking, juggling, restaurant greetings and seating, marching and drilling exhibition, etc., etc., etc. . . . What I really have a sense of dismay about is that there is a *center* of anything. . . . It isn't that one is *better* than the other, but simply that it is *different* from the other.

Schuman conceded—in a way. "Okay—we'll change the name to Lincoln Center for Some of the Performing Arts."[48] Considering the impulse of the major constituents to treat Lincoln Center less as a partner and more as a landlord, Loesser's list would have only exacerbated their displeasure with Schuman's industry. He was either doing too much or too little; he was bound to displease many. But his dream for the center was far larger than Taylor's and Rockefeller's dreams, and though the movers and shakers of Lincoln Center professed that "greater emphasis should now be placed on the program functions of the Center" when they tapped Schuman, their changing attitudes during Schuman's tenure suggest that they did not know what they were asking for. Certainly Schuman gave them far, far more than they wanted, and they would let him know that in due course.

Among his papers, Schuman had a quote attributed to Pablo Picasso that appeared in *Le Figaro Littéraire* of January 1962.

> Always strive for perfection. For instance, try to draw a perfect circle, and since you can't draw a perfect circle, the involuntary flaw will reveal your personality.
>
> But if you want to reveal your personality by drawing an imperfect circle—your circle—you will bungle the whole thing.[49]

So it was that, for the next seven years, Schuman tried to draw his perfect circle around Lincoln Center. The first year, unsurprisingly, was spent learning the ropes and getting Philharmonic Hall completed and opened. That's when Schuman faced his first crises as head of Lincoln Center.

The first, and small, crisis concerned the premiere of the Eighth Symphony. The commission for the work had been extended well before Schuman had any inkling that he would be president of Lincoln Center. All the same, Winthrop Sargeant, music critic for the *New Yorker*, found it unseemly that the work appeared as part of the opening festivities. Sargeant felt that Schuman should have used his influence to have Bernstein remove the symphony. Schuman's lawyer contacted Sargeant to clarify that each Lincoln Center constituent was free to program whatever music its management chose and that the central administration had no business interfering with that fundamental right. Sargeant understood but held his ground, arguing that "the degree of his scrupulousness—or even of the appearance of scrupulousness—should increase in direct porportion [*sic*] to the power that [Schuman] wields." Sargeant's answer assuaged Schuman enough to keep him from bringing a libel suit against Sargeant and the *New Yorker*, but the accusation stung.[50]

The acoustics of the new hall was a far larger crisis that created a slew of headaches. The opinions after "Tuning Week," when different musicians tried out the hall prior to its official opening, were mostly positive, and a recording of Brahms's Symphony no. 2 made during that week by Bernstein and the Philharmonic was well received by all who heard it.[51] Opening week, in contrast, brought out opposing camps who alternately praised and panned the clean, crisp sound of Philharmonic Hall. Some musicians—Samuel Barber among them—were "enthralled with the sound of the hall." Others, such as conductor George Szell, considered it a "world scandal," as the hall lacked the *gemütlich* sonic ambiance that marked other great halls.[52] Harold Schonberg summarized the concerns in an article in the *New York Times*.

> It is true, of course, that some musicians have many reservations about the acoustics. (Others think them wonderful.) But from the way some self-appointed experts are carrying on, you'd think that Philharmonic Hall was a great big, yellow, $15,000,000 lemon. Well, it isn't. It does have some defects, as the acoustician in charge and the Lincoln Center officials are readily prepared to admit. The big trouble remains the

> lack of bass response, and a secondary one is unequal distribution of sound throughout the hall. These defects are, of course, under intensive study.[53]

The New York City newspaper strike that began the day before Schonberg's article appeared meant that many had no chance to see his more sober assessment, and for the duration of the strike—it would not end until the end of March—rumor overtook reality. It was decided to "soft-pedal this touchy subject," leading Schuman to ask a writer to kill a story he was about to publish on the matter.[54] The acoustical experts themselves were divided in what they recommended. Young offered an analogy in a memo to Schuman. "We are going to be in the position of the family who has received widely differing medical views from several doctors. We're going to have to decide which doctors or group of doctors we have confidence in, and go ahead, or else call the whole business off."[55] Volunteer fundraisers resigned. Musicians threatened never to play the hall again. And throughout the tumult, Schuman sailed a steady course, projecting a message that the administration was aware of the problems and would do everything necessary to fix the problem while, at the same time, neither overreacting nor overpromising. The question of acoustics would plague Lincoln Center over the course of its history, but in this first foray in the sound wars, Schuman's public silence and private resolve helped the center to win the battle at hand.

Schuman knew that bigger battles were ahead. Negotiations with City Center over whether the New York City Ballet and the New York City Opera would join Lincoln Center continued in an on-again, off-again fashion during Schuman's first years. The incorporation of the Music Theater of Lincoln Center presented a temporary problem: by March 1963, all parties agreed that the ballet would join Lincoln Center but that discussions needed to continue over whether the opera would follow.[56] The zigzag nature of the talks, however, almost guaranteed that what was decided one day would be nullified the next, and City Center would make the acoustic problem seem like child's play.

Amid the ongoing strife, Schuman achieved some unqualified successes. He invited the duo-pianists Arthur Gold and Robert Fizdale to perform an opening week recital. He had hoped the "boys," as the partners in life as well as music were known, would be allowed to premiere Milhaud's Concerto no. 2, op. 394, for two pianos and four percussionists, a work that was commissioned to celebrate the opening of Juilliard at Lincoln Center and which Milhaud delivered well in advance of the school's completion. Schubart, acting president of Juilliard at the time, must have dissuaded Schuman from pilfering the score, as Gold and Fizdale performed a program of Debussy, Bartók, Brahms, and Haieff. The mutual affection the pianists and Schuman shared is evident in their communications. "Words can never tell you how deeply touched we are that you invited us to participate in the historic opening of

Lincoln Center. We felt it to be a great privilege for which we shall always be most grateful." Schuman replied, "Your concert at Lincoln Center was the great success that I knew it would be, and I couldn't be happier about your having participated."[57]

If Schuman could not finagle a new piece for Gold and Fizdale, he did manage to get three new pieces for the dedicatory concert of Philharmonic Hall's organ. Schuman initially hoped to engage the services of the organists at St. Patrick's Cathedral and Temple Emanuel to join Virgil Fox, then organist at the Riverside Church, in a great ecumenical demonstration of the new organ. That idea was quickly abandoned in favor of bringing in E. Power Biggs and Catherine Crozier as guest organists to appear alongside Fox, but another facet of Schuman's original vision for the dedicatory concert remained. "I should like to suggest that we commission three new works for the occasion. These commissions should be awarded at once. Once the three institutions have been selected with their representative organists, we should discuss these commissions with them. Time is of the essence if we are to have any new works."[58] Within weeks, Schuman had lined up Persichetti, Cowell, and Thomson, with the understanding that they would deliver their works by June 1.[59] Thomson expressly requested that Biggs play his piece; Crozier got the Cowell, and Fox the Persichetti. All three men received $1,000 each for their efforts, and all of them delivered their works on time. When it was all over, Schuman wrote an omnibus letter to the composers. "I want to thank you, dear friends and colleagues, for helping make the inaugural organ concert in Philharmonic Hall the great success that it was. Each of you came through handsomely, vindicating not only my confidence in you as composers, but also in the commissioning idea for this special event."[60]

With commissions being fulfilled, with plans for festivals being hatched, with film emerging as a major component, with musical theater looking to be a rewarding addition (fiscally and aesthetically) to the constituents, with a major article in the *New York Times Magazine* laying out the events and institutes yet to see the light of day, with Schuman appearing on the television show *What's My Line?* to trumpet the opening of Philharmonic Hall, the promise—the dream—of Lincoln Center enriched Schuman immeasurably in those first years.[61] He (or his amanuensis) wrote to the school newspaper of Marine Park Junior High School in Brooklyn about how Lincoln Center represented the full flowering of American culture throughout the nation.

> America has been long, perhaps, in coming to maturity in the arts. Maturity is now evident, not only in the great performing organizations that form a Lincoln Center, but even more fundamentally in the emergence of creative American artists of stature. . . . The prestige of our country has reached its greatest heights the world round through the outstanding achievements of our performing artists and creators of art.[62]

And he was hardly alone in his reveries about the center. Anne Hobler, a colleague from his Sarah Lawrence days, wrote to Schuman shortly after visiting Philharmonic Hall. She apologized for taking so long to write, hoping instead that she would run into Schuman and tell him in person her impressions. When she did sit in front of her typewriter, it was at a time when all the other buildings were at most skeletons. Ground hadn't even been broken yet for Juilliard. But Hobler looked beyond the physical to the metaphysical.

> Those Abramovitz stately columns, the shimmering Lipold mobile and the listening to the Strauss "Zarathustra" were only part of the thrill. The other part was seeing as well as believing that this great idea is now a reality, and to thousands of people like me. One doesn't walk through those columns for the first time, and come away being quite the same. Intangible things happen—spiritual, intellectual and emotional. Maybe Lincoln Center happened now because of the real need all over the world for solid structures signifying the permanence of creative expression.

Schuman highlighted this passage and thanked Hobler for her letter. "It was worth waiting for, and is certainly one of the finest letters we have received on Lincoln Center."[63] In those early years, Lincoln Center demanded a lot from Schuman. In those early years, it repaid Schuman handsomely. He had a dream, and Lincoln Center was fulfilling it.

TWENTY-THREE

SOMETHING OLD, SOMETHING NEW, SOMETHING BORROWED

Near the end of his life, Schuman described how he balanced the many demands on his time as an administrator with his vocation as a composer.

> I determined that, for me, if I wanted to be a composer, I had to have between 600 and 1,000 hours alone, per year, in a room. That's all. I just had to have 600–1,000 hours alone in a room. Anything else wouldn't work for me. And how did I accomplish that? I would get up in the morning. If there were no early morning appointments at school, I would call in, and I'd say look, "There's no fire down there, I'll arrive around 11:00." If I happened to have a 9:00 appointment, I would arrive at 9:00. So, I would start working in the morning at composition, early in the morning, and if I worked from 8:00 to 9:00 or 8:00 to 10:00—say, two hours; I would put on my calendar "two hours"—at the end of the week I would add up: six hours, or twelve hours. . . . During the summertime I could work twenty or thirty hours a week, but during the course of the winter I could only work six or eight or ten, sometimes twelve. So I always made my 600, I never made my 1,000.[1]

He gave Knud Meister of the Danish newspaper *Berlingske Aftenavis* some added information of the system as he used it in his first year as Lincoln Center president. "When I start to compose, I write in a book what time it is. If I am interrupted by the telephone, I make a note of the time I start the conversation and one as soon as I hang up. Let us say that the telephone in a day has stolen 16 minutes from me—well, then, I transfer the 16 minutes to other workdays. I do not give a second away."[2] He was monstrously efficient and may have usually made his 600 hours at Juilliard, but his 1962 datebook reveals that he didn't always make them once Lincoln Center came into the picture. The opening page of the datebook has the calculation for two seasons:

> Total composition
> 1960–61 438:20
> 61–62 361:13
> Sym No VIII 655:13

(The discrepancy between this number for the Eighth Symphony and the number on the title page of the manuscript may be due to adjustments he made after the work was first completed.) At the end of the datebook, Schuman gave a more plaintive account of the year. "No music written for last months of '62 (since June 14 really—except for proof reading) a fantastic year of great actions & satisfaction of Lincoln Center. Now to do both!"[3] He received nearly 20 requests for commissions during his Lincoln Center years; he only accepted five and struggled to find the time to complete these.[4] Composition remained a priority for him at Lincoln Center, but the muse, as Schuman might have said, did not always cooperate.

Lightning did strike at the dedication of the Philharmonic Hall organ, for beyond the satisfaction Schuman could take in providing three new numbers to the organist's repertoire, the concert bore compositional fruit for himself. Biggs had asked early on if he could program an oddity of sorts, according to Schuman's associate Reginald Allen. "[Biggs] feels that Charles Ives's 'Variations on America' (approximately seven minutes) would be a diverting number to have on his program, assuming that it fell properly into context. I told him that I would pass this on to you and that we would, under any circumstances, await the completion of the commissioned works."[5] The Ives did make it onto the program, and it so stimulated Schuman that he immediately began to imagine how he might recast the work for orchestra. He asked his publisher to obtain the score for him and to secure permission to orchestrate it, a matter that was complicated because the rights were held jointly by the Ives estate and the work's publisher, Mercury Music, and the folks at Mercury were slow in responding to Schuman's publisher's entreaties. "Any news on permission to orchestrate Ives' 'America'?" Schuman impatiently wrote in late January. "I can't stop my mind from thinking how to do it.[6] By July 1963, the contracts were drawn up, and Schuman set out to score the organ piece.[7]

The *Variations*, like *New England Triptych*, was an instant hit. The premiere took place at the first of the New York Philharmonic's "Promenade Concerts" for 1964, with André Kostelanetz conducting. The concerts themselves were something of a spectacle, with fancy lighting and exotic dance accompanying the music as patrons enjoyed light fare at the tables set up in Philharmonic Hall. Schuman invited Cowell, whose book on Ives was already a classic, to the gala event. While the critic for the *New York Times* decried the kitschy quality of the evening and considered the "irreverent jauntiness" of the Ives-Schuman "moderately amusing," Cowell was unabashed in praising the brilliance of Schuman's effort. "The Ives is delightful—the scoring strong, but witty and deft as Ives would have liked. I thought as it went on how glad that you gave it a sense of fun—Ives did not make it for Queen Victoria, nor did you make it for Queen Elizabeth! I liked the instrumentation better than anything on the program, except perhaps the first movement of the Ravel [Concerto in G major]."[8]

Schuman was touched. "I am so pleased to have your okay on my Ives effort. Next to having the composer there himself, you are the ranking authority."[9] Lukas Foss performed the work with the Buffalo Symphony less than a year later. "As a conductor, let me say that I owe you a special vote of thanks for making this delightful, touching, naive, naughty work available for orchestral performance. And as a composer, all I have to say is 'hats off'; the orchestration is superb."[10] Irving Kolodin similarly praised "the composer's irreverent thoughts on a reverent subject."[11] And André Previn relished the prospect of bringing the work, whose tune is the same as "God Save The King," to the British. "I am also looking forward to the London Symphony's reaction to your 'America' Variations. I am sure they will be genuinely amused, as was [English conductor Sir John] Barbirolli when he heard me conduct it in Houston. He loved it, especially (to quote him) 'the jiggy parts.'"[12]

Schuman himself repeatedly called the Ives "amusing."[13] But others were not so amused. The irreverence and naughtiness and jiggyness led to cancelations of performances and to irate letters, as some felt that Schuman was making fun of America. One educator was "quite shocked at this reaction but apparently war thoughts are in the minds of our students more than we realized."[14] A retired Army colonel fired off a telegram to Howard Mitchell, conductor of the National Symphony, to express his outrage that they would play the piece; his wife wrote Schuman an impassioned three-page letter, denouncing the sacrilege to which he treated this unofficial national anthem.[15] Schuman chose not to assert that he found humor in the original, which he sought to retain and amplify. His response was diplomatic.

> You must understand that had I felt there was anything disrespectful to our American ideals in the musical variations on a theme which has so often served as an expression of those ideals, I would never have transcribed the Ives' piece. I'm a little dismayed, I must confess, that a person of such obvious good will as yourself could interpret the composition as unpatriotic, and I can only report to you that the work has been widely performed in many parts of the country, and certainly your reaction was quite special.
>
> I did want you to have this word of reassurance from me. And I suppose that there we must let the matter rest—in the knowledge that men and women of good will have the privilege of disagreeing.[16]

Schuman's patriotism could stand a good joke or two, but during the turmoil of the Vietnam era, other people weren't laughing. And one can easily imagine that, at other times of national dissension, not all auditors hear the Ives-Schuman with favor. For Schuman, though, recasting the Ives was a labor of love of both music and country. "About all that I will get from my orchestration is the pleasure of doing it. This was considerable. The contract, as I recall it, was four ways: The Ives estate, Mercury Music, Presser and WS."[17] Though he had to split the royalties, Schuman nevertheless did not do poorly with this piece, much to the chagrin of at least one organist. "I still hope one day you will tackle the organ. It is only fair, now that you have stolen Ives from my repertoire. Frankly, to play it on the organ after ANYONE having heard the transcription would only guarantee Instant Demise. I ask not penance, only a replacement of one of my party pieces!"[18]

The orchestration, like *New England Triptych*, was also destined for a band version. Schuman himself did not have the time to do this, but just as he turned his thoughts to hiring a collaborating transcriber, William E. Rhoads, director of bands for the University of New Mexico, wrote to ask whether Schuman was planning to reorchestrate the work for band. Schuman was delighted to hear from him. "It is my thought that the collaborating transcriber would send me his version and then could be responsive to my suggestions. The principal problem will be to find a way of simplifying the string figures in some of the variations. In other words, I should like the variations to be as practical as possible for bands below the 'A' level."[19] After the catastrophe of such an arrangement with "Be Glad Then America," one would think that Schuman would be chary in allowing someone else to recast his music, but Rhoades, unlike Cal Bean at Presser, composed original music for band. He worked quickly and skillfully, and Schuman was impressed. "I want to say again that I think you have done a first-rate job. . . . I am perfectly willing that the printed version be listed as 'William Schuman in collaboration with William E. Rhoads.'" Schuman also sent Rhoads scores of *Credendum* and the Third Symphony to see if he might be interested in trying his hand at these.[20] Nothing came of this, in part because Rhoads was incensed that, in his mind, he was not given ample credit on the publication of the band version and felt that Schuman and Presser had deliberately slighted him. Schuman was nonplused: "While what took place may have been questionable in judgement, it was certainly never meant, in any way, in bad faith. As for my own part, I can only say that I have worked with many collaborators in a long career, and this is the first disagreement I have ever experienced."[21] Overstatement or not, Schuman acquiesced to change the legend to read: "Transcribed for Band by William E. Rhoads / Based on the Orchestral Version by William Schuman."[22]

Only one original composition was begun and completed in Schuman's first two years at Lincoln Center, and that work was written in a flash. In January 1963, William Skelton, the conductor of the Colgate University Glee Club, wrote to Schuman to see if he would be willing to compose a work that could be performed as part of the inauguration ceremonies on April 19 for incoming Colgate president Vincent Barnet. Schuman had received an honorary degree from Colgate in 1960, and Skelton suggested that Schuman owed this to his "alma mater." Skelton, however, was realistic, as his request came with only four months to spare, and he felt that his request would be in vain.[23] Schuman, however, was intrigued by the challenge.

> Where on earth would I suddenly find a text to set, and the time to set it, in the time you indicate? Having said this, I will surprise you by telling you I would like to try. Here is my problem—find me the words you want, and if I find they are sympathetic for me as a composer, I will try to oblige. Brass accompaniment appeals to me, although I might prefer a cappella. Do you have in mind three or four minutes?[24]

Skelton and his colleagues were flabbergasted. "Your tentative acceptance of a commission . . . threw this university into a complete panic. The thought of a talent of your stature composing for us immediately got every dean, director, committee chairman, committeeman into the act of selecting a text." In mid-February, he sent Schuman two versions of a passage from chapter 28 of the book of Job, whence the university's motto, "Deo ac Veritati," came.[25] A month later, Schuman had nothing to show. "Hopefully, I will turn out a short choral work to celebrate the occasion. At this writing I confess that I am stuck, but hope the week end will give me the time to become unstuck."[26] That letter went out on a Thursday; by Tuesday of the following week (March 26), he was done, and on April 3, Schuman wrote to Skelton to make sure that he had received the music.[27] Skelton was understandably elated and wrote to Schuman after the ceremonies had passed. "I would not deceive you by stating that every grandmother, housewife and teenager stood up cheering madly, but I can honestly report that the critics, and there are quite a few, were pleased and impressed. Certainly none of them topped my enthusiasm."[28]

Deo Ac Veritati, a canon with coda for three-part chorus of men's voices, uses only the three Latin words for the text, repeated over and over again, in typical Schuman style for his vocal settings. The piece itself is in three parts. A two-voice canon at the minor third, in $\frac{3}{4}$ time, begins "full voice, with dignity and strength," as a vocal fanfare, never dropping below mezzo forte in volume. The canon is highly chromatic to the extent that Schuman may have constructed a 12-tone row and freely elaborated around it, as every note in the chromatic scale appears within the first 12 bars of the 33-bar canon. After a two-bar codetta, the canon repeats, stopping two-thirds of the way to generate a climax, using contrary motion and an accelerando, to the three-part non-canonic coda that makes feints toward triads before oscillating between B major and D major in the final 17 measures. D major, with its high A in Tenor I, wins the argument on the word "Deo." It is truly an occasional piece, and its salience outside of the Colgate campus is questionable, although when Harry Langsford, the conductor of the Wayne State University Men's Glee Club, asked Schuman for guidance on interpreting the work, Schuman stated that the words were Colgate's motto and then gave the conductor a general insight into the anthem. "If they feel the melodic nature of the separate lines and know that the music is meant to soar, I am sure—and especially under your guidance, that they need no written words from me."[29]

If *Deo Ac Veritati* was all new material, and somewhat dissonant material at that, another composition from this time was based on old music that provided no harmonic clashes whatsoever. Schuman presented his idea in early August 1963 to his copyist Anthony Strilko, who had expended much time and effort on the last two symphonies, *A Song of Orpheus*, and the orchestration of the Ives.

> Some years ago (1943, or before), I arranged a traditional Austrian song—"The Orchestra Song"—for any combination of changed or unchanged voices. It has now occurred to me that a version of this little piece for band—"The Band Song"—and one for orchestra—"The Orchestra Song"—would be an attractive addition to the repertory, and would meet the added goal of taking me away from work that I should be doing. The song itself is a series of 8-bar melodies. Each melody will be played by a section of the orchestra so that one has Melody #1, then Melody #2; and then #1 and #2 combined; then #3 along and #1, 2 and 3 combined, etc. until all five or six melodies are playing together, at which time there is a grand tutti. My new version of this will not stick completely to the choral piece.
>
> Here is what I propose: I will send to A. Strilko the following: Melody #1, with instructions as to its exact instrumentation, and similarly all the way along the line. From this instruction sheet I would ask you to make a full score for band, and when you finish that, for orchestra. (A different version.) We will not worry about parts until I send the score off to Presser. In terms of time, I would say that the band score will take you longer because there are so many instruments to fill in. I will, of course, send you the instrumentation that I would like to use for band. But first, tell me whether you would be able to take on these chores for me during the weeks ahead. I can send you the band version right away.
>
> Seriously, although I do not like to give my work to anyone else but you, I will be most understanding if you tell me you would prefer not taking it on at this time.[30]

Strilko himself was a composer and was tied up until mid-October, but Schuman decided to wait for him to execute his scheme. Though Schuman thought that he would create the band version first, it was the orchestra version that he sent to his publisher in late February. Soon both men were thinking up ways to approach Arthur Fiedler, the conductor of the Boston Pops Orchestra, to see if he would premiere the work. "It should be made clear in any approach to Fiedler (soon I will write some program notes) that the 'Orchestra Song' is based on traditional Austrian melodies, freely adapted, to which I have added a percussion section, trusting it is in the spirit of the original."[31] But André Kostelanetz, who was slated to introduce the Ives–Schuman *Variations*, saw the score in early spring and persuaded Schuman to let him have the premiere with the Minnesota Symphony Orchestra on April 11. He sent a telegram the next day. "THE 4700 AUDIENCE CHEERED THE PREMIERE OF YOUR DELIGHTFUL ORCHESTRA SONG STOP WE ENCORED TO GREAT ENJOYMENT OF AUDIENCE ORCHESTRA AND MYSELF WILL

PHONE YOU TONIGHT LOVE TO YOU BOTH FROM US ANDRE"[32] Schuman's chief concern with the work was that Presser was hoping to sell it as part of the company's School Orchestra Series. If professional orchestras were also to buy it, Schuman reasoned, there would be no way to track performances of it, which could be done if those orchestras rented parts.[33] Schuman's worries proved to be unfounded, for while *The Orchestra Song* is popular, in no way has it achieved a standing anywhere close to the Ives–Schuman or *New England Triptych*.

At the same time, its appeal led Schuman and Presser to create a band version. Once again, Schuman relied on others to make the transcription. Unlike with Rhoads, however, the transcriber's name was left off of the published version, for, in Schuman's opinion, "the transcription is serviceable, and is merely a literal translation of my orchestration." Some adjustment would be necessary, he noted, since the unnamed transcriber "miscalculates the weight of horns in a band. The horns in the orchestra predominate quite easily. In a band they do not, but are, in fact, quite weak when compared to the trumpets and trombones." These details, Schuman told his publisher, he would correct over the phone.[34] Thus *The Band Song* has an even more detached history than its orchestral predecessor, and both of them together show Schuman focused yet again on writing and arranging pieces that would reach a wide audience. He joked about it with his publisher. "I presume that I have to get you a hit for every symphony I write. I am at a loss to know how I can atone for the string trio I now seem to be composing—at least the parts are inexpensive to print."[35]

Schuman's passive description of his trio echoes the history of the work's genesis, for it did not begin as a string trio. The commission for the work came in the summer of 1962, requesting

> a piece of chamber music of major proportions for an ensemble not to exceed six instruments. One or two voices may be substituted if you prefer a vocal-instrumental combination. . . . The work is being commissioned for performance at the next Elizabeth Sprague Coolidge Foundation Festival scheduled to take place in Washington, D.C. on and about October 30, 1964, which will mark the hundreth [*sic*] anniversary of the birth of the late Elizabeth Sprague Coolidge.[36]

More than a decade had passed from the time Schuman last received a commission from the Coolidge Foundation. Both *Night Journey* and the Fourth String Quartet were Coolidge commissions; perhaps Schuman's service with Harold Spivacke on the State Department advisory board in the 1950s gave Spivacke reason to avoid the appearance of nepotism. This festival, though, was special; commissions went to "composers in whom Mrs. Coolidge had a personal interest." Schuman thus joined Luigi Dallapiccola, Howard Hanson, Walter Piston, the Malipieros (Gian Francesco and his nephew Riccardo), Darius Milhaud, Virgil Thomson, Giselher Klebe, Juan Orrego-Salas, Aurelio de la Vega, and

Alberto Ginastera as one of the stars of the Thirteenth Festival of Chamber Music at the Library of Congress.[37]

It took him more than a year to settle on which instruments he would use in his featured work. The Ford Foundation had turned down his proposal to write a duo concertante for violin and cello, so Schuman had written *A Song of Orpheus* for cello and orchestra instead. The concertante idea, born in the thwarted Philadelphia commission, had a long half-life in Schuman. He discussed his ideas for the new chamber work with Leonard Rose, the cellist for whom he wrote *A Song of Orpheus* and who, Schuman believed, would be asked to perform at the Library of Congress. "I now begin to think of a work for your Trio in which the first movement would be for piano solo (a separate work which also would serve as the first movement of the Trio); then a duo for violin and cello (a separate work which would also serve as the second movement of the Trio); and finally a culminating movement for the whole trio."[38] Rose's trio had two other well-known musicians in it: violinist Isaac Stern, who premiered Schuman's Violin Concerto; and pianist Eugene Istomin. Rose wrote back to say that the conception of the work "sounds interesting and unique," that Stern and Istomin also liked the idea, and that, if it was at all possible, it would be wonderful if the work could be completed by the summer of 1963, since "we have had a request to do an American work at Edinburgh. So far we have not been too happy with the works we have investigated."[39] The work was not completed by then, and Spivacke probably would not have allowed the premiere to take place prior to the Coolidge festival, but six months after his exchange with Rose, Schuman told Spivacke that his ideas for the work hadn't changed much.

> The composition I have begun for your October 1964 celebration is a Duo for Violin and 'Cello. Leonard Rose is interested in performing this work, and he tells me also that Isaac Stern would like to play it with him. My thought was also to write a first movement which would be for piano, and a final movement which would be for violin, cello and piano. However, as my ideas now appear to be developing, the work may simply turn out to be the extended duo. I write now in case you wish to retain the services of these two superb artists and, should piano be added, those of Istomin as well.[40]

But they had changed enough that the notion of using a piano was now considered optional.

They were only ideas, though, as concurrent letters to his publisher reveal that Schuman hadn't made much headway on the new piece. He was much more focused on the Ives *Variations*, waiting for word that the legal issues had been settled. The summer was approaching, though, and he had arranged his Lincoln Center schedule to resemble the one he enjoyed at Juilliard, with the summer months reserved for intense composition. He laid out his plans to his publisher, whose headquarters were in Bryn Mawr, a suburb of Philadelphia.

> For your information, I have begun to think about a new piece called Violin and Cello Concertante. I hope to write it over this summer and early fall. It will be performed at the Library of Congress celebration in October, 1964. Next year I then hope to write a band piece for the St. Louis celebration in 1964 that I mentioned to you. The other big work will be the Ninth Symphony for Philadelphia, but I don't expect to start that for at least a year. If you mention this fact in Philadelphia, feathers will fly and breasts will be beaten, and we'll have all sorts of problems. I do have some ideas for the work. But I want to think about it a long time.[41]

The St. Louis piece would be postponed until 1968, the same year Schuman completed the Ninth Symphony. The only work on his composing desk he needed to address that summer was the chamber music work for the Library of Congress. And the muse, Schuman said in a letter to a friend, was virtually silent: "My Duo for Violin and 'Cello proceeds at a snail's pace, literally and figuratively, since the opening tempo is adagissimo."[42] Seven months later, he continued to despair about how slowly the work was going, but it had taken a more definite shape by the winter. "I do hope that I am successful in writing the Trio for the Coolidge Festival. It goes slowly and badly, but maybe the spring will bring rejuvenation."[43] He had established the instrumentation: violin, viola (not piano), and cello, so Rose's trio would no longer be needed. Progress, however, continued at a snail's pace. He took a month off after the opening of the New York State Theater in April 1964 to devote to composing, and at the end of his working holiday, he reported to Spivacke that, almost two years after he had accepted the commission, he had completed just shy of half of the work. That was the bad news. The good news was that Schuman believed that "long weekends in Connecticut will supply the time and atmosphere for the remaining pages." He also had a name for the work: *Amaryllis, Variations for String Trio*.[44]

Although the original commission allowed the substitution of one or two voices for instruments, Schuman's next letter to Spivacke suggests that he may have forgotten the possibility of substitution, for his latest idea fit snugly within the terms of the commission.

> Now, dear Harold, sit tight and hear this one. The piece opens with a statement of the round "Amarylis," [*sic*] treated in terms of its original spirit—first literally and then with some minor changes. The next variation is a contemplative one, curiously vague, I think, in tonality, but I hope not in meaning. The variation which follows is a good solid rhythmic piece with the round melody always appearing in altered but, I trust, recognizable forms against faster music in the other voices—at least for the most part. Now I am struggling with the next section, which will be a free fantasy, I think, then will come the next-to-the-final section, which will be scherzo-fuguish, followed by the return of the theme. And here, I have a thought.
>
> I would like to introduce three female voices at this point. They would sing the round. The strings would continue. I believe that the voices would sound so fresh and

> welcome after the other portions of the material that their inclusion is worthwhile, at least on an optional basis. But what I would like is to have the three singers (two sopranos and a mezzo) either off-stage or behind a screen on stage. The point is that at the first performance I would not want their presence known. They would not be listed in the program. I want to have the surprise of their sounds. Actually, what I want are three lovely and pure voices—the kind that Rose Marie has in her madrigal group. [Rose Marie Grentzer, Spivacke's wife, taught choral music at the University of Maryland.] Opera singers would be completely out. The three singers could also turn, if you wish, into three sections of singers, but since it is a chamber work I think the three solo voices are better. Their part could be taught to them in about ten minutes. Furthermore, they would only have to attend the final rehearsal of the Trio. Please tell me you will play along with my folly.[45]

Though he was still composing the work, the remainder of the piece was firmly in his mind. Even so, in the letter Schuman admitted that the idea of using voices came to him after he had decided on the materials he would develop into *Amaryllis*; the beginning was written before the end was in sight. The women's voices were as much a surprise to him as a composer as he wanted them to be for the members of the audience.

And they were a surprise. In his lengthy and enthusiastic description of *Amaryllis*, Paul Hume of the *Washington Post* wrote the kind of review that Schuman longed to see, not solely because of its positive opinion of the work but because of its ability to put the reader in the auditorium at the time the work was being played.

> Of the three new works heard Saturday afternoon, only one had a high degree of originality in thought and presentation. This was William Schuman's variations for string trio on the old English round, Amaryllis. [The other two works were by Gian Francesco Malipiero and Milhaud.]
>
> At the outset of the work and for a considerable number of minutes thereafter, you might reasonably have thought Schuman was concerned chiefly with an examination of Amaryllis from every angle. In purposeful simplicity he let the three players walk all around the tune, seting [*sic*] it forth in a variety of direct ways. Gradually, however, and almost always at a soft, softer, or softest level of sound, Schuman began to carry the ancient melody into regions of harmonic thought far removed in actuality, if not in implication, from those in which it began.
>
> It is a technical tour de force of surprising vitality, expressed in a refined, disciplined economy which is dictated by no means soley [*sic*] by the restrictions of the string trio. Having dissected the minutest fragments of the tune, Schuman sprang a surprise. The doors at the back of the Library's stage swung open to disclose three lovely young damsels all dressed in modish black. These advanced, while the music continued, to a place just behind the members of the string trio.
>
> Then, in the same slow mood in which the work had begun, they sang the original version of Amaryllis. From this point to the conclusion, they continued their song while around them the strings wreathed old and new harmonies, those that were new now

> sounding strangely right with the older melody. In future performances the element of surprise will be missing, but the closing will not lose its remarkable sense of unity.[46]

Spivacke, apparently, helped to man the doors. "I can tell you now that the most nervous among the performers were the two door openers. Everything worked well, however, and it had the effect and the piece was well received."[47] Also there in Washington to hear the premiere of *Amaryllis* that Saturday afternoon in October was Schuman's old teacher Charles Haubiel. Almost a year elapsed before he wrote to Schuman, as he waited until he had some works to send in the hopes that his former student would show them around Lincoln Center. "I liked the STRING TRIO which I heard at the Coolidge Festival in Washington D.C. last November. I seem to hear, therein, some echoes of the contrapuntal work you did with me so many years ago. Do you feel there is any connection whatever?"[48] Certainly Haubiel's training is in evidence in the score. So is another one of Schuman's "tutors" whom Harold Schonberg perceptively named. "Schuman's 'Amaryllis,' a set of variations for string trio and three female voices on an old English round, combined his well-known rhythmic and technical traits with something new, a venture into a type of pointillistic writing that suggested a tonal Webern."[49]

If the critics on the East Coast were generally upbeat in their appraisal of Schuman's latest effort, the writer for the *Los Angeles Times* was far less supportive. Several of the Coolidge festival pieces were exported to that city's famed Monday Evening Concerts. Spivacke had told Schonberg that this particular Coolidge festival was for the "old-timers." The L.A. concert series celebrated the avant-garde—it was the first venue in America to present the music of Boulez—and old-timer music was considered, to use critic Walter Arlen's word, dreary. Here was an entire evening of it, and Arlen, like Hume, felt that *Amaryllis* was the centerpiece of the concert he heard. But Arlen's take was as far from Hume's as Washington is from Los Angeles.

> [The concert] reached its unhappy climax with the "Amaryllis" Variations for string trio by William Schuman, positively the dullest, gloomiest, awkward piece of music imaginable. From the tonal or, more correctly, modal beginning which exposed the Old English round with a total lack of charm, through the stylistically clashing, dissonant and unidiomatic variations that went on forever and a day, to the finale for which three muses in white blouses suddenly appeared from the wings to sing the old tune in mournful tones, there was not a redeeming feature.[50]

Roy Travis, a professor in the Music Department of the University of California at Los Angeles, wasn't nearly as dyspeptic as Arlen. After giving Schuman his commentary on how one section reminded him of the opening of Schubert's "Unfinished" Symphony and another "made a rhetorical effect in the best Bartokian manner," Travis undercut Arlen with one simple sentence: "The piece was well received by the audience."[51]

Yet *Amaryllis* became one of Schuman's star-crossed compositions. Its New York premiere wasn't covered by the *New York Times*, which was all for the best, Schuman thought, since "the first violinist left some of his music at home, and so the work had to be played minus an enormous chunk—an entire variation—one of the meatiest of the composition."[52] Its neglect in the years immediately following its completion led Schuman to think about recasting the material in some way. Then the members of the Juilliard String Quartet reprised the work in Washington in a recital given in tandem with an exhibit of Schuman's manuscripts at the Library of Congress. The concert was a success, and the *Washington Post* critic on hand wrote that even "the effectiveness of its surprise ending has not been dulled by the passage of time."[53] Schuman was elated. "The performance was absolutely great, and I felt that for the first time I really heard the work. In fact, it is so good with the Juilliard boys that I no longer feel the need of making a larger work out of it. They are going to speak to [RCA] Victor about recording it."[54] The work, as of this writing, has never been commercially recorded.

As for making a larger work out of it, shortly after the trio's premiere Schuman volunteered, "I am beginning to think of making a symphony out of "Amarylis" [*sic*], but that's a long way off, and I'll wait and see if the idea sticks."[55] The *Concerto on Old English Rounds* could be that symphony, although the proximity of Schuman's remarks to the necessity of fulfilling the commission for the Philadelphia Orchestra suggests that he was thinking in more immediate terms. But even with the concerto finished by 1974, Schuman was not finished with *Amaryllis*. Kostelanetz came to Schuman in 1976 asking for a work, and to Schuman *Amaryllis* fit the bill. Schuman wrote to Strilko on May 18: "André Kost must have revised score at NYC address May 30. He leaves on trip May 31."[56] And so, as he had done with "Be Glad Then America" and *The Orchestra Song* and *The Band Song* and the band version of the Ives–Schuman *Variations*, Schuman supervised someone else who constructed his composition for him. Strilko dutifully followed Schuman's direction on how to distribute the instruments for a string orchestra and even postdated the score "22–24 April '76." (Schuman was very busy that April: the National Symphony had an all-Schuman festival on April 6 and 7 with three new works, and the New York Philharmonic gave the New York premiere of the *Concerto on Old English Rounds*, another score that drew upon the round "Amaryllis.") What exactly Kostelanetz played at the Philadelphia premiere that July—or at the New York premiere in May 1977—is unknown, as Schuman's copy of Strilko's score contains a cut of 23 measures that was made before the published version of the score appeared. As it stands, *Amaryllis: Variants for Strings on an Old English Song* lasts less than ten minutes. In terms of forces, it is certainly larger, but as a composition it is much smaller, even slighter, than the trio from whence it came. As for how Kostelanetz played it, Schuman had mixed feelings after hearing it in New York. "The Kostelanetz' Amaryllis I didn't think turned out so well in performance—it is really not his kind of piece, although, of course, I am delighted that he loves it."[57] Schuman most certainly felt that the piece deserved wider play, a sentiment he expressed to his publisher.

> It is my belief that the new version for strings of Amaryllis should be promoted in a very special way. I would suggest that a personalized letter be sent not only to the major orchestras, but, even more particularly, to the many small organizations that performed Variations on American and New England Triptych during the bicentennial years. It seems to me that the latter should say that you are happy to enclose a score (or, if you prefer, that you will send one at their request) of the new work about which Peter G. Davis wrote in The New York Times of May 22, 1977, "during its brief course the set of Variations remains on an appropriately tender and subdued level, marked by Mr. Schuman's bittersweet melodic phrases . . . the piece makes its points concisely and attractively." The letter might mention that the work was introduced by Andre Kostelanetz, who commissioned and gave the premiere of New England Triptych and the premiere of Variations on America.[58]

As with the string trio, the string orchestra version has neither been commercially recorded nor widely played.

In the first three years of his presidency at Lincoln Center (1962–64), Schuman managed to finish a large orchestral work he had begun in June 1960, toss off a choral piece for Colgate University, orchestrate two bonbons—one long and one short—and compose a 620-measure string trio that uses women's voices in 43 of those measures and that took him more than two years to write. He had negotiated his contract to ensure that he would have time to compose. No one could accuse Schuman of wasting time, but he didn't have time enough to compose. He set out the challenge and the possible solution in early 1964.

> I must make a determined effort to continue giving the Center everything I have, but, at the same time, finding the discipline of schedule which permits me to continue as a composer, albeit a less productive one in quantity. My resolve of keeping two hours free each weekday morning has not proved satisfactory, partly because there is rarely a week without one or two morning meetings, and also because the telephone keeps ringing. Now I have asked my colleagues to try to hold off from disturbing me these first two hours of the day if they can.[59]

If Schuman was concerned that he couldn't find the time to compose in his first two years at Lincoln Center, which weren't exactly a honeymoon, the next two years would make him long for the relative freedom he had enjoyed in 1962 and 1963. The entire world would soon find out not only that the honeymoon was over but that some were calling for a divorce.

TWENTY-FOUR

ONE NIGHTMARE AFTER ANOTHER

By the spring of 1963, the demands of Lincoln Center had become so great that Schuman could no longer afford the time it took to commute from New Rochelle. Tony was away at Wesleyan University, Andrea was heading into high school, and Frankie was ready to move back to New York City, where she could find new opportunities to use her experiences in social work and volunteerism. So Schuman regretfully put the Elk Avenue house on the market and bought a Fifth Avenue apartment, into which the family moved at the end of August.[1] The loss of Schuman's retreat away from the city was quickly redressed when they built a "little prefabricated house" on land in Greenwich, Connecticut, that they purchased from James Warburg, the Juilliard trustee and good friend of the Schumans.[2] The goal thus became spending long weekends and summers in Greenwich, where Schuman would have time to compose. Six hundred hours, though, continued to be elusive; on the last page of his 1965 desk diary, Schuman indicated that he managed 149 hours, 6 minutes, for the year.[3]

Lincoln Center was relentless. Schuman had to develop a vision for the entire complex, manage the expectations of the constituents already there, and nurture the possibility of bringing new constituents into the fold. Rockefeller admitted that "all of us realized the job was a rougher and tougher one than we had imagined in the beginning," but Schuman was not only meeting the challenges before him but was enjoying them.[4] That background, however, didn't make the perfect storm of problems that arrived in December 1964 any less difficult.

That storm gathered together an accumulation of concerns that were going unmet. At the beginning of 1964, only one of the major constituents—the New York Philharmonic—was in its new home at Lincoln Center. The Metropolitan Opera would have to wait until the middle of 1966 for its new house to be completed. Two other buildings would open before then: the New York State Theater (later renamed the David H. Koch Theater), designated as a major performing arts venue for the World's Fair taking place in the summers of 1964 and 1965; and the Library-Museum building with its Vivian Beaumont Theater surrounded by books and records and archives and exhibits. The State Theater gave Schuman the greatest headaches, not only in fighting over who would take to the stage but also in fighting over who would hold the lease.

The New York State Theater opened in April 1964, with the World's Fair programs, the musical theater shows that Rodgers's group produced, and the New York City Ballet offerings anchoring the space for the first year. Other groups were also recruited to use the hall and help underwrite its operation. The first such group ignited a controversy. Schuman had left on a monthlong vacation to make progress on *Amaryllis*, leaving his deputies in charge as the visiting Royal Shakespeare Company and its director Peter Brook came to New York. The theater company immediately ran into problems with the acoustics. Architect Philip Johnson indicated that the hall "has the perfect reverberation time for music, 1.7 [seconds], which is not fitted for the human voice." In response to that, Brook said that he felt that he had "been taken for a ride."

> I'm extremely angry because—despite the marvelous enthusiasm from the audience and the wonderful reception from the critics—of the irresponsibility of permitting a guest company to play Shakespeare in a building that was not properly tested for dialogue. When I discovered on opening night that neither the architect, Mr. Johnson, nor the acoustical expert, Wilhelm L. Jordan, had bothered to come to listen to the dialogue my amazement was complete.[5]

Senior Lincoln Center administrators pushed back, stating that the Shakespeare company was offered an opportunity to conduct a dry run in the theater and had decided against it. While there were complaints from some patrons about an inability to hear the actors on opening night, many of the reviewers chose not to comment at all about acoustical difficulties in the new theater.[6] But with the Lincoln Center staff still smarting from the black eye they received from the acoustical problems in Philharmonic Hall, this new round of accusations compounded their task of making the older constituents feel at home in the new buildings.

Bringing in the new constituents also was filled with drama. The New York City Ballet was ready to join Lincoln Center—the State Theater was designed with dance in mind—but the New York City Opera eyed warily its upscale cousin, and the Met management was suspicious of its more populist relative. Even bringing the ballet company had hurdles of its own. Talk of a smaller modern dance company at Lincoln Center led Lincoln Kirstein, general director of the New York City Ballet, to hesitate, but he was clear in his communications with Schuman that he hoped that "we can evolve into the constituent dance company at Lincoln Center. But I am terrified of the fixed costs, the building maintenance, the rising spiral of inflation."[7]

If Kirstein was ready to move his company to the State Theater, Morton Baum wasn't ready to do it unless he controlled the theater. Baum cofounded the New York City Center of Music and Drama in 1943, and he believed the original documents establishing the State Theater entitled City Center, and not Lincoln Center, to control its operations. Having been lukewarm to the entire idea of Lincoln Center, now Baum hoped to purloin a brand-new building in exchange for relocating from West Fifty-fifth Street. Baum insisted that control of the building was necessary to maintain City Center's affordable-price policy, a claim Schuman and the other officers at Lincoln Center dismissed as demonstrably false.[8] Baum also had a Rockefeller in his corner: New York Governor Nelson Rockefeller, the younger brother of the chairman of Lincoln Center. Nelson's lieutenant governor, Malcolm Wilson, was called upon to settle the dispute between Baum and Lincoln Center, but although Wilson agreed that Baum had no claim to the State Theater, negotiations with City Center, which began in December 1962, continued to go nowhere.[9] By October 1964, John D. Rockefeller III wrote to New York City Mayor Robert F. Wagner, who had also been involved with settling the dispute between the centers.

> When Bill Schuman and I met with you last week, we agreed that we would confer directly with Morton Baum, and we would make every effort to resolve the differences that have developed between Lincoln Center and The City Center of Music and Drama. We have had three such meetings with Mr. Baum during this week and it is a matter of great regret to Bill and me that these meetings have failed to result in agreement.[10]

Baum had counted on people taking umbrage at the notion that Lincoln Center was not capitulating, and the following month witnessed the rise of citizens groups that protested against Lincoln Center; they were convinced that Rockefeller, Schuman, and the rest of the cultural elite were trying to snatch the theater from the people.[11]

By the end of November 1964, the fate of the New York State Theater weighed heavily upon Schuman. So did the fate of the Repertory Theater of Lincoln Center, a constituent conceived by the original Lincoln Center exploratory committee. There was no institutional history on how this particular constituent should behave, but there certainly was a vision for what the Repertory Theater ought to be.

> Although there have been a number of attempts in the United States to establish permanent repertory companies, and from time to time some of these efforts have been on a high artistic level indeed, there has been no single company which has achieved for this country a theater comparable in stability and artistic excellence to the Comédie Française, the Old Vic, or the national Theater of Greece, to mention but three. . . . The new company will develop a body of players fused into a working unit of artistic cohesion committed to the company for long periods of time.[12]

The directors of the company, Robert Whitehead and Elia Kazan, had assembled a troupe that would be ready to play the 1963–64 season, but the company's permanent home, the Vivian Beaumont, wouldn't be ready until the fall of 1965, its opening delayed by the same construction difficulties and cost overruns that plagued all of the Lincoln Center edifices. Rather than reconstitute the company, Whitehead and Kazan and their board approved plans for a temporary structure on New York University's Washington Square campus.[13] The reviews from the first season were generally poor, but Schuman told both directors not to be discouraged. "I battle all comers in your behalf. Of course you are not satisfied with the first season, but these people who are so quick to criticize have no concept of the problems, or of the time it takes to do the thing properly."[14]

Doing things properly also meant keeping people apprized of plans, and Schuman was distressed to open up the *New York Times* and learn things about the Repertory Theater that not only were news to him but that also contradicted agreements Whitehead and Kazan had made with Schuman and others.[15] At the same time, Schuman received word that the Beaumont would be ready by the spring of 1965 but that the Repertory Theater did not want to occupy it midseason. Schuman suggested the possibility of bringing to New York other regional theater companies—the Tyrone Guthrie Theater in Minneapolis; the Alley Theater in Houston; the Arena Stage in Washington, D.C.; the Actors Workshop in San Francisco; the American Shakespeare Festival Theatre and Academy in Stratford, Connecticut; the Association of Producing Artists in Ann Arbor; the Theater Group in Los Angeles; and the Seattle Repertory Theater—but scheduling and funding fortuitously killed the idea, since construction problems delayed the opening until the fall.[16] When it came to the Repertory Theater, in mid-1964 Schuman was simultaneously attempting to solve occupancy problems and nurture a sickly constituent who at times refused his advice. It did not help when playwright Arthur Miller sent Schuman an accusatory letter suggesting that Lincoln Center wanted the Beaumont to become just another Broadway theater, an accusation not grounded in the facts.[17] But in a world-weary letter that he delivered by hand, Kazan explained one of the reasons why the Repertory Theater had struggled to find its footing: Kazan himself, still mourning the loss of his wife the previous December, had not found his own footing. He wanted to get back to film, and the demands of the Repertory Theater made it impossible for him to do so. Therefore, he informed Schuman that, once the Beaumont opened, he would leave the company and Lincoln Center.[18] Schuman fully understood, but at the same time he wanted not to do any injury to the fledgling company. He wrote to Kazan:

> You and Bob [Robert Whitehead] discussed an announcement. It seems to me that such an announcement would be premature, and should not be made at this time.

> When it is made, I propose that it be a positive one, stressing your belief in the Repertory Theater, and the fact that you are relinquishing the co-directorship so that you may have time to pursue your work in film. In any case, the announcement would come from the Repertory Theater, rather than Lincoln Center.[19]

By November 1964 negotiations with City Center had come to a standstill, and the leadership of the Repertory Theater was coming undone. Schuman sought to continue the talks with the one and to shore up the other. He inadvertently drew the Metropolitan Opera into the picture, and when he did, all hell broke loose.

Above and beyond the frustrations that Rudolf Bing, the Met general manager, encountered with the vagaries of construction, he was also not at all happy with the progress being made on Lincoln Center Festival '67. To begin with, he did not believe that Schuman and his staff should have a programming role at all. "As far as I know, Lincoln Center is not supposed to be a producing unit."[20] Rockefeller's 1963 year-end letter flatly contradicted Bing. "Your service as President of Lincoln Center has been outstanding, particularly in relation to program development—the lifeblood of the project. You have brought to it imagination, vision, enthusiasm and untiring energy; also, may I add, courage and determination."[21] Though the chairman of Lincoln Center apparently disagreed with him, Bing nevertheless remained adamantly opposed to the idea of a visiting foreign opera troupe coming into his new opera house that very first summer. Comparisons would be inevitable, and Bing felt that he did not want to place his company in that position. Schuyler G. Chapin, vice president for programming at Lincoln Center, recalled that "John Rockefeller finally had to be brought into the situation because he had received an enormous gift from the German government for the opera house and in return the Germans had indicated that they hoped the first foreign company to visit the new theater might be a German one."[22] The Met board eventually overruled Bing and cleared the way for a foreign company to be one of the star attractions for the festival. But no one expected the West German government to act as swiftly as it did. Just hours after Chapin arrived in Bonn to discuss the possibility of the Hamburg Opera being that troupe, the authorities agreed to give one million marks (approx. $250,000 in 1964 money) to help underwrite the project. Chapin was stunned but encouraged, and he left Bonn for Hamburg to make further arrangements and discuss repertoire.

When he returned to the States, however, the Met administrators were furious with Chapin for (in their minds) acting so precipitously.[23] Later, Bing would insist that the Met had the right to have veto power over which productions the Hamburg Opera would present and who would be involved with those productions. Rolf Liebermann, the general director of the Hamburg Opera, told Chapin: "I have the feeling the Met wants us to fail."[24] At issue for Bing was the likelihood that one of the productions would be by Walter Felsenstein, one of the leading proponents of *Regietheater* (director's theater), where musical values are subordinate to dramatic ones. For all of the Met's conservatism, Bing had attempted to bring Felsenstein to the United States to discuss the possibility of directing a new Met production. The State Department, however, refused to issue Felsenstein a visa, most likely because, in addition to working with Hamburg, he was a director at the Komische Oper of East Berlin and was an official in the arts hierarchy of the German Democratic Republic (aka East Germany). The idea that a Felsenstein production would take place on the Met stage but not with the Met's singers was galling enough, but the fact that Schuman had dreamed up this audacious idea of bringing cutting-edge opera to New York City further angered Bing. Schuman's role as über-administrator had moved beyond that of benevolent landlord and was encroaching upon the artistic visions and financial well-being of the constituents. At least this was how not a few non–Lincoln Center administrators saw matters. And in Bing's case, the fact that the Broadway Association had formed a committee to save the old Metropolitan Opera House, both as a landmark and in the hope that another opera company might find a home there, only increased the agitation that surrounded the Met's move to Lincoln Center.[25]

A month after the premiere of *Amaryllis* in Washington, Schuman wrote to New York City Mayor Wagner to tell him that "our intensive efforts to establish a permanent or even an interim relationship between Lincoln Center and City Center have been unfruitful."[26] During that month, Schuman had spoken with some of the board members of the Repertory Theater to address their impending leadership vacuum. Herman Krawitz handled business affairs for the Met and seemed to have the right set of skills and the right temperament to work with the Repertory Theater. With Schuman's knowledge, one of the Repertory board members had talks with Krawitz to see if he might be persuaded to leave the Met and join the Repertory. Krawitz was flattered by the solicitation but was convinced he needed to stay where he was.[27]

Tensions around Lincoln Center, however, were so great that this action, traceable to Schuman, was viewed as an unfriendly raid of constituent personnel. When word about the attempt to poach Krawitz reached Bing, he was apoplectic. Whitehead, feeling that his board had lost faith in him, resigned as director of the Repertory Theater. Kazan felt he had no choice but to join his business partner. Kirstein, though he was unaffected by "the Krawitz affair" (Schuman's name for the events of December 1964),[28] nevertheless inserted himself and his company in the middle of the crisis of confidence. A *New York Herald Tribune* reporter covered the story:

> "They hate us here," said Lincoln Kirstein, general director of the [New York City Ballet]. "They've treated us in the same shameful way they've treated Bob Whitehead. William Schuman wants us to go back, and we are going back." . . . Mr. Kirstein

> accused Mr. Schuman of seeking absolute control in the instances of both the State Theater and the Repertory Theater. "If they lose Whitehead as well as us, they're going to have two empty houses up there, and I'd like to know how Schuman is going to fill them."[29]

In his notes for a Lincoln Center board meeting to discuss all of these events, Schuman indicated that he had received word secondhand that "Opera and City Center Ballet officials [were] stating that I was on my way out and they were proposing other names." Bing, though he continued to calumniate Schuman in the press, was not part of this particular cabal, according to Schuman's notes. Schuman, in contrast, chose to remain quiet and did not make any public statements until mid-January: "L.C. [Lincoln Center] to succeed only if there are no splits in its public presentations—family arguments settled in private."[30] The Lincoln Center board stood behind Schuman to a man, even as Schuman denounced Bing's remarks as "inexcusable and reprehensible." Despite the support that Schuman received from his staff and board, though, Baum sensed that Schuman was weakened by these events and sought yet again to wheedle out of Schuman and Rockefeller an agreement to turn the New York State Theater over to City Center. The Lincoln Center men held their ground.[31] Further negotiations with Baum and City Center were so inconclusive that Lincoln Center's Public Affairs Office prepared competing press releases, some indicating that the City Center had decided to join Lincoln Center and others stating that the marriage could not be consummated. On January 11, 1965, word went out to the press that City Center would indeed become a constituent of Lincoln Center, and Schuman held a press conference to talk about that good news as well as about the events that had been given such prominent play the month before.

Morton Gould composed a list of things that he thought indicated that the worst had passed.

> 1. I see that Viet Nam is back on the front pages.
> 2. The real problem with Lincoln Center has not been touched upon—namely—how do you cross Columbus Avenue and Broadway to reach the place—or is this a way to control population explosion?
> 3. This past year I had trouble with my Center too. . . .

Schuman joked with Gould in answer. "I think the trouble you have had with your Center is really the End."[32] Throughout the storm, Schuman remained optimistic. "Fantastic days, these, at Lincoln Center. But everything will come out well if we just stick to our knitting and broaden our shoulders."[33] Nevertheless, the strain took its toll. Lincoln Center's general counsel was admitted to the hospital for exhaustion; John D. Rockefeller III and one of his deputies were down with sore throats; and the January executive committee meeting was canceled because of illnesses and prior commitments.[34]

Frankie, Bill, and Morton Gould. Photo by Bob Serating.

It was just as the clouds began to lift that Schuman began seriously to contemplate writing his memoirs.

> I am bringing up the subject in my own mind again because I would like very much to say in writing what has taken place in the last three weeks at Lincoln Center and its Repertory Theater, as distinguished from what has been reported in the press. This, I can assure you, would make fabulous reading given an interest in the subject—and this is something of course that I cannot assess.[35]

Equally noteworthy is that, though his projected table of contents for his memoirs included at least one chapter on Lincoln Center, he chose either not to draft that chapter or to withdraw it from public view. In his extended interviews he similarly eschewed talking at length about the "rhubarb" (another favored term of his) of December 1964. Many of the remaining documents—the memoranda to the files, the letters from irate conspirators, the accounts that made it to the press—tell enough of the story to understand that Schuman's crucifixion and resurrection were inevitable.

The gales that buffeted Schuman professionally during "the Krawitz affair" probably seemed inconsequential in light of the news he received shortly after it was all over. He disclosed the news to John D. Rockefeller III, who was in Tokyo.

> You may recall that we decided not to take our few days' holiday after the City Center announcement because it seemed important to remain here for the press. This

> certainly proved to be the case. We had then planned to get away for a few days following the Board meeting on February 8th, but we again had to postpone our trip. I am sorry to have to report to you and Blanchette that Frankie had to enter Lenox Hill Hospital last week for a mastectomy. The prognosis is excellent; there is no sign whatsoever that the malignancy spread, and she is making a rapid recovery. Hopefully, if all continues to go well, we will be able to get away toward the end of the month, although of course this is not at all certain.[36]

Frankie, who was treated for a carcinoma of the right breast, was in the hospital for 11 days.[37] They did manage to take a week's vacation in mid-March. Both Frankie and Bill received best wishes from many, including notes from Bing and Krawitz; Bing's was handwritten.[38]

The other demands of Lincoln Center all seem minuscule when set next to "the Krawitz affair," the City Center negotiations, and Frankie's cancer. An attempt to bring in a festival of avant-garde music never got off the ground.[39] The bookings of Philharmonic Hall and how they compared with the bookings at Carnegie Hall remained a matter of intense interest to Schuman. "I consider this monthly report on Philharmonic Hall in the nature of vital statistics."[40] The challenges of the Film Festival extended beyond complaints about its being scheduled across the Jewish holidays and about people answering the ads in the papers getting their tickets ahead of the local Lincoln Center devotees who waited for the flyer in the mail.[41] The festival ran a considerable deficit in its first year and was projected to run an even greater deficit going forward. Schuman had to figure out a way to turn the Film Festival over to a constituent that had not been created.[42]

Then there was Juilliard. Dealings with Peter Mennin, the new president of Juilliard, were particularly prickly. Mennin let it be known, according to Schuman, that "Juilliard–Lincoln Center relations . . . have been irritating, and from your [Mennin's] point of view far from satisfactory."[43] Mennin had been obdurate during discussions about the possibility of a modern dance constituent at Lincoln Center. Schuman and other administrators had sought his opinion and advice as they contemplated this development; Mennin viewed it as a play for Juilliard space and money. Much of the tension between the two men stemmed from Mennin's awareness that Schuman never championed him as his successor at Juilliard. Schuman had recommended several other men to follow him—Vincent Persichetti, Richard Franko Goldman, Norman Lloyd, Jacques Barzun—but not Mennin.[44] During Mennin's tenure at Juilliard, he kept Schuman at arm's length and chose not to involve his predecessor in the life of the institution. During Schuman's tenure at Lincoln Center, some of their conflicts became so acute that Schuman would turn to Schubart to act as referee. But in the larger scheme, the challenges that Juilliard presented to Schuman as Lincoln Center president were small.

By August 1965, Schuman was in high spirits. He recounted for the general manager of the Philadelphia Orchestra the number of things on the docket for the upcoming months.

> Just to give you some idea of what's ahead, we have the regular fall openings of the Philharmonic and the Ballet, separate events for the opening of the new Library-Museum and the Vivian Beaumont Theater buildings, not to mention the opening of the Repertory Theater's first season under its new directors, and unveilings of two important sculptures.[45]

The Library-Museum, in fact, was ready to open in April, but a dispute between the library and the city over who would cover certain operating costs led to an indefinite delay.[46] As a result, the Beaumont, which was finished later, opened earlier, with an audience of 700 movers and shakers present for the dedicatory ceremonies on October 14, 1965. Its official opening occurred one week later when the new artistic directors of the Repertory Theater, Herbert Blau and Jules Irving, brought Georg Büchner's *Danton's Death* to cheer the New York public. Alexander Calder's stabile *Le Guichet* (The Ticket Window) generated some controversy, as New York City Parks Commissioner Newbold Morris fought against its installation in front of the Library-Museum. "If the Municipal Art Commission voted to accept the sculpture, I must be wrong. I'm a product—or maybe a prisoner—of the 19th century." The other sculpture, Henry Moore's *Reclining Figure*, also had its detractors, less for its artistic merit and more for the nationality of its creator. Schuman, who never failed to defend the need to place more American composers on the programs of American orchestras, must have found it somewhat ironic to be called upon to defend the decision to go across the pond to commission a work of art for Lincoln Center from a British citizen.

> "It would be an insult to American artists to commission them or to buy their works merely because they are Americans," he said. "Our artists are among the best in the world and have no need of the protectionism that would be afforded by a narrow, chauvinistic, artistic tariff against foreign artists.
>
> "The only criteria that Lincoln Center recognizes are those of excellence and in its choice of works of art, the outstanding works of American artists have won an important place. The presence here today of Alexander Calder attests to that.
>
> "If we were to follow the line of reasoning of the picket who protested against the Moore work, our American composers would have to picket Lincoln Center every time a work of Beethoven was performed."[47]

(One person, an artist, had picketed the Moore on the opening night of the Beaumont. Schuman's remarks gave that picketer greater prominence—and everlasting, if anonymous, recognition—than he would have likely received had Schuman chosen to stay silent.)

Schuman's anticipation of all these events during the summer was not only meant to impress his Philadelphia correspondent with all of the activity happening at Lincoln Center. Schuman also hoped to excuse himself for not having begun work on the Ninth Symphony that summer. He had earlier told Ormandy that "I think a great deal about your symphony these days. My mental process is slowed by the fantastic administrative pressures of my post here, but there will come some calmer moments towards summer and I am going to devote myself to nothing else compositionally but this work."[48] He was not fallow as a composer during the summer of 1965, but the Ninth did not yet win his devotion. Instead he stitched together two works, both of which he later withdrew, during his working vacation.

The first sprang from a request Schuman received from the New York Philharmonic's general manager. Schuman wrote to his publisher with an idea.

> I need your permission for the following. Carlos Moseley called to ask, at [conductor] William Steinberg's request, whether I would compose a fanfare which the Philharmonic would use to open its Park Concerts series this summer. Three composers are invited, and I was the first, since he asked my suggestions for the other two. I want to comply, since the Philharmonic has for many years been close to my heart. I told Carlos that because of other commitments, I did not want to take precious time for composing a new fanfare—an impossible assignment to begin with—but I did have a thought. I can extract about 50 bars—plus one new bar of ending—from the second movement of my Seventh Symphony. It will be good for the purpose and should run about 1–1/2 minutes. I told Carlos that the Philharmonic would have to defray the copying of these few bars, to which he readily agreed. Would you agree to let the Philharmonic have this fanfare—which I would call "Philharmonic Fanfare"—for this summer? Any performances beyond this summer would, of course, be subject to terms. I would also send Presser, without charge, the tissues of the fanfare, which it could then have in its catalogue. Carlos and I agreed that the derivation of the material from the Seventh Symphony need not be mentioned.[49]

Schuman's description is reflected in the "manuscript" he left behind. It consists of two items: a marked-up score of the Seventh Symphony, from which Schuman extracted mm. 1–33, 45–50, and 85–98; and a scrap of paper containing the concluding three bars of the fanfare, on which Schuman wrote the instruction "Bar 98 chord hold 3 bars" as well as three measures of figures for percussion (bass drum, cymbals, snare drum, and timpani).[50] The higgledy-piggledy nature of the *Philharmonic Fanfare* may have gone unnoticed for its outdoor performances—at least one of which was nearly rained out—but it didn't pass Schuman's muster.[51] He later wrote to Moseley: "I am unhappy with the Fanfare I did for you last summer. If you want to use it again, I would fix it up. The playing time would probably be about 2–1/2 to 3. In effect, I would use the entire second movement from my 7th Symphony, with perhaps a different introduction, and definitely a newly composed ending. If you don't need it again, never mind."[52] Apparently, Moseley didn't need it again, but it was the first of four fanfares Schuman would compose over the next quarter-century, if one considers the *Philharmonic Fanfare* a composition as opposed to a construction.

The other work from the summer of 1965 was most definitely a composition, his longest for orchestra alone and, outside of his two operas, his longest work in any genre. It came about when Schuman was attending a party honoring Martha Graham on the occasion of her seventieth birthday.

> And nice speeches were being made, and I made a speech about Martha, and I said, "Someday I'll think of a birthday present to give you." So she got up before this whole crowd and said, "Bill, I want a birthday present, and it's in the form of a new score. You can't deny me in front of all these people." I said, "I wouldn't deny you publicly or privately."[53]

Judith (1949) was Schuman's last score for Graham. He allowed her to use *Voyage* (1953) after she had given him the eye treatment. Now a decade later, she once again manipulated Schuman into capitulating. He wrote to Hauser, "I have been weak enough to tell Martha Graham 'yes' that I will do another work with her. If she sends me the material in time, I will begin the middle of June. If not, hopefully, I will be working on the next symphony."[54] Schuman's wording makes it unclear if he was hoping that Graham would not come through or that he would be able to work on Ormandy's symphony. One thing, however, he had made clear to Graham: she was not to dance in whatever work he would write for her. When Virginia Katims, whose husband, Milton, was the conductor of the Seattle Symphony, asked some years earlier if they might engage Graham to reprise *Judith*, Schuman was frank in his assessment. "Although it is not for me to say, my judgment would be that it is out of the question for [Martha Graham] to do an extended solo performance. . . . While she is remarkable for her age, there is no use pretending that she is not past her prime."[55] Now, having been cornered into writing for Graham, Schuman extracted a promise of his own in private. "I said, 'Martha, I'm going to say something to you that's very tough, but I'm an old, old friend now; it's our fourth work together. I'll write it for you if you don't dance it. Just be the choreographer.'"[56] Graham agreed at the time, but the performance was months away.

Getting to the performance required Graham getting to Schuman the synopsis for the dance, something she did before Schuman's artificial mid-June deadline.

> I am attaching a quick resume of our work. I cannot yet give you the exact timing of the incidents and sequences, but I will do so shortly—and I believe also that you[r] sense of the dramatic will fulfill that for me perhaps. In any event, I fly from London the night of June 17th, arriving in New York on the 18th. The attached is what I have envisioned as the sequence. I know this is subject to your approval, and also I know you don't trust me at all—because you know I may change it.[57]

The story comes from 1 Samuel 28. King Saul, having expelled all mediums from the land of Israel, feels compelled to consult a seer. Saul's servants take him to the witch of Endor, who conjures up Samuel for Saul. Samuel in turn denounces Saul and confirms that young David, who has been gaining in stature and acclaim, will supplant the king. Schuman marked up the resume Graham had sent him, identifying sections that could have similar music and thus simplifying his task. He also received confirmation from Graham's office that the terms of the commission were very advantageous: $5,000 for the work, split evenly over two fiscal years, with the costs of score, parts, and copies—which amounted to an additional $2,321.16 in expenses—borne by Graham's organization.[58] She had provided the motivation in terms of both story and money; now she had to wait for Schuman.

Just after the national holiday, Schuman wrote to Graham to bring her up to date. One idea he had seems to have sprung from his successful coup de théâtre with *Amaryllis* the year before.

> The music goes slowly, but I hope to have some sizeable chunks for you by the middle of next month. I keep thinking about the ending. Today I began sketching this section. It does need a singer, but I have a new thought. No words. But a vocal line. I keep seeing (on stage) and hearing someone of the caliber of Adele Addison. Do you know her? She is a magnificent artist, and is usually in residence at Aspen. If she is there this year, perhaps you will meet her. The vocalise (without words, but humming ah's and perhaps other syllables) appeals to me because its abstract nature is to be preferred to word meanings, and yet we have the human element. Please agree. (— or not!)[59]

The correspondence between the two doesn't reveal whether it was Graham who nixed the singer, but Schuman ended up writing a purely orchestral score, one which he completed in its entirety by August 1, less than a month after telling Graham that "the music goes slowly."

He ended up producing nearly 45 minutes worth of music in as many days. The timing of the music is easy to determine because a recording was made prior to the premiere of the work. Schuman and a member of Graham's staff both wrote to the head of the Ford Foundation to see if the foundation would underwrite the prerecording of the score. Schuman laid out his reasons in full.

> The piano reduction is about the equivalent to an orchestral score that a pencil sketch is to a painting by El Greco. But now with Martha Graham we have a different problem. Let us face it, she is no longer young. The fact that she is taking on this new project at all is characteristic of her courage, her artistic vitality and her unwillingness to halt her magnificent work. This particular score will be even more difficult to reduce to the piano than most. Without exaggeration, I would say that if she had the benefit of being able to listen to the sounds while she imagined her dance, which she could do in private, without a rehearsal pianist at hand, her labors and her problem would be reduced during the creative process by an astonishing percentage—75 is not too high a figure.

> The second point I wish to make is that this proposal is solely for the benefit of Martha Graham. In no way does it benefit the composer, nor is it of importance to the composer. I just wanted you to know that the project is for Martha only. I thought you might want to know this as you consider the project.[60]

The Ford Foundation did come through with funding, but in fact the recording turned out not to be "for Martha only," as Schuman was in negotiations with Columbia Records to release the work after it was recorded in late September. Schuman envisioned an all-Graham album, incorporating the soundtrack from the 1961 film of *Night Journey* with his new score trimmed by "judicious cuts in repeated sections, which could bring the recorded version (similar to a concert version) to within a 30-minute span."[61] Between the recording and the end of the negotiations came the work's premiere on November 2, 1965.

Graham reneged on her promise not to dance. "She looked at me and said, 'Have I been naughty?' I said, 'You can never be naughty,' and this was after the performance."[62] But the ramifications of her decision were felt by the cast and were seen by the audience. Bertram Ross, one of the dancers in the production, recalled later:

> Martha was "The Witch" in *The Witch of Endor*. I was "King Saul." She said with such relish in rehearsal, "I beat him and beat him," but then onstage she forgot what to do. I was saying, "Beat me," and Bob Cohan, as "King David," was yelling across the stage, "Beat him, beat him."[63]

Gus Solomons, who played Samuel, painted an even bleaker picture.

> By 1965 Martha could only do about three steps herself. . . . And she couldn't always remember what came next or where she was supposed to be. The men would literally move her from place to place, where she'd do her three steps.[64]

Few would say it out loud, including *New York Times* critic Clive Barnes, but as Schuman had noted to the Katimses, Graham was past her prime. Barnes was circumspect in his assessment. "This is a very great dance company indeed, and if this first performance was a foretaste of the season to come, then they are dancing, corporately, probably better than at any time before."[65] If Graham's dancing individually was worse than at any time before, another aspect of her company transcended terpsichorean issues. "When Graham's *The Witch of Endor* was performed in 1965, half of the male cast were people of color, an extraordinary casting decision for its time."[66]

Schuman's retinue was there in force and let him know how much they appreciated his contribution. Composer Carlos Surinach praised Schuman, saying that the score had "a stunning theatrical drama and it is full of invention."[67] Amos Vogel, codirector of the New York Film Festival, wrote and said that *The Witch of Endor* was far superior to Fellini's "opulent, garish and ultimately shallow" *Juliet of the Spirits*.[68] Claire Reis, one of Schuman's earliest champions, had both praise and criticism to offer. "There were three elements which made the 'Witch of Endor' so impressive—your music, the set and Martha—the eternal stage personality—this was my impression. I can add to you what I did not like: the choreography. I found it confused, too repetitious, too seldom dramatic for the subject and for your music."[69] Joseph Machlis, Reis's companion at the premiere, had added an analysis of Schuman's Third Symphony to his revised *The Enjoyment of Music* just a few years before. Of the new Graham piece, he said, "I think it is one of your strongest works, full of tension and theater atmosphere, and richly evocative of that nightmare world inhabited by Martha, or the Witch of Endor, or both."[70]

Despite the encomia his score received, Schuman waffled on what he would do with *Endor*. He said shortly after the premiere, "I am not issuing it as a work, but will be using the materials in the next big opus," which, in another letter, he made clear was the Ninth Symphony.[71] But the following spring, he renewed his idea of issuing a shortened version of the recorded material with *Night Journey* on the other side, and in the fall he pushed for a coupling of *Judith* and *Endor*.[72] The quality of the existing recordings, the challenges of reconvening the musicians for *Endor*, and the lack of money to rerecord these scores all scuttled the plan of coupling two Graham dances onto one record at that time.[73] In a replay of the events surrounding the near publication of the Second Symphony, Schuman withdrew a work toward which he had some misgivings but came to esteem highly enough that he was ready and eager to send it out into the world. In this instance, the finest recording engineers could not reclaim a performance that was nearly lost forever.

As for the music itself, Schuman borrowed another idea from the Second Symphony: slow music takes up more time. He added to that experience the fact that sparsely scored music is easier to notate. The middle section of *The Witch of Endor* is a slow eight-minute (70-bar) duet between the first violins and the violas and celli in unison, and much of the score uses tempi on the slower side of the spectrum. The faster sections are often built on ostinati that Schuman notated once and then wrote measure repeat signs as they continue, so they, too, are handled economically in terms of their expansion. Whole sections are repeated verbatim, so much so that three of the manuscript's 135 pages have no musical notes on them whatsoever but have instructions as to which earlier measures are to be played at that point in the score.

Bar 710 = Bar 183 (Page 42)
711 —— 184
712 —— 185
713 —— 186

---

714 —— 306 (P. 60)
715 —— 307 (etc.)[74]

In terms of its harmonic and melodic language, Schuman draws upon his emancipated palette of dissonance. The opening chord contains all but three notes of the chromatic scale, and unaltered triads are almost nonexistent in the score. The plaintive duet at the center of the work comes to rest on a perfect fifth, but throughout most of its meanderings it avoids consonant intervals and any allusions to tonality. It is thus noteworthy that, in his race to complete this score in a timely fashion, Schuman used his most contemporary tonal arsenal and did not call upon the modal or populist strain that suffuses the works he wrote immediately before *Endor*. He also was adventurous timbrally, with the virtuosic xylophone part adding an unusual (for Schuman) coloristic effect. Perhaps most stunning is the fact that, though he stated more than once that he would recycle the score into the Ninth Symphony, Schuman chose to leave *Endor* virtually untouched. A percussion duet near the end of the Ninth Symphony recalls the dialogue between the timpani and snare drum near the beginning of *Endor*, and the chords that open *To Thee Old Cause* find their source in this Graham dance. But other than those two sonic references, there is little of *Endor* that shows up in other pieces. Schuman's comments about reusing the material preceded his reawakened interest in issuing a recording of the work, and by January 1966, when he confided that "I have already committed a few sketches [for the Ninth Symphony] to paper [and] am optimistic that by the end of 1966, the work might be completed," the implication is that the sketches were of new material and not of *Endor* redux.[75] Given that both the sound recording without video and the video recording without sound exist, it may be possible to reconstruct *The Witch of Endor* for future generations to study a work that both Schuman and Graham felt was not their best.[76]

Schuman would write other works with dances in them—the waltz in particular appears frequently in his compositions from the 1980s—but *The Witch of Endor* was the last of Schuman's five scores designated for the dance. Antony Tudor, who commissioned *Undertow* in 1944, would seek another ballet score from Schuman, sending him a poem that Tudor thought would appeal to him. Schuman answered: "It contains many sentiments, ideas and visions that strike a responsive chord (no pun). It is clear to me, however, that I can not really launch a musical work calculated both for concert and ballet use unless I have from you the aural atmosphere you seek, the timings you envision and those marvelously suggestive Tudor descriptions for emotional climate." Tudor also asked whether the *Three Colloquies* for French horn and orchestra (1979) might be suitable for dancing. Schuman didn't answer, stating instead that he still hoped one day to write another dance work, although he did not state whether he hoped to collaborate with Tudor again.[77] Graham similarly asked Schuman for yet another score, but the year was 1975 and Schuman had inviolable deadlines he had to meet for works that were to be premiered during the bicentennial year.[78] His final dance score is far finer than may seem to be the case, given

Schuman's decision to withdraw it. But as with the Second Symphony, that decision was made as other works were growing in importance. Though he used very little of *Endor*'s material in the Ninth Symphony, the later work would prove to be an emotional highpoint for Schuman. In many ways Schuman shared the same propensity he attributed to Graham.

> One of the things I love about Martha, which is one of her great things, when she has something that doesn't work; forget it. Over and out. You don't talk about it, you don't try to keep it in; you try to fix it if you can. She does that. She was not profligate with her work; she would try to fix it up. But if she didn't fix it, she didn't, you know, go around moaning about it: so what, that didn't work. It was a great experiment.[79]

Neither she nor Schuman sought to fix *The Witch of Endor.*

In her ninety-first year, Graham wrote to Schuman to express her disappointment in being unable to participate in the celebrations surrounding his seventy-fifth birthday. "You've meant a great deal to me in my life. Your courage and the many things you've done, along with your gifts of music to the world, will be thought of and treasured always. I wish for another birthday where I might be with you."[80] If anything, Schuman was more generous in his reply.

> There has been nothing else in my professional life remotely resembling the unique qualities that you bring to a composer. To have you utter such kind words to me about our association and friendship gives me the utmost satisfaction—but satisfaction is such an inadequate word to describe my feelings about the repeated opportunities I have had of experiencing your art as it was aborning.[81]

As 1965 drew to a close, Schuman had good cause to feel good about life. His wife had survived a bout with cancer. His son had graduated from Wesleyan "and, if I may brag a little–cum laude and Phi Bete–and is now a graduate student at Columbia in French."[82] Andrea was in her third year at the Dalton School on the Upper East Side and was proving every bit as precocious—and challenging—as Schuman had predicted she would be. He continued to see the big picture even as he got down in the weeds, griping about ushers with beards, inquiring about candles after a Consolidated Edison power outage, and railing about the Goldilocks-like situation of their corporate offices being either too hot or too cold.[83] These, too, fell to the president of Lincoln Center to navigate. As for Schuman the composer, his international profile had not dimmed. His fame was spreading through the Soviet Union as Ukrainian conductor Igor Blazhkov premiered the Third Symphony with the Leningrad Philharmonic Orchestra and championed his music.[84] His advice was sought by a group of industrious young men who formed the American Recorded Music Society in London and asked Schuman to lend his name as honorary president, which he did.[85] Within the United States, his opinion was sought on matters of composers-in-residence for orchestras—an idea then considered a novelty—and on the role of the avant-garde within the larger music scene.[86] The weight of his responsibilities had not killed his love for the occasional practical joke, as when he tricked Mark Schubart, a heavy smoker, into thinking that Lincoln Center offices would soon become smoke free.[87] He was featured on the National Educational Television series, *The Creative Person*, talking about his role as a composer, teacher, and administrator, in that order.[88] For Schuman, the future looked bright.

The year 1965 also saw the escalation of the war in Vietnam, the assassination of Malcolm X, the confrontation at the Edmund Pettus Bridge in Selma, the beginnings of campus unrest at the University of California at Berkeley, and a riot in Watts (south-central Los Angeles). The World's Fair had failed to meet its financial targets, and John V. Lindsay became mayor at a time when New York City was sliding into the abyss. A six-minute song by Bob Dylan released as a single in July 1965 reached no. 2 on the charts. At the end of 1965, Schuman felt fairly secure. Aside from having time enough to compose, he had just about everything. That meant, of course, that he had a lot to lose, and the next three years would see a different parade of nightmares, not as explosive as "the Krawitz affair," but nightmares all the same, coming at Schuman almost as if in slow motion.

TWENTY-FIVE

THE POTEMKIN CENTER

Schuman surely must have heard rumblings that, after the Metropolitan Opera's success with his *Vanessa* in the winter of 1958, Samuel Barber was being courted to provide a work for the Met's first season in its new Lincoln Center opera house.[1] When "the great news reached the papers" in May 1964, Schuman felt "simply overjoyed" for Barber, hopeful for American opera, and vindicated in his efforts to get American institutions to commission and perform American music.[2] Schuman wanted as many people as possible to witness the event. He wrote to Rudolf Bing and Anthony Bliss, the Met's general manager and president, respectively, to tell them that National Educational Television was willing to broadcast four hours of the Met's opening and that all expenses would be paid through the underwriting that the broadcasting company was securing from the Met's longtime radio sponsor, Texaco.[3] Live video broadcasts would have to wait, though, as the Met decided instead to rely on "the miracle of radio" to share with the nation the excitement that attended the opening of the new house and Barber's new opera.[4]

The premiere of *Antony and Cleopatra* on September 16, 1966, has since entered the annals of music history as a colossal failure, what Barber biographer Barbara Heyman called "the monumental misfortune of Barber's career."[5] But the verdict at the time was much less definite. Harold Schonberg wrote that the opera "enjoyed a lukewarm success" but only after declaring that the opera house itself was an acoustical marvel.[6] Given Barber's earlier success at opera and Lincoln Center's earlier failures with acoustics, Schonberg's words augured well for both the composer and the opera company. Another critic of sorts, Jacqueline Kennedy, widow of assassinated President John F. Kennedy, wrote privately to Schuman to thank him for sending her the opening night program, since she was unable to attend the opera on that evening. In a handwritten postscript, she expressed her views. "I saw 'Anthony [*sic*] and Cleopatra'—and I loved every second of it—really critics are most unfair. It was beautiful to hear and to see."[7]

Samuel Barber and Schuman. Photo by Bob Serating.

Whether Schuman shared Schonberg's or Kennedy's opinion of the opera cannot be determined, as he chose not to repeat whatever words he shared with Barber on the night of the premiere in a follow-up letter. But given his own treatment at the hands of the newspapers, Schuman likely affirmed Kennedy's other observation: Critics are most unfair. Schuman was in his fifth year at the helm of Lincoln Center. By the end of that year, all but one of the original constituents were in their new spaces, the ballet and opera companies from City Center had joined the others, and new constituencies for film and chamber music were almost ready to be launched. Not everything went smoothly, of course: musical theater and repertory theater were struggling, and the idea of a constituent in modern dance was slowly being abandoned. But Lincoln Center as a whole was steadily developing a record of success. The criticism, however, continued, both from without and within.

"Bill Schuman's Festival," Bernstein's playful name for Lincoln Center Festival '67, continued to generate a fair share of controversy.[8] At one point, Schuman and Chapin, vice president for programming, explored the possibility of bringing the Prague National Opera to the festival in addition to the Hamburg Opera, but Bing "expressed concern that the addition of the Prague Opera would, in view of the participation of the Metropolitan and the Hamburg

Opera, result in too many opera performances during the Festival," according to the minutes of a Lincoln Center Council meeting. The idea was dropped.[9] Then, in his formal announcement of the festival, Schuman voiced the belief among the Lincoln Center staff that "this is the first [festival] of its kind in the United States, or in the world, to take in all the performing arts in an urban center." Given that the staff had in mind the festivals in Salzburg, Edinburgh, and Bayreuth, Schuman's comments were unremarkable. The problem was that Expo '67 in Montreal was also in the planning stages, and the Canadian authorities did not appreciate Schuman's snub, regardless of whether it was deliberate or unintentional.[10] A snub of a different sort occurred when Schuman appeared on television with Irving Kolodin, music critic for the *Saturday Review*. Schuman thought that he was being invited to talk about Lincoln Center generally and the festival specifically. Kolodin, in contrast, thought that the two men were going to have a conversation about the state of music at Lincoln Center, and when he started asking Schuman some pointed questions and raised doubts about the festival program, Schuman became defensive and turned the discussion into a monologue. In a letter Schuman wrote to Kolodin later, purportedly an "apology" for monopolizing the conversation, he concluded in a supercilious manner: "Lincoln Center is not in very good shape when one of our leading and most influential critics is something less than thoroughly informed on the workings of the performing arts center of this city." Kolodin fired back: "I am well informed on the content of the Festival, but do not agree that it is all equally creditable to Lincoln Center, or, of course, all discreditable to Lincoln Center. I will, naturally, not presume to have a total judgement until it has been revealed as a totality. Then, perhaps, we can have another discussion at greater length and with different ground rules, on the net of it all."[11] Schuman certainly fought to protect "his" festival from those who would seek to whittle it down to size.

He also sought to promote the festival as widely as possible. There were numerous attempts—and a few successes—in bringing both the government and private enterprise on board to support the festival. With his background as an advisor to various agencies in the federal government, Schuman conceived the festival as an artistic weapon in the ongoing cultural battle for hearts and minds in Europe. The New York Film Festival had already resulted in partnership with the British Film Institute, and when Schuman was in London in 1964 to solidify that partnership, he also met with officials in the United States Information Agency based there. As recorded in the minutes of Lincoln Center's Executive Committee, Schuman reported back that "little is known about Lincoln Center by members of the USIA abroad, but there is great interest in Lincoln Center. . . . The members of the British press were interested but seemed to know very little about Lincoln Center. Dr. Schuman recommended that this program be handled by the development of a thorough information program in each foreign country with people in performing arts groups."[12] A year before the festival got under way, Leonard Marks, the director of the USIA, expressly asked that all information about Festival '67 be sent to him personally so that he could coordinate the overseas stories and broadcasts.[13] Marks thus furthered Schuman's longstanding desire to convince the Europeans that Americans weren't uncultured country cousins.

Ironically, one way the festival organizers set out to prove that America had culture was to invite foreign performing arts groups to perform at the center and then to draw foreign audiences to see and hear these groups at the festival. Schuman dispatched Chapin to meet with representatives of the U.S. Travel Service as well as the Department of Commerce to convince their offices that the festival had the potential of attracting foreign visitors, and further talks with these and other federal agencies were encouraged.[14] And before he himself set out on an April 1967 tour of various European cities "to underscore the international character of the Lincoln Center Festival '67 and to capture European interest in this major artistic and cultural event," Schuman filmed two extended clips in the Washington studios of the United States Information Service, in which both he and Vice President Hubert Humphrey appeared. Humphrey represented President Lyndon B. Johnson, who had been promoting a "Discover America" program, which Humphrey chaired.[15] Schuman would have something of a tough sell in Europe, however, as the impression among the Europeans was that New York was an unsafe city.[16] So not only was Schuman going to the major European cities to tell them about Lincoln Center and its inaugural festival. Not only was he stumping for the White House and its initiative to bring more tourists to the United States. He also had to allay fears that visitors to New York would be the target of criminals.

Then there was the matter of finding a corporate sponsor. They approached Joseph C. Wilson, chairman of the board of the Xerox Corporation, asking for $500,000. Wilson was sympathetic but doubtful, given the company's budgetary constraints; Schuman recalled him asking, "How can I cut some research project back when we are spending $500,000 for an arts festival?"[17] They turned to American Express, once again to be told that "we simply could not fit this additional substantial commitment into our plans this late in the game."[18] The following year, for Festival '68, they would go to Henry Ford II of the Ford Motor Company and Juan Trippe of Pan American Airlines, and again they would be turned away. Mercedes-Benz underwrote a reception for the Hamburg Opera in 1967, while Olivetti Underwood Co. played a much more substantial role in bringing the Rome Opera to New York in 1968.[19] But both festivals were funded primarily through the Lincoln Center Fund, which in turn relied heavily on private donors, some of the same people that the fundraisers for the Met and the New York Philharmonic approached for gifts. For Festival '67, the staff estimated that the festival could pay for itself with full houses but prudently budgeted for 75 percent occupancy and a maximum loss of approximately $535,000.[20] The actual deficit came close to the budgeted figure: "$533,411 exclusive of further income anticipated from 'Unknown Soldier and His Wife,'" the new Peter Ustinov play that premiered during the festival.[21] For Festival '68, Schuman came up with a brilliant idea: focus a portion of the festival around the twenty-fifth anniversary of the Koussevitzky Music Foundation.[22] Not only would this bring together "a representative cross-section of works of the past together with chamber music and orchestra works which may now be in the process of being written under Koussevitzky commissions," but it also had a potential built-in source of additional funding through the foundation itself. Given that Schuman was one of the directors of the Koussevitzky Foundation, its contribution of $50,000 toward the cost of "a kind of 'Festival within a Festival'" was all but assured once Schuman had hatched his idea.[23] Had Schuman and his staff been as successful in finding other corporate money for Bill Schuman's festivals, they likely would have continued beyond 1968 and would not have been moribund for nearly 30 years.[24] Then again, as Chapin noted in his memoirs, the Met and the New York Philharmonic discovered that there truly was an audience for summer performances and that these constituents did not need to rely on the Lincoln Center administration to reach this audience.[25] The festivals were, in a way, the victims of their own success.

They also played an indirect role in Schuman's life as a composer. As early as 1963, he began to solicit ideas for a work to celebrate the nation's bicentennial. That year he asked Alicia Smith, the choral conductor Gregg Smith's wife at the time, if she could arrange a text for a major work based on American themes and ideals.[26] Three years later, he met with his publisher, who asked him if he had thought about composing a piece for the bicentennial. Schuman wrote Alicia, "He was, I know, enormously pleased (and, I am sure, surprised) not only to learn that I am interested, but that I have already begun work."[27] Schuman tentatively named the work *Nineteen Seventy-Six*—he preferred words instead of numerals—and in a June 1966 letter to his publisher, he laid out his ideas for the work.

> To celebrate the 200th anniversary of the signing of the Declaration of Independence, I envision music for soloists, mixed chorus (children's chorus may also be used), and orchestra. The length of the work will be the normal running time of a concert. It is my plan to use as texts words of American authors. It will be my intention to give the feeling and spirit of some of the facets of "The American Dream." If I am successful, I will achieve this goal by indirection and implication rather than a head-on assault conceived either chronologically or in terms of subject matter. No one can encompass the scope and meaning of America in a single work. It is my ambition, in this work, to give expression through words and music to some of the feelings that are so

> deep within me. If I can succeed in expressing these feelings to my own satisfaction, then I have no doubt that the work will have meaning for others.

In addition to recycling some of his earlier compositions, he envisioned new settings of Emerson that Smith was arranging and "a dramatic scene for soprano and orchestra" based on the drowning scene in Dreiser's *An American Tragedy*, the source of Schuman's hoped-for opera.[28]

Three things kept Schuman from painting on such a large canvas in the 1960s. First, he and his publisher could not line up a commission to underwrite the work; Schuman estimated that the cost would be anywhere from $70,000 to $125,000.[29] The second was that, for the second time in his career, Schuman forfeited an entire summer's worth of composition because of illness. In June 1966, he came down with a "miserable throat" that lasted for the entire month.[30] The throat problem may have been related to a hiatal hernia, which can cause acid reflux and heartburn, but it wasn't until early August that the hernia, which had been causing Schuman periodic discomfort, was discovered.[31] A few weeks later, he was in "a good deal of pain—due to some strange neuro-muscular mystery which, hopefully, will be explained or will disappear." Taken in sum, the health problems left Schuman with what he called a "punk summer."[32] Not only were the plans for *Nineteen Seventy-Six* curtailed but his promise to the manager of the Philadelphia Orchestra to have the Ninth Symphony completed by year's end also was rendered impossible. In the case of the symphony, the delay would prove propitious, but the loss of composing time further stymied Schuman's efforts to be as much a composer as an administrator.

The third reason why the bicentennial piece failed to materialize at this time was Alicia Smith. Schuman found that their working styles were incompatible, and he reluctantly informed Smith that, on this project at least, they would need to go their separate ways.[33] Schuman tabled *Nineteen Seventy-Six* for a number of years, but he would revive it in time to obtain a bona fide bicentennial commission, albeit one for a work not quite as splendiferous as *Nineteen Seventy-Six* would have been. But he had begun to look far into the future of the Lincoln Center Festivals and saw a confluence of his own projected composition and the likely theme of the festival in the bicentennial year. "It is the thought that these Festivals would normally include distinguished foreign organizations, but thinking ahead to 1976 we are contemplating devoting the entire Festival period to America as a land of the arts."[34] Perhaps Schuman hoped the bicentennial festival would have also been the site for the premiere of his *Nineteen Seventy-Six*.

A different festival at Lincoln Center proved to be far more popular and durable than the international extravaganzas that Schuman summoned into being. Schuman went to the Lincoln Center Executive Committee in March 1966 with a proposal for a festival of Mozart's music in August at Philharmonic Hall. The minutes of the meeting give the fundamental details:

> 27 concerts are planned, and he reviewed briefly the nature of certain of these concerts. He discussed the proposed budget of $183,000, which will include $68,000 rent to Philharmonic Hall. The tickets for the concerts will be at the fixed price of $3.00 per ticket, so that at 81% of rental capacity the Festival will break even.[35]

Schuman and his staff approached the Martha Baird Rockefeller Fund for Music for help in meeting the anticipated deficit. No one at Lincoln Center imagined that attendance in August would reach the break-even point of 81 percent; the officers at the Rockefeller Fund had their own doubts concerning the festival and turned down the request for funding.[36] But when all of the money came in from the first "August Mid-Summer Serenades: A Mozart Festival," the staff discovered that the deficit the festival ran was only $12,000 more than it would have cost the center to leave Philharmonic Hall dark for those concerts. To William W. Lockwood Jr., executive producer of programming at Lincoln Center, the progenitor of the Mostly Mozart Festival "was an unqualified success from every standpoint and must rank not only as the surprise of the year on the New York concert scene, but also as one of the most successful projects yet to be undertaken by the [Lincoln Center] Programming Department."[37]

The festivals were one of the few high points for Schuman during his final years as president of Lincoln Center. Just about everywhere else he turned, the glittering façades of the sparkling new buildings barely disguised the disorder and discord roiling behind them. The problems of the Repertory Theater seemed well nigh insoluble. The team of Blau and Irving failed to capitalize on the blank slate that was handed to them after the departure of Whitehead and Kazan. T. E. Kalem, drama critic for *Time* magazine and president of the New York Drama Critics Circle, wrote Schuman a blistering letter at the end of Blau and Irving's first season, not in his official capacities in either post but "in the light of what I regard as responsibilities entailed by those posts. The path to excellence is never certain. What is certain about the work of Blau and Irving is that if permitted to continue, they will leave no abyss unplumbed."[38] But Kalem's complaint was addressed to the wrong person; it was as though Kolodin had written to Schuman to object to the programming at the Met. Though the Repertory Theater was brought into being by Lincoln Center, it had become a separate constituent with its own board of directors. Schuman forwarded Kalem's letter to Robert Hoguet, the president of the Repertory Theater, and could only hope that Hoguet and his board would do something. Some months later, after a meeting with Hoguet, Schuman committed his thoughts to a memorandum for the files.

> My personal reaction from the conversation was one of discouragement. I do not feel that a success can be made under the present arrangements, and I do not believe that creative minds cannot come up with a better answer. On the other hand, as an institutional matter, I feel that Lincoln Center must be very careful not to trespass. In view

> of Mr. Hoguet's invitation for other ideas, I think we should sit down with him after the third production of this season.[39]

A month later, Blau resigned, leaving his partner Irving to run the Repertory Theater without him.[40] The Repertory Theater would limp along until it was disbanded in 1973.

The Music Theater of Lincoln Center also started to come apart around the same time as Blau's resignation. It, too, was an independent constituent, and like the Repertory Theater, Lincoln Center sired it, so the administration was forced to deal with its problems whether it wanted to or not. Hoyt Ammidon, the chairman of the board for this constituent, was having difficulty in getting Richard Rodgers, its president, to come to "the recognition of a budget as a budget and a firm intention to live by it."[41] Ammidon had taken on a new role to oversee the center's capital fundraising, so he and Schuman both were particularly eager to bring the Music Theater to heel so that Ammidon could focus his attention to the needs of the entire center. Schuman drafted a letter to Rodgers and asked Ammidon to read it over. Ammidon apparently recommended that Schuman not send it, electing instead to meet with Rodgers and express in person some of the concerns that Ammidon and Schuman shared. Whether the meeting itself went well is unknown, but Ammidon's letter to Rodgers summarizing their meeting greatly disturbed Rodgers. In the midst of all the turmoil with the various constituent problems and reports of cost overruns, Schuman somehow was able to see the silver lining. He wrote to Ammidon:

> This has been a tough week at the Center, filled with too many major disappointments. But, while I can't help but feel dismayed about the overages and let down about American Express, et al. I still feel the same sense of dedication, encouragement and optimism. Also, I believe that under your leadership we will raise the funds required to complete this enterprise and keep it going.[42]

Just about every week in 1967 was a tough week at the center. Construction costs for the Juilliard building were more than $1.5 million over budget, and the building wouldn't be ready for occupancy until the winter of 1969 at the earliest, meaning that the money Juilliard was expected to generate at Lincoln Center was now lost for a year more than the staff had anticipated.[43] Mennin and Juilliard's Board of Directors were threatening to do away with the proposed Drama Division, saying that they could not see their way clear to fund it, even as Schuman and his pencil pushers sent one proposal after another up to Morningside Heights in an attempt to convince the Juilliard officers that they were mistaken.[44]

The fledging of the Film Society of Lincoln Center during this year is all the more remarkable, and Schuman knew how unlikely its creation was. In looking for ways to tighten the center's belt, the executive committee was contemplating the termination of the film festival. Schuman stood athwart that move.

> The only new art that Lincoln Center has added to the traditional ones is film. Film is the great innovative art of the Twentieth Century[,] and a center for the performing arts without a strong film program is incomplete.
>
> The Directors have been remarkable in going along with me in the launching of a film program. Several have told me quite frankly that they supported it because of my personal enthusiasm—despite their reservations.[45]

No doubt some of those directors feared that the Film Society would go the same direction as the Repertory Theater and the Music Theater. (The latter closed its doors in 1974.) But unlike the other new constituents, the Film Society thrived, and those close to its genesis and workings never hesitated to name Schuman as the founder of the film center. Certainly Schuman saw himself that way.[46]

The challenges with the constituents may have come to Schuman unbidden, but he occasionally courted trouble on his own. It is worth noting that, from his 1934 polemic on Wagner and Judaism to his 1961 love letter to Vincent Persichetti in the *Musical Quarterly*, Schuman saw his writings published at the rate of one every six months. Often, they were letters to the editors of newspapers or magazines. Other times, they were reprints of keynote addresses he gave at conferences. Some are book reviews; a few are journal articles; and occasionally, as is the case with the *Proceedings of the American Society of Newspaper Editors*, they were transcriptions of his extempore remarks as a panelist.[47] Before he assumed the presidency of Juilliard, the quality and quantity of his prose made him one of the most widely read composers in American history, with roughly 50 published items to his credit in 28 years.

In the seven years he steered Lincoln Center, no fewer than 28 pieces—one every three months—appeared. Clearly Schuman did not have the time to write all of these himself. He now had more help in drafting and crafting his ideas than he had at Juilliard, and in his speeches, especially, he directed his staff to lift whole passages from one and embroider around the edges to make it serve a different audience. (Dartmouth College's Hopkins Center for the Performing Arts, a New England test run for the architects designing their much larger efforts on the Upper West Side, elicited a dedicatory speech from Schuman that he cannibalized repeatedly throughout the decade.)[48] As the visible leader of the nation's premier performing arts center, his words (and words attributed to him) were in great demand.

In his public speaking, Schuman preferred to take a list of questions given to him by the host institution and weave his answers in such a way that he demonstrated the breadth of his knowledge, the depth of his thinking, and the quickness of his wit. This was easier for him to do when he was at Juilliard; most of his talks were to community groups, university students, and others in the fields of music or education (or both). His improvisational skill was on display in mostly low-stakes venues. Now that he was at Lincoln Center, the stakes were considerably higher. Businessmen and politicians and their wives made up his audience now, making the need to stay on script much greater. It was a small price to pay in exchange for the opportunity of running such a vast enterprise. But on occasion the improvisatory and impish Schuman would momentarily take center stage. On one of those occasions, the appearance proved to be fateful.

In December 1966, he was invited to Princeton University to give a speech as part of a conference. Schuman asked Henry Bessire, the executive director of development at Lincoln Center, whether the conference was worth his time.

> There is no question in my mind that . . . you should be there. Not only should you be present, but hopefully you would make a major address . . . on "The Role of the Cultural Center". This is the kind of forum for you. There will be representatives of industry and philanthropy at this meeting and it is these people with whom we must communicate.[49]

So with the help of Bessire and others, Schuman crafted his Princeton speech, "The New Establishment."[50]

> When I use the word "establishment," I mean any center of power—real or imagined. In using the term "new establishment," I refer specifically to the so-called cultural centers; the ones existing, the ones under construction, and the ones being planned. These are new institutions on the American scene. Mostly they are only partly functioning, and mostly we have to look to their future. But already, real or imagined, they are viewed as "the Establishment."

Schuman was trading on the currency of the day, as charges of belonging to or fighting the Establishment—the social and political norms—filled the air in 1960s America.[51] By labeling Lincoln Center and its ilk as "the New Establishment," Schuman sought both to criticize the tendency of these cultural centers to engage in the hidebound ways of their predecessors and to spur the representatives of industry and philanthropy to look to create something truly novel. To do this, Schuman offered what he called "Schuman's Law and Its Postulates."

> The law: "Nonprofit institutions in the performing arts compromise their reason for being in direct proportion to the programs and policies which are adopted for fiscal reasons extrinsic to artistic purpose."
>
> Translation: The bottom line cannot drive the choices performing arts institutions make.
>
> Postulate #1: Timidity in programming comes from "catering to the social and esthetic predilections of those who buy the tickets," focusing on "the percentage of the budget which must be met by voluntary contributions," and letting the institution get too large for its own artistic good.

> Postulate #2: "Imagination in programming concept tends to increase in direction proportion to: A. The clarity of institutional mission; B. The sophistication of the trustees; and C. The convictions of the professional leadership."
>
> Translation: Cowardice does not lead to artistic and aesthetic excellence.

As provocative as the law and postulates were in themselves, Schuman went further as the Lawgiver became the Prophet.

> Earlier I stated that all of us in the performing arts swam in the same sea: the sea of deficit. This sea is obviously a red sea, and only a p-r-o-f-i-t profit can part it. Now, as deep as that red sea is, I think it should be deeper. Basic to our problem is not that our deficits are too large, but that they are too small.

The remainder of the speech strongly suggests that the pillar of cloud and fire that will allow the people of the new musical nation to walk on dry ground to the new artistic promised land and that will smite the boorish Egyptians-cum-Philistines nipping at the heels of the harassed but enlightened aesthetic chosen people are those very representatives of industry and philanthropy who managed to enshrine the old Establishment against which Schuman was railing. Schuman as Moses was announcing to the Pharaohs before him: Let my (contemporary) music go!

Whoever actually wrote the speech, Schuman eagerly delivered it and felt no shame in doing so. He was secure enough in the words he spoke that he sent John D. Rockefeller III "a copy of the speech I gave at your alma mater last week."[52] He seemed caught off guard when Rockefeller's response came over the next few weeks. First, Rockefeller and Schuman met for lunch along with two other Lincoln Center directors "to look ahead into the future and face up frankly to the problems which are before Lincoln Center," Rockefeller wrote in his diary. "The lunch was responsive to the concerns . . . as to whether Bill Schuman's leadership has been as effective as it should be."[53] Then, in a lengthy end-of-the-year letter that Schuman characterized as "unfriendly," Rockefeller spelled out what Schuman would need to do to set right the course of the center, the implication being that, should Schuman not do so, his days were numbered.[54] Thus were the seeds sown that would eventually flower into what Schuman came to describe as his "retirement" from Lincoln Center (a description that had implications for his medical coverage later in life).[55]

Rockefeller's letter laid out the road to success. At Princeton, Schuman advocated for bold action; at Lincoln Center, Rockefeller made it clear that Schuman would have to cut back on the ambitious programs he envisioned. "While our primary objective is of course cultural, it was recognized that we would have to slow up our rate of progress in that direction in order to do a really effective job in relation to day-to-day management problems."[56] Schuman also needed to give greater consideration about the role that deficits play. Schuman's Princeton speech, in Rockefeller's mind,

> is subject to misinterpretation. You emphasized the desirability of larger deficits if art institutions are to attain artistic heights without equally emphasizing that such deficits must be within the bounds of obtainable contributions if the project is to survive. This kind of deficit philosophy can be the downfall of Lincoln Center or any other artistic institution unless as much attention is given to sound financial planning and effective fund-raising as to the creation and development of programs.

It may not have occurred to Rockefeller that Schuman had no clear sense of what the bounds of obtainable contributions was. At Juilliard, Schuman was spared the arduous task of fundraising to some degree because of the presence of the generous endowments that kept the school and its various enterprises running. Those endowments had to be replenished, and there were times of austerity and retrenchment, but the fundraising required at Lincoln Center was of a different magnitude than what Schuman knew in his time at Juilliard. It did not help matters that Schuman believed that the funding problem stemmed from the niggardly support that, in his mind, the arts received from people and institutions of means. Rockefeller, in contrast, felt that the representatives of industry and philanthropy were already being generous and that the demands of the center were colliding with a Zeitgeist that was starting to redirect corporate coffers away from cultural concerns and more toward economic revitalization of urban communities. Lincoln Center was billed as such a project, but American cities in the mid-1960s were in upheaval, and a cultural playground for the upper middle class had decreasing cachet to the money men of the day. So Rockefeller placed the situation in the starkest terms he could. "Lincoln Center is in fact at a crossroads. The construction has been completed except for one building [Juilliard] and now we can give our attention to making Lincoln Center succeed, to determine whether our original goals and objectives are sound and obtainable.... The months ahead are crucial ones. It is your leadership that will be the determining factor." In his own memo to himself, Schuman wrote about the meeting he had with Rockefeller within days of receiving the letter. Schuman, according to his memo, made the point "most strongly" that if he had lost the support of Rockefeller and the other senior members of the board, then "I could not continue effectively in the post, and that I would not. As always in my meetings with the Chairman, the exchange of views was completely and utterly frank, and I left with the feeling that I had made my points. But I cannot in all candor say, even in a confidential memorandum to the files, that I was completely satisfied."[57] He was right to be dissatisfied, for less than two years later, Rockefeller would determine that Schuman's effectiveness as a leader had come to an end.

Schuman also appeared to be tone-deaf when it came to hearing Rockefeller's concerns. He laid out the increasingly dire financial situation to Rockefeller, but his diagnosis of the problem focused on the wrong aspect of what was ailing Lincoln Center.

> I believe that management has lived within its means as they have been anticipated, and undertaken constant review and refinement of budgetary planning. However, the capital overages in the past year have substantially increased our problems in planning for the future. I hope that, with your help, the seriousness of this problem fully be reviewed by the Lincoln Center Fund Committee at its meeting on Friday, and that we can reach some general agreement with our principal fund-raisers on our ability to meet the new goals.[58]

From Schuman's vantage point, his staff had been responsible with the handling of the monies it had received, but the fundraisers simply hadn't raised enough. But Rockefeller had said that Schuman was responsible for the fundraisers as well as the administrative staff. From Rockefeller's point of view, Schuman didn't require his help, and he wasn't inclined to offer any.

But finding money for Lincoln Center was no easy prospect. Mayor Lindsay was offering no help for 1967 and gave no indication that future appeals to the City of New York would be favorably received even as the senior leadership of Lincoln Center was determined to "get into the City budget."[59] After he returned from Europe to promote Festival '67, Schuman traveled to Washington to deliver a speech to the Friends of the John F. Kennedy Center for the Performing Arts. He used the platform to excoriate Congress for its "appalling stinginess . . . It is true that private patronage is and should continue to be the backbone of support for the arts in America. Government should complement that patronage in meaningful amounts if it is to discharge its own obligation to our artistic heritage."[60] But Schuman could browbeat the lawmakers only so much. It wasn't the fault of the federal, state, and city administrations that escalating costs and shrinking sources of potential income necessitated drastic measures at the center.

Rockefeller's seriousness about Schuman's need to cut back on projects extended to one of Schuman's fondest dreams: the Chamber Music Society. After having reviewed a progress report on the gestation of the Society, Rockefeller wrote Schuman in the plainest manner possible. "I am sympathetic to moving forward with the development of the project, but I am unsympathetic to Lincoln Center's making any further financial commitments in relation to it. . . . Until we have proven that we have a substantial fund-raising potential for ongoing annual needs, I believe we must not take on added responsibilities which have ongoing financial obligations." To underscore the importance of his position, Rockefeller invoked a parallel from history. "You will remember that Winston Churchill once said that he did not wish to preside over the liquidation of the British Empire. Neither you nor I want to preside over the liquidation of Lincoln Center. My belief is that we are moving in that direction unless we stop now the making of new commitments for programs involving substantial amounts of money." Rockefeller also had copies of the letter sent to directors who had been privy to the year-end luncheon and its ensuing letter;

he was not going to push back against Schuman by himself.[61] Less than a week later, Schuman wrote to Alice Tully, asking her to "enable us to make a firm beginning by assuring the funds required to plan and launch the Chamber Music Society."[62] He also wrote to Rockefeller, pushing back against the suggestion that any of the programming aspects of Lincoln Center should be curtailed. "One of the principal arguments advanced in all our fund-raising efforts was our repeated assertions that Lincoln Center was to be more than buildings.... The fact that we have to meet building overages should not lead us into the trap of tacitly reasoning that educational and artistic programs are, after all, postponable."[63] The battle lines were emerging: Rockefeller wanted to hold the line on any and all expansion of Lincoln Center programs until the money for them was in hand; Schuman wanted to promote the programs in the belief that "if the programs were imaginative enough there would be enough money for the needs of the constituents and Lincoln Center."[64] It was the Princeton speech all over again. A phone conversation in early March and a dinner gathering before Schuman departed for Europe temporarily assuaged both men, but they would soon be respectfully adversarial as the fiscal problems of Lincoln Center became even more extreme.[65]

Those problems dwarfed all concerns about whether the maw of Lincoln Center would be fed by public or private funds. By the summer of 1967, the center's appetite for money far outstripped the ability of the fundraisers to satisfy it. In his history of the center, Edgar Young, Rockefeller's deputy, succinctly sketched the dilemma facing anyone who had eyes to see.

> During that summer of 1967, in spite of the artistic and public success of the 1967 summer activities, there was growing anxiety over the operating budget and fund raising. For the fiscal year of 1967 and 1968 a gross expenditure of $7 million was budgeted, offset by estimated income of $4 million, leaving a deficit of $3 million. Of that need, $1.3 million could be met if the goal of the Lincoln Center Fund could be reached; the balance of $1.7 million was to be drawn from the income and the reserves of the Lincoln Center Fund. The key to this plan was the reality of the plan to raise $1.3 million, an increase of 160 percent above the $.5 million raised in the previous fiscal year. There were serious doubts that such a rapid increase in giving could be attained.[66]

In fact, Young was quietly building up a case against Schuman that would make it easier for his boss to eliminate the programming department altogether and to throw Schuman overboard.[67] But if Schuman shared Young's doubts about fundraising, he gave little evidence of it in his letters and speeches. Nor did he alter his schedule to address more aggressively the growing shadow between the essence of the center and its pending financial descent. At a time when Schuman might have been reasonably expected to devote more of his time in the office, he felt a second wind blowing through his studio. It was the wrong time for him to be a composer. But the muse was insistent.

In looking back at this period in Lincoln Center's history, Bessire distilled the tensions of the moment as a difference of opinion about the fundamental purpose of the center. Was Lincoln Center first and foremost a gathering of performing arts organizations whose collective efforts were greater than anything any one individual constituent could imagine? Or was Lincoln Center a glorified landlord that gave the individual constituents free rein to do as the constituents pleased? Schuman strove for the former; some of the constituents' leaders held out for the latter.[68] This difference of opinion led Schuman's opponents to try to get Rockefeller to fire Schuman in late 1964. They failed. But four years later, without much effort, they succeeded, in part because Schuman refused to focus on real estate. He focused instead on three large orchestral canvases that portrayed loss and grief, death and commemoration, each without a word being sung or spoken. Each testified to events in Schuman's life and to those in the lives of people whom Schuman had never met. In a way, Schuman returned to the kind of compositional engagement that drove him during the late 1930s and early 1940s, when he enlisted in faraway wars through his pen. The strife was closer now, appearing on college campuses, disrupting kitchen conversations, and igniting city ghettoes. Schuman addressed none of these conflicts directly. Yet it seems more than a happy accident that his Lincoln Center separation, which started slowly in late 1966 and ended two years later, coincided with these three scores.

TWENTY-SIX

THE DEATH OF THE DREAMERS

In writing to fellow composer Halsey Stevens, Schuman turned on their head the sentiments he expressed in his Princeton speech:

> I have always been amazed in our time by the prophets of doom who have stated that the symphony qua symphony was a thing of the past, and had no place in contemporary music. This makes as much sense as saying that the novel is a thing of the past. The symphonic approach—the discursive musical essay of multiple characters and characteristics—is basic to expressivity in music. I firmly believe that in one form or another it will endure. Furthermore, it is my conviction that the 20th Century is extraordinarily rich in symphonic literature, even though much of it does not bear the symphonic nomenclature.[1]

It was not only that performing arts ensembles were blinkered in their unwillingness to program contemporary music. Composers themselves were also exhibiting cowardice by not writing for the traditional ensembles, not the least of which was the symphony orchestra. What also infuriated Schuman was that prominent supporters of contemporary music weren't helping matters by suggesting that the orchestral concert itself had become passé and that artists using non-orchestral instruments, computers, and electronics were composing the truly important music of the day. Leonard Bernstein's remarks to the *New York Times* particularly raised Schuman's dander. "The symphony," Bernstein opined in 1965, "is not really in the mainstream of what is being written now in the world. . . . If this is true, it means that symphony orchestras have a museum function. A conductor is a kind of curator. He hangs symphonies up in the best possible lighting."[2] Schuman refuted Bernstein's views in a speech titled "Higher Education and the Avant-Garde" that he gave a few weeks later at Sarah Lawrence College.[3] A few years later, he extended his counteroffensive in an introduction he wrote for *The Orchestral Composer's Point of View*, edited by Robert Stephan Hines.

> There *is* a viable contemporary symphonic literature. . . . The symphonic literature of the twentieth century is a rich one. Yet, its exposure is anemic. The real problem comes from the lack of willingness of conductors to continue successful works in the repertory—especially, although not exclusively, the works of American composers. . . . The fact remains that it is usually the shorter and more easily playable and accessible compositions that are programmed time and time again at the expense of the larger statements in the longer and more difficult compositions.[4]

In the late 1960s, Schuman was still in demand as a composer, and the time from the summer of 1967 to the fall of 1969 were banner years when it came to "larger statements in the longer and more difficult compositions."

The recrudescence began with a smaller score that had occupied Schuman's attention for more than five years. Elizabeth Gentry Sayad, a sixth-generation Missourian and founding president of the New Music Circle of St. Louis, contacted Schuman in November 1962 to see if he might consider writing a piece for the festivities surrounding the dedication of Eero Saarinen's "Gateway to the West," situated in the Jefferson National Expansion Memorial in St. Louis. In the spring of 1963 Schuman named three pieces he would be working on over the next few years: "a new piece called Violin and Cello Concertante," which would become *Amaryllis: Variations for String Trio*; "a band piece for the St. Louis celebration in 1964"; and "the Ninth Symphony for Philadelphia."[5] Delays in the dedication of the monument and indecision on the part of Sayad and her associates as to the forces Schuman should deploy resulted in an almost comic concatenation of ideas for the piece. First it was to be a "work of fanfare character for about twenty brasses." Then it became a "band piece." Then Sayad suggested a work for chorus and orchestra, going so far as to send texts for Schuman to consider. "The texts do more than leave me cold," Schuman wrote; "they bring on a deep freeze. Let us relax. Why don't I agree to make an orchestral version of my band overture, 'Chester.' This would be a wonderful premiere and I will treat the work in such a way that it will be based on my band overture."[6] Sayad wanted a new piece, though, so Schuman came up with a different idea: "Prelude and Fanfare for St. Louis: (a) Reflection; (b) Declaration."

> "Reflection" will be a setting of an old Missouri tune of the same name, for solo cornet or trumpet, and strings, which should play about three minutes.
>
> "Declaration" will be a fanfare, drawn from "Credendum" in the same manner that I will be doing "Philharmonic Fanfare" from Symphony No. 7. I find that, unintentionally, I seem to have fanfares in my symphonies, but if anyone asks me to write one, I must say, as I have, that it is impossible.[7]

He had begun to ponder the tune from the 1837 *Missouri Harmony* in November 1964, but it wasn't until the summer of 1965 that the bipartite idea came to him.[8] Postponement after postponement led Schuman eventually to shelve all of his plans for the St. Louis piece. He imagined that the delay would give him more time to think about the Ninth Symphony, but even that work would have to wait until 1967.[9]

By the fall of that year, Schuman's interest in the St. Louis piece was rekindled. He traveled to the Gateway City and received a tour of the Arch, but the commission wasn't the reason for his journey to the Midwest. William Shea, owner of the New York Mets, had persuaded R. D. Brown, CEO and president of the Rawlings Corp. in St. Louis, to send Schuman two tickets to the third game of the World Series. (Tony, who was 23 years old, joined his father.) Schuman thanked Brown for his generosity and added: "Please join me in prayers for fair weather. It would be beyond even this baseball buff to travel all the way to St. Louis and have the game postponed."[10] The gods smiled twice on St. Louis: Game 3 went on as scheduled, and the hometown Cardinals beat the Boston Red Sox, 5–2. Schuman wrote to thank Shea. "My son and I had a wonderful day in St. Louis on Saturday. I sat next to Mr. Brown, who couldn't have been nicer, and in fact the whole jaunt was one which neither pere nor fils will ever forget."[11] Clearly a copy of the Shea letter did not accompany the letter Schuman sent to Sayad. "I am back at the office, after that perfectly marvelous day in St. Louis. What made the day for my son and me was not so much the game (after all, the Red Sox lost) but the wonderful tour you gave us during the morning. The Arch is truly exciting, and I felt inspired. If only some time appears."[12] By then, Schuman's inspiration was being poured into the symphony whose genesis was even longer than the St. Louis piece.

In the spring of 1957, Alexander Hilsberg, the music director of the New Orleans Philharmonic-Symphony Society, wrote to Schuman to ask him if he could "write a work in the coming year which will fall within the definition of Tranquil Music."[13] The source of the commissioning money was Edward B. Benjamin, who had previously underwritten an entire disc of "Music for Quiet Listening," conducted by Howard Hanson, "a recording of some compositions that have won my awards for restful music at Eastman School."[14] Schuman wrote to Hilsberg to tell him that "I now do have some material that I have sketched for a short work which I believe would fill the bill of particulars. My problem is that I do not believe I can have it ready for next season because of other prior commitments."[15] Complications arose as to which season would be workable for the New Orleans people as well as for Schuman, and whether Hilsberg, who was hospitalized in the late fall, would be able to conduct the work. After years of negotiations for a tranquil work, the manager of the New Orleans Philharmonic-Symphony stopped pressing Schuman, in part because Hilsberg had returned to Philadelphia, where he had once served as concertmaster and assistant conductor to the Philadelphia Orchestra.

Hilsberg died unexpectedly on August 11, 1961. He was 61 years old. His widow, Neya, started a fund, and Ormandy told Schuman how she wanted it used: "to commission a work of major symphonic proportions, to be written

Father and son.

for and performed by our orchestra in memory of her late husband. Both Mrs. Hilsberg and I would be very happy if you could accept this commission."[16] At first, Schuman rejected the commission, thinking that it came directly from Hilsberg's widow. Schuman had an aversion to commissions from specific patrons rather than from institutions or foundations. His experience with Samuel Dushkin and the Violin Concerto no doubt colored his views on such arrangements, but he had vowed to himself early on that he would never "have to go to society women for support."[17] Ormandy reassured him that the commission was coming from the Philadelphia Orchestra Association and that Mrs. Hilsberg and friends of her late husband made the money available for a commission. That clarification prompted Schuman to change his mind, and shortly after having received the news of Schuman's acceptance of the commission, Neya Hilsberg passed away.[18]

Schuman had no idea at the time that the symphony he would compose would commemorate the dead beyond Alexander and Neya Hilsberg. His early ideas for the work only hint at its final form. There was no question that he viewed the Ninth as his work for the Philadelphia Orchestra, and, as in the case of the *Celebration Concertante*, he heard a particular sound when he thought of Ormandy and his men. "I have a special idea for my Ninth Symphony which will feature the string orchestra. There is no body of strings in the entire world that I have heard which is superior to the Philadelphia Orchestra." Ormandy balked, thinking that Schuman was talking about another symphony for strings alone, and made it clear to Schuman that "I am just as proud of my woodwind and brass sections as I am of my strings." Schuman quickly corrected Ormandy, stating that a work that featured the strings would not necessarily omit the other choirs of the orchestra.[19] But some years later, he did state that Ormandy's fears were legitimate.

> The symphony is slow in coming. I have given it a great deal of thought, and have recast my original concept of scoring it for strings alone. Your cogent arguments were most helpful. Truth to tell, there is not yet one note on paper (there were some last spring, but they have been torn up) and I can't blame all of this on Lincoln Center, although of course my administrative duties here are horrendous. I want this work to be the best I have ever done.[20]

All of these ideas—including the "thought to use the basic materials of [*The Witch of Endor*] in my Ninth Symphony"[21]—surrounded the work years before Schuman traveled to Rome and saw the monument at the Ardeatine caverns in memory of the 335 Italians killed by the Nazis in 1944.

It was shortly after returning from his European trip to promote Lincoln Center Festival '67 that Schuman wrote Ormandy with his first good news about the commission.

> You will happy to learn that I am deeply in through [*sic*: thought?] concerning "our" piece. I have set time aside this summer, and hope by the fall of the year to be able to report real progress. As I believe I mentioned to you, I lost all of last summer because I wasn't well—but I am pleased to report that my health at the moment is excellent.[22]

Prior to this news, Ormandy needled Schuman about the work. He sent Schuman a letter he had received from an admirer of Schuman's music along with his response to it. "I agree with you that he is one of the outstanding contemporary composers," Ormandy wrote. "I wish his Symphony No. 9 were ready so that we could program it, but it is difficult to be a composer and, at the same time, the President of one of the most colossal undertakings in the field of the arts."[23] He rebuffed an invitation from Schuman's publisher in the winter of 1966 for the Philadelphia Orchestra to be included as one of the commissioners for Schuman's imagined magnum opus, *Nineteen Seventy-Six*. "It is never too soon to start making plans," Ormandy wrote Arthur Hauser in response, "and it was a very good idea that you asked William Schuman to write a large-scale work for chorus and orchestra. At the rate that he and some of his colleagues are working on commissions I don't think you have started too soon."[24] Ormandy's decision two years later to ask Bernstein, not Schuman, for a bicentennial work may have stung Schuman, who saved the clipping of the announcement and filed it with his papers for *Nineteen Seventy-Six*.[25]

But Schuman waited months before he told Ormandy why, for the first time since he had contemplated the symphony for the Philadelphia Orchestra in

1961, he was brimming with ideas. He did, however, share his enthusiasm with Hugo and Nathalie Weisgall. Hugo was a composer-in-residence at the American Academy in Rome in 1966 and 1967, and Bill and Frankie saw the Weisgalls during their stay in Rome.

> Never in my life have I been so affected by a monument as I was my [*sic*] the Nervi. I keep thinking of it all the time. At the moment, it is leading me to write a symphony with a programmatic starting point. This I have never done before, but it appears to be happening to me now. The work will not be any attempt at a realistic musical summary of those horrible events, but it will certainly reflect my feelings as they have evolved from the experience of visiting the memorial.[26]

Nathalie quickly became one of Schuman's principal pen pals during the summer of 1967 as he peppered her with questions. How many were killed? What motivated the massacre? Who were the men? Were they intellectuals, or did they come from all walks of life? What is the exact title of the monument? Is it by Nervi or by his pupils? Nathalie answered all of his questions, sent him books and pamphlets—including Attilio Ascarelli's *Le fosse Ardeatine*, with its graphic photographs of the dead—and lent her suggestions, one of which seemed to get lost in Schuman's focus on the monument itself. "The actual title of the monument is 'Fosse Ardeatina'. Ardeatina is a section of Rome. Fosse (the plural of fossa) means pit, ditch or grave. My dictionary says that in Dante 'fosse' refers to the 'Circles of Hell'."[27] In Schuman's lengthy program notes for the symphony, he never mentioned the multiple meanings of *fossa*, even though they significantly enrich one's understanding of the monument and the event.

Nathalie also sent to Schuman an excerpt from *The Blue Guides: Rome and Central Italy*, one of the standard travel guides a tourist of the time would use.

> On March 24, 1944, by way of reprisal for the killing on the previous day of 32 German soldiers by the resistance movement in Via Rasella, the Germans shot 335 Italians. The victims, who had no connection with the killing of the Germans, included priests, officials, professional men, 100 Jews, dozens of foreigners and a boy of 14. After the incident the Germans buried the bodies under an avalanche of sand artificially caused by the exploding of mines. Local inhabitants, who had taken note, provided a medical-legal commission with the means for exhuming and identifying the bodies after the retreat of the Germans. The 335, reinterred after identification, are commemorated by a simple cement structure placed in 1949 over their mass grave.[28]

Nathalie was also exercised by the massacre and shared with Schuman information she received from the local watch repairman, who, she said,

> was one of those rounded up in the Gestapo prison, where most of the victims came from. He was never taken out to the sand pits because he escaped by asking to use the bathroom, leaving all his papers and identification with a guard as security and then squeezing through the rails of the bathroom window (he is the tiniest man I have ever

> seen).... He told me that practically all of the victims came from the Gestapo prison, not an Italian prison. This would, of course, explain the disproportionate number of Jews, and also the impression that most were very prominent and influential intellectuals who were thrown in the German prison for their anti-Nazi activities and their possible alliance with the resistance.
>
> Other recollections mention that members of the resistance touched off the killing by carefully timing the movements of the German troops which daily passed by the Via Rasella, and by, one day, throwing a bomb in their midst, killing them all. It is said that orders came directly from Hitler to kill 10 Italians for every German soldier killed, and so the easiest place to get enough Italians was at the nearby Gestapo prison. In their haste they got more than the number they needed. This order was never made public and the hostages were gathered in secrecy. There seems to be no singling out of what sort of people the victims should be. Alberto promised to put me in touch with the families of some of his Jewish friends who were victims but I've called him again and again and he's always too busy repairing watches. He used up all his family's money and property paying bribes to get out of prisons and buying false identification papers. The prices were very high. It seems that the monks at the adjacent Catacombs of Callixtus heard the mine explosions and traced the sound, thereby discovering the bodies. As far as I know, none of this above information is in any book.[29]

Having decided that he must somehow associate his symphony with the memorial, Schuman wrestled over how the title page for the work should look. He enlisted the help of both Nathalie and Frankie.

> You and my good wife agree on the use of three words for the title. My own feeling is that the decision could be based on whether I mention the symphony first, or the title first. For example, one way would be to say:
>
> Symphony IX
> (Le Fosse)
> The other way would be:
> Le Fosse Ardeatine
> Symphony IX
>
> The question to me is whether I want the title to be indicative of Le Fosse, as a generic idea, or Le Fosse Ardeatine as a specific. Please help me think a little more on this one.[30]

At that point, Hugo, who had been staying out of the correspondence in order to finish his Holocaust-influenced opera, *Nine Rivers from Jordan*, chimed in and gave the work its final identification: "Symphony IX (Le Fosse Ardeatine). To my way of thinking, this puts it into the series of your symphonies and also gives a clue as to the specific idea behind it."[31] By the end of the summer, Schuman estimated that he was "about half way" on the symphony, an estimate that remained unchanged a few weeks later.[32] It wasn't until February 1968, though, that Schuman, who had given three-fourths of the symphony to his copyist Anthony Strilko, was ready to tell Ormandy about the new work and its programmatic content. "The title, which I will explain fully to you and in an extended program note, is that of an extraordinary monument in Rome which commemorates the massacre of some 320 Italians in reprisal for the killing of 30 German soldiers."[33]

Though his numbers were off, his choice of identification was precise and concerned nationality, not ethnicity or religion. If Schuman ever singled out the slaughter of Jews in the hell of Ardeatina, it was mostly in private conversation. His program notes for the symphony are already unusual in the amount of musical detail they contain given that "I really do not like to talk about the music I've written and much prefer to leave this to others."[34] But the extramusical portion of the notes contains only one explicit reference to the Jewish victims: "the Germans murdered 335 Italians, Christians and Jews from all walks of life." His surviving letters are silent about the ethnic identities of the murdered. His use of Latin terms for the three sections of the symphony—Anteludium, Offertorium, and Postludium—not only solemnizes the work but does so with the archaic language of the pre–Vatican II Catholic Church. Perhaps Schuman was taking a page from Stravinsky's late works, with their hieratic atmosphere; Schuman wrote to Stravinsky in February 1965 to thank him for the remarks he prepared for the America-Israel Cultural Foundation dinner the month before and to reminisce about their previous encounters and Schuman's work on the final preparation of the parts of *Jeu de cartes*.[35] Perhaps, in titling the sections as he did, Schuman was acknowledging his own audience with Pope Paul VI at the Vatican in April 1967. One thing he was not explicitly doing was to spotlight the massacre of the Jews over the killing of the other victims in the Ardeatine caves.

Yet at least one correspondent was quick to seize on "the element of recent Jewish history tied into this piece."[36] The association of the symphony with the Ardeatine monument led to a torrent of contributions to the Alexander Hilsberg Fund in Philadelphia; without looking at a list of the donors, it is impossible to know what motivated this outpouring of money.[37] It is certainly easy to draw a line from the Germans committing this atrocity in Italy to the enormity of the Holocaust, whose primary target was the Jewish people. Schuman himself drew it in his notes. "Our visit was at the Easter and Passover season and each grave had fresh flowers. Somehow, confrontation with the ghastly fate of several hundred identifiable individuals was more shattering and understandable than the reports on the deaths of millions which, by comparison, seem abstract statistics." But Schuman seemed to leave the act of recollection to the individual who encounters his symphony. "My reason for using the title is not then, musical, but philosophical. One must come to terms with the past in order to build a future. But in this exercise I am a foe of forgetting. Whatever future my symphony may have, whenever it is performed, audiences will remember." Remember the escaped watch repairman, who was Catholic? The viciousness of the German soldiers, most of whom were nominally Christian?

The large number of Jewish victims? The larger number of non-Jewish ones? Like the music itself, which "does not attempt to depict the event realistically," the symphony's subtitle and Schuman's essay about the work are more evocative than determinative.[38] In this he followed the lead of Nathalie Weisgall, whose first letter to Schuman about the monument contained the kernel of Schuman's essay.

> Your idea of doing a symphony based on this tragedy will surely produce as impressive a monument. I feel so strongly that those days should never be forgotten . . . much less forgiven. Histories, documents, etc. .are there for the facts which are too horrible and too numerous to be comprehensible. It is only through a work of art that one can feel the impact of the madness of those days.[39]

Schuman was also enthralled with some of his own effects in the new symphony. In his notes, he brought the reader's attention to the fact that the opening melody, which "continues its development over a span of 33 bars," is joined by a second voice at the twelfth bar, which repeats the same melody one-half step higher. It is the same technique Schuman used in both the passacaglia and fugue of the Third Symphony, but here Schuman is drawing upon the highly dissonant linear writing that he developed in the late 1950s and that appeared in the previous two symphonies. The melody traverses all 12 tones by the end of measure nine, flexibly repeating earlier notes when the music repeats the exact melodic idea that used those notes. Still, though the serially inflected melody marks it as a product of the 1960s, its stepwise reiteration and lengthy development are reminiscent of Schuman's contrapuntal training with Haubiel and embrace of autogenesis under Harris.

Another musical feature that Schuman pointed out in his program notes was the "sonorous climax [of the Offertorium] for full orchestra, with three pairs of struck cymbals employed in rhythmic patterns." He tried to reassure his publisher when he sent him the instrumentation of the symphony.

> I hope you are not alarmed at the 3 pairs of large cymbals, but I have an effect in this symphony at a certain point of climax which will not only be startling to hear, but will be sensational to see. . . . I'll bet Ormandy is going to claim it is too much for the Philadelphia ladies. Let's gird for a battle, and suggest that two of the three cymbal players be Hauser and Schuman.[40]

Since Ormandy had complained about "the excessive percussion" in *Credendum*, Schuman figured that this effect would bother Ormandy as much as, if not more than, it would the Philadelphia ladies. But Ormandy said not a word about the cymbal passage (mm. 521–26) in his letters to Schuman, and its effect is somewhat muted aurally by the tutti orchestra.

Ormandy did comment on the symphony prior to its January 1969 premiere. "Last summer I studied your symphony but didn't have enough time to really work on it, but I will do this during my Christmas holidays. What I have already noticed is that it is one of your finest works and I really look forward to performing it."[41] He did not change his opinion after having performed it. "I consider your Symphony IX your best and most inspired creative accomplishment to date."[42] Schuman told Sheila Keats, who in 1971 was writing program notes for a recording of the Seventh Symphony, that "the Seventh, Eighth and Ninth are somehow connected in my mind, perhaps because they represent the efforts more or less of a single decade."[43] Symphonies nos. 3–6 similarly represent the efforts of a single decade in even more compressed form (1941–49 versus 1959–68), but he did not speak of those four symphonies as a group. It is more their approach to dissonance, their expanded timbral palette (such as the use of harps in the Eighth), and their subterranean serial passages that yoke the Seventh, Eighth, and Ninth together. The final chord of the Ninth, for example, is a barbaric fortississimo yawp that contains all 12 notes of the chromatic scale, as though in that chord Schuman exorcised once and for all the serial daemon that possessed his works for a decade. Further support for this reading can be found in the works that follow the Ninth, almost all of which abandon highly concentrated and sustained dissonance in favor of more eclectic musical materials set cheek by jowl. At least once in the symphony—midway through the Postludium—the dissonance abates, and a chain of consonant triads accompanying a seemingly distracted melody appears, sounding at first reminiscent of *Prayer in Time of War* or *Judith* but, upon reflection, serving as a harbinger for the harmonic direction of the works from the 1970s and beyond. Strikingly, the two works for solo vocalist and accompaniment—*The Young Dead Soldiers* (1975) and *Time to the Old* (1979)—are among Schuman's most dissonant pieces in his later years, suggesting that Schuman's newly acquired serial skills continued to inform his melodic writing.

The physical act of completing the symphony held special meaning for Schuman. He wrote to Hauser: "I am now sketching the last pages of the symphony and expect to complete the entire work in Monte Carlo the end of this month. We will be staying with a friend for six days and I think that should do it. If it doesn't, I hope to complete it in Rome the following week."[44] The manuscript indicates that the work was completed on March 27, 1968, and gives four locations where Schuman worked on the symphony: Greenwich, New York, Monte Carlo, and Rome, though this last location seems more of a symbolic gesture to the Ardeatine monument itself, which Schuman had visited the day before. March 27 also had an additional significance for Schuman: it was his wedding anniversary, and the symphony was something of a present to Frankie in celebrating in Rome their 32 years together. As for the symphony, his diary reveals that he spent a total of 306 hours and 25 minutes composing the work, less than half the time he spent writing the Eighth Symphony.[45] Considering that the Eighth recycled musical material from the Fourth String Quartet and that the Ninth was almost wholly new, the speed with which Schuman composed this work is astonishing. His return to the one-movement structure that the Second and the Sixth Symphonies employ shows that his conception of what constitutes a symphony was fluid. The use of orchestral choirs pitted against each other make the work recognizable as Schuman by its timbre and texture, its high dissonant quotient place it at the pinnacle of his experiments with tonality, and its sociopolitical engagement objectify the liberal tendencies that motivated much of his work for most of his career. In many ways, then, the Ninth is Schuman's symphonic *summa musicæ*.

Shortly after his return from Europe, Schuman returned to work on the fanfare he promised the folks in St. Louis. The on-again, off-again dedicatory ceremony was on again and scheduled for May 25, with the United States Army Band set to premiere the work and show off the Herald Trumpets, "the official fanfare ensemble for the President of the United States," which was not yet a decade old.[46] Schuman managed to finish a short score of the *Dedication Fanfare* by May 5, apparently leaving the creation of a conductor's score and the parts to the Army Band's associate conductor.[47] If Mother Nature showed favor to Schuman once in St. Louis for the World Series, she was disinclined to repeat herself for the ceremony, which was washed out by driving rain.[48] Sayad gave Schuman the option of having the work premiered either by the St. Louis Symphony's brass section at its final concert or at an Independence Day celebration under the Gateway Arch by a group yet to be selected. She also needed to know whether the Army Band and the Herald Trumpets were necessary; Schuman assured her that they were not but that the brass section of the symphony would be insufficient.[49] So it was that on July 4, 1968, the local Laclede Band under the direction of Laurent Torno

> played [the work] without a fumble. . . . Can you believe that 650,000 people on both sides of the Mississippi River heard your work? [Schuman later inflated the number to 750,000.] The amplification system was excellent. Where we sat we couldn't even see the band, but heard everything very clearly. The light of sunset playing on the Arch at 8:15 when your work was programmed, was fantastically dramatic.[50]

Notwithstanding his earlier intentions to use the opening of *Credendum* as the skeleton for the fanfare, Schuman had composed an entirely original work, harmonically indebted more to the bitonal *George Washington Bridge* than the Ninth Symphony, and ending it with a blaze of E♭ major glory. At first he called the piece *Dedication Prelude*—both his sketches for the work and his short score bear that title—but come publication time, he thought differently. He wrote to Presser's director of publications:

> On the DEDICATION PRELUDE, let us change the title to DEDICATION FANFARE, or at least wouldn't you like to consider this? My reason is three-fold. Firstly, people who heard the piece in St. Louis kept referring to it as DEDICATION

> FANFARE. Secondly, it is undeniably "fanfarish." Thirdly, its musical content is slight, and it might be preferable to understate this ahead of time by the word fanfare, rather than overstate it by the word prelude.[51]

Far from slight was the next major orchestral score that Schuman composed in 1968. Once again the New York Philharmonic came to him with a commission, this one to celebrate the orchestra's 125th anniversary year (1967–68). Bernstein's original idea was to premiere a new work every week, but the management convinced him that "some fifteen to twenty composers from various parts of the world" composing works from ten to 20 minutes in length would be more than sufficient for the anniversary celebration.[52] Schuman accepted the commission with the understanding that other commissions took precedence—one could never guess when that archway might actually be dedicated, and how would Ormandy have responded had Bernstein's work displaced Philadelphia's in Schuman's queue?—and by the end of 1966 he made clear that he couldn't deliver the piece in time for the anniversary season.[53] In fact, it wasn't until June 1968, after the completion of the commissions for St. Louis and Philadelphia, that Schuman turned his attention to the New York piece.

This is not to say that he had not been thinking about its form and materials. Midway through its composition, Schuman wrote to Bernstein to tell him about his progress and the new direction the piece had taken.

> Let me say a word about it, because it differs greatly in spirit from the proposed work that you and I discussed last February at our home. You may recall that I was toying with the idea of an opening work to be called "New York, New York." It was to be in three movements, the last a fugal treatment of the opening theme of your great song of the same name. But, understandably, my mood now is very different from what it was last February. The day we left Europe this spring we read of the assassination of Dr. King as we boarded the 'plane in London. And then, of course, later this spring there was the additional tragedy of Robert Kennedy.[54]

Death once again darkened Schuman's compositional mien, and he wanted the audience to share in his sorrow by asking them not to applaud at the first performance, which Schuman dedicated to the memory of King and Kennedy. (The work itself bears no dedication.) Schuman turned once again to Whitman, the poet whose words he had set in *Pioneers*! and *A Free Song* and the *Carols of Death*, this time for an epigraph to convey the spirit of his Evocation for oboe, brass, timpani, piano and strings, which he called *To Thee Old Cause*.

> "To Thee Old Cause!
> Thou peerless, passionate, good cause,
> Thou stern, remorseless, sweet idea,
> Deathless throughout the ages, races, lands,
> . . . Thou seething principle!

Anyone who knows the poem from *Leaves of Grass* might wonder if Schuman was telegraphing more than a lament for two fallen men. The stanzas skipped over by Schuman's ellipsis are these:

> After a strange, sad war—great war for thee,
> (I think all war through time was really fought, and ever will be really fought, for thee;)
> These chants for thee—the eternal march of thee.
> Thou orb of many orbs!

Whitman's words could be appropriated either in support or in opposition of war, and Schuman's use of them on the surface may be meant to be as multivalent, as are his remarks on the Ninth Symphony. But at the time Schuman composed the work, the United States was embroiled in a strange, sad war halfway around the globe, one that led American soldiers on March 16, 1968, to kill more Vietnamese civilians in My Lai and My Khe than the Germans slaughtered two dozen years earlier in the Ardeatine district of Rome. (The My Lai massacre would not come to the public's attention until 1969.) Both King and Kennedy had advocated for the American withdrawal from Vietnam as early as the spring of 1967, so Schuman's invocation of their memory, Whitman's poem with its comments on war, and the specter of Bernstein as conductor—his opposition to the war in Vietnam had led him to be an outspoken and energetic campaigner for Eugene McCarthy, the Democratic senator whose September defeat in Chicago to Humphrey led to riots by antiwar protestors—all these factors suggest that *To Thee Old Cause* was a musical rebuke of the direction in which the country was headed.[55]

> Thou seething principle! Thou well-kept, latent germ! Thou centre!
> Around the idea of thee the strange sad war revolving,
> With all its angry and vehement play of causes,
> (With yet unknown results to come, for thrice a thousand years,)
> These recitatives for thee—my Book and the War are one,
> Merged in its spirit I and mine—as the contest hinged on thee,
> As a wheel on its axis turns, this Book, unwitting to itself,
> Around the Idea of thee.

As he had done with *A Song of Orpheus*, Schuman "sets" the words he excerpted from the poem, indicating in the score that the first trumpet's "melodic line [is to be] played clearly, as though the words were sung" (beginning in m. 258, with the words "Thou seething principle!" repeated three times by the entire orchestra). The melody itself is a full flowering of the opening oboe solo, which slowly expands upward and which itself is developed when the string choir entered, double speed, after the oboe falls silent. *To Thee Old Cause* overall relies less on dissonance than does the Ninth Symphony, but it has its share of craggy harmonies—"Thou seething principle!" eventually embraces all 12 tones, and the final F♯ major halo emerges after a thunderous instrumental

Schuman and Leonard Bernstein, June 25, 1978. The inscription reads: "Thank you forever, dear Bill. Lenny '78." Photo by Richard Braaten, Kennedy Center.

tutti that includes two-octave forearm tone clusters on the piano. As with the Ninth, the timpani has many opportunities for virtuosic display, with the performer here instructed to employ "hard sticks for maximum penetration." But where the Ninth seemed to express rage and anger, even in its slow and quiet moments, *To Thee Old Cause* expresses steely resolve and, by the end, an uneasy confidence that, somehow, all will be made right. It is as though Schuman updated *Prayer in Time of War* 25 years later in a sadder-but-wiser piece. (The third major orchestral score of 1967–69, *In Praise of Shahn*, is covered in chap. 28.)

A few of Schuman's friends wrote to tell him how moved they were by this new work, which, though it was completed after the Ninth Symphony, was premiered before it.[56] (Ormandy had scheduled the Ninth for January 1969; *To Thee Old Cause* was completed on August 17, 1968, and premiered less than two months later.) Robert Sour, vice chairman of BMI's Board of Directors, was impressed by both Schuman works on the program—the Third Symphony and Berlioz's *Symphonie fantastique* rounded out the evening—and confidently assured Schuman that he agreed with Schuman's assessment of his career going forward: "I don't blame you for wanting to devote all your time to composition." Perhaps Schuman feared Sour would share his assessment with others, for Schuman quickly knocked it down.

> Permit me to make a minor correction to an incorrect impression you must have received from me. I do not want to devote all my time to composition. I never have wanted to. As a young man, when I was given two Guggenheim Fellowships in successive years, I petitioned the foundation to permit me to teach at the same time. I always needed a "public life" as well as those hundreds of hours of solitude that go into composition. What I do fervently seek, in whatever number of years may be ahead, is a situation which will give me more time for writing. My hope is that, as the Center continues to improve the efficiency of its operations, this will come about.[57]

Schuman, in fact, had been approached to see if he would be willing to be considered as the next president of BMI after Robert J. Burton died from a fire in his hotel room ignited by an unextinguished cigarette.[58] Schuman indicated to Sydney Kaye, BMI's legal counsel, the sole circumstance that would tempt him to leave Lincoln Center. "I find my post here both stimulating and fascinating, and have every intention of staying. If I ever did change, the only foreseeable reason would be my inability to work out sufficient time for composition."[59] That was his opinion in April 1965, not long after Krawitz affair that remained his opinion in October 1968, less than a month before Rockefeller invited him to step down.

TWENTY-SEVEN

THE DEATH OF THE DREAM

It wasn't the need for more time to compose that led to Schuman's resignation as president of Lincoln Center. As the *Dedication Fanfare*, the Ninth Symphony, and *To Thee Old Cause* demonstrate, under the right situation he could compose quite a bit in a year's time. Ultimately his insistence on expanding Lincoln Center, at a time when budgetary constraints threatened the center's very existence, led to his firing.

Young's warnings and Rockefeller's entreaties concerning the well-being of the center were met repeatedly by Schuman with resistance if not out-and-out defiance. He had dreamed of starting the Lincoln Center Teachers Institute in 1966, according to his blueprint for the center, which appeared in the *New York Times Magazine* in September 1962. In 1967, the institute remained on the drawing boards, but despite the discouraging economic environment Schuman lobbied hard for its creation.

> In discussing the Teachers Institute I emphasized that this was beginning a major educational institution, and we should not start it unless we had promise of adequate financing for the next six years. I was pleased by the enormous enthusiasm for the Teachers Institute. For example, Mr. Ames said, "I would not dream of postponing the Lincoln Center Teachers Institute." He said that to his mind the Institute, the Lincoln Center Student Program—all the things that we do for Education—are absolutely the basic programs.[1]

The institute, in a much curtailed version of what Schuman originally imagined, was finally unveiled in 1976.

On the eve of Lincoln Center Festival '67, Schuman had to face down those who wanted to curtail dramatically the programming that the central administration did. Schuman not only refused to back down but came close to calling Rockefeller a hypocrite if the chairman of the board wasn't willing to support the president in these programming efforts.

> It is one thing to question the wisdom of an annual festival of the scope of our current one—and on this subject we all have open minds—but it is quite another to say that Lincoln Center itself should not be in programming. What follows from such a stand is that Lincoln Center is a group of buildings occupied by great performing arts organizations; each going its own way and renting its facilities as it sees fit to other users during off-seasons. Such an approach means the Lincoln Center qua the Center as an artistic force would not exist. The separate organizations could then have functioned just as well if separately housed geographically. What happened to the dream of cross-fertilization and all the other beautiful statements that we made? I personally believe in them as much now as I did when I first began. It was heartening to me to have you say at yesterday's meeting of the Board that you too believed in our programs. Given this belief on your part and mine, I now ask your help in finding some way to reach a rededication of these principles on the part of our Board.[2]

In a follow-up meeting to discuss further Schuman's position, Father McGinley, the former president of Fordham, "turned out to be the best champion of Lincoln Center programming."[3] Catholic priests and celebrated composers, however, could not reverse the sea of red ink that was washing over the center, and under Schuman's watch, the undesignated reserves for Lincoln Center continued to drop until there was only $500,000 left by October 1968. In facing the prospect of bankruptcy, John Mazzola, the center's lawyer, wrote in a report, "Analysis of the Disappearing Net Worth of Lincoln Center Fund": "We can no longer accept any deficits as our funds, for all practical purposes, are exhausted."[4]

Young's history of Lincoln Center fully covers the financial numbers that led him to describe these years as "crisis and resolution."[5] What he failed to do was to reflect on how larger forces, including the decision to offer Schuman the presidency in the first place, led to the crisis. No one in 1961 could have fully predicted the financial and political upheaval that enveloped the center in 1968, but it was relatively easy to imagine the internecine battles that would surface once all of these creative artists were brought together onto one campus. The impulse to hire Gen. Taylor as president in 1960 was born from pragmatism; the impulse to hire Schuman as president a year later was born from idealism. By the end of the 1960s, many of the dreams of the idealists had died, and many of the dreamers perished alongside their dreams.

Schuman was nearly a casualty himself. Not long after he returned from Europe to promote Festival '68, not long after he had completed the Ninth Symphony and the *Dedication Fanfare*, he had "a piece of disappointing news" to share with Ormandy. "It seems that I have been working too hard and have gotten myself a fine case of fatigue. Nothing of any concern, but the doctors are not permitting me out all week."[6] At that point, Schuman thought he might return to the office no later than early June. In fact, he did not return until early September. A diagnosis of "coronary artery insufficiency" that was first made in

July 1966—midway through his second "lost summer"—was reaffirmed on May 23, 1968.[7] Both prior to and after his triple bypass surgery in 1983, Schuman referred to his "heart attack" of 1968, but the contemporaneous medical records and correspondence suggest that Schuman had an episode of angina: one notation expressly states that there was no evidence of infarction (i.e., permanent heart damage), and the *New York Times*' story on his resignation from Lincoln Center indicates that "he was away from his work for four months for what he said his physicians called 'mild heart spasms.'"[8] His distress was serious enough, however, that his doctors remanded him to give up his Lincoln Center duties for the entire summer, which he did. They apparently said nothing about composing, though, as Schuman began and finished *To Thee Old Cause* during his recuperation.

He also gave away Andrea's hand in marriage on May 30 in a ceremony in the living room of their apartment on Fifth Avenue. Andrea recalled that "it was a smallish group (much to the dismay of my in-laws). Ruth and Norman Lloyd played the wedding march. My father was shaky, and sat mostly on the couch."[9] Schuman had been right in predicting that Andrea would be the first one truly to strike out on her own: she had just turned 19 when she married Donald Weiss, a doctoral student at Princeton who went on to teach philosophy at the State University of New York at Binghamton, whereas Tony would not marry until Andrea's son Josh, who was born in 1974, was already a teenager. Despite the challenges that both children gave their parents—and that, because of their celebrity, the parents gave their children—the Schuman family managed to weather the various storms of life relatively intact.

But 1968 was, without question, one of Schuman's most difficult years. The intrigue and conniving at Lincoln Center far eclipsed what he had experienced at Juilliard, and the further up the corporate ladder he climbed, the more he risked being out of touch with the artistic flow. The best he could do was to establish institutions that would honor that creativity and artistry. Once he returned from his summer of rest, he pushed through the inauguration of both the Film Society of Lincoln Center and the Chamber Music Society of Lincoln Center, the latter a dream from the time he first began planning to lead the center, the former a dream that others had but that he quickly adopted as his own. His determination to found these constituents at a time when money was scarce and when the Repertory Theater was taking on water only exacerbated Schuman's standing among the members of the board and the leadership of the other constituents that had to trim budgets.[10] After he left in December of the year, he fought strenuously not only to preserve the fledgling constituents but also to counter the revisionism that already was attempting to undermine the two societies by suggesting they were artistically and financially unviable.[11] But during the fight to found them, Schuman never gave any public indication that he considered his days numbered.

The death knell sounded in November. Schuyler Chapin, who was in charge of programming at Lincoln Center, wrote Schuman a desperate memo on the first of the month. Morale was down, and uncertainty and disorganization seemed the order of the day, according to Chapin. Some extremely practical questions also needed to be answered about the next two Lincoln Center Festivals; contracts were being signed for Festival '69, and Chapin was hearing rumblings that the program itself was in jeopardy. He also hoped to bring Schubart, who was running the education programs at the center, into the conversation, since he "shares my concern and undoubtedly has an equal number of unresolved questions."[12] On the twelfth of the month, the executive committee voted "upon motion duly made and seconded . . . that no further programming would be undertaken unless the funds to meet the direct and indirect costs are in hand, pledged or guaranteed" and that Festival '69 and the August Mid-Summer Serenades would be scrapped. According to the minutes, "Mr. Schuman voted for the motion to discontinue the Mid-Summer Serenades during 1969, but asked that his abstention in voting for canceling Lincoln Center Festival '69 be noted."[13] Chapin was so stunned by the action that he was unable at first to respond, but when he did, he argued forcefully that the executive committee's decision was not only "damaging to me personally in a professional sense, but even more important, it is damaging in a permanent manner to the name and reputation of Lincoln Center." Schuman understood Chapin's reading of the decision,

> but as an organization man I am going not only fully to support it, but to do everything in my power to see that its public presentation is turned to our advantage. Perhaps, after all, it will be only through this kind of action that the true state of our financial situation will be driven home. And, while I am wholly sympathetic with the sentiments of your letter, and understand the embarrassment and unprofessionalism of the action you must now take, I do not see that there is a choice.[14]

Impresario Sol Hurok weighed in, as some of the contracts for Festival '69 were with him. Hurok was incredulous that the commitment to Festival '69 was only $150,000. "I have on several occasions been involved with far less powerful groups who were able to raise this sum or greater in a single evening, and that without the pressure and obligation of commitments already executed in good faith."[15] But what Hurok didn't know was that Festival '68's deficit was greater than anticipated, and the executive committee felt it had no choice. Not only was Festival '69 abandoned, but Schuman's plans for Festival '70—an all-Bartók extravaganza 25 years after the composer's death, with Antal Doráti as curator—were also aborted.[16] Chapin's distress over the cancelation of the festivals would pale in comparison with the news that he delivered in mid-December to the gathering of representatives from the board and the various constituents. The minutes read: "Mr. Chapin reported to the [Lincoln Center] Council the Lincoln Center Executive Committee decision to discontinue the

Programming Department at the Center and the consequent discontinuance of the office of Vice President, Programming."[17] In other words, he was charged with telling his peers of the elimination of his own job. (Chapin wasn't the only one to go. The *New York Times* reported that two other vice presidents "resigned": John L. Bauer, vice president of operations; and Jack DeSimone, vice president of public relations. "The aim was to reduce costs," the *Times* said.)[18]

Chapin was out, but Schubart was still in. Had Schuman followed through on the opera subject that Herman Wouk had proposed 20 years earlier, he might have seen that he was living a modern-day version of the dreams of Pharaoh's chief butler and chief baker, with Schuman as the patriarch Joseph, the seer who brought the men together and helped to interpret their dreams. Like Joseph, Schuman's own circumstances were straitened. The day after Schuman assured Chapin that he was an organizational man, Rockefeller had breakfast with two Lincoln Center directors. "We agreed that the circumstances were such that it would appear that Bill Schuman could no longer be effective as President of Lincoln Center," Rockefeller said. "It was felt that I was the one to talk with him and that the meeting should take place as soon as possible." Rockefeller had lunch that very day with Schuman to convey the news. "Bill was fine throughout our discussion, reiterating several times his desire to be cooperative in whatever was best for Lincoln Center. . . . He indicated that he continued to have the same deep interest in Lincoln Center and hoped that it would be possible for him to continue a relationship of some form."[19] After further discussions it was decided that "we would make him President Emeritus which seems to mean a lot to him. In addition, we agreed that he would be given one year's salary which is generous under the circumstances." Schuman also asked that the termination date be moved to June instead of January 1, anticipating that "such an early date would indicate to the public that he had been fired." Rockefeller was unmoved by Schuman's request, stating that such a delay "would be complicated . . . in terms of its practicality."[20]

Schuman spent the next few days celebrating Thanksgiving and composing no fewer than eight drafts of his resignation letter, sending them to Rockefeller for suggestions.[21] (The press caught wind of the story before Schuman and Rockefeller could agree on the language, and Schuman granted an interview with the *Times* reporter to make sure the story was both accurate—from Schuman's perspective—and sympathetic.) As for a "relationship of some form," Schuman would have to settle for the title of emeritus; he was never tapped in any special advisory way. He was passed over in helping out with a special educational grant that the Carnegie Corporation was giving to the center, even though he had helped to secure the grant and was so certain that he would supervise the study that he told the *Times* reporter it was typical of the part-time work he planned to do. The Carnegie people, however, told

Schubart that he "must hold off on any commitment to anyone." Schubart ended up supervising the study and writing the report, "The Hunting of the Squiggle," which was published in 1972.[22] Schuman would make a virtue out of necessity in his omnibus letter sent to those who wrote to him on the occasion of his resignation. "I am greatly looking forward to having time to compose and to taking on special assignments that interest me. But no more big administrative posts. I feel that I have done my stint. It has been wonderful, but I expect the future to be even more so."[23] The patriarch Joseph also looked to a more wonderful future and later told his brothers, who sold him into slavery in the first place, that although they had meant it for evil, God had used it for good. Schuman did not have religion to rely upon to buoy him at the time, but he, too, could look around him and see that some people, Chapin among them, had it far worse; that others, including Schubart, had it far better; and that he, for better and for worse, owed his fate in part to the treachery of others.

He also had his own intransigence to account for his being put out to pasture. Some months after he had left Lincoln Center, he attended the Second International University Choral Festival at Lincoln Center. Despite all of the cutbacks, this Schuman brainchild went forward in 1969, perhaps because its expenses were relatively modest and its cancelation would have had international ramifications. Though he no longer held any institutional post, Schuman still wrote the occasional memorandum for the files to remind him of the events and people he encountered. Schuman was generally optimistic, but in his memo on attending one festival concert a tinge of bitterness crept into his remarks.

> NOTE: John D. Rockefeller 3rd was seated several rows in front of us at the last concert. I made a point of going over to shake his hand. He told me how much he admired the evening. I was, naturally, pleased by this reaction, since last spring and summer he refused funds from the John D. Rockefeller 3rd Foundation even though his professional staff had urged the grant. He also would not contribute personally. Hopefully, another time around, the situation may be different. It is my own speculation—and purely that—speculation—that he withheld funds last spring because I was unwilling to cut Lincoln Center's budget which, in my view, would emasculate the Center's programming mission.[24]

In fact, he did cut Lincoln Center's budget, but not drastically enough. He also voted to rein in the center's programming mission, but again not drastically enough. He fathered ideas and programs and constituents during his tenure as president of Lincoln Center that have enriched generations of concertgoers for decades. But at the end of 1968, as *Time* [magazine] editorialized; "what the center needs now is a fiscal wizard rather than a gifted artist as its next president."[25] Schuman was not interested in mastering the finances or asking for the big gift. His raison d'être to head Lincoln Center had evaporated.

Schuman's summer illness had serendipitously resulted in the creation of a leadership team that had functioned so well during his absence that the office of the president was deliberately left vacant after Schuman was squeezed out. Young wrote in his history, "Executive leadership was now placed in the hands of [Amyas] Ames, as chairman of the Executive Committee, and of Mazzola, who had been functioning as chief executive officer since the preceding June."[26] Mazzola became the fourth president of Lincoln Center in 1977.

Years later, Ames diagnosed Schuman's error.

> He and I have always been friends. But, he made a mistake, I think, in dramatizing a separate activity by Lincoln Center before he had accomplished the marriage of Lincoln Center to the separate artistic entities. Now they're solidly married and the world knows there's an advantage in coalescing the arts in one place. . . . John Rockefeller and . . . the founders made a mistake in putting a man in charge to do more programming—seemingly in competition with the constituents. When they picked me they were picking an administrator who had the same outlook as the constituent leaders. I was their co-equal. Bill Schuman was introduced as the head of a superimposed organization—seeming a new performing art rival—and it blew Lincoln Center apart. My strength was that I was an administrator and I was able to pull it all together because I was one of the constituent leaders.[27]

Not only had Ames served as the president of the Philharmonic Society. He was also one of the two Lincoln Center board members who went to Rockefeller on November 14, 1968, and called on him to cashier Schuman for the good of the center.

A decade later, Schuman wrote to congratulate Ames on his ten years as chairman, to congratulate himself on having the foresight to start the Chamber Music Society and the Film Society, and to "raise a small point, but one that is important to me": the omission of his name and honorific title from the programs and general stationery of Lincoln Center. Ames's response serves as an epilogue to Schuman's years at the helm. The letterhead, Ames told him, was "limited to those who are participating directly in the procedures of Lincoln Center, attending Directors' meetings, etc." Schuman no longer fell into this category. But Ames ended his letter by noting Schuman's unique and ongoing service to the center.

> As I look back over the history of this institution, it is more and more evident how valuable the procedure and the image established by you in the early years have been to its successful development. You contributed a style and a breadth of function which, even though we have been unable to find the funds to continue, were the real cause of the worldwide reputation that we enjoy.
>
> With thanks to our President Emeritus.[28]

After Lincoln Center, there would be no more big administrative posts for Schuman. But he was only 58 years old. He still had lots of time to dream a lot of dreams.

PART 5

THE YEARS OF COMPLETION

TWENTY-EIGHT

THE ADMINISTRATOR REINVENTS HIMSELF

Two letters from his last day as president of Lincoln Center—one outgoing, the other incoming—adumbrate the days and weeks ahead for Schuman. The first is a note Schuman sent to the chairman of the board of Lincoln Center, John D. Rockefeller III.

> Dear John:
>
> On this my last day as President of Lincoln Center I do want to send you a brief personal word. Working with you this past decade has been a fascinating experience, in which we have shared the satisfaction of many achievements, as well as the pain of some trying and difficult situations. During this time I have come to know and appreciate your very special qualities.
>
> Although the welfare of the Center will remain close to my heart and interests, there is only one way to leave an institution—and that is to leave. But you must know that, on a personal basis, I want always to be available to you, should you feel the need of my guidance in the areas of my professional competence.
>
> With every good wish to you for continuing health, happiness and progress in the worthy endeavors which enjoy your allegiance, I am, as always,
>
> Faithfully,[1]

The second was likely received sometime after Schuman left the Lincoln Center campus, but it, too, was composed on the eve of the New Year. Marshall Bartholomew ("Barty"), the retired conductor of the Yale Glee Club, had known Schuman longer—and probably better—than Rockefeller had.

> Dear Bill:
>
> Thanks for your note of December 20th and the enclosed article from the New York Times "Schuman Quitting Lincoln Center Post." I don't like that word "quitting" because you are not in any sense quitting, but retiring with honor to concentrate upon full time creative achievement in composition. You have probably forgotten that many years ago I protested your over-extended activities, first at Sarah Lawrence, then at G. Schirmer, Inc. and later at the Juilliard, climaxed by your heavy responsibilities at

> the Lincoln Center. Composition is a full-time occupation and creative work is not something that can be sandwiched into spare time.
>
> You have done a magnificent work in guiding the Lincoln Center along its path to greatness and you can certainly resign with a good conscience. . . .
>
> Hearty good wishes—sempre più![2]

Schuman never imagined that he would be a full-time composer; that was the dream of others. At the same time, he had always insisted that his proper title was "Composer and President," whether he was at Juilliard or Lincoln Center. Now shorn of the second identifier ("emeritus" notwithstanding), he would have to do everything possible to maximize the first and nurture the shards of the second. With no steady source of income available to him for the first time in more than 33 years and with the prospect of many more years of life ahead, Schuman had to reinvent himself.

Even before he had left Lincoln Center, options had begun to come in for Schuman's next act. The chairman of the Music Department at the University of California at Los Angeles wrote to Schuman on the very day that his resignation from the center was announced to ask if the university might entice him with a position. Schuman responded that he was not going to make any decisions for a few months. He was more frank with John Vincent, a composer on the UCLA faculty who was retiring that year. "It will take me a little time before I make any commitments, and in all candor, moving to the West Coast would seem to this old easterner a somewhat drastic decision, despite the many attractions that I am sure I would find."[3] His first three weeks away from Lincoln Center were punctuated by his coming down with "the bug," blacking out, falling, and breaking two of his ribs. "But I am cheerful because I feel so happy about the new work [the Ninth Symphony] and my new freedom to write more music."[4] That freedom also translated into time away, as he and Frankie spent two weeks at the end of January in Florida with Jim and Joan Warburg. Then they continued on to San Juan, Puerto Rico, for a meeting of the Board of Directors for National Educational Television, given that, as Schuman told friends, "one of the first things I did on leaving Lincoln Center was to accept a long-standing invitation to join the Board of National Educational Television."[5] (In 1970, NET was replaced by the Public Broadcasting Service, and Schuman's board service effectively ended and was replaced by his brief association on the National Programming Council.) Florida and Puerto Rico combined add up to three weeks Schuman spent away from his desk without a composition deadline on the immediate horizon or the demands associated with running an institution bearing down upon him; it is hard to find a similar hiatus in his schedule prior to this gift of time. Upon his return, he wrote to fellow composer Gail Kubik: "I have never been better, happier, or more relaxed."[6]

The time with the Warburgs was particularly valuable. It was Jim, as chairman of the board of directors for Juilliard, who had been most eager to hire Schuman as president in 1945 and who, in 1961, was reluctant to see him leave to become president of Lincoln Center. "Of one thing I feel sure: if anyone can make Lincoln Center into what it ought to be—if anyone can so fill its Byzantine shell with such content that the shell will be forgotten and the 'carriage trade' will become lost in the throng—that person is you. I hope to live long enough to see you succeed and, if we drink enough Martinis together, I think I shall."[7] Warburg died on June 3, 1969, less than six months after Schuman had left Lincoln Center, less than three months before Juilliard began its first year in its Lincoln Center home that Warburg had considered an appropriate place for him to be memorialized as someone associated with the enterprise. "I don't care about plaques," he wrote to Schuman, "but, if my name in bronze anywhere in the Center would really mean anything, it would be more appropriately there than as a patron of whole complex." More than a decade later, Warburg's widow would find another way to memorialize both her husband and Schuman, her neighbor on Richmond Hill Road in Greenwich, Connecticut. In the early days of Schuman's self-reinvention, loyal friends and colleagues surrounded him. Little changed on that front for the man who "was widely regarded as the most powerful man in American musical life."[8]

Notwithstanding his happiness with his newfound circumstances, he was eager to find outlets for his non-compositional talents. He signed with Herbert Barrett Management as a speaker (his fee: $1,500) and traveled to deliver lectures.[9] But the occasional speech hardly gave Schuman the platform he had once enjoyed, and his interest to an audience waned the more that time separated him from his post at Lincoln Center. Besides, he hated doing it. "I realized that I couldn't give a set speech. I would improvise, and you can't be a professional talker and give a different speech. I realized that whatever success I had as a public speaker had to do with my conviction about what I was talking about. But I hated doing it for money. I just didn't enjoy that at all."[10]

The NET Board brought Schuman far greater satisfaction than public speaking did. His decision to join the board was actually made in October 1968, one month before his forced resignation, leaving one to wonder if Schuman saw the handwriting on the wall sooner than he later admitted.[11] In NET, he saw the kind of artistic ferment he had tried to bring to Lincoln Center. He pledged to Peter Herman Adler, the music and artistic director of NET Opera, to "do everything in my power to move public television in the direction of greater and more imaginative programming in the arts. . . . As my own plans in my 'new career' develop, I hope that, as time permits, I may have some involvement with public television. At the moment, this is nothing more than a general thought, but I mention it to you to emphasize my understanding of its importance."[12] His board service also brought him into contact with other prominent supporters of public television, such as Norman Cousins, the editor of the *Saturday Review* (which Schuman read religiously), and Glenn Seaborg, chairman of the United States Atomic Energy Commission, who sent Schuman copies of his commission's annual report to Congress for bedtime reading.[13] Though his time on the board was short—he stepped down in late 1970 because of possible conflict of interests with another organization with which he had associated himself—Schuman had a profound influence on NET.[14] Just as he had done with the performing arts high schools, with the International Society of Contemporary Music and the League of Composers, and with the Academy and the Institute of Arts and Letters, Schuman preached the merger gospel to all who would listen at NET and Channel 13 (the New York City public television station where Frankie had done exceptional volunteer work throughout the 1960s and started the precursor of the Friends of National Public Television). Ward B. Chamberlin Jr., vice president and managing director of Channel 13, wrote to Schuman after the two institutions came together in 1970. "The history of public television may not even footnote your role in the NET/13 merger, but those of us who really care and who realize its importance know the critical nature of your efforts. It would probably have gone off the track without your patience and your wise counsel." Schuman was flattered at the praise but, despite his past merger mania, he felt it important to give credit where credit was due: the idea for the merger, Schuman insisted, was Frankie's.[15]

Schuman also considered developing and possibly heading a graduate program in arts administration at New York University. He had entered into discussions with David Oppenheim, the dean of NYU's School of Arts and Schuman's erstwhile sparring partner when Oppenheim worked for Columbia Records and Schuman tried to get the label to do more for serious music. Schuman proposed to undertake a feasibility study for the university, offering his services for $25,000. "Although we naturally hope and expect that my work will result in the establishment of the project at the University with my participation in a leadership role, neither party is so committed."[16] That study would have to wait, though, as Schuman took on a study for the electronic video recordings division of the Columbia Broadcasting System.[17] He met in Chicago with William Revelli, the director of bands at the University of Michigan, and Robert S. Hines, who was teaching at Wichita State University, both of whom were highly enthusiastic about the prospects of using this new technology in music education.[18] He continued to work on this study until yet another prospect captured his imagination: Videorecord Corporation of America.

A far-sighted graduate student working in the midst of the video sunrise cast doubt on the grandiose predictions that accompanied the dawn of the age of the videocassette. Even so, he felt obliged, as do all doctoral students, to repeat the wisdom of the sages.

> The material written so far about home video systems may have already used up an entire forest of trees. Yet throughout the avalanche, one assumption persists virtually unanalyzed—that cartridge TV means a communications *revolution*. . . . Industry insider Stafford L. Hopwood believes: "It will usher in the world's third communications revolution. The first came when man learned to record written words. The second came with the printing press. But the impact of this device will change the world more than the printing press."[19]

In the late 1960s, Hopwood served as vice president of business development and professional products for CBS Laboratories, a division of the Columbia Broadcasting System. According to his unfinished memoir, Schuman abandoned his study on electronic video recordings shortly after his friend William Bernbach, a leader in the advertising field, asked Schuman why he was trying to answer business questions for CBS when he could get his feet wet in the business itself.[20] Schuman met Hopwood and the other men "Hoppy" had assembled as part of the enterprise, and in early March 1970, an announcement appeared in the *New York Times* that Schuman had been elected the chairman and Hopwood named the president and chief executive officer of "Videorecord Corporation of America, a newly formed company for electronic programming and publishing and creative production services."[21] (Bernbach also joined the board of directors.) Hopwood's vision for the future of the videocassette appealed to Schuman, who sent friends the Videorecord press release on the eve of his March 1970 travels to Japan for the State Department. And Schuman sounded a bit like Hopwood in his assessment of the videocassette: he was quoted as saying that it was "the most important advance in communications since the invention of movable type."[22]

Schuman had reason to feel heady about the possibilities of Videorecord and its potential. His "growing interest in the efficacy of new technologies for teaching" led him to tap contacts old and new to see if they would become "engaged in developing programs which employ a variety of technological innovations without being committed to any system or particular piece of hardware."[23] He spoke to Bernstein about the possibility of creating "software—pre-recorded video program packages which can be played over any ordinary television set for viewing at any time and location by an individual or group"—for the company.[24] The New York Philharmonic approached Schuman to see if there were any ventures that might develop between the orchestra and Videorecord. He met with Joan Ganz Cooney, one of the founders of the Children's Television Workshop, about the possibility of bringing their six-month-old show *Sesame Street* to the new company.[25] Mark Schubart hitched the Lincoln Center education programs to the company's rising star, signing a contract "under which [Videorecord] with the support of Lincoln Center will produce education programs specifically designed for the videocassette format."[26] And people at the Smithsonian Institution spoke with Schuman about "a specific proposal in which the Smithsonian and Videorecord would collaborate in funding some beginning experiments."[27]

There was also a financial incentive for Schuman to be bullish about Videorecord. The 20,000 shares of stock he was issued were worth $45,000, almost as much as his salary at Lincoln Center.[28] The continuing growth and value of Videorecord was tied to the willingness of the major companies developing the hardware (Sony, Matsushita/Panasonic, RCA, et al.) to agree, in a timely fashion, upon an industry standard. Videorecord tried to avoid the format wars and was unwilling to promote one technology over another, but the delay in industry concurrence hurt the company's ability to generate programs and interest. As of early 1971, Videorecord had produced only one piece of software: a history of the abacus.[29] Still, Schuman was so convinced of the potential of Videorecord that he devoted more pages in his dictated memoirs to his time with the company than to any other period of his life.

Schuman had talked about writing his memoirs before and had tried to interest a publisher in his story, but in the years after Lincoln Center he took a greater interest in setting down his story as he saw it. "Not just the Lincoln Center side of my career, not just personal experiences, but things of general interest. The book will take the form of an autobiography and I haven't found any reasonable way to apologize for that."[30] Of the chapters he listed in his projected table of contents, he managed to cover nearly all aspects of his life up to that time, but just as fascinating are the chapters that are either lost, were never dictated, or were destroyed: one on his high school years, another on his life as a Tin Pan Alley composer, and a third on his days at Lincoln Center. The absence of a chapter on the latter passage in his life appears to be more than an accident or a loss of interest in the memoirs themselves. In September 1969, he drafted a seven-page outline of a book that would cover nothing but the Lincoln Center years "with full regard for all its facets, its success and its seaminess."[31] But for reasons known only to Schuman, he decided against setting out his side of the Lincoln Center story. In a letter he drafted and chose not to send, he challenged Elia Kazan and Kazan's retelling of the history of the Repertory Theater at Lincoln Center as found in Kazan's 1988 autobiography *Elia Kazan: A Life*.

> Although these events took place over twenty years ago, I have never commented upon them or written about them publicly, and as far as I can recall, even privately. I have no desire now to deviate from this course, but at the same time with the publication of your book, I think some private clarification is required to be left with my effect [*sic*]. Hence, this letter.[32]

In fact, Schuman did mention some aspects of the Lincoln Center years in his extended interviews and in the oral history he gave as part of the Lincoln Center Oral History project. But even in the latter interview, more than half of which covers his non–Lincoln Center life, Schuman shied away from giving full accounts of the controversies that swirled around him at the center, preferring instead to focus on three aspects of his days there: fundraising, the creation of the Film Society, and the creation of the Chamber Music Society of Lincoln Center.

The latter two were his unquestioned legacies, and he did everything to defend them against those who questioned them. He was invited to join the boards of both societies after he had stepped down as president, and while he was active and interested in film, more of his energies went toward the chamber music constituent than the film constituent. At the very first board meeting of the Chamber Music Society that he attended, Schuman read into the minutes the facts that

> (a) The formation of the Exploratory Committee for Chamber Music was an official act of the Executive Committee of Lincoln Center.
> (b) The Executive Committee of Lincoln Center accepted especially contributed funds to enable the Lincoln Center administration to aid in the development of an independent organization for chamber music.
> (c) The Executive Committee of Lincoln Center understands that chamber music will not be in the Lincoln Center budget after June 30, 1969.

He was taking preemptive measures against the rewriting of the Society's history and the attempts to suspend its future endeavors. But the financial troubles of the center led to a tug-of-war as to whether the '69–'70 season should be postponed, and "a majority of those present expressed themselves in favor of total suspension of activity."[33] A month later, an announcement went forth that "a newly formed chamber-music organization will make its home in Lincoln Center and give several preview concerts there in September."[34] The shift in the society's fortunes was not due exclusively to Schuman's backroom wheeling and dealing, but the sentiments expressed in an unsent memorandum Schuman composed for the board suggests that he did join the society's professional staff in fending off both the predations of the Lincoln Center Executive Committee and the timidity of the society's own Exploratory Committee.[35] Schuman would criticize the Chamber Music Society in the future for drifting away from what he saw as its animating principles, but as with the Juilliard String Quartet, he took particular—and justifiable—pride in giving birth to this particular institution.

Schuman's dealings with Juilliard and its president, Peter Mennin, led to some of the more unsavory events in Schuman's early retirement. Mennin had been interviewed for the Juilliard presidency even before Schuman had left the position, but the board of directors decided to continue its search and selected him only after considering several other candidates. Meanwhile, Schuman had bequeathed to his eventual successor a commissioning plan for the opening of the new campus in Lincoln Square that he would fulfill with a composition of his own. Schubart described it as

> an entire evening's "entertainment" which would employ in a single work the resources of the music, dance, and drama divisions, presumably to be presented during the first year of the School's occupancy of its new building. The commissioinees would be: composer, William Schuman; choreographer, Antony Tudor; playwright, Thornton Wilder?
>
> Obviously, all of this will need a lot of discussion, though Bill Schuman has already indicated his interest.[36]

The delays in Juilliard's move to Lincoln Center delayed the implementation of the commission, and by the time Mennin wrote to Schuman in 1966 to request a piece for Juilliard's opening, Schuman had become one of more than 20 composers Mennin and his staff had considered for commissions that were considerably smaller than the *Gesamtkunstwerk* Schuman had imagined.[37] Schuman demurred on writing a work for the opening, citing his desire to compose a work "for chorus or for chorus with orchestra" but stating the likelihood that he would not find the time to complete it "in time for the dedication, which I presume you are planning in the latter part of '68 (you don't give a definite date)." With his parenthetical comment Schuman hinted at Mennin's inattention to detail. Strikingly, Mennin did not catch the hint and not only failed to mention when Schuman would need to have his work in hand but also read past Schuman's apprehension. "My primary interest was in getting you to commit yourself on the work itself. The tone of your letter of March 8 relieves me somewhat in that you do commit yourself."[38] Schuman expressly did not commit himself, giving Mennin only his hope and expectation that he would find both the time to provide a work and an appropriate text to set. He found neither, which may have all been to the good, given that Mennin fumbled the commissioning project, leaving unspent thousands of dollars earmarked for new works.

Just days before the official dedication of the Juilliard building, Mennin's differences with Schuman received wider exposure. Journalist Martin Mayer had already written about Lincoln Center and Schuman's role in it, stating in 1962 that "the odds against Schuman and the Center are high, but they are not prohibitive."[39] By 1969, Mayer's wager seemed prescient, and in a September 1969 *New York Times* Sunday feature on Mennin, Mayer inferred that the problems Mennin faced as Juilliard moved to Lincoln Center all lay at the feet of Schuman, who (according to Mayer) whipsawed the Juilliard board into moving the school to Lincoln Square and attempted to abscond with a Carnegie grant earmarked for the school to pay down the center's debt.[40] Schuman wasn't the central character of Mayer's story, but he took great umbrage at Mayer's characterization of him and the school. He wrote to Mary Smith, his former executive secretary who was working for the Boston Symphony Orchestra: "When we meet I will tell you about that misleading piece on Juilliard. In the meantime, let me just characterize it as disgusting, which I realize is much too generous."[41] As he had done when he felt he had been libeled by *New Yorker* critic Winthrop Sargeant, Schuman asked his lawyer Abraham Friedman to write to the offending party for clarification. This time, however, Friedman did not correspond with the writer but with the subject of the writer's article: Friedman asked Mennin to call him and explain how Mayer could construct such falsities, given that his chief source for the article was Mennin himself.[42] Schuman, meanwhile, was incensed enough that he called the *New York Times* and got the Sunday editor to agree to print his letter in an upcoming Sunday edition of the paper.[43] Schuman's fiery rebuttal—and Mayer's response to Schuman's remarks—appeared in the morning papers on Sunday, October 26, 1969; that evening, the Juilliard School hosted the formal dedication of its new Lincoln Center home.[44]

Schuman feigned innocence and conflated events when he recalled the dedicatory evening years later.

> When the Juilliard School dedicated Alice Tully Hall [*sic*; the Juilliard formal dedication occurred in Alice Tully Hall], Bernstein was the emcee on television, and Peter Mennin didn't want him to say all the complimentary things he wanted to say about me, and it got to be a regular fight, and Bernstein said: "I won't appear if I can't say what I want to say." Unbelievable. I mean, I found out about small people, and I never knew about this before. I should have known, of course, but I didn't. . . . Afterwards Mennin did not invite us to go on the tour of the building with the VIPs who were present, as though I had never been at the school, as though I hadn't brought him.[45]

Perhaps Mennin was being small in trying to keep Bernstein from praising Schuman on that night and in not treating Schuman as a VIP. And Schuman may have been smarting from a phone call he received weeks before the dedication from John D. Rockefeller III, in which Rockefeller indicated that he expected Schuman to write his speech for the Juilliard dedication. ("'Bill,' he said, 'You do these things so easily, why you could think up these remarks in the shower.' 'John,' I said, 'The shower is the place where they send pitchers when they're knocked out of the box.'")[46] But Schuman's decision to publicly accuse Mayer of duplicity—and thus to impugn Mayer's principal source—encapsulates a moment when Schuman failed to see the greater good. As with his campaign in the late 1950s to defend Juilliard's honor against a bumbling attempt to besmirch the school's name, so here Schuman claimed the moral high ground for what amounted to a Pyrrhic victory. In the case of the *New York Times* profile, Schuman should have known that Mayer would get the last word, and Mayer chose well. "Like much else that happened during Mr. Schuman's late incumbency at Lincoln Center, [the costs of running the Juilliard School at

Lincoln Center] presented a problem for others to solve. Now as then, I fear, Mr. Schuman is worrying about the wrong things."[47]

Even though Mayer had taken Mennin's side, he had also given Schuman and others ammunition to use against Mennin, who emerged from Mayer's profile as an effete, secretive, and dispassionate man. Schuman and Mennin jousted at least twice more, and both times Schuman bested Mennin. Shortly after the Juilliard dedication, Mennin told Schuman that it was not only inadvisable but also probably illegal for Schuman to be president emeritus of both Juilliard and Lincoln Center. This emeritus imbroglio led Schuman to speak to a lawyer who served on the Juilliard board. "I do not know whether Peter Mennin is trying to be funny or trying to make trouble—naturally, I hope the former. I can find no legal basis why a President Emeritus of any institution can not be a President Emeritus of any other institution, whether or not they have any official or other connection with each other."[48] Schuman was imperious in his letter to Mennin announcing his victory. "With the assurance that I can indeed be President Emeritus of both institutions, I know that you will want to restore my listing as such on the appropriate title page of the catalogue, as I did for my predecessor when he became President Emeritus until the time of his death."[49] Mennin predeceased Schuman, so Schuman was President Emeritus of Juilliard for many, many years.

Mere days before Mayer's profile of Mennin was published, Schuman alerted Mennin to another problem that, at first, did not draw the two men into conflict. Schuman had assumed the presidency of the Walter W. Naumburg Foundation upon Naumburg's death in 1957; he had also stepped down as president of the foundation when he went to Lincoln Center in 1962. Leopold Mannes succeeded Schuman, and after Mannes's sudden death in 1964, Mennin succeeded Mannes. Mennin's stewardship of the Naumburg Foundation was adequate if not stellar, but by 1969 Mennin's lack of attention to the affairs of the foundation was proving worrisome to some of its directors. Schuman wrote to tell Mennin of the "increasing restiveness on the Naumburg front" but also sought to allay his successor's worries. "I have taken steps to quiet questioning voices with the assurance that after Juilliard opens you will give some thought to the Naumburg Foundation, but that clearly you are wholly preoccupied with the pressing problems of the school at the moment."[50] Matters continued to deteriorate over the next 18 months to the point that, at an executive committee meeting of the foundation, Schuman turned to Mennin and told him that he must resign as the foundation's president. The foundation continued to founder after Mennin stepped down, and Francis Thorne, executive director of the foundation, appealed to Schuman for help. Schuman was willing but only to a degree. "I wanted to make it absolutely clear to the other Directors that my motives [in the Mennin affair] were not personal but institutional." As a result, he told Thorne that he was not willing to allow his name to be considered as

Mennin's successor and insisted that any Naumburg materials that Thorne felt Schuman should see should also be sent to other members of the executive committee of the board.[51]

Schuman remained close to other composers, with Copland at the head of the list. Schuman had served as the master of ceremonies for Copland's sixtieth birthday celebration in 1960; he reprised his role in 1970. Though some at the latter event complained about the commercialism exhibited by Boosey & Hawkes, Copland's publisher, everyone—including Copland—agreed that Schuman was at the top of his form in feting the man about whom Schuman enthused, "However ingenious the invention of new superlatives to describe your exploits, your response will bring the same horsy laugh and toothy smile. . . . One of the privileges of my life is being part of the Copland Era, as our time will certainly be known in the history of American music."[52]

Schuman forever had to share decadal anniversaries with Copland—their births were nine years and nine months apart—but Copland saw a way to honor Schuman and to lure him into one of Copland's causes. Copland had been a Fellow at the MacDowell Colony on eight separate occasions and assumed its presidency during the 1960s.[53] He had received the second-ever MacDowell Medal, an honor given "to an artist who has made an outstanding and lifetime contribution to his or her field." (Writer Thornton Wilder, who also attended the famous artists retreat, received the first medal.)[54] Schuman certainly knew about the colony, but he had never had occasion to travel to Peterborough, New Hampshire, to view it firsthand. Copland addressed this absence in Schuman's career by championing him for a MacDowell Medal, and in 1971, Schuman became the fourth composer (after Copland, Varèse, and Sessions) to receive the medal. Every honoree is presented on Medal Day (the second Sunday in August) by a distinguished colleague; Schuman was the only composer Copland deigned to present.

Just as Schuman had regaled the assembled guests at Copland's birthday celebrations, so he entertained them at the festivities honoring him.

> The last award . . . that I got in the summertime was at Camp Cobbossee for Boys and it was several years ago, and it was the all-around Campers Cup of 1924. I still have it on my desk.
>
> You know, from that time at camp I recall two connections which can be related to the MacDowell Colony. I was beginning to write music, my first piece was an immortal tango called Fate, (And you [Aaron] said that I didn't deal with the more serious side of life) which I composed on my violin. And I had an idea. I had never heard of the MacDowell Colony, Aaron Copland, or anything. Really, I had no knowledge of any of these things. So I made up an artists' colony. I started to write an operetta on an artists' colony which was on the ocean front. I don't remember why, but it was called Newnick, and the first line of the opening chorus, which I recall, was

> "Though we couldn't pay the rental, all our thoughts were transcendental, as we came down to Newnick by the sea." I don't recall the music, but I understand that previous recipients of these awards, who were writers, often read from their works and I thought that you might like me to sing you one of my symphonies because I'm not certain that you'll buy the records.[55]

Schuman's experience at the MacDowell Colony was so positive that he decided that he wanted to help it in some way. His keen eyes saw that they needed assistance in the areas of budget and fundraising. "I would be delighted to help with this, for I have had a good deal of experience (more than I wanted) in this particular facet of institutional life."[56] Perhaps he knew instinctively, given his experiences with the Naumburg and Koussevitzky Foundations, that he was not going to be an idle spectator once he voiced his interest. The professional staff at the artists retreat also wanted to reel Schuman in, dangling in front of him the prospect of joining the board of directors, which Schuman did. Copland saw the potential for the colony. "After 45 years the Colony remains, in its form, pose and physical setup, essentially the same. It's just great that you felt moved to pitch in–as only you can."[57] As Copland guessed, the gifts in leadership and money that Schuman would bring to the Colony profoundly affected its direction. Could one expect anything less from Schuman? But Copland would be in for a surprise when Schuman turned into the Colony's quarter-million-dollar rainmaker.

Until that time, Schuman continued to flirt with various institutions and organizations. He toyed with the idea of doing a study on American orchestras and their need, among other things, to be rescued from the hands of foreign conductors. (Pierre Boulez had already been named as Bernstein's successor at the New York Philharmonic, and Schuman was none too happy. His instincts were right when it came to his own music: Boulez performed not a single Schuman work during his directorship of the Philharmonic, and the only Copland works he performed were the more "difficult" scores: *Connotations* and the *Orchestral Variations*.) He had written a draft of the study for the staff of the Twentieth Century Fund, but although "recent well-publicized events have emphasized the importance of the Study and I hope that the Fund will do something in this field," Videorecord took up much of Schuman's discretionary time. The staff at the fund left the door open to Schuman to conduct the study, but Schuman let the opportunity pass.[58]

His time in Puerto Rico for the annual meeting of the National Educational Board in 1969 may have opened a different door for Schuman to travel to the territory two years later "to do a study and report on the Conservatory of Music of Puerto Rico and the Puerto Rico Symphony Orchestra."[59] After submitting the report, he seemed to lose track and interest in what was taking place in Puerto Rico, for in 1977 he sent a copy of the report to Eugene and Marta Casals Istomin, asking them if any of his recommendations had been followed. (Mrs. Istomin had assisted her former husband, cellist Pablo Casals, in founding the Casals Festival, the conservatory, and the symphony orchestra; two years after Casals's death in 1973, she married pianist Istomin.) Marta commended Schuman for his report again and assured him that the report had been helpful, that some of his suggestions paralleled the long-term goals of the organizations, and that other recommendations, though still valid, were slower in being implemented.[60] Schuman did not live to see it, but in 1992 Marta became the president of the Manhattan School of Music, the institution that Schuman had persuaded to buy Juilliard's old Morningside Heights campus. Decades before she came to the school, Schuman was trying to direct its future leader to adopt his ideas about music education.

Schuman also continued to be involved in governmental affairs. He received an invitation from William P. Rogers, secretary of state in the Nixon administration, to serve as a member of the Joint Committee on United States–Japan Cultural and Educational Cooperation. Schuman at first was reluctant to accept.

> Over a period of many years I have had the privilege of serving the Department and other agencies on special ad hoc assignments. Certainly, Mr. Secretary, I want to be of any assistance that I can to you, in however modest a way. In the particular instance at hand, however, I am not certain that my own professional competence is best used on the Committee. In order for me to give you an informed answer, I should appreciate further information on the Committee's work and some estimate of the time it would take.[61]

Further information quickly followed, convincing Schuman of the importance of the assignment and the impact his presence would have at the meeting in Tokyo, which the bureaucrats in Washington called CULCON. If the post-Tokyo letter from the assistant secretary for educational and cultural affairs is any indication, the meeting itself was not Schuman's dish. "Too often the conference got bogged down into EDUCON, or into administrative and financial problems. But the purpose of a cultural conference is to talk about cultural exchange, and I am so grateful you were there to remind us! . . . I want to assure you that your participation made a major difference, both for the Japanese and for ourselves."[62]

Akeo Watanabe—a Juilliard graduate, founding conductor of the Japan Philharmonic Orchestra, and conductor of the Kyoto Symphony Orchestra at the time of Schuman's visit to Japan—had known and corresponded with Schuman earlier and had performed the Fourth Symphony and the *American Festival Overture* with his Japanese musicians. Watanabe recommended various places that the Schumans should visit during their stay. The meetings prevented them from seeing much in Tokyo, but their more leisurely schedule in Kyoto allowed them to take in a Noh drama.

> Both my wife and I are absolutely fascinated by the Noh theater and, despite the fact that we understood not one word, felt nevertheless that we were sharing a remarkable experience.
>
> We did, fortunately, visit the places [in Kyoto] that you mentioned and others as well. But for us perhaps the highlight consisted of the hours and hours in which we walked the back streets of the city and went into the small art shops.[63]

The trip also had the added advantage of giving Bill and Frankie an around-the-world adventure, as they traveled to Hong Kong, Istanbul, and Rome before returning to the United States.[64]

Another unexpected benefit from the trip came from an interview Schuman had with an English-language Tokyo paper. Schuman was cautious in the States when it came to airing his view about electronic music; his most extensive thoughts on the subject are tucked away in his introduction to *The Orchestral Composer's Point of View: Essays on Twentieth-Century Music by Those Who Wrote It*, hardly a place one expects to read about electronic music.[65] For the Tokyo paper, though, Schuman felt freer not only to answer questions about electronic music but also to place it within the greater context of instrumental music in general.

> "Electronic music represents the invention of a new instrument which can exceed human limitations with conventional means. The real question is whether or not this medium can produce anything which is truly artistic." This, Schuman concludes, remains to be seen, but when more experience has been gained perhaps something significant will come. The machine, says Schuman, will never replace the man with the horn, but will be an additive. . . . "The bow drawn across the string in the hands of a master artist is to music what the hearth is to the home."[66]

Though his analogy cloys, it gives a concise image of how he viewed the international avant-garde of his day.

A different series of episodes provides insights into how he viewed some more popular musical elements of the day. In his life after Lincoln Center, Schuman continued to frequent the theater often. He became particularly interested in the younger crop of musical theater practitioners and went to see both *Company* (Stephen Sondheim, b. 1930) and *Applause* (Charles Strouse, b. 1928) in June 1970. Composer-lyricist Edward Kleban (1939–87) reentered Schuman's orbit at this time. Schuman had recommended Kleban to Rodgers as a possible collaborator, and Kleban had not forgotten Schuman's "warm interest and continued enthusiasm in my work. . . . I have many composer-collaborators now, and if, indeed, as my work matures, you felt the need for words of one kind or another for a piece of your own, I would of course be honored to join you in any such venture." Kleban wrote to ask Schuman for a letter of recommendation in support of his application to New York City's Creative Artists Public Service Program, which Schuman gladly provided.[67]

Three years later, Kleban began a collaboration with Marvin Hamlisch that resulted in the musical *A Chorus Line*.

Schuman's multifarious activities in the immediate aftermath of the Lincoln Center years point in no one direction. His work with National Educational Television and Videorecord could lead one to believe that Schuman was going to focus on music education in his later years. But he hadn't fully extricated himself operationally or emotionally from the goings-on at Juilliard and Lincoln Center, and as long as he retained a residence in New York City, it was hard to imagine how he could extricate himself fully from these organizations. Other opportunities were practically his for the asking if he were willing to relocate, but he was not so willing. Where Schuman ultimately decided to pour his energies isn't all that surprising upon reflection. All of his other pursuits had always been subservient to his self-identification as a composer. His older colleagues—Sessions, Copland, Harris—were beginning to produce less and less, and many of his younger colleagues found his music to be hopelessly out of date. Schuman didn't care. He wasn't finished composing what Walt Whitman called "music complete in all its appointments, but in some fresh, courageous, melodious, undeniable styles—as all that is ever to permanently satisfy us must be."[68]

TWENTY-NINE

THE COMPOSER REASSERTS HIMSELF

Though Schuman knew it was unlikely he would ever accept a major administrative assignment again, it took some time for him to accept the shift in priorities that resulted from this shift in possibilities. "To be happy," he once said, "I have to have a demanding job, but I also must compose."[1] His demanding job now was to learn how to promote himself as a composer. He had always prided himself that he never lobbied musicians to perform his works. Now he had to develop a set of self-promotional skills designed to bring his music to the attention of others and to get his publisher to follow suit.[2] More fundamentally, he had to change his understanding of himself and curb his tendencies to involve himself with big projects. Such a momentous change did not occur overnight. Almost three years after he left Lincoln Center, he came to a realization of what lay ahead, and, since his publisher was implicated in that future, Schuman shared his realization with him. "As I head into my 'senior' years, I want more than I can possibly tell you to free myself from having to rely on activities other than composition for my basic livelihood. And so, after a long and varied professional life, some of it by choice, much by financial necessity, I want to spend my remaining years as a full-time composer."[3] Before, he had obliquely criticized those who had relied on "society women" as patrons, insisting, "I've always been my own patron and, therefore, I can write anything I want, and every piece of music I've written is because I wanted to write it."[4] Now he was apologizing to society women Claire Reis and Minna Lederman for being "'a boob' . . . about my own relationship with the League [of Composers]. Clearly I was too young to know what it was all about and profligate in disassociating myself from it so soon after I was invited onto the Board."[5] Going forward he would accept commissions and gifts from friends of means, male and female. He had fought in the past to do his music his way, even once (in the case of the Violin Concerto) denying the person who commissioned a work the privilege of performing that work in public. Now he found he had to fight to have others do his music at all.

One of his first fights was with his recurring sparring partner, the Philadelphia Orchestra. January 1969 saw the premiere of the Ninth Symphony. In February, Schuman received word that the Philadelphia Foundation, affiliated with the orchestra, was willing to underwrite the recording of the new work. By the middle of March, the manager of the orchestra wrote to tell Schuman that the recording had been canceled because the subvention would not cover the entire cost of the recording, even though the figures the foundation received were those provided by Ormandy and the agreement was accepted by the orchestra and RCA Victor. Schuman expressed his anger in a memorandum for the files. "If great organizations conduct their business along the lines indicated by the present situation, our problems, indeed, are greater than economic. What is involved here is a pure and simple case of basic ethics."[6] Schuman refused to budge and believed that his unyielding stand "finally shamed them into sticking to the original concept."[7] But though the work was recorded in May, more than two years elapsed before the recording was released, as RCA vacillated over which piece would be coupled with the Ninth. Recording the *Amaryllis* Trio, the businessmen at RCA decided, would be too expensive, but in their determination to put a chamber music work on the other side, they hoped to reissue the 1961 recording of the Third String Quartet that had been performed by the Juilliard String Quartet and had been deleted from the catalog in 1964.[8] Ultimately they decided to put Persichetti's Symphony no. 9 (*Sinfonia Janiculum*), which Ormandy premiered and recorded in March 1971. The recording of the two American Ninth Symphonies, both of which were identified with Rome, was finally released in December of that year.[9]

The commissioning, completion, and recording of the Ninth was a protracted affair. Schuman's Canticle for Orchestra, *In Praise of Shahn*, was the polar opposite. A conspectus of Schuman's first year out from under institutional umbrellas for the first time since 1935 found him reporting "total sunshine," with his new piece, created in commemoration of the highly acclaimed American impressionist painter Ben Shahn, as evidence of his newfound freedom. "If I had still been at Lincoln Center, and anyone had asked me to write a piece on such short notice, it would have been impossible."[10] Schuman prepared program notes for the world premiere and had them reprinted in the score with the request that they be used whenever the work is performed. They give some idea of the short notice.

> In the spring of 1969, shortly after the death of Ben Shahn [Shahn had died on March 14 of a heart attack; he was 54 years of age], I received a call from Lawrence A. Fleischman of the Kennedy Galleries in New York on behalf of a group of the late artist's friends. Would I accept a commission to compose a work in Shahn's memory? Because of my admiration for the astonishing achievements of this artist, my response was immediate and affirmative.[11]

The astonishing terms of the commission may also have contributed to his immediate and affirmative answer. They included selling 200 copies of the work, all autographed by Schuman, to the Ben Shahn Foundation at wholesale rates to be resold or given away; permission to use a piece of Shahn's as cover art; a grant of $10,000 toward a possible recording ($2,600 more than the Philadelphia Foundation had promised for the recording of the Ninth Symphony); and a fee to Schuman of $8,000 for composing the work (twice as much as Schuman received from the New York Philharmonic for *To Thee Old Cause*).[12] Schuman received the contract in early May, revised and returned it on May 28, and completed the work on October 27.

On the same day he sent back the contract to the Ben Shahn Foundation, Schuman wrote to Thomas P. F. Hoving, director of the Metropolitan Museum of Art, about an idea that Schuman had brought to Hoving. The Met was undergoing a massive expansion and renovation in anticipation of its centennial, and Schuman felt that an appropriate way to celebrate the five major centennial exhibitions was to have fanfares on the opening night of each one. Hoving concurred and gave Schuman the responsibility to determine the instrumentation and composers of the fanfares. For instruments, Schuman suggested six horns, three trumpets, three trombones, one tuba, timpani and two percussionists, although his own fanfare uses four trumpets. For the players and conductor, Schuman recruited his good friend and former Juilliard colleague Frederik Prausnitz to contract and lead the ensemble. For composers who would write the fanfares, Schuman chose Bernstein, Copland, Thomson, Piston, and himself.[13] Piston had some questions about the nature of the occasion, which Schuman addressed in a humorous manner.

> Last week Virgil's piece was played at the Museum's opening event [October 16, 1969]. The procedure is simply that the fanfare is played a number of times at various intervals during the course of the evening. The great stone spaces are extraordinarily reverbant [*sic*] and so I am very much afraid that music qua music is non-existent. What one hears is a joyous and festive conglomeration of mixed sounds, if not media. Perhaps this answers your question, "Is it a concert?"[14]

Although Schuman completed his *Anniversary Fanfare* on July 14, 1969, it was not performed until April 13, 1970, the official centennial celebration for the museum. President Nixon was supposed to join the festivities, but he sent his wife, Pat, to represent him instead.[15]

The date of completion for the *Anniversary Fanfare* and the delay in its performance are both significant. In commenting on the Met fanfare commissions, *New York Times* music critic Raymond Ericson asked: "What happens to fanfares after they've served their purpose? Do they evaporate, or do the composers find a use for them in some other work?"[16] He could have asked Schuman what he proposed to do, because the opening 145 measures of *In Praise to Shahn* are little more than a reorchestration of the 140-measure *Anniversary Fanfare*. Considering that Schuman never published the fanfare, he may have intended from the beginning to incorporate it into his work for the Ben Shahn Foundation, but his letters are silent about this possibility. If anything, they suggest that in the month following the completion of the fanfare, Schuman was still struggling to give form to the Shahn work.

An undated letter from Moishe Bressler—Schuman identified him in the program notes as Morris—provides a clue into Schuman's first thoughts about the musical memorial. How Bressler came into the picture is unclear, although Schuman's liaison with the Ben Shahn Foundation was a lawyer named Martin Bressler. The letter from Moishe indicates that Moishe made a tape of melodies that he had sung to Shahn, including some of Moishe's original songs. Though he struggled for the right English words, Moishe wanted to impress upon Schuman the importance these songs held for him and Shahn.

> I promised to write to you—offering some more commentaries about the few of the melodies on my "Shahn" tape you asked for. I find the task exceedingly hard—around a table I can talk and elaborate about every one of these old song-tales I love so much, but to write about them, particularly write in English is another matter. . . . Shahn [a Lithuanian Jew] always claimed that his name stems from the Hebrew "Beit-Shan"—and I, the Ukrainian Jew, who was brought up on the Russian and Hebrew culture, wept a song. . . . He enjoyed them, he understood them (there is nobody around here I can sing them for now).

Schuman found little sympathy with the songs on the tape. He wrote to Moishe in early August to tell him of his intention not to use any of them. "The more I struggle to find ideas for the Shahn piece, the more I realize that I will not be able to use any traditional music. But please don't think that this in any way diminishes the help you have given me in describing the background and characteristics of the great artist."[17] Perhaps, by early August, Schuman had decided to use the *Anniversary Fanfare* as the opening section for his Shahn piece; a month later, he had decided on its name and informed his publisher that the work was two-thirds complete.[18] And while there is no documentation to confirm this, it would appear that Schuman also decided to delay the premiere of his *Anniversary Fanfare* until the New York Philharmonic premiered *In Praise of Shahn: Canticle for Orchestra* in late January 1970.

Ericson, who (of course) had not heard the *Anniversary Fanfare* yet, made hardly any mention of the opening section of *In Praise of Shahn*. (Schuman's program notes studiously avoid calling this section a fanfare: "it's a kind of clarion call.") Instead, he focused on the music's continuity with the rest of Schuman's oeuvre.

> It has the composer's characteristic use of orchestral choirs as opposing units, thick polyphony and healthy extraversion. Its main section begins with a quite beautiful

> melody, with some elements of Near Eastern music, which builds contrapuntally to an almost unbearable tension. The beginning and end are loud and rhetorical.
>
> As a whole, the music proceeds at white heat. Compressed within a 15-minute span, it is indeed a hymn of praise, a celebration, somewhat noisy but impressive for all that. Mr. Bernstein conducted it for all it was worth, and the orchestra responded in kind. The audience seemed to like the work, and, the composer took three bows from his place in the audience.[19]

Ericson's description of the piece could easily be transferred to depict Shahn's 1962 poster for the opening of Philharmonic Hall. The poster features an image of the hall as a Gothic organ on which a wild angel-like spirit, all head and no body save arms, gazes heavenward and plays an inaudible but palpable "hymn of praise, a celebration, somewhat noisy but impressive for all that." It was likely the Shahn image that Schuman was most familiar with—he would have seen it countless times in his first year at the center—but in the case of the canticle, not everyone was as positively inclined as Ericson. Writing for the *Christian Science Monitor*, Miles Kastendieck was thrown off by the work's opening.

> Mr. Schuman delivered his "Praise" with a fanfare of unmistakable brassy dissonance. That it should have had such a military slant perplexed one listener at least. Like so many of his pieces, this one bogged down in counterpoint in which he would seem to indulge for its own sake. There was a brightness of spirit that did herald praise; but somehow when everything has been stated, only a feeling of passing interest survives.[20]

And Harriett Johnson's review in the *New York Post* sounds almost as though she was writing about the Schuman of the late 1930s and early 1940s, whose music roiled the musical establishment, which wanted its contemporary music to be tonal and tuneful and resented the polyphonic jungle Schuman created.

> "In Praise of Shahn" starts with fireworks, and the sound literally is a series of skyrockets. All this is quite fascinating and promises a continued directness and unquestioned purpose which doesn't materialize.
>
> Apart from these fanfares (at least, on first hearing), Schuman has taken a melody which, in itself, does have a soaring, expansive quality, but which he has surrounded by such a bulwark of contrapuntal and harmonic erudition that we feel the melody went to sea with a bunch of psychiatrists.
>
> Instead of the open cheer of optimism, we enter a maze from which the music never extricates itself. Suddenly, Bang—it is catapulted into the swell, swing and stamp of military accouterments. "In Praise of Shahn," may need repeated hearings for clarification but last night it puzzled more than excited this ear and emotions.

Similar things were said by B. H. Haggin, complaining about the Second Symphony, and Lou Harrison, complaining about the Third.

The money set aside for recording the canticle expedited the promulgation of the work, and the front of the record jacket featured Shahn's artwork. Its coupling with Carter's Concerto for Orchestra likely increased its sales as well, for in 1970 Carter retained his luster, whereas Schuman was becoming passé. The 11 months from the recording studio to the record bin may have been a record for a Schuman work, but the entire experience with *In Praise of Shahn* was also a deception of sorts.[21] Never again would Schuman find it that easy to obtain a commission, to complete a work, and to realize a recording of that work. Recordings of his new works from here on would be harder and harder to come by and would take years to appear. As of this writing, some of the major works of his last 20 years have never been commercially recorded. Schuman indirectly addressed this lacuna during these years, but the lack of the prospect of a recording did not keep him from composing.

In addition to the medium- to large-scale works that Schuman continued to write, he also turned out a few shorter pieces. On June 30, 1969, before he had finished the *Anniversary Fanfare*, Schuman tossed off a variation on the tune *Happy Birthday to You*. At the head of the manuscript, Schuman wrote these words, which in turn were read when the piece was performed to commemorate Eugene Ormandy's seventieth birthday at the Philadelphia Orchestra's anniversary concert and ball.

> For Gene:
>
> The irreverent morsel below is in inverse proportion to the respect, admiration and affection I have long held for you and the superb artists of the great, great Philadelphia Orchestra.
>
> Faithfully,
> Bill Schuman

Schuman felt that the assembled audience might benefit from an explanation of his 13-measure morsel.

> For your information, my little variation is in the form of a brief two part invention. The upper line (right hand) is a combination of the Star Spangled Banner and Happy Birthday. The lower line (left hand) is Rosenkavalier plus the opening phrase of the Haffner symphony. Please tell Bill [William Smith, assistant conductor of the Orchestra] that for this to make any sense to the audience, he will have to play each line separately and then in combination.[22]

Nineteen composers submitted variations for piano solo in honor of Ormandy, but only the variations by Bernstein, Copland, and Schuman were orchestrated and performed by the orchestra at the concert.[23] The recording from that evening reveals that, though the members of Philadelphia's high society warmly applauded all three variations, only the Schuman variation, which preceded those of Bernstein and Copland, elicited audible laughter.

Schuman's variation for Ormandy was neither the first nor the last time Schuman turned to *Happy Birthday*. In the summer of 1951, Samuel Barber was compiling a folio of variations to honor the seventy-fifth birthday of Mary

Louise Curtis Bok Zimbalist, the founder of Barber's alma mater, the Curtis Institute of Music in Philadelphia. He invited composers: "[Would you] harmonize 'Happy Birthday to You' in any shape, style, or variant which might amuse you on the enclosed sheets of manuscript paper—or simply transcribe the melody in your own hand on one sheet? I am asking a few distinguished composers to join me in this gesture; and the pages, when returned here, will be bound in an album." Schuman was slow to respond, so Barber wrote a follow-up letter to tell Schuman: "Among those who joined us are Messrs. Bax, Bloch, Chavez, Copland, Dohnanyi, Harris, Hindemith, Honegger, Martinů, Menotti, Milhaud, Piston, Pizzetti, Poulenc, Sibelius, Stravinsky, Thomson, Vaughan Williams, Villa-Lobos, and Walton."[24] Schuman hurriedly composed his contribution to the folio, a single-line rendition of that tune that presents the first phrase of the song in the key of F major, the second in A♭ major, the third in D major, and the fourth in B♭ major, ending not on the new key's tonic but on its dominant, which is also the first key's tonic.[25] He apologized to Barber, for in comparison with the other composers, he had reason to be "still somewhat embarrassed by my own modest contribution. Frankly, I was so pressed at that particular time with professional duties, which included a series of personal appearances as pallbearer for any number of distinguished colleagues who decided that last spring was the time to leave us."[26]

He turned to the tune at least once more, when Mark A. Schubart turned 60. The title of this irreverent rendition—*Score Three for Mockshin at Three Score*—recalls the musical Festschrift Schuman composed for Carl Engel on the occasion of Engel's sixtieth birthday (the *Three-Score Set* of 1943). Schuman provided a "legend" for his compositional choices. "On Sunday, May 14, 1978, at our home in Greenwich, CT 06830, MAS announced that he read newspapers backward as a preferred perversion. In tribute to this exotic taste we offer the following." What follows is a three-part round on *Happy Birthday*, with Part 1 being the retrograde of the tune in F, Part 2 the inversion beginning on B♭ and ending on F, and Part 3 the retrograde inversion beginning of F and ending on B♭. For the latter two parts, Schuman also provided the text in retrograde, turning "Ma-ark" at the end of the third phrase of the melody to "Ark-Ma."[27] It is doubtful whether Schuman intended for the tribute to be sung, just as later (nonbirthday) tributes to Leonard Feist and H. Wiley Hitchcock are meant more to be musical puzzles to amuse rather than pieces to be performed (see chapter 32 for more on these pieces). But all the birthday variations, especially the ones to Ormandy and Schubart, show Schuman's wit and humanity.

The next two works Schuman composed—those after the Ormandy variation, the *Anniversary Fanfare*, and *In Praise of Shahn*—also exhibit wit and humanity. The year 1970 was a fallow one for composition. Based on the correspondence and the aborted memoir, it was more the Year of Videorecord, although he considered yet again the idea of making an orchestral version of his *Chester Overture*, which his publisher encouraged him to do.[28] In 1971, in contrast, he completed two choral works, both of which had spent years on the drawing boards. W. Douglas Pritchard, director of choral activities at Iowa State University, offered Schuman a commission for the Iowa State Singers. As with most of his choral commissions, Schuman struggled to find an appropriate text. Schuman and Pritchard discussed the possibility of using something from Herman Melville's *Battle-Pieces*—Pritchard could hear "Balls Bluff: A Reverie" with offstage flute and drum—but notwithstanding the ongoing war in Southeast Asia, Schuman wasn't inspired by Melville's words.[29] The delivery date of the end of 1970 for the new pieces had come and gone, when Schuman encountered some advertisements from the 1897 Sears & Roebuck mail-order catalog, which was republished in 1968 with introductions by veteran *New Yorker* writers S. J. Perelman and Richard Rovere.[30] The ad copy fired his imagination, and by the summer of 1971, he had completed the *Mail Order Madrigals*. He wrote to Pritchard to tell him that

> These madrigals have turned out to be bigger pieces than I had originally anticipated and I can only hope that you will not be disappointed in them. The spirit behind the absurd words that I have chosen certainly has a precedent in some very fine madrigals of the Elizabethan period, which often had nonsensical words and wonderful music.[31]

Pritchard loved the works, and on the eve of the premiere he wrote to praise Schuman for the ingenious way he had fulfilled the commission.

> I want to reiterate and amplify my previous comments about the "Madrigals." The entire idea is brilliant, but I don't know of anyone else who could have brought it off. At the hands of other fast-publishing composers the idea would predictably be another one of those "cute" pieces we use as encores. Your madrigals have too much integrity for that. What is so effective, of course, is the deliberately serious musical treatment of utterly innocuous text material.[32]

The premiere in Ames, Iowa, was arranged to take advantage of the visit that the Boston Symphony Orchestra was to make there. Schuman wrote to the manager of the orchestra to joke about this serendipity. "Surely the BSO will be giving one of the most unusual programs in its entire history. It is doubly rewarding to me that this strange affair will have a cappella music of mine on the first half [*Prelude for Voices*, the *Carols of Death*, and the *Madrigals*] and after intermission the Brahms Requiem, which I will try not to read as a second half presented as atonement for the first."[33]

The first two of the *Madrigals* are for men alone and women alone, respectively, with the remaining two for mixed chorus. Schuman's manuscript, however, reveals that he intended not only to have this distribution of voices but that he also made plans to publish the four madrigals in all-women's and all-men's versions.[34] The four act in concert as a vocal symphony in miniature. The first madrigal ("Attention, Ladies!") opens with a brief two-part fanfare followed by an explosive spoken "QUOTE!" after which the music divides into three parts and traverses various moods, not unlike the first movement of a symphony. The second ("Superfluous Hair") is a dissonant scherzo, in keeping with its text complaining of "a horrible growth of coarse hair springing up like bristles . . . repulsive to the touch and disfiguring to behold." The third ("Sweet Refreshing Sleep") functions as the slow movement, and in keeping with its text that talks about a cure for sleeplessness, its central section is set, lullaby-like, in compound meter as if to rock the insomniac back and forth. Its final cadence also emerges as something of a surprise, with quiet but dissonant chords resolving at the end to a somnolent D♭ major chord that, if the chorus has Russian-style basses, ends with a low rumble not unlike a contented snore. The final madrigal ("Dr. Worden's Pills") returns to the faster tempos of the first two madrigals and acts as a rondo-like finale. Its central section is a three-part round that, both in its words ("Women can be beautiful") and textures, echoes the *Five Rounds on Famous Words*. Later in life, Schuman made a similar observation of all the *Madrigals* that put them in a less favorable light. Someone had written to Schuman, suggesting a program that would include the *Madrigals*. Schuman advised against it. "If you want other light pieces, rather than the Mail Order Madrigals, I would suggest Five Rounds on Famous Words. I have always found my madrigals somewhat disappointing."[35] His disappointment may have been caused by the failure of the *Madrigals* to catch fire with choral groups. They are charming but are not easy, and their admixture of absurd words and serious music favors the latter. Perhaps if the music attempted to crack a joke the way that the Ormandy variation does, the *Mail Order Madrigals* would win more admirers. Even so, the four pieces are impressive and full of surprising touches, such as the final cadence that appears to end on a long-held D-major chord, only to slide at the last second up one half-step, as if the chorus had suddenly launched itself into orbit.

The *Madrigals* were completed on July 28, 1971. The month before, Schuman had completed another choral work, the *Declaration Chorale*. He composed it for Lincoln Center's Third International University Choral Festival, which was scheduled for the summer of 1972. He wrote to Tikhon Khrennikov, secretary of the Union of Soviet Composers, about his vision for the festival.

> Of all the programs undertaken by Lincoln Center during my tenure, none gave me more satisfaction than the fulfillment of the concept of an International University Choral Festival. The purpose of the Festival can be simply stated: to bring together young people from all parts of the world to meet in friendship and to sing together. While music is the medium for the gathering, the benefits in understanding and lasting camaraderie are values of equal significance.
>
> The Third Festival, in April of 1972, has my very special interest, since I accepted Lincoln Center's request to compose a short work. At the final concert, my "Declaration Chorale" will be given its first performance by the Festivals' 650 young singers from sixteen countries under the direction of Robert Shaw. The text is drawn from the writings of the American poet, Walt Whitman.[36]

It was Schuman's idea to have a commissioned piece of music for the festival; it was Schuman's decision not to accept a fee for his work. The fact that Lincoln Center had promised to purchase 700 copies had to make Schuman's publisher happy. And Schuman was happy about the piece. He sent it to Pritchard, who praised it as effusively as he had praised the *Madrigals*.

> I can't tell you how impressed I am with "Declaration Chorale." Its bold, aggressive harmonies and vigorous rhythmic properties are unmistakably Schuman. I am especially taken with the second section, "On every side." And the contrasting section, "Yet, we walk" is a perfect complement to the preceding rhythmic and angular section. This will have a very impressive sound with the large chorus at the premiere. It also would have been ideally suited for the concert here on March 12! I think you have used the Whitman texts most imaginatively—beautifully suited to the occasion for which it was commissioned.[37]

James R. Bjorge, the festival organizer, also congratulated Schuman on his chorale. "The choruses worked hard on your piece—which isn't easy, as you know—and under Bob's great leadership sang it extremely well. [Robert Shaw was music director of the festival.] I was deeply moved by what you wrote, especially the closing, the reiteration of 'Peace', leading into that magnificent E major chord; so beautiful."[38] But Robert Sherman, writing in the *New York Times*, had less kind things to say about the piece, which was sung by the 16 choirs participating in the festival (including two from the Soviet Union).

> Mr. Schuman's six-minute anthem is adapted from a gloriously appropriate Whitman text ("We of all continents, we of all castes . . . Peace!"), but the complex linear fabric made the words impossible to grasp. This probably stemmed more from the composition than from the singing—since the choir's diction elsewhere was excellent—and it was a pity, vitiating the potent emotional message the score should have delivered.[39]

Schuman had planned on composing yet one more choral work in 1971, according to a letter he sent to his publisher. "During August I expect also to complete a version for mixed chorus and snare drum of 'When Jesus Wept' and 'Chester,' using the 'New England Triptych' as a basis and employing both words and sounds. These pieces also will be for first performance next spring in Iowa."[40] No sketches or manuscript have turned up for this fantastic combination of voices and percussion.

Another vocal work Schuman contemplated in 1971 fascinates mostly in light of his decision not to incorporate Jewish folk material in his Shahn commission and his lack of interest decades earlier in working on an opera with Herman Wouk based on the Joseph story. Paul Kwartin, chairman of the Community Affairs Committee of the American Conference of Cantors and cantor at Brooklyn's Union Temple, approached Schuman to see if he might compose music for one of the Jewish High Holy Day services. Kwartin reminded Schuman that, "since the great Bloch and Milhaud services of the thirties and forties are based on the Friday eve and Sabbath morning liturgy, no major composer has concentrated on the Yom Kippur liturgy. Schoenberg wrote a stirring setting of Kol Nidrei, but we look to you for a more complete coverage of the texts."[41] Schuman made an attempt.

> The commission you offer I want very much to accept, but I have read, reread and reread again the Yom Kippur service as contained in the Union Prayer Book. To put it in the vernacular, I simply am not "turned on" as a composer. . . . I want to execute the commission. Is there another way? I simply cannot set any of these words. Would there be a possibility of using some other poems which might form a triptych, or indeed possibly of commissioning three short poems or prose statements which would be suitable for inclusion in the service, reflecting the intent and spirit of the occasion but not as specific as the text, which in English tends to be repetitive and in my view sometimes banal despite its lofty purpose.[42]

Schuman's reluctance to set the Hebrew text gains perspective when one recalls that, with the exception of his 1944 Te Deum and his short occasional piece written to the Latin words of Colgate University's motto, all of Schuman's vocal works have English-language texts, including his youthful *Adoration*, which was performed at Temple Sharaay Tefila in the early 1930s.

Schuman tentatively accepted the commission, and Kwartin sent him additional material to consider. Once again Schuman tried, and once again could not get past his lack of sympathy for the texts: "While my own faith is very deep indeed, it does not respond to the specifics of formalized worship." He then offered a suggestion. "If I can find three texts which could be appropriate for inclusion in the Day of Atonement services, would this represent to you a reasonable approach?" He further suggested that his 1958 *Carols of Death* might be "appropriate" for the Yom Kippur service, although his intent was "to find words either for one extended piece—8 to 10 minutes—or two or three shorter contrasting pieces . . . within the next several months and ask you to comment on its suitability to the purpose you have in mind before I undertake it for this particular commission."[43] Despite the fact that the stated purpose of the commission was for a liturgical service, Kwartin provisionally agreed to the poetic limitations Schuman had proposed, but with a caveat of his own. "It would be better, of course, if that poetry were by a Jewish poet, and to that end I send along some fragments by Bialik, Greenberg, Tchernikovsky, Gilboa, Trainin."[44]

Schuman tried one more time, going so far as to ask an unnamed friend to try his hand at writing a text, but Schuman found even this specially composed poetry unusable. He shared with Kwartin the disappointing news as well as further insight to his own soul. "It has become increasingly clear to me that my ardent desire to fulfill the commission has nothing to do with the artistic and intellectual sensibilities which would have made it possible. My apologies to you for what must seem unforgivable procrastination. The truth is otherwise. I have worked hard and long and now know that it is simply not my dish."

Schuman recommended that Kwartin contact Hugo Weisgall, who "understands full well the liturgy both as a practitioner himself in the Synagogue and as a member of a distinguished Jewish family long identified with Jewish artistic and intellectual life."[45] (Some years later, when he was directing synagogue choirs in Baltimore, Weisgall set the Sabbath service from the *Union Prayer Book* in his *Evening Liturgies* [1986–96].) Schuman did not say whence the "ardent desire to fulfill the commission" came, but his inability to move forward on this "cantor commission" shows how keenly Schuman felt the words he set to music. For all of his impressive craft as a composer, he was mute when the words failed to stir him, even words that perforce reminded him of his own family and heritage.

Yet another failed commission from 1971 reminded him of his own upbringing, this time of his training as a young violinist. Robert Rudié, a Juilliard graduate in violin and the head of the school of music at the Riverdale Country School, which both Tony and Andrea attended, approached Schuman in another capacity, that of project director for a commissioning idea that the Manhattan School of Music was initiating for its Preparatory Division. (Juilliard handed over the Preparatory Division to Manhattan when the latter bought Juilliard's Morningside Heights campus.) The project, in conjunction with New York City's Eleanor Roosevelt Junior High School, was to increase the number and skills of young violinists. One way of doing so, thought Rudié, was to provide a "school of violin playing" in the form of newly composed music designed to help young students and their teachers work on specific aspects of violin pedagogy. And Rudié turned to Schuman to see if he would be interested in providing that "school of violin playing."

Schuman accepted the commission in late 1971 and gave considerable thought and time to it the following year. "These pieces," he wrote to someone needing biographical information in late 1972, "aim to give the beginning student an immediate experience in playing chamber music."[46] A notebook that contains early versions of the pieces, which he ultimately named *Two-Part Violin Inventions for Student and Teacher*, begins with a preface in Schuman's hand.

> These pieces for two violins, pupil and teacher, are intended to supplement formal instruction. The aims are:
>
> 1. to give the student, from his first efforts, the experience of performing music with another player whose part is independent.
> 2. to instill a sense of pitch not related to harmonic underpinning but pure interval relationships.
> 3. to develop rhythmic sophistication.

Schuman went on to credit Rudié for the invitation to write the pieces as well as for his guidance in developing a *gradus ad Parnassum* for violin. (Schuman also jotted a note for Rudié, telling him that the "fancy notebook" was a gift from

Vera and Isaac Stern and that "this should not inhibit you from burning it if the pieces don't work.")[47]

In many ways, the *Inventions* are counterpoint exercises, and Schuman's training with Haubiel made short work out of composing these duets. Because of a change in leadership at Manhattan, the commission was reinstated in 1973. "This music is to be in the form of approximately 20 two-part inventions with both parts playable by students in the beginning stages of their studies, and is intended to proceed on a more elementary level and form a unit with the pieces you have already completed for the project under a previous commission."[48] The exact dates of composition on these *Inventions* are difficult to place, as Schuman chose not to place dates on the surviving materials, but his correspondence suggests that, although he did not receive the first half of the $5,000 commission until early May 1973, the *Inventions* were his major compositional effort for much of 1972.[49] Among his manuscripts at the Library of Congress is a bound copyist's score, annotated by Schuman, of the 20 *Two-Part Violin Inventions for Student and Teacher.* The cover page indicates that these constitute Part I of the project, with the student's part beginning on open strings and advancing to first position and the teacher's part providing a more elaborate accompaniment to the student's efforts. The surviving materials also indicate that Schuman consulted with someone (Rudié?) about the progression of the inventions, as he wrote down that he needed to compose new pieces to fit between already composed inventions to assist in the gradual development of the student violinist. Given that the surviving score is in a copyist's hand and not Schuman's own, and given that the reinstitution of the commission asked for "approximately 20 two-part inventions," it would appear that Schuman completed the commission. He did not, however, allow the inventions to go forward. On the surviving score, Schuman wrote: "July 17, 1976/not good enough—/forget/keep for reference?—WS." The Violin Concerto had vexed Schuman for a decade before he felt that he got it right. Schuman spent half that time on the inventions before deciding that he got them wrong.

In addition to the failed commissions and the completed choral works of 1971, Schuman ended that year with a major orchestral score.[50] On behalf of the Eastman School of Music, Walter Hendl, the school's director and Schuman's former Sarah Lawrence colleague, invited Schuman in early 1970 to be one of 22 composers commissioned by Eastman to compose works as part of Project 71, the yearlong festival marking the School's fiftieth anniversary. Schuman's first thoughts weren't about an orchestral work at all, as he told Hendl. "I have been toying with the idea of writing a work employing two pianos. I have never written such a composition and, since I am a great admirer of [the two-piano team of] Gold and Fizdale, I am wondering what you think. Do please let me have your thoughts."[51] Whatever Hendl thought, Schuman abandoned the two-piano idea in favor of composing "an orchestral version of my piano cycle entitled 'Voyage.' These five pieces have always seemed to me to need an entirely different setting than the keyboard, and I plan a completely new working of the materials and hope confidently that we will have a major result."[52] Schuman had misgivings, though, concerning the feasibility of transferring the music from one medium to another. As late as August of 1971, he had not completely made up his mind on what he would do, and this for a work scheduled for a February 1972 performance. But Hendl, who planned to conduct the premiere with the Rochester Philharmonic, wrote to inform him that the concert was pushed back to May. The news gave Schuman "a new lease on life. . . . If you do not hear from me again, 'Voyage' it will be. Should I change my mind about 'Voyage,' lifting the time barrier will give me the opportunity in any case to do a major work."[53]

Both the manuscript and the published score indicate that Schuman worked on *Voyage* between September and December 1971, but only the manuscript provides the completion date of December 6. An annotated score of the piano version also provides insights into the changes Schuman envisioned and adopted. On the eve of the premiere, he wrote to his friend and colleague Vincent Persichetti. "Confession: I finally did it and made an orchestral version of Voyage even though you once told me I should let it stand as a piano piece. But I don't think you will be too displeased because it turned out to be a big rewrite job."[54] Each of the five sections of the original piano piece is expanded considerably, especially in their second halves, and Schuman added new material throughout. Most notable is the expansion of the parallel material at the ends of the first and fifth sections, especially the addition of a plagal B♭ chord to complement the final F-major sonority, so that when the material returns at the end, the sense of journey is made all the more palpable and definitive.

The premiere was pushed back a second time, from May to October, which Hendl felt was necessary given the unrest at Eastman over his directorship. By the time Schuman came that autumn for his first visit to Rochester to receive an honorary doctorate and to witness the premiere of *Voyage*, neither Howard Hanson, the school's longtime director, nor Hendl, the man who had the unfortunate privilege to follow Hanson, was at Eastman, and the premiere itself had been given over to the student-populated Eastman Philharmonia as part of its annual concert in honor of the United Nations with Gustav Meier at the podium. Reviewers from both local dailies (the *Rochester Democrat and Chronicle* and the *Rochester Times-Union*) commented on the deftness of Schuman's orchestration, and one, perhaps thinking that Schuman had planned the occasion of the premiere to coincide with the U.N. celebration, wrote that "it is Schuman's rhythmic vitality that glides the listener through 'Voyage' to its final resting place on an F major chord, the end of an engrossing intellectual journey toward peace."[55] (The other reviewer called the work "virtuoso stuff, which the orchestra handled with spirit and musical competence, if not with complete polish.")[56] Neither critic was willing to pass judgment on the work itself, one calling it "at once introspective and dramatic, a seeming expression of inner turmoil," the other carping about "Schuman's pendulum swing, back and forth, from string to wind choirs."

The latter comment approaches the most remarkable notion surrounding *Voyage for Orchestra*: that Schuman felt unabashed in taking a work nearly 20 years old and recasting it as representative of his compositional language of the day. Schuman finessed this matter when he tried to interest André Previn in the London premiere of the work. "Anyone making a comparison will find the most extensive modifications, deletions, additions, new harmonizations and all manner of compositional adjustments, let alone the introduction of extensive percussion parts which of course were not in the original."[57] But the obverse was also true: anyone making a comparison would find how much material Schuman chose not to change at all. And whether he was consciously aware of it, Schuman had signaled a turning away from the dissonant style of the 1960s and toward a return to triad piles, tuneful melodies, and an unapologetic invocation of tonality. From the beginning of the 1960s to the end of the decade Schuman tried on the garb of the serialists and tailored it to his uses. From the premiere of *In Praise of Shahn* in 1970 through *Voyage for Orchestra* (1972) to his opera *A Question of Taste* (1988), Schuman's larger works would no longer bask in dissonance for dissonance's sake. He was reverting to his earlier compositional self.

Donal Henahan, in his review of the New York premiere of *Voyage*, recognized how out of step Schuman was with the times. The American Symphony Orchestra gave two premieres that afternoon, and Henahan found both works "large in scale and ambition, and both were in idioms that fell outside the pale of the avant-garde as it is usually defined these days."[58] The other new work that appeared on the program was the Oboe Concerto of John Corigliano. Though the two composers were from different generations—Corigliano was born in 1938—each admired the other's work. Corigliano and his peers began to look to Schuman as a pioneer of the kind of music they hoped to write, and Schuman looked to them as the bearers of the symphonic legacy he sought to extend. And not just symphonies: a year after the Metropolitan Opera announced that it had commissioned Corigliano to write a work to celebrate the Met's hundredth birthday, Schuman predicted that Corigliano "will be the first American composer to write a successful opera for the Met—one that will remain in the repertory."[59] That opera, *The Ghosts of Versailles* (1991), seems to be fulfilling Schuman's prophecy. Schuman was in step with the new world of American music that was emerging in the 1970s, but he remained old news to much of the musical establishment. Corigliano's Oboe Concerto would go on to be recorded by RCA Victor; as of this writing, Schuman's *Voyage for Orchestra* has not been commercially recorded.

But in the early '70s, it was too early to tell that Schuman was about to be eclipsed. In one part of the globe, his music was very much in the ascendency. Twenty-eight-year-old Ukrainian conductor Igor Blazhkov wrote to tell Schuman that "the Soviet first performance of your 3d symphony has great success. The [Leningrad Philharmonic] orchestra and conductor [Blazhkov] felt unforgettable moments of the great creative satisfaction during the working at your remarkable symphony."[60] Agnes de Mille was traveling in Russia a few years later with the American Ballet Theatre when a young composer came up to her and told her: "I love Copland and Bernstein, but William Schuman is my father."[61] And in that same city around the same time, a female conservatory student created a small scandal when her highly polished composition was discovered to be an act of plagiarism, as she tried to pass off Schuman's *Symphony for Strings* as her own.[62]

Not only were young Soviet musicians enthralled with Schuman's music. Near the end of his life, Dmitri Shostakovich came to the United States. During the course of his visit, he went to the home of David Lloyd Kreeger, a Washington, D.C., collector of impressionist and modern painting and sculpture who lived in a home designed by architect Philip Johnson to highlight Kreeger's collection. Kreeger wrote to Schuman to say that Shostakovich had little interest in visual art. "The Maestro soon made it plain that his interest was . . . in hearing the works of contemporary America. I played the Columbia recording of your Third Symphony by the New York Philharmonic under Leonard Bernstein. His comments were most enthusiastic—with such adjectives as 'formidable—powerful—marvelous.'"[63] The Ninth Symphony received similar plaudits when it was a featured work in Moscow as part of the All-Union Friendship Festival, with the writer for the Soviet news agency *TASS* saying that "this symphony, written under the impression of one of the tragic events of the past war, is intensely dramatic and lyrical and marked by complex turns of musical thinking and writing. It deeply moved the listeners."[64]

Though he no longer wore the vestments of institutional authority, Schuman remained one of the high priests of American music at home as well as abroad. For example, he traveled to Washington, D.C., for the official opening of the Kennedy Center for the Performing Arts. The conductor Antal Doráti, a dear friend of Schuman's, selected a program meant to display the various aspects of the new Concert Hall and to score sociopolitical points as well. Beethoven's Overture *Consecration of the House* opened the evening followed by Stravinsky's *Le sacre du printemps*, which showed off both the hall's acoustics and the orchestra's virtuosity. The second half of the program featured a chamber-sized orchestra that accompanied violinist Isaac Stern in the Mozart Concerto in G major, KV 216. And to close the program, Doráti chose *A Free Song*. Critic Paul Hume rightly noted that "neither [the Beethoven nor the Schuman] represents its composer at his greatest, but each one has an appropriate tone for festive occasions."[65]

Schuman had written the secular cantata to inspire his fellow Americans in the early and not altogether successful years of WWII. How different it must have sounded in 1971, as President Nixon (who attended on opening night, shared his box with Bill and Frankie, and shook Bill's hand after his composition was performed) sought to wind down the conflict in Vietnam.[66]

The conflict at Lincoln Center was also winding down. The Film Society and the Chamber Music Society were proving to be viable, and as a gesture of gratitude from the child to the father, in 1971 the Chamber Music Society commissioned Schuman to compose a work for its players.[67] The work itself would not be completed until January 25, 1978, with its premiere nine months later. But both the Chamber Music Society and Schuman were aware at the outset of the likelihood of delay. At the time, he had *Voyage* to finish, but that was not all. "There are certain other plans which are under way, and as things now stand, if I do not write your work in '72, I would not be optimistic about having the time for it for several years after that."[68] The nation's big party was not far in the future, and Schuman was going to try again to ignite interest in his *Nineteen Seventy-Six*. Little could he have guessed that another commission would not only upend his bicentennial ambitions but would help him further distill into one work many of the trends then pushing and pulling on his aesthetic universe.

THIRTY

ROUND AND ROUND AND ROUND HE GOES

Martin E. Segal's story is a classic immigrant's story. He was born in Vitebsk, Russia, in 1916, the year before the Bolshevik Revolution. His family came to the United States in 1921, settling in Brooklyn. Marty, as everyone called him, took on odd jobs as a young teen, and by the age of 16, he had left home to strike out on his own. In 1939, he founded his own company, which grew to become one of the nation's leading consulting and actuarial firms in the employee benefits field. Twenty-eight years later, he sold part of his business and started looking for other things to do. His interests in his fifties were in the arts, and he proceeded to use his influence and power as a businessman to leverage opportunities and money for artists of all kinds. He began to work with his friend Abraham Beame, who became mayor of New York City at a time when the municipality was close to insolvency. Marty showed the mayor and everyone else that the arts were part of the solution and not part of the problem, said the writer Diane Solway in a 1988 profile of Segal. "During his 1974 chairmanship of the Mayor's Committee on Cultural Policy, Segal scored a major coup when his committee issued the first report showing the impact of the arts on New York City's economy ($3 billion that year)."[1] He went on to become the chairman of Lincoln Center in 1981 and to raise more than $8 million to underwrite the First New York International Festival of the Arts in 1988, a latter-day incarnation of the festival idea that Schuman had tried to create at Lincoln Center. No wonder Solway called Segal "New York City's leading cultural power broker."

In her profile, Solway used a single sentence to knit together the selling of Segal's share of his firm, when "he took up with the arts," and his "big league advance on the city's cultural front six years later" in the Beame administration. "In 1968," she writes, "he became the founding president of the Film Society of Lincoln Center." In his correspondence with Schuman, Segal put a different spin on the importance of that particular presidency—and of Schuman's importance to his life. Schuman sent a note by hand in advance of the story in the *New York Times* that announced Segal's appointment as chairman of Lincoln Center. Segal wrote to Schuman to thank him for his thoughtfulness and for more than that. Schuman, according to Segal, steered him into his leadership in the Film Society and that, in turn, led to his service as chairman of the Lincoln Center board. An earlier letter also finds Segal crediting Schuman for bringing Segal into the world of the arts. It is not surprising, therefore, to discover that Segal looked for ways to repay Schuman for helping to make the arts his second act.[2]

In the late spring of 1972, Schuman told Segal his thoughts about a grand project he had been mulling a long time: an evening-length composition that would celebrate the nation's two hundredth birthday. In a letter in June, Schuman pursued the topic further.

> As one composer, I could only give expression through words and music to some of the feelings that are so deep within me. If I could succeed in expressing these feelings to my own satisfaction, then and only then could the work have meaning for others. It is clear to me at this juncture that any project that I might undertake for an event as important as this one would for me be the most significant and largest effort in my long career as a composer. A major stumbling block for me is the difficulty in freeing myself of all other compositional commitments from right now into 1976. Every bit of this time would be needed to develop a text and compose a work which would encompass the entire normal running time of a concert (about 70 to 80 minutes actual music).[3]

Schuman had already tried to obtain sponsorship through his publisher, but Presser couldn't get enough orchestras to agree to help commission Schuman's magnum opus. Schuman himself approached Catherine Filene Shouse, a wealthy Washington, D.C., patron of the arts and founder of the Wolf Trap National Park for the Performing Arts, to see if she or her associates might be interested in commissioning the work, but his inquiry went nowhere.[4] Now Segal was asking Schuman to clarify the scope of "Project 1976" (Schuman's alternate name for the work), and Schuman took the ideas he sketched out for Segal to create a more detailed prospectus for what he hoped to accomplish and how much time and money he would need to accomplish it: from 1972 to 1976, to the tune of $125,000.[5]

With Schuman's prospectus in hand, Segal turned to William May, chairman and chief executive officer of the American Can Company. Schuman had also brought May into the Film Society orbit, so both men were favorably disposed to Schuman. But although May believed that Schuman was the preeminent composer of the day and the logical choice to write a work commemorating the bicentennial, the American Can Company could not see its way clear to help underwrite the expenses.[6] Schuman was replaying the episode of the Lincoln Center Festivals: the grand idea was compelling, but the financial support was lacking.

In the midst of trying to find corporate sponsorship for *Nineteen Seventy-Six*, Schuman managed to secure a $20,000 commission, his largest ever, to write a bicentennial work for the National Symphony Orchestra. David Lloyd Kreeger, another Russian émigré who made good in the New World, helped to negotiate the agreement between Schuman and the orchestra in his capacity as president of the National Symphony Orchestra Association.[7] But before Schuman accepted the commission, he wanted assurance that he could seek a cosponsor for the work he envisioned, if for no other reason than to help cover the costs of copying the score and parts and paying a researcher to help him find texts. If Kreeger and the administration of the orchestra agreed, then Segal had agreed to try to find such a cosponsor.[8] Over the next year and a half, Segal and Schuman approached different institutions seeking additional underwriting; documentation shows a request for $50,000 from the Helena Rubinstein Foundation as well as a letter asking the National Symphony Orchestra to hold off announcing its part of the commission in the hope that tobacco conglomerate Philip Morris would cosponsor the work. But by the middle of 1974, *Nineteen Seventy-Six* had no cosponsor.[9]

The lack of money by itself was, in some ways, a lesser impediment to Schuman's plans than was his inability to find suitable texts. In his letter of clarification to Segal, he discussed his ideas of the sources from which he would ultimately draw the words for his composition.

> The aim of this work as I view it should be to capture the American flavor through music set to words of a wide variety of American authors known and unknown, covering a broad spectrum of time, place and content. Candidly, I approach the idea of this task as an unabashed patriot. The work you discussed with me must be an affirmation. After hearing it, the listener should have a renewed sense of some of the things that are superb about America and experience a renewal of his belief in the "American dream" as more than a cliche. To achieve such results, the textual matter cannot be spineless or Pollyannaish.
>
> If one hopes, for example, to capture something of the grandeur of the American landscape without contrasting it with what has happened to urban civilization, one loses not only a dramatically effective contrast but, what is even more serious, credibility. Similarly, if one uses the great words of a Jefferson or a Lincoln and doesn't contrast these with some of the horrors of the bigots and witch hunters that have plagued our nation in various guises ever since Salem, there is the same loss of drama and believability.[10]

As widely read as Schuman was, he was not convinced that he knew enough of American literature and poetry to construct a libretto of such sweeping scope. So he turned to others for assistance.

Arthur Schlesinger Jr. was one of the first persons he approached. Schlesinger and Schuman were members of the Century Association, a private club for authors, artists, and sympathetic amateurs. Schuman wrote to Schlesinger to see if he might be interested in helping him in considering sources in crafting a text for this grand bicentennial work. Schuman had hoped for a one-on-one meeting with Schlesinger, but Schlesinger sent him a bibliography to consider and wished him well on the composition.[11]

A few months later, he asked Richard Freed, a Washington-based freelance music critic and program annotator, to assist him in finding texts. Freed got off to a slow start because of circumstances that Schuman said "reads like a Russian novel," but over the course of eight months Freed (and possibly others) turned up "lots and lots of material" for Schuman to consider. Only one piece spoke to him. He wrote to Archibald MacLeish to tell him of his frustrations and his single success. "Although I have written much choral music, finding the text is always enormously difficult. If you agree that I may have the use of your efforts, I already know that there is one poem that moves me greatly. It is 'The Young Dead Soldiers.' I want very much to set these words for one of the movements of the symphony."[12] The text did not make it into the bicentennial symphony, but Schuman did make use of it all the same. He also wrote to Kreeger to tell him of his failure to find texts that inspired him to compose.

> Curious as it may sound, I am not the least depressed by this state of affairs, for I have often known this to be true for many months as I contemplate the structure of a large composition. By the end of this year my decks will be cleared for complete concentration on your work and I am naturally hoping for the best. In any case, my enthusiasm and dedication to the project is enormous, and I certainly want it to be the very best effort of which I am capable.[13]

He was not nearly so sanguine a few months later when he wrote again to Freed. "I am just finishing my 'Concerto on Old English Rounds' for Solo Viola, Women's Chorus and Orchestra and have already put in lots of time on research for the '76 Project with discouraging results."[14]

Instead of *Nineteen Seventy-Six*, the "Triple Concerto on Old English Rounds" (as he contemplated calling it) fired his imagination for most of 1973.[15] While the origins of the rounds Schuman used are indeed old and English—Samuel Pepys wrote in his diary on April 24, 1660, about how " after supper my Lord [Sir Edward Montagu] and we had some more very good musique and singing of 'Turne Amaryllis,' as it is printed in the song book, with which my Lord was very much pleased"[16]—Schuman first encountered them not in songbooks but through Marion Farquhar, one of Sarah Lawrence College's benefactors when it came to languages and literature. Farquhar taught a number of rounds to Schuman, who in turn taught them to the chorus during his first year of conducting the ensemble (1938–39), and at least two of the rounds Schuman would later use in his concerto were performed in concert that year.[17] Their oral transmission explains in part that, when it came to "Turn Amaryllis," no printed version comports with the version Schuman employed in the first work that drew on the round, his *Amaryllis* for string trio.[18] Shortly after that work's premiere, Schuman contemplated the possibility of expanding it "in a new format, for symphony orchestra and women's chorus. The work would be very different from the Trio variations, but would stem from them."[19] There the idea lay dormant for a number of years until it was stirred briefly when Schuman and Ormandy discussed the possibility of writing a piece for pianist Rudolf Serkin using forces similar to those Beethoven deployed in his Choral Fantasy.

> The idea of composing almost any work for Rudi Serkin has great appeal to me because of my profound admiration for his artistry. Although he has undoubtedly forgotten, some years ago he did ask me for a piece and said that it should be "impossibly difficult." . . . I must confess that I am not intrigued with the combination of solo piano and chorus with orchestra. Perhaps this is because I have written so much choral music that employs piano that I find it difficult to envision the need for this instrument along with the chorus and orchestra. But certainly I want to think about the matter.[20]

Piano "along with the chorus and orchestra" failed to appeal to Schuman, but a telephone call gave him another instrument to consider as a possibility. In 1972, violist Donald McInnes received a Ford Foundation grant that allowed him to approach a composer to gauge his or her interest in composing a concerted work for McInnes. It was the same Ford Foundation program that brought Leonard Rose and Schuman together a decade earlier and led to *A Song of Orpheus*. After speaking to McInnes, exchanging letters, and listening to a tape of his playing, Schuman agreed to be open to composing a work for him.

There were, however, some problems that needed to be overcome. The first was how soon Schuman could produce the work. Schuman's focus remained on *Nineteen Seventy-Six*, and he wanted to wait until July 1 to hear whether he could secure funding for that work. Even if funding wasn't forthcoming for *Nineteen Seventy-Six*, Schuman did not think he could start work on the viola piece until 1973, which would in turn delay its premiere realistically to the 1974–75 season. Then there was the matter of paying for copying the score and parts. At this point in his life, Schuman was unwilling to accept commissions that did not cover copying costs, and before he would agree to accept the Ford Foundation commission, he had to know how much of these expenses the foundation would cover. When told that the foundation would cover only up to $3,000 in those expenses, Schuman and McInnes drew up an agreement between themselves whereby McInnes would reimburse Schuman for half of all copying expenses beyond that amount and that the violist would "personally copy the solo viola part and piano reduction or meet the costs of copying them."[21] With the terms of the commission now protecting him from unacceptable copying costs, Schuman was ready to tackle the artistic challenges the new work presented, including integrating a women's chorus into a viola concerto.

Prior to beginning work in earnest on the concerto, Schuman composed *To Thy Love: Choral Fantasy on Old English Rounds* for women's voices. Despite its title suggesting a loosely structured work, it is highly sectional, beginning with a chorale fanfare on the syllable "la," followed by slow contrapuntal elaborations on "Turn Amaryllis." Next come sequential presentations of "Who'll Buy Mi Roses?" "Great Tom Is Cast," and "Come, Follow Me," after which these three rounds are combined in a quodlibet. The fanfare returns unchanged—in the manuscript, Schuman used his typical shorthand telling the copyist which earlier measures to insert at this point—and the work ends with a homophonic rendition of "Amaryllis" and a repeat of its first line, "Turn, Amaryllis, to thy swain," in which Schuman replaced the word "swain" with "love," thus justifying the work's title, *To Thy Love*. After the concerto was completed but before its world premiere, Schuman wrote to Harold Aks, conductor of the Sarah Lawrence College Chorus, in a humorous attempt to interest him in the choral fantasy. "When I conducted the Sarah Lawrence chorus 107 years ago, I taught these beautiful rounds to the girls and they were perennial favorites at our concerts and on tour. Recently I have completed a 'Concerto on Old English Rounds.' . . . Much of the material in the 'To Thy Love' version is used in the concerto." Schuman also suggested that he would try to prevail upon whichever performing organization agreed to do the New York premiere of the concerto to invite "the girls of SLC" to constitute the chorus. "In the meantime, if you like the pieces, please get a few of your girls together and let me hear how these rounds sound in combination (see pp. 15, 16 and 17)."[22] Schuman surely knew that Sarah Lawrence had been a coeducational institution since 1968; perhaps he did not know that the "girls" had joined the "boys" in forming one chorus. (The women of the Camerata Singers, with Abraham Kaplan conducting, sang in the New York premiere of the concerto.)

Though he derived joy from the rounds, Schuman harbored doubts about the accuracy of the rounds as he knew them. He wrote to Frederick Hart, his former Sarah Lawrence colleague and a close friend of Farquhar's. The handwritten letter, on a piece of manuscript paper, shows some of Schuman's earliest thoughts for McInnes's piece as well as his propensity for misspellings. "Are these correst [*sic*] as sung by Marion? I've got an idea for their use in a fantasy for solo viola–women's chorus—orchestral winds and pitched percussion. Please let me know as soon as possible." "These" included music for "Come, Follow Me," "Great Tom Is Cast," and "Who'll Buy Mi Roses?" Schuman also asked Hart about the words: "Me or Mi?" Hart answered back (in red pencil): "It should be Mi," and he also corrected "any old clothes" to "any old cloths," a change Schuman ignored.[23] Schuman later sent the unusual letter to Edward Waters, chief of the Music Division at the Library of Congress, asking his further help. "Enclosed you will find, in my absurdly faltering hand, three rounds which I have recently used as a basis for an extended work. Can your research people tell me whether they are anonymous or by known authors, and what general time period you think they come from. The 'Fred' on my rounds is a great friend of the late Marion Farquhar, who taught me these rounds."[24] The specialists at the Library of Congress were able to help Schuman with "Great Tom Is Cast" and "Come Follow Me," but "Who'll Buy Mi Roses?" like Schuman's version of "Turn Amaryllis," proved to be untraceable. "It is one of the many catches built out of street cries, and it sounds British all right (that is, not American). The tune is the well-known British and American folk tune 'Jenny's Baby' ('Polly Put the Kettle On'), or a variant of it. That tune dates at least from the 18th century, and was certainly widely used in the late 18th and early 19th century."[25] As for the instrumentation he sketched for Hart, Schuman decided to expand the orchestra to include both brass and strings, but he kept to his original vision of pitched percussion, omitting his trademark timpani in favor of tubular bells.

By the late winter of 1973, he was already well along with the composition. He sent a section to McInnes, who found it "not only exciting, but so well written for the viola!!!" The work occupied him for all of the spring and summer months as well. Frankie, trying out their new electric typewriter for the first time on the Fourth of July, wrote to Eddie Marks to tell him of their life in Greenwich. "Now, the summer routine has set in—we,re here most of thej time—Bill is writing in his newly enlarged study with delusion of grandeur and a large sofa on which he can sleep—but the work is coming along and he is managing to overcome hisk surroundings." McInnes wrote to Schuman two months later, expressing his incredulity that the work was nearly completed.[26] The only sour note came in an exchange Schuman had with his copyist, Anthony Strilko, who was facing severe financial straits. Out of desperation, Strilko quoted Schuman a rate of $15 per page and estimated that the work would run to 140 pages. He now wanted to know if Schuman would consider a flat rate of $2,000 for copying the score, thus saving Schuman $100 if Strilko's estimate was correct and allowing Strilko to collect some of the money up front. Schuman told Strilko that he would try to find additional copying work for him but that the quoted page rate would stand. Schuman would have been better off had he taken Strilko up on his desperate offer: the score and parts ran to nearly 250 pages, and Schuman was forced to write to the Ford Foundation to ask them to help defray the expenses that far exceeded everyone's estimates.[27]

McInnes paid the Schumans a visit during the 1973 holiday season and worked on the concerto with Bill. With the premiere scheduled for November 1974, the two men had plenty of time to iron out the various problems they encountered. Schuman was not only impressed with McInnes's artistry. He also wanted the legend on the solo part to read "Edited by Donald McInnes": "Never in my many associations have I worked with a more congenial, scholarly, and altogether wonderful colleague."[28] He also showed the score to Frederik Prausnitz, who was then the music director for the Syracuse Symphony, to get his opinion of the work. "In your second paragraph you say, 'Bill, this has to be the best (your violist had better be the best as well).' I'm delighted that you think the work is my best and can assure you that in Don McInnes we have an extraordinary soloist who will do brilliantly."[29] In nearly all of his correspondence surrounding the *Concerto on Old English Rounds*, Schuman was just as likely to promote McInnes as he was to promote his own composition. He encouraged other conductors to engage McInnes in performances of the concerto and celebrated Bernstein's decision to engage McInnes in a recording of Berlioz's *Harold in Italy*. He complained to the management of Columbia Records when the release of the concerto recording was delayed, stating (rather extravagantly) that "the only way that McInnes' career can be advanced at this point is to have a record of his performance with the Philharmonic."[30] He pushed hard to sway the Avery Fisher Artist Program to recognize the viola as a solo instrument and to award McInnes its prestigious prize.[31] He also thought of writing other pieces for McInnes. He made a start on a short piece for viola and flute and suggested that the work he was contemplating for the Chamber Music Society might be scored for a sextet, in which case McInnes's talents might be put on display again.[32] In the case of the sextet, the fact that *In Sweet Music* has a virtuoso part for the viola is testament to McInnes's forward reach into Schuman's compositional imagination.

The concerto itself, in many ways, is a lodestone for all the traits and techniques Schuman had started refining in the two most recent orchestral scores—*In Praise of Shahn* and *Voyage for Orchestra*—and it provides a compass pointing to works that lie ahead as well as the aesthetic philosophy to which Schuman subscribed. Whereas the earlier two scores incorporate other works with sections and extensions added on to make them presentable as new and original compositions, the *Concerto on Old English Rounds* unapologetically announces its borrowings and unashamedly guides the listener through the kaleidoscopic changes the music undergoes. The work neither baffles nor astounds. Fundamentally, it aims to please. Andrew Porter wrote in *The New Yorker*:

> This is a happy, witty score, which often made me smile and nearly made me laugh aloud; the composer's sleight of hand when he starts bringing the different rounds together in a wicked gallimaufry is wonderfully neat. But it is also a poetic piece. The viola begins it, "uttering" the Amaryllis melody and music on it; and elsewhere the viola is descant commentator on the other tunes.[33]

What is "tune" and what is "commentary" is clear throughout, and Schuman made clear to the violist that the opening utterance was supposed to be "sung" by having the words of "Turn Amaryllis" written beneath the notes as a reminder of its origins, just as he had done earlier in *A Song of Orpheus* and *To Thee Old Cause*. More than tune and commentary, though, is the inescapable sense that this is a tonal work, one that begins and ends in A minor and that not only has solid tonal anchors when the women's chorus sings the rounds but also when the horns bray their variant of "Great Tom Is Cast"—sounding like the seven-ton bell in Oxford, England, whose creation the round celebrates—and when the viola cadenza begins with its frolicsome version of "Who'll Buy Mi Roses?" and at other moments throughout the work. The music begs to be enjoyed, not by performers alone but by listeners as well, as though Schuman were signaling, more fully than he had previously done, that the era of total dissonance in American music was finally over. More major scores were yet to be composed, and in all of them—even the mildly dissonant *Three Colloquies*—Schuman found new ways of affirming and reaffirming the major triad, not in collisions with its kin but all by itself. In the concerto, more fully than in *Shahn* and *Voyage*, he marked his own claim to being a purveyor of the New Romanticism before that term had come into vogue, and not merely as a grandfatherly figure to whom the younger composers sent their scores for perusal but also as a stakeholder in ensuring what one newspaper writer called "new music's return to the mainstream, a look back that is a revival."[34]

Because of its length and its unusual forces, the concerto confounded as often as it delighted. Schuman had to explain to one concert promoter that "this is not a 'choral work.' It is a big stand-up concerto for the viola, and according to McInnes (I don't know) it is the biggest virtuoso viola part in the literature."[35] *Boston Globe* music critic Michael Steinberg had a difficult time pegging the concerto. After noting that the work had a precedent in scoring but not in aesthetic outlook to "Vaughan Williams's languishing, serene-sensual masterpiece of 1925, 'Flos campi,' a contemplation for viola, wordless mixed chorus, and chamber orchestra," Steinberg went on to berate Schuman for writing music he felt was uncongenial to the composer's own aesthetic.

> Schuman's most characteristic strength has always been in passionately declamatory music and in a certain fierce and broad lyricism (in the most remarkable way he has made a virtue of gracelessness), and it is from such moods that his most eloquent, masterful music has grown—works like the splendid Third Symphony and the Symphony for Strings early in his career, or the "Ardeatine Caves" Symphony more recently.
>
> Conversely, the playful and the virtuosic have been less congenial to his temperament. . . . And this new concerto I find much of the time brazenly tough, the toughness getting in the way of the intended fun, and the solo part seems awfully difficult but not brilliant.[36]

Steinberg faulted the concerto, in essence, for trying to be "serene-sensual" and for not being graceless enough; the work Porter found happy and witty, that often made him smile and nearly made him laugh aloud, Steinberg found humorless. Schuman had made a turn in the concerto, and Steinberg, at the time, wasn't turning with him.

Harold Schonberg, the *New York Times* critic who was generally becoming less and less sympathetic to Schuman's latest music, caught a glimpse of what made this work different from previous Schuman efforts.

> Here and there, there is a modal feeling or a deliberate archaism, but Mr. Schuman has not set out to be quaint, and they do not occupy an important part of the score.
>
> Altogether characteristic of the composer were the motoric sections—those fast-moving passages, often punctuated by pungent brass combinations, found in so much of Mr. Schuman's music. In the Concerto, they seemed rather mechanical. It was when Mr. Schuman was in repose that he created the memorable moments of the score.[37]

Porter similarly tired of those moments where "counterpoint is ground out in a ruthless way that recalls Hindemith at his most graceless" and also intuitively recognized that Schuman's version of the "Amaryllis" round was corrupt in some way.[38] But all three critics seemed to sense something new stirring in this work, which presaged and followed other works that were also engaging in tonality and collage [e.g., Rochberg's dramatic turn to tonality in the Third String Quartet (1972); Del Tredici's groundbreaking Alice pieces (1969–81); Druckman's use of Charpentier, Cavalli, and Cherubini in *Prisms* (1980); Corigliano's concertos for piano, oboe, clarinet, and flute (1968–81)]. Schuman was on to something new.

Some of Schuman's close friends joined with Prausnitz in praising Schuman's accomplishment. William Bergsma, one of McInnes's fellow faculty members at the University of Washington, perceptively summarized what made the work a success.

> The <u>concept</u>—always the most important thing in Schuman—of <u>only</u> chimes: the intricate happenings when Great Tom is Cast; the capitalizing on Don McInnes' characteristic strengths as a performer (has there ever been quite so good a violist?) show the canny composer at his crafty best.[39]

(Schuman wrote a fan letter to Walter Rosenberger, the New York Philharmonic's percussionist who played those chimes on both the New York concerts and the recording. "I can't let this season go by without telling you what a magnificent artist you are. . . . I am very much afraid you have spoiled me for the future. I will always have your very wonderful sounds in my ears.")[40] Frederick Hart received the recording at the same time that he was "writing a sort of memoir" about Farquhar. Understandably, the concerto took on personal connotations for him. "I congratulate you. It is a stunning work—a tour de force. You are a master of the medium and, as so often, I succumb to your music. I wish Marian [*sic*] could have heard it. She would have loved it. . . . Marian loved you both and you were fond of her."[41] And several of the Sarah Lawrence "girls" wrote to tell Schuman how much they, too, enjoyed the work.

The concerto was the highlight of 1974, but another event that year cast a shadow on one of the major concerns to which he had earlier turned his attention. One of his friends in the business world kidded Schuman about the men who composed the board of directors of Videorecord Corporation of America. To the friend, it "sounded more like that of a university rather than a business venture so he felt it could not possibly succeed but eventually would go out of business. . . . His good-natured quip," Schuman noted confidently at the end of 1970, "will prove to have no foundation either in fact or fancy."[42] But by the end of 1971, Schuman realized that Videorecord, having decided to wait for an industry format standard to emerge, was at the mercy of the hardware manufacturers. He told a friend who wanted to know whether Videorecord was a good bet that "this is a fine investment for someone who has capital funds to place in a risk venture enterprise and who can afford to forgo immediate income for a longer term go-around . . . income should come to dealers in '72."[43] Schuman was certainly right to predict, in an omnibus letter to library directors, that "the impact which videocassette programs are destined to have on forward-looking libraries is almost inestimable."[44] But there was no income coming to dealers in 1972. Meanwhile, Stafford Hopwood, president of Videorecord, was enjoying a $75,000-a-year salary, access to two company cars, a generous expense account, and the consolation that his two college-aged children and his brother were on the company's payroll. The board asked Hopwood to step down in March 1973 and discussed the possibility of merging with another company. A year later, with millions of venture capital dollars exhausted, Videorecord was liquidated. In his exposé of the company in the *Wall Street Journal*, Jonathan Kwitny restated "an obvious, but often overlooked, fact of business life: The star quality of a company's board of directors in no way guarantees success."[45] Schuman, who later claimed not to know whether the company had filed for bankruptcy, told Kwitny: "The technology was much behind what everybody thought at the time. But I never felt that anything was stated that was in fact incorrect. Obviously, [the business] was speculative."[46] To a friend who had read the *Wall Street Journal* story, Schuman put the entire affair in perspective.

> Actually, for more than a year I have had no connection with the corporation because the technology was not sufficiently advanced and there was little hope of doing the work that I hoped to accomplish in the arts. You are nice to wonder whether I was in any way harmed and I can say that I was not. There are very exciting possibilities for the video cassette form, and I hope that the medium is exploited by people of knowledge and taste.[47]

Some people lost their investments, but Schuman was looking ahead to the Next Big Thing.

Strikingly, at the time he was retreating from Videorecord, a new opportunity was dropped in his lap. Howard Klein, the head of the Rockefeller Foundation's arts programs, wrote to Schuman in June 1973 to "ask for your opinions and comments regarding a proposed project that officers of The Rockefeller Foundation are considering. The project is to attempt to document a history of American music over the past 200 or more years on 100 discs. The coming bicentennial celebration is the reason for the project, although such an effort has seemed to many long overdue."[48] Klein may not have known it, but he was tending the shoot whose seed Schuman had planted a decade earlier when Schuman suggested that the foundation do something about recording American music.[49] Not surprisingly, therefore, Schuman ended up giving much more than opinions and comments this time around: he and his junior partner Robert Sherman wrote a 54-page report focused on developing "the most logical and effective institutional format for the recording project."[50] It took them six months and earned Schuman $10,000; he called it "an enormous job—much bigger than I had anticipated, but I confidently believe worth all the effort."[51] Considering that he had to trim his own bicentennial project, it is not surprising that Schuman transferred some of his ardor for his individual work to this corporate celebration of American music, suggesting that the Recorded Anthology of American Music, as it would come to be called, "could easily become the nation's major project in music for the Bicentennial celebration. It has everything in its favor because the concept is a grand one which represents all of America's creative achievement in music."[52]

The centrality of the Schuman-Sherman report in the creation of the Recorded Anthology of American Music, which in turn would beget New World Records, is beyond dispute. When, in November 1974, Klein sent out the final version of the Project Report, he freely acknowledged that report's lineage. "The latest report builds upon previous reports, notably that done by William Schuman and Robert Sherman about which many helpful comments were solicited from the consultants." At the same time, he spoke freely of the divergent opinions and views the final report incorporated, creating "a wide variety of disparate ideas contributing toward one educational and artistic whole."[53] Schuman throughout was one of the divergent voices, stating repeatedly and emphatically to Klein, by both letter and telephone, that an anthology of "100 discs comprising not only concert art music, but everything from marching bands to bebop, film music to field hollers, symphonies to theater songs—in short, music of every genre, spanning well over 200 years of America's history and cultural heritage"—would be woefully insufficient.[54] If Schuman's ideas on how to expand the anthology were passed over in the short term, in the long term the development and philosophy of New World Records reads as though Schuman himself could have written it: "Through the production of over 400 recordings some 700 American composers have been represented. In an industry obsessed with million-unit sales and immediate profits, New World chooses artistic merit as its indicator of success."[55] As with the Dance and Drama Divisions at Juilliard, a good number of people have Schuman to thank for the visionary concepts behind New World Records.

At the same time that he was writing the Rockefeller report, Schuman was approached to see if he would be willing to serve as president of the MacDowell Colony. Ever since he received the MacDowell Medal in the summer of 1971, he had been on the lookout for a way to serve the artists retreat. But taking the role of president was not an option. In typical Schuman fashion, he created a new reality. He wrote to J. Russell Lynes, who was retiring from the post:

> I have made the proposal, which I know you have heard, that of giving the presidency to a "man of affairs" and creating the position of Chairman, which would supply the art front. In any case, I would not undertake even to be chairman without a clear understanding of precisely what my contribution could be. I have come to have great interest in the Colony and a deep belief in its effectiveness. It is for this reason that I would not accept any office without its duties being carefully delineated and within the scope of my available time.[56]

That was January 7, 1974. Two weeks later, he wrote to a friend: "Don't be shocked if you hear that I've been named Chairman of the MacDowell Colony."[57] And he was so named.

One of the first proposals Schuman made as chairman of the MacDowell Colony was to move the Medal Day ceremonies from rural New Hampshire to bustling New York, but the staff felt that this would not only offend the local townspeople but would also undercut the goal of making people aware of the unique place of the retreat in the world of the arts. Schuman quickly offered a counterproposal: give Martha Graham, who was turning 80 in 1974, a special medal, do it in New York, and (most important of all) bring the discipline of dance within the orbit of the MacDowell Colony.[58] He also persuaded Agnes de Mille to give the presentation speech for the medal. "All in all, I think the addition of choreography into the good works of the MacDowell Colony is an important step. I can report that Martha was most enthusiastic when I spoke to her on the telephone."[59] Choreography hasn't been completely added to the good works of the famous retreat—Merce Cunningham received the MacDowell Medal in 2003 as an Interdisciplinary Artist—but Schuman's attempt to make it a part of the colony resonates with his creation of the Dance Division at Juilliard and his hopes to found a modern dance constituent at Lincoln Center.

In a fascinating coincidence, Schuman was inducted into the American Academy of Arts and Letters in the spring of 1974, shortly after becoming chair of the MacDowell Colony. "Between 1923 and 1992, each Academician, upon election to the Academy, was assigned a particular chair. Fastened to the backs

Martha Graham, Schuman, and Agnes de Mille, on the occasion of Graham's receiving the MacDowell Medal, November 7, 1974. Photofest.

of each chair is a plaque listing the name and date of tenure of each previous occupant. The names of members who were no longer alive in 1923 were also included, creating an unbroken lineage of occupation going back to 1904." Schuman was assigned Chair 7, the chair once held by Edward MacDowell.[60]

Just as he had created an opportunity for Graham to be recognized, so Schuman continued to work on behalf of his fellow composers. The rotation at the MacDowell Colony for the MacDowell Medal was such that, in those days, a composer received the medal every third year. Copland (1961), Varèse (1965), and Sessions (1968) preceded Schuman as honorees. His first year as chairman in 1974 coincided with the award going to another composer, and he was delighted when the selection committee recommended that Walter Piston receive the medal. Schuman wrote to share the good news with Piston, who, not understanding the seriousness of the honor and experiencing a slow recovery from hip surgery, initially declined it. Schuman impressed upon Piston the prestige that attended the medal and suggested that, while the assembled guests in Peterborough would enjoy Piston's presence, his possible absence was not grounds for declination. Piston gladly accepted, and Michael Steinberg delivered the speech in Piston's honor and received the medal on his behalf.[61] Piston thanked Schuman for his role in the honor. "My fan mail indicates that the MacDowell ceremony was a most brilliant occasion, and that Michael outdid himself. It was good to have him. I am shortly getting back to health but still have bad days. Coming to Peterboro [*sic*] would have been risky, to say the least. Thank you for understanding." Piston died on November 12, 1976.

Schuman also continued to assist composers and musicians in other ways. He worked to get a Rockefeller Foundation grant to study the feasibility of consolidating office facilities and support services for nonprofit music organizations in New York City.[62] He tried to persuade the staff of the Chamber Music Society to program Harris's Piano Quintet in honor of Harris' seventy-fifth birthday.[63] He wrote letters of support for Otto Luening and Lester Trimble as they sought funding from the National Endowment for the Arts.[64] He wrote checks to help support Jean Morel, the conductor Schuman had brought to Juilliard, who was dying and impoverished.[65] He commended *Saturday Review* music critic Irving Kolodin for his piece on Barber and Menotti, and his letter praising Kolodin's article was printed for others to see. "In my view, Barber is not sufficiently appreciated as a composer. I believe that one reason is to be found in the mistaken belief that musical vocabulary—qua vocabulary—has a quality of its own. Many listeners and evaluators confuse expressive intent and achievement with methodology and aesthetic predilection."[66]

All of these were for persons and institutions he knew. He also reached out to those he didn't know. He congratulated Donald Martino on winning the Pulitzer Prize in 1974, calling him "a fine composer" and wishing him many years of productivity.[67] Martino was stunned by Schuman's gesture. "To receive a note from you, a composer whose music I have known and admired virtually all my adult life, gives me more pleasure than you can possibly know. I think the greatest joy I have had in the Pulitzer Prize has been the good wishes extended to me by so many people, many of whom, like yourself, I have never met."[68]

And he had his quirks. He wrote to the lottery commissioners of both New York State and Connecticut, encouraging them both to create a subscription system so that one could play the same numbers regularly without having to remember to buy tickets. When Connecticut inaugurated such a system, Schuman seemed to take credit for its implementation. "As you are no doubt aware, I made this proposal about two years ago and at that time I was told that there were some obstacles. It is good to know that they have been overcome, so I feel this is a most constructive move." He then requested several applications for friends and for himself.[69] He also urged his publisher to contact the creators of a feature film based on Robert Katz's 1967 best-selling book, *Death in Rome*, to suggest that they use his Ninth Symphony as background music for the film. The Italian producer Carlo Ponti had other ideas. The movie, *Rappresaglia* ("Retaliation"), went by the title *Massacre in Rome* in the United Kingdom and the United States, starred Richard Burton, and has original music by Ennio Morricone.[70]

Schuman had spent so much time from the middle of 1972 to the middle of 1974 trying to fund *Nineteen Seventy-Six* that he may not have seen at the time how important were the other things that happened in that same period of time. Perhaps he was not responsible for bringing the subscription lottery system to Connecticut. But he was steering the MacDowell Colony into a future of greater financial security and widening artistic influence. He provided the catalyst for the Rockefeller Foundation to move forward on an ambitious project whose reverberations would be felt for decades. He composed a multi-stylistic work that used music of the past to presage the music of the future. And he leaned on his friend Marty Segal in ways that would further prepare Marty for artistic leadership. It was an impressive stretch of work by any calculation. And the bicentennial still loomed in the near distance.

THIRTY-ONE

BICENTENNIAL FIREWORKS

The National Symphony Orchestra began to celebrate the bicentennial of the United States two years early. Conductor Antal Doráti had the inspired idea of opening the 1974–75 season with "a 'statement' about the symphony as an art form in America. I will program three American symphonies which I consider true, masterly examples of different styles. . . . I'm not aware that anything similar has been arranged in the past and think it will be a very fitting thing to do in the capital city which is in the present day so much damaged by—you know what!"[1] President Richard Nixon had been present at the inaugural concert of the orchestra in its new concert hall in 1971, with the Schumans as his guests that evening. But on the October 1974 evening that Doráti made his orchestral statement, the presidential letter of congratulation read to the audience came from the desk of Gerald Ford. Nixon had resigned the presidency in disgrace, Washington was dispirited, and Doráti believed that an opening program of three American masterpieces would bolster the hearts and spirits of the nation's capital buffeted by a crisis never before seen in American history.

Doráti later referred to the concert as "the '3 thirds' program": he performed the third symphonies of Roy Harris, William Schuman, and Aaron Copland.[2] Harris and Schuman were able to be present for all of the concerts; Copland arrived in time for the second performance. *Washington Post* music critic Paul Hume reported that the audience rose to its feet after the performance of each man's symphony, that the composers came to the stage to thank the performers and the audience, and that the playing of the Harris and Schuman was particularly fine. Hume marveled especially about Schuman's youthful work. "The quality of music throughout this symphony comes with incredible impact as you remember that the composer was 31 when he wrote it. The perceptions and ingenuity with which that quality is expressed matches the originality of thought. The finale is a triumph."[3] In a follow-up story, Hume tried to get the three composers to divulge their bicentennial plans. Copland, whose last compositions date from 1973, said that he wasn't saying. Harris, in his typical grandiose way, spoke of composing "a large score for teen-age band and chorus, a work which will tour abroad" and of traveling to Moscow at the invitation of Tikhon Khrennikov, head of the Union of Soviet Composers, to record all 14 of his symphonies as "a gesture of friendship and also it is being done there because they are not being recorded here." (The recordings were not done there, either, and the "large score" was either left incomplete—if it is his *Bicentennial Aspirations* for band—or was never begun.) Schuman was not as self-aggrandizing as Harris, but neither was he as taciturn as Copland.

> My lips are characteristically unsealed. I wanted, for sentimental reasons, to write my Bicentennial works for Washington. I am writing my 10th Symphony, which is being called "The American Muse." Then I am writing a work for chorus and orchestra. And finally I am revising my "Casey at the Bat" to be done as a cantata.... Calling my new symphony "The American Muse," I am dedicating it to the accomplishments of all American artists in our 200-year history.[4]

The sentiment, in this case, was for Schuman's country, the land that he loved and to which he had pledged his allegiance. A decade earlier, he had contemplated the meaning of patriotism as he considered working with poet Roy Villa.

> Can one sing the glories of homeland without being nationalistic or chauvinistic? I think so. In my view, there is no reason to confuse the hope of a United Nations with the identity of one's own national habitat. Is it naive still to believe in the American dream? I don't think so. Our stated code I, for one, still find inspiring, and I believe that despite all the horrors perpetrated in our country, we do keep moving ahead. Perhaps three steps backward for every four forward. But still some advance.[5]

Schuman's indefatigable patriotism resulted in the propaganda works of the early 1940s. It influenced his decisions to compose *The Mighty Casey* in 1951 and *Credendum* in 1955. It emerged in his witty orchestration of Ives's *Variations on "America"* in 1963. It compelled him for over a decade to attempt to find a way to create his *Nineteen Seventy-Six*. Now, with that evening-length work out of reach, he envisioned a trilogy of works that would "sing the glories of homeland," two of them quite literally: a new work for chorus and orchestra and a cantata version of his opera. And the premieres of all three were to take place in the nation's capital in 1976.

But just as the program of the "3 thirds" was a pre-echo of the National Symphony Orchestra's bicentennial festivities, so Schuman had already tipped his hand on some of the celebratory sounds he was creating for the orchestra. A week before the program of the "3 thirds," some of the musicians from the orchestra had joined Doráti to play for the dedication of the Hirshhorn Museum and Sculpture Garden of the Smithsonian Institution, and on that evening they premiered Schuman's *Prelude for a Great Occasion*. Doráti had contemplated adding the *Prelude* to the all-Schuman concert he was planning for

1976, but Schuman strongly counseled against it for a very simple reason. "When I decided to do a more extended piece for Hirshhorn, I used materials that will be in the first movement of Symphony No. 10, although treated quite differently. For this reason, the Hirshhorn piece should not be on the W. S. program you are planning."[6]

Like Marty Segal, Joseph J. Hirshhorn (1899–1981) was a successful immigrant whose path crossed Schuman's. He made his money first as a stockbroker and then as an investor in various mining interests. He used that money to collect contemporary art and displayed much of it at his home in Greenwich, Connecticut. (His property was on the east end of John Street; the Warburgs lived on the west end; and Schuman lived south of the Warburgs.) Hirshhorn was persuaded to give his collection to a museum that would bear his name in Washington. Hirshhorn exhibited his own patriotism in his remarks at the museum's opening. "It is an honor to have given my art collection to the people of the United States as a small repayment for what this nation has done for me and others like me who arrived here as immigrants. What I accomplished in the United States I could not have accomplished anywhere else in the world."[7]

Schuman thought that Hirshhorn would only require a fanfare of approximately three minutes—the manuscript bears the title *Ceremonial Fanfare for a Great Occasion*—but because it was the only music to be heard as part of the formal ceremonies, Hirshhorn requested a longer piece, so Schuman crossed out *Ceremonial Fanfare* on his manuscript and wrote *Prelude* instead.[8] Over the first minute or so, the music spits out stammering chords, gathering them into trademark triad piles (see the end of the Seventh Symphony) before the material for the Tenth Symphony takes over. In the *Prelude*, a dialogue between the upper and lower brass is cut by 40 percent for the similar section in the symphony, and the triad piles of the beginning reappear in the *Prelude* before the main ideas resident in the symphony are repeated. Like both the Seventh and Tenth Symphonies, the *Prelude* ends in a blaze of E♭ major, and, even more so than in either of those two works, the percussion is very active, including quick repeated strikes of the tam-tam and a peal of chimes at the end of the work. Schuman worked fairly quickly on the piece, agreeing to the terms of the commission on May 14, 1974, and finishing the work less than five weeks later, on June 24.[9] And he hoped to do a different kind of double-duty with the *Prelude*. Not only did he use its materials in the Tenth Symphony but he also offered the *Prelude* to Cincinnati Symphony Orchestra conductor Thomas Schippers as a substitute for the bicentennial fanfare that Schuman reluctantly agreed to write for that orchestra but never essayed.[10]

If the *Prelude* was a warm-up for the Tenth Symphony, other events helped Schuman reconceive the choral piece he hoped to write for the bicentennial. With no new text at hand to set, he began to consider the possibility of taking his opera *The Mighty Casey* and using it as the foundation of a work to celebrate

America. Because G. Schirmer still held the rights to the opera, he first had to receive assurances that revising the opera would not rankle his old publisher. In order to entice Hans Heinsheimer, who was still with the firm and who had worked with Schuman and Jeremy Gury on the opera, Schuman reminded Heinsheimer of another work that Schirmer could have published but chose not to—the *William Billings Overture*—and of what happened after he signed with Theodore Presser.

> Instead of the single overture, I extended the materials into three separate movements and published them under the title NEW ENGLAND TRIPTYCH. The TRIPTYCH, as you know, is an enormously popular work and has reached hundreds of performances. It could be that CASEY, reworked as a vehicle for narrator, chorus and orchestra, would have a new life.[11]

The return-on-investment Schirmer realized from *The Mighty Casey* wasn't everything that the firm had hoped for, so Heinsheimer was supportive of Schuman's attempt to do for Schirmer what he had done for Presser.

First, however, Schuman would have to obtain Gury's permission to rework the libretto. The two men had been in touch earlier in the 1970s, but their conversation had almost nothing to do with their joint creation. Gury had become involved in the world of broadcasting, and with Bill and Frankie's work in public television, the three of them discussed a project that Gury revealed further in an article for the weekly magazine *Broadcasting*.[12] All three agreed, according to Gury, that "the telecommunications field is heavily mined with destructive, but innocent appearing, objects. . . . Every time I think I have the problems solved, monstrous new ones appear." Gury also held out hope that one of his latest efforts, the *Four Canticles*, would inspire Schuman to set words Gury felt were much more poetic than the libretto he concocted for *Casey*. "I have made some changes; I now feel they should be done—even with solo flute."[13]

More than a year elapsed before Schuman actively sought to get together with Gury, this time to discuss the cantata that "should give 'Casey' a new and different life and, who knows, may even result in more performances of the opera."[14] Schuman called Gury and set up a luncheon meeting, only to have to call a second time to postpone it. Gury was at turns regretful and furious at what he perceived as Schuman's slight. Not only had Schuman raised Gury's hopes for a meeting but he also never accepted Gury's vision of what true art is, beginning with Schuman's compromises (in Gury's eyes) on the *Casey* libretto and furthered through his cold response to the *Canticles*. Gury's outburst so troubled Schuman that he wondered if Gury had all of his wits about him.[15] Gury chose to grant Schuman permission to recast the work, but he sent that news to Heinsheimer, not to Schuman, and, from that point on, Schuman went forward without engaging Gury. By the end of 1973, Schuman could see that "the project looms bigger now because I am thinking of a 'Fantasy-Overture' which could be performed as a separate orchestral piece as well as the prelude to the new cantata." To do all of this work, he needed Heinsheimer to send him a copy of the orchestral score, the vocal score, and the arrangement of his "Choruses from *The Mighty Casey*" so that he would have all of the authoritative, corrected scores at hand.[16]

He also needed to find someone to underwrite the cantata. The $20,000 from the National Symphony would cover a new symphony and the cantata, and that is how Schuman thought he would proceed at first.

> On the '76 commission, I told Denton [William Denton, managing director of the National Symphony Orchestra] that I was at work on my Symphony No. 10, which I hoped would be a short symphony of approximately 20 minutes, since I was intrigued with this particular challenge. I felt confident—given no unforeseen circumstances—that I could complete this work well in time for the '76 celebration, and further, that "Casey at the Bat" would also be ready. I am less certain about a further work for the celebration which would be for soloist and orchestra.[17]

Doráti was "more than happy" to hear about Schuman's designs on the Tenth Symphony but was far less happy about the cantata. "The other part, namely the Casey piece, gives me a vague feeling that it may not be the happiest choice, for the rather unartistic reason that the Board which has commissioned you on an unprecedented scale would expect a new piece of yours rather than a new edition of an old one."[18] Schuman turned again to Segal, first to see if Segal would approach Philip Morris a second time on Schuman's behalf—"since the scope of the project is reduced to the one work . . . the commissioning fee would be half the sum that we had originally discussed"—and then to pursue Segal's proposition of having the Martin E. Segal Company commission the cantata. "I hope you'll understand my reluctance to accept your generosity. I can only view it as an act of personal friendship, for I cannot imagine that it was a professional decision that your company would normally make."[19]

Another corporate decision made it unnecessary for Schuman to take Segal up on the offer. In May 1975, a press release heralded the creation of a new foundation.

> Norton Stevens, President of Norlin Corporation, the nation's largest musical instruments company, announced today the establishment of the Norlin Foundation, chartered to "help people discover, develop and enjoy their capacities to the fullest and specifically to recognize, encourage and reward exceptional achievement in music." "To that end, we are proud to announce the election of Dr. William Schuman as Chairman of the Board of Trustees", said Mr. Stevens.[20]

Stevens had been at the helm of the Norlin Corporation since 1962 and had deliberately expanded and diversified the company's core businesses, so much so that there seemed no longer to be a core business.

> It is a Panamanian holding company with headquarters in New York, and [in 1977] it grossed $238 million on a product line that includes Ecuador's best-selling beer, a clutch of high-technology switching devices that turn up, among other places, in commercial and military jet planes—and an assortment of electronic organs, pianos, Moog synthesizers, drums and guitars that made Norlin the biggest manufacturer of musical instruments in the United States.[21]

Stevens's core interest was music, and he had quietly been at work on the foundation well before the press knew anything about it. Certainly Schuman knew something about it. On November 21, 1974, Stevens sent Schuman three separate letters: one informing Schuman of the establishment of the Norlin Foundation, its budget of $100,000 for the coming years, and Stevens's invitation to Schuman to be a founding trustee and chairman; a second granting Schuman a commission of $25,000 to compose a "symphony" based on *The Mighty Casey*; and a third asking Schuman if he would consider serving as a consultant who would create "a record with program notes which will be interesting and informative for Norlin's many audiences" at a fee of $20,000 plus expenses for an assistant of $5,000.[22] (Schuman hired Robert Sherman, his coauthor of the Rockefeller report, as his assistant.) As with Videorecord earlier in the decade and Lincoln Center the decade before, Schuman was called upon again to help steer a new organization on its maiden voyage. And if Schuman's course for the first two institutions revealed that he saw farther into the future than the institutions could afford to see, the Norlin outing would reveal the opposite, as Schuman and Stevens developed a myopia for what lay ahead for music-making in the American home on the cusp of the digital revolution. But that was a few years down the road. By the end of 1974, Norlin's commission brought all of Schuman's ducks in order for the downsized bicentennial offering: a compact symphony, a cantata on baseball, and a third work either for soloist and orchestra (what Schuman told Doráti in January) or for chorus and orchestra (what Hume reported after the "3 thirds" concert).

The symphony was the first of the works Schuman completed. Before he had completed any of the movements, he wrote to Doráti to express his vision of the work, its character and its intent.

> I mentioned to you some words of John Adams which I may quote in part in the program book. These are as follows: "I must study politics and war, that my sons may have liberty to study mathematics and philosophy, geography, natural history and naval architecture, navigation, commerce, and agriculture, in order to give their children a right to study painting, poetry, music, architecture, statuary, tapestry, and porcelain."

He chose not to use the Adams (which he slightly misquoted) in his program notes; nor did he fully divulge the rationale behind his dedication. But just as the idea of Doráti's symphonic statement was conjured up at a time when national morale was ebbing, so Schuman articulated the raison d'être of the symphony as the ramifications of Watergate were leading inexorably to Nixon's resignation.

> It seems to me that the remarkable development of American artists in all media—music, visual arts, letters—has been truly remarkable. I want to dedicate my symphony to America's artists because I believe that they have been a complete success. They have been as diverse as the democracy that gave them birth, and their achievements have found world acceptance. At this time, when there is so much reason for doubt and re-evaluation, it is good to be reminded of positive achievements. This is especially true where our artists are concerned, and Americans have every reason to have deep pride and satisfaction in their creations. For these reasons I am subtitling my Symphony No. 10 AMERICAN MUSE.[23]

His program notes, which are not reproduced in the printed score, are more nuanced, referring to the national celebration.

> My Symphony No. 10 is subtitled American Muse because it is dedicated to our country's creative artists, past, present and future. At this time of our Bicentennial celebration, when we are assessing so many facets of our national being, we should derive enormous satisfaction from the incomparable treasure given to us in the short span of two hundred years by America's creative men and women of letters, music, visual arts and all forms of theater. This work, then, is for my colleagues, with gratitude for their achievements and joy in the identification of being one of them.

With outer movements expressing optimism and a "largely contemplative second movement," Schuman hoped that "over all, the music emerges as an expression of affirmation."[24]

The first movement, which is an elaboration of the *Prelude for a Great Occasion*, is traceable to an even earlier work: *Pioneers!* of 1937. Schuman had wavered earlier in the decade on whether to reissue "this extremely youthful work of mine [that] makes some pretty grueling demands, especially on the tenors."[25] Given that *Pioneers!* had never been a top seller—recall that the original publication was without a piano reduction of the eight-part chorus—and that Presser already had newer Schuman works to sell, one can understand the practical decision not to reissue the work. Given Schuman's proclivity in the first half of the 1970s to recycle older works, one could have almost anticipated that Schuman would find another use for the choral piece. In his notes for the Tenth Symphony, Schuman attributed the decision to use *Pioneers!* to Frankie. "My wife's instinct proved fortuitous, for recalling Pioneers and experiencing again its optimism was precisely what I needed to get me started on the symphony. Optimism is, after all, an essential ingredient in understanding America's beginnings."[26]

The manuscript of the Tenth Symphony does not reveal if the first movement preceded the Hirshhorn *Prelude*, although his August 5, 1974, letter to Doráti, indicating that "I am in the middle of the second movement of the symphony," suggests that, after the completion of the *Prelude* in late June, July was spent on the first movement.[27] Whichever work was completed first, Schuman seemed to know, as he did with the *Anniversary Fanfare* and *In Praise of Shahn*, that he was working on two pieces at once.

Doráti's familiarity with the *Prelude* made it difficult for him to appreciate the first movement. He shared his initial impressions of the symphony with Hume. While Doráti was convinced that the work "promises to be a tremendous contribution to America's <u>third</u> century," he told Hume of his reservations as well as his strong positive reactions.

> As I am studying this work, the first marvel that emerges before me is its second movement, an "Adagio" [of] almost Brucknerian concentration and haunting, gripping beauty, a slow movement the like of which I can hardly remember in American music, and in music of our century anywhere.
>
> The third movement (the finale) is witty, complex and brilliant. Of the first movement I must tell you later,—my silly illness set me back in my studies and I don't have a clear enough picture of it in my head—although, curiously enough, it is the simplest of the three movements of the symphony, almost nothing more than an extended and highly sophisticated "fanfare." But that's just it—it *must* be more than that—so back to study!![28]

When Doráti shared the same assessment with Schuman, with a slightly more cautious criticism of the first movement, Schuman reached all the way back to his first big orchestral success.

> I think the first movement will work very well despite the finality of its ending. (When Symphony No. 3 was first played, the same comment was made to me about the brilliant close of the first part.) In the instance at hand, I believe that the fanfarish nature of the concluding section gives a feeling of something more to come. Further, since a principal theme of the first movement is introduced in the last movement, I think there will be a convincing sense of wholeness to the entire work. But the performances will tell us.[29]

(The *Pioneers!* motif returns in the last movement.) Neither man wrote to the other about the *Prelude for a Great Occasion* and its place in this history, although Schuman could have reminded Doráti that the conclusion of the *Prelude* was much more final and that he had truncated the ending of the first movement to help set up the "deeply brooding second movement," "the quiet, introspective slow movement" that the reviewer for the *Washington Post* felt was the most compelling part of the work after a first hearing.[30]

The lone review in a prominent paper points to how little coverage the all-Schuman concert received. Hume wrote a Sunday focus piece on Schuman, making it clear to all that "the National Symphony Orchestra is honoring Schuman as it has no other composer."[31] But Hume allowed *Post* junior critic Joseph McLellan to review this one-of-a-kind concert. The *New York Times* did not bother sending down a critic. Schuman's major creative efforts to honor and celebrate the nation he loved were being ignored. And when the Tenth did make it to New York three years later, John Rockwell in the *Times* could barely disguise his disdain.

> The Schuman was commissioned for the Bicentennial celebrations. It is a big, serious score for a large orchestra, and at times—its Larghissimo middle movement, especially—it works up a real modicum of eloquence.
>
> It is also determinedly, blissfully old-fashioned; Mr. Schuman writes his music in calm contradiction of nearly every avant-garde musical fashion of the last 40 years. Perhaps, with the perspective of a century or two, such matters will seem unimportant, and Mr. Schuman will emerge as a truly important 20th-century American composer. Right now, however, his anachronistic qualities sound as if he simply hasn't been *listening* to the music of his time.[32]

Joseph Machlis cheekily wrote to Schuman: "The idiot who passes for a critic on the Times was sure you wrote the way you did because you had not heard what's being done these days. Did it never occur to him that you wrote the way you did precisely because you HAD heard what people are doing nowadays?"[33] But both Machlis and Rockwell were missing what was happening in American music. By 1979, the year of the Tenth's New York premiere, Schuman's music was neither *avant* nor *arrière*, and there were plenty of indications that, if anything, he was in the mainstream of a new current of American music. But in his old age he had little luck in getting his works heard beyond the occasional performance. He tried to get the Tenth recorded at least twice, once in 1979 for CBS Records with "a major orchestra and conductor," and in 1988 with Leonard Slatkin and EMI.[34] Slatkin did eventually record the Tenth, but for RCA, and it was released in 1992, the year of Schuman's death and 16 years after its premiere. But despite the lack of understanding and dissemination that the Tenth endured, it had a "very deep meaning" for Schuman.

> A layman would ask, doesn't every work have a deep meaning for its composer? My answer would be, at the time of completion and composition, yes, but after a time—at least for me—there are some works that I feel close to and others about which I have many reservations. The Tenth, for reasons I can't and needn't try to explain, evokes a strong visceral response.[35]

Though he was invited by at least one other orchestra to write an eleventh symphony, Schuman refrained from doing so.[36] The Tenth thus stands as his last symphonic testament, one that apparently spoke to the composer at the same time that it spoke for him.

The other two bicentennial works influenced each other. Schuman knew from the beginning how *Casey at the Bat* (his name for the cantata) would sound, since he was not doing a major recomposition of the score. The materials, in fact, give no clear indication on how much work Schuman himself did on reorchestrating the work. A surviving piano-vocal score of *The Mighty Casey* appears to be the source for most of the cuts and small emendations. A notebook contains an additional 20 pages of larger changes and additions (including the E♭-minor wail at the end of the cantata), and in the piano-vocal score Schuman directed the editor, Thad Marciniak, to those pages in the notebook that needed to be inserted at various points. Marciniak, however, operated under the assumption that he was hired to create an arrangement. As a result, according to Schuman, "he added things which I had not anticipated or wanted. . . . I should say that I respect Mr. Marciniak as a musician and the trouble arose because he thought I wanted an 'orchestration' rather than an expanded transcription."[37] Marciniak later recalled Schuman's words when he saw the addition of contrapuntal lines and obbligatos: "This is not my composition anymore." Marciniak scaled back his approach, expanding the orchestra, retaining Schuman's choices of instruments and inner voices, and completing the entire work for Schirmer and Schuman.[38]

Beyond the issue of editorial choices lie the larger facts that the cantata was both more popular in tone than the original *Casey* and a reworking of a quarter-century-old work, and those considerations drove Schuman's choices for the other remaining bicentennial work. He said as much to Doráti.

> Because of the nature of "Casey" following intermission, with its lighthearted Americana aura, and because Symphony No. 10, directly preceding intermission, will be such a positive and optimistic work (speaking of the two outer movements), I have found myself more and more wanting to open the concert in a wholly contrasting manner—in short, with an introductory work that would embrace a different aspect of the American Bicentennial celebration.[39]

Schuman's choice of text was the MacLeish poem he had come across in the first half of 1973.

> "The Young Dead Soldiers" [was] written during one of the darkest hours of World War II. "Everything was going wrong," Archie recalled. "The Russians were biting back, we'd lost the Philippines," he'd heard of the terrible death of young Richard Myers, son of his friends from Paris days, Richard and Alice-Lee Myers—the lad burned in the cockpit of his plane—and then a note crossed his desk asking for something to spur the sale of Victory Bonds. With this tangle of ideas running through his head, he wrote "The Young Dead Soldiers" in about seven minutes one morning. Not until he'd finished did he realize that he had created a poem, not a prose piece.[40]

It is unclear how much of the Myers story Schuman knew, but on the top of the second page of his program notes for *The Young Dead Soldiers*, he wrote "Lieutenant Richard Myers," in keeping with the dedication that appears with the poem.[41] Schuman clearly was driven in composing the work, telling Doráti in early June 1975 that he was "completely taken with the composition of this work and fully expect that it will be finished by Labor Day."[42] Labor Day that year fell on September 1; Schuman finished *The Young Dead Soldiers* on July 12.

Unlike the notes for the Tenth Symphony, those for *The Young Dead Soldiers* said very little about the music. Instead, Schuman chose to write about the "riches of Archibald MacLeish" and to reprint the poem. He did add a word to the title of MacLeish's poem: "Lamentation." "The lamentation begins with a wordless introduction, a vocalese [*sic*] by the soprano, followed in imitation by the French horn. The setting is then ushered in by the ensemble sounding a sustained chord, a harmony characteristic of the whole piece." That six-note chord, consisting of the first five notes of the D♭ major scale superimposed over an A♮ bass, recalls the sound worlds of *The Witch of Endor* (with its nine-note opening chord) and the Ninth Symphony (with its 12-note closing chord), with their substitution of sonority for tonality. For most of the work, the soprano and French horn entwine with dissonant counterpoint as the ensemble of eight woodwinds and nine strings mirrors the unfinished nature of the poem—"We leave you our deaths. Give them their meaning."—by refusing to offer any recognizable tonal center until the very end, when the soprano sings the final words, "Remember us," ten times as the music works its way to a quiet E-major conclusion. The withholding of a tonal referent until the very end gives *The Young Dead Soldiers* much of its feel as a lamentation; it also reflects Schuman's larger compositional canvas. If the *Concerto on Old English Rounds* and, to a lesser degree, the Tenth Symphony drew from deep wells of consonance reinterpreted for modern times, *The Young Dead Soldiers*, like *The Witch of Endor* and the Ninth Symphony, suggests that there is also a time in the twentieth century for unremitting dissonance. That all the works in the 1970s now find their way to a major-key final cadence reflects Schuman's own journey from polytriads through controlled dissonance to his own remembrance of harmonies past.

If 1976 was, for Schuman as a composer, "perhaps the most exciting [year] of my life," April 1976 was perhaps the most exciting month.[43] Not only did it feature the world premieres of *The Young Dead Soldiers*, the Tenth Symphony, and *Casey at the Bat*, but a few weeks after the National Symphony Orchestra performances Donald McInnes joined Leonard Bernstein and the New York Philharmonic in the New York premiere of the *Concerto on Old English Rounds*. April also saw the continuation of Schuman's hourlong radio programs, *American Muse*, which began airing on March 30 and were heard every Tuesday evening at 9:05 P.M. on WQXR-FM in New York City for 20 weeks.[44] The script for the first program—which featured Harris's Third Symphony, Copland's "Hoe-Down" (from *Rodeo*), Barber's Adagio for Strings, and the Ives–Schuman *Variations on "America"*—shows that the series was in many respects an outgrowth of his bicentennial compositions.

> The Bicentennial is a celebration, and what I intend to do here is really to celebrate our music. . . . I intend to share my own enthusiasms, calling your attention to some profoundly significant works together with some lighter fare—works I happen to enjoy and admire, and which I feel serve to define what we mean when we speak of "American" music. My comments will not be technical or scholarly; I'm not offering a course in musical analysis or music history, but simply discussing some fascinating music—among friends, as I see it—entirely in terms of its impact on the listener—its visceral, emotional and intellectual effect as felt by both the "trained" and "untrained" listener.[45]

Robert Sherman was his producer at WQXR, and Richard Freed helped Schuman write the scripts. Schuman also introduced Freed to a new dessert whose fat content was, in its day, revolutionary. "You may have helped enormously in my battle with obesity: the ice cream spoiled me, and since Haagen-Dazs is hard to find here (and to spell, possibly), I may be able to do without the stuff [ice cream] altogether."[46]

The radio series was surrounded by four other bicentennial efforts, two that were brought to term and two that were stillborn. Some of the people who commissioned the *Dedication Fanfare* for the Saarinen Arch in St. Louis were after Schuman to open a conference to be held there in June 1976 on "Americanism in American Music." He worked on his contribution from mid-October of 1975 until the conference, finding the assignment both extraordinarily difficult and highly stimulating. His essay, "Americanism in Music: A Composer's View," pleased conference organizer George McCue to no end, so much so that his letter reads almost as a paraphrase of Schuman's radio program introduction. "You succeeded beyond our most hopeful dreams in keynoting the ensuing discussions, but even more important you made a beautiful and substantial statement of the point of trying to identify American characteristics in our music—as well as the point of not becoming obsessed with this for any reason but to produce, appreciate and support all music that speaks to our feelings."[47]

Another speech-turned-article resulted from the induction of John Philip Sousa into the Hall of Fame for Great Americans. Schuman served on the Board of Electors of the Hall of Fame from 1964 on, and beginning in early 1969 he advocated for Sousa's admission. The induction itself did not take place until August 1976, though Schuman throughout his tenure on the board had been lobbying for Sousa. He was delighted, therefore, when the American Bandmasters Association asked him to deliver the induction speech.[48] Schuman turned to Howard Shanet, chairman of the Music Department at Columbia University, for many of the particulars of Sousa's career, and Schuman credited Shanet for "our Sousa speech" both privately and publicly.[49] Yet Shanet could not have known the depth of Schuman's affection for Sousa's music. Schuman wrote that same year in an article for a publication targeting musicians:

> I can recall many, many years ago, when I was a young professor, giving a course on how to listen to music. For a whole year my students were trained in the art of virtuoso listening. I remember the final examination; the students had no idea of what work I would be asking them to analyze. They were astonished when, after a full year devoted to the great symphonic masterpieces, the examination consisted of a request to analyze the *El Capitan* march of Sousa. For, within this single composition, one finds all the attributes, the niceties of form and all the other qualities that are expected of high-level music making.[50]

If personal appearances and the print media were hospitable to Schuman, broadcast media proved less so. The original idea for the WQXR *American Muse* programs was to sell them to other radio stations; there is no evidence that any other station picked up the series. Both Schuman and Walter Neiman, the president of WQXR, had floated the idea of doing a year's worth of programs, but *American Muse*'s lack of commercial success sealed its fate.[51] So Schuman turned to other media. He hoped to use the resources of the Norlin Foundation to launch a new film series that would include films about the following subjects: conductors; electronic music; jazz, featuring Dizzy Gillespie; amateur music making; and chamber music.[52] While the film series did not get far past the dream stage, a possible television series had more momentum. Schuman wrote to Peter M. Robeck, founding president and chairman of Time-Life Films, which co-produced, with the British Broadcasting Corporation, such milestones as *The Ascent of Man* and *America* and created *Masterpiece Theatre*.[53] In his 1977 proposal for *William Schuman's Musical America*, Schuman imagined that "each hour's program would contain from one-half to three-quarters of actual music" and "all the performing musicians employed in the series will, of course, be American."

A year later he tried again to ignite interest in his idea. "If the arts have been inadequately represented on television, it is because they have been treated mostly on an ad hoc basis. If this series is successfully realized, there will exist a continuity in the presentation of one of the most unusual aspects of American life."[54] Not only did Schuman envision hosting the series but he also planned on composing his own score. He quipped to his good friend Frederik Prausnitz: "The only other person I can recall who ever did his own music in his own picture is Charlie Chaplin. Charlie may be a better composer than I am, but I'll be funnier."[55] Despite his strong feelings about what he perceived as television's abandonment of the arts in favor of the demands of the marketplace, Schuman eventually decided against pursuing the television show, in part because he would have to rely on "a superb scholar and writer who has the time to devote," and no such collaborator appeared.[56] Even the print media were not universally supportive of Schuman's efforts. He wrote an article that he titled "Great American Music Snub of '76" that chronicled the lack of American compositions being programmed by the major symphony orchestras in the bicentennial year.

Schuman, the man who could place just about any article he could dream up when he was president of Lincoln Center, was snubbed himself, as the editors at the *Times* chose not to run his article.[57]

The many bicentennial fireworks that Schuman lobbed from his pen showed the depth and breadth of Schuman's love for America. His grand act in celebration of Copland's seventy-fifth birthday showed the depth and breadth of his affection for him. It was Copland who had brought Schuman into the MacDowell Colony orbit in 1971. Four years later, it was Schuman who sought to use the resources at his command to honor Copland. The artists retreat planned a major birthday celebration for Copland in New York, with Schuman vetting Terry Sanders's film *Copland Portrait* to see if it would be an appropriate contribution to the festivities (he and other directors chose not to use it) and asking choreographer Robert Joffrey to create a work using Copland's Duo for Flute and Piano as its basis (Joffrey turned Schuman down).[58] These efforts to construct an evening's program were dwarfed by Schuman's announcement that he wanted to establish a legacy. Writing to Conrad Spohnholz, general director of the MacDowell Colony, Schuman presented his grand idea.

> It is my great pleasure to inform you that the newly-formed Norlin Foundation has voted to make, as its initial grant, a contribution to the MacDowell Colony to inaugurate Norlin Fellowships for composers at the MacDowell Colony. The Foundation wishes to establish these Fellowships in honor of Aaron Copland on the occasion of his 75th birthday.[59]

The total outlay of the grant, to be administered over the course of several years, was anticipated to be $250,000 and was created to enable composers to come to the retreat.[60] A decade later, the Norlin Foundation was disbanded, at which time Schuman informed the colony that the foundation had fulfilled 80 percent of its 1975 pledge and requested that the fellowships be renamed the Norton Stevens Fellowships. "On behalf of all the Directors of the Norlin Foundation I wish to reiterate the satisfaction that we have had in honoring a great American composer at the Colony, which meant so much to him during his formative years, and with which association the Foundation has had such a happy and productive collaboration."[61]

The grandiose gesture. The great announcement. The sustained effort. The unreached goal. The same tattoo had sounded throughout most of Schuman's life, so its appearance in the bicentennial pieces, in the media attempts, and in the Norlin Foundation fellowships hardly surprises. What is surprising is how, in the years after the bicentennial, Schuman started throwing off fewer sparks. He was beginning what he would call the "years of completion."[62] The effort required to produce the bicentennial pieces had left him exhausted. He was having more and more health problems, from an "insulted hip" that plagued him for at least six months (from October 1975 to March 1976) to the doctor ordering him not to attend the Santa Fe Chamber Music Festival in the summer of 1976—a festival held partially in his honor—because of the city's altitude.[63]

Intimations of mortality were also encroaching from outside. He had delivered the eulogy for conductor Fritz Reiner (1888–1963) in part because of the prestige of the office Schuman held at the time, one of the most powerful men in music remembering one of its most important conductors. Contrast this with his eulogy for Goddard Lieberson (1911–77), who met Schuman when they were young composers in the mid-1930s and who, through his work for Columbia Records, introduced the American public to the long-playing record and the cast album. Reiner's eulogy was studded with quotes from Albert Schweitzer, Theodore Roosevelt, William Shakespeare, and Learned Hand. Lieberson's had only one quotation but one that likely meant much more to both men. Schuman called upon his beloved Walt Whitman.

> Youth, large, lusty, loving—
> Youth, full of grace, force, fascination.
> Do you know that old age may come after you
> With equal grace, force, fascination?[64]

Old age was coming after Schuman, too. He had commissions in his compositional quiver, including the one from the Chamber Music Society of Lincoln Center he accepted back in 1971, but nothing as all-engrossing as the three large shards from the fractured *Nineteen Seventy-Six* appeared on the horizon. The next few years would find Schuman hard at work, but on projects with lower profiles. His own step, physically and compositionally, was slowing. Yet Schuman the composer would soon learn again how to do something he hadn't done in decades. He would rediscover the joy of dancing.

THIRTY-TWO

REFLECTIONS AND RUMINATIONS

By his own admission, Schuman had a "ghastly habit" of working and reading when normal people were asleep. In 1941, in "the middle of the second year of his Guggenheim Fellowship, he called a friend and complained, 'I finished my Third Symphony this morning at 5 A.M. I didn't know what to do, so I started my Fourth Symphony.'"[1] Thirty-three years later he praised former Sarah Lawrence colleague Maxwell Geismar for his Twain anthology (probably *Mark Twain and the Three R's: Race, Religion, Revolution—and Related Matters*), parts of which he read between 3 and 4:30 A.M.[2] He sent author James Gollin a fan letter, saying that *The Philomel Foundation* (1980) "is a God-send to this insomniac. At the moment I am on Page 160 and am moving slowly because I don't want to get to Page 204 too quickly."[3] So it is no surprise that his first two post-bicentennial compositions found Schuman working at an hour when the owl and the lark greet each other.

Neither composition was meant for wide distribution, as both were written for performances at intimate parties. And both drew upon Schuman's long history with counterpoint. The first, *A Round for Alice*, was written for a benefit concert honoring Alice Tully held on March 15, 1977, and sponsored by the Chamber Music Society of Lincoln Center. The round was not listed on the program for the evening—the organizers wanted to surprise Tully and the audience—and "Schuman's wittily brief contribution" was "sung beautifully by three ladies from [Abraham Kaplan's] Camerata Singers."[4] The manuscript not only gives the day of composition—February 7, 1977—but also the time: "composed 4–6 A.M."[5] The text is probably Schuman's own.

Who knows ev'ry piece we play?
Alice Tully. Our fair lady knows.
Gracious, charming connoisseur, sing we la lee la lee love,
Lee la lee la lee love. Sing we love.

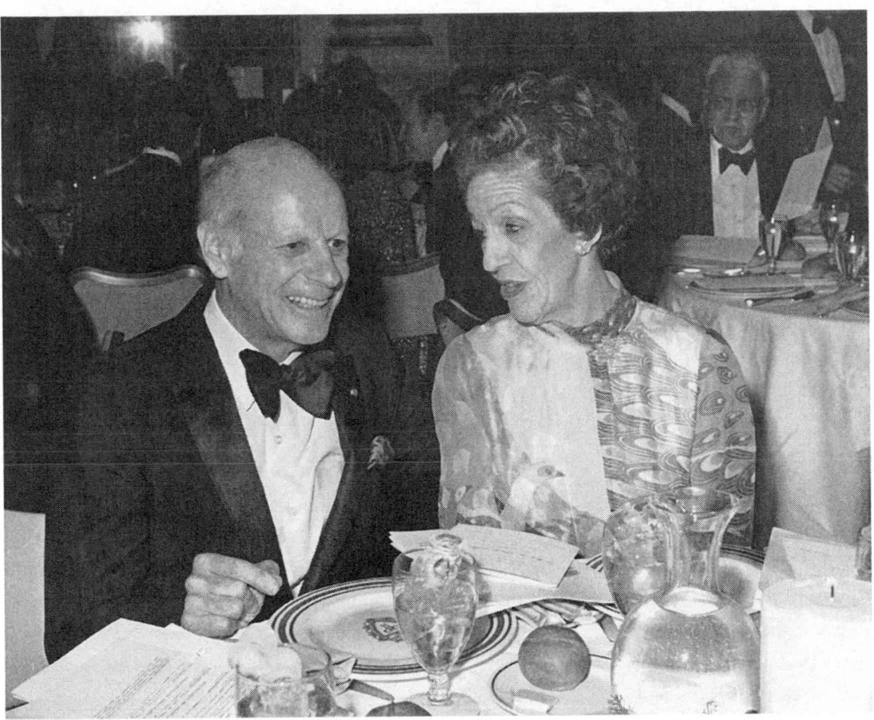

Schuman and Alice Tully. Photo by Henry Krupka of D'Arlene Studios, Inc. © C. Krupka.

The three-part round with a slower coda is unusual in at least two ways. First, each idea is five measures in length; perhaps this was Schuman's subtle way of memorializing Alice Tully by making the phrase lengths mirror the number of letters in her name. Second, the meter and tempo indicate that this E♭-major round is a waltz. Schuman was no stranger to the dance; some of his early Tin Pan Alley songs were waltzes, and the third movement of the Quartettino for Four Bassoons is a waltz. But extended works in triple time are uncommon in mature Schuman, with one notable exception: Merry's aria, "Kiss Me Not Goodbye," which Schuman had just revisited when he recast *The Mighty Casey* as *Casey at the Bat*. Here, in this *Round for Alice*, Schuman wrote the first of several compositions where triple meter makes a prominent appearance.

The second party piece is also a round in $\frac{3}{4}$ time. Two days after the party for Alice Tully, Schuman was awake at 5:25 A.M., finishing *A Round for Audrey*. His sister's birthday was on March 26, and the text celebrates the accomplishment of another woman in his life, but this time with a bit more humor.

Cheerful, cheerful grandma,
Lovable, lovable mother, mother, mother, mother, mother,
Doting wife and charming aunt and bossy, bossy sister.
Happy birthday, sweet Audrey. Many, many, many more.

Friends and family sang the round at Audrey's birthday party, and Schuman indicated on the score that they needed to be careful with this two-part round (with coda). "N.B. Folks—If you start too fast you'll get in trouble at m. 7 & 11" (the second and third "mother" are set to sixteenth notes).[6] Inasmuch as it is an echo of sorts of the Tully round, its mien as a waltz is unsurprising. Waltzes in the more serious works following these album leaves imply that his rediscovery of triple meter was not an accident.

Schuman's easy humor in these homages to Alice and Audrey takes a heartier turn in two musical tributes to male friends. Schuman had known Leonard Feist for decades. Feist had taken over the popular music publishing firm that his father, Leo, had begun in the 1890s—"You can't go wrong with a Feist song"—and on the occasion of Leonard's seventieth birthday (October 29, 1980), Schuman contributed to a roast of Feist, which was as much a chance for Schuman jovially to hoist himself on his own petard as it was for him to skewer his friend.

> [Leonard] constantly tells me that if he had been my publisher, I would have had many more performances and would not now be living in poverty on Park Avenue. There are other problems, too.
>
> Leonard, as everyone knows, is a natty dresser, a fact that he continually presses on me through criticism of my appearance. He believes that I wear the same clothes for years, that my ties are either too narrow and too long or too wide and too short, that they don't match my shirts, that the suits don't hang well, and he suspects me of patronizing cut-rate clothiers. Naturally, I don't like hearing these observations just because they are based on fact. . . .
>
> The best of Leonard is really his beautiful wife with her winning ways; she—Mary, that is—and my wife—Frankie, that is—and I often spend lovely evenings together in the theater, in restaurants, and in the country. On all of these occasions Leonard has been present and, speaking for the three of us, we have not minded at all. . . .
>
> I am pledged for life to another publisher who is also your friend and everything I write belongs to his firm. It is therefore, more than an idle gesture for me to offer you a new work which I dedicate to you with all performing rights in perpetuity.

The *Ode to Leonard* consists of three whole notes—a D♭♭, a B♯, and a C♮—with the following "Directions to performer": "The music should begin inaudibly at as fast a tempo as possible followed by a long decrescendo and accelerando. The pitch levels should be at the performer's discretion within the stated intervals."[7] Schuman's "composition" also pokes fun at aleatoric and formless pieces of the 1950s, performance art such as Fluxus from the 1960s, and other experimental approaches to music that Schuman found unconvincing. How strongly his *Ode* should be read as criticism of these movements is impossible to determine based on the *Ode* alone, but the absurdity of his work hints at his opinion of such art.

More "mainstream" in its approach as well as in its humor was Schuman's contribution to a 1987 *Festschrift* in honor of musicologist H. Wiley Hitchcock.

> It was never my plan to attempt a learned essay, but I did want to send you some special WS music which I had hoped you would find noteworthy.
>
> In the grand tradition, I searched your two names for letters which could form a theme. You have three C's and one E. I progressed only to the opening statement (enclosed) because it seemed fated for symphonic length.

Schuman then took the four notes and deployed them in conscious imitation of the motto from Beethoven's Symphony no. 5 in C minor, using some of the same "techniques" from the Feist *Ode* by introducing accidentals to add variety. "The length of this message and the affectionate irreverence of its beginning are both in inverse proportion to the debt our native composers—past, present, and future—owe to you for what you have accomplished."[8]

(Schuman wrote a similar musical signature "for A.C. [Aaron Copland] con amore," with a tune comprised entirely of A's and C's set above the lyric, "I never get tired of singing your praises."[9] And he contemplated writing a piece for Antal Doráti, who had become the music director of the Detroit Symphony Orchestra in 1977. The two talked on the phone about how to celebrate Doráti's switch from the nation's capital to the Motor City. "My mind has already hit upon an idea for my little fanfare. I won't tell you much about it except that Detroit will be in the title and the notes D and E will be used. Should you decide to program both my Third and Casey it would be great to open with my little birthday piece for you and follow it with the Symphony, and Casey after intermission."[10] As with the Schippers/Cincinnati request, the "Detroit Fanfare" ended up becoming one more of Schuman's unrealized curtain raisers.)

The Hitchcock tribute, coming a decade after *A Round for Alice*, was one of the last shavings from Schuman's composition workbench that was created in honor of a particular individual. But from the *Concerto on Old English Rounds* forward, many of Schuman's works were written with particular performers in mind. Schuman brought soprano Rosalind Rees to Doráti's attention, suggesting that the conductor engage her both for *The Young Dead Soldiers* and *Casey at the Bat*. His choice of instruments for the piece he was writing for the Chamber Music Society of Lincoln Center reflects the spell two young charismatic performers had cast upon the composer. And the concert work for French horn and the various iterations of "The Lord Has a Child" in 1980 and 1981 were the result of requests that individuals made for Schuman works.

In the case of the Chamber Music Society commission, his thoughts about writing a sextet in which violist Donald McInnes could perform soon gave way to a smaller and more unusual ensemble, but one that still included a prominent role for the viola. The decision to include the flute came from Schuman's interactions with flutist Paula Robison, who was a founding Artist Member of the Chamber Music Society. Robison had asked Schuman for a work she could premiere. While he could not bring himself to commit to writing something for flute and orchestra, Schuman assured Robison that the work he was contemplating for the Chamber Music Society "will give you a starring role."[11] Robison was so much at the forefront of his mind for the work that he wrote to conductor Leonard Slatkin in the spring of 1977 about a piece the two of them had discussed for Slatkin's orchestra. That piece, Schuman said, would have to wait until he completed the "present commission for a chamber music work (it will probably be a quintet for flute and strings) which I hope to complete this summer. [He completed the work in January 1978.] Following this, I have accepted a commission to compose a work for solo French horn (N.Y. Philharmonic) and orchestra, which will be my principal work in the summer of 1978. [He completed the work in September 1979.]"[12] By the end of August 1977, Schuman had settled on the instrumentation and the derivation of his chamber music piece, writing to Frederik Prausnitz that "I am at work again with a composition based on Orpheus With His Lute. I think I am calling it 'In Sweet Music', subtitled 'Serenade on a Setting of Shakespeare for Flute, Viola, Voice and Harp'. The text is top flight WS and I trust the music will be top flight WS—the analogy ends."[13]

He interrupted his work on *In Sweet Music* to compose a five-page memorandum in which he gave his thoughts about the Chamber Music Society on the occasion of its tenth anniversary. He praised the professional staff (Norman Singer, executive director; and Charles Wadsworth, artistic director) and congratulated himself and the other board members on the fact that "the concept of variegated programs covering a wide gamut of literature, performed by splendid resident artists with adequate periods of preparation, has been not only realized but enthusiastically received." He did, however, have "one minor point to be commented upon and one major problem to be solved." Schuman did not want the activities of the society to hinge upon the energies of the artistic director alone, so he encouraged his fellow board members that, "if there are programs which the Society wishes to undertake that Charles feels he cannot manage, then we must give him the assistance that he requires."

Schuman was even more concerned with the neglect he felt the society had shown American music. He asked Arthur Cohn—"composer, author, conductor and authority on chamber music"—to prepare a list of works that the Chamber Music Society might consider programming. Implicitly and explicitly, Schuman was calling into question the society's emphasis on commissioning new works from American composers and thinking that, in doing so, it was serving American music. "When we speak of American music, we erroneously think of the commissioned works rather than the large body of splendid music that already exists, much of which would be highly palatable to our discerning and conservative audiences. For example, the String Quartet #4 of George Chadwick would prove to be a delight."[14] Schuman's interest in older American chamber music was piqued by the Vox Records series on the American string quartet, in which the Chadwick appears. He also brought to Wadsworth's attention a newer work "not included in the Vox set": William Bergsma's Fourth String Quartet, which Schuman made available to Wadsworth via a cassette tape. Schuman described to Bergsma his futile attempts to get the quartet programmed. Bergsma responded: "How can I thank you? I'm overwhelmed. I can only think how kind Brahms was to Dvorak, and people like that."[15] In the midst of fulfilling his own commission for the Chamber Music Society, Schuman tried to expand the American repertoire by securing additional performances for works whose premieres had passed. Only one Schuman chamber music work (the Third Quartet) appeared on Cohn's list of 34 works by 30 composers. As with the Naumburg recording prize, Schuman may have benefited from the program he was promoting. But other American composers would have benefited as much if not more, and Schuman's lifelong practice was to point out to everyone the wealth of great music that American composers had produced.

Schuman's own new contribution to the chamber music repertoire gave both the flutist and the violist much to do, with the former using the alto flute and piccolo as well as the standard flute over the course of the composition. The harp for Schuman was something akin to the piano, an instrument he used infrequently and at times unidiomatically, but the harp writing in *In Sweet Music* is notable for a passage in which the composer allows the performer to choose the pitches contained within parameters that Schuman determined. While its effect is far from that of Cage or Earle Brown, the introduction of chance shows that Schuman was listening to and reading about the music around him. (In his program notes for *In Sweet Music*, Schuman wrote that "in composing the harp part, I had the considerable advantage of sympathetic editorial guidance and encouragement from the distinguished American harpist, Pearl Chertok.")[16] The treatment of the voice is conservative in comparison to the kinds of vocal writing Cathy Berberian and others made famous, but it, too, marks an advance in Schuman's conception of the voice as an instrument akin to the other players in the ensemble, so much so that Schuman and the Chamber Music Society sought and obtained a waiver to allow them to enter *In Sweet Music* for the Kennedy Center's Friedheim Awards, which had previously disqualified pieces that incorporated vocal texts but allowed pieces with vocal parts of instrumental character. *In Sweet Music* contains both, and its failure to win a Friedheim Award at least had the result of clarifying the rules for submission: that year's jury declared that "works including voice do not fall within the definition of 'instrumental' chamber music."[17]

Harold Schonberg continued to express his growing antipathy toward Schuman's music. He wrote in the *New York Times*:

> Basically the score is a setting of Shakespeare's "Orpheus With His Lute," but the words are used only at the end. Before then the mezzo-soprano has to sing vocalises and nonsense syllables. There were some sweet, lyrical things in the piece, but there

> also was a good deal of mechanical padding. Schuman never has been a distinguished melodist, and his inspiration seemed to give out after a short while. At least [Jan] De Gaetani, using her voice as another instrument in the ensemble, made a personal tour de force out of the piece.[18]

All Harriett Johnson could say in the *New York Post* is that "space limitations prevent a discussion here of the work, itself," while Bill Zakariasen for the *Daily News* aligned himself more with Schonberg, calling the work "slight" and "unpretentious."[19] But Schuman's colleagues had more favorable things to say about *In Sweet Music*. Bergsma hailed Schuman's accomplishment and was particularly impressed with how the new work was indeed that: new.

> It's a wonderfully inventive and loving treatment of material you have lovingly worked before. (I may horrify you by confessing that I have used the cello Meditations to show off Schuman to graduate students.) The newest translation, for so small a force, is richer than I could have imagined. The fancy you show—and the strength—is virtuoso composition at its best.[20]

His old colleague Norman Lloyd came to a rehearsal and wrote to thank Schuman for allowing him to hear "a beautiful, moving work—brooding, yet joyous and marvelously put together. The inventive instrumentation always *sounds*—you get a tremendous amount of mileage from such a small number! . . . Again many thanks for the beautiful sweet music."[21]

Getting *In Sweet Music* onto a disc initially proved to be a challenge. Schuman approached Nonesuch Records, but they turned him down, citing a glut of new music albums that the company was already committed to release.[22] With the addition to his work list of the song cycle *Time to the Old* a year later, Schuman had enough new works for solo vocalists to create an entire album devoted to this niche of his catalog, and those two works joined *The Young Dead Soldiers* on a 1980 release by Composers Recordings, Inc. (CRI). But the constant struggle to find an outlet for recordings of his own music gave Schuman the impetus to reenter the fray for other composers, and the 1980s would find him once again involved in visionary projects to help record the American repertoire.

Schuman was never single-minded about where money should go, and while he spent much of his lifetime in pursuit of recording opportunities for himself and his American composer-colleagues, he also served composers in other ways. The 1975 $250,000 Norlin Foundation gift to the MacDowell Colony went to composers; so did a 1978 $300,000 CBS Foundation grant Schuman helped corral on behalf of the American Academy and Institute of Arts and Letters. Named after the late Goddard Lieberson, the fellowships that the grant enabled go to "young composers of exceptional gifts." The academy and institute also administer the Richard Rodgers Awards for Musical Theater, which "subsidize full productions, studio productions, and staged readings in

New York City by nonprofit theaters of musical plays by composers and writers who are not already established in this field."[23] Rodgers gave $1 million to underwrite the award in 1978, and in both his case and in the case of the Lieberson grant, the idea "for directing the Richard Rodgers Production Award and the Goddard Lieberson Fellowships our way [i.e., to the academy]" came from Schuman.[24] According to Ted Chapin, "Dorothy Rodgers always credited/blamed (depending on her mood) Bill for steering that money in that direction."[25]

Schuman also continued his perennial role as emcee at various celebrations for his colleagues. The most prominent during this period was his role as host for a nationwide broadcast honoring Leonard Bernstein on his sixtieth birthday. Schuman related to the audience that he had first met Bernstein 40 years earlier.

> If you ask me what Lenny was like then the answer, with hindsight, would be exactly what you might have expected:
>
> What now is wise was then precocious
> What now is erudition was then promise
> What now is mastery was then technique
> And what now is wit, charm, brilliance was then wit, charm, brilliance.

Schuman's panegyric ended with naming Bernstein "an authentic American hero . . . a new breed of American hero—an Arts Hero. . . . Sixty is not old and for conductors, who work into their 90's, it is barely past adolescence. This then the first, we confidently hope, of many more birthday appreciations by all of us fortunate enough to be here in your time."[26] Bernstein was deeply moved and said so in a brief, handwritten thank-you note.

> Dear Bill:
> You were fantastic on Friday night. As always. Only more so.
> I love you & thank you—
> Lenny
> 28 Aug '78
> (I only wish I deserved your praises . . .)[27]

Copland received similar praises from Schuman. The Lotos Club, of which both men were members, gave a state dinner in honor of Copland's seventy-eighth birthday. The speakers that November evening were Harold Clurman, Copland's roommate in Paris during the 1920s and one of the founders of the Group Theater; Vivian Perlis, musicologist and founder of the Oral History American Music project at Yale University; and W. Stuart Pope, president of Boosey & Hawkes, Copland's publishing house. It was one of the last times Schuman had the delight of serving as master of ceremonies at a Copland birthday event. When the eightieth came around, Schuman wrote to Copland to express his dismay.

> This will be the first time I have missed an important birthday of yours for thirty years! In fact, it's the first time I haven't had the great joy of being Master of Ceremonies at the official celebration. But, believe it or not, even your junior seventy-year-old colleagues have birthdays, and the New York Philharmonic is doing my Ninth just when I should be with you, celebrating.
>
> Whatever I have said over the years in the way of singing your praises is nothing compared to the constantly increasing admiration and affection I feel for you as our greatest American composer.[28]

Schuman considered it a privilege to live in Bernstein's time, to work in Copland's shadow. And as old age began to overtake them all, Schuman did his best to stay in touch with them all. Roy Harris proved to be one of more intractable cases. Schuman had called Harris on his eightieth birthday (in 1978), but "the young lady who answered the phone said that you and Jo were asleep, having just returned from an exhausting RH celebration in Oklahoma." Under separate cover Schuman sent Harris the recording of the *Concerto on Old English Rounds*, whose liner notes include an interview with Phillip Ramey, during the course of which Schuman praised Harris's *Symphony 1933* and Third Symphony. "I had another wonderful opportunity of expressing my admiration for you."[29] Harris never answered, and a year later Schuman wrote again. "When I was elected a member of the American Academy a few years ago I was appalled to find that you were not a member. It gave me the greatest pleasure to set about changing this situation and I was more than gratified that this inequity has at long last been rectified and that you are now a member of the Academy."[30] In both letters, Schuman expressed his desire to hear from Harris, but no answer was forthcoming from Bel Air, California, where Roy and Johana lived and where Roy was dying. He passed away on October 1, 1979.

Four days before Schuman lost one of his composition fathers, he lost his only direct composition son. Schuman had been working with Andrew Imbrie to see that Seymour Shifrin was elected to the American Academy and Institute. They were too late. Schuman wrote to Shifrin's widow, Miriam: "The brilliant young student that I met so many years ago at the High School of Music and Art developed into a truly remarkable man and artist. The pleasure and stimulation that I had from our long association remains a vivid and cherished memory."[31]

Several of his close musical colleagues were going through passages of their own. Morton Gould was finally beginning to shed his reputation as a slick producer of quasi-classical gruel. "You have always been handicapped as a serious composer because of your great success as a popular composer. While this is unfair, I believe it has prejudiced an appreciation of your extraordinary gifts."[32] Schuman appreciated those gifts, though he wouldn't live to see how honored Gould would become.

Schuman and Roy Harris.

Schuman did outlive his two major conducting champions, first Koussevitzky, then Ormandy. Both men had unprecedented tenures at the head of their orchestras: Koussevitzky retired after 25 years with the Boston Symphony; Ormandy led the Philadelphians for 44 years. After Ormandy announced his decision, Schuman wrote to express his wonderment. "You have been very much in my thoughts these past weeks. I simply cannot believe that there will ever be a Philadelphia Orchestra without you at the helm. By giving up some of your obligations you will have greater strength to extend your active career by years, and for this reason, and this reason alone, I am happy that you have made your decision."[33] Schuman's letter in May 1979 expressed hope and not reality, for Ormandy's post-retirement career was relatively brief, as he died in early 1985 at the age of 84.

Schuman's letters to and from Samuel Barber during this time make for some of the most poignant reading. Barber had been diagnosed with cancer of the lymphatic system in 1978, and between his chemotherapy treatments and his failing health, he was less and less able to socialize or compose.[34] Schuman attended a concert by the American Composers Orchestra, a one-year-old ensemble dedicated to American music, on whose program Barber's *Souvenirs* joined works by Silvestre Revueltas, Sydney Hodkinson, Charles Tomlinson Griffes, and Ezra Laderman.[35] He wrote to Barber, telling his colleague about his impressions. "I was so sorry not to get to see you at the American Composers Orchestra concert. I always enjoy Souvenirs and, for that matter, just about everything you write. Earlier this season, when I heard the broadcast of Vanessa, I was struck again with its extraordinary beauty. Those last pages, especially, are among the finest of the operatic literature."[36] Barber was touched. "You have always been so kind about my music which I don't forget. In fact, to turn the tables, I know I will never be able to write a crescendo such as you have in your Third Symphony, about which I have been jealous for years."[37]

Now, near the end of Barber's career, Schuman found himself once more substituting for Barber, just as he had done with Christopher LaFarge and the failed opera project at the beginning of their careers. In early 1980, Schuman sent Barber one of his most recent works. "Last year Frank Taplin [president of the Metropolitan Opera] asked me if I would compose something for Mrs. Belmont's 100th birthday celebration since your original plans to do so did not materialize. The result was the irreverent but affectionate nonsense enclosed, which I send to you with warmest greetings and which I hope will amuse you."[38] Eleanor Robson Belmont (1879–1979) had founded the Metropolitan Opera Guild in 1935, and the celebration of her contributions to the Met began in her hundredth year. (She died seven weeks shy of her centennial birthday.) It is doubtful that Barber's efforts would have had as much charm, humor, and insouciance as Schuman's *XXV Opera Snatches* for solo trumpet, which he completed on Christmas Day of 1978. The manuscript twice identifies the work as *XV Opera Snatches*, and Schuman crossed out his first version of the fifteenth snatch—the "Bridal March" from *Lohengrin*—suggesting that he may have originally intended to end the piece with an extended version of the Wagner excerpt. Instead, he added ten more snatches from the operatic repertoire. In fact, Schuman began his *XXV Opera Snatches* with a nonoperatic work: the "March of the Priests" from Mendelssohn's incidental music to Jean Racine's *Athalie*. Perhaps the misdirection was deliberate; the remaining snatches are generally recognizable to any hard-core opera buff, so maybe Schuman meant to disorient by beginning outside of the expected operatic canon. Whatever the motivation for the Mendelssohn—might he have originally intended to end with the "Wedding Chorus" after the "Bridal March"?—*XXV Opera Snatches* is at turns witty and moving with its unexpected juxtapositions of odd operatic bedfellows (e.g., "Un bel dì vedremo" from *Madama Butterfly* is preceded by the main waltz tune from *Der Rosenkavalier* and followed by "The Ride of the Valkyries"). Belmont, who couldn't attend the celebration, received a tape of the performance and sent Schuman a telegram congratulating him. One of the Guild potentates who was there also effused over Schuman's success.

> Your operatic mosaic performed at the Met Guild Luncheon honoring Mrs. Belmont was an enormous hit! An enchanting composition, a musical canvas, brilliantly conceived.

> A memorable musical journey conjuring up a treasure trove of recollections. Wonderfully innovative. We all adored it and many were wondering how, when, where they could hear it again. Hopes were expressed that it would turn up on tape, for home consumption. Bravo![39]

Notwithstanding the lusty reception the *Snatches* received at its premiere, Schuman himself was dissatisfied. He shared his frustration with conductor Gerard Schwarz, who was also a first-rate trumpeter, about this work for unaccompanied trumpet.

> The first trumpet of the Metropolitan Opera told me that no one player could possibly encompass this piece and when he first read it for me he kept stopping and changing trumpets. Obviously, this would be ruinous. Rather than cancel the piece I agreed to have a second trumpet which relieved him at crucial points as you see marked on the score.
>
> Question: Can this work be played from beginning to end by one performer? And, don't be too personal, for I know that you can do it. My question is, can anyone else?[40]

Schuman's bass clarinet and timpani solos extended the realm of the possible for those instruments. Unwittingly, *XXV Opera Snatches* did the same for the trumpet. And when he later turned the piece over to Paula Robison to arrange for the flute, he was bowled over by her derring-do and her "outrageous directions in the flute version of the Opera Snatches." "And now you are my favorite diva as well! What an extraordinary virtuoso performance you gave us."[41] And virtuoso performance is precisely what the *XXV Opera Snatches* demands.[42]

Schuman had one more occasion to correspond with Barber over their overlapping concerns. During Schuman's first term as chairman of the MacDowell Colony (1973–77), the MacDowell Medal had gone to Walter Piston in 1974. Virgil Thomson was awarded the medal in 1977, and there appears to be little correspondence between the two about the honor. But when Schuman began his second term as chairman (1980–83), again it fell to him to interact with the composer selected to receive the medal in 1980. That year, the selection committee had decided on Barber. "As your great day approaches," Schuman wrote to his colleague, "I don't want to burden you with yet another telephone call on the MacDowell matter. Does Gian Carlo want to do the honors next August in Peterborough? You know that I would be happy to make the presentation but it might be nice to get someone else and I could still participate by introducing the introducer. Drop me a note when you have a minute."[43] Two months later, Schuman repeated his query for information, particularly about whether Menotti would be willing to come to Peterborough. Barber allowed Menotti to answer for the both of them.

> Sam forwarded to me your kind invitation to accept the MacDowell Medal in his absentia. Needless to say, I would have felt honored to have been able to do so, but

> August 24 is an impossible date for me as I shall be working in Europe. Thank you for asking me.
>
> It is a long time since we have seen each other and I think it is high time you paid a visit to either Charleston or Spoleto, where I would love to have you as my guest.[44]

Charles Wadsworth accepted the medal on Barber's behalf. That fall, Barber's health took a turn for the worse. Schuman visited Barber during Barber's final stay in University Hospital in New York City and probably attended the New Year's Eve concert in the hospital at which the pianist John Browning performed. Browning later told Frankie that "Bill's generous loyalty was so deeply moving to all of us."[45] Barber died on January 23, 1981, a little more than five months after he was awarded the MacDowell Medal.

The cycle of twilight events in Schuman's life after the bicentennial find a reflection in the poems to which he was drawn for a song cycle. Schuman had heard from Ursula Eastman of G. Schirmer that soprano Phyllis Curtin was "most impressed" with *The Young Dead Soldiers*, which her student Cheryl Studer performed at Tanglewood in the summer of 1977. She reminded Schuman that the two of them had talked at a gathering at Claire Reis's home two years earlier to celebrate Copland's seventy-fifth birthday. "You uttered a promising word to me about songs but also needing texts. Since then I have kept that in my mind." Remembering that conversation and reflecting upon *The Young Dead Soldiers*, Curtin suggested that Schuman look at MacLeish's 1954 *Songs of Eve* for possible inspiration. "There are 28 of them—all short and many of them seem asking for music. Ever since I've wanted to tell you. The book has been all this time on my bed table, waiting. So—Ursula and the *Soldiers* lit the fire." Schuman promised Curtin that he would look at *Songs of Eve*.[46] Two months later, he related to MacLeish the impact the *Songs of Eve* had upon him.

> I greatly admire these poems, but do not feel compelled to set them to music.
>
> I am particularly taken with some of your more recent work and am wondering whether or not an effective song cycle could not be made from Conway Burying Ground, The Old Gray Couple, both I and II, and possibly one or two others, such as Dozing on the Lawn. I am not yet certain. For example, in The Old Gray Couple, II, I am not clear yet in my mind how to handle the She/He antiphonal effect since we cannot sing each time She and He. Possibly, somehow, the music can be wrought to imply this. My tentative title for the song cycle is MacLeish. I am enormously moved by these later works of yours and wondering whether you have added anything since the publication of the New and Collected Poems. How wonderful it is to re-read all of you and come upon so many old friends.[47]

MacLeish was thrilled at the prospect of a song cycle based on his late poems. "The theme of most of them is old age, or the losses of old age (<u>Hebrides</u>, <u>Mark Van Doren at the Brook</u>) or the old memories that return to old age (<u>Family</u>

Group, White-Haired Girl). Think about it and let me know how you feel."[48] Schuman loved the poems MacLeish suggested but noted that "there is a problem of references that are so clear in the reading, but less so in the hearing. . . . On the other hand, the four that I feel so strongly about, Dozing on the Lawn, Conway Burying Ground, and The Old Gray Couple, #1 and #2, may suffice for the cycle. I just don't know yet."[49] Early in 1978, Schuman brought MacLeish up to date. "What wonderful days I am spending with your magnificent words. The music comes slowly, but I am not stuck. The deliberate pace is caused by the rich and varied possibilities your words command. Be patient and maybe by the late spring I can report better progress."[50]

Late spring should have found Schuman shifting his compositional energies to the New York Philharmonic horn piece that had been commissioned in 1977, but the muse seemed to abandon Schuman for much of 1978. He completed *In Sweet Music* at the beginning of the year, then filled the remainder of the year with false starts and unfulfilled realizations for the MacLeish songs and the horn piece. He supervised Jon Goldberg, conductor of the Endymion Ensemble, in creating a chamber music reduction of *A Song of Orpheus*, which premiered that November. He told Goldberg, "Thinking about the season to date, one of its nicest occasions by far was my association with you," but some years later he confided to Lukas Foss that he didn't think Goldberg's version worked all that well.[51] Goldberg's efforts paid off in a second collaboration between the two men, as Schuman decided to return to his 1947 ballet score for *Night Journey*, which had never been published. He retained the original chamber-music orchestra of nine strings, four woodwinds, horn, and piano, which was initially a concession to Martha Graham's budget but now had the benefit of appealing to ensembles such as the Endymion. (For the film version of the early 1960s, Schuman had written additional sections for the opening and end credits and indicated in a copyist's score that the number of strings was to be increased.) He further chose to cut some material that worked with choreography but was repetitive in the concert hall. These changes led to an unusual phenomenon in Schuman's later years: he saw *Night Journey* recorded not once but twice after its publication.

Choreographic intimations also haunted the uncomposed horn piece. Anthony Tudor wrote to Schuman in the early fall to see if he could entice Schuman into writing a work that Tudor could use for the stage. Schuman was intrigued but somewhat cool to the idea, telling Tudor that "I can not really launch a musical work calculated both for concert and ballet use unless I have from you the aural atmosphere you seek, the timings you envision and those marvelously suggestive Tudor descriptions for emotional climate." He went on to tell Tudor about the Philharmonic commission, which, by January 1979, Schuman had tackled in earnest. "I am finally into the horn piece sans choreography. But, I still do want to compose a dance work one of these days." When the piece was completed, he wrote to Tudor again to invite him to attend the premiere, adding, "I would be intrigued to know whether you might find it tempting for choreographic purposes."[52] Schuman also wrote to Oliver Smith, one of the directors of the American Ballet Theatre, to suggest that he come to the premiere. "I still believe [the horn piece] would be an interesting score for choreographic purposes. If you have a chance to hear it, do let me know what you think."[53]

Getting from the commission to the first performance, though, required more than images of dancers. The administration of the New York Philharmonic had asked Schuman to compose a work for their principal horn player John Cerminaro. Cerminaro in turn introduced Schuman to Gunther Schuller's 1962 treatise, *Horn Technique*, which in turn led Schuman to look at Schuller's second concerto for French horn and orchestra.

> This is an extraordinary work and I can't imagine anybody ever wanting to write another horn concerto—you've said it all and exploited the instrument's potentialities in a most comprehensive manner. In addition, the concerto is an absolute model of clarity, scholarship and invention. I am so glad that I told the Philharmonic my work would not be a concerto but simply a piece that used horn as a solo. Heartiest congratulations to you on this latest impressive achievement.[54]

Schuller's treatise and concerto both worked to get Schuman's juices flowing, and no sooner had he completed the *XXV Opera Snatches* late in 1978 than he had the horn piece fully under way. By early July, he had the final bar within sight and wrote to tell H. Wiley Hitchcock about his progress. "I am deep into the French Horn Fantasy and my fantasy is that I hear it some day without blurps. This is more easily accomplished with a pencil point than the embouchure."[55] The manuscript originally bore the title *French Horn Fantasy*, but Schuman at some point erased it, and nine days after he wrote to Hitchcock, Schuman sent word to Albert K. ("Nick") Webster, executive vice president and managing director of the New York Philharmonic, that he had changed the title to:

> THREE COLLOQUIES
> for French Horn and Orchestra
> I Rumination
> II Renewal
> III Remembrance
> (played without pause)

He went on in a lighthearted manner. "Ask me how it is. In a word, stunning; or, if your prefer, beautiful or any other adjectival approach that you consider appropriate for a work of such clear genius—there I go, understating things again."[56] He had completed the horn part and the piano reduction; all that remained was the orchestration, which Schuman managed to do over the next seven weeks, and the copying of all the music by Anthony Strilko.

The *Colloquies* proved to be the last work Strilko copied for Schuman. An automobile accident that November left him unable to complete work on the *Colloquies* on his own and forced him to subcontract the work out at his own expense. Schuman seemed to grow tired of the drama that surrounded his work with Strilko, and from that point on Schuman made other copying arrangements. Strilko tried on various occasions to find favor with Schuman, even going so far as to suggest (humorously?) that "this breach of time in our musical involvement will only serve to make trouble and confusion for our respective biographers." But Schuman held firm, saying that "you know that my feeling of friendship for you is much more important than any professional collaboration. The former remains pure, but the latter did bring with it some problems which I think we can both do without."[57] So ended a professional relationship that had begun with *A Song of Orpheus* 20 years earlier.

There were no problems with the *Colloquies* from the vantage point of the principal horn player of the Philharmonic, who was now Philip Myers. (Cerminaro had left New York to join the Los Angeles Philharmonic.) Schuman wrote to assure conductor Zubin Mehta that all was under control. "When I told [Myers] that you expressed some concern about the length of the work for solo horn, I asked him if there was enough time to rest and his reply was 'More than I need.' I met Aaron Copland on the street and told him Myers' reaction to which he said, 'See what an older horn player says.'"[58] Preparations continued to go smoothly, and after the premiere in early January 1980, Schuman told Mehta what he had said to Nick Webster.

> I don't know how many premiere performances I have had in my long life as a composer, but I can count them by the score (no pun). Never have I had a more satisfying and joyous experience than this last week.
>
> Zubin was a joy to work with—caring, meticulous and imaginative, with a businesslike approach coupled with artistic involvement. He made the most of every rehearsal minute. And in Philip Myers we had, of course, a horn player who has no superior. The orchestra could not have been more responsive and cooperative.[59]

The technical demands on the instrument were nowhere near as comprehensive as those surveyed by Schuller, but Nicholas Kenyon, writing in the *New Yorker*, felt that Schuman had suitably met the demands of the commission.

> If there are to be display concertos for orchestral players, let them all be as well made, pleasing, and harmless as William Schuman's "Three Colloquies," for French horn and orchestra. . . . This work is nearly perfectly constructed, and was beautifully played by Philip Myers, the Philharmonic's principal horn. Schuman struck a happy medium between exploitation of the horn's traditional "hunting" idioms (there was a rising call in the first section which recalled the Prelude to Act III of "Lohengrin") and invention of lyrical, melodic material for the instrument. The colloquies were labelled "Rumination," "Renewal," and "Remembrance," though I daresay that "Resting,"

> "Running," and "Reclining" would have done just as well. The jolly style of the second section was attractive; the sentimental chorale melody of the final pages was a little objectionable; the fading close was masterfully controlled.[60]

Schonberg was characteristically less charitable, calling the work "representative of Mr. Schuman's compositional expertise. . . . The music is even slick. But it does not really have much nourishment. The gestures sound a bit tired and routined, and the big tune of the last movement is one of those fabricated melodies that is forgotten as soon as it is heard."[61] His colleague Edward Rothstein was a bit more sympathetic three years later when the *Colloquies* were performed as part of the New York Philharmonic's series *Horizons '83—A New Romanticism?* Mehta and composer Jacob Druckman served as co-curators of the series, and Schuman's *Colloquies* was one of the newer works on the program, though to Rothstein it sounded as though it belonged to an earlier era. "It was, in fact, an intelligently written, colorful and easily accessible work, the horn's lyrical dreaming becoming the focus for fantastical weavings of dance and disruption. But there were also times when it seemed as if the work itself lacked conviction, as if it were itself looking back, with some longing, on a lost musical style."[62]

The critics failed to address Schuman's choice of title. As with *Credendum*, Schuman chose a Latinate term that simultaneously reveals and conceals. Between whom are these colloquies, these conversations occurring? One answer would mark the French horn and the orchestra as the conversationalists. But Schuman is communicating with a musical style that was in the process of rediscovery, as the whole of Rothstein's article suggested. The opening eight-note chord that combines C♯ minor with G major sounds both vaguely dissonant and, after a five-note B♭-tinged chord answers, strangely tonal. In the middle movement of the *Colloquies* ("Renewal"), Schuman twice calls upon the waltz rhythm to carry the music forward. And the harmonies on the final pages invoke memories of a Renaissance motet, with the French horn fading away before fully resolving its downward descent into the F-major chord that, almost as an echo of the *Voyage for Orchestra*, quietly ends the piece. The music converses with all of these referents and more, for at the time Schuman was composing the *Colloquies*, he was writing to and for and about longstanding friends and colleagues whose mortality was foregrounded far more than in previous years. One was Samuel Dushkin, the violinist who commissioned a concerto he never had an opportunity to perform in public. Dushkin died in 1976; the last movement of the *Colloquies* ("Remembrance") is a free reworking of the Andantino discarded from the first version of the concerto. The circumstances of Schuman's life in the late 1970s form part of the conversations embedded in his compositions at this time.[63]

The completion of the *Three Colloquies* in September 1979 freed Schuman to resume his work on the MacLeish songs. Near the end of November, he wrote to MacLeish to bring him good news and to ask for some guidance.

> I am still with the songs and hope that my settings will do justice to your magnificent words. I am using three in the following order: Dozing on the Lawn, Conway Burying Ground and The Old Grey Couple (I). This three-song set is to be performed as a unit without pause between songs. In my view, although each song will be listed by its correct title, there should be a collective title for the set. May I turn to you for a suggestion.[64]

MacLeish responded enthusiastically to Schuman's news but failed to offer a suggestion for a title, so Schuman had to suggest one of his own. The manuscript shows that his initial idea for a collective title—*Evening's End*—was drawn from a line in "The Old Grey Couple," describing how the two go off to talk yet they don't talk and how they go to bed yet lie awake. "Their lives they've learned like secrets from each other. / Their deaths they think of in the nights alone." Schuman, however, decided on a different title and shared it with MacLeish, who apologized for neglecting to answer Schuman's earlier query. "Sorry about the overall title. Of course you should have one and *Time to the Old* is grand."[65] This line comes from "Conway Burial Ground": "Time to the old is world, is will / Turning world, unswerving will / Interval until." Schuman changed the order of the songs and recomposed the ending of "Dozing on the Lawn" to extend it slightly. A month after he told MacLeish his projected order, Schuman finished his first and only song cycle. All three songs, with their slowly turning dissonances, their long-spun vocal lines, and their halting rhythms, summon a world beyond this one where time no longer matters, if time exists at all. "It was dark in the dream where I was laid. / It is dark in the earth where I will lie" ("Dozing on the Lawn"). There is no need to measure time between dream and death, as both are equally impenetrable by the human senses.

At the cycle's premiere, *New York Times* critic Donal Henahan called *Time to the Old* "an unrelentingly somber setting of three Archibald MacLeish poems about death and dying." *Washington Post* critic Joseph McLellan offered a more probing analysis of the cycle when it was performed six years later at a concert belatedly celebrating Schuman's seventy-fifth birthday.

> Schuman's music—intensely chromatic and full of vivid dramatic hushes, pauses and terror-tinged melodic leaps—intensifies the effect of the already tense words. There are moments of calm. . . . But the shadow of death hovers in the background of each poem and takes the spotlight at the end. The music is superbly dramatic and the emotions are subtly shaded.[66]

Rosalind Rees, to whom Schuman dedicated *Time to the Old*, was the soprano for both performances. Her traversal of the songs in an all-Schuman concert at

Sarah Lawrence in February 1986, with Thomas Muraco as accompanist, was her finest performance of them all, if Schuman is to be believed.

> Without exaggeration I can say to you that this was one of the greatest experiences I have had, listening to my music. And those experiences, I hardly need tell you, have involved many, many works and hundreds of performances. Your work is never on less than a high professional level, and my association with you is a constant joy. But at Sarah Lawrence you achieved a depth of projection that realized the songs in their full potential. I can only use the word "great" in describing the occurrence. You know, too, that Frankie who was seated down the aisle from me had exactly the same reaction.[67]

Schuman, the original Pangloss (according to Leonard Bernstein), had more reason to be hopeful in the winter of 1986 than he did in the winter of 1980, shortly after he finished *Time to the Old* and after the successful premiere of *Three Colloquies*.[68] The humor of the *XXV Opera Snatches* and the rounds for Alice and Audrey stand out in stark relief from the unremittingly dour works of 1977–1979. The works of these years concerned themselves with death; the music of the 1980s would celebrate life.

THIRTY-THREE

TRIPLETS

Of all the events devoted to Schuman's seventieth birthday, none was quite as expansive as the 1980 Aspen Music Festival. Schuman sensed from the start that this Rocky Mountain celebration of his music "could become the centerpiece of the story that is being planned on the various performances that have been scheduled for the birthday year." Add the fact that he found the thought of celebrating his birthday in Aspen "endearing," and the prospect of returning to the festival after a 21-year absence—the final version of the Violin Concerto was premiered there in 1959—understandably gave Schuman a thrill.[1] The programs surrounding his birthday weren't devoted to his music alone, but the number of his compositions performed over the course of one week was prodigious: the *Three Colloquies* (this time with John Cerminaro as the soloist), *Time to the Old*, the *Symphony for Strings*, the Ives-Schuman *Variations on "America," The Young Dead Soldiers*, *In Sweet Music*, the film of *Night Journey*, *George Washington Bridge*, *Four Rounds on Famous Words* ("Haste" was omitted), *Carols of Death*, the *Mail Order Madrigals*, *New England Triptych*, and two of his concertos (piano and violin). And the day before Schuman arrived in Aspen on July 30, the New York String Quartet performed the Third String Quartet.[2] It was quite the birthday bash.

The presence of the American Brass Quintet at the Festival also spurred Schuman to add to the repertoire for brass instruments. It was more than their presence, though.

> Some months ago Bob Biddlecome [bass trombonist for the ABQ] called me to ask whether I could accept a commission to do a work for the American Brass Quintet to be performed this summer at Aspen. Unfortunately, prior commitments precluded my acceptance. The offer set me to thinking, however, that I would like to find some way of expressing my appreciation to all of you for the handsome retrospective festival you are mounting on the occasion of my seventieth birthday. A few days ago I completed

THREE PIECES FOR FIVE BRASSES
1. Ladies and Gentlemen!
2. The Lord Has a Child
3. Look Before You Leap!

These modest pieces, which are approximately 1'20", 3', and 2'20" respectively, totaling about 6'40", are being mailed directly to Bob.[3]

Schuman went on to suggest on which of the concerts the *Three Pieces for Five Brasses* might best work. The organizers chose to include the short suite on the birthday concert, which also included an 8-by-4-foot cake with an image of New York City on the top.[4] Writing for the *Aspen Times*, local reviewer Jon Busch gave a capsule review of various concerts. He had little to say about the cake and only a trifle more about the world premiere he witnessed. "The second half of the very long program opened with Schuman at his best in Three Pieces for Five Brasses again featuring the American Brass Quintet. The performance was excellent."[5]

In his notes for the *Three Pieces for Five Brasses*, Schuman informed the audience that all three modest pieces were derived from earlier works: "the cry of the circus barker enticing 'Ladies and Gentlemen' to come to the sideshows" from the *Circus Overture* (1944); "a free adaptation" of his contribution to *American Hymns Old and New* (1956); and a reworking of "Caution," the third of his *Five Rounds on Famous Words* (also from 1956), which, "while based on the original tune, is largely new music far removed from the choral setting."[6] All three movements were far removed from their original settings, but Schuman may have been right to single out "Look Before You Leap!" as the arrangement that traveled the farthest distance musically. Not only does it give up some of its character as a round but it also breaks out of its foursquare rhythm twice in the movement to engage in an unabashed waltz, one more musical fractal pointing to Schuman's reincorporation of this particular dance into his compositional aesthetic.

Though the recording of the premiere gives ample evidence that the players of the American Brass Quintet had not solved all the technical problems the *Three Pieces* posed, the audience nonetheless expressed appreciation for the suite. The witty conclusion of the final number, with its emphatic exclamation point coming after the quick rhythmic "iteration" of the last movement's title words, is a crowd-pleaser. So it is somewhat surprising that Schuman, who had contracted with Theodore Presser on July 21 to publish the new work, should write to his publisher a little more than a month later to express a change of mind. "I have decided to withdraw my Three Pieces for Five Brasses. My present plan is to make a more extended work out of the Second Movement, The Lord Has a Child. The new work will be written for full band, and I will leave open for the moment its possible suitability for brass quintet."[7] He had more to say about the withdrawn suite to Ken Godel, who would replace Anthony Strilko as Schuman's copyist.

> I think your work is first class and certainly I want to be in touch when I next have need for your services. Truth to tell, I liked your copying of my Three Pieces for Five Brasses better than the pieces themselves. Yesterday I told Bob Biddlecome that I was withdrawing them. At the moment I am doing a work for large band, but the copying will be part of the commission offered by the American Band Masters Association and the Air Force.[8]

Biddlecome followed up with a letter in which he conveyed his disappointment at Schuman's decision to withdraw the piece. "I am not going to try and get you to change your mind. I'm sure that you are the best judge of the piece in relation to why you had intended it to be. I have conveyed your greeting to the other members of the Quintet and they all asked me to please tell you how anxious we are to have a William Schuman brass quintet in our repertoire."[9]

Biddlecome and his colleagues would get their wish, and sooner perhaps than they expected, but Schuman's decision to withdraw the suite and recast the second movement wasn't driven solely by artistic concerns. He had been in discussions with representatives from the American Bandmasters Association, the same organization that had sponsored the elevation of Sousa to the Hall of Fame for Great Americans. A few days before he wrote to his publisher about withdrawing the *Three Pieces for Five Brasses*, Schuman received a formal letter on behalf of the association and the United States Air Force Band for a commission to celebrate the association's fiftieth anniversary. The commissioned work needed to be completed by January 1, 1981; the commission itself carried the fee of $5,000.[10] His decision to accept the commission not only pushed the *Three Pieces* aside but also further delayed Schuman's work for Leonard Slatkin and the St. Louis Symphony on a piece he had agreed to write the previous year that was commissioned to celebrate the orchestra's centenary.

Perhaps there was something about Missouri that caused Schuman not to produce his St. Louis commissions in a timely fashion. The various postponements surrounding the *Dedication Fanfare* (1968) had not been of his making, but now as Schuman struggled to find the materials that would serve as the basis for his new St. Louis work, he seemed to forget how indigenous Midwest music did little to inspire him. In the mid-1960s he had abandoned the idea of using a tune from the *Missouri Harmony* in his fanfare, but the greater prominence of an orchestral work—and the success Schuman had had with some indigenous New England music—led him to try again. He wrote to the director of the Missouri Historical Society, who in turn suggested Schuman contact Tilford Brooks, chairman of the School of Music at Washington University. Schuman wrote to Brooks:

> As you know from your conversation with Mrs. Frances H. Stadler, of the Missouri Historical Society, I am interested in exploring the possibility of using indigenous music from the St. Louis area in the composition I have been commissioned to write for the St. Louis Symphony Orchestra.

> My hope was to find several compositions, either folk or formally composed, which I could adapt in a manner similar to that which I followed in using the music of William Billings in my New England Triptych. If you feel that one or more of your graduate students might be intrigued with a research project along the lines I have suggested, perhaps it might be better for me to discuss the matter further by phone.[11]

Brooks put Schuman in touch with Susan Deich, who found Schuman some old Missouri tunes. He was unimpressed, finding the material "rather predictable, if not ordinary," and he told Deich that, unless "there is some reasonable chance of unearthing material of greater potential," he no longer needed her services.[12] He nevertheless imagined that his work for St. Louis would involve a chorus as well as an orchestra, and he wrote to Slatkin in April 1980—the orchestra's centennial year—to agree on a date to premiere the work. "March of 1982 sounds like a reasonable goal for me, implying as it does that the work should be in your hands for the '81-'82 season. At the moment, I have no ideas and have not been successful in finding a suitable text. In any case, we will have lots to talk about when we meet."[13]

The *Three Pieces for Five Brasses* and the new band work intervened, and the latter quickly became the vehicle for Schuman to appease the men of the American Brass Quintet. By the middle of October, he wrote to Biddlecome to tell him of his progress. "I am composing a brass quintet version as well as a version for full band of a work I have tentatively titled, The Lord Has a Child, subtitle: Variations on a Melody."[14] In fact, only the manuscript for the brass quintet version bears a completion date—October 31, 1980—and the band version is in short score, suggesting that Schuman may have worked with an editor at Presser to fill out the parts and to construct the conductor's score. With the exception of a few accompaniment figures, the two scores are identical in every feature of melody, harmony, and rhythm. Most notable about the last is that Schuman stole a page from "Look Before You Leap!" and, in the renamed *American Hymn*, altered the tune so that, for a brief passage, it could waltz.

The premiere of the brass quintet version went without a hitch, with John Rockwell's review—"the piece moves in idiom from solid Americana to a somewhat wilder style that nonetheless never betrays the composer's inherent conservatism"—placing the new work in the seeming rearguard of contemporary music.[15] In the wind band and brass quintet versions of *American Hymn*, the music makes no apologies for being doggedly tonal while at the same time the elements take flight in ways that mark the work as a product not of the 1930s or '40s, when a certain form of Americana was the vogue, but of the 1970s and '80s, when Ivesian collisions of sound worlds in the hands of Del Tredici and Bolcom became the new norm. In fact, on the same concert, the American Brass Quintet gave the New York premiere of Bolcom's Brass Quintet, "which despite its functional title is strung together from musical 'portraits' of the composer's ancestors. The device offers Mr. Bolcom a dramatically plausible excuse—if he needed one—for his normal eclecticism and colorful good cheer." Rockwell's willingness to extend the palm to Bolcom and the back of the hand to Schuman for engaging in similar musical behavior exhibits the bias that the elder Schuman had to face in his later years.

He also had to face incompetence, which marked the events surrounding the premiere of the band version. The annual convention of the American Bandmasters Association took place in Washington, D.C., that year, and Schuman's work was one of several premiere performances on the conference program that included no fewer than six concerts, four of which were given by the bands of the Army, Navy, Air Force, and Marines, respectively. The last was given *American Hymn* to premiere, and John Paynter, director of bands at Northwestern University, was given the privilege of conducting the Marine Band that evening. On the preceding day, from his hotel room at the Hyatt Regency, Paynter sent Schuman a list of editorial suggestions. His letter runs to four pages and has 37 suggestions. Schuman adopted all but four.[16] Schuman revisited the letter several weeks after the work's premiere and wrote a letter of thanks to Paynter:

> Of the approximately 40 suggestions for editorial adjustments you proposed I found virtually all of them to be practical improvements, and I am incorporating them, as you will see, in the score. I say, "As you will see", but heaven knows how long it will take the Marines and the Navy to correct the materials and forward to my publisher. I thank you wholeheartedly for these helpful suggestions, but I thank you for much more.
>
> As a veteran composer who has worked with many, many conductors over a long period of time, I rejoice always in the performing artist who is truly pleased to work with the composer in the first realization of his manuscript. You could not have been more thoughtful, cooperative and sensitive, and I was wholly delighted with what you were able to achieve.[17]

It took the staffs of the combined bands more than six months to return the materials, and when they arrived the folks at Presser discovered that they failed to include the adjustments that Paynter had recommended. Schuman was incredulous. He wrote Paynter: "Never in my entire professional life have I had so disagreeable and unsatisfactory a relationship as the one that I did not enjoy with the Air Force Band and the Marine Band! If our military is run with the same degree of disarray, no increased budgets can save us!" Schuman begged Paynter to step back "to work your magic and see that the materials are finally in acceptable shape."[18] Schuman also promised Paynter appropriate credit on the published score, an honor Paynter at first was reluctant to accept. He reconsidered when he tallied up the time he spent: "Some 150 hours of my love have gone into making the edition conform with the way we performed it with the Marine Band in Washington."[19] *American Hymn* for Concert Band bears the legend: "The composer wishes to thank John Paynter for his many useful editorial suggestions, which have been incorporated in the score."

With the commission for the American Bandmasters Association behind him, and with the premieres during the same month of the two wind versions of *American Hymn*, Schuman returned to pondering what he should do for the St. Louis Symphony. In April 1981, he wrote to Slatkin to tell him that although he had planned on composing a work for chorus and orchestra,

> I spent literally months searching for suitable text material without success. Naturally, faced with having to give up, at least for the moment, a work with chorus, I have been thinking in purely orchestral terms.
>
> Occasionally, during my long career I have had extended periods when the ideas that I sought simply were not forthcoming in a satisfactory way. Such has been the case for these past months. Now, however, I seem to be on the way to some progress.[20]

Did the premieres of *American Hymn* the previous month get Schuman unstuck, the same way that the commission from the American Bandmasters Association seemed to persuade Schuman to rethink his *Three Pieces for Five Brasses*? It is impossible to know the chain of internal events, but external ones show that what began as a slow middle movement for a suite expanded to become a ten-minute exploration for winds that, in turn, gave way to a 25-minute orchestral encyclopedia on *The Lord Has a Child.*

His program notes for *American Hymn: Orchestral Variations on an Original Melody* cover the tracks of his search for indigenous materials and make the choice of his own song sound like more of a fait accompli than the documents allow, but they accurately sketch the distance Schuman traveled from song to winds to orchestra.

> As I was contemplating the composition I would undertake for the St. Louis Centennial, The Lord Has a Child would not leave me. In my composer's ruminations I still felt the need of basing a large work on my setting of Langston Hughes. Although the present work uses some ideas from earlier versions, it is an entirely new concept, and the main body of its large form consists wholly of new material.
>
> My use of the word "melody" in the subtitle, rather than "theme", is purposeful, and a word on the subject might be helpful in an initial hearing of the composition. Traditionally, variations on a theme imply not only modifications and developments of the melodic aspect itself, but even more important, the continuation of the harmonic structure of the theme sequence. Therefore, although we may sometimes feel far-removed from the melodic content of the theme, we are sonically reassured by the consistency of the harmonic progressions and usually, too, by the length of phrases.
>
> In using the word "melody" in the title I mean to declare that all the variations spring exclusively from the melodic content.[21]

Harmony and rhythm and timbre and form, in other words, are all treated freely, with one example being the two waltz sections that occur, one a derivation from the earlier versions and the other sounding almost Sondheimesque, which is not completely surprising given Schuman's praise of *A Little Night Music* (1973) as "a classic show within the great tradition of American musicals."[22]

In November 1981, Schuman wrote to Joan Briccetti, general manager of the St. Louis Symphony, to inform her that "work is going well on the new piece, and I expect to complete my short score by the end of the year and the full orchestration by the spring of '82. . . . if my schedule holds, we will have the completed, copied score before the summer, at which time I will, of course, send it on to [Slatkin]."[23] The date of completion Schuman affixed to the manuscript is only a month later—December 7, 1981—but "completion" in this instance did not mean there was no more work to do, as Schuman's letter four days later to Briccetti reveals. "This is a happy week, for I have given the copyist the complete composition in outline with all the base orchestration in place. When he returns the score to me in one or two months, I will complete the orchestration in plenty of time to get it to our dear maestro before the summer."[24] The short score uses mostly five staves on which Schuman has indicated the disposition of the voices and the instrumentation; at points requiring more detail or that include the percussion instruments, the score expands to as many as 11 staves, and at points of lighter orchestration, Schuman has contracted to as few as three. To compose his third *American Hymn*, Schuman used up old manuscript paper, turning it upside down in order to ignore the preprinted instrument identifiers and their concomitant clefs, the latter of which he typically crossed out. Though it took Schuman more than half a year to go from the idea of revisiting his original melody one more time to finishing the short score, the materials give more than the usual evidence of second thoughts. Schuman chose repeatedly not to rewrite an entire page if he decided not to use certain measures or instructions on that page, so the short score for the orchestral version of *American Hymn* provides one of the most revealing glimpses into Schuman's methods in composing an extended work.

The correspondence also reveals that, from the start, Schuman paved the way for a recording of *American Hymn*. Earlier in 1981, Schuman's neighbor Joan Warburg decided to establish an award to honor him on the occasion of his seventieth birthday. Given Schuman's expertise in handling fundraising and endowments, Warburg allowed Schuman to assist her in setting the terms of the award and choosing the organization that would administer it. They first discussed the possibility of entrusting the capital fund to Schuman's hometown orchestra. Schuman wrote to Warburg: "In suggesting the New York Philharmonic as the possible recipient of the capital fund and the organization that would carry out the terms of the William Schuman prize, i.e., in recognition of the creation of a significant body of symphonic music, my thought was the stability and preeminence of that organization, as well as my own close association with it over many years."[25]

Before Warburg and Schuman decided on the particulars of the prize, though, another American composer received "one of the most lucrative and highly regarded awards in the world of music, the $78,500 Ernst von Siemens

Music Prize . . . on the basis of his numerous orchestral works."[26] Schuman wrote a letter to congratulate the recipient, Elliott Carter. "The success that you have had on the continent is enormously important for all those who have a deep concern for the position of the American composer." Schuman never warmed to what he charitably called Carter's "uncompromising works" and "intellectual vigor," and his not-so-subtle attempt to expatriate Carter—the von Siemens is a German prize—led Carter to respond with a correction. "Actually my work has been seldom & usually badly played in Germany, so I was as much surprised as the Munich press dismayed when the winner was announced."[27] In the United States, Schuman and Warburg worked to create an American award as lucrative and highly regarded as the European one Carter received.

Nearly a year went by before the press release went out to announce that "a $50,000 prize to an American composer for lifetime achievement, the William Schuman Award, has been created at Columbia University." Schuman, at age 71, was the first recipient of the eponymous award. The award fund of $250,000 "was established 'to recognize the lifetime achievement of an American composer whose works have been widely performed and generally acknowledged to be of lasting significance.'" (In Schuman's lifetime, the other recipients of the prize were David Diamond, Gunther Schuller, and Milton Babbitt.) The money was made available to Columbia through the Bydale Foundation, which had been created in 1965 by James Warburg; previously the foundation had made "extensive grants in education, public affairs, environmental affairs and the arts." While the press release made note of Schuman's "long and close association with Columbia University," he was dissatisfied with Teachers College while he was a student there and had sparred with the university when it twice failed in the 1960s to award a Pulitzer Prize in Music. The decision not to vest the money with Juilliard reflected the still strained relationship between Schuman and Mennin and points to a proximate reason for the choice of Columbia: the dean of the School of Arts at the time was Schuyler Chapin, Schuman's protégé at Lincoln Center.[28]

The receipt of the William Schuman Award led Schuman to write to Briccetti in St. Louis months before the premiere of *American Hymn* to help her identify funding sources for a recording. He was blunt in his suggestion. "I nominate myself. In December of 1981 I was given an award which included cash. If you were to record American Hymn, I would donate $5,000 toward the budget, and if, as I hope, Leonard would perform Symphony #10 for the other side (he gave a magnificent performance of this work with the Chicago Orchestra) I would contribute $10,000."[29] Briccetti managed to secure additional funding from the National Endowment for the Arts, which also led her to steer the recording toward works the orchestra had commissioned. Schuman bowed to the inevitable, resigned to the fact that Slatkin's rendition of the Tenth Symphony would have to wait for another time but pleased at the prospect of sharing a disc with his "honored colleague," Joseph Schwantner (1943–), whose *Magabunda* was premiered by the orchestra in 1984 and was given top billing on the recording released the following year.[30]

Schuman was not nearly as pleased with the main review of *American Hymn* when the St. Louis Symphony came to New York in January 1983 for two concerts at Carnegie Hall. Briccetti sent him the reviews.

> I was delighted that you sent the Daily News and Post, since good reviews are obviously less irritating than bad ones. I had decided not to buy them because I was willing to settle for one blast. Seriously, though, I was so happy that Leonard and the Orchestra received the kind of recognition that they both so richly deserved, especially since Rockwell of the Times was his usual mean-spirited self.[31]

In a letter to his publisher, Schuman chose stronger language to express his opinion of Rockwell. "That mean-spirited bastard on the Times said the orchestra wasn't first-rate, which obviously, as a second-rater, he wouldn't know!"[32] Rockwell did indeed criticize the orchestra but did so on the terms Slatkin himself had staked out.

> In an interview in the current Carnegie Hall program booklet, Leonard Slatkin says that he has chosen warhorse symphonies to conclude the St. Louis Symphony's two winter New York programs because he feels his ensemble is now ready to be measured against the "yardstick" of the other major orchestras that play regularly in the hall.
>
> Last night, following the first and more venturesome of the symphony's concerts . . . one was forced to conclude that while this is a very good group, and certainly capable of providing pleasure in either St. Louis or New York, it does not yet rank at the very top of this country's orchestral hierarchy.

Rockwell was similarly tempered in his assessment of *American Hymn*, calling it "a major recent statement by America's most visible and determined symphonist" but concluding that the work "sounded bland and self-importantly empty, the folkish simplicity comprised of ingenuity, yet not really attaining to genuine complexity."[33] Though Harriett Johnson and Bill Zakariasen, in the *New York Post* and the *Daily News*, respectively, had kinder things to say about *American Hymn*, Rockwell's opinion echoes those of the St. Louis critics who first heard the work in September 1982.[34] Frank Peters, writing for the *St. Louis Post-Dispatch*, found the work "a grandiose, tedious work—a big presence but an empty character." James Wierzbicki's review for the *St. Louis Globe-Democrat* was more extensive than that of any other critic, but his verdict was no less severe.

> Schuman's piece lasted 26 minutes. It contained four interesting moments: a variation that was waltz-like and another that was more or less jazzy, and two effectively paced climaxes. Everything else meandered or drifted, sounding like prologues or epilogues to the more noteworthy events but not linked to them with any apparent logic. The craftsmanship that characterizes the music of the 72-year-old Schuman was evident

> here. Still, "American Hymn" fell flat—the harmonic language was cautious, the artistic statement was vague, the "original melody" and its various permutations went too easily in one ear and out the other.[35]

Some of Schuman's friends and close colleagues held different opinions. Richard Freed obtained a tape of the St. Louis premiere and confided to Schuman that "after the first two hearings I felt the work was too long. . . . The more I heard it, though, the more I had to acknowledge that there seems to be nothing in it that could be sacrificed without damage, and the more sense it came to make in terms of overall 'weight' (if I may use such a term), balance, etc. In short, it is superb." Composer Phillip Ramey, who attended the New York premiere, was far less reserved.

> It is in every way a stunning piece. . . . The first statement of the theme in cornet with strings and bass drum is <u>inspired</u>, pure and simple; the fast parts are quite ear-catching (some of the percussion writing particularly struck me); and the ending is moving. I also like the theme, and the fact that it is never quite lost sight of (the opening is a fine preface for it). Of course, your fingerprints are everywhere; no one else could have written that music, and I think that is one of the highest tributes a composer can be paid. . . . It occurs to me that, especially since Aaron is no longer writing, you are <u>the</u> American composer. Certainly for me. . . . I hope you will forgive my unusually extravagant enthusiasm, but it is so seldom these days that I hear any new music of real quality.[36]

That cornet solo recalls the Salvation Army moment in *Undertow* nearly 40 years earlier, in which Schuman employed the same instrument to play an American hymn; there it was used in parody, here in homage. Ramey's liner notes for the recording suggest he may not have caught the internal reference, but in those notes he continued to voice his admiration for the work, calling *American Hymn* "one of the highpoints of [Schuman's] output—fresh, eloquent, continually inventive, impressive in architecture and in detail."[37] John Corigliano had to wait until the recording was released in the fall of 1984 to form a judgment. He agreed with Ramey's assessment. "I was totally knocked out by your *American Hymn*. It's a great piece! I think Phillip is right—you are producing greater and greater works. I would love to borrow a score of the work and study it—it's really amazing."[38]

Corigliano's letter came at a low point not only in Schuman's life and career but also, as far as Schuman was concerned, in the fortunes of American music. Schuman was perennially chauvinistic about American composers and American music; he once suggested to Columbia provost Michael I. Sovern that the university consider hiring Jacob Druckman, who was born in Philadelphia in 1928, if it was going to promote Mario Davidovsky, who was born in Argentina in 1934 but emigrated to the United States in 1960.[39] But as pianist and author Samuel Lipman noted about this period of music making in New York City, there were legitimate reasons for Schuman's dystopian view. "The recent tenure of Pierre Boulez at the New York Philharmonic," Lipman wrote, "intellectually and musically the most interesting such period in the domestic musical life of the past quarter century, was marked by expressed disdain for almost all our native products."[40] During the seven years Boulez served as music director (1971–77), he conducted not a single Schuman work, and between the premieres of *In Praise of Shahn* (1970) and the *Three Colloquies* (1980), the orchestra performed only five Schuman works, two of which were conducted by Bernstein in 1976 and two of which were conducted by Kostelanetz either on tour or as part of the lighter Promenade series. Schuman wasn't alone in being neglected by the hometown orchestra. Charles Wuorinen wrote an impassioned letter to the music administrator for Avery Fisher Hall, in which he complained that the Philharmonic had overlooked his works for years and asserted that the orchestra existed to serve the artistic community as an outlet rather than the general populace as an amusement.[41]

But the American symphony orchestra had become a business, and the idea that it should cater to American composers was as foreign to the conductors who led the orchestras as it was to the businesswomen and businessmen who managed them. Schuman repeatedly laid the blame at the feet of "the new crop of conductors (mostly foreigners) who inhabit the podiums of major cities between jet trips and who obviously have no knowledge or interest in our native music."[42] But his indictment was more sweeping, gathering together orchestra managers, boards, conductors, critics, and audience members. In an address to the American Symphony Orchestra League meeting in New York City in June 1980, Schuman spelled out what he viewed as the purpose of an American symphony orchestra: "1) the systematic and continuing exploration of the great literature of the past on a rotating basis over a period of years, 2) the systematic and purposeful effort to develop a repertory of contemporary works which have already found favor, and 3) the introduction of new works, both by established composers and newer ones." Those contemporary works, both established and new, were not necessarily by American composers, but Schuman went on, using the first person plural, to make his case for homegrown music. "We ask that American music be systematically and consistently programmed. We will not have a secure American repertory until every American symphony orchestra recognizes that American music must be a basic ingredient of every season's programming." Do these things, Schuman told the assembled leaders of American symphonies, and "you will have rewarded me more than I dared hope."[43]

Two years later, Schuman's hopes still awaited their reward. Zubin Mehta, Boulez's successor at the New York Philharmonic, attended to Schuman's music, conducting the *Colloquies* twice and the Eighth and Ninth Symphonies between 1980 and 1985, so Schuman, in the aftermath of his remarks to the symphony league, could take some personal satisfaction in his change of fortunes. But performances and recordings of his own music remained hard to come by, and given that he viewed himself, "along with Aaron Copland and one or two other American composers . . . [as] well represented through recordings," he found the state of affairs unacceptable for American composers.[44] As he had done from the mid-1930s on, he labored to find outlets for American music, working with record labels and producers, talking to orchestra conductors and managers, contemplating radio and television prospects, arguing on behalf of his less fortunate colleagues, and bending the ear of anyone who would listen.

Philanthropists and congressmen were not immune to Schuman's attempts to reshape the conversation. For much of 1982, he labored over a program to give people of modest means an incentive to make charitable donations. Schuman's proposal would make such giving as simple as ABCD: an Advance Bequest Certified Deposit. The final version of his proposal was published in *Philanthropy Monthly*, where he described the mechanics of the program.

> You make a deposit in an approved ABCD account in your own name and designate a specific charity as the future beneficiary. The income derived from the ABCD account would be paid to you for life. The charity would receive the principal upon your death. Furthermore, your income would be doubled; basic to the concept of ABCD is a tax reduction . . . of 50%. For example, if your contribution were $2,000, the income produced year after year would be based on that sum, yet the actual cost to you, because of the reduction in your tax, would be $1,000.

The editors at *Philanthropy Monthly* distilled Schuman's proposal into two sentences. "Somewhat like an IRA [individual retirement] account, an annual ABCD gift would encourage saving and provide a life income for the donor. On his death the principal would go to charity."[45] But Schuman originally had sought a larger audience for his idea. He submitted an earlier draft of his proposal to an editor at the *New York Times* and thought that, should the *Times* turn him down, the "My Turn" guest editorial page in *Newsweek* might be appropriate. "If *Newsweek* refuses, my next two choices would be the *Wall Street Journal* and the *Washington Post*."[46] All of these publications rejected Schuman's op-ed piece.[47] Between his vision for a wide distribution of his ideas and the narrow audience of *Philanthropy Monthly* lay an exchange of letters with two authorities: Thomas Troyer, who had served as an undersecretary in the U.S. Treasury Department; and Eli Evans, president of the Charles H. Revson Foundation. The two men helped Schuman hone his proposal and suggested that ABCD would need to find a congressional sponsor if it were to gain any serious momentum. Schuman made some fainthearted attempts to interest people who might interest people in Washington, but he flatly told Troyer: "I don't know anyone in Congress."[48]

By then, Schuman's health had caused him to reevaluate his priorities, and non-compositional efforts drew less and less of his attention. Before giving up on ABCD, he completed the last version of *American Hymn* in December 1981 and turned to two smaller commissions for choral music. A larger project was in the works, as Nick Webster at the New York Philharmonic was pulling together a coalition of orchestras to commission Schuman to write a large work for chorus and orchestra, but all the details hadn't been ironed out. One of the choral commissions was quite lucrative at $6,000; the other, quite modest at $1,000; together they would comprise all of the music Schuman would write in 1982.

The first to be completed was *Perceptions*. Choral conductor Gregg Smith, on behalf of his Gregg Smith Singers, the Dale Warland Singers, I Cantori, and the Philadelphia Singers, applied to the National Endowment for the Arts for money to commission Schuman to write a work for these professional singing groups. Schuman left behind very little correspondence to unravel how he came to choose the Walt Whitman texts he did and when he started work on the commission, but by mid-April the work was completed, and by mid-June Schuman was clamoring for payment as a precondition to publication.[49] The manuscript is unusual, as Schuman took paper that was meant for orchestra (the names of the instruments are printed to the left of each staff), turned it upside down, and wrote the work in pencil. The homophonic choral writing in the eight movements allowed Schuman to write out the text only once for all the parts, though, unlike the printed version, he distributed the four parts onto four staves. *Perceptions* is a study in sonority and harmony, on how to connect dissonant chords to each other. As such, it marks a return to the kinds of experiments he tried in the *Choral Etude*, *Pioneers!* (both 1937), and the two versions of the *Prelude for Voices* (1936 and 1939; like the last movement of *Perceptions*, the *Prelude* uses a soprano soloist). The occasional uses of imitation and ostinato in *Perceptions* similarly call to mind the *Four Rounds* and the *Carols of Death* from the late 1950s, and the descending B♭-to-E tritone that ends the first movement of *Perceptions* is found, with the same pitches, at the conclusion of "Haste," the fifth *Round* from 1969. The choice to set Whitman further cements *Perceptions* as a compendium of Schuman's choral writing. He nevertheless hoped to expand *Perceptions* into something larger and something different. He later remarked to Rosalind Rees, who was Smith's wife and the soprano soloist Schuman had in mind when he wrote the last movement, "To You," that "I do wish we could find a way to record [*Perceptions*] again, and I will have to dream up some companion pieces. I am still toying with the idea of a song cycle based on Perceptions, which I mentioned to Gregg."[50] The song cycle never materialized.

The impetus for the other choral work from 1982 came from Joel R. Stegall, dean of the School of Music at Ithaca College. Ithaca College Chorus conductor Lawrence Doebler had started a festival at the college in 1979 "to encourage the creation and performance of new choral music and to establish the Ithaca College Choral Series," with Theodore Presser as cosponsor of the festival and publisher of some of the works premiered there.[51] Stegall approached Schuman, a Presser composer, to determine if he might write a work for them, "three to five minutes in duration, for mixed voices and suitable for performance by a high school choir. It may be unaccompanied, accompanied by keyboard or a small wind group (such as a quartet), using instruments that might be available to the high school choral director."[52] Schuman quickly accepted the commission and added that finding texts would prove to be the challenge. Stegall sent Schuman five sets of lyrics by Alicia Carpenter, author of "Ithaca Forever," the college's alma mater, as well as instructions on how to reach her. Carpenter was also Gregg Smith's ex-wife, and some 15 years earlier she had tried to construct a text for Schuman to use for his *Nineteen Seventy-Six*. Schuman thanked Stegall for the suggestion. "Without passing judgment on their worth, I simply do not find them of interest to me."[53]

Four months later, Schuman wrote to Stegall with some astonishing news about the commission.

> I have been working on your pieces, but I may be giving you more than you want. At the moment I am completing a sketch on the fourth of four pieces that I anticipate will make up the commission. When completed, I estimate the performing time (I am still composing) at about ten to twelve minutes. Since you only wanted three to five minutes, I could simply give you one piece, which could be extracted, or let you have the four.
>
> Let me warn you that I could find no text, and, having just completed a big serious choral work for professional chorus, I found myself in a more relaxed mood.[54]

Less than a week later, Schuman had completed *Esses*. As with the *Five Rounds on Famous Words*, Schuman assembled his own texts, in this instance finding words that all begin with the letter "S". The humor is not unlike that generated by the *Mail Order Madrigals*, with *Esses*' four movements—"Suggestions" built around a waiter's imaginary food recommendations, "Serenata" compiling a chain of musical terms, "Stillness" tracing moments of quietude, and "Singaling" (in his manuscript Schuman did not use hyphens to separate the syllables in the title) nonsensically stringing together a list of cities—once again tracing the choral equivalent of a compact symphony for voices. In the final piece, "the rich heritage of the spiritual and the nuances of the blues" combine to bring this charming suite of slightly silly choruses to a close.

Schuman made the four-and-a-half-hour drive from New York to Ithaca to work with the college choir on the premiere of *Esses*, which took place on November 13, 1982. He heard a preview performance of *Perceptions* at a private concert that the Gregg Smith Singers gave at the home of Mr. and Mrs. William R. Mayer on December 15, 1982.[55] And he had expected to attend the premiere of *Perceptions*, which was much closer than Ithaca: the Cole Auditorium of the Greenwich Library, less than 20 minutes from his Richmond Hill home. But that January 9, 1983, concert came less than two weeks after Schuman was discharged from Lenox Hill Hospital. He had been admitted to the cardiac unit on December 17 and was released on New Year's Eve. Marty Segal stopped by and sent flowers; "L.B. [Bernstein] came to visit and did a hilarious imitation of Sid Caesar, trying to fall asleep."[56] Frankie took on some of the duties to communicate with those who needed word from her husband. She informed one such correspondent that "[Bill's] plans for the next few months are absolutely in the hands of our physician."[57] Schuman had already begun to scale back his activities, but his unexpected holiday hospitalization hastened his resolve to "drastically curtail my activities in the months immediately ahead to realize the satisfactory prognosis I have received."[58] He tried to go to the occasional concert, making it to the St. Louis Symphony's New York performance of *American Hymn* but being thwarted in attending the New York City premieres of *Perceptions* and *Esses* because the snow that evening led the limousine service not to send a car to ferry Schuman to the concert.[59] As intent as Schuman was on following the doctor's guidance, his recovery failed to measure up to the prognosis he was given, and most of 1983 turned out to be a wash. Notwithstanding his compromised condition, he did try to compose, turning his attention to the big New York Philharmonic commission. In the fall of 1983, he summed up both his immediate past and his immediate future. "I worked very hard this summer, but what I produced was disappointing, and I am afraid I still haven't effectively begun. My health was a factor in this, and I am hoping that the open heart surgery which I am soon to undergo will be as successful as I expect."[60] Another letter went out that same October day with the same basic message. "This summer hasn't been great, but I am soon to undergo open heart surgery, and I am most optimistic."[61] Thirty years earlier, Schuman had forfeited a summer to hepatitis. Now he lost almost two years to coronary deficiency and recovery from triple bypass surgery. Back then, he had come roaring back with *Credendum*, the *Rounds*, and the *New England Triptych*. This time, he got a second chance to write the bicentennial work he had always wanted to write.

THIRTY-FOUR

THE WIND WAS WITH HIM

On the first anniversary of his triple bypass surgery, Schuman wrote to O. Wayne Isom, the cardiologist who performed his surgery. (Isom would later, in 1987, perform quintuple bypass surgery on Larry King, the American television and radio host, and would pass up the opportunity to do surgery in 2004 on former president Bill Clinton in favor of a round of golf.)[1] "There is no doubt in my mind," Schuman wrote to Isom, "that the operation was enormously successful. I would describe my condition as about 80% better than it was before the surgery. But using percentages is quibbling because it is clear to me that the procedure was a necessary, life-saving measure." After acknowledging that "not all the problems that caused the condition in the first place have disappeared," Schuman zeroed in on what the surgery meant in his life. "For me the greatest gift that I received was the ability to return to my work, which now continues to engage my full time and vigor, beginning early in the year."[2]

One sign of Schuman's gratitude for the gift Isom gave him is found in a complimentary close that he used in his correspondence around this time. Schuman dictated nearly all of his letters, and, from 1946 on, the overwhelming majority of them end with some variation of the formula "With every good wish to you, I remain, as always, Faithfully." But around 1957, he started to incorporate a more intimate formula: "All the best, Yours," which he used for friends and acquaintances. "Affectionately" was saved for those who had an almost familial relationship with Schuman (e.g., Koussevitzky, Bernstein, Copland, Harris, Martha Graham, Schubart, Persichetti, and family). But prior to 1983, Schuman rarely ended his letters with the word, "Cheers." The upbeat close never supplanted the others in frequency, and its appearance at this point in his life may also reflect the popularity of the television sitcom of the same name that began running in 1982. But in 1982 he increasingly cheered his correspondents, and why not? Frankie called her husband "a euphoric."[3] The success of his surgery increased his euphoria and good cheer.

His vastly improved health resulted in an almost unprecedented flow of music from Schuman's pencil. The New York Philharmonic commission that was initiated in 1980 still awaited Schuman's attention. Nick Webster in the Philharmonic offices proved to be an effective broker for Schuman in lining up the symphony orchestras of Albany; Atlanta; Chicago; Washington, D.C.; Portland, Oregon; Pittsburgh; and St. Louis to join with the New York Philharmonic to underwrite a major work from Schuman. (Other orchestras were discussed, but various financial and labor-related issues prompted Webster to pass them over.)[4] Robert Shaw, the conductor of the Atlanta Symphony, used the surgery and the commission as an excuse to write Schuman and wish him a speedy recovery. Schuman thanked Shaw for his thoughtfulness and told him about his progress on the joint commission.

> The new piece has not yet advanced to the point of even a blank page, but is only in the very early state of preliminary cogitation, which so far has produced precisely nothing. I'd like to blame it on the recent physical setback, but I know this is not true. In any case I have great zest for the project and only hope that over the next couple of years I can bring it to fruition.[5]

Less than a year after writing those words, Schuman completed *On Freedom's Ground: An American Cantata for Baritone, Chorus, and Orchestra.*

Schuman had, in fact, proceeded far beyond "preliminary cogitation" by the time he responded to Shaw. The month after his surgery, Schuman and Webster reviewed the particulars of the commission. "The project involves a major work, of thirty to forty minutes duration, for full orchestra and chorus, for a fee of $75,000 plus up to $15,000 for the preparation of parts. . . . In addition, we have discussed the possibility of the commission involving the Crane School of Music and the centennial celebration of the Statue of Liberty."[6] Frédéric Auguste Bartholdi's statue *La Liberté éclairant le monde* was conceived in the early 1870s, completed in France by 1884, reassembled on Bedloe's Island in April 1886, and officially dedicated on October 28 of that year. In a fascinating parallel linking Bartholdi's statue and Schuman's cantata, the former was originally intended to celebrate the centennial of the signing of the Declaration of Independence but was delayed for ten years. Schuman also had labored to commemorate that signing, but now, in focusing on a different centennial occurring ten years later, Schuman found an avenue to return to the patriotic themes that so stirred him throughout his creative career. Schuman himself had no difficulty articulating the central theme of the cantata. "Basically, the subject is America, all the things that are right about it and some that are wrong. It is a land with the possibility of change."[7]

Finding a text, however, would be the first and biggest hurdle, as it had always been for Schuman. After *Esses*, Schuman wanted some poetry with more heft. Instinctively, he telephoned Richard Wilbur. Wilbur had won a Pulitzer

Prize in 1957 for his collection of poetry *Things of This World*, and, during his tenure as chancellor and president of the American Academy of Arts and Letters, he and Schuman had worked together on merging the academy and the National Institute of Arts and Letters.[8] Wilbur had also composed a poem at Schuman's request to celebrate the opening of Philharmonic Hall; it appeared not only in the souvenir booklet distributed at the concert hall but was also reprinted in the *New York Times*.[9] When Wilbur expressed interest in Schuman's latest project, Schuman wrote him an ebullient three-page letter that made clear he already saw the entire cantata in his mind's eye.

> Supposing we are thinking of a work of approximately 30 to 40 minutes in duration, I could envision the following: Section 1.—A long, slow, mysterious build-up which begins softly in the orchestra and chorus, gaining in intensity through a long development, leading to the first climax. This is an extended section which I could imagine taking four minutes. Not too many lines of text would be needed for this, and as a composer, I would hope that you could pay attention to making some of the key words end with open vowel sounds or contain open vowel sounds within them, such as "soon". Section 2.—I would envision as a sturdy, forward-moving allegro with positive statements which carry forward the purpose of your text and that has within it several discernible mood changes. This large section would end again in a climax, as far as the words are concerned, but with an orchestral summing-up which would gradually bring us down to a moment of quiet. The third section is in a sense the centerpiece of the work and is the one that I described to you as a Requiescat. . . . What I would hope you could supply for this movement would be the most moving lines imaginable, relating to all the moments of despair which the subject matter suggests and yet somehow leads to a serene ending. You can get some idea of the length of text required of this movement, which again is an extended one, perhaps 12 minutes, by looking at the MacLeish poem ["The Young Dead Soldiers"].
>
> Finally, we come to the last section. At the beginning of the section we somehow need an opportunity for lighter music. Since the celebration is really Franco-American in origin, it occurred to me that a short madrigal-like text in French (with the famous Wilbur translation thrown in both for the composer and the public) might be a possibility.
>
> I must somehow move from the above without interruption to a long peroration, which brings everything together and gives a climax of moving and satisfying proportions. It could well be that the Emma Lazarus words, "Give me your tired, your poor," etc. (you will undoubtedly want to look up the entire poem) could serve as some passacaglia-like statement, reiterated, while other textual material proceeds. Would it be too corny to have her words sung in many different languages, first consecutively and later simultaneously?[10]

Had Wilbur known Schuman's choral oeuvre, Schuman could have described the work thus: the work opens with something akin to the first pages of *A Free Song* followed by a mirror image of the first section of the *Prologue* (don't forget the shout at the climax!), the spirit of the *Carols of Death* as the requiescat (or

Schuman's actual *Requiescat*), leaven like the *Mail Order Madrigals*, and a "passacaglia-like statement" reminiscent of the closing section of the *Prologue*. He had written all of these choral moments before. Now he would combine them in service to Lady Liberty and, by extension, to the nation she illumines.

Schuman swept up Wilbur in his torrent of enthusiasm, but the poet was concerned about his own skill at moving from idea to reality.

> I am reeling a bit still from your suggestion that, instead of providing some closing lines for the Lady Liberty, I try my hand at making a text for the whole. One reason for reeling is that your suggestion is a great honor for me. The other reasons have to do with the challenge to avoid banality, with my musical inexperience, with my inexperience as an occasional poet. . . . If it turns out that my attack upon the whole does not satisfy you or me, I shall still be glad to attempt any part that seems to you within my powers.[11]

So days before he wrote to Shaw on February 20, Schuman committed himself to write a work for the centenary of the Statue of Liberty and had persuaded Wilbur to try his hand at composing the text. All that remained was the writing.

On April 5, Wilbur sent Schuman his first stab at the words for the first two sections. He ended his letter: "Dear Bill, I have a calm ego and am not touchy. If you are discouraged by these drafts and ideas, don't hesitate to dissolve our partnership; of if you don't want to go so far just yet, do be downright about what doesn't please you." The draft was hardly that; of the twenty lines of poetry Wilbur sent to Schuman, fifteen made it into the final text without any alteration whatsoever and the other five required very little adjustment on Wilbur's part.[12] By the end of the month, Schuman was taking "unsatisfactory, faltering first steps" on the first movement and checking the mails like a forlorn lover, waiting for more words from Wilbur, and by mid-May, Wilbur hammered the first two six-line stanzas and the final couplet into their final shape.[13] Two months passed before the delivery of a polished second section and a complete draft of the requiescat. Wilbur was particularly conscious of weaving into his text the history of the 1963 March on Washington and Martin Luther King Jr.'s "I Have a Dream" speech and, hearing that Schuman had located in his own library the Negro spiritual "Free at Last," surmised that Schuman felt "no irresistible Charles Ives impulse to echo it."[14] Schuman already imagined that, for the end of this section, he would recapitulate music from earlier in the work, and both men ultimately agreed to change "invincible dream," with its clear connection to King, to "invincible hope," "because the Democrats and now the Republicans have been using the word 'dream' a bit much."[15] Schuman was bowled over by Wilbur's requiescat text. "Richard, the words for Section 3 are glorious—repeat, glorious!" He also started to look ahead.

> The big problem we have now is the fourth movement and the fifth movement. The fifth doesn't worry me because we have discussed various possibilities, but before it

> takes place we absolutely must have a fourth movement that is light and swift, of a 3 to 4 minute duration (not many verses). The word, "Dance", occurs to me. American ethnic groups have almost all kept their traditional dances. Is it worth a thought?

He also concluded that "the third movement, now that I study it, will definitely not have a female solo, but either a baritone or possibly—a fleeting thought—a narrator. I opt for the singer, but the other did cross my mind. That whopper of a text will take me all next fall, winter and spring if I'm lucky!"[16]

Both men were more than lucky. Schuman was hard at work setting the third section in early August and was contemplating a title for the entire work. Whatever else it would be called, he was clear about one element: "I rather like the sub-title, An American Cantata."[17] Meanwhile, Wilbur "found myself writing this draft of an artless ditty, prompted by your notion that our 'ethnics' brought their dances with them. . . . This may be nothing like what you're after, in tone or measure, since at one stage you spoke, as I recall, of a madrigal. If by chance it fits the bill in a general way, do fire away with suggested changes." Once again, the text was a nearly flawless 16-line poem that Schuman incorporated whole cloth as the fourth movement.[18] Near the end of the month, on a "beautiful sort of State-of-Maine day," Wilbur gloried in the joys of late summer in New England. "Before we all go off to a friend's for cocktails and croquet, I had better get down to business and send you what I've been doing." His letter contained all the remaining lines of the text. "If these lines appeal to you," Wilbur wrote, "they could of course lead right into Emma Lazarus in French or Urdu." In the margin of Wilbur's letter, in reference to incorporating the Lazarus poem, Schuman wrote: "Forget."[19] In just over four months, Wilbur had composed the entire text for the then-unnamed "American cantata." And Schuman had no need to worry that he would not finish the third section until the spring. He wrote to Brock McElheran, conductor of the choruses at the Crane School of Music in Postdam, New York, that he was "steaming ahead at a very fast rate, and I feel confident that I will finish the work before very long. . . . The first two movements are already in the works. The third is nearing completion at this end, and the final two are in the wings."[20] That was January 10; Schuman completed the cantata on February 6. "I was so hot I couldn't stop."[21]

Shortly after accomplishing his Herculean feat, Schuman wrote to Wilbur to convey how a comparison to the Augean stables was not completely far-fetched.

> It has been very difficult writing these days because I have now no sight in my right eye at all. I asked the doctor if the operation could be postponed until I finished the work. I doubled my efforts which really meant I quadrupled them because of the handicap, and I can report that the work is completed. The score is now being copied, and I very much hope that I can conclude the first batch of proofreading by April 15, when I go into the hospital. It has been a struggle sometimes to know whether it was a line or a space that I was dealing with, but I am satisfied that what I have done is the

> best of which I am capable. My music is old-fashioned enough so that there happens to be an enormous difference between the sound of a line and a space![22]

Still to be determined was the overall name for the cantata. On a slip of paper that he later tucked into the corrected score, Schuman wrote out some of the possible titles: "Praise to This Land"; "The Great Bay"; "The Same Great Bay"; "The Invincible Hope"; "Immigrants Still"; "On Freedom's Ground." One title he suggested to Wilbur quoted the last line of the poem for the title: "The Wind Is With Us." According to Schuman, his son, Tony, "who is a very good judge of these things, thought it was too nautical for the whole title."[23] In all these matters, Wilbur obliged Schuman.

> You have a genius for titles, and have thought of all of our section titles and of those for the whole, so that in pondering the matter of the general title I can't possibly be arguing against you. "The Wind is With Us: An American Cantata" has the virtue of being quite unlike other patriotic pieces in name, and I suppose it could be argued that it embodies one part of the argument; the elements, in Back Then, are seen as subjects and vassals, while toward the end of the cantata, in the peroration, they appear to partake of liberty. "On Freedom's Ground" is less oblique, a shade less fresh, but is more encompassing of the subject and suggests not only Come Dance but such a phrase as "Anchored . . . in the continent's rock." And "It came ashore," for that matter. I shall be happy with either.[24]

For all of Wilbur's deference and his willingness to adjust his text to fit the requirements of the music, Schuman never shrank from praising Wilbur and his poem to others, and on at least one occasion he read the text to someone else and began to weep, so moved was he by Wilbur's words.[25]

The music operates in a fashion similar to the orchestral version of *American Hymn* in that many of its materials are variations on the eight-bar "liberty" melody that Schuman introduces at the very beginning of the piece. The choice of instrument and its slow traversal of the melody are also reminiscent of *American Hymn*, though here it is the more penetrating solo trumpet and not the mellower cornet that Schuman calls upon. This "liberty" melody constitutes the main melodic materials for the first two sections of *On Freedom's Ground* and reappears *en toto* at the end of the third section and midway through the fourth. Its second half provides the foundation for the baritone solo in the third section, and though the final section has no immediately discernible connection to the "liberty" melody, its repeated ascending trajectory reverses the scalar descent of the fifth measure of the melody that has figured so prominently in the third section, which, like the fifth section, employs the soloist.

Two other moments in the score stand on opposite ends of the tonal landscape. One comes at the end of the third section, with its reference to the full partnership of the oppressed and dispossessed in the American dream of liberty. The contested nature of that shared dream is recapitulated in a tortured chromatic passage for the orchestra that eventually yields to a sustained D-major chord in the strings, pianississimo, a tonal benediction to the harmonic torment that preceded it. That chord is rudely interrupted by a fortissimo blast of dissonance that employs ten of the 12 notes of the scale, but the D-major chord returns, not quite as prominent but still insistent in its right to conclude this anguished section. In microcosm are the two harmonic poles Schuman traveled between: the dense—and, at times, serially derived—chromaticism most prevalent in the compositions of the 1960s, and the triadic harmonies never absent from his work but newly promoted in his most recent works.

The second of these moments telescopes into one passage Schuman's own musical emigration from the worlds of Tin Pan Alley to those of the concert hall. In a reminiscence shared with Frank Loesser's daughter Susan, Schuman spoke of how a tune from the early 1930s reappeared in *On Freedom's Ground.*

> We were writing all these songs and had modest success [Bill remembered], got very little money, not enough to live on but enough to pay our expenses. We once started on an operetta based on the life of da Vinci and Frank had some wonderful lyrics. Then a few years ago I wrote a choral work, in which I wanted to bring in some old American tunes. I felt I ought to have a waltz, and suddenly a waltz tune I had written with Frank for the da Vinci show came to mind. The work was first performed by the New York Philharmonic. There they were playing the waltz—a rousing tune—and I'll tell you what the real words were: "Here comes that drunken da Vinci again, all filled with highballs, stewed to the eyeballs."[26]

Schuman dedicated *On Freedom's Ground* to his family: "my wife, son, daughter, grandson, sister, and to the memory of my parents and brother." It was one of the first and most prominent public references Schuman ever made to Robert. The dedication also shows how, for Schuman, the connection of patriotism and family were intricately woven together. His children, especially, expressed "hatred, disdain, and other strongly negative emotions about the President and the US government" at various times of their lives, Andrea Schuman said, which "was more than he could handle."[27] In its way, then, Schuman's dedication is a benediction and gift: the country that had nurtured his family and had given them all opportunities that might well be unimaginable elsewhere was a country that had an innate capacity to change. That the work's premiere and subsequent performances across the nation took place in the shadow of the Iran-Contra arms-for-hostage debacle rebuked all who were listening closely. "Be proud at least that we know we were wrong, / That we need not lie, that our books are open." Wilbur's words rang out, even if they did not seem at the time to ring true.

Close attention is rarely paid to occasional pieces, and *On Freedom's Ground* has suffered in no small part because of its connection to a particular event in history. John Rockwell, Schuman's bête noire at the *New York Times*, likened the cantata to "those grand. empty, ceremonial pieces with which English composers of this century have favored us. . . . The score is at its most successful in its instrumental interludes, especially the quiet patter of percussion at the end of the third part and the witty dance music at the outset of the fourth. But for most of the time, this is a work more noble in its patriotic intentions than its esthetic realization."[28] Joseph McLellan, writing for the *Washington Post*, also found the dance music "the most immediately enjoyable movement" while at the same time agreeing with Rockwell, if in less damning terms. "'On Freedom's Ground' is nearly the ideal celebratory cantata—public music, not notable for deep personal feeling but well wrought, highly communicative in its gestures and instantly comprehensible and enjoyable."[29] In reviewing the Chicago performance under the baton of Leonard Slatkin, *Chicago Tribune* critic John von Rhein couldn't quite decide whether *On Freedom's Ground* deserved praise for its present-day accomplishment or for its nostalgia for music past. The cantata shared the program with Barber's Overture to *The School for Scandal* and Hanson's Symphony no. 2 ("Romantic"), two American warhorses from the early 1930s, which was a time

> when a number of native composers where flexing their musical muscles, determined to create a body of work that would be truly American in every respect, free from the stultifying restraints of an exhausted European Romantic tradition.
>
> . . . "On Freedom's Ground" is in many ways a musical embodiment of that same American vigor and optimism, a spirit that seems to burn almost as brightly in the recent works of our musical elder statesman as in the works he composed in his younger years.

But von Rhein was uncertain whether such a conjuration was appropriate in 1987.

> "On Freedom's Ground" on the surface sounds like the kind of hokey patriotic exercise one had thought American composers had stopped writing by 1950. . . .
>
> Schuman's music evince[s] a bigness of gesture as open-hearted as the nation it celebrates. The score fuses the "no-nonsense masculinity" (to quote Phillip Ramey's memorable description) and spasmodic rhythmic energy characteristic of the composer's earlier style with the severity and harmonic density of his more recent music. . . . The composer was present to share in the prolonged, and amply deserved, applause.[30]

Throughout his life Schuman would comment on the gulf between the critical and lay receptions his works received. If von Rhein never told his readers what lies beneath the "hokey" surface of the cantata, at least he acknowledged that the audience not only appreciated the performance, as did von Rhein, but also the composition.

Other noncritics did as well. The Chicago performance further cemented Schuman's connection to John Corigliano, who, in his capacity as the Chicago

Symphony's first composer in residence, gave an analytical presentation of *On Freedom's Ground* prior to the performance.[31] Schuman also paid a debt of gratitude to Nick Webster of the New York Philharmonic, who further honored Schuman by nominating the cantata for the Grawemeyer Music Award, the world's largest prize for music composition.[32] The January 1987 nomination made *On Freedom's Ground* a late entry, and unlike the similarly late entry of *A Free Song* 44 years earlier, the new cantata failed to win the prize. But the comparisons between the earlier secular cantata and the later American cantata are numerous. Both offer "praise to this land" in their somber commemoration of those who died to defend it, their steely resolve to call all to action on its behalf, and their stentorian appeals to the American values of freedom and liberty. They also join Schuman's other works for chorus and orchestra—the *Prologue* (1939), the first secular cantata, *This Is Our Time* (1940), and the revised *Casey at the Bat* of 1976—in the dubious distinction of not having ever been commercially recorded. (As of this writing, a recording of *On Freedom's Ground* and *A Free Song* is scheduled to appear in early 2011.) Schuman's patriotism as realized in choral terms repeatedly strives for universality when particularity and individual quirkiness might have won these works—and the sentiments behind them—a larger audience and a longer shelf life. Then again, as Rockwell and McLellan suggest, such music rarely transcends its occasion. (One critic opened his review of *On Freedom's Ground* with a version of Rockwell's comment. "If the United States government suddenly made the improbable decision to appoint a composer in residence—a sort of American equivalent to England's Master of the Queen's Music—William Schuman would surely be offered the job.")[33] Schuman certainly hoped his music would beat the odds, though he joked with Wilbur about the pressure he felt after Wilbur confided that his old college roommate was deeply moved by the text.

> I sympathize completely with your college roommate, for I cannot read it aloud without being emotionally aroused. This puts me in the most terrible inferior position. Suppose when the work is performed with the music, one is not moved! In any case, we could have a first in which the musical setting of the words diminishes their emotional force. Of course, I don't believe this for a minute, and the more I work, the more I am convinced that we have something here.[34]

The writer of Ecclesiastes posited, "To everything there is a season, a time for every purpose under heaven." *On Freedom's Ground* had its time and season, and perhaps a future season and time will find a way to make the cantata its own.

Schuman was so thrilled at his first collaboration with Wilbur that he was eager for another. He was still proofreading *On Freedom's Ground* when he asked Wilbur: "Do you have some other thoughts for a suitable poem of a page or a page and a half in length? . . . This time I would have in mind something far removed from the hortatory or the chauvinistic, i.e., personal." Wilbur had nothing to offer, so Schuman turned his attention elsewhere.[35] The Chamber Music Society at Lincoln Center had scheduled a black-tie party on October 1, 1985, in honor of Schuman's seventy-fifth birthday. Schuman himself chose to celebrate the occasion by writing some music of his own for the gathering of nearly 300 friends and admirers.

> This composer gratefully offers thank-you music to mark this happy occasion. Dances, composed this past summer, was completed on August 12.
>
> The tunes come from a variety of sources: The jigs are from Ryan's Mammoth Collection of 1050 Reels and Jigs, published in 1883 by Ellias Howse, Boston; the schottische and the polka were chosen from an unidentified collection, published circa 1880; the polka is credited to a Bohemian composer. Anton Wallerstein, 1813–1892; the waltz dates from circa 1932, when Frank Loesser and I started and abandoned an operetta, based on the life of Da Vinci; the waltz fragment, not previously notated, came to mind; I'll See You In My Dreams (1924) by Gus Kahn and Isham Jones and The Charleston (1923) by Cecil Mack and Jimmy Johnson are both used with permission of the copyright owners.
>
> All the tunes are treated freely, often in a manner far removed from their original habitat. The Finale recalls the Dances through juxtapositions and alterations which lead to a brief coda.[36]

Schuman's original program notes for this work for wind quintet and percussion disguise a number of facts. First, he had turned to fellow composer and percussionist William Kraft for guidance on handling the percussion demands, since Schuman was using only one percussionist for the work.[37] Second, as early as 1982 he had expressed "a desire to compose a work for conventional wind quintet," something he thought about undertaking as soon as he finished the choral pieces that then occupied his attention (i.e., *Perceptions* and *Esses*).[38] Third, in late July 1985 he was already thinking ahead to a different wind quintet. "I have accepted a commission from the Naumburg Foundation for a work which includes clarinet. It is my hope to complete this work (probably a wind quintet with percussion) during the coming season."[39] Two weeks after writing about a wind quintet with percussion to be completed sometime in the next nine months for the Naumburg Foundation, Schuman had finished his *Dances* for the Chamber Music Society birthday concert. The manuscript, in fact, shows signs of haste, with its 21 numbered pages interleaved with six additional pages that provide corrections and expansion of the musical material. Tellingly, all of these interleaved pages occur after the waltz fragment.

For the principal fact Schuman kept hidden from the birthday audience was that a significant portion of his *Dances* was a transcription for woodwind quintet of the fourth movement of *On Freedom's Ground*, which had been completed but whose premiere was still a year away. Neither "I'll See You in My Dreams" nor "The Charleston" appears in *On Freedom's Ground*, which explains the helter-skelter nature of the later pages of the manuscript, since the earlier pages were a straight wind transcription from the fourth movement. When he later revised the work, he was more forthcoming on the work's genesis.

> DANCES owes its origins to an occasion and to a previous work. Last October 1 the Chamber Music Society of Lincoln Center gave me a splendid birthday party. By way of appreciation I offered DANCES as "thank-you" music. Five of the tunes that I used in DANCES were employed in the fourth movement of the then recently completed work, ON FREEDOM'S GROUND, which had its world premiere on October 28 of this year by the New York Philharmonic. When I heard DANCES at the party, I decided to make it into a concert piece by adding an extended introduction, a new ending and a number of minor editorial changes.[40]

He made the revisions in January 1986, giving his copyist a pencil manuscript of the introduction and new ending as well as a marked-up copyist's score in which he renumbered the measures and clarified where each dance began. He also added the word "divertimento" to the title of this diverting work.

No sooner had he finished the revisions to the *Dances* than he turned his attention to another work that also owed its origins to an occasion and to two previous works. To celebrate Texas's sesquicentennial, Citicorp/Citibank provided $50,000 for fanfare commissions at the behest of the Houston Symphony Orchestra; Tobias Picker, its composer-in-residence; and Sergiu Comissiona, its music director. According to a story in the *Houston Chronicle*, "There is no limitation on the number of instruments, though they must all be part of the standard orchestra. Most composers are interested in writing pieces for a large number of instruments." Among the composers who agreed to write fanfares were Schuman, Steve Reich, Jacob Druckman, John Adams, Charles Wuorinen, Marc Neikrug, Olly Wilson, Poul Ruders of Denmark, Tikhon Khrennikov of the Soviet Union, and Aulis Sallinen of Finland.[41]

Andrew Porter of the *New Yorker* obtained a recording of the fanfares and wrote a droll story about them all.

> There was variety: romantic strains mingled with the robustly jubilant outbursts; melting episodes brought relief from insistent tantaras. The shortest piece was Wuorinen's "Fanfare," which lasts a little over a minute, and the longest was Schuman's "Showcase: A Short Display for Orchestra," which lasts about four and a half minutes. . . . Schuman is a veteran fanfaronader. The list of his works includes "Philharmonic Fanfare" (New York, 1965), "Dedication Fanfare" (St. Louis, 1968), "Anniversary Fanfare" (New York, 1970), and "Prelude for a Great Occasion" (Washington, 1974). His "Showcase" for Houston recycles some music from "American Hymn": it is a spirited piece.[42]

As Schuman had done with some of the earlier fanfares and for the *Dances*, *Showcase* sandwiches existing music—here, mm. 379–544 of *American Hymn*—between a newly composed introduction of 18 bars and a coda of 20 bars. What Porter missed was that a portion of this new music is drawn from the timpani solo that opens the second section ("Our Risen States") of *On Freedom's Ground*. With its propulsive music, its virtuosic treatment of all the families of instruments, and its final dramatic crescendo on a unison F that culminates with a tutti F-major chord splayed across the orchestra, *Showcase: A Short Display for Orchestra* is one of Schuman's most successful short compositions and one of his finest pieces that cobble together bits and pieces from other works. In many ways, *Showcase* stands at the end of his career—he completed it on February 19, 1986—the way the *American Festival Overture* (1939) stands at its beginning: as a testament to the timbral savvy, structural ingenuity, and rhythmic chutzpah of their creator.

If *Showcase* is a display piece, *Awake Thou Wintry Earth* is a curio. In 1985 the Walter W. Naumburg Foundation held what was billed as the first major competition in the United States for the clarinet. The winner, Charles Neidich, not only received sponsorship for two Alice Tully Hall recitals but was also promised compositions especially commissioned for his performance. Joan Tower wrote a clarinet concerto that Neidich premiered in 1988; Schuman's duo for clarinet and violin was completed on August 12, 1986, and premiered by Neidich and violinist Curtis Macomber in the late winter of 1987.

Schuman had been tempted to write a clarinet concerto of his own. Michael Webster, son of pianist Beveridge Webster and a talented clarinetist, wrote to Schuman in 1973 to see if he might be persuaded to accept a commission for "a clarinet concerto (or possibly even a double concerto for clarinet and piano)."[43] Over the rest of the decade, Webster and Schuman continued to explore the possibility, but the press of Schuman's other commitments and Webster's inability to secure funding for a commission rendered the clarinet concerto moot. By the time the Naumburg commission arrived in the mid-1980s, Schuman had already composed works that placed nearly every instrument of the orchestra in its own spotlight: flute (*In Sweet Music* and the arrangement of *XXV Opera Sketches*); oboe (*To Thee Old Cause*); bassoon (the Quartettino); French horn (*Three Colloquies*); trumpet (*XXV Opera Sketches*); violin, viola, and violoncello (the two concertos and *A Song of Orpheus*). A work for clarinet seemed almost preordained.

The decision to use "Awake Thou Wint'ry Earth," a seventeenth-century Dutch carol, preceded the commission by three years. Shortly after completing the choral works of 1982 and some months after he had expressed an interest in writing a wind quintet, Schuman wrote to the offices of publisher E. C. Schirmer. "Years ago when I conducted college choruses, I recall a publication of yours, based on a traditional Dutch song. It was called Awake Thou Wint'ry Earth. It was arranged for women's chorus. Is it also arranged for mixed voices? I would greatly appreciate your sending a copy of each version and billing me at the above address."[44] What precisely he intended to do with the carol at that time is unclear, and a month later he had his unexpected hospital stay. At any rate, he apparently received no response to his inquiry, for he wrote to his own publisher on July 3, 1986, asking: "Were you ever able to track down the choral arrangement from E. C. Schirmer called Awake Thou Wint'ry Earth? I really need it."[45] Just over a month later, he had finished the duo, consisting of two movements: Reverie and Variations. (He also arranged the work for flute and bassoon, which he completed in November 1986.)

His original program notes explore both the music and the impetus for their composition.

> For reasons both musical and institutional I eagerly accepted The Walter W. Naumburg Foundation commission to provide a work for the winner of its clarinet competition. To compose music for the clarinet alone or in combination with another instrument or ensemble set my creative juices flowing. . . .
>
> Reverie, as the name suggests, is basically contemplative although there are some contrasting moments of a more animated nature. The two instruments wend their separate ways but always each complements the other.
>
> Awake Thou Wintry Earth is a 17th century Dutch carol (the English title is by Thomas Blackburn). Some 45 years ago when I conducted the chorus of Sarah Lawrence College the Carol was frequently on our programs. Unaccountably this lovely melody came to mind decades later and seemed perfect as a theme for the second movement of the Duo. The Variations are mostly continuous rather than sectional. In one way or another all the music derives from the Carol melody—sometimes identifiably so and sometimes far removed from the simplicity of the original.[46]

While most of the focus on the duo falls on the second movement by virtue of its biographical overtones and tonal immediacy, the "Reverie" deserves greater scrutiny, as it contains perhaps the last example of Schuman's serial interests. The first 19 measures explore nine notes of the scale before the instruments exchange musical lines and repeat and lightly elaborate the material over the subsequent 15 measures. Then, at m. 35, the music deploys the three notes that Schuman has held in abeyance while it simultaneously introduces a new 12-tone row that is unwound over the next ten measures. The music continues in this fashion, using elaborated 12-tone rows and yielding by the final cadence to a tonal conclusion. Schuman failed to draw attention to his use of serial procedures here, just as he failed to do so in the Seventh Symphony and other works from the 1960s. He withdrew his earliest serial effort—the Fugue for Strings of 1946. With the distraction of the seventeenth-century carol, he managed to disguise one of his last nods to a quintessential twentieth-century compositional technique toward which he had a conflicted and extremely private relationship.

Even the second, more tonal movement of the duo seems more experimental than fully formed. Schuman's formidable contrapuntal skills are occasionally on display, such as in the invertible counterpoint that opens the first movement and reappears in mm. 72–104 of the second. But some gestures seem more like miscalculations, such as the imbalance between the clarinet's long held notes at the extreme top of its register and the violin's pizzicato accompaniment (Variations, mm. 60–69). Schuman's music contains numerous examples of instrumental duets, but the extended canvas of *Awake Thou Wintry Earth* seems to last longer than the musical materials warrant. Schuman himself seemed to sense this, as he revisited the duo less than a year after its completion and placed some of its ideas in more conducive surroundings.

The angularity of much of *Awake Thou Wintry Earth* makes it more at home among the pensive works of the late 1970s than among the more public and celebratory pieces he composed between 1980 and 1986. Indeed, after the rather severe works of that earlier period, the 1980s were filled with musical sunshine, occasionally brilliant, rarely obscured, usually warm and inviting. And the radiance came partly from events and awards and publications outside of the compositions themselves, all honoring one of America's great musical statesmen.

His seventieth birthday was preceded by the publication of *William Schuman: Documentary*, a collection in 53 pages of a biographical essay, a catalog of works, a selective bibliography, pictures of Schuman from age three to his late sixties, and an "introductory note" by one of Schuman's dearest companions.

> Bill Schuman and I have been close friends through four decades, and I have come to know this man and his music in a way that can be described only as loving. I have rarely met a composer who is so faithfully mirrored in his music; the man *is* the music. We are all familiar with the attributes generally ascribed to his compositions: vitality, optimism, enthusiasm, long lyrical line, rhythmic impetuousity [*sic*], bristling counterpoint, brilliant textures, dynamic tension. But what is not so often remarked is what I treasure most: the human qualities that flow directly from the man into the works—compassion, fidelity, insight, and total honesty. Compassion is the keynote; it is the mark of a man, and, for me, the mark of this man's music.
>
> Leonard Bernstein
> New York City
> Spring 1979

Schuman was deeply touched by Bernstein's words, his performances of Schuman's music, and his chairmanship of a committee to "celebrate my three score and ten." "For weeks now I have been thinking of how I could thank you for your extraordinary lifelong encouragement and support. . . . What I feel goes beyond my capability to express. But I do think you know."[47] He was also deeply appreciative of the work of the *Documentary*'s principal author, Christopher Rouse, who had written Schuman religiously beginning in 1961 and who routinely shared his compositions with Schuman for critique. Rouse had wanted to include analyses of some of Schuman's compositions; his Cornell University master's thesis focused on the Seventh Symphony, and years later he sent Schuman an analysis of the Sixth, about which Rouse commented that, "in my opinion (for whatever that may be worth) No. 6 IS his greatest symphony, and his greatest work."[48] But Schuman had a different opinion about the documentary.

> In my view, you should forget about the analysis of the music that you had before and write a general account which would not attempt the kinds of personal observations that you were previously attempting. Perhaps at some future distant date you will want to do a full biography, but I think that the present project makes it impractical. But a major statement, which could certainly run 20–30 printed pages, will give you all the room that you need. The material that you labored so hard on will not necessarily be lost, but it seems to me that what I have just described is what the need really is. Do give this some thought before you write or call.[49]

Rouse never did attempt the biography or publish his analyses, but he remained loyal to Schuman to the end, as seen in his letter of condolence to Frankie. "It simply never seemed a real possibility that Bill wouldn't be around—I expected him to outlive us all and hoped he wouldn't be too saddened when I was no longer around to wish him a happy birthday when No. 130 rolled around."[50]

The Juilliard School also reentered Schuman's life in the early 1980s as a major source of happiness. As late at November 1981, Schuman expressed sharp disappointment with his successor Peter Mennin. "I must tell you frankly that since you have been President of the School, we have been often invited to a few special events and those several occasions at which my own music was being performed. We are not, however, and have not been on any regular mailing list."[51] Schuman felt cut off from Juilliard during the Mennin years, but Mennin's sudden and unexpected death in June 1983 brought the prospect of a change in relationship to the school. The selection by the Juilliard board of Joseph W. Polisi ushered in a new wind. Schuman was positively excited about Polisi's promise, adding that "both Frankie and I (we feel like surrogate parents) are here to offer any guidance or assistance that you may request, but please know that I underline the word request."[52] Polisi extended many kindnesses to the Schumans over the next decade, including playing the bassoon part in the premiere of the *Dances* and securing a recording of Schuman's operas. Frankie expressed the depth of the connection when she answered a man who wanted to bequeath his considerable fortune to Schuman as his sole heir. Bill had died the year before, and Frankie suggested that the man will his estate to Juilliard instead. "The current President of the School is Dr. Joseph Polisi, a young man in whom my husband had great faith and whom he considered his musical son."[53] The restoration of his ties to Juilliard constituted a lifeline in Schuman's last decade.

During the 1980s Schuman continued his quixotic crusade for the recording of American music. The Rockefeller Foundation had successfully launched New World Records, but Schuman still felt that not enough was being done. Using the resources of the Koussevitzky Music Foundation and appealing to the National Endowment for the Arts for seed funding, Schuman and others proposed the American Music Recording Institute, which its founders envisioned as a permanent organization underwritten in part by corporate America (Schuman wanted to go to AT&T for the first sales pitch).[54]

> A long-term mechanism is needed to fill the gap between the lack on the part of large commercial companies to record serious American music and the inadequacies of the smaller companies to finance this important element of our cultural life.
>
> The vehicle to achieve this goal is the American Music Recording Institute (AMRI). The premise of AMRI is that serious American music cannot be recorded without subsidy. This applies to the best composers of the past and the present and takes into consideration the need to encourage emerging generations.[55]

With Polisi's arrival at Juilliard, the AMRI board sought to affiliate the proposed institution with the school, but the men behind the organization were barely able to meet the matching grant the that the National Endowment for the Arts awarded them ($11,400 by the end of 1984), and the proposal withered on the vine.

Schuman also continued his friendly skirmish with the Chamber Music Society of Lincoln Center, badgering its board and administration to do better. In 1981, he wrote in a three-page memorandum in which he tallied up the number of individual works performed by the society from its inception to the 1980–81 season. "Including the commissions, the percentage of American works presented was less that 5%, and, if we delete the commissioned works, the percentage was less than 2½%. The time has now come for the Board to establish as stated policy the development of a liberalized repertory to correct this inequity in the content of our programs."[56] By 1984, when Schuman sent the board of directors a five-page memorandum, his concerns had turned to a revolving-door policy that failed to cultivate a regular stable of performers. A draft of the memorandum shows that Schuman laid the blame at the feet of the society's administration, but he toned down his sentiments in the version he sent out. Even so, his views were not his alone: Andrew Porter remarked some months later, "The concerts of the Chamber Music Society of Lincoln Center (sometimes dubbed the Sight-Reading Society of Lincoln Center), in Alice Tully Hall, have seldom in my experience maintained a consistently high level, although individual works on a program have on occasion been well performed, with character and conviction."[57]

American chamber music was not Schuman's only concern. He also sought to address the problem of foreign conductors and the dearth of American music on orchestra programs by encouraging and promoting American conductors who were willing to perform homegrown products. He counseled Dennis Russell Davies that "it is for you as a coming maestro of international fame to schedule American music in reasonable proportion to other repertory, but to do so in a manner that requires you to champion what you consider to be the highest quality without diminishing your role as conductor of extraordinarily catholic tastes."[58] He considered Leonard Slatkin his "arm to the future," and Slatkin indicated a predilection to be just that in an interview with *Gramophone*'s Edward Seckerson in 1988.

> I ask if [Slatkin] might consider one or two of the Piston symphonies. I have happy memories of a Second from him at the Proms a few years back. "Yes, certainly. I love No. 2—it's a beautiful piece—but actually I'm more anxious to get No. 6 down—and No. 4. I think they are more indicative of Piston's best work and his time is long overdue. It's also time for people to hear other Roy Harris symphonies but No. 3. There are seven, after all [*sic*: there are 14 Harris symphonies]. The same with Roger Sessions. Only No. 2 gets done. And William Schuman. Of his ten symphonies, only No. 3 gets heard, yet the Sixth and Eighth are incredible works. Schuman is perhaps the most underrated of all. He's the man, I think, who may eventually emerge as the great American symphonist."[59]

In the early 1980s, the great American symphonist received a number of honors large and small. He accepted the Boston Symphony Orchestra's Horblit Award, whose purpose is "to foster and promote the writing of symphonic compositions by composers resident in the United States by providing for awards to be conferred in recognition of meritorious work in that field, and thus to enlarge and enrich the fund of good music suitable for rendition by symphony orchestras." The award was given in conjunction with performances

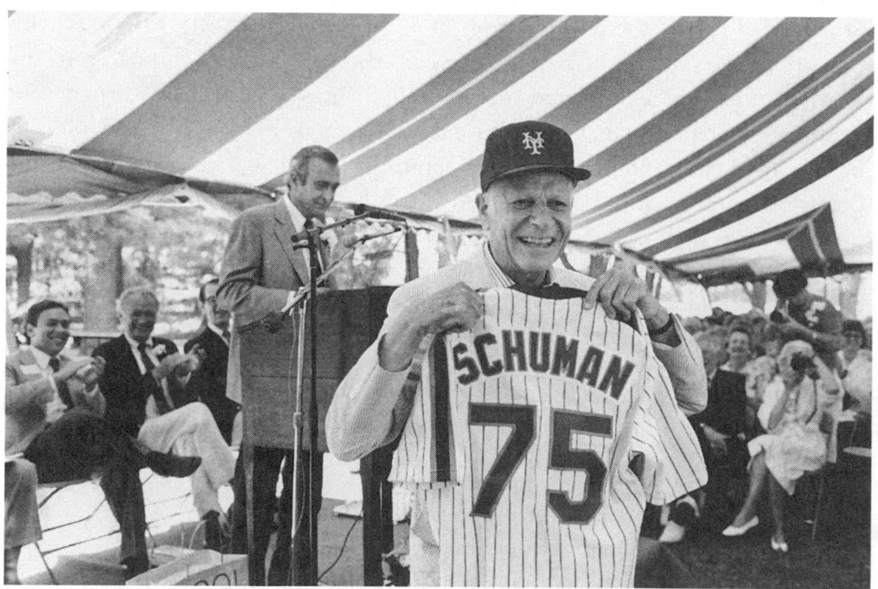

Schuman at the MacDowell Colony Medal Day ceremonies, August 1985. Left to right: Edwin Cohen, cochair of the colony board; Bill Banks; Varujan Boghosian, cochair, at podium; Schuman. Photo by Nancy Crampton.

of the Third Symphony as well as *The Young Dead Soldiers* and *Time to the Old* and came with a cash award of $5,000.[60] He and Frankie both were inducted into the George Washington High School Alumni Hall of Fame "for their outstanding contributions to the arts and humanity," the alumni newsletter said. "Mrs. Schuman claimed that she enjoyed every day of her GW career, while Mr. Schuman expressed the fear that we might have looked up his old school records. Mr. Schuman, noted composer, regaled the group with stories of his early days in the GW orchestra and his equally enthusiastic participation in the GW football team."[61] Network Communication President Steve Robinson produced a 90-minute radio program, *William Schuman: A Life in Music*, which aired in August 1982. Schuman quipped to Robinson: "Today I received an offer of a commission for a piano concerto as a result of the program."[62] Earlier that same year the American Academy and Institute of Arts and Letters awarded him its Gold Medal for Music. Bernstein gave the speech on that occasion, and Schuman returned the favor when Bernstein received the Gold Medal in 1985, the same year that the Pulitzer Prize Board awarded Schuman a Special Citation "for more than half a century of contribution to American music as composer and educational leader."

But Schuman was slowing down. On January 30, 1984, he presided over his last annual meeting as chairman of the board of the MacDowell Colony. The board's resolution reads in part: "Thanks in large measure to him, the Colony flourishes as never before, and does so on a solid fiscal foundation, surely the best point for any institution to begin its second 75 years."[63] He began to turn other responsibilities over to those who had more energy than he had. "It is a source of the greatest satisfaction to me to see such wonderful younger colleagues continuing to care and to struggle to maintain values which would be taken for granted in the Utopian society which will never arrive."[64] And he turned once again to the task of writing his memoirs. He contacted William J. Bennett, head of the National Endowment for the Humanities under President Ronald Reagan and Schuman's fellow board member for the National Humanities Center, to see if the NEH might have a grant program that would allow Schuman to hire a researcher to assist him on his memoirs. "I am determined to take on the book, once I have finished my present assignment, which should certainly take me two years."[65] Schuman finished that project—*On Freedom's Ground*—in one year. The time to compose his account of his life had been handed to him.

So had a most unexpected opportunity.

THIRTY-FIVE

A RARE VINTAGE

For years, Schuman had longed for a professional production of his sole operatic effort, *The Mighty Casey*. The 1953 premiere took place at a university that has a very fine music school, but the zeal of the young singers could not match the polish of seasoned performers. The 1955 television broadcast had high production values, but the cramped requirements of the medium (both spatially and time-wise) left much to be desired. In 1961, the Museum of Modern Art essayed the work, which was seen by a writer for *Sports Illustrated*. All he would venture about the work was a rehash of criticisms that had already been visited upon the opera, giving them the inevitable baseball twist. "The opinion of the majority of music critics was that *The Mighty Casey* struck out."[1] There was exploration in the 1960s to interest the Fujiwara Opera Company of Tokyo in doing the opera. "What I really want to hear is the tape!" Schuman exclaimed to Hans Heinsheimer at G. Schirmer.[2] But the idea came to naught. The Theater Workshop that was run by the New York City Department of Parks gave a performance in 1967 that was hailed in the *New York Times* as the local premiere of the opera. Schuman was incensed, not only listing other local performances but also stressing "the difference between works professionally presented for evaluation by regular critics and works which are used as vehicles for the benefit of the students' development."[3] But New York City had yet to see a professional troupe mount the opera. In 1981, Schuman wrote to congratulate the performers at the Manhattan School of Music for their successful production, but it was yet another school production. "Aside from a poorly mounted television show several years ago and a number of performances of my cantata version there has never been a full-fledged theatrical presentation of professional quality."[4] He was willing to travel to Indiana in 1982 for a tour of various colleges and universities provided there could be "an absolutely first class production by the forces of Bloomington (you mention the University of Indiana [*sic*]) of my baseball opera, The Mighty Casey." But no such production occurred.[5]

And then the Glimmerglass Opera Company brought *Casey* to Cooperstown, New York, the home of the National Baseball Hall of Fame and the alleged birthplace of the game. The event in the summer of 1986 elicited a letter from the White House.

> I am delighted to send greetings to everyone at the Glimmerglass Opera Theater production of The Mighty Casey.
>
> And I want to send double congratulations to the opera's composer, William Schuman: first on the opera itself, and then on his birthday. Mr. Schuman is one of our national assets. He has not only given us original music of depth and delight, but has brought us the music of so many other fine composers. And over the decades, he has trained your musicians to gladden our hearts.[6]

The person who wrote Ronald Reagan's letter for him may have scrambled which musicians Schuman had actually trained, but Schuman had worked diligently throughout his life to bring the music of other fine *American* composers to light. And now the production of *Casey* during his seventy-fifth birthday celebration gladdened his heart. The year began with a party chez Schuman with family and a few old friends on the actual day, August 4, 1985. Eddie Marks was there, and together the two sang their old Cobbossee hit, "We're Dressed Up for the Visitors."[7] And now the year ended with the first-ever professional production of the baseball opera that had taken root in the wilds of Maine some 60 years earlier, in part from Marks's recitation of the Thayer poem. B. A. Nilsson, writing for *Opera News*, said hardly anything about "Schuman's intricate writing" but affirmed what Schuman had always hoped would happen to *The Mighty Casey*: the opera "got a grand-slam treatment by [Cooperstown's] resident Glimmerglass Opera."[8]

So positive was the experience of the Cooperstown throng that Paul Kellogg, Glimmerglass's general director, saw more than a repeat performance in the future. "We would be thrilled to have the stage premiere of a new William Schuman work written to accompany *Casey*, and we could stage it when it is done—say after 1988. . . . I would be delighted to work with you again on anything."[9] And so it was, before *On Freedom's Ground* had its first performance, that the seed was planted for Schuman's last major work.

First up, though, was a smaller project that Kellogg and Schuman agreed to and that Schuman finished not long after he wrote the alternate version of *Awake Thou Wintry Earth*.

> COOPERSTOWN FANFARE [February 27, 1987] was composed for the Glimmerglass Opera Theater on the occasion of the opening of The Alice Busch Opera Theater on June 27, 1987 in Cooperstown, NY. The FANFARE (which lasts approximately one minute) was performed on the opening night, as it henceforth will be at all performances, on an outdoor balcony to summon the audience at curtain time at the beginning of the performance and at the conclusion of intermissions. Although the work is scored for but four instruments, equal multiples of each part may be used.[10]

This, the last of the fanfares Schuman wrote, shares with them the basic trait of being derived from earlier material. Here, Schuman took the opening five measures of "Whoever You Are" (from the 1982 choral work *Perceptions*) and expanded them into a 13-measure exposition that is then repeated a minor third higher and with some chromatic intensifications. A third repetition, again a minor third higher, is interrupted by a homophonic parade of chords, all of which have the first trumpet sounding a high A as the second trombone descends from G to C♯ on a whole-tone scale, which in turn is arrested by a turn to the D-major conclusion. This overall trajectory also mirrors the structure of "Whoever You Are," which (like the fanfare) begins in G major and ends with a D-major peroration. Whitman's words likely were in Schuman's mind as he transferred the choral work into this instrumental medium for the Glimmerglass Opera.

> Whoever you are! motion and reflection are especially for you,
> The divine ship sails the divine sea for you.
>
> Whoever you are! you are he or she for whom the earth is solid and liquid,
> You are he or she for whom the sun and moon hang in the sky,
> For none more than you are the present and the past,
> For none more than you is immortality.

Schuman was looking beyond the *Cooperstown Fanfare* for possible operatic properties for Glimmerglass, but his past experiences with composing an opera gave him good reason to believe that he would not succeed in finding a story or a librettist. As a result, he accepted a commission to write a work celebrating the opening of the Tampa Bay (Florida) Performing Arts Center. Incredibly, he was offered the commission in early 1987 for a center that was slated to open that summer. Schuman told the folks in Tampa Bay that he had another commission he was working on that would not be completed until the early summer, after which time he could turn his attention to Tampa Bay. "Even under the most optimistic forecast," he warned them, "it is unlikely that the work will be ready before the 1988–1989 season. For this reason, I think it unwise to make any announcement at this time."[11] But as a sign of his intention to make good on the commission, he accepted the first installment of $20,000 for the celebratory work.

The work that occupied his attention for much of the first half of 1987 was his String Quartet no. 5. His good friend Marty Segal had dreamed up the kind of New York festival Schuman had labored to establish at Lincoln Center: the New York International Festival of the Arts, "an ambitious arts undertaking that plans to attract outstanding performers, composers, choreographers and film makers from around the world, [which was] scheduled to begin on June 13, 1988, and be held in the city every two years thereafter." One of the first announcements of the new festival brought news of seven commissions; according to Segal, the seven composers selected "were based on recommendations from a panel of authorities." Ned Rorem (b. 1923) and Joseph Schwantner (b. 1943) weren't present for the announcement, but the other five composers were: Christopher Rouse (b. 1949), Gunther Schuller (b. 1925), Jacob Druckman (b. 1928), Stephen Albert (b. 1941), and the grand old man who was more than a decade older than the rest. The *New York Times* story led with Schuman's comments about his commissioned work. "I plan to compose chamber music, although I don't know what yet."[12] The *Dances* were done, *Showcase* was ready for Houston, *Awake Thou Wintry Earth* was nearing completion, and *Casey* had not yet scored its triumph at Glimmerglass. After the exertions it took to complete *On Freedom's Ground*—still unperformed at the time of the festival commission—perhaps a chamber work appeared to be a manageable prospect.

The two-movement quartet that resulted from the commission is remarkable for the scale of Schuman's self-borrowing. Previously, he would alter works that were based on earlier ones, either extending them through chains of variations (*A Song of Orpheus*, *American Hymn*) or adding substantial new portions to preexisting music (the last two movements of the Eighth Symphony, *Voyage for Orchestra*, *Chester: Overture for Band*). Even in the patchwork efforts (*Casey at the Bat*, every fanfare save for the *Cooperstown Fanfare*), new music was interwoven with the old. But the first movement of the Fifth String Quartet is a straight transcription of the slow movement of the Tenth Symphony, so much so that, at one point in his sketches for the movement, he wrote the notation "mm. 15 through 23: omit top note of chord" and did not trouble himself with writing out those nine measures until it came time to write out the manuscript. The filigree in the quartet is more elaborate than that in the symphony, especially at those points at which sustained chords in the orchestral version call out for more animation in the all-string version. But one could easily take the score of the symphony and follow the quartet, and vice versa. In preparing the symphony for its premiere, Doráti had singled out praise for the Brucknerian slow movement. Did Schuman recast the movement to ensure that it would have greater exposure? Or was this the act of a composer who was running out of ideas?

His treatment of the quartet's second movement suggests that it was a combination of both creative fatigue and repurposing music that may otherwise have gone unheard. Here, Schuman recycled some—but by no means all—of the Variations movement of *Awake Thou Wintry Earth*. The opening 24 measures of the quartet movement, for example, present all new material noteworthy for the rather straightforward presentation of the Dutch carol. The next variation is a rewriting of the duo's opening measures, with Schuman starting out with two voices but quickly adopting a four-voice texture and reharmonizing the duo's material. With the exception of a cello cadenza and a two-part variation for the violins, the rest of the movement eschews the leanness of *Awake Thou Wintry Earth* and fills out the harmonic and gestural implications of the earlier work. But equally telling is what Schuman chose to jettison or recompose, such as the violin duet in the quartet that has no immediate cognate in the clarinet-violin duo. In the earlier work, the instruments often seem to be "talking" past each other; here, there is more of a sense of the various lines working in coordination with one another.

The Variations portion of the second movement of the quartet take up 300 measures, and the Epilogue accounts for the final 62 measures, but in terms of time, the Epilogue is only slightly shorter than the Variations. With instruments muted for the rest of the work, the music first spins out a slow reminiscence of the carol, then recapitulates 33 measures from the first movement (in typical Schuman shorthand, he noted in his manuscript which measures from the first movement the copyist needed to interpolate here), and closes with a brief recollection of the carol in E major and a turn to a final cadence in E♭ major, the same key in which the first movement ends. The valedictory nature of the Fifth String Quartet, with its extensive self-quotations and pensive caste, places it alongside Shostakovich's final string quartet as a work that is both autobiographical and remote, accessible and impenetrable at the same time. It is one of Schuman's finest achievements, dedicated to the memory of Vincent Persichetti, his longtime friend, first biographer, and musical fellow traveler, who died on August 14, 1987, five days before Schuman completed the quartet.[13]

A Question of Taste, the opera Schuman composed for Glimmerglass as a companion piece to *The Mighty Casey*, is a remarkable achievement in other ways. Schuman could have easily allowed *On Freedom's Ground* to be his last major musical statement. But as with that work, once he found a way into the new opera, he was too hot to stop.

He first asked Richard Wilbur if the two of them could collaborate once again. Frankie had suggested to Schuman that he look at Roald Dahl's short story "Taste," which first appeared in the December 8, 1951, issue of the *New Yorker*. The story tells of a dinner party at the London home of Michael Schofield at which six people are present: the story's unnamed narrator and his wife; Schofield, his wife, Margaret, and their 18-year-old daughter, Louise; and Richard Pratt, "president of a small society known as the Epicures," a well-known oenophile about 50 years old whose mouth is shaped "like a large, wet keyhole." The narrator recalls that "on both Richard Pratt's previous visits Mike had played a little betting game with him over the claret, challenging him to name its breed and its vintage." Mike had wagered Pratt a case of the wine if Pratt could guess correctly; both times Pratt had won the wager. On this evening, Mike is certain he has found a claret that Pratt cannot identify, and in his overconfidence he tells Pratt, "I'll bet you anything you like." Pratt names his stakes: "I want you to bet me the hand of your daughter in marriage." After some initial confusion and vocal consternation from both Margaret and Louise, Mike presses what he thinks is his advantage. Pratt offers his two houses as a counterbid; with them, Mike tells Louise, she will be a rich woman. Louise at first is adamantly opposed to the wager, but her father wears her down with his assurances that Pratt will never identify the wine, and the bet is on. Of course, Pratt does successfully name the wine's year, vintage, and vineyard, flustering all except the maid, who overhears the entire gambit. She interrupts the dinner party by returning to Pratt his reading glasses, which he had forgotten on top of the filing cabinet upstairs in Mike's study, the same place Mike had allowed the wine to breathe before bringing it down to the table. The story ends with Margaret having the last words: "Keep calm now, Michael, dear! Keep calm!"[14]

Schuman thought the story would suit his purposes for a companion piece for *Casey*. He shared his find with Wilbur, who was less enthusiastic about the Dahl than Schuman was. "My sense of what might adapt to music is not a keen one, but I <u>think</u> I see that this tale might make for a <u>very</u> light short opera, in which the music would amuse itself especially with the gloating voice of the connoisseur as he rehearses the qualities of wines." Wilbur also asked Schuman to understand his decision not to undertake writing the libretto. "I don't think I'm the one to do it, and in any case I am (as I told you over the 'phone) very anxious at present to concentrate on recovering the habit of writing my own poems."[15] Wilbur gave him the name of another poet who might be able to work with Schuman. Two months later Schuman reported back to Wilbur.

> Thank you so much for referring me to John Hollander. We talked by phone and he couldn't have been nicer. He wanted very much to do the work with me, but was concerned with his other commitment. Since I do not have the luxury of waiting (time, you remember) I was happy to follow his suggestion that I get in touch with J. D. McClatchy. I have met with Mr. McClatchy and talked with him several times by phone. His knotty poetry seems far removed from the lyrics that would be required for the new opera, but he wants to do the work and I somehow feel that his intelligence and wit may carry the day. He has an excellent sense of theater, but the problem of the text remains. I'm optimistic, but not so foolish as to proceed just to solve the problem of finding a librettist.[16]

Wilbur agreed with Schuman about McClatchy's poetry but was equally confident that his young protégé—"a bright, talented, enthusiastic fellow with whom you should enjoy working"—would be able to turn the short story into a libretto.[17]

McClatchy (b. 1945) was eager. "I accepted at once, without ever having read the Dahl story. A few days later, when I got hold of the story, I was a little dismayed by its slickness, but could see at once its operatic possibilities. My task would be to 'translate' Dahl's one-dimensional plot into a resonant dramatic structure."[18] Within days McClatchy produced "a quick sketch of an opening for *A Matter of Taste*. Though it falls into verse, I've tried to keep it fairly clear and straightforward—i.e., singable. But because this is a quick rough draft, I'd plan to add nuances in a later version—and, of course, adjust it to your thoughts about the musical line."[19] What McClatchy did not know at the time was that Schuman was soliciting sample work from other writers, one of whom was Michael Bawtree, author of *The New Singing Theatre: A Charter for the Music Theatre Movement* (1991).[20] But McClatchy's verse and approach, Schuman felt, were superior to the efforts of the others, and soon the two were moving forward on what Schuman called *A Question of Taste*.

McClatchy originally tried turning the narrator and his wife into Louise's uncle and aunt, but neither he nor Schuman could figure out what dramatic purpose they served, so they were cut. They did agree on adding a suitor for Louise, Tom, whose middle-class background and aspirations make him, in Schofield's eyes, an unacceptable match for Louise. The maid gets a surname (Mrs. Hudson), Michael and Margaret Schofield lose their first names, and Richard Pratt is transmogrified into Phillisto Pratt, his oleaginous manner made plain in his new name. By May 1987, McClatchy and Schuman were in regular contact, shaping the details of the story, and though McClatchy was in London for much of the fall, he continued to supply Schuman with words to set. Schuman for his part began composing sometime in June 1987; by the following April, he had completed the vocal score.

McClatchy later published some of his diary entries from this period. They not only chronicle his back-and-forth with Schuman but also record some of the music Schuman heard in his mind as he wrote his opera: McClatchy should avoid using the word "tonight" because "Bernstein had patented the word"; Sondheim's lyrics for *A Little Night Music* are exemplary for what Schuman had in mind; "Là ci darem la mano" (*Don Giovanni*) came to Schuman's mind as he imagined the climactic "Tasting Song."[21] The Mozartean lightness of the score, the importance of the waltz, and the traces of Cunegonde's "Glitter and Be Gay" (*Candide*) heard in Louise's tra-la-las reverberate in McClatchy's exchanges with Schuman.

The waltz plays an especially important role in the opera. After the opening "conflict" *Klangfarbenmelodie*, the orchestra introduces the waltz that will be associated with Louise. In classic Schuman fashion, the outer voices move in opposite directions at roughly the same pace, going from the solid B♭-major beginning to more and more esoteric (but still tonally derived) chords, then erupting in what will become Louise's stratospheric flights of vocal fancy before circling back to the waltz's beginning strains. The waltz returns at various moments in the opera: at the conclusion of Louise's aria, as an intermezzo that gives the dining party time to take their seats and begin the meal, as a sad witness to the successful conclusion of the wager, and as a conduit for celebration at the opera's end. Louise herself undergoes a transformation from the story (whose time period, 1950 or '51, is contemporaneous to Dahl's own at the time of its creation) to the opera (which is set in 1910). In the story, Louise says little beyond her vehement opposition to being the object of a bet and takes a passive role in the events determining her fate. In the opera, it is Louise, over Tom's objections, who ultimately accepts Pratt's wager, an act that is reflected in the wilted waltz that follows. Schofield and Pratt also have waltz fragments: Schofield, in his apostrophe to wine at the start of the dinner; and Pratt, in his confession of obsession over Louise. Though Schuman came to the waltz independent of *A Little Night Music*, there is at least one other fascinating use of triple time in *A Question of Taste*, where Pratt's "tasting" aria continually loops back to a minuet-like feature, a fitting musical caricature of his supposed aristocratic superiority.

Before he had an opportunity to hear his new opera in a workshop performance, Schuman turned to complete two outstanding commissions and cancel a third. In February 1988, he returned the $20,000 to the Tampa Bay people, apologizing and explaining that "my long delay in writing the commissioned work was caused by an irresistible compulsion to devote my time first to a different project which continues to consume all my attention" [i.e., the opera].[22] Meanwhile, he had already conceived the piece he was asked to write as part of a birthday bouquet being gathered for Leonard Bernstein to celebrate his seventieth birthday. He wrote to Boston Symphony Orchestra conductor Seiji Ozawa in November 1987: "Your idea of asking a few composers to write variations on 'New York, New York', not exceeding 1½ minutes, is charming, and I will take part with pleasure. . . . Because of my schedule I must do the variations over the Christmas holidays which will be upon us almost immediately."[23] The variation, *Let's Hear It for Lenny!*, wasn't completed until June 24, 1988, but Schuman may have indeed completed the variation when he told Ozawa he would, for just after the New Year, he laid out his plans for the work. "In composing one of the variations for the Bernstein celebration on his tune, New York, New York, I may quote briefly from I Feel Pretty, Tonight, and possibly a fragment from the Candide Overture."[24] Not only does the work use all of these Bernstein tunes and fragments—and Schuman quoted liberally from "Tonight" and *Candide*—but it also opens with the bass drum and gong strokes that are indelibly associated with *Fanfare for the Common Man*. Schuman wasn't the only composer of a birthday variation to make the connection between the upward thrust of "New York, New York" and the similar wide-open gesture in the Copland: Corigliano's variation also begins with a reference to the fanfare. But Schuman's homage strikes a deeper emotional chord than does the Corigliano. Copland was no longer sentient enough to compose a variation in honor of Bernstein. In quoting his older and younger colleagues, both of whom he had met a half-century earlier, and in weaving their music into his characteristic triad piles, Schuman turned this musical valentine—which is also his last orchestral work—into a compendium of the three men's work. If only Koussevitzky could have conducted it.

The other commission came from the Van Cliburn Foundation in Fort Worth, Texas. The eighth Van Cliburn International Piano Competition was scheduled for 1989, and the organizers turned to Schuman in January 1987 to write the commissioned work that they would need by New Year's Eve of 1988. As with *Let's Hear It for Lenny*! Schuman knew from the start what this work would be. He told Richard Rodzinski, the executive director of the foundation: "As I discussed with Van and with you, I am planning a piano work based on the William Billings anthem Chester. The work will be based on my prior treatment of this piece in my Chester Overture for band and my New England Triptych for orchestra. Of course, the material will be greatly varied and there will be additions."[25] In fact, the music was not greatly varied: *Chester: Variations for Piano* is, like the first movement of the Fifth String Quartet, a straight transcription, this time of the *Chester: Overture for Band*. The "additions" include a "piccolo" obbligato beginning in m. 212, which is followed by rapid left-hand smears beginning in m. 220. But again, one can follow the *Overture* with the piano score and vice versa.

Given Schuman's history of writing for the piano, it is hardly surprising that *Chester: Variations for Piano* is not always idiomatic for the instrument. It resembles Musorgsky's "Great Gate of Kiev" from *Pictures at an Exhibition*, with its clumsy bass grace notes, its lurches from one part of the piano to another, its easy-to-notate-but-almost-impossible-to-execute rapid octaves, and its constant cries for orchestral color. Its difficulties became immediately apparent after Schuman delivered the score. Rodzinski gave Schuman an early verdict. Having shown the work to two former gold medalists, the general conclusion was that *Chester* "is really charming and flashy, and will present a number of challenges." Some of the challenges required editorial attention, and Schuman adjusted some of the notes to accommodate some of the more unpianistic passages. But Rodzinski's main complaint was more fundamental: Schuman indicated that the tempo for most of the work was extremely fast, quarter note = 160. "I do recall, of course, that in our last conversation you told me Beveridge Webster had played through the piece for you. Was he really able to maintain that tempo to the end?!"[26] Schuman wrote to reassure Rodzinski. "I am not concerned about my tempo mark of 160 because you will note that it is preceded by 'circa'. This would permit a certain latitude in the speed and assure that the spirit of the piece will be maintained."[27] The difficulties of the piece, however, have less to do with its tempo and more to do with its conception. Schuman may have been a Ravel when it came to orchestration, but he was no Ravel when it came to writing for the piano. Great transcriptions transcend their original source, as does Ravel's orchestration of the Musorgsky or Liszt's various reminiscences of the operas of his day. *Chester: Variations for Piano* is only an adequate transcription, and a successful performance of the piano piece rests on a familiarity with the band piece on which it is based, how that earlier work "sounds," and how to transfer those "sounds" to the piano.

With these two works off of his desk by the end of August 1988, Schuman was free to turn his entire attention to *A Question of Taste*. But before he could turn to the orchestration, he and McClatchy needed to hear their work to see what needed to be adjusted. A workshop performance was arranged by Glimmerglass and was originally scheduled to take place in Cooperstown, but Schuman's health had prevented him from traveling to Tanglewood to hear his tribute to Bernstein in mid-August, so the performers rehearsed in Cooperstown but came down to New York City to perform for Schuman and McClatchy on September 1, 1988.

The question of health shadowed the collaboration. Earlier in the year Schuman had written to his publisher about the contract that needed to be drawn up.

> Some provision should be made in case either McClatchy or I for reasons beyond our control are not able to finish the work. Should this occur in McClatchy's case the composer would be free to choose a successor with an equitable share of royalties to be determined. Should the composer be unable to finish the opera, he would like to leave the question of another composer completing the work for decision by his wife and his publisher. For your guidance I am well into the work and expect to have a completed sketch by the summer. This sketch could form the basis for some other composer to do the orchestration if I were unable to carry it out myself.[28]

He had finished the work months ahead of his own schedule, but he and McClatchy both felt that time was not on Schuman's side.

McClatchy wrote in his diary on August 4, 1988—Schuman's seventy-eighth birthday—about receiving a phone call from Schuman in thanks for the birthday greetings McClatchy had sent earlier. "Several people, closer to the Schumans than I, have hinted Bill is unwell. Whether it's a perennial bone and back problem, or something more serious, I don't know; perhaps they don't either, but no one is talking. Bill's voice *does* sound a little weaker. I hope he has the strength for the orchestration and premiere." Schuman suffered from spinal stenosis, which he believed he inherited from his mother and which impeded his work in his later years.[29] It made work on *A Question of Taste* difficult.

The workshop inevitably revealed that there was more work that the two men could and should do. Of the numerous adjustments that McClatchy felt needed to be made, the most serious was the final ensemble. Instead of ending the opera with Pratt still at the table and the others ready to do him bodily harm, McClatchy invoked the example of *Don Giovanni*, having Pratt flee the scene and the remaining characters reflect upon the events of the evening. Schuman had originally thought that the opera could end with Pratt's exit, but he came reluctantly to see the wisdom of McClatchy's dramatic expansion. It created the perfect set-up for an extended quintet along the lines of Barber's *Vanessa*, whose final pages Schuman greatly admired, and one can easily imagine a master of counterpoint writing a canon (*Così fan tutte*, *Fidelio*) or a fugue (*Falstaff*) to let both the characters and the music unwind. But despite McClatchy's pleadings for more music at this point of the opera, Schuman refused to budge. "Bill is determined to bring the curtain down as quickly as possible. Something else he said, though, struck me as his real reason for resisting any changes now. He said he just didn't want to go back to the score, that he felt 'written out.'"[30] In Schuman's defense, just two years earlier he had seen *The Mighty Casey* in a highly professional and sympathetic production and witnessed how a few judicious cuts addressed some of the longueurs in that work.[31] Lengthening his new opera may have seemed unwise, and revisions more of a distraction than a necessity.

Besides, the work was in sufficient shape that Kellogg and the staff at Glimmerglass felt confident in scheduling a summer 1989 premiere. Schuman would need to complete the orchestration in less than a year. To facilitate that process, he devised a system. "Great thick cardboard sheets about two feet long are used; he 'indicates' orchestration which the copyist will fill out, and then Bill will correct it all, making certain the sound he wants is there."[32] Once again, he defied the auguries and finished the task on the last day of February. But bad health continued to plague him. Midway through the task of orchestration, McClatchy saw him. "He seems much frailer," McClatchy wrote. "As Frankie said, just referring to their schedule though she may as well have had more in mind, 'Everything's slowing down.'"[33]

The Glimmerglass staff and artists may have initially fretted over Schuman's music, but their worries were dispelled days before the opera's premiere, according to McClatchy.

> At the end, everyone, conductor, singers, director, the odd people in the house, and I—all of us were delighted by the score. Its deft transparency, its ravishing bits, and melodic buoyancy are bound to make it appealing. And the scoring reveals the work more as the elegant comedy it was written to be; the piano had made it dark, percussive, motoric—and that's not, in fact, the effect of the score at all.[34]

McClatchy also noted the role that Schuman played at the eleventh hour.

> He reminds me, I suppose, of the old Verdi—the same shrunken, noble figure of age.
>
> At this late stage of things, tempers are rawer, patience frayed, and details nag. And arriving, as he has, at the very last minute, Bill would be bound to stir things up. The trouble is, he's usually right.[35]

The rough dress rehearsals gave way to a sparkling premiere.

Not everyone liked the work, of course. Bernard Holland (*New York Times*) opined that "Mr. Schuman, I think, is a more interesting composer than J. D. McClatchy's libretto lets him be." Holland found the characters one-dimensional and laid the blame on the librettist.

> There is villainy and virtue, love and contempt—but no people. Rather we are given characters who wear their one-idea identities like name tags at an auto dealer's convention. . . . Irony is the ability of one thing to seem to be several other, and often contradictory, things—Mr. Schuman's chameleon-like waltz tunes, for example. In "A Question of Taste," one reads the name tags and has little else to learn.[36]

When the opera came to New York, courtesy of the Juilliard School the following year in honor of Schuman's eightieth birthday, John Rockwell once again dismissed Schuman's music, calling it "merely bland."[37] In contrast, Willard Spiegelman (*Wall Street Journal*) felt that the proper context for understanding the new opera was to view it in tandem with its companion piece and found ample reason to praise McClatchy's work.

> If "Casey" shows the dark side of American exuberance, "A Question of Taste" plucks success and a happy ending from the jaws of imminent tragedy. Unlike "Casey," it is all tension and surprise. In his creative maturity, Mr. Schuman has composed a chamber opera that celebrates the triumph of youth, passion and idealism over the schemings of age, greed and money. This classic comic story is all the more touching when paired with his more energetic, more populist and more pessimistic earlier work. . . . The libretto, by the poet J. D. McClatchy, succeeds in two complementary ways: its deftly rhymed couplets and quatrains are eminently singable, and Mr. McClatchy's additions to the tale have inspired Mr. Schuman to write a score that alludes wittily to operatic comedies by Mozart and Richard Strauss.[38]

(One should add Bernstein and Sondheim to Spiegelman's list.) McClatchy's friend Wayne Koestenbaum saw a deeper truth in the two operas. "'Taste' and 'Casey' together make a marvelous double bill. Each opera hinges on a question, a wager. A man is tested; he fails the test; his failure is redeemed by love (and by your music)."[39]

The premiere of *A Question of Taste* on June 24, 1989, for all intents and purposes, marks the end of Schuman's creative life. So energized was he by the experience on his second opera that a year later Schuman was talking to McClatchy about the possibility of writing a third. After the premiere, though, there was ample evidence that Schuman no longer had the same spark that allowed him to compose both his American cantata and his period opera at breakneck speed, and McClatchy was witness to the dimming of the flame.

Schuman's eightieth year began auspiciously. Three days after his birthday, the John F. Kennedy Center for the Performing Arts released the names of the 1989 Kennedy Center honorees: singer and actor Harry Belafonte, actresses Claudette Colbert and Mary Martin, dancer Alexandra Danilova, and Schuman.[40] He and Martin went all the way back to the ill-fated 1944 production of *Henry VIII*, and though his relationship with the Kennedy Center wasn't as long, it was far deeper. Closer to the heart was the memories that the ceremony and subsequent telecast created and elicited. Upon his arrival in Washington, D.C., Schuman was handed a telegram from Bernstein: "DEAR BILL, AT LAST . . . HUGS AND KISSES TO YOU BOTH. LENNY." Schuman responded, "I knew then that the weekend would be wonderful, and it was! I can't thank you enough for the support I know you lent to my candidacy."[41] Bill and Frankie did not travel alone, and he wrote to another acquaintance about how meaningful the events were for his family. "We had a lovely visit at the White House with a minimum of ceremony in which Frankie and I were joined by our son and his bride of two years, and our daughter and her son, Josh, who turns 16 next week."[42] He also expressed his amazement at how the telecast had allowed him to reconnect with his Cobbossee campmates. One, Sandy Krasner, not only helped Schuman recall the names of some of the kids as well as the words to some of his songs but also reminded him of some of his shenanigans back in the 1920s.

> You were quite manipulative, and far more sophisticated than I was. One night, for some reason, some of us were across the lake at a place I think was called "The Colony". We were seated opposite a group of girls. The girl opposite me was pretty. The one opposite you was not. You stood up and suggested that we all play a game—that each girl was to move up two chairs—just like checkers or chess. Needless to say, the pretty girl wound up opposite you and you made sure it remained that way. I, of course, in my stupid, naive way did not know what to do about it. I should have known that you would do well in life.[43]

"Isn't it amazing," Schuman wrote back to Krasner, "the hold that Cobbossee has on us even to this day. To have been there was truly an extraordinary experience."[44]

A dear friend who had known Schuman only since the 1940s gave him another opportunity for retrospection. Greenwich neighbor Joan Warburg turned to him in the fall of 1989 with a request for a commission. Schuman had already written a work of sorts for Warburg: the little *Round for Emily Joan Warburg* to celebrate the birth of Warburg's granddaughter on September 2, 1981. Now she wanted a larger, more public work as part of the celebrations surrounding the 350th anniversary of the establishment of Greenwich, Connecticut, that were taking place in 1990. Schuman accepted an $8,000 commission for a three- to six-minute unaccompanied choral work that needed to be completed by the spring of 1990. He even identified the source of his text: McClatchy.[45] The two men had spent the summer and fall discussing different texts that McClatchy brought to Schuman's attention: Elizabeth Bishop, Anthony Hecht, Randall Jarrell, the dramatic poems of Robert Frost (particularly "Home Burial" and "The Death of the Hired Man"), Thoreau and Muir and Audubon and others. Ideas swirled about creating an American *Histoire du soldat*; McClatchy thought that the legend of Johnny Appleseed lent itself particularly well to the kind of setting Stravinsky gave to his hapless Russian soldier. Now, with an actual commission with a fixed deadline in front of them, surely both men could either find or adapt a text that would meet the modest requirements that Warburg put forth.[46]

But none of McClatchy's ideas quickened Schuman, including the poem that McClatchy had attempted for the Greenwich Founders' Day celebration. Schuman asked McClatchy to start all over again. Schuman wasn't the only one who was stuck, though, and with loving exasperation McClatchy volunteered that it was time for them both to move on.

> I've two suggestions. One is for you just to plunge ahead, trust yourself to the text and to your ability to have what you've already written inspire what's to come. The second suggestion is for you to look elsewhere for a text—and preferably one by a dead poet with whom you can't argue. (I don't mean to be facetious; there's a whole different psychology at work with a text that's fixed rather than fluid.) I'm enclosing a few of the very last poems by Connecticut's greatest poet, Wallace Stevens. Have you thought of him? It's an obvious connection for the ceremony; and there are other poems than these to consider.[47]

A month later, Schuman wrote to Warburg to tell her that he had found a solution to the commission, courtesy of Richard Vogt, director of the Greenwich Choral Society. The year before, Vogt and the society performed the 1956 choral arrangement of *The Lord Has a Child* at a concert celebrating Schuman's installation as an artist laureate by the Greenwich Arts Council. It was Vogt who suggested that Schuman rework the text for chorus with instruments.[48]

Vogt offered Schuman an artistic reprieve, but in his letter to Warburg, Schuman revealed his own desperation and creative drought.

> Richard's suggestion that I do a new version of the hymn is in line with similar projects that I have undertaken in the past, as is traditional with so many composers. For example, I first was commissioned to write the song, Orpheus With His Lute, for a production of Henry VIII, and later I accepted several commissions, using the song as the basis for the compositions of new works; i.e., A Song of Orpheus—Fantasy for Cello and Orchestra, and In Sweet Music for flute, viola, harp and voice. I also made choral arrangements of the original song. . . . While I can report progress, in many ways remodeling older material is even more difficult than writing something completely new, but I am now happy in the endeavor, whereas previously I felt frustrated, given the unresolved problem of a text.[49]

Schuman failed to tell Warburg about the commission that led to his original setting of the Langston Hughes poem. Nor did he mention the commissions from the American Brass Quintet, the American Bandmasters Association, the St. Louis Symphony Orchestra, and the Houston Symphony Orchestra, each of which he fulfilled by parceling out that hymn. But the decision to recycle the hymn once more freed Schuman to fulfill the Greenwich commission, and despite spending ten days in the hospital earlier in the year, he finished what would be his last complete score on March 15, 1990.[50] Warburg was gracious and grateful.

> You must know how thrilled all of us connected with the 350 Commission are with your hymn for brass quintet and chorus. It is sure to be the highlight of the Greenwich

> Pops/Greenwich Choral Society Concert on June 9th. To have had you dedicate it to Richard Vogt's Greenwich Choral Society as well as your "ole friend Joan" is very special.[51]

Heavy rains in May led to a postponement of the outdoor concert, which took place on June 16. "It was like a bigger-than-life celebration. . . . There were friends and neighbors with their children, approximately 5,200, the biggest crowd ever." No music critic would mar such a spectacular festival with a negative review. The writer for the *Greenwich Time* said scant little about *The Lord Has A Child* beyond how the work sounded to him. "The Schuman work . . . uses a hymn-like melody to which he adds polytonal harmonies and modulations, ending with a gentle amen."[52] The *Greenwich News* critic chose a polemical line of argument, decrying what happened to American music during the 1940s when "a flood of German intellectuals swept into the country and soon occupied leading positions in our music schools, bringing with them their severely atonal, dissonant, Serialist theories." True American music was temporarily lost. "Fortunately, there came a shift in popular opinion and those lost American composers are at last being rediscovered. The entire evening's program was a tribute to them all. William Schuman was present at the concert and must have been gratified by the tumultuous applause offered to him with love by his Greenwich admirers."[53] It was his last premiere, and the Manhattan-born kid was hailed as a Connecticut hero.

Later that summer McClatchy tried again to stir up whatever embers of creativity remained in Schuman. The two discussed once more a work for the stage.

> By all means, if you want to work on a new opera, you must. And I will do anything I can to help—at the low level of suggestion or the best level—collaboration. Of course I'd be thrilled to work with you again, but if you'd prefer to try someone else, fine. The main thing is for you to work. . . .
>
> On the drive to and from [Cooperstown], I thought of a couple of operatic possibilities to toss out to you. One is Mary Baker Eddy. Another would be to adapt some folk plays—Japanese, or American Indian, say. A third idea (this could be an oratorio with narrator, or an opera) is Johnny Appleseed—a wild fantasy of his adventure, with a Chorus of Saplings, etc., full of the Open Road. (Would this hit the environmental nerve as well!)[54]

McClatchy later called the Appleseed story "an effort to play to [Schuman's] strengths at vigorous and plangent American lyricism," but another stage work would likely have taken both men at least two years to complete.[55] The talk was the thing.

Autumn brought the deaths of two of Schuman's closest colleagues. His fellow academicians in the American Academy of Arts and Letters called upon Schuman to write the commemorative tribute to Bernstein, who died on October 14.

Schuman himself was not well enough to attend the meeting at which the tribute was read, so he asked Hugo Weisgall to read it on his behalf.

> On the deeper personal level there are not words for me adequately to express what his enduring friendship meant to those he loved and who loved him. In the final analysis it was his capacity to interact fully with his fellow human beings which was the underlying factor from which all else emerged.
>
> If music, as Aaron Copland has written, is one of the glories of mankind, then surely our Leonard Bernstein will ever be one of the glories of music.
>
> We are fortunate to have lived in his time.[56]

Five days before Weisgall read Schuman's tribute on December 7, Copland had died. Schuman attended a luncheon in memory of Copland, at which he revealed what was on his reading table. "The quotation that I used [at the luncheon] . . . is by Joseph Addison and appeared in The Spectator of May 17, 1712. It is used in John Hersey's new book, 'Antonietta', in his dedication to his wife, Barbara. 'Cheerfulness keeps up a kind of daylight in the mind, and fills it with a steady and perpetual serenity.'"[57] Schuman shared with Vivian Perlis the joy he had had in one of his last visits with Copland, one that Perlis arranged.

> As I told you on the telephone, it was wonderful visiting Aaron last week. Although he is frail physically and his memory is virtually non-existent, two things came through which were so heartening. When a subject was introduced which didn't require him to remember the past, one had flashes of the giant intellect undiminished. The other reassuring aspect was the Copland wit. It came through at so many points during the visit. I still feel the warmth of his hand on my shoulder, and those slaps on the back just as though it was back when he was an old man of 35 and I an old man of 25. But now we are younger, and our age differences seem not to matter so much.[58]

As 1990 drew to a close, Schuman's older colleague and younger protégé had left him.

Schuman, however, was intent on forging ahead. If there was not to be another opera, other commissions vied for his attention. Gerard Schwarz approached him about a composition for the Seattle Symphony, but nothing more came from that conversation.[59] Stuart Altman, president of Brandeis University, also approached Schuman—the first recipient 34 years earlier of the school's Creative Arts Medal in Music—with an idea for a commission: Would he consider writing a work for the Lydian String Quartet, the university's resident ensemble, in memory of either Bernstein or Copland? Altman tried to strengthen his hand by asking Robert Koff, the founding second violinist of the Juilliard String Quartet and now retired from Brandeis, to second Altman's request. It was Koff who had persuaded Brandeis to underwrite the Lyds, as they are known, and who coached and advised the quartet in its early years. But Schuman was resolute.

> Whether I could find the time and when I can find the time are the two basic questions. Only recently have I completed my String Quartet No. 5 which you might

> look at since it is published by Theodore Presser, and I am sure is in the University Library. In addition to this fact (meaning I may not be ready to compose another quartet soon) I have accepted one small commission for a choral work and a larger commission for an unaccompanied opus for violin.[60]

William Ferris, founder of the William Ferris Chorale, invited Schuman to join other composers in writing a vocal fanfare using the words "Amen" and "Alleluia" for the Chicago-based choir. The length, complexity, and accompaniment were all left to Schuman's discretion. And he had ample time: Ferris made his request in September 1990 for a work to premiere during the choir's 1991–92 season. Schuman accepted Ferris's proposal.[61]

The commission for the opus for violin took longer to germinate. Schuman had spoken to Donald Leavitt, chief of the Music Division at the Library of Congress, about the possibility of "a commission for a work for violin (perhaps it was viola; I do not recall) with piano or it might have been a small ensemble of other instruments." Leavitt stepped down in 1985, and James W. Pruett took his place in 1987. The commissioning idea got lost in the change of administrations, but Schuman wished to revive it on behalf of a particular performer. "An extraordinary young violinist by the name of Robert McDuffie has just recorded my Concerto for Violin and Orchestra. . . . I have great confidence in young McDuffie, and I would pursue with enthusiasm writing a work which he could introduce." Pruett apologized for the oversight and doubly agreed with Schuman: McDuffie's career was developing splendidly, and a work for violin under the aegis of the Library of Congress was something meriting further discussions.[62] The question that nagged at Schuman was the instrumentation. The initial commissioning agreement called for a work for violin and piano, but Pruett must have forgotten Schuman's earlier proposal: "While I am not averse to writing a work for violin and piano, I am intrigued with Robert McDuffie's suggestion of a work for unaccompanied violin."[63] The commission was redrafted. "The plan is for you to compose a new work for solo violin under the auspices of our Elizabeth Sprague Coolidge Foundation, with additional support of $7,500 from Mrs. Cameron Baird." All totaled, the commission was worth nearly $16,000.[64]

In early January 1991, Schuman joked with his copyist Ken Godel. "Be warned. I hope to have a short a cappella work within the next month or so, and then we'll be beginning work on a commission for solo violin. I'll give you notice in time for you to buy a double-stop pen."[65] But the ideas weren't flowing for either work. In April, Schuman informed Ferris of his progress. "You should know that I have written about four measures for you, but do not think for a minute that I have a 'writer's block'—merely suffering from a lack of ideas, but we do have some time, and your demands are modest which seem to coincide with my current level of productivity. Amen, Alleluia."[66] Schuman filled four pages with ideas for the *Alleluia*, but none of them gelled. On the day after

Christmas, he wrote Ferris to say that his health had precluded his ability to complete the work. "I would like to hope that somehow I can find a way of helping you celebrate, for such certainly has been my intention. But let us agree that if I cannot finish the work (which after all is to be of modest length) by February 1 of 1992, my withdrawal from the project will be definite."[67] The *Alleluia* was left incomplete.

No sketches have been found of the violin piece. In fact, the agreement between Schuman and the Library of Congress was almost left unconsummated. Pruett wrote in September 1991 to see if the commissioning letter had gone astray. It had not. Schuman was mulling it all over. "Should I accept it? My answer is an enthusiastic 'yes'. It is my hope and expectation to begin work before too long. Will I complete the project? I certainly hope so, and, barring unforeseen circumstances, I'm cautiously optimistic."[68]

There is something fitting in the fact that Schuman's last commission was for an unaccompanied work on his own instrument. With the Violin Concerto spanning 12 of his middle years, the violin traverses the arc of Schuman's life. Blanche Schwarz Levy, his childhood violin teacher, shared a treasured memory with Schuman of those early days with the fiddle. "I can only recall when you played on my second pupils' recital in N.Y. (my salad days!) in Wurlitzer Hall that an unknown elderly gentleman came to me and made his prophetic statement: 'Who is this boy? Remember—he will make his mark in the world.' What a mark!"[69] In that second recital, Schuman played with piano accompaniment. It was at his debut recital a year earlier that his sister developed stage fright. She joked about it in the handmade card she gave "to my kid brother" on his eightieth birthday.

> Congratulations on your many significant contributions to a brighter and better world, on your high standards in every aspect of life, and, not the least, on your indomitable optimism and sense of humor.
>
> —BUT—
>
> Did you have to play "To a Wild Rose" so loud that no one could hear the piano? HUH?[70]

At the end of his life, no one but Schuman heard the violin music he heard.

Both his older sister and his violin teacher outlived the unlikely prodigy. Frankie wrote to Schwarz Levy that Bill "had really been in poor health for some time and had experienced a rapid decline in the last six months. I think all who saw him felt that his time had come. You must know how much you meant to him and how touched he was by your letters over the years."[71] In his book on Schuman, Joseph Polisi relates the details of Schuman's last public celebration: the opening of the exhibit "An American Triptych: The Dynamic Worlds of William Schuman" at the New York Public Library for the Performing Arts on October 25, 1991. He also chronicles Schuman's final hours: the complaint of angina; the breaking of his left hip and hand after falling while using his walker; the discovery of blockage in his heart; the successful hip surgery; the code blue; the pronouncement of death at 11:43 A.M. on February 15, 1992.[72]

Midway between those two events, Schuman passed the torch to a new generation. Poor though his health was, he rallied to attend the world premiere of *The Ghosts of Versailles.* Earlier in 1991 he wrote to Susan Feder, who worked for G. Schirmer, the same publisher he once worked for, the house that still publishes the Third and Sixth Symphonies, the *Symphony for Strings*, and dozens of other works. "I want to congratulate you on being the publisher of John Corigliano's opera. He and his librettist played the work for us a few weeks ago, and I think it's terrific. In fact, I dare hope and even predict that it may well be the first American opera to succeed at the Met. Let's keep our fingers crossed."[73] A fortnight before the curtain went up, Schuman offered his congratulations to his younger colleague and quipped about both his health and the price of tickets. "Naturally, we plan to be present and it will mark my first truly venturesome outing after an unpleasant summer both for Frankie and me, involving what seemed like a high percentage of the medical profession of this area. We did manage to get good seats for your premiere, and all we had to do in return was to mortgage our Connecticut home!"[74] Attend they did, with the virile Schuman confined to a wheelchair. McClatchy was there, too. "I was delighted to get a glimpse of you the other night at the Met. (Quite a production they gave the piece, no?) Almost worth the ten-year wait, I'd say. I don't imagine it will encourage the Met to do more new opera, but maybe it will encourage others."[75] Schuman had spent much of his life encouraging the Met in this direction. His presence that evening was undoubtedly meant to serve as a reminder to all of his commitment and passion for new American music.

And he was not done. On the day before he died, he dictated a number of letters. One went to Richard Dufallo, a conductor of contemporary music based in New York, reassuring him that Schuman would write a letter on his behalf to the National Endowment for the Arts. Another went to composer David Del Tredici, thanking him for sending him the article from *Modern Music* in which Paul Rosenfeld praised the Second Symphony. Del Tredici had placed the date of the article as 1930. "Somehow the date seems wrong, for I had not yet composed any of the music to which he refers. I look forward to seeing you on the 26th."[76]

No man gets to finish everything that he starts in this life. Schuman finished more than most men dream of starting. McClatchy caught the essence of Schuman's zeal.

> He was a man almost *driven* to happiness: an outsize life and career, the innovations and institutions he started, the buoyant optimism of his personality and convictions,

> the dramatic flair of his music. Underneath it all—and this is true of every great artist—was a strong, serious, stubborn streak that knew what he wanted, that listened to the voice he'd had in his mind's ear since childhood, and that time and again cannily found ways to let that voice sing out.[77]

Schuman tended to destroy his sketches and the manuscripts of his unpublished pieces. It is a wonder that the occasional sketch survives, and the existence of a handful of unpublished and unheralded pieces is a greater wonder still. More sketches and more pieces may await discovery. But there is at least one unfinished work that speaks volumes about Schuman the man and Schuman the composer. Gathered together with his compositions from the late 1970s and 1980s is a short score for a song. There is no date, but the handwriting is strong, suggesting that it comes well before the *Alleluia*, in which the penmanship is visibly enfeebled. The first page of the sketch contains an introduction and the first five measures of the vocal line, the latter of which Schuman repeated on the second page. It is on that second page that he indicated the forces he intended to use: voice, oboe, and strings. The instruments give out before too long, and the obbligato oboe only occasionally resurfaces, but the five-page draft presents a complete melody down to the final bar. Not only that, but Schuman wrote out all the words of the poem that stirred his creativity and trumpet his beliefs. In nine lines, the poem manages to trace his entire life. Unsurprisingly, these lines come from *Leaves of Grass*.

> Not from successful love alone,
> Nor wealth, nor honor'd middle age, nor victories of politics or war;
> But as life wanes, and all the turbulent passions calm,
> As gorgeous, vapory, silent hues cover the evening sky,
> As softness, fulness, rest, suffuse the frame, like freshier, balmier air,
> As the days take on a mellower light, and the apple at last hangs
> really finish'd and indolent-ripe on the tree,
> Then for the teeming quietest, happiest days of all!
> The brooding and blissful halcyon days!

EPILOGUE

WILLIAM SCHUMAN AND THE SHAPING OF AMERICA'S MUSICAL LIFE

Paul Wittke's vivid portrait of Schuman for the readers of *Schirmer/News* captures the complexity and the humanity, the odd combinations, that made Schuman who he was:

> Schuman was a multifarious man. His family (particularly his wife, Frances) and its traditions were paramount; he believed in an all-inclusive political, moral, and artistic democracy; he was tough-minded, aggressive if need be, thoroughly urban; he gave serious thought to serious things; he was a master of public speaking, spontaneous, funny, lucid; he was very witty. To be in a room with him and Morton Gould (another fantastic speaker) was like attending a Neil Simon play; he was intensely interested in all the minutiae of life and art. But he was not stuffy—the last word one could apply to him. He was the odd combination of a hard-headed businessman and an artist of deep insight into the mysteries of his craft and human nature. He had the best of both worlds. And lest we forget—he is one of the few true artists the city of New York has given us. He loved his city and it loved him. I don't think he would want us to forget that.[1]

Most of Wittke's readers knew of the various administrative posts that Schuman had held; fewer knew of the many maneuvers Schuman conducted behind the scenes to promote American composers and American music, including his own.

The quotation says little about Schuman's music, and it was as a composer that Schuman wanted first and foremost to be remembered. Copland memorably stated, "Schuman's work reflects his personality—full of drive and conviction, not lacking in emotional content, with a love of the grandiose and a wonderful eloquence."[2] Copland's description squares with part of Wittke's. What about the humor, the wit, the spontaneity?

In his review of the world premiere of Schuman's original version of the Third Symphony, *Washington Post* music critic Tim Page tried to take the measure of Schuman's music in the early twenty-first century.

> There may be some purely musical reasons for his present obscurity. The Symphony No. 3 is so ambitious, so unrelentingly proclamatory that it wears the listener down by sheer assertion. Lotsa brass, lotsa fugues, lotsa energy, lotsa lotsa—for almost 40 minutes. At times, Schuman reminds me of one of those windy German contrapuntalists of the late 19th century—Max Reger, say—with hard, modern American muscles. At other times, he seems a Shostakovich with nothing to bear witness to.[3]

Page may be overly harsh in both his judgment of Schuman's music and his allegation of its obscurity. For starters, the music has never been totally absent from the concert hall. Schuman himself joked about the ubiquity of the *New England Triptych*. "I guess it has become my C-Sharp Minor Prelude."[4] Neither Rachmaninoff's piano piece nor Schuman's orchestral piece has fallen completely out of favor with performers or audiences.

But most of the music—and particularly the works for orchestra—exhibits a sobriety that is rarely leavened by the drollness for which Schuman was justly lauded. At times, the music barely avoids falling into aural quicksand. Consider how the fugue in the second section of *A Free Song* and the repeated timpani strokes that precede the ballplayers' speeches in *The Mighty Casey* bog down the proceedings in those works. (Jeremy Gury suggested the timpani thumps; Schuman eliminated them in the cantata version of the tale, and the 1989 production at Glimmerglass cut them from the opera.)[5] Rarer still are moments that turn into aural quicksilver: the passage in the orchestral *American Hymn* that is later recast as *Showcase* is one of the few sustained scherzos in Schuman's catalog. (The manuscript dispenses with an article for the latter work's subtitle, calling it "Short Display for Orchestra.") The one thing there is not a "lotsa" in Schuman's music is levity, save for those choral works—the *Five Rounds*, the *Mail Order Madrigals*, *Esses*—expressly designed to elicit chuckles. And as for a light touch? *New York Times* music critic Harold Schonberg asserted that Schuman decidedly lacked it, though *A Question of Taste* might have given Schonberg second thoughts.[6]

Schuman's music (to use one of Schuman's favorite phrases) isn't everyone's dish. His compositional voice is unquestionably recognizable, but the long melodic statements, the polytonal harmonies, the nonrepeating rhythms, and the autogenetic forms make his music less memorable than the music of many of his peers. His best music deserves a wider audience, and Schuman knew that developing such an audience depends largely on the quality of recordings available. As long as recordings are hard to find or are by performers other than those of the first rank, Schuman's music will likely languish.

His compositions were central to his self-identity, and he understood clearly that others eclipsed him in this area. "One of the privileges of my life," he volunteered at one of the events where he assumed his accustomed role as master of ceremonies, "is being part of the Copland Era, as our time will certainly be known in the history of American music."[7] But the twentieth century in

America would look quite different had Schuman not exercised his formidable skills: the businessman, who was tutored by his father and maternal grandfather and obtained a brief but consequential education in its application; the public speaker, who discovered that talent by chance and honed it through practice; the power broker, who expressed this flair in the athletic outing clubs and summer camp activities of his teenage years and in nearly every facet of his adult life. He didn't speak Yiddish, but he understood himself to be a *macher*, a person who gets things done and makes things happen. And he was a composer, "one of the most glorious pursuits imaginable in terms of inner satisfaction and most absurd in terms of a worldly career!"[8]

In 1987, Tim Page asked 20 leading musicians "to name one composer of the past they thought underrated and one they believed overrated, and to explain their reasons." Schuman was unique in choosing two American composers. Equally noteworthy is how he chose to be identified, nearly 20 years after he had left Lincoln Center.

> William Schuman
>
> *Composer and administrator.*
>
> Underrated: Roy Harris is a composer often cited for technical shortcomings. But his best music has a grandeur and eloquence which, in the course of time, will ensure the acceptance it deserves.
>
> Overrated: Charles Ives is a glorious American original who composed few successful works. Overall, however, his compositions do not succeed because of their crude, haphazard forms and undistinguished materials.[9]

(Page: "Charles Ives led the category of the overrated, with three negative votes": Peter Schickele and Ransom Wilson joined Schuman.) But "IVES THRIVES," as H. Wiley Hitchcock thundered to Schuman upon reading Schuman's verdict. Schuman reveled in Hitchcock's turn of phrase and typographical vehemence. He also reminded Hitchcock: "I was one of the original incorporators of the Ives Society because I believed it imperative that his music be issued in authoritative editions. I also have long recognized his extraordinary qualities and the fact that he has produced some music of unquestionable worth."[10] Even without the trappings of power bestowed on him at Juilliard and at Lincoln Center, he was and remained an administrator, butting heads and cutting deals with all and sundry.

The sheer breadth of his interests—and his willingness to go against his own tastes and interests—set Schuman apart. He attended the premiere of Charles Wuorinen's *Two-Part Symphony*. Like much of Wuorinen's music, the symphony is nearly impossible to grasp at first hearing. Schuman wrote to Wuorinen to congratulate him on the performance and the work itself ("a stunning accomplishment"). Schuman freely admitted his own shortcomings when it came to understanding what Wuorinen was doing but also demonstrated his *macher* inclination to try to shape people and things into the image he imagined was best. "It is good news that the work will be recorded, for, obviously, it will take many hearings to become fully acquainted with its subtleties. Please do write a long work which has the serenity of the slow introduction to the second movement. It seems to me to be a new developing facet of your gift which I, for one, believe deserves deep mining." Wuorinen wrote back not only to assure Schuman that the symphony represented, in Wuorinen's own mind, a step forward in his own compositional aesthetic but also to thank Schuman for the generosity of his remarks. "I value your judgment greatly, and have always admired your humane and balanced response to music—and to human affairs as well."[11]

Schuman had an eye and ear for talent. Robert Ward, one of the young composer-administrators whom Schuman hired for Juilliard, later went on to win the Pulitzer Prize for his opera *The Crucible* and to lead the North Carolina School of the Arts. Ward's daughter Melinda had seen Schuman in a wheelchair and looking frail at the premiere of *The Ghosts of Versailles*. Ward wrote to Frankie after Bill's death to share a vision very different from his daughter's.

> One of my earliest memories of Bill was [him] pacing up and down the sixth floor corridor of the old Juilliard while a faculty party was in progress. He was filling me in on his ideas for converting the Carnegie Mansion into a grand music center and his ideas were moving as fast as his feet. His vision was embracing something which would be exciting and fine for the entire musical community. This reflected Bill's way.[12]

Not everyone appreciated Bill's way. Schuman had—and has—his detractors. W. McNeil Lowry, vice president of the Ford Foundation, helped to make that institution a major player in the arts world. He called Schuman a "flâneur" and a "tame castrate for Rockefeller" and felt that having to interact with Schuman was, for him, a "penalty."[13] Schuman's grand designs for the Carnegie mansion and his forward remarks about a composer's development can easily be read, both at the time and in retrospect, as manipulative and intrusive. In his unpublished memoirs, Phillip Ramey opined that Schuman "was a perhaps unique combination of serious artist and glib politician.... Once, I mentioned to Copland that Bill seemed a charming guy. His reply: 'Yes—so long as he sees a purpose to it.'"[14]

What one sees in Schuman depends on what one brings to the seeing. Filmmaker Errol Morris contemplated the meaning behind various famous photographs that appear to be unaltered representations of reality but that, upon closer inspection, reveal the possibility that the photographs were staged. After discussing the opposing views of two other scholars, Morris offered his own opinion.

> Is one right? The other wrong? I don't think so. Their views show the many different ways that a photograph can be seen. The different functions it serves. A photograph can display evidence from a patch of reality it records, but also leaves a strange footprint. An impression of an instantly lost past around which memories collect. For whatever reason, I am thinking of the myth of "Orpheus." The attempt to bring the dead back into the world of the living. But in "Orpheus," there is a warning. In journeying to the underworld, Orpheus must walk in front of Eurydice and never look back. Eternally trapped in the present, we are doomed to perpetually walk "in front" of the past.[15]

The past that Schuman occupied is forever lost. Different men and women will have different Schumans that they see, ones not necessarily right or wrong. But the fact of his presence and the facts and myths that emanate from, and adhere to, him all mark Schuman as an uncommonly powerful and influential man of the arts. And his scores show him to be a composer of unquestioned skill and compelling force. Both he and his music have left a sizable footprint on the paths they have traversed.

At the same time, it is in the eternal present that Schuman strove to be remembered. Unlike Orpheus in the underworld, Schuman—an Orpheus in Manhattan—never looked back. He did not dwell on the past. He saw and planned for the future. Most of all, he lived in the present. For him, life is the present.

NOTES

List of Abbreviations

All Schuman manuscripts and sketches, unless otherwise indicated, are held by the Library of Congress, Washington, D.C.

For archival materials, box and folder numbers are provided thus: 150/2 = box 150, folder 2.

Autobiography — William Schuman, Autobiography, ca. 1970. Chapters 1–5, table of contents, and related correspondence courtesy of Anthony Schuman. Additional chapters and materials, William Schuman, biographical files, Juilliard School Archives, Juilliard School, New York, NY.

The chapter titles listed in the table of contents are:

1. April 4, 1930
2. Three-Score Set
3. Second Symphony (alternate version titled "Boston")
4. Englewood et sequens
5. Sarah Lawrence College

*6. George Washington High School
*7. Tin Pan Alley
8. G. Schirmer, Inc.
9. Juilliard School of Music
*10. Lincoln Center
11. Videorecord
*12. Grand Design
*13. My Music
* either never dictated, missing, or lost

The 30-page chapter in Anthony Schuman's possession titled "Sarah Lawrence School" differs from a 24-page chapter fragment (missing the first 18 pages) at the Juilliard School titled "Sarah Lawrence." The titles of the other chapters held at Juilliard are:

(8) G. Schirmer
(9) The Juilliard Years
(11) Videorecord
A. Performance
B. Post Lincoln Center

AWS	Materials courtesy of Anthony Schuman, Schuman's son.
CCNY	Carnegie Corporation of New York Records, Columbia University Rare Book and Manuscript Library, series III.A (Grant Files).
COB	Cobbossee Scrapbook, courtesy of Anthony Schuman.
Columbia-A	Central Files, University Archives and Columbiana Library, Columbia University in the City of New York.
Harris-CSULA	Roy Harris Papers [unprocessed], Special Collections, John F. Kennedy Memorial Library, California State University, Los Angeles.
JIG	Materials courtesy of Judith Israel Gutmann, Schuman's niece.
JS	Office of the President, General Administrative Records, ca. 1932–1962, subseries I: Subject Files, Juilliard School Archives, Juilliard School, New York, NY.
JS-Comm	Office of the President, General Administrative Records, 1933–1985, box 55, folder 2, Juilliard School Archives, Juilliard School, New York, NY.
LaF '41	Christopher LaFarge, diaries, 1941, MS Am 2118 (5), Houghton Library, Harvard University.
LaF '42	Christopher LaFarge, diaries, 1942, MS Am 2118 (6), Houghton Library, Harvard University.
LCPA	Lincoln Center for the Performing Arts Archives, New York, NY.
LCPA-City	Box ID 090398, folder "[The] City Center of Music and Drama — Negotiations re: Constituency, 1964–1965," Lincoln Center for the Performing Arts Archives, New York, NY.
LE-Yale	Lehman Engel Collection, box 16, folder "Schuman, William," Irving S. Gilmore Music Library, Yale University.
LoC-AC	Aaron Copland Collection, ML31.K66, Performing Arts Reading Room, Library of Congress, Washington, D.C.
LoC-LB	Leonard Bernstein Collection, ML31.B, box 50, folder 4, Performing Arts Reading Room, Library of Congress, Washington, D.C.
LoC-PA	Performing Arts Reading Room, Library of Congress, Washington, D.C.
LoC-SK	Serge Koussevitzky Collection, ML31.K66, box 54, folder 18, Performing Arts Reading Room, Library of Congress, Washington, D.C.
LoC-WS-A	William Schuman manuscripts, sketches, and other materials, ML96. S414, Performing Arts Reading Room, Library of Congress, Washington, D.C.
LoC-WS-Z	William Schuman manuscripts, sketches, and other materials, unprocessed and/or uncatalogued prior to October 1, 2009, Performing Arts Reading Room, Library of Congress, Washington, D.C.

MN-Penn	Margaret Naumburg Papers, Rare Book and Manuscripts Library, University of Pennsylvania.
NYPL	Research Collection, Music Division, New York Public Library for the Performing Arts, Astor, Lenox and Tilden Foundations.
NYPL-A	The Papers and Records of William Schuman, JPB 87-33, New York Public Library for the Performing Arts, Astor, Lenox and Tilden Foundations.
NYPL-B	William Schuman Collection, Additional Material Received, July 1995 (Location: Rose Bldg.), New York Public Library for the Performing Arts, Astor, Lenox and Tilden Foundations. Originally not a part of NYPL-A. Accessed before June 1, 2009.
NYPL-C	William Schuman Papers, Addenda from Rose Building. A reorganization of NYPL-B. Accessed after June 1, 2009.
NYPL-Smallens	Alexander Smallens Papers, ca. 1900–1970, JPB 89-88, series I, folder 50, New York Public Library for the Performing Arts, Astor, Lenox and Tilden Foundations.
NYPL-VP	Vincent Persichetti Papers, 1901–1996 and undated (bulk 1930–1987), JPB 90-77, New York Public Library for the Performing Arts, Astor, Lenox and Tilden Foundations.
OHAM	William Schuman, transcript of 12 interviews with Vivian Perlis, February 1, 1977, to November 16, 1977, American Music Series, Oral History American Music, Yale University. Interview no. 46 a-hh.
QP-Yale	Quincy Porter Papers, MSS 15, subseries I.H, box 11, folder 139, Irving S. Gilmore Music Library, Yale University.
RAC	Series 200, record group 1.1, Rockefeller Foundation Archives, Rockefeller Archive Center, Sleepy Hollow, NY.
RFA-1	Rockefeller Family Archives, record group 5, series 1, subseries 1, Rockefeller Foundation Archives, Rockefeller Archive Center, Sleepy Hollow, NY.
RFA-2	Rockefeller Family Archives, record group 5, series 3, subseries 1, JDR III Papers, Rockefeller Foundation Archives, Rockefeller Archive Center, Sleepy Hollow, NY.
SLC	Sarah Lawrence College Archives, Bronxville, NY.
SLC-CW	Constance Warren Papers, Sarah Lawrence College Archives.
SLC-WS	Faculty folder, Schuman, William H. 1936–1994, Sarah Lawrence College Archives.
S-W	William Schuman, transcript of 16 interviews with Heidi Waleson, November 2, 1990, to June 17, 1991. Transcript courtesy of Heidi Waleson, New York, NY. Pagination on transcript is inconsistent; pagination used is that of the 1,166-page pdf. Numbers in brackets indicate tape and side number, e.g., 3/2 = tape 3, side 2.
Taggard-DC	The Papers of Genevieve Taggard, Rauner Library, Dartmouth College.

VMB	Materials courtesy of Vera Marks Barad, second wife of Edward B. Marks Jr.
VP	Vincent Persichetti, unpublished biography of William Schuman, ca. 1948, in Vincent Persichetti Papers, 1901–1996 and undated (bulk 1930–1987), JPB 90-77, New York Public Library for the Performing Arts, Astor, Lenox and Tilden Foundations. Chapters 1–4 are in box 101, folder 4; chapter 5 is in box 101, folder 5.
WS-Gruen	William Schuman Interview, May 7, 1975, Oral History Project, Dance Collection, New York Public Library for the Performing Arts, Astor, Lenox and Tilden Foundations, (JPB 87-33 box 152, folder 9)
Zinsser	"Dialogue between William Zinsser and William Schuman," April 3, 1989, to July 11, 1989, transcript courtesy of Anthony Schuman.

Introduction: "The Impact of a Single Symphony"

1. Chalmers to Schuman, October 5, 1962, NYPL-A, 72/5.

2. See "The Long Hard Road Ahead," full-page advertisement for the NAACP Legal Defense and Educational Fund, *New York Times*, October 18, 1962: 33.

3. Chalmers to Martin Luther King Jr., March 6, 1960, as cited at http://www.stanford.edu/group/King/about_king/encyclopedia/chalmers_allanknight.html, accessed March 24, 2009.

Chapter 1: "The Family Tree"

1. OHAM, 1. The transcript of the tape erroneously focuses on the first syllable, suggesting a shorter or longer "u," but the tape itself finds Schuman focusing on the second syllable.

2. The manifest information is found in the Manifest Header Data File, 1834–ca. 1900, of the National Archives. According to a "Death Record" in Anthony Schuman's possession, Rosa Kramer was born on February 14, 1840.

3. Personal communication with Dr. Gerhard Immler, July 2, 2009.

4. S-W, 121 [3/1].

5. Oral history of Audrey Schuman Gerstner, June 30, 1994, JIG. Moritz Schuhmann is listed as a seller of "hats and caps" in the *1869 Williams' Cincinnati Directory*, but does not appear in the 1868 or 1870 editions.

6. Fanny Schuhmann to Peßla Schuhmann Sänger, January 9, 1868, JIG.

7. NYPL-A, 150/12.

8. S-W, 125 [3/2]. Schuman didn't specify when this occurred other than it took place before Sam married Ray in 1906.

9. Schuman's Spanish-American War papers, JIG.

10. Schuman to Max Welker, December 5, 1950, 150/13.

11. See Steve Swayne, "William Schuman, World War II, and the Pulitzer Prize," *Musical Quarterly* 89, 2–3 (Summer–Fall 2006): 291–95.

12. VP, chap. 1, pp. 2–3.

13. Clinton Adams, *American Lithographers 1900–1960: The Artists and Their Printers* (Albuquerque: University of New Mexico Press, 1983), 20.

14. Schuman to Leonard Burkat, October 26, 1983, NYPL-A, 125/12.

15. Stephen Birmingham, *"Our Crowd": The Great Jewish Families of New York* (New York: Harper & Row, 1967), 292–93.

16. Michael A. Meyer, *Response to Modernity: A History of the Reform Movement in Judaism* (New York: Oxford University Press, 1988), 287.

17. Ibid., 306.

18. Howard Sonn to Schuman, August 9, 1980, NYPL-A, 124/9.

19. Samuel Schuman to William Schuman, July 22, 1942, NYPL-A, 150/12.

20. Gertrude M. White to Schuman, November 30, 1960, NYPL-A, 43/7.

21. Schuman to Merrill A. Pitcher, January 13, 1950, NYPL-A, 150/12.

22. Louis Heilbrunn's history comes from a family history given to the author on August 6, 2006, by Henry Heilbrunn, Louis' great-grandson.

23. S-W, 122 [3/1].

24. OHAM, 5. The bill of sale for the cow, on which Louis penned Bill an explanation of the transaction, is dated April 10, 1916, and is in the possession of Anthony Schuman.

25. S-W, 128–29 [3/2]. He also recalled summer rentals at Molyneaux in Big Indian (in the Catskills) and at Smith Farms in Cedarhurst. See S-W, 131 [3/2] and OHAM, 7. Schuman clearly recalled living at 112th Street in 1930—see OHAM, 40—but it is unclear from Schuman's recollections and a January 17, 1991, letter from his sister Audrey Schuman Gerstner (NYPL-C, "Correspondence G, 1991–1993") whether the first two Manhattan addresses occurred before or after the move to Far Rockaway. VP, chap. 1, p. 6, gives 107th Street as the address the Schumans went to after Far Rockaway.

26. From Henry Heilbrunn's family history.

27. OHAM, 5–6.

28. Schuman to Bernard Stollman, January 21, 1966, NYPL-A, 83/3.

Chapter 2: "A Kid Grows in Queens and Manhattan"

1. The recollections of Robert come from OHAM and S-W, 125–28 [3/2]. Bill Schuman stated in S-W that the family was "living in Far Rockaway; I remember all those days very well" (S-W, 127 [3/2]). Yet in the same interview he said that Robert was "about nine years old, ten years old" at the time, which is not possible. The 1920 U.S. Census puts the three children in Far Rockaway; the 1930 Census does not list Robert with the family.

2. These songs were made into a medley for the Sarah Lawrence College Chorus, identified as "Medley No. III" and performed on a concert in New York Times Hall on April 2, 1945. CD PH 017, SLC.

3. The last four songs, along with "I Don't Want to Get Well" and "How 'Ya Gonna Keep 'Em Down on the Farm," are listed as one of five groups of songs Schuman suggested for a benefit concert given on behalf of the American Composers Orchestra in the fall of

1990. See Schuman to Francis Thorne, February 23, 1990, and Thorne to Schuman, "Sept. 27," both in NYPL-C, "Correspondence T, 1989–1990."

4. OHAM, 2.

5. Personal correspondence with Anthony Schuman, July 19, 2006.

6. Ibid.

7. NYPL-B "Box 12–Programs." A program for a second recital on May 24, 1925, is in NYPL-C, Scrapbook 3. At that recital, Schuman played last on the program, suggesting he was one of the better students. He performed Adoration (Borowski) and Son of the Puszta (Keler Bela). The ensemble finale was Carnival of Venice (Dancla), with Schwarz and student violinists Ruth Stein and Raymond Schuler.

8. See the subject clippings file for "Violin, Viola, Violoncello. Teachers Guild, Inc.," NYPL.

9. S-W, 130 [3/2].

10. For evidence of this familiarity, see a series of articles in the *Campus* (Sarah Lawrence College's newspaper): "Versatile Schumann [*sic*] Holds Music Hour" (November 2, 1936, 6); "Schuman Further Reveals Self as a One Man Orchestra" (November 9, 1936, 6); and "Schuman Plays Four 'Fiddles' at Music Hour" (November 16, 1936, 6).

11. NYPL-B, 13/"Milray Outing Club for Boys." Penciled above the card is the date 1926–7.

12. S-W, 131 (clarinet), 134–35 (double bass; both 3/2), and 158–74 [4/2] (Alamo Society Orchestra). See also OHAM, 7–9 (violin), and 31–35 (Alamo Society Orchestra).

13. Zinsser, April 9, 1989, 3.

14. S-W, 159 [3/2].

15. S-W, 162 [3/2].

16. Schuman to David Ewen, September 20, 1946, NYPL-A, 14/8.

17. See http://www.luckyshow.org/ice hockey/Crescents.htm, accessed January 23, 2009.

18. VP, chap. 1, p. 5.

19. Edward B. Marks, *Still Counting: Achievements and Follies of a Nonagenarian* (Lanham, MD: Hamilton Books, 2005), 28.

20. VP, chap. 1, p. 9.

21. OHAM, 5.

22. Autobiography, chap. 1, p. 5.

23. See Schuman's February 18, 1960, speech at Town Hall, esp. p. 2, NYPL-A, 182/1.

24. Schuman to Harold Ickes, U. S. Secretary of the Interior, August 6, 1940, NYPL-A, 20/12.

25. See William Schuman, "Cultural Confidence Game," *Lincoln Center Journal* 1, 1 (October 1967): 15.

26. See Schuman to Bonnie Zitofsky, July 19, 1985, NYPL-A, 143/11.

27. Schuman to Anthony Schuman, July 20, 1957, NYPL-A, 150/10.

28. Schuman–William Shea correspondence, NYPL-A, 82/7; Schuman to R. D. Brown, CEO and president of the Rawlings Corp. in St. Louis, NYPL-A, 79/4.

29. Schuman to Samuel J. Shure, September 20, 1950, NYPL-A, 149/15; Schuman to Harlow Parker, May 18, 1961, NYPL-A, 33/2.

30. William B. McCourtie, *Where and How to Sell Manuscripts: A Directory for Writers* (n.p.: The Home Correspondence School, 1920), 102.

31. See Schuman to L. Hayman, president, Rogers Peet Co., February 28, 1980, NYPL-A, 139/2. In 1956, Rogers Peet ran an ad in the *New York Times* featuring testimonials from former Ropecs, including "Well do I recall when this magazine meant glorious days reading," September 25, 1956, 15. For more on the Order of Ropeco, see the Rogers Peet ad in the *New York Times*, October 9, 1956, 15.

32. Schuman to Thornton W. Burgess, March 5, 1954, NYPL-A, 149/4.

33. S-W, 151 [3/2].

34. See Schuman to Goddard Lieberson, July 22, 1954, NYPL-A, 10/14; and Gertrude Martin to Robert Mann, July 30, 1954, in JS, 7/9.

35. Schuman to Nathan Broder, September 19, 1956, NYPL-A, 8/6. The book was *The Energies of Art: Studies of Authors Classic and Modern* (New York: Harper, 1956).

36. Schuman to James P. Warburg, August 13, 1947, NYPL-A, 44/3; Schuman to Glenn Seaborg, April 20, 1970, NYPL-A, 92/1; and Schuman to Herman Wouk, April 29, 1947, NYPL-A, 44/10.

37. Thomas H. Briggs, *The Junior High School* (Boston: Houghton Mifflin, 1920), 327. For photographs of the school, its benefactor James Speyer, and activities at the school, see Eric K. Washington, *Manhattanville: Old Heart of West Harlem* (Charleston, SC: Arcadia, 2002), 58–60.

38. *The Speyer School Curriculum* (New York: Teachers College, 1913). See esp. pp. 11 and 134 for more about the "junior secondary school," as it was called.

39. OHAM, 26–27; S-W, 135–37 [3/2].

40. S-W, 136–37 [3/2].

41. William H. Schuman, *College Chums* (ca. 1923), typescript courtesy of Anthony Schuman. For Bill's denigration of the play, see OHAM, 27.

42. Meyer, *Response to Modernity*, 286. For Gamoran, see Mayer, 299–300; and Emanuel Gamoran, *A Survey of 125 Religious Schools Affiliated with the Union of American Hebrew Congregations* (Cincinnati: Union of American Hebrew Congregations, 1925), esp. 40–45. See also OHAM, 15.

43. OHAM, 16–17.

44. S-W, 139–40 [3/2].

45. See Schuman from William A. Shea, September 27, 1982, NYPL-A, 141/12.

46. S-W, 136 [3/2].

47. The certificates are among the papers in COB.

48. S-W, 135 [3/2]; VP, chap. 1, pp. 7–8.

Chapter 3: "Camp Cobbossee (and a Summer Abroad)"

1. OHAM, 8. For an overview of American summer camps at the turn of the twentieth century, see: Leslie Paris, *Children's Nature: The Rise of the American Summer Camp* (New York:

New York University Press, 2008); Abigail A. Van Slyck, *A Manufactured Wilderness: Summer Camps and the Shaping of American Youth, 1890–1960* (Minneapolis: University of Minnesota Press, 2006); and Gary P. Zola, "Jewish Camping and Its Relationship to the Organized Camping Movement in America," in *A Place of Our Own: The Rise of Reform Jewish Camping*, ed. Michael M. Lorge and Gary P. Zola (Tuscaloosa: University of Alabama Press, 2006), 1–26, esp. 2–11.

2. Advertisement in *Good Housekeeping*, June 1917, 15.

3. Porter E. Sargent, *A Handbook of American Private Schools* (Boston: Geo. M. Ellis Co., 1917), 273. The institutes accommodated 200 students. See *Automobile Blue Book 1921*, Vol. 1: *New York State and Adjacent Canada* (New York: Automobile Blue Book Publishing Co., 1921), 478.

4. David Lyon Hurwitz, "How Lucky We Were," *American Jewish History* 87, 1 (March 1999): 34.

5. Henry Wellington Wack, *Summer Camps, Boys and Girls* (New York: Red Book Magazine, 1923), 73.

6. OHAM, 8.

7. Schuman to Abraham Friedman, January 6, 1965, NYPL-A, 16/13.

8. C. Randolph Fitzhugh, "Josh Junior," *Almanak*, August 6, 1928, 5, COB.

9. Abbott Baum, "Looking Out," *Red and White Almanak*, n.d., 2, COB.

10. OHAM, 21.

11. OHAM, 11; and Edward Marks, *Still Counting: Achievements and Follies of a Nonagenarian* (Lanham, MD: Hamilton Books, 2005), 36.

12. OHAM, 43.

13. Autobiography, chap. 4, p. 6.

14. The age range for the boys is given in an undated and unidentified clipping, "Parents Jam Pier when School Tourists Return," COB.

15. S-W, 139–40, 142 [both 3/2].

16. Schuman to Clarence Francis, July 30, 1963, NYPL-A, 56/2.

17. Schuman wrote the following notation: "Pictures of My 'First' Trip Abroad! (for souvenirs, programs, diary, post-card pictures, etc. see box on top shelf of closet marked) France!" COB.

18. OHAM, 43.

19. "Minstrel," *Almanak*, n.d., n.p., COB.

20. The unsigned and undated article, "Minstrel Show Is Successfully Given" (COB), most likely appeared in the *Daily Kennebec Journal*.

21. Schuman to Abraham Friedman, January 6, 1965, NYPL-A, 16/13; Schuman in fact turned 17 the same month the minstrel show was performed. See also Composers' Forum Transcript, October 21, 1936, Record Group 69.5.3; National Archives and Records Administration II (College Park, MD), 4 ("I started composing when I was 15 and it was a tango for a show"); and S-W, 99 [3/1] ("I was probably sixteen, maybe fifteen, about sixteen, with a lyric by Edward B. Marks, Jr.").

22. "Minstrel," *Almanak*, n.d., n.p., COB.

23. Marks, *Still Counting*, 289. See also p. 35.

24. "It's Up to Pa," *Almanak*, August 6, 1928, 1, COB.

25. I.H.B. Spiers, "To My 1905 'Extra-French' Class in the William Penn Charter School," introduction to Eugene Labiche and Edouard Martin, *Le voyage de Monsieur Perrichon* (Project Gutenberg eBook #9453), downloaded January 25, 2009.

26. The lyrics for the song, with a handwritten annotation attesting that it was the 1927 prize-winning song, are in COB.

27. Marks, *Still Counting*, 35.

28. "Winthrop: Camp Cobbossee Presentation," *Daily Kennebec Journal*, clipping in NYPL-A, 162/1.

29. "It's Up to Pa," *Almanak*, August 6, 1928, 2, COB.

30. Zinsser, April 10, 1989, 10.

31. Marks, *Still Counting*, 36.

32. See Woodrow Sandler to Schuman, September 3, 1933, NYPL-A, 37/2; and the program for *Fair Enough: A Revusical*, presented by the Brant Lake Players of 1934, in NYPL-B, Box 12, "Programs."

33. Schuman to Harold Friedman, March 10, 1952. Both the letter and the mimeographed invitation to the reunion are in NYPL-A, 10/2.

34. Autobiography, chap. 4, pp. 21–22.

35. David Straus to Frances Schuman, March 2, 1992, NYPL-C, "Condolence Letters"; "It's Up to Pa," *Almanak*, August 6, 1928, 1, COB.

Chapter 4: "A Flash in Tin Pan Alley"

1. The paper is in COB. The grade on the paper is actually an "A+," but the plus was added later and is in black ink, while the grade of "A" is in red pencil and is underlined. Whether the plus was added by the teacher or by Schuman cannot be known.

2. See OHAM, 34.

3. Ferdinand Nauheim to Persichetti, undated (probably early 1948), NYPL-VP, 17/18.

4. Edward B. Marks, *Still Counting: Achievements and Follies of a Nonagenarian* (Lanham, MD: Hamilton Books, 2005), 35. This may be in reference to their stint as counselors in 1929, when Schuman apparently brought a car to Maine. Schuman wrote about purchasing a "flivver": "I hope we can aFord it." Schuman to Marks, June 4, 1929, VMB.

5. See Olin Downes, "Toscanini Honors [Cosima] Wagner Memory," *New York Times*, April 4, 1930.

6. Nathan Broder to Persichetti, July 8, 1948, NYPL-VP, 19/20.

7. Ferdinand Nauheim to Persichetti, undated (probably early 1948), NYPL-VP, 17/18.

8. Zinsser, April 10, 1989, 21.

9. Schuman saved a business card from Paramount and wrote above the card "1928–9." See NYPL-B, Box 13. For his work as a salesman, see Schuman to David Ewen, September 20, 1946, NYPL-A, 14/8.

10. Schuman to Marks, October 31, 1928, AWS.

11. Schuman to Marks, December 10, 1928, VMB.

12. Schuman to Marks, May 18, 1931, VMB.

13. Schuman to Marks, February 13, 1929, VMB.

14. Schuman to Marks, undated, VMB.

15. Schuman to Marks, March 17, 1929, AWS.

16. Schuman to Marks, June 7, 1929, AWS. This letter is on Paramount Advertising Co. stationery.

17. Schuman to Marks, May 29, 1929, VMB.

18. Malkin Conservatory of Music catalog for 1925–1926, p. 11; this is repeated in the 1927–1928 catalog, p. 7, in the Malkin Conservatory of Music folder, NYPL.

19. S-W, 182–83 [179–80]; Zinsser, April 9, 1989, 4. See also David Ewen's recollection of his interactions with Persin, March 23, 1980, NYPL-A, 129/1.

20. Cf. the Deuxième Trio des Parques ("Quelle soudaine horreur ton destin nous inspire!") in act 2 of *Hippolyte et Aricie* (1730).

21. "New 'Moon' Song Called Rhythmic Fox-Trot Triumph," unidentified clipping in NYPL-A, 188.

22. The songs, both circa 1930, were *Doing the Dishes* and *Where the Grass Grows Green*. See Thomas L. Riis, *Frank Loesser* (New Haven, CT: Yale University Press, 2008), 25 and 283 n. 25.

23. Flora Rheta Schreiber and Vincent Persichetti, *William Schuman* (New York: G. Schirmer, 1954), 6. An earlier profile of Schuman lists the number as "some 30 or 40 songs." See Ronald F. Eyer, "Meet the Composer: (4) William Schuman," *Musical America* 64, 2 (January 25, 1944): 8.

24. Frank Loesser to Persichetti, April 10, 1948, NYPL-VP, 17/18.

25. See Arthur Loesser, "My Brother Frank," *Music Library Association Notes* 7 (1949–1950), 224.

26. Eyer, "Meet the Composer," 8.

27. Schuman to Marks, May 18, 1931, VMB.

28. Marks to Nauheim and Schuman, July 22, 1932, VMB.

29. The script for *With All Due Respect*, VMB.

30. Eyer, "Meet the Composer," 8.

31. Marks, *Still Counting*, 37.

32. Schuman to Isaac Stern, March 18, 1990, NYPL-C, "Correspondence S, 1990."

33. See Riis, *Frank Loesser*, 259–60. The four-page August 18, 1965, entry is in NYPL-A, 68/6 (uppercase in original).

34. "Part of [his attitude] was a presumed snobbery; he didn't want to be thought of as an intellectual. He was obviously fighting something deep inside." S-W, 114 [3/1].

35. See Robert M. Yoder to Schuman, October 1, 1948, and Schuman to Yoder, October 29, 1948, NYPL-A, 26/2. See also Robert M. Yoder, "He Put That Tune in Your Head," *Saturday Evening Post*, May 21, 1949, 42–57.

36. Schuman to Edward N. Waters, August 21, 1962, NYPL-A, 65/13.

37. Vera Marks Barad gave the author the manuscript as a gift. The song stylistically is not quite as harmonically advanced as "Lovesick" but engages in similar word-painting gestures

(e.g., within a major-mode context, setting the word "sad" with a diminished chord). The song is attributed to "William H. Schuman" with no mention of a separate lyricist, and it is in a copyist's hand, with some mistakes rubbed out of the parchment and others (spelling a chromatic chord incorrectly) remaining.

38. Nauheim to Persichetti, undated (probably early 1948), NYPL-VP, 17/18. On the cluelessness of Schuman's parents, see OHAM, 37.

39. See Bernstein to Schuman, May 13, 1967, and Schuman to Bernstein, May 20, 1967, NYPL-A, 49/5.

40. S-W, 101–2 [3/1]; Zinsser, April 10, 1989, 21.

41. OHAM, 37–38.

Chapter 5: "Frankie"

1. On the "Births Reported in 1913—Borough of Manhattan" (microfiche in the New York Public Library), the name is spelled "Francis." No middle name or initial is indicated.

2. Frances Prince to her parents, Leonard and Gertrude Prince, August 4, 18, 20, and 22, 1927, AWS.

3. Schuman to Frances Prince, November 16, 1931, AWS.

4. S-W, 136 [3/2]. See "Fast Learners," *Time*, November 8, 1937, accessed January 21, 2009; Harry L. Hollingworth, *Leta Stetter Hollingworth: A Biography* (Lincoln: University of Nebraska Press, 1943), esp. chap. 20, "The Special Opportunity Class (P.S. 165)," 148–54; Leta S. Hollingworth, *Gifted Children: Their Nature and Nurture* (New York: Macmillan, 1926), 70–71; and Leta S. Hollingworth, *Children above 180 IQ (Stanford-Binet): Origin and Development* (Yonkers, NY: World Book Co., 1942), 106.

5. Nina Jones, "Beautiful and Organized Apt for Frances Schuman," (*Yonkers, NY*) *Herald Statesman*, April 14, 1962, AWS.

6. Information about the Prince family comes from a private communication with Anthony Schuman, August 18, 2005; information about Frankie's academic career is in S-W, 199 [4/2].

7. Frank Loesser to Persichetti, April 10, 1948, NYPL-VP, 17/18.

8. S-W, 196 [4/2].

9. Nauheim to Persichetti, undated (probably early 1948), NYPL-VP, 17/18. For an overview of Prohibition in New York City, see Michael A. Lerner, *Dry Manhattan: Prohibition in New York City* (Cambridge, MA: Harvard University Press, 2007), esp. 138–40 on speakeasies.

10. OHAM, 46, and Frances Prince to her parents, August 20 and 22, 1927, AWS.

11. J. Brooks Atkinson, "The Play: Strange Images of Death in Eugene O'Neill's Masterpiece," *New York Times*, October 27, 1931, 22.

12. S-W, 197 [4/2].

13. Schuman to Blanche Levy, October 5, 1989, NYPL-C, "Correspondence L, 1989." For Martha's Vineyard, see Schuman to Connie and Lester Trimble, July 19, 1978, NYPL-A, 118/7.

14. A short history of the Vocational Advisory Service is found in Joseph Samler, "The Vocational Advisory Service: Mission Accomplished?" *Vocational Guidance Quarterly* 19, 2 (December 1970): 131–32.

15. Leta S. Hollingworth to Frances Schuman, April 15, 1937, NYPL-A, 19/10.

16. Jones, "Frances Schuman," AWS.

17. S-W, 157 [3/2].

18. Frances was working part time as late as 1945; see "The William Schumans," *Mademoiselle*, February 1945, 152.

19. Inge Heckel, interview with the author, December 12, 2005.

20. Jones, "Frances Schuman," AWS.

21. See http://www.nul.org/mission.html, accessed February 8, 2009.

22. Personal communication with Anthony Schuman, August 18, 2005.

23. OHAM, 98–99.

24. S-W, 229 [5/2], and Schuman to Frances Schuman, September 22, 1952, AWS.

25. Mark Schubart's remarks, Frances Prince Schuman memorial service, JIG.

Chapter 6: "An Unconventional Education"

1. Edward B. Marks, *Still Counting: Achievements and Follies of a Nonagenarian* (Lanham, MD: Hamilton Books, 2005), 285.

2. See the travel documents in NYPL-C, "Misc. Papers: Cruise Lines Passenger Lists, 1931–1935"; "Ship to Visit 33 Nations," *New York Times*, May 18, 1930, S11; and "Hamburg-American Cut Rates," *New York Times*, March 6, 1931, 47. For a history of the *Resolute*, see Frederick E. Emmons, *American Passenger Ships: The Ocean Lines and Liners, 1873–1983* (Newark: University of Delaware Press, 1985), 38–39.

3. S-W, 194 [191]. For the average weekly wage in 1932, see Scott Derks, *The Value of a Dollar: Prices and Incomes in the United States, 1860–2004* (Millerton, NY: Grey House Publishing, 2004), 201.

4. Though the song bears a publication date of 1933, Schuman indicated, in a June 17, 1932, letter to a "Mr. Austin" with the Arthur P. Schmidt Co. that the song had been completed by that date. See Arthur P. Schmidt Company Archive, General Correspondence, 67/19, LoC-PA.

5. Both of the two vocal-piano scores for *Adoration* are dated October 24, 1932; the string quintet arrangement has no date. See OHAM, 17, for his description of the piece and its performance at Shaaray Tefila. An item in the Shaaray Tefila *Messenger* of June 1, 1943, "Pulitzer Prize in Music," states that "as a member of our Young Folks League, [Schuman] composed music for the Adoration at a Youth Service" (NYPL-C, Scrapbook 2). For the discussion of the Yom Kippur service, see chap. 29.

6. James Robertson to Schuman, March 25, 1968, NYPL-A, 87/12.

7. The firstborn's name was Sue; see Schuman to Hazel Wittner, September 9, 1946, NYPL-A, 43/9.

8. Scalero to Haubiel, September 14, 1922, bMS Mus 261i (temporary), Houghton Library, Harvard University. A March 1, 1928, letter similarly presents Haubiel as eager and demanding. For the recommendation from Blanche Schwarz, see OHAM, 41.

9. S-W, 181 [4/2].

10. See Schuman to Donald S. Fuller, June 1, 1942, NYPL-A, 15/5.

11. The *Préludes* are one of the earliest examples of Schuman's use of a copyist to give his manuscripts a professional look. Other scores this particularly florid copyist rendered are: the *Four Canonic Choruses* (1934); the Canon and Fugue for violin, cello, and piano (1934); the two pastorales (1934); the *Choreographic Poem for Seven Instruments* (1935); the First Symphony (1935); and the First String Quartet (1936).

12. The foreword is with the manuscript of the *Préludes*.

13. Marks, June 28, 1933, and July 12, 1933, and Frankie, August 3, 1933, all in AWS; Sandler, July 15, 1933, and September 8, 1933, NYPL-A, 37/2.

14. Fred Everett Maus, "Recent Ideas and Activities of James K. Randall and Benjamin Boretz: A New Social Role for Music," *Perspectives of New Music* 26, 2 (Summer 1988): 217 (italics in original). For Schuman on Dykema's course, see OHAM, 48; and Schuman to Helen Dykema Dengler, February 5, 1979, NYPL-A, 98/13. For an overview of Dewey's aesthetic philosophy, see Harold B. Dunkel, "Dewey and the Fine Arts," *School Review* 67, 2 (Summer 1959): 229–45.

15. Peter W. Dykema to Schuman, May 21, 1936, NYPL-A, 10/16. See also Schuman to Engel, July 24, 1936, LE-Yale.

16. See program, NYPL-A, 168/1.

17. Haubiel to Persichetti, September 27, 1947, NYPL-VP, 17/18.

18. Schuman to Haubiel, August 29, 1945, AM 18 Carton 5, Houghton Library, Harvard University.

19. See the correspondence in NYPL-A, 19/4.

20. Haubiel to Marian MacDowell, November 6, 1946, bMS Mus 261 (514), Houghton Library, Harvard University.

21. Schuman to Haubiel, September 30, 1965, NYPL-A, 60/4.

22. Mason to Schuman, March 21, 1935, NYPL-B, "Mason, Daniel Gregory."

23. "American Music Concert Attracts Enthusiastic Audience at Salzburg," unidentified clipping in NYPL-A, 188.

24. *Treizième concert de La serenade*, M.D.E. Inghelbrecht, conductor, June 28, 1935, NYPL-C, "Programs, Music: 1924–1959."

25. "Thoughts on Lincoln Center" (WS—Memo to Himself), September 29, 1961, NYPL-A, 67/5.

26. Schuman to Marks, July 27, 1935, AWS. For the location of Schuman's flat, see Hanna Dansky to Schuman, April 29, 1964, NYPL-A, 54/1.

27. Schuman to Frances Prince, August 14, 1935, AWS.

28. See Composers' Forum-Laboratory program, October 21, 1936, NYPL-A, 168/1.

29. Mason to Schuman, March 20, 1936, NYPL-B, "Mason, Daniel Gregory."

30. Susan Loesser, *A Most Remarkable Fella: Frank Loesser and the Guys and Dolls in His Life* (New York: Donald I. Fine, 1993), 96; and Nathan Broder, "The Music of William Schuman," *Musical Quarterly* 31, 1 (January 1945): 25. Broder also mentioned the opinion of Mason, although he left Mason unnamed.

31. Composers' Forum Transcript, October 21, 1936, Record Group 69.5.3; National Archives and Records Administration II (College Park, MD), 1, 2, and 4, courtesy of Melissa de Graaf.

32. Jules Werner to Schuman, October 25, 1936, NYPL-A, 44/11. Werner is the junior project supervisor for the Composers' Forum-Laboratory.

33. Howard A. Murphy to Schuman, October 31, 1936, NYPL-A, 27/8.

34. Undated letter cited by Marion Knoblauch-Franc, in "Manuscript Excerpts," 1 and 3, NYPL-A, 133/9. Knoblauch-Franc interviewed Schuman on May 3, 1982, for a prospective book on the Federal Music Project; he apparently showed her letters from the era. See also Roy Rosenzweig and Barbara Melosh, "Government and the Arts: Voices from the New Deal Era," *Journal of American History* 77, 2 (September 1990): 601.

35. See Claire Reis, *Composers in America: Biographical Sketches of Living Composers with a Record of Their Works 1912–1937* (New York: Macmillan, 1938), 215.

36. Schuman to Frances Prince, August 14, 1935, AWS.

Chapter 7: "Sarah Lawrence and the Beginning of the Decade of War"

The opening poem for this chapter is taken from Murray Kempton and David Remnick, *Part of Our Time: Some Ruins and Monuments of the Thirties* (New York: New York Review of Books, 2004), 316.

1. Sarah Lawrence College, 2008 CORE Survey on Alcohol and Drug Use, courtesy of Abby Lester, Sarah Lawrence College archivist.

2. "Samuel Levinger Killed in Spain Fighting as Volunteer for Loyalists," *Campus*, October 11, 1937, 1; "Samuel Levinger Honored by Memorial Rites," *Campus*, February 21, 1938, 3; "Levinger Asks Ambulance as Memorial for Son," *Campus*, March 7, 1938, 3; "Loyalist Ambulance Attracts Attention on Campus," *Campus*, March 14, 1938, 1. The last article does not mention Samuel, but the ambulance appears to be the one requested by his father as a memorial to his son.

3. See William Schuman, "Sarah Lawrence College, Final Exploratory Course Reports 1936–1937, Volume I: Arts," 19–20, SLC.

4. S-W 208 [5/1].

5. Leah Levinger, "Genevieve Taggard as a Don," April 29, 1950, 2, 6–7, Taggard-DC, 2/35.

6. Ibid., 7.

7. S-W, 226–7 [5/1]. The quota on the number of Jewish students admitted to Sarah Lawrence, "instituted in 1928–29 and adhered to (with modifications) at least until 1956," is treated matter-of-factly in Constance Warren, "Personal Reminiscences of the Early Days of Sarah Lawrence College," 8, SLC, and much more sensationally in Louise Blecher Rose, "The Secret Life of Sarah Lawrence," *Commentary* 75, 5 (May 1983): 52–56, and "Letters from Readers," *Commentary* 76, 2 (August 1983): 4–17.

8. See Steve Swayne, "William Schuman, World War II, and the Pulitzer Prize," *Musical Quarterly* 89, 2–3 (Summer–Fall 2006): 273–320. For works labeled as propagandistic, see chap. 10.

9. For Copland, see Elizabeth B. Crist and Wayne Shirley, ed., *The Selected Correspondence of Aaron Copland* (New Haven, CT: Yale University Press, 2006), 89, 106. For Blitzstein, see Leonard J. Lehrman, *Marc Blitzstein: A Bio-Bibliography* (Westport, CT: Praeger: 2005), 104, 106–9.

10. Woodrow Sandler to Schuman, June 1935, NYPL-A, 37/2.

11. "34 Ex-U.S. Aides Linked to Reds," *New York Times*, December 14, 1955, 30.

12. NYPL-C, Scrapbook 3.

13. See Birmingham, *"Our Crowd,"* 292–93, 296.

14. Arthur Mendel to Schuman, August 5, 1947, NYPL-A, 28/6. Mendel followed the letter with an explanation (August 7, 1947), Schuman called the letter "impressive" but gave no answer to Mendel (August 12, 1947), and Mendel responded in a handwritten note on August 17, 1947: "The purpose of my letter was to persuade, not to impress. But since (as I gather) it failed in the one purpose, I'm glad it succeeded in the other." The earlier event, organized by the Cultural Division of the National Negro Congress, was reported in "Group Discusses Fight on Race Bias," *New York Times*, March 17, 1947, 16. A March 16, 1947, story of the event in the *New York Herald Tribune*, "Fannie Hurst Speech Off, Hits Red Sponsorship," indicated that Schuman, Robeson, and Fredric March were sponsors of the event. This article is referenced in Schuman's FBI file, as is the fact that the National Negro Congress itself was investigated for un-American activities.

15. Barbara Kaplan, "Becoming Sarah Lawrence," http://www.slc.edu/about/History_of_the_College.php, accessed February 18, 2009.

16. Constance Warren, April 1, 1935, memorandum "In re: William Howard Schuman–music," SLC-WS.

17. Warren, April 22, 1935, handwritten note, SLC-WS.

18. OHAM, 51–53; and Warren to Schuman, June 3, 1935, NYPL-A, 38/9.

19. "Versatile Schumann [*sic*] Holds Music Hour," *Campus*, November 2, 1936, 6 (at which Schuman lectured on orchestration and played woodwinds); "Schuman Further Reveals Self as a One Man Orchestra," *Campus*, November 9, 1936, 6 (brass and percussion); and "Schuman Plays Four 'Fiddles' at Music Hour," *Campus*, November 16, 1936, 6 (strings).

20. Horace Grenell and William Schuman, introduction to *Sounds: A Study of Orchestral Color* (New York: Musicraft Records, 1937), 1. For the business dealings between Schuman and Musicraft, see Henry Cohen to Schuman, March 8, 1937, and September 20, 1937, NYPL-A, 27/8. See also David Bonner, *Revolutionizing Children's Records: The Young People's Records and Children's Record Guild Series, 1946–1977* (Lanham, MD: Scarecrow Press, 2008), 57. I thank Mr. Bonner for making a photocopy of the manuscript of *Sounds* available to me.

21. "Madrigal Singers Give Concert Here," *Campus*, March 8, 1937, 1.

22. Warren to Engel, September 29, 1937, Correspondence, SLC-CW.

23. Engel to Schuman, June 2, 1936, LE-Yale.

24. Engel to Schuman, November 23, 1938, LE-Yale.

25. Engel to Schuman, January 29, 1939, LE-Yale.

26. K. Gary Adams, *William Schuman: A Bio-Bibliography* (Westport, CT: Greenwood Press, 1998), 68.

27. Schuman to Warren, March 27, 1938, SLC-WS.

28. The December 8, 1934, issue of *Campus* is filled with stories and editorials about the Sarah Lawrence College Chorus, its organization, its financial status, and its role on campus. Most important among them is "The Chorus History" by Nancy Garoutte (4), in which she devoted half as much space to the chorus from 1929 to 1938 (pre-Schuman) as to the years 1938–1943 (the Schuman era).

29. "Fellowships Awarded to S. L. Faculty," *Campus*, March 28, 1939, 1.

30. See the rosters for the chorus in Chorus Box, Folder "Lists & Conductors," SLC.

31. "They Had Knute, But We Have Bill," *Campus*, December 8, 1943, 2.

32. Lehman Engel, *This Bright Day: An Autobiography* (New York: Macmillan, 1974), 88–89, 118.

33. William and Frances Schuman to Samuel and Ray Schuman, July 11, 1937, NYPL-B, "1932–39."

34. See the Schuman-Porter correspondence from July to September 1938, QP-Yale, 11/139.

35. Schuman to Eleanor Schuetze, March 26, 1956, NYPL-A, 16/8; "Schuman Will Be Honored," *Los Angeles Times*, April 22, 1956, D6.

36. "Cellist Fred Sherry Talks with Composer William Schuman," *Lincoln Center/Stagebill*, October 1986: 20C, NYPL-A, 176/2. See also OHAM, 102.

37. Frances McFarland to Schuman, March 2, 1938, NYPL-A, 44/11; Schuman to Harold Spivacke, May 21, 1957, NYPL-A, 148/5; and notation on last page of manuscript.

38. Frances McFarland to Schuman, October 4, 1937, NYPL-A, 44/11. A second letter from McFarland bearing the same date indicates that a scheduled concert of Schuman's chamber works and solo compositions had been postponed.

39. Schuman to Sam Dennison, January 25, 1981, NYPL-A, 127/7. According to a March 2, 1938, letter from McFarland to Schuman (NYPL-A, 44/11), Schuman had believed that the Composers' Forum-Laboratory staff could copy the symphony. McFarland told him it would not be possible for them to undertake this work.

40. Schuman to various composers, October 16, 1937, NYPL-B, "Composers Forum Laboratory–American Composers Project."

41. For more on the American Composers Alliance, see "The Composers Organize: A Proclamation," *Modern Music* 15, 2 (January–February 1938): 92–95. Schuman attempted a merger between the ACC and the ACA, but it came to naught. See Schuman to Engel, May 10, 1938, LE-Yale.

42. Davidson Taylor to Schuman, March 24, 1938, NYPL-B, "American Composers Committee."

43. Chalmers Clifton to Schuman, January 25, 1938, NYPL-A, 44/11.

44. "Schuman Wins Prize Given by Committee for Spanish Aid," unidentified clipping in NYPL-A, 188. Much of the same information is found in "Notes of Musicians," *New York Times*, April 17, 1938, X6.

45. "Schuman's Symphony to Be Played," *Campus*, May 23, 1938, 1.

46. Mary Lee Gildart, "Schuman's Symphony Included in Concert," *Campus*, June 8, 1938, 6.

47. "Graham Dances with Others for Spain," *Campus*, January 17, 1938, 3.

48. "Schuman Addresses Music Institute," *Campus*, October 31, 1938, 1.

49. Gerald Strang to Schuman, January 14, 1939, NYPL-A, 31/3.

50. The cover page for the Quartettino manuscript is dated "Jan. 20, 21, 1939." For more on the recording, see David Hall, "New Music Quarterly Recordings—A Discography," *Journal* [Association of Recorded Sound Collections] 16, 1–2 (1984): 21. Adams gives 1939 as the year Peer International published the work (see p. 30), but the earliest print publication appears to occur two years later, when the Quartettino was included in the *suplemento musical* of the October 1941 issue of the *Boletín latinoamericano de música*. The earliest Peer edition comes from 1956. See also OHAM, 110–11; Otto Luening, *The Odyssey of an American Composer: The Autobiography of Otto Luening* (New York: Charles Scribner's Sons, 1980), 423; and Alfred Frankenstein, "American Composers XXII: William Schuman," *Modern Music* 22, 1 (November–December 1944): 24.

51. Schuman to Engel, May 13, 1939, LE-Yale.

52. OHAM, 71.

53. Schuman to Copland, September 6, 1938, LoC-AC. 262/13. As for Sessions' judgment on the Second Symphony, Schuman told the story in two versions. In both, Schuman requested to meet with Sessions, who had voted against giving Schuman the prize. In one version, Sessions convinced Schuman that the other judges were wrong; see Schuman to Sessions, June 15, 1961, NYPL-A, 39/8. In the other version, their conversation ended with Sessions believing that he was in error in voting against the work and Schuman believing that Sessions was right originally and that the Symphony should not have been awarded the prize; see OHAM, 70–71.

54. One sign of affiliation between the North American Committee to Aid Spanish Democracy and the American Communist Party is a flyer published in June 1937 by the Communist Party of New York calling people to a rally that was being sponsored by the committee. See http://digitalcollections.mcmaster.ca/north-american-committee-aid-spanish-democracy-and-affiliates-leaflet-june-1937, accessed September 4, 2009. See also Merle Curti, *American Philanthropy Abroad: A History* (New Brunswick, NJ: Rutgers University Press, 1963), 396.

Chapter 8: "'The pupil is outdoing the master'"

1. Paul Rosenfeld, "Current Chronicle: Copland–Harris–Schuman," *Musical Quarterly* 25 (1939): 372.

2. Ibid., 379.

3. Ibid.

4. Ibid., 380.

5. See Beth Ellen Levy, "Frontier Figures: American Music and the Mythology of the American West, 1895–1945" (Ph.D. diss., University of California–Berkeley, 2002), 133.

6. See Paul Rosenfeld—"Harris Before the World," *New Republic* 77 (February 7, 1934): 364–65; "Early European Music," *New Republic* 78 (April 11, 1934): 244–45; "Tragic and American," *New Republic* 81 (November 21, 1934): 47—and John Tasker Howard, *Our American Music* (New York: Thomas Y. Crowell, 1931), 572.

7. Levy's discussion of Harris's mythic trajectory in "Frontier Figures" (97–219) is de rigueur reading on the topic.

8. Harris's 1937 arrangement of *The Art of the Fugue* for string quartet was published by G. Schirmer and recorded by the Roth String Quartet. See Nicolas Slonimsky, "Roy Harris: Cimarron Composer" (manuscript, University of California–Los Angeles, Music Library, Special Collections, 1951), 50. Royalty statements found in Harris-CSULA, "Recordings–1947," show gross royalty earnings of $227.84 from 1942 to 1946. Most of this income came from the Bach recording, although the statements also show royalties from: *Symphony 1933*; the Third Symphony; "4 min & 20" ("a four-minute piece for string quartet and flute to finish out the eighth side of the records," according to Harris. See Slonimsky, "Cimarron Composer," 43; and Slonimsky's 1934 recording of Varèse's *Ionisation* (1931), for which he recruited various composers to play the piece, since it was beyond the abilities of the percussionists of the New York Philharmonic. One of the composers in the ensemble was Schuman; "Harris was in the recording booth, supervising the acoustics." See Nicolas Slonimsky, *Perfect Pitch: A Life Story* (Oxford: Oxford University Press, 1988), 138–39, and http://www.ubu.com/sound/slonimsky.html, accessed March 14, 2007.

9. Rosenfeld, "Current Chronicle: Copland–Harris–Schuman," 379.

10. Nicolas Slonimsky to his wife, Dorothy Adlow, July 21, 1933, in Slonimsky, *Perfect Pitch*, 140.

11. Levy, "Frontier Figures," 133–45 and 199–203.

12. Koussevitzky to Erskine, November 10, 1933, Harris-CSULA, "Letters, 1937, A–L."

13. Harris to Schuman, January 29, 1937, NYPL-A, 20/2.

14. Dan Stehman, "Harris, Roy," *Grove Music Online*, edited by Laura Macy (accessed March 14, 2007), http://www.grovemusic.com. See also Levy, "Frontier Figures," 147–59.

15. See Dan Stehman, *Roy Harris: An American Musical Pioneer* (Boston: G. K. Hall, 1984), 52–57, for an analysis of this work.

16. As quoted in Levy, "Frontier Figures," 129.

17. Ibid., 130.

18. Olin Downes, "Harris Symphony Has Premiere Here," *New York Times*, February 3, 1934, 9.

19. Levy, "Frontier Figures," 132.

20. Arthur Mendel and Olin Downes, "An American Work," *New York Times*, February 11, 1934, X8.

21. Harris to Schuman, February 15, 1937, NYPL-A, 188. The review of the Harris Quintet is also pasted into this scrapbook.

22. Schuman to Harris, February 17, 1937, NYPL-A, 188.

23. Levy, "Frontier Figures," 148 n. 58.

24. Ashley Pettis to Roy Harris, April 15, 1937, Harris-CSULA, "Letters, 1937, A–L."

25. Both letters—an undated one from Lucien Paul Capron, and a May 20, 1937, one from Schuman—are in Harris-CSULA, "Letters, 1937, A–L" and "Letters, 1937, M–Z," respectively.

26. A reference to the last movement of the Symphony for Voices, titled Inscription ("The Modern Man I Sing").

27. Schuman to Harris, April 20, 1938, Harris-CSULA, "Letters, 1938."

28. Schuman to Engel, March 23, 1937, LE-Yale.

29. "Schuman, Student of Harris, Tells of Composer's Life," *Campus*, November 21, 1938, 4. See also: "Mr. Roy Harris, Modern Composer, to Discuss Music," *Campus*, May 10, 1937, 1; "Harris Lectures on American Music and Real Masters," *Campus*, May 17, 1937, 1–2; "Roy Harris Honors S. L. Chorus," *Campus*, October 17, 1938, 1; "Harris Completes First Piece for Chorus," *Campus*, January 17, 1939, 4. This last article states that Harris was composing "a short suite of three pieces," which Harris scholar Dan Stehman dubbed the "Whitman Triptych." See Stehman to Schuman, August 25, 1988, NYPL-C, "Correspondence S, 1988."

30. Slonimsky, "Cimarron Composer," 59–61. Harris's article, "Sources of a Musical Culture," *New York Times*, January 1, 1939: 101–2, is less combative than Slonimsky's characterization would lead a reader to believe, and nowhere in the article does Harris write about his inability to interest a conductor in his Third Symphony.

31. See Howard Pollack, *Skyscraper Lullaby: The Life and Music of John Alden Carpenter* (Washington, DC: Smithsonian Institution Press, 1995), 354–55.

32. Leonard Bernstein, "The Latest from Boston," *Modern Music* 16, 3 (March–April 1939): 182–84.

33. Schuman to Koussevitzky, October 18, 1938, LoC-AC, 54/18.

34. Schuman to Frances Schuman, February 14, 1939, NYPL-B, "1932–39." The letter is handwritten in pencil.

35. Moses Smith, *Koussevitzky* (New York: Allen, Towne & Heath, 1947), 269–70.

36. Warren Storey Smith, "Myra Hess Soloist at Symphony; Work by Schuman Is Received Rather Coldly," *Boston Post*, February 18, 1939, NYPL-A, 188.

37. Moses Smith, "Symphony Concert: Miss Hess as Soloist, and 100 Men to Follow," *Boston Evening Transcript*, February 18, 1939, part 4, p. 5, NYPL-A, 188. Another clipping of the review appears in NYPL-C, Scrapbook 3, with an identification by Schuman's wife, Frances, on the clipping.

38. Moses Smith, "Music: Flute Players' Third Concert," *Boston Evening Transcript*, February 20, 1939, 18. A clipping of the "Second Thoughts" portion of this review is found in NYPL-A, 188. See also Schuman to Sheila Thomas, September 26, 1967, NYPL-A, 86/5.

39. Moses Smith, "Symphony Concert: Roy Harris's New Third Symphony Receives Its First Performance," *Boston Evening Transcript*, February 25, 1939, part 4, p. 6.

40. OHAM, 69.

41. Moses Smith, in introducing his readers to the Third on the eve of its premiere, volunteered that the work "was completed last month [i.e., January 1939]" and that his information about the symphony came "from a conversation with the composer and

from a perusal of the score with the composer at one's side." Moses Smith, "Music: Foreword to New Symphony by a Seasoned American," *Boston Evening Transcript*, February 23, 1939, 18.

42. OHAM, 105.

43. Flora Rheta Schreiber and Vincent Persichetti, *William Schuman* (New York: G. Schirmer, 1954), 19.

44. The proposal itself—titled "Musical Survey"—is in RAC, 252/3009.

45. His letter of resignation is in Harris-CSULA, "Letters, 1938"; the "List of Undesirable Conditions, and possible remedies" is in "1937—M–Z."

46. Schuman to David H. Stevens, February 21, 1941, RAC, 252/3009. Stevens was director of humanities for the Rockefeller Foundation.

47. Roy Harris and Jacob A. Evanson, *Singing through the Ages* (New York: American Book Co., 1940).

48. Lorna Dietz, American Book Co., to Harris, December 30, 1941, Harris-CSULA, "Letters, 1941, A–L."

49. See Levy's discussion of Harris's 1940 article for *Modern Music*, "Folksong—American Big Business," in her "Frontier Figures," 163–71.

50. Levy traces the problems that beset him and his decline as a composer of influence to the *Folksong* Symphony. See Levy, "Frontier Figures," 171–79.

51. Harris to Schuman, October 22, 1942, NYPL-A, 20/2.

52. Olin Downes, "Harris Symphony Has Premiere Here," *New York Times*, March 12, 1943, 12.

53. Frank D. Fackenthal, provost of Columbia University, to Harris, February 4, 1943, in Columbia-A, 126/10.

54. As quoted in Slonimsky, "Cimarron Composer," 78. Slonimsky stated that Harris told him this in August 1950.

55. Schuman to Copland, March 31, 1943, NYPL-A, 11/6. In a May 14, 1952, letter to Harris, Schuman gave Harris permission to be his proxy vote on matters pertaining to a festival Harris was arranging for Pittsburgh. He continued: "I do hope that your Fifth is performed and if the Committee considers one of mine, I would like it to be my Sixth (the latest and hence the best), although Steinberg did a fine job in Buffalo on No. IV." NYPL-A, 20/2.

56. In an October 22, 1942, letter to Schuman, Harris remarked: "I was delighted to learn of your lectures on my music." The location of these lectures is not mentioned in the letter or the other extant Harris-Schuman correspondence. NYPL-A, 20/2.

57. Schuman to Igor Buketoff, August 6, 1957, NYPL-A, 5/5. Buketoff had written to Schuman two days earlier, asking for Schuman's immediate attention. On the back of Buketoff's August 4, 1957, letter, Schuman wrote his initial recommendations. For Harris, he chose the Third and Seventh Symphonies (1937 and 1955, respectively); on the final list he sent to Buketoff, Schuman included Harris's 1954 cantata, *Abraham Lincoln Walks at Midnight*, for mezzo-soprano and piano trio.

58. Alfred Frankenstein, "American Composers XXII: William Schuman," *Modern Music* 22, 1 (November–December 1944): 23.

59. Ibid., 27.

60. OHAM, 239.

61. Levy, "Frontier Figures," 203.

62. B. H. Haggin, "Records," *The Nation*, July 29, 1939, 131. Haggin's comments come at the end of the review. The final paragraph begins: "That leaves two singles. . . . The other ($1) offers Charles Ives's 67th Psalm and William Schuman's Choral Etude, sung by Lehman Engel's Madrigal Singers. Much has been written . . ." Haggin actually said nothing about the Schuman work he was ostensibly reviewing!

Chapter 9: "Schuman, Copland, Koussevitzky, and Bernstein"

1. See Howard Pollack, *Aaron Copland: The Life and Work of an Uncommon Man* (Urbana: University of Illinois Press, 2000), esp. chap. 11, "Copland among His Peers" (159–77), and chap. 12, "Copland and Younger American Composers" (178–215). Copland's relationship with Schuman is discussed on pp. 191–92.

2. For a recounting of this anecdote, see Nicolas Slonimsky, *Slonimsky's Book of Musical Anecdotes* (London: Routledge, 2002), 133–34.

3. Aaron Copland, "Scores and Records," *Modern Music* 15, 4 (May–June 1938): 245–46.

4. See: "Chester," *Music Trade Review* (London), March 1, 1938, in NYPL-A, 188; Schuman to Reis, November 20, 1937, NYPL-A, 36/5; Schuman to Engel, May 10, 1938, LE-Yale.

5. See the December 17, 1948, letter and royalty statement from J. & W. Chester to Schuman, NYPL-A, 180/1.

6. Schuman to Copland, September 6, 1938, LoC-AC, 262/13.

7. Schuman to Isadore Freed, September 4, 1958, NYPL-A, 16/11. In addition to the *Three Moods for Piano*, Schuman's published works for piano are *Three-Score Set* (1943), *Voyage* (1953), and *Chester: Variations for Piano* (1988).

8. Schuman wrote, "The Three Studies take about 8 to ten minutes in performance." Schuman to Porter, July 22, 1938, QP-Yale, 11/139.

9. Schuman to Copland, September 24, 1957, NYPL-A, 11/6.

10. Schuman to Calvert Bean Jr., November 20, 1961, NYPL-A, 179/2.

11. Schuman to Engel, May 13, 1939, LE-Yale.

12. Schuman to Copland, July 29, 1942, NYPL-A, 11/7.

13. Schuman to Copland, September 1, 1942, NYPL-A, 11/7.

14. Aaron Copland and Vivian Perlis, *Copland: 1900 through 1942* (New York: St. Martin's, 1984), 282.

15. OHAM, 72. In another interview, Schuman said the headache lasted three days. See Zinsser, April 4, 1989, 9.

16. Letters in NYPL-A, 188.

17. See Hugo Leichtentritt, *Serge Koussevitzky, The Boston Symphony Orchestra, and the New American Music* (Cambridge, MA: Harvard University Press, 1946), esp. 3–10; José A. Bowen, "Koussevitzky, Sergey," in *Grove Music Online: Oxford Music Online*, http://www.oxfordmusiconline.com/subscriber/article/grove/music/15431, accessed March 4, 2009; and "The History of the BSO," available at http://www.bso.org/.

18. See Koussevitzky's rejection of Copland's 1939 recommendation of Elliott Carter's *Pocahontas Suite*, in Copland and Perlis, *Copland: 1900 through 1942*, 282–83.

19. October 18, 1938, and February 1, 1939, letters from Schuman to Koussevitzky, as well as the correspondence between Schuman and Koussevitzky's secretary, are in LoC-SK.

20. Autobiography, chap. 3, p. 7.

21. Schuman to Koussevitzky, February 20, 1939, LoC-SK.

22. "Boston Symphony Orchestra Plays Schuman Work," *Campus*, February 28, 1939, 1, 4.

23. Warren to Schuman, February 28, 1939, NYPL-A, 38/9.

24. OHAM, 80 and 83; Leonard Bernstein, "The Latest from Boston," *Modern Music* 16, 3 (March–April 1939): 182–83.

25. Autobiography, chap. 3, p. 14.

26. Margaret Naumburg, *The Child and the World: Dialogues in Modern Education* (New York: Harcourt, Brace, and Co., 1928), 31–32, as quoted in Blythe Hinitz, "Margaret Naumburg and the Walden School," in *Founding Mothers and Others: Women Educational Leaders during the Progressive Era*, ed. Alan R. Sadovnik and Susan F. Semel (New York: Palgrave, 2002), 38.

27. Hinitz, "Margaret Naumburg and the Walden School," 42–43.

28. Douglas Martin, "Walden School, at 73, Files for Bankruptcy," *New York Times*, June 23, 1987, B1.

29. Jewish Women's Archive, "Margaret Naumburg." http://jwa.org/encyclopedia/article/naumburg-margaret; (accessed March 5, 2009).

30. See Schuman to Claire Reis, May 1, 1938, NYPL-A, 25/6.

31. Copland and Perlis, *Copland: 1900 through 1942*, 351.

32. Schuman to Naumburg, September 7, 1938, postcard, MN-Penn.

33. Naumburg's October 20, 1938, and May 29, 1939, letters to Schuman, and Schuman's May 27, 1939, and June 3, 1939, letters to Naumburg, are in NYPL-A, 31/1. See also John Burk, "Symphony No. 2, in One Movement by William Howard Schuman," *Boston Symphony Orchestra Concert Bulletin, 58th Season 1938–39*, 734. After Schuman's reversal, Naumburg turned first to Lincoln Kirstein for advice and then separately asked Roy Harris and Douglas Moore to write the music for *Playground*. Their letters to Naumburg as well as the dance synopsis for *Playground* are in MN-Penn.

34. John Burk, "American Festival Overture by William Howard Schuman," *Boston Symphony Orchestra Concert Bulletin, 59th Season 1939–40*, 245. The biographical portion of Burk's note continued to list "Playground" as a work in progress.

35. Schuman to Robert Beckhard, March 21, 1942, in *Letters of Composers: An Anthology, 1603–1945*, ed. Gertrude Norman and Miriam Lubell Shrifte (New York: Alfred A. Knopf, 1946), 411.

36. Schuman to Koussevitzky, September 19, 1939, LoC-SK.

37. Schuman to Koussevitzky, September 22, 1939, LoC-SK.

38. Autobiography, chap. 3, p. 16.

39. Flora Rheta Schreiber and Vincent Persichetti, *William Schuman* (New York: G. Schirmer, 1954), 19.

40. Schuman to Mr. and Mrs. Max Geismar and Guest, November 17, 1939, NYPL-B, "1932–39."

41. Schuman to Henry Allen Moe, January 18, 1940, NYPL-A, 18/13. "Everybody in that orchestra knew that nobody could sight-read this. They yelled bravo, and [Koussevitzky] couldn't figure. . . . It never occurred to him to ask anybody what had happened." S-W, 359 [8/1].

42. Schuman to Koussevitzky, November 16, 1940, LoC-SK.

43. Schuman to Moe, January 18, 1940, NYPL-A, 18/13; Constance Warren to Schuman, June 3, 1940, NYPL-A, 38/9; and class lists from 1939–40 and 1940–41, SLC.

44. "Transit Difficulties for Metropolitan—Tryouts for American Work," *New York Times*, November 16, 1941, X7.

45. See Pollack, *Aaron Copland*, 205–6.

46. "Tanglewood," handwritten notes on mimeographed program from July 18, 1941, in NYPL-A, 188.

47. Schuman to Copland, July 21, 1941, NYPL-A, 11/7.

48. Pollack, *Aaron Copland*, 546.

49. William Schuman, "Aaron Copland," *Perspectives of New Music* 19, 1–2 (Autumn 1980–Summer 1981): 52.

50. Copland and Perlis, *Copland: 1900 through 1942*, 350.

51. Schuman to Copland, March 21, 1942, LoC-AC, 262/13.

Chapter 10: "Populism, Progressivism, and Politics"

1. Genevieve Taggard, "Arts and the War," speech delivered to the students at the High School of Music and Art, New York, NY, March 27, 1942, in Taggard-DC, 4/62 (underlining in original).

2. Schuman to Engel, January 16, 1937, LE-Yale. The manuscript bears the date "December 19, '36" and the notations "1st version" and "never performed—should not be." See LoC-WS-A for a copyist's rendition of this version.

3. Frederic Cohen, review of *The Princess and the Pea: A Fairy Tale in One Act*, Op. 43, by Ernst Toch, in *Notes* (Music Library Association), 2nd ser., 11, 4 (September 1954): 602. See also "Marion Jones Farquhar," obituary, *New York Times*, March 16, 1965, 39; and May 1, 1947, letter from Farquhar to Harold Taylor, president of Sarah Lawrence College, in Frederick Hart faculty folder, SLC.

4. OHAM, 149. For Schuman's personal reminiscence of Farquhar, see OHAM, 274–77.

5. See N.S. (Noel Straus), "Concert Is Given by Trapp Family," *New York Times*, December 11, 1938, 60.

6. As quoted in Jennifer D. Rector, "American Proletarianism in Two Collaborative Works by William Schuman and Genevieve Taggard," masters of music thesis, University of Missouri–Kansas City, 1996, 61–62.

7. A fuller analysis of *Prologue* may be found in Rector, "American Proletarianism," 64–73.

8. Benjamin M. Steigman to Winthrop Parkhurst, May 1, 1939, NYPL-A, 19/7.

9. Aaron Copland and Vivian Perlis, *Copland: 1900 through 1942* (New York: St. Martin's, 1984), 285–86.

10. Parkhurst to Steigman, May 8, 1939, NYPL-A, 19/7.

11. Alexander Richter to Schuman, May 9, 1939, NYPL-A, 19/7.

12. Irving Kolodin, "American Works Heard; Shulman [*sic*] Debut," *New York Sun*, May 8, 1939, n.p.; W., "Music by Guggenheim Fellows Played," *Musical America* 59, 10 (May 25, 1939): 28; and N.S. (Noel Straus), "Composers' Forum Opens Music Week," *New York Times*, May 18, 1939, 20. All clippings are in NYPL-A, 188.

13. Moore to Schuman, May 7, 1939, NYPL-A, 30/6. No year is on the letter.

14. Schuman to Alexander Smallens, May 11, 1939, NYPL-Smallens.

15. Yvette Weintraub (6th term, High School of Music and Art), Programme Notes, "All American Program: 'American Music for American Youth,'" May 13, 1939, NYPL-A, 188.

16. Statement by Alexander Richter, head of the music department, during intermission of school concert, evening of May 13, 1939, NYPL-A, 19/7.

17. "Many thanks for thinking of me in connection with music for the Soviet Pavillion [*sic*]. I'll have a piece for Piano and 'Cello by July and will send it along then if you're still interested." Schuman to Engel, May 13, 1939, LE-Yale.

18. See "Concert and Opera Asides," *New York Times*, August 6, 1939, X5. I thank Rika Asai at Indiana University for directing me to this article.

19. Schuman to Alexander Smallens, November 3, 1939, NYPL-Smallens; and Schuman to Henry Allen Moe, January 18, 1940, NYPL-A, 18/13.

20. Schuman to Genevieve Taggard, December 29, 1939, postcard, Taggard-DC, 2/47. The date comes from the undated card's postmark.

21. See Taggard-DC, 4/24.

22. For Durant, see the Senate subcommittee minutes for Tuesday, September 15, 1953; for Young People's Records, see David Bonner, *Revolutionizing Children's Records: The Young People's Records and Children's Record Guild Series, 1946–1977* (Lanham, MD: Scarecrow Press, 2008), 99–104.

23. William Schuman, "Writing for Amateurs and Pros," *New York Times*, June 30, 1940, X5.

24. Neil W. Levin, "Max Helfman," from the Milken Archive of American Jewish Music, http://www.milkenarchive.org/artists/artists.taf?artistid=280, accessed March 8, 2009. See also Hugh J. Riddell, "Music in Praise of Democracy," *Sunday Worker*, June 30, 1940, in NYPL-A, 188; and JPPC (Jewish People's Philharmonic Chorus) Milestones 1923–2006, http://thejppc.org/_wsn/page5.html, accessed March 8, 2009.

25. Marion S. Jacobson, "From Communism to Yiddishism: The Reinvention of the Jewish People's Philharmonic Chorus of New York City," in *Chorus and Community*, ed. Karen Ahlquist (Urbana: University of Illinois Press, 2006), 212. See also Philip Moddel, *Max Helfman: A Biographical Sketch* (Berkeley, CA: Judah L. Magnes Memorial Museum, 1974), 24–27.

26. Schuman, "Writing for Amateurs and Pros."

27. Henry W. Simon, "Workers Sing the Way Valkyries Ought To," *PM*, December 3, 1940; and Bruno David Ussher, "William Schuman Cantata 'This Is Our Time,'" *Los Angeles Daily News*, May 3, 1941, both in NYPL-A, 188.

28. Colin McPhee, "Records and Scores," *Modern Music* 18, 1 (November–December 1940): 57.

29. Schuman to Louis G. Wersen, September 17, 1959, NYPL-A, 43/7. For an analysis of *This Is Our Time*, see Rector, "American Proletarianism," 75–100.

30. "Vital Music of U.S. Composers Lauded," *San Francisco Examiner*, March 26, 1940, in NYPL-A, 188.

31. Roy Harris, Ashley Pettis, and William H. Schuman, "The Composer's Economic Status," p. 1, and "Recommendations," p. 2, in Musical Survey, submitted to the Rockefeller Foundation, May 1, 1940, RAC, 252/3010.

32. See February 21, 1941, letter from Schuman to David H. Stevens, RAC, 252/3009.

33. See May 1, 1940, internal memo by David H. Stevens, director of humanities; and November 20, 1940, interoffice memo from John Marshall, assistant director of humanities, to Stevens, both in RAC, 252/3009.

34. This material is adapted from Steve Swayne, "William Schuman, World War II, and the Pulitzer Prize," *Musical Quarterly* 89, 2–3 (Summer–Fall 2006): 273–320.

35. "Ickes Asks Scorn for 'Superior Race,'" *New York Times*, July 5, 1940, 8.

36. "Americans Arm against Hitler's Ideas as France Drifts Away from Democracy," *Life*, July 15, 1940, 26.

37. Schuman, "Writing for Amateurs and Pros."

38. Schuman to Harold Ickes, August 6, 1940, NYPL-A, 20/12.

39. See Schuman to the United States Senate Appropriations Committee, April 22, 1955, NYPL-A, 2/2; and Schuman to Claire Reis, February 9, 1962, NYPL-A, 79/8. Also see Clayton D. Laurie, *The Propaganda Warriors: America's Crusade against Nazi Germany* (Lawrence: University Press of Kansas, 1996), 1–2.

40. Schuman to Archibald MacLeish, July 23, 1943, Box 20, Folder "Schuman, William, 1943, 1975–77," Archibald MacLeish Papers, Manuscript Division, Library of Congress, Washington, D.C. MacLeish's July 30, 1943, response is in NYPL-B, "1943."

41. There is a February 15, 1942, letter from the text's poet, Arthur Guiterman, to Schuman, in NYPL-A, 17/8. It is unclear from the letter, though, if Schuman and Guiterman are talking about this particular text, which was published as "Land of Hope" in *Hearst International Combined with Cosmopolitan* 115, 2 (August 1943): 6.

42. See Schuman to R. L. F. McCombs, March 10, 1947, NYPL-A, 34/4.

43. Samuel Schuman wrote to his son: "By the way why not elaborate on the Parade of the Newsreel and you have a fine military piece—Think it over." July 22, 1942, NYPL-A, 150/12.

44. OHAM, 145–6. According to a story in the *Pittsburgh Press*, "high school bands throughout Pennsylvania will be given a piece he has written at the request of their state director—'News Reel,' his first piece for high school bands." "Nation at War Still Needs Music, Composer Says," *Pittsburgh Press*, December 10, 1941, NYPL-A, 189.

45. Walter Onslow to Schuman, August 14, 1940, 20/12.

46. See Swayne, "William Schuman, World War II."

47. Schuman to Koussevitzky, September 18, 1942, LoC-SK.

48. John Samuel Wannamaker, "The Musical Settings of the Poetry of Walt Whitman: A Study of Theme, Structure, and Prosody," Ph.D., University of Minnesota, 1972, 117–18.

49. Arthur Berger to Copland, April 12, 1943. "Berger would have heard [the work] in the BSO's [Boston Symphony Orchestra's] New York City concert of April 3." Wayne D. Shirley, "Aaron Copland and Arthur Berger in Correspondence," in *Copland and His World*, ed. Carol J. Oja and Judith Tick (Princeton, NJ: Princeton University Press, 2005): 195–97.

50. Copland to Schuman, March 27, 1943, and Schuman to Copland, March 31, 1943, NYPL-B, "Copland, Aaron."

51. Charles Dollard to Eliza Gaylord and Walter A. Jessup, December 23, 1941, CCNY, 220/8.

52. Schuman to Alfred V. Frankenstein, April 13, 1953, 16/9.

53. Alfred Frankenstein, "American Composers XXII: William Schuman," *Modern Music* 22, 1 (November–December 1944): 26.

54. Anne Wolfson Livingstone, "Very Personally Remembered," 3, Taggard-DC, 2/37.

Chapter 11: "World War II and the Prize-Winning Composer"

1. Claire R. Reis, *Composers, Conductors and Critics* (New York: Oxford University Press, 1955), 70–71. Reis's July 12, 1939, letter informing Schuman of the honor is in NYPL-A, 25/6.

2. Copland to Schuman, May 6, 1943, NYPL-B, "Copland, Aaron."

3. Alfred Frankenstein, "American Composers XXII: William Schuman," *Modern Music* 22, 1 (November–December 1944): 23.

4. Reis to Schuman, July 12, 1939, NYPL-A, 25/6.

5. Schuman to Bernstein, December 7, 1939, postcard, LoC-LB.

6. Schuman to Pearl Kroll, March 25, 1980, NYPL-A, 133/3.

7. Olin Downes, "Coolidge Quartet of Strings Heard," *New York Times*, February 28, 1940, 16.

8. Vivian Perlis, CD notes for *William Schuman (1910–1992): Three String Quartets*, Lydian String Quartet (Daniel Stepner, Judith Eissenberg, violins; Mary Ruth Ray, viola; Rhonda Rider, cello (Harmonia Mundi HMU 907114, 1994), p. 6.

9. See "Chorus Will Travel by Bus in April," *Campus*, February 14, 1940, 1; Chorus Box, Folder "Chorus Programs 1929–1970," SLC; and Constance Warren, President's Report, May, 23, 1940, sec. "Publicity," p. 9, in *President's Reports: November, 1938 to May, 1941* (book 3), SLC.

10. See SLC-WS.

11. OHAM, 63–65; S-W, 231–33 [5/2]; Olin Downes filed two *New York Times* reviews of the Debussy: "Boston Symphony Aided by Chorus," February 14, 1943, 51; and "Dr. Koussevitzky Conducts Mozart," February 15, 1943, 10.

12. John W. Arant to Standard Symphony Broadcasts, September 27, 1942, NYPL-A, 27/4. W. J. Held of the Standard Oil Company of California forwarded Arant's letter to Edwin McArthur, conductor of the Standard Symphony Hour, along with a personal cover letter from Held, on September 29, 1942. "We thought you might be interested in the attached fan letter, to which we replied from this office, concerning the 'American Overture' of Schumann [*sic*]. While we do not necessarily share his sentiments, we are passing it on to you with the thought that it might be taken into consideration in planning future programs."

13. John Briggs, "Barlow, Rubinstein Heard in Philharmonic Concert," *New York Post*, November 6, 1942, 46.

14. Schuman to Harold Spivacke, December 11, 1953, Music Division, Old Correspondence, "Schuman, William 1950–1956," Library of Congress. Emphasis in original.

15. Leonard Bernstein, "Young American—William Schuman," *Modern Music* 19, 2 (January–February 1942): 98.

16. OHAM, 118.

17. Richard Freed, "Notes on the Program," National Symphony Orchestra, Leonard Slatkin, music director, seventy-fourth season, 2004–2005, concerts for February 3–5, 2005, pp. 8, 10. I thank two members of the National Symphony Orchestra administration for making available to me the program notes for this concert and for allowing me to hear a live recording of the symphony: Patricia O'Kelley, managing director of Media Relations, and Louise Niepoetter, executive assistant.

18. OHAM, 118.

19. Olin Downes, "Boston Orchestra Offers New Work," *New York Times*, November 23, 1941, 55; Schuman to Downes, November 23, 1941, and Downes to Schuman, December 1, 1941, NYPL-A, 12/4.

20. Robert Lawrence, "New Symphony Is Directed by Koussevitzky," *New York Herald Tribune*, November 23, 1941, 40.

21. Anonymous, "Roland Hayes Is Orchestral Guest," *New York Sun*, November 24, 1941, in NYPL-C, Scrapbook 1.

22. Lou Harrison, "First-Time Fashions, New York, Fall 1944," *Modern Music* 22, 2 (November–December 1944): 33.

23. Henry Simon, "An American Gets a Break for Once," *PM*, November 24, 1941, in NYPL-C, Scrapbook 1.

24. "Music Critics Give Award," *PM*, May 15, 1942, in NYPL-C, Scrapbook 3.

25. Virgil Thomson, "A Tasty and Nourishing Repast," *New York Herald Tribune*, April 8, 1942, in NYPL-C, Scrapbook 3.

26. Both reviews are in NYPL-C, Scrapbook 1.

27. Donald Fuller, "Forecast and Review: New York, Spring, '42: Music of the Americas," *Modern Music* 19, 4 (May–June 1942): 254.

28. The Schuman-Fuller correspondence is in NYPL-A, 15/5.

29. Schuman to Sidorsky, March 28, 1939, courtesy of Karl Miller. The other letter, also courtesy of Miller, is dated May 30, 1941. In it, Schuman states: "It seems particularly stupid to me this morning that any of us should ever allow personal riffs of any description to

interfere with art associations. . . . Should you feel this way collaboration at a future moment would still be possible."

30. Robert Sabin, "Review of Symphony no. 4 and *Prayer in Time of War*," *Music Library Association Notes* 8, 1 (December 1950): 130.

31. David Ross Baskerville, "Jazz Influence on Art Music to Mid-Century," Ph.D. diss., University of California–Los Angeles, 1965, p. 369.

32. OHAM, 144.

33. "Nation at War Still Needs Music, Composer Says," *Pittsburgh Press*, December 10, 1941, 30.

34. Copland to Schuman, September 3, 1942, NYPL-A, 11/6; Bernstein to Schuman, October 1, 1941, NYPL-A, 6/10.

35. Edward B. Marks, *Still Counting: Achievements and Follies of a Nonagenarian* (Lanham, MD: Hamilton Books, 2005), 31–32.

36. On the question of life insurance, see Harry I. Kapp to Schuman, March 30, 1942, NYPL-A, 149/15. For Schuman's attempts to secure a commission with the Army Specialist Corps, see Steve Swayne, "William Schuman, World War II, and the Pulitzer Prize," *Musical Quarterly* 89, 2–3 (Summer–Fall 2006): 291–95.

37. Schuman to Eric T. Clarke, December 19, 1942, CCNY, 220/8.

38. Smallens to Schuman, February 6, 1942, NYPL-A, 37/9.

39. Engel to Schuman, July 23, 1942, NYPL-A, 14/5.

40. See Barry H. Dremes to Schuman, July 18, 1946, NYPL-A, 12/5; and Arthur Loesser to Schuman, November 9, 1946, NYPL-A, 26/2.

41. Schuman to Sister M. Paula, February 8, 1949, NYPL-A, 33/2.

42. OHAM, 104.

43. For more on the opera with LaFarge, see chap. 18. For more on the film score, see Carl Winston to Schuman, May 25, 1942, NYPL-A, 44/15. Though the letter does not provide Carl's last name, the *Index to Register of Voters, Los Angeles City Precinct No. 1628, Los Angeles County, 1942* lists Carl and Florence Winston as registered Democrats living at the same address that appears on this letter: 8551 Lookout Mountain Ave. She is listed as a housewife; he is listed as a producer. For more on Winston, see Ursula Hardt, *From Caligari to California: Erich Pommer's Life in the International Film Wars* (Providence, RI: Berghahn Books, 1996), 122 n. 35.

44. Schuman to Copland, September 1, 1942, NYPL-A, 11/7. See also Schuman to Bernstein, January 31, 1942, LoC-LB.

45. Daniel Saidenberg to Kenneth Klein, from a December 21, 1942, letter from Klein to Schuman, NYPL-A, 22/5.

46. See the first page of the 1942 manuscript.

47. Louis Biancolli, "Audience Turns Critic at Town Hall Forum," *New York World-Telegram*, January 14, 1943, in NYPL-C, Scrapbook 3.

48. Paul Bowles, "Schuman Music Topic of Forum at Town Hall," *New York Herald Tribune*, January 14, 1943, in NYPL-C, Scrapbook 3.

49. Arthur Berger, "Forecast and Review: 'Once Again, The One-Man Show, 1943,'" *Modern Music* 20, 3 (March–April 1945): 175–76. For Berger's comment on "a real low," see chap. 10, note 49.

50. Schuman to Koussevitzky, September 18, 1942, LoC-SK.

51. See Waring's and Oscar Levant's autographs in NYPL-B, 13/"Milray Outing Club for Boys."

52. Robert Shaw to Schuman, December 23, 1942, NYPL-A, 37/7. Ellipsis in original.

53. Louis Biancolli, "Audience Turns Critic," in NYPL-C, Scrapbook 3.

54. See G. Wallace Woodworth to Schuman, December 21, 1944, memorandum, NYPL-A, 143/4.

55. Douglas Moore to Schuman, January 22, 1943, NYPL-A, 30/6.

56. Frank D. Fackenthal to Schuman, February 4, 1943, NYPL-A, 33/8.

57. "Schuman's Works Prove Popular," *Campus*, January 27, 1943, 3.

Chapter 12: "The Modern Meteor I Sing"

1. Schuman to Copland, July 29, 1942, NYPL-A, 11/7.

2. Copland to Frances Schuman, April 3, 1941. NYPL-B, "Copland, Aaron." Schuman's February 18, 1941, letter to Koussevitzky is on Fifth Avenue Hotel stationery. See LoC-SK.

3. Copland to Schuman, March 27, 1943, NYPL-B, "Copland, Aaron."

4. Schuman to Copland, March 31, 1943, NYPL-A, 11/6.

5. L.A. Sloper, "Three Novelties Heard at Symphony Concert," *Christian Science Monitor*, March 27, 1943, 4.

6. George E. Judd to Schuman, March 1, 1943, NYPL-A, 7/2.

7. Schuman to Copland, April 5, 1943, NYPL-A, 11/7.

8. Carl Engel to Schuman, May 19, 1943, letter, NYPL-B, "1943."

9. Olin Downes, "Schuman Song Led by Koussevitzky," *New York Times*, April 4, 1943, 43.

10. Virgil Thomson, "Superficially Warlike," in *The Musical Scene* (New York: Alfred A. Knopf, 1945), 125. According to Thomson biographer Anthony Tommasini, Thomson titled his own reviews. *Virgil Thomson: Composer on the Aisle* (New York: W. W. Norton, 1997), 336.

11. Schuman himself referred to *A Free Song*, *Prayer in Time of War*, and *Steel Town* as "three works composed as propaganda pieces during the war." See Schuman to R. L. F. McCombs, March 10, 1947, NYPL-A, 34/4.

12. See Schuman to Harold Spivacke, October 17, 1942, NYPL-A, 21/7; and Constance Warren, "Supplement to President's Report," December 11, 1943, pp. 7–8, in *Sarah Lawrence College President's Reports*, November 1941 to May 1945 (Book 4), SLC.

13. Fritz Reiner to Schuman, November 9, 1942, NYPL-A, 36/4.

14. Judith Colt to Schuman, August 23, 1945, NYPL-B, "1945."

15. Schuman to Else Bickel, September 28, 1960, NYPL-A, 4/6.

16. Ralph Lewando, "Ovation Is in Order at Schuman Premiere," *Pittsburgh Press*, February 27, 1947, in NYPL-C, Scrapbook 3.

17. Leopold Stokowski to Schuman, December 22, 1943, NYPL-B, "Stokowski, Leopold (1943)."

18. Irving Gifford Fine, "Boston Opens an Exciting Season," *Modern Music* 22, 2 (November–December 1944): 43; and Hunter Johnson to Schuman, December 12, 1943, NYPL-B, "1943." See Phillip Ramey, *Irving Fine: An American Composer in His Time* (Hillsdale, NY: Pendragon Press, in association with the Library of Congress, 2005), 239 and 288n for more on Fine's attitude toward Schuman's music.

19. Harrison Engle, "Thirty Years of Social Inquiry: An Interview with Willard Van Dyke," *Film Culture* 3, 2 (Spring 1965): 26 (italics in original).

20. William Alexander, *Film on the Left: American Documentary Film from 1931 to 1942* (Princeton, NJ: Princeton University Press, 1981), 268. See also Mary Losey to Schuman, October 11, 1938, SLC-WS.

21. Douglas C. McGill, "Willard Van Dyke, Ex-Head of Films at Modern Museum," *New York Times*, January 24, 1986: A17; J. Hoberman, *Village Voice*, December 9, 1981; "Big Want-to-See Impulse Brought 'Em Out for Underground 'Scorpio,'" *Variety*, February 23, 1966, 25. All these articles are in the clippings file "Van Dyke, Williard" at the Margaret Herrick Library of the Academy of Motion Picture Arts and Sciences, Beverly Hills, California.

22. Charles A. H. Thomson, *Overseas Information Service of the United States Government* (Washington, DC: Brookings Institution Press, 1948), 66 and 80–81 n. 32. The word "propaganda" was not universally maligned in the 1940s. Thomson distinguished between "propaganda" and "information"; see pp. 10–13.

23. Harrison Engle, "Thirty Years of Social Inquiry: An Interview with Willard Van Dyke," *Film Culture* 3, 2 (Spring 1965): 36.

24. Yuka Tsuchiya, "Imagined America in Occupied Japan: (Re-)Educational Films Shown by the U.S. Occupation Forces to the Japanese, 1948–1952," *Japanese Journal of American Studies* 13 (2002): 200.

25. WS-Gruen, 8.

26. Philip Dunne, "The Documentary and Hollywood," *Hollywood Quarterly* 1, 2 (January 1946): 167–68.

27. Harrison Engle, "Thirty Years of Social Inquiry: An Interview with Willard Van Dyke," *Film Culture* 3, 2 (Spring 1965): 26; and Jonas Mekas and Edouard Laurot, "The American Documentary—Limitations and Possibilities: An Interview with Williard van Dyke," *Film Culture* 2, 3 (1956): 7. See also Williard Van Dyke, "The Interpretive Camera in Documentary Films," *Hollywood Quarterly* 1, 4 (July 1946): 405–9.

28. See WS-Gruen, 9; and "Chapter B: Film and Lincoln Center," p. 7, from "Composer in America: William Schuman Talks about His Life and Works," chapter drafts from a proposed memoir with David Wright, in William Schuman, biographical files, Juilliard School Archives, Juilliard School, New York.

29. Schuman to Copland, May 18, 1945, NYPL-A, 11/7.

30. See the various letters and memos between Schuyler Chapin and Schuman about Van Dyke in NYPL-A, 57/1. See also Schuyler Chapin, *Musical Chairs: A Life in the Arts* (New York: G. P. Putnam's Sons, 1977), 174.

31. OHAM, 188 and 190.

32. As quoted in Eric T. Clarke to Charles Dollard, August 25, 1942, CCNY, 220/8.

33. Barbara A. Zuck, *A History of Musical Americanism* (Ann Arbor: University of Michigan Press, 1980), 196–97. Zuck here quoted Boris Schwarz, *Music and Musical Life in Soviet Russia, 1917–1970* (New York: W. W. Norton, 1973), 180.

34. Artur Rodzinski to Schuman, April 14, 1943, NYPL-B, "1943"; Schuman to Rodzinski, April 23, 1943, NYPL-A, 36/10; and Serge Koussevitzky to Schuman, May 11, 1943, in NYPL-A, 189 [BK desk].

35. Rudolph Elie Jr., "Symphony Concert," *Boston Herald*, November 13, 1943, in NYPL-C, Scrapbook 3.

36. Moses Smith, "Boston Goes All-Out for Premieres," *Modern Music* 21, 2 (January–February 1944): 103.

37. Koussevitzky to Schuman, December 27, 1943, NYPL-B, "1943."

38. Schuman to Arthur A. Hauser, July 20, 1956, NYPL-A, 178/3.

39. Juan Orrego-Salas to Schuman, November 17, 1947, NYPL-A, 32/9; José Limón and Lynn Garafala, *José Limón: An Unfinished Memoir* (Middletown, CT: Wesleyan University Press, 2001), 142; Vladimir Ussachevsky to Schuman, November 4, 1975, NYPL-A, 118/10; and Ned Rorem to Schuman, November 20, 1985 postcard, NYPL-A, 139/12.

40. Artur Rodzinski to Schuman, May 6, 1943, NYPL-B, "1943"; and Schuman to Rodzinski, May 16, 1943, NYPL-A, 36/10.

41. John Tasker Howard, *The Music of Washington's Time*, chap. 2. (The footnote was Schuman's.)

42. Unidentified paper fragment, in NYPL-B, Box 15, Folder "Publications/Writings undated." The paper likely comes from one of three courses that Schuman took at Teachers College: Cultural Development of the American people (Winter 1934); The Historical Development of Modern Education (Spring 1935); or The Arts in Education and Life (Spring 1936).

43. Program notes for February 17, 1944, in copyist's score, LoC.

44. "Yale and S. L. to Hold Concert This Saturday," *Campus*, December 2, 1942, 1, 4; and Marga Kent, "Joint Glee Club Concert Proves Great Success," *Campus*, December 14, 1942, 1, 6.

45. Robert Bagar and Louis Biancolli, "Notes on the Program," *New York Philharmonic-Society Orchestra Program*, February 17–18, 1944. The notes on the *William Billings Overture* were provided by Schuman.

46. Olin Downes, "Rodzinski Offers Schuman's Music," *New York Times*, February 18, 1944, 15.

47. Thor Johnson to Schuman, September 17, 1955, NYPL-A, 21/6; "City Tenders Fete To U.N. Assembly," *New York Times*, September 24, 1955, 11; and the 1954–55 correspondence between Schuman and Hans Heinsheimer of G. Schirmer, in NYPL-A, 180/5.

48. Eugene Goossens to Schuman, September 21, 1942, NYPL-A, 17/5.

49. The correspondence about the Goossens variation is in NYPL-B, "Goossens, Eugene."

50. Robert Tangeman, "Variations for a Jubilee," *Modern Music* 22, 4 (May–June 1945): 261.

51. Schuman to Copland, October 11, 1944, NYPL-A, 11/6.

52. For a contemporaneous review of the Te Deum, see Paul Hume's review in *Notes*, 2nd ser., 3, 2 (March 1946): 184.

53. OHAM, 215–20. The "corrected script #1" of "The Famous History of the Life of King Henry VIII," dated July 27 (no year), is in NYPL-A, 147/4. Stephen Walsh does not mention Schuman in his telling of the Rose-Stravinsky conflict; see *Stravinsky: The Second Exile: France and America, 1934–1971* (New York: Alfred A. Knopf, 2006), 164–66. In his telling of the story, Alexandre Tansman identified the person who would do the "*quelques retouches à l'orchestration*" as "Mr. X," who "*arrange* même *les œuvres de Cole Porter*," all of which suggests Robert Russell Bennett and not Schuman. See Tansman, *Igor Stravinsky* (Paris: Amiot, Dumont, 1948), 288.

54. Fritz Reiner to Schuman, January 26, 1945, NYPL-B, "1945."

55. Schuman to Aaron Copland, October 11, 1944, NYPL-A, 11/6.

56. "Memorandum of Meeting with William Schuman and GWW," December 21, 1944, NYPL-A, 143/4.

57. For more on William Schuman and the *Musical Quarterly*, see Steve Swayne, "American Musicology at the Crossroads, Contemporary Music in the Crosshairs: The Ideological Battle at G. Schirmer, Inc. at the End of World War II," paper presented at the annual meeting of the American Musicological Society, Quebec City, Quebec, Canada, November 2, 2007. Available at http://www.orpheus.dartmouth.edu.

58. Samuel Barber to Schuman, September 27, 1944, NYPL-B, "1944."

59. Zinsser, May 1, 1989, 10.

60. Schuman to Lukas Foss, January 19, 1989, NYPL-C, "Correspondence F, 1989–1990".

61. David Diamond to Schuman, March 17, 1991, and Schuman to Diamond, May 2, 1991, NYPL-C, "Correspondence D, 1991."

62. See Autobiography, chap. 8, pp. 2–3.

63. OHAM, 153.

64. See Autobiography, chap. 8, pp. 7–8.

65. G. Wallace Woodworth to Schuman, August 5, 1945, NYPL-A, 143/4.

Chapter 13: "Wringing the Changes"

1. See "Transcript of the Forum on Contemporary Music Held under the Auspices of the Associate Members of the *New School for Social Research*, December 17, 1944, Mr. Copland Presiding," *Musicology* 1, 1 (Autumn 1945): 61–91. The transcript includes some of Schuman's remarks about Erskine's speech. On p. 84 of his copy, where his remarks begin, Schuman wrote: "Obviously a poor transcription; funnier at the time." NYPL-B, "Articles 1943–1948."

2. OHAM, 229–30.

3. John Erskine, *My Life in Music* (New York: William Morrow, 1950), 254–56.

4. James P. Warburg, *The Long Road Home: The Autobiography of a Maverick* (Garden City, NY: Doubleday, 1964), 217.

5. Ernest Hutcheson, *While I Live I Must Work: Writings of Ernest Hutcheson: Memoirs, Addresses, and Excerpts from His Journal of Letters to His Wife, In Coeli*, edited by Thomas W. Hutcheson (Glenn Falls, NY: Quisisana Press, 2003), 294, 370.

6. William Schuman, "Unconventional Case History," *Modern Music*15, 4 (May–June 1938): 222.

7. Hutcheson, *While I Live*, 296.

8. Schuman to Serge Koussevitzky, June 17, 1945, and June 19, 1945, LoC-SK. Schuman's meeting with the Juilliard board took place on Wednesday, June 27, 1945; see Hutcheson, *While I Live*, 295–96.

9. January 16, 1946, press release, written by Emily S. Nathan, in NYPL-A 45/1.

10. OHAM, 168, 236.

11. OHAM, 232.

12. See Andrea Olmstead, *Juilliard: A History* (Urbana: University of Illinois Press, 1999), 142–70; July 15, 1993, letter from Frances Schuman to Rainer Böhlke, in JPB 87-33 Add'l Materials. Folder "Correspondence B, 1992–1994"; Joseph Polisi, as quoted in Maro Chermayeff and Amy Schewel, *Juilliard* (New York: Harry N. Abrams, 2002), esp. 50–51; and Polisi, *American Muse: The Life and Times of William Schuman* (New York: Amadeus, 2008), 89–105.

13. John Erskine to Schuman, January 24, 1946, JS, 1/11.

14. Agenda for November 30, 1945, board of directors meeting, in JS, 1/11.

15. Schuman to John Erskine, January 25, 1946, JS, 1/11. See also Schuman to Julia Smith, February 14, 1963, NYPL-A, 82/8, in which Schuman corrected Smith's account of Friedberg's retirement in her book *Master Pianist: The Career and Teaching of Carl Friedberg* (New York: Philosophical Library, 1963), 104–6.

16. Schuman to Fritz Reiner, September 13, 1945, and Reiner to Schuman, September 14, 1945, NYPL-A, 11/6.

17. Thor Johnson to Schuman, May 26, 1947. JS, 15/18.

18. Serge Koussevitzky to Schuman, June 30, 1948, letter, NYPL-A, 7/2.

19. Olmstead claimed that Schenkman was fired (see *Juilliard*, 158); Schuman told Koussevitzky that Schenkman resigned (see Schuman to Koussevitzky, July 7, 1948, NYPL-A, 23/8). It would appear that Schuman, in light of Koussevitzky's comments, intended to reassign Schenkman.

20. Ellen Highstein, *The New Grove Dictionary of American Music*, ed. H. Wiley Hitchcock and Stanley Sadie (London: Macmillan, 1986), s.v. "Lloyd, Norman," III/95.

21. "Oral History with Mark Schubart," Sharon Zane, interviewer, Lincoln Center for the Performing Arts. Oral History Project, 18.

22. Schuman to Frederik Prausnitz, May 15, 1961, JS, 11/5.

23. Memorandum from Steve Novak to Jane Gottlieb, May 24, 1994, regarding the history of choral conducting at Juilliard, courtesy of Jane Gottlieb, vice president for library and information resources, the Juilliard School.

24. Frederic Cohen has been rightly identified as the first director of the Juilliard Opera Theater; see http://www.juilliard.edu/press/kit/articles/History-of-Opera-at-Juilliard.html, accessed March 6, 2010. Schenkman was listed as a new appointment on the November 30, 1945, agenda for a meeting of the Juilliard board of directors. Also, in a July 18, 1946, letter to Charles Haubiel, Mark Schubart identified Schenkman as the school's opera director. (See JS, 1/11, and JS, 15/18, respectively.) See also the December 1946 picture of Schenkman as conductor of *Der Freischütz* in Chermayeff and Schewel, *Juilliard*, 42. When Cohen was appointed as head of the Opera Theater Unit for the 1947–1948 year, the duties between Cohen and Schenkman were clarified, with Cohen supervising and directing all productions with the exception of those requiring orchestra, in which case Cohen acted as stage director and Schenkman as musical director and conductor. See Schuman to Cohen, May 7, 1947, Office of the Vice President for Finance and Administration, Faculty Contracts, 1927–1948, 1/24, Juilliard School.

25. Schuman to Robert L. Shaw, June 13, 1947, JS, 15/18.

26. For "the second thing," see OHAM, 249: Schuman's recollection of the creation of the Juilliard String Quartet continues to p. 251. For "the very first item," see Harriet Gay, *The Juilliard String Quartet* (New York: Vantage, 1974), 5.

27. Gay, *The Juilliard String Quartet*, 5–6. Ellipsis in original.

28. Robert Mann, as quoted in Chermayeff and Schewel, *Juilliard*, 55.

29. Schuman to Robert Mann, October 22, 1959, JS, 7/9. Bad grooming and sartorial inappropriateness often sent Schuman into a rage. He complained to Schubart after one choral concert about "the different colored socks worn by the boys," this after noting that "a man across the aisle from me was sitting in shirt sleeves and I asked him please to put on his coat, which he sullenly did after deciding seethingly not to give me a black eye first." Schuman to Mark Schubart, November 22, 1957, JS, 14/3.

30. See Gay, *The Juilliard String Quartet*; Helen Epstein, "The Juilliard Quartet: Scenes from a Marriage," in *Music Talks: Conversations with Musicians* (New York: McGraw-Hill, 1987), 162–75; and Andrew L. Pincus, "The Juilliard String Quartet: Long Live the Revolution," in *Musicians with a Mission: Keeping the Classical Tradition Alive* (Boston: Northeastern University Press, 2002), 185–228.

31. Schuman to Louise Rood, March 19, 1946, JS, 15/18.

32. Schuman to Julia Smith, December 16, 1955, JS, 18/6.

33. S-W, 640 [13/1].

34. Schuman to Bernstein, October 21, 1941, LoC-LB.

35. OHAM, 251.

36. William Schuman, "On Teaching the Literature and Materials of Music," *Musical Quarterly* 34, 2. (April 1948): 159, 160, 167.

37. William Schuman, introduction to *The Juilliard Report on Teaching the Literature and Materials of Music* (New York: W. W. Norton, 1953), 14–15.

38. See JS, 8/4, for thank-you notes from the various individuals and school officers who received complimentary copies of *The Juilliard Report on Teaching the Literature and Materials of Music*.

39. Occidental College, my alma mater, was one of the institutions that saw the light. In the 1970s, the sequence of four music history courses was called "The Literature and Materials of Music."

40. Minna Lederman to Schuman, May 6, 1948, NYPL-A, 24/3.

41. Schuman to Paul Henry Lang, November 11, 1949, NYPL-A, 25/3.

42. R. F. Goldman, "The Juilliard Review," *Juilliard Review* 1, 1 (Fall 1954): 6.

43. OHAM, 252. For more on this aspect of Schuman's industry and influence, see Steve Swayne, "American Musicology at the Crossroads, Contemporary Music in the Crosshairs: The Ideological Battle at G. Schirmer, Inc. at the End of World War II," paper presented at the annual meeting of the American Musicological Society, Quebec City, Quebec, Canada, November 2, 2007. Available at http://www.orpheus.dartmouth.edu.

44. See chap. 11.

45. See the correspondence between Schuman and Naumburg, as well as between Hutcheson and Naumburg, in WWN, 8/9.

46. Walter W. Naumburg to Schuman, October 21, 1947, WWN, 8/8.

47. Minutes, November 7, 1946, meeting of the board of the Walter W. Naumburg Foundation, WWN, 8/9.

48. Minutes, May 17, 1948, special meeting of the board of the Walter W. Naumburg Foundation, in WWN, 8/8.

49. Daniel Gregory Mason to Schuman, February 9, 1949, WWN, 9/14.

50. See http://www.naumburg.org/previous-winners.php for a list of the recording awards (accessed April 5, 2009).

51. See the December 7, 1949, draft and the December 9, 1949, final letter from Schuman to Elise and Walter W. Naumburg, WWN, 10/1.

52. Schuman to David Oppenheim, February 17, 1954, WWN, 10/1.

53. OHAM, 169.

54. See Nathan Broder to Persichetti, July 8, 1948, NYPL-VP, 19/20; and VP. For the comment on Schuman and Barber being the firm's "white-haired boys," see Schuman to Rudolph Tauhert, April 11, 1961, NYPL-A, 180/17.

55. Hutcheson, *While I Live*, 297–98.

56. Lazare Saminsky, "New Faces among Our Composers: An Appraisal," *Musical Courier*, February 1, 1945, 13.

57. Hutcheson, *While I Live*, 383. See p. 372 for the remark about Schuman's rage.

58. Erskine, *My Life in Music*, 255.

59. As quoted in Chermayeff and Schewel, *Juilliard*, 49.

Chapter 14: "Dancing in the Dark"

1. Walter Piston to Schuman, June 15, 1934, NYPL-A, 34/7. See John Nathaniel Vincent, *The Diatonic Modes in Modern Music* (Berkeley: University of California Press, 1951).

2. On Piston's attitude toward Schuman's Sixth, see Piston to Schuman, December 2, 1953, NYPL-A, 34/7; and Piston to Schuman, June 29, 1954, JS, 3/5 (whence comes the

quotation). On Schuman's recommendation to Morel of Piston's Fourth, see the 1951 correspondence between Schuman and Piston in NYPL-A 34/7.

3. WS-Gruen, 6.

4. WS-Gruen, 26.

5. WS-Gruen, 6.

6. OHAM, 221.

7. As quoted in Judith Chazin-Bennahum, *The Ballets of Antony Tudor: Studies in Psyche and Satire* (New York: Oxford University Press, 1994), 115.

8. Donna Perlmutter, *Shadowplay: The Life of Antony Tudor* (New York: Viking, 1991), 132.

9. As quoted in Chazin-Bennahum, *Ballets of Antony Tudor*, 119.

10. Ibid., 107.

11. WS-Gruen, 19.

12. Schuman to Samuel Barber, November 7, 1956, NYPL-A, 6/3. See also Ned Rorem to Schuman, October 30, 1991, NYPL-C, "Correspondence R, 1990–1993"; and Schuman to John Corigliano, June 20, 1981, NYPL-A, 126/4.

13. WS-Gruen, 11.

14. Perlmutter, *Shadowplay*, 164.

15. See J. Alden Talbot to Schuman, July 17, 1944, NYPL-A, 6/1; Talbot was managing director of the Ballet Theatre.

16. Schuman to Virginia Wallenstein, December 17, 1945, NYPL-A, 44/1.

17. This overstatement originated with Tudor himself. See John Gruen, *The Private World of Ballet* (New York: Viking, 1975), 261–62.

18. Schuman to Tudor, January 13, 1945, in answer to Tudor, January 7, 1945, NYPL-A, 41/14.

19. Gruen, *Private World of Ballet*, 261–62.

20. Tudor to Schuman, February 21, 1945, NYPL-A, 41/14.

21. John Martin, "New Tudor Ballet in Premiere Here," *New York Times*, April 11, 1945: 18.

22. Tudor to Schuman, July 1, 1964, NYPL-A, 87/2.

23. Schuman to Alexander Smallens, April 20, 1945, NYPL-Smallens.

24. OHAM, 222; Tudor to Schuman, August 31, 1944, NYPL-A, 41/14.

25. For more on the critical reception of *Undertow* as well as a description of the dance, see Chazin-Bennahum, *Ballets of Antony Tudor*, 135–43; and Perlmutter, *Shadowplay*, 164–69.

26. Isabel Morse Jones, "Soviet Work Highlight of Music Event," *Los Angeles Times*, November 30, 1945, A2.

27. Virginia Wallenstein to Schuman, December 9, 1945, NYPL-A, 44/1.

28. Virgil Thomson, "Crime in Music," *New York Herald Tribune*, October 4, 1946, in NYPL-C, Scrapbook 3.

29. WS-Gruen, 14.

30. Schuman to William Vacchiano, September 12, 1946, JS, 6/2.

31. Frances Schuman to Rosalie Calabrese, July 3, 1993, NYPL-C, "Correspondence C, 1992–1993."

32. WS-Gruen, 29–30.

33. Harold Spivacke to Schuman, July 29, 1946, NYPL-A, 25/9.

34. Martha Graham to Schuman, August 12, 1946, in Music Division Old Correspondence, "Graham, Martha: Scripts for William Schuman," LoC.

35. Graham to Schuman, August 30, 1946, NYPL-A, 18/10.

36. See Ernestine Stodelle, *Deep Song: The Dance Story of Martha Graham* (New York: Schirmer Books, 1984), 145–50, for a lengthy discussion of the dance.

37. See Graham to Schuman, October 28, 1946, NYPL-A, 18/10. Graham's eight-page scenario for the dance, dated October 26, 1948, is also in this folder.

38. Schuman to Graham, January 17, 1947, NYPL-A, 18/10.

39. Flora Rheta Schreiber and Vincent Persichetti, *William Schuman* (New York: G. Schirmer, 1954), 129.

40. WS-Gruen, 33–34.

41. Helen McGehee, in Robert Tracy, *Goddess: Martha Graham's Dancers Remember* (New York: Limelight Editions, 1997), 127.

42. John Martin, "Graham Dancers in Harvard Event," *New York Times*, May 5, 1947, 32; and Martin, "Graham Company Offers New Dance," *New York Times*, February 18, 1948, 34.

43. Robert Sabin, *Martha Graham* (New York: Theatre Arts Books, 1961), (10; pages not numbered). The Clive Barnes quotation appears in the notes on the DVD *Martha Graham in Performance*, Kultur D1177 (n.d.); I have been unable to find another source for this quotation.

44. John Martin, "Graham Dancers in Harvard Event," *New York Times*, May 5, 1947, 32; Cyrus Durgin, "Dr. Lang, Olin Downes in Tilt as Harvard Symposium Ends," *Boston Globe*, May 4, 1947, 48; "The Music Box: Symposium: Third Concert," *Harvard Crimson*, May 5, 1947, http://www.thecrimson.com/article.aspx?ref=208514, accessed April 17, 2009; and John Rockwell, "Concert: Music Today, Series at Goodman House," *New York Times*, October 16, 1984, C4. *Night Journey* originally premiered on May 3, 1947; erroneous dates are given in K. Gary Adams, *William Schuman: A Bio-Bibliography* (May 7, 1947) and Schreiber and Persichetti's *William Schuman* (February 17, 1948).

45. In his book, Polisi provides a useful descriptive analysis of the work (403–4). However, his statement that "the original 1947 version of *Night Journey* was adapted by Schuman for an ensemble of fifteen instruments" is misleading. While the 1980 version is shorter, both versions employ the same ensemble.

46. Schreiber and Persichetti, *William Schuman*, 39.

47. Schuman to Fanny Brandeis, November 30, 1949, NYPL-A, 26/6.

48. Schuman to Graham, May 29, 1949, NYPL-A, 18/10.

49. Jeanne Belfy, "The Commissioning Project of the Louisville Orchestra, 1948–1958: A Study of the History and Music," Ph.D. diss., University of Kentucky, 1986: 31–69.

50. Jeanne Belfy, *The Louisville Orchestra New Music Project: An American Experiment in the Patronage of International Contemporary Music* (Louisville, KY: University of Louisville, 1983), 10.

51. Belfy, *The Louisville Orchestra*, 11. Belfy reproduced the grant proposal as an appendix to her dissertation (218–26).

52. John R. Woolford to Schuman, February 11, 1950, NYPL-A, 26/6. "Branch water" is plain water, as opposed to soda water, but specifically refers to a particular kind of plain water common in Kentucky.

53. See the Woolford-Whitney-Schuman correspondence in NYPL-A, 26/7 (the cited letter is dated February 27, 1950); the Hall-Schuman correspondence in NYPL-A, 27/4; and William Schuman, "Louisville Policy," *New York Times*, December 24, 1950, 47.

54. Graham to Schuman, June 14, 1949, NYPL-A, 18/10.

55. See Belfy, "The Commissioning Project," 42–52. Belfy derives her four-part division from Doris Hering, "The Season in Review," *Dance Magazine* 25, 2 (February 1951): 12.

56. Schuman to Graham, June 15, 1949, NYPL-A, 18/10.

57. As quoted in Stodelle, *Deep Song*, 168–69.

58. Graham to Schuman, June 14, 1949, NYPL-A, 18/10.

59. Robert Sabin, "Martha Graham Created Dance with Louisville Orchestra," *Musical America* 70, 2 (January 15, 1950): 67, 87. See also Sabin, "The Dance Concerto: Martha Graham and William Schuman Create a New Form for the Theatre," *Dance Observer* 17, 2 (1951): 22–23.

60. R. S. [Robert Sabin], "Louisville Orchestra Has Martha Graham as Soloist," *Musical America* 71, 2 (January 15, 1951): 13, 24.

61. Virginia Wallenstein to Schuman, February 17, 1952, NYPL-A, 44/1; Robert Russell Bennett to Schuman, December 31, 1952, NYPL-A, 31/6; and Lucia Dlugoszewski to Schuman, June 10, 1965, NYPL-A, 54/2.

62. Agnes de Mille, *Martha: The Life and Work of Martha Graham* (New York: Random House, 1991), 304.

63. Paul Kresh to Schuman, December 29, 1965, NYPL-A, 64/3.

64. Anna Kisselgoff, "Dance: Martha Graham's New 'Judith' in Premiere," *New York Times*, May 1, 1980, C19.

65. Schuman to Graham, September 7, 1984, and Graham to Schuman, November 10, 1984, NYPL-A, 130/8.

66. Graham to Schuman, January 23, 1951, NYPL-A, 18/10. See also Robert Whitney to Schuman, February 12, 1951, NYPL-A, 26/7.

67. Norman L. Johnson, "The Louisville Orchestra's Best Work Is Displayed in 'Judith' and 'Undertow,'" *Louisville Courier-Journal*, April 18, 1951, 9. For more on this chapter in the history of the Louisville Orchestra, see Allen J. Share, *Cities in the Commonwealth: Two Centuries of Urban Life in Kentucky* (Lexington: University Press of Kentucky, 1982), 110–19.

68. See Polisi, *American Muse*, 114–17, for a history of the formation of the Dance Division and Chermayeff and Schewel, *Juilliard*, 76–91, for insight into the early founders.

69. Schuman to Mark Schubart, January 11, 1951, JS, 13/2.

70. Schuman to de Mille, January 15, 1951, and de Mille to Schuman, January 18, 1951, NYPL-A, 12/9.

71. Pearl Lang, in Tracy, *Goddess*, 87.

Chapter 15: "Family Matters"

1. Schuman to Marks, July 27, 1935, AWS.

2. S-W, 393 [8/2].

3. Schuman to Copland, September 17, 1943, NYPL-A, 11/7; and Copland to Schuman, September 22, 1943, NYPL-A, 11/6.

4. Schuman to Margaret Boni, October 14, 1947, NYPL-A, 6/13; and Josef Marais to Schuman, February 2, 1948, NYPL-A, 27/2.

5. Schuman to Frank Loesser, May 2, 1949, NYPL-A, 26/2.

6. Schuman to Harry Robin, September 17, 1948, JS, 12/5; and Schuman to Hans Heinsheimer, August 10, 1950, NYPL-A, 180/6.

7. Autobiography, chap. 4, pp. 8–9.

8. OHAM, 6.

9. S-W, 149–50 [3/2]; S-W, 419 [9/1].

10. Schuman to Jack Morrissey, September 24, 1947, NYPL-A, 27/7. For the description of Ray as "quite lame," see Schuman to Bruno Zirato, September 21, 1946, NYPL-A, 32/3.

11. OHAM, 6.

12. S-W, 124–25 [2/2].

13. Schuman to Harold Spivacke, June 22, 1950, NYPL-A, 25/9.

14. Schuman to William H. Cassebaum, December 4, 1950, NYPL-A, 150/13; and Schuman to Charles K. Hamilton, December 6, 1950, NYPL-A, 19/2.

15. William H. Cassebaum, M.D., to Schuman, November 30, 1950, NYPL-A, 150/13.

16. Julian J. Fried to Schuman, December 6, 1950, NYPL-A, 150/3.

17. Schuman to John R. Woolford, November 30, 1950, telegram, NYPL-A, 26/7.

18. Schuman to Bernstein, October 21, 1949, NYPL-A, 6/10.

19. Personal correspondence with Andrea Schuman, January 22, 2009.

20. Schuman to Mary F. Langmuir, May 26, 1949, NYPL-A, 150/14.

21. Schuman to Harold Spivacke, June 22, 1950, NYPL-A, 25/9.

22. Schuman to Jeanne Mossige, November 8, 1951, NYPL-A, 30/7.

23. S-W, 204 [4/2].

24. Frances Schuman to Leonard and Gertrude Prince, May 1, 1952, AWS.

25. See: Schuman to Randolph B. Smith, September 11, 1950, NYPL-A, 150/10 (about the Little Red Schoolhouse); Schuman to James M. Hubball, September 18, 1950, 19/13 (about the Buckley School); and Schuman to Alan V. Tishman of Tishman Realty & Construction Co., October 10, 1950, NYPL-A, 41/3 (about the apartment).

26. Personal correspondence with Anthony Schuman, June 14, 2009.

27. Personal correspondence with Anthony Schuman, November 19, 2007.

28. See chap. 2, n27.

29. Schuman to Anthony Schuman, August 3, 1960, NYPL-A, 150/10.

30. Personal correspondence with Anthony Schuman, April 1, 2009.

31. Schuman to Arthur A. Hauser, May 19, 1961, 179/2.

32. Schuman to Harlow Parker, May 18, 1961, 33/2.

33. *Three Star News*, AWS.

34. Personal correspondence with Andrea Schuman, June 15, 2009.

35. Frederick Steinway to Schuman, November 14, 1962, NYPL-A, 40/8.

36. Personal correspondence with Anthony Schuman, April 23, 2009.

37. Ibid.

38. Schuman to Robert Lawrence, August 27, 1964, NYPL-A, 25/5.

39. Personal correspondence with Anthony Schuman, June 14, 2009.

40. Personal correspondence with Andrea Schuman, June 15, 2009.

41. See Margaret D. Barnett to Schuman, February 21, 1962, NYPL-A, 4/2 (Andrea's birthday); and Schuman to Harold Friedman, March 10, 1952, NYPL-A, 10/2 (Cobbossee reunion).

42. Personal communication with Judy Israel Gutmann, June 15, 2009.

43. Schuman to Bernstein, September 1, 1957, LoC-LB.

44. OHAM, 2.

45. Schuman to Paul Henry Lang, June 24, 1959, NYPL-A, 25/3.

46. Schuman to Frances Schuman, September 21, 1952, postcard, AWS.

47. Schuman to Frances Schuman, September 24, 1952, AWS.

48. Schuman to Frances Schuman, December 25, 1956, note, AWS.

Chapter 16: "An Old Religion, Two Champions, and a New Symphony"

1. Olin Downes, "Hanson Conducts Premiere of Work," *New York Times*, January 16, 1949, 70.

2. Serge Koussevitzky to Schuman, January 4, 1945, NYPL-B, "Koussevitzky, Serge."

3. Schuman to Koussevitzky, April 4, 1949, NYPL-A, 23/8.

4. Schuman to Artur Rodzinski, May 16, 1943, NYPL-A, 36/10.

5. Leonard Bernstein to Schuman, November 14, 1948, NYPL-A, 6/10. For an account of the Israel Philharmonic Orchestra concert at Beer Sheba, see Stephen J. Whitfield, *In Search of American Jewish Culture* (Hanover, NH: Brandeis University Press, 1999), 102–3; and the Web site for the Israel Philharmonic Orchestra (http://www.ipo.co.il/history/timeline.asp, accessed April 24, 2009).

6. Bernstein to Schuman, September 28, 1949, and Schuman to Bernstein, October 7, 1949, NYPL-A, 6/10.

7. See: Schuman to Franz M. Joseph, February 4, 1946, NYPL-A, 21/4 (American Youth Orchestra); Luening to Schuman, November 1, 1948, and Schuman to Luening, November 3, 1948, NYPL-A, 1/11 (American Music Center); Louise Fillmore to Schuman, December 15, 1948, NYPL-A, 28/1 (MacDowell Association); Merle Bateman, director of certification, accreditation, and publications for the State Department of Education for Maryland, to Schuman, January 27, 1949, NYPL-A, 4/1 (Baltimore Institute).

8. The Mendel-Schuman correspondence is in NYPL-A 28/6.

9. Schuman to J. S. Chaikoff, August 25, 1949, NYPL-A, 9/2.

10. See the Esco Foundation for Palestine Inc. to Schuman, March 26, 1951, NYPL-A, 14/3.

11. Schuman to Anneliese Landau, February 20, 1946, NYPL-A, 24/1. See also Anneliese Landau, *The Contribution of Jewish Composers to the Music of the Modern World* (Cincinnati, OH: National Federation of Temple Sisterhoods, 1946), 78–79.

12. Whitfield, *In Search of American Jewish Culture.*

13. Schuman to Anis Fuleihan, March 2, 1958, JS, 6/17.

14. See Alessandro Portelli, *The Order Has Been Carried Out: History, Memory, and Meaning of a Nazi Massacre in Rome* (New York: Palgrave Macmillan, 2003), 179–81. See Schuman to Ormandy, September 19, 1966, NYPL-A, 78/4, about Schuman's early work on the symphony, and Schuman to Felicia Bernstein, May 10, 1967, NYPL-A, 49/5, about the Nervi monument to the victims of the massacre. Schuman visited Rome in April 1967 as part of a European tour to promote the Lincoln Center Festival '67.

15. Personal correspondence with the author, January 9, 2007.

16. William H. Schuman, "Richard Wagner Alias 'K. Freigedank,'" *American Hebrew and Jewish Tribune*, March 2, 1934, 304. This article was a reworking of a paper Schuman wrote for Teachers College; see Joseph W. Polisi, *American Muse*, 29–30.

17. Karl F. Miller, "William Schuman, 1910–1992," *American Record Guide* 55, 4 (July–August 1992): 30.

18. Antal Doráti, *Notes of Seven Decades* (London: Hodder and Stoughton, 1979), 206. Doráti's account of his tenure as conductor of the Dallas Symphony Orchestra is covered in pp. 194–216.

19. Peggy Louise Jones, "Composer to Hear Symphony Again in Federation Concert," *Dallas Morning News*, February 28, 1949, 14.

20. In a March 22, 1949, letter to Doráti (in NYPL-A, 13/1), Schuman sent the revised ending as well as instructions on various tempos that Doráti had taken too slowly in the premiere performance. Schuman returned to Dallas for the second performance in April 1949.

21. William Schuman, untitled document, November 14, 1951, p. 1, in NYPL-A 146/5.

22. John Rosenfield, "William Schuman's Symphony Premiered," *Dallas Morning News*, February 28, 1949, 14.

23. Doráti, *Notes of Seven Decades*, 206.

24. Schuman to Persichetti, July 22, 1948, NYPL-A, 34/2.

25. The three letters from Spender to the Schumans—April 14, 1948, May 2, 1948, and September 6, 1948—and Spender's hand-copied poems are in NYPL-A, 40/4.

26. Schuman to John Fitch, October 28, 1948, NYPL-A, 16/5.

27. Schuman to Serge Koussevitzky, December 1, 1948, NYPL-A, 23/8.

28. Robert Sabin, "Twentieth-Century Americans," in *Choral Music*, ed. Arthur Jacobs (Baltimore: Penguin, 1963), 380.

29. Karl F. Miller, "William Schuman, 1910–1992," *American Record Guide* 55, 4 (July–August 1992): 30.

30. William Schuman, interview in John W. Clark, "The One-Movement Symphony in America, 1937–1976: With Analyses of Works by Roy Harris, William Schuman, Vincent Persichetti, and Peter Fricker," Ph.D. diss., University of California–Santa Barbara, 1982, pp. 233, 242.

31. Richard Pye, "'Asking about the Inside': Schoenberg's 'Idea' in the Music of Roy Harris and William Schuman," *Music Analysis* 19, 1 (2000): 70; the analysis of the Sixth is on pp. 76–89. See also Richard C. Pye, "Models of Unity and Diversity in the Symphonies of William Schuman: An Exploration of Genera Theories in Relation to Stylistic Change and the Dynamics of Form," Ph.D. diss., University of Newcastle, 2000 (the analysis of the Sixth appears on pp. 196–271); and "The Construction and Interpretation of Bespoke Pitch-Class Set Genera as Models of Harmonic Duality in William Schuman's Sixth Symphony," *Music Theory Spectrum* 25 (2003): 243–74.

32. Peter Dickinson, "William Schuman: An American Symphonist at 75," *Musical Times* 126, 1710 (August 1985): 458.

33. Karl F. Miller, "William Schuman, 1910–1992," 30.

34. Vincent Persichetti to Schuman, February 1, 1949, NYPL-A, 34/2.

35. Ormandy to Hans Heinsheimer, September 23, 1949, NYPL-A, 180/5. Heinsheimer's June 28, 1949, letter, in which he offered Ormandy the Philadelphia and New York premieres, is missing, but it is mentioned in his September 28, 1949, letter to Ormandy, also in 180/5.

36. See Ormandy to Schuman, January 11, 1950; Schuman to Ormandy, January 12, 1950, telegram; and Ormandy to Schuman, January 16, 1950. All are in NYPL-A, 34/4.

37. Ormandy to Schuman, September 14, 1951, and Schuman to Ormandy, September 18, 1951, NYPL-A, 34/4.

38. Schuman to Ormandy, October 24, 1951, NYPL-A, 34/4.

39. Mary S. Waterbury to Ormandy, November 14, 1951, NYPL-A, 34/4.

40. Roger Sessions to Schuman, November 21, 1950, NYPL-A, 39/8.

41. Bernstein to Schuman, May 14, 1958, NYPL-A, 6/10.

42. Letters about the challenges surrounding the recording of the Sixth Symphony are found in NYPL-A, 34/4 and 34/5 (Schuman-Ormandy); 10/14 (Columbia Records and Mitropulos); and 8/1 (BMI).

43. Schuman to Ormandy, December 3, 1953, NYPL-A, 34/5. See also Schuman to Ormandy, December 11, 1951, NYPL-A, 34/4.

44. Ormandy to Schuman, December 31, 1958, NYPL-A, 34/6.

45. Mary H. Krouse to Schuman, April 27, 1959, and Schuman to Ormandy, April 29, 1959, NYPL-A, 34/6.

46. Schuman to George Rochberg, June 22, 1959, NYPL-A, 178/6.

47. Schuman to Al Boss, July 17, 1959, NYPL-A, 7/1.

48. Schuman to Ormandy, July 22, 1959, NYPL-A, 34/6.

49. Ormandy to Schuman, November 11, 1959, NYPL-A, 34/6.

50. Schuman to Arthur A. Hauser, December 4, 1959, NYPL-A, 178/6. This was not the first time Ormandy and the Philadelphia staff tangled with Schuman and his publisher over

a performance fee. See Arthur A. Hauser to Schuman, October 3, 1957, NYPL-A, 178/4. (See pp. 288-89 of chapter 19.)

51. Schuman to George Rochberg, December 21, 1959, NYPL-A, 178/6. See also Schuman to Rochberg, May 31, 1960, NYPL-A, 179/1.

52. In a June 11, 1960, letter to Rochberg (in NYPL-A, 179/1), Schuman wrote that the original date was September 23, 1959.

53. See Ormandy to Schuman, April 11, 1974, and Schuman to Ormandy, April 16, 1974, NYPL-A, 111/6.

54. Phyllis White Rodríguez-Peralta, *Philadelphia Maestros: Ormandy, Muti, Sawallisch* (Philadelphia: Temple University Press, 2006), 41.

Chapter 17: "Delays and Diversions"

1. Kenneth L. Bovee, president of the Michigan School Band and Orchestra Association, to Schuman, February 12, 1945, NYPL-B, "Michigan School Band and Orchestra Association." For more on Schuman's involvement with the association and its aims during this period, see James Burnham Hause, "A History of the Michigan School Band and Orchestra Association: The First Twenty-Five Years 1934–1959," Ed. D. diss., University of Michigan, 1969, 154–236.

2. Schuman to Dale C. Harris, supervisor of Department of Instrumental Music for the Pontiac Public Schools, March 2, 1945, NYPL-B, "Michigan School Band and Orchestra Association."

3. Schuman to Harris, September 11, 1945, NYPL-B, "Michigan School Band and Orchestra Association."

4. Schuman to Edwin Franko Goldman, January 13, 1950, NYPL-A, 18/4. In S-W, 1066 [21/2], Schuman mentioned Goldman traveling to Ann Arbor with Gould and him.

5. Undated document in NYPL-A 148/5.

6. Le Corbusier, *When the Cathedrals Were White: A Journey to the Country of Timid People*, trans. Francis E. Hyslop Jr. (New York: Reynal & Hitchcock, 1947), 75.

7. Richard Carney, "Pilgrims to the Colossus," *Sunday Record* (Bergen County, NJ), October 18, 1981, A-12.

8. S-W, 1069–71 [21/2 and 22/1].

9. Frederick Fennell to Schuman, October 14, 1952, NYPL-A, 16/2.

10. Fennell to Schuman, March 10, 1953, NYPL-A, 16/2.

11. Fennell to Schuman, May 23, 1953, NYPL-A, 16/2.

12. Marshall Bartholomew to Harold Spivacke, February 22, 1942, in Marshall Bartholomew Papers MSS 24, 7/1, Yale University. The Bartholomew-Spivacke correspondence is in this folder.

13. Bartholomew to Schuman, January 21, 1943, 6/4. Schuman's letter is not among his papers or among the Bartholomew Papers at Yale.

14. Bartholomew to Schuman, January 11, 1951, NYPL-A, 6/4.

15. Schuman to Frederick P. Hart, April 7, 1965, NYPL-A, 60/4.

16. Schuman to Bartholomew, January 15, 1975, NYPL-A, 93/8.

17. Schuman to Claire Reis, June 14, 1946, NYPL-A, 25/6.

18. Schuman to Reis, July 8, 1946, NYPL-A, 25/6.

19. Schuman to Reis, June 14, 1946, NYPL-A, 25/6.

20. The October 17, 1945, commissioning letter from Dushkin is in NYPL-A, 13/8.

21. Schuman to Serge Koussevitzky, February 4, 1946, NYPL-A, 23/8.

22. Schuman to Samuel Dushkin, May 17, 1946, NYPL-A, 13/8.

23. Schuman to Arthur A. Hauser, March 26, 1956, NYPL-A, 178/3.

24. Schuman to Beveridge Webster, September 10, 1946, NYPL-A, 44/4.

25. S-W, 88 [2/1].

26. M.A.S., "Samuel Dushkin Plays," *New York Times*, March 13, 1946, 25.

27. OHAM, 288, italics in original.

28. S-W, 90 [2/1].

29. Unnamed officer at G. Schirmer (Nathan Broder?) to Dushkin, February 9, 1949, NYPL-A, 13/8.

30. Schuman to John N. Burk, Boston Symphony Orchestra program annotator, January 25, 1950, NYPL-A, 7/2.

31. Cyrus Durgin, "Isaac Stern Performs Mendelssohn, Schuman Concerts at Symphony," *Boston Daily Globe*, February 11, 1950, evening ed., 14.

32. R. P. (Ross Parmenter), "Stern the Soloist in Schuman Work," *New York Times*, March 16, 1950, 50.

33. Schuman to Rafael Druian, June 7, 1950, NYPL-A, 13/6.

34. Dushkin to Schuman, July 9, 1950, NYPL-A, 13/8.

35. Schuman to Isaac Stern, March 13, 1951, NYPL-A, 40/9.

36. Schuman to Betty Sawyer and Stanley Wolfe, July 7, 1954, NYPL-A, 37/2.

37. Schuman to Edward R. Wardwell, September 9, 1977, NYPL-A, 118/12.

38. Schuman to Rafael Druian, August 20, 1958, NYPL-A, 13/6.

39. Polisi, *American Muse*, 392; his analysis of the concerto begins on p. 389.

40. See note 33 in chapter 6.

41. See Schuman to Spivacke, May 2, 1949, and Schuman to Spivacke, May 26, 1949, NYPL-A, 25/9.

42. Schuman to Spivacke, June 22, 1950, NYPL-A, 25/9.

43. Personal correspondence with Anthony Schuman, January 9, 2007.

44. Schuman to Hans Heinsheimer, August 10, 1950, NYPL-A, 180/6.

45. Schuman to Samuel J. Shure, July 12, 1950, NYPL-A, 149/15. In his September 20, 1950, letter to Shure, also in 149/15, Schuman identified the precise nature of the injury.

46. Schuman to Morris Hastings, November 14, 1951, NYPL-A, 10/14.

47. Olin Downes, "Annual Music Fete Starts in Capital," *New York Times*, October 29, 1950, 96.

48. Also on the program that evening was the U.S. premiere of Boulez's Second Sonata, with David Tudor at the piano. See C. H., "Boulez' 2d Sonata Heard in Premiere," *New York Times*, December 18, 1950, 35.

49. Schuman to Spivacke, December 15, 1950, NYPL-A, 25/9; and Schuman to Alexandre Moskowsky, January 23, 1951, NYPL-A, 27/7. Schuman identified the date of the league's concert in his November 6, 1950, letter to Spivacke, NYPL 25/9.

50. Aaron Copland, "Current Chronicle: New York," *Musical Quarterly* 37, 3 (July 1951): 394–96.

51. Raphael Hillyer to Schuman, October 11, 1955, JS, 7/9.

Chapter 18: "Striking Out"

1. Martin M. Goldsmith to Schuman, October 25, 1942, NYPL-A, 17/4.
2. Countee Cullen to Schuman, January 16, 1943, NYPL-A, 9/6.
3. Lillian Smith to Schuman, December 6, 1944, NYPL-B, "1944."
4. Elmer Rice to Schuman, June 26, 1945, NYPL-Smallens.
5. See Maurice Abravanel to Eric Walter White, February 28, 1981, Eric Walter White Correspondence, Box 20, Harry Ransom Humanities Research Center, University of Texas at Austin.
6. Personal correspondence with Herman Wouk, August 24, 2009.
7. Wouk to Schuman, March 29, 1947, NYPL-A, 44/10.
8. Schuman to Wouk, April 29, 1947, NYPL-A, 44/10.
9. Schuman to Wouk, June 12, 1947, NYPL-A, 44/10.
10. Wouk to Schuman, June 30, 1952, and Schuman to Wouk, August 7, 1952, NYPL-A, 44/10.
11. Schuman to Douglas Moore, February 23, 1948, NYPL-A, 30/6.
12. Schuman to Flora Rheta Schreiber, April 19, 1948, NYPL-A, 39/5.
13. Schuman to Schreiber, March 19, 1951, NYPL-A, 39/5.
14. Marion Bauer to Schuman, February 27, 1949, and Schuman to Bauer, March 9, 1949, NYPL-A, 4/4.
15. Schuman to Lincoln Kirstein, April 13, 1954, JS, 18/3.
16. Schuman to Evelyn B. Gundy, January 24, 1963, NYPL-A, 59/7.
17. Schuman to Claire Reis, April 9, 1965, NYPL-A, 79/8.
18. Eric T. Clarke to Frederick P. Keppel, July 16, 1941, CCNY, 220/8.
19. Christopher LaFarge, September 30, 1941, LaF '41; and May 27, 1942, LaF '42.
20. LaFarge, October 28, 1941, LaF '41.
21. LaFarge, December 17, 1941, LaF '41.
22. LaFarge, December 23, 1941, LaF '42.
23. See Sarah Lawrence College letter of agreement, May 22, 1941, NYPL-A, 38/9.
24. Christopher LaFarge, *Mesa Verde* (New York: J. Laughlin, 1945). See also an announcement about *Mesa Verde* in *Desert Magazine*, September 1945, 2.
25. LaFarge, May 27, 1942, LaF '42.
26. Schuman to LaFarge, June 25, 1942, NYPL-A, 24/1.
27. Clarke to Charles Dollard, August 25, 1942, CCNY, 220/8.

28. LaFarge to Schuman, July 3, 1942, NYPL-A, 24/1. See also J. D. McClatchy, "William Schuman: A Reminiscence," *Opera Quarterly* 10, 4 (1994): 26.

29. Clarke to Schuman, September 23, 1942, NYPL-A, 27/4.

30. Clarke to Schuman, August 6, 1942, NYPL-A, 27/4.

31. Clarke to Robert Lester, March 11, 1943, CCNY, 220/8.

32. McClatchy, "William Schuman," 32.

33. Schuman to Alex North, June 28, 1985, NYPL-A, 136/12.

34. See *New York Times*, February 27, 1949, SM5. For more on Schuman and Young People's Records, see Bonner, *Revolutionizing Children's Records*, esp. 21, 82–83 (where Bonner discusses the Moore opera), and 166–67.

35. The *New York Times* carried an advertisement for the North/Gury musical (February 13, 1949, X2). For more on the musical, see Sanya Shoilevska Henderson, *Alex North, Film Composer* (Jefferson, NC: McFarland, 2003), 31. For Schuman's calendar, see NYPL-A, 153.

36. OHAM, 380; Ross Parmenter, "The World of Music," *New York Times*, May 13, 1951, X7; S-W, 612 [12/2].

37. Jeremy Gury to Schuman, August 24, 1950, 18/15.

38. Gury to Schuman, July 10, 1950, and August 24, 1950, NYPL-A, 18/15.

39. See Gury to Schuman, August 1, 1951, August 13, 1951, September 4, 1951, and February 4, 1952, NYPL-A, 145/2; and LaFarge, December 28, 1941, LaF '41.

40. Gury to Schuman, August 13, 1951, NYPL-A, 145/2.

41. Gury to Schuman, May 23, 1951 and February 4, 1952, NYPL-A, 145/2.

42. Schuman to Saul Schechtman, July 7, 1952, NYPL-A, 37/3.

43. Hans Heinsheimer to Alfred de Liagre, November 8, 1951, NYPL-A, 145/2.

44. Peter Filichia, notes for *Wish You Were Here* (original cast recording), reissued as BMG 09026–68326–2 (compact disc), © 1996, p. 10.

45. Schuman to Bernstein, November 12, 1951, NYPL-A, 6/10.

46. Gury to Schuman, August 1, 1951, NYPL-A, 145/2.

47. Gury to Schuman, August 13, 1951, NYPL-A, 145/2.

48. W. S. Cutchins, executive with Louisville-based cigarette company Brown & Williamson, to Ford Frick, president of the National Baseball League, June 25, 1951, NYPL-A, 145/2.

49. Walter Hendl to Schuman, undated [possibly early summer 1952], NYPL-A, 20/7.

50. Schuman to Hendl, July 18, 1952, NYPL-A, 145/2.

51. For the University of Michigan, see Schuman to Hans Heinsheimer, August 15, 1952, NYPL-A, 180/5; Schuman to Esther E. Pease, November 5, 1952, NYPL-A, 33/3; and Frederick Dorian to Schuman, December 8, 1952, Schuman to Dorian, December 11, 1952, and Schuman to Dorian, December 12, 1952, all in NYPL-A, 13/2. The correspondence between Schuman and Moshe Paranov about the premiere is in NYPL-A, 20/4.

52. Andrew Stiller, "Devil and Daniel Webster, The," in *The New Grove Dictionary of Opera*, ed. Stanley Sadie, *Grove Music Online*. Oxford Music Online, http://www.oxfordmusiconline.com/subscriber/article/grove/music/O008545 (accessed June 7, 2009).

53. Douglas Moore to Schuman, May 5, 1953, NYPL-A, 30/6.

54. Schuman to Douglas Moore, May 6, 1953, NYPL-A, 30/6.

55. Schuman to Sara White Dreiser, December 14, 1951, NYPL-A, 13/3.

56. Schuman to Alvin Manuel, January 8, 1952, NYPL-A, 13/3.

57. Schuman to Harold J. Dies, April 18, 1952, NYPL-A, 13/3.

58. See correspondence between Schuman and Harry Brown, NYPL-A, 13/3; correspondence between Schuman to Norman Rosten, NYPL-A, 36/14; correspondence between Howard Sackler and Schuman, NYPL-A, 37/1; and Schuman to Lincoln Kirstein, December 1, 1953, NYPL-A, 23/6 (mention of both Sackler and Agee).

59. Schuman to Harold J. Dies, November 19, 1965, NYPL-A, 16/13.

60. Ivan Spear, "Hollywood Report," *Boxoffice*, August 14, 1954, 20.

61. The August 31, 1954, contract for *The Last Notch* is in NYPL-A, 18/3.

62. Frank D. Gilroy to Schuman, April 1, 1955, NYPL-A, 18/3.

63. Gilroy to Schuman, April 18, 1957, NYPL-A, 18/3. See also Frank D. Gilroy, *Writing for Love and/or Money: Outtakes from a Life on Spec (The Early Years)* (Hanover, NH: Smith & Kraus, 2008), 58.

64. "Baseball in Cold Blood," *Time*, May 18, 1953, 60.

65. Gury to Schuman, May 25, 1953, NYPL-A, 18/15.

66. William J. Krebs to Alfred de Liagre, September 8, 1953, NYPL-A, 145/2.

67. Schuman to Richard Rodgers, March 2, 1955, NYPL-A, 36/9.

68. Schuman to Louis Gesensway, February 21, 1955, NYPL-A, 17/3.

69. Schuman to Robert Saudek and Schuman to Paul Feigay, both March 7, 1955, NYPL-A, 16/7.

70. Alfred de Liagre to Schuman, March 7, 1955, NYPL-A, 145/2.

71. Schuman to Moshe Paranov, March 17, 1955, NYPL-A, 20/4.

72. Saudek to Schuman, March 10, 1955, NYPL-A, 16/7.

73. "H.C.S." [Harold C. Schonberg], "There Is No Joy in 'Casey' Opera," *New York Times*, March 7, 1953, 34. Schuman mentioned the positive reviews to Elizabeth Sonn ("Aunt Lizzie"), March 17, 1955, NYPL-A, 38/1.

74. Harold C. Schonberg, "Casey Bats Again with Same Result," *New York Times*, May 5, 1953, 34.

75. See Robert U. Nelson to Schuman, December 17, 1958, NYPL-A, 42/1; Don Gillis to Schuman, July 22, 1959, NYPL-A, 18/2; and Linda Madden to Schuman, May 8, 1974, NYPL-A, 145/3.

76. William Bergsma to Schuman, March 7, 1955, JS, 19/2.

77. Rose Marie Grentzer to Schuman, November 29, 1950, NYPL-A, 17/7.

78. LeRoy Leatherman and Martha Swope, *Martha Graham: Portrait of the Lady as an Artist* (New York: Alfred A. Knopf, 1966), 55.

79. For a description of Graham's insinuating herself into the work, see WS-Gruen, 53–56. The "eye treatment" and "perfectly well" quotations come from p. 54.

80. Schuman to Kathleen Davidson, December 17, 1952, NYPL-A, 39/13.

81. John Martin, "The Dance: Novelty," *New York Times*, May 10, 1953, X2.

82. Gertrude Macy to Schuman, April 10, 1953, JS, 18/2. The Graham score for *Voyage* is in the Martha Graham Collection, Box 187, Library of Congress. For Schuman's declaration that it is "the composer's orchestration," see Schuman to Harold Spivacke, January 25, 1958, Spivacke-Schuman correspondence file, Music Division, Library of Congress. For more on Brant and *The Mighty Casey*, see the correspondence in NYPL-A, 7/7.

83. Bertram Ross, in Robert Tracy, *Goddess: Martha Graham's Dancers Remember* (New York: Limelight Editions, 1997), 159.

84. John Martin, "Martha Graham Begins Dance Engagement at Alvin Theater with Premiere of 'Voyage,'" *New York Times*, May 18, 1953, 25.

85. Schuman to Graham, May 18, 1953, NYPL-A, 18/10.

86. Schuman to John Marshall, May 18, 1953, NYPL-A, 18/10.

87. Leatherman and Swope, *Martha Graham*, 55.

88. Schuman to Kathleen Davidson, June 15, 1953, NYPL-A, 39/13.

89. Reprinted in *Pan Pipes of Sigma Alpha Iota* 45, 4 (1953): 4–5.

90. Schuman to Lillian Steuber, October 2, 1953, NYPL-A, 40/10.

91. Steuber to Schuman, October 15, 1953, NYPL-A, 40/10.

92. See K. Gary Adams, *William Schuman: A Bio-Bibliography* (Westport, CT: Greenwood Press, 1998), 79.

93. Schuman to Hans Heinsheimer, September 14, 1954, NYPL-A, 180/5. For Gustave Schirmer's approval of Schuman's affiliation with BMI, see Schuman to Robert J. Burton, September 11, 1952, NYPL-A, 8/1.

94. Gustave Schirmer to Schuman, December 27, 1955, NYPL-A, 180/5.

Chapter 19: "The (Mostly) Off-Stage Ambassador"

1. Robert J. Burton to Schuman, August 26, 1952, NYPL-A, 8/1.

2. Schuman to Copland, January 17, 1946, NYPL-A, 11/6.

3. Schuman to Kenneth Levy, March 30, 1965, NYPL-A, 84/7.

4. Seymour Shifrin to Schuman, December 10, 1956, NYPL-A, 39/11.

5. Shifrin to Schuman, October 9, 1953, JS, 3/5.

6. For a summary of the contest between BMI and ASCAP, see Kerry Segrave, *Payola in the Music Industry: A History, 1880–1991* (Jefferson, NC: McFarland, 1994), 94–97, 120–21.

7. Schuman to Mrs. R.I.C. Prout, July 19, 1957, NYPL-A, 8/1.

8. http://www.bmi.com/foundation/program/bmi_student_composer_awards/, accessed June 16, 2009.

9. The complete list is at http://www.bmi.com/genres/detail_basic/535120, accessed June 19, 2009.

10. Schuman to Edward M. Cramer, April 1982, NYPL-A, 125/9.

11. James G. Roy Jr. to Schuman, April 13, 1983, and Schuman to Roy, January 5, 1984, both NYPL-A, 125/9.

12. *The Juilliard Report on Teaching the Literature and Materials of Music* (New York: W. W. Norton, 1953), 27.

13. Autobiography, chap. A, pp. 24, 27.

14. See Turner Catledge to Schuman, April 25, 1961, and Harold Schonberg to Schuman, May 9, 1961, both NYPL-A, 3/5; and the thank-you letters for his Economic Club speech, NYPL-A, 55/3. (The quotation comes from John O'Keefe's January 18, 1968, letter.)

15. K. Gary Adams lists most, but not all, of Schuman's published writings and speeches. See Adams, *William Schuman: A Bio-Bibliography* (Westport, CT: Greenwood Press, 1998), 229–44.

16. Schuman to Olga Naumoff Koussevitzky, December 20, 1951, NYPL-A, 23/9.

17. OHAM, 251–52. For more on Schuman's desire to shape the *Musical Quarterly* and to create his own journal, see Steve Swayne, "American Musicology at the Crossroads, Contemporary Music in the Crosshairs: The Ideological Battle at G. Schirmer, Inc. at the End of World War II," paper presented at the annual meeting of the American Musicological Society, Quebec City, Quebec, Canada, November 2, 2007. Available at http://www.orpheus.dartmouth.edu.

18. See Schuman to Margaret Grant, October 13, 1953, NYPL-A, 23/10, for Schuman's "strong recommendation" of the commission to Hall Overton that resulted in Overton's Symphony no. 1 (1956).

19. Mark Schubart, June 13, 1947, memo for the files, Office of the Dean, General Administrative Records, 1946–1962, Juilliard School Archives, The Juilliard School, New York, NY, 1/1. See correspondence in 1/2 and 1/3 for the pieces commissioned and the composer's reasons for not fulfilling the commissions.

20. Schuman to Walter Piston, January 28, 1953, JS, 3/5.

21. See the Harris-Schuman, Harris-Schubart, and Harris-Prausnitz correspondence in JS, 3/5.

22. Harris to Schuman, September 14, 1955, JS, 3/5.

23. Schuman to Copland, June 15, 1951, JS, 3/5.

24. Copland to Schuman, June 22, 1954, JS, 3/5. For a description of the Whitman cantata, see Schuman to Copland, September 26, 1951, JS, 3/5.

25. Copland to Schuman, December 15, 1955, JS, 3/5.

26. Howard Taubman, "Copland Fantasy for Piano Heard," *New York Times*, October 26, 1957, 18.

27. Schuman to Copland, September 24, 1957, NYPL-A, 11/6.

28. Schuman to Carl Haverlin, February 3, 1953, NYPL-A, 8/1.

29. Schuman addressed to George A. Sloan, unsent letter, ca. March 1953, NYPL-A, 28/10.

30. See Schuman to Courtlandt D. Barnes Jr., March 30, 1953, and Anthony Bliss to Schuman, April 24, 1953, both NYPL-A, 28/10.

31. See Barbara B. Heyman, *Samuel Barber: The Composer and His Music* (New York: Oxford University Press, 1992), 380–94, for the compositional history of *Vanessa*. For the list of American operas at the Met up to 1968, see Francis Robinson to Schuman, May 27, 1968, NYPL-A, 70/7.

32. Schuman to Barber, November 7, 1956, NYPL-A, 6/3.

33. Schuman to Floyd G. Blair, April 1, 1955, JS, 10/11.

34. Blair to Schuman, April 18, 1955, JS, 10/11.

35. Olin Downes, "Philharmonic Year, Closing at Carnegie Hall Today, Marked by Eclectic Programs," *New York Times*, April 17, 1955, X9.

36. Schuman to Ralph F. Colin, May 2, 1955, JS, 10/11.

37. Nora Shea, undated interoffice memo, New York Philharmonic Archives, Box 005–01–21, Location 3/32, Folder "Board of Directors, Blair, Floyd G., General Correspondence, January/May 1955."

38. See Schuman to Ralph F. Colin, May 9, 1955, JS, 10/11; and Ralph F. Colin to Floyd G. Blair and Arthur Judson, May 10, 1955, letter, New York Philharmonic Archives, Box 005–01–21, Location 3/32, Folder "Board of Directors, Blair, Floyd G., General Correspondence, January/May 1955."

39. Harold C. Schonberg, "New Job for the Protean Mr. Bernstein," *New York Times*, December 22, 1957, 31.

40. Ross Parmenter, "Leonard Bernstein Heads Philharmonic," *New York Times*, November 20, 1957, 43.

41. Schuman to Copland, February 4, 1974, NYPL-A, 98/6.

42. Schuman to Marc Connelly, February 17, 1954, NYPL-A, 31/10.

43. September 30, 1954, minutes of the meeting of the Policy Committee for the National Institute of Arts and Letters, NYPL-A, 31/10.

44. See the correspondence in NYPL-A, 92/8.

45. Life at the High School of the Performing Arts served as the model for the film *Fame*. See http://www.imdb.com/title/tt0080716/, accessed June 20, 2009.

46. "Merger Proposed for Arts Schools," *New York Times*, December 12, 1958, A2.

47. Suzanne Daley, "400 Gather to See La Guardia H.S. Get Cornerstone," *New York Times*, October 18, 1982, B1; William R. Greer, "Music and Arts Merge in High School—Finally," *New York Times*, September 10, 1948, B5.

48. Schuman to Cece Waserman, August 14, 1982, NYPL-A, 134/4.

49. For Schuman on aesthetic and personal predilections, see Schuman to Seymour Shifrin, January 15, 1951, NYPL-A, 39/11; Schuman to George Rochberg, December 13, 1956, NYPL-A, 178/3; Schuman to Gerald Freund, December 12, 1963, LCPA, Box ID 090400, Folder "Rockefeller Foundation, 1963–1964"; Schuman to Oliver Daniel, August 18, 1964, letter, NYPL-A, 50/1; Schuman to David Epstein, April 14, 1978, NYPL-A, 99/11; Schuman to Samuel Adler, September 23, 1983, 123/5; and Schuman to Marks, February 27, 1986, AWS.

50. Anton Haefeli and Reinhard Oehlschlägel, "International Society for Contemporary Music," in *Grove Music Online, Oxford Music Online*, http://www.oxfordmusiconline.com/subscriber/article/grove/music/13859, accessed June 20, 2009.

51. Carol J. Oja, *Making Music Modern: New York in the 1920s* (New York: Oxford University Press, 2000), 290–91.

52. See Frederick Prausnitz to Milton Babbitt, January 29, 1951, JS, 11/1; and Frederic Cohen to Babbitt, January 30, 1951, NYPL-A, 20/16.

53. Schuman to Babbitt, February 5, 1951, NYPL-A, 20/16.

54. Schuman to Seymour Shifrin, February 21, 1951, NYPL-A, 39/11.

55. Schuman to Max McCullough, October 17, 1952, in Old Correspondence, Schuman, William 1950–1956, Music Division, Library of Congress.

56. "Draft Resolutions Submitted by the Music Committee," submitted September 25, 1952, UNESCO International Conference of Artists, Venice, 1952 [UNESCO archives].

57. Schuman to Babbitt, March 10, 1953, NYPL-A, 20/16.

58. Babbitt to Schuman, March 22, 1953, NYPL-A, 20/16.

59. Ross Parmenter, "The World of Music," *New York Times*, June 13, 1954, X9; "Two Music Groups Announce Merger," *New York Times*, December 2, 1954, 38.

60. Schuman to McCullough, October 17, 1952, in Old Correspondence, Schuman, William 1950–1956, Music Division, Library of Congress.

61. Schuman to Alfred V. Frankenstein, December 30, 1957, NYPL-A, 16/9.

62. See "Notes and Comment," *Juilliard Review* 3, 1 (Winter 1955–56): 53.

63. McCullough to Schuman, July 13, 1955, NYPL-A, 42/2.

64. Schuman to Dorothy Norman, June 15, 1955, NYPL-A, 31/4. For more on Norman, see Roberta Smith, "Dorothy Norman, 92, Dies; Photographer and Activist," *New York Times*, April 13, 1997, 38.

65. André Kostelanetz to Schuman, February 25, 1954, NYPL-A, 23/7; Charles Munch et al. to Schuman, October 29, 1954, NYPL-A, 7/2.

66. Schuman to Lucien Wulsin Jr., August 17, 1955, NYPL-A, 42/2.

67. See: Schuman to McCullough, August 17, 1955, McCullough to Schuman, September 7, 1955, and Wulsin to Schuman, August 31, 1955, all NYPL-A, 42/2; Thor Johnson to Schuman, September 2, 1955, and Schuman to Johnson, September 10, 1955, both NYPL-A, 21/6.

68. OHAM, 124.

69. Schuman to Hazel Wittner, September 9, 1946, NYPL-A, 43/9.

70. Ward Wheelock, "The Power of an Idea," in *This I Believe: The Living Philosophies of One Hundred Thoughtful Men and Women in All Walks of Life—As Written for and with a Foreword by Edward R. Murrow*, ed. Edward R. Murrow (New York: Simon & Schuster, 1952), xvii.

71. "Bonell Critical of 'This I Believe'," *New York Times*, February 21, 1955, 19.

72. Dan Gediman, "Afterword: The History of *This I Believe*: The Power of an Idea," in *This I Believe: The Personal Philosophies of Remarkable Men and Women*, ed. Jay Allison and Dan Gediman (New York: H. Holt, 2007), 267.

73. Schuman to Bill Little, February 28, 1972, NYPL-A, 113/7.

74. Schuman to Thor Johnson, September 22, 1955, NYPL-A, 21/6.

75. Henry Brant to Schuman, October 5, 1955, NYPL-A, 7/7.

76. Thor Johnson to Schuman, October 20, 1955, and Schuman to Johnson, November 7, 1955, both NYPL-A, 21/6. For the reviews of the concert, see Arthur Darack, "A Premiere for UNESCO," *Cincinnati Enquirer*, November 5, 1955, clipping in NYPL-A, 190; and Mary

Leighton, "Schuman Work Given Premiere in Cincinnati UNESCO Concert," *Musical America* 75, 16 (December 15, 1955): 31.

77. Schuman to John Evarts, December 21, 1955, NYPL-A, 14/3.

78. Schuman to Ormandy, November 22, 1955, NYPL-A, 34/5.

79. Ormandy to Schuman, December 12, 1955, NYPL-A, 34/5.

80. Schuman to Ormandy, December 13, 1955, and December 18, 1955, NYPL-A, 34/5.

81. Ormandy to Schuman, February 24, 1956, NYPL-A, 34/5. Other statements in this paragraph come from correspondence in 34/5.

82. Arthur A. Hauser to Schuman, October 3, 1957, NYPL-A, 178/4. Schuman's handwritten response on the letter is dated October 7, 1957.

83. Aaron Copland, "Current Chronicle: New York," *Musical Quarterly* 37, 3 (July 1951): 395.

84. Henry Cowell, "Current Chronicle: New York," *Musical Quarterly* 42, 3 (July 1956): 386–89.

85. Howard Taubman, "Copland Fantasy for Piano Heard," *New York Times*, October 26, 1957, 18.

Chapter 20: "With an Eye on the Marketplace"

1. Schuman to Arthur A. Hauser, July 16, 1956, NYPL-A, 178/3.

2. Albert Christ-Janer to Schuman, July 21, 1955, NYPL-A, 10/7.

3. Schuman to Christ-Janer, June 11, 1956, NYPL-A, 10/7.

4. Schuman to Christ-Janer, July 27, 1955, NYPL-A, 10/7.

5. Schuman to Christ-Janer, October 11, 1955, NYPL-A, 10/7.

6. Schuman to Langston Hughes, January 5, 1956, NYPL-A, 19/13.

7. Hughes to Schuman, January 20, 1956, NYPL-A, 19/13.

8. Schuman to Hughes, January 25, 1956, NYPL-A, 19/13.

9. Schuman to Hughes, April 5, 1956, Langston Hughes Papers, JWJ MS26 Box 143, Folder 2662, Beinecke Library, Yale University. The eight Schuman-Hughes letters among the Schuman papers are also among Hughes's papers at Yale.

10. Albert Christ-Janer, Charles W. Hughes, and Carleton Sprague Smith, eds., *American Hymns Old and New* (New York: Columbia University Press, 1980), 140. Hughes wrote the biographies and the notes on the hymns. The hymn itself is on pp. 802–3.

11. Schuman to George Rochberg, April 10, 1956, NYPL-A, 178/3.

12. Schuman to Arthur A. Hauser, April 30, 1958, NYPL-A, 178/5.

13. Schuman to Hauser, July 16, 1956, NYPL-A, 178/3.

14. Schuman to Rochberg, November 6, 1956, NYPL-A, 178/3.

15. The manuscript for "Haste" bears the date of October 18, 1969, and unlike the other Rounds, it is not written out as a choral arrangement. For an order of the *Five Rounds* that differs from Schuman's suggestion, see the order on the compact disc *I Hear America Singing* with Gregg Smith and the Gregg Smith Singers (VoxBox CD3X 3037, © 1996); and Joseph McLellan, "William Schuman's Vivid Vocal Works," *Washington Post*, May 8, 1986, C13. For the request for an additional round, see Schuman to Calvert Bean Jr., September 5, 1969, NYPL-A, 111/9.

16. Schuman to Nathan Einhorn, November 20, 1969, NYPL-A, 104/8.

17. Bean to Schuman, August 11, 1969, NYPL-A, 111/9.

18. Schuman to Ned Rorem, December 7, 1970, NYPL-A, 112/6.

19. See André Kostelanetz to Schuman, February 25, 1954, March 19, 1954, and March 26, 1954, NYPL-A, 23/7.

20. Schuman to Kostelanetz, April 27, 1954, NYPL-A, 23/7.

21. Schuman to Kostelanetz, July 16, 1954, NYPL-A, 23/7.

22. Schuman to Copland, July 20, 1954, NYPL-A, 11/7.

23. Kostelanetz to Schuman, July 23, 1954, NYPL-A, 23/7.

24. Schuman to Kostelanetz, February 1, 1955, NYPL-A, 23/7.

25. Schuman to Kostelanetz, August 2, 1955, NYPL-A, 23/7.

26. Kostelanetz to Schuman, August 19, 1955, NYPL-A, 23/7.

27. Schuman to Kostelanetz, December 14, 1955, NYPL-A, 23/7.

28. Schuman to Hans Heinsheimer, September 14, 1954, NYPL-A, 180/5.

29. Schuman to Heinsheimer, September 15, 1954, NYPL-A, 180/5.

30. Thor Johnson to Schuman, September 17, 1955, NYPL-A, 21/6. See also "City Tenders Fete to U.N. Assembly," *New York Times*, September 24, 1955, 11.

31. Ormandy to Schuman, May 10, 1955, NYPL-A, 34/5.

32. See notations on Hauser to Schuman, December 6, 1955, NYPL-A, 178/3.

33. Schuman to Kostelanetz, March 1, 1956, NYPL-A, 23/7.

34. Thor Johnson to Schuman, July 25, 1956, and Schuman to Johnson, July 27, 1956, both NYPL-A, 21/6.

35. Hauser to Schuman, February 21, 1957, NYPL-A, 178/4.

36. Hauser to Schuman, May 20, 1959, NYPL-A, 178/6.

37. Undated fragment of a term paper, NYPL-B, 15/"Publications/Writings undated."

38. See Charles Hammond to Schuman, May 17, 1952, and Schuman to Hammond, May 28, 1952, and July 30, 1956, NYPL-A, 26/8.

39. Schuman to Hauser, July 20, 1956, NYPL-A, 178/3.

40. As quoted in Hauser to Schuman, May 3, 1957, NYPL-A, 178/4.

41. William Mootz, "Band Overture Highlights Winter Concert at U. of L.," *Louisville (KY) Courier-Journal*, January 11, 1957, sec. 2, p. 8.

42. See the correspondence in NYPL-A, 26/8. The letters that are quoted from Schuman to Ernest E. Lyon, director of bands at the University of Louisville, are June 7, 1957, and February 4, 1958.

43. Percy Grainger to Schuman, June 20, 1957, NYPL-A, 18/11.

44. For an analysis of this work, see Joseph Machlis, "William Schuman," in *American Composers of Our Time* (New York: Thomas Y. Crowell, 1963), 146–48.

45. Schuman to Hauser, January 15, 1965, NYPL-A, 179/6; and Schuman to Arnold Broido, September 9, 1970, NYPL-A, 111/9.

46. The correspondence on the *Piping Tim Fantasy* is in NYPL-A 179/2.

47. Hauser to Schuman, August 2, 1961, NYPL-A, 179/2.

48. Schuman to Hauser, August 4, 1961, NYPL-A, 179/2.

49. Schuman to Hauser, August 7, 1961, NYPL-A, 179/2.

50. See the Bean-Schuman correspondence in NYPL-A, 179/2.

51. William Revelli to Schuman, January 16, 1962, and Schuman to Revelli, January 22, 1962, NYPL-A, 36/6.

52. Schuman to Revelli, March 20, 1962, NYPL-A, 36/6.

53. Schuman to Joseph Albright, March 6, 1974, NYPL-A, 145/4. Albright conducted the Scarsdale High School Band in Scarsdale, NY.

54. See Walter Lowendahl to Schuman, November 20, 1956, NYPL-A, 41/12; and Abraham Friedman to Hauser, December 5, 1956, NYPL-A, 178/3.

55. Schuman to Imogene Boyle, March 6, 1957, NYPL-A, 5/3.

56. Undated memorandum from Schuman to Harold Spivacke—"Information on Manuscript Gifts to The Library of Congress"—in NYPL-A, 148/5.

57. Albert Boyars to Schuman, May 20, 1958, NYPL-A, 41/12. For the Venice Film Festival, see more at http://asac.labiennale.org. The Venice Festival had a rule that films shown there could not be played elsewhere during that festival season. Personal correspondence with Michele Mangione, ASAC Film Library, July 29, 2009.

58. Personal correspondence with Bill Hooper, June 27, 2007, reprinted with permission.

59. See "Composer in America: William Schuman Talks About His Life and Works," in Schuman, William: Chapter drafts from proposed memoir with David Wright & correspondence, 1986–87, The Juilliard School Archives; and J. Robert Paxton to Schuman, November 14, 1946, NYPL-A, 40/5.

60. Schuman to Isadore Freed, May 30, 1955, NYPL-A, 16/11.

61. Schuman to Freed, October 24, 1955, NYPL-A, 16/11.

62. Schuman to Freed, April 3, 1956, and February 15, 1957, NYPL-A, 16/11; and Schuman to Hauser, April 16, 1958, NYPL-A, 178/5.

63. Schuman to Freed, September 4, 1958, NYPL-A, 16/11.

64. Schuman to Freed, October 15, 1958, NYPL-A, 16/11.

65. Freed to Schuman, October 28, 1958, NYPL-A, 16/11.

66. For an analysis of the *Three Piano Moods*, see Frances Dillon, "Reviewed Work(s): *Three Piano Moods: I. Lyrical. II. Pensive. III. Dynamic* by William Schuman," *Notes*, 2nd ser., 18, 3 (June 1961): 489.

67. Kenneth Munson to Schuman, May 31, 1958, NYPL-A, 38/6.

68. Munson to Schuman, September 4, 1958, NYPL-A, 38/6.

69. S-W, 1048–49 [21/2].

70. Schuman to Steven O. Boehlke, February 28, 1973, NYPL-A, 144/11; Schuman to Jane Hardester, September 2, 1976, NYPL-A, 92/11.

71. Schuman to Peter Kermani, December 8, 1976, NYPL-A, 92/4.

72. Christopher Rouse, *William Schuman Documentary: Biographical Essay, Catalogue of Works, Discography, and bibliography* (New York: G. Schirmer, 1980), 18.

Chapter 21: "International Man of Music"

1. Harris to Schuman, April 16, 1952, NYPL-A, 20/2.

2. Schuman to Harris, May 26, 1952, NYPL-A, 20/2.

3. Ray Moremen et al., "In Quest of Answers: An Interview with William Schuman," *Choral Journal* 13 (February 1973): 8.

4. OHAM, 139. Schuman made these comments after attending the premiere of Carter's Symphony for Three Orchestras (1977); he also related Copland's reactions to the Carter.

5. Kyle Gann, *American Music in the Twentieth Century* (New York: Schirmer, 1997), 127. For the audience's response to *4'33"*, see Philip Gentry, "The Cultural Politics of *4'33"*," chap. 5 of "The Age of Anxiety: Music, Politics, and McCarthyism, 1948–1954," Ph.D. diss., University of California at Los Angeles, 2008, pp. 174–75. I thank Dr. Gentry for making this chapter of his dissertation available to me.

6. Minutes, Music Panel for ANTA, October 26, 1954, p. 1, NYPL-A, 2/1 (upper case "music" in original). For the founding of ANTA, see "National Theatre Is Authorized by Congress to Advance the Drama," *New York Times*, June 30, 1935, 1.

7. Emily Abrams Ansari provides a comprehensive and insightful account of the activities of the Music Panel. See her "'Masters of the President's Music': Cold War Composers and the United States Government," Ph.D. diss., Harvard University, 2009. I thank Dr. Ansari for sharing with me drafts of her dissertation and for entertaining my questions and observations about this period in Schuman's life.

8. Cage to Schuman, January 10, 1955, JS-A, 18/5.

9. See John Cage, "Juilliard Lecture," in *A Year from Monday: New Lectures and Writings by John Cage* (Middletown, CT: Wesleyan University Press, 1963), 95–111. I thank David Patterson for making me aware of this lecture.

10. Grenell to Schuman, May 17, 1949, NYPL-A, 17/7.

11. Minutes, Music Panel for ANTA, February 8, 1955, p. 4, NYPL-A, 2/2; and Minutes, Music Panel for ANTA, April 20, 1960, p. 6, NYPL-A, 3/1.

12. Minutes, Music Panel for ANTA, December 8, 1954, p. 5, NYPL-A, 2/1, and Minutes, Music Panel for ANTA, March 8, 1955, p. 2, NYPL-A, 2/2.

13. Schuman to Virginia Inness-Brown, September 20, 1955, NYPL-A, 2/2.

14. Minutes, Music Panel for ANTA, February 28, 1956, p. 2, NYPL-A, 2/3.

15. Minutes, Music Panel for ANTA, December 8, 1954, p. 4, NYPL-A, 2/1.

16. Minutes, Music Panel for ANTA, February 19, 1958, p. 5, NYPL-A, 2/5.

17. Minutes, Music Panel for ANTA, May 3, 1955, p. 4, NYPL-A, 2/2. Marshall Stearns, founder of the Institute for Jazz Studies and author of *The Story of Jazz* (1956), was added to the panel.

18. Minutes, Music Panel for ANTA, October 17, 1956, p. 4, NYPL-A, 2/3.

19. Edward Mangum, "Third Tour of Asia for I.E.P.," January 25, 1957, report to Robert C. Schnitzer, p. 5, in Robert C. Schnitzer Papers, T-Mss 1999-028, Box 5, Folder 10, NYPL.

20. Minutes, Music Panel for ANTA, April 15, 1959, pp. 3–4, NYPL 2/6.

21. Much of this information can be found in Edgar B. Young, *Lincoln Center: The Building of an Institution* (New York: New York University Press, 1980), chaps. 1–3 (see esp. p. 25 for a description of the "appropriate educational instrument" for the Lincoln Square project). See also Mark Schubart to Schuman, September 8, 1955, JS, 14/1; Schuman to David M. Keiser, June 21, 1956, JS, 19/2; and Schuman to Schubart, July 12, 1956, NYPL-A, 12/4.

22. Schuman to Copland, February 14, 1956, NYPL-A, 11/6; and February 21, 1957, Minutes for Regular Meeting of Board of Directors of Metropolitan Opera Association Inc., p. 4, NYPL-A, 29/2.

23. Mark Schubart, "Moscow Rolls Out Red Carpet," *New York Times*, April 20, 1958, X9.

24. Minutes, Music Panel for ANTA, December 8, 1954, p. 3, NYPL-A 2/1.

25. Schuman to Cliburn, May 19, 1958, JS, 2/16.

26. Max Frankel, "U.S. Pianist, 23, Wins Soviet Contest," *New York Times*, April 14, 1958, 18.

27. Schuman to Gilels, October 28, 1955, JS, 18/6.

28. Schuman to Mary Stewart French, December 5, 1955, NYPL-A, 15/4.

29. William Schuman, "Juilliard Goes on Tour," *Juilliard Review* 5, 3 (Fall 1958): 3.

30. Minutes, Music Panel for ANTA, September 8, 1957, p. 2, NYPL-A, 2/4.

31. E. W. Doty to Schuman, December 19, 1958, JS, 9/7.

32. Ewald B. Nyquist to Schuman, November 19, 1959, JS, 9/7.

33. Schuman, "Juilliard Goes on Tour," 4. See also Robert C. Schnitzer to Aleck Gingiss, June 12, 1958, NYPL-A, 2/4.

34. Howard Taubman, "On Coming Home," *New York Times*, September 14, 1958, X11. See also "Excerpts from the Press," *Juilliard Review* 5, 3 (Fall 1958): 5–8.

35. Minutes, Music Panel for ANTA, August 27, 1958, p. 2, NYPL-A, 2/5.

36. "Juilliard Orchestra Tour: Repertory," *Juilliard Review* 5, 3 (Fall 1958): 8.

37. David S. Cooper to Schuman, May 12, 1958, NYPL-A, 9/5.

38. Cooper to Schuman, February 3, 1956, NYPL-A, 11/5.

39. See Ansari, "'Masters of the Presidents' Music.'"

40. See January 15, 1960, announcement, "Agency Music Advisor," and Angelo Eagon to Schuman, March 9, 1960, both NYPL-A, 42/3; and Ansari, "'Masters of the Presidents' Music.'"

41. Schuman to Virginia Inness-Brown, November 21, 1960, NYPL-A, 3/2.

42. Schuman to Herbert E. Marks, April 18, 1959, NYPL-A, 180/3.

43. Schuman to Herbert E. Marks, February 29, 1960, NYPL-A, 180/3.

44. Schuman to Karl Korte, December 17, 1964, NYPL-A, 64/3.

45. Schuman to Rochberg, December 31, 1955, NYPL-A, 178/3.

46. Schuman to Rochberg, November 13, 1956, NYPL-A, 178/3. For Rochberg's account of the audition of the *Sonata-Fantasia*, see George Rochberg, *Five Lines, Four Spaces: The World of My Music*, edited by Gene Rochberg and Richard Griscom (Urbana: University of Illinois Press, 2009): 258–59.

47. Schuman to Rochberg, May 21, 1957, NYPL-A, 36/8.

48. Rochberg to Schuman, May 24, 1957, NYPL-A, 36/8.

49. Schuman to Rochberg, February 17, 1960, NYPL-A, 179/1.For Rochberg's appreciation of Schuman's enthusiasm for the Second Symphony, see Rochberg, *Five Lines, Four Spaces*, 20.

50. Schuman to Copland, September 24, 1957, NYPL-A, 11/6.

51. Schuman to Copland, October 28, 1957, LoC-AC, 262/13.

52. Mark Swed, "Theater: The Passages of 'Candide,'" *Los Angeles Times*, November 5, 1995, 7.

53. Schuman to Bernstein, September 1, 1957, LoC-LB.

54. Schuman to Etzel Willhoit, See January 8, 1957, NYPL-A, 43/8.

55. Howard Taubman, "Juilliard Group Gives Three Premieres," *New York Times*, February 2, 1957, 13.

56. Schuman to Arthur A. Hauser, April 30, 1958, NYPL-A, 178/5.

57. Schuman to Leonard Feist, June 4, 1959, JS, 21/3.

58. Schuman to Benjamin V. Grasso, June 11, 1959, NYPL-A, 17/6.

59. Schuman to Milton Katims, April 28, 1959, NYPL-A, 23/1.

60. The envelope containing the manuscript bears the inscription, in red pencil, "Pencil Sketch/Variation on 12 Note Theme/William Schuman." The inscription does not appear to be in Schuman's hand, though the sketch itself is.

61. Christopher Rouse, "Expansion of Material in the Seventh Symphony of William Schuman," MFA thesis, Cornell University, 1977, 51.

62. For more on this work, titled *Masquerade*, see JS, 3/6. The Juilliard Library also possesses a videotape of the performance and a score of the work, with variations by Bergsma, Weisgall, Druckman, Persichetti, Lloyd, Starer, Aitken, and Giannini.

63. William Bergsma to Schuman, July 8, 1960, JS, 3/6.

64. Schuman to Hauser, May 16, 1960, NYPL-A, 179/1.

65. Schuman to Rochberg, May 31, 1960, NYPL-A, 179/1.

66. Christopher Rouse, "Seventh Symphony of William Schuman," 71.

67. See S-W, 358–59 [8/1].

68. Karl Kroeger, "Review of William Schuman, *Symphony No. 7*," *Music Library Association Notes*, 2nd ser., 20, 3 (Summer 1963): 407.

69. Leonard Burkat to Schuman, February 20, 1957, and Schuman to Burkat, May 8, 1957, NYPL-A, 7/2.

70. Schuman to Carleton Sprague Smith, June 6, 1957, NYPL-A, 40/1.

71. Schuman to Thomas D. Perry Jr., March 10, 1959, NYPL-A, 7/2.

72. Perry to Schuman, March 19, 1959, NYPL-A, 7/2.

73. Carlos Moseley to Schuman, February 2, 1960, NYPL-A, 32/3. See also Howard Shanet, *Philharmonic: A History of New York's Orchestra* (Garden City, NY: Doubleday, 1975), 371–72.

74. Schuman to Moseley, February 4, 1960, NYPL-A, 32/3.

75. Schuman to Hauser, July 20, 1960, NYPL-A, 179/1.

76. See Datebooks: 1960, NYPL-B, Box 16.

77. See W. McNeil Lowry to Schuman, February 17, 1959, and Schuman to Lowry, February 18, 1959, NYPL-A, 16/7; Schuman to Michael Rabin, March 4, 1959, NYPL-A, 35/2. Correspondence with Leonard Rose is in NYPL 36/12.

78. William Schuman, program notes for *A Song of Orpheus*, NYPL-A 146/1. In his book, Polisi has a more extended Schuman quotation about the work and cites this folder as the location for the document in question. I have not been able to find that document, and Polisi has since been unable to locate the document.

79. Schuman to Ormandy, February 14, 1961, NYPL-A, 34/6.

80. Schuman to Walter Piston, March 23, 1955, JS, 3/5.

81. Richard Franko Goldman, "Current Chronicle: New York," *Musical Quarterly* 49, 1 (January 1963): 92.

82. Ibid., 93.

83. Schuman to Edward Downes, August 21, 1962, NYPL-A, 146/7.

84. See Barbara Heyman, *Samuel Barber* (New York: Oxford University Press, 1992), 410–20.

85. OHAM, 76.

86. Schuman to Janet D. Schenck, November 22, 1961, JS, 17/4.

87. Schuman to Robert Whitehead, March 9, 1961, and Schuman to Edgar B. Young, June 20, 1961, NYPL-A, 21/9.

88. See the comments of Polisi and Edward Bilous in Maro Chermayeff and Amy Schewel, *Juilliard* (New York: Harry N. Abrams, 2002), 96, 98.

89. Schuman to Spivacke, July 25, 1960, NYPL-A, 25/10.

90. Schuman to Schubart, July 5, 1961, JS, 14/6.

Chapter 22: "The Dream Defined"

1. Paul Goldberger, "Robert Moses, Master Builder, Is Dead at 92," *New York Times*, July 30, 1981, A1.

2. Robert C. Weaver, "Class, Race, and Urban Renewal," in *Urban Analysis: Readings in Housing and Urban Development*, edited by Alfred N. Page and Warren R. Seyfried (Glenview, IL: Scott, Foresmand, 1970), 347. I thank Will DeKrey Dartmouth College Presidential Scholar (2006–7), for his inestimable help in understanding the context for urban renewal generally and the Lincoln Square project specifically.

3. Robert A. Caro, *The Power Broker: Robert Moses and the Fall of New York* (New York: Vintage Books, 1975), 1013–14. For Moses's account of the Lincoln Square project, see Robert Moses, *Public Works: A Dangerous Trade* (New York: McGraw-Hill, 1970), 513–33.

4. Charles Grutzner, "Lincoln Sq. Unit Spurs Relocation," *New York Times*, November 9, 1958, 51.

5. See "Notes of Conversation with Mr. Ammidon following Meeting about Programming," June 23, 1967, NYPL-A, 47/3 (also in NYPL-A, 67/6).

6. Charles Grutzner, "Suit Begun to Bar Lincoln Sq. Plan," *New York Times*, December 3, 1957, 37.

7. William Schuman, "The Idea: 'A Creative, Dynamic Force,'" *New York Times Magazine*, September 23, 1962, 38.

8. See Ralph G. Martin, *Lincoln Center for the Performing Arts* (Englewood Cliffs, NJ: Prentice-Hall, 1971), 21.

9. Edgar B. Young, *Lincoln Center: The Building of an Institution* (New York: New York University Press, 1980), 51.

10. Ibid., 18.

11. Ibid., 109.

12. John M. Taylor, *General Maxwell Taylor: The Sword and the Pen* (New York: Doubleday, 1989), 2.

13. Ibid., 230, 234–36. See also Albin Krebs, "Maxwell D. Taylor, Soldier and Envoy, Dies," *New York Times*, April 21, 1987, A1.

14. Young, *Lincoln Center*, 110.

15. Schuman to Harry R. Wilson, October 3, 1961, NYPL-A, 43/8.

16. John D. Rockefeller III, diary entries for August 8, 1961, and August 15, 1961, RFA-1, 9/72.

17. Schuman to Dorothea and Vincent Persichetti, September 12, 1961, NYPL-VP, 15/3.

18. Alma Lane Lesser to Schuman, September 17, 1961, NYPL-A, 24/4.

19. Marc Blitzstein to Schuman, September 16, 1961, NYPL-A, 5/1.

20. Schuman to Blitzstein, September 19, 1961, NYPL-A, 5/1.

21. Harold Taylor to Schuman, September 13, 1961, NYPL-A, 41/7.

22. William Schuman, "Thoughts on Lincoln Center (WS–Memo to Himself)," September 29, 1961, NYPL-A, 67/5. Quotations in this section come from this memorandum.

23. Arthur Gelb, "10 Million Lincoln Center Fund to Be Headed by Mark Schubart," *New York Times*, June 14, 1962, 25.

24. Schuyler G. Chapin, "Festival '67—Some Afterthoughts," *Lincoln Center Journal*, October 1967, 3.

25. Heidi Waleson, "A New Season and a New Hand at Mostly Mozart," *New York Times*, July 11, 1982, H1.

26. Gelb, "10 Million Lincoln Center Fund," 25; "How 'La Traviata' Gets to Civics Class," *New York Times*, July 24, 1976, 50.

27. Richard P. Shepard, New Plan for Young at Lincoln Center," *New York Times*, January 12, 1976, 33.

28. Raymond Ericson, "14 Lands to Send Choruses To City," *New York Times*, February 4, 1965, 23; Raymond Ericson, "Rumania Is Out . . . But Ghana Is In," *New York Times*, February 16, 1969, D17; Robert Sherman, "Choirs from 16 Countries Stir Audience at Festival Finale," *New York Times*, May 2, 1972, 50; and "Memorandum of Meeting with William Schuman and GWW," December 21, 1944, NYPL-A, 143/4.

29. See the spring 1963 letters between Schuman and Agnes de Mille, NYPL-A, 54/9; the materials in LCPA, Box ID 090398, Folder "American Dance Theater, 1965–1966"; and the materials in NYPL-A, 47/4 ("American Dance Theater"). For Rebekah Harkness's role in scheming to head the new constituent, see Sasha Anawalt, *The Joffrey Ballet: Robert Joffrey and the Making of an American Dance Company* (New York: Scribner, 1996), 167, 171, 182–83.

30. See the materials in the folder "Choral Society of Lincoln Center, 1963–1964," LCPA, Box ID 090398.

31. Schuman to George T. Delacorte, April 22, 1965, NYPL-A, 67/3.

32. Schuman, "The Idea," 38.

33. Schuman to Rockefeller, March 31, 1967, NYPL-A, 81/10.

34. Elia Kazan to Schuman, November 13, 1961, NYPL-A, 64/5.

35. Bosley Crowther, "Our Film Festival," *New York Times*, September 22, 1963, 115.

36. OHAM, 345.

37. Schuman to Schuyler G. Chapin et al., September 28, 1964, NYPL-A, 58/2; Young, *Lincoln Center*, 230, 285.

38. Young, *Lincoln Center*, 240.

39. September 26, 1962, memo from John W. Mazzola to Schuman, LCPA, Box ID 090394, Folder "[The] Music Theater—Legal Matters, 1962–1964." See also "Oral History Interview with William Schuman," Oral History Project, LCPA, 157–61.

40. Minutes of the Meeting of the Lincoln Center Executive Committee, September 20, 1962, NYPL-A, 90/2.

41. Milton Esterow, "Rodgers Is Named Head of Music Unit By Lincoln Center," *New York Times*, October 22, 1962. For the change of name, see Minutes of Special Committee of the Executive Committee, June 20, 1963, NYPL-A, 90/3.

42. Richard P. Leach, "New York Music Theater—A Record of Conversations and Conclusions," October 3, 1962, LCPA, Box ID 090394, Folder "[The] Music Theater—Legal Matters, 1962–1964."

43. Schuman to Rodgers, May 29, 1963, NYPL-A, 56/3. See also Schuman to Rodgers, September 15, 1964, LCPA, Box ID 090394, Folder "[The] Music Theater, 1962–1965."

44. S-W, 754 [15/2].

45. January 7, 1962, press release prepared by John W. McNulty, NYPL-A, 56/3.

46. Schuman to Harry Allen Feldman, July 1, 1964, NYPL-A, 56/1. Schuman wrote in praise of Feldman's article, "Jazz: A Place in Music Education?" (*Music Educators Journal* 50, 6 [June–July 1964]: 60, 62–64), in which Feldman excoriated educators for bringing jazz into the classroom.

47. See Schuman to Gordon J. Davis, November 1, 1990, NYPL-C, "Correspondence D, 1990," for Schuman's opposition to forming a jazz constituent at Lincoln Center.

48. Schuman to Loesser, August 13, 1965, Loesser to Schuman, August 18, 1965, and Schuman to Loesser, August 20, 1965, NYPL-A, 68/6.

49. Pablo Picasso, as told by Marie-Alain Couturier, O.P., translated from *Le Figaro Littéraire*, Paris, January 1962, in NYPL-A, 181/13.

50. Abraham Friedman to Sargeant, November 16, 1962, Sargeant to Friedman, November 30, 1962, and Schuman to Friedman, December 15, 1962, all in NYPL-A, 16/13. Polisi joins the possibility of a libel suit to Sargeant's criticism of the Seventh Symphony and of commissioning organizations, which came two years before the exchange of these letters ("The Inside Track," December 10, 1960, pp. 231–32). Sargeant did not review the Eighth Symphony for the *New Yorker*, but he wrote a critique of the Lincoln Center enterprise on the occasion of the opening of Philharmonic Hall ("Culture, Inc.," October 6, 1962, 94–98).

51. Minutes of the Meeting of the Board of Directors and Members of Lincoln Center, June 11, 1962, pp. 2–3, NYPL-A, 90/2; John McClure (Columbia Records) to Schuman, July 11, 1962, and Schuman to McClure, August 8, 1962, NYPL-A, 32/1.

52. Barber to Schuman, October 3, 1962, NYPL-A, 49/1; and March 14, 1963, William Schuman memorandum to file, "Phone call from George Szell, March 14, 2 p.m., for at least half an hour," in LCPA, Box ID 090398, Folder "Acoustics—Philharmonic Hall, 1963." For the *Ungemütlichkeit* of the hall, see Goddard Lieberson to Schuman, January 3, 1964, NYPL-A, 66/1.

53. Harold C. Schonberg, "Acoustics Again," *New York Times*, December 9, 1962, 61.

54. Schuman to Irving Kolodin, February 13, 1963, LCPA, Box ID 090398, Folder "Acoustics—Philharmonic Hall, 1963."

55. Young to Schuman, June 17, 1963, LCPA, Box ID 090398, Folder "Acoustics—Philharmonic Hall, 1963."

56. See March 28, 1963, press release by Jack McNulty, in LCPA, Box ID 090398, Folder "[The] City Center of Music and Drama—Metropolitan, 1962–1963."

57. Schuman to Schubart, February 14, 1962, NYPL-A, 63/4; Raymond Ericson, "God and Fizdale, Duo-Pianists, in Concert at Philharmonic Hall," *New York Times*, September 30, 1962, 82; and Arthur Gold to Schuman, October 8, 1962, and Schuman to Robert Fizdale and Gold, October 11, 1962, NYPL-A, 59/5.

58. Schuman to Reginald Allen, January 29, 1962, NYPL-A, 76/2.

59. Schuman to Allen, February 14, 1962, NYPL-A, 76/2.

60. Schuman to Cowell, Persichetti, and Thomson, December 21, 1962, NYPL-A, 76/2.

61. Schuman appeared on *What's My Line?* on September 30, 1962 (episode #632). His prominence is marked by the fact that the panelists, who were blindfolded, had to identify not only his line of work but also his name. I thank Paul Doherty, Hollywood talent agent and self-described "#1 *What's My Line?* fan," for allowing me to view this episode.

62. William Schuman, "What Will Lincoln Center Mean to Our Young People?" *Marine Currents*, March 1963, 1–2, in NYPL-A, 186/10.

63. Anne Hobler to Schuman, November 11, 1962, and Schuman to Hobler, November 20, 1962, NYPL-A, 19/9.

Chapter 23: "Something Old, Something New, Something Borrowed"

1. S-W, 83–84 [2/1].

2. Knud Meister, "Larmen giver mig den nødvendige stilhed" ["Noise Gives Me the Necessary Silence"], *Berlingske Aftenavis*, December 29, 1962, 7.

3. 1962 Datebook, end page, NYPL-B, Box 16, Datebooks: 1962.

4. See the "Commissions (Pending)," NYPL-A, 53/2.

5. Reginald Allen to Schuman, April 3, 1962, NYPL-A, 76/2.

6. Schuman to Arthur A. Hauser, January 24, 1963, NYPL-A, 179/4.

7. Schuman to Hauser, July 25, 1963, NYPL-A, 179/4.

8. Henry Cowell to Schuman, May 22, 1964, NYPL-A, 53/10.

9. Ross Parmenter, "First Promenade for Philharmonic," *New York Times*, May 22, 1964, 40; Schuman to Cowell, June 4, 1964, Henry Cowell Papers, 1851–1994, JPB 00–03, 14/10. NYPL. Also in NYPL-A, 53/10.

10. Lukas Foss to Schuman, February 25, 1965, NYPL-A, 59/2.

11. Irving Kolodin, "Recordings Reports I: Orchestral LPs," *Saturday Review*, June 25, 1966, 52.

12. André Previn to Schuman, June 30, 1967, NYPL-A, 77/10.

13. Schuman to Frank Brieff, June 10, 1964, NYPL-A, 49/15; Schuman to Arthur Fiedler, March 9, 1965, NYPL-A, 56/1.

14. Martha McCrory to Marny Michel, July 6, 1966, NYPL-A, 179/7.

15. Marcella Palmer Blanchard to Schuman, November 1, 1966, NYPL-A, 48/6.

16. Schuman to Blanchard, November 14, 1966, NYPL-A, 48/6.

17. Schuman to Cowell, July 1, 1964, Henry Cowell Papers, 1851–1994, JPB 00-03, 14/10. NYPL. Also in NYPL-A, 53/10.

18. Frederick Tulan to Schuman, July 12, 1966, NYPL-A, 86/6.

19. Schuman to William E. Rhoads, September 9, 1966, NYPL-A, 78/8.

20. Schuman to Rhoads, December 13, 1966, NYPL-A, 78/8.

21. Schuman to Rhoads, February 17, 1969, NYPL-A, 81/3.

22. See the cover page of the 1968 Merion Music score of the *Variations*.

23. William Skelton to Schuman, January 4, 1963, NYPL-A, 52/8.

24. Schuman to Skelton, January 15, 1963, NYPL-A, 52/8.

25. Skelton to Schuman, February 15, 1963, NYPL-A, 52/8.

26. Schuman to John Arons, March 21, 1963, NYPL-A, 47/3.

27. Schuman to Skelton, April 3, 1963, NYPL-A, 52/8. The date of March 26, 1963, is on the manuscript.

28. Skelton to Schuman, April 22, 1963, NYPL-A, 52/8.

29. Schuman to Harry Langsford, October 24, 1966, NYPL-A, 144/4.

30. Schuman to Anthony Strilko, August 1, 1963, NYPL-A, 86/2.

31. Schuman to Hauser, March 20, 1964, NYPL-A, 179/5.

32. Kostelanetz to Schuman, April 12, 1964, NYPL-A, 179/5.

33. Schuman to Hauser, April 3, 1964, NYPL-A, 179/5.

34. Schuman to Calvert Bean, September 9, 1966, NYPL-A, 78/8.

35. Schuman to Hauser, April 13, 1964, NYPL-A, 179/5.

36. Harold Spivacke to Schuman, July 12, 1962, NYPL-A, 65/13.

37. Harold C. Schonberg, "A Really Cosmopolitan Festival," *New York Times*, November 8, 1964, X13.

38. Schuman to Leonard Rose, October 11, 1962, NYPL-A, 36/12.

39. Rose to Schuman, December 23, 1962, NYPL-A, 36/12.

40. Schuman to Spivacke, May 22, 1963, NYPL-A, 65/13.

41. Schuman to Hauser, May 9, 1963, NYPL-A, 179/4.

42. Schuman to Hauser, July 25, 1963, NYPL-A, 179/4.

43. Schuman to Earl V. Moore, February 17, 1964, NYPL-A, 69/4.

44. Schuman to Spivacke, June 1, 1964, NYPL-A, 65/13.

45. Schuman to Spivacke, July 1, 1964, NYPL-A, 65/13.

46. Paul Hume, "Dallapiccola Work Highlights Coolidge Festival," *Washington Post*, November 1, 1964, A12.

47. Spivacke to Schuman, November 10, 1964, NYPL-A, 65/13.

48. Charles Haubiel to Schuman, September 23, 1965, Charles Haubiel Papers, Cage 482, Box 1, Folder 4, Washington State University.

49. Schonberg, "A Really Cosmopolitan Festival," X13.

50. Walter Arlen, "Museum Concert Dreary," *Los Angeles Times*, December 15, 1965, E14.

51. Roy Travis to Schuman, December 14, 1965, NYPL-A, 87/1.

52. Schuman to Warren De Motte, October 25, 1965, NYPL-A, 54/1. The performance took place on October 15, 1965, in a Paul A. McGhee Washington Square Chamber Music concert and was broadcast live. See "Radio," *New York Times*, October 15, 1965, 91.

53. Alan M. Kriegsman, "Juilliard Performs Shuman [*sic*] to Cheers," *Washington Post*, November 11, 1967, C22.

54. Schuman to Hauser, November 15, 1967, NYPL-A, 78/9.

55. Schuman to George Middleton, November 4, 1964, NYPL-A, 69/3.

56. Note on manuscript.

57. Schuman to Paul Snook, October 7, 1977, NYPL-A, 117/8.

58. Schuman to Arnold Broido, July 22, 1977, NYPL-A, 111/11. See also Peter G. Davis, "Concert: Plangency and Exotica," *New York Times*, May 22, 1977, 52.

59. Schuman to Young, February 26, 1964, NYPL-A, 89/3.

Chapter 24: "One Nightmare after Another"

1. Schuman to The Hon. Christopher J. Murphy, April 11, 1963, NYPL-A, 150/5.

2. Schuman to Arthur A. Hauser, July 29, 1964, NYPL-A, 179/5.

3. Notation on December 31, 1965, in 1965 desk diary (blue cover), NYPL-A, 156.

4. Rockefeller to Schuman, July 1, 1965, AWS.

5. See Louis Calta, "Acoustics Scored at State Theater," *New York Times*, May 20, 1964, 36.

6. See LPCA, Box ID 090400, Folder "Royal Shakespeare Company, 1962–1964."

7. Schuman to Lincoln Kirstein, December 24, 1963, LCPA, Box ID 090398, Folder "[The] City Center of Music and Drama—Metropolitan, 1962–1963."

8. Schuyler G. Chapin to Schuman, January 31, 1964, and Schuman to Newbold Morris, September 29, 1964, LCPA-City.

9. See Schuman to Morris, July 13, 1964, LCPA-City; and Schuman to Rockefeller, August 6, 1964, NYPL-A, 81/8.

10. Rockefeller III to Robert F. Wagner, October 30, 1964, LCPA-City.

11. See John S. McNulty to Schuman, November 24, 1964, LCPA-City.

12. William Schuman, "The Idea: 'A Creative, Dynamic Force,'" *New York Times Magazine*, September 23, 1962, 34.

13. For a short history of the Repertory Theater of Lincoln Center, see Edgar B. Young, *Lincoln Center* (New York: New York University Press, 1980), 243–47. Kazan also wrote about the Repertory Theater from his perspective. See *Elia Kazan: A Life* (New York: Alfred A. Knopf, 1988), 687–700.

14. Schuman to Robert Whitehead and Elia Kazan, April 9, 1964, LCPA, Box ID 090400, Folder "[The] Repertory Theater (Vivian Beaumont Theater), 1961–1966."

15. July 13, 1964 "Notes for Meeting with Whitehead and Kazan," LCPA, Box ID 090400, Folder "[The] Repertory Theater (Vivian Beaumont Theater), 1961–1966."

16. Schuman to W. McNeil Lowry, June 10, 1964, NYPL-A, 80/7. See also Schuyler Chapin, *Musical Chairs* (New York: G. P. Putnam's Sons), 196.

17. See Arthur Miller to Schuman, October 22, 1964, and Schuman to Miller, January 27, 1965, LCPA, Box ID 090394, Folder "Miller, Arthur—Lincoln Center Repertory Theater, 1964–1965."

18. Kazan to Schuman, October 23, 1964, NYPL-A, 64/5.

19. Schuman to Kazan, November 2, 1964, NYPL-A, 64/5.

20. Rudolf Bing to Schuman, December 7, 1963, NYPL-A, 70/5.

21. Rockefeller to Schuman, December 31, 1963, NYPL-A, 81/8.

22. Chapin, *Musical Chairs*, 178. Chapin vividly recounts this entire episode in his memoirs in chap. 11, "Lincoln Center Festival," 170–204.

23. Chapin to Schuman, June 19, 1964, and June 29, 1964, NYPL-A, 56/3.

24. Chapin to Schuman, April 23, 1965, NYPL-A, 56/3.

25. Arno C. Zeyn to Young, December 9, 1964, LCPA, Box ID 090394, Folder "Metropolitan Opera—Miscellaneous General Matters, 1964–1968."

26. Schuman to Robert P. Wagner Jr., December 4, 1964, NYPL-A, 67/3.

27. Herman E. Krawitz to Robert L. Hoguet Jr., December 2, 1964, LCPA Box ID 090394, Folder "Personnel—"Coming/Going," 1962–1968." See also Krawitz's letter of the same date to Schuman in this folder.

28. See Anthony A. Bliss to Schuman, December 23, 1964, NYPL-A, 70/6; and Schuman to Abraham Friedman, January 6, 1965, NYPL-A, 16/13.

29. William Bender, "Now the Ballet Is Pulling Out of Lincoln Center," *New York Herald Tribune*, December 12, 1964, 8.

30. December 14, 1964 "WS Notes for Board Meeting," NYPL-A, 67/5.

31. See "Meeting of Messrs. Rockefeller, Schuman, Baum and Dr. Ronan," December 15, 1964, memorandum for the files, NYPL-A, 67/5.

32. Morton Gould to Schuman, January 5, 1965, and Schuman to Gould, January 7, 1965, NYPL-A, 59/11.

33. Schuman to Hauser, December 17, 1964, NYPL-A, 179/5.

34. Schuman to Clarence Francis, January 8, 1965, NYPL-A, 56/2.

35. Schuman to Abraham Friedman, January 6, 1965, NYPL-A, 16/13.

36. Schuman to Rockefeller, February 8, 1965, NYPL-A, 81/9.

37. See Lawrence P. Shea, M.D., to Frances Schuman, March 1, 1965, invoice, NYPL-A, 150/11.

38. The Bing and Krawitz notes are in NYPL-A, 70/6.

39. Mark Schubart to Schuman, February 7, 1963, NYPL-A, 84/1.

40. Schuman to Chapin, June 5, 1963, LCPA, Box ID 090394, Folder "Philharmonic Hall [Avery Fisher Hall]—Bookings, 1964–1968."

41. See the letters in NYPL-A, 58/1.

42. Schuman to Stanley Reed, October 10, 1963, NYPL-A, 58/2.

43. Schuman to Mennin, June 2, 1965, NYPL-A, 63/6. This letter is marked: Not Sent.

44. For Persichetti, see Schuman to David M. Keiser, October 23, 1961, JS, 7/10; for Goldman, see Schuman to Keiser, January 29, 1962, NYPL-A, 59/10; for Lloyd, see Schuman to Keiser, February 14, 1962, NYPL-A, 21/9; for Barzun, see Barzun to Schuman, April 16, 1962, NYPL-A, 6/5.

45. Schuman to Stuart Louchheim, August 20, 1965, NYPL-A, 78/3.

46. Minutes of the Board of Directors and Members of Lincoln Center, March 8, 1965, NYPL-A, 91/1.

47. November 16, 1965, press release by Peter D. Franklin, NYPL-A, 71/4. A portion of these remarks appeared in a newspaper story covering the Calder dedication; see Grace Glueck, "A 'Knockout' Ends Sculpture Fight," *New York Times*, November 16, 1965, 59. The Newbold Morris quotation comes from this article. See also Young, *Lincoln Center*, 188–93 (openings) and 212–18 (sculptures).

48. Schuman to Ormandy, December 11, 1964, NYPL-A, 78/3.

49. Schuman to Hauser, May 26, 1965, NYPL-A, 179/6.

50. As of this writing, this uncatalogued "manuscript" is in a large box of materials that Schuman's heirs sent to the Library of Congress after Schuman's death. Also included in the box are early works, such as the Canon and Fugue and the First Symphony, as well as late works, such as the 1985 *Dances* and the 1990 version of *The Lord Has a Child*.

51. See Harold C. Schonberg, "Park Crowd Gets Double Feature," *New York Times*, August 12, 1965, 29; and Richard D. Freed, "Steinberg Leads Concert in Rain," *New York Times*, August 14, 1965, 11.

52. Schuman to Carlos Moseley, February 25, 1966, NYPL-A, 75/2.

53. WS-Gruen, 42.

54. Schuman to Hauser, May 26, 1965, NYPL-A, 179/6.

55. Schuman to Virginia Katims, November 15, 1963, NYPL-A, 23/1.

56. WS-Gruen, 42–43.

57. Graham to Schuman, June 8, 1965, NYPL-A, 59/12.

58. Gertrude Macy to Schuman, June 22, 1965, and October 15, 1965, bill from Anthony Strilko for "The Witch of Endor by William Schuman," NYPL-A, 59/12.

59. Schuman to Graham, July 6, 1965, NYPL-A, 59/12.

60. Schuman to W. McNeil Lowry, August 18, 1965, NYPL-A, 59/12.

61. Schuman to John McClure, October 11, 1965, NYPL-A, 52/9.

62. WS-Gruen, 45.

63. Bertram Ross, in Robert Tracy, *Goddess: Martha Graham's Dancers Remember* (New York: Limelight Editions, 1997), 167.

64. Gus Solomons Jr., in Tracy, *Goddess*, 280.

65. Clive Barnes, "Dance: Martha Graham," *New York Times*, November 3, 1965, 43.

66. Tracy, *Goddess*, 287 n. 3.

67. Carlos Surinach to Schuman, November 4, 1965, NYPL-A, 83/3.

68. Vogel to Schuman, November 4, 1965, NYPL-A, 146/14.

69. Reis to Schuman, November 3, 1965, NYPL-A, 79/8.

70. Machlis to Schuman, November 7, 1965, NYPL-A, 69/5. See also Joseph Machlis, *The Enjoyment of Music: An Introduction to Perceptive Listening*, rev. ed. (New York: W. W. Norton, 1963), 642–44.

71. Schuman to Persichetti, November 23, 1965, NYPL-VP, 15/4. See also Schuman to Richard Killough, November 23, 1965, NYPL-A, 52/9.

72. Schuman to Killough, April 4, 1966, and November 4, 1966, NYPL-A, 52/10.

73. See Killough to Schuman, the April 22, 1966, and May 20, 1966, NYPL-A, 52/10.

74. This is an excerpt from p. 125 of the manuscript of *The Witch of Endor.*

75. Schuman to Boris Sokoloff, January 28, 1966, NYPL-A, 78/4.

76. The video of *The Witch of Endor* is in the archives of the Martha Graham Center of Contemporary Dance, 316 East Sixty-third Street, New York, NY 10065. I thank Bethany Roberge, center administrator, for giving me the opportunity to view the video.

The Witch of Endor inspired another musician to essay the same topic for Graham. Louis Thomas Hardin, who adopted the pseudonym Moondog, released his first third-stream album with Columbia in 1969. One of the pieces on that album is titled "The Witch of Endor." According to Moondog's original notes, "This piece is part of a ballet that I wrote for Martha Graham. It begins and ends in 5/4 time, danced by the witch. The trio consists of three parts: I. The witch's prophecy of Saul's death; 2. An idealized depiction of the battle on the mountain, and Saul, realizing he is losing it, decides to take his own life by falling on his own sword, held by a soldier; 3. The death of Saul." (See Moondog, liner notes for *Moondog/Moondog* 2, compact disc, BGO Records BGOCD510, [p. 10].) His biographer Robert Scotto, who finds the six-and-a-half-minute suite "somewhat academic and conventional," wrote that Moondog "was likely to have composed it around 1965, perhaps a little before or after" and that it may have been an original work or a repurposing of an existing piece. [Personal correspondence, July 24, 2009, with Robert Scotto, author of *Moondog, The Viking of 6th Avenue: The Authorized Biography* (New York: Process Media, 2007).] Moondog may have written his "Witch of Endor" for Martha Graham, but there is no evidence that Graham ever knew about Moondog's efforts or that Moondog made his score available to Graham. (Personal correspondence with Aaron Sherber, music director and conductor, Martha Graham Dance Company, January 16, 2009.) How Moondog came to know about *The Witch of Endor* is unclear, but it is doubtful that he stumbled upon the idea independently of Schuman's collaboration with Graham. I thank Karl Miller for making me aware of the connection between Moondog, Graham, and Schuman.

77. The quotation comes from Schuman to Tudor, October 2, 1978. See also Schuman to Tudor, January 4, 1979, and December 19, 1979, all NYPL-A, 118/8. The poem Tudor sent Schuman is not now identifiable.

78. WS-Gruen, 46.

79. WS-Gruen, 45–46.

80. Graham to Schuman, October 4, 1985, NYPL-A, 130/8.

81. Schuman to Graham, October 31, 1985, NYPL-A, 130/8.

82. Schuman to Helen Cowen, October 19, 1965, NYPL-A, 9/5.

83. Schuman to Young, December 19, 1962, LCPA, Box ID 090400, Folder "Philharmonic Hall [Avery Fisher Hall] Operations, 1961–1962"; and Schuman to Chapin, June 10, 1964, LCPA, Box ID 090394, Folder "New York State Theater—Operations, 1962–1964" (beards); Schuman to John W. Mazzola, November 15, 1965, NYPL-A, 70/2 (candles); Stephen R. Steinberg to Herbert Oppenheimer, November 18, 1964, LCPA, Box ID 090394, Folder "Office Space, 1962–1965" (offices).

84. See the correspondence between Blazhkov and Schuman, NYPL-A, 48/6.

85. See NYPL-A, 47/8, "American Recorded Music Society."

86. Schuman to Gerald Freund, December 12, 1963, LCPA, Box ID 090400, Folder "[The] Rockefeller Foundation, 1963–1964" (composers-in-residence); Schuman to Benjamin Boretz, October 21, 1963, NYPL-A, 77/8 (the avant-garde).

87. Schuman to Schubart, January 22, 1964, and Schubart to Schuman, January 24, 1964 (on which Schuman wrote to Young: "Ed–My j-o-k-e worked! Please return. WS"), NYPL-A, 67/5.

88. "William Schuman and His Music," Program Information for WNDT-13, September 22, 1965, NYPL-A, 55/5.

Chapter 25: "The Potemkin Center"

1. See Barbara Heyman, *Samuel Barber* (New York: Oxford University Press), 428–60.

2. Schuman to Barber, June 1, 1964, NYPL-A, 49/1. Heyman quoted all but the first sentence of the letter; see *Samuel Barber*, 434.

3. Schuman to Anthony A. Bliss and Rudolf Bing, January 10, 1966, NYPL-A, 70/6.

4. Allen Hughes, "Radio. U.S. Heard Premiere of Met," *New York Times*, September 17, 1966, R15.

5. Heyman, *Samuel Barber*, 428.

6. Harold C. Schonberg, "Music: After It All Was Over," *New York Times*, September 25, 1966, D17.

7. Jacqueline Kennedy to Schuman, November 1, 1966, NYPL-A, 64/2.

8. See Schuman to Copland, February 10, 1967, NYPL-A, 53/6.

9. Minutes of the Lincoln Center Council Meeting, January 17, 1966, NYPL-A, 66/3.

10. Richard F. Shepard, "World Arts Festival Planned Here in '67," *New York Times*, June 15, 1966, 1; "Schuman Remark Irritates Expo '67," *New York Times*, June 20, 1966, 19; and Milton Esterow, "Viennese Slate U.S. Concert Tour," *New York Times*, June 23, 1966, 30. The

writer of the June 20 story was Charles Lazarus, a stringer who did not disclose his sources and used innuendo to make Schuman look bad. See Jack deSimone to John W. McNulty, June 24, 1966, NYPL-A, 56/3.

11. Schuman to Irving Kolodin, February 13, 1967, and Kolodin to Schuman, February 17, 1967, NYPL-A, 83/7.

12. Minutes of the Executive Committee of Lincoln Center, June 23, 1964, NYPL-A, 90/4.

13. Jack deSimone to Tom Mathews, August 1, 1966, NYPL-A, 56/3.

14. Minutes of the Executive Committee of Lincoln Center, February 14, 1966, NYPL-A, 91/2.

15. Minutes of the Executive Committee of Lincoln Center, March 13, 1967, NYPL-A 91/3. See also Schuman to Hubert H. Humphrey, March 20, 1967, NYPL-A, 56/4.

16. Schuman to deSimone, March 15, 1967, and Richard M. Rosen to Schuman, March 22, 1967, NYPL-A, 74/5.

17. "Memorandum for the Files," December 20, 1966, NYPL-A, 89/2; and Joseph C. Wilson to Schuman, January 20, 1967, NYPL-A, 56/3.

18. Howard L. Clark, president of American Express, to Schuman, February 28, 1967, NYPL-A, 47/5.

19. Hoyt Ammidon to Henry Ford II, February 7, 1968, and Schuman to Gianluigi Gabetti, president of the Olivetti Underwood Corporation, April 8, 1968, NYPL-A, 56/7; Schuman to Hoyt Ammidon (re: Pan American Airlines), October 4, 1967, NYPL-A, 47/3; and Robert M. McElwaine to John O'Keefe (re: Mercedes-Benz of North America), June 27, 1967, NYPL-A, 56/4.

20. Minutes of the Executive Committee of Lincoln Center, March 30, 1965, NYPL-A, 91/1.

21. Minutes of the Executive Committee of Lincoln Center, October 9, 1967, NYPL-A, 91/3.

22. Schuman to Chapin, February 1, 1967, NYPL-A, 56/5.

23. Schuman to Olga Koussevitzky, May 5, 1967, and Abraham Friedman to Schuman, June 28, 1967, NYPL-A, 56/5.

24. Anthony Tommasini mistakenly stated that the Lincoln Center Festival's inaugural summer was 1996. See Tommasini, "Festival Doesn't Sound Very Musical This Time," *New York Times*, June 28, 2009. For more on the lack of underwriting for the festivals specifically and Lincoln Center's financial period generally, see Howard Taubman, "Lincoln Center Reorganizing in Crisis," *New York Times*, January 14, 1969, 39.

25. Schuyler Chapin, *Musical Chairs* (New York: G. P. Putnam's Sons, 1977), 203.

26. Schuman to Alicia Smith, October 29, 1963, NYPL-A, 85/3.

27. Schuman to Alicia Smith, January 28, 1966, NYPL-A, 77/1.

28. Schuman to Arthur A. Hauser, February 15, 1966, NYPL-A, 77/1.

29. Schuman to Harold Weill, November 25, 1972 ($75,000 figure), and undated proposal, ca. spring 1972, "Project 1976" ($125,000 figure), NYPL-A, 147/10.

30. Schuman to Shirley Gould, June 22, 1966, NYPL-A, 59/11; and Schuman to Gregg Smith, June 28, 1966, NYPL-A, 85/3.

31. Schuman to Charles M. Spofford, August 10, 1966, NYPL-A, 85/8.

32. Schuman to Alicia Smith, September 8, 1966, NYPL-A, 77/1.

33. Schuman to Alicia Smith, June 21, 1967, NYPL-A, 77/1.

34. Schuman to Carlisle H. Humelsine, February 6, 1968, NYPL-A, 77/1.

35. Minutes of the Executive Committee of Lincoln Center, March 31, 1966, NYPL-A, 91/2.

36. Schuman to Donald L. Engle, April 1, 1966, and Engle to Schuman, July 7, 1966, NYPL-A, 71/7.

37. William W. Lockwood Jr. to Schuman, September 9, 1966, NYPL-A, 71/7.

38. T. E. Kalem to Schuman, April 13, 1966, NYPL-A, 80/4.

39. "Memorandum for the Files," December 13, 1966, NYPL-A, 80/4.

40. Milton Esterow, "Herbert Blau Quits Lincoln Repertory," *New York Times*, January 14, 1967, 1.

41. Hoyt Ammidon to Schuman, March 7, 1967, NYPL-A, 72/4.

42. Schuman to Ammidon, February 24, 1967, NYPL-A, 72/4. Also in this folder are Schuman's draft letter of the same day; Ammidon's February 28, 1967, letter to Rodgers; and Rodgers's March 2, 1967, reaction letter to Schuman.

43. See William F. Powers to Carl A. Morse, February 10, 1966, and Schuman's March 27, 1967, "Confidential Memorandum," LCPA, Box ID 090393, Folder "Juilliard School—Building, 1963–1968."

44. See especially: Schuman to Peter Mennin, October 5, 1967, NYPL-A, 62/6; and Schuman to John W. Drye Jr., October 10, 1967, NYPL-A, 63/2.

45. Schuman to William F. May, June 29, 1967, NYPL-A, 57/7.

46. See Martin E. Segal to Schuman, December 1, 1975, NYPL-A, 116/9; and Schuman to May, March 23, 1980, NYPL-A, 135/2.

47. Alice Fox Pitts, ed., "Problems of Journalism: Proceedings of the 1961 Convention [of the] American Society of Newspaper Editors," Statler Hilton Hotel, Washington, D.C., April 20–22, 1961. Schuman's remarks are on pp. 124–28.

48. William Schuman, "The Arts in Our Colleges," delivered November 18, 1962, reprinted in *Dartmouth Alumni Magazine* 55, 4 (January 1963): 16–17.

49. Henry E. Bessire to Schuman, October 14, 1966, NYPL-A, 79/1.

50. "The New Establishment," address by William Schuman at the Princeton University conference "The Performing Arts: Their Economic Problems," December 8–9, 1966, Princeton, NJ. An offprint of the speech is in NYPL-A, 183/13.

51. For an overview of the term, see Henry Fairlie, "Evolution of a Term," *New Yorker*, October 19, 1968, 173–206.

52. Schuman to Rockefeller, December 13, 1966, NYPL-A, 81–89.

53. John D. Rockefeller III diary entry for December 23, 1966, RFA, 11/79.

54. Rockefeller to Schuman, December 30, 1966, and Schuman's "Memo for the Files," January 9, 1967, AWS. According to the memo, Schuman met with Rockefeller on January 4, 1967, to discuss the year-end letter.

55. On the use of the word "retirement," see Schuman to James A. Barthelmess, February 20, 1970, NYPL-A, 146/15; and Schuman to Tikhon Khrennikov, September 22, 1971,

NYPL-A, 147/6. For its medical coverage ramifications, see Schuman to Martin E. Segal, January 27, 1983, NYPL-A, 141/10.

56. Rockefeller to Schuman, December 30, 1966, AWS.

57. Schuman, "Memo for the Files," January 9, 1967, AWS.

58. Schuman to Rockefeller, January 12, 1967, NYPL-A, 81/10.

59. See "Memorandum for the Files," January 30, 1967, NYPL-A, 74/5; and "Memorandum for the Files," March 31, 1967, NYPL-A, 81/10.

60. "Friends of Kennedy Center Speech," May 19, 1967, NYPL-A, 64/7.

61. Rockefeller to Schuman, February 22, 1967, LCPA Box ID 090400, Folder "Rockefeller, John D. 3rd, 1962–1964, 1967–1968."

62. Schuman to Alice Tully, February 28, 1967, AWS.

63. Schuman to Rockefeller, March 2, 1967, LCPA, Box ID 090400, Folder "Rockefeller, John D. 3rd, 1962–1964, 1967–1968."

64. "Memorandum for the Files," March 31, 1967, NYPL-A, 81/10.

65. "Memorandum for the Files," March 6, 1967, and "Memorandum for the Files," March 31, 1967, NYPL-A, 81/10.

66. Young, *Lincoln Center*, 292.

67. See Schuman to Henry E. Bessire and John W. Mazzola, May 1, 1967, and Schuman to Rockefeller, June 6, 1967, NYPL-A, 81/10. Also see Young to Rockefeller, July 24, 1967, LCPA, Box ID 090398, Folder "Board of Directors, 1962–1967," in which Young stated that programming and institutional development accounted for one-third of the Lincoln Center budget.

68. Henry Bessire, "Oral History Interview with Henry Bessire," Sharon Zane, interviewer, July 3, 1991, Oral History Project, LCPA, 54.

Chapter 26: "The Death of the Dreamers"

1. Schuman to Halsey Stevens, February 9, 1965, NYPL-A, 83/2.

2. "Bernstein Lists Season's Music," *New York Times*, April 28, 1965: 38.

3. William Schuman, "Higher Education and the Avant-Garde," speech given at Sarah Lawrence College, May 9, 1965. A transcript of the speech is in NYPL-A, 183/1.

4. William Schuman, introduction to *The Orchestral Composer's Point of View*, ed. Robert Stephan Hines (Norman: University of Oklahoma Press, 1970), 8–9.

5. Schuman to Arthur A. Hauser, May 9, 1963, NYPL-A, 179/4.

6. Harold Blumenfeld to Schuman, November 18, 1962; Schuman to Elizabeth Gentry, February 7, 1963; and Schuman to Elizabeth Gentry Sayad, May 4, 1964, all in NYPL-A, 148/1.

7. Schuman to Hauser, May 26, 1965, NYPL-A, 179/6.

8. Schuman to Paul Glass, November 5, 1964, and Glass to Schuman, November 8, 1964, NYPL-B, Box "Annotated Published and MS Scores," Folder "Gateway to the West" 1964.

9. Schuman to Calvert Bean Jr., October 5, 1965, NYPL-A, 179/6.

10. Schuman to R. D. Brown, October 4, 1967, NYPL-A, 79/4.

11. Schuman to William Shea, October 11, 1967, NYPL-A, 82/7.

12. Schuman to Sayad, October 9, 1967, NYPL-A, 144/10.

13. Alexander Hilsberg to Schuman, May 3, 1957, NYPL-A, 31/3.

14. Edward B. Benjamin to Schuman, undated, JS, 1/9. Schuman answered on October 29, 1959.

15. Schuman to Hilsberg, May 7, 1957, NYPL-A, 31/3.

16. Ormandy to Schuman, April 27, 1962, NYPL-A, 78/4.

17. Ray Moremen et al., "In Quest of Answers: An Interview with William Schuman," *Choral Journal* 13 (February 1973): 9.

18. Sol Schoenbach to Schuman, May 24, 1962, NYPL-A, 78/4. For Schuman's vacillation and ultimate acceptance, see the early May 1962 Schuman-Ormandy correspondence in this folder.

19. Schuman to Ormandy, September 22, 1961; Ormandy to Schuman, September 26, 1961; Schuman to Ormandy, September 28, 1961, NYPL-A, 34/6.

20. Schuman to Ormandy, January 27, 1964, NYPL-A, 78/4.

21. Schuman to Richard Killough, November 23, 1965, NYPL-A, 52/9.

22. Schuman to Ormandy, June 12, 1967, NYPL-A, 145/4.

23. Ormandy to Eric Bromberger, September 27, 1965, NYPL-A, 78/3.

24. Ormandy to Hauser, February 4, 1966, NYPL-A, 77/1.

25. "Ormandy Selects Bernstein to Write Bicentennial Piece," *New York Times*, January 12, 1968, 21. The clipping is in NYPL-A, 77/7.

26. Schuman to Hugo Weisgall, June 16, 1967, NYPL-A, 146/8.

27. Nathalie Weisgall to Schuman, August 3, 1967, NYPL-A, 146/8.

28. *The Blue Guides: Rome and Central Italy*, ed. L. Russel Muirhead (London: Ernest Benn, 1956), 224. In her August 3, 1967, letter to Schuman (NYPL-A, 146/8), Nathalie Weisgall did not include the last sentence.

29. Nathalie Weisgall to Schuman, August 3, 1967, NYPL-A, 146/8. Two-dot ellipses are in the original.

30. Schuman to Nathalie Weisgall, August 31, 1967, NYPL-A, 146/8.

31. Hugo Weisgall to Schuman, September 7, 1967, NYPL-A, 146/8.

32. Schuman to Robert S. Hines, August 24, 1967, Robert Hines Papers, JPB 06–35, 5/1, NYPL; and Schuman to Hauser, September 29, 1967, NYPL-A, 78/9.

33. Schuman to Ormandy, February 21, 1968, NYPL-A, 78/9.

34. Schuman to Fred Sherry, June 4, 1990, NYPL-C, "Correspondence C, 1990."

35. Schuman to Igor Stravinsky, February 10, 1965, NYPL-A, 83/3.

36. Stanley Wolfe to Schuman, October 7, 1967, NYPL-A, 88/11.

37. Sol Schoenbach to Schuman, April 23, 1968, NYPL-A, 82/6.

38. William Schuman Symphony No. 9, Le Fosse Ardeatine, Program Notes for Philadelphia Orchestra, dated November 19, 1968, NYPL-A, 146/9.

39. Nathalie Weisgall to Schuman, August 3, 1967, NYPL-A, 146/8. Two-and three-dot ellipses are in the original.

40. Schuman to Hauser, March 6, 1968, NYPL-A, 78/9.

41. Ormandy to Schuman, October 3, 1968, NYPL-A, 146/8.

42. Ormandy to Schuman, March 19, 1969, NYPL-A, 78/3.

43. Schuman to Sheila Keats, June 11, 1971, NYPL-A, 103/5.

44. Schuman to Hauser, March 6, 1968, NYPL-A, 78/9.

45. See the entries for March 26 and 27 in the 1967 Desk Diary (Black), NYPL-A, 156.

46. See http://www.usarmyband.com/herald_trumpets/the_us_army_herald_trumpets.html, accessed August 17, 2009.

47. Schuman to Major Gilbert H. Mitchell, Jr., April 24, 1968, NYPL-A, 144/10.

48. Max Frankel, "Humphrey Gains Missouri Votes," *New York Times*, May 26, 1968, 58. In his book on the Gateway Arch, W. Arthur Mehrhoff failed to note the cancelation of most of the ceremony. See *The Gateway Arch: Fact and Symbol* (Bowling Green, OH: Bowling Green State University Popular Press, 1992), 82.

49. Gillian Schacht to Schuman, May 27, 1968, NYPL-A, 144/10.

50. Sayad to Schuman, July 9, 1968, NYPL-A, 144/10. For the 750,000 figure, see Schuman to C. A. Wiley, October 2, 1970, NYPL-A, 111/9.

51. Schuman to Calvert Bean Jr., September 4, 1968, NYPL-A, 78/9.

52. Carlos Moseley to Schuman, August 9, 1966, NYPL-A, 75/2.

53. Schuman to Moseley, December 16, 1966, NYPL-A, 75/2.

54. Schuman to Bernstein, July 13, 1968, NYPL-A, 146/11.

55. For Bernstein's antiwar views, see Barry Seldes, *Leonard Bernstein: The Political Life of an American Musician* (Berkeley: University of California Press, 2009), 110–14.

56. See the letters from Anne Hobler (October 6, 1968, NYPL-A, 83/5), Robert Rudié (October 10, 1968, NYPL-A, 79/6), and Vincent Persichetti (October 19, 1968, NYPL-A, 78/2).

57. Schuman to Robert B. Sour, October 28, 1968, NYPL-A, 50/4.

58. "Robert J. Burton, B.M.I.'s President," *New York Times*, March 30, 1965, 47.

59. Schuman to Sydney M. Kaye, April 15, 1965, NYPL-A, 50/2.

Chapter 27: "The Death of the Dream"

1. "Memorandum for the Files," March 31, 1967, NYPL-A, 81/10.

2. Schuman to Rockefeller, June 6, 1967, NYPL-A, 81/10.

3. "Notes of conversation with Mr. Ammidon following meeting about Programming," June 23, 1967, NYPL-A, 47/3 (also NYPL-A, 67/6).

4. Edgar Young, *Lincoln Center* (New York: New York University Press, 1980), 296.

5. Ibid., 282–304.

6. Schuman to Ormandy, May 13, 1968, NYPL-A, 77/7.

7. See "Statement of Claim for Group Health Insurance Benefits," May 23, 1968, NYPL-A, 55/8.

8. He mentioned his "heart attack" in OHAM and S-W. The May 1, 1970, "Group Insurance Enrollment Card and Health Statement" (NYPL-A, 121/3) carries the notation "May 1968 acute coronary insufficiency with no evidence of infarction." See also Clarence Francis to Schuman, June 10, 1968, NYPL-A, 56/2; Ferd Nauheim to Schuman, December

9, 1968, and Schuman to Nauheim, December 11, 1968, NYPL-A, 80/9; and Richard F. Shepard, "Schuman Quitting Lincoln Center Post," *New York Times*, December 5, 1968, 61.

9. Personal correspondence with Andrea Schuman, March 28, 2008.

10. See Frank E. Taplin to the Chamber Music Society Exploratory Committee, December 26, 1968, NYPL-A, 51/8.

11. See Schuman's annotations on the January 6, 1969, "Minutes of Meeting of the Board of Directors and Members" and the January 21, 1969, "Minutes of Meeting of the Executive Committee," NYPL-A, 91/5.

12. November 1, 1968, memorandum from Schuyler G. Chapin to Schuman, NYPL-A 68/2.

13. November 12, 1968, "Minutes of Meeting of the Executive Committee," NYPL-A, 91/4.

14. Chapin to Schuman, November 13, 1968, and Schuman's same-day response, NYPL-A, 52/1.

15. S. Hurok to Schuman, November 25, 1968, NYPL-A, 67/6.

16. For more on Festival '70, see NYPL-A, 56/9.

17. Minutes of the Lincoln Center Council Meeting, December 18, 1968, NYPL-A, 66/4.

18. Howard Taubman, "Lincoln Center Reorganizing in Crisis," *New York Times*, January 14, 1969, 39.

19. Rockefeller, diary entry for November 14, 1968, RFA-2, 12/81.

20. Rockefeller, diary entry for November 21, 1968, RFA-2, 12/81.

21. For the resignation letter drafts, see NYPL-A, 80/8.

22. See Margaret E. Mahoney to various, December 4, 1968, and Mahoney's "Record of Interview: Subject: Lincoln Center for the Performing Arts: Proposed Education Study," December 10, 1968, CCNY, 658/4. Other materials in this folder cover this grant from the Carnegie Corporation. For Schuman's remarks, see Shepard, "Schuman Quitting," 61.

23. Schuman to various, December 10, 1968, NYPL-A, 80/9.

24. "Lincoln Center Choral Festival" (for the files), April 1, 1969, NYPL-A, 147/6.

25. "Cultural Centers: Wanted: A Fiscal Wizard," *Time*, December 13, 1968, 67.

26. Young, *Lincoln Center*, 300.

27. Amyas Ames, "Oral History Interview with Amyas Ames," Sharon Zane, interviewer, October 17, 1990, Oral History Project, LCPA, 41–42 and 56.

28. Schuman to Ames, January 5, 1978, and Ames to Schuman, January 12, 1978, NYPL-A, 105/3.

Chapter 28: "The Administrator Reinvents Himself"

1. Schuman to Rockefeller, December 31, 1968, NYPL-A, 80/8.
2. Marshall Bartholomew to Schuman, December 31, 1968, NYPL-A, 80/9.
3. Schuman to John Vincent, December 20, 1968, NYPL-A, 80/9.
4. Schuman to Arthur A. Hauser, January 17, 1969, NYPL-A, 146/9.

5. Schuman to David and Sylvia Keiser, June 10, 1970, NYPL-S, 103/1.

6. Schuman to Gail Kubik, March 25, 1969, NYPL-A, 51/6.

7. James P. Warburg to Schuman, July 22, 1965, NYPL-A, 88/1.

8. Donal Henahan, "Schuman Now Basking in 'Total Sunshine,'" *New York Times*, January 28, 1970, 43.

9. Herbert Barrett to Richard Franko Goldman, June 20, 1969, NYPL-A, 113/6. In a letter to Eddie and Margie Marks (March 9, 1970), Schuman told them that "I have been writing music, lecturing and preparing my memoirs. . . . I've just come back from the Midwest for lectures." NYPL-A, 107/8.

10. William Schuman, "Oral History Interview with William Schuman," Sharon Zane, interviewer, July 10, 1990, Oral History Project, LCPA, 9.

11. Schuman to John F. White, October 8, 1968, NYPL-A, 73/2.

12. Schuman to Peter Herman Adler, March 13, 1969, NYPL-A, 73/2.

13. For more on Cousins, see the Schuman-Cousins correspondence, NYPL-A, 108/7–9; for more on Seaborg, see Schuman to Glenn T. Seaborg, April 28, 1970, NYPL-A, 92/1.

14. Schuman to Peter G. Peterson, December 17, 1970, NYPL-A, 114/1.

15. Ward B. Chamberlin Jr. to Schuman, October 6, 1970, and Schuman to Chamberlin, October 26, 1970, NYPL-A, 108/8. See also Schuman's June 1, 1970, memorandum in this folder, in which he outlines the contours of the consolidation of NET and Channel 13.

16. Schuman to David Oppenheim, dean of the School of the Arts, New York University, March 4, 1969, NYPL-A, 76/7.

17. Schuman "for the files," April 3, 1969, NYPL-A, 76/7.

18. William D. Revelli to Schuman, May 2, 1969, Correspondence, Box 2, William D. Revelli Papers, Bentley Historical Library, University of Michigan; and May 16, 1969 letter from Robert S. Hines to Schuman, Robert Hines Papers, JPB 06–35, 5/1, NYPL. I thank Danielle Fosler-Lussier for making me aware of the Schuman-Revelli correspondence at the University of Michigan.

19. Cliff Christians, "Home Video Systems: A Revolution?" *Journal of Broadcasting* 17, 2 (Spring 1973): 223.

20. Autobiography, chap. 11, p. 34.

21. "Dr. Schuman Heads Electronic Concern," *New York Times*, March 3, 1970, 83.

22. Alan M. Kriegsman, "From Lincoln Center to Video Tape Cassettes—With Gusto," *Washington Post*, October 25, 1970, H1.

23. Schuman to Abbott Kaplan, August 14, 1970, NYPL-A, 121/8.

24. David E. Moore, "Videorecord's Dr. Hopwood Calls for Innovation," *Southern Connecticut Business Journal*, October 27, 1970, 20.

25. Schuman to Stafford L. Hopwood Jr., May 6, 1970, NYPL-A, 121/7. See also Schuman to Mike Dann, January 12, 1971, and the 11-page report "A Proposal to Adapt Sesame Street Programming for Videorecords," NYPL-A, 121/4.

26. Mark Schubart to Bertrand M. Lanchner, September 9, 1971, NYPL-A, 122/5; and Minutes of the VCA Board of Directors, September 14, 1971, NYPL-A, 120/3.

27. Schuman to S. Dillon Ripley, May 21, 1971, NYPL-A, 122/8.

28. "Summary of Qualified Stock Option Plan," August 1, 1970, NYPL-A, 120/2.

29. Schuman to Arnold Broido, March 11, 1971, NYPL-A, 111/9.

30. Henahan, "'Total Sunshine,'" 43.

31. William Schuman, "Lincoln Center Book," September 30, 1969, p. 2. The document is marked, in Schuman's hand, "Rough Draft I." AWS.

32. Schuman to Elia Kazan, undated letter draft, NYPL-C, "Correspondence K, 1988."

33. Minutes of the Exploratory Committee for Chamber Music at Lincoln Center, January 8, 1969, NYPL-A, 51/9.

34. "Lincoln Center to Get New Music Unit," *New York Times*, February 24, 1969, 32.

35. January 13, 1969, unsent memorandum from Schuman to the Exploratory Committee for Chamber Music at Lincoln Center, NYPL-A, 101/2. He also called the committee's actions "ill-considered in content and most unfortunate in form." See also Amyas Ames to Alice Tully, January 12, 1969, NYPL-A, 51/9, in which Ames expressed his concerns that "the 'Resident Artist Concept' may not work and may lead the Society into deep trouble." Schuman was very much in favor of the Resident Artist Concept.

36. Mark Schubart to William Bergsma et al., May 15, 1962, JS-Comm.

37. Details on the commissions can be found in JS-Comm. An undated list contains the following composers (strikethroughs in the original): Barber, Berio, ~~Bernstein~~, Boulez, Carter, Farberman, ~~Ginastera~~, Kay, ~~Kirchner~~, Overton, Penderecki, Persichetti, Petrassi, Rochberg, ~~Schuller, Schuman~~, Searle, Sessions, ~~Shchedrin~~, Wolfe, Wolpe. Other lists have fewer composers on them.

38. Schuman to Peter Mennin, March 8, 1966, and Mennin to Schuman, March 11, 1966, JS-Comm.

39. Martin Mayer, "New York's Monument to the Muses," *Horizon* 4, 6 (July 1962): 11.

40. Martin Mayer, "Are the Trying Times Just Beginning?" *New York Times*, September 28, 1969, D17, D20.

41. Schuman to Mary Hunting Smith, October 10, 1969, NYPL-A, 94/7.

42. Abraham Friedman to Mennin, October 3, 1969, AWS.

43. Schuman to Seymour Peck (*New York Times*), October 14, 1969, AWS.

44. "William Schuman Protests a 'Completely False History,'" *New York Times*, October 26, 1969, D29; and George Gent, "Juilliard School Dedication Marks Completion of Lincoln Center," *New York Times*, October 27, 1969, 1, 57.

45. OHAM, 331, 355.

46. William Schuman, "Lincoln Center Book," September 30, 1969, 3–4, AWS.

47. "William Schuman Protests a 'Completely False History.'"

48. Edward Wardwell to Schuman, February 2, 1970, NYPL-A, 105/2.

49. Schuman to Mennin, February 20, 1970, NYPL-A, 105/4.

50. Schuman to Mennin, September 26, 1969, NYPL-A, 105/4.

51. Schuman to Francis Thorne, June 25, 1971, NYPL-A, 109/5. See OHAM, 349–58, for Schuman's account of his relationship with Mennin.

52. William Schuman, birthday tribute for Aaron Copland, November 14, 1970. Schuman actually wrote the tribute by June of that year. See both the tribute and Schuman's June 25,

1970, letter to Claire Reis, NYPL-A, 98/7. For the responses to Schuman's role in the Copland celebration, see the letters from Carlos Moseley (November 17, 1970; NYPL-A, 109/7); Copland himself (November 21, 1970; NYPL-A, 98/6); and Minna Lederman Daniel (November 27, 1970; NYPL-A, 98/15: she was especially critical of the commercialism as well as insightful on the role Reis played in Copland's career). See also Schuman to Stuart Pope of Boosey & Hawkes, December 7, 1970, NYPL-A, 98/7.

53. Bridget Falconer-Salkeld, *The MacDowell Colony: A Musical History of America's Premier Artists' Colony* (Lanham, MD: Scarecrow Press, 2005), 112–13; and Copland and Perlis, *Copland since 1943* (New York: St. Martin's Press, 1989), 323.

54. "Medal Day," http://www.macdowellcolony.org/md.html, accessed August 27, 2009.

55. William Schuman, Address for the MacDowell Medal, August 8, 1971, NYPL-A, 184/11.

56. Schuman to Russell Lynes, August 19, 1971, NYPL-A, 106/5.

57. Copland to Schuman, September 7, 1971, NYPL-A, 98/6.

58. The criticism of Schuman's draft is found in M. J. Rossant to Schuman, August 18, 1969, NYPL-B, Folder "Twentieth Century Fund Study (1969) 2 of 3." For his decision not to complete the study, see Schuman to John E. Booth (whence the quotation comes), April 28, 1970, Booth to Schuman, May 4, 1970, and Rossant to Schuman, May 11, 1970, NYPL-A, 118/1.

59. Schuman to Stafford L. Hopwood Jr., February 12, 1971, NYPL-A, 121/7. The 47-page report "Music in Puerto Rico: The Next Decade (1972–1982)" is dated March 15, 1971, and is in NYPL-A, 95/12.

60. Marta Casals Istomin to Schuman, March 15, 1977, NYPL-A, 102/7.

61. Schuman to The Hon. William P. Rogers, May 12, 1969, NYPL-A, 102/12.

62. John Richardson Jr. to Schuman, April 3, 1970, NYPL-A, 102/12.

63. Schuman to Akeo Watanabe, April 28, 1970, NYPL-A, 102/12.

64. Schuman to Marks, March 9, 1970, NYPL-A, 107/8.

65. William Schuman, introduction to *The Orchestral Composer's Point of View*, ed. Robert Stephan Hines (Norman: University of Oklahoma Press, 1970), 5–7. See also Ray Moremen et al., "In Quest of Answers: An Interview with William Schuman," *Choral Journal* 13 (February 1973): 5.

66. Donald P. Berger, "On the Tokyo Music Scene: Interview With U.S. Composer William Schuman." unidentified paper. The clipping is in NYPL-A, 102/12. In a May 14, 1970, letter to Berger (also in this folder), Schuman called the write-up of the interview "excellent."

67. Edward Kleban to Schuman, January 25, 1971, and Schuman to Naomi Thaler, February 3, 1971, NYPL-A, 113/1. See also the June 1967 correspondence between Schuman and Richard Rodgers about Kleban, NYPL-A, 72/4.

68. Walt Whitman, "Democratic Vistas" (source volume, 1871; electronic edition, Cambridge: Chadwyck-Healey, 1999), 76.

Chapter 29: "The Composer Reasserts Himself"

1. "Mixing Business and Art," *Business Week*, August 3, 1963, 45.

2. Schuman to Eugene Moon, June 11, 1971, NYPL-A, 111/9.

3. Schuman to Arnold Broido, November 23, 1971, NYPL-A, 11/9.

4. Ray Moremen et al., "In Quest of Answers: An Interview with William Schuman," *Choral Journal* 13 (February 1973): 9.

5. Schuman to Minna Lederman Daniel, December 7, 1970, NYPL-A, 98/15.

6. Schuman to Boris Sokoloff, March 18, 1969, NYPL-A, 146/10. For the underwriting of the recording, see Schuman to Roger Hall, February 20, 1969, NYPL-A, 79/6.

7. Memorandum for the files, April 1, 1969, NYPL-A, 146/10.

8. On the possible couplings, see Schuman to Broido, March 26, 1971, NYPL-A, 111/9. Schuman wrote to Copland to say, among other things, "Ormandy recorded the Ninth two years ago last May but RCA Victor has yet to release it." (August 19, 1971, NYPL-A, 98/6.) See also Carol Oja, ed., *American Music Recordings: A Discography of 20th-Century U.S. Composers* (Brooklyn, NY: Institute for Studies in American Music, 1982), 269.

9. Jerome F. Weber, "A William Schuman Discography," *Journal of the Association for Recorded Sound Collections* 8 (September 1976): 81. For a review of the recording, see Lester Trimble, "Two Ninths by Two Contemporary Americans," *Stereo Review* 28, 2 (April 1972): 70–71.

10. Donal Henahan, "Schuman Now Basking in 'Total Sunshine,'" *New York Times*, January 28, 1970, 43.

11. William Schuman, program notes, reprinted in *In Praise of Shahn: Canticle for Orchestra* (Bryn Mawr, PA: Merion Music, 1971), iv.

12. Martin Bressler to Schuman, May 7, 1969, NYPL-A, 53/2. For the recording costs for the Ninth Symphony, see Schuman to Boris Sokoloff, March 18, 1969, NYPL-A, 146/10; for the commission for *To Thee Old Cause*, see Carlos Moseley to Schuman, August 9, 1966, NYPL-A, 75/2.

13. Schuman to Thomas P. F. Hoving, May 28, 1969, NYPL-A, 144/15. For the choice of composers, see Schuman to Nathan Einhorn, November 20, 1969, NYPL-A, 104/8.

14. Schuman to Walter Piston, October 24, 1969, NYPL-A, 144/15. See also Grace Glueck, "Metropolitan Museum Opens Big Centennial Show," *New York Times*, October 17, 1969, 37.

15. Schuman to Calvert Bean Jr., September 5, 1969, NYPL-A, 111/9. In her coverage of the celebration, Grace Glueck did not mention the fanfare. See her "For Museum Birthday, Good Cheer and Cake," *New York Times*, April 14, 1970, 52.

16. Raymond Ericson, "Salvos from Rooftops," *New York Times*, November 2, 1969, D19.

17. Moishe Bressler to Schuman, undated, and Schuman to Bressler, August 7, 1969, NYPL-A, 144/13.

18. Schuman to Bean, September 5, 1969, NYPL-A, 111/9.

19. Raymond Ericson, "Shahn's Portrait Painted in Music," *New York Times*, January 30, 1970, 29.

20. Miles Kastendieck, "Carter, Schuman Works Receive World Premieres," *Christian Science Monitor*, February 11, 1970, 6.

21. Jerome F. Weber, "A William Schuman Discography," *Journal of the Association for Recorded Sound Collections* 8 (September 1976): 81. Weber states that the recording was done in February 1970 and that the LP was released in December 1970.

22. Schuman to Stuart Louchheim, October 17, 1969, NYPL-A, 145/9.

23. A score of the Variations can be found in NYPL-A, 90/1. The composers who submitted variations are Barber, Theodor Berger, Bernstein, Copland, Creston, Dello Joio, Diamond, von Einem, Finney, Nicolas Nabokov, Orff, Persichetti, Piston, Rochberg, Rózsa, Schuman, Sessions, Thomson, and Zádor.

24. Samuel Barber to Schuman, June 12, 1951, and July 30, 1951, NYPL-A, 6/3.

25. The score, marked "For Mary Curtis Zimbalist" and dated August 6, 1951, is in NYPL-A, 142/9.

26. Schuman to Barber, September 17, 1951, NYPL-A, 6/3.

27. The Schubart "Happy Birthday" is in LoC-WS-Z.

28. Schuman to Broido, September 9, 1970, and Broido to Schuman, September 11, 1970, NYPL-A, 111/9.

29. Personal communication with W. Douglas Pritchard, January 13, 2010.

30. *1897 Sears Roebuck Catalogue*, introductions by S. J. Perelman and Richard Rovere, ed. Fred L. Israel (New York: Chelsea House Publishers, 1968). See pp. 32, 34, and 45 for the ads Schuman used for his texts.

31. Schuman to Pritchard, August 3, 1971, NYPL-A, 147/4.

32. Pritchard to Schuman, March 3, 1972, NYPL-A, 147/7.

33. Schuman to Thomas D. Perry Jr., February 28, 1972, NYPL-A, 94/7.

34. See also Schuman to Bean, July 22, 1971, NYPL-A, 111/9.

35. Schuman to John Boatner, July 3, 1986, NYPL-A, 139/2.

36. Schuman to Tikhon Khrennikov, September 22, 1971, NYPL-A, 147/6.

37. Pritchard to Schuman, March 3, 1972, NYPL-A, 147/7.

38. James R. Bjorge to Schuman, May 19, 1972, NYPL-A, 147/6.

39. Robert Sherman, "Choirs from 16 Countries Stir Audience at Festival Finale," *New York Times*, May 2, 1972, 50.

40. Schuman to Bean, July 22, 1971, NYPL-A, 111/9.

41. Paul Kwartin to Schuman, May 10, 1971, NYPL-A, 148/2.

42. Schuman to Kwartin, May 21, 1971, NYPL-A, 148/2.

43. Schuman to Kwartin, December 10, 1971, NYPL-A, 148/2.

44. Kwartin to Schuman, January 4, 1972, NYPL-A, 148/2.

45. Schuman to Kwartin, March 9, 1972, NYPL-A, 148/2.

46. Schuman to Dan Patrylak, September 14, 1972, NYPL-A, 147/3.

47. This uncatalogued notebook, with its colorful striped cover, is in LoC-WS-Z.

48. Robert Rudié to Schuman, February 28, 1973, NYPL-A, 144/8.

49. See: Schuman to Dan Patrylak, September 14, 1972, NYPL-A, 147/3; Schuman to Larry Diefenbach, October 19, 1972, NYPL-A, 98/14; and Rudié to Schuman, February 28, 1973, NYPL-A, 144/8.

50. I thank David Peter Coppen, Special Collections Librarian and Archivist, Sibley Music Library, Eastman School of Music, for providing background and additional archival materials for *Voyage for Orchestra* (1971).

51. Schuman to Walter Hendl, March 9, 1970, NYPL-A, 147/3.

52. Schuman to Hendl, February 17, 1971, NYPL-A, 101/2.

53. Schuman to Hendl, August 19, 1971, NYPL-A, 146/15.

54. Schuman to Persichetti, October 19, 1972, NYPL-VP, 15/4.

55. Theodore Price, "Interesting 'Voyage,'" *Rochester Democrat and Chronicle*, October 28, 1972, clipping preserved in Sibley Music Library Special Collections, Rochester Scrapbook October–November 1972, p. 120.

56. George H. Kimball, "Philharmonia Adept in Premiere," *Rochester Times-Union*, October 28, 1972, clipping preserved in Sibley Music Library Special Collections, Rochester Scrapbook October–November 1972, p. 121.

57. William Schuman, program notes for *Voyage for Orchestra*, NYPL-A, 146/15.

58. Donal Henahan, "Music: The American Symphony Opens with Two Premieres," *New York Times*, November 10, 1975, 40.

59. Schuman to John Corigliano, June 20, 1981, NYPL-A, 126/4.

60. Igor Blazhkov to Schuman, March 1, 1965, NYPL-A, 48/6.

61. Agnes de Mille, "Russian Journals," *Dance Perspectives* 44 (Winter 1970): 22. Emil Yevgenyevich Zakharov (1934–) suggested to Svetlana Savenko, professor of musicology at the Moscow State Conservatory, that the composer who spoke to de Mille may have been Iosif Arshakovich Andriasov (1933–2000) or Givani Konstantinovich Mikhailov (1938–95), Armenians who, like Zakharov, were passionate admirers of Schuman's music. (Mikhailov was professor of American music at Moscow State Conservatory.) Personal correspondence with Savenko, January 17, 2010.

62. See Solomon Volkov, *Testimony: The Memoirs of Dmitri Shostakovich* (New York: Limelight: 2004), 172–73. Mario di Bonaventura, director of publications at G. Schirmer, sent an excerpt from *Testimony* to Schuman, writing, "I thought you'd like to read about a very famous scandal that shattered the Union of Composers in Moscow a few years ago that 'involved' you. This is the first time I have read about it in a western source. This affair was talked about often in Moscow but I could never get the 'lady's' name. I still know don't know [*sic*] who it was" (undated letter, NYPL-A, 116/3). Savenko identified the woman as Lyudmila Yasonova.

> Yasonova was really a student of Rodion Shchedrin but by the time of her theft she was already a postgraduate in the class of Tikhon Khrennikov. She had 'used' William Schuman's 5th Symphony for strings ('The slow movement is really great, it's a work of a composer of genius'—I quote Mr. Zakharov). 'Her' work was introduced for a performance abroad as she was a very proper candidate: young, woman, from Kazakhstan. The score of the 5th Symphony was in the Library of the Composers Union and Mr. Zakharov went there, took it and showed to the members of the session. Khrennikov was furious and turned Yasonova out of his postgraduate class and out of the Composers Union (she was just accepted in the Union). She returned to Almaty and later nobody in Moscow heard anything about her." (Personal correspondence with Savenko, August 19, 2009, and January 17, 2010, used by permission)

63. David Lloyd Kreeger to Schuman, June 22, 1973, NYPL-A, 147/10.

64. "American Music at Moscow Festival," May 10, 1982 [*sic*], dispatch for the *TASS* news agency, NYPL-A, 136/2. See also Schuman to Tikhon Khrennikov, December 18, 1980, and April 5, 1981, NYPL-A, 133/2.

65. Paul Hume, "Flawless Acoustics," *Washington Post*, September 10, 1971, B1.

66. Richard M. Nixon President's Daily Diary, September 9, 1971; White House Central Files: Staff Member and Office Files: Office of Presidential Papers and Archives; Richard Nixon Presidential Library and Museum, National Archives at College Park, Maryland. See also "Concert Hall Opening Night," *Washington Post*, September 10, 1971, B2.

67. Charles Wadsworth to Schuman, August 18, 1971, NYPL-A, 97/1.

68. Schuman to Wadsworth, September 9, 1971, NYPL-A, 97/1.

Chapter 30: "Round and Round and Round He Goes"

1. Diane Solway, "The Stages of Marty's Festival," *New York Times Magazine*, April 24, 1988, 20–21, 36–38.

2. Martin E. Segal to Schuman, March 13, 1981, NYPL-A, 141/10; Segal to Schuman, December 1, 1975, NYPL-A, 116/9.

3. Schuman to Segal, June 2, 1972, NYPL-A, 116/9.

4. Schuman to Catherine Filene Shouse, March 9, 1972, NYPL-A, 147/10.

5. "Project 1976," undated four-page prospectus, NYPL-A, 147/10.

6. William F. May to Segal, July 20, 1972, NYPL-A, 147/10.

7. See Glenn Fowler, "David Lloyd Kreeger Dead at 81; Insurance Official and Arts Patron," *New York Times*, November 20, 1990, B10.

8. See August 23, 1972, note, in Schuman's hand, on Kreeger to Schuman, August 15, 1972; and Schuman to Kreeger, September 22, 1972, NYPL-A, 147/10.

9. All these letters are in NYPL-A, 147/10. For the Helena Rubinstein Foundation, see Segal to Schuman, October 4, 1972; Schuman to Harold Weill, November 25, 1972; and Diane K. Corbin to Schuman, June 11, 1973. For Philip Morris, see Schuman to Segal, February 4, 1974.

10. Schuman to Richard Freed, January 12, 1973, NYPL-A, 147/10; and Schuman to Segal, June 2, 1972, NYPL-A, 116/9.

11. Schuman to Arthur M. Schlesinger Jr., September 14, 1972, and Schlesinger to Schuman, October 2, 1972, NYPL-A, 147/10.

12. Schuman to Archibald MacLeish, February 26, 1973, NYPL-A, 147/10.

13. Schuman to Kreeger, September 17, 1973, NYPL-A, 147/10.

14. Schuman to Freed, November 20, 1973, NYPL-A, 100/6.

15. See Schuman to Neil Butterworth, January 14, 1975, NYPL-A, 152/4; and Schuman to Arnold Broido, February 15, 1975, NYPL-A, 107/9.

16. http://www.pepysdiary.com/archive/1660/04/24/, accessed September 7, 2009.

17. "Chorus, Dance, Scheduled for Parents' Day," *Campus*, February 14, 1939, 1; "Chorus Sings over Radio on WOR," *Campus*, March 28, 1939, 1.

18. Schuman to John A. Benaglia, April 19, 1965, NYPL-A, 48/5.

19. Schuman to Harold Spivacke, November 5, 1964, NYPL-A, 65/13.

20. Schuman to Ormandy, January 18, 1971, NYPL-A, 145/9.

21. See Donald McInnes to Schuman, February 22, 1972; Schuman to W. McNeil Lowry, Ford Foundation, March 31, 1972; and letter of agreement between McInnes and Schuman, August 1, 1972, NYPL-A, 107/9.

22. Schuman to Harold Aks, April 11, 1974, NYPL-A, 144/8.

23. Schuman to Frederick Hart, October 2, 1972, "Adoration—Notebooks," LoC-WS-A.

24. Schuman to Edward Waters, December 18, 1973, NYPL-A, 104/8.

25. Alan Jabbour to Waters, January 8, 1974, NYPL-A, 144/8. Jabbour also sent photocopies of "Great Tom Is Cast" and "Come Follow Me" as they appear in Mary C. Taylor, ed., *Rounds and Rounds* (New York: William Sloane Associates, 1946), 39 and 57. A version of "Who'll Buy My Roses?" quite different from the one Schuman used, appears in Haig and Regina Shekerjian, eds., *A Book of Ballads, Songs, and Snatches* (New York: Harper & Row, 1966), 134.

26. See McInnes to Schuman, April 4, 1973, NYPL-A, 107/9; Frances Schuman to Marks, July 4, 1973, AWS; and McInnes to Schuman, September 6, 1973, NYPL-A, 118/12.

27. See Anthony Strilko to Schuman, September 20, 1973, and Schuman's September 25, 1973, handwritten note on this letter, NYPL-A, 117/14; and Schuman to Richard P. Kapp, January 7, 1974, and Strilko to Schuman, January 15, 1974, NYPL-A, 144/8.

28. Schuman to McInnes, July 19, 1974, NYPL-A, 144/8.

29. Schuman to Frederik Prausnitz, June 14, 1974, NYPL-A, 111/8.

30. Schuman to Marvin Saines, June 20, 1977, NYPL-A, 95/8.

31. Schuman to Schubart, December 29, 1978, NYPL-A, 105/3.

32. Schuman to McInnes, July 2, 1976, NYPL-A, 107/9.

33. Andrew Porter, "Musical Events: Opera Prima," *New Yorker*, May 3, 1976, 114.

34. Edward Rothstein, "Concert: New Romanticism at the Philharmonic," *New York Times*, June 9, 1983, C16. See also Arthur Berger, *Reflections of an American Composer* (Berkeley: University of California Press, 2002), 101.

35. Schuman to Herbert Barrett, January 14, 1974, NYPL-A, 144/8.

36. Michael Steinberg, "BSO Plays New Viola Work," *Boston Globe*, November 30, 1974, 13.

37. Harold C. Schonberg, "Music: Two Premieres," *New York Times*, April 16, 1976, 13.

38. Andrew Porter, "Musical Events: Opera Prima," *New Yorker*, May 3, 1976, 117. Porter mused: "Incidentally, surely the fourth line of 'Amaryllis' should end with 'hie,' not 'hide;' 'hie' both rhymes—with 'nigh'—and makes better sense." A John Playford publication from 1659 gives a more likely emendation: "Here is a pretty, pretty, pretty arbor by / Where Apollo, where Apollo cannot spy." See John Wilson et al., *Select ayres and dialogues for one, two, and three voices* (London: W. Godbid for John Playford, 1659).

39. William Bergsma to Schuman, "December 17" (no year), NYPL-A, 93/20.

40. Schuman to Walter Rosenberger, June 30, 1976, NYPL-A, 112/6.

41. Frederic P. Hart to Schuman, September 27, 1978, NYPL-A, 102/1.

42. Autobiography, chap. 11, p. 41.

43. Schuman to Robert M. Keane, November 24, 1971, NYPL-A, 121/8.

44. Schuman to "Dear Library Directors" (omnibus letter), March 20, 1972, NYPL-A. 122/6.

45. See "Notice of Meeting of Board of Directors [of Videorecord Corporation of America],'" March 28, 1973, NYPL-A, 120/5; and Jonathan Kwitny, "Before Collapse Sky Seemed to Be Limit for Videorecord Corp. and Its Franchisers," *Wall Street Journal*, April 12, 1974, 24.

46. OHAM, 438; Kwitny, "Before Collapse," 21.

47. Schuman to Ely Haimowitz, April 25, 1974, NYPL-A, 101/1.

48. Howard Klein to Schuman, June 28, 1973, NYPL-A, 114/1.

49. Schuman to Henry Romney, July 23, 1976, 114/1.

50. Schuman to Klein, October 27, 1973, NYPL-A, 114/2.

51. Schuman to Klein, May 14, 1974, NYPL-A, 114/2.

52. Schuman to Klein, June 14, 1974, NYPL-A, 114/2.

53. Klein to Schuman, November 11, 1974, NYPL-A, 114/1. For a sample of the disparate views, see H. Wiley Hitchcock to Klein, June 2, 1974, NYPL-A, 114/2.

54. Elizabeth Ostrow, preface to *Index to the New World Recorded Anthology of American Music: A User's Guide to the Initial One Hundred Records* (New York: W. W. Norton, 1981), vii. See also Klein to Schuman, June 19, 1974, NYPL-A, 114/2. This letter has annotations, in Schuman's hand, of a "long conversation" the two men had on June 24, 1974. See also Schuman to Klein, November 25, 1974, and Klein to Schuman, November 26, 1974, NYPL-A, 114/1.

55. http://www.newworldrecords.org/about-us.shtml, accessed September 9, 2009.

56. Schuman to Russell Lynes, January 7, 1974, NYPL-A, 106/7.

57. Schuman to Edward M. Cramer, January 22, 1974, NYPL-A, 94/13.

58. Schuman to Arthur Levitt Jr., February 4, 1974, NYPL-A, 106/7.

59. Schuman to Agnes de Mille, March 6, 1974, NYPL-A, 106/7.

60. http://www.artsandletters.org/about_history.php, accessed September 9, 2009; and "Schuman Honored," undated and unidentified clipping, NYPL-A, 108/6.

61. See Walter Piston to Schuman, April 21, 1974; Schuman to Piston, April 25, 1974; Piston to Schuman, April 27, 1974; and Piston's acceptance address, August 10, 1974, NYPL-A, 111/7.

62. See the correspondence in NYPL-A, 110/5.

63. Schuman to Charles Wadsworth, February 9, 1973, and William Schuman, "Statement on Roy Harris," February 11, 1973, NYPL-A, 102/1.

64. Schuman to Walter Anderson, June 22, 1973 (Luening) and June 27, 1973 (Trimble), NYPL-A, 108/10.

65. See the correspondence between Schuman and Ralph Affoumado, NYPL-A, 108/4.

66. Schuman to Irving Kolodin, June 14, 1974, NYPL-A, 103/8. See Irving Kolodin, "Farewell to Capricorn," *Saturday Review/World*, June 1, 1974, 44–45. Schuman's letter was published on page 6 of the September 7, 1964, issue.

67. Schuman to Donald Martino, June 18, 1974, NYPL-A, 106/1.

68. Martino to Schuman, September 1, 1974, NYPL-A, 106/1.

69. Schuman to John F. Winchester, September 13, 1974, NYPL-A, 104/2.

70. Schuman to Arnold Broido, March 13, 1973, and Broido to Carlo Ponti Productions, April 23, 1973, NYPL-A, 111/10.

Chapter 31: "Bicentennial Fireworks"

1. Antal Doráti to Schuman, April 5, 1974, NYPL-A, 147/10.

2. Doráti to Schuman, April 18, 1976, NYPL-A, 99/4.

3. Paul Hume, "An 'Impressive' Trio of Thirds," *Washington Post*, October 9, 1974, E1.

4. Paul Hume, "A Talk with Composers," *Washington Post*, October 10, 1974, B13.

5. Schuman to Roy Villa, April 19, 1965, NYPL-A, 87/9.

6. Schuman to Doráti, August 5, 1974, NYPL-A, 147/10.

7. "History of the Hirshhorn," http://hirshhorn.si.edu/info/column.asp?key=92, accessed September 15, 2009.

8. Schuman to Doráti, August 5, 1974, NYPL-A, 147/10. See also Schuman to Joseph Hirshhorn, October 23, 1974, NYPL-A, 101/2. For the other music that evening, see Barry Hyams, *Hirshhorn: Medici from Brooklyn* (New York: E. P. Dutton, 1979), 186–89.

9. Schuman to Hirshhorn, May 14, 1974, NYPL-A, 147/5.

10. See Thomas Schippers to Schuman, April 15, 1974, and Schuman to Schippers, April 25, 1974, NYPL-A, 97/9; Schippers to Schuman, August 21, 1975, NYPL-A, 98/8; and Schuman to Schippers, September 16, 1975, NYPL-A, 116/2. The only Schuman piece Schippers is known to have conducted in Cincinnati is *Credendum* (October 16 and 17, 1970). Personal correspondence with Christina Eaton, associate principal librarian of the Cincinnati Symphony Orchestra, September 21, 2009.

11. Schuman to Hans W. Heinsheimer, September 17, 1973, NYPL-A, 147/10.

12. Nearly all articles in *Broadcasting* have no byline; I could not find an article with Gury's byline in the issues of *Broadcasting* from January 1971 to June 1972. The "lead story" on television advertising for the May 1, 1972, issue may be by Gury; its title is "Ad Controls: Road to Truth or Invitation to Disaster?"

13. Gury to Schuman, June 27, 1972, NYPL-A, 100/10.

14. Schuman to Gury, October 11, 1973, NYPL-A, 147/10.

15. Gury to Schuman, October 17, 1973, NYPL-A, 147/10.

16. Schuman to Heinsheimer, November 20, 1973, NYPL-A, 147/10.

17. Typed telephone memo on Doráti to Schuman, January 25, 1974, NYPL-A, 147/10.

18. Doráti to Schuman, April 5, 1974, NYPL-A, 147/10.

19. Schuman to Segal, May 14, 1974, NYPL-A, 145/3; and Schuman to Segal, August 13, 1974, NYPL-A, 147/10.

20. April 15, 1975, press release, NYPL-A, 110/2.

21. Stan Luxenberg, "Norlin Seeks to Scale Up Profits," *New York Times*, April 23, 1978, F1.

22. Norton Stevens to Schuman, November 21, 1974, NYPL-A, 147/9.

23. Schuman to Doráti, April 16, 1974, NYPL-A, 147/10.

24. William Schuman, composer's notes on Symphony no. 10 (April 6, 1976), NYPL-A, 109/4.

25. Schuman to Calvert Bean Jr., July 22, 1971, NYPL-A, 111/9.

26. William Schuman, composer's notes on Symphony no. 10 (April 6, 1976), NYPL-A, 109/4.

27. Schuman to Doráti, August 5, 1974, NYPL-A, 147/10.

28. Doráti to Paul Hume, February 13, 1976, Paul Hume Papers, 1/68, Georgetown University.

29. Doráti to Schuman, February 21, 1976, and Schuman to Doráti, February 28, 1976, NYPL-A, 99/4.

30. Joseph McLelland, "Brilliant Versatility," *Washington Post*, April 7, 1976, F1.

31. Paul Hume, "Honoring Schuman the Composer with Three World Premieres," *Washington Post*, April 4, 1976, 114.

32. John Rockwell, "Music: Schuman by Skrowaczewski," *New York Times*, April 22, 1979, 61.

33. Joseph Machlis to Schuman, April 27, 1979, NYPL-A, 107/6.

34. Schuman to Thomas Frost, October 4, 1979, NYPL-A, 95/8; and Schuman to Leonard Slatkin, November 5, 1988, NYPL-C, "Correspondence S, 1988."

35. Schuman to Stanislaw Skrowaczewski, May 4, 1979, NYPL-A, 108/3.

36. Peter Kermani (Albany Symphony Orchestra) to Schuman, November 2, 1976, and November 11, 1978, NYPL-A, 92/4.

37. Schuman to Mario di Bonaventura, September 16, 1975, NYPL-A, 99/4.

38. Telephone conversation with Thad Marciniak, October 14, 2009.

39. Schuman to Doráti, June 4, 1975, NYPL-A, 145/3.

40. Scott Donaldson, *Archibald MacLeish: An American Life* (Boston: Houghton Mifflin, 1992), 374.

41. William Schuman, composer's notes on *The Young Dead Soldiers* (April 6, 1976), NYPL-A, 109/4. See Archibald MacLeish, *Actfive and Other Poems* (New York: Random House, 1948), 60.

42. Schuman to Doráti, June 4, 1975, NYPL-A, 145/3.

43. Schuman to Edward M. Cramer, February 28, 1976, NYPL-A, 94/14.

44. Walter Neiman to Schuman, March 12, 1976, NYPL-A, 119/6. See also the listings in the *New York Times* radio section.

45. William Schuman and Richard Freed, "Program 1 (American Muse)," October 24, 1974, NYPL-A 119/7.

46. Freed to Schuman, November 18, 1974, NYPL-A, 119/6.

47. George McCue to Schuman, June 28, 1976, NYPL-A, 115/5. See also William Schuman, "Americanism in Music: A Composer's View," in *Music in American Society 1776–1976*, ed. George McCue (New Brunswick, NJ: Transaction Books, 1977), 15–25.

48. Schuman to Frederik Prausnitz, June 19, 1976, NYPL-A, 111/8.

49. Schuman to Howard Shanet, July 19, 1976, NYPL-A, 116/9.

50. William Schuman, "Semper Fidelis," *School Musician* 48 (October 1976): 43.

51. Neiman to Schuman, October 2, 1974, NYPL-A, 119/6.

52. William Schuman, "Relationship between Education and the Projected Norlin Television Music Series," September 16, 1975, NYPL-A, 110/2.

53. Information is from Peter Martin Robeck's paid obituary in the *New York Times*, April 4, 1999.

54. William Schuman, proposal for *William Schuman's Musical America*, August 26, 1977, NYPL-A, 118/6; and "William Schuman on American Music," April 26, 1978, NYPL-A, 142/8.

55. Schuman to Prausnitz, August 31, 1977, NYPL-A, 111/8.

56. Schuman to Peter M. Robeck, July 3, 1978, NYPL-A, 118/6.

57. See the article and correspondence in NYPL-A, 109/11.

58. See Schuman to Terry B. Sanders, June 12, 1975, NYPL-A, 107/1; Schuman to Robert Joffrey, May 5, 1975, NYPL-A, 102/11; and Schuman to Conrad S. Spohnholz, June 6, 1975, NYPL-A, 107/1.

59. Schuman to Spohnholz, October 16, 1975, Norlin Foundation folder, MacDowell Colony offices, New York, NY.

60. "$250,000 to Colony to Mark Copland's Day," *New York Times*, November 13, 1975, 51.

61. Schuman to Edwin C. Cohen and Varujan Boghosian, March 5, 1985, Norlin Foundation folder, MacDowell Colony offices, New York, NY.

62. Schuman to Dennis Russell Davies, June 13, 1981, NYPL-A, 128/1.

63. See Schuman to H. Wiley Hitchcock, October 22, 1975, and February 28, 1976, NYPL-A, 102/5; Schuman to Sheldon Rich, June 10, 1976, NYPL-A, 115/5; and Schuman to Bernice and Milton Woll, March 7, 1985, NYPL-A, 143/8.

64. William Schuman, eulogy for Goddard Lieberson memorial service, June 3, 1977, NYPL-A, 104/8. The November 18, 1963, eulogy for Fritz Reiner is in NYPL-A, 36/4.

Chapter 32: "Reflections and Ruminations"

1. "Book Proposal © 1990 by William Schuman and Heidi Waleson," p. 1, in "William Schuman memoirs (with H. Waleson): Correspondence & background material re: this project, 1990–1992," William Schuman, biographical files, Juilliard School Archives.

2. Schuman to Maxwell Geismar, January 7, 1974, NYPL-A, 110/9; in this letter Schuman referred to his nocturnal patterns as a "ghastly habit." The book itself is "an anthology of Mark Twain's radical social commentary dealing with race, religion and revolution, but also covering a wider range of social and historical matters." See Maxwell Geismar, ed., *Mark Twain and the Three R's: Race, Religion, Revolution—and Related Matters* (Indianapolis: Bobbs-Merrill, 1973), xv.

3. Schuman to James Gollin, October 15, 1981, NYPL-A, 130/2.

4. Leighton Kerner, "Chamber Music Society Salutes Alice Tully," *Voice*, April 7, 1977, 2; Harriet Johnson, "Chamber Tosses Garland for Tully," *New York Post*, March 16, 1977, 42.

5. The manuscript and copyist's score are in NYPL.

6. The score of *A Round for Audrey*, JIG.

7. The score and written tribute are found, respectively, in NYPL-A, 129/9, and Leonard Feist Papers, JPB 02-7, 1/31, NYPL.

8. William Schuman, *For Wiley H.*, in *A Celebration of American Music: Words and Music in Honor of H. Wiley Hitchcock*, ed. Richard Crawford, R. Allen Lott, and Carol J. Oja (Ann Arbor: University of Michigan Press, 1990), 12–13. The manuscript and tribute both bear the date September 1, 1987.

9. *For A.C. con amore* is dated January 16, 1981, and is in NYPL-A, 142/1.

10. Schuman to Antal Doráti, October 16, 1979, NYPL-A, 99/4.

11. Schuman to Paula Robison, April 1, 1976, NYPL-A, 112/6.

12. Schuman to Leonard Slatkin, April 26, 1977, NYPL-A, 117/5.

13. Schuman to Frederik Prausnitz, August 31, 1977, NYPL-A, 111/8.

14. Schuman to the Board of Directors of the Chamber Music Society of Lincoln Center, August 31, 1977, NYPL-A, 97/3.

15. Schuman to Charles Wadsworth, February 1, 1979, NYPL-A, 97/3; and William Bergsma to Schuman, May 1, 1979, NYPL-A, 93/20.

16. William Schuman, program notes for *In Sweet Music*, October 29, 1978, NYPL-A, 97/3.

17. Clytie M. Salisbury to Schuman, August 7, 1979, NYPL-A, 103/6.

18. Harold C. Schonberg, "Music," *New York Times*, November 6, 1978, 55.

19. Harriett Johnson, "Music Society Earns Its SRO," *New York Post*, November 1, 1978; and Bill Zakariasen, "They Asked for It, Musically" *(New York) Daily News*, November 1, 1978, clippings in NYPL-A, 163/2.

20. Bergsma to Schuman, February 25, 1979, NYPL-A, 93/20.

21. Norman Lloyd to Schuman, October 28, 1978, NYPL-A, 105/5.

22. Teresa Sterne to Schuman, November 29, 1978, NYPL-A, 108/6.

23. See http://www.artsandletters.org/awards2_all.php, accessed September 25, 2009.

24. Minutes of a meeting of the board of directors of the American Academy and Institute of Arts and Letters, March 8, 1978, NYPL-A, 166/1.

25. December 1, 2009, e-mail from Theodore S. Chapin to the author, used with permission.

26. "Statement by William Schuman for Leonard Bernstein Program, Wolf Trap Farm, August 25, 1978," NYPL-A, 94/2.

27. Bernstein to Schuman, August 28, 1978, NYPL-A, 94/2.

28. Schuman to Copland, October 27, 1980, NYPL-A, 127/12.

29. Schuman to Roy Harris, September 11, 1978, NYPL-A, 102/1.

30. Schuman to Harris, February 26, 1979, NYPL-A, 102/1.

31. Schuman to Miriam Shifrin, October 4, 1979, NYPL-A, 117/2.

32. Schuman to Morton Gould, May 4, 1979, NYPL-A, 100/14.

33. Schuman to Ormandy, May 4, 1979, NYPL-A, 111/6.

34. Barbara Heyman, *Samuel Barber* (New York: Oxford University Press), 506.

35. Raymond Ericson, "Concert: An All-American Program," *New York Times*, May 16, 1979, C26.

36. Schuman to Barber, May 30, 1979, NYPL-A, 93/15.

37. Barber to Schuman, June 2, 1979, NYPL-A, 93/15.

38. Schuman to Barber, January 18, 1980, NYPL-A, 93/15.

39. Elaine Felt to Schuman, January 11, 1979, NYPL-A, 99/13. See also Eleanor Robson Belmont to Schuman, January 15, 1979, NYPL-A, 93/19.

40. Schuman to Gerard Schwarz, March 7, 1979, NYPL-A, 115/1.

41. Schuman to Paula Robison Nickrenz, November 7, 1985, and October 6, 1985, NYPL-A, 139/2.

42. Alan Siebert gives a fine performance of the piece on his 2007 recording *Stargazer*, Equilibrium 83.

43. Schuman to Barber, March 7, 1980, NYPL-A, 107/5.

44. Gian Carlo Menotti to Schuman, May 17, 1980, NYPL-A, 135/3.

45. John Browning to Frances Schuman, April 4, 1992, NYPL-C, "Condolences—A–B." See also Heyman, *Samuel Barber*, 508.

46. Schuman to Phyllis Curtin, September 7, 1977, Curtin to Schuman, September 11, 1977, and Schuman to Curtin, September 23, 1977, NYPL-A, 98/12.

47. Schuman to Archibald MacLeish, November 14, 1977, NYPL-A, 107/7.

48. MacLeish to Schuman, November 16, 1977, NYPL-A, 107/7.

49. Schuman to MacLeish, December 12, 1977, NYPL-A, 107/7.

50. Schuman to MacLeish, February 10, 1978, NYPL-A, 107/7.

51. See Schuman to Jon Goldberg, February 5, 1979, NYPL-A, 100/12 (this folder contains the correspondence about the chamber music version of *A Song of Orpheus*); and Schuman to Lukas Foss, January 19, 1989, NYPL-C, "Correspondence F, 1989–1990."

52. Schuman to Anthony Tudor, October 2, 1978, January 4, 1979, and December 19, 1979, NYPL-A, 111/8.

53. Schuman to Oliver Smith, December 19, 1979, NYPL-A, 92/1.

54. Schuman to Gunther Schuller, September 19, 1978, NYPL-A, 115/1.

55. Schuman to H. Wiley Hitchcock, July 10, 1979, NYPL-A, 102/5.

56. Schuman to Albert K. Webster, July 19, 1979, NYPL-A, 109/7.

57. See "A Statement by William Schuman," undated document composed by Anthony Strilko; Strilko to Schuman, August 18, 1983; and Schuman to Strilko, March 21, 1985, NYPL-A, 141/21.

58. Schuman to Zubin Mehta, December 18, 1979, NYPL-A, 109/7.

59. Schuman to Mehta, January 30, 1980, NYPL-A, 109/7.

60. Nicholas Kenyon, "Musical Events: Testimony," *New Yorker*, February 11, 1980, 93.

61. Harold C. Schonberg, "Music: A New Schuman," *New York Times*, January 25, 1980, C10.

62. Edward Rothstein, "Concert: New Romanticism at the Philharmonic," *New York Times*, June 9, 1983, C16.

63. See also Joseph W. Polisi, "The William Schuman Violin Concerto: Genesis of a Twentieth-Century Masterpiece," *Music Library Association Notes*, vol. 66, no. 3 (March 1, 2010): 463–66.

64. Schuman to MacLeish, November 28, 1979, NYPL-A, 107/7.

65. MacLeish to Schuman, December 6, 1979, NYPL-A, 135/8; and MacLeish to Schuman, December 18, 1979, NYPL-A, 107/7.

66. Donal Henahan, "Concert: Gregg Smith Singers Present Four World Premieres," *New York Times*, May 21, 1980, C25; Joseph McLellan, "William Schuman's Vivid Vocal Works," *Washington Post*, May 8, 1986, C13.

67. Schuman to Rosalind Rees, March 5, 1986, NYPL-A, 139/6.

68. On Pangloss, see Schuman to Norman Singer, July 7, 1982, NYPL-A, 141/15.

Chapter 33: "Triplets"

1. Schuman to Gordon Hardy, January 9, 1980, NYPL-A, 124/4.

2. The repertory list was constructed with the assistance of Shelby Murphy, music production coordinator, Aspen Music Festival and School, October 1, 2009.

3. Schuman to Gordon Hardy, Jorge Mester, Richard Dufallo, and Robert Biddlecome, July 11, 1980, NYPL-A, 124/4.

4. "A Cake Surprises the Composer William Schuman," *New York Times*, August 6, 1980, B4.

5. Jon Busch, "Aspen Music," *Aspen Times*, August 7, 1980, B26, clipping in NYPL-A, 163/4.

6. William Schuman, notes for *Three Pieces for Five Brasses*, NYPL-A, 124/4.

7. Schuman to Arnold Broido, August 25, 1980, NYPL-A, 138/5. See also Schuman's July 21, 1980, letter in this folder, in which he granted Broido permission to publish the *Three Pieces for Five Brasses*.

8. Schuman to Kenneth M. Godel, September 29, 1980, NYPL-A, 130/7.

9. Robert Biddlecome to Schuman, September 26, 1980, NYPL-A, 138/5.

10. Arnald D. Gabriel to Schuman, August 20, 1980, NYPL-A, 147/2.

11. Schuman to Tilford Brooks, October 18, 1979, NYPL-A, 148/3. See also Schuman to John H. Lidenbusch, director of the Missouri Historical Society, October 1, 1979, in this folder.

12. Schuman to Susan Deich, December 19, 1979, NYPL-A, 148/3.

13. Schuman to Leonard Slatkin, April 21, 1980, NYPL-A, 140/6.

14. Schuman to Biddlecome, October 14, 1980, NYPL-A, 138/5.

15. John Rockwell, "Music: American Brass Quintet," *New York Times*, April 1, 1981, C21.

16. John P. Paynter to Schuman, March 4, 1981, stored with the score of *American Hymn*, accession number USMB-R-5503, United States Marine Band Library, Washington, D.C.

17. Schuman to Paynter, March 27, 1981, NYPL-A, 137/8.

18. Schuman to Paynter, October 15, 1981, NYPL-A, 137/8.

19. Paynter to Laurence Broido, February 21, 1982, NYPL-A, 137/8.

20. Schuman to Joan T. Briccetti, April 5, 1981, NYPL-A, 140/6.

21. William Schuman, program notes for *American Hymn: Orchestral Variations on an Original Melody*, April 25, 1982, NYPL-A, 129/12.

22. OHAM, 35.

23. Schuman to Briccetti, November 8, 1981, NYPL-A, 140/6.

24. Schuman to Briccetti, December 11, 1981, NYPL-A, 140/6.

25. Schuman to Joan and James Warburg, December 30, 1980, NYPL-A, 143/1.

26. "Notes on People," *New York Times*, February 27, 1981.

27. Schuman to Elliott Carter, March 1, 1981, and Carter to Schuman, April 28, 1981, NYPL-A, 126/8.

28. November 27, 1981, press release from the Office of Public Information, Columbia University, NYPL-A, 163/5.

29. Schuman to Briccetti, February 4, 1982, NYPL-A, 140/6.

30. Schuman to Briccetti, February 10, 1983, NYPL-A, 140/6.

31. Ibid.

32. Schuman to Arnold Broido, February 20, 1983, NYPL-A, 138/5.

33. John Rockwell, "Concert: Slatkin Leads St. Louis Symphony," *New York Times*, January 29, 1983, 16.

34. Harriett Johnson, "America's Musical Pride," *New York Post*, January 31, 1983; and Bill Zakariasen, "Saint Louis Symphony with Its Golden Tones," *(New York) Daily News*, January 31, 1983, 40, clippings in NYPL-A, 163/7.

35. Frank Peters, "Slatkin, Orchestra Shine," *St. Louis Post-Dispatch*, September 25, 1982, 2–3; and James Wierzbicki, "Symphony Opening Sustains Festive Mood of 'Grand Affair,'" *St. Louis Globe-Democrat*, September 27, 1982, B8, clippings in NYPL-A, 163/6.

36. Phillip Ramey to Schuman, January 29, 1983, NYPL-A, 139/4.

37. Phillip Ramey, notes for Joseph Schwantner, *Magabunda: Four Poems of Agueda Pizarro*, and for William Schuman, *American Hymn: Orchestral Variations on an Original Melody*, Nonesuch 79072–1 (LP) © 1984.

38. John Corigliano to Schuman, October 15, 1984, NYPL-A, 126/4.

39. Schuman to Michael I. Sovern, June 18, 1980, NYPL-A, 127/8.

40. Samuel Lipman, "American Music: The Years of Hope," *Music and More: Essays, 1975–1991* (Evanston, IL: Northwestern University Press, 1992), 51–52.

41. Charles Wuorinen to Frank Milburn, May 3, 1981, New York Philharmonic Archives, Box/Folder 478-01-17, New York, NY.

42. Schuman to Eugene Moon, March 8, 1982, NYPL-A, 138/5. See also Schuman to Stanley Wolfe, May 29, 1983, NYPL-A, 143/7; and Schuman to Peter G. Davis, December 9, 1983, NYPL-A, 128/1.

43. William Schuman, "The Purpose of a Symphony Orchestra," *Symphony Magazine*, August 1980, 11–17.

44. Schuman to John Kiermaier, May 19, 1978, NYPL-A, 95/7.

45. William Schuman, "An Advance Bequest Certified Deposit Is Simple as ABCD," *Philanthropy Monthly*, May 1983, 28–29.

46. Schuman to Martin E. Segal, March 8, 1982, NYPL-A, 123/3.

47. Schuman to Eli Evans, May 8, 1983, NYPL-A, 123/4.

48. Schuman to Thomas A. Troyer, December 28, 1983, NYPL-A, 123/4.

49. Schuman to Michael Leavitt, June 14, 1982, NYPL-A, 134/2.

50. Schuman to Rosalind Rees, March 5, 1986, NYPL-A, 139/6.

51. Personal correspondence with Lawrence Doebler, October 5, 2009.

52. Joel R. Stegall to Schuman, March 8, 1982, NYPL-A, 132/4.

53. Schuman to Stegall, March 28, 1982, NYPL-A, 132/4.

54. Schuman to Joel R. Stegall, July 16, 1982, NYPL-A, 144/10.

55. The invitation and the program for the concert are found in NYPL-A, 130/9.

56. Schuman to Segal, January 13, 1983, NYPL-A, 123/4; and Schuman to Chapin, February 20, 1983, NYPL-A, 127/3.

57. Frances Schuman to Jerome Bunke, January 10, 1983, NYPL-A, 127/11.

58. Schuman to Ellis J. Freedman, January 20, 1983, NYPL-A, 129/13.

59. Schuman to Arnold Broido, February 20, 1983, NYPL-A, 138/5. On a program for the concert, Schuman wrote: "WS could not attend—snow—car didn't come here. Damn. Andie, Tony & Audrey went. FPS & WS home with [grandson] Josh." NYPL-A, 174/1.

60. Schuman to Peter Kermani, October 13, 1983, NYPL-A, 123/6.

61. Schuman to Herbert A. Arnold, October 13, 1983, NYPL-A, 123/2.

Chapter 34: "The Wind Was With Him"

1. Tom Watkins, "Heart Surgeon Makes Tee Time, Misses Clinton," *CNN.com*, September 6, 2004, http://www.cnn.com/2004/HEALTH/09/06/clinton.doctor/index.html, accessed October 10, 2009.

2. Schuman to O. Wayne Isom, M.D., October 25, 1984, NYPL-A, 132/4.

3. Norton Stevens to Frances Schuman, February 25, 1992, NYPL-C, "Condolences—S-T."

4. See, for example, Schuman to Rainer Miedel, conductor of the Seattle Symphony, March 17, 1983, NYPL-A, 136/4.

5. Schuman to Robert Shaw, February 20, 1983, NYPL-A, 141/11.

6. Albert K. Webster to Schuman, December 13, 1983, NYPL-A, 147/8.

7. As quoted in Nan Robertson, "A Musical Collaboration in Homage to America," *New York Times*, January 2, 1986, C16.

8. See Richard Wilbur, "Discussions of Amalgamating the Academy and the Institute," March 7, 1975, report; and Schuman to Wilbur, October 14, 1975, NYPL-A, 92/8.

9. "Poet Summons Muses in Dedication Greeting," *New York Times*, September 24, 1962, 32.

10. Schuman to Richard Wilbur, February 2, 1984, NYPL-A, 145/7.

11. Wilbur to Schuman, February 17, 1984, NYPL-A, 145/7.

12. Wilbur to Schuman, April 5, 1984, LoC-WS-Z, 13/1.

13. Schuman to Wilbur, April 26, 1984, and Wilbur to Schuman, May 11, 1984, NYPL-A, 143/3.

14. Wilbur to Schuman, July 11, 1984, LoC-WS-Z, 13/1.

15. Wilbur to Schuman, August 26, 1984, LoC-WS-Z, 13/1.

16. Schuman to Wilbur, July 23, 1984, NYPL-A, 145/7. For "invincible dream," see Wilbur to Schuman, August 2, 1984, LoC-WS-Z, 13/1.

17. Schuman to Wilbur, August 6, 1984, NYPL-A, 145/7.

18. Wilbur to Schuman, August 9, 1984, LoC-WS-Z, 13/1.

19. Wilbur to Schuman, August 26, 1984, LoC-WS-Z, 13/1.

20. Schuman to Brock McElheran, January 10, 1985, NYPL-A, 145/7.

21. Nan Robertson, "Artists in Old Age: The Fires of Creativity Burn Undiminished," *New York Times*, January 22, 1986, C10.

22. Schuman to Wilbur, February 21, 1985, NYPL-A, 145/7.

23. Karen T. LeFrak, "Conversations on Commissioning," Vol. 2 of "Forty Years of Commissioning by the New York Philharmonic, 1945–1985," M.A. thesis, Hunter College, New York, NY, 1986, 302.

24. Wilbur to Schuman, October 13, 1984, NYPL-A, 145/7.

25. See LeFrak, "Conversations on Commissioning," 303; and the correspondence between LeFrak and Schuman, NYPL-A, 134/2. See also Albert K. Webster to Schuman, May 19, 1985, NYPL-A, 145/7.

26. In Susan Loesser, *A Most Remarkable Fella* (New York: Donald I. Fine, 1993), 14.

27. Personal correspondence with Andrea Schuman, January 9, 2007.

28. John Rockwell, "Music: Liberty Potpourri," *New York Times*, November 2, 1986, 78.

29. Joseph McLellan, "The NSO, All American," *Washington Post*, September 18, 1987, D1.

30. John von Rhein, "Slatkin, CSO Team Up to Give All-American Salute to Music," *Chicago Tribune*, November 13, 1987, sec. 2, p. 10.

31. Schuman to John Corigliano, December 3, 1987, NYPL-C, "Correspondence C, 1987."

32. Schuman to Webster, February 9, 1987, NYPL-C, "Correspondence N, 1987."

33. Peter G. Davis, "The American Way," *New York*, November 17, 1985, 90.

34. Schuman to Wilbur, November 21, 1984, NYPL-A, 145/7.

35. Schuman to Wilbur, February 21, 1985, and Wilbur to Schuman, March 1, 1985, NYPL-A, 145/7.

36. William Schuman, program notes for *Dances (1985) for Wind Quintet and Percussion*, NYPL-A, 127/2. See also Nan Robertson, "William Schuman Offers a Birthday Gift to Friends," *New York Times*, October 2, 1985, C16.

37. Schuman to William Kraft, October 20, 1985, NYPL-A, 133/11.

38. Schuman to Aubert Lemeland, March 26, 1982, NYPL-A, 134/2.

39. Schuman to Fred Jacobowitz, July 27, 1985, NYPL-A, 132/9.

40. William Schuman, program notes for *Dances: Divertimento for Wind Quintet and Percussion*, NYPL-A, 127/2.

41. Charles Ward, "Fanfares Commissioned as Sesquicentennial Project," *Houston Chronicle*, February 14, 1986, 1.

42. Andrew Porter, "Musical Events: Fanfarrado," *New Yorker*, July 20, 1987, 72.

43. Michael Webster to Schuman, May 19, 1973, NYPL-A, 118/13.

44. Schuman to E. C. Schirmer Co., November 17, 1982, NYPL-A, 141/1.

45. Schuman to Arnold Broido, July 3, 1986, NYPL-A, 125/10.

46. William Schuman, program notes for *Awake Thou Wintry Earth*, NYPL-C, "Correspondence N, 1988."

47. Schuman to Bernstein, December 10, 1979, NYPL-A, 94/1.

48. Personal correspondence with Christopher Rouse, October 11, 2009.

49. Schuman to Rouse, February 5, 1979, NYPL-A, 114/5.

50. Rouse to Frances Schuman, February 16, 1992, NYPL-C, "Condolences—O–R."

51. Schuman to Peter Mennin, November 22, 1981, NYPL-A, 136/2.

52. Schuman to Joseph W. Polisi, July 23, 1984, NYPL-A, 138/3.

53. Frances Schuman to Rainer Böhlke, July 15, 1993, NYPL-C, "Correspondence B, 1992–1994."

54. Schuman to Ellis J. Freedman, June 7, 1984, NYPL-A, 132/10.

55. William Schuman et al., "American Music Recording Institute 1985," six-page proposal, NYPL-A, 132/10.

56. Schuman to the Executive Committee of the Chamber Music Society of Lincoln Center, January 15, 1981, NYPL-A, 127/1.

57. Andrew Porter, "Musical Events: Voices of Rome," *New Yorker*, May 21, 1984, 123. See also Schuman to board of directors of the Chamber Music Society of Lincoln Center, January 26, 1984 (with drafts dated September 19, 1983, and January 12, 1984), NYPL-A, 127/2.

58. Schuman to Dennis Russell Davies, June 13, 1981, NYPL-A, 128/1.

59. Leonard Slatkin, "Walton Won: Leonard Slatkin Talks to Edward Seckerson," *Gramophone* 66, 783 (August 1988): 267. See also Schuman to Slatkin, April 26, 1977, NYPL-A, 117/5.

60. Thomas W. Morris to Schuman, March 14, 1980, NYPL-A, 94/7. See also Schuman to Archibald MacLeish, September 16, 1980, NYPL-A, 135/8.

61. Sharon Panulla, "Alumni Reunion A Success," *George Washington High School Alumni and Scholarship Association, Inc. Newsletter*, Summer 1982, 1 (NYPL-A, 163/6).

62. Schuman to Steve Robinson, August 23, 1982, NYPL-A, 141/4.

63. Trevor Cushman III, "Annual Meeting Highlights," *[MacDowell] Colony Newsletter*, Winter 1983/1984, 2.

64. Schuman to Fred Lerdahl, July 19, 1982, NYPL-A, 134/6.

65. Schuman to William J. Bennett, February 26, 1984, NYPL-A, 136/14.

Chapter 35: "A Rare Vintage"

1. "Scorecard: Casey's Baton," *Sports Illustrated*, May 29, 1961, 8.

2. Schuman to Hans W. Heinsheimer, July 13, 1962, NYPL-A, 180/8.

3. Schuman to *New York Times*, September 5, 1967, NYPL-A, 72/6.

4. Schuman to Cynthia Auerbach, May 10, 1981, NYPL-A, 123/2.

5. Schuman to Roger Briggs, October 4, 1982, NYPL-A, 124/9.

6. Ronald Reagan to various, July 18, 1986, NYPL-A, 145/3.

7. Schuman to David Straus III, August 17, 1985, NYPL-A, 140/4.

8. B. A Nilsson, "In Review: Cooperstown, New York," *Opera News*, November 1986, 57.

9. Paul Kellogg to Schuman, September 23, 1986, NYPL-A, 145/3.

10. Schuman to Laurence Broido, July 20, 1987, NYPL-C, "Correspondence P, 1987."

11. Schuman to Janette Hickin, March 12, 1987, NYPL-C, "Correspondence T, 1987."

12. Dena Kleiman, "7 Composers to Write for '88 Festival," *New York Times*, June 25, 1986, C23.

13. William Schuman, String Quartet No. V Program Notes, April 7, 1988, NYPL-C, "Correspondence T, 1987–1988."

14. Roald Dahl, "Taste," *New Yorker*, December 8, 1951, 36–41, reprinted in Roald Dahl, *Collected Stories*, edited by Jeremy Treglown (New York: Everyman's Library/Alfred A. Knopf, 2006), 270–83.

15. Richard Wilbur to Schuman, April 6, 1987, NYPL-A, 145/10. For Frankie's suggestion, see J. D. McClatchy, "William Schuman: A Reminiscence," *Opera Quarterly* 10, 4 (1994): 22.

16. Schuman to Wilbur, June 17, 1987, NYPL-C, "Correspondence W, 1987."

17. Wilbur to Schuman, June 26, 1987, NYPL-C, "Correspondence W, 1987."

18. McClatchy, "William Schuman," 22.

19. McClatchy to Schuman, April 27, 1987, NYPL-A, 145/10.

20. Michael Bawtree to Schuman, May 2, 1987, NYPL-A, 145/10.

21. McClatchy, "William Schuman," 23–24.

22. Schuman to Richard Cormier, February 25, 1988, NYPL-C, "Correspondence T, 1987–1988."

23. Schuman to Seiji Ozawa, November 19, 1987, NYPL-C, "Correspondence B, 1987."

24. Schuman to William K. Sisson, January 17, 1988, NYPL-C, "Correspondence B, 1988."

25. Schuman to Richard Rodzinski, February 21, 1987, NYPL-C, "Correspondence R, 1987." See also Van Cliburn Foundation to Schuman, January 30, 1987, NYPL-C, "Correspondence V, 1987–1992."

26. Rodzinski to Schuman, January 2, 1989, NYPL-C, "Correspondence V, 1987–1992."

27. Schuman to Rodzinski, January 12, 1989, NYPL-C, "Correspondence V, 1987–1992."

28. Schuman to Arnold Broido, January 17, 1988, NYPL-C, "Correspondence T, 1987–1988."

29. McClatchy, "William Schuman," 28 (August 4, 1988) and 32 (October 5, 1988).

30. Ibid., 31 (September 15, 1988). See also McClatchy to Schuman, September 17, 1988, NYPL-C, "Correspondence M, 1988."

31. This observation is based on my viewing of the 1986 performance of *The Mighty Casey*, Glimmerglass Opera videotape 001.

32. McClatchy, "William Schuman," 32 (October 5, 1988).

33. Ibid., 32 (December 8, 1988).

34. Ibid., 33 (June 19, 1989).

35. Ibid., 34 (June 21, 1989).

36. Bernard Holland, "'Casey,' New Schuman Work, As Glimmerglass Opens," *New York Times*, June 26, 1989, C14.

37. John Rockwell, "Juilliard Demonstrates Its Up-to-Dateness," *New York Times*, December 16, 1990, 78.

38. Willard Spiegelman, "Opera: Schuman at Glimmerglass," *Wall Street Journal*, July 7, 1989.

39. Wayne Koestenbaum to Schuman, July 10, 1989, NYPL-C, "Correspondence K, 1989."

40. "The Kennedy Center Announces '89 Awards," *New York Times*, August 8, 1989, C14.

41. Bernstein to Schuman, November 10, 1989, and Schuman to Bernstein, December 28, 1989, NYPL-C, "Correspondence B, 1989."

42. Schuman to Audrey Brentlinger, February 8, 1990, NYPL-C, "Correspondence B, 1990."

43. Sanford Krasner to Schuman, August 17, 1990, NYPL-C, "Correspondence K, 1990–1992."

44. Schuman to Krasner, September 27, 1990, NYPL-C, "Correspondence K, 1990–1992."

45. Schuman to Joan Warburg, November 9, 1989, NYPL-C, "Correspondence W, 1988–1989."

46. See McClatchy to Schuman, July 19, 1989, NYPL-C, "Correspondence M, 1989"; and McClatchy to Schuman, July 26, 1989, and July 31, 1989, NYPLA, 145/10.

47. McClatchy to Schuman, January 8, 1990, NYPL-C, "Correspondence M, 1991–1992."

48. John S. Sweeney, "'Pops' Concert This Weekend to Highlight Music of America," *Greenwich Time*, June 11, 1990, B3.

49. Schuman to Warburg, February 8, 1990, NYPL-C, "Correspondence G, 1990."

50. For the hospital stay, see Schuman to Mary Heller, April 19, 1990, NYPL-C, "Correspondence C, 1990."

51. Warburg to Schuman, May 9, 1990, NYPL-C, "Correspondence G, 1990."

52. John S. Sweeney, "Spirited All-American Pops Concert Evokes Appreciative Cheers," *Greenwich Time*, June 20, 1990, B6.

53. Leatrice Gilbert Fountain, "Review," *Greenwich News*, June 21, 1990, 29.

54. McClatchy to Schuman, August 13, 1990, NYPL-C, "Correspondence M, 1990."

55. McClatchy, "William Schuman," 37.

56. Schuman to various, December 7, 1990, NYPL-C, "Correspondence A, 1990–1992."

57. Schuman to Daniel R. Gustin, May 16, 1991, NYPL-C, "Correspondence B, 1991."

58. Schuman to Vivian Perlis, August 8, 1986, NYPL-A, 137/13.

59. Ken Haas to Costa Pilavachi, Boston Symphony Orchestra interoffice memorandum, April 1, 1987, NYPL-C, "Correspondence B, 1987."

60. Stuart Altman to Schuman, May 10, 1991, and Schuman to Altman, May 16, 1991, NYPL-C, "Correspondence B, 1991"; Gloria Negri, "Obituary: Robert Koff, Violinist, Professor, Cofounded Juilliard Quartet; at 86," *Boston Globe*, February 27, 2005; and Schuman to Koff, May 16, 1991, NYPL-C, "Correspondence K, 1990–1992."

61. William Ferris to Schuman, September 28, 1990, NYPL-C, "Correspondence F, 1989–1990."

62. Schuman to James W. Pruett, September 21, 1989, and Pruett to Schuman, October 2, 1989, NYPL-C, "Correspondence L, 1991."

63. Schuman to Pruett, October 12, 1989, NYPL-C, "Correspondence L, 1991."

64. See Pruett to Schuman, February 5, 1991, NYPL-B, "The Library of Congress" (original commission); and Pruett to Schuman, April 5, 1991, NYPL-C, "Correspondence L, 1991" (revised commission).

65. Schuman to Ken Godel, January 3, 1991, NYPL-C, "Correspondence G, 1991–1993."

66. Schuman to Ferris, April 25, 1991, NYPL-C, "Correspondence F, 1991–1993."

67. Schuman to Ferris, December 26, 1991, NYPL-C, "Correspondence F, 1991–1993."

68. Schuman to Pruett, October 31, 1991, NYPL-C, "Correspondence L, 1991."

69. Blanche Schwarz Levy to Schuman, October 31, 1980, NYPL-A, 134/9. In a November 6, 1989, letter, Schwarz Levy related to Schuman the same anecdote, this time remembering the event as her first students' recital (NYPL-C, "Correspondence M, 1989").

70. Audrey Gerstner to Schuman (handmade card), NYPL-C, "Correspondence G, 1990."

71. Frances Schuman to Schwarz Levy, May 14, 1992, NYPL-C, "Correspondence L, 1992–1994."

72. Joseph W. Polisi, *American Muse: The Life and Times of William Schuman* (New York: Amadeus, 2008), 374–75.

73. Schuman to Susan Feder, February 10, 1991, NYPL-C, "Correspondence G, 1991–1993."

74. Schuman to John Corigliano, December 8, 1991, NYPL-C, "Correspondence C, 1991."

75. McClatchy to Schuman, December 21, 1991, NYPL-C, "Correspondence M, 1991–1992."

76. Schuman to Richard Dufallo and Schuman to David Del Tredici, both February 14, 1992, NYPL-C, "Correspondence D, 1992–1993."

77. McClatchy, "William Schuman," 37.

Epilogue: "William Schuman and the Shaping of America's Musical Life"

1. Paul Wittke, "William Schuman Remembered," *Schirmer/News*, Spring 1992, 7.

2. Aaron Copland and Vivian Perlis, *Copland 1900 through 1942* (New York: St. Martin's, 1984), 350.

3. Tim Page, "National Symphony Dusts Off and Polishes Obscure Pieces," *Washington Post*, February 4, 2005, C1.

4. Schuman to David Bar-Illan, June 14, 1974, NYPL-A, 93/8.

5. Jeremy Gury to Schuman, February 4, 1952, NYPL-A, 145/2.

6. "H.C.S." [Harold C. Schonberg], "There Is No Joy in 'Casey' Opera," *New York Times*, March 7, 1953, 34.

7. Schuman, "For Aaron Copland," November 14, 1970, NYPL-A, 98/7.

8. Schuman to Dan Gustin, November 13, 1980, NYPL-A, 125/6.

9. Tim Page, "Judging Composers: High Notes, and Low," *New York Times*, March 22, 1987, 28.

10. H. Wiley Hitchcock to Schuman, March 21, 1987, and Schuman to Hitchcock, May 20, 1987, NYPL-C, "Correspondence H, 1987."

11. Schuman to Charles Wuorinen, December 13, 1978, and Wuorinen to Schuman, December 16, 1978, NYPL-A, 119/8.

12. Robert Ward to Frances Schuman, February 20, 1992, NYPL-C, "Condolences—U–Z."

13. W. McNeil Lowry, "Oral History Interview with W. McNeil Lowry," Sharon Zane, interviewer, January 11, 1991, Oral History Project, LCPA, 63.

14. Phillip Ramey, from chapter 27 of his unpublished autobiography. I thank Ramey for making passages of his book available to me.

15. Errol Morris, "Opinionator: The Case of the Inappropriate Alarm Clock (Part 7)," *New York Times*, October 24, 2009.

BIBLIOGRAPHY

I divide my bibliography into three parts: articles and books that pertain to Schuman scholarship; reviews of his published music and recordings; and writings by Schuman. It is serendipitous that the first entry in my bibliography is itself a bibliography, one so complete that, with a few exceptions, I have excluded from my bibliography those works that appear among the 900-plus annotated entries contained in this earlier bibliography. I therefore invite scholars to treat my bibliography as an amplification of Adams's essential work. (For archival collections, see the list of abbreviations.)

Articles and Books

Adams, K. Gary. *William Schuman: A Bio-Bibliography*. Westport, CT: Greenwood Press, 1998.

Anawalt, Sasha. *The Joffrey Ballet: Robert Joffrey and the Making of an American Dance Company*. New York: Scribner, 1996.

Ansari, Emily Abrams. "'Masters of the President's Music': Cold War Composers and the United States Government." PhD diss., Harvard University, 2009.

Automobile Blue Book 1921, Volume 1: New York State and Adjacent Canada. New York: Automobile Blue Book Publishing Co., 1921.

Baskerville, David Ross. "Jazz Influence on Art Music to Mid-Century." Ph.D. diss., University of California at Los Angeles, 1965.

Baumol, William J., and William G. Bowen. *Performing Arts—The Economic Dilemma: A Study of Problems Common to Theater, Opera, Music, and Dance*. New York: Twentieth Century Fund, 1966.

Berger, Arthur. *Reflections of an American Composer*. Berkeley: University of California Press, 2002.

Birmingham, Stephen. *"Our Crowd": The Great Jewish Families of New York*. New York: Harper & Row, 1967.

Bonner, David. *Revolutionizing Children's Records: The Young People's Records and Children's Record Guild Series, 1946–1977*. Lanham, MD: Scarecrow Press, 2008.

Booth, John E. *The Critic, Power, and the Performing Arts: A Twentieth Century Fund Essay*. New York: Columbia University Press, 1991.

Caro, Robert A. *The Power Broker: Robert Moses and the Fall of New York*. New York: Vintage, 1975.

Chapin, Schuyler. *Musical Chairs: A Life in the Arts*. New York: G. P. Putnam's Sons, 1977.

Chazin-Bennahum, Judith. *The Ballets of Antony Tudor: Studies in Psyche and Satire*. New York: Oxford University Press, 1994.

Chermayeff, Maro, and Amy Schewel. *Juilliard*. New York: Harry N. Abrams, 2002.

Copland, Aaron, and Vivian Perlis. *Copland: 1900 through 1942*. New York: St. Martin's, 1984.

———. *Copland since 1943*. New York: St. Martin's, 1989.

Crist, Elizabeth B. *Music for the Common Man: Aaron Copland during the Depression and War*. New York: Oxford University Press, 2005.

Crist, Elizabeth B., and Wayne Shirley, ed. *The Selected Correspondence of Aaron Copland*. New Haven, CT: Yale University Press, 2006.

Crossman, Richard H., ed. *The God That Failed*. New York: Columbia University Press, 2001.

de Mille, Agnes. *Martha: The Life and Work of Martha Graham*. New York: Random House, 1991.

Dewey, John. *Art as Experience*. New York: Minton, Balch, 1934.

Doráti, Antal. *Notes of Seven Decades*. London: Hodder & Stoughton, 1979.

Duberman, Martin. *The Worlds of Lincoln Kirstein*. Evanston, IL: Northwestern University Press, 2008.

Dunkel, Harold B. "Dewey and the Fine Arts." *School Review* 67, 2 (Summer 1959): 229–45.

Engel, Lehman. *This Bright Day: An Autobiography*. New York: Macmillan, 1974.

Erskine, John. *My Life in Music*. New York: William Morrow, 1950.

Ewen, David, "Discovery in American Music: William Schuman Is Hailed as a Major Composer." *National Jewish Monthly* 57 (January 1943): 170.

———, ed. *The New Book of Modern Composers*. 3rd ed. New York: Alfred A. Knopf, 1961.

———. "What's Going On . . . in Music." *Deb* 1, 7 (September 1946): 62, 63, 130.

Eyer, Ronald F. "Juilliard's Literature and Materials Report." *Musical America* 74, 4 (February 15, 1954): 26, 146.

———. "Meet the Composer: (4) William Schuman." *Musical America* 64, 2 (January 25, 1944): 8, 25.

Falconer-Salkeld, Bridget. *The MacDowell Colony: A Musical History of America's Premier Artists' Colony*. Lanham, MD: Scarecrow Press, 2005.

Freed, Richard. "Composer William Schuman at 70." *Washington Post*, August 3, 1980.

Gamoran, Emanuel. *A Survey of 125 Religious Schools Affiliated with the Union of American Hebrew Congregations*. Cincinnati, OH: Union of American Hebrew Congregations, 1925.

Gann, Kyle. *American Music in the Twentieth Century*. New York: Schirmer, 1997.

Gatti-Casazza, Giulio. *Memories of the Opera*. New York: Charles Scribner's Sons, 1941.

Gay, Harriet. *The Juilliard String Quartet*. New York: Vantage, 1974.

Gentry, Philip. "The Age of Anxiety: Music, Politics, and McCarthyism, 1948–1954." Ph.D. diss., University of California at Los Angeles, 2008.

Gilroy, Frank D. *Writing for Love and/or Money: Outtakes from a Life on Spec (The Early Years)*. Hanover, NH: Smith & Kraus, 2008.

Glock, William. "The Music of William Schuman." *Listener*, September 4, 1947, 408.

Goodman, Peter W. *Morton Gould: American Salute*. Portland, OR: Amadeus Press, 2000.

Graham, Martha. *Blood Memory*. New York: Doubleday, 1991.

———. *The Notebooks of Martha Graham*. New York: Harcourt Brace Jovanovich, 1973.

Gruen, John. *The Private World of Ballet*. New York: Viking, 1975.

Heyman, Barbara B. *Samuel Barber: The Composer and His Music*. New York: Oxford, 1992.

Hinitz, Blythe. "Margaret Naumburg and the Walden School." In *Founding Mothers and Others: Women Educational Leaders during the Progressive Era*, edited by Alan R. Sadovnik and Susan F. Semel, 37–60. New York: Palgrave, 2002.

Hollingworth, Harry L. *Leta Stetter Hollingworth: A Biography*. Lincoln: University of Nebraska Press, 1943.

Hurwitz, David Lyon. "How Lucky We Were." *American Jewish History* 87, 1 (March 1999): 29–59.

Hutcheson, Ernest. *While I Live I Must Work: Writings of Ernest Hutcheson: Memoirs, Addresses, and Excerpts from His Journal of Letters to His Wife, In Coeli*. Edited by Thomas W. Hutcheson. Glenn Falls, NY: Quisisana Press, 2003.

Hyams, Barry. *Hirshhorn: Medici from Brooklyn*. New York: E. P. Dutton, 1979.

Jacobson, Marion S. "From Communism to Yiddishism: The Reinvention of the Jewish People's Philharmonic Chorus of New York City." In *Chorus and Community*, edited by Karen Ahlquist, 202–20. Urbana: University of Illinois Press, 2006.

Kazan, Elia. *Elia Kazan: A Life*. New York: Alfred A. Knopf, 1988.

Kempton, Murray, and David Remnick. *Part of Our Time: Some Ruins and Monuments of the Thirties*. New York: New York Review of Books, 2004.

Kriegsman, Alan M. "From Lincoln Center to Videotapes—With Gusto." *Washington Post/Times Herald*, October 25, 1970.

Kwitny, Jonathan. "Before Collapse, Sky Seemed to Be Limit for Videorecord Corp. and Its Franchisers." *Wall Street Journal*, April 12, 1974.

Labiche, Eugene, and Edouard Martin. *Le voyage de Monsieur Perrichon*. Project Gutenberg eBook #9453, downloaded January 25, 2009.

LaFarge, Christopher. *Mesa Verde*. New York: J. Laughlin, 1945.

Landau, Anne L. *The Contribution of Jewish Composers to the Music of the Modern World*. Cincinnati, OH: National Federation of Temple Sisterhoods, n.d. (ca. 1946).

Laurie, Clayton D. *The Propaganda Warriors: America's Crusade against Nazi Germany*. Lawrence: University Press of Kansas, 1996.

Leatherman, LeRoy, and Martha Swope. *Martha Graham: Portrait of the Lady as an Artist*. New York: Alfred A. Knopf, 1966.

LeFrak, Karen T. "Conversations on Commissioning." Vol. 2 of "Forty Years of Commissioning by the New York Philharmonic, 1945–1985." M.A. thesis, Hunter College, New York, NY, 1986.

Lehrman, Leonard J. *Marc Blitzstein: A Bio-Bibliography*. Westport, CT: Praeger, 2005.

Leichtentritt, Hugo. *Serge Koussevitzky, the Boston Symphony Orchestra, and the New American Music*. Cambridge, MA: Harvard University Press, 1946.

Leighton, Mary. "Schuman Work Given Premiere in Cincinnati UNESCO Concert." *Musical America* 75, 16 (December 15, 1955): 31

Lerner, Michael A. *Dry Manhattan: Prohibition in New York City*. Cambridge, MA: Harvard University Press, 2007.

Levy, Beth Ellen. "Frontier Figures: American Music and the Mythology of the American West, 1895–1945." Ph.D. diss., University of California, Berkeley, 2002.

Limón, José, and Lynn Garafala. *José Limón: An Unfinished Memoir*. Middletown, CT: Wesleyan University Press, 2001.

Lipman, Samuel. "American Quartet Music, Old and New." *New Criterion* 7, 7 (March 1989): 15–21.

———. *Arguing for Music, Arguing for Culture*. Boston: David R. Godine, 1990.

———. *Music and More: Essays, 1975–1991*. Evanston, IL: Northwestern University Press, 1992.

Loesser, Arthur. "My Brother Frank." *Notes*, 2nd ser., 7, 2 (March 1950): 217–39.

Loesser, Susan. *A Most Remarkable Fella: Frank Loesser and the Guys and Dolls in His Life*. New York: Donald I. Fine, 1993.

Luening, Otto. *The Odyssey of an American Composer: The Autobiography of Otto Luening*. New York: Charles Scribner's Sons, 1980.

Marks, Edward B. *Still Counting: Achievements and Follies of a Nonagenarian*. Lanham, MD: Hamilton Books, 2005.

Martin, John. "Martha Graham Begins Dance Engagement at Alvin Theatre with Premiere of 'Voyage.'" *New York Times*, May 18, 1953.

Martin, Ralph G. *Lincoln Center for the Performing Arts*. Englewood Cliffs, NJ: Prentice-Hall, 1971.

Mayer, Martin. "New York's Monument to the Muses." *Horizon* 4, 6 (July 1962): 4–11.

McClatchy, J. D. "William Schuman: A Reminiscence." *Opera Quarterly* 10, 4 (1994): 21–37.

McClellan, Joseph. "Brilliant Versatility." *Washington Post*, April 7, 1976.

McGlinchee, Claire. "American Literature in American Music." *Musical Quarterly* 31, 1 (January 1945): 101–19.

Meister, Knud. "Larmen giver mig den nødvendige stilhed" [Noise gives me the necessary silence], *Berlingske Aftenavis*, December 29, 1962, 7.

Meyer, Michael A. *Response to Modernity: A History of the Reform Movement in Judaism*. New York: Oxford University Press, 1988.

"Mixing Business and Art: Schuman's Job at Lincoln Center Shows Skills Needed to Run Cultural Project." *Business Week*, August 3, 1963, 42–45 (cover story).

Moddel, Philip. *Max Helfman: A Biographical Sketch*. Berkeley, CA: Judah L. Magnes Memorial Museum, 1974.

Moremen, Ray, et al. "In Quest of Answers: An Interview with William Schuman." *Choral Journal* 13 (February 1973): 5–15.

Moses, Robert. *Public Works: A Dangerous Trade*. New York: McGraw-Hill, 1970.

Nash, Dennison J. "The Socialization of an Artist: The American Composer." *Social Forces* 35, 4 (May 1957): 307–13.

Nicholas Louis. *Thor Johnson: American Conductor*. N.p.: Music Festival Committee of the Peninsula Arts Association, 1982.

Oja, Carol J. *Making Music Modern: New York in the 1920s*. New York: Oxford University Press, 2000.

Olmstead, Andrea. *Juilliard: A History*. Urbana: University of Illinois Press, 1999.

Paris, Leslie. *Children's Nature: The Rise of the American Summer Camp*. New York: New York University Press, 2008.

Parmenter, Ross. "Music: A Happy Mixture by Serkin." *New York Times*, March 14, 1956.

———. "Webster, Pianist, Offers 'Voyage.'" *New York Times*, April 7, 1954.

Pegolotti, James A. *Deems Taylor: A Biography*. Boston: Northeastern University Press, 2003.

"The Performing Arts: Problem and Prospects." *Rockefeller Panel Report on the Future of Theatre, Dance, Music in America*. New York: McGraw-Hill, 1965.

Perlmutter, Donna. *Shadowplay: The Life of Antony Tudor*. New York: Viking, 1991.

Polisi, Joseph W. *American Muse: The Life and Times of William Schuman*. New York: Amadeus, 2008.

Pollack, Howard. *Aaron Copland: The Life and Work of an Uncommon Man*. Urbana: University of Illinois Press, 2000.

———. *Skyscraper Lullaby: The Life and Music of John Alden Carpenter*. Washington, DC: Smithsonian Institution Press, 1995.

Pye, Richard. "'Asking about the Inside': Schoenberg's 'Idea' in the Music of Roy Harris and William Schuman." *Music Analysis* 19, 1 (2000): 69–98.

Pye, Richard C. "The Construction and Interpretation of Bespoke Pitch-Class Set Genera as Models of Harmonic Duality in William Schuman's Sixth Symphony." *Music Theory Spectrum* 25 (2003): 243–74.

———. "Models of Unity and Diversity in the Symphonies of William Schuman: An Exploration of Genera Theories in Relation to Stylistic Change and the Dynamics of Form." Ph.D. diss., University of Newcastle, 2000.

Ramey, Phillip. *Irving Fine: An American Composer in His Time*. [Hillsdale, NY]: Pendragon Press, in association with the Library of Congress, 2005.

———. "William Schuman at Seventy: A Talk with the Composer." *Ovation* 1, 8 (September 1980): 17–21.

Rector, Jennifer D. "American Proletarianism in Two Collaborative Works by William Schuman and Genevieve Taggard." M.M. thesis, University of Missouri, Kansas City, 1996.

Revelli, William R. "The Challenge of the High School and College Band to the American Composer: A Panel Discussion, Part One." *Etude* 63, 5 (May 1945): 259–60.

———. "The Challenge of the High School and College Band to the American Composer: A Panel Discussion, Part Two." *Etude* 63, 6 (June 1945): 319–20.

Riis, Thomas L. *Frank Loesser*. New Haven, CT: Yale University Press, 2008.

Robertson, Nan. "Schuman Attacks Congress on Arts." *New York Times*, May 20, 1967.

Rochberg, George. *Five Lines, Four Spaces: The World of My Music*. Edited by Gene Rochberg and Richard Griscom. Urbana: University of Illinois Press, 2009.

———. *The Hexachord and Its Relation to the Twelve-Tone Row*. Bryn Mawr, PA: Theodore Presser, 1955.

Rockwell, John. "Concert: Music Today, Series at Goodman House." *New York Times*, November 16, 1984.

———. "Concert: Slatkin Leads St. Louis Symphony." *New York Times*, January 29, 1983.

———. "Music: The Endymions." *New York Times*, November 10, 1978.

Rosenthal, Peggy Z. "Whitman Music: The Problem of Adaptation." *Books at Brown* 20 (1965): 71–97.

Sabin, Robert. "The Dance Concerto: Martha Graham and William Schuman Create a New Form for the Theatre." *Dance Observer* 17, 2 (1951): 22–23.

Saminsky, Lazare. "New Faces among Our Composers: An Appraisal." *Musical Courier*, February 1, 1945, 13, 34.

Sargent, Porter E. *A Handbook of American Private Schools*. Boston: Geo. M. Ellis, 1917.

Seldes, Barry. *Leonard Bernstein: The Political Life of an American Musician*. Berkeley: University of California Press, 2009.

Shanet, Howard. *Philharmonic: A History of New York's Orchestra*. Garden City, NY: Doubleday, 1975.

Share, Allen J. *Cities in the Commonwealth: Two Centuries of Urban Life in Kentucky*. Lexington: University Press of Kentucky, 1982.

Shepard, Richard F. "Walter Mitty Fulfilled." *New York Times*, November 28, 1975.

Sherry, Michael S. *Gay Artists in Modern American Culture: An Imagined Conspiracy*. Chapel Hill: University of North Carolina Press, 2007.

Simmons, Walter. *Voices in the Wilderness: Six American Neo-Romantic Composers*. Lanham, MD: Scarecrow Press, 2004.

Slonimsky, Nicolas. *Perfect Pitch: A Life Story*. Oxford: Oxford University Press, 1988.

———. "Roy Harris: Cimarron Composer." Unpublished MS. University of California, Los Angeles, Music Library, Special Collections, 1951.

———. *Slonimsky's Book of Musical Anecdotes*. London: Routledge, 2002.

Smith, Julia. *Master Pianist: The Career and Teaching of Carl Friedberg*. New York: Philosophical Library, 1963.

Smith, Moses. *Koussevitzky*. New York: Allen, Towne & Heath, 1947.

Solway, Diane. "The Stages of Marty's Festival." *New York Times Magazine*, April 24, 1988, 20–21, 36–38.

Spender, Stephen. "We Can Win the Battle for the Mind of Europe." *New York Times*, April 25, 1948.

Stehman, Dan. *Roy Harris: An American Musical Pioneer*. Boston: G. K. Hall, 1984.

Stoddard, George D. "Art as the Measure of Man." In *Art*, 7–28. New York: Museum of Modern Art, 1964.

Stodelle, Ernestine. *Deep Song: The Dance Story of Martha Graham*. New York: Schirmer Books, 1984.

Straus, Joseph N. *Twelve-Tone Music in America*. Cambridge: Cambridge University Press, 2009.

Strauss, Andrea. "William Schuman's Legacy for Music Education." *Music Educators Journal* 87, 6 (May 2001): 24–26, 60.

Strimple, Nick. *Choral Music in the Twentieth Century*. Portland, OR: Amadeus Press, 2002.

Sutherland, John. *Stephen Spender: A Literary Life*. Oxford: Oxford University Press, 2005.

Swayne, Steve. "American Musicology at the Crossroads, Contemporary Music in the Crosshairs: The Ideological Battle at G. Schirmer Inc. at the End of World War II." Paper presented at the annual meeting of the American Musicological Society, Quebec City, Quebec, Canada, November 2, 2007. Available at http://www.orpheus.dartmouth.edu.

———. "Irresistible Vision Meets Immovable Reality: William Schuman and the Lincoln Center Festivals of the 1960s." In *Crosscurrents: American and European Music in Interaction, 1900–2000*, edited by Felix Meyer, Carol J. Oja, Wolfgang Rathert, and Anne C. Shreffler. Woodbridge, UK: Boydell & Brewer, 2011.

———. "William Schuman, World War II, and the Pulitzer Prize." *Musical Quarterly* 89, 2–3 (Summer–Fall 2006): 273–320.

———. "William Schuman's Puzzling Seventh Symphony." Library of Congress Webcast. http://www.loc.gov/today/cyberlc/index.php.

Tawa, Nicholas. *The Great American Symphony: Music, The Depression, and War*. Bloomington: Indiana University Press, 2009.

Taylor, John M. *General Maxwell Taylor: The Sword and the Pen*. New York: Doubleday, 1989.

Tischler, Barbara L. *An American Music: The Search for an American Musical Identity*. New York: Oxford University Press, 1986.

Tommasini, Anthony. *Virgil Thomson: Composer on the Aisle*. New York: W. W. Norton, 1997.

Tracy, Robert. *Goddess: Martha Graham's Dancers Remember*. New York: Limelight Editions, 1997.

Van Slyck, Abigail A. *A Manufactured Wilderness: Summer Camps and the Shaping of American Youth, 1890–1960*. Minneapolis: University of Minnesota Press, 2006.

Vincent, John Nathaniel. *The Diatonic Modes in Modern Music*. Berkeley: University of California Press, 1951.

Wack, Henry Wellington. *Summer Camps, Boys and Girls*. New York: Red Book Magazine, 1923.

Wannamaker, John Samuel. "The Musical Settings of the Poetry of Walt Whitman: A Study of Theme, Structure, and Prosody." Ph.D. diss., University of Minnesota, 1972.

Warburg, James P. *The Long Road Home: The Autobiography of a Maverick.* Garden City, NY: Doubleday, 1964.

Watkins, Glenn. *Sounding: Music in the Twentieth Century.* New York: Schirmer, 1988.

Whitfield, Stephen J. *In Search of American Jewish Culture.* Hanover, NH: Brandeis University Press, 1999.

Yoder, Robert M. "He Put That Tune in Your Head." *Saturday Evening Post,* May 21, 1949, 42–57.

Young, Edgar B. *Lincoln Center: The Building of an Institution.* New York: New York University Press, 1980.

Zola, Gary P. "Jewish Camping and Its Relationship to the Organized Camping Movement in America." In *A Place of Our Own: The Rise of Reform Jewish Camping,* edited by Michael M. Lorge and Gary P. Zola. Tuscaloosa: University of Alabama Press, 2006.

Zuck, Barbara A. *A History of Musical Americanism.* Ann Arbor: University of Michigan Press, 1980.

Reviews of Books, Scores, and Recordings

A. M. Review of William Schuman by Flora Rheta Schreiber; Vincent Persichetti. *Music and Letters* 36, 1 (January 1955): 76–78.

Cochran, Alfred W. Review of Dances: Divertimento for Wind Quintet and Percussion by William Schuman. *Notes,* 2nd ser., 45, 4 (June 1989): 857–58.

Dickinson, Peter. "Education at the Juilliard School of Music." *Musical Times* 101, 1407 (May 1960): 297–98.

———. Review of *A Song of Orpheus,* Fantasy for Cello and Orchestra by William Schuman. *Musical Times* 105, 1460 (October 1964): 759.

———. Review of *Amaryllis: Variations for String Trio* by William Schuman. *Musical Times* 108, 1494 (August 1967): 739–40.

———. Review of Symphony No. 10, "American Muse," by William Schuman. *Musical Times* 120, 1634 (April 1979): 320–21.

———. Review of *The Orchestra Song* by William Schuman. *Musical Times* 107, 1477 (March 1966): 239.

E. R. Review of *A Song of Orpheus* by William Schuman. *Music and Letters* 45, 3 (July 1964): 292.

———. Review of Symphony No. 7 by William Schuman. *Music and Letters* 44, 1 (January 1963): 96–97.

———. Review of Symphony No. 8 by William Schuman. *Music and Letters* 46, 2 (April 1965): 182–83.

Harris, Simon. Review of *In Praise of Shahn* and Symphony No. 9 *(Le Fosse Ardeatine)* by William Schuman. *Music* and *Letters* 55, 3 (July 1974): 373–74.

Hitchcock, H. Wiley. Review of the Juilliard Report on Teaching the Literature and Materials of Music, by Richard Franko Goldman; William Schuman." *Notes,* 2nd ser., 11, 2 (March 1954): 299–300.

Howard, George S. Review of *Newsreel in Five Shots (Horse-Race, Fashion Show, Tribal Dance, Monkeys at the Zoo, Parade)* by William Schuman. *Music Educators Journal* 29, 1 (September–October 1942): 50.

Hume, Paul. Review of *Te Deum for Four-Part Chorus of Mixed Voices a cappella.* (For the Coronation Scene of Shakespeare's *Henry VIII*), by William Schuman. *Notes*, 2nd ser., 3, 2 (March 1946): 184.

Jensen, Byron. Review ofViolin Concerto by William Schuman; Philip Quint; Charles Ives; José Serebrier; Bournemouth Symphony Orchestra. *American Music* 21, 4 (Winter 2003): 530–32.

Johnson, Bret. Review of Herrmann: Symphony No. 1 and Schuman: *New England Triptych* by Phoenix Symphony; James Sedares; Bernard Herrmann; William Schuman. *Tempo*, new ser., 184 (March 1993): 50–51.

———. Review of William Schuman: *The Mighty Casey; A Question of Taste* by Juilliard Opera Center and Orchestra; Gerard Schwarz; William Schuman. *Tempo*, new ser., 191 (December 1994): 60, 62.

Kroeger, Karl. Review of *American Hymn: Orchestral Variations on an Original Melody* by William Schuman. *Notes*, 2nd ser., 42, 1 (September 1985): 151–52.

M. C. Review of *Amaryllis: Variations for String Trio* by William Schuman. *Music and Letters* 48, 2 (April 1967): 183–84.

Morgan, Robert P. Review of Symphony No. 10, "American Muse," by William Schuman. *Notes*, 2nd ser., 35, 2 (December 1978): 413–15.

Ottaway, Hugh. Review of Symphony No. 8 by William Schuman. *Musical Times* 106, 1472 (October 1965): 786.

P.A.E. Review of Concerto [for Violin and Orchestra]. Piano Reduction by William Schuman. *Music and Letters* 42, 2 (April 1961): 193–94.

Parker, Craig B. Review of *Three Colloquies for Horn and Orchestra* by William Schuman. *American Music* 5, 2 (Summer 1987): 229 30.

Rouse, Christopher. Review of *Three Colloquies for French Horn and Orchestra* by William Schuman. *Notes*, 2nd ser., 39, 1 (September 1982): 209.

Talley, V. Howard. Review of *Samuel Barber* by Nathan Broder and *William Schuman* by Flora Rheta Schreiber, Vincent Persichetti. *Journal of Research in Music Education* 3, 1 (Spring 1955): 65–66.

Wright, David. Review of String Quartets Nos. 2, 3, and 5 by William Schuman; Lydian String Quartet. *Musical Times* 136, 1823 (January 1995): 45.

Articles by William Schuman (arranged chronologically)

"Richard Wagner Alias 'K. Freigedank.'" *American Hebrew and Jewish Tribune*, March 2, 1934, 304.

"Music of All Times." *Music Journal* 4, 5 (1946): 7, 44–46.

"William Schuman." *Sarah Lawrence College Alumnae Magazine*, Summer 1948, 13.

"Certification for Private Music Teachers." *Music Journal* 10, 1 (January 1952): 11, 52–54.

"It Happened in Philadelphia." *Music Educators Journal* 38, 6 (June–July 1952): 24–28, 33–34, 36, 38 (with Frances Elliot Clark, Ernest O. Melby, and William M. Cruickshank).

" . . . Very Important, But Very. . . ." *Sarah Lawrence Alumnae Magazine*, January 1953, 10–11.

"A Suggestion [about merging the high schools of music and art]." *Playbill*, ca. 1959.

"Naumburg Tribute." *New York Times*, November 1, 1959.

"Aim of Naumburg Competition to Be a 'Constructive Musical Force.'" *New York Times*, November 13, 1960.

"William Schuman Discusses Problems in the Field of Music Education." *International Musician*, Special Music Education Issue (March 1961): 22–23.

Problems of Journalism: Proceedings of the 1961 Convention [of the] American Society of Newspaper Editors, Statler Hilton Hotel, Washington, D.C., April 20–22, 1961, 124–28.

"What Will Lincoln Center Mean to Our Young People?" *Marine Currents* [Marine Park Junior High School, Brooklyn, NY], March 1963, 1–2.

"Profile: The Education of an Artist." *Educational Theatre News*, April 1963, 2–3.

"In the Light of Experience." In *Behind the Baton*, edited by Charles Blackman, 119–20. New York: Charos Enterprises, 1964.

"From the East Coast a Watchful Interest." *Los Angeles Times*, December 6, 1964, N38.

"['The Composer Is the Key'] Was Koussevitzky's Motto." *New York Times*, June 23, 1968.

"'On First Hearing': The Act of Creation in Music." In *The Joys of Research*, edited by Walter Shropshire Jr., 86–100. Washington, D.C.: Smithsonian Institution Press, 1981.

COMPOSITION INDEX

Adoration (1932), **65**, 66, 440
Amaryllis, Variations for String Trio (1964), **351–56**, 359, 363, 370, 431, 451
Amaryllis: Variants for Strings on an Old English Song (1976), **356–57**
American Festival Overture (1939), 14, 102, **116–19**, 120, 125, 139, 144, 156, 204, 225, 427, 523, 583n12
American Hymn (brass quintet; 1980), 292, **499–501**, 543
American Hymn (concert band; 1981), 292, **499–502**, 543
American Hymn (orchestra; 1981), 14, 292, 499–500, **502–6**, 509, 511, 517, 522, 533, 543, 552
Anniversary Fanfare (1969), 433, **432–33**, 435, 436, 470, 522
At Daybreak (ca. 1935), 70
At the Crossroads (1939), 128–29
Awake Thou Wintry Earth (1986), **523–25**, 531, 533, 534

The Band Song (1966), **350–51**
Be Glad Then America (concert band; 1978), **299–301**, 348

Canon (with Introduction and Coda) for Piano (1933), 109
Canon and Fugue for Violin, Cello, and Piano (1934), **69**, 569n11
Carols of Death (1958), 272, **304–6**, 315, 402, 437, 440, 497, 509, 514
Casey at the Bat (1976), 465–67, **471–72**, 473, 479, 481, 520, 533
Celebration Concertante (1959), **237–40**, 242, 250, 289, 303, **318–20**, 322, 352, 394 *See also* Symphony no. 7
Chester: Overture for Band (1956), **297–99**, 300, 436, 533, 538
Chester: Variations for Piano (1988), **538**, 577n7
Choral Etude (1937), 85, 86, 89, 109, 111, 124, 141, 168, 509, 577n62
Choral Fanfare for Women's Voices (1941), 135
Choreographic Poem for Seven Instruments (1935), 73, 75, 117, 198, 569n11
Cinq petits préludes a deux voix (1933), **67–68**, 109, 569n11
Circus Overture (1944), 171, **170–72**, 217, 225, 226, 256, 271, 498
Concerto for Piano and Orchestra (1938), 87, **109–11**, 117, 151
Concerto for Piano and Small Orchestra (1942), 110–11, **151–53**, 154, 158, 162, 165, 497
Concerto for Violin and Orchestra (1946–59), 21, 75, 203, 225, **246–51**, 271, 322, 394, 430, 442, 523, 546
  original version (1947–50), 211, **248–50**, 494
  first revision (1954–56), 246–47, **249–50**
  second revision (1958–59), **250–51**, 303, 497
Concerto on Old English Rounds (1973), 143, 233, 356, **450–57**, 473, 481, 486, 523, 637nn25 & 38
Cooperstown Fanfare (1987), **531–32**, 533
Cradle Song (piano; 1933), **66**

Credendum (1955), 236, 250, 272, **284–89**, 290, 291, 294, 295, 304, 315, 318, 348, 392, 399, 401, 464, 494, 511
"Chorale" for concert band, 300

Dances (Divertimento for Wind Quintet and Percussion), **521–22**
Declaration Chorale (1971), 335, **438–39**
Dedication Fanfare (1968), **392–93**, **401–2**, 406, 407, 474, 499, 522
Deo Ac Veritati (1963), **348–50**, 440
Doing the Dishes (ca. 1930), **49**, 566n22

The Earth Is Born (1957), **301–3**, 315, 320
Esses (1982), **509–11**, 513, 521, 552
Fair Land of Hope (ca. 1942), 135, 159, 163, 581n41
Fanfare, Song & Dance (ca. 1945; inc.), **242**
Fate (tango), 37, 425, See *Monster Minstrel Show*
Five Rounds on Famous Words (1956; 1969), 245, 293, 315, 438, 497, 498, 509, 510, 511, 552, 608n15
For A.C. [Aaron Copland] *con amore* (1981), **481**
For Wiley H. [Hitchcock] (1987), **480–81**
Four Canonic Choruses (1933–34), 68, 70–71, 73, 74, 85, 124, 193, 255, 569n11
A Free Song (Secular Cantata no. 2) (1942), 104–5, 135, **137–38**, 139, 142, 153, **158–59**, 163, 195, 197, 225, 305, 306, 402, 446, 514, 520, 552, 585n11
Fugue for Strings (1946), **245–46**, 524

George Washington Bridge (1950), 14, **241–44**, 245, 251, 298, 315, 401, 497
Glow-Worm (arr. for flute and piano, 1931), 50
God's World (1933), 50, 51, **63–65**, 66, 292

Happy Birthday to You (*Score Three for Mockshin at Three Score*) [Mark Schubart] (1978), **436**
Happy Birthday to You [Eugene Ormandy] (1969), **435**, 436
Happy Birthday to You [Mary Louise Curtis Bok Zimbalist] (1951), **436**
Holiday Song (1942), 139, 290

In Love with a Memory of You (1931), 50
In Praise of Shahn: Canticle for Orchestra (1969), **431–35**
In Sweet Music (1978), 61, 75, 171, 446, 454, 477, **481–84**, 491, 497, 523, 543
It's Up to Pa (1928), **37–40**, 41, 43, 47, 65, 83
"I Can't Say Yes to You," 38
"I Want to Be Near You," 37, 38, 46, 47, **49**
"We're Dressed Up for the Visitors," 40, 531
Judith: Choreographic Poem for Orchestra (1949), **207–13**, 219, 230, 250, 251, 268, 369, 372, 400

Let's Hear It for Lenny! (1988), **537**, 538
The Lord Has a Child (choir and brass; 1990), 292, **542–44**
The Lord Has a Child (hymn and choruses; 1956), **290–92**, 315, 498, 502, 543
Lovesick (1930), **49**, 51, 566n37

Mail Order Madrigals (1971), **437–38**, 497, 510, 515, 552
The Mighty Casey (1951–53), 24, 250, 254, **260–68**, 269, 271, 306, 315, 339, 464, **465–67**, 468, 472, 530–31, 533, 534, 540, 541, 552
"Kiss Me Not Goodbye", 479
Choruses from, 467
Monster Minstrel Show (1927), **36–38**
"Pampa" (tango), 37

New England Triptych (1956), 14, 75, 236, 250, 272, 285, **293–97**, 299, 300, 301, 314, 315, 316, 324, 346, 348, 351, 357, 439, 497, 500, 511, 538, 552
Newsreel in Five Shots (1941), 14, **135–36**, 151, 581n43
"Parade," 581
Night Journey (1947), **204–7**, 210, 211, 212, 214, 230, 250, 253, 257, 351, 372, 491, 593nn44 & 45
film version (1961), 270, 371, 497

Ode to Leonard [Feist] (1980), **480**
On Freedom's Ground (1985), 14, 20, 163, **513–20**, 521–22, 529, 531, 533, 534
Once More (ca. 1930), 54, **566–67n37**

The Orchestra Song (orchestra; 1963), **350–51**
The Orchestra Song (voices; 1939), 125, 143
Orpheus with His Lute (1944), 75, 171, 322, 483, 543

Parade of the Wooden Soldiers (arr. for flute and piano, 1931), 50
Pastorale no. 1 (1934), **69**, 569n11
Pastorale no. 2 (1934), **70**, 569n11
Perceptions (1982), **509–11**, 521, 532, 646n59
Philharmonic Fanfare (1965), **368–69**, 392, 522
Pioneers! (1937), 108–9, 124, 137, 253, 305, 402, 469–70, 509
Potpourri (Impressions of Bohemian Life) (1932), **65–66**
Prayer in Time of War (1943), 135, 153, 158, **159–60**, 163, 165, 204, 225, 226, 230, 323, 400, 404, 585n11
Prelude and Fugue for Orchestra (1937), **87–88**, 89
Prelude for a Great Occasion (1974), **464–65**, 469–70, 522
Prelude for Voices (1936; 1939), 85, 98, **124**, 142, 143, 305, 437, 509
Prologue for Chorus and Orchestra (1939), 94, **124–29**, 131, 137, 139, 154, 305, 514, 515, 520, 580n7

Quartettino for Four Bassoons (1939), **91**, 271, 479, 523, 573n50
A Question of Taste (1986–88), 444, **534–37**, **539–41**, 552

Requiescat (1942), **138–39**, 515
A Round for Alice [Tully] (1977), **478–79**, 480, 481, 496
A Round for Audrey [Gerstner, Schuman's sister] (1977), **479–80**, 496
Round for Emily Joan Warburg (1981), 542

Serenade Appassionato (1932), 22, 66
Showcase: A Short Display for Orchestra (1986), 292, **522–23**, 543, 552
Side Show. *See* Circus Overture
A Song of Orpheus (Fantasy for Cello and Orchestra) (1961), 75, 171, 233, 300, 318, **321–23**, 326, 350, 352, 403, 451, 455, 493, 523, 533, 543
chamber music version (1979), 491, 643n51
Sonnet (1935), 70
Steel Town (1944), 135, **160–62**, 163, 303, 585n11
String Quartet no. 1 (1936), 74, 76, 88, 569n11
String Quartet no. 2 (1937), 87, 91, 94, 98, 109, 143
String Quartet no. 3 (1939–40), 119, **141–43**, 147, 431, 483, 497
String Quartet no. 4 (1950), 75, 87, 208, **251–54**, 351, 400
String Quartet no. 5 (1987), **532–34**, 538, 545–46
Symphony for Strings (1943), 75, 142, **164–67**, 186, 211, 217, 225, 271, 305, 314, 445, 455, 497, 548, 635n62
Symphony no. 1 (1935), **72–76**, 85, 88, 102, 117, 148, 193, 251, 569
Symphony no. 2 (1937), 88–92, 94, **100–102**, 107, **111–15**, 139, 141, 166, 186, 234, 237, 372, 374, 434, 548, 573n53
Symphony no. 3 (1941), 104, 119–21, 125, 135, 142, **144–48**, 152, 194, 204, 225, 226, 235, 271, 320, 348, 372, 374, 399, 404, 434, 445, 455, 463, 470, 478, 481, 528, 529, 548
original version, **146–47**, 551–52
Symphony no. 4 (1941), 120–22, **148–50**, 156, 167, 211, 225, 226, 427, 478, 576n55
Symphony no. 5. See *Symphony for Strings*
Symphony no. 6 (1948), 194, 197, 203, **230–37**, 246, 250, 253, 271, 287, 525, 528, 548, 576n55, 597n20
Symphony no. 7 (1960), 110, 121, **238–40**, 250, 285, 303, **318–21**, 324, 368, 392, 399–400, 465, 525 See also *Celebration Concertante*
Symphony no. 8 (1962), 3, 4, 6, 75, 121, 233, 254, 300, **321–24**, 341, 345–46, 399–400, 507, 528, 533
Symphony no. 9, "Le fosse Ardeatine" (1968), 236, 238, 244, 368, 372–74, **392–401**, 403–4, 406, 416, 431, 432, 445, 455, 461, 507, 597n14
Symphony no. 10, "American Muse" (1975), 14, 465, 467, **468–71**, 473, 504, 533

Te Deum (1944), 171, 440, **588n52**
Tell It to the Judge (1928), 38, 43, 52
Tell Me Where I Stand (1931), 51
Theater for a Voyage (1953), **268–70**, 304, 369
This Business of Loving You (1929), 48
This Is Our Time (Secular Cantata no. 1) (1940), 119, **129–31**, 132, 137, 139, 142, 151, 520
Three Colloquies for French Horn and Orchestra (1979), 250, 373, 455, **491–95**, 496, 497, 507, 523
Three Moods for Piano (1958), 109, **303–4**, 315–16, 319, 577nn7
Three Pieces for Five Brasses (1980), 292, **497–99**, 500, 502, 644n7, *See* also *American Hymn* (brass quintet; 1980)
Three Pieces for Piano (1938), **109–10**, 117, 577n8
Three Songs Without Words for Violin and Piano (ca. 1926), **21–22**, 38
Three-Score Set (1943), 75, **164–65**, 436, 577n7
Time to the Old (1979), 400, 484, **490–91**, **495–96**, 497, 529
To Thee Old Cause (Evocation for Oboe, Brass, Timpani, Piano and Strings) (1968), 373, **402–4**, 406, 408, 432, 455, 523
To Thy Love: Choral Fantasy on Old English Rounds (1973), **452**
Truth Shall Deliver (1946), **244–45**, 246
Undertow (1944–45), 162, **198–203**, 206, 207, 210, 213, 214, 225, 241, 255, 373, 506, 592n25
  Choreographic Episodes for Orchestra, 200, 202–3

Variation on a Theme of Eugene Goossens (1944), **169–70**
Variations on a 12-tone Theme for Piano (1959–60), 110, 306, **318–19**, 320
Variations on America (1963), 236, 324, **346–48**, 350, 464, 473, 497
Voyage (piano; 1953), **268–71**, 290, 304, 442–43, 577n7
Voyage for a Theater. See Theater for a Voyage
Voyage for Orchestra (1972), **442–44**, 446, 454, 494, 533

Waitin' for the Moon (1932), **49**, 50, 64, 316
When Jesus Wept: Prelude for Solo Cornet, Solo Baritone (Euphonium) and Band (1958), **299**, 301
Where the Grass Grows Green (ca. 1930), 566n22
William Billings Overture (1944), 75, **167–69**, 226, 271, **294–97**, 466
The Witch of Endor (1965), **369–73**, 374, 395, 473, 622n76
XXV Opera Snatches (1979), **488–89**, 492, 496, 523
The Young Dead Soldiers (1975), 400, 450, **472–73**, 481, 484, 490, 497, 514, 529

INDEX

Abravanel, Maurice, 171
Adams, John (composer), 94, 274, 522
Adams, John (president), 468
Adams, Stanley, 47
Adler, Peter Herman, 417
Ailey, Alvin, 336
Albany Symphony Orchestra, 306, 513
Albert, Stephen, 274, 533
Albright, William, 274
Alice Tully Hall, 5, 423
Altman, Stuart, 545
American Academy of Arts and Letters, 104, 281, 418, 459, 484, 486, 514, 544
American Bandmasters Association, 474, 499, 501–2, 543
American Brass Quintet, 497–500, 543
American Choral Directors Association, 306
American Composers Alliance, 89, 157
American Composers Committee, 89, 109
American Composers Orchestra, 20, 487, 488
American Hymns Old and New, 292, 301, 498
American National Theatre and Academy, 279, 308, 310, 313–15
American Society of Composers, Authors, and Publishers, 47, 117, 237, 271, 273–74
Ames, Amyas, 412
Ammidon, Hoyt, 383
ANTA. *See* American National Theatre and Academy
Antheil, George
  This I Believe and, 287
Appalachian Spring. *See* Copland, Aaron and Graham, Martha
Arensberg, Walter Conrad, 70
Argento, Dominick, 274
Arrow Press, 86, 87, 88, 110
ASCAP. *See* American Society of Composers, Authors, and Publishers
Asia, Daniel, 274
Aspen Music Festival, 370, 497
Atlanta Symphony Orchestra, 513

Babbitt, Milton, 275–76, 283–84, 310, 504
Bach, Johann Sebastian, 48, 89, 95, 144–45, 152–53, 258, 319
Balanchine, George, 214
Baltimore Symphony Orchestra, 111
  Symphony no. 2 (1937), 91
Barber, Samuel, 199, 271, 307, *377*, 487–90
  Adagio for Strings, op. 11 (1936), 473
  Antony and Cleopatra, op. 40 (1966), 376–77
  Concerto for Piano and Orchestra, op. 38 (1962), 324
  early opera project, 258, 279
  G. Schirmer book on, 195
  Juilliard commissions, 276
  Juilliard Orchestra and, 314
  Kolodin on, 461
  Koussevitzky and, 113
  LaFarge on, 258
  MacDowell Medal, 489
  Metropolitan Opera Guild commission, 488
  on Philharmonic Hall acoustics, 341

Barber, Samuel (*continued*)
on Schuman, 488
on Schuman's appointment to G. Schirmer, 173
Overture to *The School for Scandal*, op. 5 (1931), 519
Pulitzer Prize (1963), 324
Scalero as teacher, 66
Vanessa, op. 32 (1956–57), 278–79, 281, 376, 539
Zimbalist *Happy Birthday* Variations (1951), 435–36
Bard College, 85
Barlow, Howard, 90–91, 111–12, 116
Barnes, Clive, 206, 371
Bartholdi, Frédéric Auguste, 513
Bartholomew, Marshall ("Barty"), 244–45, 415
Bartók, Béla, 280, 307, 342, 355, 409
Concerto for Orchestra (1944), 146
Barzun, Jacques, 26, 84, 366
Baum, Morton, 360, 364
Bawtree, Michael, 536
Bax, Sir Arnold, 436
Bay of Pigs invasion, 330, 332
Bayreuth Festival, 72, 334, 378
Bean, Calvert, 293, 301
Beethoven, Ludwig van, 166, 229, 331, 367, 445
Choral Fantasy, op. 80, 451
Fidelio, op. 72, 71, 540
Overture to *The Consecration of the House*, op. 124, 445
Plaisir d'aimer, WoO 128, 58
Symphony no. 2 in D major, op. 36, 112
Symphony no. 4 in B♭ major, op. 60, 231
Symphony no. 5 in C minor, op. 67, 164, 481
Symphony no. 9 in D minor, op. 125, 267
Belafonte, Harry, 541
Belmont, Eleanor Robson, 488
Ben Shahn Foundation, 432–33
Bennett, Robert Russell, 172, 212, 588n53
Bennett, William J., 529
Bennington College, 85, 119, 214
Berberian, Cathy, 483
Berezowsky, Nicolai, 89
Berg, Alban, 280, 307
Berger, Arthur, 137–38, 153, 195
Bergsma, William, 268, 273, 276, 319, 456, 483–84
Berlin, Irving, 14, 135
Berlioz, Hector, 188, 229, 404
Harold in Italy, op. 16, 454
Bernbach, William, 419
Bernstein, Leonard, 402, *404*, 419, 445, 541
"New York, New York" (*On the Town*, 1944), 537, 539
advocacy for American music, 144
American Academy of Arts and Letters and, 529
as reviewer, 100, 102, 114, 146
at Juilliard opening, 423
birthday celebrations, 485, 537
birthplace of, 14
Candide (1956), 317, 537
correspondence with Schuman, 142, 152, 156, 190, 217, 219, 224, 262
death of, 544–45
Fancy Free (1944), 106
first encounter with Schuman, 114–15, 485
friendship with Schuman, 121, 240, 512
G. Schirmer and, 271
humor, 511
Jewish life and culture, 226–28
Juilliard commissions, 276
Koussevitzky and, 119–22, 226
Latin American tour (1958), 237
letter from Israel, 226
Metropolitan Museum of Art commission, 432
NAACP and, 5
New York City Symphony and, 226, 280
New York Philharmonic and, 341, 402, 426, 454, 473, 507
on Schuman, 377, 423, 485, 496, 525, 542
on Schuman's music, 114, 121, 434
on the symphony, 391
opposition to Vietnam War, 403
performance of *American Festival Overture*, 120, 156
Philadelphia Orchestra commissions, 395, 435
profanity and, 54
Schuman on, 120, 157, 485
selection as New York Philharmonic conductor, 280–81

serialism and, 316–17
Symphony no. 1 ("Jeremiah") (1942), 234
Symphony no. 2, *The Age of Anxiety* (1949), 106, 230
This I Believe and, 287
West Side Story (1957), 317, 536–37
World War II and, 150
Bessire, Henry, 385, 390
Biddlecome, Robert, 497, 499–500
Biggs, E. Power, 343, 346
Billings, William, 75, 167–69, 294–97, 500
Chester, 168, 299, 538
When Jesus Wept, 299
Bing, Sir Rudolf, 334, 362–64, 366, 376–77
Bizet, Georges, 262
Bjorge, James R., 439
Blackwood, Easley, 334
Blau, Herbert, 367, 382–83
Blazhkov, Igor, 374, 445
Blitzstein, Marc, 82, 333
Airborne Symphony (1946), 234
Arrow Press and, 87
politics of, 81
Sacco and Vanzetti (1959–64), 333
Bloch, Ernest, 14, 48, 170, 187, 199, 307, 436, 439
BMI. *See* Broadcast Music, Inc.
Bolcom, William, 274, 500–501
Brass Quintet (1980), 500
Boosey & Hawkes (publisher), 87, 150, 425, 485
Borodin, Aleksandr, 262
Boston Pops Orchestra, 350
Boston Symphony Orchestra, 100, 117–19, 189, 206, 225, 238, 423
A Free Song (1942), 139
American Festival Overture (1939), 118, 225
Barber's music and, 324
Concerto for Violin and Orchestra (1946–59), 248
early history, 112
Harris's music and, 95
Horblit Award, 528
in Ames, Iowa, 437
Koussevitzky's tenure with, 113, 487
Let's Hear It for Lenny! (1988), 537
Night Journey (1947), 206
reviewed by Bernstein, 100
Sarah Lawrence Chorus with, 87, 143
Symphony for Strings (1943), 166
Symphony no. 2 (1937), 91, 101, 112–13, 116
Symphony no. 3 (1941), 119, 320
Symphony no. 7 (1960), 238, 250, 285, 303, 318–21
Tanglewood (summer music festival), 120, 156, 204, 225, 490, 539
Boulanger, Nadia, 94
Boulez, Pierre, 307, 316, 355, 426, 507
Boult, Sir Adrian, 72
Bowles, Paul, 153, 158, 160
Brahms, Johannes, 143–45, 166, 184, 342
Ein deutsches Requiem, op. 45, 437
kindness to Dvořák, 483
Symphony no. 2 in D major, op. 73, 341
Symphony no. 4 in E minor, op. 98, 97
Brandeis University, 273, 545
Brant, Henry, 269, 287, 296
Bressler, Moishe (Morris), 433
Briccetti, Joan, 503–5
British Film Institute, 378
Britten, Benjamin, 257, 262, 307
Broadcast Music, Inc., 237, 271, 273–74, 278, 326, 404–5
Student Composer Awards, 6, 274, 275
Brook, Peter, 359
Browning, John, 490
Büchner, Georg, 367
Butler, Nicholas Murray, 183
Bydale Foundation, 504

Cage, John, 212, 308–10, 316–17, 483
Calder, Alexander, 367
Camp Cobbossee, 31–43, 45, 83, 333
Almanak (camp newsletter), 33, 37–40, 42, 45
Marsans, R. L. (camp director), 31–33, 36, 39
reminiscence of, 425, 531
reunions, 39, 223
Schuman's friends from, 50, 542
Schuman/Marks shows at, 52, 292
Carnegie Corporation, 257–60, 410
Carnegie Hall, 117, 128
Boston Symphony Orchestra at, 225
Federal Music Project at, 127
Harris's music at, 96, 105
in comparison to Philharmonic Hall, 366

Carnegie Hall (*continued*)
Isaac Stern and, 52
Juilliard Orchestra at, 186
Louisville Orchestra at, 209, 213
New York City High School of Music and Art at, 124
New York Philharmonic at, 336
recording from, 95
Sarah Lawrence College Chorus at, 87
Schuman at, 45, 52–53, 65, 68, 179
Schuman's music at, 124, 159, 236, 248
St. Louis Symphony at, 505
Carnegie, Andrew, 4
Caro, Robert A.
Pulitzer Prize (1975), 329
Carpenter, Alicia. *See* Smith, Alicia
Carpenter, John Alden, 89, 100–101, 147
Carter, Elliott, 284, 308, 504
Concerto for Orchestra (1968–69), 435
FMP Choral Contest winner, 90
CBS Symphony Orchestra, 90–91, 111
Century Association, 449
Cerminaro, John, 492–93, 497
Chabrier, Emmanuel, 71
Chalmers, Allan Knight, 5, 3–6
Chamber Music Society of Lincoln Center, 421, 446, 461, 481
criticism of, 527
genesis of, 335–36
Schuman benefit, 521–22
Schuman commission for, 446, 454, 477, 481–83
Schuman's founding of, 5, 388–89, 408, 412, 421
skirmish with Schuman, 482, 527
skirmished with Schuman, 421
Tully benefit, 478
Chamberlin, Ward B. Jr., 418
Channel 13 (New York's public television station), 62, 418
Chapin, Schuyler G., 362, 377, 379, 409–11, 504
memoirs, 380
Chapin, Theodore S., 485
Chaplin, Charlie, 27, 475
Chaucer, Geoffrey, 139, 245
Chávez, Carlos, 94, 280, 307, 436
Chicago Symphony Orchestra, 513, 519
Chopin, Frédéric, 66, 108
Etude in E major, op. 10, no. 3, 65
Christ-Janer, Albert, 290–91
chuman, Ray (Rachel, née Heilbrunn) (mother), 217–18
Churchill, Winston, 133, 388
Cincinnati Symphony Orchestra, 169, 170, 286, 295, 465
Clarke, Eric T., 259–60
Cleveland Orchestra, 120
Cliburn, Van, 312, 315
Clinton, Bill, 42, 512
Clurman, Harold, 485
Cohan, George M., 94
Cohen, Frederic, 188, 283, 590n24
Cohn, Arthur, 482–83
Colbert, Claudette, 541
Colgate University, 348–49, 357, 440
Collegiate Chorale, 153–54, 158
Columbia Broadcasting System (CBS), 89, 94, 418, 419
Columbia Records, 86, 237, 371, 418, 454, 471, 477
Columbia University
Alice M. Ditson Fund, 278
Douglas Moore at, 127
Howard Shanet at, 474
Intercollegiate Music Forum and, 85
John Erskine at, 180
Joseph H. Bearns Prize in Music, 71, 73, 128
Lincoln Center and, 311
Nicholas Murray Butler at, 183
Paul Henry Lang at, 308
Peter Dykema at, 69, 71
Teachers College, 27, 45, 51, 67–71, 74, 83, 103, 128, 167–68, 191, 251, 297, 504
William Schuman Award and, 504
Comissiona, Sergiu, 522
communism, 13, 70, 79, 81–82, 90, 227, 232
American Communist Party, 92, 129–30
Yiddish choruses and, 130
Composers Recordings, Inc. (CRI), 484
Composers' Forum-Laboratory, 74–76, 89, 103, 109, 126, 134
Ashley Pettis and, 84, 89, 98
Harris and, 95
Schuman and, 87–89, 109, 152
student compositions and, 85
Conlon, James, 186

Cooney, Joan Ganz, 419
Cooper, David S., 315
Copland, Aaron, *99*, 106, *157*, *170*, 179, 307, 429, 445, 545
advocacy for American music, 108
American Composers Alliance and, 158
American Composers Committee and, 89, 109
An Outdoor Overture (1938), 93, 125–28
Appalachian Spring (1944), 106, 162, 205
Arrow Press and, 87, 110
Arthur Berger and, 137
as old-guard composer, 289
at Sarah Lawrence, 85
bicentennial plans, 463–64
Billy the Kid (1938), 93
birthday celebrations, 121, 425, 476, 485–86, 490
birthplace of, 14
borrowings in, 168
childhood of, 82
compared to Schuman, 107
Connotations (1962), 121, 321, 323–24, 426
Copland on Music, 253
correspondence with Schuman, 105, 120, 152, 156–59, 166, 171–72, 217, 294, 311
criticism of Schuman, 180–81
death of, 545
Duo for Flute and Piano (1971), 476
Fanfare for the Common Man (1942), 170, 537
final illness of, 144
friendship with Schuman, 109, 119, 121, 156, 240, 425, 512
Goossens variation (1944), 170
Harris and, 103
humor, 545
influence on Schuman, 110, 115
introduction of Schuman to Koussevitzky, 100, 102, 112
Jewish life and culture, 228
Juilliard appointment, 138, 273
Juilliard festival and, 187–88
Juilliard Orchestra and, 314
Koussevitzky and, 113
Leaves of Grass cantata, 277
Lincoln Portrait (1942), 121, 157, 158
MacDowell Colony and, 425–26, 476
MacDowell Medal, 460
Metropolitan Museum of Art commission, 432
Moses Smith on, 101
Music for a Great City (1964), 121, 324
Music for the Theatre (1925), 199
Musicians' Committee to Aid Spanish Democracy and, 90, 111
Naumburg Foundation and, 193–94
Norlin Fellowships in honor of, 476
on Schuman, 142, 425, 551, 554
on Schuman's music, 61, 92, 108–12, 116, 120–22, 138, 142, 156, 253, 289, 493
Orchestral Variations (1957), 426
orchestration, 146
Passacaglia (1921–22), 145
Paul Rosenfeld on, 93–94, 107, 108
Philadelphia Orchestra commission, 435
Piano Fantasy (1957), 110, 121, 277, 289, 317
piano music of, 109
piece by Schuman in tribute to, 481
politics of, 81
Rodeo (1942), 106, 259, 473
Schuman on, 122, 135, 508
Schuman's MacDowell Medal and, 425
serialism and, 110, 277, 316–17
Statements (1935), 148
Symphony no. 3 (1944–46), 144, 234, 463
Tanglewood and, 120, 156
The City (1939), 93, 161
What to Listen for in Music, 121
World War II and, 150
Zimbalist birthday variation (1951), 436
Corigliano, John, 199, 444, 456, 506, 519, 548
homage to Copland, 537
Oboe Concerto (1975), 444
The Ghosts of Versailles (1991), 444, 548, 554
Cornell, Katharine, 204
Cousins, Norman, 418
Cowell, Henry, 91, 148, 289, 343, 346
This I Believe and, 287
Cramer, Edward, 274
Crane School of Music, 513, 516
Creston, Paul, 13, 14, *170*
Crowther, Bosley, 337
Crozier, Catherine, 343

Crumb, George, 274
Cullen, Countee, 255, 260
Cunningham, Merce, 160, 309, 336, 459
Curtin, Phyllis, 490
Curtis Institute of Music, 66, 436

d'Harnoncourt, Rene, 84
Dahl, Roald, 534–36
Daily Worker, 81, 130
Dallapiccola, Luigi, 316, 351
  Cinque Canti (1956), 318
  favorable view of *Credendum*, 318
Dallas Symphony Orchestra, 230, 263, 287
Danish National Symphony Orchestra, 235–36
Dartmouth College, 45, 309, 384
Davidovsky, Mario, 274, 506
Davies, Dennis Russell, 186, 527
de la Vega, Aurelio, 351
de Liagre, Alfred Jr., 262, 266
de Mille, Agnes, 212, 214, 336, 445, 459, *460*
Debussy, Claude, 307, 342
  Jeux (1912–13), 113
  La damoiselle élue (1887–88), 143
Del Tredici, David, 456, 500, 548
Dello Joio, Norman, 13, 209
Detroit Symphony Orchestra, 481
Dewey, John, 83
  Art as Experience, 68
Diamond, David, 120, 167, 173, 212, 276, 504
  FMP Choral Contest winner, 90
  Koussevitzky and, 113
  Musicians' Committee to Aid Spanish Democracy award, 90
Dlugoszewski, Lucia, 212
Dodge, Charles, 274
Doebler, Lawrence, 509
Dohnányi, Ernő, 436
Doráti, Antal, 445, 533
  "3 thirds" program, 144, 463
  Bartók and, 409
  Dallas Symphony Orchestra, 230–31, 263
  Detroit Symphony Orchestra, 481
  National Symphony Orchestra, 463–64
  Schuman as Brucknerian, 470
  Schuman bicentennial commission, 467–70, 472, 481
Doty, E. W., 313–14
Downes, Edward, 324
Downes, Olin, 97–98, 104, 143–44, 147–48, 159, 169, 225
  in defense of the New York Philharmonic, 279–80
  Music Advisory Panel of ANTA, 308
Dreiser, Theodore, 265, 266, 381
Druckman, Jacob, 456, 494, 506, 522, 533
Druian, Rafael, 249, 250
Dufallo, Richard, 548
Dushkin, Samuel, 246–49, 394, 494
Dvořák, Antonín, 89, 483
Dykema, Peter, 68–69, 71
Dylan, Bob, 375

E. C. Schirmer (publisher), 523
Eastman School of Music, 243, 393, 442–43
  Eastman Philharmonia, 313, 443
Edinburgh International Festival, 72, 334, 378
Eliot, T. S., 69, 305
Elizabeth Sprague Coolidge Foundation, 204, 207, 251, 285, 351, 546
Engel, Carl, 106, 159, 164, 173, 195, 271, 436
  death of, 172
  dedication of *Three-Score Set*, 164, 436
Engel, Lehman, 85–87, 109, 124, 128
  Arrow Press and, 87, 91, 110
  FMP Choral Contest judge, 90
  Madrigal Singers, 85, 87, 168
  on *Newsreel*, 151
  Sarah Lawrence and, 85
  Soviet Pavilion (1939 World's Fair), 128
Ericson, Raymond, 432–34
Ernst von Siemens Music Prize, 503
Erskine, John, 95, 179–85, 195–96
  Bruno Walter and, 180
Ewazen, Eric, 274
Expo '67 (Montreal), 378

Farquhar, Marion, 125, 245, 450, 452–53, 456
fascism, 79, 82, 92, 124, 134, 135, 140, 229
Feder, Susan, 548
Federal Music Project, 74, 76, 127, 141
  Choral Contest, 90
Feigay, Paul, 266
Feist, Leonard, 318, 436, 480, 481
Felsenstein, Walter, 362–63
Fennell, Frederick, 243–44

Ferris, William, 546–47
Fiedler, Arthur, 350
Film Society of Lincoln Center, 24, 446
  genesis of, 338
  May's role in, 448
  Schuman's founding of, 5, 338, 383–84, 408, 412, 421
  Segal's role in, 447–48
Fine, Irving, 160
Fiorello H. La Guardia High School of Music & Art and Performing Arts. *See* New York City High School of Music and Art *and* New York City High School of Performing Arts
Flanagan, William, 249
Ford Foundation, 318, 321–22, 352, 370–71, 451, 453, 554
Ford, Gerald, 463
Ford, Glenn, 254, 266
Fordham University, 329, 330, 407
Foss, Lukas, 173, 347, 491
Fox, Virgil, 343
Franco, Ferdinand, 81, 92, 124
Frankenstein, Alfred, 105, 139, 142
Freed, Isadore, 109, 303–4
Freed, Richard, 450, 474, 506
Friedberg, Carl, 184–85
Friedman, Abraham, 423
Fuleihan, Anis, 170, 228, 259

G. Schirmer (publisher), 125, 237, 490
  Barber and, 324
  biography on Barber, 195
  biography on Schuman, 53, 195
  Carl Engel and, 172
  Corigliano and, 548
  Heinsheimer at, 234, 252, 262, 466, 530
  Musical Quarterly and, 173
  Schuman as director of publications, 106, 121, 142, 154, 172–75, 335, 415
  Schuman as special consultant, 192, 241
  Schuman's salary at, 174
  skirmish with Schuman, 271, 290
  William Billings Overture and, 169
George Washington High School, 29, 30, 41, 43, 529
Gershwin, George, 14, 49, 118, 222
  An American in Paris (1928), 66, 310
  Koussevitzky and, 113
  Porgy and Bess (1935), 126
Gerstner, Audrey (sister), 216, 518
  as mother, 216
  as pianist, 21
  birthday composition for, 479–80, 496
  care for her brother Robert, 224
  care for her mother, 218
  Carnegie Hall and, 43
  doting on her brother Bill, 23, 547
  early years, 13–15, 17
  in Europe, 63
Gesensway, Louis, 266
Giannini, Vittorio, 273
Gilbert and Sullivan, 30, 38, 43, 220
Gilels, Emil, 312, 313
Gillespie, Dizzy, 339, 475
Gilmore, Edwin L. K., 38
  Pulitzer Prize (1947), 39
Gilroy, Frank, 266
Ginastera, Alberto, 352
Glass, Philip, 274
Glimmerglass Opera, 531–33, 534, 539, 540, 552
Godel, Ken, 498, 546
Gold (Arthur) and Fizdale (Robert) (duo-pianists), 342–43, 442
Goldberg, Jon, 491
Goldman, Edwin Franko, 242
Goldman, Richard Franko, 193, 323, 366
Goodman, Benny, 339
Goossens, Sir Eugene, 169–70
Gould, Morton, 3, 240, 241–42, 364, 486, 551
Graham, Martha, 84, 198, 199, 204–14, 230
  Appalachian Spring, 270
  birthday celebrations, 369
  budgetary constraints, 491
  Dance Committee to Aid Spanish Democracy, 90
  friendship with Schuman, 374, 512
  Jocasta as dance, 204–6, 257
  MacDowell Medal, 459–60
  modern dance constituent at Lincoln Center, 336
  naming of Schuman works, 304
  request for a fifth Schuman score, 373
  Schuman's advocacy for, 270
  story of *Judith*, 210
  Tam Lin, 204–5

Graham, Martha (*continued*)
The Witch of Endor, 369–74
Theatre for a Voyage, 268–70
This I Believe and, 287
Grainger, Percy, 298
Grawemeyer Music Award, 520
Great Depression, 63, 129
Grenell, Horace, 84, 85, 149
on Cage, 309–10
Grieg, Edvard, 89
Griffes, Charles Tomlinson, 487
Grofé, Ferde, 294
Gruenberg, Louis, 89
Guggenheim Fellowship, 126
Guggenheim Fellowships, 119, 138
Gury, Jeremy, 260–63, 265, 266, 268, 466, 552
The 'Round and 'Round Horse (1943), 260
The Hither and Thither of Danny Dither (1941), 261

Haggin, B. H., 107, 434
Haieff, Alexei, 342
Hamburg Opera, 362, 377, 379
Hamlisch, Marvin, 429
Hanson, Howard, 307, 351, 393, 443
American Composers Committee and, 89
birthplace of, 14
dispute with Schuman, 313
FMP Choral Contest judge, 90
Goossens variation (1944), 170
Koussevitzky and, 113
Pulitzer Prize (1944), 234
Symphony no. 2 ("Romantic") (1930), 519
Symphony no. 4 ("Requiem") (1943), 234
Harbison, John, 274
Hardin, Louis Thomas. *See* Moondog
Harding, Warren G., 13
Harris, Roy, 89, *99*, 102, 307, 429, *487*
advocacy for American music, 108
American Composers Committee and, 89
as Boulanger pupil, 94
as festival organizer, 117, 307, 318
as publisher, 103–4
at Sarah Lawrence College, 98
autogenesis, 96–97, 165, 399
bicentennial plans, 464
birthday celebrations, 461
birthplace of, 14
borrowings in, 168
career of, 95, 106
compared to Schuman, 105–6, 107, 120, 165
compared to Sibelius, 102
Composers' Forum-Laboratory and, 74
correspondence with Schuman, 96, 98, 102
cowboy myth, 94, 97
death of, 144, 486
FMP Choral Contest judge, 90
Folksong Symphony (1940; '42), 104
fondness for Whitman, 137
friendship with Schuman, 109, 512
Goossens variation (1944), 170
in Colorado, 76
influence on Schuman, 74, 98, 115, 122, 144, 191
Jascha Heifetz and, 99
Juilliard commissions, 276–77
Juilliard presidency inquiry, 106
Juilliard Summer School and, 95, 103
Koussevitzky and, 99, 113
love of counterpoint, 95
manipulation of Schuman, 97, 102, 119
Musicians' Committee to Aid Spanish Democracy and, 90
New York Times tirade, 99
number of symphonies, 528
on Schuman, 114
on Schuman's music, 61, 74, 102, 117
opinion of self, 95, 104, 108
orchestration, 146
Paul Rosenfeld on, 93–94, 107, 108
piano music of, 109
Prelude and Fugue for Strings and Four Trumpets (1939), 125–28
Quintet for Piano and Strings (1936), 97–98, 102, 104, 461
Rockefeller Foundation study, 103, 132
Sarah Lawrence commission, 85
Schuman on, 99, 135, 553
Slatkin on, 528
Soliloquy and Dance (1938), 93, 95
Symphony 1933, 95–97, 486
Symphony for Voices (1935), 98

Symphony no. 2 (1934), 99, 126
Symphony no. 3 (1939), 93, 95, 101, 99–102, 104, 118, 144, 234, 463, 473
Symphony no. 5 (1942), 104, 158, 164
technical shortcomings, 95
This I Believe and, 287
war with Downes, 97–98
When Johnny Comes Marching Home (1934), 169
Zimbalist birthday variation (1951), 436
Harrison, Jay, 308
Harrison, Lou, 148, 434
Hart, Frederick, 245, 452–53, 456
Hart, Lorenz, 16–17, 38, 43, 51, 222
Hartke, Stephen, 274
Hartt School of Music, 264, 315, 530
Harvard University, 158, 175
Bernstein at, 100, 114
Harvard Crimson, 206–7
Harvard Glee Club, 158, 173, 335
Piston at, 197
symposium on music criticism, 206–7
Vincent at, 197
Harvard-Radcliff Chorus, 139
Harvard-Radcliffe Choral Series, 173, 335
Haubiel, Charles Trowbridge
correspondence with Scalero, 66, 69
correspondence with Schuman, 69, 355
influence on Schuman, 115, 319, 399
instructor at New York University, 70
New York University and, 66, 70, 298
on Schuman, 69
Schuman on, 70
Schuman's studies with, 43, 51, 63, 66–69, 74, 95, 191, 293, 442
Hauser, Arthur, 169, 295
affirmation of Schuman, 297–98
correspondence with Schuman, 290, 295, 300, 369, 400
disagreement with Ormandy, 288, 395
joke with Schuman, 399
on *New England Triptych*, 297
Hawkins, Erick, 213, 269
Hearst, William Randolph, 11
Heifetz, Jascha, 99
Heilbrunn, Julia (née Kahn) (maternal grandmother), 14, *15*
Heilbrunn, Leopold (Louis) (maternal grandfather), 14, *15*, *16*, 24, 25
Heinsheimer, Hans, 234–35, 262, 264, 290, 466–67, 530
correspondence with Schuman, 252, 271
Helena Rubinstein Foundation, 449
Helfman, Max, 130
Henahan, Donal, 444, 495
Hendl, Walter, 263–64, 442–43
Dallas Symphony Orchestra, 263
Herbert, Victor, 14, 43
Hill, Martha, 214
Hillyer, Raphael, 189, 254
Hilsberg, Alexander, 393–94, 398
Hilsberg, Neya, 393–94
Hindemith, Paul, 235, 280, 307, 456
as Juilliard president candidate, 181
Juilliard festival and, 187
Mathis der Maler (1933–34), 180
Symphony Serena (1946), 231
Zimbalist birthday variation (1951), 436
Hines, Robert S., 391, 418
Hirshhorn Museum and Sculpture Garden, 464
Hirshhorn, Joseph J., 465
Hitchcock, H. Wiley, 436, 492, 553
Schuman composition in honor of, 480–81
Hobbes, Thomas, 69
Hobler, Anne, 344
Hodkinson, Sydney, 487
Hoguet, Robert, 382–83
Holland, Bernard, 540
Hollander, John, 535
Hollingworth, Leta S., 56–57, 59
Holocaust, 397, 398
Holst, Gustav, 14, 199
homosexuality, 62, 199–200, 202, 214
Honegger, Arthur, 307, 436
Hoover, Herbert, 90
Hopwood, Stafford L., 419, 457
Horst, Louis, 206, 214
Houston Symphony Orchestra, 522, 533, 543
Hoving, Thomas P. F., 432
Howard, John Tasker, 94
Hughes, Edwin, 181, 308
Hughes, Langston, 291, 502, 543
Street Scene, 256, 262, 291
Hume, Paul, 354–55, 445, 463, 468, 470
Humphrey, Doris, 198, 214

Humphrey, Hubert, 379, 403
Hurok, Sol, 203, 409
Hutcheson, Ernest, 181–83, 193, 195–96

I'll See You In My Dreams (Gus Kahn and Isham Jones) (1924), 521
Ickes, Harold (U.S. Secretary of the Interior, 1933–46), 132–36, 173
Indiana University, 530
Inness-Brown, Virginia, 308
International Society of Contemporary Music, 282–84, 310, 418
Irving, Jules, 367, 382–83
ISCM. *See* International Society of Contemporary Music
Isom, O. Wayne, 512
Israel, Audrey (sister). *See* Gerstner, Audrey
Istomin, Eugene, 352, 426–27
Istomin, Marta Casals, 426–27
Ithaca College, 509–10
Ives, Charles, 94, 307, 515
  as "authentically American composer", 107
  orchestration, 146
  Psalm 67, 86
  Schuman on, 553
  Variations on America (1891–92; c1909–10; c1949), 324, 346–48, 350–52, 356, 464, 473, 497

Jacobi, Frederick, 89, 273
Janáček, Leoš, 307
jazz, 150, 310, 317, 339, 475
Jewish life and culture, 228, 366, 440
  Eastern European immigrants, 13, 82, 433
  German-American Jewish life, 13, 21, 32, 57, 82, 180
  masscre in Italy (1944), 396–99
  Ormandy and, 240
  prejudice against Jews, 70, 80
  response to World War II, 226
  Schuman and, 46, 80, 227–28, 229
  socialism and, 80, 130
  Taggard and, 140
  trades in the 1800s, 10
  Weisgall and, 441
Jewish People's Philharmonic Chorus, 130
Joffrey, Robert, 476
John F. Kennedy Center for the Performing Arts, 121, 147, 388, 445, 483, 541
Johnson, Harriett, 434, 484, 505
Johnson, Hunter, 160
Johnson, Lyndon B., 379
Johnson, Philip, 359, 445
Johnson, Thor, 169, 186, 286, 287, 289, 291, 295, 296
Joplin, Scott, 19
Josten, Werner, 89
Judaism
  anti-Zionism and, 13
  Camp Cobbossee and, 32
  Judith and Holofernes, 210
  Reform Judaism, 29, 65
  Reform Sunday School, 28
  Richard Wagner and, 229–30, 384
Juilliard Orchestra, 186, 188, 197, 228, 303, 313–15
Juilliard School, 337, *See also* 179–326
  compared to Lincoln Center, 408
  Dance Division, 5, 190, 199, 213–15, 325, 459
  disagreements over Lincoin Center, 421, 24
  Drama Division, 5, 325, 383, 459
  Erskine as president, 95
  fundraising at, 387
  graduates from, 427, 441
  Harris at, 95, 103
  Harris presidency inquiry, 106
  Institute of Musical Art, 181, 183–84
  James Warburg and, 358, 417
  Juilliard Summer Institute, 51, 65, 68, 71, 83, 96
  Koussevitzky's counsel to Schuman, 121
  Lincoln Center dedication, 342, 423
  Lincoln Center Teachers' Institute and, 335
  Mennin as president, 366, 421, 424, 526
  Morningside Heights campus, 427, 441
  move to Lincoln Center, 329, 344, 422
  Polisi as president, 526–27
  Prausnitz at, 432
  race-blind admissions, 5
  relations with Lincoln Center, 366
  Schubart at, 62, 342
  Schuman after, 429
  Schuman as composer at, 345, 352
  Schuman as president, 5, 6, 53, 69, 142, 415–16, 553
  Schuman as President Emeritus, 424
  Schuman commission for, 422

  Schuman's music at, 541
  Schuman's support for black artists, 82
  Schuman's tenure at, 334
  Shaw at, 154
  speechmaking at, 384
  The Literature and Materials of Music (L&M), 191–92, 195, 275
  Ward at, 554
Juilliard String Quartet, 5, 188–90, 253, 336, 356, 421, 431, 545

Kabalevsky, Dmitri, 309
Kalem, T. E., 382
Kaplan, Abraham, 452, 478
Kastendieck, Miles, 434
Katims, Milton, 318, 369, 371
Kay, Ulysses, 275
Kazan, Elia, 337, 361, 363, 382, 420
Keats, Shiela, 400
Kellogg, Paul, 531, 540
Kennedy, Jacqueline, 376
Kennedy, John F., 4, 332, 376, 541
Kennedy, Robert F., 402, 403
Kermani, Peter, 306
Kernis, Aaron Jay, 274
Khrennikov, Tikhon, 438, 464, 522
King, Larry, 512
King, Martin Luther Jr., 4, 6, 402, 403, 515
Kirstein, Lincoln, 257, 311, 359–60, 363
Kleban, Edward, 428–29
Klebe, Giselher, 351
Kleiber, Erich, 72
Klein, Howard, 458
Koestenbaum, Wayne, 541
Koff, Robert, 189, 545
Kolodin, Irving, 127, 347, 378, 382, 461
Kostelanetz, André, 507
  Amaryllis for Strings and, 356–57
  New England Triptych and, 250, 285, 293–97
  Promenade Concerts and, 346
  The Orchestra Song and, 350
  This I Believe and, 287
Koussevitzky Music Foundation, 278, 380, 426, 526
  Copland's influence with, 158
  influence on Schuman, 276–78
  partnership with Lincoln Center, 380
  Rouchberg commission from, 317
  Schuman commission from, 142, 164
Koussevitzky, Olga, 276
  This I Believe and, 287
Koussevitzky, Serge, 537
  American music festival in New York, 117
  attitude toward Harris, 95, 99–100
  correspondence with Schuman, 114
  counsel to Schuman about Harris, 118–19
  death of, 276
  development of career, 112
  influence on Schuman, 115
  Juilliard Orchestra and, 186
  Juilliard String Quartet and, 189
  on Schuman's music, 120, 159, 164
  recommendation of G. Schirmer post, 182
  Robert Shaw and, 153–54
  Sarah Lawrence Chorus with, 87, 143
  Schuman's fondness for, 512
  Schuman's music with, 91, 116, 141, 144, 146, 166, 204, 225, 233, 246
  support for Schuman, 100–102, 121, 137, 172, 226, 235, 240, 487
  tribute to, 247
Kraft, Victor, 111
Kraft, William, 521
Krasner, Sandy, 542
Krawitz, Herman, 363, 366
Kreeger, David Lloyd, 445, 449, 450
Krenek, Ernst, 100
Kroeger, Karl, 320, 323
Kubik, Gail, 416

La Guardia, Fiorello H., 117, 281
Laderman, Ezra, 265, 334, 487
LaFarge, Christopher, 152, 163, 257–59, 261, 278–79, 488
  on Barber, 258
  on Schuman, 258
Lambert, Constant, 199
Landon, Alf, 79
Lane, Burton, 23
Lanfer, Helen, 206, 213, 214
Lang, Paul Henry, 224
  editor of the *Musical Quarterly*, 192
  Music Advisory Panel of ANTA, 308
Lang, Pearl, 214

Le voyage de Monsieur Perrichon, 37
League of Composers, 141, 157, 253, 418
  founding in 1923, 115
  loss of *Modern Music* (1946), 192
  merger with ISCM, 282, 284, 310
  Schuman's relationship with, 430
  Town Hall/League of Composers Award, 142
  tribute to Koussevitzky, 225
Leavitt, Donald, 546
Lederman, Minna, 430
Leinsdorf, Erich, 179
Leningrad Philharmonic Orchestra, 374, 445
Leo Feist Music, 50, 51, 480
Levine, James, 186
Levinger, Leah, 80
Levinger, Samuel, 79, 80, 92
Lewis, Sinclair, 79
Lewisohn Stadium
  Stadium Concerts, 128, 129
Lhevinne, Rosina, 185, 312
Library of Congress, 146, 325
  Coolidge commissions, 204–5, 207, 251, 285, 353, 546–47
  Festival of Chamber Music, 352
  final Schuman commission, 546–47
  research for Schuman, 452–53
  Schuman's holographs at, 54, 146, 293, 302, 356, 442
Liebermann, Rolf, 362
Lieberson, Goddard, 477
  Goddard Lieberson Fellowships, 484–85
Limón, José, 167, 214, 319, 336
Lincoln Center for the Performing Arts, 284, 553, *See also* 329–412
  acoustic problems, 3, 240, 341–42, 359
  Andrea and, 222
  as "eighth constituent", 337, 407
  Chapin at, 504
  commissions for, 324, 334
  complaints against, 330, 339
  conflicts at, 446
  early forays into jazz, 339
  Great Performers at Philharmonic Hall, 338
  in comparison to Carnegie Hall, 366
  International University Choral Festivals, 335, 411, 438–39
  Juilliard dedication, 423
  Juilliard move to, 214, 303, 312, 325–26, 422
  Lincoln Center Festivals (1966–70), 72, 334, 339, 362, 377, 379–80, 388, 395, 406–7, 409, 448, 532
  Lincoln Center Fund, 334, 379, 389
  Lincoln Center Student Program, 336
  Lincoln Center Teachers' Institute, 335, 406
  Metropolitan Opera move to, 358, 363
  modern dance constituent at, 336, 359, 459
  Mostly Mozart Festival, 5, 334, 381–82
  New York City High School of Music and Art adjacent to, 281
  New York Philharmonic move to, 321, 322, 358
  on Schuman at, 417
  organ dedicatory concert, 343
  Philharmonic Hall, 4, 5, 329, 330, 334, 341, 343–44, 346, 381–82, 434, 514
  programming at, 5
  Schubart at, 62, 187
  Schuman after, 416–17, 428–29, 430, 553
  Schuman as correspondent, 197
  Schuman as president, 3, 6, 163, 416, 468, 476
  Schuman as president emeritus, 424
  Schuman's last day as president, 415
  Schuman's memoirs and, 420–21
  Schuman's salary at, 420
  Segal as chairman, 447–48
  speechwriters at, 26
  time demands at, 431
  Videorecord and, 419
Lincoln Square, 311–12, 315, 325, 329–30, 336, 422
Lindsay, John V., 375, 388
Lipman, Samuel, 506–7
Lippmann, Walter, 281
Lloyd, Norman, 186–87, 190–91, 366, 408, 484
Loesser, Arthur, 74, 148
Loesser, Frank, 24, 54, 65, 74
  Baby, It's Cold Outside (1944), 217
  collaboration with Schuman, 49–52
  criticism of Lincoln Center, 339–40
  Da Vinci Opera Comique, 50, 52, 518, 521

Guys and Dolls (1950), 55, 321
in California, 60
introduction of Frankie and Bill, 58
on Schuman, 53
Loesser, Susan, 518
Loos, Armin, 90
Los Angeles Philharmonic Orchestra, 202, 493
Lotos Club, 485
Louisville Orchestra, 207–11, 213, 214–15, 219, 263
Lowry, W. McNeil, 322, 554
Luening, Otto, 89, 227, 310, 461
Prelude on a Hymn Tune by William Billings, 168
Lydian String Quartet, 545
Lynes, J. Russell, 459

Maazel, Lorin, 240
MacDowell Colony, 425–26
MacDowell Medal, 197, 425, 459, 460, 487–90
Norlin Fellowships at, 121, 476, 484
Schuman as chairman, 6, 197, 459, 462, 489, 529
MacDowell, Edward, 460
"To a Wild Rose", 21, 547
MacDowell, Marian, 70
Macero, Teo, 274
Machiavelli, Niccolò, 69
Machlis, Joseph, 372, 471
Mackey, Steven, 274
MacLeish, Archibald, 14, 134–35, 450, 472–73, 490–91, 495, 514
Malipiero, Gian Francesco, 307, 351, 354
Malkin Conservatory of Music, 44, 45, 48
Manhattan School of Music, 427, 441, 530
Mann, Robert, 35, 188–89, 196
Mannes School of Music, 5
Mannes, Leopold, 5, 424
Marciniak, Thad, 472
Marks Music (Edward B. Marks Music), 38, 49, 50, 51, 64, 108
Marks, Edward B. Jr. (Eddie), 24, 45, 63, 67, 72, 216, 453, 531
at Cobbossee, 33, 36–38, 40, 42, 43
college-age collaboration with Schuman, 46–48, 54, 62
correspondence with Schuman, 48, 72
lifestyle habits of, 68
memoirs, 37
work and education, 42, 45
Marks, Herbert, 46, 47, 67
Marks, Jean Carolene, 67
Marsans, R. L., *See* Camp Cobbossee
Martha Baird Rockefeller Fund for Music, 382
Martin, John, 201, 206, 269
Martin, Mary, 171, 541
Martino, Donald, 274
Pulitzer Prize (1974), 461
Martinů, Bohuslav, 212, 436
Mason, Daniel Gregory, 71, 73, 76, 193–94
Masselos, William, 277
May, William, 448
Mayer, Martin, 422–24
Mazzeo, Rosario, 119, 320
Mazzola, John, 407, 412
McCarthy, Eugene, 403
McClatchy, J. D., 535–36, 539–44
Johnny Appleseed idea, 542, 544
on Schuman, 539, 540, 548
on *The Mighty Casey*, 260
McDonald, Harl, 89
McDuffie, Robert, 546
McElheran, Brock, 516
McGinley, Laurence J., 329, 330, 338, 407
McInnes, Donald, 453, 451–56, 473, 481
McLellan, Joseph, 470, 495, 519, 520
McPhee, Colin, 131
Mehta, Zubin, 493, 494, 507
Melville, Herman, 437
Mendel, Arthur, 97, 227
attitude toward Harris, 97
Mendelssohn, Felix, 229, 488
Mennin, Peter, 276
as Juilliard president, 184, 366, 383, 526
as Naumburg president, 424
conflicts with Schuman, 421–25, 504
death of, 526
on Juilliard commissions project, 422
Schuman's hiring of, 273
Menotti, Gian Carlo, 262, 263, 436
Kolodin on, 461
on behalf of Barber, 489
Schuman's greetings to, 199
Meredith, James, 4–5
Messiaen, Olivier, 307

Mester, Jorge, 186
Metropolitan Museum of Art, 432
Metropolitan Opera, 265, 329, 336, 337, 379, 380, 382
  Barber and, 278, 280, 376
  Bing at, 334, 362
  broadcast of Lincoln Center opening, 376
  Carnegie Corporation and, 257–59
  compared to Broadway, 261
  Corigliano and, 444, 548
  exploration for new home, 311, 329
  Krawitz at, 363
  Lincoln Center Festival '67 and, 362–63, 377
  musicians at, 489
  old Metropolitan Opera House, 363
  on New York City Opera, 359
  on tour, 336
  Schuman and, 265
  Schuman's commissioning plan for, 278–79
Metropolitan Opera Association, 265, 276–78, 311
Metropolitan Opera Guild, 488
Metropolitan Opera Studio, 337
Milhaud, Darius, 280, 307, 342, 351, 354, 436, 439
Millay, Edna St. Vincent, 51, 64, 65, 70
Miller, Arthur, 361
Miller, Karl, 233, 234
Mitchell, Howard, 347
Mitropoulos, Dimitri, 190, 237, 279, 280
  This I Believe and, 287
Modern Music (journal), 105, 166, 548
  Bernstein and, 146
  demise of, 26, 192
  Schuman and, 115, 141, 282
Moe, Henry Allen, 119, 138
Monteux, Pierre, 112–13, 226
Moondog, 622n76
Moore, Douglas, 154, 276
  American Composers Committee and, 89
  correspondence with Schuman, 128, 154, 256, 265
  Guggenheim Fellowship, 127
  on *The Mighty Casey*, 264, 267
  Prayer and the Land (1940), 161
  The Devil and Daniel Webster (1939), 264
  The Emperor's New Clothes (1948), 260
Moore, Henry, 367
Morel, Jean, 186–87, 197, 461
Morricone, Ennio, 461
Morris, Errol, 554
Morris, Newbold, 367
Moseley, Carlos, 322, 368
Moses, Robert, 329–30
Mourning Becomes Electra (Eugene O'Neill), 59, 233, 234
Mozart, Wolfgang Amadeus, 143, 166, 381, 435, 445, 536, 541
  Così fan tutte, 71, 540
  Die Entführung aus dem Serail, 71
  Don Giovanni, 71, 536, 539
  Le nozze di Figaro, 71
MuCullough, Max, 283–86
Munch, Charles, 225, 238, 248
Munson, Kenneth, 304–5
Murphy, Howard, 71, 74–75
Murrow, Edward R., 286, 287
Museum of Modern Art, 84, 163, 247, 530
Music Educators National Conference, 300
Music Theater of Lincoln Center, 338–39, 342, 383, 384
Musical Quarterly, 173, 191–93, 289, 384
Musorgsky, Modest, 152, 538
Myers, Philip, 493
Myers, Richard, 472

National Association for the Advancement of Colored People (NAACP), 4, 5
National Association of Music Schools, 313
National Educational Television, 375, 376, 416–18, 429
  NET Opera, 417
National Endowment for the Arts, 461, 504, 509, 526–27, 548
National Endowment for the Humanities, 529
National Institute of Arts and Letters, 104, 142, 281, 514
National Public Television, 418
National Symphony Orchestra, 144, 347, 513
  "3 thirds" program, 463, 464
  all-Schuman festival (1976), 356, 449, 467, 470, 473

Copland and, 121
premiere of original version of Symphony no. 3 (1941), 146
Nauheim, Ferd (Ferdinand), 24, 63
as lyricist/librettist, 49, 52
introduction of Frankie and Bill, 58, 62
Marks and, 51
on Schuman, 45, 54
post-high school career, 42, 151
Naumburg, Margaret, 116, 115–17, 141
Naumburg, Walter W., 141, 193–94
Nazism, 82, 396–97
Neidich, Charles, 523
Neikrug, Marc, 522
New Masses, 81
New World Records, 458–59, 526
New York City Ballet, 311, 336, 337, 342, 359, 363
New York City Center of Music and Drama, 342, 360, 377
affordable-price policy, 360
negotiations with Lincoln Center, 342, 360, 362, 363–66
New York City High School of Music and Art, 123–26, 273–74, 281, 486
New York City High School of Performing Arts, 281
New York City Library-Museum for the Performing Arts, 359, 367
New York City Music Critics Circle Award, 148
New York City Opera, 337, 342, 359
New York City Symphony, 226, 280
New York Film Festival, 337, 366, 371, 378
New York Giants, 25, 221
New York Philharmonic Orchestra, 127, 379, 380
"3 thirds" program, 144
Bernstein and, 280, 473
Boulez and, 426, 507
contemporary American music and, 279–80, 309
exploration for new home, 311, 329
Horizons '83, 494
Kostelanetz and, 346
Lincoln Center Student Program and, 336
Mehta and, 507
Moseley and, 322, 368
musicians of, 456, 482, 492
Philharmonic Hall and, 358
Rodzinski and, 164, 167
Schuman's first encounter with, 43, 52, 62
Schuman's music with, 5, 202, 237, 321, 356, 402, 432, 433, 445, 486, 491, 511, 513, 518, 522
substitute for the Boston Symphony, 118
Videorecord and, 419
Webster and, 492, 509, 520
William Schuman Prize and, 503
New York State Theater, 338, 353, 358–60, 364
New York University, 12, 42, 45, 46, 66, 298, 311, 361, 418
Nielsen, Carl, 307
Nixon, Richard M., 427, 432, 446, 463, 469
Nonesuch Records, 484
Nordoff, Paul, 126, 127
Norlin Foundation, 467, 475, 476, 484
North, Alex, 260–61

Odets, Clifford, 81
Oenslager, Donald, 262, 266
Office of War Information, 135, 154, 161–62, 285
Olmstead, Andrea, 184–85
Omnibus (television program), 267, 266–67, 530
Oppenheim, David, 418
Oregon Symphony, 513
Ormandy, Eugene, 402, 451
Bernstein and, 395
birthday variations, 435, 436, 438
bluntness of, 235
Celebration Concertante/Symphony no. 7 and, 238–40
correspondence with Schuman, 197, 226, 322, 407
criticisms of Schuman's music, 288
Danish Symphony Orchestra and, 236
death of, 240, 487
disagreements with Schuman's publisher, 288–89
fan mail, 236
friendship with Schuman, 240
on Schuman's music, 239, 288, 400
Persichetti and, 431

Ormandy, Eugene (*continued*)
pride in entire orchestra, 395
promised premiere to, 237
recordings of Schuman's music, 236, 431
retirement of, 487
Schuman's music and, 234, 238, 288, 295
Schuman's Ninth and, 368, 369, 393–95, 400, 404
support for Schuman, 226, 240
Orrego-Salas, Juan, 167, 351

Page, Tim, 478, 551–53
Paranov, Moshe, 264, 267
Parker, Henry Taylor, 96–97
Parmenter, Ross, 248–49
Paynter, John, 501
Peabody Conservatory, 181
People's Philharmonic Choral Society. *See* Jewish People's Philharmonic Chorus
Pepys, Samuel, 450
Perlis, Vivian, 143, 163, 339, 485, 545
Persichetti, Vincent, 276, 343
analyses of Schuman's music, 53
death of, 534
first biographer of Schuman, 12, 23, 53–54, 195
friendship with Schuman, 512
Juilliard and, 191, 273
on Schuman's Symphony no. 6, 234
Orpheus with His Lute and, 322
Psalm for Band (1952), 297
Schuman on, 366, 384
Symphony no. 9 (*Sinfonia Janiculum*) (1970), 431
Voyage and, 443
Persin, Max, 44–45, 48–49, 63, 65, 68, 191
influence on Schuman, 115
Peters, Frank, 505
Pettis, Ashley, 75, 84–85, 98
American Composers Committee and, 89
Rockefeller Foundation study, 103, 132
Philadelphia Orchestra
commissions for, 235, 238, 318, 321, 356, 381, 394–95
Hilsberg and, 393–94
management of, 237, 367, 431
Ormandy celebration, 435
Ormandy's tenure with, 487
Schuman's music and, 240, 288
strings of, 320
Philip Morris, 449, 467
Pi Kappa Omicron, 297–98
Picasso, Pablo, 341
Picker, Tobias, 265, 274, 522
Piston, Walter, 9, 101, 276, 307, 351
birthplace of, 14
commissions for, 197
Concertino for Piano and Chamber Orchestra (1937), 126, 127
correspondence with Schuman, 89, 197, 276
death of, 461
Goossens variation (1944), 170
Juilliard Orchestra and, 314
Koussevitzky and, 113
MacDowell Medal, 197, 460–61, 489
Metropolitan Museum of Art commission, 432
modal effects in his music, 197
on Schuman, 138
on Schuman's music, 197, 198
Schuman's music compared to, 166
Slatkin on, 528
Suite no. 2 (1948), 231
Symphony no. 4 (1950), 194
Symphony no. 5 (1954), 197, 323
Zimbalist birthday variation (1951), 436
Pittsburgh Symphony Orchestra, 513
Pizzetti, Ildebrando, 436
Polansky, Larry, 274
Polisi, Joseph W., 184–85, 250, 526, 527, 547
on *Night Journey*, 593n45
Pollack, Daniel, 312
Porter, Andrew, 454, 522, 527
Porter, Cole, 14
Porter, Quincy, 87, 89, 110, 193
Poulenc, Francis, 436
Prague National Opera, 377
Prausnitz, Frederik, 302, 432, 456, 475, 482
at Juilliard, 188
ISCM and, 283
Syracuse Symphony and, 454
Previn, André, 347, 444
Princeton University, 167, 310, 385–86, 389, 391, 408
Pritchard, W. Douglas, 437, 439
Prokofiev, Sergei, 199, 232, 267, 307, 309

propaganda, 324
connotations of, 134
film as, 161–62
music as, 134, 311
Odets plays as, 81
Schuman's music as, 131, 135, 151, 154, 159–62, 200, 288, 464
Pruett, James W., 546–47
Public Broadcasting Service, 416
Puccini, Giacomo, 488
Pulitzer Prize, 104, 137, 154, 504
Copland on, 142
first prize in music (1943), 137

Rabin, Michael, 322
Rachmaninoff, Sergei, 112, 312, 552
Rakowski, David, 274
Ramey, Phillip, 486, 506
on Schuman, 519, 554
Ravel, Maurice, 145, 199, 307, 538
Concerto in G major (1929–31), 346
Daphnis et Chloe (1909–12), 113
RCA Victor, 194, 356, 431, 444, 471
Reagan, Ronald, 275, 529, 531
Rees, Rosalind, 481, 495, 509
Reese, Gustave, 172
Reich, Steve, 13, 522
Reiner, Fritz, 153, 159–60, 171–72, 186, 226, 477
Reis, Claire (Raphael), 109, 115–16, 141–42, 193, 245–46, 257, 371–72, 430, 490
Repertory Theater of Lincoln Center, 337, 360–65, 367, 382–84, 408, 420
Revelli, William, 300–301, 418
Revueltas, Silvestre, 487
Rhoads, William E., 348, 351
Rice, Elmer, 256
Richter, Alexander, 126–28
Riverdale Country School, 441
Robbins, Jerome, 214, 336
Robeson, Paul, 82
Robinson, Steve, 529
Robison, Paula, 481–82, 489
Rochberg, George, 316–18, 320
correspondence with Schuman, 239, 292
defense of serialism, 317
director of publications at Presser, 238
Second Symphony (1956), 317
Sonata-Fantasia (1956), 316
turn to tonality, 456
Rockefeller Foundation
Composers' Institute study, 103, 132, 133, 172
Louisville Orchestra and, 209
Norman Lloyd and, 187
Recorded Anthology of American Music, 458–59, 462, 526
Sarah Lawrence College and, 84
Schuman and, 132, 270, 288, 461, 468
Rockefeller, John D. III, 338, 365, 387, 415, 554
Ames on, 412
artistic philosophy, 330
diary entries, 332, 386, 410
evaluation of Schuman, 362, 386, 388, 410
firing of Schuman, 387, 390, 405, 410, 412
first president of Lincoln Center, 330
Juilliard and, 325, 423
Lincoln Center exploratory committee, 311
Maxwell Taylor and, 331–32
negotiations with City Center, 360, 364
perception of Lincoln Center, 340, 358, 388
sparring with Schuman, 386–90, 406, 411, 423
Rockefeller, Nelson, 360
Rockwell, John, 207, 471, 500–501, 505, 518–19, 520, 541
Rodgers, Dorothy, 485
Rodgers, Richard, 49, *340*
"Mountain Greenery", 17
"My Heart Stood Still", 38
and Hart, 16–17, 38, 43, 51, 222
birthplace of, 14
Carousel (1945), 338–39
friendship with Schuman, 38
Kleban and, 428
Music Theater of Lincoln Center, 338–39
Music Theater of Lincoln Center and, 359, 383
Oklahoma! (1943), 106, 214, 259
Richard Rodgers Awards for Musical Theater, 484–85
The King and I (1951), 339
The Mighty Casey and, 266

Rodzinski, Artur, 9, 120, 164, 167, 202, 226, 294, 538
Rodzinski, Richard, 538
Rogers, Bernard, 170
Rood, Louise, 189, 190
Roosevelt, Franklin Delano, 61, 63, 79, 180
Roosevelt, Theodore, 13, 477
Rorem, Ned, 167, 199, 293, 334, 533
Rose, Billy, 170–72, 256, 322
Rose, Leonard, 318, 321, 322, 352, 353, 451
Rosenfeld, Paul, 93–94, 95, 93–95, 102, 105, 107, 108, 548
Rosenthal, Meyer aka Anthony Ross, 29, 31, 33, 37, 38, 49
Ross, Bertram, 269, 371
Rothstein, Edward, 494
Rouse, Christopher, 274, 306, 319, 320, 533
  on Schuman, 525–26
  Pulitzer Prize (1993), 3
Ruders, Poul, 522
Rudié, Robert, 441, 442

Saarinen, Eero, 392, 474
Sabin, Robert, 149–50, 206, 211–12, 233
Saidenberg, Daniel, 152
Saint-Saëns, Camille, 65
Sallinen, Aulis, 522
Salzburg Festival, 72, 334, 378
Sandler, Woodrow (Woody), 52, 68, 81
Sänger, Peßla (Pauline, née Schuhmann) (paternal great-great aunt), 10
Sarah Lawrence College, 54, 273, *See also* 79–175
  Campus (school newspaper), 79, 80, 87, 90, 114
  educational philosophy of, 181
  Farquhar and, 125, 450
  film on, 161
  Frederick Hart and, 452
  Geismar and, 478
  Grenell and, 309
  Harold Taylor and, 333
  Harris and, 98
  Hendl and, 263, 442
  Hobler and, 344
  influence on Schuman, 191–92
  James Warburg and, 180
  MacLeish and, 134
  Norman Lloyd and, 186
  political views at, 79, 90
  quota on Jewish students, 80
  Rees at, 496
  Schuman speech at, 391
  Schuman's departure from, 172
  Schuman's role at, 6, 44, 87, 89, 260, 415
  Schuman's salary at, 174, 216, 258
  Sidorsky and, 109, 149
  Spender and, 231
  Taggard and, 123, 139
  the Chorus, 61, 85–87, 99, 124, 139, 143, 197, 214, 244, 452, 457, 524
  This I Believe and, 287
Sargeant, Winthrop, 341, 423
Saudek, Robert, 266–67
Sayad, Elizabeth Gentry, 392–93, 401
Scalero, Rosario, 66, 69
Schenkman, Edgar, 100, 186, 188, 589n19
Schippers, Thomas, 465, 481
Schirmer, Gustave, 172, 174, 192, 271
Schlesinger, Arthur Jr., 449–50
Schmid, Adolf, 65–66
Schnitzer, Robert, 308, 313
Schoenberg, Arnold, 48, 199, 307, 440
  Verklärte Nacht, op. 4 (1899), 198, 201, 203
Schonberg, Harold, 355, 552
  on *Antony and Cleopatra*, 376
  on Bernstein, 280
  on *Concerto on Old English Rounds*, 456
  on *In Sweet Music*, 483–84
  on Philharmonic Hall acoustics, 341–42
  on Schuman, 275
  on *The Mighty Casey*, 268
  on *Three Colloquies*, 494
Schreiber, Flora Rheta, 53, 102, 118, 257
Schubart, Mark, *188*, 409–11
  acting president of Juilliard, 342
  as Schuman's deputy, 187, 193, 366
  Carnegie Corporation study, 411
  first encounter with Schuman, 187
  friendship with Schuman, 326, 512
  Lincoln Center Fund and, 335
  Moscow article, 312
  on Frankie, 62
  on Juilliard Dance Division, 213
  on Schuman's Juilliard composition, 422
  practical jokes and, 375
  sixtieth birthday composition, 436
  Videorecord and, 419

Schubert, Franz, 143, 355
Schuhmann, Abraham (Anton) (paternal great-grandfather), 10
Schuhmann, Franziska (Fanny) (paternal great-grandmother), 10
Schuhmann, Henry (paternal uncle), 10, 12, 29, 35, 42
Schuhmann, Moritz (Morris) (paternal grandfather), 9–10, *11*, 15
Schuhmann, Rosa (née Kramer) (paternal grandmother), 9–10, *11*
Schuhmann, Sophie (paternal aunt), 10
Schuller, Gunther, 334, 339, 492, 493, 504, 533
Schuman, Andrea Frances (daughter), 229, 518, 542
- adoption of, 219, 251
- Dad "borrows" knee socks, 222
- Frankie on, 220
- high school, 358, 374
- marriage of, 224, 408
- musical tastes, 222
- neighborhood newspaper, 221
- Riverdale Country School and, 441
- summer camp, 222
- Suzy (cocker spaniel) and, 223
- third birthday, 220

Schuman, Anthony William (Tony) (son), *394*, 518, 542
- birth of, 166
- Camp Cobbossee experience, 220–21
- Dad singing to, 217–18
- Dad's stories and, 25
- FDR and, 61
- marriage of, 408
- musical tastes, 217, 222
- nicknames, 224
- on Andrea, 220
- on Dad's lap pool, 222
- on household pets, 223
- on Martha's Vineyard, 252
- on names, 517
- on Robert, 20
- politics of, 61, 163
- Riverdale Country School and, 441
- shared love of baseball, 24–25, 221, 393
- shared love of trains, 221
- sibling for, 219
- Wesleyan University, 221, 358, 374

Schuman, Audrey (sister). *See* Gerstner, Audrey
Schuman, Frankie (Frances, née Prince) (wife), *57*, *88*, *365*, 480, 518, 526, 542, 554, *See also* 56–62
- at Sarah Lawrence, 79
- belated honeymoon, 87
- birthplace of, 61
- breast cancer, 61, 366
- confidant to husband, 61, 76, 224, 490
- Copland and, 156–58, 180–81, 217
- dating Bill, 68, 73, 84, 216, 233
- early married life, 216
- family planning, 175, 219
- George Washington High School Alumni Hall of Fame, 29, 529
- health issues, 548
- home life, 218, 220, 224, 551
- husband as "a euphoric", 512
- marriage to Bill, 84
- Nixon and, 446
- on Bernstein, 115
- on music, 85, 496
- on Robert, 19
- on Schuman's music, 61
- on *Undertow*, 203
- Polisi and, 184, 526
- pregnancy, 155, 166, 167, 216
- protection of Bill, 511, 540, 547
- public television and, 418, 466
- reentry into the work force, 358
- role in NET/Channel 13 merger, 418
- Rorem and, 167
- suggestion for composition, 397, 469, 534
- the Spenders and, 232
- the Weisgalls and, 396
- typing of, 453
- vacation with Bill, 239, 416, 428
- wedding anniversaries, 39, 400
- work life, 190, 216
- working life, 84

Schuman, Ray (Rachel, née Heilbrunn) (mother), *17*, 63, *64*, 518
- as pianist, 17–18
- death of, 218
- family background, 14
- marriage to Sam, 13
- poor health of, 224, 539

Schuman, Robert (Monroe) (brother), 15, 18, 19, *20*, 29, 223–24, 518
Schuman, Samuel (father), *12*, *17*, 29, 32, *64*, 518
  career as bookkeeper, 12, 13, 15, 42, 63, 183
  escapades of, 10
  family background, 9
  final accident and death, 218–19, 251
  legal change of last name, 13
  religious practices of, 13
  Spanish-American War and, 18
Schuman, William (Howard), *16*, *20*, *34*, *46*, *64*, *72*, *88*, *99*, *157*, *170*, *174*, *224*, *325*, *331*, *340*, *365*, *377*, *394*, *404*, *460*, *479*, *487*, *529*
  "When Jesus Wept" and "Chester" for mixed chorus and snare drum (1971), 439
  adoption of autogenesis, 144, 399, 552
  advocacy for American music, 279, 310, 506–8, 526–27
  Alleluia (1990-91), 546–47, 549
  allowance from his father, 63
  American Academy of Arts and Letters Gold Medal for Music, 529
  American Muse (radio program on WQXR-FM), 473–74, 475
  American Music Recording Institute and, 526–27
  An American Tragedy (opera), 265, 381
  as bandleader (Alamo Society Orchestra), 22, 29, 41, 73, 83
  as clarinetist, 22
  as conducting student, 68, 71
  as contrapuntalist, 552
  as double bassist, 22, 30, 529
  as emcee, 121, 485
  humor, 338
  as *macher*, 553
  as optimist, 140, 218, 364, 373, 383, 411, 469, 472, 511, 514, 547, 548
  as prankster, 27, 375
  as speaker, 26, 275, 384, 417
  as vocalist, 23
  attitude toward Jewish causes, 226–30
  audience with Pope Paul VI, 398
  baseball, 23–25, 28, 33
  birthday celebrations, 374, 495, 497, 503, 521, 531, 541
  borrowings in, 168, 454
  boxing, 23, 28
  Brant Lake Camp, 39, 51, 81, 84
  Brucknerian music, 470, 533
  business school (1928-29), 42, 45, 195
  calculating composition hours, 321, 322, 345, 357, 358
  Camp To-Ho-Ne, 39
  canoeing, 33–34
  Charles Ives Society and, 553
  childhood violin lessons, 21
  choice of music paper, 162, 165, 201, 246, 293, 503, 509, 521, 522
  choral writing, 124, 139, 305, 510
  collaboration with Herman Wouk, 256
  College Chums (original play), 28
  commission to write a sacred service, 439–41
  commissioning other composers, 183, 187, 276, 343
  compared to Knute Rockne, 87
  compared to Max Reger, 552
  compared to Sibelius, 114
  comparison of ballet to modern dance, 198
  complimentary close for letters, 512
  composer and president, 416
  composition for Juilliard opening, 422
  Concertino for Bass Clarinet and Chamber Orchestra (ca. 1940), 119, 320, 579n41
  contemplated move back to NYC (1950), 220
  coronary artery insufficiency, 407
  correspondence with Harold Ickes, 132–36
  counterpoint lessons with Haubiel (1932-34), 67, 70
  Creative Arts Medal in Music (Brandeis University), 545
  Da Vinci Opera Comique (ca. 1931), 50, 52, 518, 521
  dates of completion as opus numbers, 110
  death of, 240
  difficulty in writing for the piano, 109, 538
  director of publications at G. Schirmer, 172–75, 182, 198

disagreements over Lincoln Center history, 421–24
disinclination to revise works, 75
drive to compose, 76, 430, 553
early life in Englewood, NJ, 15
early morning work habits, 478
embellishment of stories, 44, 55, 179
emeritus imbroglio, 424
exercise regime, 222, 326
feelings toward his brother, Robert, 19
feminist attitudes, 189
film and television series ideas, 475
FMP Choral Contest winner, 90
football in high school, 529
forays into Jewish music, 65, 439
forays into serialism, 246, 319, 399, 400, 403, 518, 524
Four One-Minute Songs, 86, 87
friendship with Copland, 109
friendship with Harris, 109
George Washington High School Alumni Hall of Fame, 529
German-Jewish heritage of, 5, 9
Guggenheim Fellowship, 86, 93, 104, 117, 120, 129, 142, 150, 156, 405, 478
harp writing, 323, 483
health issues, 381, 416, 476, 511, 516, 539, 540, 547–48
Henry VIII (1944), 171, 322, 541, 543
hepatitis (1954), 25, 241, 249–50, 271, 285, 294, 511
homosexuality and, 61, 199, 342
Horblit Award, 528
household pets and, 223
Howard Music as holding company, 271
humor, 322, 399, 437, 475, 480, 492, 551
in Japan for the State Department (1970), 427–28
in Puerto Rico, 416, 426
in Salzburg (summer 1935), 71–73, 76, 84
injured leg while playing softball (1950), 25, 252
interest in dance, 73
jazz inflections in his music, 49, 150, 289, 505
Juilliard presidency, 25
Koussevitzky and, 113
Li'l Abner (opera), 260, 261
life in Far Rockaway, 16, 19, 23, 50
love of vaudeville, 17, 62
MacDowell Medal, 425
memoirs and autobiography, 26, 174, 365, 420, 529
Mesa Verde (opera), 258–60
Milray Outing Club for Boys, 23, 38
Music Advisory Panel of ANTA, 308–9, 311, 312, 313, 314, 315
music appreciation handbook, 84
musical style, 552
Musicians' Committee to Aid Spanish Democracy, 90, 111
Musicians' Committee to Aid Spanish Democracy award, 90
National Humanities Center board member, 529
Naumburg American Composers' Recording Prize and, 194
New Romanticism and, 455, 494
New World Records and, 458–59, 526
New York Music Critics Circle Award, 104, 142
Nineteen Seventy-Six (bicentennial piece), 380–81, 395, 446, 449–50, 451, 462, 464, 477, 510
on *Appalachian Spring*, 162
on Barber, 461, 488
on Bernstein, 120, 485, 486, 525, 545
on Blitzstein, 333
on Copland, 121, 425, 545, 552
on Corigliano, 444, 548
on gender, 190
on George Whitefield Chadwick, 482
on grooming, 590n29
on Harris, 98, 104–5, 158, 486
on Loesser, 53
on Morton Gould, 486
on Ormandy, 236, 487
on Paul Bowles, 158
on Polisi, 526
on race, 190
on serialism, 317
on the videocassette revolution, 419
orchestration, 65, 146, 165, 503, 538, 540
paper on Shakespeare), 69
paper on William Billings, 168, 297
patriotism of, 163, 347, 518
Paul Rosenfeld on, 93–94
philanthropic proposal, 508

Schuman, William (Howard) (*continued*)
piece for piano and 'cello (1939), 580n17
piece for unaccompanied solo violin (1990-92), 21, 546–47
Piping Tim: Fantasy for Band, 300
Playground (drama/ballet) (1938-39), 116–17, 141, 578
pronunciation of last name, 9
Pulitzer Prize (1943), 104, 105, 137, 142, 155, 158, 159, 167, 256
Pulitzer Prize Special Citation (1985), 529
race-blind admissions, 5
rate of published articles, 384
reading habits, 25–27
Recorded Anthology of American Music and, 458
reflection on religious upbringing, 228
reorganization of the Juilliard School of Music, 183
representation through recordings, 508
resignation from Lincoln Center, 410
Rockefeller Foundation study, 103, 132
self-borrowing, 75, 87–88, 162, 164, 254, 319, 356, 368, 373, 442–43, 465, 469–70, 483, 499, 521, 522, 532, 533, 534, 538, 543
shared love of baseball with son, 221, 393
similarity between democracy and baseball, 133
Slatkin on, 528
sparring with Rockefeller, 386–90, 406
special consultant to G. Schirmer, 192, 193
special meaning of Symphony no. 9, 400
Strange Fruit (opera), 255
studies at Juilliard Summer Institute (1932–33), 51, 65, 68, 71, 83
studies with Harris (1936–38), 95, 96, 97
study of Webern's music, 318
subscription lottery system and, 461
Tampa Bay Performing Arts Center commission, 532, 537
the Krawitz affair, 363, 365, 366, 375, 405
The Last Notch (opera), 266, 306
This I Believe and, 287
time on Martha's Vineyard, 25, 59, 204, 224, 251–52, 263, 285–86, 287
trip to France, 1925, 34–36
triple bypass surgery, 408, 511, 512–13
Two-Part Violin Inventions for Student and Teacher (1972-76), 441–42
use of bass clarinet, 66, 146, 323, 489
visiting Loesser in California, 60
waltz rhythms in his music, 54, 171, 373, 479–80, 494, 498, 500, 502, 505, 518, 521, 536–37, 541
What to Listen for in Music (Copland), 121
What's My Line? and, 343
William Schuman: Documentary, 525
With All Due Respect (Marks-Nauheim-Geldman-Schuman) (1931), 52
work on *Jeu de cartes* (Stravinsky), 398
writing for young people, 124, 136
WWI songs, 20
Schumann, Clara, 184
Schumann, Robert, 44, 108, 167
Schwantner, Joseph, 274, 533
Magabunda (1983), 505
Schwarz Levy, Blanche, 21, 59, 66, 70, 547
Schwarz, Gerard, 240, 489, 545
Seaborg, Glenn, 26, 418
Sears & Roebuck, 14, 437
Seattle Symphony, 318, 369, 545
Segal, Martin E., 447–49, 462, 465, 467, 511, 532–33
serialism, 306, 316
Babbitt and, 310
Bergsma and, 319
Bernstein and, 317
Cage and, 309
Copland and, 110, 277, 317, 323–24
Dallapiccola and, 318
Rochberg and, 316–17
Schuman on, 110
Schuman's forays into, 110, 246, 319–21, 323–24, 349, 400, 518, 524
Stravinsky and, 317
Webern and, 318
Serkin, Rudolf, 451
Sesame Street, 419
Sessions, Roger, 101, 307, 310, 429
birthplace of, 14
correspondence with Schuman, 89
MacDowell Medal, 425, 460
Musicians' Committee to Aid Spanish Democracy, 90
on Schuman's music, 92, 237
Symphony no. 2 (1944–46), 173, 528

Shaaray Tefila (temple), 17, 18, 28–29, 65
Shahn, Ben, 431, 433, 434
Shakespeare, William, 69, 171, 322, 359, 477, 482, 483
Shaw, Robert, 153–54, 159, 513, 515
  Billy Rose and, 171–72
  Juilliard and, 188
  Lincoln Center and, 335, 438–39
  on Schuman's music, 305
  Robert Shaw Choral Series, 173
Shepherd, Arthur, 89
Sherman, Robert, 439, 458, 468, 474
Shifrin, Seymour, 273–74, 275, 276, 283, 486
Shostakovich, Dmitri, 156, 232, 280, 307, 309, 445, 534, 552
Shouse, Catherine Filene, 448
Sibelius, Jean, 102, 114, 436
  Symphony no. 3 in C major, op. 52 (1907), 101
  Symphony no. 4 in A minor, op. 63 (1910–11), 307
Sidorsky, Judith, 109, 149
Sigma Alpha Iota, 268–70
Slatkin, Leonard, 146, 186, 240, 471, 482, 499, 500, 502, 503, 504, 505, 519, 528
  on Schuman, 528
Slonimsky, Nicolas, 99
Smallens, Alexander, 126, 128, 129, 130, 151, 202, 256
Smith, Alicia, 380–81, 510
Smith, Carleton Sprague, 290
  Music Advisory Panel of ANTA, 308
Smith, Gregg, 306, 380, 509, 510
Smith, Julia, 189, 589n15
Smith, Moses, 96, 101, 102, 104, 114, 166
Smith, Warren Storey, 100–101
Smithsonian Institution, 419–20, 464
socialism, 80, 90, 123
Sokolow, Anna, 212, 336
Solomons, Gus, 371
Sondheim, Stephen, 428, 541
  A Little Night Music (1973), 502, 536, 537
Sonn, Howard (cousin), 14
Sonn, Lucille (cousin), 14, 17–18, 63
Sousa, John Philip, 261, 474–75, 499
Sowerby, Leo, 120
Spanish Civil War, 81, 82, 92
  Battle of Belchite, 79
  Republican cause, 80, 90, 92, 124, 141
Spanish-American War, 10, 12, 18
Spender, Stephen, 231–32
Speyer Experimental Junior High School, 27–30, 50, 56
Spivacke, Harold, 204, 355
  Bartholomew and, 244
  Coolidge Foundation and, 208, 251, 352
  correspondence with Schuman, 253, 325, 353
  position at the Library of Congress, 204
  State Department and, 351
  wife of, 354
St. Lawrence University, 304, 306
St. Louis Symphony, 401, 499, 502–3, 505, 511, 543
St. Louis Symphony Orchestra, 513
Stegall, Joel R., 509–10
Steinberg, Michael, 368, 455–56, 460
Stern, Isaac, 52, 246, 248, 249, 352, 442, 445
Stern, The Rev. Dr. Nathan, 29
Steuber, Lillian, 270, 304
Stevens, Halsey, 391
Stevens, Norton, 467–68, 476
Stevens, Wallace, 543
Stockhausen, Karlheinz, 307, 316
Stokowski, Leopold, 160, *170*
Strang, Gerald, 91
Straus, David III, 39–40
Straus, Noel, 97
Strauss, Richard, 212, 344, 541
  Der Rosenkavalier, 71, 435, 488
Stravinsky, Igor, 74, 93, 119, 172, 246, 257, 276, 280, 307, 316, 317, 398, 436, 542
  Agon (1953–57), 316
  Apollon musagète (1927–28), 97
  influence on Schuman, 74
  Le sacre du printemps (1913), 113, 308, 445
  Petrushka (1910–11), 113
  Scènes de ballet (1944), 172
  Symphony in Three Movements (1944), 146
Strilko, Anthony, 350, 356, 397, 453, 492–93, 498
Strouse, Charles, 428
Studer, Cheryl, 490
Swinford, Jerome, 83–84
Szell, George, 154
  on Philharmonic Hall acoustics, 341

Taft, William Howard, 13

Taggard, Genevieve, 130, 137, 139–40
  address to high schoolers, 123–24
  as advisor, 80
  collaboration with Schuman, 80, 91, 123–25, 127–31
  husband as communist, 130
  Sarah Lawrence and, 84
Taubman, Howard, 314, 318
Taylor, Deems, *170*
Taylor, Harold, 333
  This I Believe and, 287
Taylor, Maxwell D., 331–32, 333, 334, 335, 340, 407
Teachers College. *See* Columbia University
Thayer, Ernest L., 14, 34, 267, 531
The Charleston (Cecil Mack and Jimmy Johnson) (1923), 521
The Juilliard Report on Teaching the Literature and Materials of Music, 27, 191, 275, 311
The Juilliard Review, 26, 193, 276, 313
The Seven Lively Arts, 170, 256
Theodore Presser (publisher), 298, 350, 509
  band music for, 300, 348, 351, 501
  choral music for, 293, 306, 510
  editorial assistance from, 500
  Hauser and, 290
  Isadore Freed and, 109, 304
  Ormandy and, 239, 288
  promotion of Schuman's music, 351, 430, 448, 469, 546
  Rochberg and, 238, 292
  Schuman's contracts with, 326, 347, 368, 401, 498
  Schuman's defection to, 169, 288, 290, 295, 466
Thomas, Dylan, 305
Thompson, Randall, 32, 89, 118
Thomson, Virgil, 212, 343, 351
  Arrow Press and, 87
  as moderator, 152
  Four Saints in Three Acts (1934), 126
  Harris and, 103
  MacDowell Medal, 489
  Metropolitan Museum of Art commission, 432
  Music Advisory Panel of ANTA, 308
  on Schuman's music, 148, 159, 202–3
  The River (1938), 161
  Zimbalist birthday variation (1951), 436
Thorne, Francis, 20, 424–25
Tin Pan Alley
  Marks Music and, 108
  Rodgers and Hart, 16
  Schuman and, 17, 21, 45, 46, 51, 54–55, 62, 64, 68, 316, 420
  Schuman as arranger, 50, 125
  Schuman's memoirs and, 43, 44
  Schuman's paper on, 30
  Schuman-Loesser collaboration, 49–50, 518
  waltz songs and, 479
Toscanini, Arturo, 52, 71
Tower, Joan, 190, 523
Town Hall, 249
  Copland's music at, 157–58
  Dushkin at, 247
  Naumburg Foundation and, 194
  Reis and, 141
  Sarah Lawrence Chorus and, 87, 244
  Schuman's music at, 142–43, 152, 154
  Shaw and, 153
  Town Hall/League of Composers Award, 142
Tudor, Antony, 198–203, 207, 210, 214, 213–15, 373, 422, 491–92
  Pillar of Fire, 198
Tudor, David, 309
Tully, Alice, 389, 478, *479*, 480, 496
Tureck, Rosalyn, 111, 152–53

U.S. Air Force Band, 499, 501
U.S. Information Agency, 288, 315, 378, 379
U.S. Marine Band, 501
U.S. State Department, 228, 279, 309, 312, 313, 363
  criticisms of, 285
  Schuman's work for, 284, 308, 351, 419
UNESCO (United Nations Educational, Scientific, and Cultural Organization), 6, 224, 283–85, 287–88
University of California at Los Angeles (UCLA), 87, 197, 416
University of Miami, 315
University of Michigan, 264, 300, 301, 418
University of Washington, 456
urban renewal, 329–30
Ussachevsky, Vladimir, 167, 310
Ustinov, Peter, 380

Van Cliburn International Piano Competition, 538
Van Druten, John, 199
Van Dyke, Willard, 160–63
  collaboration with Schuman, 161
Van Vactor, David, 120
Varèse, Edgard, 94, 212, 282, 289, 307
  MacDowell Medal, 425, 460
Vassar College, 85
vaudeville, 17, 18, 50, 53, 66, 206
Vaughan Williams, Ralph, 307, 436
  Flos campi (1925), 455
Velucci, Paul, 85
Verdi, Giuseppe, 262, 540
  Falstaff, 71, 540
Videorecord Corporation of America, 418–20, 426, 429, 436, 457–58, 468
Vietnam War, 163, 347, 364, 375, 437, 446
  My Lai massacre, 403
Villa, Roy, 464
Villa-Lobos, Heitor, 262, 307, 436
Vincent, John, 197, 416
  FMP Choral Contest winner, 90
Vivian Beaumont Theater, 359, 361, 367
Vogel, Amos, 338, 371
Vogt, Richard, 543–44
von Rhein, John, 519

Wadsworth, Charles, 482–83, 490
Wagenaar, Bernard, 89, 273
  Musicians' Committee to Aid Spanish Democracy and, 90
Wagner, Richard
  "Judaism in Music", 229–30, 384
  Die Walküre, 488
  Lohengrin, 488, 493
  Tristan und Isolde, 71
Wagner, Robert F., 360, 363
Waleson, Heidi, 339
Wallenstein, Alfred, 212, 226
Walter W. Naumburg Music Foundation, 141, 193, 424–25, 426, 521, 523
  American Composers' Recording Prize, 194, 209, 235, 483
Walter, Bruno, 72, 180
Walton, Sir William, 436
Warburg, James, 26, 180, 184, 358, 416–17, 465, 504
Warburg, Joan, 416–17, 465, 503–4, 542–44
Ward, Robert, 273
  Pulitzer Prize (1962), 554
Warfield, William, 276
Waring, Fred, 153–54, 173
Warren, Constance, 80, 84
  first meeting with Schuman, 83
  Sarah Lawrence Chorus and, 86, 114, 143
  This I Believe and, 287
Watanabe, Akeo, 427
Watergate, 163, 469
Webern, Anton von, 307, 318, 355
Webster, Albert K. ("Nick"), 492, 493, 509, 513, 520
Webster, Beveridge, 247, 523, 538
Webster, Michael, 523
Weill, Kurt, 71, 199, 256, 262
Weingartner, Felix, 72
Weisgall, Hugo, 396–97, 441, 545
Weisgall, Nathalie, 396–97, 399
Weiss, Donald, 408
Weiss, Joshua (grandson), 223, 408, 518, 542
Werner, Jules, 74
Westminster Choir College, 85, 98, 103
Whitehead, Robert, 361, 363–64, 382
Whitman, Walt, 98, 403
  A Free Song and, 138, 158
  Carols of Death and, 305
  Cooperstown Fanfare and, 532
  Copland and, 277
  Copland on, 108
  Declaration Chorale and, 402–3
  Harris's choice of, 98
  Koussevitzky's recommendation of, 137, 156
  on music, 429
  Perceptions and, 509
  Schuman's choice of, 14, 65, 135, 139, 477, 549
  To Thee Old Cause and, 402–3
  World War II and, 137
Wierzbicki, James, 505
Wilbur, Richard, 513–18, 520, 534–35
  Pulitzer Prize (1957), 514
Wilder, Thornton, 422, 425
William Schuman Award, 504
Wilson, Olly, 522
Winograd, Arthur, 189
Winston, Carl, 152, 584n43
Wish You Were Here (1952), 261–62

Wittke, Paul, 551
Wolfe, Thomas, 98, 124
Woodworth, G. Wallace ("Woody"), 158, 173, 175, 335
Works Progress Administration, 74, 76, 111, 285
World War II, 10, 123
  Harris and, 95
  response to, 226, 234
  Sarah Lawrence Chorus and, 87
  Schuman and, 81, 146, 150, 160, 169, 446, 472
  Whitman and, 137
Wouk, Herman, 26, 256, 410, 439
WQXR, 97–98, 473, 475
Wulsin, Lucien, 286, 287
Wuorinen, Charles, 274, 507, 522, 553–54
  Two-Part Symphony (1978), 553

Yaddo Festival, 87, 110
Yale University, 193, 246, 485
  Yale Glee Club, 168, 244–45, 415
Yasonova, Lyudmila, 635n62
Young People's Records, 130, 260–61
Young, Edgar, 330–32, 338, 342, 389, 406–7, 412

Zimbalist, Mary Louise Curtis Bok, 436
Zwilich, Ellen Taaffe, 190